CASS SERIES ON SOVIET (RUSSIAN) MILIT

THE SOVIET HIGH COMMAND

CASS SERIES ON SOVIET (RUSSIAN) MILITARY INSTITUTIONS

Series Editor: David M. Glantz

ISSN 1462-1835

This series examines the nature and evolution of Soviet military institutions in peace and war and the human dimension of the Soviet Army.

1. Aleksander A. Maslov, translated and edited by David M. Glantz, *Fallen Soviet Generals: Soviet General Officers Killed in Battle, 1941–1945*. (ISBN 0 7146 4790 X cloth, 0 7146 4346 7 paper)
2. Aleksander A. Maslov, translated and edited by David M. Glantz and Harold S. Orenstein, *Captured Soviet Generals: The Fate of Soviet Generals Captured by the Germans, 1941–1945*. (ISBN 0 7146 5124 9)
3. John Erickson, *The Soviet High Command: A Military-Political History, 1918–1941*. (ISBN 0 7146 5178 8)

CASS SERIES ON SOVIET (RUSSIAN) STUDY OF WAR

Series Editor: David M. Glantz

ISSN 1462-0960

This series examines what Soviet military theorists and commanders have learned from the study of their own military operations.

1. Harold S. Orenstein, translator and editor, *Soviet Documents on the Use of War Experience*, Volume I, *The Initial Period of War 1941*, with an Introduction by David M. Glantz. (ISBN 0 7146 3392 5 cloth)
2. Harold S. Orenstein, translator and editor, *Soviet Documents on the Use of War Experience*, Volume II, *The Winter Campaign 1941–1942*, with an Introduction by David M. Glantz. (ISBN 0 7146 3393 3 cloth)
3. Joseph G. Welsh, translator, *Red Armor Combat Orders: Combat Regulations for Tank and Mechanized Forces 1944*, edited and with an Introduction by Richard N. Armstrong. (ISBN 0 7146 3401 8 cloth)
4. Harold S. Orenstein, translator and editor, *Soviet Documents on the Use of War Experience*, Volume III, *Military Operations 1941 and 1942*, with an Introduction by David M. Glantz. (ISBN 0 7146 3402 6 cloth)
5. William A. Burhans, translator, *The Nature of the Operations of Modern Armies* by V. K. Triandafillov, edited by Jacob W. Kipp, with an Introduction by James J. Schneider. (ISBN 0 7146 4501 X cloth, 0 7146 4118 9 paper)
6. Harold S. Orenstein, translator, *The Evolution of Soviet Operational Art, 1927–1991: The Documentary Basis*, Volume I, *Operational Art, 1927–1964*, with an Introduction by David M. Glantz. (ISBN 0 7146 4547 8 cloth, 0 7146 4228 2 paper)
7. Harold S. Orenstein, translator, *The Evolution of Soviet Operational Art, 1927–1991: The Documentary Basis*, Volume II, *Operational Art, 1965–1991*, with an Introduction by David M. Glantz. (ISBN 0 7146 4548 6 cloth, 0 7146 4229 0 paper)
8. Richard N. Armstrong and Joseph G. Welsh, *Winter Warfare: Red Army Orders and Experiences*. (ISBN 0 7146 4699 7 cloth, 0 7146 4237 1 paper)
9. Lester W. Grau, *The Bear Went Over the Mountain: Soviet Combat Tactics in Afghanistan*. (ISBN 0 7146 4874 4 cloth, 0 7146 4413 7 paper)
10. David M. Glantz and Harold S. Orenstein, editor and translator, *The Battle for Kursk 1943: The Soviet General Staff Study* (ISBN 0 7146 4933 3 cloth, 0 7146 4493 5 paper)
11. Niklas Zetterling and Anders Frankson, *Kursk 1943: A Statistical Analysis* (ISBN 0 7146 5053 8 cloth, 0 7146 8103 2 paper)
12. David M. Glantz and Harold S. Orenstein, editor and translator, *Belorussia 1944: The Soviet General Staff Study* (ISBN 0 7146 5102 8)
13. David M. Glantz and Harold S. Orenstein, editor and translator, *The Battle for L'vov, July 1944: The Soviet Staff General Study* (ISBN 0 7146 5201 6)

THE SOVIET HIGH COMMAND

A Military-Political History

1918–1941

THIRD EDITION

JOHN ERICKSON

Emeritus Professor,
Honorary Fellow Defence Studies,
University of Edinburgh

FRANK CASS
LONDON • PORTLAND, OR

This edition published in 2001 in Great Britain by
FRANK CASS PUBLISHERS
2 Park Square, Milton Park,
Abingdon, Oxon, OX14 4RN

and in the United States of America by
FRANK CASS PUBLISHERS
270 Madison Ave, New York NY 10016

Transferred to Digital Printing 2006

Website: www.frankcass.com

First published in 1962 by Macmillan & Co. Ltd.
Second edition published in 1984 in the United States of America
by Westview Press Inc.

British Library Cataloguing in Publication Data

Erickson, John, 1929–
The Soviet high command: a military-political history, 1918–1941. – 3rd ed. – (Cass series on Soviet (Russian) military institutions)
1. Union of Soviet Socialist Republics. Armiia – History – 20th century 2. Soviet Union – History, Military
I. Title
355'.00947'09041

ISBN10:0-714-65178-8 (hbk)
ISBN10:0-415-40860-1 (pbk)

ISBN13: 978-0-714-65178-1 (hbk)
ISBN13: 978-0-415-40860-8 (pbk)
ISSN 1462-1835

Library of Congress Cataloging-in-Publication Data

A catalog record for this book is available
from the Library of Congress

Typeset in 10.5/12 pt Bembo by Cambridge Photosetting Services, Cambridge

The Socialist island will never have peaceful frontiers with the bourgeois state. That will always be a front, even though it may be in a latent form.

M. N. Tukhachevsky to G. Zinoviev, 1920.

The army of a socialist country, an army standing guard over the gains of the working masses — all experience teaches us — can only be an army led and educated by the Communist Party.

Kommunist, November 1957.

International News Photos

THE FIRST FIVE MARSHALS OF THE SOVIET UNION

Seated, left to right: Tukhachevsky, who was shot in 1937; Voroshilov, who died in his bed in 1969; Yegorov, who disappeared, presumably later shot, in 1939. *Standing:* Budenny, who died of natural causes in 1973; and Blyukher, who was shot in 1938.

CONTENTS

CHAPTER PAGE

LIST OF MAPS ix

SERIES EDITOR'S FOREWORD xi

PREFACE TO THE THIRD EDITION xiii

PREFACE TO THE SECOND EDITION xxi

PREFACE TO THE FIRST EDITION xxxi

ACKNOWLEDGEMENTS xxxv

INTRODUCTION

I. THE ORIGINS OF A NEW ARMY 3

PART ONE

The Revolutionary Military Command, 1918–1920

II. THE CREATION OF THE SOVIET MILITARY MACHINE 25

III. THE FORMATION OF THE SOVIET COMMAND, 1918–1920 53

IV. BEFORE THE GATES OF WARSAW, 1920 84

PART TWO

Military Debates and Political Decisions, 1921–1926

V. THE STRUGGLE FOR CONTROL OF THE ARMY 113

VI. TOWARDS COLLABORATION WITH THE REICHSWEHR 144

VII. THE REIGN OF FRUNZE AND THE RISE OF VOROSHILOV, 1924–1926 164

PART THREE

Foreign Adventures and Strategic Priorities

VIII. THE SOVIET RE-ENTRY INTO THE FAR EAST: THE PROBLEM OF JAPAN AND CHINA 217

IX. MILITARY AND NAVAL TRAFFICKING WITH GERMANY 247

X. SOVIET PREOCCUPATIONS WITH WAR 283

PART FOUR

The Politics of Mechanisation

XI. THE REACTION TO THREATS FROM EAST AND WEST 325

XII. A BRIEF TRIUMPH, 1934–1935 366

XIII. PLOTS AND COUNTER-PLOTS 404

PART FIVE

The Military Purge and the Reconstruction of the Command

XIV. THE KILLINGS, 1937 449

XV. EXEUNT OMNES . . . 474

XVI. THE RACE WITH TIME, 1939–1940 510

PART SIX

The Beginning of the Ordeal, 1941

XVII. 'WE ARE BEING FIRED ON. WHAT SHALL WE DO?' 565

XVIII. THE BATTLE FOR MOSCOW: NOVEMBER–DECEMBER 1941 628

THE PROSPECT 666

NOTES 671

GENERAL APPENDIX 763

APPENDIXES I–IV 776

SOURCE MATERIALS AND BIBLIOGRAPHY 809

BIOGRAPHICAL INDEX TO LEADING MILITARY PERSONALITIES 835

INDEX 849

LIST OF MAPS

THE EASTERN FRONT 62
August 1918–March 1919

COUNTER-OFFENSIVE AGAINST DENIKIN 72
October–November 1919

THE RED ARMY DRIVE ON WARSAW 1920 96

OPERATIONAL PLAN OF THE TRANS-BAIKAL GROUPS,
FAR EASTERN ARMY 243
(For 17 November, 1929)

THE SOVIET FAR EAST 359

LAKE KHASAN (CHANGKUFENG) OPERATIONS 496
31st July–13th August, 1938

RED ARMY OPERATIONS, KHALKHIN-GOL 535
20th–31st August, 1939

SOVIET DEPLOYMENT AGAINST FINLAND 546

THE BREACHING OF THE WESTERN AND NORTH-WESTERN FRONTIERS 594
Situation 21st June–9th July, 1941

THE KIEV ENCIRCLEMENT 611
(August–September 1941)

GENERAL SOVIET PLAN FOR TIKHVIN-VOLKHOV OPERATIONS 636

THE MOSCOW COUNTER-OFFENSIVE 652

SERIES EDITOR'S FOREWORD

No historian has contributed more to Western understanding of the intricacies of Soviet military development than John Erickson. Beginning in the early 1960s, and continuing into the four decades succeeding, Professor Erickson, virtually single-handedly, created, shaped, and validated the historical genre of Soviet military studies. In the finest traditions of modern historiography, as articulated in the early nineteenth century by the father of the discipline, Ludwig von Ranke, he did so by skillfully pursuing, developing and applying the basic tenets of modern scientific historical investigation to his study of the Red Army in peace and war. While inspiring others, including myself, to work in the same field by his example, he also equipped them with the methodologies, tools, and will to do so.

A thorough researcher and prolific writer, Professor Erickson has, in the course of over 40 years of work, authored a prodigious number of books and articles on nearly every aspect of Soviet military development. Although military in focus, these works are unique in that they study the military within the oft-neglected but essential context of political, economic, and social developments. The most important of these books are *The Soviet High Command, The Road to Stalingrad*, and *The Road to Berlin*. Together, this trilogy of seminal studies on the Red Army has provided the starting point and intellectual basis for almost every other work Erickson and other Sovietologists have written during the past four decades.

A military classic in its own right since its publication in 1962, *The Soviet High Command* was and remains Erickson's single most important historical work. Forty years later, it is still the most accurate and perceptive work in its field and will likely remain so for some time in the future. As Professor Erickson acknowledges in his Preface to this new edition, the book's accuracy and perceptiveness are, at least in part, a direct by-product of a unique historical circumstance in the form of the 'Khrushchev thaw' in Soviet historical scholarship. This period, during which the Soviet political leadership briefly loosened the fetters on military investigation of the Red Army's past and encouraged greater historical candor, did indeed provide unique openings for a scholar as keen as Erickson. Above and beyond this, however, it took the author's own unique research methodology, characterized by a particular combination of persistence, perceptivity, and energy, to exploit those unprecedented opportunities. This Erickson did, by thoroughly scouring pre-war archives, closely studying German, available Soviet, and a vast array of other sources, and by skillfully capitalizing on the chance to interview key wartime Soviet military figures.

A product of this prodigious research effort, *The Soviet High Command* is a study whose 'stream-of-consciousness' approach captures the immense and elusive intricacies of a system that few then, and even now, fathomed. Most remarkable of all, despite the growing volume of 'modern' research on the Red Army, precious little has been published that credibly challenges or invalidates Erickson's facts, judgments, or conclusions. On the contrary, recent research has tended to confirm or embellish what Erickson has written. This fact, in and of itself, demands that the book be reprinted and occupy a vital place on the bookshelves of those interested in military history and the Red Army's role in it.

Finally, and personally, this Foreword represents a heartfelt and humble testament to the decisive role and influence *The Soviet High Command* and Professor Erickson's other works have had on my decision to work in this field. While his work has served as impetus and inspiration for me, my over 20 years of labor in the same field has profoundly underscored the difficulties he has had to overcome and the uniqueness, accuracy, and permanence of his scholarly work.

DAVID M. GLANTZ
Carlisle, PA
January 2001

PREFACE TO THE THIRD EDITION

THE *Soviet High Command: A Military-Political History, 1918–1941* (first edn, London, Macmillan, 1962) was indubitably a product of the early stages of the Cold War, though not in any sense supportive of the burgeoning propaganda war or the myths which surrounded discussions of Soviet military organisation and capability, suppositions that the Russians were ten feet tall, and that all they needed to reach the Channel was boots. Quite the contrary. The function of the book was expressly one of 'de-mythologising' the Red Army, taking up where D. Fedotoff White had left off during the Second World War with his pioneer work utilising Russian sources: *The Growth of the Red Army* (Princeton, NJ, Princeton University Press, 1944).

Mention of Russian sources has a particular relevance in outlining the fate of the *Soviet High Command*. The questionable availability of sources, even their supposed total absence, coupled with notions of some impenetrable screen of secrecy pervading East and West alike, almost sealed the fate of the book, raising serious doubts about its viability. This was disconcerting to the point of active discouragement, ending in initial rejection of the proposed book, accompanied by a certain *frisson* in some academic circles that the Red Army was somehow not quite a 'respectable' subject.

There is perhaps no greater incentive to do something than to be told that it cannot be done. The problem of sources was far from insuperable, overcome partly by footwork in libraries, partly by fortunate coincidence. Library holdings here and abroad proved to be extensive, many of their Russian military acquisitions dating back to the 1920s and 1930s, both monographs and periodicals, much of it largely ignored or unexploited. There were promising omens of things to come, such as lighting upon the *Provisional Field Service Regulations (PU-36)*, Tukhachevsky's own *chef d'oeuvre* and a key Soviet publication; unmarked, intact, provenance an English second-hand book shop, price one shilling and three pence (old money).

It was also fortunate that embarking on the book coincided with the post-Stalin rejuvenation and resurgence of Soviet military thought and military-historical investigation under Marshal Zhukov. This rendered greater access to captured German diplomatic and military records, with selectively edited but far from valueless Soviet documentary and memoir materials published on the occasion of the 40th anniversary of the October Revolution. Inter-Library Loan also penetrated the 'Iron Curtain'. The Lenin Library in Moscow responded very generously to loan requests, forwarding rare Soviet military journals dating back to the 1920s. Bookshops in eastern and central Europe were well stocked with translations of Soviet military publications. In Belgrade, Soviet military-theoretical studies, such as General A. A. Svechin's 1926 classic *Strategy* (Moscow, Military Herald, 1926 and 1927), were to hand. Svechin's book was reprinted in 1956 (Belgrade, 'Vojno Delo', 1956) in the Yugoslav military series 'The Military Library of Foreign Authors'. Though there is now an English translation of *Strategy* (Minneapolis, East View Publications, 1992) we have yet to see full Russian reprints of General Svechin's work, even if there is greater reference to his publications. The availability of the *Japanese Special Studies on Manchuria*, a multi-volume series prepared in 1955 by the Military History Section, Headquarters, Army Forces Far East and distributed by the Office of the Chief of Military History, Washington, furnished invaluable material on Soviet strategy, military organisation and operations in the Soviet Far East, Soviet reaction to the Japanese Kwantung Army and the hitherto virtually unknown Soviet–Japanese military conflicts at Lake Khasan in 1938 and Nomonhan in 1939.

What in other contexts might appear to be a pedestrian task, what Professor Mark von Hagen in his preface to *Soldiers in the Proletarian Dictatorship: The Red Army and the Soviet Socialist Sate, 1917–1939* (Ithaca and London, Cornell University Press, 1990) called the reconstruction of 'the most basic outline of events', proved to be formidably difficult, not least in uncovering the origins of the Red Army. It is a problem which even now remains to be fully resolved, complicated from the outset by the overlap in personalities, institutions and military practices between the Tsarist Army and the Red Army. It was certainly an excess of revolutionary fervour which caused the Red Army to be described as 'quite different from any previous army in history', issuing as it did from the October Revolution, in the Introduction to Erich Wollenberg's *The Red Army* (first published, London, Secker & Warburg, 1938; here, London, New Park, 1978).

By the mid-1950s, the massive Stalinist log-jam of obliteration and distortion had begun to break up, 'un-persons' were being restored and rehabilitated. Soviet military historians referred to archives, albeit prudently, though *Historical Archive* produced increasingly valuable documentary evidence. Soviet biographical questionnaires of leading Bolshevik political and military leaders first compiled in 1927 now saw the light of day. In short, Soviet historians had embarked on their own 'de-mythologising' campaign, sufficient to furnish the bulk of a bibliography extending to 25 pages in the first edition of *The Soviet High Command*. One singular contribution to establishing that indispensable 'most basic outline of events' was Colonel Kuzmin's *Guarding Peaceful Labour, 1921–1940* (Moscow, Voenizdat, 1959), a basic account of military developments from the close of the Civil War to the 'Winter War' with Finland in 1940. It is a work that has not entirely lost its utility, and is still cited from time to time. One remarkable study of the key military reforms of 1924–25, the 'Frunze reforms', was I. B. Berkhin's *Military Reform in the USSR, 1924–1925* (Moscow, Voenizdat, 1958), referring to Trotsky without further ado, delving into the archives, furnishing extensive data on military organisation, the central, regional and local military administration, troop establishments, re-organisation of arms and services, 'command cadres', training, recruitment and Party-political work. The year 1957 had already seen the publication of a two-volume edition of Frunze's collected papers, military documents, submissions on military organisation and military doctrine, first published in a three-volume edition in 1927, the origins of what became a virtual iconography of Frunze. Slowly but surely major publications of the 1920s, sometimes in curtailed form, began to creep back into circulation, or at least were noticed, notably the absolutely indispensable three-volume history of the Civil War, *Civil War, 1918–1921* (Moscow, Military Herald, 1928–30), edited by A. S. Bubnov, S. S. Kamenev and R. Eideman, the three volumes covering Red Army actions, military art and an 'operational-strategic outline' of Red Army operations.

To say that the problem of sources had been entirely overcome would be presumptuous. No study or investigation of the former Soviet system is ever replete with sources. Nevertheless, by combining material from the 1920s with that produced in the 1950s and early 1960s, it proved possible to furnish a sturdy version of a 'basic outline of events'. The battle over proving the viability of attempting a study of the formative years of the Red Army is now decades away but it was one won on points. It is the habit of books to take on a life of their own, and the first edition of *The Soviet High Command* was no exception. It appeared in Italian as *History of the Soviet General Staff* (Milan, Feltrinelli Editore, 1963) and, much to my own surprise, received a not wholly unfavourable reception in Warsaw Pact military publications.

In 1963 the book turned itself into a passport, in a manner of speaking. Discussions at a high level had arranged for Cornelius Ryan, author of *The Longest Day*, to visit Moscow in order to write a book on the battle for Berlin in 1945. It was agreed that he could be accompanied by a second person, but not an American. I was selected to be that second person by virtue of being the author of *The Soviet High Command*, adjudged to be a serious work of military history free from propaganda.

The visit fortunately coincided with yet another 'mini-thaw' on the Soviet scene; indeed, it was one of the products of this change in temper. Here was an opportunity to view the Soviet military system from the inside, and meet Marshals of the Soviet Union: Rokossovskii, the master of mobile warfare, the formidable Koniev, and Chuikov, the famed defender of Stalingrad.

It was also the occasion for me to be introduced to the Soviet archives under the tutelage of Col. I. I. Rustunov, a Soviet military historian in his own right, much of his work devoted to the Tsarist Army and the Russian Army in the First World War and, equally important, to the specialists from the Military-Historical Section of the Soviet General Staff, headed by Lieutenant-General S. P. Platonov.

Lieutenant-General S. P. Platonov was the chief editor of *The Second World War 1939–1945: A Military-Historical Outline* (Moscow, Voenizdat, 1958), a collective work which engaged numerous Soviet military historians. It would be more than a decade, 15 years to be precise, before that book title, referring to the Second World War at large, surfaced once more in the Soviet Union in the 12-volume *History of the Second World War 1939–1945* (Moscow, Voenizdat, 1973–82), a development not without political significance. The General Staff section was in effect the 'powerhouse' of Soviet military history, its function to prepare historical analyses of Red Army operations in order to establish 'numerical norms' for future operations. This was also intended to contribute to military doctrine and to systematise the documentation on separate fronts and armies, for example, documents pertaining to all six Soviet wartime tank armies. The result was a huge data bank.

If the General Staff historical section was the powerhouse, then the workshop was provided by the Institute of Marxism-Leninism and the historians connected with the ambitious six-volume history, *The Great Patriotic War of the Soviet Union 1941–1945* (Moscow, Voenizdat, 1960–65), compiled under the editorial chairmanship of P. N. Pospelov. This was a marked and deliberate departure from association with the wider history of the Second World War, 1939–45, in favour of the specific 'Great Patriotic War of the Soviet Union, 1941–45'. It also signalled a genuine, professional divide between 'technical' military history and one that was avowedly military-political, not least in its celebration of N. S. Khrushchev's significance in the war. Though much criticised, the volumes released valuable data and represented a major multilingual research effort. I was invited to attend one of the later editorial meetings at which proof copies were discussed. The military made it abundantly plain they would vouch for the accuracy of the data but not for what was described as 'narrative', namely the political gloss. On the anguished question of Red Army losses Marshal Koniev ordered the removal of casualty figures, observing that as long as he was alive he would not permit this. Strangely enough, not much later at a press conference he publicly announced Red Army losses of 10 million men, killed and missing. The recent work edited by Colonel-General G. F. Krivosheev, *Soviet Casualties and Combat Losses in the Twentieth Century* (London Greenhill, 1997), has now clarified the deliberate confusion.

Given this rather intensive introduction, it was inevitable that my own attention should turn increasingly to the 'Great Patriotic War of the Soviet Union', to continue the history of the Red Army into the war years. Though the 'most basic outlines' were different, the fundamental questions remained the same, namely, what were the characteristics of the Soviet military system, this time under conditions of maximum stress, and what constituted 'Soviet military performance'. Much of the early part of this work was compiled in Moscow amidst a growing furore over the cause and course of the tragedy of 1941 and Stalin's role throughout the war; a furious controversy that, if anything, has intensified since the collapse of the Soviet Union. The interchanges with Soviet historians grew more interesting and more complex, with the inescapable consequence of my being identified (often mistakenly) with particular Soviet schools and becoming involved in the dualistic politics of Soviet military history. The history of the Soviet Union's cruel war *was* politics, no holds barred. One benefit of these contacts, however, was to facilitate the contribution of Soviet military historians to the British *History of the Second World War*, published by Purnell, whose Editor-in-Chief was Sir Basil Liddell Hart and Editor was Barrie Pitt – one crack in the Cold War ice which steadily widened.

The 1984 reprint of *The Soviet High Command* (Boulder, CO and London, Westview Press, 1984) offered the opportunity to review the state of the Soviet military after the lapse of 20 years and to survey what had been achieved in Western literature. One notable feature was the appearance of substantial documentary publications, those pertaining to Soviet military theory and practice, in particular two volumes published during 1965–70 on 'questions of strategy, operational art' and tactics in Soviet military publications 1917–40.

A significant addition to the literature on the origins of the Red Army was S. M. Klyatskin's study of the 'formative years of the Red Army', *In Defence of October* (Moscow, Nauka, 1965), especially valuable for its elucidation of the complicated evolution of Red Army structures and Soviet military-political arrangements at all levels. Pride of place, however, must go to the two documentary publications, *High Command Directives 1917–1920* (Moscow, Voenizdat, 1969) and the massive four-volume *Front Directives 1917–1922* (Moscow, Voenizdat, 1971–78), the final volume being a virtual statistical handbook of the Soviet military machine covering the Civil War years, exposing the very innards of the Red Army. Meanwhile, 12 volumes of the post-Khrushchev 'official' *History of the Second World War 1939–45* (Moscow, Voenizdat, 1973–82) trundled their rather humdrum way through a substantial portion of Leonid Brezhnev's stay in the Kremlin.

That 'most basic outline' of Soviet military developments had filled out appreciably over two decades, expanding to detailed studies with substantial documentary support. But it was not only historical studies, interest in current Soviet military affairs increasingly commanded the attention of the United States Army, notably in the matter of Soviet military theory, and, above all, in that great mystery, operational art. This gave a fresh cast or twist to the work I was doing. Colonel David Glantz has initiated and pursued the most profound studies in Soviet military theory, prime examples being *Soviet Operational Art: In Pursuit of Deep Battle* (London, Frank Cass, 1991) and the two-volume documentary collection *The Evolution of Soviet Operational Art, 1927–1991* (London, Frank Cass, 1995). In his Foreword to Volume I of the latter work, Colonel Glantz highlighted the Americans' 'frustration over the perceived poor performance of the US Army in Vietnam, where simple tactical approaches failed to produce positive strategic results' (p. viii). This brought about growing interest in what the Imperial Russian Army and the Soviet Army called 'the operational level of war'.

For those who had mocked the supposed lack of sophistication in Russian military theory, the discovery of a Russian storehouse of theoretical innovation came as a complete surprise. Since the late nineteenth century, Russian theorists had closely examined the relationships between mass, mobility and firepower. In 1961, operational art had been rejected in American military circles as 'conceptually irrelevant'. Almost 30 years later the 'operational level of war' suddenly provided the United States Army with the framework for new operational concepts embracing the 'intermediate level of combat between the more traditional levels of strategy and tactics'. The 1930s Soviet theories of 'operations in depth' and 'deep battle' and its progenitor, M. N. Tukhachevsky, commanded great and growing attention. They were brought to the forefront of British attention by the late Brigadier Richard Simpkin's 1987 study *Deep Battle: The Brainchild of Marshal Tukhachevskii* (London, Brassey's, 1987), a professional soldier's appraisal, with which I was pleased and privileged to be associated. It would be an exaggeration to say that the theory and practice of 'deep battle' has now become a commonplace but Russian military theory is now firmly implanted in the West.

More recently, the doors of the Soviet military archives have opened, though not without much creaking of hinges. Of the much-anticipated 'revelations' there is little appreciable evidence. The Russian preoccupation has been largely with filling in the so-called 'blank spots', most of them involving Stalin's crimes against his own people. The history of the Red Army, as it has been generally perceived, has not been substantially altered, but much illuminating detail has been divulged. We now have a mountain of material on Stalin's military purges, the procedures, the victims and their numbers, in both the pre- and the post-war military purges. We also have extensive data on Soviet losses for all operations from 1918 to 1989, from the

Red Army's first engagement at Narva in 1918 to the Soviet Army's final withdrawal from Afghanistan. But what has added great depth to studies of the pre-1941 evolution of the Red Army, particularly of military theory and many aspects of its 1941–45 wartime operations, has been the declassification of previously secret General Staff studies, 'future war and threat assessments 1927–1941', many hundreds of volumes from the library of the General Staff Academy, treatises on mobilisation, the military economy, and, above all, a treasure trove of Soviet military thought.

What, more than 40 years ago, would I have found most illuminating and fundamentally important from this assembly of archive materials and secret military studies, had they been to hand? The military studies which have now been declassified reveal not only the bedrock of the Red Army as it evolved before 1941 but also the basic building blocks of a military-political and military-economic system that endured for three-quarters of a century. The archives, brilliantly exploited by specialists such as Lennart Samuelson in *Plans for Stalin's War Machine: Tuchachevskii and Military-Economic Planning, 1925–1941* (Basingstoke and New York, Macmillan, 2000) and David R. Stone's most recent work *Hammer and Rifle: The Militarization of the Soviet Union 1926–1933* (Lawrence, University Press of Kansas, 2000), lay bare the origins of the huge transformation which engulfed the Soviet Union between 1926 and 1933 and which finally sealed its doom. The massive Stalinised militarisation of Soviet society in which Soviet military theorists played a key role was nothing short of a huge military-industrial revolution. The military demanded the absolute centralisation of the economy, the total integration of state and society.

Though this military-political and military-industrial system was instrumental in winning a gigantic war, the horrendous cost in blood and treasure notwithstanding, the victory eventually proved disastrously Pyrrhic. With survival assured, the conviction of infallibility, the pervasiveness of military domination of society and the 'military-industrial complex' induced obsolescence and 'stagnation'. Top-heavy 'military weight' finally accelerated the collapse of the very state the system had been designed to defend. This overweening military fixation was rooted in what Andrei Kokoshin, the distinguished Russian First Deputy Defence Minister in the 1990s, identified in his Introduction to *Soviet Strategic Thought, 1917–91* (Cambridge, MA, MIT Press, 1998) as an implanted 'sort of code' ('*geneticheskii kod*', 'genetic code' in the original Russian), which informed all military-political and military-strategic concepts. It was an endemic condition, generating a viral form that steadily undermined the regime's security at home and abroad.

The end of the Soviet system was with its beginning. In *The Collapse of the Soviet Military* (New Haven and London, Yale University Press, 1998)

Lieutenant-General William Odom uttered an apt requiem: 'Arm-in-arm the Communist Party and the generals went to their demise.' Forty years ago the effort to reconstruct even 'the most basic outline of events' in the evolution of the Red Army in the 1920s and 1930s disclosed fear of an abrupt, cataclysmic failure of the system. It had stalked the regime from its inception. *The Soviet High Command* had no predictive function, nor was one intended, but it did convey, and I submit still does, the sense of a fate hanging in the balance, at times precariously so, whatever the propagandistic chest-beating.

The system lived perpetually on a narrow knife-edge. How frighteningly narrow was brought home to me in a singular exchange with Chief Marshal of Artillery N. N. Voronov. He asked me if I was satisfied with the assistance I had received in investigating the events of June 1941. I relayed what I had learned but, knowing he was present at very centre of events during the early hours of Sunday 22 June, I asked him for his interpretation. His final remark was quite astonishing. He said that at about 7.30 am the High Command had received encouraging news: the Red Army was fighting back. The worst nightmare had already been overcome. Red Army soldiers had gone to war, 'the system' had responded and would respond.

JOHN ERICKSON
Edinburgh
February 2001

PREFACE TO THE SECOND EDITION

BOOKS sometimes have secret lives of their own, lives dominated by a form of predestination that may owe more to Caxton than to Calvin but that nevertheless steers them and their authors along unintended and unimagined courses. Twenty-two years ago, when this book was in its original format, it was unexpectedly and unaccountably transformed into a kind of passport, which facilitated my access to the Soviet Union. There followed a series of close encounters of a military kind with a diverse array of Soviet officers, ranging from grandee marshals to stolid, veteran riflemen. What had hitherto been constricted research suddenly and startlingly came alive. The environment was made tangible and the men whose careers reached back to the infancy of the Red Army, to the early days of the Soviet military system, and to the heady triumph over the *Wehrmacht*, emerged from arid print and pallid documentary stereotypes as real personalities.

Since 1962, the picture has changed almost beyond recognition, largely because of the diligence and application of historians on both sides of the East-West divide. In brief, what was the Red Army has become much more accessible so that it is no longer necessary to scrabble for information or to rely upon a curious collection of myths. Immediately evident is the convergence, however accidental, of interests shown by both Soviet and non-Soviet historians in the final, fateful days of the Red Army's precursor, the Imperial Russian Army. That interest is broadly based and runs the gamut from the high command to the common soldier.

Professor Allan K. Wildman provides a searching analysis in his major work *The End of the Russian Imperial Army: The Old Army and the Soldier's Revolt, March–April 1917* (Princeton: Princeton University Press, 1980), a study complemented by *Voenno-revolyutsionnye komitety deistvuyushchei armii* (Moscow: NAUKA, 1977). This documentary collection takes the tale up to March 1918. An astonishing and unique accumulation of archival *richesse.* Professor M. Frenkin's monumental *Russkaya armiya i Revolutsiya 1917–1918* (Munich: 'LOGOS' Verlag, 1978), utilises material that can only leave the reader agape. The high command and in particular those key figures the *Genshtabistyi*—the General Staff officers who then, as now, could wield immense power within the machine—are treated in depth by Professor Matitiahu Mayzel in *Generals and Revolutionaries, The Russian General Staff During the Revolution: A Study in the Transformation of*

Military Elites (Osnabrück: Biblio Verlag, 1979). If there is yet room for further investigation and analysis, it must lie with the Russian and Soviet General Staff, though this is not to disparage the useful outlines of institutional development provided by Colonel Kavtaradze and Colonel Danilov in an invaluable source, *Voenno-istoricheskii Zhurnal* (Moscow: *Krasnaya Zvezda,* 1971, no. 12, and 1977, no. 9).

Thanks to the impressive labours of Soviet historians such as V. I. Miller, L. S. Gaponenko, and many others, the ordinary Russian soldier is emerging from the cloak of anonymity history seemed to have thrown over him. In *Slavic Review* in 1971 Professor Marc Ferro draws upon Soviet archives to paint one picture of the Russian soldier—'Undisciplined, Patriotic and Revolutionary'. We can peer even more closely at him in Professor Tatyana Kuzmina's studies based on materials from the Moscow Military District, *Revolutsionnoe dvizhenie soldatskikh mass Tsentra Rossii nakanune Oktyabrya* (Moscow: NAUKA, 1978). These are not just historical curiosities. One of the greatest developments of the time was the creation of the Red Army, which fused the old Imperial and the new Soviet styles. This was the search for an 'army of a new type' that would be distinctively class based and that would pursue the struggle between political requirement and military efficiency as well as the compromise between utopianism and pragmatism with the kind of ruthlessness that wins on the battlefield, where the Bolshevik regime had to survive or perish.

The dying days of the Imperial Army are indeed crucial to understanding the first stirrings of what became the Workers and Peasants Red Army (RKKA) and the creation of a rudimentary but workable Soviet military system. This turbulent and desperately dangerous interlude is examined at length by S. M. Klyatskin in *Na zashchite Oktyabrya* (Moscow: NAUKA, 1965), which should be required reading for any student of the Soviet military system between 1917 and 1920. The bones of that book can be picked clean with profit. But the Red Army was also a composite of numerous revolutionary Red Armies. As I was writing in 1968 of the origins of the Red Army (in *Revolutionary Russia,* Cambridge: Harvard University Press, 1968) and looking at Richard Cobb's mighty study, *Les Armées Révolutionnaires* (Paris–The Hague: 1961) on French revolutionary armies, I was obliged to note the paucity of material on the several Soviet revolutionary armies, not to mention key fronts. That situation has been steadily rectified over time, starting with A. N. Nenarokov's *Vostochnyi front 1918* (Moscow: NAUKA, 1969) and followed by biographies (if they can be called that) of armies, divisions, and brigades. Real close-ups, however, appear in works such as A. L. Fraiman's study of the defence of Petrograd in the spring of 1918, *Revolyutsionnaya zashchita Petrograda v fevrale-marte 1918* (Moscow-Leningrad: NAUKA, 1964). Although the Bolshevik sailor squads still receive close attention, the development of the Red Navy has been examined through a Leninist prism by B. I. Zverev in *V. I. Lenin i Flot (1918–1920)* (Moscow: VOENIZDAT, 1978) and A. K. Selyanichev in *V. I. Lenin i stanovlenie Sovetskovo Voenno-morskogo Flota* (Moscow: NAUKA, 1979).

There has been surprisingly belated appraisal of Lenin's *military* role, as opposed to political myth-making, but Colonel N. N. Azovtsev has made some amends with his bibliography of Lenin's military writings, *Voennye voprosy v trudakh V. I. Lenina,* 2nd edition (Moscow: VOENIZDAT, 1972), and a formal monograph, *V. I. Lenin i sovetskaya voennaya nauka,* 2nd edition (Moscow: NAUKA, 1981). Meanwhile, the horizon of the history of the Red Army in the Civil War and the fight against 'foreign intervention' expanded appreciably with the publication of two major documentary collections: *Direktivy Glavnovo Komandovaniya Krasnoi Armii (1917–1920)* (Moscow: VOENIZDAT, 1969) and the four massive volumes of *Direktivy komandovaniya frontov Krasnoi Armii (1917–1922)* (Moscow: VOENIZDAT, 1971, 1972, 1974, 1978), the final volume being virtually a statistical handbook of the Red Army for these war years. If this material does not actually supersede the Trotskii papers, at least it vastly supplements them, for here are the very innards of the Red Army.

Though the war was won, conflict of a different order faced the Red Army and its heterogeneous command, not the least significant being the running battles over *military doctrine*—a theme fixed in its historical context but with obvious contemporary relevance. Lenin himself, who in 1917 had expressed his skepticism about some special mystique pertaining only to military affairs—*kakoe zhrechestvo!*—now warned against 'Communist swagger', since 'our military Communists are still insufficiently mature to lay claim (*pretendovat'*) to the leadership of all military affairs'. The duel in the 1920s between Trotskii and Frunze, with Stalin lurking in the shadows, continues to reverberate even today. In spite of Trotskii's derisive assault on Frunze's jejune views, it is the latter who passed into Soviet military-political tradition and became a kind of military legend. Frunze's impetuosity, which prompted Lenin's remarks on the need for caution, seemed to transform him into a zealot pleading the cause of a distinctive 'proletarian military doctrine'. The symbol and the substance of this doctrine are fully explored in Walter Darnell Jacobs, *Frunze: The Soviet Clausewitz, 1885–1925* (The Hague: Martinus Nijhoff, 1969). Trotskii appears as the cold pragmatist cast in the dubious mould of a mere functionary—a strange transformation indeed of a man who was the fiery, ferocious phrase maker of the Civil War.

The fundamental debate on the relationship between war and politics, as well as the fashioning of a strategy best suited to the available military means, still bears further investigation. We come back to the role and importance of what ultimately became the General Staff (which did not assume this formal designation until 1935), One intriguing feature of this debate concerned the actual need for a superior staff organ. Frunze insisted on the necessity of a 'military brain' (*voennyi mozg*) to serve the entire Soviet state, but that apparently was too straightforward. The more sophisticated and convoluted premises for the emergence of 'Soviet military science' and the direction of Soviet military thought are explored by Colonel I. A. Korotkov in *Vestnik voennoi istorii* (No. 2, Moscow: VOENIZDAT, 1971). A more extensive treatment is found in a detailed and indispensable monograph, *Istoriya Sovetskoi voennoi mysli Kratkii ocherk 1917-iyun 1941* (Moscow: NAUKA, 1980).

During the early 1930s the Red Army began to gulp down the first products of the industrialisation drive, launched during Stalin's Five Year Plans, that furnished the true sinews of war—tanks, guns, and aircraft. The secret collaboration with the German *Reichswehr,* many details of which remain secret to this day, had already initiated the Red Army into the mysteries of modern warfare, particularly the potential of the tank. In 1929 K. B. Kalinovskii, the chief of the infant Soviet armoured force, produced a preliminary work on tank operations, 'High speed tanks in the meeting engagement' (Moscow-Leningrad: *Gosudarstvennoe voennoe izdatelstvo,* 1929). In the same year the Soviet command set up its first 'mechanised regiment', a unit designed for independent operations, followed by the 'mechanised brigade' formed in May 1930. V. T. Vol'skii, who was to become the wartime commander of the formidable 5th Guards Tank Army, played a leading part in these early experiments with tank units. But more than field experimentation was afoot. Slowly but surely the idea took root that in any future war the destruction of large enemy forces would depend upon systematic and sequential successes across the entire face of the front. Operations would have to be connected not only in space but also *in time.*

Thanks to two Soviet documentary collections we can now scan the whole array of these ideas and formulations, which embraces strategy, operational art, and tactics. *Voprosy strategii i operativnogo iskusstva v sovetskikh voennykh trudakh, 1917–1940* (Moscow: VOENIZDAT, 1965) and *Voprosy taktiki v sovetskikh voennykh trudakh, 1917–1940* (Moscow: VOENIZDAT, 1970) are publications I assume owe much to Marshal Zakharov's prompting when he was restored to his post as chief of the Soviet General Staff. Those less inclined to toil through these massive compilations can best turn to *The Soviet Art of War: Doctrine, Strategy, and Tactics,* edited by Harriet Fast Scott and William F. Scott (Boulder: Westview Press, 1982) or use the Soviet survey provided in *Ocherki sovetskoi voennoi istoriografii,* edited by General Zhilin (Moscow: VOENIZDAT, 1974). The footnotes in the latter are especially useful.

In the course of time Soviet ideas on strategy, operational art, and tactics converged to produce a coherent doctrinal position, 'the theory of operations in depth' (*teoriya glubokoi operatsii/boya*). In 1925 the first draft of the *Field Service Regulations* had begun to trace the outline of the 'combined arms' doctrine, the essence of which was to combine fire with movement; the *Regulations* of 1929 were more explicit. The combined arms concept gradually approached the notion of 'operations in depth', producing the distinctive doctrinal formulation set out in the provisional *Field Service Regulations* for 1936 (PU-36). This bears all the hallmarks of M. N. Tukhachevskii's insight and foresight. There is no better example of continuity in Soviet military thought than the fortunes of the theory of operations in depth, a theme that has been expertly explored by Professor Earl Ziemke in *Parameters* (Carlisle Barracks: U.S. Army War College, June 1983). As Professor Ziemke points out, not only has this theory been rehabilitated, but it is now 'lodged in a position of high esteem in the corpus of Soviet military thought' and promises even further advances. To summarize, the operations-in-depth theory envisaged a four-echelon offensive. With air elements in the first echelon and combined-arms shock armies in the second echelon, the third echelon would consist of exploitation forces, supported by reserves in the fourth echelon. Professor Ziemke correctly notes that I was not able to make specific reference to the *theory* of operations in depth as such because it was not until 1965, in *Voenno-istoricheskii Zhurnal* (Nos. 1 and 3), that G. Isserson—'father' of operations in depth—produced a firsthand account of his theoretical work of the 1930s.

The spectre of operations conducted to great depth at high speed is one of NATO's nightmares, though the concept of striking in depth has also been considered as part of NATO's countervailing strategy. We observe here a form of military jujitsu that turns enemy strength back on itself by attacking the exposed echelons, moving at high speed with 'deep strike' formations, and using the most advanced weaponry. What links past, present, and future is the emphasis on the initial period of hostilities. It is here that Soviet anguish begins. In 1937 Stalin aimed his great sundering blow at the high command of the Red Army, accomplishing no less than the decapitation of the Soviet military, to use Isserson's phrase.

Even after almost half a century has passed, the military purge still retains many gruesome mysteries, though the official 'rehabilitations' have disposed of the grotesque charges of treason and other concocted infamies. But the whole muddied and bloodied spectacle of mass repression, its methods, mechanisms, and bureaucracies—the latter making it more horrible—is the essential background to the decimation of the Soviet military. A comprehensive analysis of it is supplied in Robert Conquest's massive dossier of a murder machine, *The Great Terror* (New York: Macmillan, 1968). One particularly pertinent feature, among many others, is the revision of the tally of losses from the military purge, which by Khrushchev's own admission reached even battalion and company commanders. Half the Soviet officer corps, or some 33,000 to 40,000 men, suffered either death or imprisonment. This is no exercise in statistical niceties, but rather, a bleak illustration of the impact of the losses. These losses virtually wiped out the 'high command'—three out of five marshals, fourteen of sixteen army commanders, eight out of eight admirals—and emptied the ranks of regimental commanders, whose replacements came not from the Frunze Academy but from the lowlier officer schools. Nor was the fate of the survivors wholly enviable. They were pushed up through depleted senior ranks to take over brigades and divisions, where they could only flounder and fumble until taught some terrible lessons by the German Army.

No less horrible in its impact, the strategic views and operational assessments of many of the dead commanders ironically proved to be utterly valid, not least with respect to appraisals of the German threat and the military form it might take. Perhaps by way of overcompensation, or even as a kind of idealisation of a vanished military elite, something like a cult of Tukhachevskii developed. It began formally with an edition of his selected works, *Izbrannye proizvedeniya* (Moscow: VOENIZDAT, 1964, in two volumes). There were also earlier compelling firsthand accounts of Tukhachevskii's role and insights, such as Isserson's recollections of Tukhachevskii's role in the major war games of 1936 *(Voenno-istoricheskii Zhurnal*, 1963, No. 4). But Tukhachevskii's lessons in sound military practice were ignored, as well as his warnings of possible enemy concentration on the frontiers and his insights into shortcomings of the Red Army. Inherent military skills perished with those commanders who were executed. There is also Lieutenant General Todorskii's personal lamentation over Tukhachevskii's fate, also published in 1963. If anything, the naval command suffered even more calamitously. It was sacrificed on the altar of Stalin's 'big ship' fixation, which inhibited the short-range, defensive capabilities of the navy and led in turn to the loss of control over key sea lanes. The further fate and fortune of the Soviet navy and air forces are treated in two quite separate works of some importance, A. V. Basov, *Flot v Velikoi Otechestvennoi voine 1941-1945. Opyt operativno-strategicheskovo primeneniya* (Moscow: NAUKA, 1980) and M. N. Kozhevnikov, *Komandovanie i shtab VVS Sovetskoi Armii v Velikoi Otechestvennoi voine 1941-1945 gg.* (Moscow, NAUKA, 1977). The latter was translated and published under the auspices of the United States Air Force as volume 17 in the Soviet Military Thought series, entitled *The Command and Staff of the Soviet Army Air Force in the Great Patriotic War 1941–1945* (Washington, D.C.: U.S. Government Printing Office).

There has been a steady flow of memoirs and the accumulation of official biographies of previous 'nonpersons'. This material amply confirms that these manic killings went on far beyond those first shattering blows of 1937, spilling over into 1938 and into the period leading up to and even beyond the German attack. A trickle of officers returned from the cells and cellars of the NKVD, but others were trundled off to death. Shtern, Loktionov, and Smushkevich, air defence and air force commanders, were all shot on October 28, 1941, condemned for 'treasonable activity'. Other officers, condemned for failing to hold the Germans, also faced the executioner at this time. But the role of personal whim—the jerk of Caesar's thumb—was illustrated by the fate of Pavlov, commander of the Western Front in 1941, who was listed among those shot but was rumoured to have been reprieved by Stalin himself, thus becoming a hale if less than hearty survivor. The purges generated stories both macabre and monstrous. The fate of Pavlov formed only a minute particle, while events in the Far East built up a murk that is even more durable and more difficult to penetrate. Some light is shed on these circumstances by General G. S. Lyushkov's report after his defection to the Japanese (*Most Secret. Interrogation of Lyushkov, G. S.*, London: Public Record Office, November 1938) and by Professor Alvin C. Coox in 'L'Affair Lyushkov: Anatomy of a Defector' in *Soviet Studies* (Glasgow: 1968, Vol. 19). We still do not understand what really happened in the Red Army operations at Lake Khasan and Nomon-Han in 1938 and 1939 nor do we know what Richard Sorge did or did not know and what he reported to Stalin. Sorge, a German journalist working in China and Japan and senior operative Soviet intelligence agent, warned Stalin of impending German attack in 1941 and of the Japanese plans in 1944. He was named posthumous Hero of the Soviet Union in 1964.

Thanks to the availability of captured German documents, particularly the files of *Fremde Heere Ost*, it is now possible to examine the Soviet military establishment more closely. We also have such materials as *Grosses*

Orientierungsheft Russland Stand 1.3.1939, Finnish and Rumanian intelligence materials, and the massive files dealing with *BARBAROSSA*. Soviet accounts make the most of the reorganization introduced after the poor performance of the Red Army in the 'Winter War' with Finland. The 'official histories' (the six-volume *Istoriya Velikoi Otechestvennoi voine,* Moscow: VOENIZDAT, 1961–1965, and the twelve-volume *Istoriya Vtoroi Mirovoi voiny,* Moscow: VOENIZDAT, 1973–1982) cannot disguise the fact that a vast amount remained to be done in the way of retraining and reequipping the Soviet armed forces. In *Stalin and His Generals, Soviet Military Memoirs of World War II* (1969; reprint ed., Boulder and London: Westview Press, 1984) Professor Seweryn Bialer provides an ample selection of Soviet memoir literature depicting the constrictions and contradictions that abounded in the days before June 1941. In fact, memoir literature remains the main source for any detail on the command conference held in December 1940 and the major war games that followed early in January 1941. The former was marked by confusion and indecision over the organisation of Soviet armoured forces. The latter are notable for Zhukov's map exercise in which he smashed the 'defenders' with that 'local superiority in forces' that the German Army employed with such brutal effectiveness in June 1941.

At this juncture in Soviet history, politics and current security preoccupations all seem to fuse into a single mass, shifting backwards and forwards through time but pivoting on the *survivability* of the system. In terms of historical analysis Colonel V. A. Anfilov has expanded his earlier monograph, published in 1962, into two substantial volumes, *Bessmertnyi podvig* (Moscow: NAUKA, 1971) and *Proval 'Blitskriga'* (Moscow: NAUKA, 1974). These are important contributions to an understanding of the course of planning (or the lack of it) before June 1941. The memoirs of Marshal A. M. Vasilevskii, *Delo vsei zhizni* (Moscow: POLITIZDAT, 1975, 2nd Ed.) are more explicit, perhaps the most explicit information on war planning at that time. Together with N. F. Vatutin and G. K. Malandin, Vasilevskii worked under the direction of Marshal A. M. Shaposhnikov on a revised defence plan in the early autumn of 1940. The essence of this plan was to counter a major German concentration running northward from the mouth of the river San, necessitating Soviet deployment in strength from the Baltic to the Polesian marshes. For reasons unexplained by Vasilevskii, Stalin personally and peremptorily altered Shaposhnikov's operational draft, changing the lines of the main German thrust from a northerly to a southwesterly axis. He assumed that Hitler's objective would be the concentrations of Soviet industry, the grainlands, and the deposits of key raw materials. Marshal Zhukov, in his memoirs, added that Stalin did provide some justification for this major change by arguing that 'without these vital resources' Hitler would be quite unable to wage a protracted war. However, the historians (and ideologues) had already fought a pitched battle ten years earlier over the issue of Stalin's responsibility and Russia's general preparedness when debating Professor A. M. Nekrich's book *1941 22 iyunya* (Moscow: NAUKA, 1965). This was a turbulent encounter with 130 participants. I was subsequently given a copy of the notes of these proceedings, which demonstrate the passions aroused and articulated. A version of this debate appears in *Survey*, No. 63, April 1967.

After three decades of discussion, debate, and not a little digression—beginning with the breaking of the Stalinist mould itself—some further answers to the crucial questions of threat assessment, war planning, the role of the surprise factor, the responsiveness of the system, and the responsibility of individuals, military and political alike, have been carefully formulated. Neither the military as a body nor Stalin as an individual escapes unscathed. Stalin blundered in dismissing, distorting, or ignoring what was known of German intentions and operational plans. But the military professionals failed to grasp the essentials of the German 'war doctrine'. The 'new methods' demonstrated by the German Army were either ignored or unrecognised. The Defence Commissariat and the General Staff assumed that a Soviet-German war would follow an orthodox pattern, with the main forces engaging only after several days of frontier battles and with similar conditions for the concentration and deployment of both German and Soviet forces. The roots of disaster—and disaster it speedily became—lay with the inability of all concerned to grasp the essence of German military doctrine in a tactical, operational sense and of the German 'war-waging doctrine' in its widest strategic framework. As a result, effective operational planning was unhinged from the start and accurate intelligence was too easily construed as disinformation.

What is interesting is how historical events have been arranged to fit present conditions. The framers of current doctrine obviously have the problem of working around the conundrum 'When is a surprise not a surprise?' Clearly, when examining German strategic intentions, Russian analysts can point to more or less correct anticipation of German moves. Cataclysmic surprise erupted with the reality of the German Army's astonishing performance and its capacity to inflict immediate, devastating, near fatal damage. Accepting the analogy that 1941 was the equivalent of a medium-size nuclear blitz, the relevance of warding off any repetition becomes all too plain. Never again those hapless, pathetic, incredible, wailing signals: 'We are being fired on, What shall we do?' Hearing the crack of doom once and only once must be made to suffice at all costs and for all time.

John Erickson

PREFACE TO THE FIRST EDITION

THE Red Army, together with Soviet military leadership and its relations with the Communist Party, have been since the Russian Revolution the object of intense interest, varying degrees of scrutiny and frequent generalisation. Since 1945 Soviet military power has intruded itself directly upon Europe, and the year of Germany's defeat provided a maze of conflicting and paradoxical impressions, as the Soviet armed forces came under a wider, more immediate and sustained observation. The aim of this book is to furnish a history of the origins and development of this leadership, together with a survey of its relations with the Communist Party and the governmental apparatus, within the chronological limits of the first attempts to organise the Red Army and a military command to the near-destruction of both in the first stage of the Soviet-German War in 1941. German military and diplomatic files, become available as a result of their capture, have added one additional avenue of explanation. The other has been provided by the faster flowing tide of explanation following on the 20th Congress of the Communist Party and the reaction to the 'cult of the individual', although much remains mere confirmation of what had hitherto been adduced or astutely reconstructed.

Unlike the German Army with its celebrated General Staff, the product of continuity and tradition, the Soviet military leadership cannot be depicted in terms of a single powerful military organ, and identified with that institution. Although several senior Red Army officers held high hopes for the eventual ascendancy of the Red Army Staff, and while this did become the Red Army General Staff, these professional ambitions remained unsatisfied. Formal arrangements were made for the relationship of military and civil power, but these scarcely constituted the crux of the matter. Not infrequently the scheme of 'Army-Party relations' has been employed to characterise the operation of the Soviet system, and though having its uses, this becomes too stereotyped when what is at stake is represented by the ill-defined and shifting relationships of some fifty military-political leaders. The idea has great relevance in the earlier stages of the evolution of the military command, and at points of crises, but in itself remains too narrow a platform upon which to place the whole process of higher command. For the space of one military generation the Soviet armed forces operated under a command which lacked a physical unity, due to the presence of influential members of the officer corps of the Imperial Russian

Army within it. That dichotomy, over which furious political and personal struggles raged, requires explanation in terms of frustrated ambitions and private animosities as much as through Party decisions.

In addition, there is one dimension of command which is not a feature of more orthodox military organisation and which demands attention, the Political Administration and the military commissars. Over its origins and early form there is much dispute, and this among Soviet military-political historians also. The Red Army was founded as and remains an avowedly political army, the sword and shield of the Revolution. While the commissar was originally an instrument of control over Red Army officers whose loyalty might be questionable, at an early stage he was enticed by the appeal of command, so that there ensues an elaborate criss-crossing of functions and positions. For the reason that political command within the Soviet armed forces is both complicated in operation and questioned as to its history, more space has been allotted here to an explanation of its general working down to a comparatively low level in the command chain. The device of commissars is not new. The armies of the French Revolution knew them, and a form of commissar or political officer has been introduced into more modern armies. But the role of the Political Administration and the function of the military commissar in the Soviet armed forces can be connected with an awkward dilemma with which the Soviet command is faced even now. The requirements of political reliability and the claims of military efficiency frequently clash. As upon the occasion of the dismissal of Marshal Zhukov in 1957, the Communist Party asserts its claim to be the sole leader and educator of the Soviet armed forces. As will be seen, the problem of control and reliability is not solved when a greater proportion of the members of the Soviet forces are Party members. It is then that the watchers of the watchers come to the fore. Unitary or one-man command, over which many bitter struggles were fought, is hailed as a great achieveinent. The fact that it is not an inevitable feature of a Communist military organisation, for which reason its particular Russian career invites closer inspection, is borne out by the recent criticisms made of this boast by Marshal Chu Teh of the Chinese Communist armed forces.

The military factor in Soviet foreign policy can also be seen through the processes of the command, although with many obscurities as yet unclarified. In so far that a considerable element of the history of the Red Army was determined by the failure of the attempts to achieve a compromise between socialism and militarism, so in the struggle of revolutionary internationalism with Great Russian nationalism bitter dissensions arose among the military and political leaders. The idea of war as a social phenomenon produced special convolutions of theory, planning and organisation. In the contact between the Red Army and the *Reichswehr*, however, the military leadership played a vital and unique role in an arrangement about which the Soviet Union to this day maintains an iron silence. In the Far East, in addition to lending professional help to revolution in China, Soviet senior commanders were faced with a most demanding military task after the Japanese march into Manchuria; a far from unimportant part of these tasks brought the Red Army to the battlegrounds of Lake Khasan and Khalkhin-Gol. For more than a decade after the Civil War the Soviet armed forces suffered from technical deficiencies and backwardness. The strategic aspect of industrialisation lent new features to Soviet military power and added a range of military possibilities, not least an increased defensive capacity. On Voroshilov's admission, no Soviet war plan in the accepted sense had existed before 1927.

While the Red Army, that is the ground forces, enjoyed a hegemony over the naval and air arms which is maintained even now, the development out of technical and professional obscurity of the latter is a matter of considerable interest. Although the Soviet naval command, learning its faith in the submarine from the German Navy, made slower progress, the technical achievement and performance standard of Soviet aviation came to impress contemporary Europe.

The pre-1941 climax in both those services occurred when they ran foul of Stalin's own notions of what ought to constitute an air force and a navy. The havoc wreaked on Soviet aviation in 1941, as well as the reversion by the naval command to the ideas for which their predecessors had been shot, only served to underline the incorrectness of those notions. For the formulation of military doctrine between the end of the Civil War and the military purge, it is possible to draw upon a professional literature of considerable richness, flecked at times with real imaginativeness. Of late Soviet military monographs have been directing more of their attention to these writings and their authors, as the modern Soviet Army attempts to catch up on its past, hitherto almost blotted out but for Stalin's 'military genius'.

Inevitably, any account of a Soviet institution or command group within this period becomes increasingly concerned with Stalin and the consolidation of his power. Perhaps the most intricate item of what was a brutal and tyrannous business was the affair involving the liquidation of almost the entire high command and a large segment of the officer corps, in the years 1937–8. Its murderousness notwithstanding, the purge of the armed forces remains an extraordinary episode in the history of the Red Army and the Soviet state, if for no other reason than Stalin's success in carrying out this dangerous undertaking. In insuring himself and his regime against a threat from the military, potentially real but difficult enough to prove in fact, Stalin visited a terrible weakening on the defensive capacity of the Soviet Union. That instance, together with the total effect of his almost uninhibited personal rule, brought dire results in 1941.

While this book is much indebted to many varied sources, it might perhaps not be invidious to single out Captain N. Galay's writings on Soviet military affairs and Dr Raymond L. Garthoff's invaluable pioneer work on Soviet strategy and military doctrine, which command the attention of the student of Red Army history, Soviet military development and military-political affairs in the Soviet Union. It is as a contribution to the objective enquiry into these matters that the present work is also directed.

A NOTE ON THE SPELLING OF NAMES

Where a generally accepted rendering of a name exists, even as a contravention of the rules of transliteration, this has been employed in order to facilitate recognition (as, for example, with Budenny, Yegorov, Tukhachevsky). Both the accepted and transliterated renderings will be supplied in the index.

ACKNOWLEDGEMENTS

THE bulk of the research for this work was completed during the tenure of a Fellowship at St Antony's College, Oxford, for which I wish to express my appreciation to the Warden and Fellows, and also for the special travel grant made to me by the College for the purpose of collecting material. To Dr Margaret Lambert I owe a special debt for her patient guidance through the intricacies of the captured German documents. I am indebted to Mr D. C. Watt of the London School of Economics and Political Science for furnishing me with items which would have otherwise escaped me. Mr David Footman of St Antony's College, Oxford, kindly placed numerous pieces of his own research into the Civil War period at my disposal, and Dr Alvin D. Coox in Tokyo lent me painstaking assistance in enquiring into the organisation and operations of the Red Army in the Far East. For the opportunity to discuss Soviet military organisation and Soviet military sources, as well as to draw on his first-hand acquaintance with the Soviet armed forces, I am much indebted to Mr J. M. Mackintosh. To Mr L. Schapiro of the London School of Economics and Political Science I owe the considerable profit derived from his written and verbal analysis of Soviet politics as a whole. To Vernon J. Harward Jr., of The City College, New York, go my thanks for his advice and assistance with the proofs. Not least in the scale of valuable assistance comes the efforts of the staff of the libraries and institutions who spared no pains to track down documentary publications and specific editions. I would also wish to thank my wife for placing her knowledge of Russian, and her time and patience at my disposal.

The individuals and institutions named are, however, in no way associated with the views and conclusions incorporated here, for which the responsibility is mine.

J. ERICKSON

October, 1960

INTRODUCTION

All types of arms; such as rifles, machine-guns, armoured cars and the like have to be put at the disposal and under the control of the company and battalion committees and under no circumstances to be issued to the officers, even if they demand them.

Point 5 of *Order No. 1*.

Brothers, we beg you not to obey an order that is meant to destroy us. An offensive is planned. Take no part in it. Our old leaders have no authority now. The papers have said that there should be nowhere an offensive. Our officers want to make an end of us. They are the traitors. They are the internal enemy.

Razlozhenie Armii v 1917 godu.

But everyone knows, Russia and the army remain! In these great and difficult historical moments they need courageous, firm and experienced leadership, which would save them from complete dissolution. Remember those men, who remain at their posts, carrying out their infinitely difficult task, not complicating the situation . . .

General Novitskii to General Dukhonin. Letter, 19th November, 1917.

CHAPTER ONE

The Origins of a New Army

In the revolutionary year 1917, by casting off authority and abandoning discipline, the Imperial Russian Army carried through a mutiny of such vast proportion that no military or political group could either control it or be held responsible for the final disintegration. The Army, Lenin was to observe somewhat cynically, voted with its legs.

During the major upheavals in March 1917, when the Provisional Government and the Petrograd Soviet of Workers and Soldiers Deputies attempted to rule after the Tsar's abdication, the soldiers on the five Russian battlefronts tasted for the first time the hitherto forbidden fruits of political activity and the delights of pressing their various claims. For the majority, this expressed itself only in the crudest manner. The multi-million mass of peasant infantrymen wished to be done with a war which had exacted so fearsome a toll of Russian dead and maimed. Their attention was riveted on the land and their minds possessed with the idea of remaining alive to claim their share of the agrarian spoils. Demoralisation did not come quite so swiftly to the technical units and the artillery men, nor to the troops of the élite battalions who had distinguished themselves in a war which, even with its opening, brought catastrophe. Great Britain and France were now forced to bend their efforts to keep Russia in the war and to hold her to her solemn word, while the German High Command schemed to knock away this weakened link in the *Entente* chain.[1]

The March Revolution had quickly granted the armed forces their charter of personal and political rights with the famous 'Order No. 1'. The Order itself was penned by N. D. Sokolov, surrounded by soldiers 'half-dictating and half-suggesting' the contents.[2] The Order authorised the election in all military units and naval formations of 'committees' drawn from the lower ranks. Representatives to the Petrograd Soviet were also to be chosen by units. Orders issued by the Duma Military Commission were to be obeyed only if they were sanctioned by the Soviet. The elected 'committees' would also assume responsibility for all arms, which were not to be issued to officers. Soldiers henceforth would enjoy all the rights of an ordinary citizen; saluting when off duty was abolished. Officers would no longer enjoy their previous exalted form of address, and rudeness to soldiers was prohibited.[3] Although the product of a considerable provocation, the Order constituted a deadly threat to the authority of the officers. In addition, from this point forth the concealed social struggle leapt into the light of day, so that officers came to be regarded only as 'the land-owner in military uniform'.[4]

All of this had been brought to pass on the streets of Petrograd, beginning on 8th March, when the factory workers had pressed themselves into the ranks of the soldiers, murmuring that brother should not fight with brother. The fraternisation of the numbed soldiers with the impassioned and hungry workers had brought the first Revolution into full flower. The Petrograd garrison had first stared sullenly at the demonstrators, then muttered and mumbled away the chances of bringing them to heel by force. The peasant troops finally went over to the 'internal enemy', the workers. The rank and file of the army accepted the Revolution, looking upon it with some pride as a part of their own accomplishment. The officers were less inclined to do so, placed as they were in an impossible situation. Excesses against officers were not uncommon in the early days of insurrection, although it was the sailors of the Baltic Fleet who displayed an extreme of ferocity, hurling the more detested of their superiors beneath the ice — atrocities which wedded them irrevocably to the party of extremists, the Bolsheviks.

The Provisional Government, as yet only nominally master of the state, sent out its commissars to military units and installations, so that its will might carry some expression. An abortive attempt to undo the damage of 'Order No. 1', by issuing 'Order No. 2', and also confining the sweeping changes to the Petrograd Military District only,[5] did not succeed in bringing about the desired effect. The soldiers would not be brought back under the authority of the officers in this manner. The problem of the front was especially difficult, for here Russian troops began to fraternise with the Germans, holding impromptu 'front-line meetings'. On such occasions, primitive gifts were exchanged, and there were shouts from the Russian lines of 'Germani nicht Feind. Feind hinten.'[6] Although the Russian troops held their positions, opposition to any kind of offensive mounted. As the year advanced, desertion and 'loitering in the rear' assumed vast proportions. Now, as in the earlier days of the war, the infantry sold its military items, including tent canvas which was quickly made up into skirts for village women. A flourishing trade in Army boots existed. In France the Russian brigade on the Western Front raised shouts of 'Down with the war!' and proceeded to elect a soldier-committee as an expression of solidarity with the Revolution at home.[7] As a punishment for mutiny sections of the brigade were transported to North Africa; among them was a Corporal Rodion Malinovskii,* who later made his escape.[8]

* The present Marshal Malinovskii, successor to Zhukov as Soviet Defence Minister.

In many simple minds the opposition to the war stiffened. The soldier-peasants, presenting a monotonous picture huddled in their grey army great-coats at meetings of the Petrograd Soviet, followed avidly the schemes for bringing them land. Land and peace were the outstanding issues. During the early stages of 1917 it was Menshevik and Socialist-Revolutionary propaganda which made its mark on the armed forces. The Bolsheviks, quite belying their name at this time, were a small extremist minority who had been as much surprised by the triumph of the swift and anonymous March Revolution as many other professional revolutionaries who had dreamed of this day. Lenin languished as yet in Switzerland, negotiating his return to Russia in the notorious 'sealed train' arranged by the German General Staff. The latter were anxious to take advantage of any measure which would draw or knock Russia out of the war. Lenin's advocacy of peace favoured him in German eyes. In Petrograd itself a temporary Bolshevik 'Military Commission' had been set up and attached to the Party Central Committee.[9] This 'Commission' boasted three members, plus one representative from each military unit which chose so to be represented.

* * * *

Bolshevik 'Military Organisations' were set up to talk, not to fight. The Bolshevik view circulated among the disaffected or passive soldiers through three main channels, those of organisation, agitation and propaganda.[10] Apart from winning influence in any section willing to listen to them, the Bolsheviks came to aim primarily at neutralising the armed forces, whereby the mass of soldiery would not be used — nor be capable of being used — to effect a thorough-going counter-revolution. As one means of propaganda a soldiers canteen flourished in the editorial premises of the Petrograd *Pravda*, where refreshment and political talks were freely dispensed.[11] In Moscow, soon after the March Revolution, the city Bolshevik Committee organised its own 'Military Bureau', in which some 200 Party members and sympathisers worked among the soldiers of the garrison and units from the Western Front. On the South-western Front the Bolshevik Ensign Krylenko was elected to the Committee of the XIth Army, while units of the Northern Front (centred on Petrograd) fell quickly under pronounced Bolshevik influence.

The Petrograd garrisons stood at the heart of the Revolution. The Northern XIIth Army was looked upon as 'the first line of defence of the proletarian revolution', though the overweening pride on the part of these rough and dirty soldiers at 'their' revolution repelled not a few including Sukhanov himself. The 436th Novoladozhskii Regiment set up a Bolshevik committee with close ties fastened upon Riga, where the Bolsheviks had also opened a soldiers club called 'The IIIrd International'. The Latvian and Siberian Rifle Regiments of the XIIth Army counted for a great deal; numbering about 40,000 men, the Latvian Regiments had organised Bolshevik cells in their reserve units situated in and about Petrograd. In this manner the Latvian riflemen — the future nucleus of the first Bolshevik professional armed force — fell under Bolshevik sway at a relatively early stage of 1917 and passed under actual Bolshevik control as the year advanced.[12] In the great naval base of Kronstadt sailors of the Baltic Fleet formed a naval soviet[13] designated *Tsentrobalt*, from which some 3,000 rebellious sailors set about defying the Provisional Government and harrying the right wing in general. In Sevastopol and Odessa the blue-jackets of the Black Sea Fleet similarly made their presence felt. Nearer to Moscow M. V. Frunze and Myasnikov raised Bolshevik cells among the soldiers of the Western Front. In this welter of committees* and disordered agitation a cavalry sergeant by the name of Budenny found himself elected to the soldiers organisation in his regiment.

The rumours of the circumstances in which Lenin finally arrived in Russia caused a certain patriotic resistance among the soldiers to Bolshevik propaganda as the work of 'German agents'. Nevertheless at the end of June 1917 the Bolsheviks held the first large-scale conference of their military members and organisations; the conference assembled in Petrograd under the name of the 'All-Russian Conference of Front and Rear Military Organisations of the RSDRP(b)'. In all, according to Soviet sources, this conference represented 26,000 Party members among the military or in 'military organisations'.[14] More than that, it was here that the initial thought and preliminary planning which had gone into the business of raising or rallying a force loyal to the Bolsheviks began to show the first results. The conference, while affirming that the Bolsheviks did indeed have adherents in the armed forces, turned to considering the ways and means of armies as a whole, as well as the further work of the 'Military Organisations'. Over the question of standing armies and their relation to the State, the Bolsheviks, as well as other revolutionaries, had decided views. They abhorred the standing army, preferring the armed militia as the definitive type of proletarian military organisation. This expressed not naiveté but the deepest consideration of the military experiences of the proletariat to date — the Paris Commune or insurgent Russia fighting on the streets in 1905–6. It is the

* Major-General Sir A. Knox, the British military observer with the Russian Army, indicates the loss to the army of 'fighting men engaged in talk' with his figures of the membership of the committees of the South-western Front. Front-line, depot and rear units had no less than 84,948 officers and men engaged in this 'talk', so that there is some justification for the category of 'desertion by election' to the committees, as well as a prime illustration of the ramifications of these activities. See General Sir A. Knox, *With the Russian Army, 1914–1917*, Vol. II, pp. 699–700.

very consciousness of the purpose of these June debates which mark them out as a precise step in the Bolshevik ideas of 'their' armed force.

Not merely in theoretical questions but in organisation as a whole the June Conference provides some test of Bolshevik activity. Accepting the Soviet figure of 26,000 Party members, and assuming, as is not unlikely, that this doubled by November 1917, there were some 50,000 active Bolsheviks at work in the armed forces;[15] to off-set this, a one-day census of the army in April 1917 set the strength at over nine million.[16] It is therefore not in numbers but in the purposefulness and intensity of Bolshevik activity that the key to their role in the army must be sought. Out of the June Conference came the 'All-Russian Bureau of Military Organisations', whose members included men soon to be prominent as a preliminary leadership group in the Civil War — Podvoiskii, Krylenko, Nevskii, Kedrov, Cherepanov, Bubnov, Antonov-Ovseenko, Mekhonoshin. The Party's military-political experts were fast learning the business of exploiting the break-down of an army, for Podvoiskii himself made it clear that pressing for 'democratisation' as well as peace hastened that over-all incapacity within the army, which was itself insurance against the army being used to crush the Bolsheviks.

The Russian High Command was also preoccupied with the decline within the army and turned to schemes for the moral and physical regeneration of the Russian troops. By mounting an offensive it was hoped to restore some sense of purpose and discipline into the mass of troops. Kerensky's oratory whipped up a momentary enthusiasm among the soldiers. The Provisional Government would also through these actions be able to carry out Russia's obligations to her allies, themselves about to embark upon great offensive actions on the Western Front. But the Russian offensive, ordered for 29th June, flopped and fizzled away, merely sacrificing the last of the spirited and disciplined troops who acted within the army as the very final barrier to disintegration. Russian soldiers deserted *en masse*. Having taken the first line of trenches, they refused to move on. Soldiers called out to advancing comrades to halt, or else dragged away the field kitchens to prevent others moving up. The commissars of the Provisional Government reported the soldiers, now streaming away from the front, to be '. . . armed and unarmed, in good health and high spirits, certain they will not be punished'.[17] Many took themselves and their arms home, so that the influx of deserters could not but aggravate an already seriously disturbed agrarian situation.

First opposition to the idea of an offensive and then discontent at the subsequent disaster raised fresh disturbances in Petrograd. Lenin's apprehension over the ultimate attitude of the army resulted in the Bolsheviks holding back from an attempted seizure of power during 'the July days'.[18] Bolshevik vacillation and weakness discredited them. The Government rallied, re-imposing the death-sentence in the army and replacing Brusilov by Kornilov as commander-in-chief. The Bolshevik leaders, including Lenin, went into hiding. Punitive action was taken in army units; 900 soldiers of the fractious 'Dvinsk troopers' of the Vth Army were transported to the east.[19] But as General Khlembovskii had earlier observed, it was impossible to lock up the whole army — and even if it were possible, this would not go against their wishes, for the soldiers would at least emerge alive from their penal rigours.

When, however, in the first fortnight in September Kornilov launched and failed to consummate his *coup d'état*, the final breach between the officers and men in the armed forces was sealed. The latter, desperate for peace, looked upon the 'counter-revolutionary' officers as their first enemy. Desertion took another upward swing.[20] Soldiers commandeered trains, ordering the drivers to take them where they wished. More of the Russian Army went home from the war on foot.

The fright over Kornilov helped to raise the political stature of the Bolsheviks. The Petrograd Soviet seized upon the device of 'special defensive measures' to ward off the threats implied in the *coup*, thus setting a precedent for the creation of the 'Military-Revolutionary Committees'. The Bolsheviks in their turn lighted upon these new bodies, hastening the disintegration in the army by brushing away the relatively stable regimental committees and trying to replace them with 'provisional revolutionary committees'. The stampede was quickened with shouts for full 'democratisation' of the army, for full rights to the soldier, for the end of the war. The whole embodied the anguish and desperation of '. . . the huge, weary, shabby and ill-fed mob of angry men'.

Meanwhile in the streets, factories and squares of cities, in the dust and muddle of small towns and villages, the Bolsheviks went about setting up their private army, the Red Guard. During the March Revolution in Petrograd substantial quantities of arms had found their way into various hands. General Kornilov demanded later the return of 40,000 rifles to the plundered arsenals.[21] By the end of March ten per cent of the Petrograd workers had been mobilised to form a militia for 'the defence of the revolution'.[22] The temporary Bolshevik Military Commission soon occupied itself with organising its own small bands, the *Voenki*.[23] Already during the disturbances of 1905–6 Bolshevik 'combat squads' had fought on the streets. At this date, such was the weakness of the Provisional Government, that it could not prevent the formation of what were in effect private proletarian miniature armies. By the end of April 11,000 workers had been enrolled in some kind of para-military unit. In Moscow, in Reval, in the Urals, Red Guard detachments sprang up, or had their counterpart in the 'Fighting Detachments of the People's Militia' (*BONV*).* Numbers, however, were a very uneven guide to the real state of affairs.[24] The distribution of weapons was casual and disorganised. When rifles and revolvers failed to appear, staves and pikes took their place. The raw workers not infrequently needed training in the use of such arms as were available; sympathetic soldiers would impart the rudiments of military training to the men from the factories.

By August there existed a real need to centralise and organise the staffs of the Red Guards in Petrograd. To this end a joint staff, the *Buro Tsentralnoi Komendatury*, came into being; a little later a similar body was set up in Moscow.[25] In the provinces K. Voroshilov laboured on the Lugansk town-committee for 'defence against the counter-revolution'. In Minsk Frunze built up the nucleus of a pro-Bolshevik force. Nevertheless the network remained thin and fragile when viewed against the turbulence at large. The Party questionnaire to delegates to the 2nd Congress of Soviets (held in October) asked, under Item 21, about the formation of Red Guard detachments. Few reported any positive results. More often the answer ran: 'Wanted to organise. No weapons.'[26] In spite of the special Bolshevik attention to the 'Factory committees for munition-plants', which helped to supply arms, there was never an adequate supply. Smuggling and theft added a little to the stocks.

Yet not a few names upon the rolls of the Red Guards were to become famous in the Red Army. On the eve of the rising in Petrograd approximately 20,000 Red Guards — variously armed, if at all — could be mustered.[27] Less than 10,000 stood by in Moscow. Some Chinese, part of the labour imported into Imperial Russia for railway construction, took up their position in the Petrograd and Moscow Bolshevik detachments. In addition to the cosmopolitan touches, not a few rogues, ruffians and adventurers found places in the ranks of 'fighters in the class struggle'.

Riga fell to the advancing German troops in September. The Allied Military Missions continued to press for information about Russia's strengths and weaknesses,† all the while urging her to continue in the war. On the Russian side, mistrust of the Allies appeared frequently in an open and unconcealed form.[28] In France drastic action had been taken against the mutineers of the Russian brigade. In the Far East the Americans and the

* *BONV* forces were not raised by the local soviets but were a fighting force raised and responsible to the Communist Party, that is, the Bolsheviks alone.

† General Verkhovskii, now War Minister, reported the military strength of the Russian Army at the beginning of October to be: 1,500,000 infantry, 500,000 specialists (mostly artillery), 3,500,000 in rear establishments, 2,900,000 engaged on para-military duties, and 1,500,000 in the rear areas as a whole, of whom only 400,000 were fit for any kind of military duty.

Japanese cast frequent and anxious glances at Vladivostok, where disaffection was spreading and where also 662,000 tons of war supplies awaited shipment into European Russia along the Trans-Siberian Railway — a task manifestly beyond the capacity of the railway.[29] The colonies of German and Austro-Hungarian prisoners lodged in the Russian east also gave the Allies cause for acute anxiety.

* * * *

By late October the issue of power was about to be decided in Petrograd, while the Bolsheviks completed many of their preparations for the seizure of power. On 20th October the Petrograd Soviet voted to form a Military-Revolutionary Committee; due to a sharp left swing, many of the soviets throughout Russia gradually slipped out of the hands of the Mensheviks and the Socialist-Revolutionaries and into the grasp of the Bolsheviks. Reports poured into the government about the low morale of the army; the commissars cited the prevailing chaos in supplies and the utter war-weariness.*

The Petrograd Military-Revolutionary Committee, soon a thoroughly Bolshevised instrument, stood out as the head-quarters of insurrection. This body proceeded to send out its own commissars to the Petrograd garrison, a complex operation which was co-ordinated by the special Bureau of Commissars. On 2nd November the actual preparations for the seizure of power were put in hand. On 4th, under the guise of a demonstration the Bolsheviks reviewed their armed man-power in Petrograd. In the Smolny, the girls' finishing school commandeered as Bolshevik head-quarters, a conference of regimental committees agreed that no unit should be sent to the front before the consent of the Petrograd Soviet had been obtained for such a transfer. General Cheremisov, the Northern Front commander, provoked a head-on clash by proposing to do this very thing. The thought of being sent to the front roused the Petrograd garrison to what fury it could muster; six months of 'holiday' in the rear had brought about a considerable decline in spirit. Such a situation did, however, place the garrison in the hands of the insurrectionists, and the Bolshevik commissars proceeded to elbow the last representatives of governmental authority out of the way.

Trotsky, Podvoiskii, Antonov-Ovseenko, Mekhonoshin and Lashevich, together with the commissars in the regiments and in installations, began

* Lieutenant Dolgopolov, Assistant Commissar Vth Army reported deterioration of morale; Richenko, Chairman of the Commissars/126th Division, Special Army, reported disintegration; Alekseyevskii, Commissar to the IVth Army, reported food and clothing supplies bad and morale sinking. The same tone was struck in the reports of Posnikov (IIIrd Army), Grodskii (IInd Army), Tiesenhausen (Rumanian Front), Chekotilo (XIth Army).

to play their appointed parts. By brilliant oratory Trotsky won over the machine-gunners of the vital Peter and Paul fortress. The Military-Revolutionary Committee denounced the government and the General Staff for having 'broken with the Petrograd Soviet'. Colonel Polkovnikov, the Petrograd garrison commander, was warned that his orders would be invalid without the counter-signature of the Military-Revolutionary Committee. The Colonel answered, not unnaturally if a little optimistically, that he was capable of dealing with his own troops. The Government struck back by closing the Bolshevik printing presses and cutting the telephone link with the Smolny. The Bolsheviks responded by calling upon the soldiers of the garrison to re-open the presses and counter-manding the order for the cruiser *Aurora* to put to sea.[30]

At 2 a.m., on 7th November, 1917, the Bolshevik bid for power began in all earnest. The less-spirited members of the garrison were detailed to watch the movements of the officer-training battalions and keep an eye upon the Cossack barracks. Meanwhile telephone exchanges, banks, railway stations and bridges fell with only a scanty show of resistance to the insurgents. In the evening at 9 p.m., the Winter Palace — the seat of government — was assailed by Kronstadt sailors and Red Guards from the Vyborg district of the city; they were covered by the guns of the rebel cruiser *Aurora*. An armoured car company joined in the assault, while the cruiser fired blank-shot to intimidate the defenders. In the closing scene Antonov-Ovseenko arrested the remaining ministers and escorted them through a crowd intent upon lynching them.

To take power in the capital was one thing. To register the victory throughout Russia remained another. Kerensky left for the front, hoping to rally resistance in the Army. Insurrection in Moscow met with sterner resistance; five days of heavy fighting followed upon the first rising.[31] Artillery and armoured car units moved up to the assistance of the Bolsheviks. The Kremlin had to be stormed to clear it of its officer-cadet defenders.[32] Red Guard detachments poured in from the outlying districts, though their operations were hampered by the lack of trained officers. Frunze hurried to help with a force of 500 soldiers under his command. On the morning of 15th November Lenin instructed Podvoiskii of the Petrograd Military-Revolutionary Committee to order Raskol'nikov to proceed to Moscow with his force of Baltic sailors. Finally the insurgents shattered the resistance to them, but not before both sides had incurred heavy losses.

While the fighting flared and finally faded in Moscow, the 2nd Congress of Soviets, which had assembled in Petrograd, tried to give substance to this new Soviet power. As for the force actually at their command the Bolsheviks could count the 3,000 blue-jackets who had been brought into the capital by destroyer as reinforcement for the armed detachments. A further 1,500, with artillery, moved up to Petrograd. The Latvian Rifle Regiments of the Petrograd reserve and a Machine-Gun and Armoured Car force formed the military nucleus of the land 'army'. Otherwise the Red Guards had to bear the brunt of the responsibility, yet they were not real 'military units' either in training or armament. During the fighting at the Pulkovo Heights on 10th November, when General Krasnov tried to break into the city with his Cossacks, 20,000 people had been mobilised to dig trenches and set up defences around the city. Baltic Fleet sailors stiffened the ranks of the armed workmen and finally prevailed over Krasnov's Cossacks.[33]

The sailors were indispensable, and yet at the same time they represented a strange liability to their masters; unlike the soldiers of the Petrograd garrison, who had lounged and talked for six idle months, the sailors itched for a fight, ready to vent their fury on the 'bourgeoisie'. The difficulty lay in imposing even a rudimentary external discipline on these free-booters, inflamed as they were by political phrases and lust for action. They were led by Pavel Efimovich Dybenko, head of *Tsentrobalt*. Dybenko came of a poor family in Chernigorsk; he joined the Party in 1912 and had been one of the ring-leaders of the mutiny on the battleship *Imperator Pavel I* in 1915. Early in 1917 he had occupied himself with organising sailor-squads in Helsingfors.[34]

The new government, having taken the name of the Soviet of People's Commissars, settled to its frenzied work under the chairmanship of Lenin. The decrees on 'immediate peace' and the land question were rushed through. At the same time a Committee for Naval and Military Affairs took over the old Ministry of War.[35] This Committee, composed of three veteran Bolsheviks—Antonov-Ovseenko, Krylenko and Dybenko—became heir to the vast Imperial administrative machine of the War Ministry, which had far to go before it outlived its usefulness to the new incumbents. Antonov-Ovseenko, in addition to his extensive political activities, had enjoyed some military training as an officer-cadet in 1904; by now a specialist in the matters of insurrection, he had now to apply himself to more orthodox military matters. Dybenko represented the navy, while Krylenko — described by Bruce Lockhart as 'an epileptic degenerate'[36]— changed his role as erstwhile Imperial Ensign and agitator on the South-western Front for a brief career as Bolshevik Commander-in-Chief. It was a crude jest. Podvoiskii, another of the Party's military experts, showed remarkable talent; a Party member since 1901, he had been one of the driving forces behind the Red Guards, taken a major part in directing the propaganda to the soldiers and worked on the planning of the seizure of power.

As the new Committee took stock of its position, and the Military-

Revolutionary Committee kept watch on the revolutionary actions unfolding beyond Petrograd, the 2nd Congress of Soviets addressed itself directly to the front. This body requested that 'provisional revolutionary committees' be appointed in the armies, a move which was designed to disrupt the older committees — on which various shades of political opinions were represented — and replace them with Bolshevised groups. To replace the agents of the old government, new commissars stood ready to journey to the units and military installations.[37] Five days after the Petrograd *coup*, the Western Front telegraphed:

> . . . the 21st and 57th Infantry Divisions at combat readiness. Rifles in hand, they stand for the defence of the Soviets at the first call of the Committee. 94th and 75th Siberian Divisions [are] for the rising and the Soviets. . . .[38]

Once again the fronts stirred and trembled with new agitation, but none as yet embodied serious and concerted threats against the new regime.*

Nevertheless the Bolsheviks came face to face with stiff resistance from time to time. In Kiev on 10th November officer-cadets attacked the local Military-Revolutionary Committee, located in the former Imperial Palace; fourteen Bolsheviks, including Yan Gamarnik, N. N. Lebedev and S. Bakinskii were arrested. Two days of heavy fighting ensued in an attempt to restore the Bolshevik fortunes. N. A. Rudnev organised the soldiers of the 30th Regiment in Kharkov into a fighting detachment which co-operated with the local Red Guards. This combined force later linked up with Voroshilov's 'fighting detachments' from Lugansk.[39] Sporadic fighting continued and the first shots were exchanged in what was to become a bitter and protracted civil war. Detachments were surrounded and disarmed, first by one side and then the other. 'Counter-revolutionary' officers found themselves under arrest; strong points and railway links fell into various hands, though the pro-Bolshevik forces managed to retain or recapture numerous key positions. Red and 'White' forces thus played out the first scenes of the Civil War in the Ukraine.

* * * *

The consolidation of Soviet power in the northern and central regions of Russia proceeded throughout the month of November and into December 1917. The army was in no condition to be used against the Bolsheviks. At the end of November 1917 the Chief of Staff of XIIth Army, General Posokhov, reported that '. . . the army just doesn't exist'.[40] At the same

* A not uncommon reaction, although it would be impossible to describe any stand as being typical, was demonstrated by the Army Committee of VIth Army, which demanded an end to the civil war and adopted the slogan: 'Not a single soldier for Kerensky, not one soldier for the Bolsheviks.'

time the XIIth Army held an extraordinary session of the Army Congress, when a new Executive Committee was elected; the new committee had a Bolshevik majority and a Bolshevik president, S. M. Nakhimson. On 19th November General Novitskii, Commander of the XIIth Army, wrote to General Dukhonin, seeking permission to enter into an agreement with the new government. Novitskii wrote that

> I know that many will reproach me for this, but I am taking this step with the deep conviction that such a decision can weaken that anarchy which exists in the army. . . . In view of this I have decided to approach you in the name of the army which was entrusted to me, with a request to conclude an agreement with the new governmental power, so that by setting up a unity of power in the army and the country the difficult consequences, which follow disorganisation in the ranks of the soldiers, will be averted.[41]

From the Vth Army E. Sklyanskii, later to achieve fame as Trotsky's deputy during the Civil War, wrote that they were ready to resist the 'counter-revolutionary elements' gathering about the *Stavka*, Supreme head-quarters.

At the centre of their new-found power the Bolsheviks set about taking over the War Ministry and the existing military machinery. On 27th November Order No. 11 proclaimed that all military schools, together with their personnel, should be taken over for the purposes of the new government.[42] Not only the buildings and administrative machinery fell to their hands, but the Bolsheviks also had at their disposal the vast stocks of war-material which had been delivered by the Allies to Russia through the northern and far eastern ports. Yet mere occupation of the War Ministry did not signify that the threat from the old General Staff had been removed. The generals represented a very definite threat in being,[43] for here in the actual head-quarters was a rallying point for the 'underground' ex-government and for those officers who had been associated with Kornilov in his abortive *coup d'état*.

The Bolsheviks struck first at the Commander-in-Chief, General Dukhonin. Following upon Lenin's Peace Decree, the General was ordered to begin preparations for arranging local armistices with the Germans. Dukhonin refused. In the course of a telephone conversation on the evening of 22nd November, 1917, Dukhonin was relieved of his post.[44] A radio message gave the news of the change of command, informing the soldiers that 'the work of peace is in your hands'. Ensign Krylenko assumed the position of Commander-in-Chief, with a former Imperial officer, M. D. Bonch-Bruevich, as Chief of Staff. Dukhonin remained at the *Stavka* in Moghilev until he could be replaced by his successor.

The heads of the Allied Military Missions present at the *Stavka* questioned Dukhonin about the possibility of a separate Russian peace with Germany, reminding him that Russia had bound herself by treaty not to act in this manner. Trotsky flew at the Allies for this interference in Russia's 'internal affairs', but on neither side did threats mean much at this stage. Krylenko meanwhile advanced steadily if leisurely upon the little town of Moghilev, knotting up the cord of Soviet power as he went, using for this purpose a storm-group of Baltic sailors. The generals failed to rally the army. In Petrograd the Northern Front commander General Cheremisov frustrated the efforts to use the troops against the Bolsheviks. In Minsk General Boldyrev found himself incapable of physical resistance to Krylenko and his murderous sailors; he was placed under arrest. On the Western Front General Baluyev was forced out of his command and his place taken by a lieutenant-colonel. In the *Stavka* hapless efforts were made to rally the forces of a new anti-Bolshevik government. Chernov, the designated head of this body, retired to a couch where he remained, in Chamberlin's words, '. . . lying . . . with a compress on his head.'[45]

The brutal climax came swiftly to Moghilev. The Allied Military Mission left. Krylenko and his sailors arrived as the Moghilev soviet surrendered to the insistent demands of the Left extremists and took over the town. Dukhonin did not flee with the Socialist-Revolutionary leaders who returned to Petrograd, nor would he go with the shock-battalion who did not stay to face the sailors. A mob lynched him, although Krylenko spoke out against harming the general. According to Chamberlin, a burly sailor roused the crowd, who dragged Dukhonin out of the railway carriage, into which he had been taken with Krylenko, and killed him.[46] A 'provisional revolutionary committee' took over the running of the *Stavka*, the occupation of which finally smashed the old army into pieces. From this point on there were only those bitterly hostile anti-Bolshevik senior officers who travelled to the south, there to set about the formation of the Volunteer Army.

The Imperial Russian Army trundled out of existence with its mammoth desertions, its 'democratisations' and stood finally upon the eve of its demobilisation by the Bolsheviks. In the garrisons and the rear at large the insurrectionists' grip tightened slowly but perceptibly. In Voronezh the Bolsheviks and Left S.R.s set up a Military-Revolutionary Committee which took power into its own hands. In Samara a Bolshevik enclave was established by V. V. Kuibyshev and V. K. Blyukher. The latter it was who later developed into one of the outstanding Red military commanders during the Civil War. From Samara, units were smuggled to Chleyabinsk by Blyukher, who hurried his scratch force into railway waggons freely chalked with the words 'Demobilised troops'. These he later employed against the Cossack General Dutov.[47]

On the battle-fronts local armistices heralded the approach of peace negotiations with the Central Powers. The new Soviet government had tried and failed to draw the Allies into general peace negotiations,[48] so that they were obliged to tread the road to Brest-Litovsk alone. Whatever its insurrectionary origin, the new government had to face the responsibilities connected with the armed forces and the defence of the country. On the one hand, because of political tactics and since it could not now be stopped, the process of 'democratisation' was allowed to run its full course. Yet there is evidence that the Bolshevik leaders had already begun to turn their attention to constructive measures aimed at the creation of a new armed force.[49]

On 23rd November, 1917, the decree of gradual demobilisation appeared, declaring that this step would be so administered out of the interests of avoiding the disorganisation of transport and stripping the fronts too precipitately of their holding units. Doing away with the old army in such a formal manner was a necessary step towards organising a new one. At the end of December two further decrees — 'On elective command and the organisation of discipline in the army' and 'On the equalisation of rights among serving soldiers'[50]— were promulgated; both were designed to convince the soldiers that the old order would be completely swept away. By the decree on command, the regimental, battery and squadron commanders were to be elected by the existing committees; higher commands were conferred by the nearest higher committee (division and army). In theory chiefs of staff could not be elected by personnel without 'specialist training', and the same reservation applied to all other specialist staff–doctors, technicians and engineers. The second decree put an end to all Tsarist insignia and distinctive orders, abolished officer-organisations and swept away the decorations awarded by the Imperial Army.

Elections to the command posts took on the aspects of farce, primitive revenges and low cunning. Rejected officers had the right to resign, for upon being stripped of their command they reverted to the ranks. The anti-Bolshevik forces in the south drew not a few embittered recruits from this substantial pool of dismissed officers. Many NCOs were elevated to the lower command positions. The principle of elective command was also applied in the Red Guard, whose members found it much to their taste. Although on the whole elections seem to have been taken seriously, enormous blunders were made. An ensign commanded the 6th Siberian Corps (though, by the same token, a former ensign was now Commander-in-Chief); a corporal reigned as Chief of Staff in the 35th Infantry Division.[51] Politically acceptable and not infrequently competent officers retained their posts. Major-General Novitskii, who had earlier addressed himself to Dukhonin, survived this time of troubles. Colonel Boris Shaposhnikov, who was tinged with a slight radicalism, not only survived but found himself promoted to the command of the Caucasian Grenadier Division with which he served.

These final consequences of a course scored out so deeply by 'Order No. 1' also formed part of the background to the All-Russian Demobilisation Congress which was assembling in Petrograd. Yet the ring of Russia's enemies tightened. In the Ukraine, anti-Russian separatism seized its chances. On a larger scene Lenin and the Central Committee of the Party were cornered between the Germans, who threatened if no peace were concluded, and the Allies, who threatened if it were. German armies stood almost at the threshold of Petrograd and Japanese troops at Russia's Far Eastern gate. Antonov-Ovseenko had already left for the Ukraine with a mixed force of some 7,000 men with the aim of destroying the anti-Bolshevik General Kaledin. With civil war becoming every day a more substantial prospect, the Bolsheviks withdrew from Kiev to the comparative safety of Kharkov, where they set up the 'Ukrainian Soviet government'. This body was duly recognised in Petrograd as the 'proper government' of the Ukraine, but such an exchange of paper rights and courtesies did not dispose of the existence of the *Rada*, the initial Ukrainian nationalist body. This would have to be reduced by force.

Against a darkening backcloth of growing strife and chaos, the Demobilisation Congress set about its work. Fedotoff White declares that shortly after the November revolution Lenin and Trotsky were deep in consideration of the question of reorganising the Russian armed forces. Lenin did indeed take a great interest in the proceedings of the Congress, which was in effect carrying out a vast inquest on the death of the army.[52] The new government also proceeded to a quick modification of the machinery at least nominally handling the affairs of the armed forces. The Collegiate of People's Commissars for Military Affairs replaced the initial Committee for Naval and Military Affairs. The War Ministry (under its new Collegiate name) concerned itself with the demobilisation, dealing at the same time with supply problems and the storage of weapons. Staff organisations continued to function.

The rebuff administered by the Central Powers to Russia's advocacy of a just peace based on 'no annexations and indemnities' caused the idea of a guerrilla or 'revolutionary war' to possess the minds of the members of the Central Committee. Lenin was well aware of the fact that if the army would not fight for Kerensky, it would not do so for him. Yet, as if by way of devious exploration of this idea, he circulated an odd questionnaire to the delegates of the Demobilisation Congress; the final point inquired whether the army (assuming it could vote) would support an immediate peace with drastic annexationist and economic consequences for Russia, or choose to fight the 'revolutionary war'.[53] It is not a little ironic that this should have been asked of a Demobilisation Congress working on the problems of disbanding an army which had been so persistently weakened by Bolshevik propaganda and agitation. 'Revolutionary war', however, gained adherents far beyond the confines of the Central Committee, and became an issue round which much bitter controversy centred.

* * * *

In addition to the work of demobilisation, the Congress began work on the formation of a new 'Socialist Army', in which only proletarians recommended by factory-committees or the affidavit of 'socialist-revolutionary parties' would be enrolled.[54] Here was the root of the short-lived experiment of the volunteer army. In addition, on 19th December, 1917, the All-Russian Collegiate for the Formation of the Red Army was elected and two days later began work at its first session on the principles of the organisation of the Red Army and the programme to be followed by the special Bureau of the Collegiate.[55] A multitude of ideas, however, flourished at this time. Not even the name of the new army had been properly fixed, for contemporary announcements refer to the 'National-Socialist Army', a 'Red Socialist Army' or just an unadorned 'Socialist Army'.[56]

After the confused deliberations of late December 1917 Lenin wrote on 14th–16th January, 1918, to the Demobilisation Congress, assuring the participants that he considered 'the foundation of a socialist army an important question', and one which he believed that the Congress would successfully solve. By early January 1918 a definite programme of agitation designed to produce recruits was already being put into operation. Lenin, however, was not deceived as to the real issue. He saw with singular clarity where the real danger to the Bolsheviks lay in the matter of raising a new fighting force. To rally an army to fight a defensive war against the Germans could not fail at the same time to rally anti-Bolshevik forces throughout Russia. This most pertinent political consideration necessitated a very circumspect approach to the new army.

To add to the confusion, what had been the old *Stavka* and what was now incorporated into the Bolshevik apparatus took its own action to form new units both at the front and in the rear. Northern Front Command Signal No. 2090 of 11th January, 1918, alerted all committees in the army, from platoon upwards, to watch for volunteers for what was called 'the Red Revolutionary Army'. Army and corps commissars must submit reports each Saturday on the progress being made in this matter.[57] Krylenko on 16th January addressed a second directive to the army on the formation of what were called 'National-Socialist Guards', which were to be set up in divisional reserve areas and units lodged near the front. Recruitment was to be on a volunteer basis. In the XIIth Army (Northern Front) this produced the organisation of a 'congress of instructors' for the proposed new Guard, while the front-line newspaper *Okopnaya Pravda* announced the times and places where men might sign up.[58]

Official opinion seemed to waver between holding the present positions with a screen of Red Guards or trusting everything to the creation of a new army. The much publicised 'Declaration of the Rights of the Toiling and Exploited Masses' (17th January, 1917) referred in its fifth paragraph to a 'Socialist Red Army of workers and peasants'.[59] At the 3rd All-Russian Congress of Soviets Lenin argued the case for a 'Socialist army', hinting that Red Guard detachments alone would not suffice. Simultaneously the All-Russian Collegiate for the Formation of the Red Army intensified its activities. Local and regional organs to handle recruitment began to appear. Fighting units were re-formed, supplies and equipment came under stricter supervision.[60] The Collegiate branched out into an organisation-agitation section, and recruiting, outfitting, mobilisation, weapons, supplies, transport, medical and financial departments.[61] On 29th January, 1918, 20 million roubles were put at the disposal of the Collegiate for Red Army affairs.

The retention of the previous administrative machinery had been an act dictated by necessity. In the matter of actual units and formations the Bolsheviks neither planned nor managed to receive substantial elements of the old army into the new. The complete destruction of the old was a necessary prelude to the creation of the new army. Apart from two Latvian brigades and a reserve regiment, only the 436th Novoladozhskii and the 479th Khadnikovskii Regiments passed intact into the Red Army.[62] Nevertheless the Bolsheviks were in urgent need of men, which caused them to cast about for recruits among the prisoners of war held in the Russian interior and to examine that other untapped source of manpower, the Chinese labourers.

On 28th January, 1918, the decree signed by Lenin brought the 'Red Army' into formal existence. The new army was called 'The Workers and Peasants Red Army' (RKKA); no man younger than eighteen was to be enrolled, pay was fifty roubles per month, and a recommendation of true proletarian loyalty was required of prospective entrants.[63] At the date of this decree Cherepanov estimates that the Bolshevik forces — counting Red Guards, 'revolutionary sailors' and troops drawn into the early Red Army units from former Imperial Army units — amounted to 50–60,000 men.[64]

A most prominent feature of the new military system was the emphasis upon decentralisation. In view of the prevailing political and economic conditions this could scarcely have been avoided, yet it also accorded with the make-shift arrangements which were everywhere prevalent. The local soviets took the responsibility for the new units created in their area, hence the flurry of signing up in Moscow, Ivanovo-Voznesensk, Saratov and elsewhere. In the case of men recruited from the ranks of soldiers as yet still not demobilised, responsibility passed to the Army and Corps Committees. In fact the first Red Army units as such formed up near Petrograd from men of the XIIth Army, when on 7th February, 1918, under Order No. 4124/1811 the 437th Sestoretsk and the 9th Siberian Regiments became the 1st and 2nd Red Army Regiments respectively.[65] Commanders were elected and not appointed. The Red regiments had each 3 battalions, 3 platoons to a battalion and 3 sections to a platoon. The platoon consisted of 150 men, giving the regiment 1,350 men. In the rear areas of XIIth Army the creation of other units was hurried along.[66] In the Ist Army 1,606 men signed up with the Red Army on 13th February and 917 from the Vth Army by 18th February. On 15th February a national unit, the 1st Tallin Red Army regiment, was organised, with 12 companies, a machine-gun detachment and light artillery.

The brunt of this decentralised activity fell on the local Military Commissariats which employed three officers. To stimulate recruiting the Red Army Collegiate's agitation section, run by L. M. Kaganovich, sent out 140 administrative assistants and 300 agitators to various parts of Russia. Nevertheless the decision in favour of a regular army, rather than complete reliance upon a militia, reflected an over-riding interest in the defence of the Party and its hold upon the newly-won power. The aim was to ensure that 'the dictatorship of the proletariat' remained a dictatorship. On 24th February Lenin warned the advocates of 'revolutionary war' that they were merely playing into the hands of the bourgeoisie; such phraseology only acted as 'a provocation to the bourgeoisie'.[67] To keep power over the state it was necessary for the Bolsheviks to create their own well-organised army rather than make an *indiscriminate* appeal to workers, peasants and other brands of revolutionaries.

The Russians stood in mortal peril. They had need to defend themselves, for the Central Powers had shown their teeth at the second meeting at Brest-Litovsk. Either the Soviet delegates must accept the dictated terms, or the German army would resume its advance into Russia. In reply to the Soviet tactics of dragging out the negotiations, the Central Powers concluded a separate peace with the Ukrainian *Rada* on 9th February. This ignored the fact that the Bolsheviks had succeeded in driving the *Rada* out of Kiev by force. On 15th the German armies stood ready with 58 divisions and 13 brigades to resume full-scale military operations against Russia. A Bolshevik appeal to the Allies fell on unreceptive ears. As the German columns advanced, Petrograd Radio announced Russia's acceptance of the Central Powers' terms. Bitterly divided, the Central Committee finally voted to sign the peace with its devastating demands upon Russia. On 3rd March, at the signing, Russia surrendered 400,000 square miles of territory and one-third of her population to the Central Powers.[68]

The decree of 21st February ('The Socialist Fatherland is in danger') had evoked no mean response of volunteers to bear arms, a demonstration that the Russians were far from being morally down-at-heel. But the 'volunteer army' proved a failure from the beginning, largely because internal political threats to the Bolshevik regime made a popular appeal politically inexpedient. Such an appeal might have been made on the platform of 'revolutionary war', for which Lenin's opponents in the Party clamoured. Those Bolsheviks who suspected that the military position had been painted in colours more sombre than the facts would justify were slow to see the consequences which would have followed from the 'provocation to the bourgeoisie'; to proclaim a defensive war would have supplied that very 'provocation'.

In the Far East, Japanese troops stood ready for the signal to move into Russia's Maritime Provinces. Already in Siberia White Cossacks had struck at the scattered Bolshevik groups, with the aim of detaching Siberia from European Russia. German troops moved deeper into the Ukraine, where anti-Bolshevik Cossacks harried the flimsy Red units. The latter, caught between the field-grey hammer and the White anvil, broke into scattered and disorganised bands without commanders and without aims save escape. At this juncture Voroshilov decided upon the bold plan of drawing his motley group of fighters away from Lugansk and across the steppes of the Don to the Volga and Tsaritsyn. Overnight, amid scenes of nightmare confusion, Voroshilov became the commanding general of the Vth Ukrainian Army, such as it was.

As one shaky and improvised Red force went to pieces in the Ukraine, while hastily formed and untried Red Army units formed up in Petrograd and at a few points on the Western Front, Trotsky exchanged his post as Commissar for Foreign Affairs for that of Commissar for War. The struggle for the creation of a real army had begun, but the effects of military anarchism still made themselves manifest in the innumerable committees, the elective commanders, the total inadequacy of the volunteer system and the chaotic decentralisation. For many, such a state of affairs represented not military inefficiency but privileges for which they had fought hard and which they intended to retain. They would fight for them against Trotsky's regimentation, but the expansion of the Civil War and the looming shadow of intervention by Russia's former allies made it imperative that definite steps be taken to establish a centralised military machine, that some method be found to unify Red strategy and that a programme to find officers for the Red Army be devised and implemented.

Above all, the new Red Army had to be moulded in absolute subservience to the interests of the Party, so that even by its very composition it should be made to serve the 'dictatorship of the proletariat'. The interests of military efficiency enjoyed an inferior place against this absolute requirement. From the first obscure weeks of its existence, the Workers and Peasants Red Army was primarily a political instrument, destined to serve a specific political cause. Should the army's desire so to serve falter in any way, then it would be pressed into following this path. The Soviet state established as its aim first political reliability and only in second place came the actual efficiency of the military machine, for the former was absolute and the latter only relative. For one of the principal elements of the Red Army, the new officers of the 'command staff' (since the name 'officer' was eschewed), this fundamental bias, dictated by the circumstances of the Bolshevik political requirement, was to have sweeping and ultimately devastating effects.

PART ONE

THE REVOLUTIONARY MILITARY COMMAND, 1918–1920

The most important task in the business of creating the army consists of the training of a new command staff, completely imbued with the ideas of the workers' and peasants' revolution.

Point 10 of the 5th Congress of Soviets (July 1918) resolution on the Red Army.

Partisanism, its vestiges, remnants and survivals, have been the cause of immeasurably greater misfortune, disintegration, defeats, disasters and losses in men and military equipment in our army and the Ukrainian army than all the betrayals of the military experts.

V. I. Lenin, *All out for the fight against Denikin* (1919).

For the good of the work, I need military powers . . . I shall myself, without any formalities, dismiss army commanders and commissars who are ruining the work . . . and, of course, not having a paper from Trotsky is not going to deter me.

J. V. Stalin, letter to V. I. Lenin, 10th July, 1918.

The psychological change-over from the destruction of the old army to the creation of a new one was achieved only at the price of continued friction and conflict.

L. Trotsky (*KVR*, Vol. 1, p. 15).

CHAPTER TWO

The Creation of the Soviet Military Machine

Although the fundamental importance to the Bolshevik leadership of preserving the existence of their dictatorship had precluded the possibility of setting up and organising a national army to fight a defensive war, the same prior claim of self-preservation demanded that the Revolution should be able to defend itself. Within the ranks of the Party leadership itself a bitter struggle raged over the ratification of the peace treaty with the Central Powers.[1] Taking one road of desperation, tentative approaches were made to the *Entente* on the question of their attitude if the Germans resumed hostilities in Russia.

The Red Army had by this time come into nominal existence, while the bulk of what military effort there was followed the strictly decentralised course which Krylenko's directives both suggested and approved. Local soviets conceived grandiose plans for organising their own armed units, formidable paper armies, or else they relapsed into muddle or dilatoriness.[2] Such Red units as did exist, composed usually of enlarged Red Guard detachments sometimes stiffened with sailors, showed alarming weaknesses. In the Ukraine, Petrov's Bolshevik force numbered little more than 1,000 men. In Petrograd, nine battalions of the 1st Army Corps, with a strength of 12,000 men, made up the city garrison. No Red Army units had been organised in Siberia or deep in rural Russia. Where detachments of newly enlisted men were formed, they frequently inflicted substantial damage on the discipline of the few regular units in being, since all the lawlessness of elective command failed to settle.

The search for trained men led into the prisoner-of-war camps. In January 1918 a Prisoner of War Congress held in Samara petitioned that it might be allowed to form Red Army units. From this point forth the Soviet command did not neglect the possibilities for winning recruits to their army from this man-power pool.[3] The result was the formation of the 'International Battalions' of the Red Army, as well as the Chinese Battalion, which drew its recruits from the labour reserve of Chinese in the rear areas. San Fu-Yan's Red detachment formally entered the Red Army in May 1918.[4]

The volunteer basis of the new army produced only an anarchic and badly organised force, drastically short of officers, a body enjoying a holiday from discipline. Plundering and marauding formed a conspicuous part of the activities of these ill-clad, ill-equipped and mutinously-disposed men.[5] The new units not infrequently merged quite haphazardly with the remnants of the old army which were still in existence. Differing notions of how these contingents should be organised produced an odd assortment of establishments. Although Krylenko's directive advised that 150 men should form the basic unit, the Moscow district organisations followed a scheme designed to give them regiments consisting of 3 battalions (with a total strength of 1,200 men). In Baku the choice fell upon the basic unit of 13 men, four such 'thirteens' making up a section with a strength of 53.[6] Many of these units went to man the holding 'screens' (*Zavesy*), the improvised or shakily organised armed detachments used to contain the Germans. The theory was that more substantial forces could be organised behind these provisional defences.

It was in connection with defence against the Germans that the first significant Bolshevik command centre was set up to deal with operational questions. This body was the Supreme Military Soviet, which was set up on 4th March, 1918, in Petrograd by *Sovnarkom* (Soviet of People's Commissars). General Bonch-Bruevich was put in command, with P. P. Prosh'yan* and K. I. Shutko as his commissars.[7] The group was given a much more extensive frame-work at the end of the month, when the staff was made up of the Commissar for War, the Commissar for the Navy, a member of the Collegiate of the Commissariat for Military Affairs, two 'military specialists' and a 'naval specialist'.[8] The term 'specialist', whether military or naval, has a major significance for the early history of the Soviet command at all levels, which the euphemism was designed to hide. The specialists were ex-Imperial officers, who saw no compromise to their martial or political honour in assisting in the defence of their country. Admiral Al'tfater had seen his activity in this light, and there was some justification for it. The 'screens' did provide a way whereby the ex-officers were introduced to Soviet military service, incongruous though it may have seemed, and defence against the Germans secured the services of a number of senior commanders for the regime.

The principal military adviser to the Bolsheviks at this time was Krylenko's Chief of Staff, the ex-Imperial General M. D. Bonch-Bruevich. In the Bureau of the Revolutionary Committee for the Defence of Petrograd, this

* On 18th March, at Ya. M. Sverdlov's suggestion, Left S R P. P. Prosh'yan was excluded from membership and replaced by Podvoiskii. On 10th April, however, Prosh'yan was re-appointed (announced in *Pravda*, No. 76, 16th April). Trotsky had also attempted to have this body re-named the Supreme Soviet for National Defence, but this suggestion was rejected, the date of the decision being given as 19th March, 1918.

ex-Imperial General worked with Sverdlov, M. M. Lashevich (himself an ex-Imperial NCO), Ya. M. Fishman, M. Levin, M. A. Spiridonova and M. S. Uritskii. These in turn collaborated with the Party's military experts, ex-Ensign Krylenko, Podvoiskii, K. A. Mekhonoshin, K. E. Yeremeyev (commander of the Petrograd Military District) and ex-Ensign V. M. Smirnov.[9] Two operational centres, Moscow and Petrograd, acted as the focal points for the 'western' and 'northern' screens, and within these large zones were smaller areas or districts so constituted for ease of administration.

Manning the 'screens' frequently meant nothing more than pushing a rifle into the hands of a Red Guard coming from his factory or work-place, and sending him out with little or no formal training. Of much greater importance was the pressing need to obtain a command and administrative staff for these provisional units. That problem was to be the cause of a protracted struggle, but at least by 10th February, 1918, ten training courses for officers had started to function.[10] In their own way, these first Red officer schools were quite distinctive, but their real importance emerges at a slightly later stage of the problem of officering the Red Army. Between two extremes of the completely haphazard and the attempt at some element of planning, the volunteer army did enjoy one brief moment of success. When the German troops began their advance on Petrograd on 22nd February, recruitment figures leaped up in the capital. The workers hurried to man the improvised units and a hasty mobilisation in Moscow produced an enthusiastic response.

The crisis of arms went side by side with a deepening rift in the Party itself. The 'Left Communists' had emerged during the furious debates on the peace question as the protagonists of the 'revolutionary war', which Lenin so feared as a political peril to the survival of the Bolshevik regime. Bukharin spoke out for a war waged with mobile partisan detachments (which was exactly how the Ukrainian peasants were fighting off the Germans). The guardians of the Socialist conscience hated and feared the idea of a regular military establishment, for this smacked too much of the military instrument of a state-system which they had so recently helped to destroy. At the 7th Party Congress, which met on 6th March, Lenin used the argument that newly-signed peace with the Central Powers gave the Bolsheviks a breathing-space, during which time a sense of discipline might be restored and the masses given some military training. What had now become the 'military question' took on an artificially composed aspect, as Lenin sought at all costs to deflect further conflict, and put the establishment of a regular military system in the category of a temporary measure only. This concession was to recoil upon the Red Army and its command somewhat later. Meanwhile, on 9th March, *Sovnarkom* decreed that Yu.

Danilov, V. Al'tfater and A. Aledogskii — 'experienced and knowledgable military specialists'— should prepare not later than 15th March plans for the organisation of a military centre and army and for the creation of 'a powerful armed force on the principles of a socialist militia' and the general arming of workers and peasants.[11]

None could place great faith in the durability of the Peace of Brest-Litovsk. Bolshevik Russia assumed the cramped and cordoned size of well-nigh the original state of Muscovy. The Bolshevik government removed the capital once more to Moscow, where Trotsky, in his new capacity of People's Commissar for War, set about his tasks. Trotsky's appointment marks a new and drastic approach to the problem of organising the Red Army and turning it into a fighting machine. From his efforts developed the centralised military and political machinery which rammed the Red forces through to victory in the Civil War, and which provided the Red Army with certain basic institutions and attributes.[12] It was an achievement which provoked many vehement protests at the manner of its execution and made many intractable enemies for Trotsky.

* * * *

The new War Commissar had never been the recipient of a formal military education. His professionalism was that of the revolutionary rather than the dedicated or specialist military man. Nevertheless, as he admits himself, he found an absorbing interest in military matters, in the mystique which held men together in the company of arms and in the detail of running an army.[13] It would be unwise to suggest that the absence of a formal military education necessarily implied a totally untutored approach to military matters,[14] or one unacquainted with ways of handling men. Out of the accident of personality Trotsky carried within himself many of the attributes for success in his new assignment. Although arrogant and inclined to over-dramatisation, he displayed a remarkable distaste for the impractical and the unreal, combined with a lashing energy and a ruthlessness which bordered on the fanatic.

He took power when volunteerism had failed at every turn. In Nizhni Novgorod only 174 men signed up. Smolensk mustered 2,000, but in Voronezh recruits found themselves without an officer to command them. Wild confusion prevailed in what purported to be the military administration. Discipline in the field had vanished, and those who tried to restore it often took their lives in their hands. Local Soviets hoarded for their own particular use every scrap of military equipment they could find. And all over Russia the Bolsheviks scrabbled for men.

In the two months of April and May 1918 a stream of decrees set in motion the first machinery which was to transform the Red Army into a substantial, cohesive and regular military force. Endangered by weakness, when the Soviet republic lay exposed to its enemies at the end of March 1918, Trotsky played with the idea of seeking Allied military help to re-organise the Russian armed forces.[15] Aware that the peace would not last, it was therefore reasonable to suggest that British and French instructors should lend their assistance in re-forming the forces which would contain the Germans. In the Far East, the Japanese were ready to advance into the Russian lands at the first opportunity. 'Intervention by invitation', however, passed away as a hope but briefly entertained, and with it went all idea of Allied instructors and technical assistance being used to re-build the army.

The great storm of the Civil War, which had already partly broken over Russia, was finally unleashed, not by the immediate machinations of the 'Imperialists', but by Trotsky's own precipitate action in dealing with a body of men which the war had cast into east-central Russia. Here the Czechoslovak Legion, former prisoners of war and some 50,000 strong, struggled with the amazing scheme to make its way home via Siberia and Vladivostok. In the spring of 1918, thanks to its discipline and its fighting spirit, the Legion represented the most formidable fighting force in the whole of Russia. By May 1918 as a consequence of involved agreements with many parties, Czech troops were strung out at various points along the Trans-Siberian Railway. On 25th May Trotsky directed that these Czech troops should be disarmed. At this signal breach of faith the Legion faced no alternative but to submit, or to fight its way out of the situation, declaring simultaneously its enmity towards the Soviet regime.[16] Round this tightly-knit body of sorely-tried men, who for the moment retained the full exercise of military efficiency, the Civil War blazed up as the anti-Bolshevik White forces in Siberia gathered at this juncture to seize their chance also.

Throughout this critical period the first effects of Trotsky's re-organisation made their appearance, bringing a new and coherent policy for the entire military administration, man-power, the supply of officers and the enlistment of NCO's. From the beginning Trotsky had persuaded himself that nothing could be really accomplished without calling in the professional military men; the decision of 9th March had marked a deliberate step in this fateful direction. He further disassociated himself from the ruinous and extremist propaganda which had worked such havoc in the ranks of the Imperial Russian Army. Nor was Trotsky prepared to tolerate the anarchy which existed in the lower levels of the military-administrative system.[17] The early decisions of March 1918 marked out the vital processes of re-creating the Red Army, even after such a short period of life, and must have been made with Trotsky's full cognisance, if not at his insistence.

To remedy the administrative chaos the decree of 8th April, 1918, set up standardised Military Commissariats, organised at the various administrative levels throughout the territory under Soviet control. Commissariats were to follow the distribution of *Okrug* (region, corresponding to the Military District), *Guberniya* (province), *Uyezd* (district), *Volost'* (small rural township) and urban commissariats. According to the Instruction of 8th April, they were to be manned by two military commissars and a 'military specialist'. The commissariats were linked in a chain of command corresponding to their distribution and connected with the local Soviets at their respective levels. The local authorities were invested with the right to promote the candidature of one of the posts for military commissar and for the post of military director in the existing commissariat.[18] The speed with which these bodies were organised varied greatly, with more rapid progress being made at the upper levels than in the depths of the country. The standard of efficiency also was far from uniform, and the severe criticism which was levelled at the Petrograd Military Commissariat suggests that if a hopelessly disorganised state of affairs could exist in a major centre, then deep in the country literally anything could choose to happen — or not to happen. These commissariats at the lowest level were organised without fixed establishment and very much in the light of local conditions.

As for the organisation of military units, at the end of April the principle of elective command went on to the rubbish heap, although in practice a number of units retained it until the end of 1918. Command appointments henceforth rested with the appropriate military bodies. What is more remarkable, however, is that the elective principle crept back into the Red Army through the strangest and most unlikely crevice of all, provoking a new crisis in 1919. To one further April decree Trotsky himself attached the greatest importance, namely the measure which introduced compulsory training for the 'toiling masses'. On 22nd April, the All-Russian Central Executive Committee adopted at Trotsky's persuasion a resolution which prescribed military instruction for school-children, 'preparatory or pre-military service training' for youths of 16–18 years of age, and compulsory training for all males between 18 and 40 years.[19] Not less than twelve hours of instruction, spread over eight weeks, were to be given. In this way trained reserves could be prepared on a very large scale.

The man-power situation demanded in its turn a reversal of the existing policy. Trotsky vehemently defended the 'class composition' of the Red Army, under which arms were placed only in the hands of true proletarian elements, workers and poor peasants (that is, those employing no hired labour). This was all very orthodox, a product of necessity as well as a means to coercion. But the failure of the volunteer experiment meant introducing organised mobilisation.[20] The first phase of this remained, however, only a partial and selective mobilisation. On 29th May, the Central Executive Committee decreed the formal transition from a volunteer army to one of mobilisation among 'workers and poor peasants', a step dictated by the pressing need to fight 'internal and external counter-revolution' and famine, the latter dubbed 'the struggle for bread'.[21] Trotsky had his own mobilisation plan for the 'toiling masses' introduced on 26th June. While adhering very firmly to the notion of a distinctly proletarian composition for the Red Army, he did not mean that the regime would permit 'the bourgeoisie' to escape from some form of service. Corresponding 'bourgeois' age-groups were liable for mobilisation for labour service, an astute if vicious propaganda move, which produced more personal misery and dislocation than it brought efficient labour-battalions into existence.

On 12th June *Sovnarkom* decreed the mobilisation of the workers and poor peasants in the Pri-Volga, Urals and Siberian Military Districts (those immediately threatened by armed anti-Bolsheviks).[22] Separate decisions of 17th and 19th June, 1918, mobilised the Moscow and Petrograd workers, a partial call-up which paved the way for the full mobilisation of the 1893–7 age-classes. Soviet sources tend to considerable exaggeration in estimating the strength of the Red Army in the summer of 1918. Movchin, in the official history of the Civil War, admits that the first drive for volunteers produced only a limited response; by 10th May, 1918, the Red Army numbered 306,000 men drawn mostly from the urban proletariat.[23] Recently Shatagin has set these figures at 263,780 on 20th May and 362,435 by 1st July — not including Red Guards and partisans.[24]

Superficially impressive, these statistics do not accord with the situation at large, for *trained* men counted for the real strength of the armed forces. The acute shortage of these would account for the acquisitive eyes cast upon the Czech Legion, and the high priority for prisoner-of-war recruitment. Using this yard-stick, the Soviet regime in the early summer of 1918 did not command more than 50,000 trained men (excluding parts of the old army as yet still held in the 'screens'). This was the hard core of the Red Army upon which the subsequent expansions were made. The peasants were not interested in fighting; only the youth, unacquainted with war, provided willing recruits.

Providing the men did not solve the problem of officers. Trotsky's officer-policy set him upon a course destined to bring him into violent collision with a large part of the Party rank and file, as well as provoking clashes higher up the scale. The Commissar for War resolved to bring back the ex-Imperial officers — in the guise of 'military specialists' — to man the command positions in the Red Army.[25] The very name 'officer' evoked feelings of hostility and resistance on the part of the soldiers, Bolshevik and non-Bolshevik alike. The disorders of 1917 had eroded the sense of discipline, and once authority had fallen to pieces it was mocked, degraded and frittered away by the anarchistic dealings in 'elective command'. Between the Bolsheviks and the ex-officers not a shred of mutual respect remained, for the former identified the Tsarist officers with the old regime and the latter regarded the Bolsheviks as hired enemy agents and the instigators of the destruction of the old army.

The genealogy of the Soviet officer-corps cannot be traced without reference to the Imperial Russian officer-corps. The latter did not by any means present a united front. Lacking social homogeneity, in its structure the officer-corps had divided itself into the intellectual officers, the personnel of the General Staff and the field officers of diverse and often humble social background. The war-time officers represented an even greater social diversity, and the sense of division was accentuated by the discriminations practised against them as 'hostilities only' officers by the career men. The break widened in 1917 when the new officers played politics or intervened in the political movements in the Army. Already a few ex-Imperial officers had worked with the Bolsheviks in running the 'screens', and while this may have prepared them for later co-operation during the Civil War, this preliminary phase was on a very small numerical scale.

In addition Trotsky formulated a variation on his 'military specialist' policy which included the ex-NCOs of the Imperial Army; in these men he espied the future personnel of the Soviet officer-corps as such.[26] The average NCOs conformed more closely to the required class qualification of the Red Army, since they were often of very humble origin and yet skilled in the military arts and practised in command. Budenny, the future Soviet cavalry commander, had been an NCO in the Imperial Army, learning his trade during the Russo-Japanese War. The special inducement of being promoted into junior command positions openly appealed to these men, and Trotsky, unabashed, held this out to them.

The recognition of the seriousness of the command problem had occurred at an earlier stage, when it had been critical even under the volunteer system. For the supply and training of 'Red commanders' an Instruction of 10th February, 1918, laid down the first principles, prescribing four months of 'preparatory training' (three months for specialists). The candidates undertook to remain in the army for not less than one year upon completion of their course. The Red 'candidate-commander' should be able to read and write fluently, have a knowledge of arithmetic which covered addition, subtraction, multiplication and division. The curriculum for 'preparatory training' included the Russian language, arithmetic, geometry, history and hygiene. The specialist groups studied tactics, fortification, artillery, military topography and administration, as well as drill. A commissar nominated by the Main Directorate of Military Education supervised the administrative and political side of the pupils' life.[27]

Over the burning question of the 'military specialists', Trotsky could command very precise arguments. The April plan for the Red Army envisaged 30 divisions, a figure expanded in May to 88; 28 first-line divisions would be raised first, followed by two groups of 30 of the second line. It was calculated that each infantry division would need 600 officers as command staff (88 divisions absorbing 52,800 officers).[28] Even the preliminary first-line divisions would require a minimum of 16,800 officers and the likelihood was that 18,000 would be needed. In the summer of 1918, the All-Russian Supreme Staff worked out the estimated requirement of the Red Army in officers as 55,000.[29] In spite of the statistics (which were worked out by ex-Imperial officers), Trotsky's opponents also mustered arguments of by no means negligible weight.[30] Apart from being *a priori* class enemies of a most dangerous brand, already some of the ex-Imperial officers had dealt out treason and conspiracy to the Soviet regime. An ex-Imperial lieutenant had incited the Destroyer Division of the Baltic Fleet to mutiny. On the Eastern Front, where the very existence of the regime was at stake, senior ex-officers holding responsible positions had betrayed these trusts. Even Trotsky felt the tremors of the lack of support, and threatened the ex-officers with reprisals against their families if they betrayed the strange confidence which was thrust upon them.[31]

Notwithstanding the grave risks and the excited outcry, after bringing the decision before *Sovnarkom* on 29th July, 1918, Trotsky began his general mobilisation of ex-officers with Order No. 228. By the end of November 1918, 22,315 such men had entered the Red Army. With similar orders 128,168 ex-NCOs were mobilised, as well as 2,409 of the former military-administrative personnel, whose offices had been commandeered in 1917.[32] Now it was the turn of their very persons. With doctors, veterinary surgeons and auxiliary medical personnel, the first great mobilisation of ex-Imperial command and administrative staff brought — including the NCOs — 165,113 men to the Red colours.[33] For the period of the Civil War, from 12th June, 1918, to 15th August, 1920, no fewer than 48,409 ex-officers were taken into the Red Army, with 10,339 of the military-administrative staff and 214,717 ex-NCOs.[34]

By stark comparison, in 1918 the command courses for 'Red commanders' passed out 1,753 qualified candidates (43·3 per cent infantry). For the period 1918–20 a grand total of 39,914 'Red commanders' proceeded to the Red Army. Their total did not meet even the number of ex-officers,[35] leaving aside any qualitative comparisons. By December 1920 the command staff of the Red Army numbered 130,932, to which must be added 315,797 of the military-administrative staff. The total strength gained by conscripting the 'specialists' (including doctors) amounted to 314,180 — a mighty percentage of the 446,729 command and administrative staff of the Red Army at the close of the Civil War.[36]

The quantitive argument alone justified Trotsky's policy. Yet the very fact of being right did not diminish the vigorous opposition to Trotsky for bringing back 'the old men'. Lenin showed visible surprise on being told by Trotsky that more than 30,000 ex-officers now served with the Red Army.[37] This was Trotsky's reply to his opponents' attempt to make political capital out of the undeniable but thinly-spread cases of treason and conspiracy.[38]

* * * *

The setting up of machinery to unify the strategic direction of the Civil War roused a no less fervid resistance. The Soviet defence effort had been originally vested in a variety of bodies — the All-Russian Collegiate for the Formation of the Red Army, the Main Directorate of the General Staff, the Supreme Military Soviet and the Commissariat for Military Education. In May a new body, the All-Russian Supreme Staff, was organised, with a chief of staff and two commissars at its head; its role was primarily one of planning and co-ordination, a task which increased as the Civil War fronts emerged and expanded. Already by 4th May, 1918, the territory under Soviet control was divided into Military Districts which had been suggested in the first place by the general divisions of areas for the 'screens'. The new districts consisted of the Northern Commune (White Sea)* Yaroslavl, Moscow, Orlov, Pri-Volga and the Urals.[39]

Uniting the various commissariats into a single People's Commissariat for Military Affairs was the logical outcome of the very considerable extension of the work imposed upon the departments by the stress of widening war. Decreed on 19th August, 1918, the new commissariat had sections for recruiting, administration, training, arms, and the supervision of the training of reserves.[40] The most far-reaching innovation, however,

* On 8th April, 1918, A. A. Samoilo was appointed chief of staff to the White Sea Military District, arriving at Archangel towards the end of May. At the end of June, Samoilo became commander of land and naval forces, with R. Kulikov as his commissar, and Rear-Admiral Ya. E. Vikorist as flotilla commander. M. S. Kedrov had earlier been despatched at the head of a forty-man commission (with 33 Latvian riflemen) to supervise the affairs of the Archangel district. Allied fears for Murmansk led to the landing, early in March, of a small party of Royal Marines; a joint Anglo-American expedition later took part in what George F. Kennan has called 'one of the most futile and luckless of military undertakings'. Any idea of linking up the Siberian with the northern anti-Bolshevik front was doomed to failure. See George F. Kennan, *The Decision to Intervene*, Ch. II, Ch. XI and Ch. XVI. M. S. Kedrov wrote up his side in *Bez bol'shevistskovo rukovodstva* (Iz istorii interventsii na Severe), Leningrad 1930.

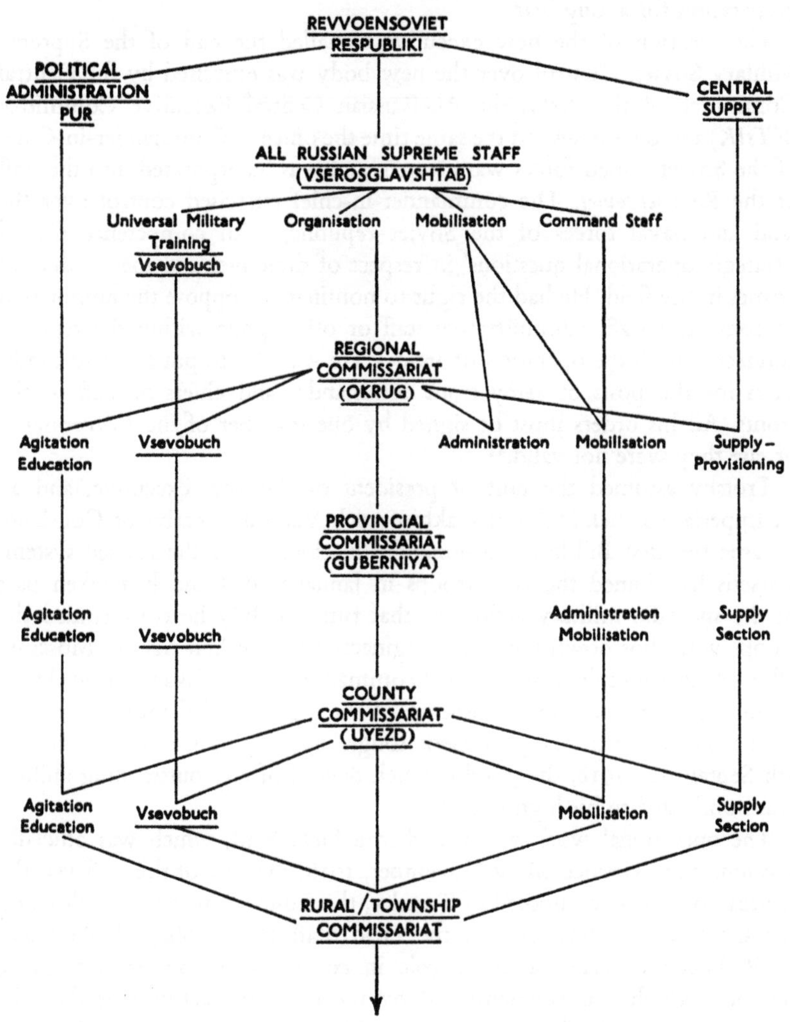
MILITARY-ADMINISTRATIVE-SUPPLY ORGANISATION: CIVIL WAR
REVVOENSOVIET
RESPUBLIKI
POLITICAL
ADMINISTRATION
PUR
CENTRAL
SUPPLY
ALL RUSSIAN SUPREME STAFF
(VSEROSGLAVSHTAB)
Universal Military
Training
Vsevobuch
Organisation
Mobilisation
Command Staff
REGIONAL
COMMISSARIAT
(OKRUG)
Agitation
Education
Vsevobuch
Administration
Mobilisation
Supply-
Provisioning
PROVINCIAL
COMMISSARIAT
(GUBERNIYA)
Agitation
Education
Vsevobuch
Administration
Mobilisation
Supply
Section
COUNTY
COMMISSARIAT
(UYEZD)
Agitation
Education
Vsevobuch
Mobilisation
Supply
Section
RURAL/TOWNSHIP
COMMISSARIAT

came with the formation of a central military executive, the *Revvoensoviet Respubliki* (Revolutionary Military Council of the Republic)* which started upon its momentous career on 6th September, 1918, following on the announcement of the Soviet Republic as 'an armed camp'. This signalled preparation for a long war.

The creation of the new executive signalled the end of the Supreme Military Soviet. Control over the new body was exercised by the Central Committee of the Party, the All-Russian Central Executive Committee (*VTsIK*) and *Sovnarkom*. At the same time the office of Commander-in-Chief of the Soviet armed forces was created, and was incorporated into the staff of the *Revvoensoviet*. The commander-in-chief exercised control over the land and naval forces of the Soviet republic, with competence for all 'strategic-operational questions' in respect of directives and the conduct of armies in the field. He had the right to nominate or oppose the nomination of command staff, administrative staff or other posts within the republic connected with the operation of armies. He was also to put forward candidates for the posts of army front commander and chiefs of staff of the fronts. All his orders must be signed by one member of the *Revvoensoviet* or else they were not valid.[41]

Trotsky assumed the post of president of the new executive, and an ex-Imperial colonel, Ioakhim Ioakhimovich Vatsetis, a native of Courland, became the first Bolshevik commander-in-chief under the revised system. Vatsetis had joined the Red troops in January 1918 and had taken part in the sporadic military actions at that time. In July he commanded the troops who shot down the rising engineered by the Left SRs in Moscow, after which triumph he was named commander of the Eastern Front. Here, raising the Vth Red army (consisting of three divisions) from the remnants of the old Siberian Army, Vatsetis fought against the Czech Legion. On 4th September, 1918, the good colonel, devoid of any outstanding ability, was nominated to his high post.[42]

The operational work was vested in a Field Staff, which was officially brought into existence on 1st November, 1918; the core of this staff was the 'Bureau of Three' composed of Trotsky, the trusted commissar Aralov and the Commander-in-Chief. On the Field Staff B. M. Shaposhnikov and P. P. Lebedev played a major role in co-ordinating Soviet strategy, a function which was supplemented by the extensive activity of the All-Russian Supreme Staff — also under the firm hand of the senior ex-Imperial officer General A. A. Svechin. The Supreme Staff concerned itself with

* Translated as the Revolutionary Military Council or the Revolutionary War Council. The abbreviated form *Revvoensoviet* has been here retained, in the same way that there has been no substitution of 'council' for 'soviet'.

ORGANISATION OF THE ALL-RUSSIAN SUPREME STAFF (VSEROSGLAVSHTAB)

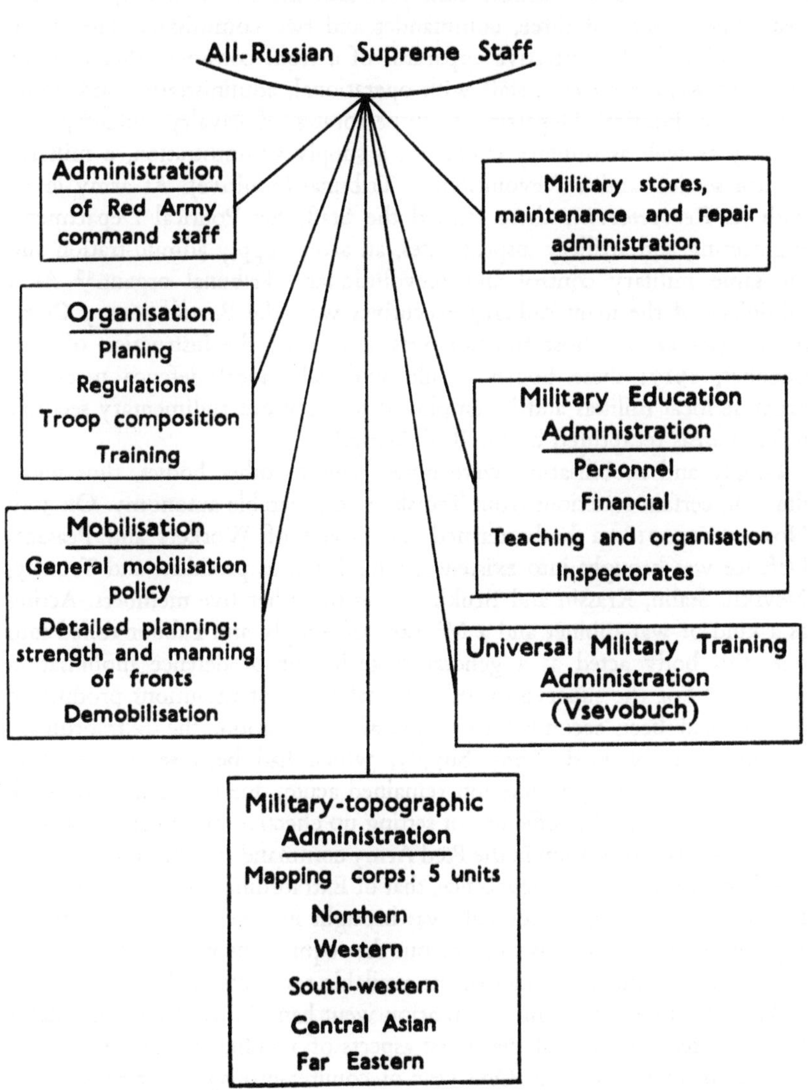

general defence matters, recruiting, the manning of the fronts and military training (including *Vsevobuch*). To complete the chain of command the same pattern of the military executive was transferred downwards to front and army level. Fronts and armies each possessed the *Revvoensoviet*, with the basic membership of three, commander and two commissars. The entire command and administrative apparatus of a front consisted, therefore, of the front *Revvoensoviet*, a staff with operational, administrative and signal sections, a Political Department, Inspectorates of cavalry, infantry and artillery as well as military engineers, a supply administration, a military control section and a Revolutionary Tribunal (punitive). At army level, with its *Revvoensoviet*, there existed the Staff, the Political Department, engineering and artillery inspectorates, an army supply administration and the same military control and Revolutionary Tribunal organs.[43] As a subsidiary of the main military executives were the Revolutionary Committees (*Revkom*), whose function was defined by the Instruction of 24th October, 1917; these bodies would undertake local defence measures, organise local militias and be employed to carry out rudimentary security tasks in areas recaptured by the Red Army.[44]

Supply and mobilisation were given over to other bodies, thus withdrawing certain functions from Trotsky's considerable autonomy. On 30th November, 1918, a body termed the Soviet of Workers and Peasants Defence was brought into existence, with Lenin as president and Trotsky, Nevskii, Stalin, Krassin and Brukhanov as the other five members. Acting as a kind of war-cabinet and a Ministry of Supply and Labour rolled into one, this body acted as a general co-ordinator of defence mobilisation policies.[45] For the supervision of the vital work of munitions production Krassin had been seconded to a special organisation, the Extraordinary Commission for Red Army Supply, which had been set up on 10th November. The supply question remained acute, due to the disastrous fall in production and the difficulty of setting up effective machinery; not until 1924–5 was this confusion in the Red Army command system more precisely regulated. In July 1919 a new office, that of Extraordinary Plenipotentiary of the Red Army Supply Council, was brought into being and entrusted to Rykov, whose task it was to carry out the requisitions which were nothing short of an organised plunder of the available resources of the country.

Trotsky's innovations in organisation went hand in hand with an intense policy to reduce some of the worst aspects of a military anarchism which was far from vanquished. One year of counter-propaganda against being 'partisan-minded' — *partizanshchina* — failed to still the opposition to these new-fangled Moscow innovations.[46] Trotsky adopted the slogan of 'Exhortation, organisation and reprisals' to bring a sense of cohesion and reality into the Red Army. More often than not reprisals played the greater and more effective role, with Trotsky ostentatiously placing 'the death-penalty in the arsenal',[47] arguing that an army cannot be built without reprisals. In a printed order he promised the retribution of shooting for the commissar and the commander of any unit which retreated without orders.[48] Thus, when the 4th Lettish Regiment refused to go into action — this was mutiny in a trusted Red regiment — two members of the regimental Party collective went before the Revolutionary Tribunal. In a notorious case Trotsky personally intervened when a unit of Petrograd workers seized a steamer and ordered it to take them to Nizhni-Novgorod; an improvised gun-boat intercepted the deserters, who offered no resistance.[49] Trotsky instituted a field tribunal which passed sentence of death upon the commander, the commissar and every tenth man.[50]

None of this, or indeed the whole policy, passed without violent criticism, and part of the history of the formative stage of the Soviet military machine is the appearance of a sustained and altogether highly vocal opposition to Trotsky. There was undoubtedly an opposition to the prevailing policy based on first principles, to which was added the dissensions of men seeking to attack Trotsky himself. The left-wing Utopian Communists had already demanded a military organisation more suited to the requirements laid down by Socialist principles. During 1918 Trotsky had defined their position and subsequent defiance as having centred upon a defence of elective command, hatred of the 'military specialists' and distaste for the policy of centralisation.[51] The dispute also reached into the matters of military theory. 'Positional warfare' was conducted by regular orthodox armies, such as were possessed by capitalist states; the Revolution needed to fight its war with small, mobile independent detachments combining various arms. So ran one argument. Trotsky swept this aside as being merely '. . . the idealisation of our weakness'.[52] He showed the greatest impatience with theoretical speculation when the actual task was to defeat the White armies in the field; he bluntly stated that if anyone cared to consider the business of teaching men how to wind on their puttees, keep their rifles clean and grease their boots as 'military doctrine', they were welcome to do so.[53]

On the other hand, excessive opposition to the 'military specialists', manifested by handling them roughly, could seriously prejudice the operation of Trotsky's policy. Stalin lashed out repeatedly and insolently over the ex-officers. Running what amounted to a private war in Tsaritsyn in the company of Voroshilov, Stalin embodied the opposition at the front.

Sent originally upon a mission to organise food supplies for the centre, Stalin telegraphed to Lenin on 7th July, 1918, blaming the breakdown of rail communications upon '. . . our military "specialists" (*Cobblers!*)'.[54] The

Tsaritsyn group simply refused to comply with the new method introduced by Trotsky; on 5th October he managed to obtain the recall of Stalin,[55] at the same time threatening Voroshilov and Minin with court-martial unless they followed regular procedure over reconnaissance and battle reports. It is quite plain that Trotsky had formed a low opinion of Voroshilov's military ability, and on 14th December, 1918, he had him transferred to the Ukraine.

Nevertheless, although this was perhaps an extreme example, feeling against the ex-officers ran high. In his life of Chapayev, the brilliant partisan commander, Commissar Furmanov described Chapayev muttering under his breath about the old officers — 'Have a chair, please, General . . .' — for the man who had formerly kept him standing in the frost for twenty-four hours.[56] On the Northern Front Red regiments shot their new officers, with the result that capable Red privates or NCOs took over effective command and the ex-officers were withdrawn. Trotsky made few friends by suggesting that the complaints against the ex-officers frequently hid incompetence on the part of Communists themselves — 'frustrated Red "marshals" ' — not even knowing their own jobs but propounding some witless theory which failed to work. Trotsky therefore turned over to his critics some regiments to organise as they saw fit; by their ultimately adopting the War Commissar's own methods, his point was vindicated. Yet, in the long run, this early discontent was to have a considerable effect upon the Soviet command.

* * * *

The purely operational command system was only one aspect of the structure which developed during the Civil War. Control of the widely differing and often deeply antagonistic elements was the vital issue. Even a brief survey of the whole scene would suggest the necessity for strict control; an ex-Imperial colonel and a dedicated revolutionary held command over a command staff, the overwhelming majority of which came from the derided and detested 'officer class'. The vitally important 'class composition' of the new army rested on the resilience and loyalty of a comparatively weak industrial proletariat, which, in turn, would finally lead the peasants, without whose man-power preponderance the main army could not be formed. Between the ex-officers and the ex-NCOs of the former Imperial Russian Army, now in Soviet service, there existed a certain inevitable professional rivalry over promotion, as the latter were ushered into junior command posts. Control was exercised indirectly by the selective recruitment and the avoidance of any kind of national army, that is, a Russian army. This is how Trotsky distinguished the Red Army and the Imperial Russian

Army — alike in many of their features, but set apart by the difference in their political aims. However, the agency of positive control, setting thereby the ground-work for a second great command chain, was provided by the Bolshevik Military Commissar.[57]

The commissar, a term apparently produced by Menshevik Braunstein in March 1917, played a vital part in army politics under the Provisional Government.[58] The Bolsheviks freely availed themselves of this device of personalised control both during and after the seizure of power.[59] After November 1917 the functions of the commissar do not seem to have been made at all clear. Commissars there certainly were, taking part in the varied 'political activities' and the spate of army congresses. The first deliberate direction of the commissars came with the setting up of the Organisation-Agitation Bureau of the Collegiate for the Formation of the Red Army on 7th February, 1918.[60] The bulk of the work consisted of sending out agitators to help in the recruiting drive for the Red Army, for which a special course trained commissars in agitation techniques, taking 150 men at a time.[61]

The commissars acted as the supervisors of the 'military specialists', guarding against treasonable activity, but in this capacity they were assuming the status of agents of the government and not representatives of the Party. Nevertheless, in this supervisory capacity, they conformed even at this early date to Trotsky's subsequent picture of the 'military specialist' flanked to left and right by two commissars with revolvers in their hands. Clearly, then, supervision of a politically unreliable command staff must be connected with the first phase of the commissars' place in the Red Army. Counter-signature of orders introduced strict 'dual command', whereby the ex-officer took the responsibility for the military-operational work, and the commissar for its revolutionary probity, but without the warrant to interfere in operational matters.

On 3rd April, 1918, the All-Russian Bureau of Military Commissars was set up and began to function five days later. The Organisation-Agitation section of the Red Army Collegiate remained the same, but was attached to the new Bureau of Commissars (*Vseburovoenkom*). Soviet military historians did and still do dispute the origin of the military commissar as he emerged during the Civil War, and whether he owed his lineage to the early section of the Red Army Collegiate or to the Bureau of Commissars.[62] The question is much complicated by the fact that on 2nd May, 1918, the presidium of the *VTsIK* brought out a decree authorising the creation of an All-Russian Agitational Bureau of the Red Army attached to the *VTsIK*;[63] this meant that commissars were to be centrally appointed and might now perhaps be regarded as more than government agents. As to the person of the commissar, however, the resolution of the 5th Congress of Soviets referred to him only as an 'unimpeachable revolutionary' — not specifically a Party member. Yet when the commissar became the direct representative of the Party in the armed forces, this presumably demanded that he be a Party man. The actual practice contradicts this, for, of 500 commissars sent out from 1st July to 10th October, 1918, 300 were Communists, 93 Communist 'sympathisers', 35 Left SRs, 3 'Internationalists', 1 Anarchist, 1 SR-Maximalist and 68 belonged to no party whatsoever.[64]

Political activity and its organisation seem to have hurried far ahead of any authorisation or regulation. Red Army men in the summer of 1918 were not in the habit of waiting for decrees, and the political temper, fanned by many months of congresses, meetings and agitation, remained hysterically high. In July 1918 Political Sections were in existence in armies and at the fronts, that is, several months before their actual authorisation. In mid-January 1919 Political Sections at divisional level were organised and it was these bodies which carried the brunt of the political work during the Civil War.

Once again it was a cardinal point of Trotsky's policy to knit up these diverse powers and functions into a more effective centralised organisation. The Republic *Revvoensoviet* had its own Political Department, but there was still a great deal of diffusion of office in the matter of the military commissar. In May 1919 the Main Political Administration (*PUR*) was set up after the 8th Party Congress, to direct the political work and the political personnel of the Soviet armed forces centrally. The distinctive feature about this organisation was that it did *not* come under the direct control of the Central Committee, although it was run by a member of the Central Committee. This very significant arrangement lasted until 1925, but during the Civil War period Trotsky had demanded and obtained the complete independence of the army political organs from control by the civilian Party machine.[65]

With respect to the commissar, two questions had to be thrashed out — his status and his function. Reasons of military efficiency suggested that 'dual command' could not be regarded as a permanent arrangement. In the Red Army Disciplinary Code of January 1919 all reference to the military commissar was omitted, presumably from the conviction that he would not long remain as a feature of Red Army organisation once 'dual command' had been replaced by unity of command. Trotsky himself suggested this in his statements about the commissar, dwelling on the ideal arrangement whereby the commander would direct his attention increasingly towards an intelligent appraisal of the importance of political work and the commissar cease to be a supervisor of suspect loyalties and become a military help-mate. This, however, obviously depended on vast developments in the command staff.

During the Civil War it would appear that the commissar came to be connected with the developing theory of *morale*, for his was the greatest test of responsibility in the final resort. Trotsky early discovered that by stiffening a weak or wavering unit with Party members, imbued with the spirit to fight and die, he could work wonders.[66] These calculated switches, plus the support derived from the commissar, saved many a perilous situation, but brought their own criticism; S. I. Gusev, writing to Stasova, the secretary of the Central Committee, commented acidly:

> Trotsky sets the tone for the whole of this system. Frequent changes of the political workers and commanders, crowding the Southern Front *Revvoensoviet* with a great number of Party members and Trotsky's princely journeys along the front. . . . All this is a symptom of the system of organised panic.[67]

No doubt the principle, which did away with the need to set up special shock-troops, could also be interpreted as excessive interference on the part of the centre.

Out of an apparently spontaneous generation of political will at the *lowest* levels of the Soviet armed forces there grew up one of the most intricate problems of regulation which continued to stare the Political Administration and the Communist Party in the face long after the Civil War had ceased. Among the various contestants for power in and over the political machinery in the Red Army, the Communist 'cell' (also known as the 'Party collective') was perhaps the most bizarre; the 'cell' was made up of a hard core of Communists in the regiment or military installation and had developed by mid-June 1917. It was at this time that the All-Russian Conference of Front and Rear Organisations of the RSDRP(b) laid down a form of rudimentary organisation for 'cells', which operated presumably under the aegis of the Military Organisations attached to the RSDRP(b). During the phase of construction of the Red Army on volunteer lines, many units lost their Party nuclei either through the effects of demobilisation or because very few were created to replace those in the process of disappearance or dissolution. On the other hand, the delegates of the Petrograd Conference of Soldier-Communists, which met in April 1918, devoted a great deal of attention to the question of this kind of organisation. They produced a solemn document — 'Instructions to the collectives of the RKP(b) in Red Army units, aviation units, ships and coastal commands' — which advised the immediate formation of such 'cells' and defining the function of these small but energetic bodies. They were to organise meetings in the units, guard 'revolutionary discipline', purge 'undesirable elements from the detachment' and supervise the 'political, cultural and economic life of the detachment'.[68] This at once placed them in a position both competitive with and complementary to the military commissar, whose duties were slowly but surely evolving in a similar direction.

During the winter of 1918–19 these 'cells' seemed to have mushroomed at an enormous speed. Party mobilisations, whereby stiffening forces were sent to threatened sectors of the fronts, favoured their growth; over a period of three months Petrograd sent 2,000 Party members to the front at the end of 1918.[69] The weavers of Ivanovo-Voznesensk departed for the front as a Party cadre. By February 1919 more than 1,500 'cells' flourished in Red Army units, consisting on the average of 15–30 Party members and 40–50 sympathisers or candidate members, although on the Southern and Western Fronts the average fell slightly to 12–20 and 15–30 for the same type of adherents.[70] At this time, the same winter which had seen such phenomenal growth of 'cells', witnessed also their frequent interference in the operational and administrative life of the units to which they belonged. Not content with interference, there were cases of actual usurpation of command. Following the accepted styles of 'empire-building', these groups set about electing their members in a chain of organisation which ran up to divisional and even army level. Thus, running all the way up from detachments, through companies and regiments, to the division (or army level, in some cases), extended a rapidly-expanding, widely-ramified political organisation free from any centralised control whatsoever. In fact, it represented the very antithesis of central control.

The 'cells' exhibited other strange features. It was obvious that they complicated the functions of the military commissar. The co-existence of Party members with non-Party men in this group meant that non-Party elements participated in debates and discussions of Party affairs. The very core of the 'cell' was a small praesidium or Party committee, made up of 3–5 Communists, who not infrequently came to be the real power behind the throne of unit command. Something not unlike the pre-November 1917 conditions was beginning to creep into the Red Army afresh, threatening the disorders which had so visibly affected the Imperial Russian Army. *Partizanshchina*, which was being stamped out, re-appeared in the political sphere as 'army syndicalism'; this placed immense emphasis on the power and the integrity of the local political organs and energy in the Soviet armed forces.

This state of affairs had to be brought to an end. In January 1919 the Instruction on Party 'cells' in the Red Army severely circumscribed the powers of this kind of organisation, banning the 'cell' from any interference in operational matters and confining it to its original function, the care of the unit's political spirit, but only in co-operation with the commissar. This step raised howls of protest, but the wide scope and intensity of the activity of the 'cells' (7,000 of them flourished by the end of the Civil War) raises the important question of whether the organisation from the top or the bottom played the decisive role in establishing the political work which was carried on in the Red Army. This is also a subject upon which Soviet military historians have found it hard to agree.[71] Controlling the Party nucleus in military units provided the political administration with a very difficult task, for here lay the dilemma of wishing to effect central control of political activity in the Red Army without losing the very considerable advantages afforded by the presence of such a powerful reservoir of spirit and loyalty. Trotsky seems to have held firmly to his ideas of a strict military and political centralisation, the effective separation of the Army's political organs from the civilian Party apparatus, yet emphasising the role of the individual Communist and the Party nucleus in sustaining and hardening the will to fight in the many units where they existed. The advantage derived from moving these Communist squads to points where they were needed justified a central control of political as well as military matters; equally, groups grown too influential could be broken up and effectively dispersed.

The third chain of control and command concerned the security apparatus in the Red Army. This took the form of organising Special Sections (OO) of *Cheka* men and units to maintain army security. These agencies came under the special command of the *Cheka*, but the decree of 21st February, 1919, removed them from this authority and placed the apparatus of internal security under the Republic *Revvoensoviet*[72]— a signal acquisition for the Red Army, which did not, however, remain permanent.

* * * *

A very pertinent if unmistakably anti-Trotsky document was produced on the operation of the military system at the beginning of 1919 when Stalin and Dzerzhinskii investigated, on behalf of the Central Committee, the catastrophe which had overtaken Soviet arms at Perm (Eastern Front) and especially the IIIrd Army. The report breathes militant detestation of the Republic *Revvoensoviet* and the organs associated with it. In the report to Lenin, the opening indictment — for it reads as nothing less — attacked the *Revvoensoviet* '. . . whose so-called instructions and orders disorganised the control of the front and the armies'.[73] The lack of co-ordination between the IInd and IIIrd armies resulted from the 'isolation of the Republic *Revvoensoviet* from the front' and the 'ill-considered instructions of the Commander-in-Chief'.

In the actual report on the defeat, the co-authors attacked the All-Russian

Supreme Staff for having neglected to form a *Red* Army, since they merely utilised the Tsarist procedure to assemble a 'popular army'.[74] Due to the negligence of the Bureau of Commissars 'whipper-snapper commissars' only were sent to the front — therefore, let the personnel of the bureau be replaced.[75] The ill-prepared directives from the centre demanded that it should be re-fashioned into a 'narrow group', consisting possibly of five persons: two experts and three supervisors of the supply administration, the General Staff and Bureau of Commissars.[76] The sting came in the tail — these men must be 'sufficiently experienced not to act arbitrarily and light-mindedly in the control of armies'. The reference to Trotsky was quite plain. This report, in addition to the ferment over the political organisation in the army, and the bitterness over the 'military specialists' formed the background to the intensive struggle which was waged over military policy at the 8th Party Congress, where Trotsky's innovations came under heavy fire.

The conflict over military policy, embodying as it did the most critical issues of the defence of the Revolution, brought about an upheaval in the leadership and then in the ranks of the Party. According to Trotsky, Lenin accorded him massive but conditional support.* This had helped to quieten one revolt over the 'military specialists', when Larin suggested that the ex-officers should be replaced by Communists. Lenin, on being assured by Trotsky that concentration camps and the acid tests of the Eastern Front guaranteed a rigorous selection, did not press the point. Similarly, nothing came of the proposal to replace Vatsetis as Commander-in-Chief by Lashevich, himself a former NCO of the Imperial Army. Beyond these much disputed details or aspects of the military policy, there were wider consequences which affected policies concerned with the regulation of the supposedly autonomous regions of the Soviet republic. Political and economic centralisation followed inevitably upon military centralisation. In April 1919 the control of the Baltic Fleet, based then on Riga, did not pass to the nominally autonomous Soviet Republic of Latvia, but was lodged with the Muscovite centre.[77] Likewise Ukrainian military units, nominally under the control of the Soviet Government of the Ukraine and the Ukrainian Communist Party, were not free to pursue military

* There is no doubt, however, of the tone of Lenin's July statement on the ex-officers. The Party was committed to opposing the '. . . ignorant and self-conceited belief that the working people are capable of overcoming capitalism and the bourgeois order . . . without learning from bourgeois experts, . . . without going through *a long schooling* of work side by side with them'. The known cases of treason would not themselves justify 'changing the fundamentals of our military policy'. In Lenin's phrase, 'hundreds and hundreds' of ex-officers are committing treason, but 'thousands and tens of thousands of military experts have been working for us systematically and for a long time, and without them we could not have formed the Red Army . . .' (see *All out for the fight against Denikin!*).

policy dictated more by provincial interests, however extensive these might be. From this point of view, vital political interests were at stake in the struggle over the control of the military machine and the degree to which it might pursue its centralisation without inhibition.[78]

The 8th Party Congress had not assembled when Kolchak's White troops broke open the Eastern Front, precipitating a grave situation. The Central Committee decided that Trotsky should straightway leave for the front and the military delegates return to their units. This raised vehement protest that Trotsky was evading the criticism which his policy so richly deserved, so that the military delegates were permitted to stay and argue in Moscow and Sokol'nikov presented Trotsky's theses in the latter's absence at the front. The opposition, which became known by the name of the Military Opposition, was compounded of Left-wing Communists and elements dissatisfied with the prevailing military policy as a whole. V. M. Smirnov led for the opposition, which demanded the widening of the scope of the responsibility of the members of the *Revvoensoviet*, attacked the retention of the 'military specialists', sought increased military power for the commissars and required a greater place for local Party organisations in the centrally directed political work of the armed forces.

On the evening of 20th and the morning of 21st March, 1919, the military delegates — numbering 85, 57 with voting rights — thrashed out policy in a particularly heated debate. Lenin intervened to justify the present policy, upholding the status of the 'military specialists' and chiding the opposition for their intransigence which disturbed the general Party line.[79] In spite of this admonition, the majority voted against the official programme by 174 votes to 95;[80] to resolve the dead-lock a special committee was established to undertake a thorough examination of the military question.

Trotsky claims that the 8th Congress was a triumph for his policy and Stalinist historiography declares it a defeat. The contradiction is comprehensible in so far that Trotsky is referring to the public vote, which finally upheld him, and the Stalinists to the defeat dealt out in secret. Stalin himself adopted a very equivocal position at the Congress, appearing to support the official line, rejecting Smirnov's arguments as dangerous for the establishment and maintenance of discipline in the army, yet apparently supporting Voroshilov in his criticism of Trotsky. Trotsky himself charged Stalin with being the leader of an organised and sustained opposition at the Congress, where he skilfully and patiently directed the Tsaritsyn group, unleashing the 'vilest kind of personal attack' on Sokol'nikov, the official spokesman for Trotsky's policy.[81] Resistance to the Party line collapsed in the end, but Zinoviev took the opportunity to convey the opposition's strictures as a 'warning' to Trotsky — which the latter brushed quickly aside.[82] Although the opposition had to yield ground and did not succeed in altering the Party line, the 8th Congress did effect certain substantial and influential changes in the military and political establishment. Trotsky's own theses invite some inspection, for they are themselves an important commentary on the assumptions of long-term military policy at this time.

Trotsky argued that a regular standing army, centrally directed and properly disciplined, was absolutely essential to fight the battles of the Civil War — and to win them. Although the Red Army might look suspiciously like the old Imperial Russian Army, the real point was that the Red Army was serving quite different political ends. Considering the future army of the Soviet state, Trotsky pressed for the adoption of the militia form, on the basis of a huge improvement in industrial strength and the triumph of the proletariat. This force would not be trained in the standard barracks of a typical standing army, but under conditions not much divorced 'from normal working circumstances'.[83] He even envisaged a return to elective command, through a possible combination of elective procedure applied to trained military cadres and a wider application of the principle to the future army.[84] Over this programme, where the political logic is undeniably firm but the details of organisation inevitably obscure, a major struggle was to develop at the close of the Civil War, the conflict bursting out when the 9th Party Congress once again endorsed this scheme and even set about enlarging it. The conversion of the Red Army into a militia force caused the bitterest of many rancorous and heated debates.

For the machine, the 8th Congress requested strict class mobilisation, a powerful Party-political control — centralised and operated by the commissars — over the 'military specialists', the organisation of a system of attestation over the command staff, energetic efforts to create a proletarian command staff, the setting up of a Political Administration (*PUR*) with a member of the Central Committee at its head, the issue of military regulations and finally the regulation of the commander-commissar relationship.[85] A rider to these quite considerable proposals demanded more specific and detailed changes — a set of points suggestive of the extreme demands of the opposition and the criticisms of Stalin's report on the Perm catastrophe. The re-organisation of the Field Staff was suggested, so that it would maintain closer ties with the fronts, the work of the Republic *Revvoensoviet* was to be regulated, the All-Russian Staff overhauled in the light of deficiencies uncovered and strengthened with Party representatives, and periodic meetings with 'responsible Party workers' from the various fronts were to be arranged.[86]

If public confidence had not been visibly disturbed, Trotsky's opponents in the higher echelons of the Party had the satisfaction of knowing that

Trotsky had not come out of the struggle unscathed. Nevertheless, the 8th Congress resulted in the organisation of the centralised Political Administration and the closing down of the Bureau of Commissars, when this decision went into effect in May 1919. In the same month Attestation Commissions were set up to screen officer-candidates; these operated under the control of a Higher Attestation Commission, which was made up of five members, two military commissars, two representatives acting as military experts, and the Chief of the Personnel Section of the All-Russian Staff. Similar commissions were set up at all levels from the local to the regional, and were usually made up of a small board of commissars and experts and the representative of the local Soviet. These boards played a substantial part in controlling officer-selection and continued their career after the end of the Civil War.

The tide of criticism had been unable to make any drastic modification in the operation of the military establishment, but the 8th Congress was notable as the point of the formal emergence of the Military Opposition, and the confirmation of the fundamental contradiction in this phase of Soviet military organisation. While the machinery most vitally needed for the operation of a powerful standing army was strengthened and amplified, and that distinctive political apparatus was formally centralised and buttressed against civilian or local interference, the very idea of a standing army, or even an orthodox military force, was still an open question and one liable to be opened still wider.

The problem of the organisational form of the Soviet armed forces was further complicated by the activities of the personnel and instructors of the Universal Military Training (*Vsevobuch*) command. By the summer of 1919 this training was organised to a plan which divided Soviet territory into regimental districts, corresponding to the *guberniya* or parts of it, depending upon the density of population. These areas were further divided into battalion, company and section districts, so that the unit and its particular parts corresponded to specific areas for recruitment and training. Where a *guberniya* could not be divided, due to sparseness of population, into many sub-divisions, there a militia brigade would be organised. Only very weak regular units formed the backbone of these preliminary organisations, which played a dual role — to provide the Red Army with reinforcements and a reserve of trained man-power, and to serve as the basis for the ultimate creation and emergence of the class militia.[87]

At the 7th Congress of Soviets, in December 1919 Trotsky again referred to the prospect of doing away with the standing army and introducing the militia, a statement which had greater force, since his address was being delivered at a time when the question of Soviet victory in the Civil War was no longer in doubt, although hard fighting still lay ahead. The struggle to retain the regular Red Army gradually intensified as the possibility of a transition to the militia system became more real, and less of a utopian fantasy.

Although the Military Opposition tried to shift its ground from a criticism of the form and management of the military machine to objections over matters of strategy and operational questions, the months following upon the 8th Congress were taken up with heavy fighting which occupied the forefront of all attention. In spite of this, however, what later emerged as a very distinctive doctrine began to take shape at this time, arising out of the insistence that this special revolutionary war fought by the Red Army had produced equally distinctive tactical features and strategic innovations. A handbook of the methods to be used in the revolutionary war was issued.[88] Positional warfare had given place to a war of manœuvre; Trotsky's critics therefore suggested that the rigid social and military experience of the ex-Imperial officers rendered them fundamentally incapable of fighting a revolutionary war of manœuvre to a successful conclusion. Trotsky swept this aside once again, largely because he discerned yet another assault upon the 'military specialists' — although in this he was partially deceived.

Certain of the new doctrinal fumblings hit very accurately at the military essence of the Civil War. Fronts did not correspond to what had come to be understood by that term as a result of the gigantic and sustained operations of the 1914–18 War. A front began by spreading out with the advance of whichever side was momentarily victorious — a huge widening and lengthening space, with the troops living off the land, and fighting taking place along the communication lines, accompanied not infrequently by deep penetrations into the enemy rear with pulverising raids. Both Red and White cavalry scored spectacular, if brief successes after this manner. The straggling fronts, with their chaotic rear, could be crumpled by thunderbolt blows, smashing like a fist through stretched paper. Once the blow lost its momentum, however, and the forces became spread ever more thinly across a greater space, a counter-blow sent them reeling away in disorder. Weak organisation in the rear constantly hastened this process of dissolution and disintegration.

The opposition to Trotsky, fervid exponents of a growing belief in a 'proletarian' method of waging war, produced workable and valuable schemes, such as cavalry using horse-drawn artillery, mobile machine-gun units, and the *tachanka* — a light peasant cart with a machine-gun mounted upon it. The suggestions for innovations in the use of armoured-car squadrons and the employment of armoured trains (particularly effective weapons) enjoyed considerable success, although one day Trotsky would be able to round on these unsophisticated military innovators with the charge that when the Red Army wanted to do anything in advance of the *tachanka*, it had to turn to bourgeois military science to achieve it.

Trotsky did himself untold damage by his arrogant rebuffs, for not all of his critics were fools or knaves. The Tsaritsyn group hated him for his handling of them, although they supplied endless provocation. Voroshilov no doubt smarted under the charge that he was capable of handling a regiment only, not 50,000 men.[89] After visiting Budenny's cavalry squadron in the summer of 1919, Budenny relates that Trotsky, on his return to Moscow, remarked:

> Budenny's corps — a horde, and Budenny — their ataman ring-leader. . . . He is the present-day Stenka Razin. And where he leads his gang, there will they go; for the Reds to-day, to-morrow for the Whites.[90]

The Red cavalry, which had been difficult to organise since Cossacks did not take willingly to the Soviet regime and industrial workers were not born to the saddle, finally combined the hardiest and most spirited fighters in its ranks, well sprinkled with practised free-booters. It was not above cutting its own commissars to pieces. After the sack of Rostov in the winter of 1920, Dumenko, one of Budenny's corps commanders, shot down Commissar Mikeladze, who protested at the pillage. Trotsky fumed at reports of the disorders. When the *Cheka* finally led Dumenko out and shot him, there ended an extraordinary and turbulent career.

★ ★ ★ ★

In considering the formative stage of the Soviet military establishment as a whole, it is impossible not to record it as a singular achievement. Yet from the first moments of its existence, a struggle for control over this machine had begun in all earnest. The conscious and deliberate inclusion of warring and contradictory elements at all levels offset the gains in centralised organisation and increased administrative efficiency. The command system was cumbersome and its particular unwieldiness was increased by the inescapable necessity of dual command. The control organs and their directors added a whole new dimension to the emergent military-political system. The truly distinctive feature of the operation of the Soviet military system during the Civil War was that the Red Army possessed centralised, independent control of its political and security organs. It still remained, however, to provide satisfactory definitions for such matters as the role of the commissar and the commander-commissar relationship. The administration of supply was still exceedingly crude and liable to large-scale breakdown, although the finest administrative system in the world could not have improved upon the steadily deteriorating economic situation throughout the whole of Soviet Russia.

It would appear that the Red Army was the product of expediency, and that the introduction of fundamentally opposed elements into the military system is comprehensible in the light of their being regarded as temporary features, innovations designed to bring victory in the field. Such expedients were therefore both justifiable and acceptable, in certain quarters, since a powerful control mechanism had been provided from the outset and was being steadily developed. Yet the army and the command were inexorably captured by the machine, which, by Trotsky's own admission, bore a striking resemblance to that of the old order. Socialism had as yet to try conclusions with the particular brand of militarism which the Civil War developed. For the aggravation of the inevitable tensions Trotsky cannot be absolved from a measure of the responsibility. For the deliberate perpetuation and political exploitation of these same dissensions the blame lies with the more militant of the Military Opposition. Although losing its importance as a component of Party politics towards the end of the Civil War, that group, compounded of malice, frustration, excessive idealism and undeniable talents and political skills, achieved ultimate significance as the heart of the movement within the Red Army and the command against Trotsky. Before this gathered its full momentum a host of other experiences, which further defined the several interest-groups within the Soviet command, added themselves out of the circumstances and enmities of the Civil War battle-fronts.

CHAPTER THREE

The Formation of the Soviet Command: 1918-1920

From the first days of its existence the Soviet high command was not a unified body of men, nor was it destined so to become until the passage of many years. It possessed no distinctive name of its own. The term 'officer corps' conjured up a body detested with singular intensity by military and civilian alike in the Communist camp. The contrasting terms of 'military specialist' (*Voenspets*) and 'Red commander' (*Kraskom*) set off two mutually antagonistic elements within the command group as a whole, with the latter thinning out very rapidly at the higher levels of command and planning. In the whole history of the Civil War, the ex-Imperial Russian officer occupied a strange and often tragic place. The White armies fielded an excess of officers, so that capable and fanatical 'Officer battalions' were sent into countless attacks. The Red Army found itself continually and drastically short of officers, for combat losses as well as the burden of incompetence and inferior training, not to mention treachery on several occasions, aggravated what from the outset had been an almost insurmountable drawback.

The inner-Party disputes over the form and function of the centralised military machine had been resolved at the 8th Party Congress in a manner which suggested that the cracks had only just been papered over. The bitter and inescapable struggles over strategy and the operation of the fronts, which were merely another dimension of the basic struggle over and within the military machine, took place against the background of the evolution of a number of very uncertain relationships. Among the more precarious of these was that between the higher command echelons and the senior 'military specialists'. Here conflict and rivalry had rapid and enormous consequence.

The Supreme Military Soviet acted as the first conscious command centre, where Trotsky acted as chairman, together with Podvoiskii, Sklyanskii and Danishevskii as members of the group and a staff of 'military specialists' working under the direction of the ex-Imperial General Bonch-Bruevich. Efroim Markovich Sklyanskii, then twenty-six, was an asset to the

Bolshevik cause and subsequently an extremely capable deputy to Trotsky. A Kiev medical student who had joined the Bolsheviks in 1913, become an army doctor and a member of the Bolshevik military organisation of the Imperial Russian Vth Army, Sklyanskii shouldered an ever-increasing burden during the Civil War.[1] Podvoiskii, a Bolshevik well acquainted with the problems of military organisation, had worked as the president of the Collegiate for the Formation of the Red Army. After a number of important military-political assignments to the fronts, he came to take charge of the universal military training (*Vsevobuch*) command. It was to this preliminary command group that Lenin's telegram of 1st April, 1918, assigned definite but limited tasks.[2]

Also in April something akin to a General Staff was re-formed with the setting up of the All-Russian Supreme Staff, which concerned itself with planning the requirements and organisation of the Red Army. Although engaged on working out the man-power and officer requirements of the new force, as well as the composition of the first proposed Red Army divisions, the ex-officers were faced with a situation in which discipline had collapsed and cohesion vanished. A regiment could not be represented merely by its number, table of ranks and establishment — a style to which the former officers had been accustomed. The new and feeble Red regiments varied widely in strength; equipment and uniforms were conspicuous by their absence, elective command encouraged anarchy, weapons combined a multitude of styles and systems — and it was thus that the regiment went off to fight its bit of a local war.

In the early summer of 1918 the revolt of the Czech Legion changed the Soviet military scene from one of haphazard muddling to a frenzy of mobilisation and the committing of Red units to life-and-death battle. The advancing summer drew with it a pestilence of violence and terrorism. The Left SRs, the one legal party left with the Bolsheviks, were desirous of bringing Russia once more into war with Germany and incidentally ending Bolshevik rule. To this end they engineered the killing of the German Ambassador, von Mirbach, and raised the standard of dubious revolt. Muralov, veteran Bolshevik and Moscow Red Guard commander, with Podvoiskii acted with despatch to crush this, assisted by Colonel Vatsetis.[3] Boris Savinkov's conspirators struck separately at Yaroslavl, seizing and holding the town for two weeks. The Soviet commander of the Volga front, Colonel M. A. Muraviev — who had fought with the Bolsheviks in Petrograd and the Ukraine — turned traitor to his masters, swinging his troops round to face west and proposing an armistice with the Czechs.[4] The manner of Muraviev's end is uncertain; it may have been suicide or summary execution, or else his plan for gathering leading Bolsheviks into the town of Simbirsk mis-carried when he attempted to seize the person of ex-Imperial Lieutenant M. N. Tukhachevsky, Ist Red army* commander.[5] Simbirsk, however, fell to Czech and White troops. On 16th July a Bolshevik group put to death in squalid and horrible circumstances the Russian Imperial family, lodged at that date in Ekaterinburg. On 30th July Lenin fell grievously hurt with bullets in the chest and left shoulder, fired into him by a young SR woman, Fanya Kaplan. There followed an orgy of killing in the name of Bolshevik retribution.

The critical military situation, imperilling the very existence of the Bolshevik regime, had built up furiously on the Eastern Front; treason, of which some warning had been given, speeded up the collapse.[6] On 7th August, 1918, Trotsky left Moscow for the scene of operations, where Vatsetis had taken command, after the defection of Muraviev on the Upper Volga. On 10th July Vatsetis had been named front commander. Trotsky describes Vatsetis variously as a man 'who never lost himself in the chaos of the revolution'[7] and elsewhere as 'irascible'.[8] From his armoured train, which took on the character of a mobile head-quarters, Trotsky assumed personal control of the operations from Sviyazhsk, the nearest main railway station to Kazan. Red Army troops fell back from Simbirsk and Kazan, laying open the road to Moscow to the White forces. Disorder and defeatism prevailed. To Trotsky it appeared that the 'soil itself seemed to be infected with panic'. By a show of calculated brutality and by furious attention to detail, the Red units were brought up to a state of combat readiness by Trotsky and his assistants during this most critical month.[9] At one moment Trotsky himself stood in extreme danger. A White raiding party, led by Colonel Kappel, had penetrated deep into the Red rear and was moving dangerously near to Trotsky's own HQ. It was, from the Soviet point of view, a very fortunate accident that the White colonel did not possess any accurate information about the true state of the Red defences, else he could have seized not only the HQ but the Soviet Commissar for War.

On this miniature testing ground Trotsky tried out not a little of his theory and practice of war. He saw how demoralised units could be hammered back into shape. He had evidence of how an injection of Communists, willing to fight and sacrifice themselves, could stiffen up dispirited front-line fighters eager to seek the rear. Vatsetis, after a brief consultation with Trotsky, left for Vyatka to put the same methods into operation there. Meanwhile Stalin, who at this time found himself in the south, had written to Lenin, raging at the effects which Trotsky's early

* To distinguish between 'the Red Army' (*RKKA*) and individual Red armies, and to avoid confusion between 'Red' and 'White' armies Soviet armies are shown by a roman numeral followed by 'Red army', as above. To assist translation, Soviet use of the arabic numeral for army designation after 1939 has also been retained here.

efforts were producing. It needed, wrote Stalin, a firm hand to stop Trotsky from handing out credentials to all and sundry. It must be knocked into his head — such was Stalin's tone — that appointments made must be with the knowledge of the local people. Finally, 'not having a paper from Trotsky' would not deter Stalin from arrogating the necessary military rights to himself, including dismissing army commanders and commissars.[10]

★ ★ ★ ★

Throughout the autumn the shaky Red power in the east solidified into a recognisable military force. The command organisation took shape. On 4th September, 1918, the Republic *Revvoensoviet* took over the central direction of the Red Army and its attendant affairs. Vatsetis assumed the post of Commander-in-Chief, Trotsky took the leading position in the *Revvoensoviet*, with Sklyanskii as his deputy and a staff which included I. N. Smirnov, Rosengoltz, Raskol'nikov, Muralov and Yurenev. All of these counted themselves 'Trotsky's men', and the appointments reflected the first fruits of victory, for here were its architects. These men were attached to Trotsky in a firm personal manner as well as being collaborators in the business of war. Between Trotsky and Vatsetis there existed a certain understanding; as for Vatsetis, although this ex-Imperial Colonel showed but average ability, he was ably assisted by a Field Staff which included notable talent. Boris Shaposhnikov, subsequently Stalin's military mentor, was seconded to the Operations Branch of the Staff. This ex-officer had completed the course at the General Staff Academy in 1910, holding staff appointments with a cavalry division during the World War. His official biography tends to confirm the view that since May 1918 he had been acting as one of the main props in the early Soviet Operations Branch.[11] In the person of P. P. Lebedev, another ex-Imperial senior officer who added his services to those of Shaposhnikov, the Soviet command gained very considerably with the acquisition of this professional talent.

The Bolshevik substitutes for senior commanders were shovelled away with rude but understandable haste as their manifest incapacity for the positions which they occupied became all too plain. Only Raskol'nikov, in the naval command, showed the requisite degree of ability, yet the reduced scale of naval operations — confined to river actions with small flotillas and using sailors as special infantry — made his task easier. To handle the ships which were left to the Bolsheviks, it was necessary to rely once again upon the ex-Imperial officer.

The Eastern Front, as well as being the crucible in which the Red Army found its shape and won its first victories, played a vital role in developing both a system of command, crude as it was, and a concentration of command personnel. By the end of 1918 this front numbered five armies and had passed under the command of the ex-Imperial Colonel S. S. Kamenev. The first Bolshevik victories, however, owed less to military mastery and efficiency than to the operation of a natural law, as the first impetus of the White troops exhausted itself and the Reds were able to thrust them back sufficiently to avert disaster. But the new White armies, mustered under the leadership of Kolchak, proved to be a formidable enemy.

Until the White Siberian troops came into action in mid-December, the Red armies encountered little stiff resistance. Of the latter forces, the IVth Red army was commanded first by A. A. Baltiiskii and subsequently taken over by T. S. Khvesin. The IInd came under V. I. Shorin[12] (with S. I. Gusev as his commissar), Zh. K. Blyumberg commanded the Vth, M. M. Lashevich the IIIrd and M. N. Tukhachevsky the Ist. This first consolidated Eastern front command was a pertinent illustration of the role of the Imperial officer. Khvesin, Baltiiskii and Shorin came from the fold of the Imperial Army. To represent the Party and to watch for the tell-tale signs of unreliability and disaffection, Gusev held his all-important watching brief. It was not to be long before Gusev began to play a very active role in the operational as well as the political affairs of the Eastern Front. The magic and the mystique of command completely ensnared him, to the degree that he ultimately played the role of an additional, if at times somewhat irresponsible, military adviser. In the person of Lashevich,[13] the ex-NCO was represented, the whole ensemble of pasts and varied talents producing inevitable clashes and bizarre relations. To Lashevich no greater contrast could be found than the young Mikhail Tukhachevsky, Ist Red army commander.

Tukhachevsky came of an impoverished but aristocratic family. Born in 1893 and hailing from Penza, Tukhachevsky was first a page in the Imperial Cadet Corps, and then went on to a military academy, from which he was gazetted a junior lieutenant in 1914. The military fame which Tukhachevsky avidly sought eluded him not long after the war had begun, for he was taken prisoner by the Germans on the Eastern Front in February 1915. Tukhachevsky had no intention of allowing a prisoner of war cage to hold him. Five times he attempted to escape. His captors finally lodged him in the fortress of Ingolstadt.[14] In 1917 Tukhachevsky made good his escape and arrived back in Russia in the late autumn. It was to the Bolsheviks that Tukhachevsky gave his allegiance. From his work in training troops in the Moscow area Trotsky singled him out for a more responsible post. In April 1918 Tukhachevsky became a member of the Communist Party, proceeding in the early summer to the Eastern Front to take up command of a Red division. It was under the patronage of Trotsky that Tukhachevsky took over the Ist Red army. Trotsky's opponents did not neglect to observe that the War Commissar had not been slow in appointing a former aristocrat to a responsible command post in the Red Army.

Of all the Red Army commanders in the Civil War, Tukhachevsky displayed strategic talents and tactical abilities of a conspicuously high order. In these he was matched perhaps only by his rival and fellow ex-Imperial officer Boris Shaposhnikov. His lack of years set off his military achievements in a manner all the more striking and breath-taking. Brilliant, quick of mind, with a streak of cruelty allied to an impetuousness which bordered on the rash, the young Red Army commander cultivated a certain hauteur and an arrogance which was not calculated to ease all his friendships. Although a Party member, in no accepted or acceptable sense of the word was Tukhachevsky a Marxist. Radical inclinations he may have possessed, but they were of a peculiar order. His passion was his patriotism, of such an order that he appeared to be more the opportunist than the loyal adherent. His support for the Bolshevik regime seems to have derived less from any political idea than his realisation that they were demonically active, that they would serve the fading fortunes of Russia most with their doctrine of expanding revolution. It was no accident that he laboured also to provide a military theory and a form of organisation which would fit in with the political doctrines of his new masters in the field of dynamic expansion. Reputedly a slavish admirer of Napoleon (whose style of orders he consciously imitated),[15] the young ex-lieutenant took few pains to conceal his ambitions. His abilities nevertheless matched his aspirations and made him on more than one occasion the saviour of the Eastern Front. From these spectacular triumphs he moved, at the age of twenty-seven, to command of the entire Soviet forces arrayed against Poland in 1920. He thus accomplished his ambition of achieving by the age of thirty either fame or death.

In the east fortunes fluctuated wildly, reflecting the instability of the forces engaged on both sides. On 24th December, 1918, Perm fell to the White troops; it was a catastrophe produced out of faulty co-ordination among the Soviet commanders, and to make matters worse, many prisoners and considerable productive power fell into the enemy's hands. Lenin despatched Stalin and Dzerzhinskii on a fact-finding mission to the IIIrd Red army. Seizing upon this opportunity Stalin lost no chance of finding the kind of facts which were themselves a severe criticism of the centre and the Commander-in-Chief. Nevertheless, in spite of its invective aimed at Trotsky and Vatsetis, the report was a model of incisiveness in its display of the present weaknesses, and action taken in the light of these recommendations produced a noticeable strengthening of the Soviet left wing to the north.[16]

As a consequence of the re-shuffle in command M. V. Frunze proceeded to take command of the IVth Red army at the end of January 1919. A veteran Bolshevik, Frunze, now aged thirty-four, had a long record of political activity before 1917; during the First World War he had worked extensively among the soldiers of the Western Front, winning what influence he could. He had formed a detachment of pro-Bolshevik soldiers and during the seizure of power marched on Moscow to help the Bolshevik insurgents. In August 1918 Frunze joined F. F. Novitskii, an ex-Imperial senior officer, in organising Red Army formations for the Eastern Front from the Yaroslavl Regional (*Okruzhni*) Military Commissariat.[17] Both men soon tired of rear work, and after fruitless application and finally a visit to Moscow, Frunze went to his new command, with Novitskii as his chief of staff. Frunze, who has become one of the archetypal images for the modern Soviet Army, represented the Communist Party intellectual turned soldier and succeeding at a very difficult task. He displayed considerable administrative ability, high personal courage and an iron will, though perhaps lacking in imagination. The evidence of Frunze's military career suggests that he worked most intensively to master the military trade, both in theory and practice.

Frunze found the IVth Red army in a parlous state, verging on open mutiny.[18] Having re-imposed a certain discipline upon the troops, not without some difficulty, Frunze took up his station on the southern flank of the Eastern Front, while preparations went ahead for the coming offensive. It so happened that Kolchak's forces were the first to strike; with four armies, numbering some 130,000 men, with 210 guns and 1,300 machine-guns, the White blow struck out in a double direction, splitting the Soviet front. By way of comparison, and as a measure of the forces which the Soviet commanders were handling, Vatsetis's reports to Lenin on the *actual* combat strength of the Red Army and the strategic tasks assigned to it are of some value.[19] In February 1919 on six fronts (including the independent VIth army), the Red Army deployed 343,100 infantry, 40,060 cavalry, 6,561 guns and 1,697 machine-guns. The Eastern Front absorbed 76,400 infantry, 8,750 cavalry and 372 guns. Vatsetis's total for the White forces on 15th February, 1919, amounted to 511,190.[20] An indication of the material deficiencies is given in the statement of the Artillery Inspectorate of the Field Staff, which reported a deficiency of 3,791 guns, 13,416 machine-guns and 233,378 rifles.[21] This was measured against the establishment laid down by Directive No. 220 of 13th November, 1918, setting out the strength and equipment table for regular divisions and brigades.

The breaching of the Eastern Front presented the high command with a new crisis, the severity of which was fully recognised in Moscow. To the north the White attack faded, but in the south Ufa fell and the way to the

Combat strength on fronts and in armies for period 25 January–15 February 1919

		Infantry	Cavalry	Machine-guns	Guns
I	Independent VIth Army	17,500	160	312	70
II	Western Front:				
	VIIth Army	22,700	830	282	309
	Lettish Army	11,900	180	196	39
	Western Army	43,700	2,150	548	145
	Total/Western Front	78,300	3,160	1,026	493
III	Ukrainian Front	43,500	3,520	606	124
IV	Southern Front:				
	Donets Group	12,800	400	150	26
	VIIIth Army	22,700	1,250	402	62
	IXth Army	31,800	6,500	730	152
	Xth Army	32,100	9,500	758	220
	Total/Southern Front	99,400	17,650	2,040	460
V	Caspian-Caucasian Front:				
	XIth Army	19,000	6,800	847	159
	XIIth Army	9,000	200	259	19
	Total/Caspian-Caucasian Front	28,000	7,000	1,106	178
VI	Eastern Front:				
	Ist Army	10,500	300	254	39
	IInd Army	17,900	760	439	72
	IIIrd Army	13,600	3,360	355	59
	IVth Army	18,100	2,300	253	98
	Vth Army	5,400	50	170	67
	Turkestan Army	10,900	1,800	?	37
	Total/Eastern Front	76,400	8,570	1,471	372
	Combined total	343,100	40,060	6,561	1,697

Chief Operational Directorate/Field Staff *V. Mikhailov*
Military Commissar Op. Direc. *Vasil'ev*
For Chief Naval Operational Directorate *Men'shov*

Volga opened. Trotsky had left hurriedly for the front, thereby missing the 8th Party Congress where his opponents were gathering to hack away at his whole position and policy. The main problem was to prevent the collapse of the entire front and to stem the kind of panic which weak rear organisation and a relatively ineffectual command system only encouraged. The critical situation led to sharp exchanges between the front and the central command,* in which, according to Trotsky, the Communists at the front sided with S. S. Kamenev, while the commissars of the Operations Branch not unnaturally took Vatsetis's part.[22] These verbal passages at arms took place at the conference of the regional with the central military organs in the east itself. Trotsky and Vatsetis re-organised the army commands; Frunze took over command of the Turkestan Red Army (previously under G. V. Zinoviev) and the IVth, G. D. Gai took the Ist, while Tukhachevsky assumed command of the Vth from Blyumberg, V. I. Shorin was sent to the IInd and S. A. Mezheninov to the IIIrd.[23] At a joint meeting of 10th April, 1919, at Simbirsk, where Trotsky, Aralov, Vatsetis, Gusev and Kamenev participated, it was decided to divide the front into two parts, with a southern group made up of the Ist, Vth, IVth and Turkestan Armies. Command of this was invested in Frunze, with V. V. Kuibyshev and F. F. Novitskii as the members of his *Revvoensoviet*.[24] Frunze proceeded to work out a plan to check the White advance, basing it on the assumption that the greatest danger came from General Khanzhin's advance on Samara.[25]

Trotsky seems to have had misgivings about entrusting the command of the southern army group to Frunze; at a meeting of the *Politburo* in the latter half of April[26] he proposed withdrawing the command from Frunze, on the ground of the latter's inexperience, and sending Vatsetis to take over the front so that S. S. Kamenev could control the southern group. This was defeated and Frunze proceeded to put his plan into effect. Whatever Trotsky's fears about Frunze, which proved to have no basis, the new commander enjoyed brilliant professional advice and support, and had some 71,000 men under his command. P. P. Lebedev acted as Chief of Staff for the Eastern Front, and was a 'military specialist' of considerable talent; F. F. Novitskii worked as head of Frunze's staff, while an ex-Imperial Lieutenant-Colonel of Engineers, D. M. Karbyshev, supervised the erection of defensive positions. Making careful preparation, Frunze gathered his forces near Buzuluk for his counter-offensive. On 28th April, 1919, the southern army group went over to the offensive. The heaviest fighting of the Civil War had begun.

* G. K. Eikhe (later Vth Army commander) has intervened over the history of the Eastern Front with a new monograph *Ufimskaya avantyura Kolchaka* (*Mart-Aprel'* **1919**) (Kolchak's Ufa gamble, March-April, 1919), Moscow 1960. Based entirely on Red Army archives, this work is meant to replace the studies of Ogorodnikov (1938), Boltin (1949) and Spirin (1957).

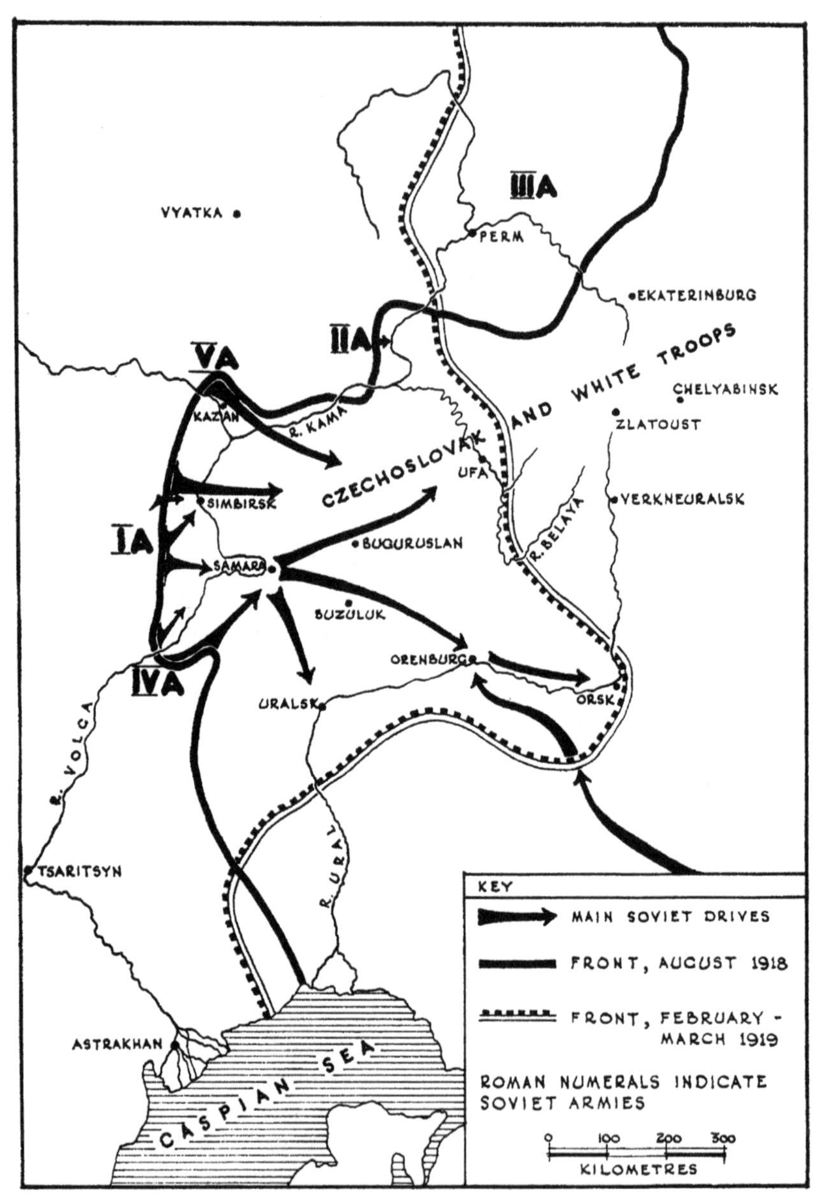
VYATKA
IIIA
PERM
EKATERINBURG
IIA
VA
CZECHOSLOVAK AND WHITE TROOPS
CHELYABINSK
KAZAN
R. KAMA
ZLATOUST
UFA
SIMBIRSK
VERKNEURALSK
IA
BUGURUSLAN
SAMARA
R. BELAYA
BUZULUK
ORENBURG
IVA
ORSK
URALSK
R. VOLGA
R. URAL
TSARITSYN
ASTRAKHAN
CASPIAN SEA
KEY
MAIN SOVIET DRIVES
FRONT, AUGUST 1918
FRONT, FEBRUARY - MARCH 1919
ROMAN NUMERALS INDICATE SOVIET ARMIES
0 100 200 300
KILOMETRES

THE EASTERN FRONT
August, 1918 - March, 1919.

Frunze's counter-offensive met with great success, coming as it did at a time when the White troops had exhausted their reserves and their momentum was waning. Tukhachevsky's Vth army, minus two divisions, was detached from Frunze's group, yet this local re-shuffle was a trifle compared with the major changes wrought in the senior ranks of the Eastern Front command. At Vatsetis's insistence,[27] S. S. Kamenev was replaced as front commander by A. A. Samoilo, another ex-Imperial senior officer who had commanded the VIth Red army in the Northern Commune, and organised defence against the Intervention there.[28] With the new commander came a new plan. To Tukhachevsky's disgust he was obliged to change his direction to the north and the north-east on to the flank of the White Siberian Army. In ten days Tukhachevsky received five directives from Samoilo, each one altering the direction of the main blow. Gusev of the Eastern Front *Revvoensoviet* protested vehemently against the activities of Samoilo, which were flinging the whole operation into confusion. To add to the general chorus of protest, Stalin chose this moment to protest from Petrograd about the behaviour of another 'military specialist', Kostyayev;[29] a White attack launched upon the city had succeeded in taking Yamburg on 17th May, but the drive was repulsed.* In the Ukraine Denikin's power was increasing and threatening the tenuous Soviet hold upon that area.

From Kiev, Trotsky agreed that S. S. Kamenev should be re-instated as commander of the Eastern Front, but admitted that he was ignorant of the colonel's present whereabouts. Samoilo's commissars in the north had begun to argue heatedly in favour of their former chief,[30] whatever the Eastern Front might think of him, but on 29th May Samoilo relinquished his command in the east. In his recent memoirs Samoilo entered a bitter note about Gusev's animosity and intrigue against his person. [31] At the end of May, however, a general offensive of the Eastern armies had been ordered, with Frunze's forces playing a major part and the Vth army being assigned to deep penetration of the enemy rear. The drive was concentrated on Ufa, which fell on 9th June.[32] This triumph, erasing all the White gains, touched off a storm of argument in the Soviet command about resuming the advance across the Urals.

Lenin had urged every effort to conquer the Urals.[33] Vatsetis opposed any extension of the line of operations across the Urals, arguing that the troops could be better employed on the Southern Front. S. S. Kamenev, supported by Smilga and Lashevich, contended that troops could be detached from

* In the middle of June, Stalin was faced with a treasonable outbreak at the Krasnaya Gorka fort, which was recaptured on 16th. Lenin referred to this incident at the opening of his July 1919 remarks on the ex-officers, calling it 'a vast conspiracy . . . whose purpose was the surrender of Petrograd'. Stalin's effort at the direction of operations to recapture the fort was later glorified as one of the first conscious and successful attempts at 'co-ordination'.

the Eastern Front and the offensive still be maintained. On 6th June Vatsetis's directive ordered that operations should be suspended at the line of the Belaya and Kama rivers and defensive positions taken up.[34] On 9th June the Eastern Front *Revvoensoviet* signalled its complete disagreement with this to Lenin. On the following day S. S. Kamenev sent off his personal appraisal of the situation, emphasising that the favourable situation should be exploited with all speed.[35]

Trotsky feared this idea, suspecting that beyond the Urals the Red armies might be moving into deadly trap. There were other strategic commitments and possibilities to be considered, which reduced the safety margins very markedly. Troops were badly needed on the Southern Front, where Denikin was hammering into Soviet-held territory. At the same time Lenin was urging upon Vatsetis the idea of trying to effect a military link-up with the newly-created Soviet Republic of Hungary — which would have meant forcing the barrier of Polish-occupied territory and warring upon Rumania.[36] On 15th June, however, the Central Committee decided that the advance into the Urals must continue and instructions to that effect were passed to the Eastern Front on 16th.[37] The Eastern Front command plan was completed by 22nd and passed to the Commander-in-Chief for approval, although Vatsetis still kept up his attitude of reserve towards the proposed operations.[38]

Tukhachevsky had already made his plans for forcing the mountain barrier. The Vth army was split into three groups, with the centre made up of I. D. Kashirin's cavalry[39] and infantry. By the first week in July these troops, taking a daring but arduous passage, infiltrated into the enemy rear. Benefiting from the speed and surprise of their advance, they fell upon and massacred the 12th White Division. The IInd and IIIrd Red armies advanced in support of the Vth and by the end of the month moved down from the heights and ravines into the Western Siberian plain, consummating an important strategic and tactical victory.[40] The capture of Zlatoust yielded substantial acquisitions of military stores and control over the arms factories. The fight for Western Siberia continued through August and September, when Blyukher's 51st Division played an outstanding part.

The Red armies in the east derived considerable assistance from the various partisan groups. Divided roughly into the Western and Eastern Siberian partisan areas, these irregulars played a major part in harrying Kolchak's Siberian hinterland and have a history made up of manifold tales of horror and ferocity.[41] The Urals-Siberian Bureau, run by F. I. Goloshchekin, acted as an important military-political centre and was fiercely proud of its authority. In September 1919 the 'Supreme Staff of the Partisans of the Red Army' was elected by the Siberian partisans, with the non-Party

Kaban peasant E. M. Mamontov as president of this assorted body. Zhigalin has left one of the numerous stark pictures of the Western Siberian partisan movement.[42] With the prevailing shortage of weapons, one partisan regiment issued a single rifle between three men, and yet another one rifle to fifteen men. The 'Peasants Red Army of Western Siberia' included, in December 1919, 24 partisan regiments with signal and engineering companies; some 16,000 men had 9,000 rifles, 60 machine-guns and about 90 grenades.[43] Mamontov, described as 'weak in political matters', met Commissar I. N. Smirnov of the 26th Division of the Vth Red army to arrange for the subordination of the partisans to regular military command. This was formally effected by Order No. 1117 of 26th December, 1919.[44] In addition to the peasant army, from one armed detachment operating in the Urals a brilliant commander passed to the Red Army from the Eastern Front.

This man was Vasili Konstantinovich Blyukher, whose official biography declares that he was born in 1889 of a poor peasant family in the province of Yaroslavl. He started his revolutionary activity in the Mytishchinskii machine-shops in 1910 and became a Bolshevik in 1916. In 1914 Blyukher had been mobilised but was seriously wounded in 1915 and invalided out. Taking part in the revolutionary disturbances in Samara in 1917, and becoming chairman of the Chelyabinsk Soviet, Blyukher on 18th March, 1918, took command of all units fighting the White leader Dutov. On 2nd July the Red forces abandoned Orenburg, and Blyukher's force and I. D. Kashirin's Southern Detachment arrived on 11th–12th at Beloretsk. Here the two forces were combined, with the result that on 2nd August, 1918, Blyukher was chosen to command the Composite South-Urals Detachment and worked out a plan for linking up with the Red Army.[45] Blyukher repeatedly broke through White encirclement in a series of spectacular raids and finally smashed his way through to the IIIrd Red army, where his forces were re-organised into the famous 51st Division. His conspicuous military ability prompted the rumour, doubtless helped by his strange name, that he was a former German or Austrian prisoner of war gone Bolshevik.* Blyukher led the 51st to fresh triumphs against Wrangel in November 1920, after which he was transferred to the Far East; here his real career began, culminating in his long command of the Special Red Banner Army of the Far East.

* * * *

At the centre, however, intrigue and dissension brought about a radical

* In all the speculation over Blyukher's name, it has proved possible to find only one actual alternative and that was put forward by General Niessel, whose information was to the effect that Blyukher's real name was Gurov. If Blyukher did give himself this *nom de guerre*, then it indicates at least an acquaintance with military history, if also a rather bizarre personal taste.

alteration in the high command. Against the background of hostility to Trotsky, a double struggle was being played out — the first being the final phases of the struggle over the Eastern Front and the second a mounting tension over the measures to be adopted against Denikin in the Ukraine. The enraged commissars of the Eastern Front had the ear of Stalin, who had already made plain his opinion of Commander-in-Chief Vatsetis in his report on the Perm catastrophe. Stalin had just conducted the successful defence of Petrograd against Yudenich's first blow, and with this increased prestige at his back, he pressed for the dismissal of Vatsetis. On 3rd July, 1919, Vatsetis was relieved of his command and replaced as commander-in-chief by S. S. Kamenev. On the morning of the same day it was further resolved to re-organise the membership of the Republic *Revvoensoviet.* These multiple thrusts at Trotsky accomplished the displacement of his old friends by the new men — Gusev, Smilga, Rykov and S. S. Kamenev — although Trotsky retained the presidency.[46] Trotsky and Kamenev clashed straightway over the strategic plan for dealing with Denikin in the south. S. S. Kamenev proposed a plan which aimed at dealing a blow designed to eliminate Denikin and his base in the Kuban. Trotsky very correctly saw that this did not take proper account of the Ukrainian political situation — sound as Kamenev's ideas might appear militarily. Coming so quickly upon the clash over the Eastern Front feud between Trotsky and Kamenev, Trotsky's enemies were given the chance to suggest that this was nothing but a continuation of an old struggle. Trotsky denies this, although he does not appear to have held Kamenev in much affection. Subsequent events justified Trotsky in his opposition to the original plan, but at this point Trotsky felt impelled to offer his resignation as an expression of his disquiet — but this was rejected on 5th July, 1919.[47] Trotsky acquiesced in this and proceeded to the Southern Front.

Trotsky had seen for himself the weakness in the Ukraine, in marked contrast to the Eastern Front, where the Soviet republic had made a heavy military investment. His pleas for reinforcements and supplies suggested an attempt to modify the Kamenev plan by shifting the balance of the military build-up to a line which he himself favoured. But no sooner had Trotsky returned to the scene of these giant and unrewarding labours in the south when a new blow fell upon him. At Kozlov he received a signal, dated 8th July and signed by Lenin, Sklyanskii, Dzerzhinskii and Krestinskii, intimating that Vatsetis was implicated in a military conspiracy and consequently under arrest. A certain Domozhirov, who had been proved a traitor, implicated Isayev, who had been attached to Vatsetis's staff.[48] Trotsky, doubtless shaken by the turn of events, later referred to Vatsetis's crime as being one of 'reckless talk' only, prompted possibly by resentment at his recent dismissal, or by perhaps just a little too much reading of Napoleon. Certainly the charges against Vatsetis were never substantiated (or even acted upon), while Stalin had long shown his ill-will towards the man and now used Dzerzhinskii of the *Cheka* to cut him down in order to strike afresh at Trotsky. Vatsetis lived to enjoy responsible posts in the Inspectorate, the Military Academy and the Militia Inspectorate of the Red Army after the Civil War.

The momentous turn of events in the south had tended inevitably to produce serious problems of command and threw up a spirited group of military leaders who rivalled the tenacious commanders of the east. In the south the historic clash between Trotsky and Stalin, played partly over the fortunes of the Xth Red army, led to an early conclusion of personal alliances which bedevilled command relationships long after the end of the Civil War. It was here that the 1st Cavalry Army was organised, and while it enjoyed a unique record during the Red-White struggle, this force fell under the increasingly powerful political patronage of Stalin. That scheming triumvirate of war and politics — Stalin, Voroshilov and Budenny — cast a giant shadow across the military and political destiny of Russia. It is this bitter and ugly partisanship which must be considered in connection with the dramatic and critical strifes of the summer of 1919 and Denikin's drive on Moscow.

While on the Eastern Front a relatively substantial Soviet force had been established during the winter of 1918–19, the same consolidations had not been worked in the Ukraine and Southern Russia. The centre's Directive No. 4 of 11th September, 1918, envisaged raising 47 divisions and 4 cavalry divisions; 11 would be formed in the east and originally 12 were planned for the south.[49] In the Ukraine itself the German occupation had driven out the thin Bolshevik forces, who had also to contend with anti-Bolshevik bands. Out of a desire to avoid a head-on clash with the Germans in the baleful summer of 1918 the Russian Central Committee had adopted the policy of underground resistance, rejecting Bubnov's and Pyatakov's plea for armed insurrection. Meanwhile the White General Krasnov was clearing the region of the Don of Bolshevik forces. Voroshilov, at the head of a motley force of Red Guards and armed workers, cut his way to the east from Lugansk, fighting off Krasnov's men until he came within striking distance of Tsaritsyn on the curve of the Volga.

In May 1918 Stalin proceeded under orders to the North Caucasus and to Tsaritsyn to organise food supplies for the hinterland. On 13th June Lenin received a signal from Stalin to the effect that the situation in Tsaritsyn had deteriorated owing to White Cossack attacks, and he would not now be proceeding to Novorossiisk to deal with the scuttling of the Black Sea

Fleet.[50] Stalin had no senior military appointment; he later rejected the place proffered by Trotsky in the Republic *Revvoensoviet*,[51] but turned himself into what Trotsky termed a 'manager of all the military forces at the front'.* In Tsaritsyn itself Voroshilov converted the town into 'the Red Verdun', the praises of which were sung in the political mythology which grew up to glorify Stalin's part in the Civil War. Trotsky set Voroshilov's military talents at only a point or two above zero, describing him as a 'hearty and impudent fellow' and as 'a gifted brow-beater'.[52] His military company — the ex-tailor Shchadenko, the local orator Minin — inspired even less of the War Commissar's confidence. The Tsaritsyn group carried on its own private war, less real *partizanshchina* than downright insubordination; Stalin seems to have lent his encouragement to this. On 5th October, 1918, Trotsky counter-attacked by setting up a formal military command for the Southern Front under the 'military specialist' Sytin, with Shlyapnikov, Lazimir and Mekhonoshin as commissars.

Trotsky managed to gain the re-call of Stalin, but faced a much aggravated situation when Stalin returned to Tsaritsyn. Trotsky finally travelled to the front, where he faced Voroshilov — who temporised.[53] Commissar Okulov was sent to the Xth Red army to keep a watch upon Voroshilov and his men. On 14th December, 1918, Trotsky telegraphed to Lenin that it was imperative that Voroshilov be transferred to the Ukraine and cease to work his particular havoc with the Xth. But once Voroshilov was in the Ukraine there was reason to suspect him of disrupting the staff work and of attacking the 'military specialists'. The violence of the polemic or the extremes of the eulogy in the writings of Trotsky and the Stalinist historians respectively on the Stalin-Voroshilov stand over Tsaritsyn make clarification difficult. There were not infrequently sound reasons for over-ruling the 'military specialists'. Yet to convert this into a policy, and to follow an intimidating course designed almost to force the ex-officer to be counter-revolutionary, was entirely without justification. And it is an open question whether Voroshilov's own military talents justified this calculated arrogance.

As for the general situation, Trotsky desired to press on with the investment of the Ukraine and seize the opportunity afforded by the collapse of German power. Lenin was more concerned with the Northern Caucausus and the region of the Don, which he wished to see denied to the White forces as their base. When Kolchak had driven to Perm, there was a danger of Denikin striking up the Volga and effecting a junction. Tsaritsyn barred

* The *Pravda* note (31st May) on Stalin's appointment mentioned the 'general direction of supply questions in the south of Russia', also 'special powers'. There was nothing to stop Stalin becoming a 'military manager', although Stalin did gradually work his way into the military command, the climax to which occurred in 1920 in the Polish campaign.

the road for him, but Kolchak was beaten back in the east.[54] The Soviet forces were able to mount something of an offensive in the Ukraine in the spring of 1919. Antonov-Ovseenko played a substantial part in these victories,[55] and by April the Ukrainian nationalist forces under Petlura were being scattered. Having swept to the west, the militant Communists were planning to take the offensive against Rumania and thus internationalise the Revolution.[56] Podvoiskii and Bubnov, in company with Antonov-Ovseenko, acted as the general command in the Ukraine, and their manner of doing it went right against Trotsky's centralised methods. Trotsky accused Antonov-Ovseenko of actually encouraging the independence and guerrilla-ism of the Ukrainian troops.[57] Lenin wanted full concentration on the vital task of assisting the Don region and the second mission of forming '. . . solid connections by rail with Soviet Hungary'.[58]

Denikin gradually mobilised his strength in the Kuban. In the Ukraine the peasants in the Soviet rear became increasingly disillusioned with the realities of Soviet rule and harried the Bolsheviks with raids in April 1919.[59] In the following month Ataman Grigoriev, with whom the Bolsheviks were in precarious alliance, raised a serious rebellion, which was finally crushed but added greatly to Soviet difficulties and weakness as Denikin's armies were beginning to strike. Trotsky was appalled at the Ukrainian situation, which needed an iron hand and massive reinforcement of men and materials. It was evidently his intention to change the command of the Ukraine in favour of a person or persons who would deal very vigorously with the guerrilla-ism which was rampant.[60] These proposed changes remained unrealised as Denikin struck at the end of May 1919, dealing heavy blows to the four Red armies in the south. Vsevolodov, commander of the IXth Red army, deserted to the White troops. By the end of June the White army, supported by the Cossacks, had taken Tsaritsyn, occupied the Donets Basin and taken Kharkov, all against a not very serious Soviet resistance.

On 3rd July, 1919, Denikin issued his 'Moscow Directive', prescribing a triple drive on the capital. This was the moment when Trotsky, harried by his own enemies, was on the point of resigning. At the front anti-Soviet guerrillas impeded the Red troops, but the greatest danger was presented by the splendid White cavalry, which was virtually free to raid as it pleased. The Soviet military build-up for a counter-offensive went hand in hand with what Trotsky viewed as a disastrous strategic plan for the use of this strength. S. S. Kamenev proffered a scheme for striking at the eastern end of the front, into the Don and at Tsaritsyn, aiming at Denikin's base; this had the added advantage of keeping Kolchak and Denikin completely separated. The real disadvantage was that it meant fighting along a line of poor communications and in the midst of a population — Cossacks — who would resist. Although the Cossacks formed a part of Denikin's forces, Trotsky saw correctly that they could be split off from the White Guards; attacking rather towards Kharkov, the Red Army would have behind it a sympathetic population and excellent communications, and could drive a wedge between the Cossacks and the White Guards.

V. N. Yegor'ev* on 27th July, 1919, had pointed out the unsoundness of the Kamenev plan, which as Southern Front commander, he was asked to put into effect. Trotsky at once communicated this fact to Lenin.[61] The offensive on the eastern sector of the front began early in August, with Shorin and Selivachev struggling with their forces to make any substantial progress; in effect, the offensive broke down and at the end of September Trotsky could in all truth write that the situation was worse than at the beginning of the action.

* * * *

Besides the plan, the Red Army urgently needed cavalry to parry the devastating White raids. Semyen Mikhailovich Budenny made the largest contribution to answering this problem. Born in 1883, Budenny was a professional cavalryman, having served in the Russo-Japanese War and in the First World War. His skill he had learned at the St Petersburg Riding School of the Imperial cavalry.[62] During the troubled months of 1917 he had been elected to his regimental committee and in November Budenny began organising a Bolshevik detachment to fight in the Donbas. Stalin had met Budenny for the first time in July 1918, when the ex-NCO of cavalry came out well from an encounter with General Snesarev's questions on tactics.[63] At the end of July Budenny and Voroshilov met in connection with planning a cavalry raid, which was a conspicuous success. During his trip to the south, Trotsky inspected Budenny's squadron; in response to Budenny's plea for cavalry divisions and corps, Trotsky replied: 'You don't understand the nature of cavalry. That is a very aristocratic family of troops, commanded by princes, barons and counts. . . .'[64] Nevertheless, on 28th November, 1918, Budenny's force was re-organised into a composite division, with two brigades. Dumenko held the principal command, with

* V. N. Yegor'ev is to be distinguished from A. I. Yegorov. Yegor'ev had taken over the front command from V. M. Gittis on 12th July and Yegorov was named assistant to the front commander. It was at the meeting of commanders at Kozlov on 24th July that Yegor'ev, Sokol'nikov (commissar) and Peremytov (chief of the operational staff) first came out as opponents of the Kamenev plan, a meeting which evidently turned out to be a first-class row. In spite of the obvious weight of the objections raised, and disregarding the subsequent course of events, modern Soviet accounts still accuse Trotsky of 'sabotaging Party orders' and undermining the authority of the *Glavkom*. Lenin on 28th intervened with a telegram based on a *Politburo* decision, warning against 'vacillations' and upholding Kamenev.

Budenny as chief of staff, but when Dumenko fell ill with typhus, command devolved upon Budenny.

Budenny's brigade commanders were Gorodovikov (1st) and Timoshenko (2nd). Semyen Konstantinovich Timoshenko had been born in 1895 in the village of Furmanko in Bessarabia, of a peasant family. He attended the village school and worked as a barrel-maker, but was mobilised in 1915, becoming an NCO. In 1918 he fought with partisan detachments in the Crimea and Kuban before joining up with Budenny. He later assumed command of the crack 6th Division of the 1st Cavalry Army.[65] A small reinforcement to Timoshenko's brigade at this time included a party of Red cavalry sent from Moscow, with several ex-Imperial NCOs among them. One of the recruits was Georgi Konstantinovich Zhukov, already known as a brave and outstanding soldier; he had served with distinction in the 10th Novgorod Dragoon Regiment of the 10th Cavalry Division of the Imperial Russian Army.[66] Zhukov was twenty-two when he began that long and fruitful association with the 1st Cavalry Army. Many miles removed, but also operating with the cavalry of the 30th Division on the Eastern Front, was another future Marshal of the Soviet Union, K. K. Rokossovskii.

The situation with regard to Denikin had meanwhile deteriorated drastically. In the middle of August the White cavalry leader Mamontov carried out a devastating raid in the Soviet rear, creating havoc. With the failure of the Soviet counter-offensive to the east, Denikin did what Trotsky had foreseen he would do: he struck on to the Kursk-Voronezh region in late September. Trotsky's objections and protests did not avail against the firm, fanatical intention to hold the original plan. Trotsky's proposed re-groupings were ignored. On 11th October, Yudenich in the north launched a sudden second blow at Petrograd, taking Yamburg once again.[67] Denikin took Orel on 13th, leaving only Tula (a big munitions centre) between him and Moscow. Kamenev's plan had cracked wide open, literally opening the door to Denikin through Voronezh and Orel. In the face of calamity, Trotsky's plan was finally adopted and the front split into two operating groups, under Yegorov and Shorin.[68] The groups would act to the north-west of Orel and to the east of Voronezh, where Budenny's cavalry was moving. The frantic re-grouping was complete by mid-October and the attack prepared. Trotsky had meanwhile gone to Petrograd to direct the defence of the city against Yudenich, the successful outcome of which gained him enormous acclaim and prestige.

Budenny's cavalry had moved into the Voronezh area, in defiance of orders to proceed to the south-east. Going north, Budenny had heard that Mamontov was about to stage another of his raids and sought to forestall him and bring him to battle. In the subsequent engagement Mamontov was defeated and Budenny occupied Voronezh on 24th. With the fall of Orenburgh and Voronezh to Red troops, fortune changed fast in the Ukraine. On 15th November Budenny took Kastornaya, driving a wedge between the White

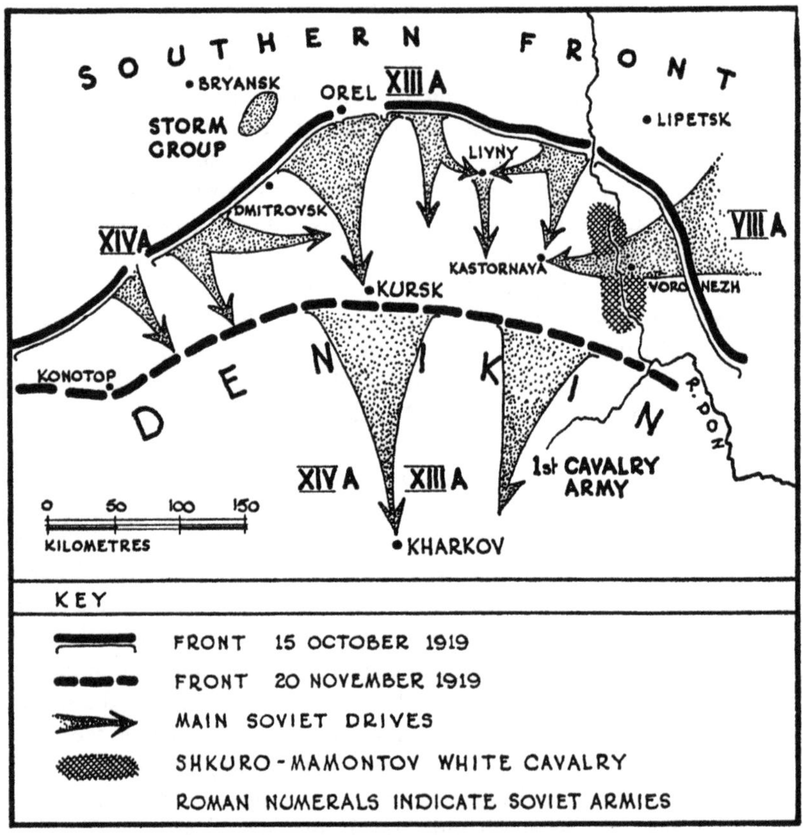

COUNTER-OFFENSIVE AGAINST DENIKIN
October-November, 1919.

Guards and the Don Cossacks. Red infantry prised White troops out of Kursk and after 17th November began pushing on to Rostov.

On 2nd December, 1919, Budenny's cavalry corps became officially the 1st Cavalry Army, with its *Revvoensoviet* staffed by Voroshilov, Shchadenko and Budenny. The first meeting was held on 6th, with Stalin, Voroshilov, Shchadenko and Yegorov in attendance.[69] Aleksander Ilyich Yegorov, the front commander, impressed Budenny as a 'military specialist' of some quality. Son of a poor family, Yegorov had distinguished himself at school and entered the army. During the First World War he showed great personal courage, being wounded five times and ending as a regimental commander. In 1917 the Provisional Government arrested him for his criticisms of its policy. After November 1917 Yegorov worked in the 'screens' and various military committees before going to the Ukraine. After the Left SR rising in 1918 he joined the Communist Party. Budenny vouched for his courage in action as well as his reticence over his technical skills — 'he comported himself modestly' — not brandishing his education like so many other ex-officers.[70]

From the Eastern Front, I. N. Smirnov reported on 4th December, 1919, that Kolchak's army had been battered into pieces. To the north Yudenich fell back from Petrograd, retiring to internment in Estonia. In the south Denikin could not stave off disaster as the 1st Cavalry Army drove the White troops back to their starting line, splitting them in two. Denikin was forced back across the Don and the Manych into the Northern Caucasus, while Wrangel was trapped in the Crimea. By Novocherkassk and Rostov, under the pale sun of winter, the Red and White cavalry joined in a mighty clash. On 8th January, 1920, Budenny's troopers clattered into Rostov-on-Don, the ultimate victors.

The Civil War fronts had meanwhile undergone modifications. Frunze's eastern command had developed into the Turkestan Front, where the paths of Malenkov and Bulganin first crossed in executing military-political and security duties. At the end of November 1919 Tukhachevsky handed over the famous Vth Red army to G. Kh. Eikhe and was transferred to the Southern Front. On 19th January, 1920, however, Tukhachevsky wired to Trotsky that he was virtually without employment in Kursk; could he not be assigned to the People's Commissariat for Military Affairs or to transportation?[71] Trotsky placed the blame for this suspiciously enforced idleness upon Stalin, and Tukhachevsky was very literally in what might be termed Stalin's territory. Stalin's ring of friends tightened visibly here and this Tukhachevsky was soon to discover for himself. He finally moved to Rostov, where he took command of the closing stages of the destruction of Denikin's forces.

As the VIIIth and IXth Red armies moved up behind the 1st Cavalry Army Budenny received orders to storm the Bataisk Heights, which had been invested by Denikin with a strong force equipped with artillery. On 16th January, 1920, the Soviet cavalry — deprived as yet of the support of the three Red armies assigned (VIIIth, Xth and IXth), which were still re-grouping — received its orders for the assault. The tornado of White artillery and machine-gun fire shattered the Soviet attack. Shorin, the new commander, refused to fall in with Budenny's modified plan. Having failed to convince Shorin of the futility of hurling cavalry against these defences, Voroshilov, Budenny and Shchadenko asked to be relieved of their commands. This was refused, whereupon they sent a telegram to Lenin, Trotsky and Stalin. After further fruitless attacks, on 1st February Budenny visited the front Field Staff, writing that same night a letter of appeal to Lenin about the waste of fine cavalry and the intransigence of Shorin who fastened them in a trap of swamp and mud.[72] On 3rd Budenny spoke to Stalin on the telephone; the latter decided to send Ordzhonikidze to join the 1st Cavalry command, and blamed Sokol'nikov (VIIIth army commander) for surrounding the 1st Cavalry Army with 'an atmosphere of enmity and malice'. On 5th Tukhachevsky and Ordzhonikidze issued orders to Budenny allowing him to take the Bataisk position from the rear.[73]

At the end of February Budenny and Voroshilov met Tukhachevsky at Bataisk, where his coach was in a railway siding. As soon as they presented themselves Tukhachevsky berated them for disobeying orders. Budenny eyed the young man, '. . . looking no more than twenty-five. He held himself firmly — even in an intimidating pose . . . a truly young man, good looking . . . one not yet accustomed to his high position.' As soon as Budenny's report was concluded, Tukhachevsky left. Budenny and Voroshilov immediately questioned Ordzhonikidze about the new commander. There was little Ordzhonikidze could tell them, except that Tukhachevsky wished to and knew how to fight, he studied Clausewitz and he was young and hot-blooded, seldom thinking out a course of action to its logical conclusion. He did not, however, conceal from his listeners that Tukhachevsky was not well-disposed towards the 1st Cavalry Army and in particular to Budenny.[74] This mutual lack of confidence was to have enormous consequences some six months later in the course of the war with Poland.

At the time of these exchanges the Soviet republic was experiencing something in the nature of a lull, confident that it now stood upon the prospect of victory in the Civil War. In December 1919 Trotsky had spoken of the achievements of the regime and its military men at the 7th Congress of Soviets, singling out Frunze, Sokol'nikov and Tukhachevsky for special mention as commanders of merit and distinction. It was here that Trotsky spoke once again of the transition to a militia, and this programme went forward to the 9th Party Congress in March 1920.[75] It was very much the inspiration of optimism and was at the mercy of a change in circumstances. At the beginning of 1920, although relations with Poland were troubled and involved, the weight of the military momentum was beginning to shift, not to the west, but to the east, into the Russian border-lands. In his Turkestan operations Frunze retained F. F. Novitskii as his chief of staff until October 1919, when Baltiiskii took over this post; Piotr Ionovich Baranov, a future commander of the Red Air Force and associate of Frunze, joined the *Revvoensoviet* of the front. Kuibyshev detached himself to control the establishment of Soviet military and political power in the Trans-Caspian area, a task which was completed by February 1920 with the occupation of Krasnovodsk. In the same month Frunze arrived in Tashkent and proceeded to try to implement a policy designed to win the native population by concessions.[76] The next stage meant a sustained military effort in Central Asia to reduce the remaining White bands and the several native populations.

Denikin's retreat and collapse had also hurried Red troops back into the Northern Caucasus and brought within sight the possibility of reducing the independent Caucasian republics to Soviet rule. After the opening of friendly relations between Soviet Russia and Kemalist Turkey, the three states of Georgia, Armenia and Azerbaidzhan were gripped in a vice from which there was no escape. Tukhachevsky was given the military command of the Northern Caucasus, with Ordzhonikidze and Kirov as the commissars of the new Caucasian Bureau.[77] The first move was made against Azerbaidzhan in April with the XIth Red army, but by this time the gravity of the situation in the west, where full-scale war with Poland was imminent, caused Tukhachevsky's transfer to the Western Front and a heavy shift in the military emphasis to the west once more. The resumption of these operations at the end of 1920 was motivated not by reasons of defence but rather by aggressive designs, carried out by men who owed not a little of their advancement to Stalin and upon whose support they could rely.

* * * *

In view of the fact that the Civil War had been dominated by land engagements, the naval and air arms had contributed relatively little to the scale of the operations. Consequently their place in the command organisation was markedly subordinated to the basic interests of the Red Army. Soviet aviation could muster few machines. Pre-1917 aircraft production had amounted to only forty machines from three factories. An Aviation Technical Council had been set up after November 1917, and on 20th December it was decided to form squadrons from the available aircraft. At the bidding of *Sovnarkom* the Main Administration of the Workers-Peasants Military Air Fleet was set up in May 1918, and on 10th August the Field Administration of Aviation Units (*Aviadarm*) was organised for the control of squadrons. There were 349 machines at the fronts on 1st February, 1919; of the 1,100 machines on hand, 719 were in store (163 had no engines and 363 were unserviceable).[78] Nevertheless, some 30 Red flights each of six aircraft took part in operations, and there was a small number of machines for naval aviation. But not until the mid-1920s did the Red Air Force receive any systematic attention to its command, organisation, personnel and equipment.

The Baltic sailors had already played an outstanding part in the Bolshevik seizure of power, but the basic problem was to organise an effective and

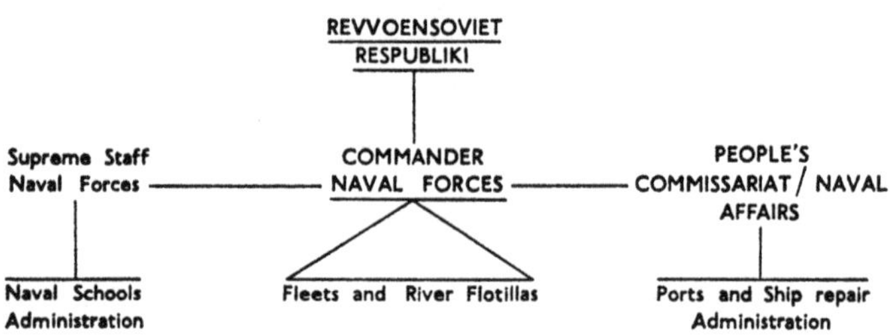

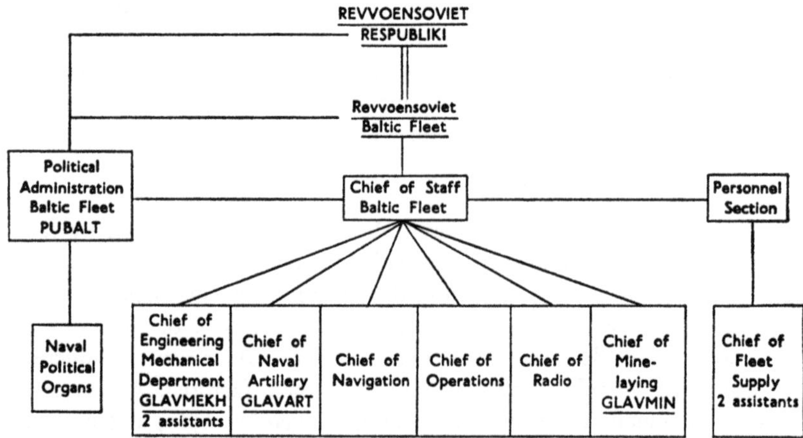

reliable naval command. As with the Red Army, taking over the former Imperial administration for the Russian Navy provided the means for keeping naval affairs under control. The Central Committee of the All-Russian Naval Forces (*Tsentroflot*) had acted, immediately after the seizure of power, as an initial command group with Dybenko and Raskol'nikov as the Bolshevik commissars working with Admiral Al'tfater to supervise the fleet from a Naval Collegiate. The All-Russian Congress of Fleet

Sailors, which held its meetings in Petrograd in middle and late November, pushed forward other changes for operations on a wider scale. The Congress elected P. E. Dybenko as People's Commissar of the Naval Ministry, Captain 1st Class Modest Vasil'evich Ivanov (former commander of the 2nd Cruiser Squadron of the Baltic Fleet) as director of the Naval Ministry and the Black Sea sailor V. V. Koval'skii as a second member of the Collegiate. The Political Section of the Naval Collegiate was also organised, with I. I. Vakhrameev, Zheleznyakov, Zedin, Maksimovich and Sherstobitov as its members. Ivanov was promoted to rear-admiral and chief petty officers Vahkrameev and Raskol'nikov made lieutenants.[79] Legal functions and regulations were lodged with the Supreme Naval Committee of Enquiry[80] and the staff organisations in the fleet placed under the control of the Naval Collegiate.

Order No. 113 of 12th February, 1918, set up the People's Commissariat for Naval Affairs, retaining Dybenko as head and adding Saks to the persons of Vakhrameev and Raskol'nikov as commissars. The administration of the Baltic Fleet was vested, by the *Sovnarkom* decree of 20th February, in the Soviet of Baltic Fleet Commissars, while the operational aspects were placed under the Military (Operational) Section of *Tsentrobalt*. This arrangement lasted until 6th December, 1918, when the *Revvoensoviet* of the Baltic Fleet took over the administrative control and operational command of the Baltic Fleet, and *Tsentrobalt* was officially closed down on 18th.[81] The principal operational commitment in the first half of 1918 was to deny the ships of the Baltic Fleet and in the Black Sea to the Germans. After an arduous struggle, in which the ice-breaker squadrons played an important part, the ships of the Baltic Fleet were successfully transferred from the Finnish station of Helsingfors to the naval base at Kronstadt. Disaffection among the officers, without whom the ships could not be run, was widespread. Admiral Shchastnyi, who had played a large part in the operation transferring the ships of the Baltic Fleet, was later executed — the object lesson which this deed provided far out-weighing the actual issue of the charge of counter-revolution. In June 1918 the scuttling of the Black Sea Fleet units was also intended to deprive the Germans of possible prizes.

Large naval units played little or no part in the subsequent Civil War operations.* Baltic Fleet sailors were sent to man the river flotillas on the

* In the Baltic, Russian naval units were opposed by ships of the Royal Navy. After indecisive engagements in May 1919, a surprise British attack with aircraft and torpedo-boats on Kronstadt on 18th August succeeded in disabling two Soviet battleships and other smaller vessels. The Soviet cruiser *Oleg* had been torpedoed in June. The result of these actions was to cause the virtual cessation of Soviet naval operations, and there was no challenge to British naval hegemony in the Baltic, itself established to prevent the Baltic States falling under Bolshevik power. In 1939, Stalin was to recall those torpedo-boat raids in arguing with the Finns over a concession for a Soviet naval base at Hango.

Volga and the Caspian, or made up the storm-squads sent to the Ukraine early in 1918. Ships of the Baltic Fleet were used to transport supplies and small naval units were employed in Stalin's operations for the defence of Petrograd in May 1919; Stalin took the opportunity to rail once again about the ex-officers, this time in the guise of 'naval specialists', although with some justification, for treason was not uncommon.[82] Both officers and seamen, rather than the ships, presented the major difficulties of the new Workers-Peasants Red Fleet. The use of the Imperial officers was quite essential and there was little hope of creating any kind of Red naval command except over a long period. The naval commissars tended to side with the ratings against the officers. The original men of 1917 became widely scattered throughout Russia on *Cheka*, military, and detached flotilla duties. The signs of indiscipline, which had shown themselves from the outset, grew stronger; peasant replacements fell under the influence of considerable and prolonged political agitation. The culmination was the Kronstadt rebellion of February 1921, when the sailors took up arms and manned the gun-batteries against the regime. This further retarded the development of the Red Navy, adding political unreliability to the technical stagnation and command difficulties. The lag in development continued until 1926, when the Soviet naval command approached the German *Reichsmarine* for assistance in training and technical re-construction.[83]

* * * *

In the course of some eighteen months the Red Army had surpassed the original figure of three million men set by Lenin. Sixteen Red armies had operated around a perimeter of 5,000 miles. Approximately a million deserters had been apprehended or returned to their units; at one point in 1919 the number of deserters almost equalled the combat strength of the Red Army as set down in Vatsetis's strength returns.[84] In an army composed mainly of peasants, the proportion of workers rose only slowly; the Mobilisation Section of the All-Russian Staff reported that at the end of the Civil War the Red Army included in its strength 630–760,000 workers, or 15–18 per cent of the total strength.[85] Over this strangely-assorted company of arms and politics was ranged a command group which had also developed considerably since the first days of the mobilisation of the 'military specialists' in mid-1918. It was obvious from the first that Communist man-power, while it may have been liberally and often heroically expended at the fronts, could not hope to fill the growing number of important command posts and those at a lower level. Somewhere in the region of 30,000 of the ex-Imperial officers had taken over staff and command positions in the various Red armies in the field, while the remainder manned the military administration and instructor branch. At the same time a heavy, if uneven programme of training courses had been put into operation to raise up a proletarian officer cadre. From the original 18 courses in 1918, they had grown to 63 in 1919 and 153 by the end of 1920.[86] By a reflex of professionalism, the ex-officers seem to have tried to turn out passable products from their courses, although the reception of the junior 'Red commander' might be marked by a lack of enthusiasm in his new unit. Here the commander, himself not infrequently an ex-officer, looked askance at men turned out 'by a bunch of political agitators', while the commissar probed the social and political background of the young man. The unit commander would submit the junior to his own personal and private examination.[87] In general, the products of the latter-day courses — late 1919–20 — did not secure so firm a niche in the military hierarchy as the men of 1918, who had passed the tests of war and unit loyalties at an earlier stage.

The Red Army General Staff Academy was formally opened by Ya. M. Sverdlov on 8th December, 1918, by which time 183 pupils were chosen from the 435 candidates to attend the shortened courses. The teaching plan called for a seven-month course, with 280 hours of the total of 940 devoted to practical instruction. Short staff courses were also organised at the fronts in April 1919; 22 pupils were enrolled on the Southern Front on 13th April and 30 on 23rd May.[88] Academies of Artillery, Military Engineering, Military Medicine, Supply and Naval studies were also organised from the frame-work of the old Imperial military academic system. Only a very small number of trained higher commanders could be turned out, and it is difficult to assess the impact which this had. Taking the case of Chapayev, the commander of the 25th Division, his guerrilla-ism was far from subdued by his attending such a course. Furmanov's comments in his life of Chapayev make it clear that, if anything, the turbulent commander was further confirmed in his opposition to the ex-officers by his closer contact with them.[89] It was not until after the Civil War that a real start could be made with large-scale training of the higher command staffs — rendered difficult by the low level of general education possessed by the student-commanders.

In spite of the discrepancy in numbers when comparing the ex-officers and the Communist commanders, it is still possible to speak of a Soviet command, albeit one still in the difficult stages of emergence and cohesion. The battle-fronts were a powerful factor in throwing up men of talent who had a capacity for military command and were loyal to the Bolsheviks. Yet this company contained many different elements; the Chapayev type was an invaluable asset but difficult to incorporate into a regular command. Blyukher is, perhaps, in a class on his own, a many-sided talent who rendered long and valuable service to the Soviet government. Frunze was in his person equally exceptional, but his type did conform to the generation of good, painstaking middle- and senior-grade command staff who came from the Party and were sufficiently endowed with native ability to carry through their tasks. The divisional commanders of the type of V. I. Kikvidze, Kotovskii, E. I. Kovtyukh and I. S. Kutyakov were those who formed a spectacular, if nevertheless capable group of men who were later educated for more senior positions.

Discernible also is a small group of what might be called 'the young professionals', with Tukhachevsky as the best example, or I. E. Yakir, another representative. Yakir was by origin a Bessarabian Jew, born in 1896 and a member of the Party since 1917. He had been a member of the Bessarabian Soldiers Committee, and had taken part in the campaigns against Denikin, and later against Poland. The two figures of Primakov and Putna, both successful cavalry and infantry divisional commanders, had a similar representation. By association a number of the 'military specialists' who held senior field commands — Yegorov, Shorin, Samoilo, S. S. Kamenev — might well be included in the circle of Soviet command proper; what was of supreme importance was the political alliances which they contracted at this turbulent stage. At the highest command level, the regime was fortunate in having the services of senior ex-officers who were content to carry out their functions to the best of their not inconsiderable abilities. S. S. Kamenev possessed talent above the average — if also a little recklessness. P. P. Lebedev was an invaluable acquisition to the Red Army Staff, and Shaposhnikov made similar large contributions.

The political command furnished in addition a second source of men versed in military affairs yet having a further dimension of responsibilities. At the highest levels there developed what might be called the super-commissar, figures such as Ordzhonikidze, Kuibyshev and Kirov, or Gusev, Shvernik and Mekhlis. Stalin himself represented a unique development in this.* They were closely associated with the work of the armies in the field, with higher command functions and military planning. The collegiate system of command raised their role to great importance and provided the Red Army with a grade of men much experienced in the war which it was fighting and later very active in formulating the political lessons of such warfare.

*In an article in *Kommunist* (No. 2, 1958) Marshal Bagramyan listed the outstanding commanders and commissars of the Civil War. Of the commissars, Stalin came third on a list of 19 names, but he was preceded by Kalinin and Sverdlov. Kalinin was a mere figure-head and Sverdlov died soon after the Civil War began, so that Stalin emerges as the leading commissar, in effect. Khrushchev was listed seventeenth. Of the outstanding commanders, Frunze heads the list, with Blyukher fifth; Voroshilov, Budenny and Apanasenko precede him. Uborevich, Yakir and Timoshenko are listed, but there is no mention of Tukhachevsky, Yegorov, Eideman. None of the 're-habilitations' or recent historical accounts devote either space or accuracy to Tukhachevsky. Of the 're-habilitated' commanders, only Blyukher has emerged from the obliteration visited upon the military command, with any effective presentation.

Conflict and tension, however, quickly gathered about the person and status of the military commissar, who was already making his career out of participation in many of the duties usually associated with military command in the normal and accepted sense. A certain amount of this had been envisaged by Trotsky's early remarks on the reconciliation of the commander and the commissar which he hoped for, but beyond hints of how

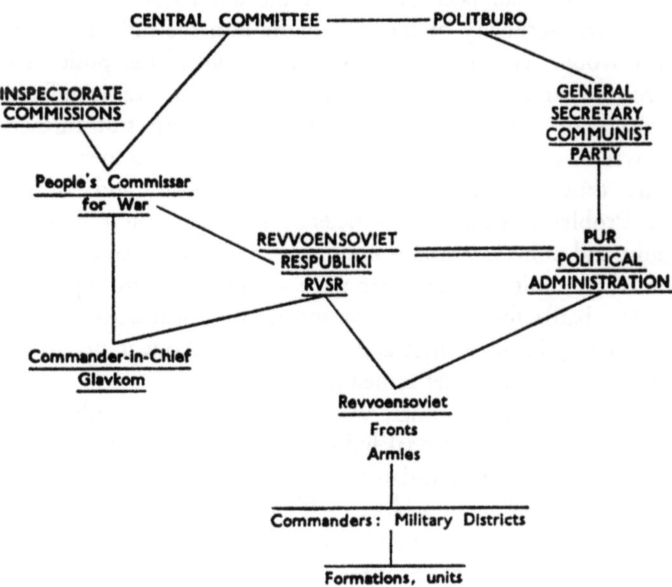

the relationship might develop, Trotsky did not commit himself to a programme which either relegated or advanced the commissar. If anything, the whole division of command seemed to exist as a feature distinctly temporary and produced out of a very visible necessity. It had proved impossible, not unnaturally, to foresee how the military commissar would develop his position in the Soviet military system. At the First All-Russian Assembly of Political Workers in 1919 the problem took a startling turn, when no less a person than the head of the Political Administration — Ivan Smilga — opened the campaign for the abolition of dual command. Smilga's remarks, made no doubt with the full cognisance of Trotsky, showed under what strain the whole system of command was labouring.

Smilga advocated that military commanders of proved loyalty should be divested of their commissar chaperones — this had been heard before — but his point was that the present command system should be reviewed in its entirety. Out of the stress and innovations of war, the original schemes and institutions were taking some punishment and parts of the military-political scheme had already outlived their usefulness.[90] Coming as it did from the top level of the Political Administration, the charge was a grave one and suggested that the principle of military efficiency was taking a strong hold, supported by pressures from the military command. Smilga's views clashed head-on with some of the opinion within the Military Opposition, which had been arguing at the 8th Party Congress for the extension of the authority of the commissar into the military-operational field. This would have led to the normalisation of the position of the military commissar within the whole military structure, yet it suffered from the drawback of complicating the command system still further. The problem was not merely that the Red Army could absorb or eject its commissars, thus regularising the business of authority and command at one blow. Problems of military proficiency and education, the place of the Communist and non-Communist commander and the level of the military education of the military commissar were all entwined into separate sets of interests. The battle for 'unity of command', one-man authority (*edinonachalie*) had begun in all earnest and the struggle about it was waged for many long years in the Soviet armed forces.

Beyond the fronts and armies, where the stresses of combat produced alliances of interests and personal links common to all such situations, the early divisions within the Russian Communist Party over military policy accelerated the formation of a bloc, itself sharing certain opinions and experiences, and this gave 'the Red command' its first definite outline as a political force. Directed at Trotsky, two issues were at stake — what Trotsky had done to the Red Army and what he now purposed to do with it. After the 8th Congress, the opposition to Trotsky shifted its attack from the organisation of the Red Army to discussions of strategy and tactics as used in the Civil War. The notion that there existed a 'proletarian science of war', that the Red Army was employing it and that here lay the secret of its success began to gain ground. The supporters of this idea included the inevitable number of extremists, but there is no doubt that among men of the stamp and inclination of Frunze the conviction was growing that they — the Red commanders, self-taught and battle-tested — were devising something quite new in the history of warfare, and waging war with a unique military instrument, the Red Army. This art they had fashioned for themselves, while they had helped fashion the military machine. There was, as it were, a special ingredient to their victories. It is more correct to say that the Red command was experiencing the first onset of professionalism and pride of achievement, rooted in ambition both for themselves and the Red Army for and in which they were fighting.

In a rudimentary form this had already provoked clashes with Trotsky and new storms were brewing over the creation of the proposed militia. Trotsky was beginning to occupy himself increasingly not with military but economic affairs. Military policy was about to be set upon by the various feuding interests, all of which showed remarkable vitality. Stalin had on more than one occasion utilised momentary grievances to fashion a clique of calculated malevolence and self-seeking discord against Trotsky. Voroshilov and Budenny of the 1st Cavalry Army could be expected to foster discontents and lend their aid in a struggle with Trotsky and the 'military specialists' identified with him. Stalin had tried to topple Trotsky from the leadership of the Red Army; it had been a notable victory when Trotsky's protegé Vatsetis had been trundled out of the post of Commander-in-Chief. There can be no judgement but that Trotsky had made a massive and unique contribution to Soviet victory in the Civil War, and that the Red Army was his creation, but the off-shoot of his methods and his long-term policy were leading to a situation of acute conflict. The diversion of Trotsky's attention to matters other than military provoked a crisis, which might otherwise have been kept in check. On the other hand, Trotsky had made it plain that his mission was to organise victory, not to become the ultimate arbiter of the destiny of the Soviet armed forces. His ideas remained linked with those notions of the potentialities of Soviet society which he had continually entertained, and the emphasis of his thought was political rather than military. This was the key to his success in the Red Army as well as the factor contriving his withdrawal. The great difficulty in estimating Trotsky's final contribution to the history of the Soviet armed forces is to distinguish between what he regarded as merely temporary innovations and what limitations he would ascribe to a temporariness which necessity transformed into a curious permanence.

This war of 'little valour and no mercy' opened in the winter of 1919–20 into its final tormented stage, to which was added a new and dramatic twist with the war against Poland and the Soviet advance to the outskirts of Warsaw. Inter-command feuds were further intensified by this operation, while at the same time, the re-organisation of the military establishment and the radical solution proposed for a transition to the militia system appeared to split the command wide apart. Trotsky's plans were a political as well as a military challenge, which his opponents on the Central Committee and at the highest levels of the military command were not unwilling to accept and exploit.

CHAPTER FOUR

Before the Gates of Warsaw: 1920

The capacity in which the Red Army would or could support the external revolutionary aspirations of the Russian Communist Party had begun to occupy the minds of the military-political leadership over the question of Hungary and possibly Rumania. In 1920 this issue occupied even more attention on the part of Lenin, Trotsky, Stalin and the Red Army leadership. The connections between the military and political offensive were far from being clear. The absence of definite limits and firm conditions rendered this speculation not so much unrealistic as especially removed, as it were, from the more orthodox relationship of military factors to foreign policy planning. In the Soviet view, war brought in its wake social eruptions which favoured revolution. The general post-war ferment was sufficiently advanced in the winter of 1919–20 for this issue to be argued optimistically. Eastern and Central Europe had been flung into a post-Versailles turmoil in which the traditional order wavered and all but collapsed. Germany showed brilliant revolutionary promise. In the east, colonialism roused and stirred bitter passions, which the Russian Communists hoped to turn to their advantage. The *Komintern*, dedicated to the cause of organising revolution on a world-wide scale, flourished in cosmopolitan hands.

Yet the Red Army's major offensive action upon non-Soviet soil proved to be a chastening and much debated experience. It added one real illustration of how far revolution could be carried on bayonets, but its very frustration did not provide a final and conclusive demonstration in futility to the 'internationalists' in the Red Army and Party leadership. The relation of foreign and military policies was most imperfectly understood in the early Soviet state, and the clarification of this issue — vital for any state — occupied many troubled years. Lenin and Trotsky constantly looked over their shoulders at the European scene and later at the east. In the general business of recovering her old frontiers, a *Realpolitik* which escaped the internationalists and mollified the ex-Imperial segment of the military command, Soviet Russia had not been wholly unsuccessful in her piecemeal settlements.

With the absence, however, of official Russian representation at the

Peace Conference, it was inevitable that only a tentative solution could be found for the involved question of the Russo-Polish frontier.[1] In December 1919 the 'Curzon line' set up a minimum demarcation between the two countries, but while the diplomats bickered and bartered, Piłsudski of Poland acted energetically to accomplish his own settlement for the western border areas. Polish troops occupied Vilno in April 1919 and drove out Soviet forces. Piłsudski aimed to detach Russia's former western border provinces from Soviet grasp by creating a 'federation' of new states, whose leader could only be Poland. Russian imperialism, whether Red or White, remained for Piłsudski the principal enemy. This consideration weighed with his calculated refusal to launch an all-out offensive against the Bolsheviks in 1919, when such an action would have rendered Denikin substantial assistance and may perhaps even have brought him to Moscow.[2]

In pursuit of Polish interests, fighting had broken out between the Polish and Ukrainian Nationalist troops as the Poles strove to keep the vitally important area of Eastern Galicia under their rule. By July 1919 Polish forces had completed the military occupation of this region. The cause of Ukrainian independence itself crumbled away before the onset of the Russian Bolsheviks, the imperialist claims of the Russian anti-Bolsheviks and the vacillations of the Allied Supreme Council. At the end of that year Petlura, the nominal head of the Ukrainian separatist government, saw that salvation might be won by turning to the Poles, at a time when Poland — though by no means a French satellite — found itself under increasing pressure from some French quarters to adopt a more aggressive anti-Bolshevik position.

During the first few weeks of 1920 the Bolsheviks were aware that matters had advanced to crisis point.[3] In his telegram of 11th March, 1920, to Unshlikht on the Western Front, Lenin asserted that the Poles would fight.[4] This front, to which V. M. Gittis had been appointed as commander in July 1919, was weakly held, and military weakness was accentuated by economic dislocation and exhaustion. Elsewhere, Budenny's 1st Cavalry Army was fighting out the last desperate encounters with White units in the Northern Caucasus. Trotsky, in an effort to assist the enormous work of reconstruction, had seen fit to try to apply military methods to organising labour; as a result, on the Eastern and on parts of the Western Fronts individual Red armies were converted into 'Labour Armies'[5]— an experiment which was not attended by a very conspicuous success.

To the south of Russia the last White redoubt was now located in the Crimea, whence the remnants of Denikin's troops were being ferried from the port of Novorossiisk. As the Soviet command hurried to reinforce and to man the weakened defences in the west, it had not escaped the attention of Lenin that the successful withdrawal by land of the White forces to the

Crimea owed not a little to a serious Soviet blunder in not blocking the approaches to the peninsula. Lenin made no secret of this in his telegram to Sklyanskii on 15th March, 1920, demanding at the same time energetic measures of reinforcement for Soviet troops and blockade of the Whites.[6] There was some cause for alarm, for this gathering White army represented qualitatively, if not quantitively, the finest body of anti-Soviet troops to be arrayed against the Red Army. Coming under Baron Wrangel's full command early in April, they were, to quote Stalin's own description, veterans and 'splendidly enregimented' — an achievement which owed much in the last resort to Wrangel's own colossal labours to perfect the forces under his command.

Faced also with Poland, the Soviet government had shown itself in March 1920 to be not indisposed to concluding a settlement with the Poles, even at the price of a fairly generous territorial settlement in the latter's favour. Necessity rather than sentiment dictated this policy, for economic strain gave an uninviting prospect to a new and external war. The military command, however, had occupied itself with the preparation of a preliminary operational plan for use against the Poles, for in February *Glavkom* had instructed the Field Staff to draw this up.[7] Commander-in-Chief S. S. Kamenev had travelled to Smolensk, where on 10th March he discussed the plan with the front commander, V. M. Gittis. This basic plan envisaged two phases, one of which would be the conquest of the Minsk area, and the other would be based upon the co-operation and co-ordination of the northern and southern groups of the Soviet armies.

* * * *

With the break-down of Soviet-Polish talks for a local cease-fire, Piłsudski gathered himself finally for an offensive into the Ukraine. Having previously concluded an agreement with Petlura, on 25th April Polish troops launched their attack, overcame scattered Soviet resistance, occupied Kiev on 6th May and a small stretch of the left bank of the Dnieper, then turned immediately to the defensive.[8] The military situation had altered enormously — although on 8th April S. S. Kamenev had ordered front commanders to plan for a possible Polish offensive. To counter the move into the Ukraine now meant introducing a greater complexity of factors into the first plan drawn up by Shaposhnikov. At the end of April *Glavkom* began to work out the variations which would have to be incorporated; S. S. Kamenev, Chief of Staff P. P. Lebedev and Shaposhnikov discussed the alternatives. One involved transferring Budenny's cavalry from the Northern Caucasus to the Soviet Ukraine. This had the advantage of bringing up a formidable Soviet striking force to the right bank of the Dnieper, and at the same time being in possession of that force to use it against the numerous anti-Soviet partisan groups which were operating in the rear of the Soviet armies facing the Poles.[9] One of the most serious threats to security was presented by Makhno,* the outstanding Ukrainian peasant leader,[10] with whom the Soviet command had earlier entered into an alliance of convenience in order to accomplish the defeat of Denikin.

A wave of chauvinism and Russian patriotism began to sweep many ex-Imperial officers into the orbit of the Red Army. A tide of enthusiasm moved not a few Communists into extravagant forecasts about the blows soon to be delivered against the capitalist world, although there was a strong and genuine feeling that some major crisis was to hand, when oft-defended bastions might topple. Trotsky struck out at unfounded optimism and especially against the political fancies which saw revolution in Poland opening the national gates to the Red Army. No reason existed to suppose that the war would open with a Polish revolution, although it might conceivably end that way.[11] Meanwhile the plan of campaign was being considered by the Central Committee, and on 28th April approval was given to the basic plan devised by the Field Staff. Stalin was assigned to specify the exact nature of the variants to be introduced in consultation with *Glavkom*. As previously envisaged, the main blow was to be mounted by the Western Front in Belorussia and North Polesia. A supporting blow would be provided by the South-western Front, driving in the general direction of Rovno-Brest. Both fronts were to co-operate as closely as possible—with the single aim of destroying the enemy in *the direction of Warsaw*. The South-western Front operations, although in a subsidiary role, were to bear a 'broad and decisive character' — for which reason Budenny's cavalry would be assigned as reinforcement. The offensive was timed for 14th May in Belorussia.[12]

The first task was to raise the strength of the Soviet armies in the west. The 'Labour Armies' reverted once again to their purely military function in Belorussia. For the south-west, the transfer of Budenny's cavalry had been decided upon. By 15th May, according to Tukhachevsky's own figures, 92,393 infantry and cavalry had been assembled on the Western Front.[13] Transport facilities were, however, bad. In the initial plan, the main blow was to be mounted by the XVIth Red army moving in the direction of Igumen-Minsk; a supporting role was allotted to the XVth Army operating to the north of the XVIth. Since this meant in fact opening the offensive by

* Nestor Makhno was the guerrilla leader in whose territory a peasant-anarchist republic was set up. He co-operated with the Red Army, only to turn and fight against it as an occupying power. In October 1920 his military aid was enlisted against Wrangel, and he gained thereby momentary recognition of his 'army' and his 'republic'. Very strict precautions were taken, however, to keep Red Army and Makhno units carefully segregated, and on the liquidation of the threat from Wrangel, Frunze issued immediate orders for operations against Makhno. Makhno himself escaped abroad after the crushing of his movement.

forcing the River Berezina, the left bank of which had been heavily invested by the Poles, the plan was at once modified by Tukhachevsky.

Tukhachevsky had assumed command of the front on 29th April, having left the Northern Caucasus, to which V. M. Gittis was sent. The new commander's modification involved allotting the main operational task to the XVth Army, which would strike in the general direction of Vilno, with the XVIth fighting supporting actions in a line with Minsk. In addition, right flank units of the XVth were separated into a 'Northern Group' under the command of E. N. Sergeyev, with the mission of forcing the River Dvina in the Disna-Polotsk area, and then striking on into the enemy rear.[14] While this was sounder in approach, the pre-attack changes brought new and hidden dangers with them, for technical units were badly below strength, and the very idea of a 'non-stop offensive' was seriously prejudiced by the inadequate supply of reserves.

The Polish 4th Army in the meanwhile prepared to drive on Moghilev, the offensive being timed for 4th May. Soviet reinforcements[15] were rushed to the west, accompanied by the usual mobilisation of Communists. Mass-agitation, conducted under the direction of A. F. Myasnikov, went on in the pre-front areas. On the eve of the Soviet offensive, Red forces were disposed into the 'Northern Group', the XVth Army (under A. I. Kork) to its south, and the XVIth (commanded by N. V. Sollogub) on the eastern bank of the Berezina. The total strength deployed for the offensive, according to Tukhachevsky's figures, amounted to 92,400 officers and men. There were adequate supplies for the first days of the offensive — 180 rounds per man, 400 shells to each gun — but this optimistic view could not cover up the fact that the whole supply system was confused and amounted to a major weakness on the Soviet side. It is worth noticing that the Red Army — which Polish Military Intelligence estimated at 70 divisions on 1st March, 1920[16]— had the greatest difficulty in first strengthening and then servicing its western striking force. The major part of this effort had been expended on forming a concentrated striking force at the centre of the front, but the secondary areas — Bobruisk and Mozyr — were held with relatively thin units.

At dawn on 14th May, as directed, the XVth Army and units of the 'Northern Group' went over to the offensive. The XVIth had to delay its advance, since the re-grouping of newly-arrived units was not yet completed. During the first days of the offensive the 43rd Regiment (15th Rifle Division), commanded by V. I. Chuikov,* distinguished itself in heavy fighting.[17] On 16th the XVth Army drove north-west, and then re-grouped as a prelude to changing its line of advance to the south-west. Three days

* Now Marshal Chuikov, famous for his command of the 62nd Army at Stalingrad in 1942.

later the XVIth finally went into action, at that point when the blows of the XVth were beginning to slacken. Soviet troops were consolidating their gains on the western bank of the Berezina by 21st, but the exploitation of the success required much greater strength. That strength lay with the reserves which had been expressly committed at the very beginning of the operation. In spite of Tukhachevsky's own defence of these actions, the inconclusive outcome confirms Shaposhnikov's view that this was a premature undertaking.[18]

On 1st June the Poles began to fight back very vigorously, and the Soviet position deteriorated. Lenin telegraphed to Stalin on 2nd that '. . . the situation on the Western Front is worse than Tukhachevsky or *Glavkom* think'.[19] Therefore the divisions which Stalin had requested must be diverted to this front, while Trotsky would see that Stalin received troops from the Crimea. No more units could be moved from the Northern Caucasus without exposing that area to serious dangers.[20] But as the Western Front offensive slowed down, showing in the process deficiencies in the co-ordination of the XVth and XVIth armies, new blows were in the process of being aimed at the Poles from the south-west of Russia, where Budenny's cavalry played a notable part on this scene of operations.

Budenny and Voroshilov had been summoned to Moscow by *Glavkom* early in April to discuss the transfer of their cavalry to the Soviet Ukraine. Lebedev and Shaposhnikov suggested moving the cavalry by train. Budenny refused outright, pointing out that this would impose insoluble problems of fodder and water. What had by now become a dispute was settled ultimately in Budenny and Voroshilov's favour.[21] The Central Committee also appointed Stalin to the South-western Front *Revvoensoviet*, with Dzerzhinskii as 'chief of the rear', a sinister sign that disaffection in the rear would again be settled by execution and intimidation. This appointment was made on 26th May, while on the previous day advance units of the 1st Cavalry Army had entered the district of Uman, having travelled from Maikop, Rostov-on-Don, through Ekaterinoslav and into Uman. The cavalry army by now numbered upwards of 16,000 men, possessing in addition to its rifles and sabres 304 machine-guns and 48 guns. Further reinforcements included I. S. Kutyakov's powerful 'Chapayev Division' and a Bashkir cavalry brigade under M. Murtazin.[22]

Yegorov commanded the South-western Front, with its XIIth and XIVth armies, the 1st Cavalry Army and the 'Fastov army group' (commanded by I. E. Yakir of the 45th Division). To Yegorov on 9th May S. S. Kamenev had sent a directive, signed by Kurskii and Lebedev, laying down the aims of the forthcoming offensive on this front. XIIth Army was to drive on Kiev. XIVth Army would mount its blow on the right flank and 1st Cavalry was to pierce the Polish front and operate in its rear and upon its flanks. S. S. Kamenev journeyed to Kharkhov on 10th May to discuss the plan in detail with Yegorov (front commander), R. I. Berzin (*Revvoensoviet* member) and N. N. Petin (Chief of Staff).[23]

The front directive of 23rd May laid down the final tasks of the front forces.[24] The XIIth Army (commanded until 10th June by S. A. Mezheninov and thereafter by G. K. Voskanov), XIVth Army (under I. P. Uborevich) were to act with the cavalry to smash the Polish front in the Ukraine. Although timed for 26th May, only the XIVth and the 'Fastov army group' took the field that day; XIIth Army's re-grouping was not yet complete, and the Poles succeeded in beating off small units from that force. On 31st May Yegorov ordered XIIth Army to stage a frontal attack on Kiev, while the XIVth attacked along its right flank.

On 3rd June Stalin in a special telegram analysed the failure of units of the 1st Cavalry to achieve any substantial results. The enemy had made skilful use of trenches to hinder the cavalry, so much so that Budenny's men could not make progress without infantry support to reduce Polish strongpoints.[25] Yegorov simultaneously assigned to the 1st Cavalry the task of breaching the Polish front about Kiev, for which purpose the cavalry was deployed in multi-echelon form.* Budenny's request for more artillery was answered by moving up special units from Taganrog. On the evening of 3rd and throughout 4th the Soviet cavalry took up its positions for the coming offensive. The entire Soviet front at this juncture stretched from the Western to the South-western Fronts, with the 'Mozyr group' acting as a link between them. Amounting to less than two divisions, this physical weakness in the chain was offset to some degree by the fact it stood upon ground very difficult for any kind of movement.

At dawn on 5th June, opening with blinding machine-gun and artillery fire, the 1st Cavalry Army swept into the attack. Their success was accompanied by a general offensive of the XIIth, XIVth and 'Fastov group' armies. The rear of the 3rd Polish army was seriously threatened by the onrush of Budenny's cavalry,† which began its attack on Kiev on 9th; by 10th it was ordered to press on to Zhitomir. In ten days the Ukraine had been cleared on a line running from Zhitomir through Kazatin to Vinnitsa. The 1st Cavalry split into two groups‡ commanded separately by Budenny

* First echelon: 4th Cavalry Division, Second: 14th and 11th Cavalry Divisions, Third: 6th Cavalry Division and the Special Cavalry Brigade.

† Kotovskii's cavalry brigade penetrated the rear and cut the Kiev-Zhitomir road. The 58th Rifle Division (XIIth Army) under P. E. Knyagnitskii attacked Polish troops holding the Dnieper, the Dnieper River Flotilla being used to advance the Soviet troops.

‡ Voroshilov took the 4th and 14th Cavalry Divisions, objective: Korosten. Budenny took the 6th and 11th Divisions, objective: Zhitomir.

and Voroshilov, as Polish troops fell back continuously. On the Western Front Tukhachevsky carried out a rapid re-organisation of his forces. On 18th June Polish troops withdrew from their positions facing the 'Mozyr group'; without waiting for orders T. S. Khvesin advanced to occupy the town of Mozyr itself. The prime factor was now the co-ordination of the two Soviet fronts; as the south-western forces drove forward into Eastern Galicia, the western command re-opened its offensive operations on a large scale, defeating the Polish forces on the Berezina river line. But as the south-western troops failed to surround and annihilate the Polish forces, so did the western armies find it impossible to drive the Poles southward to destruction in the marshes.

★ ★ ★ ★

British and French pessimism deepened about the ultimate outcome of the Soviet-Polish war,* but in the midst of moves to end the war developments in the rear of the Soviet South-western Front made a sudden impact on the whole war-situation. On 6th June 'the black Baron' Wrangel lunged at the Soviet rear. Although the British Government had tried to bring about a negotiated end to the Civil War,[26] Wrangel was almost obliged to take the field if for no other reason than the disintegration which prolonged inactivity would bring to his army. Striking at I. Kh. Pauka's ill-prepared XIIIth Red army,[27] Wrangel's 2nd Corps achieved substantial success. Nor did the XIIIth Army have an agreed and co-ordinated plan of defence against Wrangel's incursion. Bursting out through the Isthmus of Perekop, the 2nd Corps descended on the shore of the Sea of Azov and drove on to Melitopol. By the end of June Wrangel accounted himself master of the Northern Tauride, which was a signal increase in the territory originally under his control. Yegorov on 10th June ordered XIIIth Army to halt the break-out and sent cavalry and infantry reinforcement. By way of reply, Wrangel's veterans ripped Zhloba's 1st Cavalry Corps and the whole weakened Soviet force to pieces on 28th. The 'Wrangel front' had grown into serious proportions, and also acted as a menace to the rear of the Soviet armies operating against Poland.[28]

'The march on Warsaw' began to make itself heard as a final objective for the Soviet armies. Trotsky himself opposed this idea since an extension of the military operations would impose an intolerable strain on Soviet resources and capacities. An extension of the military operations brought with it the attentions of the other European powers, both victors and

* A Franco-British mission left for Poland on 22nd July, 1920. General Paul Henrys was already in command of the strong French military mission operating in Poland; on his arrival, General Weygand took up the post of adviser to the Polish Chief of Staff, General Rozwadowski, but ultimate responsibility lay with the Polish officers, as Weygand himself has freely admitted.

vanquished. On 17th July the Soviet government rejected the idea of a 'Peace conference' (which would have included Wrangel also), choosing to ignore French and British warnings about an expansion of Soviet military operations on to territory indisputably Polish.[29] Rumania also threatened the security of the south-western armies' flanks, and in view of the uncertainty of her attitude, Yegorov was ordered to take precautionary measures. For Germany, the prospects for Poland were of vital importance. Already with the exchange of Kopp and Hilger between Berlin and Moscow as representatives for prisoner of war repatriation, a purposeful diplomatic traffic had been set in motion.[30] Soviet defeat of Poland would simultaneously destroy the whole basis of the Versailles settlement and bring Soviet troops on to — or over — the German frontier.

To Seeckt of the German *Reichswehr*, who was seeking contacts with Moscow with a view to outwitting the Versailles settlement upon Germany, a Soviet victory implied that the long-term interests of Germany would triumph, although the *Reichswehr* could not guarantee the integrity of the old German-Russian frontier. Apart from these sanguine views, however, there is no real evidence that there was any arrangement for a joint Soviet-German 'war of revenge' on Poland.[31] While admittedly seeking contacts with Moscow, Seeckt had no illusions about Bolshevism, which had already tried its fortunes in defeated Germany, nor did he abandon his view that Germany must be kept out of any armed clash at this moment. On 26th July, Seeckt wrote to the German Foreign Ministry that 'the complete victory of Russia can no longer be called into question'.[32] Six days earlier the German declaration of neutrality had agreeably affected the Soviet chances; the *Truppenamt* memorandum of 24th left no doubt that this was to be a benevolent neutrality.[33]

The events which led up to the drive on Warsaw and the subsequent Soviet defeat before the city became the inevitable subject for violent controversy in the Soviet high command. Apportioning or avoiding the blame produced a military literature of some bulk, marked invective and asperity as well as searching analysis. In itself the operation provides the one isolated example of Tukhachevsky's military art in handling armies and fronts. As a disaster which mesmerised the Red commanders for a decade, the whole process of planning and executing the Warsaw operation merits some examination to uncover its course and end. Nor is it likely that Stalin chose to forget the harsh words and unfavourable judgements which fastened about his name and the part his friends played in the final débâcle.

There can be no doubt that a high degree of optimism influenced S. S. Kamenev's decision to fall in with the proposed offensive against Warsaw. The Republic *Revvoensoviet* commanded that the Soviet armies should not halt their drive on the 'Curzon line', but proceed into Poland for the destruction of the Polish army. Kamenev accordingly altered his strategic dispositions to this end. On 21st July he reported to the centre that Grodno had been taken and the river Niemen forced, thus depriving the enemy of a position from which they might further resist the advance of the Red Army. The whole affair could be finished within three weeks.[34] In a second long report, written on the same day, Kamenev examined the wider strategic implications of the advance, suggesting the delimitation of the role of the South-western Front in the event of Rumanian intervention against Soviet Russia. Nevertheless, by utilising *only three* armies on the Western Front, Kamenev counted on crushing Poland if she were not assisted either by Rumania or any one of the Baltic states.[35]

A spirit of intense optimism prevailed. The two principal tasks were to ensure an adequate supply and reinforcement of the front, and also to co-ordinate in the most effective manner the actions of the Western and South-western Fronts. With the conclusion of the preliminary stage of the Western Front build-up, early in June, Soviet effectives had increased to 104,075.[36] Kakurin states that in June the west received 70,000 additional men, of whom 37,000 went into the line.[37] A significant commentary on this, however, is XVIth Army signal No. 823 that from 14th May–15th June, there had been 24,615 deserters, of whom 10,357 had been apprehended and 14,258 had surrendered voluntarily.[38]

The whole Soviet front stretched some 200 miles, running from the north-east to the south-west. Tukhachevsky's western armies consisted of the IVth, XVth, IIIrd, XVIth and Gai's 3rd Cavalry Corps. In the south the XIIth, XIVth and the 1st Cavalry Army fought under Yegorov's command. Between the two fronts the 'Mozyr group' still acted as the link, with a strength of approximately 8,000 infantry and cavalry.[39] In view of this disposition much depended on S. S. Kamenev's directive of 23rd July, which was based on the assumption that the Polish armies were incapable of further serious resistance,[40] and issued — as Piłsudski's commentary acidly observes — at that very moment when the activities of the two Soviet fronts were beginning to diverge.

Kamenev had evidently fallen under the spell of the idea of imminent victory while visiting the Western Front head-quarters in Smolensk. It was here that on 19th July, Smilga (of the Western *Revvoensoviet*) announced that the left wing of the Polish forces had ceased to exist and that Warsaw itself was completely demoralised.[41] To Yegorov on 23rd July Kamenev directed an order that by 4th August his right wing should attain the line Kowel-Włodzimierz-Wołyński, thus bringing the Southern right wing into contact with the Western left wing. In Paragraph 2 it was further laid down that the 1st Cavalry Army (and the XIVth) should press their actions against the Polish 6th Army; the 1st Cavalry, having covered itself from the Lwow side, should concentrate on a narrow front and continue the operations 'in the properly decided direction'.

That phrase in the directive produced great diversity of interpretation. Shaposhnikov attempted to argue, a little ingenuously, that the 1st Cavalry Army's true aim was masked by a massive feint in the direction of Lwow, while it was ready to swing up to Lublin. Kakurin denies this explicitly. Svechin criticised the directive for its startling impreciseness of language. The directive must also be related to Kamenev's simultaneous order to the Western armies, which were ordered to maintain the pursuit, to reach the line of Prasnysz-Modlin and the Vistula by 18th August, on which date *Warsaw also was to be occupied*.[42] There can be little doubt that the final blow was to be delivered by the Western Front.

By the end of July *Glavkom* embarked upon its re-organisation of the entire command relationships, a move necessitated by the speed of the Red Army advances and the greater chances of success. Under the new arrangement the Western and South-western Fronts were detached, with Yegorov being instructed to concern himself with Wrangel and the situation which would be created by Rumanian intervention, should it materialise. Having allotted Yegorov a rather ambiguous strategic assignment, Kamenev proceeded on 31st July to ask Tukhachevsky for the 48th Division, for use against Wrangel. On 2nd August, he asked for two more divisions, but this time Tukhachevsky refused outright.[43] Yegorov, in his turn, demanded these reinforcements. They were finally taken from the XIIth Army, a deliberate weakening of this force to which Kamenev consented by extending the operational control of the Western Front into this sector of the South-western Front.

On the other hand, the necessity of making an effective stand against Wrangel had to be pressed upon South-western Front HQ in Kharkov. This obvious division of function in the tasks assigned to the forces under Yegorov led Kamenev to another consideration, namely, that a substantial element of the South-western Front forces should pass under Tukhachevsky's command. This could not fail to displease Yegorov and the command staff of the 1st Cavalry Army, which had fought bitterly and not unsuccessfully against the Poles and without whose successes the Western Front armies could not have mounted their spectacular drive. On 3rd August, an independent decision on the part of Tukhachevsky set in motion the passage of his 'secret army' into the northern bottle-neck running up to the frontier of East Prussia and from which subsequently there was to be no escape. This action contributed most effectively to detaching more completely the two

Soviet fronts both in purpose and relative position, as well as working against Kamenev's original scheme of controlling and co-ordinating them. Yet the *Glavkom* had shown itself to be singularly confused in its approach to the problem of the two fronts and their co-ordination for the final action.

★ ★ ★ ★

The 6th August was a day of great consequence for both the Soviet and Polish high command. Although the Polish troops were still falling back and about to do battle for Warsaw, in Piłsudski's mind there arose an interesting speculation about the significance of the physical divergence of the two Soviet fronts.* His attention fell upon that void between Dęblin (Ivangorod) and Lublin. Having taken a fateful decision upon the consideration that pushing through this joint would bring Polish forces into Tukhachevsky's rear, Piłsudski issued the order for the assembly which would bring him into this very position.[44] On the same day Tukhachevsky was given command of the whole Polish front.[45] Yegorov was ordered to replace the 1st Cavalry with infantry, so that the cavalry might be readied for new offensive action.

Yet between Tukhachevsky and Kamenev there developed a grave difference of opinion about the proposed Warsaw operation on the eve of its execution. Like Piłsudski, Kamenev found his attention drawn increasingly to that 'gap' between the fronts. Tukhachevsky argued that he must be in a position to strike at the left wing of the Polish defenders of Warsaw, and this justified the risk of the arduous northerly passage. As for a Polish counter-attack — should it materialise — Tukhachevsky maintained that it would be mounted from the Vistula area which he now threatened. Having based his arguments upon the strength of his northern blow, nevertheless he demanded control of the XIIth and the 1st Cavalry Army.[46]

In making such a demand, Tukhachevsky must have realised that, even with its acceptance, the delays imposed by deficient rail communication would not have brought him immediate control of these formations. This did not lessen Kamenev's misgivings about the weakness in the front; nor was he encouraged by Tukhachevsky's failure to co-ordinate the northern armies in the light of a not impossible serious resistance to them. To add to the unreality the IIIrd Red army captured a copy of Piłsudski's order of

* Piłsudski was not unique in considering the idea of a northerly blow mounted from the right flank. Weygand, Rozwadowski and Piłsudski had all been struck by this possibility, but the great difference occurred in the manner in which this blow was to be mounted; General Weygand maintained that the true difference lay in the tactical-operational aspects of the idea, where Piłsudski found a method and position well suited to the capabilities of the Polish troops. In brief, General Weygand favoured establishing a fixed defensive line on the San-Vistula rivers before launching a counter-attack, General Rozwadowski was thinking of a counter-attack launched from both Polish flanks, and Piłsudski was pondering his own 'bursting into the joint' plan.

6th August which clearly indicated the direction in which the counter-blow would be made. Tukhachevsky dismissed it as a bluff, anticipating serious resistance only at the northern points.[47]

Confident of victory, and with many substantial reasons to justify it, Tukhachevsky on 10th August issued his directive for the final 'battle of

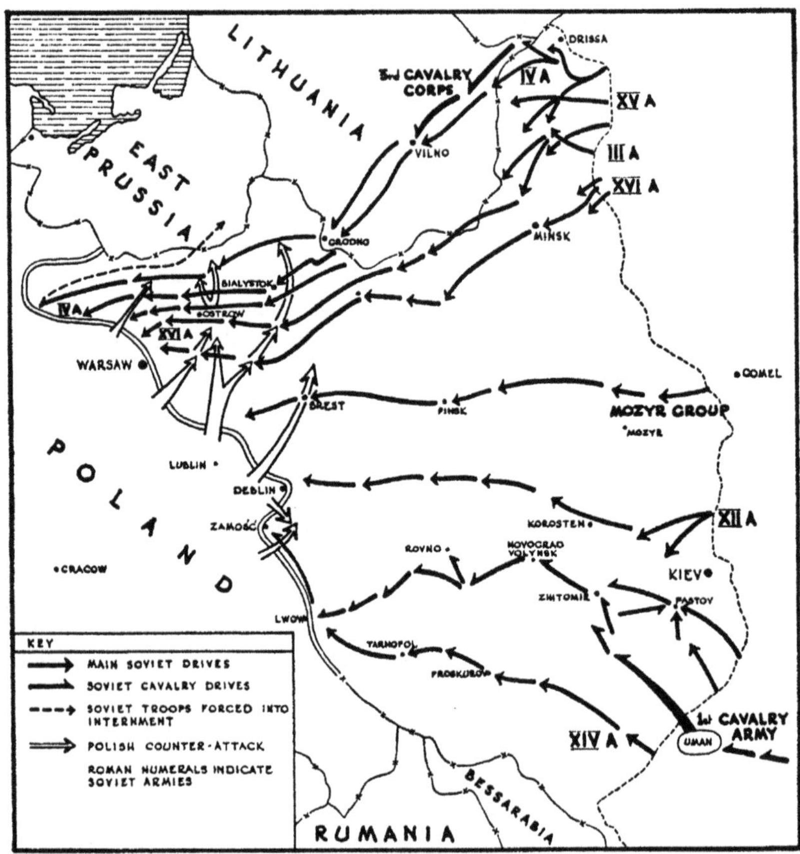

THE RED ARMY DRIVE ON WARSAW 1920

Warsaw',[48] the absolute confirmation of his intention to take the enemy in the rear, cutting the Polish capital off from its communication with Danzig, simultaneously forcing the Vistula to the south and pushing the 'Mozyr group' on to Deblin. At the eleventh hour *Glavkom* woke up to the significance of the Polish concentrations in the south. Tukhachevsky had assumed that the rear, his XVIth Army, would be covered by the XIIth —

but this had already been weakened to draw forces for use against Wrangel. The way to Tukhachevsky's rear armies lay exposed and undefended.

On 11th August *Glavkom* ordered Yegorov to break off the Lwow operations (Shaposhnikov's suggested 'feint') in which the 1st Cavalry Army was engaged and swing his effort towards Lublin, with the cavalry moving on Zamość.[49] Yegorov began to argue. He submitted that Timoshenko's 6th Cavalry Division (the best in the 1st Cavalry Army) should be sent against Wrangel and the XIVth Army could relieve the 1st Cavalry.[50] Kamenev had put the whole question in a very tentative way to Yegorov, but Tukhachevsky would not agree with the proposed modifications, demanding control over the south-western forces and making the despatch of these forces to his command a matter for Yegorov himself. The 1st Cavalry Army, having been withdrawn from action, had meanwhile been re-committed to heavy fighting near Brody, where it found itself in the thick of a prodigious battle against stubborn Polish defence.

On 13th August *Glavkom* sent an unmistakable order to Yegorov which, while making it clear that actual subordination of command was not involved but merely the breaking off of the Lwow operations, demanded that:

> (1) from 12.00 hours on 14th August Commander SW will place under the operational control of Commander W XIIth and 1st Cavalry Army (minus 8th Cav. Div.) at the line of demarcation, set at the present moment between 1st Cavalry and XIVth Armies.[51]

Of the stream of instructions sent out, Shaposhnikov claimed that of the three directives sent after 11th August the last one arrived first and little could be done about any of them.[52] Delays in deciphering, whether by design or accident, added to the loss of time. On 14th Yegorov passed on to 1st Cavalry Army the order about their passing under Tukhachevsky's command, yet neglected to order the complete cessation of action for the capture of Lwow.[53]

On 15th, however, Tukhachevsky signalled to Budenny of the 1st Cavalry Army and Voskanov of the XIIth Army that they were to begin moves designed to co-ordinate them expressly with Tukhachevsky's plans.[54] Budenny at once queried the validity of this order. By a quirk of fate the order carried only Tukhachevsky's signature since it was a copy of the original despatched in error. With only a single signature the order was not valid. The confirmation which Budenny inevitably demanded arrived only on 17th, by which time the 1st Cavalry was deeply committed to new engagements for the capture of Lwow, having resumed its action on 16th. Not until 20th could it be extricated.[55] Stalin had very definitely opposed the order to come under Tukhachevsky, insisting that such a transfer '. . . only held things up and inevitably meant an unnecessary, harmful hitch in the operations'.[56] 'The operations' signified the capture of Lwow and the 1st Cavalry command developing its own military-political campaign in Eastern Poland.

Yegorov and the 1st Cavalry played their obstructionist roles perfectly. *Glavkom* had to resort to threats in order to have its order passed to Budenny, and only in this instance would Yegorov and Berzin sign the transfer order. The distance of the various head-quarters from the fronts added delays, and the ambiguity of *Glavkom*'s own crucial instructions contributed to the whole confused outcome. It was with these arguments and insubordinations for its background that the battle for Warsaw reached its climax. Tukhachevsky's armies wheeled in their northerly encircling movement. Radzimin, only twenty-three kilometres from Warsaw, fell to advancing Soviet troops on 13th–14th August. On the following day the battle for the Wkra, where Tukhachevsky engaged Sikorski, raged with such intensity that General Haller urged upon Piłsudski the necessity of counter-attacking at the chosen point twenty-four hours in advance of the selected time. Piłsudski reluctantly agreed.

The 16th opened with the 1st Cavalry Army many miles from the scene of the decisive operations. General Sikorski was in danger of being taken in the rear. It was the day when the Polish counter-offensive opened in to that weak Soviet joint — the day, Piłsudski writes, when '. . . I opened my attack, if one can call that an attack'.[57] But after two days Tukhachevsky's left wing was rolled away under the Polish blows. The XVIth Red army, attacked in flank and rear, already weakened to the point of being skeletal, fell back in utter disorder. The IVth Red army, trapped in the north, received its orders much too late. The dilapidated state of rail communications deprived Tukhachevsky of the chance to bring up 50,000 reinforcements.[58] Only on 20th did Budenny tear himself away from Lwow and turn in the direction of Lublin. It was, by this time, much too late. By 21st Piłsudski struck deadly blows at the XVIth, the IIIrd and XVth Red armies. The IVth was trapped beyond hope, some of its elements being forced over the German frontier into internment.[59] Sikorski on 12th September launched his offensive which recovered Rovno and Tarnopol; on 20th Piłsudski hammered the IIIrd Red army into pieces, taking Grodno on 26th.

To the south Budenny had to fight his way out of threatened encirclement, all the while harassed by enemy aircraft and shelled ceaselessly by Polish guns. The tardy move to support the Warsaw operation had been completely abortive. Both Soviet cavalry forces — Budenny's 1st Army and Gai's 3rd Corps — had to cut their way out. Only Budenny finally succeeded, although Gai, imprisoned in the northern passage, fought skilfully and tenaciously in order to stave off defeat and surrender.[60] By this time, however, the demoralised Red armies streamed back across the lines which had been so furiously contested.

It was inevitable that the defeat in the field, with its enormous political consequences, should touch off a new conflict in the Soviet command as a whole. Trotsky, who at times had faced the opposition of the majority to suggest sensible and realistic policies, pointed out that Stalin, in the secret debates at the 10th Party Congress tried to put the blame on Ivan Smilga, whom he accused of having failed to adhere to the date which had been 'settled' by him for the capture of Warsaw. Therefore, the blame was Smilga's — and by implication, Tukhachevsky's. Trotsky refuted the absurdity of this accusation with characteristic heat.[61] Stalin's alibi could not fail to draw attention to the fact that the South-western Front had first ignored and then disobeyed the Central Committee's decision about the unification of the fronts. Lenin sought to avoid settling the blame on individuals, so that the internal breaches caused by the defeat might be more speedily sealed up. According to M. D. Bonch-Bruevich, Lenin could only observe of the 1st Cavalry Army — 'Eh! Who on earth would want to get to Warsaw by going through Lwow!'[62] The military men, however, attended more assiduously to their honour, re-fighting throughout the next ten years the abortive campaign, searching for culprits both real and imaginary. Out of this there developed in the high command a virtual 'Vistula complex', which could not easily be shaken off.

In 1922 S. S. Kamenev produced his explanation. His view of the 1st Cavalry Army's activities led him to the conclusion that this force — the ace up the Red Army's sleeve — was completely neutralised at the vital stage of the war. However, the planning and conduct of the actual drive on Warsaw could not be exempted from certain technical criticisms.[63] Nor could the effect of Wrangel's offensive be discounted because of its effects on the Soviet rear. It was evident that the decision of who should be given priority, the Poles or Wrangel, had been difficult to arrive at. On 11th July, 1920, Stalin had dismissed the idea of an advance on Warsaw as ridiculous while Wrangel still haunted the Soviet rear, a menace not yet '. . . countered by any special or effective measures against the growing danger . . .'.[64]

Tukhachevsky lectured to the War Academy in 1923 on the campaign. The diversion of the 1st Cavalry from the Lublin-Brest line towards Lwow was condemned by him as a major factor in determining the fate of the operations at a decisive stage. Tukhachevsky defended his northern right hook, maintaining that the decision to move troops from the south to the aid of the north was taken in time adequate enough to leave a margin for the successful fulfilment of the move. This is questionable. While criticising considerable mal-administration in the Western command — failure to move reserves, feebleness of technical means — Tukhachevsky in conclusion insisted that the export of revolution was feasible, and next time the bourgeoisie might not find so automatic a salvation and so easy an escape from the Bolshevisation of Europe.[65]

Tukhachevsky took risks which lacked uniform calculation; his sweep to the north (in the style of the Imperial Russian Army's movement in the 1830 Polish Rising) had given rise to misgivings among the high command as a whole. The IVth Red army and Gai's 3rd Corps lay stretched upon a dangerous limb. Yet perhaps the greatest weakness was in his rear, which was an ill-assorted jumble of peasant-carts, ammunition trains, artillery parks and straining locomotives. With an improvised army, with wide variances of divisional strengths — falling as low as 500 men — Tukhachevsky's 95,000 effectives advanced 550 kilometres and occupied 190,000 square kilometres of territory.

In his lecture Tukhachevsky delivered his points about the behaviour of Budenny's cavalry with some asperity. These arguments found massive expression in the huge publication by two military-political experts, N. E. Kakurin and V. A. Melikov, although the fallibility of the northern drive did not escape criticism. In 1924 Shaposhnikov wrote up his account, from the point of view of a member of the Field Staff; though he confirmed the main outlines of Tukhachevsky's analysis, he argued that the main error lay in the false estimations of relative strengths. In short, he challenged Tukhachevsky's view that the front command 'had a right to be optimistic' about the eventual outcome. With his generalisations, Shaposhnikov took up what he hoped was an unexceptionable stand, imitating Lenin's view that the Soviet armed forces had, if anything, over-reached themselves. This was a calculated orthodoxy which foreshadowed his later exposition of the relationship of military to political command, fashioned to meet the prevailing political fashion — and again in opposition to Tukhachevsky.

V. Triandafilov in 1925 produced, when Deputy Chief of Staff, his own view; with a reasoning not too heavily bludgeoned by political considerations, he argued that the Warsaw operation failed precisely because it lacked adequate force, an inadequacy which was increased by bad co-operation. The latter Triandafilov blamed on *Glavkom* and the South-western Front command; the Lwow operations should have been counter-manded *quickly*, and the South-western Front acquainted most precisely with the new tasks assigned to 1st Cavalry.[66] Yegorov waited until 1929 before making a public reply to his critics; invoking the aid of a large documentation, he sought to show that Tukhachevsky and S. S. Kamenev ought to take the blame. Obliged to admit that by then '. . . the legend of the fateful role of South-western Front in 1920' had passed into military and political history, Yegorov's argument that the timely movement of the 1st Cavalry would not have affected the outcome was refuted by General Sikorski himself,[67] by no means an interested party in the disputes of the Soviet high command. The third volume of the official Civil War history, which appeared in 1930, gave little support to the position defended by Stalin-Voroshilov-Budenny and Yegorov, arguing that the decisive point was Warsaw not Cracow.[68] Major-General Svechin, in his major work on strategy, did not include a particular study of 1920, but used it extensively as a negative proof of how not to wage war, arguing a thesis of the integration of military and political activity in war-making. *Glavkom* did not escape severe implied criticism, though in the final analysis Svechin seemed to favour Wrangel's incursion as the ultimate tip in the scales against the Soviet fortunes.[69]

The employment, or more precisely, the lack of employment of military man-power in 1920 provides an illuminating example of the difficulties facing the high command in the Polish campaign. It is all the more remarkable that reinforcement against Wrangel had to come from a heavily-committed front when the Red Army numbered over 5,000,000. On the two decisive fronts, Western and South-western, 360,000 and 221,000 men respectively were mobilised, the combined 581,000 representing only 10 per cent of the total Soviet military strength. At the decisive *point* only 50,000 men could be mustered, and that with difficulty. In fact the true Red Army which lay at the disposal of the command was made up of only 7–800,000 men out of 5,500,000 mobilised. A basic force of 4–500,000 riflemen was available, on paper at least, for operational use. Taking the figures for 1st October, 1920, of 5,498,000 'mouths to be fed' (ration strength), there were 2,587,000 men clustered in the reserve armies, which meant that half of the total strength lay immobilised in the interior.[70] Putting 159,000 men into the line on two active fronts proved to be a task of almost overwhelming proportions for the multi-million army. This suggests that improvisation was at a premium, and would account for the difficulties of accurate military assessments even on the part of the most professional of the Red Army's temporary professional assistants.

The outcome could not persuade the 1st Cavalry Army command, either then or later, that it had been mistaken in pursuing secondary objectives and had acted with shameful insubordination. Yegorov naturally tried to minimise the importance of the failure to dis-engage and support Tukhachevsky's XVIth army by shielding it with the XIIth. Even that bad solution was better than none at all. The select group of the 1st Cavalry Army—Budenny, Voroshilov (with Yegorov), Timoshenko, Bakhturov, Zotov,

Gorodovikov and Tyulenev — gathered more closely round the Stalin banner. Even as recently as 1957 General Tyulenev defended the decision to march on Lwow as being unmistakably correct, and explained the failure of the 1st Cavalry Army to withdraw and transfer to Western Front command as a consequence of the XIIth Army's own failure to take up the positions then held by the 1st Cavalry Army.[71] But this is still an admission in principle of the necessity for the cavalry army's move.

* * * *

With the Soviet armies turning to the defensive in the face of the Polish successes in their counter-offensive, it was obvious that the main weight of the Soviet military effort would be switched to the south in order to accomplish the destruction of Wrangel. By examining the course of the efforts to contain and finally destroy Wrangel, it is possible to look a little more closely at the proofs of those arguments which saw in Wrangel that final straw which broke the back of the whole Red Army drive on Warsaw — a secondary yet urgent military commitment which could not be ignored. It helps to clarify the admittedly awkward predicament in which the South-western Front command found itself, faced with this considerable responsibility of holding Wrangel in check.

After his successful break-out in June and his defeat of the Soviet counter-offensive at the end of that month, Wrangel made his choice not to proceed with any kind of attempt to subdue the Ukraine, but rather to concentrate upon the areas of the Don and the Kuban. If his investment of these areas went according to plan, he could then evacuate the Northern Tauride, hold the Crimea by controlling the Isthmus of Perekop, but develop his base in the Kuban — the original home of the first Volunteer Army in 1918. There was to be no wild adventuristic 'drive on Moscow' in the Denikin manner, without having first secured a stable rear. The Don Cossacks were possible allies. His immediate overtures to Makhno were less successful, however, for his envoy was promptly hanged.

To break into the Don, Wrangel organised a sea-borne landing at a point thirty kilometres to the east of Mariupol; the South-western Front command ordered the Azov flotilla and a cavalry brigade to deal with this. Dated 15th July, the general command of the operation was entrusted to R. P. Eideman, XIIIth Red army commander.[72] The Soviet attempt to destroy the invaders succeeded upon this occasion, but a second landing by Colonel Nazarov was not prevented without the intervention of the IXth Red army from the Caucasus.

At the end of July the White troops mounted an offensive to break through into the Donbas and on to the Don. The blow was aimed through Orekhov to Aleksandrovsk and Ekaterinoslav; at the same time a new expedition was prepared to land on the sea-coast of the Kuban, with the idea of linking up with a guerrilla movement organised behind the IXth Red army and making contact if possible with General Khvostikov, whose anti-Soviet troops were fighting in the Caucasian foothills.[73] Wrangel's offensive took the Red Army off balance in the north; on 26th July the South-western Front command ordered an immediate offensive to halt the break-out, with the 2nd Cavalry and XIIIth armies combining to hold the line. Command of the XIIIth Red army had passed to I. P. Uborevich on 16th July, and the front command ordered the 2nd Cavalry to adopt the tactics which had been tested in action against the Poles.[74] The main point is, however, that at the beginning of August the Soviet command was obliged to reinforce the troops holding Wrangel in order that he should not accomplish his aim of transferring himself to the Don lands and the Kuban.

The South-western command now tried to crush Wrangel by trying to push its offensive to the point of surrounding the White troops in the Northern Tauride and cutting them off from the Crimea. On 11th August Lenin sent the front command a signal, urging maximum efforts for the defeat of Wrangel, so that 'complete victory' could be won in Poland.[75] The Red troops had succeeded in gaining a bridge-head at Kakhovsk on the right bank of the Dnieper, to the line of which Wrangel had advanced, but a White cavalry raid to the rear of these forces caused them to break off the action and withdraw to the bridge-head — although all efforts to dislodge the Soviet troops failed, and the bridge-head was held. This fact played a considerable role in the final defeat of Wrangel's forces, and did, in fact, prevent his further penetration to the north. The attempt to encircle Wrangel, however, had failed — a fact attributed by Kuz'min to the failure to reinforce the divisions striking down from the north, which itself was due to the imperfect reinforcement policy of the *Glavkom* and the Field Staff.[76] Yet at this critical juncture of both the Polish and the Wrangel operations, there were not enough men available for all the operations, and this lack of man-power was exacerbated by the bad state of the communications.

At this point, Wrangel organised and despatched his second but major expedition to the Kuban; three landing groups were organised to land in the Akhtyr region, on the Taman peninsula and finally at Novorossiisk. The Cossack General Ulagai took command of the first group, with the task of striking to the rail-junction of Timoshevskaya and on to Ekaterinodar, the capital of the Kuban.[77] The White landings began on 14th August and by 18th Ulagai had taken Timoshevskaya, thereby threatening Ekaterinodar — and creating the possibility of a link-up with the anti-Soviet partisans in the rear of the XIth Red army. Despite the serious situation, Ulagai's hesitation and the heavy concentration of Soviet reserves in the Kuban — a restless area which needed watching — proved to be factors which saved the day for the Soviet command. The Caucasian command, under V. M. Gittis and G. K. Ordzhonikidze, reacted quickly enough, using troops of the IXth Red army and small naval units to liquidate the invasion; the operation was completed by 10th September.[78] Similarly Colonel Nazarov's White force, which had landed previously to the west of Taganrog, was finally chased down and destroyed at Konstantinovskaya; his expedition into the Don had attracted few recruits, nor had Wrangel been able to break out and take possession of the area.

Meanwhile energetic efforts were being made to reinforce the South-western Front once again to deal with Wrangel. By the end of August, strong detachments of workers were moved in to stiffen the available forces; the usual mobilisation of Communists took place, and S. I. Gusev was attached to the front command, with V. P. Potemkin, Chief of the Political Department of the South-western Front, being attached to the Crimean sector of the front.[79] At the same time, Wrangel's position had changed in view of the fact of the retreat of the Soviet armies from Polish territory. The success of the Polish counter-offensive once more raised the possibility of linking up by driving through the barrier of Soviet troops which so far held him. Throughout September the Soviet forces were strengthened against Wrangel, while the issue of peace or further war between Poland and Soviet Russia hung in the balance. The provisional peace treaty which the Poles and Russians signed on 12th October marked the death of Wrangel's hopes and signalled the beginning of the end.

The Russo-Polish provisional agreement of 12th October had not been gained without heavy resistance to it by interested parties on both sides wishing for a renewal of war. Tukhachevsky seems to have thought of a possible winter campaign, while Piłsudski tried to hold up the signing of the agreement. Trotsky bitterly contested any attempt by the Bolsheviks to re-open the war; he found himself consequently out-voted by the majority still intent upon war, either out of motives of revenge or the conviction that the peace would not be observed. To make his stand quite plain, Trotsky threatened to appeal to the mass of the party if this course were taken up. Lenin, prompted perhaps by the recollection that Trotsky had opposed the march on Warsaw and his view had been justified, abandoned his previous position and withdrew his support from those who wished for a continuation of the war.[80] The threatened outbreak of further hostilities with Poland did not materialise, and the peace was concluded on 23rd October.[81]

Reinforcements against Wrangel were moved in from far and near — from the Caucasian Front, from Turkestan, and from Siberia, from which were drawn Blyukher's famous 51st Division and the 30th Division under I. K. Gryaznov. The 1st Cavalry Army, which had completed its withdrawal from Polish operations, was also destined as a reinforcement. By mid-September the Soviet forces amounted to 38,400 infantry, more than 7,000 cavalry, 288 guns, 1,067 machine-guns, not more than 45 aircraft and six or seven armoured trains.[82] By the first week in September reinforcement had enabled the VIth Red army to be reformed, with K. A. Avksent'evskii in command, and V. P. Potemkin and L. Z. Mekhlis as his commissars. On 21st September the gradually mounting forces were placed under an entirely new command, with the creation of the Southern Front on that same day. The front was to be made up of the VIth Red army, the XIIIth (under I. P. Uborevich, with Yu. Yu. Mezhin as commissar), and the 2nd Cavalry Army (commanded first by F. K. Mironov and subsequently by O. I. Gorodovikov, with Shchadenko among his commissars). Simultaneously the command of the Southern Front was vested in M. V. Frunze, possibly at Lenin's own insistence.[83]

Frunze, who had held command in Turkestan, evidently had a talk with Lenin on 20th September before his departure to the new front. According to Frunze's adjutant, S. A. Sirotinskii, Lenin urged upon the new commander the necessity for dealing a final blow to Wrangel and avoiding the possibility of a winter campaign — an interesting comment on Lenin's line of thought at a time when the Russo-Polish issue was still in doubt.[84] On the following day Frunze again met Lenin before leaving for the front; on 28th September Lenin talked with Bela Kun, who had been attached to Frunze's staff as commissar. Frunze's second commissar was Gusev, who had been sent to the erstwhile South-western command.

On 24th September Frunze arrived at his new head-quarters, Kharkov, where, five days later, a conference of commanders was held to decide upon the strategic plan to be used for the defeat of Wrangel.[85] Frunze had arrived at a time when Wrangel was undertaking a new drive to break away to the north, still motivated by the possibility of that link up with the Poles. At the beginning of September Wrangel had re-organised the whole of his forces in the Northern Tauride into two main striking forces; a break-out might be effected to the north-west, cutting through the VIth and 2nd Cavalry armies, and bringing himself into the line of a possible Polish advance. This move, however, exposed his right flank to serious danger from the XIIIth Red army to the east; it was imperative to remove this threat and to this end Wrangel on 14th September opened an offensive against the XIIIth Red army, driving north to Aleksandrovsk and east to

Mariupol, both of which he gained on 19th and 28th–29th September respectively. By turning his northerly drive against the 2nd Cavalry, he hoped to break this barrier and burst into the rear of the VIth Red army, thus eliminating the Kakhovsk bridge-head.[86]

Frunze ordered Uborevich of the XIIIth, to which he sent reinforcements, to hold the White troops from any further northerly penetration, cutting them off from the Donbas. On 3rd October Frunze reported to Lenin that the threat to the Donbas had been eliminated, but requested that Budenny's 1st Cavalry Army be urged to speed up its progress to the Southern Front. Checked to the east, Wrangel struck up to the Dnieper on 6th, beginning to force a crossing in the region of Aleksandrovsk on the night of 8th — and the operation reached its climax on the eve of the conclusion of the Russo-Polish provisional agreement. After very heavy fighting, the initiative was wrested from Wrangel — although Lenin detected a note of 'excessive optimism' in Frunze's signal to him on the results of the fighting.[87] But the balance had swung in Frunze's favour; the conclusion of the Russo-Polish agreement was a discouraging sign, however tenuous the peace may have seemed. The Soviet troops, with a number of bridge-heads on Wrangel's perimeter, were in a good position to carry out a large-scale encirclement. Soviet strength reached nearly 100,000 infantry and 33,600 cavalry, outnumbering Wrangel by four to one. Yet Wrangel could still escape by retiring to the Melitopol fortified positions, which would mean he would escape annihilation in the Northern Tauride and re-gain the Crimea. Speed was essential, and Frunze desperately urged that the 1st Cavalry Army be speeded on its way. On 27th October it arrived at the front and the following day the Soviet offensive opened.

On the morning of 28th October, in 15 degrees of frost, the attack began; by 3rd November it had still failed to achieve the complete destruction of Wrangel in the Northern Tauride, for White troops had slipped back into the Crimean 'bottle'. At the neck of this bottle lay the lines of fixed defences — the Turkish Wall — with considerable entrenchment and barbed wire. Although under-manned and somewhat neglected, this formidable barrier had to be broken. The task of storming the defences of Perekop, the 'White Verdun', was assigned to Blyukher's 51st Division; timed for the morning of 8th November, the assault was delayed by fog until midday. A savage battle followed, and only after the fourth full-scale attack on the night of 9th November did Blyukher's troops breach the defences. At the same time, by means of a brilliantly conceived but hazardous operation, units of the 51st had turned the White defences; by a trick of the climate, a strong wind opened up the sea-bed by a small stretch of the shallow water, and the frost froze a path along the sea-shallows and the river mouth of the Sivash. It took three hours to get the men across and all nearly came to horrible grief as the wind changed at the end of the perilous crossing. Taken in the rear, however, and with the crumbling of the Turkish Wall, Wrangel's last stand drew to a close.[88] Forcing the bottle-neck, Red troops burst in pursuit into the Crimea, taking Kerch at the eastern end of the peninsula on 16th November. Frunze on that day reported the liquidation of the Southern Front. What remained were scattered actions against White pockets in the south, but, much more important, the reduction of Makhno, whose help had been enlisted against Wrangel. He was now declared an enemy of the Soviet regime and his Agrarian-Anarchist republic sought out for destruction.[89]

The Wrangel operations, beginning with the June raid, his successful offensive and the July-August crises which he thrust upon the South-western Front command, would appear to have had such direct and indirect influence upon the formulation of Soviet strategic intentions that it would not be unjust to regard them as a decisive factor in their own right. Even when Wrangel's troops were diluted with raw recruits, and the crack units were more thinly spread, the strain of containing him placed the Soviet command in an unenviable position regarding their own reserves. The South-western Front command was burdened with a divided strategic assignment, for sufficient troops were not available to set up the separate anti-Wrangel front which ultimately brought him to heel. Even that frenzied and savage phase, not without its moments of crisis, reflected on the reinforcement and equipment problems which plagued the Red Army Field Staff and front commands.

* * * *

The failure of the Warsaw operation and the subsequent tussle over the question of renewing hostilities set up further antagonisms which settled about the involved points of 'exporting revolution with bayonets'. It was against this doctrine that Trotsky resolutely set his face and worked to provide adequate warnings against such dangerous recklessness. Persuaded of the ultimate triumph of revolution in Western Europe, Trotsky did not wish to see this development disastrously complicated by Red Army military operations usurping the role of the indigenous proletariat. It was not to be expected that Tukhachevsky, the sword but not the conscience of the Revolution, should feel bound by these considerations of ideological orthodoxy. The spirit of the military had been inflamed by the war with Poland, and the military argument was that 'next time' would see better preparation to accomplish this export of revolution, with bayonets properly sharpened to the task. At the height of the operations against Poland, Tukhachevsky had written to Zinoviev from Smolensk about the military problems inherent in 'the means of resistance to the bourgeoisie in the period of the socialist revolution'.* None of this, either in theory or in practice, had been investigated. What Tukhachevsky wanted was a 'special investigation of the theory of civil war', an enquiry into the 'science of civil war'. Tukhachevsky made a sharp distinction between the strategy of the class or civil war, and that of 'imperialist war'.

Tukhachevsky set out his main ideas which would dominate the 'strategy of civil war'; the 'universal dictatorship' of the proletariat would be its final aim, to which end the socialist state must create adequate military power, recruit its fighters from the ranks of the world proletariat 'independent of nationality', and postulate the permanent absence of a peaceful frontier with the bourgeois state. The role of the *Komintern*, in Tukhachevsky's eyes, would be to prepare the proletariat of the world for this coming civil war, for 'the moment of the world attack with all the armed forces of the proletariat on world armed capital'. A 'proletarian army' must be prepared for its first operations; the *Komintern* must find a place in its programme for the definition of the requisite military principles. Working on the assumption of 'a world-wide civil war in the very near future', Tukhachevsky wanted to see an international General Staff set up under the *Komintern*, which would occupy itself with studying the potential capitalist enemy, as well as working out a mobilisation plan for the working classes. This would avoid the difficulties which the Red Army itself encountered in fighting a civil war, the duration and intensity of which had come as a shock to the command. In addition, a number of military training centres and staff academies should be opened in Soviet Russia to train a revolutionary military officer corps 'of all nationalities in their languages'.

It was the more ironical but none the less inevitable that the defeat in Poland, which facilitated a Red Army build-up in the south and south-east of Soviet Russia, should have contributed thereby in an indirect but unmistakable manner to the formulation of plans in December 1920 for further military conquest in the name of the Revolution, this time into Georgia. This operation, which was also as much a plot, began without the knowledge or authorisation of the Field Staff in February 1921. While the differences over the exact form of Red Army military assistance to expanding revolution became more marked and were to play some part in the subsequent arguments over the organisation and role of the Red Army, the Warsaw débâcle had finally sealed the bitterness between the 1st Cavalry Army command and Tukhachevsky, revealing Budenny and Voroshilov in

* The full text of this letter is given in Appendix I. This was the Tukhachevsky who, in his own words, would 'pass over the corpse of Poland' on the road to the world revolution, the destinies of which would be settled in the West.

all their guerrilla-ist insubordination, backed by Stalin's political weapons. Shaposhnikov and Yegorov had their own views on the Field Staff. On the credit side, however, the show of patriotic fervour which was skilfully exploited by Bolshevik propaganda, had brought the 'military specialists' into a closer relationship with the Red Army and its command. General A. Brusilov, the former Imperial Commander-in-Chief in 1917, had offered his services to the Soviet government and sat at the head of a number of special advisory committees. But the martial honeymoon was brief, for already at the 9th Party Congress, which began its deliberations on 19th March, 1920, a resolution supported by Trotsky on the transition to a militia system had been adopted. Towards the end of the year Trotsky spoke out vigorously in defence of the new idea, which would guarantee the satisfaction of defence needs without prejudice to the productive processes of the state, and would provide the Soviet state with the ideal form of military organisation suited to it.[90] A gathering storm of criticism hovered over this project; the senior 'military specialists' were uneasy about it, and for different reasons, a rapidly consolidating group of the 'Red command' took exception to the idea of abolishing the Red Army as they knew it. The first skirmishes of a major clash were being fought at the end of 1920.

It was with every justification that Lenin urged upon Frunze the need to avoid a further winter campaign. Soviet Russia had suffered the desperate measures of 'War Communism' in the name of survival but could no longer support them as a sign of victory. Protracted war brought economic ruin and demoralisation in its train. Trotsky had every reason to attempt to revive production and reconstruction by applying military methods, but this drew him into furious political controversies. Already the peasant had begun to strike back at a regime which, while it safeguarded him against the return of the White land-lords, nevertheless exacted its own toll of requisitions from him. In Tambov peasant rebellion had raised its head — and any alienation between the worker and the peasant was fateful for the Red Army in its present form and for the militia in its projected form. As one further reflection of the dissatisfaction with the bureaucracy and the centralism a new storm was also drawing about the second military command chain, the organs of political control; the civilian Party apparatus demanded that control of the political activity in the armed forces should pass to them and the centralised chain be broken.

Out of the context of 1920, a further series of events, deeply overlaid with secrecy and wrapped in mistrust as yet unresolved, were slowly taking shape, which would have a material and far-reaching effect upon the Soviet military élite and the development of the Red Army. Throughout 1920 Germany and Soviet Russia had advanced towards a closer relationship, although there were still suspicion and heavily mixed motive at work.[91] For both, Poland was the arch-enemy, and not a few German hopes were centred on a Soviet victory. None was more intimately concerned than Seeckt of the *Reichswehr*, who entertained no illusions about Bolshevism, yet as a cold, nimble-minded and far-seeing strategist understood that *rapprochement* with the Russians could provide a way out of the restrictions imposed upon Germany by defeat and the Allied conditions. The seclusion afforded by the east could mean the re-habilitation of German war-industry and the provision of a training ground for the *Reichswehr*.

Trotsky was not opposed to such a move. In December 1920 Lenin, in a plea which did not go unheard in Germany, advocated coming to a working understanding with the German bourgeoisie and pointed out the necessity for Germany to come to an agreement with Soviet Russia.[92] Seeckt moved with calculated and astonishing care. He sought neither to frighten the French into occupying the Ruhr nor to stiffen resistance in German financial and industrial circles to his proposed special understanding with the Russians. With characteristic foresight in the late winter months of 1920 or early in 1921 Seeckt organised within the *Reichswehrministerium* a highly secret group of officers, gathered into *Sondergruppe R*; the purpose of this body was to explore the prospects for the proposed military-industrial collaboration.[93] Seeckt himself did not assume command, but entrusted this to Colonel Nicolai, thereby pursuing his aims in the deepest background, while the long work of negotiation in Germany and exploration in Russia went on.

The Civil War had nominally come to an end with the destruction of Wrangel, although fighting went on sporadically until 1922, when the Russian Far East fell under complete Soviet domination. Economic matters came to the fore, and political dissensions occupied the stage. With the new militia proposals and the shift to reconstruction questions, the existence of the Red Army was threatened both directly and indirectly. Peasant dis-affections posed grave problems. The prolonged hardships drove the workers to strike. Protests over bureaucracy and inequality brought the sailors of Kronstadt out in armed rebellion. The most terrible commentary upon this tense situation was that Tukhachevsky's next military assignment was to lead Red officer-cadets and *Cheka* units across the ice of the Neva to silence the heavy guns and the protests of 'the ornament of the Revolution', the sailors of Kronstadt. Against this background of economic strain and political pro-test, a furious struggle for control of the army had begun to be waged behind the scenes. This was no new contest, for it had overshadowed much of the period of the Civil War. The military dangers to the Revolution had put it into temporary abeyance, after the first great clash in the spring of 1919, but now the prospect of victory brought the certainty of discord.

PART TWO

MILITARY DEBATES AND POLITICAL DECISIONS, 1921–1926

. . . the new ruling class must have in all respects a distinct military system: it remained only to create it.

L. Trotsky, *The Revolution Betrayed.*

The situation of our Red Army is especially serious and we cannot consider the army fit for combat.

M. V. Frunze, 1924.

Of course, if we could have chosen between a 1½–2 million strong cadre army and the present militia system, then from the military point of view all the facts and figures would have been in favour of the first solution. But, you see, we have no such choice.

M. V. Frunze, 1925.

CHAPTER FIVE

The Struggle for Control of the Army

The defeat of Wrangel marked the final stage in the military engagements of the Civil War. It was a victory, however, which brought little respite to the Soviet armed forces and none of the realities of peace to the Soviet state. Throughout the latter half of 1920 a political and economic crisis, of an intensity and duration which involved the regime in the gravest dangers, began to occupy an increasingly dominant part in the problems evolving from the newly-won victories. That precarious alliance between the worker and the peasant, upon which the man-power policies of the Red Army were based and realised, suffered grievous deterioration, leading to eventual rupture. The shift in the centre of gravity towards the problems of the shattered economy and the urgency of economic reconstruction markedly affected the status of the military who ceased to be, in Fedotoff White's phrase, 'the petted child of the government'. As 'War Communism' displayed to an alarming degree its unsuitability as a governmental and administrative method, in the Party itself a fateful struggle opened into a simultaneous fight for leadership at the top and the efforts by the upper sections for control over the lower and oppositional elements of the Communist Party. The Red Army and its command could not long remain isolated and immune from these involved and menacing circumstances.

It was an uneasy peace which was in the act of descending. In the west, where the broken Red armies had been finally pulled back in the face of the Polish counter-offensive, Trotsky was striving to silence the exponents of carrying revolution abroad on the bayonets of the Red Army, substituting the separate political developments and their movement towards, if not as yet into revolution by direct Soviet military action. The idea died hard, when there was hope of a next time and when there would be better military preparation and more concise planning. It so transpired, however, that this second chance was snatched on Russia's south-eastern border and not in Europe. Far to the east, the collapse of Kolchak had not been followed by an immediate Soviet military expansion into all Siberia[1]. The road to the Pacific was barred by Japanese troops, landed in 1918 as part of the Intervention. A buffer state, the nominally if precariously independent 'Far

Eastern Republic', was therefore decided upon as a means of separating the Soviet and Japanese forces. Brought into existence on 6th April, 1920, the new Republic was 'recognised' by Moscow on 14th May; provisionally established at Verkhneudinsk, the Republic set up its capital at Chita later in the year. Japanese and White troops co-existed in the Russian Maritime Province, but a considerable build-up of Bolshevik military power and political influence was a pre-condition of facing up to the challenge posed by physical occupation by well-equipped Japanese troops.

In Western Siberia the peasants demonstrated most unmistakably their acute dissatisfaction with the methods adopted by the Soviet regime. With the knowledge that internal victory for the Red Army had secured his land from sequestration by the White Guard officer-landlord, the peasant nevertheless found the realities of Soviet power little to his liking, with the demands which requisition made upon him. While a determined effort was made to liquidate Makhno in the autumn of 1920, in Tambov serious rural disturbances marked the temper and displeasure of the populace. Led by Antonov, a former chief of the local militia, the peasants unleashed guerrilla warfare and rebellion upon the Soviet administration in late 1920, thereby presenting the Red Army with a further problem in 'pacification'. Likewise in the towns and cities the removal of the acute danger from the internal armed threats swept away the justification for the systematic plunder of material resources by the military in the name of victory and survival. The workers would suffer their deprivations no longer.

For the military command the advent of the transition period presented acute problems, accentuated by the lack of homogeneity in the command staff itself. In no real sense did the Red Army belong to the 'Red command', which had made its appearance during the Civil War. Numerically the new command group was hopelessly outclassed by the predominance of 'military specialists'. While the 'short command courses' were passing out more Red officers, a start had been made with the higher education of senior officers. Voroshilov characterised the structure of the officer corps with three main categories: the 'revolutionary commanders' drawn from the industrial workers, the ex-NCOs and ensigns of the old Imperial Army in Soviet service but drawn from the revolutionary peasants and finally the former field and staff officers of the Imperial Army.[2] In the newly constituted General Staff Academy, now housed in what used to be the Hunt Club building in Moscow, 400 pupils were preparing for higher command duties. At first under Tukhachevsky's direction, the Academy staff numbered some of the famous names of the Imperial Russian Army and its administration: Verkhovskii (a former War Minister), Velichko, Martynov, Gatovskii (an expert on cavalry), Svechin (who had worked on the Soviet All-Russian

Supreme Staff) and not least Vatsetis.[3] In addition to their teaching, the ex-Imperial instructors also took part in the growing controversy over a matter of major significance, the organisational form which the Red Army would adopt after the demobilisations. This question involved the military and the political commands, the 'specialist' and the 'Red commanders' alike, and drew Trotsky into a welter of acrimonious debate and antipathetic reactions to his own plans.

Already the 9th Party Congress, which met from 29th March–5th April, 1920, had accepted Trotsky's plan for a transition to the militia system as that method of military organisation which '. . . preserved in itself all the hall-marks of the dictatorship of the working class'.[4] In view of Trotsky's embattled defence of the idea of a centralised control over a regular army, his advocacy of a militia system would at first sight appear strange. Trotsky, however, had not considered the regular army the basic organisational form of the armed forces of the Soviet state, once its victory in the Civil War was assured.[5] The 9th Party Congress resolutions, which had been adopted, reflected Trotsky's ideas on the organisation of the socialist militia and the means by which the requirements of labour and defence would be met simultaneously. Stiffened with cores of regular Red Army formations, the territorial-militia would be made to correspond with the location of industrial enterprises and their agrarian peripheries. The Party resolution quoted the example of a mining centre as the location of such a formation. Although referring to the 'Workers-Peasants Militia', the scheme envisaged the closest possible collaboration between the local economic undertakings, the trade unions and the corresponding type of militia unit. A division would be located with a large undertaking, the regiments and brigades being equated with its sub-sections; the 'best elements' of the industrial, administrative or urban personnel would be transformed into a military cadre, fitted for their military responsibilities by following the requisite command courses. Thus, an active and influential trade-union official might become a regimental or company commander. In short, the plan was designed to implement, very literally, the physical dictatorship of the proletariat, with worker-soldier cadres spreading the Party control into the whole country.

The scheme, produced out of a spirit of optimism and utopianism, raised up a vociferous and vigorous opposition. Trotsky would not admit that the militia was basically a weaker form of military organisation than the regular army; he insisted that with universal military training and the wide range of para-military activity, the militia would furnish the Soviet state with an armed force conforming very closely to its economic, political and ideological requirements. A section of the senior 'military specialists' attacked the idea on the grounds of its inefficiency. Svechin skilfully suggested that among the motives behind such a scheme was a repetition of the errors of the Second International and its appraisal of 'the nation in arms'.[6] In rejecting the improvisation implied in the militia system, Svechin put forward the claims of professional and military efficiency, suggesting in effect the organisation of a 'national army' — and thereby providing a powerful justification for the retention of the 'military specialist'. Trotsky rebuffed Svechin's arguments with some heat, chiding him for his 'political blindness' in ignoring the lessons of the Revolution and for supposing that a Red barrack-regime for the production of Red cannon-fodder would now take the place of the old Imperial system dedicated to that same purpose.[7]

Certain of the 'military specialists' did nevertheless adjust their positions to fit that taken up by Trotsky, with whom they identified their professional security. The Field Staff drew up a plan for a militia devised on the lines suggested by Trotsky; it was proposed that the militia should be organised, not by the Soviet government, but by '. . . special organs (Soviets), in which local government institutions and the population would be represented, for a broad realisation of the idea of the armed nation and the militarisation of labour'.[8] That an extremely optimistic opinion concerning the work of transition had prevailed in the contemplation of these early schemes is perhaps best demonstrated by the All-Russian Supreme Staff report, which estimated that '. . . all the work of reorganisation ought to be completed in 4–6 months after the receipt of the corresponding instructions in the districts'.[9]

In the Political Administration the problems of the transition phase were added to those which had been developing throughout 1919. At the 9th Party Congress Trotsky's system of centralised control in political matters came under attack, when local civilian Party organisations demanded control over the military political organs in the place of the authority exercised by the *PUR*.* In view of the fact that the Party Central Committee did not possess either extensive or effective control over the activities of these scattered civilian bodies, then such a transfer of authority would have been calamitous. This demand was not met, but this by no means diminished the clamour for a thorough revision of the control system of the armed forces' political administration.[10]

The personnel of the Political Administration contributed to no small degree to the prevailing tensions. In practice, it began to appear as if the

* The *PUR* was basically a dual organ, coming under the Republic *Revvoensoviet* and the Central Committee, although the latter exercised as yet only an indirect control. This was at once an involved and delicate relationship. With the appointment of Gusev as successor to Smilga as head of the *PUR*, it is apparent that the balance had definitely tilted towards the group in opposition to Trotsky.

military commissar were being eclipsed, due partly to the commissar turning to tasks of a military-administrative or operational nature. Replacing the cumbersome machinery of 'dual command', a 'modified duality'[11] had become much more extensive and was the product either of the commissar's

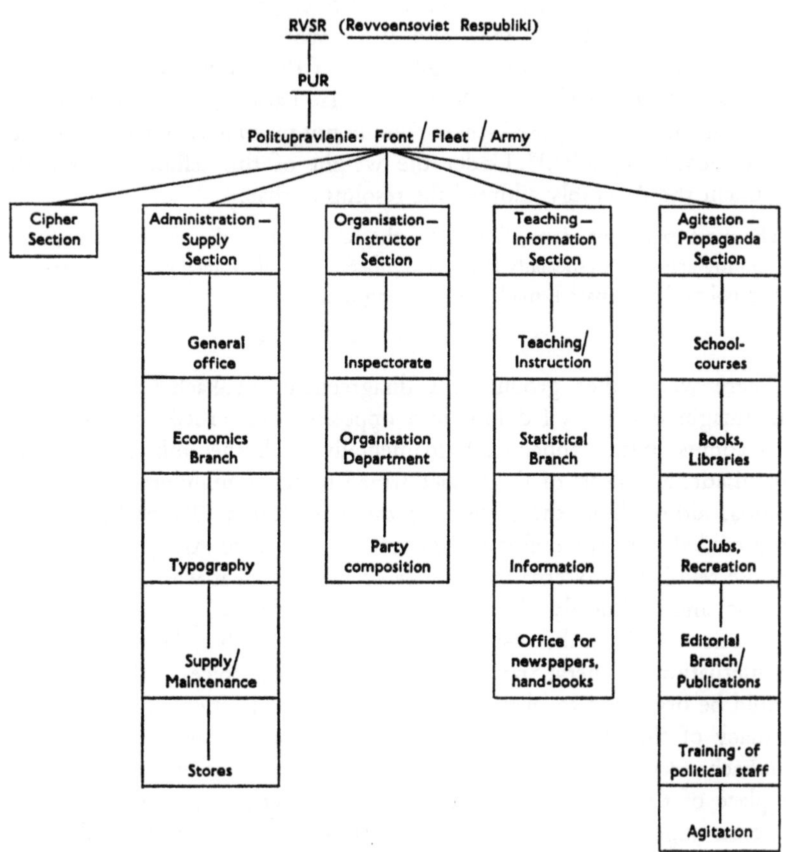

taste for military duties or of arrangement between the commander and the commissar. The feeling was nevertheless abroad that the political apparatus was undergoing liquidation, both voluntary and involuntary. During the meetings of the Second All-Russian Assembly of Political Workers, in December 1920, both the question of the transition to a militia and the future of the political apparatus in the armed forces was fiercely debated.

At this gathering, where the qualification of the 9th Congress resolutions on the militia system was urgently requested, Smilga came out strongly against the proposed scheme. He argued that there were virtually no safeguards that the industrial elements in the militia, thinly spread as they were in comparison with the predominance of peasants, would not become completely isolated. It was a principle of Bolshevik military organisation that worker elements were distributed effectively, and the proposed scheme flatly contradicted this. In view also of the weakness of the Russian communications system, effective mobilisation of the militias was doubtful in the event of an attack upon Soviet Russia. Lacking in addition a firm industrial base, the proposed scheme would not provide an adequate defence of the Soviet republic.[12] Under the weight of this telling and realistic argument the Assembly adopted the resolution that:

> The most expedient form of army for the RSFSR is at the present moment the standing army, not especially large in numbers, but well trained in military respects and politically prepared, made up of young men.[13]

★ ★ ★ ★

There were other grounds for disagreement. Tukachevsky's original and imaginative ideas led him into opposition to Trotsky's schemes on two counts, both connected fundamentally with the military tasks and organisational aspects of the Soviet armed forces. Uninhibited by Marxist dogma, although in the service of the Revolution, Tukhachevsky had propounded after the defeat in Warsaw that the Red Army could indeed impose revolution externally by force of arms. That it was both militarily feasible and politically desirable conformed exactly to Tukhachevsky's conception of the military-political offensive.[14] Further, he proposed that an international General Staff, organised under the auspices of the *Komintern*, should be organised to plan these military-political actions. In view of the primacy of the offensive in this scheme of things, it was inevitable that Tukhachevsky should at once oppose the establishment of a militia system in place of the regular army. In a brilliantly written pamphlet,[15] whose contents suggest that Tukhachevsky was supplying a great deal of the intellectual ammunition to the opponents of the militia, the argument sought to show that a militia was basically better suited to the capitalist society, with its superior rail communications and mobilisation techniques. Rejecting the notion of the militia and the 'nation in arms', Tukhachevsky suggested that such schemes were fostered by the errors of the 2nd International, which had blundered in conceiving of the struggle between the bourgeoisie and the proletariat taking place only within the limits of one nation-state. Expanding revolutions must fight, or expect to fight offensive actions, and would therefore require the necessary military power to accomplish their purposes. The army of the revolutionary state must inevitably be constituted with a view to the political tasks which face it. Workers and poor peasants would provide the ideal material for the revolutionary army, which would carry out missions — offensive, defensive and punitive — far beyond the capacity of any militia.

As the Civil War fronts were officially liquidated, and the decision to demobilise the giant army taken,[16] the struggle over the form of the Red Army after its demobilisation intensified. The resolutions of the Moscow Party Committee for 18th January, 1921, showed marked reservations about the militia plan. Suggestive of the strong influence of Smilga's views, the resolution described the chief feature of the proposed militia as its territoriality — which was itself a political question. The numerical weakness of the industrial proletariat made 'proletarian leadership' doubtful. Moreover, the Civil War had shown that only a regular army could effectively guard the interests of the Soviet state. Desertions especially weakened militias; weak rail links prevented their rapid mobilisation and effective deployment. It was recommended that a few militia units, stiffened with regular troops, should be set up in industrial areas as an experiment, which would provide valuable data on the future military policy of Soviet Russia.[17]

While Trotsky did not dispute the incontrovertible facts of Soviet industrial weakness, he placed great emphasis upon the militia idea. This conformed at the time to his plans for a solution of the severe economic crisis by the application of military methods to the labour front.[18] His 'Labour Armies' were an attempt to apply mobilised military man-power, where not engaged in military operations, to the work of reconstruction and production. This experiment was devoid of any substantial success. Militarisation, with its attendant evils of bureaucracy and the economics of requisition, was ceasing to have any immediate justification in the eyes of either the Party or the country as a whole. Trotsky's application of military methods to the transport problem, besides bringing the accusation of further 'militarisation of labour', roused the fears of the workers and the trade unions. It lead, as a result of Stalin's and Zinoviev's attacks, to a weakening of Trotsky's position. Zinoviev used Trotsky's centralised-militarised policy in the Transport Trade Union movement (*Tsektran*, under Trotsky's presidency) to attack him politically on a course which had nevertheless been approved by the Central Committee.[19] Stalin and Zinoviev were able to effect Trotsky's removal from his post in transportation. This was a pattern of intrigue which repeated itself, with direct and indirect example, in matters concerning the Red Army and military policy as a whole.

Swelling the ranks of opposition, Gusev and Frunze drew up a comprehensive scheme of reform for the Red Army, in the form of twenty-one points which were to be presented at the 10th Party Congress, to be held from 8th–16th March, 1921. Trotsky's opposition* prevented the presentation of the Frunze-Gusev theses, but they are worth examining as the platform of the emerging 'Red command'.[20] The blend was a curious one of realism and a utopianism particular to the group of senior 'Red commanders' who had risen with the Red Army. The Frunze-Gusev programme viewed the introduction of a unified military doctrine as a necessity; this doctrine would be applied by a Red Army of monolithic unity, commanded by a military and political staff fully experienced in the Civil War. It was important that educational and training standards should be raised, and that a recognised General Staff, operating with a heavy reinforcement of political workers, should be set up to direct the Red Army.[21] Technical improvement was equally important, backed by the incorporation of the successful tactics and innovations of the Civil War. The joint programme spoke out strongly against a militia, which, in such a localised form, might become '. . . the support of particularist elements, to the detriment of the general interests of the Workers-Peasants Republic'.[22] Under the prevailing conditions, the militia could embrace only the proletariat and the 'semi-proletariat' of the towns and villages.

It was obvious that the uttermost confusion prevailed in the planning and execution of military policies. The Tambov peasant risings were a material factor in dampening the optimism of early 1920. The events in Kronstadt in February–March, 1921 completely exposed the fallacies of the proposed new system, as well as illuminating the grave *impasse* which had fallen upon the entire internal policy of the Soviet government. It was this situation which the 10th Party Congress had to resolve. Hunger and privation had stirred the Petrograd workers to strikes in protest against the prevailing conditions. The blue-jackets had at a very early date shown that they were not readily amenable to discipline. Many of the men who took part in the actions of 1917 had been scattered throughout the country and the ranks of the naval forces had been reinforced with peasants from the Ukraine and elsewhere. To see in this particular social composition of the fleet personnel the mainspring of the Kronstadt rebellion — as Trotsky attempted to do — is scarcely justifiable in the light of the prevailing social composition of the Soviet armed forces as a whole.[23] The new Soviet navy had presented the regime with two enormous difficulties from the first days of its existence;

* The Frunze-Gusev theses were not presented on the formal agenda of the Congress. Frunze was evidently persuaded to drop his programme as a result of a private talk with Lenin, himself prompted by certain reservations about these new 'proletarian theories'.

the first was the actual control of the lawless blue-jackets, the second the problem of command organisation. Ex-Imperial officers were wholly indispensable for the technical control of the ships and installations, and whereas in the Red Army the commander-commissar conflicts had been blurred by compromise and modification, the naval commissars inevitably sided with the ratings in what was still a revolt against the officers.

Since the turn of the year the arrangements for the political work in the Baltic Fleet had also been subject to considerable tension. 'The fleet opposition', at a conference of Party organisations belonging to the Baltic Fleet, had in February attacked the present arrangements for their lack of contact with the masses and their increasing bureaucratic tendencies. A return to 'democratism' was demanded and the modification of the central control exercised by *Pubalt*, the Baltic Fleet Political Directorate. Zinoviev had played a substantial part in raising this temper; Raskol'nikov and Batis, two of Trotsky's protagonists in the naval political administration, accused Zinoviev of conducting a campaign designed to display Trotsky as the source of bureaucratic compulsion and himself as a support of 'democratism'.[24] This kind of political manœuvre could only worsen a situation already sensitive enough by virtue of weak discipline and the growing influence of the Anarchists among the blue-jackets.

On 28th February, 1921, the crew of the battleship *Petropavlovsk*, incensed at the repression of the Petrograd strikers, issued a resolution which attacked the regime and demanded secret and free elections to the Soviets, thereby guaranteeing a return to the triumphs of 1917.[25] A mass meeting of 1st March, addressed by Kalinin in the role of mediator, proceeded nevertheless to discuss and draw up a rigorous programme of reform, aiming at free elections to the Soviets and the abolition of privileges.[26] A 'Temporary Revolutionary Committee' took charge, and although Kalinin had been allowed to go free, two Soviet government officials, Vasiliev (Chairman of the Kronstadt Soviet Executive Committee) and Kuzmin (senior commissar) were placed under arrest. After rumours of armed intervention, the government did indeed decide on suppression of the Kronstadt mutineers, every effort being made to blame the situation on 'White Guard-ists' and 'counter-revolutionaries'.[27]

The motives for armed reduction of Kronstadt were multiple. The initial attempt to win the rebels from their leaders having failed, and in view of the widespread oppositions and discontents, then a drastic solution would have recommended itself. Zinoviev's magnifications of the Kronstadt situation may have contributed to the decision to strike hard, and yet another pertinent argument was that an attack could be made upon the fortress while the ice was still solid on the river Neva and the warships of the Baltic Fleet immobilised. The Kronstadt rebels had, for their part, rejected the suggestions of the ex-officers that they should move on Petrograd, to develop a bridge-head, seize military stores and make contact with Red Army units. For the forthcoming action the Soviet government placed Tukhachevsky in command; instead of the VIIth Army, which was in a 'demobilisation mood', picked men from the Red officer-cadets were to lead the assault. Dybenko, Fedko, Uritskii left the General Staff Academy for the new front;[28] delegates from the 10th Party Congress were hurried to assist in the work of political agitation.*

Tukhachevsky's first attack opened at dawn on 7th March, when his assault troops, roughly camouflaged against the ice and protected by covering fire from the land batteries, moved up against the rebel positions. The Kronstadt artillery and machine-gun fire broke up the assault across the ice. The second wave was cruelly handled by the rebel guns, and the troops refused to advance across the ice. They were forced to do so at revolver point. Borshchevskii, according to Barmine, took out two of his men sheltering by an ice-bound barge and shot them in front of the others, after which he pressed home his attack.[29] A number of the ordinary men of the line employed in this operation went over to the rebels.[30] With the failure of his first plan, on 17th March Tukhachevsky used a different approach. Opening with an evening artillery barrage, his camouflaged troops were concentrated and then moved forward in columns, drawing their machine-guns and light guns with them. Discovered by the Kronstadt search-lights as they moved forward, the advance columns were met with heavy fire. Finally storming the forts, with heavy loss of life on both sides, and over-coming the sailors at their guns, Kronstadt fell to the Red troops and *Cheka* units on 18th. What had distinguished the behaviour of the rebels had been their leniency in dealing with prisoners — a striking sign in view of the previous record of the Baltic sailors. The regime showed no such comparable humanity in its dealings with the rebels, but by way of reprisal put to death an undetermined but possibly very large number of prisoners.

* * * *

Against this background of internal turbulence, a section of the Soviet command proceeded to execute a further operation of the 'export of revolution with bayonets', selecting as the scene of this activity the south-eastern area of operations, the Caucasus. In Armenia, the order for Red

* On 5th March, 1921, the commander of the Petrograd Military District Avrov was relieved of his duties and Tukhachevsky named commander of the VIIth Army. The Stalinist *History of the Communist Party of the Soviet Union/Bolsheviks/*, Short Course (Moscow, 1951 Edn., p. 386) gives pride of place to Voroshilov at Kronstadt, so that he shares this dubious honour with no one else. See also Voroshilov in *Krasnaya Zvezda* for 17th March, 1961.

Army troops to cross into Armenian territory had been initiated by Stalin's telephone call of 27th November, 1920, to Ordzhonikidze in Baku. Since September Turkish troops had already been in action against the Armenian Republic. With all the appearance of friendship, the Soviet regime rendered real assistance to the Turkish command with the despatch of Soviet agents to work in the ranks of the Armenian National Army.[31] Soviet military intervention with the XIth Army had as its aim the prevention of a Turkish penetration into Trans-Caucasia, which would have been facilitated by the complete collapse of Armenia.[32] After the signature of a Soviet-Armenian agreement, however, the Soviet regime made no attempt to regain for the Armenians those territories lost to the Turks and fastened Soviet rule upon the unfortunate Republic.

The operational centre of the Soviet military-political forces in the Caucasus was the *Kavburo* (Caucasian Bureau), which had been set up in February 1920. Attached to the XIth Red army, Ordzhonikidze acted as the president of this body, with Kirov as his deputy and the Georgian Communists Mdivani and Stopani as political members. Until his transfer to the Western Front to participate in the operation against the Poles, Tukhachevsky was military commander; Mikhail Karlovich Levandovskii finally assumed the military command after Tukhachevsky's departure.[33] Although Moscow had established formal and friendly relations with Georgia, there is ample evidence that an eventual armed overthrow of the existing Georgian regime was both intended and planned.[34] This is not to say, however, that complete agreement existed between the Muscovite centre and the frontier periphery; as later events showed, there was a considerable degree of deception and arbitrary action on the part of the *Kavburo* and acute discomfiture, not to mention disagreement, in Moscow. The cessation of Red Army operations against Poland and the smashing of Wrangel provided a general military situation which favoured the military-political offensive against Georgia plotted by the *Kavburo*. The military aspects were discussed within the *Kavburo* on 3rd December, 1920, and on 18th Gekker, the ex-Imperial officer then in command of the XIth Red army, reported to Ordzhonikidze on the detailed military planning which would be necessary. The crucial point was the attitude of the Turkish command. Even if reinforced by the IXth and 2nd Cavalry armies, the XIth Army could not muster sufficient forces 'to form a firm barrier against the Turks'.[35] The pre-requisite of success was that the Turkish command should preserve a friendly neutrality. In addition, seven rifle divisions and the 2nd Cavalry Army should be moved in, plus food for December-January. This, together with an agreement with the Turkish command, would mean a six-weeks war.[36]

Soviet-Turkish relations were not of the best at this juncture. The Turkish mission which had travelled to Moscow in June 1920 had failed to make any substantial progress. In view of this strain, aggravated by Soviet policy in Armenia, and in line with Lenin's current policy of disengagement from revolutionary situations, the centre was anxious to preserve the present Soviet-Georgian *status quo*. In spite of this, the invasion of Georgia went ahead. There is again sufficient evidence to suggest that this came as a bolt from the blue to Lenin and Trotsky. Technically it was not invasion but an armed intervention to assist a rising which had broken out on 11th February, 1921 at Borchallo. The idea of intervention after this fashion may have been Stalin's, who sought in this manner to soften the blow of the breach of the Georgian frontier. The XIth Red army intervened on 17th, although on 14th the *Politburo* had expressly decided against military action in Georgia.[37] Communications between Lenin and Ordzhonikidze had unaccountably broken down on 5th; Trotsky was occupied with an inspection trip in the Urals, and only on 21st February did he signal to Sklyanskii that he required information on the nature and the origin of these new operations in Georgia.[38] The Field Staff was similarly bereft of information.[39] At the end of February, A. Samoilo was seconded to the Soviet-Turkish talks* in Moscow as military adviser on the status of Kars; on 5th March Turkish troops struck out and occupied Batum on 18th, on which date the Georgians surrendered to the Soviet troops.[40]

Lenin could do no more than accept the situation, but on 2nd March he communicated with Ordzhonikidze, who had shown his ruthlessness in the investment of Baku, recommending that 'special policies' be enacted towards the Georgian intelligentsia and that 'the Russian model' should not be arbitrarily fastened upon Georgia.[41] To the XIth army commander on 17th March Lenin sent a signal which ordered him to take particular care towards the population and sovereign organs of Georgia, to adhere strictly to the directives of the Georgian *Revkom*, and inform Lenin of any infringments of these directives.[42] The weakness of the Georgian Communist Party, however, made it virtually inevitable that the real power should pass into the hands of Ordzhonikidze and the XIth Army commander. It was equally inevitable that Ordzhonikidze's abuse of his power should create a dangerous situation as early as 1922, so that by 1924 the 're-conquest' of Georgia was a necessity.

* * * *

In view of the internal unrest and the several agitations for new policies

* This was Samoilo's second diplomatic mission. His first had been as military adviser to the Soviet delegation at Brest-Litvosk in 1918: an account of this and his exchanges with Hoffman he gives in his recent autobiography, *Dve Zhizni*, Moscow 1958, pp. 188–201.

in the Red Army's organisation and political apparatus, the decisions of the 10th Party Congress mark an important point in the attempt to develop a coherent and politically realistic programme for the Red Army during the transition phase. It was obvious that the risings in Tambov and Kronstadt indicated the need for substantial modifications in the plans for a militia. The unrest in the political apparatus, exacerbated by oppositional trends in the Party and fractional intrigue at the higher levels, reached a climax. The demand for civilian control of the military's political organs was repeated. A compromise form of this drastic step envisaged that the existing machinery should be retained, but that the elective practice would be re-introduced into the Party commissions; the actual work of political indoctrination would be handed over to the *Glavpolitprosvet* (Directorate of Political Education), whose military section would then act independently of the commissars and the *PUR*.[43]

The 10th Congress, concerned basically with the introduction of the New Economic Policy (*NEP*) and stemming the wave of oppositions which had appeared both within and to the Party, witnessed the consolidation of the position of the men in the military command who were associated with Stalin. Frunze, Voroshilov, Molotov, Ordzhonikidze and Petrovskii, among others, were elected to the Central Committee. Gusev, Kuibyshev, Kirov and Chubar, also Stalin's men, were among the new candidate members to the Central Committee. Although Frunze and Gusev were unable to obtain the adoption of their programme of reform, the Congress decisions did mark some progress in this direction. It was resolved to speed up the organisation of technical units (artillery, armoured-car detachments, aviation and engineering), and to rectify the deteriorations in the supply system.[44] The Congress condemned the agitation of 'certain comrades' for the liquidation of the regular Red Army and agitation for a speedy transition to the militia system. For the immediate future, the basis of the Soviet armed forces would be the regular Red Army, while a partial transition to militia might be effected only in those districts with a pronouncedly proletarian population, that is, Moscow, Petrograd and the Urals.[45] In fact only a full militia brigade was organised in Petrograd, and the plans for militia divisions had to wait upon the solution of other problems such as recruitment, establishment and training.[46]

The demand for modification in the political administration was met in so much that it was decided to strengthen the ties between the local Party and the military organs. Any idea of drastic change was cut short by the insistence that the *PUR* would continue in the form which it had possessed during the previous three years. Resolution No. 18 roundly condemned those 'certain groups and individual comrades' who sought to re-introduce the elective system and wished to see the subordination of the commissar to the rule of the 'cell'.[47] This condemnation by no means put an end to the decentralising or even the abolitionist activity on the part of political personnel; the heated debate on the introduction of unitary command displayed grave doubts and fears,[48] while on 17th March, 1921, the military delegates to the 10th Congress conferred with the political workers of the centre on the question of the election of Party commissions and the position of the commissars.[49]

The 'Red command' had, nevertheless, begun to emerge as a distinct body of men with their own political support and pursuing the paths of ambition with only faint concealment. That assembly of discontent over Trotsky's policy in the Red Army was now moving to a position from which it might open a heavy assault on the War Commissar and his theories. It would be too much to describe the 10th Congress as any defeat for Trotsky's ideas; he had been able to check the advance of schemes in opposition to his own — schemes which were admittedly as deficient in the formulation of practical ideas as some of his own — yet this was only a prelude to a protracted debate on matters of military theory and doctrine. This debate, one of the most intensive and unconcealed about fundamentals as has ever taken place in the Soviet command,[50] played its part in the political manœuvres during and after 1921, and as such it must be distinguished from the controversies which had raged in 1919.

Meanwhile the 1st Cavalry Army and the central command had been in conflict over very practical matters. Stationed in the Ukraine, where it had been used to reduce Makhno's irregulars, the 1st Cavalry was apparently in dire straits due to the lack of forage and the decline in training.[51] On 30th March, 1921, Voroshilov and Budenny signalled the extent of the calamity, requesting permission to move to the Northern Caucasus. Frunze, as commander in the Ukraine and the Crimea, supported the application. By way of answer, on 5th April, 1921, the Republic *Revvoensoviet* decided to reduce the 1st Cavalry Army to one-third of its present size, detaching what remained to Kremenchug and Nikolayevsk, and sending one division to Tambov.[52] This naturally aroused the 1st Cavalry Army command. On 17th April, Budenny and Voroshilov protested by telegram; three days later the *Politburo* rescinded the orders, transferring the 1st Cavalry to Manych,[53] and on 28th established the North Caucasus Military District, with Voroshilov as its commander. This area would act as a cavalry training and re-mount centre. The *PUR* despatched 15 political officers and 500 Communists to man the political apparatus; Order No. 924/163 of 30th April set up the administrative sub-divisions of the Military District and staff and field connections with the Caucasian front.[54] It was also at this time that the Red Army operating against the Tambov insurgents was strengthened; command of over a score of rifle divisions was entrusted to Tukhachevsky and military-punitive operations continued throughout the early summer.[55]

The debates on doctrine, into which the Soviet command had entered, embraced a very wide field, the intrinsic issues being complicated by the fact that many of the arguments were only a very thin screen for personal or group ambitions. The contrived artificiality of the debate was part of the process of political combination, through which Trotsky suffered some hard blows. The theme of the military factor in Soviet external policy was being discussed intensively at a time when the foundations of that policy were still imperfectly understood and its course was undergoing important changes of emphasis and direction. Actual military doctrine roused similar passions also at a time when the question of the organisational form of the Red Army had not been settled and military strength was being substantially reduced. Trotsky had already come face to face with the critics of his military method, who advocated a 'proletarian military doctrine'.[56] This was now revived, not by embittered dissidents or the zealots of 'partisanism', but by successful Red Army commanders of the stamp of Frunze, experienced in large scale operations, yet alarmed, disappointed and frustrated by the apparent trend towards defensivism and a possible lasting military conservatism. Although Trotsky's majority had triumphed at the 10th Congress, the subsequent polemics were aimed at undermining that support and whittling away at his position.

Frunze, after the defeat of the 10th Congress, enlarged and clarified his ideas in a paper, published in July 1921, on a unified military doctrine and the Red army.[57] His argument opened platitudinously enough, with statements to the effect that a given military art cannot be divorced from the general development of that state; military doctrine will follow the general political line of the ruling class of that state, with the material and spiritual resources at that same state's command exerting strong influence. The experiences of the Civil War provided the Red Army with a wealth of material on the principles upon which it ought to be trained—'manœuvre operations on a large scale'.[58] The Soviet staff ought to concern itself with the problems of the 'small war' with potential opponents possessing a higher technical level than the Red Army. In connection with the predominantly 'manœuvre character' of Red Army operations, and as opposed to the 'positional character of past imperialistic wars', the Red cavalry had a decisive role to play. And the organisational form which would apply this new doctrine would be, in the near future, only a regular Red Army.

The planning sections, to which Frunze addressed part of his remarks, had changed their form in February 1921 when the Red Army Staff took the place of the Field Staff and the All-Russian Supreme Staff, which had been responsible for operational and planning matters respectively during the Civil War.[59] It is from this point that the history of the Soviet General Staff as such begins, manned as it was by an overwhelming complement of 'military specialists'. A month previously, at a session of the Higher Academic Military-Pedagogic Soviet of the Red Army, a commission had been nominated to collect and collate the combat experience of the Civil War; army and front staffs were requested to make available for publication non-secret materials, and the newly-established Military Literature Section would handle this, as well as the new military journals — *Voennaya nauka i revolyutsiya* (Military science and Revolution), and *Voennyi Vestnik* (Military Herald), devoted to the problems of military art and military training and organisation respectively.[60]

Trotsky never minimised the experiences of the Red Army during the Civil War. Although his opponents charged him with this, the accusation lacked any foundation in truth. Trotsky carried on a strenuous campaign to persuade the 'military specialists' that they ought to abandon their theoretical rigidity, and include the very valid lessons of the Civil War in their lectures and writings; he rejected out of hand such a view as that of Svechin, who dismissed the revolutionary period as one in which no basic doctrine could be formulated, since its chief characteristic in military matters was improvisation.[61] It would appear that two distinct ideas dominated Trotsky's approach to these doctrinal issues; in opposing the 'military specialists', he engaged himself to prevent the spread of reactionary views into the Soviet military organism, and in criticising the 'Red command' he strove to check a one-sided interpretation of a single set of military operations becoming the dominant element in Soviet war doctrine.

Trotsky met Frunze's arguments head-on. Having already at the 10th Congress dismissed the proposed theses as 'ridiculous nonsense', Trotsky proceeded to subject certain of the basic assumptions of the new doctrines to a merciless and frequently uncomplimentary examination. In his discussion of doctrine at the Military Scientific Society of the General Staff Academy he did not deny that the Soviet government did not turn its face against a revolutionary war where this would lead to the actual liberation of the proletariat. However, the present task of the Soviet government was defensive in nature — not to arm and train for the offensive which Tukhachevsky recommended.[62] As for the Civil War and its special lessons, the manœuvre principle was not a Soviet invention — 'we did not invent manœuvre-ism' — but the product of the intrinsic features of the war, large areas and weak communications, common to Red and White alike.[63]

In a piece of ferocious prose, with deadly ridicule implicit in its title,[64] Trotsky proceeded to the demolition of his opponents' arguments. Trotsky argued that unity to the Soviet military effort was supplied by the consistent attempts of the worker-state to survive, and then to develop. Neither uninspired improvisation nor dogmatic insistence upon certain arbitrarily selected principles, but a realistic elasticity, were necessary to Soviet military doctrine. 'Proletarian war', or indeed any other emphasis upon the distinctiveness of a special aspect of war, became mere metaphysical idea-spinning. The Red Army, speaking out of its experience, had meant two things — inducing the peasant to follow the industrial worker into the armed struggle, and providing this body with a command staff. In examining the historical evolution of the art of war certain basic and fixed characteristics appeared, which were subject to technical, social and political influences. Erecting this, however, into a structure of 'unalterable truth' was dangerous and misleading. A Marxist approach could not mean blind support of a 'Communist war doctrine', but rather the avoidance of military doctrinairism.* It was this latter charge which Frunze sought subsequently to refute.

Gusev, dubbed at one time 'a strategic cockerel' by Stalin, also devoted much attention to expounding the new doctrine, occupying as he did the important post of chief of the *PUR*. Through Gusev it is possible to see the new doctrine in terms of its application in political work, although Gusev did not refrain from actual military commentary. In his substantial study of the lessons of the Civil War[65] there emerged a skilful criticism of the present military regime; the territorial principle (such as Trotsky wished to apply to the militia) was a blunder, for units so formed were unsuitable for use in offensive operations. Positional warfare had been a rarity in the Civil War; manœuvre warfare played the principal role, with the regular army acting as the 'basic and principal force', to which partisan units were very properly subordinated. Experience showed that a transition to the militia system needed very careful planning. This hindsight was most carefully arranged to suit the Frunze-Gusev programme.

Yet this hindsight provides a certain revelation of the mentality of the new commanders. Trotsky displayed an energetic impatience with what he

* In view of the subsequent development of ' "Stalinist" military science', and the deadening effect which this had on Soviet military development, Trotsky's arguments received a posthumous confirmation. Although Trotsky did not foresee this particular form of dogmatism, he was fully alive to a very real danger which did finally materialise. It would be too much to inject an element of prophecy into Trotsky's statements on military matters at this time, but it is remarkable that many of the warnings he gave at this time proved themselves valid long after the so-called 'debate on doctrine' had ceased.

regarded as these conceits, which were born of cumulative ignorances. Gusev displayed an inclination for demanding the concise planning of political work in the armed forces, with a persistent effort to improve the political machinery, weakened as it had become with the demobilisation of skilled political workers.[66] Full of faith, however, in the prospects of the 'revolutionary war', Gusev proposed as his programme of political work in the Red Army:

> . . . (1) education in the spirit of internationalism; (2) education in the spirit of overcoming village cohesion and petty-bourgeois narrow-mindedness; (3) struggle with the restorationist tendencies of the peasant; (4) anti-religious propaganda.[67]

In their 1921 writings and programmes, both Frunze and Gusev displayed a deal of vagueness in their discussion of points of doctrine, and Trotsky swooped upon the discrepancies; it is nonetheless strange that he did not — or would not — also recognise the degree of compulsive faith such men held in the Red Army and its future. Frunze's first arguments were clumsy, but they were scarcely ridiculous. Gusev, with his political programme, was attempting to solve the problems raised by demobilisation and the problem of the peasant in the Red Army. His 'planned political programme' did not differ radically from that operated finally in the tense years of the first attempt at industrialisation.

At the close of 1921 there were dilemmas other than the theoretical to beset the military command. Turkey, quasi-ally of Soviet Russia, was facing the advance of Greek troops into Anatolia. To accede to the Turkish request for Soviet help might bring the danger of a rapid deterioration of relations with Great Britain, supporter of the Greeks. Nor had the Kemalist Turks shown themselves to be such guileless friends of the Soviet regime. The Stalin-Ordzhonikidze group, who had so recently engineered the invasion of Georgia, had less cause to pretend to a desire to buttress Turkish power, the deflection of which had been a necessary pre-condition for the success of the Georgia operations. This tactical view evidently did not prevail at the centre, which commanded the despatch of Frunze to Angora in December 1921. Nominally Frunze travelled as representative of the Ukrainian Republic, military command of which he held; the specious diplomatic show was the conclusion of the Ukrainian-Turkish Treaty. In the space of less than a month, however, Frunze the military expert arranged for military assistance to the Turks. That Frunze worked out the plans, which resulted in Kemal Ataturk's success in his summer offensive, is impossible to prove.[68] But the military assignment included the arranging for Soviet military supplies to reach the Turks — and the stocks seized from the White troops would have been an immediate reservoir upon which to draw. This was a mission which Frunze, even if he were not the architect of the Smyrna victories, brought to a successful conclusion.

★ ★ ★ ★

In 1922 the controversy within the Soviet command took a serious turn. Trotsky was gradually forced into a position where he could be made to appear as the champion of reactionary policies — the very fact that the 'military specialists' chose to applaud him was taken as proof of his deliberate stand against the 'progressivism' of the Red commanders. Frunze, fresh from his Turkish venture, made an important statement of the new 'unified doctrine', presented at an assembly of the command and political staff of the Ukrainian and Crimean forces on 1st March, 1922.[69]

At the outset Frunze declared that such an address on training problems could be made only now, when '. . . one might consider our work of re-organisation complete in its basic features'. Of 'certain comrades' who made great play with the word 'doctrine', Frunze had two observations to make; it was essential that the Red Army should be trained to have unified views, and that unity must be reflected in every aspect of the Red Army, whether in peace or war. Nevertheless, Trotsky's criticisms had registered, for it was most obvious that Frunze was very careful to define his position about 'revolutionary war'. In addition, Frunze admitted that to prosecute successfully a war of manœuvre, positional warfare also had to be studied and even practised as an aid to manœuvre-ism.[70]

As a conclusion Frunze enumerated fifteen points, which became the basis for the platform which he and his supporters presented at the forthcoming 11th Party Congress. The theses propounded the necessity for a resumption of training, consistency of political work, the supremacy of the principle of manœuvre, the validity of the combat experience of the Civil War, the recognition of the primacy of the offensive and the need for technical advance in the Red Army.[71] In short, this represented as attractive and inspiring a programme as any Red commander, reared and practised in Civil War, could wish for. It gave the 'small war', much despised by the professionalised ex-Imperial officers, a military and doctrinal significance, anchored in quite careful qualification and bereft of a top-heavy doctrinairism.

This address marked a very considerable advance in Frunze's military thought. Proof of his ability as a military planner of calibre was supplied by his paper 'The Regular Army and Militia';[72] this was a skilled and detailed examination of the militia system, backed by a strength embodied in regular formations. The idea of the 'mixed military establishment'* — the militia and the cadre army — emerged as a possible and workable system, although Frunze pointed to the misgivings which were felt in some quarters that a regular force of only 600,000 men would not be adequate. In the equally important matter of the location of divisions and elements of divisions, Frunze enumerated five basic factors which would determine this; political considerations, the nature of the communications network (rail and telegraphic), the respective wealth of regions in human and material resources, a guarantee of barracks and billets, and a minimum of additional means of transportation.[73] The first factor was decisive in its own right, for although there would be oscillations, the general arrangement must be that the proletarian element in units should not fall below an average of 20–25 per cent of the total unit strength.

Detailed planning was not the centre of the fierce dispute that flared up at the 11th Party Congress, which opened its proceedings on 27th March, 1922. Although no open resolution was moved against Trotsky, and while Frunze and Voroshilov did not succeed in winning official acceptance of their theses, Trotsky's opponents were closing in. Although ostensibly a discussion of 'military doctrine', raising the issue of the applicability of the Marxist tenets led to doubts or enthusiasms for its extension to other fields. It became a sounding-board for opinions and a test of loyalties. In his incisive attack upon the fifteen theses presented by Frunze-Voroshilov, Trotsky did not spare his opponents. Trotsky again questioned the entire basis for the offensivism which the new doctrine so ardently advocated. It was not enough merely to re-hash the French *Field Service Regulations*. In the event of an attack upon Soviet Russia by a capitalist power or powers in possession of superior technical means, there was no alternative for the

* The relevance of these first explorations of a territorial system to the modern Soviet military establishment may be seen in the law of 15th January, 1960, covering a reduction in the strength of the Soviet armed forces. As in the Frunze period, economic retrenchment is one reason for the adoption of the territorial-cadre unit system. There is also the point that the actual military re-organisation of the army is difficult when it is 'over-manned'. On 14th January, 1960, Khrushchev reported to the Supreme Soviet that the question of a transition to the territorial system was being studied; the territorial units could train without any interruption to the productive capacity of their members, while the cadre units equipped with nuclear weapons and missiles would guarantee the defence of the USSR. Save for the mention of nuclear weapons, this is a reiteration of the arguments of the 9th Party Congress and subsequent modifications upon it. If the experience of 1922–4 is any guide (and certain institutional problems remain the same), then the problem is more difficult than Khrushchev makes it sound. In his article 'Social Problems in the Reorganisation of the Soviet Armed Forces' (*Bulletin*, Munich April 1960, pp. 3–16), N. Galay also adds a third reason for this possible change. This (comparable to the 1922–4 position) is connected with altering the social composition of the Soviet forces, for the existing form is alien to the social structure defined as 'socialist in the stage of the transition to Communism'. The officer caste is to be broken in so far as this is possible; with Malinovskii's statement that one out of every four in the armed forces is an officer being presently true, the probable figure for officers due to be demobilised might reach 250,000.

Soviet forces but to adopt a defensive posture, thereby providing the requisite time for a mobilisation which must be imperfect and difficult owing to the state of the Soviet communications. To attack first, merely because the articles of the offensive spirit so dictate, would be foolish in the extreme.[74] To accomplish the physical destruction of the enemy, which is the aim of war, it is necessary to employ the offensive — but only under those conditions which will bring about a successful accomplishment of this aim. Any initial withdrawal, in the event of attack, would be planned in accordance with temporal and spatial needs imposed by Soviet mobilisation factors; to resort to an immediate offensive, unsupported by effective mobilisation, might mean a set-back which could wrest the initiative irrevocably from Soviet hands. As for even the best of military principles, it was necessary to look only at the Civil War, where the weakness and deficiencies of the Soviet middle and junior grade commanders had made it necessary to fight the same war not once but two or three times. And, essentially, the idea of sustained defence put a premium upon that positional warfare which Frunze — and Tukhachevsky — were quick to despise.[75]

Trotsky came out powerfully against Point 5 of the theses — that which envisaged future Red Army actions in terms of the 'revolutionary war', repelling a possible capitalist attack or joining with the toiling masses of other countries in a common struggle. He had maintained that to train an army with the emphasis wholly upon the advantage conferred by offensive action was incorrect. To train an army, composed predominantly of peasants, with a doctrine founded in offensive war to support world proletarian revolution, was impossible.[76] It was, indeed, doubtful if the idea of 'revolutionary war' could be approached with the confused priorities embodied in Point 5. Fundamentally, it was defence of the Soviet state, not external revolutionary ventures, which would keep the Soviet armed forces, with the vital structural point of the worker leading the peasant, intact.

Trotsky's opponents had hammered away at their own points, voicing the exception which they had taken to his views. Voroshilov and Budenny, Minin and Kashirin, and Tukhachevsky sought to minimise the War Commissar's ideas. Voroshilov took quite the opposite line in considering the possible course of events in the case of an attack upon Soviet Russia; his was the offensive solution, yet his concern was less to state the case for offensivism than to charge Trotsky with something which was quite untrue — preventing the planned reconstruction of the Soviet armed forces.[77] Tukhachevsky occupied a distinctive place in the ranks of this kind of opposition; he was essentially less concerned with justifying the offensive doctrine out of a conviction that the proletarian leadership had produced a distinctive proletarian doctrine, than with his own views which were drawn from Napoleon. Trotsky had earlier exposed the fallacies of fitting the circumstances of the French revolutionary wars into a Soviet context; Tukhachevsky's proposal for his international general staff had been rejected, ostensibly on the grounds that such a staff would merely be the sum of the national staffs composing it, but the basic objection would seem to have been rooted in the fear of placing so substantial a power in the hands of the *Komintern*.[78] As was to be expected, Tukhachevsky rejected Trotsky's remarks about the middle and junior command staff, insisting that the chief problem was the training of the higher command staff of the Red Army, as well as concentration upon the provision of material resources. As for the assertion that the principle of manœuvre was not an exclusive Soviet preserve, Tukhachevsky maintained that, on the contrary, the Red Army had been self-taught and no borrower from the Whites.[79]

Frunze's riposte was a little blunted. Basically it was an enlargement of his lecture to the Ukrainian commanders. What is interesting about it is the modification which Trotsky's criticism had already imposed. Frunze opened by disputing Trotsky's charge of doctrinairism;[80] it was important to define the foundations of the doctrine, so that military training could proceed. The distinction which Frunze was making lay between a discussion in terms of the possibility of the offensive, as opposed to Trotsky's exclusive emphasis upon the defensive, which was quite inadmissable as a basis upon which to train. Yet this was not the core of the dispute, serious though it was. Trotsky had claimed that the Frunze group had failed to define properly its strategic and tactical position, and that 'idealisation of the previous experience of the Red Army' was the root cause of this. Frunze replied:

> I think that Trotsky is deeply mistaken. Is it possible to say that we, commander-Communists and political staff, idealise the experience of the Red Army? If one looks at our assemblies, our congresses — consider only the last congress of the Ukrainian command staff — then it will be seen that to charge us with excessive admiration for the past is not seemly. On the contrary, we said that in the past there had been a mass of blunders, that we were badly prepared, that we must study, study and study.[81]

It was not true that Lenin in his address to the Congress had come out against Frunze's position;* when Lenin spoke about 'Communist conceit' Trotsky said to Frunze, 'The whole of Vladimir Il'ich's speech is beating you'. Nor was there any analogy with Larin's remarks about the trade

* Although Frunze maintained this, and it was strictly speaking correct, there is little doubt that Lenin was cautious over this 'proletarian military science', much as he was over 'proletarian literature' and 'proletarian art'. Trotsky was right in pointing out to Frunze that Lenin was in earnest over the dangers of 'Communist conceit'. Over the precise form of Lenin's intervention, Frunze is understandably very reticent.

unions — nor indeed any analogy with the problems of the economic front.[82]

What was striking was Frunze's precise and careful disassociation of himself and his ideas from the extremists of a 'proletarian doctrine' of strategy and tactics, thereby admitting that an extreme wing did exist.[83] The new doctrine did not — and it was understood that it could not — claim the mantle of absolute innovation and invention. Yet, continued Frunze, manœuvre and mobility are the characteristics of operations hitherto conducted by a Red Army with 'proletarian elements' at its head. As for fortified positions, in view of their very cost, these would be precluded from the Soviet military picture. Finally, in spite of Trotsky's and Tukhachevsky's observations to the contrary, Frunze argued that new proletarian military methods — in contradistinction to the bourgeois — were possible; the next war would not be dissimilar from the Civil War, in which positional warfare occupied little place. At the same time, with the expansion of proletarian revolution, there will be no stable rear and hence no front-line in the recognised sense — thus further diminishing the importance of positional warfare.[84]

There is no doubt that Trotsky was fully justified in his two basic criticisms of the Frunze group — their imprecise definitions and their idealisation of past experience. Yet the programme commanded increasing support among the 'Red command', attracted as they were by ideas which promised to deliver the Red Army into their hands. Trotsky's motivation in his sustained resistance to the introduction of such a programme is not easy to define. Certainly he reacted violently, as he had done in 1918–9, to the palpable conceit which seemed to possess the new 'doctrine-mongerers'; his realisation of the unfavourable turn which the fortunes of world revolution had taken, the temporary recovery of the bourgeoisie, and the internal problems posed by the peasant in Soviet Russia, were all real factors. He was acutely aware of the technical weakness of the Soviet forces in the face of possible capitalist attack. It is possible that he understood the contact with the German military command and the assistance which they offered in reconstructing the Red Army as the signal for a decisive turn to defensivism. Nevertheless, he was mistaken in treating that idealisation by the Red command of their Civil War experience as a complete indication of either ignorance or crass conceit. Behind it, admittedly well entrenched with substantial ignorance, lay a powerful morale factor, which Trotsky ignored at his cost. It was, for Trotsky, the tragedy of this conflict that being right brought no reward, but, on the contrary, identified him with a conservatism and reactionary way of thinking which were totally unacceptable in this climate of opinion. It is significant that not all Trotsky's most trenchant remarks and searching arguments were able to displace the offensive from its lofty pinnacle or dampen that enthusiasm for 'activism' which accompanied it.

It is perhaps the most ironical commentary upon the doctrinal debates that while they reached their wordy climax, the military policy of the transition period was well on the way to breaking down. The debates and polemics were symptomatic of the tension in the political situation and of the strain in and upon the command as a whole. The reduction of the size of the Red Army had led to serious interruptions in its training, and to a deterioration in the supply situation; the artillery was largely obsolete, in short supply and with only five per cent of the guns in working order. The assorted stocks of primitive tanks and armoured cars, many of which were trophies taken from the White forces, showed similar signs of obsolescence and mechanical deficiency.[85] During the demobilisation, a series of adjustments and innovations were made in the structure of the Soviet infantry. Almost each stage of the man-power reduction produced modifications in the form of the infantry organisation, beginning with the infantry division, the establishment of which was set at 16,000 in 1921.

Two changes in organisation concerned the liquidation of the brigade and the independent brigade within the division, which had been preceded by the introduction of the corps as the tactical unity of the rifle divisions.[86] In July 1922 the new scheme was generally introduced, with the classification of three divisional types; the first was the frontier division, the second for internal garrisons and the third was made up of the rifle divisions in the Independent Caucasian Army (*OKA*). The Turkestan front divisions in reality accounted for a fourth type.[87] The strength of the frontier division was fixed at 8,705, and the internal division at 6,725, with the percentage of combat troops to the total strength set at 75·17 and 70·76 respectively. The new arrangements brought further disadvantages in their train; the diversified establishment prevented standardisation in organisational structure, while the plan did not take account of the need to set up effective artillery strength at regimental as well as divisional level.[88] The deficiencies of equipment made the innovations merely an exercise of theory, so that in effect the Red Army gained very little. The clearest demonstration of this lay in the decision, formulated in Order No. 28 (1922), to set up 'mechanised companies' — with one such company in all regiments in every rifle division.[89] Armed with automatic weapons, these companies were to be trained in 'group tactics'; yet no automatic weapons were forthcoming to equip them.

Similarly, while the heated arguments went on about a possible Soviet response to an attack, it does not appear that any workable mobilisation plan existed, nor could one be so formulated until the position of military obligations and man-power availability had been clarified. If the chief problem with the regular army (apart from equipping it) was to settle the questions of structure and organisation, the introduction of militia divisions demanded considerable planning for recruitment and training. It was, however, generally accepted that the political factor, which Frunze had enumerated, was vital to secure a proletarian control of the militia. The decree of the 28th September, 1922, was the first attempt to regularise the miniumum periods of service in the Soviet armed forces;[90] the decree fixed the obligation of military service upon all males, with the exception of men

Composition of Red Army, 1922

Arm or service	*Percentage of personnel*
Riflemen	44·3
Cavalry	11·4
Artillery	1·4
Armoured units (armoured trains, armoured cars)	1·5
Military aviation	1·6
Military communications	2·6
Military training establishments	13·2
Other military units	24·2

Total strength relative to demobilisation:

1921 1st January	4,110,000
1st May	2,614,000
1922 1st January	1,590,000

(*Note:* the 1922 total fell to 703,000 in the first half of 1923.)

who, by virtue of their class affiliations or active hostility to Soviet power would not bear arms but be called up for military service 'in a special way'. In this way a start was made with the complicated problems of re-arranging the available and potential military man-power, after which the next step was to settle the detailed plans for recruitment to the militia.

While there is a sufficiency of evidence to suggest that the Soviet military machine was grinding to a halt, if not actually breaking down, and the welter of debate pointed to a severe crisis in a command which had never enjoyed any noticeable measure of unity, the political administration was the scene of struggles both at the top and at the lower levels. Gusev, of whom Trotsky spoke slightingly and not always with justification, had defined very aptly the role of the political apparatus in the 13th point of his joint programme with Frunze; the only way to secure the Red Army, composed of tens of thousands of peasants, from 'Bonapartist projects' was to maintain the Civil War pattern of political controls. In addition, and this was Gusev's theme in his speeches and writing during his period as head of the *PUR*, a planned programme of political work was essential. Many able political workers had been lost to the army through demobilisation, although in 1922 there was some reinforcement of the strength of the political personnel.[91] With Antonov-Ovseenko's appointment to the head of the *PUR* in 1922, the leadership of the political apparatus passed to a man sympathetic to Trotsky and under whom a form of democratic decentralisation of political work took place—bringing with it substantial tactical advantages in the mounting political struggle.

* * * *

Not until 1923 is there any noticeable sign of the stabilisation of the Soviet military machine in the demobilisation period. It could be argued, and with justification, that one of the decisive factors permitting this was the possibility of making a fixed budgetary allocation to the Soviet armed forces, which had hitherto been lacking. In January–February 1923 a definite start was made with the realisation of the territorial-militia scheme, under which only the Petrograd militia brigade had so far existed. This was a sign that opinion had worked to the conclusion that the acutely dangerous stage in worker-peasant relations was past. In the beginning, ten regular divisions were converted to a territorial status with a regular core of 1607, and effectives (made up of men who would pass through the division with the mobilisation of their age-groups) of 10,959.[92] By the summer this conversion was complete, and the final stages were accompanied by a series of decrees and authorisations for the whole range of territorial establishments.

On 18th June, 1923, the Central Committee sent to Party organisations a circular on the role of the territorial divisions; it was explained that budgetary restrictions made the maintenance of a large standing army impossible, but the territorial formations would enable the toiling masses to receive the requisite amount of military training. Party organisations were urged to help to achieve that 'proletarian patronage' by working actively in the divisional political organs and bringing in the trade unions. At the end of the month the *PUR* issued its directive on the political organs in territorial divisions; the rights and responsibilities of political organs in the cadre division were also reserved to the same organs of the territorial divisions. In addition, political work would be carried on among recruits (that is, outside their annual mobilisation) in divisional recruiting areas. 'Cells' were not permitted to be formed below battalion level before mobilisation, but upon mobilisation they might be set up in regiments and companies where conditions were favourable.[93] On 8th August, 1923, the conditions of service in 'territorial military units' were formally laid down by decree; the cadre force in the division would serve under conditions conforming with the regular Red Army, with the territorial complement undergoing three months of military training of an extra-divisional nature and an annual mobilisation (all service in units coming under military law). Assigned to a division for four years, and called up by age-group, the territorial recruit would spend not more than five months of his service in mobilisation, and not more than two months in any one year.[94]

The first critical mobilisation of the territorial divisions took place in the autumn of 1923. Although marred by some desertion, by reversion to 'banditry' and subject to rumours of war and general mobilisation, the territorial divisions passed the test well enough. Though great room for improvement of all kinds was left, this system was to serve the Soviet Union for many years until it gave way to the mass army. The autumn mobilisation marked the end of serious stagnation and indecision which seemed to have settled so heavily upon the transition period. For Trotsky, it was an opportunity to claim that his plans were justified, which was partly true, although the territorial formations were much in advance of the ideas of a militia which had first prevailed. The line of attack, however, had been switched and other instruments were being employed to gain control of the army.

The direct attempt to oust Trotsky from his position as head of the Red Army and the consistent moves designed to effect a capture of the military machine were both carried out at the top levels of the leadership. They also formed part of the intensive as well as bitter struggle for power which followed on Lenin's relapse into illness. The prospect of the succession passing to Trotsky had occasioned the formation of a political combination between Zinoviev, L. Kamenev[95] and Stalin, the triumvirate whose existence was first publicly revealed by Stalin during the debates of the 12th Party Congress in April 1923. Both Stalin and Zinoviev had openly demonstrated their animosity towards Trotsky, while Kamenev lent his aid in this struggle less out of a passion directed against Trotsky than from friendship for Zinoviev and a sense of belonging to the veteran Bolsheviks, the Old Guard of pre-October 1917 affiliations and loyalty. Zinoviev had no cause to fall on Trotsky's shoulder. It was he who had failed dismally in 1917 to rise to the test of the seizure of power, when Trotsky, so new a recruit to the Bolsheviks, had carried out his splendid feats. There was 1919, when Zinoviev panicked at the White drive on Petrograd and Trotsky took over the defence, or the days of Kronstadt, part of the blame for which Trotsky placed on Zinoviev's tactless and provocative behaviour.

Stalin, who had conducted his campaign against Trotsky with increasing pressure since the grim days of Tsaritsyn, stood himself at a great crisis in his career. Since April 1922 he had held the post of General Secretary, but whatever benefits accrued to him from his position as a purveyor of privilege and a source of patronage, they paled at Lenin's realisation of the disastrous course of events in Georgia and the ruthlessness of Stalin's Great Russian policy. Lenin resolved to cut down this over-mighty subject, entering early in 1923 into a compact with Trotsky to eliminate Stalin's excessive role and to cut him out of the political appointments which provided the power to his elbow. Stalin had no positive information about the direction of this blow, just as Trotsky had yet to discover in the early weeks of 1923 that there was a fully-fledged political combination at work against him. Lenin opened his attack on 4th March, printing in *Pravda* a castigation of the work of *Rabkrin* (Workers and Peasants Inspectorate) with which Stalin had been closely associated. On 6th, L. Kamenev approached Trotsky on behalf of the seemingly crushed triumvirate, to speak of surrender terms. These were surprisingly and dangerously moderate, lacking all the ferocious punishment which Lenin had himself intended to inflict upon Stalin, Dzerzhinskii and Ordzhonikidze.

At the 12th Party Congress Trotsky likewise failed to use the opportunity to fire off Lenin's deadly ammunition, rather husbanding this for future use should the triumvirate once again lose their heads and break the parole which they had undertaken only very recently.[96] Trotsky's sense of security was false indeed, although his triumph could perhaps have been very complete. The remainder of Trotsky's performance did nothing to strengthen his position; his exposition of the necessity for a transition to a properly planned economy raised fears that *NEP*, with its momentary benefits, might be swept away for a re-imposition of the rigours of War Communism. The defence of the small nationalities, in particular the Georgians, fell flat, helped by Stalin's own volte-face which had been part of his surrender to Trotsky. In disarming his opponents, Trotsky had lowered and finally demolished his own defences. Stalin remained General Secretary, and a new tool was sharpened by the re-organisation of the Central Control Commission (*TsKK*) as an instrument of Party supervision over the state apparatus.[97] Stalin had not been removed from his vantage point which assured him of the possibility of dispensing his political spoils, and a close supporter of his, V. V. Kuibyshev, commanded the new apparatus of investigation.

The struggle for the control of the military machine was henceforth dictated by the circumstances of the politics of the triumvirate, in both its struggle within itself and against Trotsky. The first line of attack was opened with the decision of the plenum of the Central Control Commission, made on 2nd June, 1923, to carry out a thorough investigation of the Soviet military establishment, and to appoint for that purpose a special Military Commission. The commission received its mandate for the enquiry on 23rd August, and in September Gusev took over the presidency of the Military Commission from V. V. Kuibyshev, who had had N. M. Shvernik as his deputy. Sub-commissions were then set up, each with a member of the Central Control Commission at their head, and the whole action co-ordinated with the Military-Naval Inspectorates of the Workers and Peasants Inspectorate, a group of military experts and the local military inspecting commissions.[98]

There was more to this, however, than a simple investigation. Zinoviev was concerned to bring into the Republic *Revvoensoviet* Stalin himself, and if that could not be managed, then Voroshilov or Lashevich.[99] Although it was to the obvious advantage of the triumvirate to have control of the army, Zinoviev's other manœuvres against Stalin seem to suggest that his main idea was to use this as a manner of increasing his own strength and as part of the re-couping of his fortunes, damaged at the 12th Party Congress. This would get Stalin out of the post of General Secretary and cut away much of his power in the Party apparatus. Zinoviev's conclave in September 1923 at Kislovodsk, the Caucasian spa, had drawn Voroshilov, Ordzhonikidze, Lashevich and Bukharin, with Evdokimov, into a discussion of the General Secretariat, but it was a move which brought not one whit of the desired result. An attempt by Zinoviev and L. Kamenev to enlist the help of Trotsky in drawing Stalin into military affairs, and thus neutralising him politically, failed in October 1923.[100] This was, in fact, a tactic which had been tried by Trotsky himself during the Civil War and it had likewise failed. The issue could not be settled by shunting Stalin out of his Party holdings, and during the course of these involved and unscrupulous exchanges, yet another aspect of the political crisis impinged very heavily on affairs of the Red Army.

The strain in the military leadership had its counter-part in the tensions developing in the political apparatus. The promulgation of the famous Circular No. 200 in 1923 had marked a new turn in the political activities of the Soviet armed forces. The Circular had made its appearance without the permission of the Central Committee (the *PUR* was as yet only under the indirect control of the Central Committee), and, as such, was described by Geronimus as part of the 'fractional attack on the Central Committee'. The new order made substantial concessions to the demands for a form of democratic decentralisation in army political work — in a sense, it unmuzzled the army. The military Party organs were authorised to discuss *all* problems connected with Party work in the army, that is, it was possible for 'oppositional elements', as Geronimus has it, to introduce their own proposals at meetings of the military 'cells' and to carry out full discussion of political programmes. By this device the political organs were ripe for the failure to carry out the functions for which they were expressly designed — to gain support for the ruling group.[101]

A real crisis was provoked by the action of the Forty-Six, this being an oppositional group of forty-six prominent Communists, who protested outright against the present policy of the Party leadership. A much greater significance was given to this, since Trotsky on 8th October had presented a challenge to the triumvirate, and now seven days later the Forty-Six oppositional programme bore a striking similarity to this first threat to the political security of the triumvirate.[102]

This protest, made by men of no mean calibre and standing, could not be peremptorily silenced, or easily discredited. In the 'cells' of the Moscow garrison Antonov-Ovseenko, confidant of Trotsky and head of the *PUR*, was able to gather substantial support for the platform of the opposition. The furore over the issue of inner-party democracy revealed how widespread and deep was the discontent. There was nothing to stop the military political organs taking up direct political issues under the new regulations which they enjoyed; and in so doing they could muster support and marshal criticism against the ruling group. Although Trotsky had not — and could not have, by the rules against factions imposed by the 10th Party Congress in 1921 — organised this opposition, he was doubtless in close touch with such men as Antonov-Ovseenko of the *PUR* and his friend of the Civil War days, Muralov, now Moscow garrison commander. Whether consciously enjoying Trotsky's backing or not, this political ferment constituted a powerful political counter-attack and a danger to the triumvirate. It was upon this note, of mounting inner-Party tension and the apparent inconclusiveness of the assault upon the leadership of the military machine, that 1923 closed.

It was out of these circumstances that the subsequent changes in the leadership of the military machine and the consolidation of the high command were made. Such is the introduction to what Soviet military historians perforce call the period of 'military reform', which is more accurately a period of sustained and purposeful purge, which played a dual role, firstly to bring the Soviet armed forces back under the strictest control of the ruling group and secondly, to open the way for the Red command, alienated as this was from Trotsky and the policy for which he stood, or for what his opponents claimed by frequent mis-representation was this 'reactionary' policy. While there were real consolidations and certain reforms in the institutions and command organisation of the Red Army, this fact does not dispose of the existence of a grave crisis, through which the Soviet armed forces and especially the political apparatus passed. The trials and political necessities which developed inexorably from the situation of the triumvirate, both in its collective struggle against Trotsky and its own inner contradictions, emphasised once again that the basic factor in Soviet military organisation and the choice of men to run it was decisively political.

Yet in addition to these strained and potentially dangerous developments hovering about the military establishment and cutting into the command, there was one further dimension of activity upon which, to the present day, Soviet sources prefer to maintain the maximum silence, and which concerned the secret links with the German *Reichswehr*.[103] While the Soviet command in Caucasia had been pressing revolution with bayonets, as Kronstadt was shot down, during the heat and tension of the military debates, the exchanges between Soviet military and diplomatic personnel and corresponding German military, industrial and diplomatic figures had intensified, bringing certain agreements in their wake. Such arrangements, which owed not a little to Trotsky, stand as an indirect commentary on the military policy of the Soviet command during the period nominally labelled one of transition by Soviet military historians and as a feature of Soviet military-political commitment vitally relevant to the subsequent period of reform. Certain of the captured German documents make it possible to break the silence; the Soviet archives retain their secrets. Nevertheless there is some piquancy in the situation where in public Trotsky duelled with the garbled ideas of strategy brought up by the Red command, and in private considered the exchanges with the greatest professionals of the military art, the representatives of the German Army.

CHAPTER SIX

Towards Collaboration with the 'Reichswehr'

Russo-German collaboration in the military field was not, strictly speaking, an innovation introduced by the Soviet regime. Before the outbreak of the First World War Russian artillery specialists had lent their assistance to the Krupp works for the development of German artillery. This activity had been both theoretical and practical according to the information supplied by a brochure published in 1912 to mark the centenary of the Krupp concern. For the production of large-calibre guns Russian aid had been invaluable, and tests had been carried out on the artillery proving grounds near St Petersburg. When, however, the German government threatened to cancel the order for heavy guns and place it with the British firm of Armstrong, Krupp used the argument of the successes already gained with Russian help to have this decision postponed for one year.[1]

The years of bitter fighting in the east, the Treaty of Brest-Litovsk thrust upon Russia and that of Versailles fastened upon a defeated Germany, had produced a new and confused situation. The origins and course of the early contacts between Germany and Soviet Russia remain, as yet, covered in obscurities and contradictions. A plurality of purposes and the activities of numerous groups each following self-contained interests showed markedly on the German side; at an early stage Soviet Russia embarked upon the road which forked repeatedly into revolution or *Realpolitik*. With the collapse of German military power in 1918 — in which Bolshevik propaganda lent some of its demoralising aid — the prospect for revolution in Germany seemed especially bright. Karl Radek arrived in Berlin in December 1918 and was at once much impressed by what seemed to be a general and genuine movement of revolution by the workers against the government.* Moscow had substantial justification for nurturing its high hopes for the triumph of Bolshevism in Germany. The German military, however, assisted by the internal divisions in the German revolutionary movements

* Radek's own account of his doings in Germany, and one not altogether edited with too much discretion, is to be found in *Krasnaya Nov*. (1926), p. 139 f. The first part begins with 'The days of the crushing of German Imperialism'.

itself, put paid to these ambitions in the early weeks of 1919, when the *Freikorps* units systematically and effectively routed out and destroyed the insurrectionists with artillery, machine-gun, mortars and even flame-throwers.[2] There German forces were combined into the Provisional *Reichswehr*, and while they were evidently adequate to maintain that kind of internal order which crushed out street-fighting rebels, in the mind of Quartermaster-General Wilhelm Groener they had yet another potential role to play.

Groener hoped to avert the consequences of a dictated peace for Germany by developing inter-Allied differences and by offering German aid for the purpose of eradicating Bolshevism in the east. In the Baltic provinces, German troops were holding the line against Bolshevik incursions and might well be offered to the Allies as a force which would take the offensive in the cause of Intervention.[3] In the event, no such parrying was possible, but the full force of the blow fell with the Versailles *diktat* of the limitation of the German armed forces to a volunteer strength of 100,000 (of which 4,000 were permitted as officers), the banning of aircraft, tanks and weapons of an offensive type to the German army, and the restriction of naval forces to vessels of no more than 1,000 tons and no submarines. The German General Staff, the War Academy and officer-training schools were to be closed and disbanded. When General Hans von Seeckt failed in 1920 to obtain the 200,000 man army, or even an extension of the period for this reduction in military man-power, the idea of concessions from the Allies faded, and in the ensuing attempts to evade the Allied provisions, the idea of a military concordat with Soviet Russia took greater hold.

Although the notion of an approach to Russia gained ground in 1919 in Germany, the terms in which this was conceived owed not a little to the political orientation of the various interested parties. The German Left saw *rapprochement* in terms of the triumph of revolution in Germany and hence automatic connection with the Bolsheviks. The extreme Right rested its hopes in the troops of General von der Goltz in the Baltic provinces, winning back Russia to its pre-1917 position in alliance with the Russian monarchists.[4] Seeckt could see in the von der Goltz venture the way to the confirmation of Soviet-German hostility and the erection of a dangerous barrier between the two countries;* the *Reichswehr* accordingly acceded to the Allied request for the withdrawal of von der Goltz in the late summer of 1919, although money still flowed to the Baltic troops from the coffers of

* A recent East German study of German-Soviet relations, Günter Rosenfeld's *Sowjetrussland und Deutschland 1917–1922* (Akademie-Verlag, Berlin 1960), finds it a difficult proposition to explain certain of the original contacts. Seeckt is labelled (p. 299) a 'typical representative of the reactionary Junker-caste of Germany', but praised for his perception in looking to Soviet Russia.

German heavy industry, interested as it was in removing the Bolsheviks and opening up the lucrative Russian market once again.[5]

In his report of the 7th August, 1919, General Malcolm, writing to Colonel Twiss, was concerned to show that the 'eastern orientation' among the Germans was gaining strength at this time, but there seemed to be no evidence of any connection between the German government and Lenin. On the other hand a German 'Industrial Commission' had evidently made a visit to Soviet Russia in the summer of 1919, returning with what appeared to be a discouraging report upon conditions to be found there.[6] The inspiration behind this mission was Walter Rathenau, German industrialist and visitor to Karl Radek who had been arrested and imprisoned in the Berlin Moabit Prison after the abortive rising of 1918 and was subsequently lodged — after powerful intervention on his behalf — in quarters less punitive and rigorous. Radek was by no means an official spokesman for the Soviet government. The conversations pursued with his callers were not those of deliberate and precise commitment. Nevertheless, the conversations pursued with Radek form an important link in the chain of events which led up to the eventual agreement with Soviet Russia.

Among the earliest of Radek's callers were two Turks, Enver and Taalat Pasha, both of whom had left Turkey after the end of hostilities, and found shelter in Berlin. Enver Pasha and Seeckt had met during the latter's service with the Turkish staff during the war. Since a Soviet-Turkish *rapprochement* was in the air, and vitally affected Soviet military strategy during this stage of the Civil War in the south, it was not unnatural that Radek hastened to send Enver Pasha on his way to Moscow as one of the means of creating a Soviet-Turkish united front against the British.[7] Arrangements were made for the Turkish emissary to use a new Junkers aircraft, in which a senior official of that firm was also flying to Moscow to explore the possibilities of selling machines to Soviet Russia. On 17th October, 1919, Colonel Rowan Robinson, British Military Representative in Kovno, reported on the forced landing of the machine at Abeli on 15th. Hesse, the pilot, stated that he was commissioned to find out if there was a possibility of selling this type of aircraft in Soviet Russia. With Hesse was Abraham Frankel, included as 'interpreter', being also a Russian Jew and an engineer in the employment of the Junkers firm. Under a false name Enver Pasha travelled with a fellow Turk, both concealed as delegates of the Turkish Red Crescent. Hesse's instructions were to look into the question of trade relations with the Soviet government, and to convey 'an important person' from Germany to Moscow — that person being Enver Pasha. Among other papers was a letter, originating in Dessau but without a specific date for October 1919, laying out questions on patent rights in Russia, aircraft manufacture and general points (including the selling of this particular machine, either outright or for spares, if this appeared to be necessary).[8] Enver Pasha did not on this occasion reach Moscow, but finally made his way back to Berlin, renewing his attempt in 1920.

As signal proof that bars do not a prison make, Radek was meanwhile holding political court for his callers. The representative of the military was General von Reibnitz, who had recently become a dissenter from Ludendorff's violent anti-Bolshevism. Colonel Max Bauer called, as did Admiral Hintze, who had formerly acted as German Naval Attaché in Imperial Russia and who had also come to speak the language of Soviet-German *rapprochement*. Radek listened to Rathenau on his first visit speaking of the perspectives of revolution and developing faint but interesting ideas of technical help by Germany to the Bolsheviks. Radek's second session with Rathenau took place beyond his nominal prison, this time in the apartment of Reibnitz and in the company of Feliks Deutsch, manager of the *AEG*, the giant electrical combine of which Rathenau's father had been the founder. Deutsch's inclinations were all for a western orientation of German industry, yet he seems to have been won over to a certain acceptance of trade with the east — provided this included the *AEG*.[9]

While Radek's conversations produced no formal results, and Radek was by no means the formal representative of the Soviet government, the turn to the east had become more pronounced in the winter of 1919. In November the German government agreed to the arrival of a Soviet representative in Berlin to take part in the prisoner-of-war repatriations and exchanges. In this way Viktor (or Vigdor) Kopp, former Menshevik and associate of Trotsky in Vienna before the First World War, entered this strangely-assorted company. Germany did not commit herself to the policy of blockade of Soviet Russia, which was a feature of the Allied Intervention and in which she was invited to participate.[10] Although German industry was by no means won over to the idea of linking itself with the east, Rathenau took the forward-looking step of setting up an industrial 'Study Commission' to investigate the Soviet scene. Radek himself seems to have been convinced of both the desirability and the feasibility of a Soviet-German exchange which would gain for Soviet Russia the services of a country second only to the United States of America in its technical advance and would provide Germany with an outlet which would lighten the consequences of defeat.

Although too discreet to venture in person to Radek's political salon, Seeckt cannot have remained in much ignorance of the course which these verbal exchanges were taking. Not until the latter half of 1920 is there any clear indication of the final trend which Seeckt's thought upon collaboration with Soviet Russia was taking, although developments in the attitude of

German heavy industry were of prime importance, for here was the source of capital and the basis of Germany's real might. At the end of 1919 arrangements were put in hand for Radek's own repatriation, and on 10th January, 1920, Hey, Deutsch and Simons met with Radek and Kopp to discuss both the final arrangements for the journey, and economic relations between Germany and Soviet Russia. Radek made it plain that the Soviet government was 'over the hump' in the Civil War; in the spring an attempt would be made to conclude a peace with Great Britain, which, if rebuffed, would result in Soviet Russia pitting her forces against Central Asia. There did not exist, asserted Radek, any intention of forcing Bolshevism on Germany. The immediate future of Soviet-German economic relations would be marked — not by an exchange of goods — but rather by '. . . the reconstruction of Russian industry with German aid'.[11] With his bags sealed, and packed with his manuscripts and Communist pamphlets — by his own admission the records of his negotiations with representatives of the Baltic States and confidential agents of the *Entente* had been sent ahead — Radek thus rounded off his first parleys and was conveyed, not without a certain honour, over the frontier.

* * * *

Kopp, without official status or recognition, stayed on in Berlin. There is substantial reason for assuming that Kopp enjoyed Trotsky's confidence. In the light of this, Kopp's blunt questions to Maltzan, in the course of a conversation on 16th April, 1920, take on a certain significance. Kopp asked outright about the possibility of collaboration between the Red Army and the German army.* Maltzan brushed this aside, with serious allegations about Soviet propaganda in Germany.[12] Nothing more was evidently said of this idea of collaboration at this time. The only positive result was the signing, three days later, of an agreement on the repatriation of prisoners-of-war. On 22nd June Gustav Hilger arrived in Moscow as the German representative for this question — an occasion used by the Soviet government formally to assure the Germans that all the rumours of a hostile Soviet intention towards Germany, developing out of the circumstances of the Soviet-Polish war, were without foundation.[13] That same war marked a

* The memorandum on the conversation (Serial K281/K095851–853) records what was obviously a spirited exchange. When Kopp tried to ascertain the possibility of organising a 'combination between the German and Red Armies with a view to proceeding against Poland together', Maltzan told him that current Soviet propaganda, which included calling the Supreme Head of the *Reich* a 'hired ruffian', hardly made this likely. Somewhat embarrassed, Kopp replied that Soviet propaganda, which contained a few extravagances, should not be taken too seriously. Kopp asked for and obtained police protection for the personnel dealing with the prisoner-of-war exchange; in thanking Maltzan for this, Kopp indicated that he expected a Soviet government to be set up here (in Berlin) 'in the not too distant future', when he would be glad to show a return favour to Maltzan and 'to take me [Maltzan] under his particular protection'.

rapid acceleration in the drawing together of interested circles in Germany and Soviet Russia, and, as usual, there were the devious ways of indicating this interest.

Actual Soviet-German collusion over and in the war with Poland must be discounted, even on the general evidence that neither side held to a hard and fast position which would have made such a division of function possible. Seeckt had earlier made his position clear with respect to Poland, and was prophesying a Soviet victory as the Red Army swept into Poland. German professional military circles sat up to take notice of this new military machine, so recently created, which was cutting its way to outstanding success. The Soviet Chief of Staff, P. P. Lebedev, himself a professional, evidently enjoyed a high rating among his German counter-parts.[14] As for the apparent extent of this Soviet military success, notice had been given to the Germans that Soviet Russia would, in fact, respect Germany's present frontiers, but the problem set by the possible revision of the Versailles limits was not so easily solved.[15]

In Moscow Enver Pasha, who had finally succeeded in reaching Soviet Russia, not without hazards even in his second attempt, had contacted Soviet military-political leaders and reported to Seeckt about a conversation, recorded in a letter written on 26th August, 1920, with a person who most probably was Sklyanskii.* Enver Pasha concluded that the idea of an understanding with Germany was indeed most acceptable to the ruling group,† and that any gesture signifying German willingness to the same end would be well worth making.[16] There were, at about this time, hints of plans to consolidate the German and Russian positions vis-à-vis Poland; it is not impossible that Seeckt contacted Kopp in July 1920, although Seeckt very deliberately removed himself on leave at the end of July, which would not suggest any serious co-ordination of plan. On the other hand, there exists in the German archives a letter, hand-written and purporting to be from Trotsky, despatched in August to Viktor Emmanuelovich (Kopp?); the letter suggests the intensification of propaganda activity among the German Communists and other Socialist parties '. . . to prepare public opinion for the presence of the Red Army on German territory'. Such political activity must be co-ordinated with the missions assigned to the Red Army. Men, if needed, could be sent and the most urgent need was for more information on the situation in Germany.[17] While this may not

* Rabenau's life of Seeckt (p. 306) speaks of Enver Pasha being visited by a 'Russian staff officer', which could also indicate Lebedev.

† Enver Pasha's oft-quoted letter, taken from Rabenau (p. 307) and dated 26th August, 1920 runs: 'Hier ist eine Partei, welche richtige Macht besitzt, und Trotzki auch diese Partei gehört, ist für eine Verständigung mit Deutschland. Die Partei wäre bereit, der alte deutsche Grenze von 1914 zu anerkennen.'

be genuine, there is, nevertheless, ample evidence in the same records of persistent German interception of material passed to Kopp and, later, to other Soviet personnel. The only positive step, which can be adequately confirmed, was the despatch of Major Schubert to the Soviet field command as liaison officer.

The prospect of a Soviet-German *rapprochement*, brought about by the military collapse of Poland, did not materialise. Yet the German Right had been caught by the implications of the situation. On 6th August, in a letter to Brockdorff-Rantzau, Maltzan reported that by now the anti-Russian German banks were beginning to show increased interest in the idea of contact with Soviet Russia.[18] Although there were fears in Germany that the defeat in Poland might conceivably saddle the Soviet regime with grave internal troubles, if not the prospect of collapse, the tempo of quasi-negotiation speeded up towards the end of the year. Altogether, the outcome of the Polish war had been a near thing, near enough to implant the idea of the eventual establishment of collaboration at a heavy price to Poland. It was a time, also, when Seeckt had failed to gain Allied acceptance of the 200,000-man army and amelioration of the drastic military provisions for Germany. It was in the east, and through a long-term policy, rather than in the west and with resistance which was merely foolish, that Seeckt saw the future direction of German military policy. To this end, late in 1920 he organised his highly secret but remarkably efficient *Sondergruppe R** to examine the basis of collaboration with the Red Army.

* * * *

Seeckt's initiative corresponded in time with decisions relevant to this same matter which were taken in Moscow and which bore out the truth of Enver Pasha's observations on the temper and inclination of the Soviet military leadership. Kopp, in the first weeks of 1921, discussed in Moscow with Trotsky the possibilities of obtaining much-needed German military-industrial assistance to re-build the Red Army. Kopp was instructed to proceed to Germany and develop these contacts still further. Trotsky kept Lenin and Chicherin informed of the course of events, though whether Lenin actually made a formal application for German assistance in building up the Red Army and Soviet war-industry, as indeed Gessler claimed he did sometime about March 1921, seems a questionable point.[19] On 7th April, 1921, Kopp was able to report to Trotsky that the Krupp concern, Blohm und Voss and the Albatross Werke, supplying artillery, submarines

* Waldemar Erfurth, *Die Gesch. des deutschen Generalstabes 1918–1945* (Musterschmidt-Verlag, 1957), p. 89, reports that 'Gruppe R' soon became 'Abteilung R' under Major Fischer, one of Seeckt's former staff officers. Major Tschunke, Colonel Thomsen (*Luftwaffe*), General Wurzbacher (*Chef des Heereswaffenamtes*) conducted the negotiations under Seeckt's guidance.

and aircraft respectively, were willing to co-operate.[20] A small German technical mission could be sent to Moscow to discuss the details, while in Berlin Krassin, Karakhan, Kopp, Radek and other individuals carried on similar discussions about the nature and the scope of this activity. From the Soviet side there seems to have been a relatively efficient method of ensuring the necessary secrecy while informing the necessary number of individuals. The *Reichswehr*, however, carved out its own policy in virtual independence, leading to early protest and by a subsequent running battle with the diplomats who also had interests in Soviet Russia.[21]

The first German technical mission to Soviet Russia produced no visible result. The plan to re-organise the shattered plants and shipyards of Petrograd had to be abandoned, although general progress was made with the setting up of an organisation under the name of *Gesellschaft zur Förderung Gewerblicher Unternehmungen* (*GEFU*) — a 'Trade Enterprises Development Company'. The name conveyed nothing, but this body was to handle the military-industrial arrangements which were being developed, opening its offices in Berlin and Moscow in the latter months of 1921. In September 1921 Lenin and his colleagues had considered a report which emanated from an unidentified but sympathetic member of the German mission, advising that it would be sound policy to encourage confidence in the stability of the Soviet regime among German financial and industrial elements, and also to develop the approach on the Polish question which would best fall on German ears.[22] Lenin agreed upon the wisdom of joining the military and economic discussions, and the general result was to disguise the establishment of German war industry on Soviet soil as part of the policy of 'concessions' which had been generally applied to the capitalist world.

During the same month intensive negotiations were opened in Berlin and held for the most part in the private quarters of Major Kurt von Schleicher,* with the participation of General Paul von Hasse (head of the *Truppenamt*, now that Seeckt was chief of the *Reichswehr*), Niedermayer and Colonel von Thomsen. Krassin and Kopp acted for the Russians.[23] The military-industrial undertakings were built around *GEFU*, which was supplied with a capital of seventy-five million German marks (which figure, however, seems to be related to the settlement of 1923) and placed under the management of Fritz Tschunke. The plans which were being drawn up envisaged the concessions to Professor Junkers of Dessau for the manufacture of metal aircraft, spare parts and aircraft engines near Moscow, a joint Soviet-German company for the manufacture of poison-gas near Samara, and the production

* The negotiations were transferred from Schleicher's apartment in the *Matthäi-Kirchstrasse* in Berlin to the *Reichswehrministerium*. Waldemar Erfurth (p. 89) writes that, while Seeckt entered on to the Russian road with 'no light heart', General von Stülpnagel informed him personally in 1952 that Schleicher was opposed to the idea of a connection with the Red Army.

of artillery ammunition and grenades in Soviet plants under the supervision of German technicians.[24] It needed time, however, and further intensive negotiation before these plans became reality and the financial arrangements were firmly settled.

In the autumn of 1921 General Hasse of the *Truppenamt* paid a visit to Soviet Russia at the head of a German military-industrial mission, which included a high official of the firm of Junkers. It is possible that Admiral Hintze also accompanied this group. The military side centred on talks with P. P. Lebedev, Soviet Chief of Staff, and concerned strategy as much as technical help. The issue was Poland and the problem it presented to both sides. If an agreement of any kind was suggested, then Hasse had no alternative but to refer this to his superior, Seeckt.[25] The inconclusiveness of these first conversations would be suggested by the fact the Soviet command evidently decided upon a direct approach to Seekt at the end of 1921. The state of the Red Army and its actual combat efficiency would not lend support to the idea that the Soviet command was seeking a military commitment, but rather making a test of *Reichswehr* intentions. The question of commitment over Poland was quickly re-opened in early 1922, this time by Radek.

The *Reichswehr* had not been idle in exploring the ground for itself with its own agents. Major (retired) Niedermayer, who used the name of Neumann or was referred to as 'N', was in Moscow in early October, for the German diplomat Wiedenfeld reported on his presence in Russia and speculated about the nature of his mission, which, however, remained a mystery to the man from the *Auswärtiges Amt*.[26] The Hasse mission, somewhat abortive from the strategic side, did not slow up the discussions over strategic industry. At the end of 1921 Niedermayer and Schubert, acting for the *Reichswehrministerium*, and Spalock and Sachsenberg for Junkers, were evidently in Moscow making almost final arrangements for the setting up of the aircraft plant. Before the departure of this mixed commission, Junkers had been assured that they would be in receipt of adequate financial backing from the *Reichswehrministerium*; in Moscow the Russians were willing to place industrial installations at their disposal, and Junkers assessed the cost of this installation process at some twenty-one million gold marks, and upon this basis a written offer was made to the Russians as they had requested in the beginning.[27]

Krupp had also obtained a concession in Soviet Russia, which was signed in January 1922, for the establishment of an experimental tractor-station on the river Manych by Rostov-on-Don; even this apparently purely commercial deal had important military connotations, for work on heavy tractors was not far removed from experiments on tank-prototypes.[28] It is significant that the first models of tanks were designated 'Grosse Traktoren' and there is no evidence of any substantial Soviet manufacture of tanks before 1927. The problem of Soviet-German collaboration over tank design and manufacture is a difficult one, but a certain military significance must be accorded to this first Krupp concession.

The first high peak of achievement and commitment was to be approached in the spring of 1922, by which time the diplomats were also preparing their own *rapprochement* with Soviet Russia in the Treaty of Rapallo. This was an act which caused the soldiers no displeasure, nor could it affect the previous arrangements, to which one new dimension was added in the planning of the peaceful collaboration of the Red Army and the *Reichswehr* in matters of training-grounds, training-procedures and an exchange of personnel and information.

★ ★ ★ ★

The first conference between Seeckt and Soviet military experts had taken place on 8th December, 1921, if the evidence supplied by Hasse's diary is correct.[29] Seeckt does not appear to have provided any conclusive military guarantee over Poland, and in this respect, there was little advance over Hasse's first exchanges with P. P. Lebedev. On 17th January, 1922, Radek returned to Germany, in the company of Oskar Niedermayer and with the aim of talking to Seeckt. It was not until 10th February that Radek was finally able to gain access to Seeckt, when he repeated the Soviet request for German help in reconstructing Soviet armament plants and suggested to Seeckt that German assistance would be welcome in training the Soviet officer corps.[30] Radek spoke about the possibility of convening meetings of the Soviet and German General Staffs, an idea which he urged upon Seeckt, as well as introducing German military literature to the Soviet command. Radek was evidently at no pains to conceal the backwardness of the Red Army officer corps. The idea of direct German participation in the training of the Red Army was a very new element in the situation, and it is from this point that the project of joint training and experimental establishments, operated by the *Reichswehr* and the Red Army, can be admitted into the general Soviet-German schemes.

Radek did not confine himself to training, but complained to Seeckt that Germany also co-operated with the British, to which Seeckt replied that, in order to block France, a certain alliance with the British was necessary for Germany. As for Radek offering once more to join in an attack upon Poland in the spring with Germany, provided that Soviet Russia obtained this German assistance, there is little reason to suppose that this embodied a serious Soviet military intention.[31] This supposed desire would not explain the speed with which Junkers became established on Soviet soil — not because the Red Army needed its aircraft (which would have taken time to build), but rather that the financial side had been speedily settled. The agreement between Junkers and *Sondergruppe R* was signed on 15th March, 1922; the contract, signed by 'Neumann' (Niedermayer), disguised all the contracting parties by initials or false locations. Dessau became Leipzig, the Soviet government 'R.R.' and Junkers 'Firm N.N.'; aircraft were not mentioned.[32] During the month of March German officers were proceeding to Soviet Russia to begin work; before April was out German technicians were busy at the Fili plant near Moscow, where the Junkers machines would be built. In time, and after the final ratification with the Russians, this became Factory No. 22, with Factory No. 24 destined for the manufacture of aero-engines.

On 16th April, 1922, Soviet Russia and Germany signed the famous Treaty of Rapallo, a diplomatic *tour de force* which both astonished and alarmed Europe. Ioffe had telephoned Maltzan at 1.15 a.m., on Easter Sunday morning; by 6.30 p.m., that same evening the treaty had been signed.[33] In spite of rumours and prevalent fears about secret military agreements, a search of the German files of Rapallo reveals nothing in the nature of any such secret military provision.[34] Although concluded independently of the military, the German soldiers were delighted with this diplomatic achievement, which could in no way bar the way to the kind of military collaboration which had been discussed previously. Rather it appeared that the time had come to press for that final consolidation of the plans and arrangements, which had been so carefully examined. If French Intelligence was correct, the two-way traffic in missions and inquiry groups intensified on the morrow of Rapallo. Admiral Hintze and an officer named Bauer were reported as being *en mission* in Soviet Russia,[35] while Svechin travelled to Germany with a Soviet military mission, to which was attached a Soviet senior officer — named as Lazarev — in the capacity of head of Soviet aviation. This latter person may well have been Lazarevich, who occupied in the following year a high post in Soviet military education. The subject under discussion was aviation and the implementation of the Junkers agreement.[36]

Krestinsky, the accredited Soviet representative in Berlin, had meanwhile conducted further negotiations with Hasse, as a result of which increased financial backing was forthcoming from the coffer of German heavy industry for use in connection with the Russian ventures. Financial backing played a vital part in the establishment of these special relations, although it will shortly be seen that there was perhaps a significant difference in the Soviet and German approach to this factor. At the beginning of July Seeckt was visited by a Soviet agent named Rosenblatt and on 29th of the same month a preliminary commercial agreement was signed, in the deepest secrecy, between the Soviet and German negotiators of this strange commercial traffic.[37] It is important to notice that this was a preliminary agreement, and there remained a fair stretch of the road to implementation to be travelled.

The Central Committee plenum of 7th August, 1922, follows with suggestive rapidity upon the conclusion of this agreement, and it was on this date that the first budgetary allotment was made to the Soviet armed forces which showed some evidence of long-range planning. Frunze had admitted that the financial problem was especially important in the plans drawn up for the re-organisation of the Red Army. In the absence of a definite budgetary decision, the planning lost much of its reality. For aviation, the Central Committee appropriated the sum of thirty-five million gold roubles, which were to be used for purchases in Russian factories, with only a bare and indispensable minimum made available for the purchase of spares in factories abroad. With Junkers established in a Soviet plant, then the distinction about Russian factories could be finely drawn.[38]

On 11th August, 1922, a provisional agreement was concluded in Moscow on the nature of the collaboration between the *Reichswehr* and the Red Army. The German requirements were very comprehensive; the *Reichswehr* asked for facilities to gain continuous experience in tactics, training and technical matters, to develop the theory and practice of forbidden weapons, to train higher personnel in the use of such weapons, to carry on weapon testing in battle conditions as an extension of the experiments in Germany, and finally to develop theoretical conclusions from such tests which would assist the planning of training and recruitment policies. Specifically there were three requests to be made of the Red Army. The first was for the use of military bases to exercise aviation, motorised troops and chemical warfare techniques. The second concerned freedom of action to conduct weapon tests and carry on tactical training. Thirdly the *Reichswehr* asked for a full exchange of the results of work in the military field.[39] Soviet agreement to this was forthcoming, receiving in exchange an annual financial payment for the lease of these bases, as well as full participation in the technical, tactical and theoretical results gained in the tests and training on the Soviet sites. Viewed against the background of the inner Soviet struggles over tactical doctrines and training programmes, this was a handsome gift.

* * * *

While 1922 was a year of great promise in this sphere of Soviet-German contact, it had not yet yielded up any of the positive results of real achievement. The question of the appointment of a German ambassador to Moscow sparked off a dispute which itself throws some light on the way in which these initial agreements were viewed. Seeckt tried to block the appointment of Count Brockdorff-Rantzau as ambassador, out of fear for the consequences upon his *Ostpolitik* with the appointment of this man and from remembrance that the same individual sold the German Army so cheaply at Versailles. In a 'Pro-Memoria', dated 15th August, 1922, the Count gave his views on the prospects of Soviet-German relations. For him, the grave disadvantage of Rapallo lay precisely with the military fears which the treaty evoked. By giving Great Britain cause to suspect a Soviet-German 'war of revenge', or possible agreements to this end, Germany could be made to suffer most grievously as a consequence. The only serious supposition is that Soviet Russia may attack Poland; therefore Germany should labour to divert the Russians from such bellicose schemes. Such is the Soviet internal situation that an attack on Poland may be used to divert domestic strifes. In the event of war, Germany must be kept neutral, so that should Poland collapse, she might recover Upper Silesia. Defeat of the Red Army might precipitate internal strife and cause the downfall of the Soviet regime.[40]

Seeckt, in his answer of 11th September, 1922, to Chancellor Wirth, exposed the myth of supposed 'military agreements'. Seeckt had already denied the existence of military agreements in a letter to Hasse in May, 1922.[41] The core of the Eastern question was — Poland. To crack Poland, and thus strike at France must be a constant of German policy and was possible only with Soviet assistance. Seeckt once again denied any military agreement or the intention to conclude one. The German aim in Soviet Russia was to strengthen her ally by increasing her economic, political and ultimately her military capability. The common military arrangements existed to further Soviet desires in the military-technical field, and could be adjusted as the need arose. If war should come — and a potential war-situation was not so far distant — then Germany's statesmen must put her on the winning side. Neutrality was either unattainable or suicidal.[42] For Seeckt the policy of military alliance alone was an admission of despair.

Brockdorff-Rantzau finally proceeded to Moscow, where he subsequently became a supporter of the *Ostpolitik* and a vital figure in the military collaboration. In December 1922 Moscow requested that one of the top figures of the *Reichswehr* should proceed to discuss the actual arrangements which were to be made under the terms of the initial agreements which had been concluded. Hasse of the *Truppenamt* accordingly undertook this journey in February 1923 at the head of yet another German military mission. The end product was a considerable German blunder, in the opinion of Brockdorff-Rantzau. Hasse had committed the indiscretion of speaking of the coming 'War of liberation', to be fought in the next three or five years.

It was an indiscretion reddened into danger since Hasse had written a letter, in very compromising terms, to A. P. Rosengoltz, one of the principal Soviet negotiators.[43] The Count, inclined to exaggerate, foresaw the ruin of the *Reich*. Nevertheless, such indiscretions could be dangerous.

At about the same time final agreement between Junkers and the Soviet government had been reached over the terms of the manufacture of aircraft at the Fili factory. In February 1923 *Sovnarkom* finally ratified the agreement which had been drawn up previously between Junkers and the *Reichswehrministerium*, with 'R.R.' as the third party. An annual production of 300 machines was fixed, of which the Russians would take 60, from a plant which was equipped and manned with technicians by Junkers, while the raw materials and labour force were supplied by the Soviet government.[44] It is possible that a dispute over finances had held up the completion of the contract, for with regard to the production of aero-engines Junkers required certain adjustments of the financial terms. To the Russians this was not acceptable, and it is therefore interesting to notice that subsequently the arrangement broke down over the question of the manufacture and supply of aero-engines.

The military-industrial activity represented an important and expanding line of Soviet-German collaboration, but it was plagued almost from the beginning with serious difficulties. Krupp succeeded in setting up Factory No. 8 for the production of 30-mm. infantry weapons.[45] If French Intelligence was accurately informed, the Germans had already succeeded in transmitting certain quantities of war materials to the Red Army — 100 aircraft, 3–400,000 rifles, and stocks of explosives.[46] The joint Soviet-German company for poison-gas manufacture — *Bersol* — did commence work, but the failure of the technical processes caused the project to be abandoned ultimately. Ammunition, large-calibre artillery shells and grenades were manufactured in Soviet plants, at Zlatoust (Urals), the Tula arms plant, in Leningrad at the former Putilov works, with German technical assistance.

This industrial activity did not preclude progress with the programme of military collaboration. Even that, however, was arrived at only after protracted negotiation, which re-opened with the despatch of a second German mission to Moscow in April 1923, headed by Lieutenant-Colonel Mentzel and Tschunke. These *Reichswehr* representatives seem to have followed the familiar path of making lavish promises to the Russians and yet failing to achieve either concrete agreement or satisfaction of German interests. After this second virtual failure, Brockdorff-Rantzau suggested inviting Soviet negotiators to Berlin to hammer out the scope and exact commitment of the arrangements.[47] Showing signs of a certain wariness, Rosengoltz, accompanied by Krestinsky and Ustinov, arrived in Berlin at the end of July 1923, although Rosengoltz finally fell in with the revised plans for the expansion of the war industry on Soviet soil and the production of military supplies for Germany, promising the written answer of the Soviet government.[48]

What emerges from these exchanges is that the capital sum involved in these undertakings had not been previously fixed. *GEFU* had been organised, presumably on the understanding that the money would be forthcoming but without a fixed capital. What the German military mission in April 1923 had offered by way of capitalisation in the ventures was thirty-five million gold marks.[49] The Soviet military-political command had now so far committed itself to the point of conveying a written proposal in support of the German overtures. To cover the expenses of the joint undertakings, Germany provided the sum of seventy-five million gold marks, although that figure was not reached without certain internal struggles.

The question of *Reichswehr* representation in Soviet Russia was also the subject of considerable dispute and contrivance. It was obvious that the arrangements envisaged in the compact of August 1922 between the *Reichswehr* and the Red Army would necessitate close liaison. On these grounds it would seem likely that the report of the French Military Attaché in Warsaw, which maintained that a standing German military mission operated in Soviet Russia from 1922–3, was largely correct. The head of this mission was named as Bauer, with 'Neumann' (Niedermayer) and 'Teuchmann' (Schubert) as members.[50] Not until the autumn of 1923 did the *Reichswehr* complete its arrangements for a permanent representation in Moscow, by which time the *Zentrale Moskau* (*Z.Mo.*) was set up to co-ordinate the passage of German personnel and the programme of the training installations in Soviet Russia. The German ambassador had singled out Major Fischer as his candidate for the director of *Zentrale Moskau*. The *Reichswehr* managed to retain Niedermayer for this position, in spite of Brockdorff-Rantzau's grave misgivings about this officer's suitability.[51]

There is no evidence of a reliable nature to support the view that German officers were even in 1922 acting as instructors in the Red Army. The original agreement had called for facilities for training aviation units, motorised troops and chemical warfare tests. The first of these installations to be set up was the flying-school at Lipetsk, some 250 miles to the south-east of Moscow. Lipetsk was the location of one of the Red Air Force's own training bases, Kiev and Yegorievsk being the other two.[52] The re-birth of the Red Air Force (if the experiences of 1919–21 are considered part of its history) thus coincides with the development of the Lipetsk station as a joint Soviet-German venture. In 1924 work proceeded on transforming the huge and primitive air-field into a well-organised training-station.

General Helm Speidel supplies a certain amount of information on the work and organisation of Lipetsk.[53] Hangars, repair shops, communication facilities, an administration block, an engine-testing shop and a well-equipped hospital were constructed at the air base. The first machines to be used were Fokker D-XIII types, flown in by a mixed Soviet-German company called *Dereluft*.* The basic flight staff was made up of 60 German military and civilian instructors, with a further 100 German technicians. Soviet troops formed the aerodrome guard.[54]

As the organisation gradually developed, German and Soviet flight and technical staffs co-operated freely. Not until 1925 did regular flying training courses take place, but the pattern became one of the Soviet ground crews following German technical courses and Soviet air staffs receiving instruction in every aspect of flying from their German counterparts. Gradually Lipetsk-Voronezh-Borisoglebsk developed into a full air-training and combat-testing organisation. The Air Staff was located at Borisoglebsk, where one German officer at least — Captain Schöndorff — took service in the Red Army and remained with the Air Staff until 1931.[55] In this way, disguised as No. 4 Squadron of the Red Air Force, German pilots established themselves at Lipetsk.

★ ★ ★ ★

In view of the contemporary speculation about a possible Soviet-German military alliance, the events at the beginning and in the autumn of 1923 take on a special significance, providing perhaps the most searching test of the *Ostpolitik* as a feature of German policy, and revolution in Germany as an item of Soviet intentions. The French invasion of the Ruhr precipitated a major crisis in January, at which time the Soviet government declared its support for Germany. The key to the situation in terms of the incipient collaboration of the *Reichswehr* and the Red Army was once again Poland. Poland was given to understand in no uncertain terms that an attack on East Prussia or in Upper Silesia would be considered as a blow against Soviet Russia. Yet to speak of 'definite arrangements' contracted between Hasse and Lebedev in the event of Polish action in Upper Silesia — with two Soviet army groups concentrated in White Russia and the Ukraine — runs contrary to actual events and the available evidence.[56] During the critical period of the strategic dilemma imposed upon the German command, equally critical negotiations were still in progress to establish the exact terms of the military collaboration. In view of the inflamed situation, however, Hasse's indiscretions are the more comprehensible, and the fact

* Günter Rosenfeld (pp. 346–54) has a passage on the formation of the mixed Soviet-German companies, of which *Dereluft* was one, and his account is based on a consultation of the Soviet Ministry of Foreign Trade archives, where the records are presumably held.

that he spoke of a war of liberation at a future date does not suggest that he was the agent of an immediate collusion. The compromising letter to Rosengoltz might well have concerned future terms and not a few fantastic military promises.

Essentially, the events in the early part of 1923, in their international context, displayed the strategic limitations of the Soviet-German arrangements and robbed them of any but the most long-term strategic reality. The tension did contribute to an acceleration of the existing plans and to the sudden conclusion of the Junkers contract; direct military results were quite lacking. One significant factor was the diminished combat effectiveness of the Red Army, engaged as it was in an extensive transformation to the mixed military establishment, and troubled with internal dissensions in the command. It was at that moment a sorry military support for any of Seeckt's two-front calculations. And, indirectly, the Germans had it from Trotsky that the Red Army would not be used in the event of a conflict between the Germans and the Poles.[57]

Exhibiting the converse of the coin, the Soviet repudiation of its alliance with the German bourgeoisie led to the abortive Communist rising in the latter half of 1923. During the Ruhr crisis the *Komintern* had refrained from turning the situation to its advantage. The subsequent decision to ally with the German proletariat to effect the destruction of the Weimar Republic made the Red Army, in one sense, operational. Red Army Intelligence officers attempted to make contact with the elements of opposition in the *Reichswehr*. Using the facilities of the *OMS* (International Communication Section) of the *Komintern*, a highly secret organisation, Red Army officers were sent into Germany.[58] Krivitsky, then a Red Army Intelligence officer, states that a group of four or five Soviet officers, including himself, had been sent to Germany on receipt of the news of the French invasion of the Ruhr. Three types of organisation were set up; working within the framework of the German Communist Party, these were the Party Intelligence Service (working under Red Army Military Intelligence), fighting groups as the core of a future German Red Army, and infiltration groups to penetrate the police and the *Reichswehr*.[59]

The blueprint of the German Red Army was based on units organised into one-hundred-strong groups, with German Communists with war service listed by their former rank and serving as the foundation of a German Red Army officer corps; technical personnel were also organised, even to the point of a potential aviation group. The military plan, also conceived by Soviet staff officers, ruled out action against the French, with a planned withdrawal into Central Germany, where German Communist military units could link up with the greater strength of the Communists as a whole.

Bad organisation, the divisions of opinion in Moscow and Germany, fatal hesitations and the resolute action of the *Reichswehr*, notwithstanding the infiltrations, meant that the Ruhr Red Army would never be used.

Such political and strategic contortions did not cause any break in the illicit armament activities. The political paradoxes were built into the situation; as Seeckt dealt separately with 'inner and outer Bolshevism', so Soviet policy was inflicted with this political and strategic dualism. At a lunch-time conversation on 14th December, 1923, Brockdorff-Rantzau took issue with Chicherin, Radek and Krestinsky over the activities of the German Communist Party, demanding 'cards on the table' (*reiner Tisch gemacht*). In spite of attempts to disassociate the Soviet government from the *Komintern* as such, Chicherin and his colleagues had difficulties in soothing the ambassador, who threatened resignation.[60]

An attempt was made in the spring of 1924, from the German side, to reduce the scale of the commitments in Russia, a move directed by Brockdorff-Rantzau against the *Reichswehr's* independent negotiations. To his manifest alarm, the ambassador shortly discovered that such extensive agreements had been entered into by the *Reichswehr* with the Soviet command that withdrawal would spell equal catastrophe.[61] Any intention of transforming the whole arrangement into primarily economic terms was crushed by the fact that the *Reichswehr*, with the assistance of the Red Army, was pressing forward with the training installations, and the military-industrial arrangements were beginning to break down, even after so short a life. The constructions at Lipetsk marked, then, a new phase in the collaboration.

The Junkers undertaking soon ran into difficulties. Money, and the question of aero-engines, produced the crisis; early in 1924 Junkers was ordered to associate with the *BMW* (*Bayerische Motorenwerke*) in the production of aero-engines at Fili. *Sondergruppe R* and Junkers clashed; Seeckt intervened on 18th August, 1924, to explain to the aircraft manufacturer that politics and strategy, not economics, were the mainspring of the industrial activities in the east.[62] The Red Air Force had, meanwhile, been ordering its engines from Germany; at the end of 1923 60 aero-engines of 280 HP had been delivered and a further 220 of 240 HP were on order. At the same time 50 tractors of 100 HP were delivered and a further 50 ordered.[63] This had presumably sparked off the Junkers-*BMW* row. Brockdorff-Rantzau's talk with Trotsky on 9th June, 1924, however, indicated that matters were reaching a serious pass; Junkers had failed to gain any Soviet orders, although they had finally agreed to manufacture engines. Without such orders, the Fili factory was doomed (and did close in 1925 when the *Reichswehrministerium* refused a further subsidy). The

German ambassador complained that a foreign commission (either British or American) had inspected the Tula plant which was under German management. Trotsky promised to investigate what he hoped was a false report. Finally Trotsky was counselled to have nothing to do with Colonel Bauer, with whom negotiations were evidently proceeding over chemical plants, for Bauer was an ally of Ludendorff — Seeckt of the *Reichswehr* would not countenance working with such men. Trotsky thanked Brockdorff-Rantzau for this advice.[64]

Both with respect to the aircraft plant, and the industrial installations as a whole, in 1924 and subsequently there are indications of a change in the Soviet attitude, whereby advantage was taken of the financial difficulties of *GEFU* to curtail its work and develop an indigenous Soviet arms industry. It was easier, cheaper and ultimately more rewarding to hire technicians rather than finance factories. Arms shipments and ammunition manufacture had tided the Red Army over the crisis of 1922–3, but a long-term solution was in the making, and owed much to the work of Frunze. *Bersol*, committed to the manufacture of poison-gas, failed also as no answer was found to insuperable technical problems connected with the manufacturing processes.

Viewed against the prevailing background of the struggles over a military policy and the pressing problem of the supply and equipping of the Red Army, the developing contact with the *Reichswehr* forms a consistent policy. In terms of collaboration between the armies, the Soviet command was merely exchanging one set of specialists for another; the Tsarist 'military specialist' helped the Red Army through the Civil War, the professional German soldier would lead it into modernisation and enlarged training facilities. If, under Trotsky, Soviet military policy was considered as a paradox — based on rigid political assumptions, but free to be quite eclectic in parts of its application — then the collaboration with the *Reichswehr* was neither inconsistent nor even basically an innovation. The second stage of this arrangement, however, was introduced and expanded during the period of the intensive re-fashioning of the Red Army, the command system and the Soviet military establishment. It is a tribute to Trotsky that his opponents in the military debate, Frunze, Voroshilov and their intimates, continued his policy and even enlarged upon it. Excepting the fundamental debates of 1920–1, the subsequent organised polemics, weighted with military jargon, are exposed as a political manœuvre only.

* * * *

During the trial of the 'Anti-Soviet "Bloc of Rights and Trotskyites" ', which was held in Moscow from 2nd–13th March, 1938, Krestinsky and

Rosengoltz were among the accused. Both, during their cross-examination, produced versions of the first stages of the contact with the *Reichswehr*. Krestinsky stated that Seeckt contacted Kopp in July 1920; 'as early as 1920', to use Vyshinsky's phrase, Trotsky 'sent out feelers through Kopp' and approached Seeckt. Krestinsky distinguished between 'official' and 'criminal' (Trotskyite) contacts; referring to a volume of the preliminary investigation, prosecutor Vyshinsky stated that Krestinsky had named June 1920 as the first date. About actual negotiations, Krestinsky testified that these took place '... in the spring and summer of 1922'; the indictment was incorrect in naming 1921, for '... this first meeting of an official nature ... occurred in the winter of 1921–2'. Speaking of the financial arrangements, Krestinsky stated that 250,000 gold marks ($60,000) were provided as an annual subsidy by Seeckt, who had agreed to this figure '... after consulting with his assistant, the chief of staff'. The latter would be Hasse. It was in 1923 that 'the agreement with Seeckt' was carried out 'mainly in Moscow and sometimes in Berlin'— nor was it an agreement which remained unchanged. Rosengoltz admitted to establishing contact 'with Seeckt directly' in 1923, to approaching 'German military circles' in 1923 'in connection with a business contact I had ...'—Junkers.[65]

So did official policy become political damnation at this later date. Enough lies had been told about some of the truth to make it passingly plausible. In 1923 the German collaboration was only beginning to enter into the Soviet high command's involved life. It had much further to travel, bringing further political complications in its wake, but before these materialised, the Red commanders had fierce internal struggles to wage.

CHAPTER SEVEN

The Reign of Frunze and the Rise of Voroshilov: 1924–1926

The Military Commission, which had been authorised and appointed by the Central Control Commission, carried on with its investigation of the Red Army and the Soviet military establishment until January 1924. With its apparatus of sub-commissions and experts drawn from the various military and naval inspectorates, this investigating body poked, pried and questioned in the internal and frontier Military Districts selected as the basis of the investigation, as well as in the corps, divisional and regimental staffs also singled out. By the end of 1923, the Commissions had evidently assembled a very considerable body of material on the state of the Red Army, most of which indicated a parlous state of affairs covering man-power and material deficiencies, and all of which — by manipulated implication — reflected the most damaging criticism of Trotsky's management of the country's military and defence activities.

This attack launched upon Trotsky by his opponents on the Central Committee, however, was indirect in comparison with the direct political struggle, which was reaching flash-point as the Military Commission was gathering up the results of its labours and submitting its report. The 'Forty-Six', the loose combination of political opposition to the policy and purposes of the Stalin-Kamenev-Zinoviev triumvirate, had triggered off a dangerous situation. In their demand for the restoration of inner-Party democracy, this group had forced the triumvirate to open the discussion of Party policy in the Moscow 'cells', and subsequently in the provinces. The day went badly with the triumvirate, who were subject to a torrent of criticism and hostile verdicts. In the military 'cells' of the Moscow garrison, Antonov-Ovseenko, head of the *PUR*, delivered an address, in which he declared that the military 'cells' were solidly behind Trotsky.[1] It was this fervid political discussion, aimed against the ruling group, which gave Circular No. 200 of the *PUR*, issued without the knowledge of the Central Committee and promulgated on 24th December, 1923, its particular political potency. The political organisations within the armed forces were now fully authorised to discuss matters of Party policy at meetings of the 'cell' and, indeed, to initiate such discussion in terms of inner-Party democratic procedure. While Antonov-Ovseenko had obviously and dramatically over-simplified the position of the support for Trotsky in the military organisations, there can be little doubt that the younger political workers (like the students of the University of Moscow) were sympathetic to the cause of this phase of opposition. One-third of the military 'cells' of the Moscow garrison had come out in support for the programme of the 'Forty-Six', and hence underwritten Trotsky's own position.[2] This was the beginning of calamity indeed, when that instrument of control which had been specifically designed to achieve outright loyalty to the ruling group — the political administration of the Red Army — sided with the opponents or critics of that very group.

At this juncture the Military Commission began to present the first of its conclusions upon the workings of the Soviet military system. The Commission found that the Red Army Staff was not properly solving the problems concerned with the defence of the Soviet Republic and the administration of its armed forces. No effective division of function existed at the highest level, where the Main Supply Administration (*Glavnachsnab*) had combined within itself a variety of planning and administrative processes, thus solving none and lowering its general efficiency. The present organisation in the field forces did not correspond either to their operational needs or to the tasks which they might have to perform. In particular, the existing infantry and cavalry units and over-all organisation scarcely conformed to the needs imposed by modern training in peace-time, or to combat roles. No proper plan existed for the co-ordination of the construction of defence works, and there was no particular body responsible for the supervision of defence construction in and for the Soviet Union. As for the technical troops of the Red Army, these also showed marked deficiencies, both in organisation and training. In their present condition, Soviet naval forces could likewise not be spoken of as units capable of any kind of combat role.[3]

The Military Commission set out its detailed findings. In view of the composition of the Commission, there was never any reason to suppose that it would attempt any endorsement of Trotsky's military mandate. On the contrary, it looked for and found 'a great deficiency' in the militia and the regular command staff, amounting in some places to a 50 per cent shortage of officers. In specific arms, there were serious failings of quality as well as quantity, the gravity of this varying from unit to unit. 'Instability' in the army was assuming dangerous proportions. The majority of units in 1923 had changed their officers at frequent intervals. This constant chopping and changing had become — in the opinion of the Commission — one of the chief plagues of the Red Army.

Equipment and military supplies were conspicuous mostly by their absence. As for the training and education of the men to use these items, as yet missing, these presented similar failings. The root cause was to be found in the low level of qualification — both in matters of theory and in military instruction — of the command staff as a whole; this could be traced right through the military establishment, from the poor level of marksmanship in infantry units to the lack of a unified view of the Red Army and its combat unities as a whole. And with that point, the exponents of the 'unified military doctrine' could not resist delivering yet another thrust at Trotsky.

Dealing specifically with the command staff, Gusev and his fellows of the Commission found great numerical deficiency, especially in the junior levels, and a general instability. Up to 45 per cent of the Soviet commanders did not conform to the requirements of social origin; 5·3 per cent had been officers in the White Army.[4] A third of the officers were without combat experience and 12 per cent were lacking in any formal military education. Nor was the Commission at pains to hide what was indeed an all too obvious fact, that the material lot of the Soviet commander in peace-time had steadily deteriorated, thereby adding an economic penalty to the loss of prestige during the transitional period. The same flood of criticism was applied to the political apparatus of the Red Army and the methods which it had been pursuing in its work.

This calculated indictment of Trotsky and his policy had taken some time to prepare. The activities of the Military Commission were essentially an extension into the field of applied politics of the motives which lay behind the protracted military debates which had reached their climax at the 11th Party Congress. It was not, however, a sheaf of papers from an investigating committee which decided the triumvirate upon the necessity of Trotsky's removal from his military post, but the turn which the acute political crisis had taken. At the very end of 1923 Trotsky had openly challenged the new bureaucratic masters of the Party, who manipulated the machine in the interests of their own power. The ferment in the 'cells' of the Moscow garrison and the inclinations of the head of *PUR* made it plain that action must be taken. At no time, however, did Trotsky make any move which suggested that he planned to use either his position or his influence in the Red Army to bring about any military pressure on the triumvirate. Antonov-Ovseenko, with his challenging statements, acted upon his own initiative with a flamboyant disregard for the consequences.

The mine which had been laid beneath Trotsky as the head of the military machine was now primed and prepared. The work of the Military Commission could be utilised to justify the impending changes. At the October plenum of the Central Committee in 1923 Frunze had already burst out

Composition of the Red Army: Arms and Services, 1923–4

	For 1st October, 1923		For 1st October, 1924	
	Numbers	%	Numbers	%
Riflemen	243,282	42·91	232,795	43·96
Cavalry	60,650	10·71	66,842	12·62
Artillery	8,529	1·5	9,151	1·72
Air Force	9,420	1·67	10,264	1·94
Signals (outside corps)	15,585	2·76	15,361	2·9
Railway troops/Military transportation	21,562	3·81	21,272	4·01
Engineer troops	12,384	2·2	10,014	1·89
Armoured units	8,635	1·52	2,107	0·44
Fortified districts	12,940	2·28	8,706	1·64
Guards, sentry troops	19,986	3·53	23,246	4·38
National formations	8,724	1·55	12,859	2·42
Administration	21,463	3·79	19,012	3·59
Military Training Establishments (Staff)	80,084	14·14	65,004	12·27
Supply	16,000	2·82	13,676	2·58
Medical/Veterinary	12,593	2·22	10,288	1·94
Topographic	1,960	0·34	1,467	0·28
Instructors for training outside military units	1,505	0·27	1,400	0·26
Special Assignment Detachments*	7,932	1·40	346	0·06
Miscellaneous	3,283	0·58	6,066	1·14
	566,517		529,865	

with views of the rapid deterioration of the Red Army and its unfitness for any combat role. The triumvirate was facing not a military but a political challenge. For the Red commanders, the opportunity was heaven-sent. Under the guise of 'military reform' (although there were genuine measures of improvement to be undertaken) the emergent command group could capture the military machine for itself and its political masters. With

* Known as *ChON*: organised in 1918 as armed detachments of selected Party workers. Adopted this name in April, 1919, and after the Civil War used in various 'pacifications'. Almost completely disbanded after the first phase of the military reforms.

testimony and explanation, condemnation and interlocking suggestion, Frunze, Voroshilov, Ordzhonikidze, Shvernik, Bubnov — with Gusev — waited to deliver their blows at the January plenum of the Central Committee in 1924.

* * * *

While Trotsky, weakened by bouts of a malarial fever contracted during a hunting trip in the autumn of 1923, now made preparations to leave Moscow in order to recuperate in the south, further steps were being taken to bring about the end of his rule over the Red Army. Six days before the death of Lenin, the Central Committee plenum of 14th–15th January, 1924, had decided to appoint yet another special military commission, endowed with very considerable authority.[5] As its first members, this commission included Frunze, A. A. Andreyev, Gusev (acting as president), Ordzhonikidze, Unshlikht and Shvernik. A little later Bubnov and Voroshilov joined this body, together with Yegorov and others un-named.[6] The mandate of the commission was to investigate the instability of the personnel of the Red Army and to look into the state of military supply; one month was allowed for the investigation. Speed, not to say an indecent haste, was vital to the success of this operation.

To seize control of the Political Administration was even more urgent. Before the discussions had been prohibited, the military 'cells' of the Moscow garrison had swung to the support of the oppositionists and Trotsky. In the month of January the Central Committee took the decisive step of placing the highest post in the *PUR* in the hands of one of its own men, the veteran Bolshevik Andrei S. Bubnov.[7] Bubnov had been a Bolshevik since 1903; in 1917 he had been one of the organising brains behind the seizure of power. In the Civil War, after first fighting against Kaledin, Bubnov finally entered the Ukrainian Soviet administration, and was elected to the Central Committee of the Ukrainian Communist Party. After taking part in the suppression of the Kronstadt rising, Bubnov proceeded to the Northern Caucasus Military District and the staff of the 1st Cavalry Army.[8] In 1923 Bubnov had worked in the Agitation-Propaganda Section of the Central Committee, so that he was not unfamiliar with the scope of his new duties.*

* In view of the fact that Bubnov had been an adherent of the 'Forty-Six', his appointment as head of the Political Administration at first sight seems surprising. The 'Forty-Six', however, were far from being a unified faction, although containing a pro-Trotsky group. Bubnov, Kossior, Sapronov and V. Smirnov held views which diverged rather sharply from those of Trotsky's supporters. Certainly a strong and capable personality was needed as successor to Antonov-Ovseenko, and Bubnov, his adherence to a dissident group notwithstanding, fitted the need. A very skilled act of political manipulation was called for, in which the head of the administration would have to be no mere figure-head. Bubnov had the requisite experience and it cannot be said that he failed to give satisfaction.

The Central Committee commission, meanwhile, was on the point of presenting its report. On 3rd February, 1924, a Central Committee plenum heard and considered the evidence.[9] S. I. Gusev, in his capacity as head of the Military Commission appointed in 1923 and the Central Committee commission so recently set up, presented the final reports. The Central Committee commission, in its brief work of a single fortnight, had come to the conclusion that the instability in the Red Army had reached 'unprecedented proportions', that 'in its present aspect the Red Army is unfit for combat'.[10] A whole series of shortcomings and deficiencies could be found at every level of the Soviet military establishment. The very highest directing body simply did not work. Trotsky did nothing in the *Revvoensoviet*; the running of military affairs had been left in the hands of Sklyanskii and P. P. Lebedev,* who were not qualified to ensure the proper ordering of the Soviet forces. Into the military administration as a whole, unsuitable and dangerous elements had worked their way, so that the remedy was to stiffen the Staff of the Red Army and the Naval Administration with a strong contingent of Party workers.[11]

The verbal evidence which was given before the Central Committee was meant to reinforce these conclusions with all the righteous passion of men indignant at the degeneration of the Red Army. In fact, such witness was a repetition of the 11th Party Congress debates, although upon this occasion there was no rebuttal. Gusev opened with his castigation of the military bureaucrats:

> In all of our chief administrations there exists the domination of the old specialists, the generals, enjoying a very sturdy development. . . . The *Revvoensoviet* has not followed a policy, whereby the old specialists could be changed and replaced by new workers, who were turned out by us during the Civil War, who were trained after the Civil War and who would be capable of occupying higher posts and managing their duty better than the old specialists. . . .[12]

Of the 87,000 men trained as officer material during the Civil War, 30,000 had been killed in action; only 25,000 remained now, after the losses to the command staff incurred by demobilisation. It was therefore imperative to make proper use of this trained man-power to restore the cadres of the Red Army.

Gusev read out a letter from Uborevich, a commander of considerable talent recently employed in the Far East. The letter criticised the central

* This was crude slander against Lebedev, to whom the Red Army owed a great deal both during the Civil War and the transitional period. Lebedev was certainly removed from the Staff, but he was given quite a responsible post in the Ukraine and remained an important figure in the command until his death in 1933.

military administration, where, wrote Uborevich, '. . . the "benumbing" spirit of the old Tsarist specialists is all-pervading. . . . The spirit of the old bureaucrats (the Sukhomlinov-ites) wafts over the decrees of the Republic *Revvoensoviet*.'[13] Unshlikht, native of Russian Poland, professional revolutionary, participant in the actions of 1917 and subsequently on the Western Front, had formerly been assigned to the Security Service (*OGPU*) in Belorussia. Now he spoke up with the general chorus of denunciation, in no way belying Trotsky's description of him as an 'ambitious but talentless intriguer'.[14] He was followed by Lashevich, who singled out the Red Army Staff as an organ which '. . . to a considerable degree cuts itself off from the Red Army, it does not understand the psychology of the Red Army. There they have planted old generals, the commissar staff is weak, and with them nothing counts.'[15]

Frunze delivered himself of a very searching criticism of the whole Soviet military structure. There was, Frunze argued, ample evidence from the preparatory work done in the autumn enquiry, to show that neither the supply side nor the organisational aspects of the Red Army were in a fit state to be used in a major war. The post-demobilisation planning of the army had been unsystematic and quite mechanical. In the methods adopted by the Staff and the *Revvoensoviet* far too much paper-work and bureaucracy prevailed. There was no alternative but to change the personnel in charge of the direction of military affairs.[16] Ordzhonikidze followed with his own censure, quoting in support of it a letter which Tukhachevsky had written to the secretary of the Central Committee, setting out views similar to those of Uborevich. Yegorov had spoken to Ordzhonikidze of the need for a thorough-going reform.[17] Voroshilov, no friend to Trotsky, emphasised that Trotsky's blunder had been to remove the organs of military administration from the control of the Party, and to put the naval administration on a special basis, thus isolating it from the control of the Central Committee.* Thus spake the political soldier.†

On 3rd March, by the decision of the *Politburo*, Sklyanskii was abruptly removed from his post as Trotsky's deputy and Trotsky informed of this by the summary despatch of a special delegation to give him this news. The next step involved settling the new choices for the command positions which

* This charge of 'de-politicalising' the Red Army was brought against Trotsky in 1923–4, Tukhachevsky in 1937 and Zhukov in 1957. In no case is there proof that this was really intended, but rather that the ruling group felt their hold upon the army to be slipping. It is not, therefore, that there is a positive drive to free the army, but a negative reaction that the army is slipping out of control. Voroshilov, in putting what he called his case, announced that he could see 'complete catastrophe', for the Red Army and the country, if this 'abnormality' were not removed. To charge Trotsky with this, after he had initiated the whole system and seen it through four years of war, was complete nonsense.

† Stalin's contribution appears to have been on the lines of his comment: 'If we should be involved in war, we would be broken to pieces and ground to dust.'

were falling vacant and to implement the programme of reform which had been the ostensible justification for the purge of the 'old men'. A new commission was now to draw up this plan for reform in detail and to recommend the change in personnel to the Central Committee; on 6th March this step had been taken.[18] The proposed reforms could proceed on the lines which had been suggested by the Military Commission, which finally completed its work in January 1924. In order to link up with the latest developments, the business of making a detailed estimate of the military administration was prolonged until April 1924, by which date Frunze submitted to the plenum of the Central Committee a draft of the proposed measures to be undertaken.[19]

Mikhail Vasil'evich Frunze, on 11th March, 1924, was named as the successor to Sklyanskii, and effective power over the Soviet military establishment thereby passed to him.[20] Voroshilov was named commander of the vitally important Moscow Military District, thereby displacing from that position Trotsky's friend and supporter, the heroic giant Muralov. The Praesidium of the Central Executive Committee on 21st March, and *Sovnarkom* on 25th formally confirmed the new appointments to the *Revvoensoviet* staff. Bubnov, Budenny, S. S. Kamenev, A. F. Myasnikov, Ordzhonikidze, Unshlikht, Sh. E. Eliava, Frunze and Voroshilov took up the main positions.[21] The triumph of the 1st Cavalry Army and those who had served or been associated with that distinctive command was noticeably substantial. Trotsky had been effectively ousted from the leadership of the army and his hold on the political apparatus through Antonov-Ovseenko was broken for the moment.

Frunze had not waited upon the formality of these official announcements to begin the work of re-moulding the Red Army into the pattern so vociferously advocated by the Red commanders. On 4th February the *Revvoensoviet* had been used to give Frunze, as president of a special commission, full powers to draw up the reform plan. On the following day this commission held its first meeting, when five sub-commissions were appointed to draw up specifications for organisation, supply, political work, reports on the command staff and conditions of service. Commanders of military districts and heads of central and local military administrations were also to assist in preparing suggested reforms in the system of administration and supply. On 8th–9th February, 1924, an extraordinary session of these commissions, supplemented by senior commanders, departmental chiefs, sections of the Red Army Staff and unit commanders, was held. Further reports were delivered on this occasion; they covered the present organisation of the Red Army, the organisation of foreign armies, Gusev's report on the work of the Control Commission's Military

Commission, the re-organisation of the military administration and a study of the structure of the supply system at present used in the Red Army.[22] It was at this meeting that the sub-commissions were given detailed instructions; and doubtless the command staff of the Red Army was fully acquainted with the justifications, both real and imaginary, for the present changes.

The reform plan which finally emerged settled the outlines of the innovations, and grouped the proposals into modifications in the military establishment as a whole, the necessary alterations to the structure of the military administration, the new adjustments arising out of the adoption of the territorial-militia system, and the fundamental changes which must be wrought in the command staff of the Soviet armed forces. The basic motivation was summed up in Frunze's own slogan — 'Make way for the Red commanders'. The result of the elephantine labours of the numerous investigating commissions had never been in doubt. But to blame the entire situation upon Trotsky, quoting either his policy or lack of it, was patently absurd. It was from this point forward that Trotsky's own capable military theories were deliberately distorted. Trotsky had never denied the need for reform, but he had consistently questioned the basis upon which this might be conducted. Under these new conditions, however, and with the emergence of the new command group, the first phase of 'military reform' was a thorough-going and faintly-concealed purge, motivated by political considerations and the surge of personal ambitions. For Mikhail Frunze, nevertheless, the opportunity had presented itself for modernising and stabilising the Red Army. It was a measure of his innate capacity that he achieved not a little of this.

* * * *

The old *Revvoensoviet* of the Republic, which Frunze and his new command had rushed to man, had during this frenzied phase undergone both a change of name and a definition of its functions under the first Constitution of the USSR, which took effect from 21st January, 1924. This Constitution, which was introduced by Stalin with a self-advertising flourish, detailed the Military and Naval Commissariat as one of ten such commissariats, and one of the five centralised All-Union Commissariats. The *Revvoensoviet* of the USSR (*RVS SSSR*) was formally established as the governing body of the Military Commissariat, with the executive and administrative organs of the Soviet armed forces subordinated to the *RVS*, as was the Political Administration (*PUR*), which remained as yet only under the *indirect* control of the Central Committee. The new Constitution made no striking change in the regulation of the relation between the organs of government and the military command, emphasising once again the principle of centralisation and gathering the military-political instruments ever more tightly to the centre. No military control was decentralised to the separate nationalities of the Soviet Union.[23]

Apart from this very general re-definition, on 28th March, 1924, Frunze issued Order No. 446/96, which laid down the details of the re-organisation of the Military Commissariat and the central military organs. Functions were given a much more rigid definition. The Staff of the Red Army would be concerned with comprehensive planning for national defence. The Inspectorates (Army, Navy and Air Force) were responsible for combat efficiency and training. The Red Army Administration would take over the day-to-day running of Red Army affairs. *PUR* had the function of directing all the political and agitational work in the Soviet armed forces and of directing the commissar apparatus. The Chief of Red Army Supply dealt with all aspects of provisioning, while the Military Research Commission undertook examinations of defence requirements. Medical and veterinary administrations were concerned with regulation of medical and hygiene conditions.[24]

Frunze's attention narrowed to the vitally important Red Army Staff. Since its formal inception in 1921, the Staff had developed into an unwieldy group dealing with combat training, routine Red Army affairs and defence policy — all without real definition. Staff functions, Administration and the Inspectorate of the Red Army had been combined into this body. Frunze's own appointment to the post of Chief of Staff, by Order No. 78 of 1st April, 1924, marked a deliberate step in emphasising the authority and prestige of the Staff. In the summer Tukhachevsky and Shaposhnikov were both appointed assistants to the Chief of Staff,* thus incorporating both prestige and talent in the Staff. S. S. Kamenev, former Commander-in-Chief, took over the Inspectorate, N. N. Petin (a senior 'specialist') the Red Army Administration, and Unshlikht the post of Chief of Supply.[25] Frunze was freed, with the limitation of functions in the administration, to develop the Staff as the 'military brain' of the Red Army and ultimately the Soviet state. It is from this date that the old *Glavkom* finally disappeared, and the history of the Soviet General Staff — as it was to become — begins.

Frunze stressed the high priority which must be given to the development of the Staff. In his speech of 1st August, 1924, to the War Academy graduates

* The office of First Deputy Chief of Staff comprised supervision over the Operations Section, and Intelligence, Military Training and Military Topographic Sections. The Second Deputy Chief of Staff supervised organisation, mobilisation and personnel (cadres).

(the future incumbents of the Staff), Frunze suggested the manner in which he saw the widest political and strategic tasks falling into its orbit:

> The Red General Staff will fulfil its task only when it succeeds in raising itself above the point of view of the nation-state. With you [the graduates] we must look upon ourselves as a potential core, as the potential centre of a much broader Red General Staff. With you, there lies upon us the task of helping the proletariat of those countries, which until now were unable to vanquish their internal class enemy — helping them to win the victory over that enemy.[26]

The international and political implications of this statement make an interesting comparison with Tukhachevsky's letter of 1920 to Zinoviev.

The Staff was placed at the very centre of the military establishment. Its functions were connected with the working out of questions related to the defence policy of the state, the formulation of mobilisation and operational plans which accorded with the material resources at the disposal of the Soviet Union, and finally analysis and co-relation of the combat experience of the First World War, the Civil War and other wars. Although this marked a considerable step forward, Frunze was forced to admit that it did not prove possible to free the Staff from all military minutiae, even though the basic step had been taken.[27]

In addition to separating out the operational and planning, the administrative and inspectorate functions, Frunze turned his attention to the problem of 'militarising' certain state organs, with the aim of preparing the Soviet Union for a full-scale, modern war. In his summary of the reforms of 1924, Frunze referred to the same measure of militarisation which had been carried out in the United States, in France and Japan;[28] in this manner the educational process was geared to the preparation of officer-material, and thus saved a separate budgetary outlay. Similarly, the Soviet Commissariats of Education, Communications, Posts and Telegraphs, and the National Economy could be brought into line with the general requirements of the military policy of the Soviet high command. Only a systematic and planned introduction of this policy could bring full effectiveness when Soviet military policy was geared to the territorial-militia system and the small cadre army.[29]

Order No. 564 of 15th April, 1924, set in motion a thorough revision of the conditions of the administration of military districts. This went hand in hand with a purge of the staff of the military bureaucracy as a whole, in fulfilment of Frunze's aim of 'Communising' the military administration, both central and regional. The personnel was cut from 3,732 as the establishment for the central administration on 1st October, 1923, to 2,885 by the same date in 1924.[30] The avowed aim of this decision was to open up posts, so far invested by older 'military specialists', to the younger Soviet commander. In the same manner a greater percentage of Party members could be introduced into the corners of the military machine; the social disparities, shown in the excess numbers of non-proletarian elements, were corrected, and the percentage of Communists in the central military administration rose quickly from 12 to 25 per cent. The age classifications altered, so that the new staff would consist of men either below thirty years of age, or between thirty and forty.

The greatest muddle existed in the supply organisation of the Red Army. This was a Civil War legacy of a distinctly disadvantageous kind. Supply and administrative functions had been roughly divided between *Glavkom* and *Glavnachsnab* (Supply Administration); at regional levels, the same confusion had existed between the chief of supply and the field commander, if a proper regional controlling body was lacking or worked badly. The Frunze reforms put supply questions (military and naval) firmly into the hands of a Chief of Red Army Supply, to whom the various supply branches — artillery, technical, provisioning, combat requirements and the financial — were clearly connected. A system of planned supply was initiated, beginning at the centre, and ending with the military unit. The norms, tabular requirements and estimation of requirement were invested in the *RVS* Planning Commission, the head of which was the Chief of Red Army Supply.[31] A noticeable stress was laid on drilling into the junior commanders the principles of unit administration and supply procedures, a task in which the *PUR* lent the aid of a particular propaganda campaign. The aim was to bring the supply chain, based on 'the centre', the military district, the regiment, into a state of working efficiency.

Beyond the structural alterations in the military edifice, and the drastic re-composition of its personnel, Frunze's reformist policies brought about the first effective command organisation and policy decisions which set the Red Air Force (*VVS*) and the Navy (*VMF*) apart from the land-warfare predilections of former administrators. The investigations of the Military Commission had revealed grave deficiencies in the technical aspects, the organisation and the personnel of *VVS*. The Air Force was supplied with not less than thirty-two different types of machines and engines.[32] Land-based aviation possessed only twenty-eight per cent of its establishment of machines, while 'hydro-aviation' had no combat machines at all. The Red Air Force in 1923 was at the same stage as the Red Army in 1918, since '. . . there are men, knowing only the bare minimum about flying, there are aircraft, with the organisation run on semi-partisan lines — no firm discipline, instruction or the possibility of administering.'[33] It is, therefore, not surprising that the Soviet command showed the greatest interest in acquiring aircraft and aero-engines from Germany — plus a flying-school.

Up to 1924 Soviet military aviation was generally divided into land-based and naval arms. The former, divided into reconnaissance, fighter and training squadrons and flights, possessed 286 machines (without reserves). On 1st October, 1923, naval aviation had exactly 36.[34] The re-organisation of the military air forces proceeded in 1924–5 on the lines of differentiation by combat functions. Air command and administration was divided into 'combat' and 'rear' spheres; under the first came the squadrons (military and naval), under the latter aerodrome service, specialist branches, repair and supply facilities, training and research. Army aviation was divided into army 'strategic' and 'corps' aviation. The 'strategic' was further divided into interceptor, combat or 'storm' squadrons, light and heavy bombers and reconnaissance forces. The squadron was the basic unity; interceptors possessed up to 31 machines, heavy bombers up to 8 'ships', and the rest 19. 'Corps aviation' had the function of army co-operation, tactical reconnaissance and artillery observation, with a tactical unit in the 'corps aviation flight' of 6 to 8 machines. Naval aviation was planned with interceptor, reconnaissance and mine-laying units.[35] The matter of filling up the empty spaces in military aviation took time, although by 1st October, 1925, the official return signified that personnel was now at the level of establishment, while in the technical services for aviation 83·5 per cent of the fitters and 78·6 per cent of the specialist ancillary services had been found.

The naval forces presented much more than a technical difficulty. Both command staff and seamen presented aspects of a dangerous political unreliability which had reached its climax during the Kronstadt rebellion. Trotsky had managed to persuade Lenin that the drastic step of scuttling the Baltic Fleet need not be taken.[36] The new naval force was heavily injected with the more reliable Young Communist elements; the *Komsomol* thus fell heir to the Red Navy.[37] In April 1924 the old office of Naval Assistant to the Commander-in-Chief was abolished, and was replaced by a separate Chief of the Naval Forces of the Workers and Peasants Red Fleet, with its operational organ built on the Naval Staff.[38] Simultaneously the re-attestation of the naval command staff was carried out in the spring of 1924, resulting in a purge and the removal of 750 officers at least. In spite of this, 30 per cent of the naval command staff was still made up of officers of aristocratic origin, more than half had had no proper naval training and only 22·5 per cent were members of the Communist Party.[39] Much remained to be done to bring the naval forces up to any kind of combat effectiveness, and the Soviet approach to the German naval command in 1926 seems to point to certain political consolidations and a real beginning upon technical development and doctrinal progress.

Frunze's basic reforms in the Soviet military structure, the definition of staff and administrative functions, and the delineation of forms of naval and aviation command set the Soviet armed forces upon the path of modernisation and a transition to greater orthodoxy. They were modifications which stood the test of ten years of wear and tear, and were not fundamentally altered until the transition to a mass army. It was plain from the tenor of many of Frunze's remarks that budgetary considerations played a vital part in setting out certain of the limits of the reforms. In addition to providing vacant places for the rising generation of Red commanders, a limited budget demanded a maximum of efficiency and the exploitation of any resource. Much, however, depended upon the men called to the senior command positions and Frunze's command group was as distinctive as his reformist policy.

* * * *

With the loosening of Trotsky's grip on the central command positions and the displacement of Sklyanskii, the independent Red commander was advanced to the forefront of the scene. Frunze himself took P. P. Lebedev's place on the staff, just as in the following year he formally succeeded Trotsky as Commissar for War. In Frunze the Red Army had a man of proven ability and considerable talent, who had handled operations of war with skill and success. His arguments were solid and even pedestrian where Trotsky's were fiery and brilliant. Unproductive of the imaginative flights of which Tukhachevsky was capable, Frunze nevertheless hammered out a consistent and eminently practical military philosophy — in its own a way, a surrender to those very necessities which Trotsky had constantly emphasised. Although not entirely free of the inevitable tendency to fight the future war in terms of the last one, Frunze came to be a fervid exponent of modernisation and higher technical competence in the Red Army.

The aspect of Russian military sociology which fascinated Frunze, and which he presumably investigated personally, centred on the high fighting qualities of Russian troops in the age of Suvorov, who had moulded his soldiers into excellent fighting machines.[40] Suvorov placed the highest premium upon intelligent discipline and arduous training; Frunze's own frequent, if didactic, lectures on the same theme suggested that he wished to exploit his peasant soldiers in the fashion of the earlier Russian master. Equally Frunze possessed a comprehensive view of the Red Army, which was to play an important part in Soviet society as well as in its war-making. For this reason, his statements on the political aspects and apparatus of the Soviet armed forces are the most coherent of any and his understanding of the role of commander and commissar clarified by an awareness of the political limits which had to be imposed. If anything, Frunze finally came down on the side of the military commander, but it is not without significance that the transition to 'unity of command' was first effected under him.

On 18th July, 1924, Tukhachevsky was appointed Assistant Chief of Staff and Staff Commissar, having served to that date as commander of the Western Military District. The compilation of the first Red Army regulations, as opposed to those which were merely modifications of Imperial manuals, owed much to the work of Tukhachevsky and his collaborators. Shaposhnikov was retained in his former position of first assistant to the Chief of Staff. The commander of the Western Siberian Military District, senior 'military specialist' N. N. Petin was moved in as head of the Red Army Administration. The ex-Commander-in-Chief S. S. Kamenev took over the Inspectorate, and somewhat later another ex-Commander-in-Chief, Vatsetis, joined the Militia Inspectorate. Unshlikht, who had been nominally attached to the Staff as a commissar, became Chief of Red Army Supply. Budenny not unnaturally was named head of the Cavalry Inspectorate, having previously enjoyed the position of assistant to *Glavkom* on cavalry matters. Yakir, commander of the 14th Rifle Corps, took over the command of the Military Education and Training Administration. With the reorganisation of the naval forces, E. S. Pantserzhanskii was appointed Chief of the Naval Forces, with V. I. Zof as his first commissar; on 9th December, 1924, these two exchanged posts, Zof becoming in turn Naval Chief.[41] To the Red Air Force came P. I. Baranov, who had served on the Turkestan *Revvoensoviet*, and who now became Chief of the *VVS*, a post which he combined with close supervision of the formative stages of the indigenous Soviet aviation industry.[42]

The nerve-centre of the command, the *Revvoensoviet* of the USSR, had been carefully packed with men acceptable to the ruling group of the Central Committee. Zinoviev had not succeeded in capturing this body with his own nominee, and the balance had swung heavily in the favour of the political cohorts drawn from the 1st Cavalry Army and loyal to Stalin. Voroshilov was installed as Moscow Military District commander, thus putting a check on the disturbances in the garrison. On 10th May, 1924, Yegorov, associate of Stalin, Budenny and Voroshilov, was formally confirmed as a member of the *Revvoensoviet*, in addition to his duties as commander of the Ukrainian and Crimean forces, in which post he was Frunze's successor.[43] P. P. Lebedev, erstwhile Chief of Staff, was subsequently appointed Chief of Staff and military assistant to the Ukrainian commander.[44] The talented Blyukher was meanwhile detached from his duties in the Leningrad Military District and seconded for 'special duties' to the Central Committee — duties which took him to China as Soviet military adviser to Chiang Kai-shek.[45]

The senior 'military specialists', who had enjoyed the protection of Trotsky, were swept out of the operational-command posts and, in the cases where certain selected services were retained, the ex-Imperial officers found themselves confined to positions of administrative responsibility. Every effort was made, since a part of the cause of Trotsky's opponents could be identified with unsatisfied ambition, to replace the 'military specialist' by the products of Red Army training and combat experience. In July 1924 the *Revvoensoviet* officially terminated the distinction between 'the military specialist' and the 'Red commander'; in future, the single title of 'Red Army commander' would be used.[46] The new staff of the *Revvoensoviet* demonstrated the success of a military clique, in the formation and moulding of which Stalin had played a substantial part and where he now enjoyed a commanding position. Out of this clique came the new style of political soldier, the ex-NCO associated with Stalin, possessing only a rudimentary military education, a superficial understanding of Marxism combined with a readiness to run off its phrases, but a ruthless power of estimating situations in terms of narrow loyalties. This clique erected into power was not, however, the single source of military policy. With the concentration upon the Red Army Staff, a second group, associated with Tukhachevsky, Yakir and Shaposhnikov, was closely connected with planning processes and a major source of military ideas. Past enmities divided even this association into camps of divergent opinion. This general array of differing temperament, inequality of professional training, and separate political loyalties — to persons or ideas — represented the first results of winning the Red Army for the erstwhile Red Commanders. These disparities, awkward at any time, were of particular significance when viewed against the background of the 'mixed military system' — the territorial militia backed by a cadre army — which Frunze's reforms developed, regulated and stabilised.

* * * *

In his discussion of the military reforms and the setting-up of the 'mixed military system', Frunze did not conceal that no real choice had existed for the Soviet command. They were not presented with a set of alternatives. The ideal military solution would have been the retention of a 1–1½ million regular Red Army, for the existence of which Trotsky's opponents had battled furiously in 1921–2. Economic conditions and financial considerations had ruled this out completely.[47] The plenum of the Central Committee had fixed at its session of 18th December, 1922, a final reduction of the regular Red Army to 600,000, to be effected by 1st February, 1923.[48] The ceiling of the cadre army was ultimately fixed at 562,000, and it was in November-

December 1924 that Frunze intimated that no further reductions could be envisaged.[49] By this time the territorial-militia forces accounted for 52·4 per cent of the entire infantry strength of the Red Army.

Frunze took considerable pains to stress that the 'mixed' system could and would provide the Soviet Union with an adequate defence. Military criticism of the militia system was never entirely silenced, or the misgivings quietened. Out of the primitive schemes of 1923, Frunze's modifications produced a marked degree of stability in the militia-cadre army structure. The cadre element of militia divisions was fixed at 16 per cent of the establishment, and was kept on a war-footing.[50] When the militia plan had been first discussed in detail, great and valid concern had been expressed over the problem of maintaining the proletariat in a commanding position, lest it be swamped by rural Russia and overruled by all the antagonism felt by the peasant for the regime. To guarantee this proletarian role, the recruiting bases of the territorial formations were adjusted against social-economic and political factors prevailing in particular areas, stricter social selection of recruits, closer scrutiny of the command and political staff, and by using Party members and the *Komsomol* for the administrative duties and political work in militia units. There was need of Frunze's constant exhortations to concentrate upon the village; in 1924, during the annual mobilisation of the militia, peasant demonstrations took place in every military district. Slogans — 'Workers get huge wages', 'Workers live in clover!' 'Only workers get power'— were scrawled about in Tula; peasant Red Army men jibbed at the restrictions on peasants joining the Party, set about organising special peasant groups, and, in one brigade, created the 'Corn-growers' Union.'[51] Trotsky's earlier strictures had been proved correct, and it was obvious that a harsh agrarian policy, alienating the peasant, had the direst effects on the military scene. It was, therefore, a high military priority to secure the pacification of the countryside.

The militia was mobilised once a year for annual exercises. The first such mobilisations (*Tersbor*) in 1923 had been attended by confusion, a little reversion to banditry, and administrative chaos. To raise the performance of the annual mobilisations was a serious, even critically important problem. Militia forces were henceforth given a pre-mobilisation political indoctrination; local Party organisations were drawn into the preparatory work. Meetings, special territorial conferences, leaflets, political literature were all employed to facilitate the mobilisations. Most important were the adequate administrative and supply measures which had to be taken in advance, and which had previously been lacking.[52] Although the annual camp played an important part in training and political indoctrination, the decision to base all training on barracks made it possible, in theory, to introduce a comprehensive training schedule. Thus, two age-classes were subject to 210 hours of military instruction, one age-group was given a three-month course while mobilised, in barracks or military camps, four age-groups received instruction for one month also while mobilised, command and political staff were given one month's training, and finally all territorials were subject to training in the periods between mobilisation.[53]

The basis of Frunze's military-administrative policy had been a drastic reduction of the central military bureaucracy, offset by considerable decentralisation. This was no contradiction of the necessities which arose out of the 'mixed' military system. Decentralisation, plus the strains of the administrative difficulties involved in militia maintenance and mobilisation, necessitated re-furbishing the regional and local military organs, militarising certain civilian bodies and utilising the general policy of close contact between local Party and Red Army political bodies. The lack of command staff, especially in the junior grades, presented a difficulty of another order. In part this was solved by the vigorous reforms of the methods of officer-selection and education initiated under Frunze and continued by Voroshilov.

Out of these varied measures, the Red Army, embodying the 'mixed' system, consisted of 77 divisions of infantry by 1925 — 31 cadre, 46 territorial-militia (of which 28 were the first-line type).* By April 1925 a further 14 nuclei of 'third-line' territorial formations, with a cadre of 190 men only, had been brought into existence.[54] Of the 11 cavalry divisions and 8 cavalry brigades of the regular Red Army, however, only one division had been converted into the territorial type. The remainder were retained as cadre forces, and fielded 60 per cent of their war-time strength. Red Army cavalry was located according to strict operational requirements and not in relation to its recruiting.[55] Corps artillery, specialist and technical troops were also kept on a permanent footing, with not less than 80 per cent of their war-time establishment in being. In fact, the 'mixed' system was applied almost exclusively to the Red Army infantry and was itself an economic solution, whereby the regular forces, even though reduced in size, could be maintained at a higher level and with greater expenditure on equipment.[56] It was a general application of the principle by which Frunze had raised the pay of the Red commander by cutting down on the personnel of the military bureaucracy.

* A first-line territorial division had a permanent staff of 2,400 with a strength of 10,681 territorial recruits; second-line divisions were of two types, one organised on a cadre division (permanent strength 604, territorial recruits 11,750) or on a first-line territorial division (permanent strength 622, territorial recruits 11,734). The nucleus of a first-line division was set at a permanent staff of 190. The permanent staff of a first-line territorial division (2,400) was 16 per cent of its war strength; by comparison, the permanent establishment of a cadre rifle division was kept at 34 per cent of its war strength.

It was virtually impossible to apply the militia principle to the technical arms and services of the Red Army, or even to the cavalry. The political necessity of maintaining the predominance of the industrial proletariat had resulted in the concentration of militia formations, not in strict accordance with the mobilisation plan or possible operational requirements, but from the social-economic conditions permitting this political grip to be tightened. In the Moscow Military District there were thirteen territorial-militia formations, but only one in the whole of the Siberian Military District.* In areas of heavy concentration of industrial workers — Leningrad, Ivanovo-Voznesensk, Kiev, Moscow itself, Tula, the Urals — this form of military organisation was pushed ahead. Such a political requirement therefore militated against Frunze's own declared idea of using the militia system to remedy the low level of technical training in the Red Army, and, indeed, of the most rudimentary kind of training. Yet, due to this particular configuration of recruitment and organisation, the better-trained stood to receive more training, while the un-trained — and the illiterate[57] — went less well attended. And in the last resort the efficiency and stable development of the territorial-militia depended upon the quality of the cadre army.

The regular Red Army for which Frunze and his fellows had fought so stubbornly lacked on Frunze's own admission both a unified structure and a unified tactical doctrine.[58] It was Frunze's obsession to remedy both of these considerable defects. To this end, the praesidium of the Soviet of Red Army Training and Preparation on 12th July, 1924, formally decided to initiate discussions with the commanders of military districts over the question of the new Red Army infantry. The Red Army Staff accordingly prepared an outline of a possible new form, beginning with the clarification of the role and relation of the team or small combat-group and the platoon, and the employment of the fixed and light machine-gun. In these meetings, as well as in the military press, the role of 'practical infantry' — in defence and in attack — was hotly debated. The arguments centred on three issues; how to exploit the machine-gun in the company, how far command could be detached (the combat-group necessitated this) and what would be the composition of these groups, and how far the echelon of command could be permitted to go. Finally, the heavy machine-gun was incorporated into the section and designed to cover the movement of the infantry groups.[59] This, and the subsequent decisions about the fire-power of the section and the company, were cast in terms of the 'manœuvre' principle to which Frunze and his fellows held so firmly.

* In 1925, there were 32 divisions each based on one *guberniya*, 8 based on two and 4 on three. Recruitment for such things as the regimental schools, however, was 'extra-territorial'.

The overhaul of the rifle division and the rifle corps was announced with Orders No. 1298/203 and 1297/202 respectively of 7th October, 1924.* The division consisted of three rifle regiments, a detached cavalry squadron, a light artillery regiment, a company of sappers and an engineering park, a signal company and divisional artillery up to 54 guns (the 76-mm regimental and divisional gun, the 122-mm howitzer).[60] In the cadre and territorial-militia formations alike a distinction, bearing upon the size of their staff, was made between those stationed on the frontier and the forces maintained in the interior. On 1st October, 1925, the rifle troops of the Red Army consisted of 13 cadre divisions (strengthened staff), 13 cadre divisions with diminished staff strength, 33 territorial divisions of the normal type, 3 with a reduced complement and the administrations of 17 rifle corps. By the same date in 1926, a slight adjustment had been made in the composition of the staff of the rifle corps; and 3 territorial divisions, plus 7 reserve territorial regiments, had been added to the over-all strength of the rifle troops of the Red Army.[61]

The cavalry forces of the Red Army also needed unifying, existing as they did in divisions using either four or six companies and with variations in the cavalry squadrons incorporated in infantry formations. The cavalry lacked fire power; a new organisation was needed for automatic weapons, in addition to improving the command system. More than half the cavalrymen were untrained, light machine-guns were in short supply (as everywhere in the Red Army) and in divisions as many as three-quarters of the required troop horses were missing. The real difficulty was to decide upon the role of cavalry in modern war. Not until April 1925 did a full-scale conference assemble, drawing in some 300 commanders as well as Budenny, Frunze, Voroshilov, Apanasenko and Shchadenko, in order to debate the new tactical and organisational ideas which were being worked out. The first results, embodied in the orders promulgated in October 1925, divided the cavalry into newly-organised divisions and the so-called 'strategic cavalry'.† The shortage of horses, however, necessitated re-uniting all Red Army cavalry, in October 1926, into a single organisational form, with the cavalry corps (3 cavalry divisions, howitzer-artillery force, and a signals squadron) as the major tactical unity. By the same date the cavalry forces of the Red Army had been brought up to 3 corps' administrations, 9 cavalry divisions (each with 4 regiments), 8 detached cavalry brigades (with 3 regiments apiece); in addition, there were by this time 2 territorial cavalry divisions, each made up of 6 regiments.[62] Although the Red Army's cavalry force had been rescued from the doldrums and actual degeneration, much remained

* See Appendix II on the re-organisation of the Soviet infantry.

† See Appendix II on the strength and organisation of Soviet cavalry.

to be done in fixing its role in war, exploiting the increase in fire-power and laying down a concise form of organisation.

As for armoured fighting vehicles and their place in the Red Army, all was as yet in flux. The Red Army had fought its first tank engagement on 4th July, 1920, in a combined action by the 2nd Tank Squadron, Armoured Train No. 8 and Armoured Car Squadron No. 14.[63] A few primitive tanks had been produced, and trophies of the Civil War renovated. In 1923 the first systematic study of tank design and Red Army requirements was undertaken by the War Industry Main Directorate (*GUVP*), resulting in an analysis of the tank warfare of 1914–18, preparations to train a cadre of tank-men, design-study and plans to produce an experimental model. In this manner a special Technical Bureau for tank-study came into being, and managed to produce a suggested design by May 1925. Frunze himself noted the progress in the tractor-industry (part of which was a concession to Krupp in Southern Russia).[64] Although the first plans seem to have been heavily influenced by the heavy tanks which had appeared in the 1914–18 War, in 1927 the Red Army saw the first models of a light tank, the T–18.

In addition to the militia system and the re-organisation of the cadre army, Frunze's reforms produced a further singular feature — the re-organisation of the 'national formations', units of the Red Army formed out of nationalities other than the Great Russians and recruited on a national basis. Frunze attempted to explain that the Red Army was not a *Russian* army, that is, a single-nationality force.[65] However, the principle which had been established in the Civil War had tended to produce the idea of the unity of the Soviet armed forces, partly as a result of the struggle against decentralisation and local autonomies. The need to exploit the man-power resources of the Soviet Union in every possible manner lay beneath Frunze's disclaimer about a 'Russian' army. Nor were the political dangers so noticeably absent — in a real sense, the Red Army was fully operational* in 1922–4 in its 'pacifications' of the Central Asian revolts against Soviet rule.[66] An immediate stumbling-block, however, was the shortage of command staff, for the possible political value of 'national formations' would be lost if Georgian or Caucasian units were run by Great Russians merely as an extension of the Russian Red Army. Ukrainian and Belorussian divisions could be set up with relative ease; independent squadrons of cavalry were formed in Georgia,[67] Daghestan and Bokhara. The solution to the problem

* From this front came V. K. Baranov (commander of the 1st Guards Cavalry Corps in the Soviet-German War), Colonel-General M. P. Konstantinov, Lieutenant-General V. G. Poznyak (now a professor at the General Staff Academy) and Ya. Kuliev (commander of the 21st Cavalry Division, killed at Stalingrad), as well as General A. A. Luchinskii, who took part in the Far Eastern campaign in 1945. Strictly speaking, the military operations continued until September, 1931, when attempts were made to clear the Basmachis out of the Kara-Kum.

lay in permitting only those nationalities who had been obliged to render service under the military obligations prevailing in Imperial Russia to form 'national units'; that criterion at least established that there would be a non-Russian population with certain previous military experience, thus providing a rudimentary solution to the command problem. In all others, Red Army officers went as military instructors, in a manner best typified by their presence in Outer Mongolia, training a prototype Red Army on Soviet lines.[68] In the Five-Year Plan for such formations the impetus was shifted markedly to the Far East, to the republics of Central Asia and the Pri-Volga areas. Policy in the Ukraine and Belorussia settled down to being merely a strengthening of the none too numerous existing formations.[69]

Changes were made in the over-all military boundaries in the Soviet Union and in the manner by which these Military Districts (corresponding to fronts) were run by the Military District apparatus. More than two years elapsed before the re-organisation was complete, bringing a total of eight Military Districts, but a start was made in April 1924, when the Western Front was converted into the Western Military District by Order No. 508 of the *Revvoensoviet*. In June the Western-Siberian was transformed into the Siberian Military District, controlling all military units and administrations in Siberia and the Far East. The Vth Army was disbanded—after six years of life, beginning on the early Eastern Front—and two new corps, the 18th and 19th, were created in and for Siberia. Only in 1926 did the Turkestan Front cease to exist, becoming in turn the Central Asian Military District.[70]

At the head of a Military District stood now either the District Commander or the District *Revvoensoviet*; the Staff of the District included operational, training, mobilisation and recruitment sections, and the commanders of artillery, engineers, signals and chemical warfare troops were separately identified. The District administration ran its Political Department, Military Aviation, Supply, and smaller sections for technical supply, artillery, finance and unit composition. The Civil War machinery, retained without major change, had been streamlined to facilitate a reduction of administrative staff and the representation of the new technical innovations.

The course of these reforms, many of them still in their initial stages, was designed to bring the Red Army into line with other modern European armies. The motives, however, were never far removed from finding an efficient military solution to difficulties stemming directly from the economic retardation in the Soviet Union. This predicament at once raised a storm on the degree of technical progress which could be maintained, and over whether the Red Army could compete technically with other armies. The coming to power of the Red commanders did not mean that the great military debate had ended. 'Marxism and military science' was still a flourishing debating point,[71] but of greater import was the impact of technology and technical advance on ideas about the role of the Red Army. Considerable debate and extended controversy attended the introduction of each point relating to the modernisation of the Red Army. Frunze himself became increasingly pre-occupied with the terms of a future war and the capacity of the Red Army to meet it.[72] Although certainly introducing new ideas into the reformist plans for the Red Army, the intense study of the 1914–18 War contributed most to high-lighting the importance of the rear — industrial mobilisation, strategic planning, the integration of the armed forces with the society in relation to the means at its disposal. To these points Frunze devoted more and more of his attention, and about the choice of technical and strategic priorities yet one more struggle was to be waged. In addition, the political priorities and the chain of political command had to be re-established, adding the usual extra dimension to military affairs in the Soviet establishment.

* * * *

The political organs of the Red Army had failed, in a manner which filled the triumvirate with misgiving, to withstand the strain of the inner-Party crisis. Trotsky's man, Antonov-Ovseenko, had been summarily removed from his post as head of the *PUR* in January 1924. The chief task now was to swamp the supporters of the Opposition both within the army and within the ranks of the Political Administration itself. A purge was mandatory, in order to restore the political apparatus to a position where it could carry out its main function — to secure for the ruling group the political reliability of the Soviet armed forces.

Direct and indirect methods were employed by the new political command, obedient to the wishes of the ruling faction of the Central Committee. On 3rd February, 1924, the explosive Circular No. 200 was annulled and replaced with Order No. 32, which established the principle that political workers in the Soviet armed forces would be appointed from above; this was restitution, not innovation, but the long struggle which had been waged in and about the Political Administration between 'centralists' and 'democratists' was finally brought to a close. In a special campaign of recruitment — ostensibly as a mark of respect to the dead Lenin — Party ranks were thrown open to wellnigh all comers, thus repeating the technique of January 1919 when opposition in the 'cells' had been swamped. The special Leninist recruitment brought up to 4,000 Red Army officers and men into the Party, and 800 into the *Komsomol*.[73] The staff of the Political Administration was cut — that is, purged — by 40 per cent, and a new staff, with strong pre-October 1917 affiliations brought in. Such men were more likely to support a ruling faction which took its stand upon its pre-October political bona fides. The commissar staff of divisions and detached brigades was selectively re-shuffled, with a view to putting in men of known and strong proletarian background, thus shutting out the young political workers from positions of influence.

Bringing the political organisations of the Moscow garrison to heel was no easy task, and yet one vital for the political well-being of the triumvirate. In May 1924 the military section of the Moscow Committee of the Russian Communist Party demanded, as a programme point at the 12th Moscow District Party Conference, that control over political work in all military units and training establishments should be invested in the Moscow Committee itself. In the same way, during the summer mobilisation, the same body invested in a special 'Party centre' control over the political work of units at this time. Such an action earned a heated rebuke from Voroshilov, and it was in June that Voroshilov, commander of the Moscow Military District, was appointed to lead a special commission to work out plans for the closer co-ordination of the military and local Party organs. As the 13th Party Congress had demonstrated, control of the Party machine was effectively in the hands of Stalin and his allies; by knitting up the military and civilian Party functions, they could neutralise the oppositional activity once again. On 11th August, 1924, Voroshilov presented his report, stressing the view that the rift between the military and civilian political organs had produced this situation of shortcoming in the political work and the development of factional strife. The *PUR* was accordingly instructed to draw up a plan to bring about this alignment and to suggest specific measures.[74] An official 'Instruction' gave full force to the view that it was the Political Administration, acting under the indirect control of the Central Committee as its military section, which directed political work; that this work was directed through the regional organs of the *PUR* — Political Administrations of Military Districts, of Fleets, Armies and Divisional Political Sections, and thence to the political sections of individual units. This, therefore, prevented local Party committees (such as that of Moscow) from trying to take over political work.

Frunze himself placed the highest value on the work of the Political Administration,[75] seeing in this dimension of activity a specific method of increasing the efficiency of the 'mixed' military system. Certainly the development of the militia placed new burdens on the political staff, and this was an added reason for insisting upon the co-operation of the local civilian Party and military organs. In no sense could Frunze be aligned with the exponents of the policy of 'liquidation-ism' for the political apparatus of the Red Army. The lesson which was being learnt in these hours of trial for the Red Army was that the political apparatus must be first strengthened and then packed with politically reliable men. The fundamental aim of the political apparatus — control over the Red Army, and the winning of acquiescence by indoctrination — never slipped from sight during the troubled months of 1924. Frunze's dilemma, however, emerged in the question of raising the authority of the commander and yet retaining the force of the political checks. Military necessity and political priority were about to clash.

The inner-Party strife, the disaffection in the villages and the demands made by the peculiar circumstances of the territorial-militia scheme necessitated a radical reformation of the scheme of political instruction in the Soviet armed forces.* The All-Union Conference of Heads of Political Organs, which assembled in November 1924, set out to expand the initial schemes which had been drawn up by the Political Administration;[76] the main theme was devoted to the means whereby Party strength in the armed forces could be developed on a substantial scale. Already a new course of political studies had been drawn up for the winter training programme.[77] A two-year study plan, dealing with Party history, Soviet achievements, international affairs and current Party affairs, stood as the basis of the new schemes. Such a comprehensive, systematised scheme of political education and indoctrination owed its origins to S. I. Gusev, who had been, from the time of the 10th Party Congress, a propagandist for such a state of affairs. It was Gusev who suggested aiming the programme at the peasant soldier, although the internationalist line, for which he pleaded, slipped gradually into the background. A certain sign of the success of this two-year plan was that its renewal in 1926 was attended only by minor modifications of programme.

The deliberation over programmes marked a change in the tempo of the work of the Political Administration. Whereas it had been an urgent task to seal off the political apparatus from contamination by the oppositional enemy, to fasten tight bands of immediate loyalty round the military commissars and senior political staff, henceforth — by deliberate act of the ruling faction — the Red Army was embroiled in the inner-Party struggle. Trotsky did not once attempt, during the crisis of 1924, to draw upon the support in the army, which he still enjoyed, to impose the threat of a

* The basis of the political training had been the 'political hour' (*politchas*). These took place daily, and until 1924, were separately timetabled from the general education and literacy 'hours'. Order No. 2663, 1924, issued by the *RVS*, combined both of these programmes into a single daily session of two hours duration; while *politruks* at company level had taken a large part in this, the duty was transferred to the commanders, especially platoon officers. By 1st October, 1925, two-thirds of the group-leaders in this newly consolidated programme of political education were officers.

military *coup*. In this respect the situation remained what it had been in December 1923. Yet already by the end of 1924, the All-Union Conference of Heads of Political Organs was being called upon to demand the complete withdrawal of Trotsky from even the nominal direction of military affairs.[78] Trotsky, once again incapacitated by physical ailment, made no attempt to restore his fortunes by an appeal to the commissars. Any possible regeneration rising up from the lowest military-political levels, however, was now being checked by the vigorous action of the new body of commissars. The 'cells' were swamped or silenced, and finally dragged into a tighter net of Party and military political arrangements. Trotsky's real hope had gone, or was in the process of being rapidly crushed out.

There was a grave enough danger of the army being split into two camps. The threat of Bonapartism, which was itself a political weapon, did not materialise however. By the decision of the plenary session of the Central Committee, on 17th January, 1925, Trotsky was finally removed from the *Revvoensoviet* — to ensure, the explanation ran, leadership for the Red Army untainted with Trotskyist indiscipline.[79] Trotsky, in his letter of 15th January, to the Central Committee had asked to be relieved of his military duties. Thus Zinoviev had the expulsion which he had earlier urged Stalin to carry out. Six days after the conclusion of the plenum, on 26th January, M. V. Frunze was named Trotsky's successor as Commissar for War and head of the *Revvoensoviet*. It was not so simple a choice as it on first sight seemed.

The defeat of Trotsky wiped out the *raison d'être* of the Stalin-Zinoviev-Kamenev triumvirate, weakened and torn as this had become before the end of 1924. Although Frunze did ultimately succeed to Trotsky's former posts, once again the trick of 1923 was tried on Stalin, when in January 1925 Kamenev proposed that Stalin should become Commissar for War. Thus Stalin would have been cut out of his key position in the General Secretariat.[80] As in 1923, this manœuvre came to nought, yet it marked the end of an uneasy political alliance. Decency of a most rudimentary order dictated that the triumvirate should hold its triple friendships for some months yet, not breaking open the secret of its dissolution so soon upon the event of Trotsky's abrupt dismissal. The changing face of political alignment affected the fortunes of the Political Administration acutely. Already in December 1924 the 'cells' had received new instructions and firm limitations on their activity.[81] The First All-Army Assembly of Cell Secretaries, which met from 26th February–3rd March, 1925, was a time to take stock.

The Central Committee, rather than the *PUR*, provided the initiative for this assembly. It was a political inquest, on the results of which not a little depended. On 10th February, 1925, the Organisation Section of the Central

Committee, the head of the *PUR* Bubnov, the Central Control Commission and the Central Committee of the *Komsomol* (which played a vital part in the so-called military reconstruction), met to consider the results of a deep probe into the work of the 'cells'. In general, the increase in the stability of the Red Army was noted, and the fact that the 'cells' were now broadening their activist work, but the debit side was plain; specialist units lacked 'cells', Party education was dragging, the military 'cells' did little about bringing an improvement in military discipline, *Komsomol* work was not at a high level, and the civilian Party organs still showed alarming dilatoriness in interesting themselves in the territorial-militias and the problems of political indoctrination here. The All-Army Assembly of Cell Secretaries was to look into this state of affairs.[82]

To this Assembly came the secretaries of 'cells' and regimental Party bureaux, *politruks* (political assistants) and those responsible for work among the military and naval *Komsomol*. Twenty-two reports were read to the Assembly, while Frunze delivered two addresses on the territorial system as it bore upon propaganda work in the villages, and the relation of Party organisations and military discipline.[83] Four sub-sections laboured on a study of inner-Party work, on agitation among the non-Party element and in the *Komsomol*, on the problems of militia units and on their connection with agitation among the rural populations. Frunze's resolutions, and four bearing on the items studied in the sub-sections were subsequently officially adopted. A certain intensification of Party work and indoctrination followed on this meeting, one result of which was the gradual increase in the number of 'cells' themselves, which rose from 4,318 in 1925 to 5,419 in 1926. The *PUR* Directive No. 146 of 1st August, 1925, rendered the substantial service of standardising the organisation of Party education into three grades: for candidate-members and those in the first stages of 'political literacy', and the *Komsomol*, the 1st grade Party school, followed by the 2nd grade school and 'Marxist circles' for those pursuing separate study of the required texts and classics. Here the ring had finally closed, since with the completion of a basic plan for the lowest military political levels, the standardisation of Party education and the adoption of the two-year course of political indoctrination, the reformed Political Administration, re-staffed with commissars of 'pre-October affiliations', set out on its new assignments.

A change of much greater import, however, was under preparation. It was obvious that the Central Committee, and indirectly the Central Control Commission, had taken over the virtual running of the political life of the Red Army. The *PUR* had become its executive agency, while in theory the *PUR* remained under the *indirect* control of the Central Committee, acting as its military section. Voroshilov had helped to shape some of the policies aimed at securing the lowest military levels against subversion and disaffection. What bargains, conflicts and enmities were concerned in bringing the *PUR* — department of the *Revvoensoviet* — under the *direct* control of the Central Committee are obscure. The danger of allowing the political and military apparatus to be concentrated in one body was apparent, and had nearly been the cause of disaster in the winter of 1923–4. The work of consolidation, which had been carried out during 1924–5, had been the result of the active intervention of the Central Committee in military-political affairs; the weightiest factor was certainly the exigencies of the struggle of the triumvirate with Trotsky. On 8th September, 1925, the new 'Instruction on the Political Administration of the Workers-Peasants Red Army' was issued;[84] the *PUR*, in its previous form, ceased to exist, becoming the *PURKKA* (although there was many a reference to the old *PUR*). Direct control of the Political Administration was detached from the *Revvoensoviet* of the Soviet Union and placed under the Central Committee's own tight grasp. In such a manner did the establishment of an all-powerful, centralised machinery of political control — *independent of the military* — pass to the Party. The Party dictatorship had triumphed again.

Nevertheless, on the swings and roundabouts of control over and in the Soviet military establishment Frunze had laboured to bring about a massive transformation in the status of the Soviet military command group, with the official introduction of a policy of transition to 'unity of command', hailed then, as now, as one of the great achievements of the Soviet military-political command.[85] To free the commander from his commissar watch-dogs was a delicate question, affecting the status of the commissar as much as it bore upon the problem of military efficiency. The whole matter rested upon the view taken by the Army's political masters of the reliability of the Red commanders, to whom the Red Army had been as yet but half-delivered.

* * * *

Socially, professionally and politically the Soviet officer corps, such as it was, presented an almost bewildering spectacle of divergence and division on the eve of Frunze's reforms. At the end of 1922 only a little more than a half of the officers of the Red Army had been trained in any formal manner, and then not to any high degree; this training had come from the Imperial Russian Army. In the infantry and artillery, the shortage of trained officers was acute; the situation was aggravated by the fact that the Mobilisation Section of the Red Army Staff possessed no accurate figures of the mobilisation requirements for commanding staff as a whole, nor for particular arms. The training of junior command staff was in a parlous state.[86]

One of the urgent tasks was to cut out of the Red Army command staff the 2,598 men who had served either as White officers or in the White military administrations. To bring about the monolithic unity of this body of men — through the re-ordering of the processes of their selection, professional education, military duties, political loyalties and social status — was the task which Frunze set himself. At the very heart of the problem there remained the settlement of the basis of their authority in the politicalised army, such as the Red Army was and is.

Cutting down on the numbers of the central military administration and cutting out of the command staff, at the middle and senior levels, those who were considered expendable or unreliable among the 'military specialists' amounted to nothing less than a purge of the existing Soviet officer corps. The same policy went into effect in the Soviet naval forces. None of it contradicted Frunze's declared policy of opening up command positions of some responsibility to the Red commanders; the displacement of the 'military specialists' permitted younger and heavily Communised officer groups to assume active roles in the Red Army. At the same time, along with the actual changes in personnel, the opportunity was seized to establish the legal and organisational form of the officer corps as such, a formal sign of which had been Order No. 989 which announced a single title for command staff — 'Commander of the Worker-Peasants Red Army'.

The first task meant defining the scope of the duties of the command, political and administrative-supply staffs. There were no regulations governing assignments to duty or the length of service in any particular assignment. Attestation (set up in 1919) was similarly chaotic. The territorial system made classification very urgent, for here command cadres would be rotated through several assignments, necessitating controlled changes. Selection of officers (recruiting and appointments or promotions) depended on the smooth functioning of the attestation boards, which, in turn, must be able to appeal to set and legalised categories and duration of service. These were the questions which were debated and pursued by a sub-commission on officers' service, a body which met formally on 19th February, 1924 — only a few days after the commission to prepare the major reform plans.

Order No. 1244 of the *Revvoensoviet*, dated 2nd October 1924, set out the new frame of the Red Army officer corps — divided henceforth into the command staff, political, administrative, medical and veterinary.[87] For definition of service and assignments, the command staff was divided into fourteen categories, the first three categories being junior, up to six middle, to nine senior and thereafter higher command staff. The political staff now comprised twelve categories, being without the first three junior grades, however; in composition, political staff was classified by the terms of command — political (commissars and members of a *Revvoensoviet*), political-educational, and juridical-political (members of military tribunals, military procurators and legal consultants).[88] Administrative, medical and veterinary staffs were also accorded junior, middle, senior and higher posts, each enjoying thirteen categories. As a result of these changes, the separate class of staff officers was done away with, transference to staff duties corresponding to the categories for the command staff as a whole; there was no longer a single 'staff line', separated from the command and combat duties by a special distinction of status. Lengths of duty for the categories were also stipulated; the juniors served five years, the fifth category four years, the sixth and seventh for three years, and the eighth and the ninth for four years and at the tenth and above the *Revvoensoviet* decided the length of assignment.[89]

Promotion, fixed in relation to the officer's attendance at the relevant military educational establishments, and excluding the first three categories, was entered on a list of candidates, the supervision of which lay with the attestation command. By January 1925 attestation had been fixed to three stages; compilation, the scrutinising of this record at the attestation commission and confirmation by suitable reference.* To handle this, attestation commissions were set up at regimental divisional, corps, and Military District levels and in the Higher Attestation Commission of the *Revvoensoviet* of the Soviet Union. These commissions followed a standard pattern, thus doing away with the separate examination of the specialist and officers of particular arms; political, specialist and command staff passed through the same machine, an idea which certainly owed not a little to Frunze's ideal and idea of the Soviet officer, a 'full man', a citizen of sound basic qualification.[90]

Much, therefore, depended upon the system of military education which was ultimately to bind up this body of men into the forms and frames supplied by the new edicts on the officer corps. Once again, the first preoccupation was with the creation of a standardised military school; the next and immediate task to improve the quality of students and instructors. In 1924 15·77 per cent of the cadets had failed to qualify, indicating the kind of 'instability' which the Frunze reforms were elsewhere seeking to eradicate.[91] By a decision of 26th November, 1924, arising out of the

* The 1925 *Instruction* on attestation also established that in normal circles, attestation of the officers would take place annually. A superior could attest a subordinate, but only if the latter had served with him for not less than six months. Candidates from military schools could not be attested earlier than the course of the year in which they actually began their service in a military unit. In view of the fact that attestation in the Soviet armed forces is obviously a complicated business, involving not only recognisable processes of promotion, but also political and security screening, a case of attestation, drawn from captured Soviet military records, is included in the General Appendix. Although this dates from a later period, the procedure is the same and it will be seen how far back the necessary Party and security clearances go. Both command and political staffs were attested.

plenary meeting of the *Revvoensoviet*, the minimum educational qualifications were fixed for entry into the ordinary military school; great care was taken with establishing the political education of the *kursanty*, the future Red Army commanders. In a manner not dissimilar to the discussions on political work in the armed forces, the First All-Union Meeting of Red Army Military Instruction Centres was held in Moscow in April 1925, to discuss the new programme of unified military education. This gathering made several recommendations on changes in policy, although such modifications were confined basically to details — more space for political education in curricula, officers with combat experience in the Civil War to be drafted to the instructional staffs, and officer-cadets to be sent to units — especially militia units — on probation.[92] The final form of the unified school plan was adopted by the 'Instruction on Red Army military schools', dated 30th November, 1925.

The military schools gave instruction in military and combat matters, political subjects and supplied scientific and military-political education. The unified school system was devoted to giving general rather than specialist training, but in the combat-training sections there were divisions for the separate arms — infantry with a three- or four-battalion staff, artillery with two batteries, cavalry with two squadrons, signals and engineers made up of three companies. In their composition, infantry and cavalry comprised three classes, training officer-cadets, junior and senior staff; the artillery and technical services had four such classes, training the middle-grade in addition. Great though the labour was in building up a comprehensive educational — and politically active — system for the Soviet officer, the critical test lay in doing the same for the training of the present and future senior officers of the highest command levels. The Red Army was on the verge of discovering whether or not it had its own military intelligentsia, whatever the previous military debates may have indicated about the level of military talent in the Red command. Nevertheless, there did exist the Red Army Academies — the Military Academy; the Academies of Military Engineering, Artillery, Military-Administrative, Military Aviation, and Military Medicine; the Naval Academy; and the Tolmachev Military-Political Institute — by March 1924.[93]

Such institutions, although bearing Red Army names, were founded quite literally in the Imperial Russian Academies for the most part, and the staff showed the same discrepancies in its social and political aspects. At once in 1924 177 of the 777 instructors were retired for reasons of age, political unreliability or academic failings.[94] On 19th April, 1924, Frunze himself was appointed as temporary head of the Military Academy, and on 1st October inaugurated the new programmes of instruction, upon which

Frunze had not a few ideas of his own.[95] At his bidding a Chair of Military Industry and a Faculty of Supply were both added to the Military Academy. Into the curriculum came studies of the organisation of the rear and a fuller range of instruction in the science of strategy. The Military Academy, in addition to these immediate innovations, underwent a complete re-organisation during the months of 1924–5, by which time three main elements had emerged. The first involved the three basic courses covering instruction at the regimental, divisional and corps level; the second was built round the new Faculty of Supply and the third centred on the Eastern Faculty, a military-political and linguistic course designed for officers destined for duty in the Far and Near East and Central Asia. The curriculum was designed to cater for the requirements of the combat, staff and scientific-instructor personnel of the higher command levels, to train supply specialists and to turn out the Eastern specialists needed by the Staff or for special operations in the Far East. The Red Army at that time was sending military missions to China, where they played an active part in directing the military aspects of the Chinese national revolution. By 1926 the Red Army had eight military academies, which, for budgetary reasons, were supplemented by the military faculties of state universities, such foundations as the Military-Electrotechnical Section of the Leningrad Electrotechnical Institute, the military section of the Kazan Veterinary University.[96] Most pertinent of all, perhaps, was the innovation which dated from February 1924, when the Institute of Junior Scientific Assistants was set up in conjunction with the Military Academy with the task of preparing a new corps of Red Army academy instructors to replace the ex-Imperial professors who lacked or refused to have any firm ideological conviction and training. It was a task to which Frunze, conscious perhaps of the imbalance of the Soviet military intelligentsia, assigned the very greatest importance.[97]

The very centre of the problem of the Red Army officer corps, however, did not rest with these significant but purely quantitative changes. The basic question was the limits and divisions of the officer's authority, whether senior, middle or junior grade, and hitherto, a duality of power — the commander and the commissar — had ruled the scene. Already in 1919 voices had been raised in furious support of unity of command, and during 1922 and 1923 progress had been made in this direction; in practice, however, the innovation was confined to Communist commanders finishing a course at a military academy or senior command course and being in possession of the requisite Party standing. The new Instruction on Commissars of 1922 had mentioned unity of command as an immediate prospect, and Order No. 820 by the *Revvoensoviet* in 1923 had vested in the command organisations of Military Districts the right of nominating officers (including non-

Party commanders) for unitary command appointments.[98] None of these moves approached in any way the full scope of the problem, nor did they accord with the wishes of the Red commanders, nor yet did they allay the fears of the commissar staff for their future.

Frunze, in a most important declaration of policy over unitary command, laid down the form which this transformation would take in the Red Army. He envisaged three forms: the first, where the commander was invested with the military-administrative *and* political work and responsibility; the second, where the commander was given full control over the military-administrative work, and a third — applicable to military administrations and institutions — where the command structure would be left intact, but the political organs would be withdrawn.[99] The first type, Frunze warned, would be comparatively rare, and the second much more the rule. As early as 8th April, 1924 the *Revvoensoviet* had promulgated Directive No. 533 on 'the drawing of the commander into political-educational work';[100] political staffs were to introduce commanders to the kind of work done by commissars and political staffs. In June 1924 the Central Committee gave its full recognition to the principle of unitary command, installing it as the universal principle of the structure of the Red Army; the actual execution of the form was left to the *Revvoensoviet* to decide. Frunze left little doubt as to the aim of this policy:

> We must have at the head of our units men, possessing sufficient independence, steadfastness, initiative and responsibility. . . . Our former system of dual power, called forth by political considerations, prevented the formation of such command staff. Therefore that course, which we have taken with you and started making effective by joint efforts, is the essential element in strengthening our military might.[101]

The joint efforts consisted of a controlled experiment of some six months duration, with the commander being drawn into the political work — rather than the commissar being expelled. Directive No. 1515 of the *Revvoensoviet*, dated for 15th December, 1924, announced that positive results had been obtained for the trial period and that commanders were taking an active part in the political work of units. At this point, the minimum requirements for commanders in the political field were laid down, as a prerequisite for the next step.

The November (1924) assembly of political workers, which had debated the new political programme, turned its attention to this new policy. The commissars were alarmed. Their suggestion was to restrict the new trend to Party commanders only. With this, they were only repeating what the meeting of the Western Military District divisional and corps political staff had said on 21st–22nd September, when they demanded confining it to commanders who were Party members — investing it in non-Party commanders only when the latter occupied posts (such as staff duties) removed from command over the masses.[102] These were the first signs of the protracted resistance of the senior political staff of Belorussia (the 'Tolmachev group') to any extensive increase in the independence of the commander. The commissars, the momentary prophets of their own doom, felt themselves to be fighting a rear-guard action. If the commanders took the new policy as a sign that the institution of commissars was passing away, thus setting up new conflicts, the non-Party element of the command staff felt, even at this early stage, the dangers of discrimination. Frunze attempted to close, from the moment of its opening, this very serious breach in the officer-corps, for which he had prescribed such forceful measures to accomplish their unity as an officer group. He denied that there existed any intention of 'Communising' the Red Army command staff:

> Must the question of unitary command apply only to the Party members of the command staff?
>
> That question is set in the main against the general problem of the relations between the Party and the non-Party elements of the command staff. . . . It is absolutely impossible — indeed not necessary — for us to count on the fact that the entire command staff of the army and the navy will be Party members. . . . The place of the non-Party man on the command staff in the ranks of the Red Army has been, is and will always be safe. To no degree whatsoever is unitary command connected with a general Communisation of the Red Army command staff.[103]

These encouraging but inaccurate words (there was no intention of applying this command policy to the naval forces) did little to ease the situation. Frunze's public disclaimer merely serves to illustrate how deep the cleavage ran.

The November-December 1924 plenary meeting of the *Revvoensoviet* set the frame for the subsequent changes. For the commissar was reserved his place as representative of the Party, retaining full responsibility for that; there was, ran the resolution, no intention of discrediting or liquidating the role of the commissar — only his functions would be changed. His first Civil War function — supervising the heterogeneous command staff — was now revised in favour of complete authority for Party and political affairs in the Red Army.[104] In particular, the system of collective command — embodied in the *Revvoensoviet* idea itself — was kept intact for Military Districts, Fronts and Armies; military-political combinations at these high levels suffered no change. The Instruction, which issued out of this plenum, laid down the practical measures to be taken — applied to Party members and the non-Party alike of the command staff, initially closed to the junior levels, and geared to the machinery of the Attestation Boards. These boards would scrutinise possible names and draw up the lists of candidates. On 12th January, 1925, unitary command was applied to the central military organs, thus making a start on its wider implementation. Directive No. 234, under the signature of M. V. Frunze and dated 2nd March, 1925, formally freed the Red Army command staff from supervision in combat and administrative matters; the commissar retained control over the political affairs. General orders and directives — promotions, operational or mobilisation documents — would be signed by the commander and commissar jointly; matters bearing directly on combat or routine administrative matters would be signed by the commander or military chief alone. No such transition would be permitted either in the naval forces or in the 'national formations', where commissars retained their former status and functions intact.[105]

Andreyev's letter, originating from the Central Committee, gave full sanction to Directive No. 234 and followed four days later. It formally confirmed the dual form of application of unitary command: the non-Party commander received full administrative and operational autonomy, with the commissar in charge of the political work; the Party commander could become the combined commander-commissar, attending to both the military and political work of the unit, with only a political assistant (*Politruk*). In the Red Navy and 'national formations' the introduction of unitary command would proceed 'more slowly'.[106] After this insistent sound and fury had begun to die away, the reckoning made on 1st October, 1925, showed what little progress had in fact been made. Considered at the separate levels, the figures looked impressive; 73·3 per cent of the corps commanders, 44·5 per cent of the divisional, 80 per cent of the brigade and 33·4 per cent of the regimental commanders were now masters in their own military house. Yet, by the end of 1925, taking the figures for the entire command staff, only 2·67 per cent had achieved this status (in numerical terms, 1,184 of the 44,326 Soviet officers).[107] This could hardly be taken to signify the triumph of the commander over the commissar, although not a few commanders chose to interpret these few changes as a hint of radical transformations and began to behave in a thoroughly military and self-possessed manner, often at the expense of the political staff. At the highest command levels, 14 per cent of the very senior officers enjoyed this new privilege, while at the middle grade this proportion — slight enough — petered out to an insignificant 0·83 per cent. The fears of the commissars of Belorussia, their despondency about their 'lack of prospects' (*besperspektivnost*), were without real foundation.* There can be little doubt, to judge

* It is important to note that Trotsky was never an advocate for withdrawing the commissars, and whatever his ultimate schemes for the system, this was not one of them.

from Frunze's guarded remarks, that the misgivings of the political branch had done much to induce the calculated procrastination in the application of the principle of unitary command. These, therefore, were only the preliminary skirmishes in the coming battles which would be waged for the integrity of the Soviet officer corps. The old conflicts between the 'Red commander' and the 'military specialist' were giving way to new rivalries and insecurities between the Party and non-Party commander — this in a system where all commands were ordained unified, but some of which were more unified than others.

* * * *

In the summer of 1925 Frunze fell ill. At the end of October he was dead. An announcement, signed by the Central Committee and published in *Pravda* on 1st November, 1925, gave the news that Frunze had died of heart-failure on the night of 31st October. Trotsky later made the charge that Frunze had been the victim of a medical murder; suffering from an intestinal complaint, he had been advised to abstain from surgery since his weakened heart would not stand the strain of chloroform. Stalin, nevertheless, obtained an opinion from a special concilium of hand-picked doctors that surgical treatment was very necessary; by Party edict, to which the head of the Soviet war-machine could not fail to submit, Frunze was obliged, even in the face of his complete unwillingness, to undergo this operation which ended in his death.[108] As the motive for this sinisterly-contrived killing, Trotsky adduced Frunze's determination to protect the army from the over-zealous attentions of the Security Service, and Frunze's support for Zinoviev. Certainly such an eventuality — Stalin's ex-partner of the triumvirate having power in the military machine — would have created a dangerous situation, undoing all that the triumvirate's policies had achieved by their unsavoury but effective tactics.

Control of the military machine was still and would so remain a vital aspect of the struggle for power. There were many reasons why Frunze's death would have been, at least politically, not an unwelcome event. Both Zinoviev and Stalin had manœuvred to take possession of the military apparatus, as part of the struggle to dispossess Trotsky in the beginning. The rupture of the triumvirate made new disposition most necessary. Towards the end of his career Frunze himself was showing signs of an independence of spirit and antagonism towards interference in the army. If anything, Frunze was being very gradually but finally militarised out of his Communism, and his minimum requirements for Soviet defence, cutting as they did across political alignments, anticipated in outline form the subsequent tensions and discords. But such hints alone and the inconclusiveness of the evidence as a whole leave Frunze's death an open, if a rather macabre and suggestive question.[109]

The struggle at the very apex of the military command at once took on a new intensity. Zinoviev favoured the nomination of Lashevich, senior political commissar and participant in the Red command's assault upon Trotsky, as Frunze's successor. To counter this Stalin, possibly cherishing the idea of Ordzhonikidze as Commissar for War,[110] favoured the choice of Voroshilov by way of temporary compromise. The Central Committee made what was in fact a double election, appointing Voroshilov as Frunze's successor with effect from 6th November, 1925, and choosing Lashevich as his deputy.[111] On 21st November the new membership of the *Revvoensoviet* of the Soviet Union was likewise confirmed; with Voroshilov at its head, the new command group consisted of P. I. Baranov (Red Air Force commander since 24th December, 1924), Bubnov, Budenny, Yegorov, V. I. Zof (head of the naval forces), S. S. Kamenev, Ordzhonikidze, Tukhachevsky and Unshlikht. This marked the final consolidation of previous changes, which had been taking place throughout the previous months; on 7th February, D. F. Os'kin had been appointed head of the military and naval supply branch. P. E. Dybenko — having completed a higher educational course and then appointed successively commander of the 6th, 5th and 10th Rifle Corps — on 4th May took over the Artillery Administration of Red Army Supply.[112] P. I. Baranov had been formally confirmed in his posts as commander and commissar of the Air Force on 21st March. On 13th November Vitovt Putna was appointed to command the Military-Training Administration — and on the same day Tukhachevsky's appointment as head of the Red Army Staff became effective.[113] Voroshilov's old enemy thus rose to the head of the Red Army's new and powerful staff centre. In view of the divergent political and professional loyalties embedded in it, this was not, by any means, a command group which could long remain immune to bitter internal divisions.

The choice of Voroshilov as successor to Frunze could scarcely have been made on the grounds of surpassing military merit and capacity. Apart from his insubordination at Tsaritsyn and elsewhere, and his questionable part in the 1920 Polish campaign, Voroshilov had failed to impress himself upon the military scene except as a form of political soldier. During the first critical phase of the Frunze reforms, Voroshilov's assignment had been political also, and his posting to the command of the Moscow Military District a recognition of his personal toughness rather than intrinsic military value. During the acrid debates with Trotsky, Voroshilov's remarks, even allowing for the prevailing temper of those exchanges, were not distinguished either by consistency of argument or by any clarity of conception of the future role of the Red Army in modern war. In complete contrast, Frunze's ideas, if at first undeveloped and lacking in imagination, subsequently showed striking advances in understanding and the implications for the Soviet Union of a war of machines. Trotsky's original castigation of Voroshilov — that he was capable of handling a regiment only — was to be put to a searching and fateful test, now that Voroshilov was head of the Soviet military machine.

Moreover, with his new appointment, Voroshilov, and with him the new command, stood at the centre of a political whirlpool. The former triumvirate had broken up. Stalin found new allies in Bukharin, Tomsky and Rykov. The 14th Party Congress, which met from 18th–31st December, 1925, became a hurricane of accusation, recrimination and unrestrained outburst which swept before the Party. Zinoviev and Kamenev, concerned to strip Stalin of his power, were heavily defeated. Kamenev, hitherto the chief power in the Moscow political machine, was dispossessed by Stalin, who set Uglanov, his own nominee, in Kamenev's place. Trotsky sat silent and amazed during the amazing interchanges of the 14th Congress.[114] Voroshilov, supporter of the Stalin bloc, and Lashevich, protagonist of Zinoviev, clashed head-on. Battered at the Party Congress, Zinoviev, however, could still command the support of Leningrad, where he was president of the Soviet. It was essential to prise him out of this. Stalin therefore despatched Kirov, Old Bolshevik and secretary of the Baku Party committee, to still the opposition in Leningrad. In the spring of 1926, Leningrad yielded to the will of the Central Committee and the decisions of the 14th Congress. Trotsky finally spoke out against instigating reprisals and thus came to Zinoviev's aid, a step against which he had been advised by Bukharin.[115] Lashevich, senior commissar of the Leningrad Military District and the garrison, was forced out of his position — though he remained Voroshilov's deputy still.

The 'new Opposition', which was compounded of Trotsky, Zinoviev and Kamenev, came into being after Zinoviev's defeat in Leningrad in the late spring of 1926. These startling political allies displayed to Trotsky the extremes of panic, confusion and optimism. The latter worked hard to persuade the ex-triumvirs that a struggle of some arduousness and duration faced them. While no irrevocable step was taken to breach the one-party system (and Stalin could gamble on this not taking place), there was, nevertheless, a radical departure from the oppositionist tactics of 1923–4 — when Trotsky had restrained his supporters from taking the struggle into the army. On this occasion Lashevich, enjoying a considerable power as Voroshilov's deputy, did proceed to attempt to build up strength for the opposition in the armed forces. At the July plenary meeting of the combined

Central Committee and Central Control Commission, Stalin used the tale of Lashevich's clandestine activity and semi-conspiracy, as well as a two-year-old letter seized in Baku and signed by Medvedev, to expose to full public gaze the machinations of the opposition. This provided the opportunity to remove Lashevich from his post as Deputy Commissar for War and to oust him from his candidate-membership of the Central Committee.[116] But the major target could not be passed over. While the iron was hot, Zinoviev was branded with the same infamy and expelled from the *Politburo* of the Central Committee. This decision was driven through on 23rd July, 1926. Three months later to the day, at a similar plenary session, Zinoviev was removed from his post as president of the *Komintern* and the fate which he had suffered on 23rd July was now inflicted on Trotsky.[117]

The abortive move to work within the army had ultimately played into Stalin's hands. The Zinoviev-Lashevich combination at the highest command level was erased. Zinoviev's assurance, born of having Trotsky — the founder and organiser of the Red Army — as well as Deputy War Commissar Lashevich by his side, came to nought.[118] Voroshilov's temporary or compromise appointment now took on a different aspect at this defeat of the opposition. The last scenes had yet to be played, but through the person of Voroshilov and more particularly through his growing mastery of the levers of power, Stalin had captured the army, where his opponents had many times failed. Voroshilov enjoyed Stalin's confidence, and it was this fact which could make mediocrity into power of an increasingly stern order.

* * * *

While the political battles raged, considerable progress had been made with the expansion and elaboration of Frunze's original schemes. In one sense this was inevitable, for the changes carried with them a considerable momentum. By 1st October, 1926, the military-administrative map of the Soviet Union had taken on its decidedly modern aspect. By this time the Turkestan Front, kept active by reason of the 'pacifications' of rebellious populations, was converted into the Central Asian Military District. G. D. Bazilevich commanded Moscow, the garrison and the district, B. M. Shaposhnikov had taken over the Leningrad Military District (a significant appointment of a non-Party senior commander), A. I. Kork the Western, I. E. Yakir the Ukraine and the Pri-Volga, I. P. Uborevich the Northern Caucasus, N. N. Petin the Siberian Military District and K. A. Avksent'evskii the newly-formed Central Asian Military District. The only independent army — the Red Banner Army of the Caucasus — was under the command of M. K. Levandovskii.[119]

The major changes, however, centred about the Red Army Staff. Directive No. 390 of 12th July, 1926, set out the new combination of functions, by which the Red Army Staff became the main point of concentration for *all* the functions dealing with the preparation of the Soviet Union as well as the Soviet armed forces for war. All organs which included any aspect of this within their competence, yet were momentarily split up among other Administrations, were combined into the Staff. All others were expressly excluded — as was the Military-Topographic Administration. The Staff itself was organised into four departments — Operations, Organisation-Mobilisation, Communications and Intelligence — with a very important and active section for the compilation of manuals and regulations.*

The control of combat training and the various inspectorates, as well as routine administration, was combined into the Main Administration of the Red Army. The *Revvoensoviet* of the Soviet Union had under its supervision and control the Supply Administration, the Naval, Air Force, Medical and Veterinary Administrations; and the administrations of the Commissariat for Military and Naval Affairs and that of the *Revvoensoviet* itself.[120] The Political Administration (*PU RKKA*) occupied a rather different position. Since its change of name, this body had come under the direct supervision of the Central Committee in 1925, thus doing away with the former indirect arrangement. Viewed from the military-administrative aspects, this attempt to erect a military monolith conveyed the impression of strong German influence, and it was itself an irony that such a scheme should have been introduced under the signature of Voroshilov, who had so stubbornly contested Trotsky's earlier centralisation. Essentially, however, such an arrangement developed logically (with the exception of the Political Administration, which had become a casualty of politics) out of Frunze's earlier requirements for the Staff and the extensive re-organisation needed to cope with the idea of modern war as a process involving the whole nation.

Voroshilov's inheritance, nevertheless, was a military empire already in the process of being partitioned. Of the four main branches of this military-political system — operational, administrative, political and security — the last two had been lopped off; the Political Administration had been placed under the direct supervision of the Central Committee, while the security net-work operated through the Special Sections (*OO*), subordinated to the command of the Security Service (*OGPU*). These *OGPU* (later *GPU*) organs did not operate under the control of the political authority but in co-operation with it. Both the Security and the Political organs worked

* See Appendix II on the Red Army Staff, and the administrative machine.

systematically on the control of the command staff at all levels, and on the rank-and-file, a process which was intensified by the presence of oppositional elements — both real and imaginary — in the Red Army. As the Security Service developed as a virtual state within a state, possessing its own picked armed forces, rivalry with the armed forces grew, occasioning, in particular, a bitter struggle over the control of Intelligence.

Much, therefore, depended on the outcome of the protracted business of settling unitary command into the Red Army. Progress in 1925 had been undeniably slow due to three failings; the military commander, although in certain cases entitled to take over political duties, lacked the necessary training, the commissar, where seconded to command duties lacked military training, and above all the Party membership of the Soviet officer corps increased only relatively slowly.* Speeding up the tempo of unitary command went hand in hand with an augmentation of this Party strength. The combination was not purely fortuitous, thereby giving the lie to Frunze's earlier statements about the lack of intention to Communise the officer corps. Without such an increase, unitary command would have remained more of a formula and even less of a fact. As for the commissars, they had appeared to lose ground because of their being purged, and because of their low level of military education. In November 1925 the Higher Attestation Commission had nominated by that date only one officer of the political branch to unitary command of a corps, one for a division, two for a brigade and four to regiments.[121] Yet Ivan Stepanovich Koniev, Party member since 1918, military commissar in the Civil War, brigade and divisional commissar during the transition, was able to transfer to the command line through this process, and begin by 1926 the command-climbing which made him a Soviet Marshal.[122] Although towards the end of 1926 the percentage of unitary command among senior officers, who were Party members, had begun to rise steeply, in general the later stage of the reform did not develop as straight competition between the commander and the commissar. New regulations, at that time in preparation and introduced by Voroshilov, cut at the base of unitary command.

Voroshilov's equivalent of Frunze's Directive No. 234 was the Circular Letter No. 11 of 13th May, 1927, which made unitary command sound an enormous success. Once again, the relations between the commander and the commissar had to be adjusted. The commander could now 'free the commissar' from the burden of signing all orders, *except* those dealing directly with political affairs. For a Party commander without a commissar but with a political assistant (*Politruk*) the commander retained the general supervision of the military and political training, but the *Politruk* took up

* See Appendix II for data on the Soviet officer corps in this period.

the practical side, reporting to the commander on 'the political condition' of the unit. In the case of dispute between the commander and the *Politruk* on any item whatsoever of political work, the dispute was to be referred to the higher political organ and the matter reported to the Military District *Revvoensoviet*. Thus, the question was taken to a body which was not directly responsible to the military—to the Party-supervised political machine. In effect the commander fell under two automatic censures, the one military, the other exercised by a non-military body (in addition to the Party discipline imposed as a matter of course).[123] The commander had not triumphed. In the political sphere he had only formal rights; the Central Committee supervised the political apparatus, and his 'political characterisation'* was as important as ever for his promotion.

Again as a continuation of the work of Frunze, the basic and higher military education of the command staff proceeded apace, although serious defects still remained. By 1926 the academy system had been re-formed round six major centres: the Frunze Military Academy (re-named in honour of Frunze), the Dzerzhinskii Military-Technical, the Zhukovskii Military-Aviation, the Naval and Military-Medical Academies, with the Tolmachev Institute being re-named and re-organised into the Red Army Military-Political Academy.[124] These were supplemented by a scheme for utilising university faculties for further education of the Soviet officer-corps. The annual output of these academies amounted to some 2,000 military graduates. In order to speed up the training of more senior officers, at the beginning of the academic year 1925–6 the Senior Courses, run by the Military-Political Academy and the Military Academy separately, were combined into a joint course, a senior training programme with military and political subjects. At the Military District level, as a result of extensive consultations which had begun in August, 1924, the 'repeater courses' for middle-grade officers were standardised, both in subject (infantry and cavalry only) and length—ten months duration. The idea of forming a Soviet Cadet Corps (reminiscent of the Imperial Russian Army), to train a military élite from a relatively early age, was not accepted at this particular moment.[125]

As a result of the general contest of interests, and out of the struggle between military priorities and political necessities, the Soviet command, with its re-constituted officer-corps, could look back upon a few triumphs. The Red command had succeeded in giving the Red Army a much more stable structure, by establishing the 'mixed' military system with a degree of success, and by re-ordering the establishment in the interests of efficiency and modernisation. Possibly the greatest achievement was to accomplish so

* This *Partkharakteristika* is included as part of the case contained in the General Appendix dealing with attestation.

much on a limited budget, a test which Frunze had passed adequately. Yet the inner-Party feuds and rivalries had torn gaps in the Red Army; the great shift in the ultimate control of the political apparatus can be traced directly to the exigencies of the creation and the dissolution of the Triumvirate. The prevailing instability of the high command was due, in no small measure, to factors and situations expressly political. The Red command, once so anxious to capture the Red Army, and having virtually succeeded, entered into a new captivity under new masters.

★ ★ ★ ★

Part of the complaint against the 'military specialist' had been his occupation of places which should, by rights, have gone to the Red commanders; another part concerned the same specialists' 'monopolisation of military knowledge'. Such a charge had issued from the Party 'cell' of the Military Academy itself and been addressed as a report to the Central Committee.[126] The reduction of the role of the ex-Imperial officer — although he was by no means banished from the Red Army — did not, however, mean an end to the strident debate over doctrines. The senior levels of the Soviet command were disturbed by political divergences, disputes and differences over the significance of strategy, the implications of the technical backwardness of the Red Army, the role of the different arms, and the over-all methods of organising for war.

The re-casting of the military entities, a process which had begun in 1921 and reached its first peak with Frunze's reforms, suggested that there was consistency of opinion on the new tactical roles and the functions of the various arms. This, however, was not the case. The great re-thinking over the cavalry took many months and then reached only an indecisiveness, marked by new experiments. Innovations in the infantry were based also on exploiting the fire-power of the light and heavy machine-gun, but of the former there were not enough and the latter were being worn to pieces. The fashion of 'group tactics' — using small groups of 8–12 men, detached into separate fire-groups and acting independently — caused a rumpus about the effects this would have upon the command organisation and training-techniques. It was especially fallible, not only because of the shortage of the requisite weapons, but because the professional standards of the junior officers were so low. 'Group tactics', 'strategic cavalry', even the 'unified military doctrine' itself raised storms which took place at various levels and in various places, not the least important being the pages of the professional journals and the pages of the military newspaper *Krasnaya Zvezda* (Red Star) and the discussions leading to the eventual publication of the Red Army's manuals and regulations.

At a meeting of the Chief Commission for Manuals, which had been first set up under Trotsky's rule, Frunze on 25th April, 1924, presided over the session which fixed the terms for the rapid completion and publication of the requisite manuals. It was decided to publish the manuals for the separate arms as Combat Regulations (*Boevoi Ustav*), the first part dealing with formation and deployment, the second with operations. The next decision called for a sub-commission for each arm, Budenny being appointed there and then the supervisor of the work of the cavalry commission. A three-week period was suggested for the collection of the basic ideas and guiding principles for various manuals. Finally, the task of preparing the *Field Service Regulations*, the general guide for all arms, was handed over to a special sub-commission also, which was to produce a three-part work. The first part was to be a resumé of other manuals on separate arms, this being essential for the co-ordination of military work, the second part was to be devoted to the co-operation of all arms, and the third to the leadership of large bodies of troops on a strategic scale.[127]

The resultant publications were given the deliberate qualification of 'provisional', although the Red Army Staff department handling the new manuals gave it to be known that this is in no way detracted from their authoritativeness. The infantry manual, adopted in 1924, was the first of the new documents to be affirmed and put into effect. Handbooks on camouflage, on pontoon-building and on war games for command staff followed in due course. In June 1925 the *Provisional Field Service Regulations* were affirmed by Frunze, holding their place until superseded by the *Field Service Regulations* of 1929.

The 1925 *Regulations* were devoted to a military presentation of the Red Army's combat problems; there was surprisingly small space allotted to the political explanation of war-making. In essence, the whole represented Tukhachevsky's reproof to Voroshilov that the Red Army, as yet lacking substantial technical means, must oppose any army more lavishly equipped with physical courage alone — that the Red Army could not compete, except on these terms, with bourgeois armies. The work attempted to distil the lessons of the Civil War into operational ideas and principles — the necessity of the close co-operation of all arms, the importance of 'initiative' and the danger of 'passivity' in operations, the recognition of the offensive as the basic and decisive form of combat, the value of manœuvre. There was a new emphasis upon the significance of the technical factor in modern war. To the defensive was assigned the place of winning time for the preparation of an offensive blow, holding the enemy in a given position while the main blow was elsewhere prepared against him, and the investing of occupied ground and vital points.[128]

This was by no means the last word on Red Army doctrine, and Voroshilov at once appointed a new commission to draw up the definitive regulations[129]— the result of whose labours was the adoption of the *Field Service Regulations* (*PU-29*). Such codifications, however, were a pertinent illustration of how thin the genuine Soviet military élite was, for no small amount of the labour of former Imperial officers was utilised. This did not contradict the policy of excluding them from positions in the Red Army in favour of Soviet-trained officers, for the ex-Tsarist senior officers no longer, after 1926, formed a solid bloc of opinion and influence, they had ceased to be the 'caste' of which Red commanders had previously complained. Nevertheless, certain of them, as a kind of military intellectual, made their mark on the course of Soviet doctrine, if only by raising up devils of unorthodoxy which had to be exorcised.

The storms of argument among the soldiers had begun to blow before the beginning of the Frunze reforms. The centre of those storms had been located over the unsolved question of what manner of war the Soviet armed forces might be called upon to fight, and how the defence establishment of the country might best be ordered. Trotsky had not minced his words about the Soviet military predicament, and the problems which were raised up for the Soviet command by the technical backwardness of the Red Army and the instability among those who were its chief source of man-power — the peasants. It was at once ironical and inevitable that Frunze's reforms were themselves the complete justification of Trotsky's inescapable arguments, and the surrender was made to orthodoxy at the expense of the 'revolutionary phraseology' which Trotsky had so often derided. Frunze himself was under no illusions, during the period of his full command, about the actual combat efficiency of the Red Army, nor did he conceal the state of confusion and weak co-ordination which existed in the prevailing arrangements to operate the Soviet war-machine. The whole tenor of the re-organisation of the Red Army was designed to place it in a position to compete with an orthodox bourgeois army, whatever the present technical deficiencies. It was a programme which was not as thoroughly understood as Frunze might have wished, and he spared few pains to hammer in, with repetitive phrase and recapitulation of argument, the need for training and technical advance.

Nevertheless, Frunze held that the Soviet Union was not at a total disadvantage. Certain intrinsic features of the Soviet military scene, in particular the advantage bestowed by geographic space, gave the Red Army special benefits. A technically superior enemy might force an initial retirement of Soviet troops, but this would not deprive the latter of its freedom to manœuvre, and in this fact lay the salvation that the Red Army would not be forced to fight in a manner which neutralised its principal military means and its battle-tested methods. It was at one and the same time an optimistic yet pessimistic observation on the possible military requirement. The surrender of ground might facilitate the retention of the initiative; the doctrine of the primacy of the offensive was not therefore hopelessly out of place, yet the whole remained a dilemma from which Soviet military thought never succeeded in emerging, in spite of the numerous glosses on the basic ideas. Even in its crude form, all this depended upon a number of vital factors — mobilisation, rail and road communication, integration of command and the capable execution of planned withdrawal — which were still the subject of intensive re-adjustment. Above all, it demanded notable stability in the rear, without which those memorable panics of the Civil War would only be re-enacted, this time in a fury of dislocation and destruction. Of the importance of the rear Frunze had shown himself to be acutely aware. At this time considerable attention was paid to the experience of Russia during the First World War and exhaustive examinations undertaken of the rear organisation, the supply and administrative failures and the practice of other bourgeois combatants.

Shortly before his death Frunze embarked upon rather more sophisticated interpretations of his earlier views. In his reports to the 3rd Congress of Soviets (19th May, 1925), and the All-Union Assembly of the Military-Scientific Society (*VNO*), his previous ideas of revolutionary offensivism had almost completely given way to calculations of long-term strategic and military-economic preparation.[130] From the latter exposition, it was made clear that the immediate task concerned the implications of the Baltic Powers' and Poland's capacities and intentions, the problem being the defence of the Soviet western and north-western frontiers. Air attack on the Leningrad industrial complex, or the possible entry of British ships of war into the Baltic had to be considered as real factors. Frunze proceeded to give his estimate of the stages of a future war, a view which was interesting enough in itself but had wider implications when considered as a detailed commentary on a secret speech made by Stalin at a plenary meeting of the Central Committee on 19th January, 1925. Whatever the disputes among the soldiers, Stalin came out with a lucid but absolutely reserved explanation of the priorities of Soviet defence planning.[131]

★ ★ ★ ★

Stalin, at the meeting of 19th January, spoke out in support of Frunze's request for more money for the Soviet armed forces (thereby bringing the defence expenditure to 405,000,000 roubles). As there was dissatisfaction among Soviet officers with the 'mixed' military system, so evidently was there an opinion in the political leadership which favoured paring the army down until it simply disappeared into the militia. Stalin disposed of this idea at once. What such suggestions amounted to had nothing to do with the militia system but something akin to 'a peace army', the reduction of the Red Army to a 'simple militia'. Analysing the liberation movement in the East, the complications in North Africa, Anglo-French rivalry in the Balkans, Stalin concluded that these added up to 'the pre-conditions of a new war'. In addition, the apparent development of 'something revolutionary, something new . . . in Britain' would alarm the ruling strata in that country — Soviet Russia's formidable enemy — and direct them to new aggressive acts against the Soviet Union.[132] Therefore everything pointed to the fact that 'the pre-conditions for war are maturing and that war may become inevitable'. Such a war might not break out until 'a few years' time', but the Soviet Union had to be prepared for all contingencies. Stalin then proceeded to make two observations which had a vital relevance to Soviet military planning. The first concerned the estimate of breaking the 'encirclement' which had pre-occupied Soviet politicians and diplomats. However strong the revolutionary movements in the West might be, Stalin argued, the Soviet Union would have to rely on its *own* might — thus breaking the magic circle in which Trotsky had walked for many years. Secondly, in the event of war, while the Soviet Union 'could not sit with folded arms'— a total impossibility in view of the many interests and theatres which would be involved —'we shall have to take action, *but we shall be the last to do so*.'[133] Placing the emphasis on home-grown and home-based military might and the aim of military self-sufficiency, providing thereby a new set of strategic priorities, Stalin did no more than give a military twist to an argument which had already been a part of the process of beating Trotsky out of power and prestige, opposing to Trotsky's theory of 'permanent revolution' Stalin's home-grown notions of 'Socialism in one country'.

In his addresses of the spring and early summer of 1925 Frunze did much to develop Stalin's line of argument in terms of this coming engagement. He suggested that a future war would embody four fundamental characteristics. It would be essentially a revolutionary class war, rather than a nationalistic clash of previous days. The second phase of such a war would be dominated by the relations between the social-political and the economic elements within the whole society at war (and it was here that the greatest distinction between the Socialist and capitalist-type societies would become apparent). The third involved the technical factor (including aviation and chemical warfare) and the fourth was 'mass engaged on the battlefield'. It was to the second phenomenon that Frunze accorded supreme importance. Of the fourth, when the Soviet Union engaged its military forces, Frunze offered this explanation of the relative position of the Soviet Union and its capitalist enemies:

> It is my view that if once affairs do come to an outbreak of serious conflict, then all those forces which the enemy has at his disposal will be brought on to the scene. In the final resort for us we must not conceive of a future clash being such that we will be able to win through with numerically small armed forces and without involving the broad mass of the population and without employing in this undertaking all the resources at the state's command. I say 'in the final resort for us', since bourgeois armies allow that the fact of the intensification of the inner-class struggle may prevent them from going ahead with arming the whole nation, but instead take the path of relying on technical means.[134]

Even so, bearing in mind Stalin's pronouncements behind closed doors, Frunze had still not advanced very far into the heart of the matter—what would the opening stages of a future war consist of, and how should the Soviet command react?[135] If everything hinged on the political defensive, then Red Army doctrine and strategic appraisal in terms of military-political offensivism was a mis-fit, and must conflict with the basic intentions of the Soviet command.

The general dispute was neither one-sided nor yet confined to the inner cabinets of the senior Soviet command. It was not possible, as yet, to silence the exponents of the view that strategy implied making the best possible military use of the military means to hand. In the battle to define strategic purposes a number of the very senior ex-Imperial officers — with Svechin, Vatsetis and Verkhovskii at their head — launched into expositions which clashed with the opinions of the Red Army Staff. General Svechin presented his considerable study of strategy,[136] which argued the case for the strategy of attrition as a manner of conducting war offering the greatest scope. It permitted also the employment of variety of means, both expressly military and more generally military-political. As such it was in absolute contrast with the reliance placed upon a strategy aimed basically at the destruction of the enemy through the offensive. Inevitably such disputes led to estimates of the prevailing Soviet military system, and ultimately to the raising of isolated voices, retailing the virtues of 'one-weapon' theories and advocating the small élite army such as had been suggested in bourgeois military circles.

Nor was the whole matter confined to theoretical assumptions alone. The Soviet high command was directly involved in the revolutionary actions in China, to which country Blyukher had been assigned for 'special duties' and detached from his normal command position at the end of 1924. In addition to this capable senior officer, artillery, aviation and Soviet staff officers worked in China to give the revolution a military force which would be capable of executing the tasks allotted to it. At the same time the question of the Chinese revolution became one more political battle-ground upon which Stalin and Trotsky carried on the final stage of their struggle. At the other end of the world the commitment earlier negotiated with the German soldiers and the military industrialists was about to enter into a new phase of activity. Nothing inherent in that arrangement could run counter to the specifications which Stalin had laid down in January 1925. Already by the end of 1924 the joint Soviet-German military-industrial undertakings, which covered the manufacture of aircraft, ammunition and poison-gas, had begun to come apart at the financial seams. Actual technical failure, such as occurred with the poison-gas plant, speeded up the eventual liquidation of this type of activity. There were signs in 1925 that the Soviet Union would not find this a grave disadvantage, since interest mounted in establishing a native armaments industry, and it was cheaper to hire technicians than finance factories. The liquidation of *GEFU*, however, was by no means the end of the story. For the Soviet command as such it marked much more of a real beginning as the military training grounds rather than the secret factories began to come into their own. Voroshilov took over where Trotsky had been obliged to leave off, while Unshlikht played an important role during Frunze's command in settling the details of the military collaboration. The Soviet Navy made a direct approach to the German *Marineleitung*; early in 1925 German naval officers were giving full consideration to a Soviet enquiry, covering fifteen points on the training and selection of submarine crews, the tactical and strategic use of this weapon, German combat experience from 1914–18 and a request for German submarine regulations, codes and manuals.[137] In March 1926 the first major Soviet-German discussion took place on substantial German technical assistance for the Soviet Navy; in June of that year Admiral Spindler travelled to the Soviet Union, there to hear from Zof exactly what the Soviet naval command required. Zof requested German submarine plans and three submarine experts — for command, submarine construction and engines.[138]

There can be little doubt that the Red Army passed through a grave crisis from the autumn of 1923 to the winter of 1925. This was no mere simple reform. The same political tensions, which had provided the stimulus for a particular kind of military re-organisation, nevertheless set the limits to which actual reform might proceed. The Red Army gained a little on the swings of independence of field command, but began to lose increasingly heavily on the roundabouts of political control and the penetration of the army by non-military bodies. The stabilisation of Red Army organisation was not accompanied by the establishment of a homogeneous officer corps. One anomaly of background and affiliation was replaced by another. The Red Army Staff had been erected into a powerful instrument for planning and co-ordination. Administrative functions had been more clearly defined. Yet the military had lost control over the expanding ramifications of the political apparatus. The re-organisation of the various arms and services was handicapped by the lack of modern weapons. The emergence of naval and air commands was not accompanied by any precision of opinion on the significance of the technical factor in modern war. The difficulties encountered and deliberately raised up in implementing unitary command only served to emphasise that the military commissar was at once an irregularity in, yet indispensable to, the Red Army. It was a dilemma as old as the similar crisis in 1919.

The sustained tensions in the Political Administration throughout 1923–4 made it apparent that this control apparatus might not only cease to control, but begin to work against the interests of the ruling political group in conditions of inner-Party conflict. Factional work within the armed forces carried with it the threat of splitting the Red Army into two camps. Bonapartism, while never a real threat in view of Trotsky's abhorrence of any kind of *coup*, entered on the Soviet military scene with half-suggested, half-imagined coincidences more substantial than the fancied images of the French Revolution, with which the Bolsheviks had instilled useful terrors for some six years. The Opposition was to make one more sally into the affairs of the Red Army and its leadership, this time to criticise conduct of defence policy. No blood had yet been shed, but there were lessons learned and signs detected which had immediate and terrible consequences in 1937–8.

PART THREE

FOREIGN ADVENTURES AND STRATEGIC PRIORITIES

'When the next Chinese General comes to Moscow and shouts: "Hail to the World Revolution" . . . better send at once for the GPU. All that any of them wants is rifles.'

M. Borodin to Anna Louise Strong.

Paragraph 33.

(3) *The Red Army lays the greatest value on the co-operation with the Reichswehr.*

General Werner von Blomberg. Report 231/28 T 3 V. 17th November, 1928.

CHAPTER EIGHT

The Soviet Re-entry into The Far East: The Problem of Japan and China

After the catastrophes of the Russo-Japanese War, it appeared to many that the Russian Far East and imperial claims in that area were nothing but a millstone hanged about the neck of Tsarist Russia. The way to greatness lay through an assertion of Russia's claims in Europe, particularly in the Balkans. Yet in the years immediately preceding 1914 and the outbreak of war with Germany, Russia had made an astonishing recovery of position and power in the Far East. The method chosen to accomplish this was nothing less than *rapprochement* with Japan and collaboration with that power in carving up portions of defenceless China. Russia and Japan apportioned to themselves Northern and Southern Manchuria respectively, thus going far beyond the initial interests in the Manchurian railway links. Japan developed Korea as her colony, and in exchange made reluctant recognition of Russian primacy in Outer Mongolia. It was a secret to neither party, nevertheless, that competition and not collaboration, conflict rather than settlement would be the ultimate outcome of this bizarre partnership. Each watched the other with careful eyes, Japan mindful that Russia's military strength had not been broken, Russia aware of Japan's ambition, power and steady encroachments. In 1908 Russia began the construction of the new railway running from Chita to Vladivostok, built on Russian land and termed the Amur Railway, in order to provide an alternative link with the Far East should war with Japan in Manchuria come again, when the Chinese Eastern Railway would be lost to the Russians. Before this link was completed Russia was at war with Germany, thereby giving Japan a free hand in the Far East.

War and revolution left Russia especially weak in the Far East. After the Bolshevik seizure of power in Petrograd, a move was made by insurgents in Harbin to seize the Chinese Eastern Railway, depose its Russian president and set up a workers' soviet. At the beginning of 1918 the Chinese government responded by sending troops to take over the railway. Japan, watching the degeneration of Russian power most intensely, landed the first detachment of troops as part of an interventionist force on 5th April,

1918, at Vladivostok.[1] With China, Japan proceeded to conclude a series of agreements to co-ordinate military and political action for joint operations against Siberia. In August large numbers of Japanese troops were landed, moving not only into Vladivostok but into the region of the Trans-Baikal. In the Siberian hinterland Kolchak's administration mounted its offensives directed at breaking through the Soviet Eastern Front and thence on to Moscow. The Soviet government was effectively cut off from contact with the Far Eastern provinces; what little armed force there was had retired before the Japanese and taken to guerrilla warfare and underground activity. Only the ineffectual diplomatic protest could be plied by the Soviet government against Japan. In spite of the presence of some American troops in the Far Eastern Intervention force, the initiative lay with Japan.

In the summer of 1919 the Red Army began its successful break-through into Western Siberia, pushing back and destroying Kolchak's armies. During the same summer the partisan forces of the Maritime Provinces were placed under the command of S. Lazo, the energetic and capable Bolshevik who had already played an important part in holding together the scattered pro-Bolshevik elements during a critical period.[2] The IIIrd and Vth Red armies pushed on into Siberia during the late autumn of 1919, arriving at a point some 120 kilometres east of Omsk by November. At the end of December 1919 the Eastern Front was officially liquidated, but the Vth Red army moved on eastwards, bringing all the while diverse partisan units under regular military command and pursuing White troops.[3] On 7th March, 1920, the 26th Division of the Vth Army, exhausted and ravaged by typhus, entered Irkutsk, which had been handed over peacefully and by agreement to the local Bolshevik Committee. Beyond Lake Baikal lay remnants of the White forces and the Japanese. The Soviet Republic could in no wise consider precipitating full-scale attacks on the Japanese, for in addition to the basic Soviet military weakness, at the other end of the geographic scale, on the Western Front, war with Poland appeared imminent. There was every reason to give full consideration to the idea of setting up a buffer state between Soviet Russia and the Japanese, a suggestion which culminated in the creation of the Russian Far Eastern Republic.

With the downfall of Kolchak's administration the Political Centre — a loose combination of Mensheviks and SRs — formed a temporary government. This group enjoyed the nominal support of local Bolsheviks, prominent among whom was A. Krasnoshchekov (Tobelson), former head of the Far Eastern Soviet of People's Commissars in the Amur region in February 1918. Intervention had put paid to this body and its small armed force, but Krasnoshchekov had never abandoned his ideas of the unsuitability of Communism for Eastern Siberia and his conviction that the Allied powers would never consent to the establishment of an outright Communist state here.[4] The opponents of the scheme for a democratic buffer state came from the extremist Bolsheviks, who desired nothing short of full Soviet power fastened on the liberated areas. As Red troops drew near to Krasnoyarsk, Krasnoshchekov proposed a mission to the Soviet command in order to discuss this plan. Gaining permission from Czech units still deployed west of Irkutsk, on 11th January, 1920, this mission left Irkutsk, reaching Soviet head-quarters on the 18th.[5] The plan was then discussed between Krasnoshchekov, the *Revvoensoviet* of the Vth Red army and the Siberian Revolutionary Committee (*Sibrevkom*) of the Russian Communist Party.[6]

Direct wire communication with Lenin and Trotsky gained for the Soviet command at Tomsk an eventual approval of the plan. But Krasnoshchekov returned through Krasnoyarsk to an Irkutsk which had witnessed changes during which the Bolsheviks had taken over power and swept the Political Centre away. An attempt to revive the Centre brought down the wrath of the extremists on the head of Krasnoshchekov. In a prison-car — the only transport — he moved to Verkhneudinsk, followed by Bolshevik partisans: a short-lived 'Provisional Government of the Far Eastern Republic' was set up on 25th March, but constant political friction ground it away. On 28th March, in the village of Bichura a conference met to settle the problem; this was adjourned, followed by re-assembly in Verkhneudinsk and re-presentation of the buffer-state plan. Not until 14th May, 1920, was the 'Russian Far Eastern Republic' finally accepted.[7]

Lenin justified the acceptance of the buffer state on practical grounds and a particularly frank admission of the expectation of conflict between Japan and the United States of America. War with Poland and Soviet military weakness were the governing tactical factors. Early in 1920 American troops were withdrawn from Russian territory. Subsequent Soviet policy was designed to use American pressure on the Japanese, reluctant as the former was to see any increase in Japanese power and permanent Japanese establishment in Siberia. The Far Eastern Republic, however, remained a relatively weak political force for the first months of its existence. Much depended upon the build-up of military force, for Ataman Semenov, supported by the Japanese, still remained a formidable enemy.

The Far Eastern Republic fashioned its army out of the East Siberian Soviet Army, re-named in February 1920 the People's Revolutionary Army (*NRA*), with a strength of 11,000 men, 2,000 cavalry, over 100 machine-guns, six light and four heavy guns and even four aeroplanes.[8] Elements of the former East Siberian Army around Irkutsk were formed into 1st Irkutsk Rifle Division, consisting of three brigades. The Main Operating Staff of the East Siberian Army was transformed into the Military

Soviet of the People's Revolutionary Army, and at once took measures to exert its authority over the numerous partisan units still operating in the area round Lake Baikal. All this was accomplished around the hard core of the Vth Red army, where Eikhe held command, Tukhachevsky having relinquished his post to him in November 1919.

Political tensions, however, more than off-set growing military strength in the late spring of 1920. The shaky government of Verkhneudinsk sent agents to Vladivostok to urge the full union of the entire Russian Far East in a 'democratic republic'. The Bolshevik extremists, however, were more interested in waiting for the Red Army to fight its way through to the Pacific, while the Japanese held it as a matter of vital interest to prevent such a union which would destroy all valid reason for their continued presence in the Russian Far East. A series of Japanese punitive actions in the Maritime Provinces left the inhabitants under no illusions as to who were their real masters; the events of 4th–5th April, 1920, in Vladivostok, the savage repression of partisans and political suspects, were accompanied by killing in Nikolsk, Khabarovsk and other towns. Over the location of the capital of the Far Eastern Republic new struggles developed; at a conference held in May 1920 in Verkhneudinsk not a few delegates came to try and bring about the end of the Republic and integration with Soviet Russia.[9] The Far Eastern Republic seemed to be an utter failure.

Yet Japan, in the hope of gaining hold of the Republic, signalled acknowledgement of its creation and accorded recognition on 15th July, 1920. Negotiations with General Oi resulted in the signing of the Gongota Agreement, which ensured the withdrawal of Japanese troops from the Trans-Baikal.[10] The People's Revolutionary Army had meanwhile begun its advance on Chita. On 12th May it was agreed that the People's Revolutionary Army should be supplied, with the approval of Moscow, through a Special Supply Administration, and maintained as the advance guard of the Vth Red army.[11] Chita did not fall at once to advancing Republican troops; the Gongota Agreement had provided for a neutral zone to be maintained between Republican and withdrawing Japanese troops, and Chita fell within this strip. Ataman Semenov* had long been there, but he was followed by partisan units, who invested the city and finally forced him to flee; his troops were forced out and over the frontier line into Manchuria, where they were disarmed by the Chinese. Later the Japanese transported these forces through Manchuria back to the Maritime Provinces.[12] In November Eikhe brought the Republican army into Chita.

* The Ataman (later a General) was captured twenty-five years later, when the Red Army fought its Far Eastern campaign in 1945. He was put on trial and executed at the conclusion of this, in August 1946.

This transformation had been accompanied by extensive modification in the organisation of the partisan forces. Although strikingly few in number through the Russian Far East, the Bolsheviks counter-acted this deficiency by their control of armed force, of which the partisans were the basic element. In eastern Trans-Baikal partisans operated early in 1920 against the 5th Japanese Division and Semenov troops. P. N. Zhuravlev divided the partisans into two corps, and in February 1920 succeeded in linking up with guerrillas of the Amur, who had at that date succeeded in occupying Blagoveshchensk. In the spring of 1920 Zhuravlev died of wounds, and command passed to D. S. Shilov, who had worked with Lazo and raised partisan units in the Amur region.[13] The Amur Army itself was formally brought into being early in April 1920; on 18th of that month the partisan units became known as the 1st Amur Rifle Division, consisting of nine rifle regiments and one cavalry regiment, in addition to guns, an armoured train and some tanks, belonging originally to Kolchak. This force possessed able leaders; S. M. Seryshev was a former Imperial officer, P. Postyshev a partisan leader of experience and standing, together with B. Mel'nikov, M. Gubel'man, N. Popov and G. Aizenberg.[14]

The partisan movement in the Maritime Provinces had grown slowly in strength throughout 1919. In the summer of that year Lazo had re-organised the Partisan Administration into three combat regions, counting on taking 1,500 men into action. The report submitted by the Far Eastern Regional Party Committee, submitted in January 1920 to Moscow reported on the continued expansion of these forces.[15] Catastrophe followed swiftly on this proud report. In the Japanese raids and punitive actions of early April 1920 Lazo, director of the Far Eastern partisans, A. N. Lutskii and V. M. Sibirtsev — both members of the Military Soviet — were taken prisoner. After their interrogation by Japanese Counter-Intelligence, the prisoners were handed over to White Guards under Japanese officers. The end came swiftly. Lazo, a man of great physical strength, resisted the attempt to throw him alive into the furnace of a locomotive. He was struck down by a guard and hurled in, after which his two companions were burnt alive.[16]

Nevertheless, in the face of the fundamental Russian military weakness in the Far East, the partisans played a vital role. Slowly a rising tide of force rose up against the Japanese, who acknowledged that fact in their withdrawal from Trans-Baikal, while elements of White troops were also gradually liquidated. After its precarious start the Far Eastern Republic, established by November in Chita, achieved a certain stability and entered upon a brief life of its own. Not the least important event was the Republic's contact with China. Already in June 1920 the *Komintern* had intervened directly in the Far Eastern sphere, sending G. Voitinsky as its agent to

China.[17] A month previously the Provisional Government of the Maritime Provinces despatched Agariev to China,[18] but only in July did Yurin journey to Peking on behalf of the Far Eastern Republic. Yurin, a botanist by training, and later a career soldier in the Imperial Russian Army, had earlier thrown in his lot with the Bolsheviks, rising to responsible posts on the Eastern Front. At the Tomsk meeting in January 1920 he had been favourably inclined towards the plan for a buffer state and later accompanied Krasnoshchekov as one of his principal advisers.[19] During the autumn Soviet Russia seemed to benefit from a shift in the diplomatic balances in Asia. A Chinese Military-Diplomatic Mission under General Chang Shi-lin arrived in Moscow and negotiated with Karakhan; the latter produced on 27th September, 1920, a draft of an agreement between Soviet Russia and China, including a proposal to come to an understanding over the Chinese Eastern Railway.[20] But success at this stage eluded both Soviet Russia and the Far Eastern Republic. There was no break-through into China either politically or commercially.

The door to Outer Mongolia, however, slipped open in the winter of 1920. With the destruction of Semenov's command, elements of White forces tried to make their way into Outer Mongolia. One such group under Baron Ungern Sternberg, a former Russian officer and ferociously cruel, took this way out, coming into contact with the Chinese troops who provided the small garrison. Outer Mongolia was in a state of upheaval, fomented by Soviet interest in setting up revolutionary groups. Ungern Sternberg provided an open pretext for intervention. On 11th November, 1920, Chicherin transmitted by radio a suggestion to the Chinese government that Soviet troops should intervene to reinforce the Chinese troops in the region of Urga to liquidate the 'White bands' — threat to the Chinese Republic, Soviet Russia and the Far Eastern Republic alike.[21] China refused the proffered help. Ungern Sternberg, marching on Urga, planned further war on Soviet Russia, dreaming of a fantastic regeneration of Asiatic power in the style of Attila. In the winter of 1920–21 the stage was set for the first real revival of Russian power in the east, accomplished not by the Ungern Sternbergs but by the Red Army.

* * * *

With the entry of Republican troops into Chita, and the successful conclusion of negotiations with delegates from the Provisional Government of the Maritime Provinces, the Russian Far East was once again united under a single authority. If it was nominally a political unity, the same could not be said for its territorial possessions. Japanese troops still invested areas of the Maritime Provinces, occupied Northern Sakhalin, Nikolaevsk and the mouth of the Amur. They were becoming nevertheless increasingly isolated in their interventionist adventure. As the United States of America began to interest herself in the fate of the Far Eastern Republic, so did Japan struggle to limit American influence and activity used on behalf of the Republic.

Meanwhile events in Outer Mongolia were reaching a climax. Ungern Sternberg occupied Urga in February 1921, after the false start of the winter of 1920. Chen I and other Chinese officials fled; in Troitsko-Savsk, on Russian territory, they appealed for the entry of the Red Army.[22] There were other means available to the hand of the Soviet command. A Mongolian Revolutionary Party had been organised prior to these events. Sukhe-Bator and Choibalsan, the two leaders of this group fully assisted by Soviet advisers, moved up to the Mongol frontier from Soviet head-quarters. In the frontier town of Kyakhta the 1st Congress of the Mongol National-Revolutionary Party met at the beginning of March, adopting a resolution to 'co-operate with Soviet Russia'.[23] On 13th March, the Provisional National-Revolutionary Government of Mongolia was set up — all this worked by the numerically tiny 'Mongol Party'.[24] Ungern Sternberg went ahead with his grandiose plans, working out a scheme of operations against Soviet Siberia; in May he flung an all-out offensive against the Soviet border.

After the conclusion of the operations against Wrangel in the late autumn of 1920, Blyukher, who had enjoyed his first successes on the Eastern Front and distinguished himself once again with his 51st Division against Wrangel, was free to return to the east. In the same way that the conclusion of operations against Poland and Wrangel freed Soviet military strength for further operations in the south-east, culminating in the 'export of revolution' to Georgia in the spring of 1921, so the same impetus was felt far away to the east. Blyukher assumed command of the Military Soviet of the Far Eastern Republican army, replacing Eikhe. Blyukher and Gubel'man signed the order instructing Red Army units operating against Ungern Sternberg to treat any Chinese officials or units they met as allies in the common struggle.[25] Sukhe-Bator, supported by Red Army forces, led troops of the 'National Revolutionary Army' and Mongol 'revolutionary detachments' against the White insurgents,[26] taking Urga on 6th July, 1921. A new government was formed, in which Sukhe-Bator enjoyed the position of War Minister, supported by Red Army troops. The Chinese government at once took issue with the Soviet authorities and their investing of Outer Mongolia. In a note of 15th June, 1920, Chicherin had explained that the presence of the Red Army was necessary to reduce the White forces; on the elimination of this threat, but only then, would it be withdrawn.[27]

In August the Mongol Government requested the further retention of Soviet troops. To this the Soviet government readily acceded. The manœuvre was complete, skilfully managed as it had been. Soviet Russia, although incurring the enmity of China, had made a notable strategic advance.

In July 1921 the Washington Conference, for the discussion of Pacific problems, was suggested. Japan at once countered by inviting the Far Eastern Republic to a special conference at Dairen, where outstanding problems between the two states would be settled. Assembling in August 1921, this gathering was interrupted by the Washington Conference, which opened its sessions in November. On 17th December, 1921, Blyukher returned to Chita from Dairen, and on 18th addressed the Far Eastern Republic National Assembly on military problems facing the Republic. The army had to be re-organised; up to 90,000 men had been released from service, and it was now necessary to build up an armed force based on high-quality cadres of the younger age-groups. There were not the resources or even the means of transport to maintain a large army.[28] Blyukher further advised the assembly that in a conversation with the Japanese delegate Shimada at the Dairen Congress, the latter had 'let it drop' that if the Far Eastern Republic would not recognise the claims of the Japanese, then a government would be formed to do precisely this.

The military situation had also deteriorated somewhat. The Amur District Party Committee had made a serious error in committing a numerically inferior force against White troops. Blyukher left to take personal command of the recently organised Eastern Front Staff and Military Soviet, which had S. Seryshev in command, P. Postyshev as commissar and B. Mel'nikov as the second member. In May 1921 the remnants of the Kappel and Semenov White troops had carried out, with the connivance of the Japanese command, a counter-revolution in Vladivostok and Nikolsk-Ussuriisk; Spiridon Merkulov was placed at the head of the government, and once the internecine strifes quietened, a new offensive planned against Soviet forces in the Far East.[29] In November 1921 the first actions were being fought. At the end of December White units had penetrated the rear of the Republican army in the region of the station at In, seizing Khabarovsk and investing the right bank of the Amur. Advancing on Volochaevka, the Republican army was hard-pressed at this point.

On the eve of the January 1922 offensive by the Republican army, Blyukher had his open letter to General Molchanov scattered among the White troops.[30] On 11th–12th January, 1922, Blyukher's troops began their offensive; partisan attacks and frontal attacks, however, failed. In the latter half of January the partisan command was re-organised for the whole of the Maritime Provinces, with its chief A. Flegontov and his Chief of Staff B. Rubtsov. Along the eighteen-kilometre front of Volochaevka a series of defence positions had been constructed with the object of holding Blyukher's forces. From 4th–9th February fresh attacks failed to achieve a break-through. On 10th a full-scale attack was likewise repulsed. On 12th, at 8 a.m., a new assault was mounted; opposing armoured trains carried on a duel, when at 10 a.m., the storming of Volochaevka began. Badly-armed, half-clad, in freezing cold the Republican troops finally succeeded in breaking through the fortifications. In April 1922 the advance had reached Spassk, on the road to Vladivostok.

Blyukher was recalled from the Far East in July 1922. He left with the acclaim of the Far Eastern Republic ringing in his ears — not least for his success at Volochaevka, 'the second Perekop'.[31] I. P. Uborevich, a young ex-Imperial officer, commander of the IXth, XIIIth and XIVth Red armies in the operations against Denikin and Wrangel, took over Blyukher's post on the Military Soviet of the Far Eastern army. The command change may have been prompted by the recognition by the Soviet government that the withdrawal of Japan from the Russian mainland could not be long delayed. At the Washington Conference Japan had fared badly. When the Dairen Conference between Japan and the Far Eastern Republic was resumed in the early spring of 1922, Japan encountered firm resistance to her demands; the Conference was wound up in April 1922. The United States of America lent powerful aid to the cause of the Far Eastern Republic. In June Japan informed the United States State Department that Japanese troops would complete their evacuation of the Russian mainland by October; this pledge did not apply, however, to Sakhalin.[32] The Changchun Conference over Sakhalin met in September, but confident of the support of the United States, the Far Eastern Republic delegates and Soviet representatives resisted Japanese claims for economic privilege.

Throughout the summer of 1922 partisan activity increased in the Maritime Provinces. By the middle of August Japanese preparations for evacuation were going ahead. On 13th August partisan units had completed their ring around Vladivostok, leaving the sea as the only method of access. On 8th October, at 5.30 a.m., units of the Far Eastern army began their assault on Spassk; on 9th the fortified positions and the staff of General Molchanov had been finally taken. On 19th, Far Eastern army units were nine kilometres from Vladivostok and in contact with Japanese troops. I. P. Uborevich issued an order bringing his units back to a reasonable distance from the Japanese; no kind of provocation was to be supplied.[33] On 25th, after negotiations for the evacuation of the Japanese from Vladivostok, the Far Eastern army entered the city.

The Far Eastern Republic, its tactical purposes exhausted, voted on 13th November, 1922, for incorporation into Soviet Russia. The myth of its 'independence' ended with the re-unification of Soviet Russia with its Pacific cities. Basically it was American pressure upon Japan rather than the weight of Soviet military victories which accomplished this defeat of the prolonged Japanese intervention. Lenin chose to ignore this fact in his congratulatory messages. There remained the question of Sakhalin to be thrashed out with the Japanese. Of more immediate interest was the question of relations with China, with whom Soviet Russia had become entangled over the status of Outer Mongolia, and the question of the Chinese Eastern Railway. While proceeding with the pacification of the troubled territories of Soviet Siberia and the newly-won Far East, Soviet attentions became riveted on China.

* * * *

Soviet policy towards China followed a dual track, managed as it was by two agencies; the first sought after normalisation of relations and was handled by the diplomatic apparatus, the second interested itself in the revolutionary possibilities inherent in China and fell under the *Komintern*, which had first intervened in June 1920. The Red Army command stood perforce somewhere in the middle, rendering its services to both at times, as in the affair of Outer Mongolia. Lenin himself had not been blind to the potentialities of an alliance with Asian anti-colonialism and nascent nationalism, seeing in this not merely a compensation for the frustrations of revolutionary anti-climax in the West, but a realisation of the idea that 'the shortest way to Paris is through Peking'.[34] With the assistance of the guiding hand of *Komintern* agents, in South China the first Communist nucleus was created. In July 1921 the newly raised Communist Party of China held its First All-China Conference, in which 12 delegates represented 57 Party members from various Communist groups; the *Komintern* delegate was Maring, who had already been in contact with Sun Yat-sen and the *Kuomintang*.[35]

On 12th December, 1921, after a journey beginning in October, the first Soviet official diplomatic mission to China, led by A. K. Paikes, arrived in Peking. What little progress was made came to an abrupt end when the worst fears of the Chinese government were confirmed by the publication in April 1922 of the treaty signed between Soviet Russia and the new Mongolian government which it had been instrumental in installing. The treaty, signed on 5th November, 1921, had made no mention of China.[36] In August 1922 the second Soviet delegation led by A. A. Ioffe reached Peking and Paikes left for Moscow. The status of Mongolia still prevented the conclusion of agreement, and in August 1923 a third Soviet delegation, this time under Karakhan, reached China. Ioffe went to Japan, a fact which instilled some nervousness in Peking and the fear of a Soviet-Japanese understanding at the expense of China. In 1924 agreement was finally reached, by which time the Peking government had no choice but to acknowledge the reality of the situation in Outer Mongolia. Face was saved by regarding it formally as part of the Chinese Republic, but in no way relaxing the Soviet grip. The Chinese Eastern Railway was settled between the two countries, after adjustments made by the dictator of Manchuria, General Chang Tso-lin.[37]

While Moscow strove to gain recognition of its rights from the Peking government, *Komintern* interest in the *Kuomintang* and the revolutionary movements in south China intensified. Re-organised by Sun Yat-sen, the *Kuomintang* displayed active animosity towards Great Britain in China. For the advancement of Soviet policy, the ideal combination in China was between the *Kuomintang* and the Chinese Communists, since the former provided a broader revolutionary base than the numerically weak Communists. Ioffe, while dealing with the Peking government, also spared no effort to come to an understanding with Sun Yat-sen. Such an understanding was effected, although at one point it appeared that the *Kuomintang* might turn finally to the United States of America.[38] On 27th January, 1923, the terms of the compact between Ioffe and Sun Yat-sen were announced in a communiqué about their talks. There was to be no 'export of revolution' to China, Sun Yat-sen being of the opinion that the Soviet system as such was not suitable for China — but Soviet support in the struggle against the Peking government and for the cause of the national independence of China would be forthcoming. Sun Yat-sen did not press the point about the withdrawal of Soviet power from Outer Mongolia.[39]

Throughout 1923 great strides were made in implementing this compact. At this point the matter became the direct concern of the Red Army command,* since Sun Yat-sen required both an army and military supplies — the lack of which he had felt sorely in his previous military undertakings. The situation in China was the subject of close study by senior Soviet officers in 1923. Sun Yat-sen delegated a trusted young officer — Chiang Kai-shek, who had shared the perils of his master's abortive military action when he was forced out of Canton — to proceed to Moscow, in order to present letters to Lenin, Trotsky and Chicherin and also to examine at first-hand the Soviet military system.[40] Leaving in July, Chiang Kai-shek

* The retired Lieutenant-General A. I. Todorskii, writing in the October 1958 issue of *Sovetsko-kitaiskaya druzhba* under 'Meeting with Sun Yat-sen', recalls the work of P. A. Pavlov, Red Army cavalry commander, who was seconded for duties in China. One of the earliest of the Soviet advisers, Pavlov was killed in South China on 3rd July, 1924.

arrived at his destination in August. The letters he bore were in the nature of a request for military supplies for the new Chinese allies of Moscow. In the absence of Lenin due to illness, the Chinese officer was turned over to Stalin and Trotsky, and thence to Sklyanskii, Trotsky's deputy. Chiang Kai-shek was taken on an extensive tour of Red Army units and military installations, in order that he might gather the requisite knowledge of Soviet military methods. The question of military supplies was presumably also gone into thoroughly, although it was not until the following year that the first shipment of Soviet arms reached the Chinese.

In September 1923 Mikhail Borodin* left Moscow and arrived in the following month at Canton, following Sun Yat-sen's invitation. Borodin was not either a Soviet diplomatic or *Komintern* representative, but apparently the chief agent of the Russian Communist Party itself; he was charged with the re-organisation of the *Kuomintang* and was accompanied by a staff of Soviet military experts.[41] A high-powered military mission was meanwhile being assembled from the Soviet side, which would play a vital role in this major Soviet intervention in Asian political affairs. It was a dramatic reversal of the roles of 1919–22.

★ ★ ★ ★

The principal military personality employed in the rendering of Soviet aid to China was Blyukher, who had been re-called from the Far East in July 1922. Yegorov was despatched to Peking as Soviet Military Attaché, although his real function was to co-ordinate Soviet military activity in China, since the Soviet command had contacts with Chinese war-lords, notably Feng Yu-hsiang, the 'Christian general' contacted by Ioffe and later Karakhan.[42] With Blyukher at its head, the Soviet military mission had Viktor Rogachev as its Chief of Staff.[43] For the purposes of his duties in China, Blyukher, already possessed of a name which had aroused much speculation, adopted the *nom de guerre* of 'Galin',† under which he figures in Soviet and Chinese reports.

Borodin's work had meanwhile borne fruit in the convening of the 1st National Congress of the *Kuomintang*, the first ever in that body's history. Borodin had drawn very heavily on the practice of the Russian Communist Party in re-fashioning the *Kuomintang* constitution, construction and the

* Borodin (or Gruzenberg) became a Bolshevik only in 1921, having returned to Soviet Russia from the United States of America. His first assignment was to Great Britain, where he was given a short prison sentence. On his return to Moscow, he was destined for China. Borodin was, after David J. Dallin's description, an instance of how 'historical circumstances imparted stature to a man unprepared and unqualified for it'.

† It is variously 'Galen' or 'Galin'; since the latter is found in Soviet reports, it has been used here.

creation of party organs. The Congress met in January 1924 and at once set about discussing Chiang Kai-shek's proposals for the re-organisation of the army. It was here that the Soviet military mission had to complete its first tasks. The creation of the Whampoa Military Academy was decided upon and the armed forces to be reconstructed on lines suggested by the example of the Red Army. In his address at the opening of the Academy, Sun Yat-sen openly acknowledged the debt to Soviet support, and urged the new cadets to bend every effort to become the strength of the revolutionary army — without which the cause was doomed.[44]

The collaboration between Chiang Kai-shek and the Soviet officers ran into difficulties before the Whampoa Academy actually began to function. At a preliminary meeting on 6th February, 1924, there had been a dispute over the running and programme of the Academy. The faculty included Blyukher and the Soviet military expert Cherepanov, with Chiang Kai-shek as president, assisted by Liao Chung-k'ai — the latter also having participated in the talks with Ioffe in 1923.[45] Among the Chinese faculty members were graduates of the Japanese Military Academy, Chinese military schools or those returned from travels in Germany and France. Chou En-lai belonged to the latter group, and worked in the political staff of the Academy, following the pattern of the military commissars and Political Administration of the Red Army. Chiang Kai-shek, angry at the intrusion of his Soviet military advisers, resigned from his post in the Academy. The dispute was smoothed over by Liao Chung-k'ai, and the Soviet officers modified their demands.[46]

Much of the work of the Whampoa Academy suggested the activity of the Red Army's frantic training-programmes during the critical phases of the Revolution. Great emphasis was laid on the ideological training of the officer-cadets. The Soviet system of political indoctrination was adopted for use in Whampoa. Not only Soviet methods but Soviet weapons were of vital importance at this point. On 8th October, 1924, a Soviet cargo-ship slipped into Whampoa to deliver some 8,000 rifles and ammunition.[47] Only a handful of rifles had existed when the Academy had begun work; later some 15,000 rifles, machine-guns and items of artillery were obtained from Soviet sources.[48]

The strength of the Soviet military mission continued to increase, and has been placed as high as 1,000 military and political advisers. The core consisted of 24 military experts stationed in Canton to advise the *Kuomintang*.[49] Equipped with Soviet rifles, the new Whampoa cadets, imbued with iron discipline and directed by persistent political instruction, took the field at the end of 1924 at Mien-hu, Kwangtung. Blyukher advised Chiang Kai-shek on the operation, which ended in victory for the numerically inferior Whampoa troops. Blyukher almost lost his life in the fighting, but emerged from the action full of admiration for the Chinese troops. He evidently presented his sword to the commander of the 1st Training Regiment which had so distinguished itself.[50]

The first Whampoa brigade expanded rapidly, and on these foundations the National Revolutionary Army was built up. At the head of the *Kuomintang* was the political council, which directed the activities of the military through a military council. Soviet advisers were present on both and the military council was modelled on the pattern of the Soviet *Revvoensoviet.* The political administration in the army adopted the Soviet practice of military commissars, the 'cell' type of organisation and the use of political indoctrination. Liao Chung-k'ai operated the political apparatus, first in Whampoa and then throughout the army as a whole, with political officers possessing the power to counter-sign and countermand military orders — as in the Soviet dual command. Chinese commissars, assisted by Soviet political specialists, ran the political organs in the army. Like the Red Army Political Administration, the Chinese military-political system was a delicate indicator of loyalties, and conflict over the division of authority was a contributory factor in splitting the *Kuomintang* from its Soviet mentors. Who should rule and run the vitally-important political apparatus became as critical an issue later in China as it had been in the Red Army.

Blyukher scored a great personal and professional success during the early days of Whampoa. Tough and practical, evidently dressed in Chinese uniform, together with Borodin he disposed of immense influence. Impatient of too much revolutionary phraseology, he considered his task to be the raising up of a first-class fighting machine to serve the Chinese revolution. From this the National Revolutionary Army undoubtedly benefited. To the Whampoa Military Academy Blyukher assigned Cherepanov as the resident Soviet adviser.[51] While making every effort to assist the Chinese, it would appear that the aim of the Soviet military authorities was to establish the superiority of Soviet method and advice. Rogachev, Chief of Staff, played an important part in this scheme, assiduously attending every meeting of the political and military councils. With clear and forceful advice on all military subjects, and supported by the work of an increasing number of Soviet specialists at every level in the army, it was almost impossible for the Chinese to resist this penetration. There were very few Chinese officers who were in a position to answer back, and the Chinese were absolutely dependent on the Soviet supplies of arms and ammunition. It was but a short step from Soviet advice to complete Soviet control.

In 1925 Blyukher began to revise his opinion of Chiang Kai-shek, to voice the reservations which doubtless had been raised when Chiang

Kai-shek had made his first show of resistance to Soviet authority in February 1924. Blyukher's opinion, however, was reserved for Moscow only. In China the relations of the two commanders proceeded cordially enough.[52] There were generals besides Chiang Kai-shek in the *Kuomintang* and units — those perhaps more amenable to Communist influence — who could use Soviet aid. In Northern China, as an example of how wide the Soviet military-political net was being spread, General Feng Yu-hsiang had been accorded substantial aid and even lodged in Moscow. This General drew his strength from Inner Mongolia, and plans were afoot to link Outer and Inner Mongolia through 'political developments' which had played such a large part in winning Outer Mongolia to the Soviet side in 1921.[53]

In his criticism of Chiang Kai-shek, Blyukher was beginning to tread dangerous ground, for the question of China and the course of the revolution had become, inevitably, part of the struggle between Stalin and Trotsky, part of the final deadly phase of the power struggle in Moscow. Trotsky, aware of the growing power of the Chinese Communists, began to look askance at the alliance of convenience between the Chinese Communists and the *Kuomintang* which was hardening into permanent compromise. In Shanghai and Canton, Trotsky wanted to see workers' soviets created, to have elsewhere an intensification of agrarian movements against the landowners and the Chinese Communist Party bid for power. It was to be a repetition of 1917 in Russia. The Chinese Communists themselves were uneasy about their ties with the *Kuomintang*.* Stalin advocated the tactics of collaboration and maintenance of alliances within the *Kuomintang*, which had itself been made over in the image of the Russian Communist Party. Chiang Kai-shek could be managed, and the Chinese Communists ordered into line. Blyukher's words, and so many others, were lost on the wind of history. The events of March 1926, however, proved Blyukher right. Chiang Kai-shek struck hard, on 20th March, 1926, at his Communist rivals and Soviet masters.

★ ★ ★ ★

In August 1925 the diplomatic Liao Chung-k'ai had been assassinated, thereby opening an irreparable breach in the operation of the Sino-Soviet collaboration in the military sphere. The nationalistic Right-wing Chinese officers of the *Kuomintang* found themselves without substantial restraint in putting up a show of resistance to the Leftist elements — and Soviet plans.

* According to the note on p. 321 of I. Deutscher's *The Prophet Unarmed*, the Chinese Central Committee pressed the Soviet military advisers for 5,000 rifles from the supplies arriving for Chiang Kai-shek. These arms would be used to arm peasants and prepare a counter-force against Chiang Kai-shek, whom the Chinese Communists suspected of raising civil war against them. The Soviet military advisers refused the request.

In the Whampoa Military Academy itself nationalist officers and cadets were attempting to contain Communist influence by organising the Society of Sun Yat-sen, to which Borodin replied by creating a Chinese *Komsomol*.[54] The struggle over the political organs had begun in all earnest. Chiang Kai-shek took the precaution of keeping his own 1st Corps free of Communist influence, and checking, wherever possible, the entry of the Left to key command positions.

Stalin, however, could justify his policy of retaining the alliance with the *Kuomintang* by pointing to the results of the 2nd Congress of that body, held in January 1926. The Left had won a substantial majority;[55] the tactics of a united front seemed to be paying off. At about the same time A. S. Bubnov, head of the Red Army Political Administration, member of the Central Committee and the Stalinist faction, was on his way to China, where under the name of 'Kisanka' he was to assume the post of senior Soviet military adviser to the *Kuomintang*. The despatch of Bubnov, while supplying Stalin with a trusted agent on the spot, suggested that Blyukher's criticism of Chiang Kai-shek had made him somewhat suspect from Stalin's point of view.

Bubnov arrived in Canton shortly before Chiang Kai-shek loosed his bolt. On 20th March, 1926, Chiang Kai-shek arrested a number of the commissars of the Whampoa Military Academy; his detentions did not stop at Chinese, but included some of the Soviet military advisers then in Canton. Borodin and Blyukher, who were out of the city at that time, escaped interference. Rogachev, the senior Soviet officer in charge, hurried to Peking. In his report on the *coup*, Stepanov of the Soviet staff recounted that Chiang Kai-shek, acting without the knowledge of the *Kuomintang* head-quarters, aimed at putting down a Communist strike, disarming the workers — as he had disarmed a Communist Red Guard, one of the military cadres of the Chinese Communist Party.[56] From the *Kuomintang* side the story took on a different cast. Apprised of a Communist plot, Chiang Kai-shek acted at once to quell it; the Soviet naval adviser in Canton had ordered the Communist commander of a gun-boat to move in to support the risings.

Chiang Kai-shek apologised handsomely for what had been 'a regrettable incident'. The Soviet military advisers, to whom fulsome apology was also made, went back to their jobs — but not Rogachev and Bubnov. Relations between Chiang Kai-shek and Bubnov were bad; Rogachev had kept too tight a rein on the military set-up and his power had been a little too great. The animosities were sharpened, and yet by a paradox at the same time dulled, by developments in the military situation. The Chinese Nationalists could escape from irksome restrictions imposed by the Russians and Chinese

Communists alike by striking out for the arms-depots of Shanghai and Nanking. Alternatively, defeat might be thrust upon them by a combination of war-lords — the answer to this threat being a *Kuomintang* offensive. In Chiang Kai-shek's adoption of the latter solution lay the origin of the Northern Expedition, the drive to defeat enemies encroaching on the *Kuomintang*'s base and at the same time win the unification of China.

At first Soviet and Chinese strategic requirements seemed to diverge sharply. Moscow was interested as never before in China, but as part of the world battle-ground on which to fight British imperialism. For this reason the Chinese Communists must be restrained from wreaking havoc in the *Kuomintang*, since the latter was a valuable weapon in the struggle against imperialism. Similarly, at all costs the *Kuomintang* command must be diverted from any rash military adventures which might precipitate a foreign military intervention — possibly an Anglo-Japanese combination, brought to life to crush the Chinese revolution. Basically it was a policy concerned with the security of the interests of the Soviet Union. Trotsky, in arguing for a successful Chinese *Communist* revolution, could be charged with ignoring and even damaging the prospects of the fundamental struggle. The Northern Expedition had the same implications about it. It was not surprising that Bubnov, acting presumably as the agent of the will of Stalin, opposed the plan; instead he proposed shipping troops to North China to support Moscow's other ally, General Feng Yu-hsiang, who was in receipt of Soviet military aid.[57] Chiang Kai-shek's military prospects in his proposed undertaking appeared remote. Nevertheless Bubnov's opposition was one of the factors which facilitated the acceptance of the plan by *Kuomintang* leaders. Chiang Kai-shek had also one more card to play — he had requested Bubnov's re-call from China. He obtained it.

Chiang Kai-shek's stock rose in Moscow, notwithstanding the 'regrettable incident' of 20th March. He made peace with Borodin.[58] In addition to Chiang Kai-shek's own skilful diplomacy, the war-lords helped him indirectly to remain in Stalin's favour. In the late spring of 1926 Marshal Wu Pei-fu was advancing on the *Kuomintang* base. To adopt the plan for an offensive, to assist Chiang Kai-shek to fight off his enemies and thus preserve the *Kuomintang* to serve the grand Soviet design, all became respectable. It became not only respectable but profitable. Striking north to Central China would bring the revolutionary forces nearer to Feng Yu-hsiang. The Chinese idea could be sovietised. Borodin put the essence of the plan to Chiang Kai-shek; while it was basically the Bubnov plan which had been rejected by the Chinese before, now it was accepted.[59] Retired to Moscow, Bubnov himself seems to have returned with a series of military observations, one of which was the necessity to support the Northern Expedition, which could conceivably win a broad belt of territory in China. The possibilities inherent in a link with a Soviet military satellite in the north were immense. There was, however, a political complication. The agitation for agrarian reform must be suspended during the campaign, since *Kuomintang* officers would be affected substantially by such a programme.[60]

Blyukher was reputedly not impressed by the chances of success for the expedition. Nor had his opinion of Chiang Kai-shek improved in May 1926 on that expressed by him in the previous year.[61] In spite of his misgivings Blyukher did not refrain from rendering his professional support to the Chinese command, participating in the planning of the opening stages of the operations. His advice on supply and movement questions was most valuable; his ideas constantly stressed the importance of mobility, of the surprise factor, speed of march and envelopment.[62] On 1st July, 1926, Chiang Kai-shek issued the mobilisation orders for the campaign, the first stage of which corresponded to the original Soviet advice to advance on Wuhan from Canton.

Chiang Kai-shek, nominated Commander-in-Chief, introduced a variant of his own — his own 1st Corps was detached to strike through Fukien and Chekiang at Shanghai and Nanking, two glittering prizes. The National Revolutionary Army also struck to the north of Canton, fighting with three corps towards Changsha and Hankow. Wu Pei-fu was defeated, cracking to pieces by August under the blows of the exemplary troops sent against him. The Northern Expedition was turning into a notable success. Chiang Kai-shek took over the personal direction of the armies advancing on Wuhan, only to suffer a reverse of a special order from within his own ranks. With the capture of the vital arms-depots of Hankow and Hanyang, military supplies fell into the hands of Left-wing groups.[63] The commissars, directed by Teng Yen-ta and Chou En-lai of the political administration, inevitably disseminated Communist propaganda among the troops and were the mainspring of the peasant disturbances and disorders which broke out in Chiang Kai-shek's rear.

Blyukher did not play a conspicuous part in these operations. The only evidence of his direct interference is a copy of his operational orders, issued on 16th October, 1926.[64] The few available reports of Soviet military advisers in various sections of the National Revolutionary Army do, nevertheless, testify to the scope and intensity of their activity. Sergeyev, Soviet aviation adviser, had completed the organisation of an aviation unit by 10th August, 1926; a field administration, landing fields and a supply organisation as well as an operational plan were all in existence.[65] Nikitin (A. N. Chernikov) and F. M. Katyushin-Kotov submitted reports of their work with the Northern Expeditionary Force. A. I. Cherepanov was attached to a field command. Borodin, an artillery expert, submitted a report on the work of artillery units.[66] The Soviet command however, received a rude shock when Chiang Kai-shek detached himself from Wuhan, which had fallen into the power of the 'Left *Kuomintang*' and their Communist partners, and concentrated on an easterly drive into Kiangsi.

The Soviet command reacted sharply to Chiang Kai-shek's proposed easterly drive with his reserves. Borodin attempted to change Chiang Kai-shek's plans, calling on the Chinese Commander-in-Chief to resume the joint northerly drive — all to no purpose. Blyukher, although presumably well aware that a concerted northern drive would allow war-lord Sun Chuan-fang to penetrate the *Kuomintang* rear, nevertheless supported Borodin and the call for a resumption of the drive north.[67] Chiang Kai-shek thereupon resorted to the use of the device which he had employed against Bubnov — he demanded the re-call of Borodin. This time it failed to work. Borodin, enjoying the support of the Chinese Communists, was left in Wuhan, presumably upon the express wish of Stalin.

Fighting his way eastward towards Nanchang and Nanking, Chiang Kai-shek met with a check before Nanchang, when the threat from Sun Chuan-fang finally materialised. From this predicament he was rescued by the 7th Corps, which cut its way out of encirclement and inflicted heavy defeat upon that particular war-lord.[68] After taking Nanchang, in March 1927 Nationalist troops entered Nanking. A few days after this event, on 30th March, 1927, from Hankow, centre of the Wuhan commune and stronghold of the Chinese Communists, came the massive attempts to unseat Chiang Kai-shek and to bind him and his command tightly to the *Kuomintang* as a whole, the capture of which the Chinese Communists were bent on making. The only result was to hasten the physical split in the National Revolutionary Army between the field and political commands. The former was made up largely of Whampoa cadets and non-Communists, detesting the airs and power of the commissars. The latter, directed by Teng Yen-ta, lived closer to the Communists. When the two command sections made their respective choices, the *Kuomintang* army was ripped in half.

And still the alliance between Stalin and Chiang Kai-shek endured. Support for the Chinese Communists against him might still be construed as aiding and abetting Trotsky. At the prompting of the Chinese Communists, Borodin tried to get an answer from Moscow about possible resistance to Chiang Kai-shek by the Communists in Shanghai, upon which Nationalist troops were now advancing. The answer was still the same — there was to be neither let nor hindrance from the Communists.[69] The Soviet command in China was ham-strung, aware though Blyukher and Borodin were of the power accruing to Stalin's favourite ally. Chiang Kai-shek entered Shanghai unopposed by the Communists there. On 7th April, 1927, at a secret conference he and chosen commanders planned the purge of Communists.[70] On 12th, after preliminary anti-Communist actions, his troops went into action against the Communists of Shanghai, and Canton. Steadily the Communist organisations were systematically shot down, convert and sympathiser alike. At Nanking on 18th April, 1927, Chiang Kai-shek proclaimed a government separate from that of Wuhan. The army split down the centre. Borodin and Blyukher waited in Hankow for the final débâcle.

* * * *

Stalin had been tricked, although he had been a willing victim for long enough. There still remained, however, Wuhan, upon which could be built the deception that the Left, freed from the restriction of co-operating with the Right, could embark upon revolution. Stalin explained the failure to mount an offensive against Shanghai by the fact that Wuhan could not fight north and east simultaneously, that a junction with Feng Yu-hsiang was more important, that momentarily '. . . let Chiang Kai-shek rather continue to flounder in the Shanghai area and hobnob there with the imperialists'.[71] Militarily, the situation did not seem hopeless; the 4th Corps, with its Communist backbone, continued to drive north, defeating the Manchurian Army at Honan. There was still Feng Yu-hsiang, the nominal Soviet ally in whom Borodin began to place his last desperate trust.[72] But the Christian-Soviet General also played politics. The real victors at Honan were those who showed real political discretion as the better part of valour. Politically, confusion reigned quite supreme. N. N. Roy, the Indian Marxist, had been despatched to Wuhan in April. Working against Borodin, he appealed to Moscow for the new instructions which he himself half-suggested. Sent out in May, orders reached the Soviet command in Wuhan at the beginning of June; they called for agrarian revolution, rigid terror and the raising of a new revolutionary army.[73] None of this corresponded to the realities of the situation. Mention of 'revolutionary peasants'—and Roy leaked this item with disastrous consequences—automatically inclined Chinese generals to Chiang Kai-shek. Feng Yu-hsiang as one arbiter of the situation, and Li Tsung-yen as another supported by the crack 7th Corps, retired to the side of Chiang Kai-shek. Instead of forming the basis of a new Soviet front, Feng Yu-hsiang bent his efforts to knit up Wuhan with Chiang Kai-shek.

Finally, in all defiance of Stalin, and abandoning their political serfdom in the Wuhan government, the Chinese Communists staged a revolt at Nanchang on the night of 1st August.* A Revolutionary Committee of twenty-five, including Chou En-lai, Chu Teh and Ho Lun, was formed; the insurgents amounted to sixteen regiments and four battalions.[74] Within a week the rebellion had been crushed. Borodin, who had remained head of the Soviet mission up to this bitter end, was already making his way out of China. Stalin lost little time in sending Lominadze as a replacement, with the assignment of salvaging the revolution. The Soviet military mission had been withdrawn, although at what point Blyukher returned to Soviet territory remains obscure. The attempt to keep the revolution in its new extreme form in China led only to the grim and hapless folly of futile insurrection. The rising in Canton which took place in December 1927 was crushed after three days. Successive risings in 1928 were cut to pieces in a similar fashion.

The Soviet undertaking in China from 1924–7 had not been primarily a military operation. The service of the Soviet military mission, however, was far from negligible. The very quality of the senior Soviet officers assigned for service emphasised the seriousness of their enterprise. Blyukher — or Galin — made an outstanding contribution, however much Trotsky may have disparaged his political talents and flamboyance. He proved himself to be not only an able organiser but a considerable military diplomat. Whatever his failings as a master of Marxism, he was not deluded by Chiang Kai-shek nor deceived as to the fragility of the compact with him. The few available reports of individual Soviet military advisers in China are fulsome in their praise of Blyukher. A. Khmelev in his report of 5th December, 1926, wrote that '. . . for the Chinese people the name of Galin has become proverbial. Now they call all Russian advisers "the Galins" '.[75] A. I. Cherepanov scored a similar success — to a degree that he returned in 1938 as head of a subsequent Soviet mission to Chiang Kai-shek. Bubnov, although no strategist but a skilled politician, guarded Stalin's interests well enough in China. Although apparently a failure, his mission did achieve a certain retrospective triumph with the Northern Expedition. But with the entry of the Chinese question as a vital part of the factional struggle being waged in Moscow, with the danger that events in China might strengthen one faction against another, the misgivings of the Soviet military command in China about continued reliance on Chiang Kai-shek failed inevitably to register.

As a Soviet strategic concern, revolution in China had the greatest implications. To pursue alliance with the *Kuomintang* and thereby ultimately

* This is now the official birthday of the Chinese Red Army/People's National-Liberation Army.

effect Soviet hegemony over China brought under the former's rule was a *Realpolitik* burdened with distant perspectives. Control of the military effectiveness of the *Kuomintang* — by the rule of the Soviet military directorate, by being the sole source of arms — was a realistic enough basis upon which to calculate, for military power was the key to the first stage of the Chinese nationalist revolution. The dilemma of Soviet strategy, founded as it was in a number of unproven assumptions, was revealed at the time of the opposition to the proposed Northern Expedition. By Soviet calculation it could wreck all gains. Foreign intervention would have been disastrous. Possible Soviet plans for a link-up with their north-western satellite general, for expansion into Inner Mongolia, for control over a swathe of Asia from Outer Mongolia to Canton — all would have been disrupted. The basic criterion was, however, the security of the Soviet Union itself. To *reinforce* the foreign powers in China by a deliberate act of provocation — the Japanese in Manchuria, the British as co-agents of intervention heavily involved in China, crushing out the sole basis for expanding revolution and thus forever ruining a great Soviet opportunity — however fanciful the calculation, even the remotest threat of its reality brought alarm. Its strength was sufficient to divert attention from Chiang Kai-shek's March 1926 *coup* as a matter of immediate interest.

Fighting Britain in China was to become an absurdity. But to combine Asia for a great war upon the imperialists was less fanciful. If China was to be a beginning, then steps had to be taken to ensure continuity. To judge from the limited evidence of Russian plans contained in the reports of the Soviet military mission, a fairly long view was taken of military preparations in China. Military expansion would also mean military integration. To take up the struggle with Britain in the East did also conform to a traditional Russian policy, with the exception that this time China rather than India and its Central Asian approaches had been selected as the point of pressure. Ultimately triumph in China could lead to a threat to British India. It would therefore appear that Stalin was taking 'the Asiatic view' of Russian strategic obligations. Such a view, however, while it may have been connected with possibilities of a Soviet military-political hegemony in Asia, was all the more obliged to consider the problem posed by Japan. Essentially Soviet military power in the Far East was much inferior to that of Japan. To work for Soviet primacy on the mainland of Asia, yet to ignore or miscalculate the reaction which this might provoke in Japan was a gamble.

Soviet aspirations in China were reduced to the realities of tragedy and futility. Such realities had emerged as a consequence of the refusal or inability to consider immediate issues for what they were, rather than what they should or could be. The problem of Japan remained and with it, indirectly as yet, the question of military power in the Far East.

* * * *

To intervene in China to advance revolution and yet to attempt a policy of *rapprochement* with Japan implied the balance of the knife-edge. With the conclusion of the Soviet-Japanese Treaty of January 1925, Soviet diplomacy achieved a triumph with the apparent normalisation of relations in the Far East. At the 14th Party Congress at the end of 1925 Stalin insisted that '. . . we have no interests that lead to our relations with Japan becoming strained. Our interests lie in the direction of *rapprochement* between our country and Japan.'[76] All this made for sense and safety if the analysis of the inner contradictions of capitalism, showing that Japan's main enemy was the United States of America, proved correct. Such a pre-occupation would restrain Japan from intervening in China and thus damaging Soviet prospects there. To Kopp, Soviet representative in Japan and to Litvinov himself such an optimistic evaluation, founded in the teeth of all the evidence, seemed dangerously facile. Since late 1926 Stalin had tried — and failed — to obtain a non-aggression pact or even a pledge of mutual non-intervention in China from Japan.[77] In April 1927, General Tanaka, former Deputy Chief of Staff and leader of the Japanese intervention in Siberia, took over the positions of Premier and Foreign Minister in Japan, signifying the end of Shidehara's policy of 'non-resistance' in China. Japanese railway links were pushed northwards in Manchuria. Although technically only in possession of the Kwantung Peninsula, Japanese power had swelled continuously in Southern Manchuria. Soviet re-entry to Northern Manchuria had been secured in 1924, and a joint Soviet and Chinese-Manchurian administration of the Chinese Eastern Railway set up.

Japanese troops did intervene in China in 1928 in the 'Tsinan incident'. Chiang Kai-shek's resumed Northern Expedition was on the point of effecting contact with the forces of Chang Tso-lin, dictator of Manchuria and erstwhile Japanese protégé. It was a principle of Japanese policy to keep Manchuria separate from China; it had pleased Chang Tso-lin to act in support of this (and as a check upon Soviet expansion), but now he tried too much, a simultaneous opposition to Japan and the Soviet Union. Chang Tso-lin tried to wrest the Chinese Eastern Railway from the tightening Soviet grip. At Tsinan, nominally on a mission to protect Japanese citizens, Japanese troops checked the junction of Chinese Nationalist with Manchurian troops. Intervention had finally materialised, but now the iron of revolution in China had grown cold and was no longer a crux in Soviet-

Japanese relations. Chang Tso-lin withdrew — on Tanaka's 'strong recommendation' — from North China to Mukden. But the Japanese Kwantung Army (to become one of the deadliest foes of the Soviet Union), seeing in Chang Tso-lin a great obstacle to the realisation of their plans for Manchuria, resolved to kill him. This they accomplished with despatch and cunning, dynamiting his train just outside Mukden on 4th June, 1928.[78]

Chang Hsueh-liang, son of Chang Tso-lin, continued his father's anti-Soviet policy, but momentarily succumbed to Japanese pressure to separate from Nationalist China. By the end of 1928 a vigorous campaign against Soviet rights in the Chinese Eastern Railway was in full swing. Already in December 1925 the Soviet command had discussed the possibility of military action to deter Chang Tso-lin from over-reaching himself in his lunges at the railway, the Soviet Union's speediest link between European Russia, Siberia and Vladivostok.[79] A Japanese rejoinder that this would provoke military counter-measures caused it to be abandoned. In March 1929 Chang Hsueh-liang obstructed a new Soviet attempt to negotiate by demanding the inclusion of Chiang Kai-shek. The crisis advanced apace, and in July 1929 a secret conference took place between Chiang Kai-shek and Chang Hsueh-liang; the final moves for the seizure of the Chinese Eastern Railway were co-ordinated. It was not long before the Soviet Union had to consider a resort to direct military action. To surrender the railway meant cutting the life-line with Vladivostok. But military action in Manchuria could provoke, as previous experience testified, dangerous repercussions from Japan.

* * * *

Four months elapsed before Moscow committed the Red Army. Hesitation in the face of Japan, the need to mobilise in the Soviet Far East and divisions of opinion within the Soviet leadership accounted for the delay. The huge and sprawling Siberian Military District was not mobilised and possessed only little more than a score of tanks and armoured cars. To draw on the military strength of European Russia would take time and could not proceed too far out of a fear of weakening the defences of the western frontier districts. On 7th August, 1929, the Soviet Union *Revvoensoviet* decreed the formation of the Special Far Eastern Army (*ODVA*). Blyukher, who had not been assigned to the vitally important post of Soviet Military Attaché in Berlin as expected in 1928, took command.[80] Anticipations of further trouble in the Far East or Stalin's awareness of Blyukher's attitude over Chiang Kai-shek may have prevented the Berlin appointment. Blyukher was an obvious choice for the new command — a Far Eastern specialist, and even more relevant, skilled at the swift and deadly operation. Soviet troops would not have to linger in Manchuria.

Tukhachevsky, it is reported, took over the Operations Section of the Red Army Staff.[81]

The new army was first assembled by mobilisation within the Siberian Military District. The 18th Rifle Corps was activated in the Trans-Baikal sector, the 19th in Nikolsk-Ussuriisk in the Maritime Provinces. The 21st Territorial and 12th Perm Rifle Divisions were moved up to Chita, and a company of MS–1 tanks assigned to the Trans-Baikal force.[82] Further mobilisation increased the available man-power from 30,000 to 60,000 and finally to some 100,000. The vessels of the Amur River Flotilla were placed under the command of the new force. Soviet-trained forces in Outer Mongolia were likewise placed on a war-footing.

Sporadic fighting had taken place during July and August, when raids on Soviet installations and territory took place; on 19th August the Soviet government protested officially at the eight depredations which had occurred from 18th July to 18th August.[83] Remnants of White troops were reported to be taking part in these actions. Alarmed at the prospect of a Soviet-Chinese clash, which could have had enormous repercussions, a conciliation commission had been suggested by the United States of America. Soviet intentions, however, shrank far from the prospect of war. There was indication of reluctance to embark even upon a punitive action. Moscow took care to advise the Japanese that China, not the Soviet Union, would have to precipitate war.[84] Soviet dilatoriness and extreme caution suggested divisions at the highest level. Voroshilov, having suggested military action in 1925, doubtless propounded the same course now, in spite of the risks. But not until there was substantial proof that Japan would not resist a limited Soviet expedition, one which involved no extensive Soviet operations either in Northern Manchuria or reaching into the south, was the Red Army swung into action, military operations beginning on 12th October, 1929.

The Staff of the Special Far Eastern Army was located at Khabarovsk. Two small-scale operations were mounted south-west of Khabarovsk, at the junction of the river Sungari with the Amur and south at Fukdin on the Sungari itself. The object was to destroy hostile naval units harrassing Soviet steamers and enemy concentrations. The first action, fought round Lakasus, was prepared from 7th–11th October; the Chief of Staff of the Special Far Eastern Army, A. I. Lapin, was in command of the operation and the Amur flotilla was under Ya. I. Ozolin. The naval units were to destroy hostile ships and land the 2nd Division on hostile territory near Lakasus. Aerial reconnaissance preceded the action, which began at dawn on 12th October. Soviet artillery was engaged to destroy hostile vessels and batteries; under the cover of this fire, and protected by aircraft, two advance battalions of the 2nd Division were put ashore at 6.27 a.m., followed shortly after by the bulk of the division. A little after noon the town had been encircled, with remnants of the garrison retiring to Fukdin. On the same day Soviet troops began to retire from hostile territory on the orders of the command.

Much more substantial forces faced Soviet troops at Fukdin further down the river. To block the passage of Soviet monitors down the Sungari to Fukdin, barges were sunk and the reaches covered by artillery. Fukdin was protected by a triple ring of trenches. Blyukher assigned the 5th Amur and the 4th Volochaevka Regiments to the 2nd Division, and Amur vessels. Ozolin was entrusted with command of the whole operation. Two groups — the first under Ozolin himself to deal with enemy vessels, the second to effect the landing—were composed out of the combined force. Command of the second group went to the commander of the 2nd Division. On 31st October, at midnight, the operation began. At 2 a.m., the 5th Rifle Regiment (2nd Division) was embarked, effecting a landing at 11 a.m. By the afternoon the first two lines of trenches had been taken, but fighting went on until 3rd November, when the last of the enemy ships and troops had been reduced. Soviet forces were returned to Khabarovsk.[85]

A greater military effort was mounted against the border stations of Manchouli and Dalainor, to eliminate the penetrations in the Trans-Baikal. Some 10,000 hostile troops opposed the Red Army in the region of Manchouli; to effect the destruction of this force the Trans-Baikal Group of the Detached Far Eastern Army under the command of S. S. Vostretsov was set up. Including 6,000 infantry, 1,600 cavalry, 166 light and 331 heavy machine-guns and 88 guns, this force possessed in addition a company of 9 tanks (type MS–1) and 32 aircraft.[86] The plan of the operation called for a wide outflanking move from the south by the 5th Detached Cavalry Brigade, and a drive from the north by the 35th and 36th Rifle Divisions to encircle the Dalainor enemy concentration; the next stage would mean movement to the west, linking up with the 21st Rifle Division operating from the north, and the encirclement of the Manchouli enemy group. To accomplish the first task a storm group of the 107th and 108th Regiments of the 36th Rifle Division was organised, with a tank company attached. It was at the same time proposed that this attack should now be mounted from the west, with the 106th Regiment of the 36th Division covering the operation from the direction of Manchouli. One regiment of the 35th Rifle Division was to attack Dalainor from the north and another from the south. Two infantry battalions of the 36th Division were attached to the 5th Cavalry Brigade, with the task of making a wide turning-movement about Dalainor from the south-east. The defect in this plan, according to a

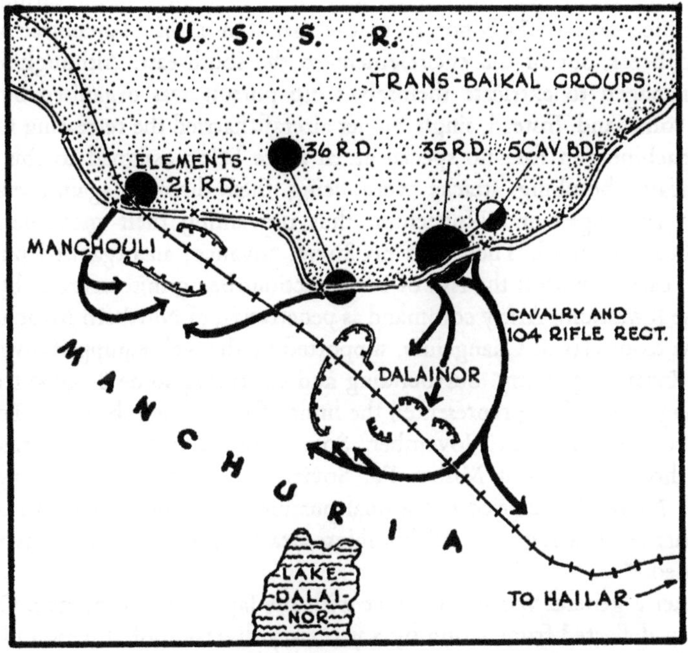

OPERATIONAL PLAN OF THE TRANS-BAIKAL GROUPS, FAR EASTERN ARMY
(For 17 November 1929)

Soviet critic, lay in the fact that the artillery was not directed to maintaining the security of the storm group (from the 36th Division), but was deployed on the northern and passive sector.[87]

The defects became obvious at once when the attack was opened on the morning of 17th November. The artillery lost contact with the 36th Division, which was mounting the main blow. Proper co-ordination between the infantry and the tanks was lacking. The infantry, minus its tanks, was pinned down by enemy fire; the tanks, without the infantry, attacked enemy trenches without success. While the storm-group was caught in heavy fighting, the 106th Regiment (36th Division) succeeded in breaking the resistance to it and by night fall on 17th advanced on the south of Manchouli, linking up with the 63rd Regiment of the 21st Rifle Division, moving from the west and south-west. This cut off the retreat of the Manchouli garrison, success being attained when the assaults of the

35th Rifle Division and the 5th Cavalry Brigade resulted in the turning of the fortified area of Dalainor from the east. On 18th, Manchurian units tried to break out of the encirclement to the south-east. Although some units managed to extricate themselves, no pursuit was organised by the Soviet command. Instead, single Soviet aircraft harried the retreating forces with machine-gun fire, no special aerial force being assigned to this task since heavy bombing attacks were being then directed against enemy reserves at Tsagan and Nuanchun, thus preventing their movement to assist those encircled. There was no Soviet advance; an organised pursuit by land carried with it the risk of Soviet actions being misconstrued by the Japanese Kwantung Army command as penetration of Northern Manchuria. Japanese troops lay at Changchun, supported by the well-equipped divisions of the Kwantung Army. Surrounding and disarming some 8–9,000 troops of Chang Hsueh-liang represented the limit of the Soviet objective. To the east, also on 17th–18th November, Soviet troops carried out a raid to reduce hostile troops at Mishan-Fu. Soviet forces from Outer Mongolia on 27th November carried out a final pursuit which took them to Hailar, and apart from a few isolated bombing attacks, military operations were concluded.[88]

Neither a general war nor conflict with the Japanese had resulted. China had been deflected from action by a necessary diversion of attention due to General Feng Yu-hsiang launching his own offensive against Nationalist troops in October. The Soviet action in November, sharp and effective as an object lesson, appreciably lessened China's chances of bringing Manchuria once more under Chinese sway. If the Soviet action worked as a deterrent upon the Chinese, its influence upon the Japanese command may have been curiously provocative, in spite of Soviet rectitude in not interfering in Northern Manchuria, much less posing a threat to the south. The Special Far Eastern Army's offensive, which displayed 'evidence of exceptional execution and tactical skill',[89] prompted the Japanese to ponder the significance of the evident revival of Russian military power in the Far East. No longer was it possible to calculate Japanese designs in terms of Soviet military weakness, since the restitution of military power to the Far East and the exhibition of the intention to develop it economically could mean a serious obstacle to Japan's expansionist design. The Kwantung Army,* already seriously beginning to reckon with the Soviet Union as an enemy becoming less potential and more real, could have been prompted in speeding up its plans for the absorption of Manchuria and the elimination of Chang Hsueh-liang by the calculation that this were best done before

* This army takes its name from Japan's legal possession in South Manchuria, the Kwantung Peninsula. This army base had a naval counter-part in Port Arthur.

Soviet power had expanded more fully. The apparent synchronisation of Soviet and Japanese aims in 1929 could not outweigh the development of a real division of interest, leading to the state of acute threat under which the Soviet Far East endured until 1939, when Zhukov delivered a smashing blow at the Japanese in the battles of Nomon-han (Khalkhin-Gol) in Outer Mongolia.

The Special Far Eastern Army developed apace and was constantly expanded, to become both in its organisation and the command arrangements one of the most singular of Soviet military organisations. It was an army associated completely with the name of Blyukher, who remained in command in the Far East. The First Five-Year Plan foreshadowed the subsequent attempt to achieve economic self-sufficiency and an armaments base for the Soviet Far East, while the organisation of the Special Far Eastern Army marked a serious step in the revival of Russian military power arrayed against Japan. Three years later Russian naval power staged its own similar re-entry. The increasing attention of the Japanese command towards the Soviet Union as a principal enemy intensified during 1928–9, with the idea of Manchuria as a base for war operations against the Russians obtaining a tight hold. In 1930, according to the testimony of Kawaba Torashiro (then an officer of the General Staff of the Japanese Army), a revised war-plan for operations concerning the Soviet Union was worked out.[90] The Japanese estimate of their situation had produced a concept of any future war as one in which a surprise initial blow would be vital to provide an early series of engagements which would provide an immediate decision — based on the idea that Japan could not support a protracted war in view of the level of Japanese national potential as a whole. With such emphasis upon the strategic offensive and the sudden blow, the Soviet Union faced an acute defence problem as Japanese power advanced itself, first seizing Manchuria.

Soviet power did not depend upon control of Manchuria but was based upon her acquisition in Outer Mongolia and the foundations laid in Central Asia. Moscow had resisted every attempt by the Chinese to detach Outer Mongolia from the Soviet orbit of real power. The role which Outer Mongolia played subsequently fully justified, in the eyes of Soviet military and political leaders, that policy of retention. Apart from this point of unanimity, Soviet policy in the Far East had been marked by violent spasms of disagreement and divergence of view among its manipulators. Voroshilov had distinguished himself by his advocacy of a forward military policy, and there was no reason to suppose that he might easily abandon it. Relations between Blyukher and Voroshilov, however, may well have cooled as a consequence of the publicity and acclaim given to the former's exploits in the Far Eastern actions. Voroshilov may have sensed a rival to his own carefully fostered popularity from a senior Soviet commander whose origin was quite as proletarian as his own.[91] This rivalry, if it can be dated from this point, was to have unfortunate consequences for Blyukher. Yan Gamarnik, who on 1st October, 1929, succeeded Bubnov as the head of the Red Army Political Administration, had served in responsible positions in the Party apparatus in the Far East and continued to maintain close links with the Far Eastern command, in the formation of whose political staff he played a considerable part. About the Staff of the Special Far Eastern Army a formidable concentration of Soviet military talent was gathered. In a comparatively short period Soviet striking power in the Far East was brought up to a level equally impressive. To organise military and economic power in the Far East so that it possessed the capacity to wage war independently of European Russia, thus escaping the dilemma of Tsarist Russia, was admirable in theory. While it conferred the benefit of increasing Soviet capability to deal with the difficulties imposed by geography and the handicaps exerted by relatively poor communications, it also carried with it the risk that the same power could be used for political ends — even as a threat. The difficulties of such an arrangement were shortly to be discovered. Meanwhile the Soviet command was involved in extensive dealings with the *Reichswehr*, with whom an intensified policy of collaboration and co-existence had been put into operation. It was not only in the East that complicated turns of policy involving the Red Army were being worked.

CHAPTER NINE

Military and Naval Trafficking with Germany

The upheavals of 1924–5 in the Soviet command do not seem to have gone by without leaving some mark on the operation of the secret military-industrial compact with Germany. Trotsky, under whom the first contacts had been contrived, made his last recorded appearance on this particular scene in the summer of 1924, when in June, Brockdorff-Rantzau had complained to him that there seemed to be a certain Russian dilatoriness, possibly obstruction even, in pursuing the terms of the joint undertaking. A point in question was the fate of the Junkers' subsidy for the Russian factory, which was in jeopardy since this depended on definite orders being placed. As Frunze's reforms gathered momentum, new Soviet military-industrial priorities were being worked out with a definite shift in emphasis on the development of an indigenous war-industry and military potential. Soviet intelligence was primarily concerned with industrial espionage. Stalin's speech on military policy to the Central Committee on 19th January, 1925, was an indication that sharp divisions of opinion existed over military policies, although Trotsky's policy of contact with the *Reichswehr* survived in its essentials even if operated by a new command.

From the German side, arising out of the different interests represented in the *Ostpolitik*, there was also a show of misgiving. No success attended the Soviet exploration, deviously conducted after December 1924, of the possibility of a Soviet-German alliance.[1] Such a proposition* evoked opposition from Brockdorff-Rantzau, who wished rather to see a political agreement which would confer upon Germany those definite advantages which had hitherto eluded her in spite of the liberal concessions made to the Russians as a consequence of the first understandings. The idea of turning the whole undertaking into an economic arrangement by gradual transformation of the more military aspects proved to be impractical, although such

* Kopp and Rykov had first suggested a definite commitment. Chicherin, when pressed, admitted the idea of a military agreement. Brockdorff-Rantzau did not hide his unfavourable opinion (as expressed in 1922) from Chicherin. For an excellent study of this, see Zygmunt J. Gasiorowski, 'The Russian Overture to Germany of December 1924', *Journal of Modern History* 1958, No. 2, pp. 99–118.

a scheme had recommended itself to Brockdorff-Rantzau early in 1924. Disengagement was prevented precisely by those far-reaching commitments entered into by the German military missions to the Soviet Union in 1923 — overt and deliberate withdrawal from which would have wreaked havoc in Soviet-German political relations. A form of solution was provided by the course which the collaboration itself had begun to take, for by early 1925 a new emphasis was being laid on the testing of equipment and the training of personnel on the sites envisaged by the *Reichswehr*'s agreement of 1922, rather than the actual production of war materials in factories located in the Soviet Union. One of the consequences of this shift of emphasis was to bring the Red Army and the *Reichswehr* into close, even intimate contact, an event foreshadowed by the negotiations of June 1924 and Rosengoltz's consultation in January 1925 with General Hasse.[2] The object of these conversations concerned the despatch of German flying personnel to the joint Soviet-German aviation training-centre at Lipetsk. In August 1925 a group of senior German officers was in attendance at the Red Army manœuvres — the Germans bereft of uniform and camouflaged as 'German worker-Communists' — while Soviet officers, passed off as 'Bulgarians', were present at the autumn exercises of the *Reichswehr*.[3] The second stage of the collaboration, one concerned directly with the Red Army itself and the Soviet military command, had begun.

Unshlikht and Rosengoltz played a substantial part in these negotiations for closer professional and technical contact, while Voroshilov assumed the position which Trotsky had first held when the arrangement was developed in the beginning. It was towards Voroshilov, however, that German anger was directed early in 1926, when a Soviet military publication, produced under the auspices of the *VNO* in Moscow, made available a dangerously comprehensive account of the military state of the *Reichswehr*, with embarrassing detail about German military strength, organisation, installations and para-military formations. Voroshilov himself had contributed the preface to this volume entitled *Foreign Armies*.[4] On 4th March, 1926, *Izvestiya* chose to be equally frank about German expenditure on armaments. Brockdorff-Rantzau lashed out at Chicherin over these provocations, declaring that it would be an unimaginable scandal for a power to publish from well-nigh official sources such damaging disclosures, when that same power was a declared friend of Germany and engaged with her upon a joint military conspiracy. As for Voroshilov's plea of 'naiveté', the Commissar for War should be aware that politics and naiveté do not mix, and for Voroshilov — ex-machinist in a factory owned by Germans before 1918 — it was an especially poor excuse, since he ought to be more precisely acquainted with German methods.[5] Such a calculated indiscretion may have been designed to bring pressure to bear upon Berlin by precipitating hostile reaction in the West towards which German policy was now steering in an effort to reach some understanding.

Also at the beginning of this critical year searching questions were being asked in Berlin about the implications of the Soviet-German undertakings. It was desired to establish what guarantees existed that Germany would receive her share of the war-materials manufactured in the Soviet Union; whether Seeckt was in direct or indirect contact with Radek and other leading Soviet officials, and whether the *Reichswehrministerium* (or Seeckt personally) received *political* reports from officers and technicians assigned by them to the Soviet Union.[6] Brockdorff-Rantzau specifically demanded that the *Reichswehr* be forbidden to maintain direct contacts with Soviet officials, that a single *Reichswehr* officer be appointed as representative of the military in Moscow, and that Brockdorff-Rantzau himself be invested with the control of German money disbursed on military projects in the Soviet Union.[7] The changes which were conceivably in the offing were checked, however, by the arrival of a Soviet military mission in Berlin. Led by Unshlikht (referred to as 'Herr U.' or 'Herr Untermann' in German documents) the Soviet mission brought far-reaching proposals concerning Soviet-German co-operation on armaments production, and arrived while the negotiations over a Soviet-German neutrality agreement were still taking place. At a luncheon party given by the Soviet Ambassador Krestinsky on 1st April, 1926, Unshlikht disclosed the burden of his mission to Stresemann, Seeckt, General Wetzell, Schubert and Luther.

Unshlikht launched into an explanation of the huge new Soviet plans for the production of artillery, poison-gas, optical and precision instruments. To accomplish this German financial assistance as well as a German undertaking to purchase a proportion of these war-supplies was a necessity. In looking at the widest possible implications of the new scheme, Unshlikht also pointed out that a comprehensive plan could be developed to include testing and training-courses (*Ausbildungskurse alle Arte*).[8] This project, continued Unshlikht, had already been discussed with the *Reichswehr* and his object was now to secure the approval of the German government. Such schemes and disclosures evidently fell with shattering impact on the non-military members of the party. Seeckt spoke not a word.[9] Whichever turn the conversations took, Unshlikht and his party continued to talk armaments, to the obvious discomfiture of several members of the gathering. The sequel was not favourable to the Russians. Although the proposed plan was given careful consideration and several of the advantages which it could bestow upon Germany were clearly recognised, Stresemann and Schubert finally concluded that at such a juncture of German policy — with relations towards the West visibly improving — German participation would not be justified. Unshlikht's mission had shown both the scope of Soviet plans and the degree to which fulfilment depended upon German support, if they were to be made effective on such a scale; as Soviet undertakings, however, they would become part of the Soviet armaments base, a point from which there was to be no departure in the future. Whether Unshlikht really anticipated any considerable success, or whether his mission was merely a stratagem to divine German intentions cannot be established either way. The mention of previous talks with the *Reichswehr* suggests that serious intentions lay behind his visit, and that the political objective may have been to anchor German policy once more in the east by offering military advantages. As such it conformed to the Soviet policy of 'the carrot and the stick' which was applied to divert Germany from *rapprochement* with the West and threatening the isolation of the Soviet Union. The 'military card' was being played as a trump.

A major crisis was produced later in the year as a result of the *Reichswehr*'s action in shipping to Stettin the grenades which had been manufactured under the *GEFU* contracts in the Soviet Union. Whatever precautions had been taken to ensure the secrecy of the operation, they did not suffice.[10] The 'revelations', long-feared by Brockdorff-Rantzau and others, finally made their appearance and not as a result of Soviet carelessness, deliberate indiscretion or diplomatic blackmail. On 3rd and 6th December, 1926, *The Manchester Guardian* enlarged upon the facts first supplied by the munition-ships — '. . . six in all, though some of them were sailing vessels . . .' — and mentioned the Junkers factory and the chemical works for poison-gas.[11] On 16th December, 1926, the Socialist deputy Scheidemann brought the matter into brightest glare of publicity by denouncing the traffic from the floor of the *Reichstag*. The issue was an embarrassment for the German Communists, a problem for the Foreign Ministry and the delaying tactics of promising full and satisfactory explanation to the Committee for Foreign Affairs allayed very few fears.

The 'revelations', damaging as they were, came as something of an anti-climax. Already the re-organisation of *GEFU* had been suggested in December 1925, and in their discussion of the question Wallroth and Hasse showed every sign of being aware that English and French suspicions of *GEFU* were fully aroused.[12] After the failure of the Junkers venture in the Soviet Union, the firm produced a lengthy memorandum on the nature of its commitments and its relations with the *Reichswehrministerium*[13] — the contents of which found its way to the press. By the end of 1926 *GEFU* had been liquidated, its assets exhausted and two of its undertakings — Junkers and Bersol — having come to an unsuccessful conclusion. A new firm *WIKO* (*Wirtschaftskontor*) was devised to handle the existing financial arrangements during the period of their winding-up. The termination of the contracts and the crisis produced by the 'revelations' offered to both Moscow and Berlin the opportunity to review the existing arrangements. After his conversation of 19th November, 1926, with *Reichswehrminister* Dr. Gessler, Brockdorff-Rantzau was to inform the Russians that Germany was about to adopt a new policy. In effect, this was to continue the relationship but have it gradually tail off, to sink perhaps to the level of an economic undertaking which Brockdorff-Rantzau had thought of in 1924.[14] By the beginning of 1927 only the aviation training-centre at Lipetsk and the proposed tank-school at Kazan existed as purely 'private' undertakings, aircraft manufacture and gas production had ceased, leaving only the annual exchange of officers at manœuvres as any kind of formal military arrangement. It was upon this basis that Soviet-German collaboration was re-negotiated by both sides in 1927. There was, however, one further item of the contact which had assumed increasing importance throughout 1926, and which was reaching some degree of effectiveness as the military side stagnated a little — this involved the dealings of the Soviet naval command with the German *Marineleitung*.

* * * *

Soviet-German naval collaboration was comparatively slow in reaching a stage where it might be compared with the progress in purely military affairs. There were two reasonably simple explanations for this; the German Navy had found means other than escape into Russia to outwit the restrictions of the Treaty of Versailles, and the Soviet command, faced with the stark fact of the 1921 Kronstadt rebellion, had concentrated upon the political rather than the technical reconstruction of the Soviet Navy. Nor did the course of Soviet military policy as a whole throughout the period of 'transition' permit of much attention being paid to the special problems involved in raising up the navy to a high standard of technical and combat efficiency. A German naval mission to the Soviet Union in 1922 produced little apparent result; it may, in fact, have been predominantly a technical mission with only a very few naval officers attached to it. *Kapitän zur See* Lohmann had evidently journeyed to the Soviet Union in 1923 in order to establish contact,[15] but no definite arrangement had been concluded.

Properly speaking, 'collaboration' does not seem to have been a feature of the first extensive Soviet-German naval contacts. The Soviet naval command, working through the *Zentral Moskau* (*Z.Mo.*), made a direct appeal for German naval assistance. There was little possibility of offering the *quid pro quo* of space and secrecy which the Red Army could extend to the *Reichswehr* in its illegal activities. Already at the end of 1924 or the beginning of 1925 the *Marineleitung* had received from the Soviet naval command a detailed questionnaire on submarine operations, on the administration of a submarine fleet, and all matters ranging from crew-selection to points of tactical naval doctrine. This was returned, presumably completed and with the necessary manuals which had been requested, through Major Fischer on 25th April, 1925.[16] Not until the following year, on 25th March, 1926, is there a record of the first full conversations conducted by Soviet naval representatives with the *Marineleitung*. At this meeting, which included Admiral Spindler, the naval captains Löwenfeld, Bindseil and Reimer, Colonel Thomsen and Major Fischer, the Soviet Military Attaché Luniev and the Naval Representative Oras laid before the German naval officers a formal Soviet request for technical and professional assistance. There was no question, Oras pointed out, of Germany building submarines for the Soviet Union. Russia wanted *everything*, but it would be preferable to have it built in the Soviet Union itself.[17]

One of the first results of this meeting was the despatch of a small German naval mission on a tour of inspection of Soviet ships and naval installations, at the same time taking the opportunity to hold talks with the Soviet naval chiefs. Admiral Spindler and *Kapitän zur See* Kinzel appear to have comprised the German delegation; the visit lasted from 2nd to 18th June, 1926. On 7th, at a meeting held from 11.30 a.m. to 12 noon, Unshlikht conveyed his thanks for the friendly attitude of the German Navy, and indicated the considerable Soviet interest in submarines — and possibly a capital ship. On the same day, from 2–4.30 p.m., Zof, Chief of the Soviet Navy, pursued a more particular line of enquiry; he mentioned the submarine-construction work which Germany was carrying out for Turkey and asked whether there was any possibility of obtaining access to these plans — but much more important was the question of the Soviet naval command having access to German submarine designs produced during the World War. The conversations were followed by visits to Soviet ships at Kronstadt, to the destroyer *Engels*, to the submarine *Batrak*, and the capital-ship *Marat**— whose commander appeared to be 'a sound torpedo-coxswain type'. On the afternoons of 14th and 15th the final conferences took place with Unshlikht and Zof. The latter on 15th again pressed for 'something concrete' from Germany, his suggestions taking the form of pressing for submarine plans, for the opportunity to draw on German experience and for the

* The *Marat* was a 23,000 ton battleship, completed in 1914 and possibly re-fitted by this date; mounted 12 12-inch guns in triple turrets, 14 4·7-inch, AA armament, 1 aircraft, with a speed of 23 knots. The *Engels* was a 1,200 ton destroyer, with 4 4-inch guns, 3 3-inch, 9 torpedo tubes (tripled).

assignment of three submarine experts — one for command, two to deal with construction and engines respectively — to the Soviet Navy.[18]

At 10 a.m., on 1st July, 1926, the whole question of delivering submarine plans to the Soviet Union was discussed by Admiral Spindler, the naval captains Werth, Canaris, Lahs and Dönner, *Geheimrat* Presse, Dr Moraht and other officials. It was suggested that the Russians might have — in principle — designs up to 1918; there was also the question of the Class B–III designs, the M–S Types, submarine-minelayers and the *U-Kreuzer*. On the point of submarine designs, *Geheimrat* Presse thought that this might compromise Germany — Admiral Spindler expressed his doubts about that, but Presse advised delivering the plans in parts only, to make sure that they did not fall into non-German hands. Canaris opposed the move outright. As for present German undertakings, the question was asked whether the Russians were acquainted with the activity of the *I.v.S.*,* (*Ingenieurskantoor voor Scheepsbouw*), the Dutch cover-firm for submarine construction. Other items of naval equipment came up for discussion; there were the plans for aircraft-launching catapult gear (in which the Swedes were also interested) and designs for motor-torpedo-boats.[19] In spite of the reservations and objections, it was decided to deliver submarine plans to the Russians, a decision which was made formal on 9th July, with the authorisation of the delivery of 'obsolete' plans. On 13th July, *Amtschef II* confirmed that the Russians might receive plans which had already been handed over to the Allies as a result of the Treaty of Versailles; an additional note confirmed that the plans of U–105 to U–114, U–122 to U–126, with others, would be sent to the Soviet Union.[20]

Zof's requests for further assistance evidently met with an equally favourable response. Access to the Turkish plans was to depend on permission from the Turkish contractor. As for German designs, these could well include Type B–III C, Type M–S, Type *U-Kreuzer* U–139 and mine-laying submarines; these designs had been turned over to the Allies. Moreover, the *Marineleitung* declared itself willing to send experts to Moscow to help with the designs, if this were necessary. A study of the operational value of submarine types would be sent, as well as studies of the type of submarine suited to the possible operations of the Soviet Navy. Purchase of construction materials would be facilitated with German firms. By a note of 29th July, 1926, Spindler confirmed that four German submarine designs had been despatched on 24th July, addressed to a confidential agent of the *Heeresleitung* and should thus reach 'Herr U' in Moscow.[21]

The intensified contact led also to preliminary discussions of naval

* The *I.v.S.*, was under retired naval captain Blum as commercial manager, Dr Techel as technical director and had a technical staff of 30; head-quarters were in the Hague.

questions in the event of a Soviet-Polish war, and other hostile combinations of the Powers. One form of assistance which the German Navy could provide was to 'lend' commanders for Soviet submarines, thereby increasing the effectiveness of what naval weapons the Soviet command possessed. The role of the Soviet Navy would be to blockade the Bay of Danzig in the event of Poland warring upon Germany and Russia. In the case of a Franco-Polish combination against Russia and Germany, it would be essential for the Soviet Navy to carry out attacks on French Mediterranean traffic, a strategic purpose which demanded a huge increase in the combat efficiency of the Soviet Black Sea Fleet.[22] Strategic co-operation, however, stumbled against the basic and incontrovertible fact that it could be no part of German designs to create a powerful naval rival in the Baltic. The note of caution, not to say distant hostility could not be erased entirely from German naval opinion over the question of contact with the Soviet naval command. From the Soviet side, in view of the complete inexperience of the command and the prevailing technical backwardness, such contact offered immediate and immense advantages. Technical re-organisation and initial planning of the type of naval force which would best serve the Soviet Union would have been immeasurably more difficult without this opportunity to draw on German skill and experience in naval warfare.

It was, therefore, a fact of some significance that at the end of 1926 R. A. Muklevich entered into the records of contact with the *Marineleitung*. 'Fat and sturdy and round-faced',[23] Muklevich played an outstanding part in the technical re-equipping of the Soviet Navy, having taken over the post of head of the Soviet naval forces from Zof either at the end of 1926 or early in 1927. Born in 1890, Muklevich started out as a textile worker, beginning his political activities in 1906. Called up to the navy, in 1917 he worked in the various Bolshevik military organisations in the north-west, and in 1918 was a military commissar with Red troops fighting the Germans. In the Civil War Muklevich served as commissar to the staff of the XVIth Red army, and was attached to the staff of the Western Front in 1920, under the command of Tukhachevsky. From 1921–2 he served as Deputy Director of the Military Academy, being associated thereafter for some time with the re-organisation of the Red Air Force. A man of considerable ability and independence of outlook, Muklevich soon came to occupy a leading position among the new naval commanders who took charge of naval affairs in the period of co-operation with the *Marineleitung*.

On 2nd December, 1926, Colonel von der Lieth-Thomsen and Muklevich had a talk in Moscow about the possibility of opening a submarine training-station on the Black Sea coast. Such a station would correspond to the installation set up at Lipetsk for aviation or the tank-school at Kazan.[24]

Attractive as it may have appeared in the first instance, this idea led to no positive results. The German Navy was able to make reasonably satisfactory arrangements for the re-armament activities which it considered vital,* and at no point did the *Marineleitung* appear anxious to combine too closely with the Soviet Navy in any other but a purely advisory capacity. Their caution contrasted markedly with the periodic recklessness of the *Reichswehr*, and immunity to pressure lay chiefly in the fact that the Soviet Navy had little to offer which the *Marineleitung* could not ultimately contrive for itself. Moscow nevertheless took what steps it could to safeguard the link with the German Navy. According to a German diplomatic report from London, dated 15th December, 1926, the Soviet Naval Attaché, the former Imperial officer Admiral Behrens,† had been recalled from his post for giving too free a voice to his anti-German views.[25] This was something of an encouraging sign, yet a necessity for the Soviet Navy if no cause whatsoever were to be given to alienate the vital friendship of the *Marineleitung*.

From 1926 senior German naval officers had access to the very heart of the Soviet naval command. To judge from the nature of the Soviet requests, the task of building up a modern naval force surpassed the professional and technical resources available within the Soviet Union. At an early date the submarine assumed considerable prominence in Soviet naval thought, although the question of exactly what type of naval force the Soviet Union should possess remained a question dependent on adequate technical advance and the training of a naval command staff. The two major concentrations of Soviet naval forces, the Baltic and the Black Sea, both required strenuous effort to raise the level of their combat efficiency, and both could be allotted only limited defensive roles. To judge from the evidence supplied from further contact with the *Marineleitung*, not for some two or three years did the problem of expansion and doctrine become pressing, at which point senior Soviet naval officers did not neglect to consult their German counterparts.

★ ★ ★ ★

Not long after the discussion of a possible joint naval training-station on the Black Sea, organised after the manner of Lipetsk or Kazan, the fate of those same aviation and tank schools seemed to hang in the balance early in 1927. On 24th January, 1927, Schubert, Dirksen, General Wetzell and Major Fischer met to discuss the present state of the collaboration. Wetzell made a strong plea for the retention of the tank and aviation schools, since

* See *Kapitän zur See* Schüssler, *Der Kampf der Marine gegen Versailles 1919–1935*, (79 pp.), Oberkommando d. Kriegsmarine, Berlin 1937: *IMT* Doc. 156–C, in Vol. XXXIV, p. 530 f.

† This is Berens, after the Russian spelling.

both arms would be vital in any war of the future. Schubert decided that consultation with Stresemann was essential before the risk which this involved — compromising Germany in the west and the winning of full national rights — could be run. Stresemann accordingly met with the successor to Seeckt, General Heye, to come to an understanding over military collaboration in the east.[26] Lipetsk and Kazan were saved, with the proviso that no *Reichswehr* officers on the active list were to be sent in 1927 for training; participation in 'the scientific gas-experiments' was similarly forbidden. The despatch of active-service German officers to Soviet manœuvres and exercises did not, however, present any fundamental problems. On 26th February, 1927, this agreement was adopted at a cabinet meeting held to discuss military collaboration with the Soviet Union; Dirksen despatched the text to Major Fischer.[27]

Although this clarified the German position, the Soviet attitude to a continuance of the arrangements remained a separate question. Early in February, Moscow had signified its willingness to continue, but this did not solve any of the detailed problems which were about to arise.[28] On 10th March, 1927, Niedermayer in Moscow had evidently talked with Unshlikht's deputy — named as Berzin*— on the problem presented by the actual status of training-stations. The mutual undertakings must have a completely legal form (*völlig legalisiert würden*). A full discussion of this question would exceed the limits of Berzin's special department (presumably one concerned entirely with the administration of the Soviet-German installations), so that it would have to be taken up at Krestinsky's next visit to the *Auswärtiges Amt*.[29] Fixing this matter proved to be more difficult than the first comments about it anticipated, while over the fate of the gas-experiments a similar tug-of-war was waged, with resistance to it coming from German circles. Major Fischer had conveyed General Heye's views on this subject to Schubert in April, and laid the information that a possible site in the Soviet Union was about to be inspected, although East Prussia offered very good facilities for the secrecy which was essential.[30]

On 18th May, 1927, Stresemann, Gessler, Heye, Blomberg, Schubert and Köpke convened to discuss the *Reichswehr*'s relations with the Soviet Union and to hammer out the points of the February agreement. Heye reported that there was now unanimous agreement over the principles of the latter. From the Soviet side a request had come that the German *Auswärtiges Amt* give its approval to the proposed development of the tank-school at Kasan. The tank-school had already been the subject of a discussion with Litvinov,

* Since the document mentions no initials, and since there were two men of the name Berzin in the military command, it can only be assumed that this does refer to Yan Berzin and not R. I. Berzin.

who had suggested a legal form (something like a limited liability company) and requested that Berlin give Krestinsky an undertaking that no political considerations would be raised against the proposed development. Stresemann signified that he had no objections, generally speaking, to such a declaration, but that this might best be handled by Brockdorff-Rantzau. Over the matter of the disarmament question, Unshlikht had also signified Russian agreement to work with Germany in this field, but as a political concern this fell within the sphere of the *Auswärtiges Amt*. Dr. Gessler had some pertinent observations to make on the gas-experiments; it was now the intention to set up the gas-experiment at Orenburg, and the *Reichswehr* was prepared to co-operate with the Russians, from whom far-reaching requests for full sharing of information had been received. The *Reichswehrminister* was nonetheless disturbed about siting these experiments in the Soviet Union, for the Russians might one day become Germany's enemies once again. Germany's interests might be better served by keeping the work on poison-gas locked away in East Prussia.[31]

So far the Russians appeared to have unbent considerably, and to have shown themselves as anxious to secure secrecy as the Germans. According to Major Fischer, who reacted violently to parts of the conversation of 18th May, Moscow placed a very high value indeed on the continuation of the chemical warfare experiments; for that reason, on 24th May, he urged the *Auswärtiges Amt* not to stand in the way of a policy which could only encourage the Russians.[32] Major Fischer was assured that this would not happen. Having straightened out further points of the February agreement, everything seemed set for its implementation, including permission for German officers to wear uniform while attending Red Army exercises.[33]

Information from the Soviet Union early in July indicated feverish military activity at Gomel, and the construction of a new aerodrome at Bryansk, where the munition factories were working night and day.[34] Unfortunately the Russians made no similar show of energy over the Kazan tank-school. At the end of July, von der Lieth-Thomsen reported that the Russians were dragging their feet over the 'Heavy Vehicle Experimental and Test Station', about which General Wetzell and Thomsen himself showed a great deal of concern. The Soviet attitude showed every sign of suspicion and mistrust. It was a matter of great importance for the *Reichswehr* that work should begin as quickly as possible. What appeared to have happened is that whereas formerly the Soviet Commissar for War had been responsible for decisions in this matter, now the question had to go through *Narkomindel*, the Commissariat for Foreign Affairs.[35] This observation was confirmed indirectly in the course of 1928, when Voroshilov talked in Moscow with General Werner von Blomberg, who led an important

German military mission on a tour of inspection of the joint installations. Voroshilov admitted to Blomberg that over the question of the erection of the German schools at Lipetsk and Kazan there had been a division of opinion in the Soviet government. It had been the task of Voroshilov — at least on his admission — to drive the agreement through in the face of this opposition.[36] It was curious that Voroshilov should refer to them as 'the German schools', and it may be that they were viewed in this light by persons other than the Commissar for War. Losing control of the technical military arrangements, which hitherto seemed to have been handled by selected members of the *Revvoensoviet* of the Soviet Union, may have been a sign of Litvinov's intervention and a desire to check potentially dangerous connections. According to the evidence of the German meeting of 18th May, Litvinov had already intervened over the question of the tank-school at Kazan. His object appeared to be the winning of a strict undertaking from Berlin about the scope of the activities and the deliberate freeing of them from political control. If this had so transpired, then the military collaboration from the Soviet side was also not free from the rivalry of the soldiers and diplomats which was so marked a feature of the conduct of German policy.

★ ★ ★ ★

While the more extravagant military-industrial ventures were wound up, and the question of the training-stations hung in the balance, the exchange of officers between the *Reichswehr* and the Red Army still continued after 1925. The attendance at manœuvres took place in 1926 just as it had done in the previous year.[37] In a report presented in 1928, Dirksen cited the exact figures for Soviet and German officers present in each other's army for 1926–7. In 1926 there had been 2 Red Army officers attached to the *Reichswehrministerium* itself, 3 on training trips and 8 in attendance at manœuvres or exercises. In 1927 the corresponding figures were 3, 3 and 8, making a total of 27 for the two years. During the same period the *Reichswehr* detached 39 officers for duties in the Soviet Union. In 1926 at Red Army manœuvres there had been 8 officers (6 in 1927), 14 had gone to the training-stations (none in 1927), 1 to the gas-experiments (2 in 1927), 2 in both years had been despatched on fact-finding tours and 4 in 1927 were sent on leave to learn Russian.[38]

The Soviet officers attached to the *Reichswehrministerium* followed the course of General Staff training which was conducted by the *Reichswehr*. In 1926 one of the Soviet officers attached to this course was Uborevich, while it is impossible to identify the other. In 1927 arrangements were made for the attendance of a further three senior Soviet officers. In conformity with the May (1927) protocol, Uborevich, Eideman* and Apoga were to attend the course for senior officers in Berlin, which would mean their residing in Germany for part of 1928. The *Reichswehr* took a very particular interest in Uborevich, whose second visit for command training this was to be. In German eyes Uborevich had already shown himself to be an exceptional officer, and his military ideas had shown marked affinity with German methods. For this reason Blomberg was anxious to obtain an extension of Uborevich's stay in Germany until May 1928; this was a point upon which the *Reichswehrministerium* placed great importance, for it would provide an opportunity — according to Blomberg — of bringing further influence to bear on Uborevich (*um ihn weiter in deutschen Sinne zubeeinflüssen*).[39] A former officer of the Imperial Russian Army, Uborevich had an impressive military record as a Soviet army commander — having led the IXth, XIIIth and XIVth Red armies to success against Denikin and Wrangel, and operating with Soviet forces against the Japanese in 1922. He had just passed the age of thirty on his first attendance at the German command course.

If Uborevich displayed an original turn of mind and showed signs of grasping the essentials of the military system which he was studying at first hand in the *Reichswehr*, then he was a singular exception among other Soviet officers, to whom German opinion ascribed excessive doctrinairism and learning by rote. The visiting Soviet officers applied themselves to their military lessons with conspicuous industry, when 'they took down every word they heard'.[40] In matters of its organisation, training and mobilisation methods the *Reichswehr* evidently concealed little or nothing from Soviet officers. German manuals and military literature, as Voroshilov admitted to Blomberg and as visiting German officers discovered for themselves, were in heavy demand in the Red Army. Although the principles seem to have been grasped well enough, flexibility of application evidently evaded the Soviet officers, although precisely the same phenomenon could be observed in their handling of purely Russian ideas.

In 1927 the principle of real reciprocity in the officer-exchanges seems to have been observed in the Soviet handling of the visit of six German officers to the autumn manœuvres of the Red Army, held in the region between Odessa and Beresovka. On 29th July, at the invitation of the Soviet government, Colonel Halm, Colonel Müller, Lieutenant-Colonel Schmolcke, and the majors Fischer, Crato and Hoth were selected to attend the exercises. On 3rd August, these officers received their movement orders.[41] The German Consul in Kiev, writing on 17th September, relayed news of the warm

* Referred to as 'Heidemann' in the German document, Eideman was at this time head of the Frunze Military Academy.

reception accorded to the officers and gave a brief summary of German impressions:

> The Russian Army is not yet ready. The higher command believes — what our officers nevertheless doubt — that the army will be battle-worthy in three years.[42]

The actual report on the manœuvres commented not unfavourably on the general conduct of the exercises, but observed that among the lower officer-grades there was a complete aversion to assuming responsibility and a great lack of initiative. The result was that in the absence of a formal order nothing was done.[43]

The proof that the German officers were not being hypercritical was supplied by Voroshilov's own inspection report on the troops of the Ukraine Military District. Carried out from 15th May to 2nd June, this inspection may well have been a preparation for the coming exercises. While pointing to the general progress which had been made, Voroshilov castigated serious failings, some due to unsatisfactory equipment, but others directly attributable to the failure to put the new regulations and directives into effect. Irregularities in combat training existed in divisions and regiments; there was a low level of marksmanship — with the machine-gun particularly. The light machine-gun was not properly exploited. Bad administration lowered the efficiency of some units. Discipline wavered, descending into 'democratism' and the like. Such a state of affairs, wrote Voroshilov, existed not only among the troops of the Ukraine, but to a greater or lesser degree throughout the Red Army. Voroshilov went on to prescribe a remedy:

> At the present stage of the building-up of the Red Army it is essential to organise a break-through towards the streamlining of combat training and a decisive struggle with slackness and the state of dis-organisation in the internal ordering of units. We must declare war against the systematic failure to comply with regulations, fixing the internal life of units.[44]

Voroshilov was instructing the Red Army Staff to prepare measures to deal with these shortcomings, as well as enlisting the aid of the Political Administration.

The German officers were evidently given the opportunity to see what they wished, although Voroshilov's report makes it clear that they might not always find a satisfactory state of affairs. Reporting from Kiev, the German Consul repeated the words of a senior Soviet officer in connection with the visit of the *Reichswehr* officers:

> We have received an order from Moscow, which has done more than amaze us. We are to show the German officers everything. In carrying out this order, we are showing the German officers more than we let our allies get their eyes on during the War.[45]

It was a sign that the tensions of 1927 were passing away somewhat and one of the many moves which facilitated the increasingly close contact of the senior levels of both armies. On 21st December, 1927, Major Fischer informed Dirksen that Colonel Mittelberger was arranging the postings to the aviation school at Lipetsk for the coming year; sent in separate groups, 20 trainees would travel in April, 22 in May and 2 at the beginning of June, for a stay of some four to six weeks.[46]

In the spring of 1928 Dirksen was informed that the Soviet Military Attaché, Luniev, was to be relieved of his Berlin post and assigned to a field command. This raised the question of a new Attaché in this key post. On 13th April, 1928, Dirksen talked with the Soviet representative Bratman-Brodowski about the reported choice of a Colonel Blücher (Blyukher) for Berlin. Dirksen pointed out that such a name — famous in the military history of Germany — in this post might provoke hostile press reaction or ironical remarks (*ironische Bemerkungen*). Was 'Blücher' itself a cover-name, asked Dirksen, for, if so, a different name would be needed for Germany.[47] On 23rd April, in a further talk, Dirksen enquired whether this man Blücher was not, in fact, the 'General Galen' who had recently served in China. Bratman-Brodowski confessed that this was so,* whereupon Dirksen reminded his Soviet colleague that 'Blücher-Galen' had been one of the chief propagandists of the Chinese Revolution. Bratman-Brodowski refreshed Dirksen's memory that rather Blyukher had been detached from duty in the Red Army and served as Chief of Staff to Chiang Kai-shek. Even so, with regard to the circumstances, Dirksen regarded the choice as 'very doubtful' (*sehr bedenklich*) and insisted upon further enquiries.[48] German objections may have been decisive in keeping Blyukher from Berlin, for A. I. Kork was appointed to this post, and on his re-call in 1929, Vitovt Putna finally took up the post in Berlin, having served previously as Soviet Military Attaché in Tokyo. In Moscow the *Reichswehr* post, known hitherto as *Zentrale Moskau* (*Z.Mo.*), was re-named *Heim Deutscher Angestellter Moskau*, with Niedermayer left enjoying his previous position and status.[49]

Colonel Mittelberger's report on the Red Army, compiled during a fact-finding mission in the spring of 1928, remains one of the overwhelming proofs that the *Reichswehr* did obtain access to the inner ring of the Soviet command and acquired a not inconsiderable insight into Soviet military methods as a result of the collaboration.[50] Mittelberger made as close a

* The Russians were once again playing the name-game. In 1921, the Germans had objected to one Brodowski as the proposed head of the Soviet trade delegation in Berlin. Bratman was therefore proposed, but when Brodowski did actually arrive in Berlin, he explained that his name was Bratman-Brodowski. It is not therefore surprising that the Germans were wary of 'Blücher'.

study as possible of the Soviet high command, in an army which still lacked any tradition of leadership, in spite of the role played by the ex-officers of the Imperial Russian Army. Tukhachevsky was absent upon some duty, so that the German Colonel failed to meet him, yet Mittelberger was ready with a judgement upon him. Tukhachevsky was one of the outstanding military talents of the Red Army, but 'everybody knew' that he was merely a Communist for purely opportunistic reasons; he could indeed change sides should his interests warrant it.[51] In general, Mittelberger was of the opinion that the Red Army was trying to cut away from political situations and gain the freedom to concentrate upon purely military objectives. His visits to the Frunze Military Academy and regimental command schools in Moscow made some impression upon him, and although he indulged in no fulsome praise, his comments were generally favourable.[52]

The difficulty of appraising the Soviet military system was fully indicated in a report despatched by the *Statistiche Abteilung** of the *Reichswehrministerium (Heer)* to von Moltke on 6th July, 1928, in answer to the latter's request for an opinion on whether the West was under-rating the Red Army.[53] In spite of the opportunity available to the *Reichswehr*, the report opened, of gaining 'deeper insights' (*tiefere Einblicke*) into Soviet military affairs, this was an inordinately difficult question to answer. It might be stated with some confidence that the Red Army could repel a Polish attack, but that it was not capable of mounting offensive operations on any scale at the present. The mobilisation plan had remained unchanged, apart from some adjustments in 1925, since 1922. Of 70 peace-time divisions, 35 were concentrated on the western frontier facing Poland. The mass of active divisions could be fully ready in six days (29 divisions), the 40 territorial divisions fully mobilised in ten or twelve days, and with the mobilisation of *new* divisions, some 160 divisions could be assembled within twenty-one days of initial mobilisation. The six cavalry divisions, organised into three cavalry corps, were stationed by the frontier, and existed in a state of 24-hour readiness. Adequate railway links could transport two divisions at full war-strength to the western frontier areas daily.

The level of technical efficiency was equally difficult to estimate. It appeared that the Soviet plan was to have Polish troops engage the crack Soviet troops defending the frontier, and also the well-trained troops which would support these operations. Behind this screen, the Red Army could be fully mobilised and brought into action. In the opinion of the *Statistische Abteilung*, and it adduced the tone and pronouncements of Red Army

* The disguised Intelligence branch of the *Reichswehr*, in the same way that the *Truppenamt* concealed the Staff.

opinion itself as well as service writing, Poland was *the* enemy (*Polen als* der *Feind gilt*). Every possible move was being made to popularise a defensive war with Poland, should this develop.[54]

In the autumn of 1928 General Werner von Blomberg, head of the *Truppenamt*, took up the invitation of the Soviet government to visit the Soviet Union, on which occasion he was to attend the 1928 autumn exercises of the Red Army. During the course of the visit Blomberg inspected the tank-school, the aviation training centre and the experimental gas centre; the other two objects of the journey Blomberg himself described as making personal contact with the present leaders of the Red Army, and carrying out a first-hand study of the Red Army. Blomberg's party was made up of the Colonels von dem Bussche and von Cochenhausen, Lieutenant-Colonel Köstring, the Majors Behschnitt and Hartmann, the Captains Gallenkamp and Hallmich. Split into three groups and routed differently so as to escape either observation or contact with other visitors, the mission was to assemble at Kiev for the manœuvres.[55] From Blomberg's own subsequent report — a substantial document of fifty-four pages — it is possible to see something of the high-level contact between the Red Army and the *Reichswehr*.

* * * *

Blomberg had nothing but praise for the manner in which the Red Army treated their German military guests. Luniev, so recently Soviet Military Attaché in Berlin, was assigned to the party as liaison officer. Everywhere the German officers met with a friendly reception, and on Voroshilov's own orders nothing was concealed from them. For the visits to the distant installations, a railway saloon-car was placed at their disposal. Even at brief halts the senior Soviet military authority or their representative would be on hand to receive them. On all sides there were expressions of the value of the link with the *Reichswehr* for the Red Army and an eagerness to hear the German officers' judgements upon the Soviet military establishment.[56]

Blomberg remained in Moscow from 19th–22nd August, leaving on 23rd for his inspection tour of the installations which lasted until 1st September. The *Reichswehr*'s Moscow centre, the *Zentrale Moskau*, Blomberg found to be capably directed by Niedermayer, who enjoyed Voroshilov's confidence and with whom the Soviet authorities discussed matters concerning the running of the installations. The only suggested change was to lodge the whole undertaking in a single house, in order to maintain secrecy; to this end Voroshilov would be consulted about providing suitable self-contained premises. At the tank-school at Kazan (situated to the east of the town, on the river Kama), Blomberg found the construction work almost complete. The school was well organised and the country offered excellent training facilities. Nevertheless the tactical training of the instructor-staff must be improved; the present head was not satisfactory, nor the German doctor. Even more important the despatch and fitting out of the tanks must be given the highest priority.[57]

The gas school,* located at Volsk and given the code-name 'Tomka', was well organised, with a good chief and excellent personnel. Due to the late construction of the centre, the experiments were behind schedule, and only in 1929 would they be taken up in earnest, after the necessarily late start made in the summer of 1928. The Russians showed the greatest interest in this work, and a special protocol on expansion of the work had been agreed with them; with such a fervid Soviet interest, the prospects for success were good, and the broadening of the experimental basis must be pushed ahead. The aviation centre at Lipetsk struck Blomberg favourably. For the training of fighter-pilots, a training-flight would have to be organised to work with the trainees; an instructor-staff for observers would work in its courses throughout the instructional year. Most of the trainees were soldiers (removed from the active list) and a small group of civilians; a certain amount of re-equipping would have to be carried out to keep the programmes in operation. At Voronezh German pilots and a Soviet artillery battery worked together in practice aerial observation; the Russian battery shot well and the Russians showed a high degree of accommodation and understanding.[58]

All three installations were in good shape, and in so far that they were actually functioning, they worked well. Blomberg considered that their value for Germany's arming was beyond any doubt. Russian interest was considerable, but they too were not immune from the financial strains involved in the running of the installations. For that reason costs would have to be carefully considered and watched when the various enterprises entered into an increased efficiency in 1929. Having thus viewed the question through German eyes, Blomberg reported on his discussions with Voroshilov about the collaboration and other, wider matters.

On the subject of the Soviet high command, Blomberg devoted himself at length to an account of his meetings with Voroshilov, whom he emphasised was simultaneously a military and political leader. Popular with the

* According to Colonel V. Pozdnyakov (in *The Soviet Army*, p. 384) the Central Army Chemical Polygon was set up in 1928 at Shikhany, near Volsk. The Soviet training and testing area was known as *TsVKhP*. This would correspond with Blomberg's information. Volsk itself lay some 300 kilometres south-west of Samara (Kuibyshev). At Chapayevsk, near Kuibyshev, was one of the main Soviet centres for the manufacture of toxic substances.

soldiers, Voroshilov had a tight grip on the army (*hat die Armee zweifellos fest in der Hand*).[59] Voroshilov's object was to disengage the army from politics, but to place the military point of view prominently in the foreground. For this reason Voroshilov was an enthusiastic partisan of close collaboration with the *Reichswehr*, a policy which he had pushed through in the government, though not always without a struggle. At the first meeting Voroshilov came at once to the subject, not of installations, but the Polish question, asking what help the Red Army might expect of the *Reichswehr* in the event of a Polish attack. Voroshilov went on:

> Not only in the name of the Red Army, but in the name of the Soviet Government also, I should like to state that in the event of a Polish attack on Germany Russia is ready with every assistance. Can the Soviet Union count on Germany in the case of a Polish attack?[60]

Blomberg answered non-committally, that this was a matter of high policy but Voroshilov insisted that this was, for the Soviet Union, one of the decisive questions. Only after such an opening did Voroshilov proceed to a discussion of the installations.

On the Kazan tank-school, the Soviet Commissar for War wanted an undertaking about the date for commencing operations. The actual tanks presented a difficulty, although Blomberg affirmed that it was hoped to ship some tanks in the spring of 1929. In the event of delay, Voroshilov anticipated 'serious difficulties'. Voroshilov laid special emphasis on the gas experiments, expressing a wish that the tests should go on through the winter (from 1st February, 1929) and for tests with gas-shells and gas-grenades. In return he offered to contribute half of the costs for erecting the test-centre. It was Blomberg's impression that the Soviet command put their greatest emphasis on the chemical warfare collaboration with the Germans. As for Lipetsk, the Russians were 'considerably in advance in this field' and Voroshilov expressed no preferences.[61]

Over officer-training, however, Voroshilov had precise requirements, emphasising the value for the Red Army of the study of the German Army and its training-methods. It would therefore increase this benefit if, Voroshilov suggested, five Soviet officers might attend the course for general staff officers and remain in Berlin for some time, five might be attached to technical troops during the main training period, and five proceed to the principal arms during the course of winter-training.[62] Blomberg made no promises, referring instead to the difficulties which beset the German Government as a result of the activities of the *Komintern*; it might facilitate this increased assignment if the Red Army could bring its influence to bear to ensure that no 'political difficulties' got in the way.

In Shaposhnikov, recently appointed Chief of the Red Army Staff from his command of the Moscow Military District, Blomberg discerned the personification of the reversal of a trend which had been identified with Tukhachevsky, Shaposhnikov's predecessor on the Staff. To Blomberg, the trim ex-Imperial staff officer Shaposhnikov — 'well-groomed . . . the English officer-type . . . reserved' — represented Red Army opinion which sought to avoid war with Poland, which interpreted the mission of the Soviet command in terms of the 'peaceful, systematic build-up of the Red Army'.[63] The course of the Kiev manœuvres had been ample demonstration that the Red Army was not yet fit for large-scale offensive operations, and that the tactical training of all grades of officer needed urgent attention. To these ends Shaposhnikov was now devoting himself, and the Kiev manœuvres showed that he also had a strong grip on the direction and management of the Red Army.

Blyukher, another of Blomberg's contacts, left a very strong impression on the German General. 'Every inch a soldier' (*straff soldatisch*), Blyukher was a man of 'calibre and prospects', and his activity in China spoke for his large-scale and successful exploits. Of the recent suggestions about his appointment as Military Attaché in Berlin, Blyukher said not a word.[64] His present appointment was that of Deputy Commander of the Ukraine Military District. During his stay in Leningrad (on 16th and 17th September), Blomberg met the commander of the Leningrad Military District — Tukhachevsky, who, up to the beginning of 1928, had been chief of the Red Army Staff. Blomberg adduced two versions for Tukhachevsky's removal; the first, that he advocated a preventive war against Poland and this the government would not countenance, the second, that his political reliability had been called into question and in the military chief some espied the shape of a chief of a possible subversive movement (*Umsturzbewegung*).[65] Tukhachevsky refrained from any comment on political matters, but on operational and tactical matters he showed himself to be a lively and shrewd questioner — in all, 'a personality very worthy of notice'.

Baranov, head of Soviet military aviation, was fully acquainted with the *Reichswehr* link; the advances in performance, organisation and leadership in Soviet aviation were a tribute to his obvious abilities. Fishman, head of Red Army Chemical Troops, had served at one time as Soviet Military Attaché in Berlin, where he had shown himself to be 'adroit, energetic and unscrupulous.'[66] Fishman's object, pursued with burning energy and 'a head full of ideas', was to give the Red Army a working chemical arm and to bring it to perfection as a military instrument. Fishman's interest was itself an important guarantee for German rewards in this field. In general, Blomberg assessed the Soviet high command as one packed with men pursuing their military objects through clear, practical principles. Including only a minority of ex-Imperial officers, the majority had occupied responsible positions since 1918. From their ranks the present government had drawn men for work in other fields — diplomacy, administration, the economy.

Passing to the Red Army and its officer corps, Blomberg painted a sympathetic but realistic portrait. He quickly noted the lack of homogeneity of the Soviet officer-corps, differentiated by varying levels of general and military education, personal ability and military capacity. The command personnel he divided into three sections; the 'politicals', the non-soldiers often or Civil War veterans, a second group in the ex-Imperial officers who supplied instructional and technical staff from divisional commanders downwards, and the third composed of the younger generation created out of the Red Army and filling posts from regimental commander downwards. It was the first category — men who learned their art in a war having itself 'little in common with war against a modern well-armed Power'*— which held a leading position.[67] Such diversity displayed itself most markedly at the senior command levels, and *must*, Blomberg argued with emphasis, affect the training and upbringing of the Army; the sophisticated ex-Imperial staff officer alongside the product of the elementary school, the energetic and practical mixed with the theoreticians, the strangers to troops in the field, who were carried by their betters. Much depended, in the opinion of the Soviet high command, upon the products of the Military Academies, and much upon the haste and results of using German training principles within the Red Army.[68] So it was that,

> ... The command staff finds itself with respect to us the [*Reichswehr*] in the conscious status of pupils. The knowledge of German military literature and of German writing is frequently astonishing. To have studied the German principles in practice counts as a personal distinction, and an assignment to the *Reichswehr* as something which is specially sought after.[69]

The further development of the command was the decisive question for the future of the Red Army; a favourable outcome depended upon replacing the ageing military intelligentsia of the present with a generation raised to a standard just as high, and relaxing 'Party principles' and incorporating more of the intelligentsia as a whole.

Blomberg subjected the Kiev exercises to a thorough criticism, and added his comments on the air manœuvres near Gomel which he also observed.[70] In conclusion he re-affirmed his views about the Red Army, seeing in it not the body-guard of a hated government — which aspect emigré opinion stressed — but a powerful factor in politics, a growing military force which

* Blomberg was referring to the Civil War.

it would be foolish to ignore, and a school for proselytising the whole people. The Red Army sought, in strengthening its military position, to become a-political, to 'leave the political water-ways'. The Red Army's main opponent is Poland; this the command clearly realises. Blomberg drew three main conclusions:

1. Our installations in Russia (Flying-school, Tank-school, Gas-experiments) are throughout settled on firm foundations. . . .
2. The developing Red Army is a factor which must be reckoned with. To have it as a friend can only be counted an advantage. Already now it is for Poland an opponent to be reckoned with.
3. The Red Army places the greatest value on the collaboration with the *Reichswehr* . . . the related strengthening of power of the Red Army lies in the German interest.[71]

The collaboration must go on. Meanwhile, the German Army could learn from the Red Army in matters concerning troop equipment, engineers (especially pontoons), military aviation, chemical weapons, propaganda techniques, the organisation of defence against aerial attack for the civilian population, and the mobilisation of the population for defence purposes.

* * * *

Following on Blomberg's return from the Soviet Union, the various measures which he had advocated were generally put into practice. One added feature, however — the revival of a form of the military-industrial collaboration reminiscent of the years before 1926 — was not directly related to his visit. The firm of Krupp was approached by Soviet representatives about an agreement covering the manufacture of high-grade steels for armaments. In the spring of 1929 such an agreement had been largely worked out, subject to any reservations which the *Reichswehr* might have upon the disclosure of technical military secrets, when the whole affair was dropped since it violated German regulations on arms-production.[72] But the matter did not rest here. The pre-occupation of the Soviet command, and the virtual obsession of Voroshilov himself, was the creation of a Soviet armaments base, in which the hiring of experts, foreign purchases, and collaboration with German arms firms played an important part. For the same reasons, sixty British tanks were ordered for the Soviet Union.

The winter of 1928 and the spring of 1929 did also mark preparations for the intensification of 'the phase of personnel' in the collaboration.[73] German ideas were incorporated in a memorandum dated 21st January, 1929, dealing with the despatch of active-list and retired officers of the *Reichswehr* to 'R'. Officers from the active list and their missions were divided into three categories; one active-list staff officer to proceed to the Red Army Staff for several months, to gain an insight into the organisation and training of the Red Army; field officers would be attached to separate Soviet army units (infantry, artillery, technical) to develop their skill and practise on Soviet equipment; 16 officers would be despatched to troop exercises and manœuvres, staying six weeks, but their trips so arranged that not all the German officers would be present at once in the Soviet Union. To learn the Russian language, 4–5 officers would be given the requisite leave. *None* of the officers in these categories was to come into any contact with the joint Soviet-German installations. Of officers retired from the *Reichswehr* ('retirement' being a device whereby the *Reichswehr* need not assume formal responsibility for the doings of these men) 42 (6 instructors, 36 pupils) were destined for Lipetsk for the fighter and observer courses; 10 officer-candidates were also to go as pupils, both groups staying from May until autumn. To the Kazan tank-school it was proposed to send 1 instructor and 10 pupils, who would follow the course lasting from spring until autumn.[74]

The work and organisation of the Kazan tank-school furnished a good example of this collaboration in military-technical fields. The school had three main functions — to train officers in the handling of tanks and tank-units, to test German models, and to run foreign models on the proving grounds by way of comparison. Five departments composed the school as such — training, testing, technical-tests, supply and a combined financial-billeting department. German and Soviet pupils attended the extensive courses, the curriculum of which was devised by the *Inspektion der Kraftfahrttruppen* in Berlin. Under a German instructor-staff, the subjects taught included theory, a general technical and mechanical course, weapon employment and communications. On 30th August, 1929, a joint Soviet-German conference was held at Kazan to discuss the running of the school. Colonel Lütz, Lieutenant-Colonel Malbrandt (the tank-school commandant), Major Pirner (chief of the Test Section), Captain Kühn and Lieutenant (Interpreter) Bernhardi represented the *Reichswehr*; Soviet tank-regiment commanders Polyakov and Yeroshchenko represented the Red Army.[75] True to his undertaking, Blomberg had expedited the shipment of tanks, which were transported in sections and then re-assembled at the tank-school. In addition to the German sources of supply, in the course of 1929 the Soviet government took the precaution of seeking a supply of British machines, for which a purchasing order was granted by the Board of Trade on 21st March, 1930;* altogether, some 60 machines — 12-ton, 6-ton and whippet-tanks — were

* The rather tart exchange over this deal is recorded in *Hansard*, Vol. 239 H.C. p. 1273 for 28th May, 1930.

involved, and formed part of a subsequent exchange of items of tank-equipment between the Red Army and the *Reichswehr*.[76]

It would not, therefore, appear to be pure coincidence that the first serious Soviet work on tanks and their use in war, as well as interest in the performance and potentialities of foreign machines, occurred about 1928–9. At the Kiev exercises in 1928, Blomberg had criticised the Soviet model MS–1 (T–18) for its lack of speed. Essentially an improved version of the Renault infantry-supporting machine, the MS–1 weighed 5½ tons, mounted one 37-mm gun for its main armament and one machine-gun, reaching a speed in the region of 16 kilometres per hour. A more successful vehicle seems to have been the BA–27 armoured car, incorporating the same armament. Another product of the early period of design was the T–24, weighing 18½ tons, armed with one 45-mm gun and 4 machine-guns; a modified M–6 aero engine of some 250–300 H.P., gave the T–24 a speed of 22 kilometres per hour. The Kharkov Locomotive-Construction Works was reported as having produced 25 of the Model T–24 in 1929, while in the same year tests were carried out on two 'tankette' designs, the T–19 and the T–20.[77] Since no indigenous Soviet automobile and tractor industry of any account existed, the Red Army received no quantity of Soviet-produced tanks before 1932. In addition to the early designs failing to produce any advance on the vehicles produced during the First World War, these Soviet prototypes suffered — on Soviet admission — from other defects; these included a marked unreliability of the motor-transmission units, frequent track-breakage, too great an amplitude which hindered movement by road, and an aggravation of poor performance resulting from bad handling and bad maintenance. Technical difficulties did not, however, inhibit Soviet interest in the tank, and K. B. Kalinovskii carried out some of the first studies on its role; tank-support for infantry (1927), the tank in defence (1928), high-speed tanks in the meeting-engagement (1929) and problems of anti-tank defence. In 1929 the first 'mechanised unities', created for independent operations, were set up, consisting of the 'mechanised regiment' — with a tank battalion, an armoured-car battalion, a motorised infantry battalion and an artillery battery.[78] Extensive tests were carried through by the Motorisation and Mechanisation Directorate of the Red Army throughout 1930–1, at a time when the Kazan school was reaching its peak. The exact relationship between early Soviet work on and experience with the tank, as a machine and a weapon, cannot be determined with respect to the fortunes of the Kazan tank-school, but, as with Soviet military aviation, concentration upon a highly specialised arm coincided with the intensification of work in the joint Soviet-German training and experimental centres.

The collaboration of the staffs, which had been ushered in by Blomberg's visit of 1928, was further developed in 1929. During the month of May those 'political difficulties' of which Blomberg had spoken reared their head, when the First of May Communist disturbances in Berlin roused and ruffled feelings; on 22nd May A. I. Kork was re-called from his post in Berlin and Vitovt Putna despatched as replacement with the immediate mission of calming the passions so aroused.[79] This flurry had no immediate effect upon the exchange arrangements which had been decided earlier in the year; the final apportioning of numbers to the training centres had been made on 18th February, 1929, and the decision to send 'a senior officer' to the Red Army Staff for a period of some six months confirmed. In return Uborevich was mentioned as the head of the equivalent Soviet contingent which would make the arrangement reciprocal.[80] The German senior officer selected for duty with the Red Army Staff was Colonel Halm, later promoted *Generalmajor*, whose tour of duty was to begin on 15th September, 1929; Blomberg's instruction specified that Halm would go about his duties in civilian clothes.[81] On 13th July, 1929, three officers were selected for further duties in connection with the Red Army Staff; reputedly of the *Statistische Abteilung*, in August these same officers are reported as having taken part in a joint conference with the Red Army Staff.[82] There followed an inspection of Soviet military installations, camps and the new mechanised units being organised.

According to French Intelligence, leading personalities of the *Reichswehr* travelled to the Soviet Union in August–September, 1929. General von Hammerstein-Equord, and Colonel Kühlenthal (head of the *Statistische Abteilung*) spent some six weeks on an extensive tour, participating in the autumn exercises of the troops of the Ukraine Military District — two weeks of manœuvres, which were followed by a conference with Voroshilov himself. On 5th September, accompanied by four officers, Blomberg arrived in Kiev to take part in the manœuvres which were related to the theme of the defence of the Kiev communication-network.[83] Kühlenthal's observations on his own experiences, embodied in a conversation reported by the French Military Attaché in Berlin,[84] indicated both the Colonel's admiration for the Russian soldier's accomplishment in difficult manœuvres — plagued by severe weather conditions — and the degree of that 'deeper insight' into the Soviet military machine which senior *Reichswehr* officers obtained. In no wise was this merely a one-way traffic, in which the Russians took and the Germans perforce gave. After Blomberg's first visit in 1928 as head of the *Truppenamt*, the departure of the particular head of that body for the Soviet Union and into contact with the Soviet high command became an annual event up to and including 1932. Halm's first report on his assignment was yet another witness to the extent of the German opportunity to comprehend the scope of Soviet military effort; it was evident, wrote Halm, that the Soviet command was coming to regard the capacity of the Red Army soldier in defence as the most trustworthy aspect of his military performance. Halm's extensive acquaintance both with Soviet military institutions and the Soviet command itself was an indication of how far this *rapprochement* with the Red Army Staff had gone.[85] At the centre of the Moscow reception stood Voroshilov, in contact of an unbroken kind since 1928 with Blomberg, Hammerstein-Equord, Kühlenthal (1929), Halm and Heye (1930) and General Adam[86] (1931 and 1932).

At a distance from the contact of the staffs, but nevertheless still within the confines of the very senior Soviet command, the newly-revived military-industrial collaboration achieved within the same period a remarkable intermingling of Soviet and German strategic-industrial interests. Already in 1928 German specialists were in receipt of numerous Soviet offers to work in the Soviet Union on assignments of strategic importance or for the defence industry; a Dr F. Haber is reported for that year to have worked on organising the Moscow Institute of Chemical Warfare, while German experts had a hand in the operations of the munitions-plants of Leningrad, Perm, Sverdlovsk and in the Ukraine.[87] In April 1928 the *Auswärtiges Amt* was notified of the case of Professor Schmitz of the Braunschweig *Technische Hochschule* who had been invited to pass a year in the Soviet Union working on anti-aircraft gun design and also aircraft armament.[88] It was therefore a logical outcome (and not inconsistent with the hiring of foreign experts for the non-military aspects of the First Five-Year Plan) that the services of a very senior German military-technical expert — General Ludwig, at one time *Chef des Waffenamtes* in the *Reichswehr* — should be secured for the Soviet war-industry. The effort to develop an indigenous Soviet armaments base (an idea constantly stressed by Voroshilov), was not ignored by the Germans and one of the principal personalities involved from the Soviet side — Uborevich — was well-known in German military circles.

'Herr Ludwig', on 3rd January, 1930, conveyed his impressions of the Soviet plans for the development of their war-industry to Trautmann. While pointing out that the Soviet war-industry was obliged to make virtually a clean start for the production of modern weapons, Ludwig disclosed some of the items in which Soviet interest was displayed, and their contacts with German firms to secure military equipment. 7·5 cm. AA guns, wireless equipment, experimental medium mortars, tracer-bullets — the inventory of armament went on. Ludwig made no bones about the position over tanks; the thirty tanks which the Russians possessed, reported Ludwig, simply did not work, but then neither did the German models; Krupp would have to supply caterpillar-tractors (*Raupenschlepper*). A machine-gun, manufactured by the German firm *Rheinmetall*, was now under test; part-German, part-Soviet production could be carried out, with the machine-gun barrels being shipped from Germany and concealed inside consignments of ordinary water-pipes. The Russians wanted equipment for munitions-works, for chemical plants and machine-tools for the manufacture of infantry weapons. In General Ludwig's view, this was a programme which could bring no disadvantage to Germany should the necessary financial and industrial support be forthcoming.[89] Dirksen reported from Moscow that 'a special authority' had been empowered to work on the military-industrial plans; Voroshilov and 'Herr Ulrich' (Uborevich) were prominent from the Soviet side, and conversations had been conducted with Krupp, 'Herr Ludwig' and Professor Schmitz.[90] It was, however, towards the state-subsidised German industrial and armaments concern of *Rheinmetall* that Soviet attention was increasingly directed, and in January 1930 Eltze of *Rheinmetall* rendered an account of the negotiations which he had been having with the Soviet authorities. In substance the proposed arrangement differed only slightly from that suggested to Krupp; military equipment would be produced for the Red Army through a *Konstruktionsbüro* — manned by some twenty German experts — and turned out with the assistance of German firms with establishment in neutral countries.[91]

Somewhat uneasy about the implications of this, the *Auswärtiges Amt* warned Eltze that he would have to assume a personal responsibility for such an undertaking and placed reservations on the scheme. On 7th February, 1930, Eltze advised that the Russians were making a political issue out of the conclusion of agreement; Voroshilov and Uborevich had stated that not only the collaboration of the Red Army and the *Reichswehr* would suffer if agreement was withheld, but Soviet-German relations as a whole would feel the dire consequences.[92] The *Reichswehr* itself, which had adopted hitherto a passive attitude in this question, bestirred itself to approach the *Auswärtiges Amt* — in an exchange between Schubert and General Hammerstein — with the object of ensuring that no refusal was decided on without prior consultation with the German Army. Hammerstein's views conformed generally with General Ludwig's opinions; the Soviet military posture was definitely defensive, and the likelihood of attack could be discounted — and even should it come to this, then the blow would fall on Poland. There was little likelihood of the guns manufactured with German help being fired against Germany. Moreover, advised Hammerstein, Uborevich was 'very pro-German' (*sehr deutschfreundlich*) and there would be no advantage in alienating him.[93] If Germany did not help the Soviet Union, then the latter would inevitably turn elsewhere, a point which was borne out by rumours of a Soviet contact with the Glenn Martin Company in the United States of America.

On 10th February a provisional agreement between the Soviet government and *Rheinmetall* was concluded in Moscow. Director Eltze, who returned early on the morning of 12th to Berlin, reported at once on the turn which events had taken; after the signing of the agreement, at which 'Herr Ludwig' was present, the party adjourned to an officers club, where a sumptuous meal was spread as well as festive drink. 'The mood of enthusiasm' was encouraged by the vodka, and under the influence of both Uborevich turned to his table and asked: 'Will we not be so advanced in two years that we can set about a revision of the frontiers and slaughter the Poles? Indeed, we must partition Poland once again.' In five days Uborevich, accompanied by twelve Soviet officers, would be visiting Germany to inspect items of equipment at *Zeiss Jena, Thiel Ruhla* and *Rheinmetall* plants. The question of military equipment would be handled by a *Konstruktionsbüro*, staffed by German experts and working under the direction of a Soviet chief.[94] But a hitch, arising out of the objections of the directors of *Rheinmetall* to the terms of the draft agreement concluded with the Soviet agreement, seemed to threaten once more the operation of this scheme. After further Soviet threats and negotiations, the details of which remain obscure, only in July 1930 was agreement finally reached and the Red Army at liberty to exploit its new Aladdin's cave piled with the products of German military-technical proficiency.

* * * *

The Soviet Navy meanwhile pursued its own specialised interests with the *Marineleitung*, although progress seems to have been comparatively slow. With only broken and scanty evidence for 1927–8,[95] the record resumes a certain continuity in 1929, by which time it was clear that a part of Voroshilov's over-all plan in military relations with Germany included an extension of the exchanges with the German Navy, although he recognised that this would take time. During 1929 discussions took place about installing an aircraft plant by the Sea of Azov to manufacture machines under licence from Germany; little progress seems to have been made with the German firm of *Rohrbach*, and a proposition to set up a naval air-station on the Black Sea was not more successful.[96] Personal contact between the naval commands, nevertheless, proceeded with a fair show of cordiality. At the beginning of July 1929 *Amtschef A* of the *Marineleitung* met V. M.

Orlov, commander of the Soviet Black Sea Fleet, at a lunch arranged by Krestinsky and conducted by Putna, acting as interpreter. Orlov had come in place of Muklevich, who had been unable to leave his duties.[97] Orlov was rising high in the Soviet naval hierarchy; a man of thirty-four, Orlov had been drafted into the Imperial Russian Navy as a cadet in 1916 and had taken part in a long-distance training cruise shortly after. At the end of 1917 Orlov was active in the Party organisations of Reval, and became secretary of the Propaganda Department of the Petrograd Military Committee, rising to the command of the Political Department of the Baltic Fleet. From this post he was assigned as Deputy Chief of the Political Administration of Soviet Water-ways and finally as Chief of the Volga Water-ways Political Administration. In 1922 Orlov took over the deputy command of the Naval-Political Administration of the Republic *Revvoensoviet*, assuming command of the Black Sea naval forces later and being appointed in 1928 or 1929 Chief and Commissar of the Naval Training Department and Chief of the Naval Training-Establishments Administration.[98] Orlov and Muklevich between them occupied the key posts of the Soviet naval command during the period first of its reconstruction and then its initial expansions.

At the end of 1929, at the request of Vöroshilov, arrangements were put in hand for the despatch of a senior Soviet naval delegation to Germany to inspect German naval installation and to consult with the German naval command. On 30th December, 1929, Putna, through the Soviet Embassy, thanked the *Marineleitung* for its sympathetic response to this request; on 27th January, 1930, the Soviet Embassy indicated that Voroshilov wished to despatch Orlov, Smirnov (commander of a mine-laying squadron in the Baltic Fleet), Berg (President of the Naval Section of the Military-Scientific Committee), Oras (deputy to Berg) and Leonov (Chief of the Artillery Section of the Military-Scientific Committee). On 4th February from Moscow Niedermayer confirmed this visit and the names selected (although Smirnov appears as head of the Torpedo Department of the Baltic Fleet).[99] At this time it appears that a German naval mission carried out a five-day tour of the Soviet Naval Academy and naval training-establishments.[100] At the end of February or the beginning of March the Soviet naval delegation with Orlov at its head arrived in Germany, touring in civilian clothes. On 7th March, 1930 Orlov (with Putna acting as interpreter)* had an extended interview with *Amtschef A* (Admiral Brutzer), *Fregatten-Kapitän* Schuster, and the captains Hormel and von Bonin. Orlov asked that the Soviet officers might be permitted a closer acquaintance with 'Panzerschiff A',†

* Putna spoke excellent German.

† 'Panzerschiff A' was the first of the famous 'pocket battleships'.

to which *Amtschef A* agreed, but on the strict condition that anything the Russians saw they would keep very secret. Orlov then questioned *Amtschef A* on matters of high naval policy and the problems of naval warfare and organisation:

Orlov. How could the tasks of the German Navy be defined within the present military-political framework?

Amtschef A. The present tasks of the German Navy may be considered to be linked with keeping the Baltic free of any enemy, to watch and maintain the exits and entrances of the Baltic. Lacking submarines and aircraft, in the case of war the German Navy could not attack, but, on the contrary, 'can only save its skin'.

Orlov. Was the transfer of the German Navy to the centre at Kiel a kind of rationalisation of naval command?

Amtschef A. This was the aim, as well as the stabilisation of the naval command.

Orlov. Does there exist a German naval operational plan, and if this does exist, is it applied (*a*) to the co-operation of the German Navy, coast-defence forces, the German Army and aviation, or (*b*) is it only a plan for naval forces?

Amtschef A. All operational plans (*O-Befehle*) were destroyed during the revolutionary disturbances. As for a new plan, the German Navy can reckon only upon four ships of the line.

Orlov. Would the creation of a 'battle-directorate' ('*Gefechtsanleitung*') — which provides for the co-ordination of *all* arms — be a desirable thing?

Amtschef A. Not unconditionally. The command must be fully acquainted with the working and possibilities of all arms and weapons. 'There is no formula for war.' ('*Für den Krieg gibt es kein Rezept.*')

Orlov. Bearing this qualification in mind, should nevertheless the whole Fleet be built along one line?

Amtschef A. This is so, but speaking for the German Navy this would mean much new equipment.

Orlov. How does *Amtschef A* himself feel about the 'reverse of the coin' of the present visit of the Soviet naval commission?

Amtschef A. Frankly, I think that weapon development with you interests me less, for I believe that we are more advanced in this field than you. However, there is a possibility for the training of flyers and torpedo-bomber pilots in the Soviet Union — things which are forbidden to us by the Treaty of Versailles.

Orlov. As an appreciation of the sympathetic treatment accorded to the Soviet Navy, an invitation to a German naval delegation is issued here and now.

Amtschef A. Which would be the best time for a visit to the Black Sea and Baltic Fleets?

Orlov. It would be possible to visit the Black Sea Fleet at any time throughout the year, although July and August are very hot. August would be perhaps the best, for this is the period of the naval manœuvres.

Amtschef A. May–June would certainly be the most convenient, but there is always a possibility of a visit arranged for the later months.[101]

In the summer of 1930 an exchange of naval officers did occur, and Admiral Brutzer availed himself of the opportunity to visit Soviet naval stations; he travelled in July in the company of the captains Witzell, Sieburg and von Bonin.[102] The visit might be appraised as the high-water mark of the limited collaboration which had hitherto existed, under which the Soviet Navy received the undoubted benefits of certain German technical assistance during the critical stage after 1924, when a serious effort was made to reconstruct the shattered Soviet naval forces. The desire of the Soviet command to establish a close and durable contact, both personal and technical, with the *Marineleitung* was clearly not reciprocated beyond well-guarded narrow limits. The nature of these *Amtschef A* had plainly indicated to Orlov in 1930. The divergence of Soviet and German naval designs was a factor far outweighing the constricted opportunities for co-operation. A precise account of the stiffening of the German naval attitude into downright rejection of extensive relations with the Soviet Navy would require more than the presently incomplete evidence, but on 7th August, 1931, the *Marineleitung* came out with a final declaration of policy, which was itself an indication of conflict with the *Heeresleitung* over the Russian connection. The German Navy wished it to be known that in the matter of 'Frage Russland' there was no question of carrying on a war with the *Heeresleitung* and its interests, but it was impossible to ignore the importance for the German Navy of maintaining friendly relations with the United States of America and Great Britain; the interests of Germany's mercantile marine demanded that the German Navy should concern itself over its relations with other high-seas powers. Good naval relations with the Baltic States were yet another pre-requisite of German naval policy. Brought down to its basic elements, self-interest was not served by ties with the Soviet Navy:

> . . . A closer co-operation with the Russian Navy does not enter into the question, because this can offer the *Marineleitung* nothing.[103]

And self-interest, both Soviet and German, was the arbiter of this combination. A naval equivalent of the problem of Poland, which bound the Red Army and the *Reichswehr* into a natural compact against a common enemy, never existed.

* * * *

Collaboration with the German Army was not merely incidental to Soviet military policy. In the first place, the question of a guarantee against Poland, which remained for the Soviet Union a formidable military opponent, came high on the list of military priorities; in Voroshilov's own words to General Blomberg, this was one of 'the decisive questions' for the Soviet government. Neither an alliance nor a definite military commitment were ever forthcoming, but the Soviet command seemed to be able to count on the understanding of the German military with regard to Poland. The exercises of 1928–9, in which senior German officers played a considerable part, were designed to strengthen the Soviet defences and improve Soviet dispositions in the event of a Polish attack. In view of the French assistance to Poland with the object of modernising and training the Polish Army, it was therefore both justifiable and essential that the Red Army should seek the active participation of the *Reichswehr* in bringing Soviet military performance to a higher standard; this may well have been the Soviet argument, and Blomberg indicated that the Soviet command was aware of the progress made in the Polish Army with the help of foreign military-technical aid.

What followed was an elaboration of this circumstance. The attempt at large-scale military-industrial collaboration had spent its first effort by 1925, with financial break-down and technical failure contributing to the inevitable liquidation of the enterprises. During this period only one of the training-centres, the aviation school at Lipetsk, had been brought into some kind of use, although it is not insignificant that the organisation of Lipetsk coincided with the first serious attempt at the revival and development of Soviet military aviation. The Kazan tank-school seems to have made very slow progress in comparison, its construction not being in any way complete until the autumn of 1928. Voroshilov, in his general comments to Blomberg, emphasised that the erection of these 'German schools' had not met with the unanimous consent of the members of the Soviet government. It would be too much to suppose that the misgivings, not infrequently expressed on the German side about the possible boomerang effects of the collaboration, did not have some Soviet counter-part. Lenin's lumping the arrangements with the German Army under the comprehensive heading of the 'concessions', which were then being extended to capitalist circles as a whole, had outworn its first use. During 1927, it is evident that the power of decision over the fate of the training-centres had been detached from the Soviet Commissar for War and Litvinov made a forceful entrance on to the scene. The Voroshilov-Unshlikht combination, which had taken over the work of Trotsky and Sklyanskii, was temporarily checked. Yet at a time when the military collaboration fell upon troubled circumstances and was itself being used as a means of bringing pressure to bear on German foreign policy, the Soviet Navy was actually expanding and developing its early contacts with the German naval command. While it is true to say that, in general, throughout the earlier phase of the Soviet-German dealings the Russians had shown themselves to be superior in negotiation, a superiority inevitably reinforced by internal German divisions during the critical 1926–7 phase, the hesitations and shaky improvisations of German policy had some parallel in Soviet behaviour.

In the later stages of the Soviet-German military arrangement, that section of the Soviet command which could still be identified with the 'military specialists' came to play an outstanding part. Before 1924 P. P. Lebedev had conducted a number of the military conversations with German emissaries; under Voroshilov, an 'inner command' of officers raised from within the Imperial Russian Army handled many of the contacts with the German officers. The selection was both inevitable and deliberate, for the professional German officers dealt with their senior Soviet fellows who were themselves not lacking in any acquaintance with military life in the accepted sense. This later phase also corresponded with the point when the Soviet government made a pronounced effort to win over the specialist, non-Party commander at all levels. Uborevich occupied a most singular position, being the object of considerable German attention and the bearer of heavy responsibility from the Soviet side. The obvious exception to this rule occurred in the technical arms of the Soviet armed forces, where a distinctly 'proletarian' element predominated — Baranov of military aviation, Muklevich of the naval forces, although Orlov of the naval command had had some association with the Imperial Russian Navy other than the lower deck. Tukhachevsky, whose fortunes waned somewhat with Stalin's victory over the Opposition, appears to have been excluded from the interchange to a marked degree; in spite of assertions to the contrary, his name appears only in 1931–2 as an active participant in the joint military and war-industry ventures. Collaboration with the *Reichswehr* did have noticeable repercussions on the alignments within the Soviet command, or, perhaps more correctly, these special circumstances made previous alignments all the more obvious. Voroshilov himself, on his own admission and the confirmation of other German reports, was an enthusiastic champion of the link with the *Reichswehr*, seeking wherever possible to expand and multiply the contacts; it was therefore a policy enjoying the approval of Stalin, contradicting none of the defensive stipulations which the latter had emphasised at the beginning of 1925.

Soviet-German collaboration in the training and experimental centres operated at the purely tactical level, although both sides were in a good position to extract considerable amounts of valuable information relevant to future developments. The Red Army Chemical Warfare arm, under Fishman's energetic direction, owed much to German assistance. Between the Soviet and German staffs, however, there developed a liaison which went far beyond a few tactical considerations. The figures supplied by Dirksen and also mentioned by Voroshilov as his requirement make it not unreasonable to suppose that a minimum of 120 Soviet senior officers passed through German training courses or were attached for training to German units during 'the phase of personnel'. In 1930 the French Military Attaché in Berlin had definite evidence of the attendance of three Soviet officers in the German Army *Wehrkreis No. II*, where they participated in the training course and took the relevant military examinations.[104] The *Reichswehrministerium* did not lock its secrets from Soviet scrutiny; a German major attached to the cypher-section of the *Reichswehrministerium* confirmed that Soviet officers worked there continually, and even had access to his office. The disquiet felt by other German officers, notably General von Falkenhausen, at the extent of the facilities granted to Soviet officers was an indirect proof of the scope of these activities. In 1929, according to the French Military Attaché in Berlin, von Falkenhausen was removed from his post at the Dresden Infantry School for objecting to the over-zealousness of five Red Army officers — including Uborevich — whose 'indiscretion, their desire to see and get to know everything, the propagandistic spirit . . .' caused him alarm.[105]

Yet General Speidel has complained that the Red Army supplied no reciprocal exchange whereby the German Army might follow Soviet military thought and its applications, and penetrate a little more deeply into the Soviet processes of war-making and planning. The tone and content of contemporary German reports does not wholly support this contention, suggesting that the Germans gave while the Russians took. Blomberg had and took the opportunity to make a thorough study of the Red Army and make some appreciation of the Soviet command and the intimate problems of Soviet military policy. Blomberg's trained eye detected a great deal, much of which was subsequently confirmed in Red Army development. Colonel von Kühlenthal of the *Statistische Abteilung* was in a position to present a very thorough study of the probable Soviet military reaction to a Polish attack and an assessment of its relative position. Soviet secretiveness took a heavy knock in 1927, when a deliberate policy of showing everything was introduced. Colonel Halm was closely connected with the Red Army Staff during a part of 1929–30 and evidently enjoyed a cordial relationship with Voroshilov. In April 1930 General Hammerstein talked at length in Berlin to Uborevich about the involved interests of Russo-Finnish and German-Finnish relations.[106] The *Marineleitung* availed itself of the chance to make thorough inspections of Soviet naval installations and training centres; Kinzel's report is quite lavish with its detail plus the ironic but careful observation that these were no mere 'Potemkin villages'. Over the development of Soviet war-industry and details of military equipment 'Herr Ludwig' was in possession of a wealth of intimate detail and well aware of Soviet priorities. It was with considerable confidence, founded in close observation and innumerable conversations with the Soviet command itself, that the *Reichswehr* could insist that the Red Army and the Soviet military establishment was being bent into a defensive mould.

Self-interest and a very special kind of perfidy dominated the military relationship. The Russians were confident over the attractions which the military possibilities offered to the *Reichswehr* and were perhaps inclined to over-play their hand, a contributory factor to the crisis of 1926–7. Out of this risky set of adventures arose the impression that perhaps the link with the *Reichswehr* was a means of bringing pressure to bear on Germany's international relations, above all, of checking too effective a *rapprochement* with the West through manipulations managed through the German military. It may be that the precise interpretation of the *Reichswehr*-Red Army contact touched off violent disputes in Soviet ruling circles; Voroshilov would not be averse to expressing himself with a familiar vehemence in a dispute rendered more involved by the wranglings of the respective factions of Litvinov and Chicherin. But the immediate gains could not be denied. From the German Army, senior Soviet officers could acquire close acquaintance with the technique of modern training as well as first-hand observation of the methods of organisation employed in a force dedicated to the idea of the cadre and the exploitation of ultra-modern military techniques. German military literature, not to mention Seeckt's own writings, circulated in the Red Army. As German military observers had noted, the Red Army lacked a tradition, in spite of the role played by the ex-Imperial officers and the propaganda devoted to the Civil War. While this had its general uses, both were anachronistic or irrelevant to fitting out the Red Army for the severe tests of modern mechanised war. Many of the more sinister or extravagant versions of the Soviet-German military compact may be discounted; no reliable or systematic evidence is available to support any contentions that either party at this stage entered into conspiratorial dealings concerned with internal events either in Germany or the Soviet Union. Yet there remains the hypothetical question of how the Red Army would have fared, a prey to powerful external enemies, technical backwardness and the acute problem of training the new command, without this recourse to the *Reichswehr*. Frunze stabilised the Red Army; he did not and could not effect its modernisation. With its strictly limited resources and those of the state similarly impoverished, the Red Army could not pull itself up by its own boot-straps. The same might be said of the problem of war-industry; Dirksen reported from Moscow in April 1930 that failing an agreement with *Rheinmetall*, the Soviet government had determined upon an approach to the firms of Bofors or Vickers.

Since it is difficult to assess the effect of contact with the *Reichswehr* on Soviet military doctrine, so an estimation of any influence which this may have had on Soviet ideas of organising their command for war is even more of a formidable problem. No single direct innovation can be adduced as evidence of immediate German influence. The reform of 1926 in the Red Army Staff, while suggesting something of the German command monolith, had much more in common with the policy of centralisation long pursued by the Russians since the early days of the Civil War. But this did not entirely solve the problem of war leadership and the question of how the military command was related to the government in matters of policy-making. The Red Army Staff occupied a strong position, controlling as it did its own extensive Military Intelligence organs; having combined planning, co-ordination and operational functions, it conformed to Frunze's idea of the staff being 'the military brain' of the state. Its voice had a certain independent ring to it, but there are numerous signs that a struggle over the status of the staff was taking place throughout 1927–8. The military and strategic aspects of the industrialisation plans were also an additional factor which complicated the situation. Whatever the indirect pressures of German example and admiration for the German scheme, internal Soviet evolution seemed to be the major element in deciding on the form of the relationship between the military and the government. Boris Shaposhnikov, who took up the post of Chief of the Red Army Staff in 1928, had decided views on this question, developed out of a massive examination of the working of the General Staff of the Imperial Austrian Army. By a coincidence which does not appear entirely fortuitous, Shaposhnikov's opinions fitted in conveniently with the requirements of Stalin, whose rigorous 'theory of leadership' left little room for the independence of individuals or institutions. Shaposhnikov entitled his study *Mozg Armii* (The Brain of the Army); preserving the metaphor, of which Frunze had freely availed himself, the new Chief of Staff defined the strategic bases of the relationships between the general staff, the political directorate of the state (for internal and external affairs) and the ruler (or ruling group). Arguing from the experience of 'total war', Shaposhnikov propounded the idea of 'total leadership'. Here, finally, was an exposition of command organisation which corresponded to Stalin's political methods. Shaposhnikov, as much as the *Reichswehr*, had much to do with the new Soviet strategic appreciations.

CHAPTER TEN

Soviet Preoccupations with War

War Commissar Voroshilov, whose temporary appointment to his post hardened gradually into permanent occupation, had inherited from Frunze a relatively firm outline of policy for the preparation of the Soviet Union for the economic eventualities of war. Frunze had also aimed at transforming the Red Army Staff into a powerful 'military brain' at the disposal of the Soviet state, with whose other executive and administrative instruments it could take a prominent part in the operational, mobilisation and military-economic planning intrinsic to the war he envisaged as a possibility. A further step in implementing this idea was taken in 1926 with the second great re-organisation of the Red Army Staff, now an operational and planning monolith of more impressive proportions. In the matter of the higher direction of war, Frunze had never made any secret of the fact that during the Civil War this had been not infrequently a clumsy and much improvised affair, with responsibilities and functions badly defined or not even at all defined. What applied to the particular military evil, the manipulation of supply, could be generally ascribed to the whole direction of the Soviet war-effort. It was, therefore, not surprising that Frunze devoted a great deal of attention to 'militarising' civil executive and administrative organs, in order to bring greater efficiency into mobilisation, communications and transportation. The territorial system and its extensive mobilisation requirements alone made this very necessary. Para-military and pre-military training among the population at large loomed into increasing prominence in Frunze's programme; with a characteristic repetitiveness, he took care to publicise and emphasise the importance of the various para-military groups in the defence programme of the Soviet Union. It was inevitable that the human being and the resources of the society should be so exploited, since human rather than industrial power formed the basis of strength. In his lectures on the importance of the rear, Frunze emphasised the need for economic mobilisation, but he was necessarily speaking of and for a society lacking the resources of large-scale industry.[1] Technical backwardness and only partial industrialisation formed the crucial issue round which the Soviet command had to adjust its point of view. Judging by Tukhachevsky's attacks, Voroshilov had resigned himself somewhat to the limited exploitation of the human element, lacking mechanical resources; on the other hand, throughout 1926, strategic opinions were being offered which had a basis in calculations of great increases in the technical equipping and efficiency of the Red Army. The absorption of the implications of 'total war' in military-industrial as well as purely social-political terms came with increasing speed to many sections of the Soviet command. This provoked the inevitable struggle over priorities. Factories operating under the terms of the compact with Germany produced weapons and munitions, but this itself did not create an indigenous military-industrial capacity or the economic potential needed for war.

All these questions appeared to assume critical importance in 1927, the year of the Soviet 'war-scare'. Events in China had taken an ugly turn, culminating in the Peking Raid in April, when the Soviet Embassy was looted of several of its compromising documents. On 12th May, 1927, the Soviet premises connected with the Trade Delegation and Arcos at 49 Moorgate, in London, were raided by uniformed and plain-clothes policemen; fourteen days later diplomatic relations between Great Britain and the Soviet Union were broken off, a melancholy climax to long months of strain and tension in the contacts between the two countries. Events in Poland, where in 1926 Piłsudski had dramatically gathered power into his own hands, also took a threatening turn; Soviet-Polish negotiations received a set-back with the assassination on 7th June of the Soviet minister, Voikov, by a young Russian exile. Capitalist plots and the machinations of powers bent on warring against the Soviet Union were seemingly espied on all sides. In July 1927 Stalin, seeing in Voikov's murder the Sarajevo of a new imperialist war, publicly proclaimed the threat of war:

> It can scarcely be doubted that the main issue of the present day is that of the threat of a new imperialist war. It is not a matter of some vague and immaterial 'danger' of a new war, but of the real and actual *threat* of a new war in general, and of a war against the USSR in particular.[2]

Stalin advised those comrades who advocated 'vigorous' measures to calm their nerves and cease to play into the hands of the enemy, who sought to sow disunity with his provocations. Yet this threat of war was conjured up at a time suspiciously convenient for the embarrassment of the Opposition, which in the spring of 1927 was in a favourable position to display to the full the absurdities of Stalin's policy in China. Chiang Kai-shek was dealing out his ferocious blows at the Shanghai Communists and thereby displaying the total bankruptcy of Stalin's tactics in China. It was therefore not undesirable to silence internal criticism with talk of external dangers, to transform the righteous indignation of Stalin's opponents into traitorous agitation.

The talk of impending war was not without its effects upon the population and the mood of the country. Hoarding and panic-buying occurred.[3] That the Soviet leaders took some of their own words seriously, frightened by the course which the inner contradictions of capitalism seemed to be taking, might be proved by the partial mobilisation of national resources which took place in 1927. The Soviet of Labour and Defence (*STO*) assumed once again those functions connected with defence which it had earlier exercised; mobilisation departments were expanded and brought up to a state of readiness, and a preliminary industrial mobilisation organised by the higher economic agencies.[4] In July 1927 the Germans noted an intensification of the Bryansk munition factory production and the construction of air-fields to the west of Gomel. Yet no large-scale mobilisation of the territorial divisions seems to have taken place, nor a single measure of direct mobilisation put into operation. Voroshilov carried out his inspection of the Red Army in the Ukraine, but it was to manœuvres and not military operations that Soviet troops marched out somewhat later. The situation appeared to be compounded of panic, precaution of a rudimentary kind and political calculation, and the year rolled on to reveal the basic connection between the artificial panic and the necessities imposed on the ruling group in the struggle against the Opposition. Having employed one personal coalition in the early phase of the war on Trotsky, Stalin resorted to a second combination with Bukharin, Rykov and Tomsky to accomplish the final stages of the elimination of Trotsky and Zinoviev from politics. At this juncture of the virtual collapse of the Stalin-Bukharin policies abroad, it was more than ever essential to silence critics and make it impossible for the Opposition leaders to direct an open attack on these failures during the forthcoming Party Congress. But the masquerade of war was itself caught up directly into the political brawl, and Trotsky quickly challenged the ruling group on their mis-management and incapacity, so fatal if matters did come to war. In this event, the Opposition would continue its struggle with those leaders, whom it would and must seek to replace.

First in a letter to Ordzhonikidze, dated 11th July, 1927, and then in an article prepared for *Pravda*, Trotsky broke right into the burning question of national defence. The Opposition, declared Trotsky, took its stand on the unconditional defence of the Soviet Union, and would therefore even in time of war strive to unseat those incompetent leaders — 'ignoramuses and scoundrels' — who even now blundered so badly when they declared the Soviet Union to be in danger. The organiser of the Red Army and the inspirer of the first Soviet victories in the Civil War was in a position to know what he was talking about. By way of an illustration, Trotsky produced his celebrated if violently contested analogy with Clemenceau; with France tormented by the incapacities of bad leaders, with whom Clemenceau continuously struggled although the Germans were only eighty kilometres from Paris, the latter finally took power and pursued the war with immense resolution.[5] Construed not as analogy but as a statement of intention, it was not difficult to present this view as evidence of the intention of treason on the part of Trotsky and the Opposition, who would raise up civil war even though the enemy were advancing on Moscow. This deliberate crudity would at least serve the purpose of supplying a pretext for hurrying the Opposition out of politics and for rendering harmless those who preached in the face of imminent danger the desirability and the necessity of a *coup d'état* to overthrow the ruling Soviet group.

Graver still were the implications of a secret paper directed to the *Politburo*, bearing the signatures of senior officers and criticising the Commissar for War Voroshilov as one incompetent to deal with the duties of his post. Yakir and Putna signed among others, but the document did not bear the signature of Tukhachevsky.[6] In addition, the document was a declaration of support for the Opposition. It was impossible to ignore this demonstration, which had about it a touch of the 1923 situation, although now it was a section of the military command and not the political organs which declared for the Opposition. The originators of the war-scare had been hoist with their own petard, for defence provided the ideal issue upon which to attack Voroshilov himself. But Stalin speeded up the attack on Trotsky, and early in August a joint assembly of the Central Control Commission and the Central Committee met to consider anew the question of Trotsky's expulsion from the Party. A detailed list of Trotsky's political crimes was prepared, ranging from his early political activity and running through 'crimes' against Red Army Communists and the shooting of commissars, to the present malefactions. The whole weight was hung round the 'Clemenceau thesis' so recently propounded by Trotsky, tangible evidence that in the event of war the loyalty of the Opposition seemed to be very much in question. These sessions were, in Trotsky's words, '. . . truly disgusting spectacles . . . each time it more closely resembled an obscene and rowdy bar-room burlesque.'[7] Amid this pandemonium so carefully contrived, Trotsky set out to defend himself and the Opposition against the charges of disloyalty and near treason. He pointed out that the Stalin-Bukharin bloc had much responsibility to bear for the ruin falling presently about the policies which they had initiated. It was a calamity in itself when Voroshilov, the Commissar for War, had made a speech on the Northern Expedition in China which in every way corresponded to the views held by Chiang Kai-shek;* the defeat in China was without disguise a blow at the strength of the Soviet Union, and this defeat had been contrived by the ruinous policies of the present ruling group.[8]

Viewed in its fundamentals, Soviet defence policy could be directed along two channels, either that of the revolutionary internationalism propounded by the Opposition, or in the manner of the Stalinists, which would mean crushing down the worker and applying piecemeal benefits to the richer peasants. In fact, the Stalinist idea only existed as a hopeless attempt at momentary compromise between these two themes and would not ensure the eventual triumph of the Soviet Union. Under Stalin's hand, victory would be '. . . *more difficult*'.[9] As for the Party, upon being questioned about it, Trotsky burst out — 'The Party — you have strangled it.'[10] In words full of meaning for a dilemma which was to wax more acute as the years advanced and the issue of defence became critical, Trotsky declared that the Opposition could not maintain the identity of a defence of Stalinism and the defence of the Soviet Union. In the summer of 1927, under the threat of a war proclaimed to be not far distant, Trotsky summed up the essentials of a position which could not alter except for the degree of its terrible severity. First muzzling and then liquidating opposition did not alter the basic facts of the case; Trotsky had revealed that fundamentally a grievous choice of loyalties, rather than details of strategy and tactics, would dictate the essence of considerations of the 'defence of the Soviet Union'. The expulsion which Stalin sought did not materialise. Even at this late stage, and in spite of the considerable indictment,[11] censure rather than expulsion was the punishment meted out to the leaders of the Opposition. On 23rd October, a renewed joint plenum of the Central Control Commission and the Central Committee enacted the expulsion ot the two Opposition leaders Trotsky and Zinoviev from the Central Committee. On 7th November, during the anniversary parades, Opposition demonstrations were ruthlessly dealt with in Moscow; in Leningrad less brutality was employed, but the same fate befell the demonstrations. One week later, at an extraordinary session of the Central Control Commission and the Central Committee, Trotsky and Zinoviev were expelled from the Party; the expulsion of prominent figures of the Opposition from the Central Committee and the Central Control Commission followed.[12] Rank-and-file Party members were expelled from the 'cells'. The 15th Party Congress, from which Trotsky was absent, occupied itself with two items — the question of the Opposition and the situation created by the surrender of

* Together with Chicherin and Dzerzhinskii, Voroshilov had been a member of the special committee of the *Politburo*, which early in 1926 had been assigned the task of formulating the diplomatic line which should be pursued in China. Trotsky did not take issue with this, but with Voroshilov's subsequent attitude.

Oppositionists to the Stalin-Bukharin faction. The Left cracked wide open, spilling out Zinoviev and L. B. Kamenev in abject capitulation. With this self-inflicted hurt cutting deep into the Opposition, Trotsky's deportation to Alma Ata was in early January 1928 finally decided and the date set for his despatch.

As in 1924, once the anti-Trotsky coalition had achieved its immediate ends, speedy dissolution of the combination followed. Having shattered the Left, Stalin had now to face the Right represented by the Bukharin-Rykov-Tomsky faction so recently his sworn allies. A great deal depended on the attitude of Voroshilov and Kalinin, who were a real reinforcement to Stalin's voting-power; without them, only Molotov stood immovably with Stalin.[13] In the ensuing battles, Voroshilov and Kalinin 'betrayed' their fellows of the Right, turning at the last moment to Stalin's side; Bukharin could only observe that, '. . . Stalin holds them by I do not know what special chains.'[14] With lies, cajolery and a tight hand over the dossiers compiled on the men with whom he was dealing, Stalin proceeded to cut the Right to pieces, while preparing to tackle the major re-direction of policy which was becoming more and more essential. Threats of war, Trotsky's reaction to them and the soldiers' revolt had all served him well; the political support of the military chief Voroshilov helped to complete the discomfiture of Stalin's rivals in the final and most dangerous stage of this deadly game. All aspects of Soviet society and the mainsprings of all policy were substantially affected by this victory for the exponents of 'Socialism in one country' and Stalinism in one system.

* * * *

If Voroshilov may be believed, before 1927 no comprehensive Soviet war-plan existed which covered the possible contingencies of war-situations and Soviet reaction to them. Long-term strategic planning had therefore still to receive the attention of the Soviet high command. Not a little indirect evidence supports Voroshilov's statement. Both Frunze's and Stalin's statements in 1925 on the requirements of military policy were couched in terms indicating that the question remained open. The basic form of the Soviet armed forces themselves had not been irrevocably determined. The low level of actual military performance and the comparative feebleness of military potential were the real determinants of the situation. There were no alternatives of varying suitability; the preoccupation with the problems of the technically backward Red Army meeting an enemy much superior in the technical means of war was indicative of the narrow range of choice. The Soviet Navy was a negligible factor; Soviet military aviation lacked an indigenous industrial base, trained personnel and modern machines in any number. Above all, the military outlook necessarily suffered from the divisions over the struggle between the ideas of 'permanent revolution' and 'Socialism in one country'; both had important military connotations.

The prospect of permanent peace and a 'peace-time establishment' could not enter very deeply into the calculations of a leadership imbued with the idea that the world was divided between the socialist and capitalist camps. Even the phraseology had a martial ring, being the language of uninterrupted war. Tukhachevsky's letter of 1920 to Zinoviev had put this in its starkest terms, although the practical measures which he proposed went far beyond the terms of official policy. The revolutionary content of external policies was directed increasingly towards satisfying the requirements of Soviet security by preventing the formation of anti-Soviet armed leagues; the best illustration was Stalin's Chinese policy, in which effective revolution was considered the immense danger since it automatically increased the danger of foreign intervention in an area vital to the Soviet Union. An imperialist combination leading to eventual armed intervention against the Soviet Union was a real hazard. Great Britain and France figured high on the list of intractable enemies of the Soviet Union; it was within their power to develop, directly or indirectly, armed combinations for use in their anti-Soviet policies. The military sector of the entire scope of Soviet strategy had perforce to wait upon the solution of the struggle which sought to determine the main direction in which Soviet effort should move — towards expanding revolution or into a defence of the single Socialist bastion. The latter would not preclude 'revolutionary lunges', but basically it would imply a tenacious defence of the Russian piece of the Socialist strong-hold. It was inevitable that the military sector should take over the main assumptions of the grand strategic outlook of the Soviet leadership, yet this was not achieved without some struggle. At an early stage in their military experience, the Soviet leaders had shown, quite inevitably with the cast of their political dogmas, a sharp distrust of purely 'military' solutions; S. S. Kamenev had irked Trotsky in 1919 with just such a set of ideas. Svechin's rigorous military explanations of the implications of strategy had never received any official support; there was not, in the fundamental Soviet estimate, any acceptable 'military' assumption which existed independently of the Bolshevik political strictures. War was not an object of Soviet policy.[15]

The configurations of a peculiar political geography contributed to Soviet difficulties. In the west a land frontier of some 2,000 miles conferred no advantages out of particular natural barriers or natural features to facilitate the defence problem; each sector contained a potential Soviet enemy pressed on to the existing Soviet frontiers. In the north was a lengthy land frontier with Finland, as well as the arbitrary frontiers with the Baltic States and Poland — the latter a formidable threat. The Rumanian annexation of Bessarabia seriously incommoded the Soviet Union, while Polish-Rumanian friendship amounted to a co-ordination of hostile elements on the critical areas of the western frontier. Piłsudski's *coup* of 1926 was itself a check to any considerable *démarche* with the Soviet Union; the Polish claim to the hegemony of the Baltic States acted as a further hindrance, for it was only upon these terms that Poland appeared willing to treat with the Soviet Union. Linked with France, possessing formidable military power — the Polish Army numbered some quarter of a million, assisted by French technical and professional help — Poland embodied a permanent threat to Soviet security. The treaties of 1920–1 with Poland and the Baltic States had drawn the frontiers but not settled any problems. As Frunze pointed out, the Leningrad industrial complex could be threatened by hostile naval and air action; Soviet naval power in the Baltic remained a negligible quantity. Similarly, the eastern frontiers presented difficulties no less involved. In the Middle East, Turkey, Iran and Afghanistan shared frontiers with the Soviet Union, making up yet another great belt, but this was a belt studded with natural barriers, formed of desert, mountain and sea. In the Far East, Russian power had barely escaped total eclipse, but rapid recovery had established Soviet power in Outer Mongolia, a form of influence in China and a cautious quasi-settlement with Japan. With a logic which was encouragement to Stalin, Soviet-Japanese relations improved visibly with the decline of Soviet influence in China.

The strategic objective of preventing the formation of anti-Soviet combinations connected automatically with the active diplomatic process of building up a security system designed to frustrate and out-distance armed intervention. Through such a system the buffer-state was assigned a positive role in Soviet calculations; 'non-aggression' and undertakings of neutrality were tied closely with the 'active defence' policy which seemed to be taking shape. The prototype of this security agreement was signed with Turkey in 1925, followed by similar undertakings with Germany, Afghanistan and Lithuania (which shared a common frontier with Germany and Poland, but not the Soviet Union). The heart of this diplomatic complex was the compact with Germany, which existed on the formal level of the 1926 Treaty and the illicit agreements negotiated before and after. It was indeed a vital question for the Soviet government to know the precise form which German help might take in the event of a Polish attack. The stakes of possible war were set immovably in European Russia and it was from Europe that the chief danger arose. For that reason, the activities of the *Komintern*, however much out of phase with Soviet diplomatic purpose, added the supplementary threat of insurrection in the capitalist rear and the ceaseless propaganda against imperialist war.

Conversely the Soviet Union obtained certain strategic benefits from the carefully cultivated contacts with the capitalist world. Economic and industrial requirements at home necessitated useful external contacts. In an address to the *Komintern*'s agents, Voroshilov emphasised in 1928 that the interests of the Red Army were often well served by peaceful relations with bourgeois states; a case in point was the military-chemical industry, which derived benefits from the United States of America, where Soviet technicians might have access to Edgewood Arsenal and its work on chemical warfare. It was therefore Voroshilov's opinion that 'correct relations' with the Americans were worth preserving at any cost.[16] The apparent divergence between Soviet diplomacy and the activities of the *Komintern* was not, in fact, a division of strategic purpose, and any tendency towards this was checked increasingly by the *Komintern*'s steady loss of prestige within the Soviet government. None of this interrupted a consistent strategic design which was founded on the close tie with the *Reichswehr* and Germany at the heart of European affairs, close friendship with Turkey in the Middle East and persistence with the *détente* with Japan. These inter-relations survived without fracture in spite of the strains of 1929 and the Soviet Union committing itself to military action in Manchuria. The limitations were indicated, however, by the scrupulous care taken by the Soviet leadership to confine its own active military intervention to the smallest possible degree.

Soviet military power was related to Soviet diplomacy by the obvious measure of its weakness, although by 1928–9 the Red Army was developing to a point where it could very probably contain any Polish attack. There was a marked difference in tone between German military reports in 1925, which dismissed the Red Army as a force of little consequence, and those of 1929 which detected considerable strengthening, even allowing for the optimism of the Soviet command. But another fundamental problem faced the Soviet leadership, which was relevant to any degree of military force possessed by the state. That problem was the relationship of the military, diplomatic and state organs in constituting the higher war-leadership and the planning echelons, which had hitherto developed in a haphazard manner. With control over its own powerful Military Intelligence, the Red Army Staff could develop towards an appreciable degree of autonomy in deciding and estimating the requirements of military affairs and the course of military policy. Some evidence that the army's wings were clipped by the diplomats is provided by the turn which the negotiations with the *Reichswehr* took in 1927; that there was a certain clash of view emerges from the divergence of opinion over dealing with the question of the Chinese Eastern Railway, before the military engagements of 1929. Over strategic preparation, the Red Army Staff had some voice in matters of mobilisation, man-power and material requirements, but the main economic agency of the state controlled the Main Administration of War Industry (*GUVP*). And more than once the Red Army had to struggle over the budgetary assignment for military purposes. Linking up the civil organs with the military machine widened the base of the army's activity in the state machine, but not to a degree disproportionate with that in many other countries. With the drift to narrower centralisation and the concentration of power in fewer but selected hands, the time was becoming ripe for a re-definition of the place of military command in the affairs of this state.

* * * *

The appointment of Shaposhnikov to the post of Chief of Staff of the Red Army in 1928 marked a decisive turn in its own right in military affairs. The reserved colonel of the former Imperial Russian Army had behind him a series of senior appointments in the Red Army; since 1918 he had been closely connected with the higher command positions and had served as assistant to P. P. Lebedev during the latter's service as Chief of Staff. In 1927, after command of the Leningrad Military District, he was entrusted with the post of command over that of Moscow, an assignment which carried with it certain indications of political reliability. Shaposhnikov was in effect military deputy to Voroshilov, although that position belonged formally to Unshlikht. The new Chief of Staff was not a member of the Communist Party, but this was no hindrance to his being entrusted with an even more responsible military post. For all his lack of formal political allegiance to the regime, Shaposhnikov showed deliberate political caution. His study of the 1920 campaign, published in 1924, had steered a very unequivocal course, and was in its controversial points a defence of the high command against Tukhachevsky's charges; it veered round the question of the 1st Cavalry Army by arguing in general terms and re-stating Lenin's thesis that Soviet military power had over-reached itself generally. Shaposhnikov showed signs of being a close student of Clausewitz, for whose ideas Lenin had also shown the deepest interest and a very considerable respect.[17] This intensive interest shown by Shaposhnikov in the ideas expressed in Clausewitz' *On War* was reflected in his own major work on the work of the General Staff, *Mozg Armii*. It is too much to suppose that Shaposhnikov produced this work, which expressed ideas intrinsically acceptable to men of the inclination of Stalin, merely as an act of self-advancement. On the other hand, Shaposhnikov cannot have failed to discern the trend of the times. Whatever the particular motives, Shaposhnikov's study had some resemblance to the ideas developed by Svechin, who also advocated linking the General Staff with the main policy-making centres so as to influence state policy. Through Svechin and Shaposhnikov, Imperial Russian precedents and sizeable pieces of the military legacy of the *ancien régime* were put to an attempted graft on the higher command levels of the Soviet machine.

The appointment of Shaposhnikov marked the defeat of Tukhachevsky, although both these men performed a curiously complementary role in buttressing the Soviet military command. Blomberg offered two reasons for the removal of Tukhachevsky from the post of Chief of Staff; one version involved his political reliability, the other his desire to wage preventive war on Poland. As far as can be ascertained, Tukhachevsky had not connected himself in any way with the Joint Opposition, with which Stalin was waging his ferocious struggle. Tukhachevsky was not a signatory to the protest of the senior officers about Voroshilov's incompetence, although the differences between the two had eight years of history behind them. It has been suggested that pressure, which he resisted, was put on Tukhachevsky to publish a condemnation of Trotsky.[18] Apart from personal animosities, however, Tukhachevsky remained the anomaly in the Red command which he had been since the days of 1921–2. Indisputably talented, his services were essential for the reconstruction of the Red Army. Although a fervid exponent of the offensive, and allowing for the rashness which he had displayed in 1920, Tukhachevsky could not be blind to the technical backwardness of the Red Army and its incapacity for effective offensive action against a well-equipped enemy; it is therefore difficult to credit the report of his desire for preventive war as a serious undertaking. Of his being a military and political adventurer leading an internal *coup*, there were no signs at this time. It was in all probability the personal factor which weighed the heaviest and Voroshilov contrived the banishment of his opponent from the centre of Red Army affairs. Tukhachevsky was assigned to the Leningrad Military District.

In 1927 the first volume of Shaposhnikov's three-part study *Mozg Armii* (The Brain of the Army) appeared.[19] It was an examination of the General Staff as the directorate of war, with historical reference to the work of Konrad von Hoetzendorff. The object was to discover, with respect to modern conditions, the function of the 'brain of the army', what place it should occupy in the state administration and how it should organise its own work.[20] In line with other current Soviet opinions, Shaposhnikov held that future wars would be on a vast scale, involving the struggle of whole peoples in arms. It was therefore a matter of simple deduction that political, military and economic planning should be included under the whole effort of preparing and directing the state at war. Since war is a continuation of policy by other means, then the General Staff, the instruments of diplomacy and the chiefs of the state machine only defeat their common purpose if each pursues a separate political objective. The key to the argument was that none of these agencies singly could achieve victory, if that was understood to mean the attainment of the political objectives implicit in the armed stage of the struggle. The 'war-lord' was an anachronism; diplomacy did not abandon its role merely because the course of policy had taken a stage where military force was its immediate instrument. The state in all its totality made war, and collective and unified action was absolutely essential. The military directives issued to the General Staff would themselves be an expression of the collective will and common purpose of the state-directorate in pursuit of its political objectives. The General Staff would not therefore be at the mercy of a conflict of purposes or institutions, but would carry out its basic function of preparing for a war which it would direct militarily and remain linked to the policy-making centres of government without degenerating into a restricted and isolated military organ.[21] Modern total war was no mere matter of adding up the respective military forces available to the contestants; in combining the stipulations of Clausewitz with a historical analysis of the General Staff during the World War, Shaposhnikov came down very clearly on the side of military art and strategy assuming its highest form as politics in the widest sense.*

The definition of modern war and the essentials of the planning processes connected with it were Shaposhnikov's main preoccupations in the length of his three volumes, which rarely rose above a relatively pedestrian tone. It was obvious that the formulation of the war-plan was vitally important; in this, the political and military objectives would be respectively set by their being designated basic war-aims and proposed war-aims, the latter reflecting the variable nature of the means. Shaposhnikov made his basic argument drawn from Clausewitz intelligible in terms of general Marxist theory by assuming that 'politics' carried the full implication of the economic motivation and determinant. A particular national policy would influence the form of any war undertaken, and that national policy in turn is conditioned by the economic structure of the society. Arguing from the point of military arrangements, however, these should not be so determined as to

* A recent but somewhat vulgarised version of this is to be found in E. I. Rybkin's *Voina i Politika* (War and Politics), Moscow 1959, 144 pp. The core of a not very sophisticated argument is to be found in 'Politics and Military Strategy', pp. 93–128.

interfere harmfully with the operations of other state instruments working for the full attainment of the political objectives. The same criteria would be applied in considering the manner in which Russia had fought most successfully, that is, in a coalition; here it was even more important to distinguish carefully the respective military-political positions of the partners and to achieve uniformity of political aim and synthesis of war-direction. Coalition warfare, which Trotsky had also recognised as one of Russia's successful ways to win wars, could yield satisfactory and decisive results if so calculated.[22]

The very dullness of Shaposhnikov's presentation was brought into sharp relief by a brilliantly incisive article on 'war as a problem of armed struggle' from the pen of Tukhachevsky, published in 1928.[23] Like Shaposhnikov, Tukhachevsky held the view that modern war demanded a directorate composed of the leadership of the state and not merely of the military chiefs. He made no specific plea for the General Staff as such, but he put forward an extremely coherent thesis on the role of the military factor and military requirements in a modern war-situation. Diplomacy could render substantial assistance to the war-plan by so fashioning the external relations of the Soviet Union with the capitalist world that a number of strategic objectives could be attained; one such objective was the concentration of maximum force against a capitalist enemy, or, conversely, the accomplishment of his isolation. To offset the effect of blockade, the diplomatic instrument could develop economic relations guaranteed against the effect of war, so that a portion of the capitalist world would be applying its strength towards assisting the struggles of the Soviet Union.[24] In considering the war-plan, provision must be made to develop the Soviet armed forces at a level consistent with productive capacity, with the proviso that this level of armed force provided enough strength to deal with the particular problems of the opening phase of a war. It followed that the industrial plan should itself become related to the war-plan, with special attention to the location of industry (this being the outline suggestion for strategic dispersal); the next vital link concerned transportation and communication, which would also comprise part of the national war-plan.[25] Thus, in the space of a few hundred words, Tukhachevsky sketched out the entire outline of the requirements of a modern military-political and military-industrial system.

Tukhachevsky's ideas on the shape of future military operations had undergone some notable transformation since his intervention in the military debates, when he had taken station on the flank of the Frunze-Voroshilov group. In place of complete reliance on the principle of manœuvrability (the distinguishing mark of Red Army battle experience),

Tukhachevsky had to admit that the defensive weapons available to the infantry outstripped the means of offensive action; in short, the machine-gun could still hold, but the tank could not yet supply overwhelming offensive power. A degree of positional warfare was therefore inescapable (a conclusion shared earlier by Frunze), but the recognition of this fact did not destroy the primacy of the offensive. Defeat of the enemy in the field by a series of offensive actions which would lay open his source of economic strength to seizure was a pre-requisite of war, and any qualification upon this vitiates the whole idea of the use of force.[26] Nevertheless certain factors of geography and other considerations make it impractical to produce a stereotype of action suited to all occasions. In considering the impact of the new weapons embodied in the bomber and chemical warfare, then depth applied not only to fronts but to whole war-theatres was absolutely essential.[27] The war of the future would be on a vast scale (exceeding that of 1914–18) and probably protracted; the position of the capitalist powers would be aggravated by the operation of unrest in their rear, and the very idea of mass warfare constituted a danger to the capitalist powers, since arming the mass in conditions of acute class struggle (which war itself would exacerbate) presented grave dangers. These points recalled Frunze's views on the position of the bourgeois army in the event of war and its reliance on superior techniques as an alternative to the mass army.

The essentials of Tukhachevsky's argument remained linked inexorably to the offensive. A war of attrition could only be successfully pursued if non-stop and successful offensive action had so placed the Red Army that 'prolongation of the war would favour Russian victory'.[28] An exception to this would occur when the opponents' lines of communications were severed from the very beginning of a war. Where Shaposhnikov and Tukhachevsky divided was over the question of interference in the affairs of the army while it was carrying out its operations. While accepting the view that the military operations should not themselves embody an aim but be related to the political objectives, the realising of which was the object of the war and the consecutive military operations, Tukhachevsky sought to free the army from the invasion of 'current political interests'.[29] In his assumptions about the social and economic foundations of strategy, Tukhachevsky was advancing further along the road of advocating a working autonomy of the military interest in the formulation of over-all strategic plans, even though accepting the primacy of the political objectives in pursuit of which war would be waged. While Shaposhnikov's was essentially a compromise argument, extolling the supremacy of the state-machine in its totality, Tukhachevsky had evidently not decided upon that degree of uniformity which would mean interference in the operational stages of the army's work in war. By analogy, something of Trotsky's distinction between the defence of the Socialist state and 'the Stalinist system' might be read into Tukhachevsky's identification of the military with state objectives but not with particular political schemes. Tukhachevsky's arguments were not consistent on this point; these qualifications may have reflected his experience during the Polish campaign, when interference in the military operational phase of a war, to the political objective of which the Red Army had fully subordinated itself, led to disaster. On the other hand that same military phase was imperfectly handled and the supplementary methods of struggle were grievously over-estimated.

While Shaposhnikov and Tukhachevsky were agreed on the form of a future war — its vastness, the involvement of the whole population, its duration and intensity bringing heavy losses — the whole question of war was complicated by its affiliation to ideology. Both Shaposhnikov and Tukhachevsky had shown that they could discuss detailed, technical military problems and the issues of long-term strategic planning in a highly realistic fashion; yet Tukhachevsky especially constructed several of his general arguments from ideological assumptions about war. War as a social phenomenon was itself a form of the struggle between the ruling classes of the conflicting states.[30] The imperialist epoch produced 'imperialist wars' closely linked with colonialism;[31] the armed intervention against the Soviet Union had been and could well be once again another form of contemporary war, but this could not be detached from the civil war in the capitalist rear which this might provoke. 'Revolutionary wars' and 'national-liberation wars' were other aspects, which in turn gave rise to the notion of the 'just' and the 'unjust' war. It was therefore logical for Tukhachevsky to consider the internationalist character of the Red Army a potent factor in so far that, in the course of its military operations, what might be nominally 'enemy occupied territory' would be the ground from which working-class help would spring.[32] In so saying, Tukhachevsky had shut his eyes tight to the recollection of Polish workers with rifles fighting the Red Army in 1920.

In view of these strictures on war, it is essential to see whether the idea of a Soviet turn to the defensive had any real meaning at this time. In brief, the situation had never advanced from Trotsky's basic argument of 1922 that the Red Army could only be reared in the spirit of a defence of the Soviet Union — to ask of the peasant service for the conquest of Brussels or Galicia was an impossibility, even if this conquest was explained as embodying a simultaneous defence of the Soviet state. Even in 1927 a prominent Marxist theoretician, Ryazanov, argued that the Soviet Union could only successfully adopt a defensive strategy; this was directed at those military chiefs who still held to the idea of all-out offensive against the capitalist world, and whose strategic outlook was based upon these assumptions.[33] The Red Army was still being educated in the spirit of internationalism, a fact stressed by Tukhachevsky as being itself a positive military advantage. It is reported that Vatsetis suggested the formation of a Red Foreign Legion, composed of foreign volunteers of proletarian origin who would serve the Revolution.[34] This idea, the forerunner of the International Brigades of later fame, was somewhat superfluous at a time when the Red Army trained foreign Communists as soldiers of their respective national revolutions of the future; Polish and German shadow units existed as a visible sign of the prevalent internationalist spirit. But the issue of defensivism came to narrow itself down increasingly to matters connected with the unmistakable signs of the revival of Great Russian nationalism — a feature detected by the German military observers in the Soviet Union. Here was a military-political climate to which the ex-Imperial senior officers were much accustomed; already in 1925 Stalin had made a plain statement that the Red Army must rely upon the sinews of its own strength, and that the defence of the Soviet Union must not be linked to ideas of the alleviation of 'encirclement' by revolutionary ventures beyond the Soviet frontiers. Basically, defensivism (which did not disavow the offensive as such or its political counter-part of the 'revolutionary lunge') was a matter of timing, a re-calculation of priorities and a re-statement of primary loyalties. The Red Army internationalists were moving out of phase, and Shaposhnikov, with his careful estimations and elevation of the state-command in its totality as an instrument of planning, direction and execution, moved to the centre. No longer was the 'military specialist' needed for his specialist knowledge alone; it was his temper, not his brain, which put a new premium upon his services.

* * * *

There were consequences other than the purely military and strategic in the present triumph of the Right over the Left in Soviet politics; as he had laid open the dilemma in defence and the divergence between the Stalinist system and the wider significance of the Soviet state, Trotsky now in 1928, from his place of exile in Alma Ata, produced yet another brilliant crystallisation of the problems facing the masters of the Soviet military-political machine. At almost every turn the French Revolution, either as inspiration or sinister analogy, had haunted the minds of those who fashioned revolution in Russia. Trotsky made liberal use of the historical terminology derived from the French experience to illustrate the various stages of the Russian Revolution; there could, therefore, be no escape from the problem of

'Bonapartism', when the revolution had been seized by the throat by an energetic soldier and a military *coup* had ushered in the rule of Napoleon Bonaparte. The Bolshevik Right, argued Trotsky in his 'Letter to Friends', written in October 1928,[35] lacked the courage to perpetrate a full-scale return to a form of capitalist restoration; it had protected the rich peasant, the *NEP* trader and the bureaucrat, creating the political and economic climate in which they flourished, but the Bukharin-Rykov-Tomsky Right dared no more. By-passing the Right, these reactionary elements would seek support directly from the army. In one leap, therefore, the Revolution in Russia approached its own 18th Brumaire. It remained to look more closely into the face of the Soviet Bonaparte.

Trotsky discerned two possibilities inherent in Soviet Bonapartism; it could either take the form of a straight military *coup*, or be effected through Stalin's personal rule. In the case of a military adventure, the army would rely on the support of the rich and richer property-owning peasants, in alliance with whom it would sweep away both Stalin and the present regime; on this foundation, the new dictatorship would aim to strengthen the incipient capitalism and put an end to the socialist features of the economy.[36] In suggesting this alliance of the army with the peasantry Trotsky was not expressing an original thought; Gusev, in pleading for a consistent programme of political education in the Soviet armed forces, had pointed to the danger to revolutionary conquests from peasant restorationism, and he had urged a priority of political indoctrination to reduce this danger in the Red Army. Trotsky affirmed that the conditions for a *coup* were ripening, with industrial workers dispirited under the present regime and the peasantry full of hostility towards Stalin's present leadership. It was a matter of lesser moment to Trotsky to distinguish the probable military leader, although he mentioned even the secondary talents of a Voroshilov or Budenny as being no hindrance to success if conditions were right for the venture.[37] It would be the bounden duty of the Left Opposition to fight alongside Stalin in this event, for the defence of socialism would be a common interest. In this argument Trotsky was stating the converse of the worker-peasant alliance upon which the Red Army had been originally based, and forecasting the political effects of the breach in this. It is true that Voroshilov was himself much attracted by the Right, although the mention of Voroshilov can have been no more than a figure of political speech. Treason, mutiny and insurrection there had been in the previous history of the Soviet armed forces, but Trotsky was speaking specifically of a *coup*.

Of the other form of Soviet Bonapartism, exemplified in the triumph of Stalin's rule, Trotsky advised that this would not enjoy the broad support of a possible military dictatorship, but be only narrowly based and wholly insecure. The instrument employed in this Bonapartism would be the Party apparatus rather than the military machine, and a 'chronic conflict' between all classes of society would ensue;[38] under this type of regime, the Left Opposition and Stalin could only struggle to the death. On balance, Trotsky felt that the greatest danger lay presently with a military *coup*, although the eventual triumph of Stalin's personal rule could kill off the revolution just as effectively. As it transpired, Stalin's agrarian policy, fused into a programme of massive and enforced collectivisation, smashed that base which Trotsky had suggested might serve as the foundation of a military dictatorship — the well-to-do peasant. A potential military dictator was unable, after the gigantic rural upheaval, to rally large-scale support from a class which was being broken and physically dispersed. Trotsky had nevertheless discerned the second great devil out of the machine which proceeded from the Soviet military-political system under the iron rule of Stalin, the unrelieved threat of a *coup* by the military. The idea of armed counter-revolution, against which the Red Army had fought during the Civil War, had been conceived subsequently as a threat emanating from the bottom, for which reason the 'class-composition' of the Soviet armed forces had been generally maintained. As for armed military action in the service of a political faction, Trotsky had shunned the very thought during the crisis of 1923–4, for precisely the reason that it would lead to the destruction of the gains of the Revolution, whatever immediate tactical political gains it achieved. In these arguments, and his final observations on Bonapartism, Trotsky was entirely consistent. In any society, the necessary retention by one group of the instruments of violence presents a set of peculiar and involved problems. The Soviet method devised to control those in possession of armed force consisted of direct Party and police control, a system which had received its finishing touches in 1925. And yet this became a deadly conundrum, for the greater the proportion of Party members in the armed forces, the more difficult became the question of Party control over them; this set apart troops of the *OGPU*, armed and organised on military lines, as the real repressive agent. Between the military and the security forces a destructive rivalry developed, a situation which Stalin later exploited for purposes of his own, and which itself conformed to Trotsky's prediction that the very insecurity of his rule would oblige Stalin to adopt all the tactics of 'divide and conquer'. Trotsky had isolated two of the basic conditions which could develop out of the present situation: firstly, a fateful division could be detected between the essentials of the defence of the Soviet state and the protection of the Stalinist system, and secondly Stalin's own creeping Bonapartism would produce internal conflicts of great intensity, one consequence of which must be to set the military chiefs at some time against the government. The founder and former head of the Red Army did not use generalisations about 'Army-Party relationships', but spoke of particular dividing issues between command groups, which is perhaps the most useful form of dealing with problems subsequently lumped under the vague classification of 'the Army and the Party'. In assessing his own ideas, Trotsky thought himself possibly guilty of exaggeration in his forecasts of Stalin's Bonapartism, and saw more immediate danger from 'a general on a white horse'. The Soviet Bonaparte waited in the shadows; the fact that he did not materialise at once was no proof of his lack of substance.

* * * *

The regression to neo-capitalism, which Trotsky had feared for some time, did not take place, for Stalin moved sharply to the left and initiated the large-scale, intensive industrialisation of the Five-Year Plan era. Pre-revolutionary Russia had not lacked a programme of industrialisation, but Soviet rule imposed the stamp of intensification and protractedness for what had often been spasmodic and incomplete. After the ending of the Civil War the immediate task of the Soviet government had been not expansion but restoration, to bring Russian industrial output to its 1913 level. As factories were brought to work at full capacity, Trotsky, Zinoviev and Kamenev proposed an increase in output in the region of a little less than 20 per cent annually. Stalin ridiculed this as the fancy of 'super-industrialisation'. At the 15th Party Congress in December 1927 Stalin professed himself satisfied with 'the rapid growth of our technology', with the percentage annual increase in the output of socialist industry, and with the 'direct and indubitable proof of the superiority of the Soviet system of production over the capitalist system'.[39] In 1928, swallowing his words, Stalin unleashed an attack on the lack of progress in industrialisation, demanding a substantial increase in investment and tempo.[40] The subsequent programme rammed Russia through the first stage of a violently-intensified phase of industrial expansion, the necessary precursor of which was the rigorous campaign of collectivisation on the land; famine seemed to threaten all progress at one stage, and Bukharin was forced to the conclusion that 'Stalin's policy is leading to civil war. He will be forced to drown the insurrections in blood. . . .'[41]

The change in policy (bearing an unmistakable similarity to the Left's earlier views and therefore raising doubts about the need to struggle with it) had enormous consequences for the Soviet armed forces. The Soviet military leaders had been tormented for some considerable time by the problems posed by modernisation with facilities much below the required minimum. The brave plans for re-organisation promulgated during Frunze's rule had come undone over questions of supply and the availability of military equipment. Frunze's claim for the primacy of infantry was nothing more than emphasis on the principal Soviet weapon — human man-power. Collaboration with Germany had stopped up some of the serious gaps and facilitated a start with specialist war-industry, but this was nothing more than a small sector of the total industrial front. The industrial and economic basis of military power had been quickly understood by leading sections of the Soviet command. By way of precept (apart from citing the experience of the 1914–18 War), Engels had clearly laid out the essentials of the problem:

> . . . So, then, the revolver triumphs over the sword . . . the triumph of force is based on the production of arms, and this in turn on production in general — therefore on 'economic power', on the 'economic situation', on the *material* means which force has at its disposal. . . . Nothing is more dependent on economic prerequisites than precisely the army and navy. Armament, composition, organisation, tactics and strategy depend above all on the stage reached at the time in production and on communications. It is not the 'free creations of the mind' of generals of genius that have had a revolutionising effect here, but the invention of better weapons and the change in human material, the soldiers; at the very most, the part played by the generals of genius is limited to adapting methods of fighting to the new weapons and combatants.[42]

This text the Soviet military command took for itself as the requirement of industrial and economic expansion for military purposes. Defence requirements were heavily underwritten in the first Five-Year Plan, for it was to be economic development in general but war-industry in particular, with the aim of consolidating Soviet defensive power and guaranteeing economic stability in time of war.[43]

Speaking in 1933 of the achievements of the Soviet defence industry, Voroshilov freely illustrated the Red Army's technical weaknesses and the limitations imposed by the lack of an armaments base:

> Let us begin with machine-guns. You are all aware of the importance of machine-gun fire in present day defensive warfare. To speak plainly, defence nowadays is impossible unless the various army units, down to the very smallest, have a high concentration of machine-guns. . . . As late as 1928, our Red Army had nothing in the way of machine-guns except the good old Maxim heavy standard type, and even this in comparatively small numbers. The Red Army had no light hand machine-guns of its own, and its equipment included several foreign makes (Coche, Lewis and Colt). These . . . in general did not constitute very serviceable weapons. Worst of all was the fact that we did not really possess a munition base.[44]

Consider the position with regard to tanks — 'everyone knows the significance of tanks in modern warfare' — continued Voroshilov:

> The Red Army was formerly entirely without tanks, for we cannot really count the few dozen tanks of various makes and types which we captured from Denikin, Wrangel. . . . However, up to 1929, these few dozen tanks alone had to serve as models for the whole Red Army to receive its training and 'education'. We exhibited these tanks in our parades and they naturally raised smiles from the foreign attachés. . . . But there was no smile on *our* faces. . . . In 1927 we were able to construct our own tank . . . but this tank was not a success, its fighting qualities being but little in advance of the old Renault. . . . The difficulty was that up to 1928 we had neither a tractor industry nor an automobile industry. It is quite plain that we had no cadre of skilled technicians who could implant the technique of tank production in the Soviet Union. Therefore we were compelled — and quite rightly too — to take the line of securing foreign makes. . . .[45]

The problem went far beyond a mere quantitative adjustment, and Voroshilov had hinted at some of the fundamental problems of raising an indigenous Soviet war-industry.

A whole series of complex factors had to be taken into account in estimating the defence requirements of the industrialisation programme. The development of Soviet raw materials and strategic items, the creation of a metallurgical base (iron and steel industries), priorities for heavy industry and machine-tools, the problems of the strategic location and dispersal of industry and particular plants, the training of a powerful cadre of workers for defence industries, the erection of armament plants, and the role of foreign purchasing commissions and non-Soviet technical help (such as *Rheinmetall*) — all had to be carefully considered. Transport and communications required also particular planning, and these calculations should be entered, in the opinion of Tukhachevsky, in the entire war-plan. Tukhachevsky's brief essay of 1928 did in fact sketch out the full military requirement, including the strategic location of industry. Tukhachevsky also touched on the question of economic blockade, which he imagined might be rendered less than total by diplomatic manœuvre. From an early date, however, the Soviet leadership laid considerable stress on economic self-sufficiency and strategic materials being drawn largely from sources over which there was physical Soviet control. The first stage of the military-industrial plan did nevertheless draw on foreign sources to a marked degree, and nowhere was this more clearly illustrated than in the Soviet negotiations for German technical and financial assistance in 1929–30, culminating in the highly advantageous agreement with *Rheinmetall*. By 1930 there is evidence that a highly-differentiated plan for the manufacture of many items of military equipment had been worked out, and quantity production about to be started. In the same year, at the 16th Party Congress, a resolution was adopted for the 'forced development' of industries which contributed to the defence capacity of the Soviet Union.[46] From the outset the aim was to build up heavy industry, at the expense of any other consideration; at the centre of that preoccupation was the intention to establish a powerful

Production of Basic Types of Weapons in the USSR: 1930–1937

Types	Average per year		
	1930–1931	*1932–1934*	*1935–1937*
Aircraft:			
Total	860	2,595	3,578
Fighters	120	326	1,278
Bombers	100	252	568
Tanks	740	3,371	3,139
Artillery:			
Total	1,911	3,778	5,020
Small-calibre	1,040	2,196	3,609
Medium-calibre	870	1,602	1,381
Rifles (in thousands)	174	256	397

Taken from *Ist. Velik. Otechest. Voiny Sov. Soyuza 1941–1945*, Moscow 1960, Vol. 1, p. 65.

armaments industry, which resulted in 85 per cent (or 177 of 199·5 billion roubles at current rates) being invested in these undertakings out of the whole Soviet industrial investment plan from 1929 to 1st July, 1941.[47]

The first results were only a drop in the ocean of the general requirements, but the production of pig-iron and steel rose respectively from 3,282,000 and 4,251,000 tons in 1928 to 4,964,000 and 5,761,000 tons in 1930.[48] In 1928 only 800 automobiles were produced, a figure which had risen to 23,900 by 1932; for the same period the production of tractors rose from 1,300 to 48,900.[49] To serve the Soviet East as a second coal-metallurgical base, the Kuznetsk combine was started on its development, in Sverdlovsk heavy industry was similarly organised on a great scale; in Chelyabinsk and

Kharkov tractor plants grew up with great speed, and in the latter electro-technical industry added further to the capacity of the city. At Stalingrad (once Tsaritsyn) work was begun on a giant tractor plant, and the settlement of industry in Rostov-on-Don aimed at setting up a centre for the supply of the Northern Caucasus. While output from plants, whose number increased all the while, tended to increase at first, the fall in the productivity of the Soviet worker was accompanied by a rise in production costs; in 1931 these had risen in heavy industry by 5·5 per cent, by 1·25 per cent in light industry and by 3·7 per cent in Soviet industry generally. As an indication of what could be done, in December 1931 the production costs of one tractor at the Stalingrad Tractor Works were cut to 3,328 roubles from the figure of 5,793 of January of the same year.[50] Such oddities scarcely simplified the problems of the military economics of the Soviet Union.

Transportation posed formidable problems. Inland waterways suffered from drawbacks of geography and climate. Roads without proper surfacing were useless in spring, wet summers and autumn. Only 1 per cent of the total mileage of roads was properly prepared.[51] Much depended upon an expansion and exploitation of the railways. Even after enormous efforts in restoration after the Civil War, much remained to be done. Long-distance traffic played a predominant role, and the new plans called for a change-over to the heavier type of locomotive and waggons, and greater operating efficiency. Extensions to the existing 77,000 kilometres of track in 1928 were also planned, and adjusted to the relatively high figure of annual additions of 3,500 kilometres.[52] In a country whose abundance of natural resources promised virtual economic invulnerability, transport and communications were the Achilles heel, and improvement in performance was as vital as expanding the existing links into a planned strategic road and rail programme. Transportation capacity was one of the most acute problems in settling the war-plan suggested in outline by Tukhachevsky. In detail it meant also choosing between East and West, with the signs being that the initial Soviet choice fell upon the intensive development of transportation and communication facilities in the East. The German summary of Soviet strategic intentions in 1928 implied that rail links would carry an adequate mobilisation in the western frontier areas and presumably guarantee the minimum supply.

The industrialisation programme necessitated a considerable overhaul of the machinery of administration and direction in Soviet economic life. To ease the work of administration, fourteen autonomous economic areas were set up finally, corresponding to the economic complexions of the Soviet Union. Direction was from the outset heavily centralised, thus conferring considerable advantages for economic mobilisation. The Soviet of Labour and Defence emerged as the very powerful instrument of control and direction, exercising, in addition to duties connected with national defence, functions of supervision and execution for the whole economic life of the Soviet state. With a membership rising to eleven men including Stalin himself, the Soviet of Labour and Defence combined within itself, on terms of 'close personal collaboration', the military-economic command which directed the first frenzied stages of industrialisation; Ordzhonikidze and Mikoyan (Heavy and Light Industries), Voroshilov (War), Molotov (*Rabkrin*) and Andreyev (Transport) were representative of Stalin's older personal command grafted on to the new centralised body.[53] It was therefore inevitable that Voroshilov should become the military's spokesman over the industrialisation programme, but he was in no way exceptional in recognising the need for economic strength as a military necessity. The basic idea and the outline of essentials had been freely suggested by other Soviet military authorities. The planning of the technical requirements of the armed forces was not Voroshilov's personal mission, but was entrusted to a mixed body, which included 'Herr Ludwig' during the early phases. But it was no less significant that such ideas and decisions should have to be filtered through the narrow channel at the top, where Stalin's grip was to become exceedingly tight. If it is perhaps an exaggeration to describe the First Five-Year Plan as a venture exclusively military in its significance,[54] the predominance of military interests was marked. Next to the giant physical transformation, the second revolutionary achievement was possibly that exercise of the propagandist's art, which accomplished the identification of '... things military as socialist, and [created] out of them an ostensibly new conception of the world'.[55]

* * * *

Industrialisation did not signify, however, a surrender to a technological view of war, which was paramount in bourgeois armies according to Soviet views. Both Shaposhnikov and Tukhachevsky had stressed not only the military-technical processes of war but also the fundamental place which the morale factor must take in the preparation of armed forces and population alike. One of the features about the war of 1914–18 so clearly discerned by Soviet military writers was the degree to which the civilian population was progressively involved in war-making processes, apart from actual mobilisation; the discovery of the 'civil front' had been high-lighted by the experiences of the Civil War, in which the stability of the rear and universal military training (*Vsevobuch*) were adduced as factors contributing greatly to eventual victory. The armed forces were not divorced from society; conversely, society was militarised and the civil front mobilised or kept in a state of partial mobilisation in a way which diminished many of the normal social consequences of a real division between war and peace-time states. Utilisation of the mass was a cardinal object of Soviet policy.

After the Civil War, in addition to the territorial training schemes, a number of para-military organisations were developed to strengthen the ties between the front and rear. The society for Assistance in Defence (*OSO*), the Society of Friends of the Air Force (*ODVF*), the Aviation and Chemical Association (*Aviakhim*), and the Military-Scientific Society (*VNO*) all contributed to expanding the area of military knowledge and technique among civilians, retired officers and interested persons alike. The degree to which this was a purely voluntary activity is questionable, for the trade unions were utilised as a means of bringing immediate pressures to bear on the working population to take part in para-military activity, a continuation of the mobilisation function which they had exercised during the Civil War. The para-military organisations also enabled military recruits to pursue training during their free time, being therefore a dilution of the territorial training scheme itself. In 1927 the various societies were united into a single, centrally-directed organisation under the portmanteau name of *Osoaviakhim*, the Society of Associates for Aviation and Chemical Defence. The emphasis on aviation and chemical matters was deliberate. In addition, military training and general military studies were carried on, with instruction in what came later to be called civil defence. On 1st October, 1927, *Osoaviakhim* had a membership of 2,950,000 (15·7 per cent being women); divided into 'cells', this association ran military study clubs, military rifle clubs, ordinary rifle instruction and marksmanship clubs, study groups for aviation and chemical subjects, air-sport clubs (later to include parachute training), 'Aerochemical units and commands' and chemical laboratories. In 1927 *Osoaviakhim* was made up of 37·2 per cent workers, 21 per cent peasants, 26·5 per cent employees of state organs, 6·7 per cent students and 7·1 per cent military personnel; in the same year the proportion of *Osoaviakhim* members who belonged also to the Communist Party rose to 17·4 per cent.[56]

General Blomberg had the opportunity in 1928 to observe some of the work of *Osoaviakhim* in connection with the air manœuvres and civil defence exercises. The 'passive defence', created out of municipal and voluntary bodies, used the services of the militia, fire-fighting services, the Soviet Red Cross, *Osoaviakhim*, traffic control and factory administrations, and voluntary wardens. *Osoaviakhim* personnel, acting with the military, manned observation points for reporting on aircraft movements; a warning system and observer corps, strengthened fire-fighting facilities and a rudimentary form of population protection had been given a preliminary shape, and Blomberg was quick to see the significance of these Soviet innovations.[57]

The prominent names of the Soviet military command lent their assistance to the unceasing propaganda campaign conducted in the interests of 'preparedness' and towards increasing the extent of para-military training. *Osoaviakhim* became a permanent military responsibility, control of which R. P. Eideman, the head of the Frunze Academy, assumed in 1932.

Any challenge to the principle of mass as a method of organisation carried with it a blow at the Soviet principle that the whole society, together with its potential, would be committed in a future war. In theory, the Red Army drew its strength from the mass support which was accorded it and from the careful cultivation of the bonds of the front with the rear. In the military section of the Communist Academy of the Central Committee of the Russian Communist Party a furious controversy was developing in 1929–30 over Red Army organisation. Bourgeois military theories with their 'false idealist views' of war and military organisation were under heavy fire. Tukhachevsky and B. I. Gorev, the latter a pioneer of Soviet sociological studies of war, criticised in trenchant fashion the ex-Imperial officers Svechin and Verkhovskii. Verkhovskii's advocacy of the ideas of the British General Fuller*— himself advocate of the vast importance of the aeroplane and tank as arbiters of the battlefield — brought down Tukhachevsky's condemnation, who rejected these ideas as propounding 'the small mechanised armies of the type of the Fascist police'. Tukhachevsky insisted that the idea of the small, élite army 'signifies the denial of the advantages of mass, mobile and offensively-trained armies'. There could be little support for the 'harmful programme' of Verkhovskii and Mikhailov, who propagated naive and fantastic theories derived from bourgeois sources.

Tukhachevsky and Svechin clashed over the problem of a defensive or an offensive strategy. Tukhachevsky based his arguments on the resolutions of the Sixth Congress of the *Komintern*, but in detail the dispute slipped into a fresh wrangle over the implications of the abortive Soviet offensive against Warsaw in 1920. The defeat was adduced as evidence of the danger of the foolhardy offensive; Melikov's recent study of the actions of the Marne, the Vistula and Smyrna[58] had illustrated the hazards of 'aimlessness and unreliability' when the predilection for the offensive was taken to the extreme. It was common knowledge that the Warsaw offensive had had its opponents in the Party and had the weight of serious opinion behind it. Tukhachevsky attacked Melikov as the mere 'heir-apparent' to Svechin,

* General Fuller's *Tanks in the Great War* had appeared in Russian as *Tanki v Velikoi Voine 1914–1918 gg.*, in 1923. Captain Liddell Hart's views on this question appeared in 1930 under *Novye puti sovremennykh armii*. These questions have again been raised in a recent study compiled by the Military-Political Academy and edited by Col. V. A. Vasilenko, Captain 1st Grade V. M. Kulakov and Colonel V. M. Kulish, as *Sovremennaya imperialisticheskaya voennaya ideologiya* (Contemporary imperialist military ideology), Moscow 1958, 494 pp. See Chapter Two, pp. 41–104.

who had produced the view that Denikin's drive on Moscow, rash as it was, had its continuation in the form of the Red drive on Warsaw in 1920. These ideas were the results of following the errors of bourgeois thought, Tukhachevsky argued, and nowhere was the error greater than in Svechin's advocacy of the strategy of attrition. Put into the context of the actual Soviet situation, the strategy of attrition was nothing more than a strategy overlaid with such political overtones that it militated against the possibility of the Soviet Union overthrowing the bourgeois states.[59] Eideman dealt with Verkhovskii's attacks on Engels, who had been accused by the former Imperial general of writing 'childish nonsense' in some of his military opinions.

The idea of an élite, professional army was nipped in the bud from the beginning and the protagonists of the tank or air-arm, in opposition to the all-round development of the armed forces, similarly checked. 'One-weapon theories' both contradicted the accepted theories of the social-political foundations of the Soviet armed forces and ran counter to the ideas which had been developed as a consequence of the technical inferiority of the Red Army. The results of industrialisation helped to remedy the latter in some respect, but the great social tensions produced by intensive industrialisation created fresh problems for that other important sector of command, the Political Administration. To direct the Red Army through the storms which were gathering throughout the land, the Political Administration was finally given a new head, whose mission it was to guarantee the loyalty of the military to the policy and persons of the ruling group.

* * * *

In several respects A. S. Bubnov had been an unexpected choice as the head of the Political Administration in 1924. Former Left Communist, Bubnov had been associated with the protest of the 'Forty-Six' at the end of 1923, but carried out a rapid and self-interested retraction of his support. Under Bubnov the Political Administration had been re-moulded as an instrument fully capable of supporting the ruling group during the tense political struggles of 1924–5. While Trotsky had scrupulously refrained from carrying the struggle into the armed forces, the ruling group showed no such hesitation and launched its anti-Trotsky campaign forcefully into the army. It was under Bubnov that the Political Administration passed under the direct control of the Central Committee and the conquests of the Party within the armed forces quickly consolidated. The campaign for unitary command had not led to the eclipse of the military commissar, and neither did the commander's autonomy achieve that impressive proportion which many had anticipated that it might. In the execution of high policy during his brief stay in China as Stalin's agent Bubnov served the Stalinist cause equally well.

Direct and indirect measures were employed to exercise that control

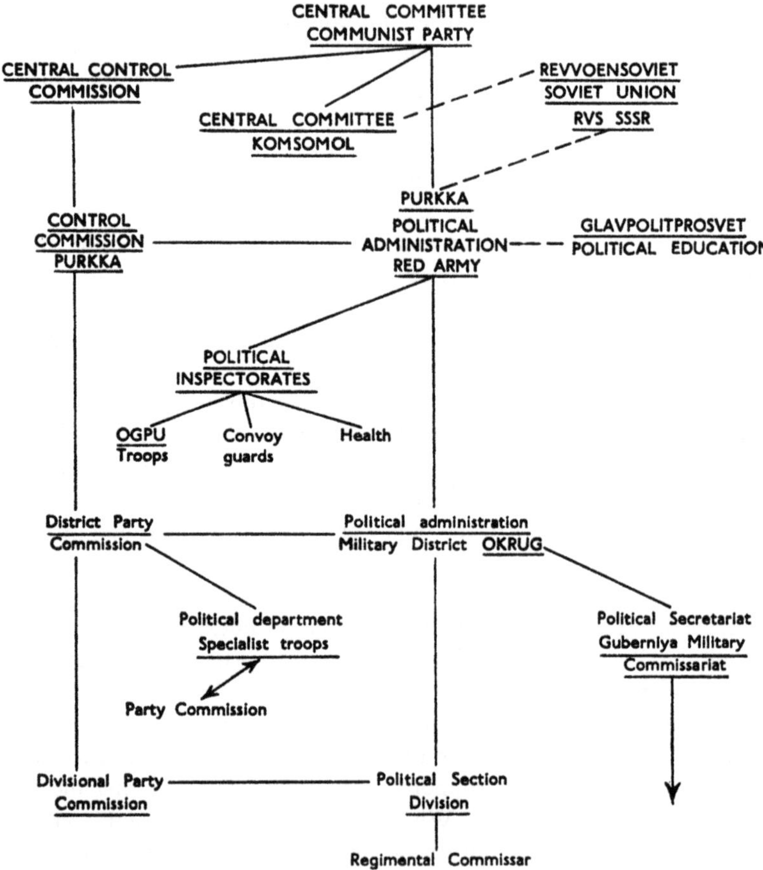

which was the primary function of the Political Administration. Indoctrination was especially important with the preponderant mass of the Red Army consisting of peasants, recruits drawn from rural areas where disaffection and unrest were rife. To maintain the loyalty of the army under these troubled conditions was no easy task and was accomplished by the close links which were maintained between the political and security organs, both of which were not under direct military control. The propagandistic activity was concerned to realise the aim of making of the Red Army not only an efficient fighting instrument but also 'the school of Socialism for millions of peasants and workers'.[60] At the end of 1928 the Central Committee issued its statement on the improvements which must be effected to bring about a satisfactory state of affairs in the 'politico-morale condition of the Red Army'.[61] The raising of the political level of the command staff and the increase in the number of Party-commanders would assist in speeding up the 'growth of the authority of Soviet power in army and navy'. A distinct lack of unity between the command and political staffs, however, 'had to be noted'.[62] In December 1928 the Central Committee pronounced on the Political Administration's report on the work of the military 'cells'. A 40 per cent increase in the membership of Party organs in the armed forces was recorded for the past three years; the rank-and-file and junior command staff accounted for the greatest proportional increase, while the proletarian content had jumped from 41·1 to 47·9 per cent.[63] In the struggle against Trotskyism and the Right deviation also the Party organs in the army had been mobilised to some effect, and there had been no mass wavering.

The technique of gathering the cell-secretaries into a central assembly was used once again to direct the political struggle into the requisite channels. Control over the 'cell' was one of the foundations of effective central control; this technique could also be used to assist certain military programmes, as was the case in 1928 when the drive for greater discipline was pushed through with the assistance of the lowest Party organs in the army. Directive No. 28015, originating from the Political Administration on 7th June, 1928, specified the military tasks which required the closest attention of Party personnel in the armed forces. The criticism of the shortcomings of Party political work in the Red Army was itself a statement of the aims of this activity. In the lowest Party organs the proletarian element remained weak, and 'comradely ties' had proved to be very slack; the 'cells' had failed to take advantage of the possibilities of 'drawing in' the worker and poorer peasant Red Army men for political indoctrination. There was slackness and lack of initiative in the 'cells' as a whole in this struggle against bureaucratism, thus contributing to the low level of material well-being in Red Army units; drunkenness, breaches of Party discipline, lack of contact with Party life, the decline of effective 'self-criticism' and cases of active resistance to developing it by the command staff, would have to be rectified. Indoctrination outside the normal political courses was unsatisfactory, and the state of inner-Party political education equally bad. Propaganda to counteract the influence of the village, the depressed rural conditions, not to mention the famine danger, had lapsed; in the 'cells' 'comradely cohesion' was not always fostered by senior political staff towards rank-and-file Party members, a situation rendered worse by cases of the command staff cutting themselves off from Red Army men.[64] To

INTERNAL ORGANISATION OF THE POLITICAL ADMINISTRATION OF THE RED ARMY (PURKKA) BY 1928

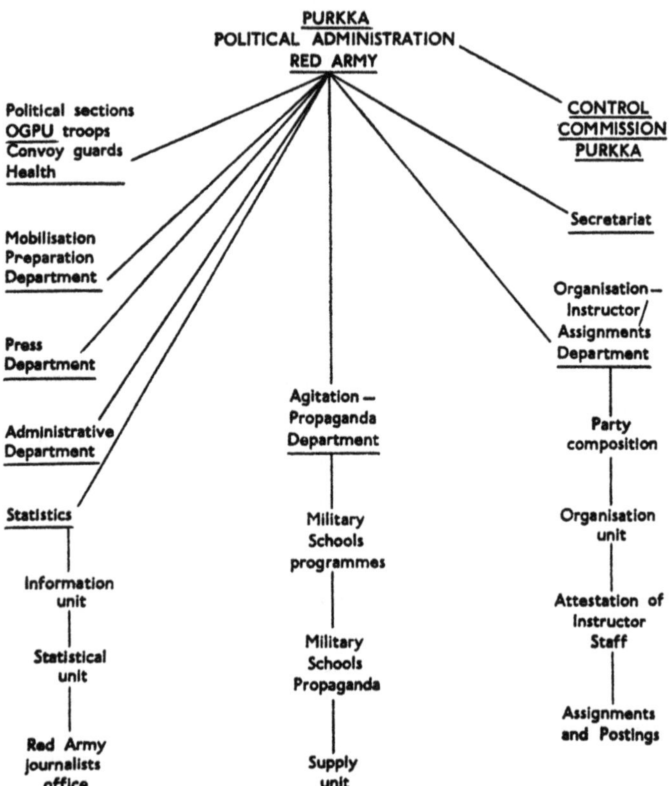

remedy this state of affairs a new campaign would be undertaken to intensify the struggle with bureaucratism, to combat deviations from the accepted Party line, to counter 'pessimistic inclinations' of those who exaggerated the backward state and the poor rate of growth of the Red Army as a whole. 'The peasant outlook' would have to be contested; 'comradely ties' must be strengthened and all Party organisations mobilised and brought into contact with the mass of Red Army men. The non-Party element of the command staff must be 'drawn in' into more political work. 'Self-criticism' must go forward in its full development.[65]

The Red Army was also used as a source of skilled man-power and indoctrinated personnel in pushing through the collectivisation programme on the land. In 1929 a set of instructions was issued to cover the release from the Red Army of not less than 15–20,000 Red Army men and junior officers, who would be assigned to the land. It was the responsibility of the Political Administration to run pre-release courses for these men destined to be 'the organisers of collective-farm (*Kolkhoz*) establishment'; the Political Administration was to prepare a mass campaign on collectivisation, at the same time instilling in the demobilised military cadres the need to assist with military training in the villages. Not later than 20th May a plan was to be prepared for the maximum utilisation of the military recruits on the land, while special financial arrangements would also be made to incorporate the Red Army men into the work of the collective farms. Tractor-crews were specially needed and must be carefully prepared in the political courses. In view of the fact that a purge of the apparatus was about to gather momentum, the men who would replace those displaced would have to be drawn in part from the Red Army; pre-training courses for this would also be necessary. A full-scale press campaign was to accompany this programme for the demobilised, who, in fact, were merely transferred from one state service to another.[66]

The summary of the position of the command and political staff of the Red Army, made in the early spring of 1929, aimed at presenting the balance-sheet of the campaign for unitary command and developments within the political staff as a whole. While paying formal respect to the policy of unitary command, the Central Committee pronouncement made a signal point of emphasising the role and importance of the non-Party commander — favourable terms which ushered in a deliberate policy of cultivating the skills and general loyalty of the non-Party officer. Harsh words were reserved for the higher sections of the political staff, where 'vacillation and political errors', the very existence of an 'inner-army opposition' were serious signs. These had been checked, but it was more than ever essential to press on with the political training of the command staff and the accomplishment of 'the maximum cohesion and full unity of the whole of the command and political staff of the Red Army'.[67] Both the political and command staff were to take an active part in training the Red Army both in the business of defending the Soviet Union and as vital organisers of the Socialist transformation of the villages. The greatest gain would be to achieve that full unity of the two staffs, the one command and the other control, in the Red Army; the small proportion of commanders enjoying the complete exercise of unitary command made it impossible to bring about the fusion in this manner, nor was it possible to prejudice the services of the non-Party commanders, who were vital to developing the military efficiency of the Red Army. Any diminution of the role of the commissar meant damaging the position of the Party in the armed forces, a step which was inconceivable. The ideal of a truly unified command was unattainable when their separate functions were so divergent, yet, if the ideal suffered, the practice of the latter half of the 1920's became increasingly the standard for the manipulation of political matters within the army. The deviations had perhaps even greater significance, for the fractures in the Political Administration occurred either at the top or at the very lowest levels. While Party membership remained comparatively low in the Red Army and in sections of the command staff, the Political Administration found less difficulty in carrying out its control function. With the increase in Party membership, the Party could less easily control the Party from without; the active role then passed increasingly to the *OO* branches, the *OGPU* Special Sections which honey-combed military units and installations.

In 1929 control of the Political Administration passed from Bubnov, who had rendered a not inconsiderable service to his masters, into the hands of Yan Gamarnik. A man in his early thirties, Gamarnik had worked during 1917 as member and secretary of the Kiev Party Committee and subsequently in Bolshevik organisations in Odessa, the Crimea and the Ukraine, becoming a military commissar in the 58th Division and ultimately a member of the *Revvoensoviet* of the XIIth Red army. In 1923 Gamarnik departed for the Soviet Far East, where he acted as secretary of the Far Eastern Party Committee; on 1st April, 1927, he was appointed to the *Revvoensoviet* of the Siberian Military District, a military-political command appointment which matched his steady ascent in the Party hierarchy. Elected a candidate member of the Central Committee at the 14th Party Congress, Gamarnik became a full member at the 15th Congress in 1927, where he distinguished himself by the vigour of his attacks on the Opposition.[68] If he adopted the general manner and tone of the Congress as a whole, then this was something of a degrading performance. The year 1928 found Gamarnik in Belorussia as secretary to the Central Committee of the Belorussian Communist Party, when his official biography mentions him beginning his activity in the Red Army.[69] On 1st December, 1928, Gamarnik was appointed a member of the Belorussian *Revvoensoviet*; on 1st October, 1929, he became head of the Red Army Political Administration and ten days later a member of the *Revvoensoviet* of the Soviet Union.

Gamarnik's appointment coincided with the purge of 1929–30, set in motion by the decision of the 16th Party Conference and directed mainly against the Rightist adherents of Bukharin, Rykov and Tomsky, with the object of cauterising the resistance to the industrialisation and collectivisation programme.[70] The Right deviation did obtain some hold over the Red Army, enough for it to be admitted by Voroshilov in February 1929 and contrasted with the Left Opposition and the problem which it presented.[71] Gamarnik was not a man of the Right, but in addition to being of Jewish origin and an intellectual, held fast to internationalist views and passionate beliefs in the mission of the Communist Party. This stood him in good stead during the early stage of the social and political crisis, but was to serve him ill later. In 1929 the extent of the purge in the Soviet armed forces never rose above a maximum of 5 per cent — less than half the figure for expulsions elsewhere. An insight into the struggle waged by the military command to limit the effects of the purge on military efficiency is supplied by a secret directive, dated 23rd September, 1929, and signed by Unshlikht (soon to be demoted himself). The 'sweeping approach' to the purge, which resulted in ex-Imperial officers being removed merely because of their connections with the former regime, was roundly condemned; even with former White officers, where a certain latitude could be permitted, the 'sweeping approach' was still out of the question and involved possible loss to the Soviet command of valuable technical skills in men whose loyalty had since been proved. 'The really corrupt elements hostile to us' must still be removed, irrespective of whether they belonged to the Soviet command staff or not, but the approach must be made 'especially carefully' in the proposed purge of technical and qualified officers, of artillery and cavalry specialists, military engineers and communications officers, the technical and flight personnel of military aviation and officers of the naval command staff.[72] The attempt at limitations seems, on the whole, to have been effective, and the Soviet command staff not to have incurred a loss on any scale.

Nothing resembling the crisis of 1923–4 in the Political Administration seems to have occurred at this later date, nor anything like a consistent oppositional trend. An outbreak of resistance to strengthening the powers of the commander by the commissars of the Tolmachev Military-Political Academy was wholly disavowed and quickly suppressed. Considerable attention was paid to raising the worker representation in the armed forces, while the peasant and 'the peasant disposition' were carefully and constantly checked during the ravages of collectivisation. During the first intensive periods of Stalin's new policies the army, immersed in a vast sea of unrest and rural agonies, remained loyal. The first pulverisings of the class of the richer peasants simultaneously broke up the foundation for any large-scale military intervention in politics; in the Red Army, the Political Administration campaigned and organised with vigour to immunise the military against possible alignment with the rural proletariat. In the face of considerable odds, the adhesion of the armed forces to the ruling group and its policies (which were to become increasingly identified with the name and person of Stalin) was achieved. The Red Army, moreover, was to become a signal beneficiary of these economic-political programmes, through which it acquired tanks, guns, more varied equipment and the means to mechanisation and motorisation. The Political Administration had to seek to disguise the price which was being paid.

* * * *

In 1929 the new *Field Service Regulations* (*PU–29*), introduced in the name of Voroshilov, marked the first great formal codification of the Soviet views of the problems of modern warfare. No longer was this labelled a provisional manual in the fashion of the earlier work, which had been either a hasty adaptation of Imperial Russian Army regulations or an equally hasty draft of ideas not fully absorbed. The 1929 *Regulations* dealt with corps, divisions and regiments; its singular feature was the special section on political education and its role in assisting the combat preparation of Soviet troops. Binding the command and political staffs through vitally important political indoctrination was meant to be the finished expression of unitary command. A future war was envisaged in terms of a 'war of manœuvre'. Pride of place went to the offensive as the only means of annihilating an opponent; defence could weaken, but not destroy him.

The 1929 *Field Service Regulations* defined the Workers and Peasants Red Army as 'the armed instrument of the proletarian state — the first and unique fatherland of the toiling masses in the world.'[73] In modern war new technical means and the deployment of the enemy in depth demanded of the commander both organisation and operation, also in depth, of the various types of troops operating in a given single direction, and, in addition, co-ordination between units operating in different directions towards various objectives. Personal initiative on the part of commanders of all grades and types of troops could have a decisive significance when applied to accomplishing the general aims of the operations.[74] Under 'Political security of the combat activities of the troops' three questions were considered: the tasks of political work, political work among the troops and also among the population (in the military rear). Political indoctrination and the political staff were henceforth formally included in the Soviet military apparatus by stipulating both as an essential and linking them directly to the combat training and readiness of the Red Army; in line with Voroshilov's view of the commissar as a vital adjunct to morale-building, it was stated that 'the basic task of political work in the Red Army consists of guaranteeing and strengthening the combat readiness of the Red Army as the armed support of the dictatorship of the proletariat'.[75] On the organisation of the military rear the new regulations laid down a specific scheme for logistical arrangements; in the rifle corps this would be handled by the Chief of Staff working through the chief of the transport services, in the rifle division also by the Chief of Staff working through the Section Chief for Rear Organisation, and in the rifle regiment responsibility would fall on the commander's assistant for supply questions, acting under the orders either of the commander or the Chief of Staff.[76]

As for operations, pride of place went to the offensive and to the role of manœuvre warfare. Great emphasis was laid on taking the enemy in the flank and at the junction of his units; the most decisive form of manœuvre, taking advantage of the mobility provided by cavalry and motorised units, was the offensive action leading to encirclement of the enemy. In the face of an extensive front which constituted a barrier to turning movements, a breach must be effected by the use of assault groups, relying especially on artillery support, exploiting the co-operation between infantry, artillery and tanks. The artillery should concentrate on reducing the enemy's own artillery resource, deployed in the first defensive echelon. If large numbers of tanks were employed, a break-through should proceed without preliminary bombardment or after short artillery preparation. Defence, under which chemical warfare and anti-aircraft items must be considered, was classified as fixed or mobile; engineering works would be used where necessary, for trenches, obstacles and communication passages. The tank was consigned to the role of direct support for the infantry storm-group; faced with a large concentration of enemy tanks, independent echelons of 'long-range tank groups' (*tankovye gruppy DD*) should be formed, the 'DD groups' taking on enemy artillery which might interfere with the infantry-support tanks. Military aviation, already initially organised into army groups in 1924–5, was to be used on a mass scale and assigned to unit or army tasks. One of the lessons derived from the 1929 Manchurian operations had been the use of air-support for amphibious landing, a point which was later incorporated into doctrine.

In 1927 new infantry regulations had been drafted to replace the provisional Frunze manual. Mobility and fire-power were the cardinal principles adduced for success in infantry combat; the aim of all manœuvre was to envelope or turn one or both enemy flanks, and failing this, the infantry accomplished the break-through. In offensive operations, Soviet infantry was to adopt three basic groupings (four with the reserve): the assault group was to be made up of not less than two-thirds of the strength deployed, and would be used for operations composing the main blow: the groups designed to pin down the enemy would consist of one-third of the strength deployed and would be employed in the second stage of the offensive movement: and a 'fire group' of artillery and heavy machine-guns would support the assault group, or the groups engaged on pinning down the enemy or laying down general supporting fire. The reserve group would be made up of one-ninth of the total strength deployed.[77] In addition to these infantry and general *Field Service Regulations*, separate manuals for individual arms were completed between 1927–9 and the naval combat regulations by 1930.[78]

In 1929 an interesting study of modern war was produced from the pen of V. Triandafillov of the Red Army Staff, who died two years later. This examination of the character of the operations of modern armies raised at once the question of the choice between a force of small motorised units or the 'armies of the millions'; the author, while briefly mentioning the theories of General Fuller, of Seeckt and of Verkhovskii, proceeded to the argument that the basic problem was still to 'secure the best conditions for free manœuvre'.[79] It would be impossible to obtain this with the small armies of armchair-strategies (*kabinetnykh voin*); but only mass armies made every possible use of transport and motorisation. Triandafillov's arguments followed logically after each other; the new productive capacities available to states (and to the Soviet Union) meant an increase in the number and diversification of weapons, giving rise to new tactical developments and important changes in the operating art.[80] Modern war demanded a high degree of perfection in the problems of supply, and the basis of Triandafillov's argument was the logistical necessities imposed by the rapidly-developing tactical possibilities and the complicated demands of the new weapons. It was still, however, war on a mass scale.

Important and influential though Triandafillov's own work was, the quantitative significance of the writing of Soviet-trained military men still did not measure up to the contribution which the officers educated and trained in the Imperial Russian Army were making. Although ex-Imperial officers were much more closely integrated into the Red Army and did not present their previous compact grouping, their invaluable knowledge and experience gave them even now a singular place in the senior Soviet commands. Of the 100 authors of the 1929 *Field Service Regulations*, 79 were ex-Imperial officers. Of the 243 military contributors to professional writing in 1929, 198 were likewise ex-Imperial officers, 29 of whom had served with the Imperial Russian General Staff.[81] A survey of the composition of the Soviet officer-corps in 1927 revealed that of 45,867 officers all told, 4,418 had obtained their entire military training in the Imperial Russian Army, 465 had passed through the former military academies (with 2,126 officers who had attended Soviet higher military centres), and 3,968 Soviet officers had received no adequate or formal military education at all. This command staff was 48·1 per cent Communist, 47·1 per cent non-Party and 4·8 per cent *Komsomol.*[82] In terms of its military intelligentsia, the Red Army therefore still owed a considerable debt to the ex-officers of the Imperial Russian Army, and there was strong justification for Unshlikht's directive to curb the 'sweeping approach' in the purge, else the Red Army's brain would have been badly damaged. Since it was impossible to expect a formidable Marxist doctrine of war to issue out of such sources, there was therefore considerable significance attached to the creation of the 'Section for Research into the problem of war' (Military Section) of the Communist Academy of the Central Committee, and such sections were set up in a number of places to carry on this study. Operational study and tactical doctrine remained the responsibility of the Red Army Staff, and with this decision the writing on military subjects tended to divide somewhat into the professional and the ideological.

The declared views of the Central Committee, embodied in a pronouncement of 15th July, 1929, on 'The State of the Defence of the USSR', summed up the general transformations which were taking place in the Soviet military establishment.[83] The internal structure of the army was changing due to the increased emphasis on technical arms; the territorial-militia system, now functioning as it should, must also be considered as one of the organisational forms of the structure of the Red Army. In organisation, the strengthening of the technical troops would continue while auxiliary units would be cut down, although the main problem remained of ordering the relations of the various arms in a modern fighting force. By 1931 it was planned to liquidate the chief material deficiencies of the Red Army, at the same time accelerating the modernisation of existing weapons and the introduction of new models of artillery, tanks and armoured cars. Military aviation, already launched in 1924–5, needed intensive development to raise it qualitatively to the level of bourgeois air-arms, a task assigned to Soviet designers, whose primary mission was the furthering of progress in aero-engines. The introduction of greater degrees of unitary command would be adopted, the Soviet officer corps having been 'thoroughly purged' of 'alien, politically unsuitable and anti-Soviet elements'; the political preparation of the command staff had also made satisfactory progress, so that, side by side with unitary command, the increase of the general responsibility of the command staff and 'raising their authority among the Red Army masses' could be fully extended. Black spots there were too: cases of 'kulak disposition', anti-Semitism, infringements of discipline, and excess of red-tape in both the military administration and the command staff.[84]

Official manuals, military monographs and general statements of policy all contributed to expanding the emergent picture of modern war, such as the Soviet Union might be obliged to wage, with the exclusion from official favour of the small school advocating the small, highly mechanised, élite army. Large-scale war, supported by intensive development of economic resources and productive capacities, waged by mass armies trained in modern techniques and steeped in political indoctrination, and directed by a unified, centralised and highly personalised military-political command — these were the objectives best suited to the necessities of state. To conjure these ideals into reality became the mission of the Soviet command in the 1930's.

* * * *

To present the state of the Soviet armed forces and the aims of the Soviet command towards the end of 1929 as the inevitable and logical outcome of the planned reforms of 1924–5 did much damage to the facts of Soviet military-political developments during the entire decade. This concealed the effect of the abrupt shifts to left and right, themselves part of the struggles of the factions, on the course of military policy. Neither the command nor the army escaped entirely unscathed from the rending political disputes which intensified on the death of Lenin. The Frunze reforms had a definite and possibly decisive effect in bringing that much-needed stability into Soviet military organisation, but that was only one half of the story. The real struggle began when defence became a play-thing for the factions, and progress in military policies depended upon the eventual triumph of a particular clique. The military, however, rendered substantial assistance to particular schemes of state policy in the Far East and with Germany; from the support of individuals of the highest military and political commands Stalin was able to derive immense tactical advantage which led to his eventual strategic victory.

The inner-command disputes revealed fundamental divisions and animosities which had their own importance. Towards Voroshilov a section of the military command had plainly displayed its full dislike and mistrust of his personal capacities as Soviet Commissar for War. As a result of these same personal tensions, and probably because of the very extremism of his views, Tukhachevsky had been banished from the centre of Red Army affairs and his place on the Red Army Staff assumed by a strict professional, Shaposhnikov, who was politically neutral yet could still direct his eye to the shape of things to come. The latter's appointment marked not so much either innovation or reversal of policy but a consolidation of the more conservative trends. Still influential, but lacking their previous coherence as a separate core of command, the senior ex-Imperial officers had not been wholly vanquished and were conducting a fighting retreat. Even if judged from the point of view of mere quantity, these men were even now incomparably valuable to the Red Army, and the subsequent cultivation of the non-Party senior commander was to be a feature of policy in the immediate future. The trend was summed up in the political parable of Shaposhnikov leading a delegation of non-Party commanders at the 16th Party Congress in 1930 to laud the present policy of increasing the defensive capacities of the country and to condemn, from the lofty heights of political neutrality but patriotic feeling, the inner-Party opposition which hindered this vital work.

The pattern of over-all command was illustrated by the developments in the control and execution of industrialisation. Real and extensive power was passing into the hands of a small, highly-centralised and much personalised group, dominated by Stalin. Shaposhnikov's forecast, couched in the language of military history, proved itself to be correct. The public and private accent was on defence, the conserving of the interests of a state rather than the abstract collaboration with Revolution. Out of this, clear signs of which were appearing towards the end of the 1920's, the formulators of military doctrine found themselves facing a difficult situation, and one complicated still further by the evident desire to erect a definitive Marxist doctrine of war. It was significant that this assignment was vested, not with the Red Army Staff, but in the theorists of the Communist Academy, who were not so intimately involved with the questions raised by the potentialities of the new weapons and the consequences of the increased delivery of new or modernised equipment to the Red Army. Tukhachevsky, who could not be accused of lacking a sense of appreciation of military ideas, must have been fully aware of the dichotomy between his stubborn defence of the mass army and the implications of the tank and military aviation. The very idea of mechanisation, with its accent on specialised equipment and the high quality of training and technical preparation, involved a challenge to the notion of quantity and some transformation of the infantry mass. The Soviet command was faced increasingly with the need for a decision which would not contradict its acclaimed principles of organisation, nor deprive the Red Army of potentially decisive military advantages. It was to discover that the politics of motorisation and mechanisation hid grievous difficulties.

Throughout the decade, military weakness had severely curtailed the role of the military factor in Soviet external policy. Soviet diplomacy had contrived an outline security scheme designed to offset this lack of strength, although the military and military action played important parts in the first expansions of Soviet power into Mongolia, the colonial-type wars to subjugate Central Asia, the military side of the revolution in China, and stemming the Manchurian crisis in 1929. A special military relationship was the cornerstone of the link with Germany, and it was here that a section of the Soviet command made its most distinctive contribution to state policy. The First Five-year Plan had set in frenzied motion measures to ensure the recovery of vital sectors of the economy and the development of an industrial-armaments base. The only consumer interest considered was that of the armed forces. This was the real transformation of the Red Army. At the service of the Socialist fatherland and its defence, in the interests of world revolution to which the internationalists of the command would still pay homage, powerful secret weapons were about to be called into operation — the internal combustion engine and the caterpillar track.

PART FOUR

THE POLITICS OF MECHANISATION

The Red Army was formerly entirely without tanks.

K. E. Voroshilov, 20th January, 1933.

. . . We must advance as far as Lake Baikal.

Kasahara Yukio (Japanese Military Attaché in Moscow) Secret report, 1931 (*IMT/FE*).

The problem is not a simple one. . . . the majority are accustomed to infantry actions, and to be able to adjust ourselves to a new level, to be able to utilise the mobility of aviation and our mechanised troops and tanks, is not so simple.

M. N. Tukhachevsky, 1935.

It is impossible to wage modern warfare without conducting independent air operations.

Deputy Air Force commander Khripin, 1935.

CHAPTER ELEVEN

The Reaction to threats from East and West

'Forward, comrades, to new victories!' The first great systematic Stalinist onslaught on all levels of Soviet society — the purge begun in 1929 and the upheavals in the countryside — was aimed at reducing opposition from those who suspected this new slogan and attempted to slow up 'the Socialist offensive'. At the end of 1930 the 'Industrial Party', accused of organised wrecking and espionage in the interests of 'foreign imperialists' planning the disruption of the Soviet national economy, stood trial for these crimes.[1] The Soviet armed forces emerged comparatively unscathed from the large-scale purge, a fact which can be attributed to the intervention of the command in the interests of military efficiency. Yet this attempt would have been of little avail if the general indulgence of the political leadership had not been behind it. A recognition of the fact that the Red Army presented no major problem of opposition, or the desire to keep interference with military morale and efficiency to a minimum, or even both together, may well have contributed to the immunity enjoyed by the military. 'Keeping the army out of politics', which the German officers had discerned as one of the main objectives of Voroshilov's leadership, paid at this time valuable dividends. Even so, the army was also used deliberately and on some scale as one of the instruments for carrying the collectivisation policies into the countryside.

At the 16th Party Congress, which opened its proceedings on 26th June, 1930, Shaposhnikov led a delegation of senior non-Party commanders which presented its own approval of the policy of industrialisation and set down a criticism of the 'Right deviationists' who sought to impede these plans. Prevailing policy at this time fostered the cultivation of the non-Party senior military experts, and this demonstration at the 16th Congress marked the affirmation of a curious alliance of interests and a gesture of support for a policy from which the Red Army had been noted down as the principal beneficiary. It was in 1930 that Shaposhnikov became a member of the Communist Party,[2] thus adding a formal political allegiance to what had been a showing of personal loyalty and professional service to the Soviet regime; Shaposhnikov had chosen his moment well, committing himself to the fortunes of Stalin when the course of the political struggle indicated the latter as the ultimate victor. Not that Shaposhnikov's Party card was a political event important in itself — the Chief of the Red Army Staff had been a non-Party man for two years in that post — but it signified Shaposhnikov's link with the Stalinist group in unequivocal terms. By the end of the period of the First Five-Year Plan the bulk of the non-Party commanders had followed the example set by Shaposhnikov and become members of the Communist Party.

Also at this point the Red Army was flung into the permanent technical revolution which marked its history throughout the 1930's. Voroshilov declared subsequently that the intensive technical progress was based on the sound work which had been accomplished in the preceding decade, and singled out 1928 as the year in which the Red Army embodied, in its organisation form and its absorption of the lessons of the World War, a modern military instrument.[3] German senior officers had observed the optimism of the Soviet command, which inclined it to over-estimate both progress and capacity, but the 1929 *Polevoi Ustav* were compiled for an army which had made striking advances in stability and the incorporation of different arms. In 1930 the Red Army possessed 70 rifle divisions (41 territorial), 13 cavalry divisions (3 territorial), 59 artillery regiments of the main artillery reserve, 16 engineer battalions and 1 'Experimental Composite Mechanised Regiment'.[4] Soviet military aviation, the *VVS*, expanded vigorously and moved away from the stagnation of the mid-1920's, an achievement which owed much to P. I. Baranov, elected a candidate member of the Central Committee at the 16th Congress and promoted in 1931 to the post of Deputy Commissar for Heavy Industry and Head of the Soviet Aviation Industry. The *VVS* disposed of an estimated number of 9 reconnaissance squadrons, 24 independent reconnaissance flights, 9 fighter squadrons, and 3 bomber squadrons by 1930; by 1st January, 1930, Soviet air strength reached an estimated 750 machines, representing a total of 310,400 H.P.[5]

The technical revolution necessitated modification in the command. Although he had become the spokesman for the policy of creating an armaments base, both in Party and wider public circles, Voroshilov's limited talents could scarcely serve as the main support for the complexity of policy which the technical innovations foreshadowed. Voroshilov had shown himself to be a keen advocate of the collaboration with the *Reichswehr*, and his technical deputy in 1930 appeared to be Uborevich; the Voroshilov-Uborevich combination carried through the highly satisfactory pact with *Rheinmetall* in the first few months of 1930. Voroshilov represented the military in that compact group, subject to ever-increasing centralisation, through which Stalin directed the major policies of the Soviet Union, in a manner which corresponded faithfully to the combined directorate which Shaposhnikov had been at such lengthy pains to depict. Gamarnik's appointment in June 1930, as Deputy Commissar to Voroshilov and deputy president of the Soviet Union *Revvoensoviet* underlined the vital part which the political command had to play in holding the army loyal during this critical period. Tukhachevsky remained the singular figure in the command. His virtual banishment from the centre of Red Army affairs, contrived under Voroshilov and relieved only by a brief restoration to the Staff as head of the Operations Directorate during the 1929 Manchurian crisis, seems to have had no effect on his influence as a leading Soviet military theoretician. Although in no way as yet specifically associated with the traffic with the *Reichswehr*, this does not suppose that he was not abreast of events and developments from that quarter. In 1929–30 Tukhachevsky had already taken serious issue over the problems of re-organising the Red Army on the lines of a small highly-mobile élite force. His personal preview of a future war, published in 1928, envisaged the employment of mass armies and total mobilisation, although it set Tukhachevsky in the midst of the quandaries of mass against mobility, quantity against quality as soon as he introduced new technical factors. In the midst of a controversy, which was in full swing by 1930 and would increase in intensity, Tukhachevsky associated himself with the younger commanders eager to develop the full potentialities of new weapons.

Tukhachevsky began his first experiments with parachute troops,[6] the first parachute detachments having been formed in 1929. His preoccupation with a combination of motor-mechanised forces and aviation, to be achieved by the use of airborne troops, brought him into close contact with men of the calibre of Alksnis, crack pilot and appointed commander of the *VVS* and member of the *Revvoensoviet* in 1931.[7] Tukhachevsky's 'group', which was in the process of being formed out of affinity of ideas and combined interests, finally included Yakir and Uborevich, Alksnis of military aviation, Khalepskii from armour and Sedyakin of artillery, Kork and Eideman. While this technical command group was marked by a membership distinguished for its collective contact with the *Reichswehr* and its admiration for German military techniques, here was not the fundamental division within the Soviet high command. The basic divergence, which took solid and ineradicable form during Shaposhnikov's tenure of the post of head of the Staff, centred round the differences in approach to the role of the military command within the state, and hence its contacts with the Party leadership and the Party machine. The one, represented by Shaposhnikov, worked within the limits of a rigid professionalism, maintaining the military point of view with all energy but rejecting any participation in 'politics'; the other — which included Tukhachevsky, to judge by his declared opinions — refused to exclude the political factor, thereby admitting the principle of struggle with the Party leadership and the possibility of criticism of the Party machine within the Red Army. Among the senior non-Party commanders the Party leadership espied the champions of professionalism at its most extreme, and had reposed not a little of its confidence in the most outstanding member of that group, Shaposhnikov. None of this was new to the Soviet command, which owed its ultimate origin to that fateful initial lack of homogeneity and the disparity of professional competence which had plagued the Red Army since its inception. Acute problems facing the Soviet leadership as a whole and arising out of the internal stresses in town and country, formidable changes in the external scene and the rupture of old friendships, as well as the considerable problems facing the military command itself, were to add fuel to the flames of this hot-burning fire.

The *Revvoensoviet* of the Soviet Union had undergone some transformation as a result of the statute of 30th January, 1929, which in no way changed the position as it had been established at the end of 1923, but was much less precise in its definitions of the powers of the *Revvoensoviet*.[8] This body continued to be the collegiate of the Commissariat for Military and Naval Affairs, with the Commissar and Deputy Commissars for War occupying the positions of president and vice-presidents respectively. These appointments were controlled by *TsIK* and the nominations of the *Sovnarkom*; in line with the practice introduced in 1929, the *Revvoensoviet* was denuded of some of its previous power in order to effect the transition to unitary command in administration. The reins of policy, however, were held tightly in the hands of the *Politburo*,[9] that compact political planning and command group in which Voroshilov was the representative of the military. Central Committee members who did not belong to the *Politburo* had access to the documents of this group, although they were otherwise secret. The *Politburo* had established a very particular control and supervision of the Commissariat for External Affairs, *Narkomindel*, so that every aspect of Soviet external relations passed under the review of the former. On 25th July, 1930, Litvinov finally succeeded Chicherin as head of *Narkomindel*, an appointment which confirmed the ascendancy which Litvinov's line in the manipulation of Soviet foreign affairs had won.

The formal arrangement of power, therefore, was of less importance than the personalised control and the close supervision of not only outlines but details of policy from the top. It was from this quarter that concessions over military policy, ranging from strategy to the running of the Red Army, had to be wrested. Stalin rested his power of policy-direction and control in this high-level group and formally linked himself with the army through Voroshilov. Although acquainted with military operations through his quasi-commands of the Civil War, and in close touch with military affairs and policy throughout the 1920's, Stalin was far from having as yet a professional grasp of military matters. Stalin had nevertheless committed himself at an early stage to political studies of strategy, in which his incorporation of Lenin's ideas assumed a not infrequently bizarre but dynamic form. For Stalin, strategy had become

> . . . the determination of the direction of the main blow of the proletariat at a given stage of the revolution, the elaboration of a corresponding plan for the disposition of revolutionary forces (main and secondary reserves), the fight to carry this plan throughout the given stage of the revolution.[10]

Tactics, which 'pursue less important objects', he defined as

> . . . the determination of the line of conduct of the proletariat in the comparatively short period of the flow or ebb of the movement . . . the object of tactics is not the winning of the war as a whole, but the winning of some particular engagements. . . .[11]

Stalin chose the occasion of the tenth anniversary of the founding of the Red Army to produce also a characterisation of the fundamentals of the army, in which both national and international features were closely mingled.[12] The Red Army was 'the army of the dictatorship of the proletariat', the army of 'the fraternity of the peoples of the Soviet Union', the army trained 'in the spirit of internationalism'. From the first followed the firm support of the rear for the front, from the second the avoidance of national disintegration (which had affected the guarantee of the Imperial Russian and the Imperial Austrian armies), and from the third the Red Army support from workers and peasants abroad in the event of an attack on the Soviet Union.

Stalin's first large-scale attempt to manipulate the strategic balance, by careful intervention in China, had fallen short of its objectives. The introduction of 'Socialism in one country' and the building up of the Soviet Union as the first socialist state complicated rather than simplified Stalinist strategy, making of this internal transformation an international factor of increasing importance. Defence of the Soviet Union, and persistent expansion of the industrial capacity and military strength of the country, amounted to a long-range attack on capitalism — but it also implied accepting Stalin's main premise that in the event of a major military clash, the Soviet Union would strive to be the last to enter. Such a scheme demanded tactics designed to forestall capitalist combinations against the Soviet Union. Stalin's crude, biased and opportunistic strategy, in which — when displayed in all its contorted complexity as in China — tactics seemed to swamp the whole, combined a certain revolutionary élan with a studied caution. Aimed at guaranteeing the minimum interests of the Soviet Union without the sacrifice of wider opportunity, it was a strategic outlook built up of reservation piled on reservation, with a special place for the tactics of the *volte-face*. Whatever its implicit contradictions (which some seek to interpret as an ultimate bias in favour of internationalism[13]), Stalinist strategy and tactics were about to be put to fierce tests.

* * * *

In 1929, although the military collusion seemed to be proving very successful, Litvinov, then Vice-Commissar for Foreign Affairs, discerned a huge crack appearing in the Soviet-German front. By making of Rapallo so effective an instrument, Russia had helped Germany to such a degree of emancipation from the Versailles Treaty that the former pariah of Europe could snap her fingers at the East.[14] Germany was turning westwards; the acceptance by Germany of the Young Plan in March 1930 and the evacuation of the Rhineland seemed fully to justify Litvinov's qualms.[15] Soviet-German diplomatic relations fell into the doldrums in the first half of 1930, but were revived officially with the publication in June of a re-affirmation of the 'spirit of Rapallo'.[16]

In addition to the military and diplomatic anchor, Stalin's policy was further embedded in Germany through the activities of the *Komintern* and the work of the *KPD*, the German Communist Party. The German Communists, after having had a more 'Moscow-directed' leadership thrust upon them, were committed to war on the other working-class party, the Social Democrats, long a thorn in the flesh of the Communists. While these tactics contrived to drive crippling limitations into any firm resistance to the Nazi-Nationalists, a negative policy turned blunders into catastrophe by throwing in the Communists on the side of the Right extremists in smashing up what was left of recognisable political life in the Weimar Republic.[17] Out of what appears to have been a miserably inadequate and hopelessly distorted view of priorities in Germany, the original miscalculation about the danger from the Right took on the proportions of a disaster and then deepened into criminal irresponsibility at the sight of Communists contriving the aid and comfort of the Nazi-Nationalists. In April 1931 so repellent had this political collusion become to many German Communists that they defected from this item of the 'Party line'.[18]

Evidence of a 'secret Stalin policy', combining a military and political insurance, is slight and open to much question. It has been suggested that Stalin instructed the Soviet officers in contact with the *Reichswehr* to offer the bait of joint resistance against the Communist Party and the hint of a mutually-arranged *coup* to set up a pro-German government in the Soviet Union, in return for the aid of the *Reichswehr* in deflecting the supposed German plans for a combination against the Soviet Union.[19] No trace of this has been left on any German record to hand, either by way of confirmation, repudiation or even vague hint. Similarly Rechberg tried to argue in mitigation at the International Military Tribunal that Stalin was the real criminal behind the advent of Nazism. A planned infiltration of Nazi combat organisations was ordered by Moscow, by which 24,000 Communists transferred their loyalty on the orders of Moscow; by 1932 this operation was brought to a climax, having been begun before 1930. At the instigation of Stalin, 40 million marks were placed at the disposal of the Nazi movement.[20] From one lacking any distinction for the reliability of his evidence, such assertions must be well-nigh discounted. Yet unfounded or misinformed rumour does not dispose of the possibility of the practice of a contorted and super-secret political warfare, conducted either to bring the situation to that rapid climax from which the Communists might profit, or insure some element of control over a power passing increasingly to the Right. By design, miscalculation or over-calculation, Stalin succeeded only in battering the life out of a political body with which he was theoretically allied. He made it more of a sacrifice than a murder.

The military contacts between the *Reichswehr* and the Red Army meanwhile proceeded apace. Uborevich and Voroshilov brought off in the spring and summer of 1930 the highly favourable deal with the German firm of *Rheinmetall*. The tank and aviation schools continued to develop their activities, and the relations between the German and Soviet commands seemed as close as ever, marked by the annual exchange of visits. From the German side, the Hammerstein-Schleicher combination showed no inclination to disavow the collaboration with the Red Army.[21] From Germany technicians, special items of machinery, engines and the equipment being prepared under the arrangement with 'Herr Ludwig' travelled to the Soviet Union. In the Red Army, whose senior commanders had expressed on many occasions their liking for the contact with the *Reichswehr*, the German command still discerned a ready ally, although one needing still substantial measures of technical and professional improvement.

But military collaboration, while admittedly involving special conditions, did not exist in a diplomatic and political vacuum. Although Soviet-German relations recovered a little from their slump in 1930 — a fact noted by

Molotov at the 6th Congress of Soviets held in March 1931 — there were signs of a possible diplomatic re-alignment which could push the Rapallo policy to one side as one of the major foundations of Soviet foreign policy. In his March speech, Molotov, full of contentment that Soviet-German relations had been restored to '. . . friendly collaboration and the further consolidation of relations',[22] nevertheless spoke of the Soviet desire to establish closer contact with France. France had been abused in Stalin's speech at the 16th Party Congress; while Molotov almost furtively waved his olive-branch, even at the same Congress of Soviets Deputy War Commissar S. S. Kamenev brandished the sword, using the evidence of the trial of the 'Industrial Party' as proof of French militaristic designs on Soviet integrity. Stalin spoke through Molotov, but he had not repudiated himself entirely as S. S. Kamenev still publicly berated the French. External requirements and internal consistency were preserved. But real inconsistency there was, perhaps most in the mind of Stalin, who would run with the German hare and aspire to hunt with the French hounds. The Soviet leadership grappled with so unique a problem, the prospects of choice. Such a luxury had long been denied to Soviet strategic and diplomatic planning; for the Soviet Union, as much as for Germany, Rapallo had been a necessity, in the same way that opposition to the Versailles settlement was a natural reaction to the violent anti-Soviet attitudes of France and Great Britain.

In the early summer of 1931 Franco-Soviet conversations were begun, and by August a non-aggression treaty was ready for signing. Not until the end of 1932 was this actually signed, by which time successful Soviet contact had been made with Poland, 'soldier of French Imperialism'. For Soviet policy to exhibit a decisive swing, it needed an indication that the Soviet Union would support the frontiers as stipulated at Versailles, that is, confirm the estrangement of Germany from Upper Silesia and the Corridor. No such indication had been produced by June 1931, and a German source affirmed the existence of a Soviet assurance that no move on these lines was intended.[23] Yet it was not only the issue of the Polish frontiers which was in doubt, but the basic motivations of Soviet and German policy — the resolution of the riddle of how long a defensivist Soviet strategy could be maintained alongside German revisionism and dynamism.

In August 1931 Litvinov travelled to Berlin to discuss Soviet policy. His press statement of 30th August, 1931, contained certain pertinent observations on the current situation, notably Poland. Litvinov denied outright that the Soviet government had approached the Poles in 1930, and denied that 'negotiations have been or are being conducted.'[24] Moreover, no third party was negotiating with the Soviet Union about Soviet-Polish relations. The

Polish Ambassador in Moscow, M. Patek, had just presented a document which was, as expressed in the Soviet press, '. . . not a step forward in Polish-Soviet negotiations but a step backward.'[25] M. Patek could scarcely have been presenting documents over non-existent contacts,[26] while Litvinov, although denying the whole thing, admitted that '. . . it is obvious that we are striving to improve our relations with Poland'.[27] The honey of continuing fidelity was mixed suddenly with the gall of stripping Rapallo of its definite pro-German tinge, for Litvinov now lumped the non-aggression pact with Germany alongside agreements with Turkey, Lithuania, Persia and Afghanistan.

Stalin merely inched his way out of Rapallo.[28] From Germany he still took all that was offered in the way of economic assistance and asked for more.[29] The military collaboration in 1931 drove ahead steadily through the troubled political and diplomatic waters. In the spring, Putna was recalled to a military command, having performed an undeniably considerable service to the cause of *Reichswehr*-Red Army collaboration. His skill, talent, (not to mention his command of German), and his avoidance of the propagandistic line of Kork contributed to his filling a vitally important post with tact and success. His successor was Yakovenko.[30] General Adam of the *Truppenamt* was scheduled to make the annual visit to the Red Army, the only abnormality being that Voroshilov asked Köstring if Adam might delay his visit until the manœuvres. French Intelligence acquired information that in July 1931 Khalepskii, chief of the Mechanisation and Motorisation Administration of the Red Army, accompanied by his adjutant, Lebedev, and Tyagunov, head of the Faculty of Mechanisation and Motorisation of the Leningrad Academy paid a visit to the tank-school at Kazan, with the object of making an exchange of tank-equipment between the Russians and the Germans. This was successfully accomplished.[31]

Stalin had more than the western frontier to occupy his mind. With tension mounting in the Far East, as Japanese pressure on Manchuria and resistance to Chinese attempts to regain her full 'national rights' increased, the Soviet command had to take account of the eastern frontier. Blyukher's troops faced formidable opposition should it come to a clash, and Soviet strength in the east was only as yet in the making. In September 1931 the Kwantung Army moved to provide its own solution to the problem of Manchuria. The threat in being had been realised.

* * * *

In 1929 Voroshilov had had his way and the newly-created Special Far Eastern Army, built up with reinforcements from European Russia, administered its sharp military lesson in the brief campaign on the Manchurian frontiers. Blyukher remained at the post of Soviet military commander in the Soviet Far East, as economic and military power grew rapidly in an area which had proved to be in a previous time the Russian Achilles heel. The building of railways, a start with the provision of an industrial base for the eastern hinterland, and strengthening of the military forces formed the elements of the policy for the Soviet Far East, the priority of which was raised by Stalin in his report to the 16th Congress in 1930. Starting up the Ural-Kuznetsk combine in the First Five-Year Plan signified the seriousness of Soviet intentions, and acted as a hint to the Japanese command that time was not altogether on their side. The link with European Russia consisted of the single-track Trans-Siberian Railway (skilful use of which had enabled the Russians in the Russo-Japanese War to mobilise a strong army, notwithstanding the single track). While building up an independent industrial-strategic base in the Ural-Baikal stretch, it was necessary to increase the capacity of the Trans-Siberian, increase strategic railways and feeder lines, and plan eventually to provide an alternative to the Trans-Siberian Railway. The significance of the military and economic decisions of 1928–30 lay, however, in the fact that the Soviet leadership had accepted the inescapable lessons of the Russo-Japanese War, the post-revolutionary crisis and the predicament of 1929, and decided to create a military force administratively and ultimately economically independent of European Russia.[32] Out of this decision there developed a unique Soviet military-political establishment.

Stalin, in so far that he had been in command of the situation, conducted in the Far East and China a political strategy the mainspring of which was hostility to British imperialism. From this fixation, allied with a pro-German policy in the west, Stalin aimed at a balance of power favourable to Soviet interests. A Soviet-Japanese *détente*, the high point of which came with the studied Japanese neutrality and refusal to participate in a conciliation during the Manchurian crisis of 1929, was marred by small differences, none of which counted so much as inevitable divergence of Russian and Japanese interests. The revival of 'Shidehara diplomacy' in 1929 by Japan seemed to augur a period of peaceful construction, but ominous hints of the real intentions and aggressive militarism of the Japanese army command could not be concealed.[33] The Japanese Siberian expedition had left behind an unsatiated appetite. A 'China party' and a 'Russian party', each pre-occupied with designs against these respective countries, elaborated their various schemes of aggrandisement.[34] Okawa, who in 1924 had spoken of the aim of repossessing Siberia and urged the development of Manchuria as a Japanese 'life-line', was closely associated with the Kwantung Army;[35] as director of the South Manchuria Railway East Asia Research Institute he worked as auxiliary intelligence, work buttressed by the activities of the Kwantung Army's own *Tokumu Kikan* (Special Service Organ).[36]

According to the testimony of Kawaba Torashiro, a war plan for use against the Soviet Union was worked out in 1930, at a time when Hata was Chief of the 1st Department of the General Staff.[37] There is little doubt that after 1929 the Japanese General Staff had to reckon seriously with growing Soviet power in the east,[38] an argument which lent force to the conspiratorial motivations to 'solve' the problem of Manchuria. Meanwhile the Russians had not been idle; in Sinkiang economic penetration pushed Soviet power further, while the Turk-Sib railway was begun, and completed by 1930.[39] In Outer Mongolia every effort was made to fasten this area into the Soviet grip, although the collectivisation programme begun in 1928 resulted in serious internal disturbances.[40] Not for nothing did Japanese officers, such as General Araki, link the question of Mongolia and Manchuria. Soviet control over Outer Mongolia gave them immense advantages, the more so as Manchuria became — looked at from the Soviet side — a mere geographical adjunct to this key position. It is therefore not surprising that Outer Mongolia, and not Manchuria, became the sensitive spot of Soviet eastern policy.[41]

The 'Manchurian Incident', which opened on the night of 18th–19th September, 1931, marked the first stage of the Kwantung Army's private conquest of Manchuria. Shidehara's protests were all in vain.[42] Attempts to limit the venture failed and the Kwantung Army rolled on. No immediate Soviet reaction was apparent, although there could be no doubt of the potential danger of the Japanese move.[43] Voroshilov was in the Soviet Far East, attending the manœuvres of the Special Far Eastern Army, and at which time he presented Blyukher with the Order of Lenin. In a speech on 6th August, Voroshilov made a pointed reference to the ability of the Soviet forces to carry out its military tasks under Blyukher's command. Blyukher replied in a speech protesting his loyalty as 'an honourable fighter of the Party and the working-class'.[44] Yet Soviet military force, unlike the position in 1929 when there was interference with the Chinese Eastern Railway, was paraded but not used. At the end of October, however, Karakhan gave the Soviet reply to Japanese charges of Soviet assistance to General Ma, and the lie direct to assertions that Soviet instructors were serving with the anti-Japanese forces at Tsitsihar.[45] On 14th November Litvinov, in a statement to the Japanese ambassador in Moscow, drove these points home with some force; he denied (in all accuracy) that no military assistance was rendered to either side by the Soviet Union, and recalled the Japanese assurance that the Soviet Union would suffer no damage to her interests through Japanese action in Manchuria — though now it appeared that

Japanese troops might advance on Tsitsihar and cut the Chinese Eastern Railway.[46] Six days later Litvinov again retorted with a statement refuting any possible analogy between the action of Soviet troops in 1929 and present Japanese military operations.[47] During this initial period of rising tensions, Soviet troops were moved up to the Soviet-Manchurian frontier, but a policy of the strictest neutrality, reputedly at the instigation of Stalin, was employed. A clash on any scale would have been a disaster not only for Soviet policy but, in the long run, for Soviet arms, for in spite of the excellence of Blyukher's troops, there appeared to be as yet neither adequate reserves nor a capable command organisation in being.

In the early spring of 1932 Litvinov carefully probed the problems of Japanese support for the remnants of White Russian elements, the intention to set up a new state in Manchuria, and the purpose of Japanese troop concentrations on the Soviet-Korean border.[48] The Japanese counter-questioned about the construction of Soviet aerodromes and troop concentrations also on the Korean border. The Soviet proposal, first made by Litvinov to Yoshizawa on 31st December, 1931, for a non-aggression pact between Japan and the Soviet Union had been abruptly rejected.[49] In January 1932 a second attempt also failed. While Litvinov, acting in close concert with Stalin, kept a tight rein on the situation, there is no reason to suppose that Voroshilov and even the confident Blyukher did not consider the possibility of military action. The Litvinov-Stalin strategy prevailed, even though the danger mounted; on the other hand, the risks inherent in military action were immense, if looked at from the point of immediate Soviet weaknesses.

What seemed like a confirmation of the worst fears of the military came with the Japanese action in Shanghai, which began on 28th January, 1932, with a truce called only on 3rd March.[50] The Kwantung Army, using Colonel Doihara who went to Tientsin to talk over the question of a puppet state with Pu Yi, was meanwhile making its arrangements to confirm its possession of a private empire which emerged as 'Manchukuo'. The emergence of what appeared to be a grand design of aggression could scarcely serve to reassure Moscow. A considerable reinforcement of Soviet troops was set in motion, effected by movements from the west. The danger from Japanese provocations by the use of White Russians operating on the Soviet-Manchurian border was real enough for the Soviet command. It is not likely that the Soviet Far Eastern Army remained in ignorance of the reconnaissance made by Colonel Suzuki, on the instructions of Hata of the 1st Department of the General Staff, involving north Manchuria and Korea, and conducted in connection with the preparation of Plan *OTSU* (against the Soviet Union) and Plan *HEI* (against China).[51] The Red Army command no doubt hankered after a more active policy to restrain the Japanese; Voroshilov, who subsequently painted the Japanese danger in very stark terms, could only propose the policy which had paid off in 1929. Blyukher made a public declaration of the danger facing the Soviet Union; at the May Day parade in Khabarovsk, the Soviet commander in the Far East proclaimed the intention to check any intrusion on Soviet territory and announced that 'the flames of a real war are beginning to flicker near our frontiers.'[52]

The urgency of the situation and the difficulties imposed by supply over such long distances and with such weak transportation facilities all combined to give the Soviet Far Eastern Army a distinctive composition.* Aviation, armoured fighting vehicles and the motor-lorry, plus strong cavalry forces were fully utilised by the Far Eastern forces — the infantry mass of the Red Army could neither be supported nor effectively employed. After 1932 every opportunity was taken to reinforce these troops, the basic shift being the transfer of three new rifle corps to the Soviet Far East. Aviation was concentrated into a Special Far Eastern Air Fleet, and supplied later with a force of long-range bombers. More than a garrison, the Far Eastern force became a severe but profitable training school, from which several senior Soviet officers gained invaluable experience. But in the summer of 1932, with peaceful perspectives dwindling away, the problem remained of how far the Japanese would go and at what point Soviet interests would be defended only by force of arms.

Worse was to come, when, at the close of 1932 Japanese troops pursued the retreating General Su Ping-wen up to the Sino-Soviet border, bringing Japanese forces once more within striking distance of Siberia. Japanese penetration into Northern Manchuria brought the Soviet command face to face with a very dangerous situation, but in the case of General Su, the path of mediation and non-commitment of troops was forced upon a military command which doubtless looked for a military solution.[53] Although the Stalin-Litvinov line had successfully staved off a crisis of arms by scrupulously careful manœuvre, taking its stand on the defence of the minimum interests of the Soviet Union, the position by the end of 1932 was that the Japanese held a line of some 2,000 miles in length running along the Soviet frontier from north-west of Manchouli to the south-west of Vladivostok. The Soviet Maritime Provinces were now a huge salient pointing to the south and a natural object of Japanese pressure. The crucial battle-ground,

* To station the main body of the Red Army in the Far East, even if this had been desired, was out of the question owing to the weakness of the rail communications and the prevailing low level of economic development at this time. These were the two governing factors in the development of the Soviet Far Eastern forces. The converse, however, for the Japanese Army was that even if it succeeded in defeating the Red Army in the east, this had by no means eliminated the Red Army as such. As Colonel Hayashi put it in *KŌGUN*, 'how to finish the war' became an intolerably difficult problem.

however, and one presenting peculiar rather than insuperable problems to Blyukher and his staff, emerged from the area where Outer (Soviet) Mongolia, Manchurian Mongolia and Chinese Inner Mongolia connected.[54]

In the spring of 1932 the formal creation of a Soviet Pacific Fleet (Naval Forces/Far East) was announced.* Soviet naval forces, which were to operate from the bases of Vladivostok, Nikolaevsk and Soviet Kamchatka, consisted only of small surface forces and a few submarines. Repair and dockyard facilities, as well as the establishment of the necessary industrial and ship construction installations, required formidable development. At the same time, exploration and trial navigation by 1931 had opened up to the passage of isolated vessels a considerable part of the Arctic sea-route, but in 1932 this remained still a tenuous link over the roof of Russia. Japanese naval power far out-stripped Soviet strength, although there is much to suggest that in the Far East the Soviet leadership pinned its faith to aviation at an early stage and to a surprising degree.

With the complete Japanese encroachment in Manchuria and her investment of the Soviet eastern frontiers drastically altering the balance of power against Soviet possessions, Stalin decided upon the re-insurance of taking up diplomatic relations with Nationalist China, broken off at the insistence of the latter; Litvinov's press statement ascribed as one of the causes 'of the present troubles in the Far East' the lack of relations between the Soviet Union and China.[55] In return for this gain, Japan not only refused a non-aggression pact offered once again but made its great displeasure over the Soviet-Chinese *rapprochement* exceeding plain, going so far as to claim that beside this fact 'the future of Manchuria [was] comparatively insignificant'.[56]

Whatever its misgivings and mortification, the Red Army command devoted to the pursuit of a more active policy was obliged to submit to the prevailing line, imposed by Stalin and carried through by Litvinov. Not only the Japanese militarists gave Stalin cause for serious concern. If some Red Army leaders doubted the wisdom of his policy, popular dissatisfactions and dissent higher in the leadership shook at the foundations of his position. Famine and terror stalked about the country; schemes to accomplish the removal of Stalin went from hand to hand among the men closest to him.[57] Syrtsov and Lominadze, who had acted as assistants to Stalin in removing Trotsky, were uncovered as the authors of a 'plot', the nature of which was merely an attempt to remove Stalin by authorised means, by voting him out of the General Secretaryship. The 'Ryutin platform', drawn up by the propagandist Ryutin, was another scheme of internal reform. How far

* In March 1939, speaking at the 18th Party Congress, Kuznetsov who then commanded the Pacific Fleet stated that this force had begun life with only one fighting ship — a submarine.

Stalin, in the midst of these plottings inspired by desperation, took the Japanese menace as signifying the advent of a major war, remains doubtful. On the evidence of the policy pursued and the restraint of the military, his point of view seems to have centred on regarding a premature, even accidental clash as being the real danger, one which would have interfered with the consolidation of the Soviet east, while he was prepared to fight only if an actual intrusion upon Soviet territory — as opposed to Soviet rights — took place. Yet 1931–2 marks the end of the attempt to balance Soviet military strength by drawing from the European forces reinforcement for the east.* The militarisation of the area east of Lake Baikal went ahead at top speed, with the rapid build-up of its economic and industrial resources.

Meanwhile, the western frontier had to be neutralised.

★ ★ ★ ★

On 14th October, 1931, Litvinov, 'on the instructions of the Government', proposed to the Polish *chargé d'affaires* the conclusion of a non-aggression pact on the lines of the recently initialled Franco-Soviet agreement.[58] The Polish government had, however, on 14th November, made it clear that the Franco-Soviet text would not serve its requirements, whereupon Litvinov signified agreement to proceed along the lines of the proposed 1926 draft. Some three weeks later Stalin took the opportunity of an interview with the German author Emil Ludwig to explain the implications of Soviet-Polish contacts. In speaking of Soviet 'likings' for any nation (the point in question was Soviet admiration for things American), Stalin added '. . . of course we must not fail to mention our liking for the Germans. Our liking for the Americans cannot be compared to that!'[59] This brought Ludwig at once to present German fears that Soviet contact with Poland might mean the recognition of the existing Polish frontiers by the Soviet Union, which would spell 'bitter disappointment for the entire German people'. Stalin flatly refuted any intention of a Soviet sanction for these frontiers — just as the Poles would never sanction the present Soviet demarcation. 'Our friendly relations with Germany will continue as hitherto. That is my firm conviction.'[60]

Another firm conviction was the policy of continuing the military collaboration, and there is no sign at this point of any break in what had

* The Soviet intention was obviously to avoid a multi-front war. In spite of their intentions, it is most difficult during this decade to decide how satisfactorily the Russians tackled this problem. Up to 1935, the western and eastern Soviet armies were still connected very definitely in terms of interior lines and inter-related. From 1941–5 the Russians were able to follow the strategy of defeating one enemy at a time, and this fact of the existence of only one 'front' has been used by one Soviet military work as the essential which enabled the Soviet command system to work as it did.

become an official Soviet policy. Yakovenko, Soviet military attaché in Berlin, occupied himself, according to French Intelligence, with arranging for the signing up of German experts in military transportation, aviation and the chemical arm, the matter being satisfactorily settled by March 1932.[61] Soviet purchases of aero-engines and aircraft parts, particularly those adapted for heavy machines, went through *Junkers* and *Bayerische Flugzeugwerke*. For the *Reichswehr*, however, the year had begun with the initialling of the Soviet-Polish pact on 25th January, 1932. This struck at the very heart of the Soviet-German military understanding, for whatever Stalin had wished the Germans to understand by his reference to talks with Poland changing nothing, to remove the Soviet military deterrent from Poland's eastern frontier altered the whole balance of force which it had been the object of the *Reichswehr* to maintain. The provisions of Article 2 of the Soviet-Polish Pact, whereby an act of aggression committed by one of the contracting parties against a third state need not mean the automatic support of the other, seemed to justify Stalin's words.[62] But the *Reichswehr* appeared to be taking its own precautions; in April 1932 Colonel Fischer travelled to Moscow, apparently to discover what the military intentions of the Soviet command in the Far East amounted to.[63] In June, the French military attaché in Berlin reported that Fischer's real object had been to dissuade the Soviet high command from denuding the vital western frontier districts in order to reinforce the garrisons of the Soviet Far East. The German argument maintained that the real enemy lay in the west and not in the east, for which reason the *Reichswehr* brought pressure to bear for the retention of the western garrisons.[64]

Fischer's reconnaissance was a prelude to extensive exchanges of views achieved by the *Reichswehr*'s invitation to Yegorov and Tukhachevsky to visit Germany to attend the manœuvres. Yegorov, ex-Imperial colonel and vigorous partisan of the collaboration with the *Reichswehr*, now occupied the post of chief of the Red Army Staff. He had succeeded to this in the summer of 1931, when Shaposhnikov had been relieved of this post and sent to the relatively unimportant command of the Pri-Volga Military District, which later acquired a certain sinister significance in connection with out-of-favour senior officers. It is generally agreed that Shaposhnikov had temporarily forfeited Stalin's favour by publishing a work on the Civil War operations which praised Trotsky unduly.[65] His period of disgrace was brief, lasting only from June 1931 until February 1932, when he replaced R. P. Eideman as head of the Frunze Academy. (Eideman thereupon took over the post of head of *Osoaviakhim*). Viewed from any angle, even that of an incident in his personal fortunes, Shaposhnikov's dismissal had been a sharp knock at the authority of the senior Soviet officers. It also indicated the tenderness of Stalin's susceptibilities. Disgrace it certainly was, for there could be no mistaking the lowly appointment to which Shaposhnikov was assigned. Equally curious was the fact that Shaposhnikov's hitherto immense caution had failed him, tumbling him into a political trap, although Stalin may have had encouragement to think the crime greater than it actually was. With Yegorov now Chief of the Red Army Staff, the talented and German-trained Uborevich took over command of the Belorussian Military District, from which Yegorov passed on his promotion.

As Chief of Ordnance (*Nachal'nik vooruzheniya*) Tukhachevsky was dealing not a little with 'Herr Ludwig', German consultant to the Red Army on military equipment.[66] The invitation to visit Germany addressed to Tukhachevsky appears to have come, however, from General Schleicher himself; the fact that Tukhachevsky had commanded the Red armies in the 1920 operations against Warsaw provoked a great deal of speculation.[67] The fact also that the Soviet officer assumed to be the commander-designate of the Red Army in the event of full-scale war in Europe was travelling to talk with Schleicher — all this with the full cognisance of the Soviet leadership — appeared to confirm the hypothesis that a German ally for the Red Army had not been ruled out. Although this was a possibility, the Soviet officers could as easily engage upon an exploration of the situation which, with von Papen as Chancellor in place of Brüning since June, caused unmistakable uneasiness on the Soviet side. The danger of a Franco-German *rapprochement*, resulting in a military alliance directed against the Soviet Union, loomed up with the advent at the head of German affairs of an outspoken opponent of the Soviet Union.[68] The German ambassador in Moscow, Dirksen, filled with gloom at the degeneration of Soviet-German relations, wrote from Moscow on 5th August, 1932, that '. . . I am extremely glad that the invitation to Yegorov has gone out; in any case it will have good political effects here'.[69] As it turned out, much greater interest attaches to what Tukhachevsky did or did not negotiate during his visit to the *Reichswehr* in the late autumn of 1932.

Tukhachevsky arrived on 18th September in Berlin, where he stayed until leaving for the manœuvres at Frankfort-am-Oder which began on 20th. His party was made up of Sedyakin (Director of Training), Feldman (Administration of Command Staff), Yakovenko and his adjutant plus a sixth officer who was not positively identified.[70] From 25th September to 7th October, having completed the visit to the exercises, Tukhachevsky accompanied by Feldman toured German factories in the west; further licences with German firms were most likely arranged during this time. Under Sedyakin, the other small party of Soviet officers betook themselves to the Dresden Infantry School. On 8th October Tukhachevsky left Berlin for East Prussia, where he stayed three days before returning to the Soviet Union.[71] The efforts of French Intelligence to ascertain whether Tukhachevsky's prime object had been the renewal of an agreement signed by Hammerstein-Equord in 1929 dealing with the exchange of intelligence were not rewarded with success. The very existence of a compact of this kind remained doubtful.[72] What, if anything, in the nature of political discussions passed between Schleicher and Tukhachevsky remains quite impenetrably hidden. Schleicher played for very high stakes in Germany; disappointed in Brüning, Schleicher had pulled the military carpet from under him and schemed for the appointment of von Papen as Chancellor. Of his ability to deal with Hitler and the Nazis, Schleicher seemed to have no doubts and had in preparation a scheme to neutralise both.[73] Whether Schleicher took the opportunity provided by Tukhachevsky's visit to dispel Soviet fears of a possible anti-Soviet Franco-German combination, or even to convey his confidence in being able to master the whole situation, cannot be even surmised. Tukhachevsky's mission, whatever service it rendered to the Soviet command and to Stalin's policy, brought no marked change in either the *Reichswehr*-Red Army collaboration or any improvement in Soviet-German relations as a whole. On 29th November, 1932, the Franco-Soviet Non-Aggression Pact was signed; the pact with Poland had been signed on 25th July, so that the Soviet Union had not delayed with carrying through first payments on a form of re-insurance against isolation from Germany. Looking at the situation in general terms, and allowing for the peculiarities of Stalin's system, it appears unlikely that Tukhachevsky did more than attend to equipment, compare German products in items which were similarly turned out under licence in Soviet military plants, and take one further look at that professionalism which commanded considerable Soviet admiration. Only in that specially restricted and unique atmosphere of *Reichswehr*-Red Army collusion would it be possible to interpret the visit as an attempt to interfere directly in German politics, to manipulate the internal scene.

With the appointment of Schleicher, not Hitler, as Chancellor at the end of 1932 it must have appeared in Moscow that the worst fears would not now be realised. The votes cast in Germany for the *KPD* rose at this time, while the Nazi vote fell. There were good grounds for believing that the *Reichswehr*, friend to the Soviet Union, would retain control. According to one who was in touch with Khinchuk, Soviet ambassador in Germany, and who discussed with the attaché Vinogradov the possibilities of combined political action against the Nazis, in January 1933 negotiations were broken off with the declaration that Moscow had become convinced that 'the road to Soviet Germany leads through Hitler'.[74] Certainly Molotov's report on the external situation, made on 23rd January, 1933, was exceedingly complacent. Seven days later Hitler came to power. The only immediate change in the military arrangements was the replacement of Köstring by Hartmann as military attaché; since Hartmann had been in close contact with Tukhachevsky's mission in 1932, and also spoke excellent Russian, his appointment scarcely signified an attempt at disruption. The change had been dictated for purely internal German reasons.[75] Von Bülow informed Dirksen on 6th February, 1933, that he did '. . . not expect any sort of change in foreign policy'.[76] Although shaken, Moscow did not seem unduly perturbed; that incompatible policy pursued by Stalin and demonstrated in all its inconsistency in the Stalin-Ludwig talk in 1931, still contained, according to Dirksen, '. . . mistrust and an attitude of watchful waiting' towards the French. On 28th February, Krestinsky told Dirksen point-blank that 'the Soviet Union would not undertake any reorientation of its policy'; but the German government might clarify the position over von Papen's proposal to the French for an anti-Soviet alliance, about which Krestinsky 'thought he recalled that Herriot himself had given information to this effect to Dovgalevsky'.[77]

Apart from an outburst on 2nd March, 1933, which drew a Soviet protest, Hitler moved carefully. Seeckt provided his personal re-statement of the military and political wisdom of Rapallo in a booklet, entitled both anachronistically but with a certain topicality — *Deutschland zwischen Ost und West*. At a Ministerial Conference of 7th April, 1933, the need for 'Russia's cover for our rear with respect to Poland' was considered vital, the more so as Polish plans for a preventive war appeared to be the reaction of Warsaw to German territorial demands.[78] Hitler's reception of Soviet ambassador Khinchuk on 28th April was marked by an exchange of views on how best to improve Soviet-German relations. From his prepared statement Khinchuk read out that the recent incidents involving Soviet persons and interests in Germany were much deplored, but wound up by suggesting the immediate ratification of the protocol providing for the extension of the Treaty of Berlin signed in 1926. For his part, Hitler intimated that he would have Khinchuk assured that he, Chancellor of Germany, '. . . was trying, and would continue to try, to order German-Russian relations on a permanently friendly basis.'[79] So far in this stilted diplomatic game, the play was a draw. The Soviet military command, meanwhile, took up its own contacts with the *Reichswehr* and set about making its explanations to fellow-soldiers.

* * * *

Tukhachevsky had extended an invitation to Lieutenant-General von Bockelberg, chief of the *Heereswaffenamt* (an appointment corresponding to

Tukhachevsky's), to visit the Red Army. The invitation was accepted and the German General arrived on 8th May.* Von Bockelberg had no complaint whatsoever of the manner in which his Red Army hosts had treated him. In particular, it appeared that Tukhachevsky was anxious to repay the friendliness which had been shown him during his own trip to Germany in 1932. Senior officers of the Red Army were anxious to impress on their German guest the value which they placed on the collaboration between the two armies and their admiration for the achievements of German technology, not to mention the *Reichswehr* itself. But in the conversations with Yegorov and Voroshilov, as well as diplomatic personnel, a slightly different note had been struck; co-operation was possible only if both states pursued the same objectives, for armies were, after all, the servants of the states which they served. The Nazi propagandist Rosenberg's virulently anti-Bolshevik speeches seemed to have set off a chain reaction of suspicion in Soviet circles, giving rise to fears of a German 'double cross'. At a small private luncheon, arranged in his office, with only a select few present, Tukhachevsky had presented rather different opinions to von Bockelberg, when he spoke repeatedly of the need for Germany to acquire in the minimum period a fleet of 2,000 bombers which would help to extricate her from the present 'difficult political situation'.[80] Voroshilov accepted Dirksen's invitation to a dinner given for the German General. The War Commissar had re-arranged his programme so as not to miss it. In a speech at the table Voroshilov emphasised his own attitude of friendship to Germany. Dirksen took him aside to have a serious conversation on the turn which relations had taken, emphasising that the distortions of the Soviet press (a reference to Radek's mordant articles) had much to do with inflaming feelings. Voroshilov repeated that 'he was a good friend of Germany', nor had he changed his point of view — and the Soviet government had likewise not turned against a policy of friendship. He asked Dirksen specifically to make it known in Germany in 'the authoritative German offices' that friendship was the Soviet object — some proof of which might be seen in the way in which General von Bockelberg had been received.[81]

In the middle of May the German military attaché Hartmann sent off his report on the discussion with Tukhachevsky about the continuation of experiments in chemical warfare; on 10th May Tukhachevsky had agreed to carrying on the '*To 1933* experiments' (presumably the programme for 1933 in station Tomka)† even though 'new material' had not arrived. The date of the exercises would be discussed with Fishman, Chief of the Chemical

* The report on this journey is to be found in Serial 8074H/E579399 f. dated 13/6/1933 and from the *Heereswaffenamt*, *No. 486/33 g.*, it is *Bericht über die Russlandreise 8/5–28/5/1933*.

† 'Tomka' is Volsk.

Warfare Administration. Hartmann seemed to find a certain obstructionist attitude among the Soviet officers with whom he was dealing. Sukhorukov of the Foreign Liaison Section of the Red Army Staff supplied only negative information. Hartmann took up the matter with Tukhachevsky, who 'at first tried to push the matter aside rhetorically' — referring to statements made in the autumn of 1932 in Berlin (where Tukhachevsky had then been) that Germany must close the stations because of the financial strain. Hartmann reminded Tukhachevsky that any suggestion of this closure applied only to the air-training station at Lipetsk — in fact, certain sections of the experiments at Lipetsk had been accordingly transferred to Tomka. Tukhachevsky responded by insisting that even if the experiments in Tomka had to be abandoned the military co-operation as a whole would not suffer; if the Germans were anxious to start up work again in Tomka, he would agree to this at once. But — interjected Hartmann — had not Fishman made it a condition that a 'new chemical warfare agent' must be provided before work could begin? Tukhachevsky evaded this point as long as possible, referring to what Fishman wanted to see in Germany, and asking that Fishman should not be shown 'just buildings'. Eventually he agreed to a resumption of work without the new agent. Hartmann pointed out that the Germans had no such new chemical agent, but neither had any other power. After fishing for information about how much the Russians knew of foreign research, and if they were ahead of the Germans in this, an officer of the Foreign Liaison let slip 'the significant admission: "perhaps" '.

Hartmann broached the subject of continuing the work in 1934. At this Tukhachevsky maintained that in 1934 the Russian budget would not, in all probability, be enough to cover the expenses of Tomka. What had been agreed upon for 1933 did not necessarily mean a commitment for any future date. If, however, 'new bases of special interest' had been added, then that elastic budget of Tukhachevsky's could be stretched to maintain Tomka even in 1934.[82]

On 15th May, von Bockelberg, Hartmann and Colonel Thomas, with Fishman and the Chief of Staff of Red Army Chemical Troops (identified as Rockinson) visited the chemical plant at Bobriki, after which a lengthy — and heated — discussion of timetables developed. Fishman, putting forward reasons of troop billeting and transportation, remarked that a certain curtailing of the experiments was inevitable. After asking about tests with the new German gas-masks, protective suits, 'new degassing media', and gas projectors, Fishman proceeded to argue about the timetable, suggesting not three but only two months. Hartmann, faced with this deadlock, feared for a moment that 'the spectre of a renewed appeal for a decision by Tukhachevsky appeared'. Von Bockelberg, however, gave Fishman to understand that the greatest effort from the German side would be made to see that all his requests were met.[83]

Summing up, the perceptive Hartmann decided that 'there *is* among the highest-placed Russians a serious and sincere willingness to deepen our military co-operation'. But only a permanent banishment of the disturbances in the political relations, accomplished in a manner which would allay Soviet suspicions, could bring the co-operation properly to life again, for at the present time the military collaboration could not play its former role of bridging the political gaps. From a military point of view, friendship with a Russia becoming industrially more powerful could be only an advantage.[84]

By the end of June Soviet obstruction was plain. In a communication of 26th June, 'in an unpleasantly noticeable way,' the Red Army released itself from its previous obligations. Hartmann met Smagin (newly appointed to Foreign Liaison) on 26th July, giving him the news that no German officers would be attending Red Army exercises during the summer. Smagin was taken aback — the German officers were expected to arrive. Did this ruling, asked Smagin, apply to manœuvres also? Hartmann said he would enquire on this point.[85] Smagin, on the staff of the Soviet Military Attaché in Tokyo from 1926–30, impressed Hartmann not a little, and the conversations seemed amicable enough. On 16th August, the Red Army was given to understand that the ban covered manœuvres as well as troop exercises. A little later (23rd September) Hartmann reminded Smagin that this decision was not so unexpected, since 'just before this' the Soviet Assistant Military Attaché in Berlin had merely picked up the telephone to say that no Red Army officers would be coming to Germany. At this, Smagin admitted the breach of military manners. Levichev (successor to Yakovenko) had also been given full information by the *Reichswehrministerium*. The break in the exchanges would appear to be, in the light of these exchanges, the primary responsibility of the Red Army command, but shared by the German command in its equally brusque response.

As for Kazan, Lipetsk and Tomka, in May Tukhachevsky had displayed a deal of deliberate obstructionism. The fate of Lipetsk seemed to be hanging in the balance anyway. On 31st October, when the installations had been closed down and the final toasts drunk by Soviet and German officers, Tukhachevsky admitted in a talk with Twardowski that the closing down had been 'a political consequence' of the conviction in the Soviet Union that German policy was taking an anti-Soviet direction. Tukhachevsky did not deny Twardowski's assertion that, although von Bokelberg's trip had gone off very smoothly, between the time of von Bockelberg's departure (28th May) and his arrival back in Germany '. . . the Red Army had suddenly made the quite unexpected demand for an immediate closing down of the establishments'.[86] Lipetsk, already partly under the axe, was the first to be formally closed, written notification of which came from the German side (*Chef der Heeresleitung*) on 26th June. Voroshilov had evidently been mollified by the way in which the negotiations had been handled by the head of *Z.Mo.*, and the manner in which the settlement had been drafted.[87] Hartmann, whose house meanwhile had been broken into on the night of 27th–28th July (apparently a straightforward burglary), received a telephone call on the evening of 15th August from Foreign Liaison, announcing that the visit of General Lutz* to Yegorov and Khalepskii (Chief of the Mechanisation and Motorisation Administration) would be quite in order. This marked the winding up of the tank-school at Kazan. The absence of friction in carrying out the liquidation of the installations evidently prompted both sides to expressions of cordial feeling and talk of renewing the co-operation in another form, although Hartmann pointed out that no '. . . *very strong* gestures for rapprochement can be expected from the Russian side in the *very near future*'.[88] The very fact that the immediate military preoccupations of the Red Army lay momentarily in the Far East, plus the inescapable fact that the Red Army could not conduct a policy on its own without reference to state policy, were added reasons, in the opinion of Hartmann, for thinking this.

On the evening of 23rd September Smagin had arranged a farewell dinner for the head of *Z.Mo.*, at which Alksnis, Fishman and Khalepskii were to be present. To the complete amazement of the German officers present, the three Soviet officers mentioned, each head of Administrations which had worked intimately with the *Reichswehr*, did not put in an appearance, although they sent representatives. As Tukhachevsky subsequently explained, these officers were unavoidably detained at the manœuvres, and Hartmann, on the actual evening of the dinner, found himself unable to think that Smagin had practised a deliberate deception. When it came to the speeches, Smagin made a very determined effort to underline — in a manner strikingly out of phase with the function itself — that the Rapallo Treaty remained the basis of friendly Soviet-German relations, and the relations of the Red and German Armies of great importance for the peace of Europe. Hartmann took Smagin on one side after the speeches for a very frank talk. Smagin stated that the reason why Soviet officers had not been detailed to exercises in Germany was out of fear that they might be molested — this had actually happened to one Soviet officer — and while in times of stress there might be incidents, and even Soviet citizens treated roughly,

* Major-General Lutz, as Inspector of Motorised Troops, was Khalepskii's opposite number. Chief of Staff to General Lutz was Colonel Guderian, who is, however, silent about the experiments in the Soviet Union.

'there were Soviet citizens *and* Soviet citizens'. Red Army officers could not be bundled about in any fashion. Hartmann pointed out that it would have been better to say this in the first place, instead of fobbing the Germans off with statements about 'official duties'; when Japanese officers could find training assignments with the Red Army (Niedermayer had mentioned this exchange in 1930), Soviet intractability in dealing with a friendly army seemed doubly hard. Smagin very heatedly told Hartmann that the Japanese assignments were over and done with.

Smagin went on, in response to Hartmann's questions, to deny any real military significance to Franco-Soviet contacts, but his remarks were punctuated by repeated reference to Rosenberg and his statements, which, if not officially disavowed, could only mean the existence of a direct threat to the Soviet Union — and hence closer ties with France and Poland. The directness of Smagin's speech impressed Hartmann, particularly since the Soviet officer had let it be known that he was close to Voroshilov. It appeared that although the desire to resume the military contacts had not diminished, powerful influences were at work to unhinge this; in the face of Soviet uneasiness, even German initiative in suggesting a resumption of military relations in some new form would have little effect without tangible assurance. 'To wait for a Russian opening move means . . . facing the fact of the progressive worsening of our present relations.'[89]

Meanwhile Voroshilov received a formal letter of thanks — in the draft of which Colonel von Stülpnagel had deleted the passage dealing with hopes for a continuation of Soviet-German collaboration. In a tale now becoming more melancholy, Tukhachevsky took up a number of points with Twardowski at the beginning of November. In a forty-five minute conversation Tukhachevsky repeated the remarks about the debt owed by the Red Army to the *Reichswehr* for its 'decisive aid'. With furious denial Tukhachevsky disclaimed reports that the Russians had leaked details of the secret collaboration to the French or Poles — besides being a breach of honour, since the *Reichswehr* knew more of the Red Army and its strategic intentions than the Red Army knew correspondingly of the *Reichswehr*, that would have been a stupid blunder. The same guarantee could be given for the Soviet government. The Red Army 'was still very reserved towards the French'. But there was a conviction in the Soviet Union that this new German government, if not hostile, was very lukewarm in its attitude to the Soviet Union. After an interruption, Tukhachevsky returned to take his leave and to remark finally (in a talk evidently conducted in French, in which Tukhachevsky was fluent):

> N'oubliez pas, mon ami, c'est la politique, seulement votre politique, qui nous sépare, pas nos sentiments, nos sentiments les plus amicaux pour la Reichswehr.[90]

A certain element of irony hung about the spectacle of Tukhachevsky making his official farewell of the *Reichswehr* in French. The first French Military Attaché to the Soviet Union, Colonel Mendras, had arrived in Moscow on 8th April. The Red Army had a new ally in the making.

★ ★ ★ ★

The fulsomeness with which the Red Army leadership acknowledged the extent of its debt to the *Reichswehr* for 'decisive' help suggests the question of how far this help had gone by 1933, and to what degree the Soviet military command had fallen under German influence. There can be little doubt that the collaboration with the *Reichswehr* enjoyed a very high degree of popularity among senior Soviet officers. Voroshilov had been a keen partisan of the arrangement, Yegorov even more so; Orlov of the naval staff had good cause to thank his German mentors. Khalepskii of the Mechanisation and Motorisation Administration had the benefit of the joint tactical and technical experimentation at Kazan. In that field for which the Red Army seemed to discern a great future — chemical warfare — Fishman and his aides had enormous German help. German technological help, admittedly augmented by particular dealings with the French, British and Americans, had played a substantial part in remedying the defects of the native Soviet industry. One of the most powerful weapons in the Red Army's arsenal was the manufacturing licence, which produced optical instruments, aero-engines, armoured fighting vehicles, chemicals and individual weapons.

During the great debate in the early 1920's on the Red Army and its doctrine, one of the principal divergencies between Trotsky and his opponents had been the former's insistence on attaining a structural and organisational homogeneity, while the latter demanded 'unified military doctrine' for first place. The Frunze reforms had been essentially a concession to Trotsky's inescapable logic. With the advent of a quantity of new weapons these two trends, at once so much at odds, began to be fused in the attempt to develop a consistent doctrinal and organisational form for the Red Army. The water-shed was 1929, at which time infantry and artillery still held pride of place in the Soviet armoury. By the following year, battle had been fully joined over the tank, and the explicit rejection of the bourgeois theories of small armies and highly-mobile élites foreshadowed growing controversy. In defending the mass army Tukhachevsky singled out its mass, mobility and offensive power as favourable attributes — but the question of reconciling the first two had yet to be solved, a point seized upon with all justification by his critics. Out of this predicament, with the help of lessons learned at Lipetsk and Kazan, the new Red Army compounded of mass and mobility was brought into being by Tukhachevsky and his group of assistants, who all the while paid formal homage to the idea of the co-operation of all arms which had become at an early stage a basic tenet of Soviet doctrine.

The close co-operation of all arms demanded the close collaboration of the various senior commanders. While the first took much time to develop and remained more of a principle than an accomplishment even after many years, the second came about through the Tukhachevsky command group, composed of young senior officers, many trained in the Imperial army — Uborevich, Yakir, Alksnis, Yegorov, Fishman, Khalepskii, Sedyakin, Eideman, Feldman. It was a command group which owed little or nothing to Stalin, unlike the Voroshilov-Budenny-Timoshenko school. No better example of the strained relations between the two could be found than the Belorussian Military District, where Uborevich was in command and Timoshenko his deputy. At the Frunze Military Academy Shaposhnikov was developing those ideas and views which predominated after 1939; Stalin and Molotov were reported to be among his listeners in 1932.

In spite of the interest shown in mechanised warfare in the mid-1920's, the lack of an industrial base restricted the introduction of armoured forces of any kind. At the beginning of 1931 the Red Army possessed only 300 MS-1 tanks and some hundred BA-27 armoured cars.[91] Skilful adaptation of British Vickers models and the American Christie designs provided the Red Army with the armoured vehicles while the Soviet tank-industry struggled to its feet; the Vickers 6-ton tank formed the basis for the T-26 and T-26A Soviet tanks, the Christie for the BT machines which later made their appearance.[92] In May 1930 the first 'mechanised brigade' was set up, with two tank and two motorised infantry battalions, artillery and reconnaissance units; in 1932 the mechanised brigades were transformed into a mechanised corps, with two mechanised and one rifle brigade, plus an independent anti-aircraft battalion. The study of armour was centred in the Stalin Academy of the Mechanisation and Motorisation of the Red Army, which opened in 1932, supported by faculties of mechanisation in Leningrad and other cities. The tank, used in co-operation with other arms, was accorded a high place as a fundamental means in the offensive. In organisation, the Soviet tank forces were divided into three types: the independent mechanised and tank unities (dating effectively from 1932), the Supreme Command Tank Reserve (*TRGK*) used to support the main blow and break-through, and tank units distributed among infantry and cavalry. With the tank, aviation was coupled with its employment of the bomber for further destruction of the enemy defence in depth, plus the use of parachute troops. The tactical role of Soviet aviation, which was to be employed on a mass scale, consisted of action as a kind of 'air artillery', working in the first operational echelon; the winning of command of the air and attack on the unprotected air flank and lines of communication were also assigned.[93]

The manœuvres held from 1931–3 marked the first attempts to develop that operationally effective combination of infantry (motorised), artillery, armour and tactical aviation; out of this arose the idea of 'the motor-mechanised unit', experiments with which had begun in 1931–2. The rejection of the 'single weapon' idea — the predominance of the tank — led to the Soviet corollary of attempting to exploit maximum effectiveness in each weapon and in combination. Voroshilov's reference early in 1934 to 'absolutely new types of units' could be explained by reference to the motor-mechanised combination, supported by artillery and aviation. The Red Army consisted of two armies in reality, the shock army — motorised and mechanised, with land and air artillery — carrying out the decisive break-through operation, while the infantry mass belonged to the older-style type of Red Army. That synthesis at which the Soviet command had been aiming ever since the days of the Civil War was achieved, in this form, by something like a military sleight of hand, by the inclusion within the mass army — which was ever vigorously defended — of a powerful, mobile armoured core, the very heart of which was the tank. On the other hand, the view of the necessity to destroy the enemy in his entire depth (hence the parachute troops and the 'Air-landing Corps' used to disrupt reserves and harry the rear) produced an organisation for the offensive of multi-echelon form; the high-speed (*BT*) tank units were also being developed for 'long-range' independent penetration in a manner which suggested certain affinities with ideas expressed in the much-scorned bourgeois military circles.* Such ideas had much in common with Tukhachevsky's ideas of the 'non-stop' offensive, although at the time when he first attempted to put them into practice he lacked the modern means to develop the manœuvre and mobility which he considered essential. His ideas on the superfluousness of strategic reserves — the advancing Red Army finding its true strategic reserve among the proletariat which it was in the process of liberating — had been rejected in favour of a system designed to set up strong reserves, a principle which was applied with equal rigour to the new tank formations which were coming into existence. During Frunze's rule

* In 1932 the *Ustav motomekhanizirovannykh voisk* appeared, as well as *Nastavlenie po samostoyatel'nomu vozhdeniyu krupnykh motomekhanizirovannykh soedinenii*: manuals on the use of motor-mechanised forces. It has proved impossible to obtain a copy of these, but the former is summarised from a *2e Bureau* report by G. Castellan, *Les Relations Germano-Soviétiques*, pp. 212–13. These have also been used by Lieutenant-General of Tank Troops N. Vedenichev to demonstrate that the German *panzer* units were using ideas already well-known to the Soviet command: see *Protiv fal'sifikatorov istorii Vtoroi Mirovoi Voiny* (Against the falsifiers of the history of the Second World War), Moscow 1959, p. 303.

over the Soviet armed forces rigid rules about the strength of reserves had been developed and appear to have remained either in force or as a guide for a very considerable period. Nevertheless, although everywhere the theme of the defence of the Soviet Union was stridently taken up, this same powerful and highly mobile shock army, serving the interests of defence, could still serve a 'revolutionary lunge' in a military-political system where the military instrument had never ceased to be both the shield and the sword of the Revolution.

Throughout the 1920's Soviet speculation about the nature, and especially the first stages of a future war, marched on from idea to idea, reinforced by the strong conviction that this was to be a 'war of machines'. With the machines now coming into the hands of the Red Army, that speculation intensified and was cast in terms of military prophecy over the possible use of the new motorised-mechanised unities with their flying artillery. One such prediction, remarkable for its prescience, envisaged a future conflict preceded by a preparatory period, during which large and powerful formations, designed to carry out the widest form of manœuvre, would be concentrated and readied. This pre-conflict period would be naturally cut to the lowest possible margin compatible with efficiency, with the aim of striking while the enemy was himself still in the process of mobilisation. Out of these first engagements would develop the battle for the frontiers. In the event of no decision being reached, then a protracted war would ensue, attritional in nature and defensive in form, until the situation developed in such a way that one side could resume offensive operations. The idea of alternate phases of intensity and lassitude was further enlarged in a study produced in 1933, which foresaw the establishment of fronts of great depth dominated by the motorised-mechanised unities which were at present in the making. Defence in depth would be indispensable to deal with the effects of break-through achieved by the new unities, and a particular consequence of this serious complication must be to make units powerful enough to fight on and continue independent operations even if cut off by hostile forces.[94] Out of the ideas of attacking an opponent in the whole depth of his front and achieving simultaneous destruction of his frontal and rear positions, the early Soviet schemes of encirclement were more fully developed and tested during the 1933 manœuvres.[95] Soviet cavalry, which had passed through a troubled and indecisive stage in the mid-1920's, took on a new lease of vigorous life; as strategic cavalry — co-operating with tanks — it was allotted an important role in carrying out tasks connected with the wide encirclement of the enemy.[96] One of the many middle-grade officers attempting to work out firm operating procedures and a stable method of command in the new mobile unities was Zhukov, who had completed a course at the Frunze Military Academy in 1931. Closely associated with Timoshenko in the 3rd Cavalry Corps in the Belorussian Military District, Zhukov was assistant to the commander of the 6th Cavalry Division in 1932 and took command of the 4th Cavalry Division in 1934. After no very great lapse of time, Zhukov's troops were singled out as a show unit and Zhukov himself advertised in the pages of the military newspapers.[97]

The defence of the western frontiers was based on the three main military districts of the Ukraine, Belorussia and Leningrad. It is difficult to find support for the fears of the Germans in 1932 that Soviet preoccupation with the Far Eastern frontiers might lead to a dangerous weakening in the west. It was in the west that the new shock armies took shape, with a preponderance of the motor-mechanised units going to the Belorussian command and the Ukraine coming a close second (tank regiments were also reported in Smolensk, Strelina, Ryazan and Kharkov). Uborevich's Belorussian command included Timoshenko's 3rd Cavalry Corps, with the 4th Cavalry Division (Zhukov's command in 1934) at Slutsk, south of Minsk. The 5th Caucasian Cavalry Division was at Novgorod-Volynskii (some forty miles north-west of Zhitomir), and the 14th in Zhitomir itself.[98] From the Baltic to the Pripet Marshes, the Belorussian and Leningrad forces (utilising the Moscow Military District as a reserve) could dispose of some 30 divisions (5 cavalry) for immediate defensive purposes. Important changes had meanwhile been taking place farther to the north, where the Baltic Fleet and fixed fortifications played a significant part. The Soviet command was ever obliged to look to the defence of Leningrad. Political prisoners, undergoing a stringent course of 're-education' by labouring on the construction of the Baltic-White Sea Canal (*Belomorstroi*), rendered signal service to their gaolers and the Soviet Navy, which expanded once again in 1933 with the creation of the Northern Fleet, with its main base at Polyarnoya. It was both to provide cover for Murmansk and act as a reserve for the Baltic Fleet. The role of the latter had to do with providing naval protection for Leningrad itself, cover the main retreat district for the Red Army and defeat attempts at sea-borne landings. With the land defence buttressed by the construction of defence lines facing Finland and farther to the north, in the event of war in the Baltic (assuming an anti-Soviet coalition but German neutrality) Soviet naval forces would carry out strategic reconnaissance in the region of enemy operations, mine-laying in the enemy operational area and destruction of observation posts and gun-batteries carried out by special detachments of cruisers and destroyers protected by submarines. Torpedo-boats would be assigned individual and tactical missions. In short the Baltic Fleet would protect the sea-borne flank of the Red Army, while the land-approaches were sealed off with a defence line running from the Chudskoi Lake, along the Estonian frontier and up to the Gulf of Finland. The northerly defence lines ran across to Lake Ladoga, and then north again to Petrozavodsk, Medvezh'egorsk and and on to the White Sea.[99] The first great problem to consume the attention of the naval command had been the possibility of French or British naval intervention in the Baltic in support of operations against the Soviet Union mounted by parts or the whole of the Baltic bloc. With the deterioration of relations with Germany, the balance of naval power in the Baltic had swung heavily against the Soviet naval forces, for while German naval power had not yet fully resurrected itself, considerations of German neutrality added to Soviet strength. It was not therefore surprising that early in 1934 the Soviet Union should seek to obtain guarantees of the independence of the Baltic States. In the Black Sea the maintenance of Soviet-Turkish friendship contributed to the lessening of Soviet difficulties, but signs of a growing Turkish-British friendship began to give rise to some concern.

The Soviet naval forces (fleets and river flotillas) did not enjoy an autonomous position but were under the control of the Commissar for War and his Commissariat. The Soviet Navy, in spite of the progress which was being made, struggled still to escape from the two burdens which had hampered the Imperial Russian Navy — geography and a marked degree of indecision about the role of sea-power. No 'school', such as the Frunze-Voroshilov group in the Red Army, had emerged from the Civil War command of the Soviet naval forces; no 'proletarian naval doctrine' had even been whispered, for while the military absurdities of stressing proletarian uniqueness had often been apparent, for the navy it would have been wholly preposterous. No doctrinal emphasis could release the Soviet Navy from the straitjacket of geography, although the White Sea Canal had been a slight loosening of the constriction. That distinctive but awkward step of setting up geographically separate fleets — Baltic, Black Sea and Pacific — could no more be avoided by the Soviet command than by the Imperial Russian Navy. The only alteration was the hazardous but profitable exploration of the Northern Sea Route (*Glavmorput*). In his conversations with the German naval staff, Orlov exemplified the Soviet Navy in search of a doctrine and an understanding of the particular significance and tactical possibilities of separate naval weapons. Voroshilov, in the declared hints which he scattered about, made it clear that the Soviet Navy would welcome the extreme in Soviet-German naval co-operation, from the training of staff to the question of ships. These hopes met with disappointment, but that Voroshilov had not abandoned them might be seen from his comments to Colonel Mendras in 1933, and the expansive invitation for the French to come to the aid of the Soviet Navy. Submarines, destroyers, even cruisers — all these, Voroshilov stated, were required by the Soviet Navy, which, if added inducement were needed, stood in some requirement of re-equipping.[100] Muklevich, meanwhile, began to search out Italy as a possible source of technical naval help.*

As far back as 1905 Captain Klado, a noted Russian writer on naval affairs, had been emphasising that the Russian Navy was plagued by an indecisiveness in answering the vital questions of '. . . not only what kind of fleet we need, but absolutely whether we need one or not'.[101] The activity of Orlov and Muklevich since 1926 was a proof in itself that the latter part of Klado's query had been taken seriously enough. While Voroshilov seemed to have grand ideas, Orlov was committing the naval forces to a strictly defensive doctrine, although losing no opportunity to expand naval power and resources where possible. 'Naval forces', as opposed to 'fleets' after the high-seas style, did exist with a certain degree of effectiveness, although the paucity of technical resources was an inhibiting factor. Orlov and his fellows appear to have lighted on the submarine, Soviet production of which began in 1927. It was exploited as a defensive weapon, although nine possible roles for the Soviet submarine were reported: reconnaissance against mine-laying, strategic reconnaissance, action against enemy merchant ships, offensive mine-laying, reconnaissance during fleet operations, the standing observation of enemy bases, the conduct of independent operations, co-operation in combined operations and the landing of agents.[102] The problems of the Pacific Fleet raised doubts about the capacity of 600-ton submarines to carry out the tasks which they might be assigned, a displacement of 1,000 tons was being suggested in the winter of 1933, and the incorporation of Italian torpedo equipment in the new Soviet ships being considered.[103]

The new schemes and forms of organisation inevitably provoked hostile criticism and disagreement within the command as a whole. Mechanisation had come to life in the Red Army to the accompaniment of a furious controversy. Tukhachevsky subsequently admitted, in 1937, that 'some comrades' had interpreted the introduction of the mechanised corps as a means to realising dreams of the 'Fuller type'. It was argued that the tank, being possessed of high speed, could scarcely be employed in co-operation with the infantry. Certainly the *BT* (high-speed) tank, assembled in the type of formation which was allotted an independent role, seemed to come dangerously near the idea of separating the tank out of the mass of the Red Army and developing a notion of its operational independence. This was not what the 'motor-mechanised' scheme implied and ran counter to a

* The destroyer *Tashkent* (2,900 tons) was one of the products.

doctrinal principle that the tank — unsupported by artillery — could not succeed. That balance between the tank and mechanised formations seemed to be an uneasy one; whichever way Tukhachevsky might argue, what was happening centred round the virtual division of the Red Army into two armies, the one verging on the élite, the other containing the mass. Participants in the disputes were the disbelievers in the tank, those who suspected that Russia provided just those physical conditions which would militate against the tank and its effective use. It was, however, in February 1933, during the course of his speech in celebration of the 15th anniversary of the Red Army, that Voroshilov made the precise claim that the problems inherent in introducing the tank into the armament of the Red Army had been solved, which is to say that the organisational form of the new unities had been stabilised in the opinion of the Commissar for War. Further intensive experimentation was to prove the reliability of this public judgement.

Krivitsky has suggested that the motorisation and the mechanisation of the Red Army came about as a result of a political bargain struck between Tukhachevsky and Stalin. The latter conceded the funds necessary to realise the fervent hopes of Tukhachevsky and his followers, in return for support (in the very nominal sense) for Stalin's general domestic and external policies.[104] This, on the face of it, seems unlikely. Until Soviet industrial capacity had increased, no extensive technical programme for the Red Army had been possible; considerable efforts had been put into the system of foreign contracts which brought the first taste of modernisation in the army. The lessons of Kazan appear to have been absorbed as rapidly as was possible. Even counting on the import of motor-transport, the Red Army had also to wait upon the construction of an indigenous automobile industry. And finally the Red Army evidently found the tank something of the indigestible item of military fare which occurred in foreign armies. The most likely explanation is that the programme was less the result of compromise with Stalin (although his authority was indispensable) than of one in the Soviet command itself, even to the extent of restraining 'the tank-men'. Similarly unsubstantiated rumours attend the reports of opposition by the high command towards Stalin's policy of collectivisation, the ruinous effect of which could gravely injure the army, with a disaffected population and a mutinous peasantry to handle. Blyukher had even taken the step in 1933 of presenting an ultimatum to Stalin that without some relaxation of the rigour of collectivisation among the peasants of Eastern Siberia, the defence of this area could not be guaranteed — thus a particular version.[105] What can be maintained is much more general and representative of the situation as a whole. Stalin, whose fortunes touched bottom in the winter of 1932, could scarcely claim to call this military command his own, although a 1st Cavalry Army stalwart stood at the head of the military machine. A truly delicate manipulation had to be made between maintaining the efficiency of the Red Army as a fighting force and ensuring its loyalty to the regime and all its impositions. The private fears and the genuine anxieties of the command, aware of the impact of collectivisation on morale, never reached at this stage the proportions of a collective protest. Concessions there may well have been, but the signal fact remains that the Red Army and its command — in the absence of evidence to the contrary — remained loyal during this period, while Stalin remained firm to his purpose.

Finally the issue was not a straight one between Stalin and the dissident military command, if this can be said to have existed as such, but involved the army's immediate rival, the *OGPU*, whose troops were also motorised on an increasing scale; the strength of this force was approximately one-third of the cadre army. Hated, feared and despised, the counter-intelligence surveillance of the army was in the hands of these men. Relations between the military and the security forces were bad, a situation which was no doubt fully exploited by Stalin in playing off the one against the other. During the period preceding the spring of 1934, the army seemed to be gaining in ascendancy. In addition to its internal intelligence service, the *OGPU* ran a vast and ramified intelligence net-work abroad, rivalling and sometimes interfering with the work of the Main Intelligence Administration of the Red Army (*GRU*), which operated under the command of Berzin. The army and the secret police were fatally entangled and fearfully taken up in a protracted struggle the one against the other. It was to become a struggle to the death.

★ ★ ★ ★

At the end of 1933, in his report on external affairs, Litvinov perforce admitted that 'Japanese policy is now the darkest cloud on the international horizon'. Throughout the preceding year, whatever the complaints of the military, the policy of avoiding being drawn into a provocative war had been successfully maintained, and as such was acclaimed as a triumph of policy. But the reality of the situation involved watching developments on the Far Eastern frontiers with minute care and evaluating possible Japanese intentions at every turn. In September 1932 the Soviet Ambassador in Tokyo, Troyanovsky, had a private talk with Koiso, Chief of Staff to General Muto, apparently on the latter's initiative. The impression gained was that the Soviet Union did not face the prospect of an immediate attack from the Japanese, yet it was recognised that the maintenance of this unsteady balance depended on the survival of the existing Japanese Cabinet, the estimated life-expectancy of which was due to run out in January 1933. It appeared that the Russians simply had not made any definite decision as to whether or not the present Japanese military preparations were directed solely against them.[106] Forced on to the strategic defensive in a situation beset with hazards and the dangers of miscalculation, the only possibility was to follow a policy of watching and waiting. Sliding, or being dragged by acts of provocation down the slippery slope of war would have exposed at once all the immediate weaknesses of the Soviet position on its eastern frontiers; the reinforcement of the Far Eastern Army was by no means complete, the frail communication and transportation links needed enormous strengthening, the proposed plan for an independent supply and production centre for Eastern Siberia and east of Lake Baikal had yet to be implemented. While in January 1933 Stalin's public tone took on a note of firmer confidence in the ability of the Soviet Union to defend itself adequately, the situation deteriorated still further. Since the summer of 1932 Japanese bombers had been harrying Jehol, technically a part of Inner Mongolia and vital for the defence of the new state of Manchukuo to seal it off from attack from the south and west. In terms of aggressive design, possession of Jehol put the Japanese in a position to penetrate deep into the Asian hinterland, to drive between Inner and Outer Mongolia and ultimately menace the Soviet under-belly in Asia. As Stalin spoke, Japanese troops and armoured cars mounted their operations for the reduction of Jehol. Serious friction over the Chinese Eastern Railway began to develop between Japan-Manchukuo and the Soviet Union. In February 1933 Japanese troops crossed on to Soviet territory by Pogranichnaya, to the accompaniment of Soviet protests; Japanese aircraft evidently made a little free with Soviet air-space, while the Russians shot up Japanese fishermen off Kamchatka.[107]

A serious clash over the Chinese Eastern Railway appeared to be in the offing, but in a conversation on 2nd May with the Japanese Ambassador Ota, Litvinov made the startling statement that the Soviet Union might consider the sale of its interests in the railway — a denial of which had been made in the Soviet press as early as 24th December, 1931. This calculated appeasement of the Japanese could not please the military, mindful of the success which had attended their arms in 1929. On the other hand, the Railway was clearly becoming a millstone about the neck of the Russians, diminishing in commercial use due to the difficulties of operation, lost to them in time of war and a flash-point for any number of explosions with the Japanese and their Manchurian puppets. Disengagement was therefore a positive advantage, and, in spite of the not altogether favourable world reaction, a move made from increasing Soviet strength. Work had already

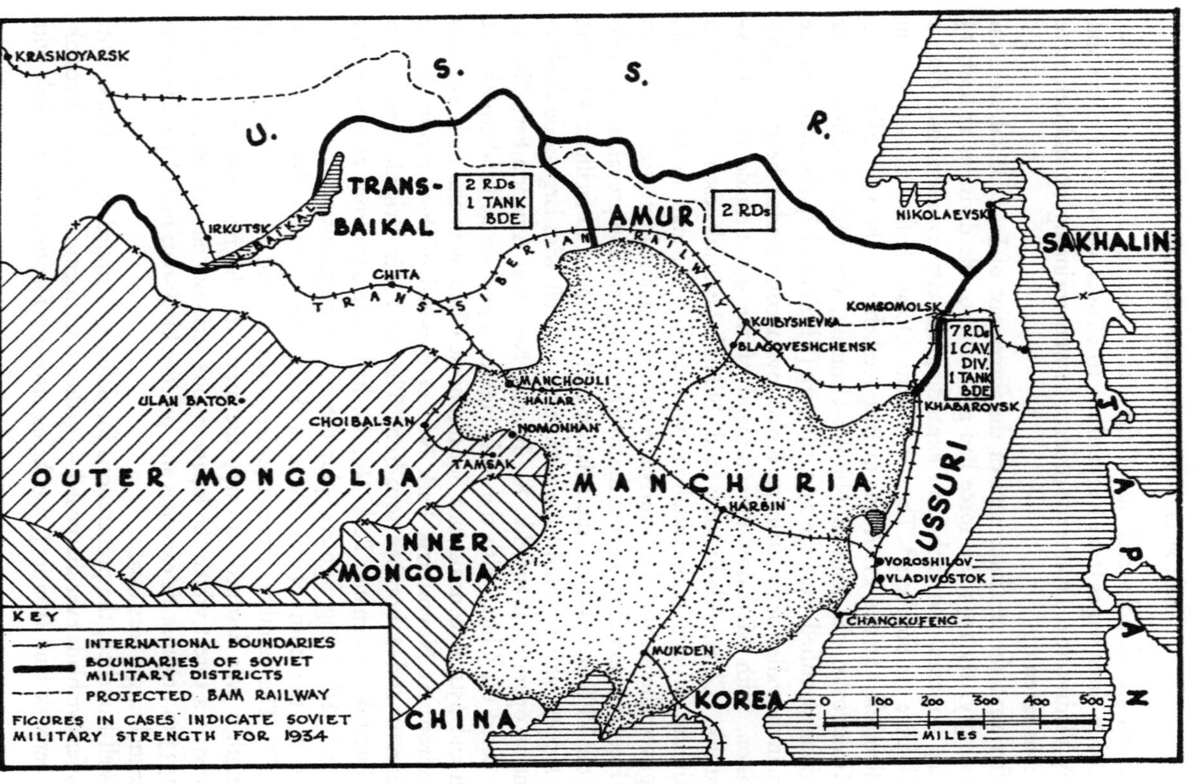

THE SOVIET FAR EAST

begun on the double-tracking of the Trans-Siberian Railway, a project worked in three stages from Karymskaya to Urusha, on to Khabarovsk and finally Vladivostok. Frontier fortifications were springing up and defensive positions taken up.

After 1932 the reinforcement of the forces east of Lake Baikal went on unceasingly. By 1933 this force had grown to 9 rifle divisions at least, 1½ cavalry brigades, 300 tanks and expanding military aviation, including a small force of bombers.* The 1st 'Pacific Ocean' Rifle Division was in Vladivostok, the 2nd Pri-Amur in Blagoveshchensk, the 12th 'Sibrevkom' in Khabarovsk, the 26th in Nikolsk-Ussuriisk, the 36th in Chita; other divisions identified were the 21st, the 57th (Vladivostok?), the 40th and the 35th. In the valley of the Dauriya, Rokossovskii commanded the 5th Cavalry Division, with Merkalov in command of the 9th Brigade in Nikolsk-Ussuriisk. Chita, Vladivostok and Nikolsk-Ussuriisk each possessed a minimum of one tank battalion, with tank companies in Khabarovsk, Blagoveshchensk and the Dauriya. Aviation, organised into the Far Eastern Air Fleet at a later date, kept to the system of organisation prevalent throughout the *VVS* at this time, the aviation park, designed to facilitate servicing and supply which would have been more difficult with large-scale deployment on operational airfields. Air Brigade No. 19 at Aviation Park No. 41 was based on Chita, with the 68th Fighter Squadron at Khabarovsk, the 18th and 25th Reconnaissance Squadrons at Chita with the 69th Bomber Squadron. At Novosibirsk Park No. 43 disposed of three reconnaissance squadrons and a bomber squadron. The 18th Air Brigade centred on Vladivostok, designated Park No. 16, had three squadrons at Spassk, the 5th and 38th being fighters, plus the 19th Reconnaissance Squadron; in addition, the 26th Naval Aviation Squadron operated from the same park.[108] The bomber force, not less than 40 and not reaching 100 in strength,† was destined to carry the attack to the mainland of Japan if necessary, a threat which the Japanese took seriously enough in the autumn of 1933 to organise air exercises and practice black-outs in Tokyo: the other potential target was Osaka.

Well-launched, the preparations for defence — tipped, nevertheless, with an offensive blade ever sharpened — gathered momentum. The Vladivostok-Khabarovsk land frontier‡ was being strongly fortified; the rail link with

* *Study of Strategical and Tactical Peculiarities of Far Eastern Russia and Soviet Far East Forces* p. 46, sets these figures at 9 rifle divisions, 1 cavalry division and 1 brigade, 350 tanks, 350 aircraft. Located: Ussuri — 5 RDs (increased to 7 in 1934), Amur — 2 RD, Trans-Baikal — 2 RD.

† During the following year, the Soviet bomber force was reported as 170 TB-5 heavy bombers.

‡ The Ussuri area was of vital importance. Mountainous and with one flank on the sea, strong concentrations of Soviet troops were maintained here and the whole turned into one great fortified district.

Blagoveshchensk was well protected. Further west the line between Chita and Krasnoyarsk had the protection of watch-points; a rail link was pushed down to connect Khiakhta on the Soviet-Mongolian frontier. Viktorov, a submarine specialist considered to be one of the most able of the senior Soviet naval staff, took command of the new naval force at Vladivostok and the Amur River Flotilla. Only a handful of submarines, with sundry light surface ships, existed to carry out the naval side of the defence, although it was reported that an immediate move had been the arming of three merchant ships with 15-cm guns to act as auxiliary cruisers. The same source conveyed information to the effect that the Soviet command had a number of fears on the score of a possible Japanese break-through at Blagoveshchensk and particularly Khabarovsk, but felt confident that any thrusts at Manchouli to the north-west and Pogranichnaya (and aimed at Vladivostok) could be safely contained.[109] In fact Blyukher had to face two threats; the first was the immediate pressure on the Maritime Provinces, about their desire to possess which there had been little Japanese reticence; and secondly was the larger threat looming up against Eastern Siberia, the back-door to which the Japanese were prising open in Jehol and the Mongolian corridor. Notwithstanding all the speculation in the military journals and the new theories of warfare, a critical struggle over the security of the frontiers in the east and the safety of the Siberian hinterland was dumped unceremoniously into the lap of the Soviet command and demanded certain solutions. The fact that the Japanese intended to make use of methods of subversion and infiltration — utilising White Russians and agents of their own selection — complicated the situation still further, making the prospect of a series of 'small wars' all the more likely.

The area of the Trans-Baikal dominated the whole of the potential theatre of war. The Russians could scarcely conceal the vulnerability of Eastern Siberia to attack, and the construction of the railway to Khiakhta pointed to the fact that the significance of the Japanese moves in the direction of Mongolia was not lost upon them. Advancing across the Mongolian plains, the Japanese could out-flank the entire Soviet defensive system even in its making. Originally, in considering military operations against the Soviet Union in the Far East, the Japanese plan had envisaged a conflict in Northern Manchuria, with the flatlands between Harbin and the Upper Sungari River and those between Taonan and Tsitsihar becoming the two major sectors.[110] To check this, in the summer of 1933 Soviet troops began work on the fixed frontier defence system based on the *tochka*, a concrete pill-box housing two or more machine-guns or 76-mm guns, protected by walls over a yard thick. The *tochka* system relied on numerous rows of fixed firing-points. With the Kwantung Army forts facing the Soviet defences, it followed inevitably that the Japanese would seek out other weaknesses in the lengthy Soviet frontier line. Behind these new defences the Russians seemed to take on a little more confidence; the climax of a summer of incidents was reached in November, when Soviet anti-aircraft guns were reported as having destroyed aircraft of a mixed flight of Japanese fighters and bombers which were flying in the direction of Possiet Bay. It was in November that the American Ambassador in Tokyo reported the opinion that the Japanese were beginning to show a real fear of the possibilities of Soviet bombing raids mounted from the Maritime Provinces against Japan. Yurenev, successor to Troyanovsky in Tokyo, did nevertheless at this same time declare his pessimism over the eventual outcome of the present critical state of Soviet-Japanese relations.[111] The Soviet search for security in the Pacific had received a psychological reinforcement with the rapid improvement in relations between the Soviet Union and the United States of America, culminating in American recognition of the Soviet state also in November. In a conversation with Nadolny in December Litvinov had been forced to admit that American naval weakness did appreciably diminish the actual effectiveness of this link with America and its bearing on the situation in the Far East.

A general pessimism in diplomatic circles and intensive preparation on the part of the military distinguished Soviet attitudes in the Far East in 1933. Already, however, certain basic facts had become plain. It was clear that Blyukher had to plan for the contingency of the Japanese striking the first blow; a Japanese attempt at a break-through of the defences at Blagoveshchensk and Khabarovsk was conceivable, but it was likely that they would try to turn the defensive lines by penetrating to the north-west of Vladivostok, the tenacious defence of which would slow down a Japanese advance. The submarine force available to the Soviet naval command, reinforced by the 'mosquito fleet' of torpedo-boats, would be occupied either with keeping Japanese aircraft-carriers at a distance or cutting communications between Japan and Manchuria. It would be a prime object of the Japanese to destroy Soviet air power with all despatch, for besides its tactical role, Soviet long-range aviation was at least in a position to mount an attack on the cities of Japan. Given the most unfavourable developments the Russians might be deprived of their military bases in the Soviet Far East, but in a calculated outburst in Tokyo, Yurenev had hinted at the possibility of Soviet offensive measures in the case of war — a reference to the possibility of a counter-offensive into Manchuria which might very well meet with some success among Japan's new 'allies'. Time dominated the space factor, formidable as that was. The Japanese could not afford to wait until the plans for the industrialisation of the east had materialised or beyond a point where Soviet military and air strength (especially the latter) had assumed its estimated grand size. The Japanese command therefore re-considered its plans for action in the event of war with the Soviet Union early in 1934, duly taking account of the change in the situation occasioned by the rapid increase in Soviet strength. Out of this a fresh approach developed, not less dangerous for the Soviet Far East, but Blyukher's larger designs were also becoming plain.

During his visit to Rome in December, Litvinov had evidently declared his fears on the score of a possible German-Polish *rapprochement* involving Poland being compensated in this event in the east (a move directed at the Soviet Ukraine), and the eventual seal being set upon a German-Polish-Japanese conspiracy against the Soviet Union.[112] If this should come to pass, one of the firmest foundations of Soviet policy for the Far East — neutralisation of the western frontiers, thereby securing the rear in this geographic reverse — would fall to pieces. In terms of the fears expressed by Litvinov the Soviet Union faced a gigantic encirclement, a grim confirmation of which seemed to make its appearance with signs of a German-Japanese *rapprochement* at the end of 1933. Soviet disquiet increased at this prospect. Even if plans had been made to make the Soviet Far East economically and militarily independent of European Russia, thus avoiding the strain of a military effort on two fronts supplied from a single source only, from Litvinov's point of view east and west could not be so easily detached. It would be some time also before the claim that they had been detached militarily could be said to have real effect, even though Blyukher's Chita and Khabarovsk army groups (plus the Vladivostok defence force) were striding along to greater strengths. A particular measure in the Soviet Far East designed to combine self-sufficiency with military readiness was embodied in Kalmykov's 'Special Kolkhoz Corps' made up of army reservists settled as collective farmers in the Special Far Eastern Army's area,* who provided ultimately some 100,000 first-line trained reserves.[113] And yet, by German calculation, in 1933 Soviet forces in the Far East (exclusive of local reinforcement measures) amounted to only one-seventh of the total military effort which was being made at that time. The Soviet command, therefore, was still playing for western stakes, advice which the *Reichswehr* had evidently offered in 1932.

* * * *

The Red Army, shuffling off the *Reichswehr* coil, was finding itself

* Owing to the lack of population, recruiting and food-production, as well as general development, was severely inhibited. Every effort was made to get more men to the east and to hold those already there. Special concessions were made (pay, agrarian concessions, higher prices for produce) to assist this.

among newly-won friends in the course of 1933, although there seems to be no reason to doubt the sincerity of Tukhachevsky and Yegorov in their statements about the good-will towards the *Reichswehr* which remained in the Red Army command. Even Voroshilov had been mollified by the manner in which the installations had been closed down. But the pleasant words could not disguise how much the situation was changing, an observation from which the Germans could not restrain themselves, as French and Polish officers seemed to spring so quickly into the shoes so recently vacated by the *Reichswehr*. In his talk with Hartmann on 23rd September at the celebrated farewell dinner, Smagin denied any 'deeper military significance' in the contacts with the French; although the French Air Minister, Pierre Cot, visited the Soviet Union in September, Tukhachevsky in his November conversation with Twardowski did not hesitate to admit that 'the Red Army is still very reserved toward the French', and, if it came to the point, 'how much had M. Cot actually seen!' General von Bockelberg, so recent a visitor to the Red Army, had seen so much more.* But Tukhachevsky explained away Pierre Cot in terms of the understandable desire of the Soviet command to get its own eyes on the French Air Force. Tukhachevsky had meanwhile taken steps, before the arrival of Pierre Cot, to explore the French possibilities. On 31st July, Voroshilov mentioned at a dinner given by the French Ambassador the possibility of French assistance to the Soviet Navy. This note of friendship and cordiality was struck from the first moments of the arrival of Colonel Mendras; at a reception on 4th May, Budenny, warmed into a positive furore of friendship through alcoholic refreshment, enlightened the French colonel to the effect that he had been originally destined to attend on a workers' delegation on the orders of Voroshilov, but having telephoned Stalin as to what he should do, received the reply, 'Join the French!'[114]

Tukhachevsky quickly followed up Voroshilov's opening move, indicating that he would like to have a talk about artillery with Colonel Mendras. The two met on 2nd August for an hour's polite but rather distant talk, when Tukhachevsky attempted to enlist the aid of Colonel Mendras in negotiations with a certain French firm, indicating that a restoration of the pre-1914 relations between the Russian Army and French industry would not come amiss now. At the end of October Colonel Mendras reported that the Russians had given it to be understood that in both economic and military terms the place vacated by Germany was there for the filling.[115] Far-reaching though the implications of this hint may have been, and allowing for a natural tendency to play down the French contacts when

* The Bockelberg report contains a very extensive list and description of the Soviet aviation and arms centres visited.

speaking to the German diplomats, Dirksen could at least claim a valid point in mentioning (in his last note from Moscow before leaving for his ambassadorship in Tokyo) on 3rd November, the waning of anti-German feeling for the moment — but as to 'the beginning of disillusion about the new friendship with France', it seemed early days so to speak.[116] It was perhaps more relevant that Dirksen had been asked 'in an unmistakable way' to bring a pacifying influence to bear in Tokyo.

French military interest in the Red Army in 1933 stopped short of considering it a potential ally in the field. The French objective concerned much more detaching the *Reichswehr* and the Red Army from their collusion, and thereby checking any attempt at a partition of Poland. In addition, it occurred to General Gamelin that Soviet aid could be utilised in weaning Turkey from German influence.[117] A mutual introduction between French and Soviet officers had so far been effected, with the first hints being dropped of closer technical collaboration as the Soviet command looked longingly at the French factories. Neither side could show any overwhelming gain. In a conversation with the German Consul in Kiev, whom Colonel Mendras consulted in the course of a motor-trip through the Ukraine, the latter declared himself in terms of some dissatisfaction over certain aspects of his stay in the Soviet Union — shadowed by security police, forbidden (it amounted to as much) to seek out former acquaintances of the Imperial Army, suspecting that MM. Herriot and Cot on their visits had been the victims of a carefully prepared 'show'.[118] And if French Intelligence could have listened in to the conversations of Yegorov and Voroshilov early in 1934, they might have had legitimate doubts that the collusion was really done.

In its internal aspect, the Red Army from 1931–3 had undergone a very marked change, worked principally with the tank. In a distinctive organisational form, Tukhachevsky and his fellows adopted the tank, shrinking, however, from full reliance upon it; the unsupported tank could not win. The 'motor-mechanised unity' was the answer, built into a shock army, itself a part of the infantry mass of the Red Army. On these terms, and yet providing an answer to the demands of mobility and new weapons, the mass army was retained. So far only a part of this development had unfolded, even though the Soviet command had some 2,000 tanks at its disposal by 1933. Military expansion as well as military experiment was in the air; the Red Army was bursting out of the old cadre seams first stitched up nearly a decade ago. Independent of the *Reichswehr*, in defiance of the Kwantung Army, under the scrutiny but not the thumb of Stalin, the Red Army and its command were about to enter into their own.

CHAPTER TWELVE

A Brief Triumph: 1934–1935

The new Red Army disposing of its mechanised brigades, motorised troops, modernised artillery and expanding chemical warfare arm, still existed under the old Frunze system of a small cadre force and territorial reserves. In all, the Frunze scheme had served the Red Army well during a troubled period. To a stable organisational form had been added the advantage of introducing the initial modifications needed to fit in varying technical changes. It had been a successful compromise with the facts of a grim economic situation, when the Red Army had been almost strangled with purse-strings. But at once it had been apparent that the system would not work very easily for technical units, not to mention aviation on any large scale. Well-suited to a large infantry mass, which could be broken down more successfully into a small cadre force and a large part-time training scheme, the technical revolution rendered it obsolete and inefficient. Nor could such a small cadre force properly carry out the defence duties connected with two long and difficult frontiers. It was not surprising that during the crises in the Far East the military command had been forced to follow dutifully, if not always willingly, in the path trodden out by Stalin and his diplomats. The props of the security of Rapallo had been rudely knocked away in the west, and it might be that the Red Army would have to face the *Reichswehr* not in the training camps but in war.

The time for a complete overhaul of the military establishment was ripe, now that the Red Army was bursting out the seams which had been stitched up some ten years ago. The old *Revvoensoviet*, the embodiment of collective control over the Military and Naval Commissariat, scarcely kept pace with the consolidation of the command which was a consequence of the advances made in expanding the arms and services of the Red Army, the *VVS* and the *VMF*. By 1933 the *Revvoensoviet* had begun to show all the signs of its age, and no attempt was made to fill the vacant fifteenth seat at this time. Flanking Voroshilov were his two most important assistants, Gamarnik of the Political Administration and Tukhachevsky, Chief of Ordnance. Yegorov occupied the position of Chief of the Red Army Staff, Alksnis head of the *VVS* Administration, Orlov the *VMF*, Khalepskii Mechanisation and Motorisation, Fishman headed the Chemical Warfare Administration,

Feldman the Red Army Administration and Eideman was the guiding spirit behind *Osoaviakhim*. Two losses the Soviet command had sustained in 1933; Baranov of the aviation industry had been killed in an air-crash and P. P. Lebedev had died in the same year. On the latter event, the *Reichswehr* sent a telegram of sympathy to Voroshilov. In the Inspectorates, Budenny ran the Cavalry Inspectorate (assisted by Tyulenev of the old 1st Cavalry Army), Rogovskii the Artillery, Vassilenko the Infantry (assisted by Alekseyev and Filipovskii), Shaposhnikov continued in his post as head of the Frunze Military Academy, while Chorkov ran the Zhukovskii Air Academy, with Indriksson as his commissar, Dubenskii his deputy, Khmelevskii Chief of Staff and Koshevnikov Chief of the Command Faculty. In the military districts, Yakir and Uborevich commanded the vitally important Ukrainian and Belorussian Military Districts respectively, while in the Far East Blyukher continued to build up his own staff; Gamarnik kept in close touch with the political officers working in the Far Eastern forces.[1]

Yet to consider the Red Army and military policy as being the preserve of the military command alone is to misrepresent the situation very considerably. The Frunze reforms, impoverished as they finally became through political pressures, were themselves a formidable illustration of the constraints laid upon the military. A formal arrangement did exist for the regulation of military affairs within the Soviet state, but this did not explain and still less did it correspond to the real state of affairs. The armed forces were an empire carved up among a plurality of powers, each possessing its own particular resources and in pursuit of its own aims. While within the military command itself there had been a protracted delay before functions were finally decided and assigned within the military establishment, on a larger scale four different agencies were at work within the armed forces to bring about certain deliberate effects. Through the Political Administration, which was directly subordinated to the Central Committee, the Communist Party directed the work of indoctrination and political preparation, aiming at ideological correctitude and unity within the Red Army and inculcating loyalty to the policies of the ruling group. By linking up political objectives with aspects of military training, the Party had thereby assumed responsibility for the state of morale — in the widest sense of the word as well as its Soviet context — which it was desired to bring about. This, then, was a positive function, the 'politicalising' of the armed forces in a manner which could and did conflict with military efficiency pure and simple. But the purity and simplicity of military efficiency had been a constant loser since the Red Army had first come into existence. Loyalty and reliability, or rather the lack of it among the military, came within the competence of the State Security services, which maintained a chain of counter-intelligence and internal espionage organs within the Red Army as far down as regimental level. The much-feared Special Sections (*OO*), inquisitor to command staff and rank-and-file alike, co-operated to some extent with the political organs, and the whole interlocking directorate of supervision and control worked outside the direct control of the military. Nor did the military operate its own instruments of retribution, the military procuracies and tribunals. Following on the 1933 reform, which modernised the system established in 1926, the Main Military Procuracy (*GVP*) was organised, with the rights of an administration, under the aegis of the Procurator of the USSR, while the courts and tribunals fell under the military section of the Supreme Court. Finally the military itself, enmeshed in this deliberate diversification of function, was vested with the responsibility of operating the Military and Naval Commissariat.

It is certainly an over-simplification to describe the main predicament of the Red Army in terms of 'Army-Party relations'. The over-all relationship was much more complex, and the lack of clear definitions of function makes the question more difficult. Gamarnik and Voroshilov each occupied simultaneously high military and political posts. Where governmental and Party functions coalesced, it was evident that what counted was not so much a clash over formal powers but a bitter personal struggle among an entire command group which operated in a very personalised manner. It was rendered more peculiar by Stalin's system of an extreme centralisation and concentration of power within the hands he himself had set at their appointed tasks. The last item it was which gave full meaning to Trotsky's forecast, made in the 1920's, of a Bonapartism advancing into greater power, a Bonapartism dispensing with the whiff of grapeshot which brought the military into dominion over the body politic, substituting Stalin's 'last word' in the *Politburo*.[2] Bonapartism without or even in spite of the soldiers created two objectives, the first being negative and pursued by the *OGPU/NKVD** and the *OO*. The other, positive to a degree, was the persistence of the effort to assimilate the armed forces into the regime. Once again, in terms of Stalin's own system, this was to present formidable problems. But a third objective could not be ignored, whatever the internal requirements of a regime slipping into total dictatorship. In the last resort, the Red Army existed to fight (the bed-rock argument which caused so much furore during the Civil War). Too much interference in the way of political manipulation and Party penetration would strike at this *raison d'être*; it might grind it out of existence. To surrender totally to that argument at once, to admit the

* The Unified State Political Administration (*OGPU*) gave way in 1934 to the People's Commissariat for Internal Affairs (*NKVD*). Contemporary accounts frequently maintain the term *OGPU/GPU* after the re-organisation.

soldiers into full and untrammelled control over their army would impede the absorption of the armed forces into the regime and its purposes, and might actually facilitate the complete alienation of the army from the regime. At all costs the army had to be rendered impotent as a contestant for power, but kept virile as an efficient fighting force. Of such dilemmas are Soviet military reforms made.

It is therefore a moot point whether the reform of 1934 might be graced by that name. Re-organisation it certainly was, but the whole process was quite internal to the military command and in no way marked any substantial re-distribution of power. Nominally a great change came over the old Military and Naval Commissariat, which was altered by the *Sovnarkom* statute of 20th June, 1934, to the People's Commissariat of Defence. To bring the military in line with recent practice, the former collective control over the Commissariat was done away with; as a result the *Revvoensoviet*, which had existed since the early days of the Civil War and acted as the collegiate responsible for the running of the Military and Naval Commissariat, was dissolved. Voroshilov became the People's Commissar for Defence, possessing all the rights of unitary command over the Commissariat. The 1934 statute did, however, make a singular definition of the functions of the new Commissariat; under the new statute Voroshilov's military administration took responsibility for these specific tasks:

the formulation of plans for the development, organisational form and arming of the army;
the organisation and structure of the land, naval and air forces;
the direction of their combat and political preparation, and the operational employment of these forces in time of peace and war;
the developing and perfecting of all weapons and military technology;
the supplying of the army with weapons and provisions;
defence works and the organisation of the anti-aircraft defence of the USSR;
the induction of contingents into active military service;
the direction of medical and veterinary services.[3]

Attached to the Commissar of Defence was a special Military Soviet, a reduction to a mere pale shadow of the former *Revvoensoviet*. Working under Voroshilov's chairmanship, the functions of this body were purely advisory; appointments to the Military Soviet were made by *Sovnarkom* on the recommendation of the Defence Commissar. The Military Soviet met and adjourned at the command of the Commissar, through whom its decisions were both made known and put into effect.[4]

The Defence Commissariat, operated by the Commissar and his eleven Deputy Commissars, possessed two main departments in the Red Army

Staff and the Main Administration of the Red Army, under Yegorov and Feldman respectively. A degree of control over the Inspectorates was vested in the Red Army Staff, although the inspectorate apparatus was controlled by an Inspector-General of Armaments. The Red Army

ORGANISATION OF THE PEOPLE'S COMMISSARIAT OF DEFENCE

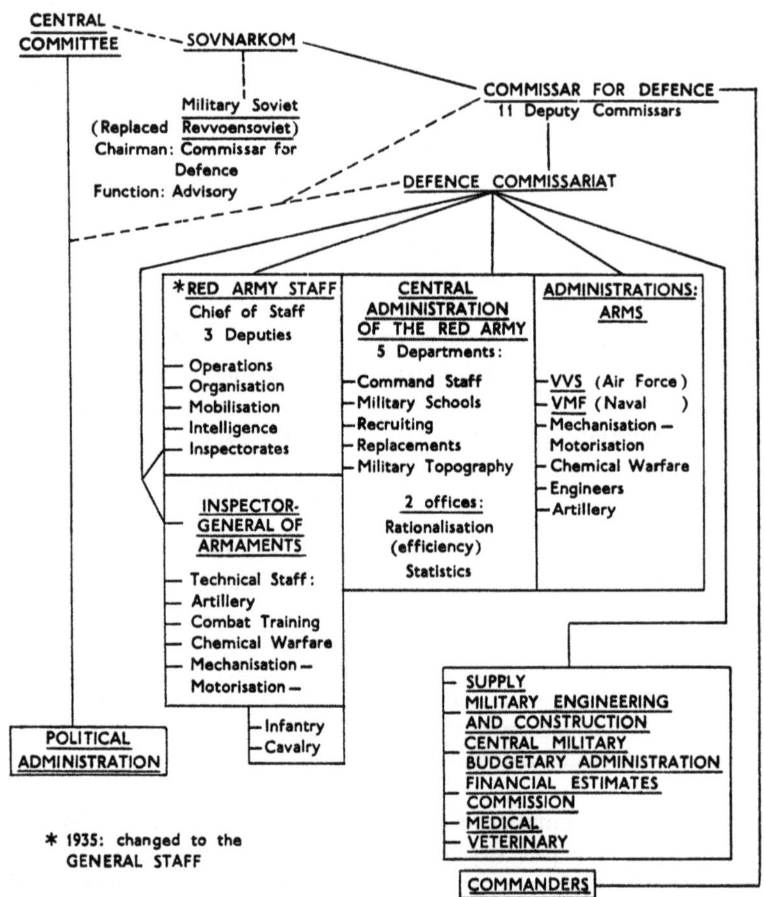

Administration had five main departments concerned with command staff, military schools, recruiting, replacements and assignments, and military topography. The *VMF* and *VVS* administrations were assembled into the Commissariat, together with the specialist chemical warfare and mechanisation administrations. Under the 1934 statute, unit commanders were formally brought under the direct subordination of the Defence Commissar. Although subordinated to the Central Committee, the Political Administration came within the orbit of the Commissariat in so far as Gamarnik was a Deputy Commissar to Voroshilov, and Voroshilov himself enjoyed membership of the *Politburo*, which concerned itself most assiduously with the activities of the Political Administration.

The 1934 re-organisation sought after increased efficiency. It was also one further step in consolidating a very highly centralised control over the armed forces, for Voroshilov emerged with powers greater than before. The weak attempt at a formal collective opinion being established in the Military Soviet showed through the conditions under which that body was set up, as well as the position which it occupied in the highest level of the command. At this time also the naval forces did not slip out of the military net into independence; from this it might be assumed that neither Stalin nor Voroshilov were much interested in granting any kind of autonomy to the naval command. The visible weakness of the Soviet Navy likewise made it superfluous at this point to set up a separate naval commissariat. The aim of the reform seems to have been twofold: first to consolidate the Stalin-Voroshilov grip over the military establishment, and second to promote the more efficient control of the military over the operational, administrative and technical aspects of the questions in which they were involved. But there was no interference with the distribution of functions which had existed prior to the advent of this new scheme. The prophets of power and glory to the Red Army Staff were doomed to disappointment; nothing like the major reforms of 1924–6 took place in 1934, and the Staff remained a kind of half-way house, undoubtedly important but still lagging in the race for prestige and power, in which some had seen it as a powerful starter. A powerful and independent Staff did not accord with the present system. Great care had always been shown to remove the independents from the staff. It was to be an executive organ in so far as it amplified the directives of the Commissar, but not a source of independent military thought. Yegorov, therefore, was eminently suited to this post. He could not be classed as an outstanding military talent, lacking that unquestionable insight into the possibilities of the technical revolution which Tukhachevsky was developing in himself, and denied that implacable if politically expedient professionalism with which Shaposhnikov shrouded himself. Yegorov worked more as a co-ordinator and general director of other talents, carrying out in unison the directives which issued from the Commissar. Yet to exact real efficiency from the centralised system, a strong Staff was an essential, and a measure of real independence could not be denied it. This lesson Voroshilov and Stalin learned quickly, for in 1935 the Staff was strengthened and diversified rather more in its activity, as well as being graced with the title General Staff.

The first intensive stage of the technical revolution in the Red Army had also produced a kind of military syndicate, formed out of the personal co-operation of the innovators in armaments, combat methods and training — Tukhachevsky, Uborevich, Yakir, Sedyakin, Khalepskii, Alksnis (and Khripin, his Chief of Staff), Fishman, Orlov and Muklevich. A real and important layer of command emerged from these relationships, which had Tukhachevsky for their centre. But whatever flexibility and mutual understanding did exist within this group, the Red Army was not permitted to be an exception to the bureaucratic rigidity which gripped the whole of the Soviet state. To the habitual sluggishness which this inevitably brings, there was added the defect of 'super-bureaucratisation' at the highest level, when the *Politburo* turned to minute scrutiny not only of policies but the minutiae also of administration and planning. Voroshilov gathered the reins of administration into the tightest possible knot; decentralisation of responsibility did not pass below his level and stopped even at the point of his two first deputies, Gamarnik and Tukhachevsky. A. Barmine, who had been assigned by the Staff to a post dealing with the export of arms (principally to the East), was in a position to observe the operation of this system at first-hand, and how exceeding small the Stalinist mills must grind. Voroshilov did not forbear to consult Stalin even on the smallest point. On a particular occasion, when Voroshilov was absent in the south, Barmine approached Gamarnik and Tukhachevsky over the implementation of some details of an arms-export deal which had already been approved. After three weeks of discussion with these senior officers over the problem, Barmine prevailed upon Gamarnik to telephone Voroshilov. At the other end of the line, by way of a solution, a secretary merely ordered Gamarnik to await the return of Voroshilov to Moscow.[5] In the degrading of Tukhachevsky from a 'leader' to a 'functionary', Barmine also witnessed a first-hand exhibition, when, on receipt of a telephone call from Voroshilov, Tukhachevsky jumped to his feet and in a 'definitely respectful voice' promised to do the Commissar's bidding.[6]

In complete contrast with the Frunze reforms, however, the 1934 measures were accompanied by a marked expansion of the Soviet armed forces. The cadre forces increased to 940,000 (almost doubling the first Frunze ceiling). The budgetary allocation also leaped up. In 1933 the expenditure on military and naval items had amounted to 1,420,700,000 roubles, with an additional 126,600,000 roubles assigned to 'Special Forces'. In 1934 the sum of 5,000 million roubles was put at the disposal of the Defence Commissariat.[7] The inference was plain. Whereas the ruling group had previously made considerable political capital out of politically expedient but largely fictitious war-scares, the inadequacy of the forces at the disposal of the Soviet command could no longer be ignored, with the Japanese pressing on the eastern frontiers and Germany throwing off the shackles of disarmament restraints in the west. The first physical expansion of the Red Army was an important factor in affecting the course of military policy, and the final jettisoning of the mixed cadre-territorial force in the following year had important consequences for the Red Army command, which found itself faced with the problem of realising on a large scale the new methods of waging war with a Red Army equipped with new and complex weapons. Already a fresh military generation, the eventual replacement to the military intelligentsia which Blomberg had observed at the centre of Red Army affairs, was taking on shape and about to press more closely upon the heels of the old.

★ ★ ★ ★

While the military complexion of the Red Army was undergoing important changes, the Political Administration, operating directly under the supervision of the Party political command, worked energetically to bring about transformations of its own within the armed forces. With the method of selective recruitment still in operation (that is, excluding 'socially alien' elements from the very start), a certain automatic control could be exercised upon the composition of the armed forces, with a specific political end in view. The military consequence of this was to deny to the Red Army the use of higher-educated and more skilled material, which an army incorporating a larger number of machines would necessarily need. At the same time, great attention was paid to increasing the proletarian contingent in the Red Army, which crept up from 18 per cent in 1921 to 43 per cent in 1933.[8] The peasant, who came from a countryside ravaged by forcible collectivisation and yet remained the largest manpower pool for the Red Army, was carefully separated from positions where he might create political havoc. The emphasis was everywhere upon the proletarian, not least in the military schools from which the reinforcements for the Soviet officer corps would come. The percentage of workers in the Red Army rose from 31·2 per cent on 1st January, 1930, to 43 per cent in 1933 and to 45·8 per cent on 1st January, 1934; for the same 1930–4 period, the percentage of peasantry fell from 57·9 to 42·5 per cent.[9] Also during the same period the percentage of Communist Party and *Komsomol* members rose from 34·3 to 49·5 per cent (of the latter, 23·9 per cent *Komsomol*), so that, by January 1934, approximately half the rank-and-file of the Red Army were officially Communists.

The officer corps presented rather more complicated problems for the political command, although the political aims with regard to the officer corps were substantially the same. In spite of the assurances given to the non-Party officers that no 'Communising' of the officer corps was intended, at the end of the First Five-Year Plan the bulk of the non-Party officers who fell into that category in 1929–30 had become Party members. Speaking in 1933, Voroshilov referred to the 'massive, decisive results' which had been achieved in the political preparation of the command staff, among whom remained only 'a small percentage' of the non-Party men. Even they, the non-Party officers were 'absolutely our people. . . . We trust in them, just as in the Communists, that they carry out and will carry out their duties equally with the Communists.'[10] Among the higher command staff in 1933 all the commanders of military districts and corps commanders were members of the Party; 93 per cent of the commanders of rifle divisions and 95 per cent of the cavalry division commanders were also Party members, with a percentage of 88 for rifle regiment commanders. What was even more significant than the membership figures, however, was Voroshilov's statement that 96–7 per cent of the divisional and regimental commanders were Civil War veterans,[11] the same men who were now being called upon to become proficient in a much more advanced art of warfare, the same which was being taught in the academies and schools to the younger vintage of officers. For the officer corps as a whole, Party membership had jumped in the period from 1930–4 to a high point of 67·8 per cent (plus 4 per cent in the *Komsomol*): by 1934 the non-Party element had fallen from 43·4 per cent in 1930 to 28·2 per cent.[12]

What lends particular interest to these figures is the remarkable immunity enjoyed by the Red Army during the purge of 1929–30 and once again, *mirabile dictu*, in the purges of 1933–4. For the first, there is tangible evidence that the intercession of the military command in the interests of a minimum interference with efficiency had been one of the important factors working for only slight interference with the armed forces, while the heavy hand of expulsion hit the civilian organisations. In 1933, an estimated 4·3 per cent of military Communists were purged, while the corresponding figures for civilian circles amounted to 17 per cent. Nothing like the 25 per cent of the 1934 expulsions among the civilians occurred in the Red Army.[13] The explanation for the restraints of 1933–4 might well lie with the fact that no extensive interference with Army Communists, and the consequent undesirable effects on morale, could be justified since the army had shown every sign of firm political allegiance during the years of acute crisis. Further, an extensive purge would have run directly counter to the aims of the Party within the armed forces; the political command was evidently greatly interested in increasing Party contingents, not only in the Red Army as a whole, but in the new technical arms of the Red Army. A step in this direction was the secret letter of 10th June, 1933, circulated in the Western *oblast*, following upon an instruction of the Central Committee, whereby the Party was to mobilise candidates for the flying and technical schools of the *VVS*. It was a matter of importance that '. . . this mobilisation be carried out conscientiously'.[14] It would therefore appear that a high priority of the political command at this time was the implementation of an extremely active and positive policy to accomplish the effective politicalisation of the Red Army.

At the 17th Party Congress, that pliant and submissive gathering which had drawn in the vanquished and was therefore graced as 'the Congress of Victors', the status of the Red Army Political Administration as the Military Department of the Central Committee was once again affirmed. It was to work '. . . on the basis of special instructions emanating from the Central Committee.' In the same regulation, the minimum lengths of service within the Party for senior commissars were also fixed; chiefs of political departments in military districts, fleets and armies were to have a minimum of ten years Party standing, those in divisional and brigade departments at least six years.[15] The senior political officers, as well as conforming to certain standards of service in the Party, were in a very different category from the military commissars who worked much lower down the military-political ladder. Not unlike Gamarnik himself, they tended to be Party intellectuals, well-versed in Marxist doctrine and 'political specialists' in the real sense of the word. In between the senior commissars and the lower ranks of the political staff, yet another group worked avidly to provide a fully comprehensive Marxist science of war — a political equivalent to the military assessments made of the technical revolution. This work went on in the military sections of the Communist Academy attached to the Central Committee. The bulk of this inspired work, which had very little military value and showed a conspicuous lack of acquaintance with military history as a whole, appears to have had little or no influence.[16] The fundamental question remained, not the clash of a few specious ideas with the basic strategic ideas being developed by the military command, but the relations between the commander and the commissar, and essentially, the contradiction between effective politicalisation and efficient militarisation of the Red Army.

In one further fundamental aspect, the work of the Political Administration had become more difficult now that the commander and the commissar were both Party members. The situation had been vastly different when Communist commissars watched over a hostile and almost totally non-Party officer corps. With the progress made in Communising the officer corps, and having used the commissars as a means to pursue an active political programme designed to align the army with the regime and its aims, the Political Administration could only function as a second-class policeman. An avowed aim had been to integrate the military and political commands; on the whole, this had met with only a poor result, since the splendid fiction of unitary command could only mean the ultimate subordination of the commissar in the interests of promoting efficient military command. At the higher levels, where the commander-commissar in one person was a more common phenomenon, and Army-Party identification supposedly complete, control was a much more difficult matter. And who, in the last resort, would watch the watchers?

From this point of view, the reforms in the security apparatus which took place in 1934 have a significance all their own. The *OGPU* changed its name to *NKVD* (People's Commissariat for Internal Affairs), with an increase in its capacities and responsibilities. In addition to its control over the organs

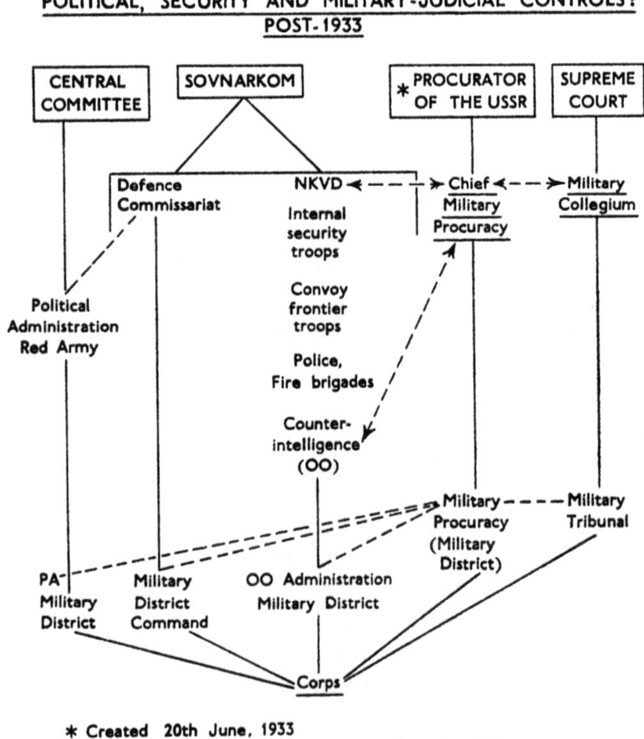

of state security, frontier guards and its own well-armed (and motorised) internal security troops, the *NKVD* united its own military forces with the militia (which carried out the functions of a normal police force).[17] The effect was to create a monolith of repression, fully supported by an independent armed force at its disposal. In the previous year, a new office had been brought into being when the Procuracy of the USSR was established, in which office the Main Military Procuracy was absorbed with all the rights of an administration. Until the 1933 re-organisation, military procuracies had been attached to military districts, fleets, corps, divisions and other formations and operated under the control of the senior assistant procurator of the Military Collegium of the Supreme Court. The Main Military Procuracy, while possessing certain connections with the Defence Commissariat and its organs, was linked 'especially' with the *OGPU/NKVD*; at lower levels, it operated in contact with 'command and political organs'.[18] Thus were the erstwhile watchers watched by a third party, whose business it was to organise internal espionage and to man the means of repression and intimidation; at its disposal lay an amalgamated military- and police-type force, the nucleus of Stalin's private army functioning independently of the Red Army military command. The re-organisation of the security apparatus had a significance all its own for the whole of Soviet society, of which the armed forces were only a part, but the reshaping of the military procuracy had little meaning except in the context of the Red Army. Certainly the problem of physical control over the armed forces had begun to change fundamentally now that large sections of the Soviet forces had become Party members. Under such conditions it was inevitable that the weight of effective surveillance should be shifted on to the secret police and its organs.

If the Red Army escaped a formidable purging during 1933–4, Krivitsky supplies a piece of evidence of his own which is an indirect confirmation of the switch from Party to secret police action in the army and suggests that the Red Army did not go scot-free. Krivitsky refers to a conversation he had with Kedrov, *OGPU* investigator, about the arrest and grilling of V. M. Primakov, deputy commander of the North Caucasus Military District. Placing this event in 1934, Krivitsky makes no mention of the charge on which Primakov was detained, although Kedrov made it clear that his branch was interested in the 'investigation', that Primakov had begun to break down and a 'confession' would have been only a matter of time if Voroshilov had not intervened to demand the release of Primakov.[19] The possibility that Krivitsky had confused the date is lessened since he has 1934 specifically under discussion, and the talk with Kedrov was evidently lengthy. It was evidently in 1935 that Krivitsky learned of the 'Primakov case', but assuming that this former member of Red Army Intelligence had heard correctly (and his disclosures later cost him his life, even in exile), then the *NKVD* was actively interfering in the senior command level of the Red Army at this time to the extent of obtaining a 'confession' from an officer detained for 'investigation'. It is to be regretted that Krivitsky did not specify the month or months of Primakov's detention in 1934, for it was at the end of that year that a strange and unexplained killing in Leningrad provided the occasion to strip off all pretence at limitation of the *NKVD*'s activities and the real Stalinist terroristic repression of society.

On 1st December, 1934, Kirov, lieutenant to Stalin in Leningrad, was shot dead by student-assassin Nikolayev in that city.[20] That same evening Stalin personally had issued the directive empowering the *NKVD* to speed up the investigation of those suspected of preparing 'terroristic acts' and to execute those so found guilty immediately after sentence had been passed. To this dead and dreadful stop came the 'liberalisation', the easing of the Stalinist rigours, which Voroshilov and Kirov himself were reported as having favoured. 'Mass repression', 'brutal acts', 'brutal wilfulness' — the terms belong to N. Khrushchev[21]— followed with bewildering speed. Yagoda,* thug and revolutionary only in the loosest sense, took command of the *NKVD* to administer the full dose of terror, first upon luckless Leningrad and then upon society at large, Party and non-Party alike. The day of even the flimsiest of immunities was over and done.

★ ★ ★ ★

While the *NKVD* looked in upon the Soviet Union (although it possessed a foreign intelligence service), the Red Army command had to look at the military security of the Soviet frontiers† and the threats gathering beyond. The year 1934 began in much the same fashion as 1933 had ended, with the Red Army keeping its foot in the German door, a position which could not have been maintained without the full approval of Stalin himself. At the time when the German Ambassador was reporting that Litvinov seemed to be fully committed to 'the decision to switch over to the French group',[22] Yegorov was singing the praises of the *Reichswehr* to Twardowski, emphasising that 'no injurious intent' had been a conscious part of the Russian withdrawal from the collaboration in the summer of 1933.[23] In the course of this two-hour talk, Yegorov clearly established that it was a Soviet first move which had led to the virtual termination of the exchanges. On 11th

* G. G. Yagoda was of Polish origin, beginning his revolutionary activity in 1907 at the age of sixteen. He took up security and espionage work after the 1917 Revolution and became deputy chief of the *OGPU* in 1924, having served as head of a Soviet intelligence and subversion department operating in America. As head of the *NKVD*, he succeeded Menzhinskii; at his trial in 1938 Yagoda was accused of killing Menzhinskii, Kuibyshev and Maxim Gorky.

† Frontier troops, as such, came under *NKVD* command.

January, at his own request, Ambassador Nadolny had an hour's talk with Voroshilov, who at once began to speak of the good relations developing between Germany and Japan — at which Soviet concern was natural, in view of the situation on the eastern frontiers. While speaking up for a renewal of relations between the two armies, Voroshilov became 'very thoughtful' and ventured no reply when Nadolny said quite frankly that 'after the Red Army had turned us out, so to speak', it was the Red Army which must now make the first move for a resumption of relations. To Nadolny it appeared that Voroshilov was basically a protagonist of the best possible Soviet-German relations, but he was momentarily under the influence of Litvinov, to whom he could find no counter-argument.[24] Litvinov's argument ran that Germany, either by taking advantage of a clash in the east between the Soviet Union and Japan or in some other fashion, would seek to make Russia 'a victim of the German militarism pursued by Hitler'.

In an inspired leak, Radek dis-avowed Litvinov's extremism and formulated to a German journalist what Stalin said publicly at the 17th Congress. Master of words and phrases, Radek came straight to the point. The Soviet Union was pursuing a policy of *raison d'état*; Litvinov represented only the man over him, a man 'hard, cautious and distrustful . . . endowed with a firm will' — Stalin, Stalin who 'does not know where he stands with Germany. He is uncertain.'[25] German armaments were growing in a striking manner, and no one could better appreciate German capabilities than the Russians. German moves in the Baltic were not reassuring. But, Radek continued, in the meanwhile the Soviet Union wished to avoid a war not only for 'tactical but also for strategic reasons, we want to extend the pause to catch our breath . . .'. Or, to put it another way, Radek pointed out that the Soviet Union had no intention of 'falling into the spokes of the wheel of history'.[26]

In his speech at the 17th Congress, Stalin did not exclude the possibility of agreement with the new regime in Germany. By way of precedent, the Soviet Union had maintained good relations with Fascist Italy, notwithstanding the differences in the internal regimes of the two countries. At the same Congress, Voroshilov and Blyukher spoke about defence measures in the Far East.[27] Voroshilov made reference to the ill-concealed Japanese designs on the Maritime Provinces, the Trans-Baikal and Siberia. Beset between east and west, it was obvious that the present state of the Soviet forces was not one designed to ensure the maximum security of the Soviet frontiers. At the beginning of the year, the Red Army existed at only a fraction above the Frunze ceiling for the regular forces. While the threat in the west still existed largely in the pages of *Mein Kampf* and Rosenberg's virulently anti-Bolshevik writings, there could be no gainsaying the Japanese forces actually on the eastern frontiers. If a large part of the re-organisation of 1934 was taken up with bringing the Defence Commissariat into being, the absolutely vital change was to put in motion a considerable expansion of the Red Army. It was that same summer of 1934, when the military re-organisation was taking final shape, which Krivitsky also selects as the critical point in the evolution of Stalin's policy towards Germany.

On the night of 30th June, 1934, when Hitler's long knives put an end to the life of a number of the Red Army's friends in the *Reichswehr* and also cut many of the rivals and opponents of Hitler to pieces, Stalin called a meeting of the *Politburo* even while the first German blood-bath raged. To this meeting were summoned Berzin of Red Army Intelligence, Litvinov, Radek and Artuzov (head of the *NKVD* foreign intelligence). Berzin, on his return from this session extraordinary, intimated to Krivitsky that Stalin understood the purge in Germany as a sign of Hitler's strength and not a portent of his early collapse. From this point forwards, after Hitler had shown himself to be a dictator capable of the extreme in ruthlessness, Krivitsky claimed that Stalin determined to come to an understanding with the German ruler.[28] Certain incidents of Stalin's 'private diplomacy' of the future were to provide some justification for Krivitsky's views. But the future did not dispose of the present unfavourable situation, viewed in terms of the strategic situation of the Soviet Union, which existed about the several gates and entries to the country. The Baltic highway seemed to lie wide open. In January 1934 Poland had come to an agreement with Germany, although the worst fears seem to have been allayed by Colonel Beck's February visit to Moscow.[29] But the through-road into Russia via Poland seemed to be guarded by a government of some fickleness. To the south, there was no firm Russian friend among the Danube states to close this path. Whatever hopes and plans for the future Stalin may have nurtured, the strength of the Red Army was his first guarantee.

It was in January 1935, in the course of a statement to the 7th Congress of Soviets, that Tukhachevsky provided an explanation of the nature of the change in the Red Army. While statements at the Congress of Soviets tended to have a set form (re-assurance over defence capacity, references to increase in equipment, and the standard warning to would-be aggressors), Tukhachevsky's statement has a number of extremely illuminating points about military decisions and problems at this critical and transitional period. It was clear that the increase to 940,000 men had been made by the end of 1934. Now was the time for the consolidation of the technical revolution, the foundation for the great expansion which was, for a second time, to transform the Red Army out of nearly all resemblance to its previous self.

Tukhachevsky at once referred to the changes in the political and social composition of the Red Army; 45·5 per cent were workers, and 90 per cent of the peasant soldiers came from farms which had been collectivised. Of the rank-and-file, 49·3 per cent were affiliates of the Party, of the command staff 68·3 per cent (90 per cent among divisional commanders, 100 per cent among corps commanders). On the technical transformation, while quoting in percentages based on the absolute figures for 1931, the Red Army Ordnance Chief singled out items in a manner which suggested the degree to which they interested the military command — tanks (small, light, medium), tank and anti-tank guns, heavy artillery, the number of machine-guns per rifle and cavalry unit, machine-guns for tanks and aircraft, and radio equipment for mobile forces.[30]

In outlining the problems which beset the command in welding quality and quantity into a fighting whole, Tukhachevsky went on,

> We are working on the problems of reconnaissance, which are of immense importance, particularly in view of the rapid development of modern operations and engagements. We are working for the development of mobility and daring, for the development of initiative, independence, persistence — to put it crudely, 'nerve'. This is a question on which everything now depends.[31]

But, continued Tukhachevsky

> . . . the problem is not a simple one. During the Civil War we became accustomed to cavalry as the most rapid arm, while the majority are accustomed to infantry actions, and to be able to adjust ourselves to a new level, to be able to utilise the mobility of aviation and our mechanised troops and tanks, is not so simple.
>
> The problem of command is becoming a very important one. It is not enough to have mobile technical equipment, it is not enough to have men individually able to use this technical equipment; we must also have men and apparatuses prepared to command battles and operations, which, with the introduction of new technical resources now develop far more rapidly, with lightning speed. The problem is a big one, and we are now working intensively on the problem of commanding engagements, on the problem of organising close and continuous inter-action, because no arm alone can give complete results. The axis of our military training in 1935 is to master the technique and art of commanding the swiftly-moving forms of engagements involving every kind of arm.[32]

Tukhachevsky made it clear, in the course of his address, that the decision to detach west and east had now been fully and finally adopted, a step necessitated because the Red Army could not operate like the German Army during the World War, switching large forces from front to front on internal lines. Even bearing in mind the role of aviation, the 'luxury' of an east-west shifting of forces could not be afforded by the Soviet command. In any consideration of the movement of large forces along the internal lines of communication there must be 'great caution' — a judgement which was itself of some interest, since the Second Five-Year Plan had been devised with a heightened emphasis on rail communication. But, essentially Tukhachevsky's defence statement merely confirmed that the command of the Red Army had committed itself absolutely to a very serious attempt to bring real military efficiency to the expanding forces at its disposal.[33] In other words, Tukhachevsky intended to make his new motorised and mechanised army battle-worthy.

The direction and scope of the re-organisations of the winter of 1934–5 raise once again the question of the possible intentions, and the relation of these to the strategic doctrines of the time, which underpinned the real intensification of modernisation and expansion in the Red Army. Certainly the formative stage had been the years 1931–3; the years of realisation now seemed to be upon the Soviet command. In no other military sphere did this seem so pronounced as in the *VVS*, the military aviation which had been nurtured at Lipetsk, but since 1931–2 had been striking out on its own. In 1935 the *VVS* was in the course of being re-equipped with the products of an indigenous Soviet aviation industry, which could supply both engines, fuselages and new designs, although it was an industry which owed much to French assistance and technical guidance. Alksnis and Tupolev, at the head of a special mission, had made a personal acquaintance with the French aviation industry.[34] The French did much to assist the development of a Soviet aluminium industry. From a force the backbone of which had been reconnaissance machines and light bombers, the *VVS* took possession of new fighters (I–15 and I–16) and bombers capable of delivering a heavier bomb-load at a greater range. While the Far East evidently had a priority call over new bombers, Alksnis and Khripin (in whom the Germans discerned an extremely able officer) especially did not ignore the potentialities of the bomber as a whole. The *VVS* had never been without an element favouring independent operations by bombers, and Blomberg at the air-manœuvres of 1928 had watched and been much impressed by Soviet performance in this field even with out-of-date equipment. A. N. Lapchinskii, a theoretician of first-rate importance during these formative years of the *VVS*, as early as 1926 had written of the possibility and the importance of strategic aerial bombardment.[35]

It is apparent that the theories of General Douhet raised in the *VVS* an effect not dissimilar to the writings of Fuller and Zoldan on the Red Army. In a study published in 1932, Lapchinskii took issue with 'Douhet-ism' to deny that airpower could be the sole arbiter of war.[36] Lapchinskii cast the role of aviation in terms of the 'inter-action of all arms' which was the positive principle of Soviet military thought, which was already denying lordship of the battlefield to the tank. In an examination of the role of aviation in support of the ground-forces (assuming that an army of 5 rifle corps, or 15 rifle divisions, were involved), Lapchinskii calculated that a total of 901 aircraft would be required for the various supporting roles — with the main force made up of 252 fighters, 312 light bombers, 76 heavy bombers and 220 reconnaissance aircraft.[37] At the same time Lapchinskii did not deny that there was a specific place for independent strategic bomber operations both in terms of the number of aircraft involved and the need for an organised command to control these operations. Such a view was forcefully rammed home by the *VVS* Chief of Staff Khripin at the beginning of 1935, when he wrote that modern warfare could not be waged without undertaking 'independent air operations'. Technique and armament both made this possible, for air defence was at an increasing disadvantage against the high-altitude and high-speed bomber.[38] The *VVS* had its eyes fixed on the industrial centres of Germany and those of Western Japan, the potential targets of potential enemies. While the principle of inter-action between all arms was maintained by assigning to aviation the role of massed support for the ground forces in their break-through operations, the importance of the 'independent air operations' of which Khripin had spoken also grew in the mind of the *VVS* command. That the main weight was gradually shifting on to the strategic bomber force was confirmed in the light of Khripin's subsequent disclosures about the composition of the *VVS*.

It was at the end of March 1935 that Tukhachevsky launched in the columns of *Pravda* (and the military newspapers) a bitter attack on the military preparations in Germany under Hitler, who had just promulgated the new law on universal military service and the fixing of the peace-time strength of the German Army at 36 divisions.[39] The growth of German air strength clearly alarmed the Soviet leaders; Radek had made the same point about German aviation early in 1934, and as Radek spoke for Stalin, so it is unlikely that Tukhachevsky's article had not first been vetted by Stalin. A real note of concern was struck in the mention of Hitler's reported statements to Sir John Simon about the retaining of freedom to act 'in the future' against the USSR, for which reason Hitler schemed to weaken the Soviet western frontiers. Tukhachevsky could not seriously believe that in the month of March 1935 Germany represented imminent peril to the Soviet Union; for this very reason there is a pronounced discrepancy between the 'political propaganda' and the more sober long-range military estimate contained in the article. Tukhachevsky agreed with Pétain that a military system which relied upon having enough time for mobilisation by stages, since the potential enemy was assumed to be incapable of bringing powerful forces into action at great speed, was not consistent with the facts.

Tukhachevsky went further in stating that the present French Army could not present an effective opposition to the German Army, and a precise part of Hitler's strategy was to keep the French in a state of military quiescence. That was the supreme danger for a Soviet command which clearly envisaged the possibility of very powerful forces being brought into action by a potential enemy in the very early stages of a conflict (Shilovskii had recently published an article on the possibility of offensive operations being opened by a potential enemy without a formal war declaration);* these enemy forces, with deep penetrations, could wreak havoc with the mobilisation processes of the state attacked. The 'battle of the frontiers' was therefore of supreme importance in denying this advantage to a potential enemy, and even assuming a considerable break-through, to meet him with a defensive strength deployed in great depth.

In terms of Hitler's intentions, Tukhachevsky aired the view that Germany was aiming primarily at revenge and aggrandisement in the west and the south — France and Belgium, Poland, Czechoslovakia and Austria.† Without the acquisition of Belgian and French ports, German naval power could not be brought into effective play. For this reason the expansion of the German armed forces aimed at the eclipse of the French and the overshadowing of the Russian. The present rate of military expansion in Germany would bring, by the summer of 1935, a 40 per cent superiority over the French and near numerical parity with the Red Army (with its augmented strength of 940,000). Tukhachevsky's article provoked an immediate German protest to both Litvinov and Gekker. In addition, it prompted a searching analysis from the German Military Attaché in Moscow;[40] this pointed out that the most obvious theme of the article centred on German aggressive preparations which were aimed at the USSR. The Soviet military command could not seriously suppose that an immediate military danger from Germany existed; rather, that part of the article reflected only the 'hysterical fear' (*hysterische Angst*) of the prevalent German attitude. Even if the article were taken as an estimate of military intentions, the fact could not be overlooked that it did not appear that the Red Army, in the opinion of its commanders, was even now in a condition to be committed to battle (*angriffsfähig*). Only the *VVS* could be considered to be an effective offensive weapon; with respect to other arms, the Soviet command was reluctant to put even the capacity for defence to the acid test of war.[41] In response to a

* One of the current criticisms made by Soviet military writers on pre-1941 theorising is that it neglected an extensive study of strategic surprise. This may have been true of the period 1938–41, but is less true of the first half of the decade. An interesting comparison of these ideas with modern Soviet notions is supplied by reference to Joseph J. Baritz's study, 'Soviet Military Theory and Modern Warfare' in *Bulletin* (Munich), May 1959, pp. 12–21.

† Tukhachevsky had the right areas but the wrong sequence.

protest made to Gekker, Voroshilov's chief of protocol in the Defence Commissariat, the only satisfaction which the Germans obtained was Gekker's comment that the Tukhachevsky article was designed to provoke a more wakeful attitude in the west to the dangers of German military expansion, and that the Third Reich could feel injured or insulted only if the cap really fitted, in which case the *exposé* had some justification.

The views put forward by Tukhachevsky (or at least bearing his name) made reference not only to German but also to French military capacities, the latter being the new-found military and technical help-mate of the Soviet Union. It was a liaison which parties on both sides viewed with marked degrees of reservation. The French military interest was largely negative, aimed at detaching Germany from the Soviet Union. While the first Franco-Soviet military contacts were being made in the early summer and autumn of 1933, senior Soviet officers did not seem to have abandoned by any means their interest in restoring connections with the German military. Voroshilov and Yegorov were counted especially firm partisans of the pro-German orientation of Soviet policy by the Germans themselves. The possibility of a split in the Soviet command over the role to be accorded to military contacts with France had been mentioned by Colonel Mendras soon after his arrival in Moscow. The proof he cited was the business of appointing a Soviet military attaché to Paris. Sedyakin and Ventsov were the two names mentioned, but Sedyakin was dropped, ostensibly for reasons of health. Litvinov favoured the candidacy of Ventsov, and Mendras interpreted the whole question as a struggle between a policy of taking up the contact and no more, and the alternative of trying to achieve a truly effective relationship with the French. [42] In the end Ventsov was appointed, and his supporters presumably triumphed. Ventsov it was who opened the first serious exchanges with Colonel de Lattre de Tassigny, member of the Staff of General Weygand.[43]

In the course of 1934 Franco-Soviet relations took on a more positive tone, and energetic efforts were made to accomplish the realisation of an Eastern Pact, which would bind up France, the Soviet Union, the Little Entente and Baltic states into arrangements of mutual assistance. The draft of 27th June, 1934, named Poland, Russia, Germany, Czechoslovakia, Finland, Estonia, Latvia and Lithuania as parties to a treaty of 'regional assistance'. An additional Franco-Soviet treaty was part of the entire scheme proposed.[44] To this suggestion of mutual assistance so arranged, Berlin reacted with great coolness; a Franco-Soviet guarantee of Germany's security seemed patently absurd. Poland provided an even greater stumbling-block, reluctant as she was to range herself with Lithuania and Czechoslovakia (against whom Poland had territorial claims outstanding) and disinclined to believe in any real Soviet change of heart. In December 1934 Litvinov and Laval recorded the determination of their respective governments to persevere with negotiations for an Eastern Pact until 'the uselessness of pursuing them further' had become apparent;[45] such 'uselessness' did indeed become apparent, and early in 1935 Laval signified to the Soviet Union and Czechoslovakia that France would engage upon a scheme of mutual assistance without the participation of Germany and Poland.[46] The first two months of 1935 were taken up with a number of separate manœuvres; France and Great Britain attempted to arrive at agreement directly with Germany, an element of which concerned discussion of a Western 'air pact'. On 20th February, the Soviet reply to the London negotiations emphasised that regional pacts organised for mutual assistance were also the Russian aim, for the whole programme for disarmament or limitation of armaments had failed; the Soviet government was interested in a security scheme working 'in its entirety' and not merely for Western Europe.[47] In Warsaw, Göring was holding some strange conversations, being 'very outspoken' to say the least, suggesting 'far-reaching plans' which seemed to imply an anti-Russian alliance and a joint attack on the Soviet Union — Poland taking the Ukraine and Germany North-western Russia.[48] Before calling on Marshal Piłsudski, Göring was tactfully constrained to be less 'over-definite' in his suggestions, but this did not prevent the point of a joint Polish-German attack being raised by the German visitor.[49] Colonel Beck, in effective control of Polish external policy, had also pushed the Eastern Pact aside, partly out of mistrust of Russia, and partly because Poland could not be considered as a guarantor of the Czechoslovak frontiers.

Tukhachevsky's article, therefore, came out in the critical month of March, 1935, at a time when the 'consistency' which Molotov had demanded in January of the Soviet Union's proto-allies seemed to be not a little doubtful, although some clarification of the situation had been obtained from the visit of Mr Anthony Eden to Moscow at the end of March, where he was received by Stalin, Molotov and Litvinov. It was at this time also that certain limited Franco-Soviet military exchanges had been and were taking place, with — according to a German military estimate — some forty French officers attached to Soviet aviation, armoured and infantry units. Their role was to prise the Russians away from the rigidity of approach (*Schematismus*), to assist with modernisation and to instruct in tactics uninhibited by over-rigidity. By the same token, some forty Red Army infantry and artillery officers were despatched to France, but this German source reported a Soviet grievance at being unable to make close acquaintance with French mechanised and motorised units.[50] As the hopes for a general scheme of security for Europe crumbled away, the conclusion of a bilateral Franco-Soviet agreement seemed imminent. On 29th April, *Pravda* published a denial of reports of Franco-Soviet disagreement over the 'automatic character' of the assistance provided for in the proposed pact. The basis was to be a decision of the Council of the League and conformity with Locarno in settling the operation of mutual assistance. The difficulty lay in finding 'appropriate formulas'. The Soviet Government desired complete reciprocity in this assistance and required the adoption of a form which would not direct it 'at any one particular party'. Moreover, any obligations had to be defined well in advance.[51] On 2nd May, the Franco-Soviet Pact of Mutual Assistance was signed, but there remained the question of ratification and 'appropriate formulas'. Article 2 of the pact spoke of immediate assistance if the USSR, and reciprocally France, became the victim of unprovoked attack.[52] On 16th May a Soviet-Czechoslovak mutual assistance pact was signed, this being dependent on French assistance to the victim of attack for the provisions of mutual assistance to come into operation. The proviso about the indispensability of French help implied at least that the Soviet Union would not find itself at war with Germany while France held back. Nor was French opinion oblivious to the danger of being dragged into a war by virtue of Russian entanglements in the Far East. The politics of the Eastern Pact, in the swiftly considered opinion of Colonel Beck, amounted to nothing more than pushing the smaller states into the orbit of Russia, to Litvinov posing as the 'innocent lamb' of Geneva, and reviving the pre-1914 traditions of Sazonov and Izvolsky. Above all, it remained to give the Franco-Soviet pact teeth, a matter which required a definite effort at military co-ordination. It was with this eventuality, as well as with problems based upon their own calculation, that the Soviet command appeared to have to reckon.

* * * *

Trotsky observed that 1935 was for the Red Army also 'a kind of twofold State revolution'[53]; it involved both the position of the command staff and the further advance to a large standing army, resulting in the eclipse of the militia system. The real revolution was the progressive normalisation of the Soviet military establishment, which resulted in the Red Army being brought into line with other European armies, conventionalised to a point where militarism seemed to be triumphant over Socialism. This could not fail to have pronounced effects on the status and prestige of the command. For many years half an army had been better than none, and a great deal had been accomplished with this reduced establishment. But the serious business of making ready for war, which included a substantial measure of re-armament and re-equipping, could not be effected by half-measures alone. The military problem was, as Tukhachevsky had stated, 'a big one' and its core the provision of effective command. To that end, the re-shuffle of March 1935 among the high command was directed, to a concentration of command effectiveness. The position of Yegorov was simplified, and the Staff invested with a direct responsibility for Red Army combat training. This department (*Boevaya podgotovka*) was run by Sedyakin, a close associate of Tukhachevsky (he had accompanied Tukhachevsky on the trip to Germany in 1932); under the new scheme Sedyakin joined Mezheninov and Levichev as deputies to Yegorov. German military observers took this re-arrangement as a sign that the Tukhachevsky-Sedyakin combination, already distinguished by their growing inclination for things French, could take over if necessary from Yegorov at the Staff.[54] The Red Army Administration, which had previously incorporated the training departments, was wound up, and in its place Feldman took over the Command Staff Administration. The *VVS* Inspectorate was also placed under the direct control of Voroshilov and thus occupied a position analogous to the command of a Military District, in its direct subordination. While involving no substantial modification in the existing chain of command, the streamlining was taken one step further.

In the summer of 1935 military preparations took on even greater intensity. To set up a large standing army and dispense with the militia system was an obvious method in increasing the efficiency of the Red Army, but it meant finding an adequate system for the preparation of trained reserves. The territorial-militia system, cumbersome and slow to develop any level of real efficiency, had nevertheless served this purpose as well as might be expected. It would not, however, provide for the wholesale propagation of a minimum of military training throughout society at large, and its existence implied that there would be time enough to mobilise a substantial force behind the thin cadre screen. Tukhachevsky patently no longer subscribed to this idea. By way of replacement to the militia, *Osoaviakhim* was overhauled to make it into an effective training organisation linked directly with the duties and commitments of the Red Army. On 8th August, 1935, a decree, signed by Stalin and Chubar, went out under confidential cover; the decree criticised the present heads of *Osoaviakhim* (R. P. Eideman held chief responsibility) for wasting their energy in all kinds of assorted activity, for having produced what amounted to a 'bureaucratic, blustering' organisation, and for shortcomings in training Soviet youth in the pre-call up period. From now on, greater attention was to be paid to pre-military training, to assisting reserve officers to keep in touch with military affairs without taking them away from production, to developing mass aviation sports, mass training in civil defence, mass markmanship, naval training, and to training short-wave radio amateurs.[55]. *Osoaviakhim* would be operated in future by a centralised command group, with its praesidium in possession of special administrative sections dealing with aviation, military training, civil defence and defence against chemical warfare, organisation for mass work and an administrative-economic section dealing with *Osoaviakhim* affairs. A ceiling of 25,000 paid workers was set for *Osoaviakhim* as a whole in the Soviet Union.[56] The Party, which was expected to assist on some scale with the work of *Osoaviakhim*, would itself be assisted by the *Komsomol* and trade-unions. The Defence Commissariat was instructed to increase its assistance to *Osoaviakhim*, to pay particular attention to raising the level of the cadres in the organisation, and to have district and unit commanders raise the standard of instruction and degree of control. Parachutes were to be provided on a larger scale. The *NKVD* was asked to look into the matter of easing restrictions on *Osoaviakhim* members and Party-*Komsomol* individuals possessing small-arms.

The Red Army, expanding all the while and climbing above the 940,000 ceiling so lately fixed, amounted in 1935 to 23 rifle corps (the corps being the largest peace-time formation in the Red Army), 90 rifle divisions,* 4 cavalry corps, 16 cavalry divisions, and 6 independent cavalry brigades, and 8 artillery brigades of the Main Reserve. The artillery strength consisted of some 100 light artillery regiments and between 30–60 heavy artillery regiments. The 20–30 engineer battalions consisted of 84 independent companies, 21 independent squadrons and 11 bridging battalions. Three independent Chemical Warfare Regiments were located on the western frontier, and 11 independent chemical warfare battalions were also organised for an arm upon which the Soviet command placed the greatest importance, not only because it was relatively inexpensive, but also it seemed to combine this advantage with that of considerable effectiveness.[57] In addition, the Red Army had substantial armoured forces, organised along the singular lines of mechanised brigades and motor-mechanised units, with tank brigades also. The precise strength of the Soviet tank-park in 1935 is difficult to ascertain, and contemporary estimates ranged from 3,000 to 10,000.[58] The The mechanised brigade, the appointed role of which concerned either the conduct of independent operations or co-operation with infantry or cavalry divisions for break-through or mobile operations, was made up of three tank battalions (32 tanks to a battalion), one light-tank battalion and a machine-gun battalion with motorised infantry. The motor-mechanised brigade substituted an extra machine-gun battalion for the loss of a tank

* Of which more than half were still on a territorial basis. The total infantry strength is given as 263 regiments of 790 battalions in *League of Nations Armaments Handbook*, Vol. 11, 1935, p. 825.

battalion. The mechanised brigades employed the *BT* type machines almost exclusively (apart from reconnaissance tanks), while the tank brigades (made up of four tank battalions with a total of 128 tanks) utilised the T–28. In addition also to these forces, since 1934 intensive training had been carried on with parachute troops, organised into air-landing units and used as such in the 1935 manœuvres in the Kiev and Belorussian Military Districts.

Motorisation, as well as mechanisation, was the second great preoccupation of the Soviet command. By the summer of 1935 (at which time Guderian supplied a provisional figure of 100,000 military lorries and 150,000 tractors for the Red Army), it was estimated that one-third of the corps artillery had been motorised, one half of the anti-aircraft artillery, and the heavy artillery of the Main Reserve also put on wheels. Three rifle divisions had been fully motorised, together with seven of the rifle divisions assigned to frontier defence. Reconnaissance and engineer units were partly motorised. Signal troops were in the process of being motorised, a process which was not fully complete until the beginning of the Third Five-Year Plan. Together with the development of Soviet aviation used for the support of ground forces, the Soviet command was beginning to have the outlines of a formidable weapon at its disposal. Already some indications had been given of the manner in which they intended to use it, and new *Field Service Regulations* were in preparation. The form of combat envisaged was reflected in the structure of the Red Army; it was assumed to be a war of aircraft and armoured forces, together with motor-mechanised units and special cavalry shock units, based on large masses of infantry and cavalry with motorised units attached. The role of artillery was heavily stressed (for the defensive, it was to be artillery fire-power and the infantry which would provide the fundamental basis). Already in 1933, the idea of echeloning in great depth had been adopted as a cardinal principle, and the picture of probable combat which emerged envisaged a series of waves — assault (with air support), break-through and support, followed by the slower moving infantry mass and the reserves. The artillery (ground and 'aerial') would open up the path for the tanks, which in turn facilitated passage for the infantry. If the whole could be summed up briefly, then all turned upon fire-power and mobility. To possess the mobility of aviation and mechanised troops and tanks was one thing, but to utilise it — 'to be able to adjust ourselves to a new level' — was, in the sober words of Tukhachevsky, 'not so simple'.

The Red Army possessed no complete monopoly of force, for Stalin had also invested the *NKVD* with the right to maintain a private army, organised on military lines. Under the command of Mikhail Frinovskii, the *NKVD* military forces were composed of rifle and cavalry forces (organised on divisional lines), mechanised units and a force of aircraft. With an expanding strength (which topped the 150,000 mark in 1936), the *NKVD* was in possession of the instruments of force under its own command, as well as militia (police) and frontier troops. Convoy or guard duty troops came under *NKVD* command, as well as railway troops used to secure the lines of communication. Such a force was in every sense the Praetorian Guard of the ruling group and in the last resort of Stalin himself. No *NKVD* military units were integrated as such with the Red Army, nor were the same units designed for use on the battle-field as first-line combat troops. Their purpose remained purely internal and repressive in the literal sense of the word. Almost invariably relations between Red Army and *NKVD* units were bad.

While the repressive and punitive capacities of the *NKVD* were undoubtedly growing and being all the more vigorously applied as the purge touched off by Kirov's assassination gathered a fearsome momentum, almost by a law of inverse proportion the latter half of 1935 saw enormous increase in the prestige and well-being of the high command and the officer corps of the Soviet armed forces. The *Politburo* sanctioned substantial concessions to the military, who seemed thereby to be set off in a world segregated from the havoc being wreaked by the *NKVD*. After the Kirov murder, over a hundred 'counter-revolutionaries' who had been arrested before the murder, were shot on the spot. After this 'demonstrative massacre',[59] the terror-machine swung first against the leftist elements, nullifying their restoration to limited grace by the trials of Zinoviev and L. B. Kamenev, first in January and then in July 1935, on charges of plotting against the life of Kirov and of Stalin. Yet, while showing signs of a certain premeditation and even planning, the purge had not yet slipped down the slope into widespread irrationality, into killing and denunciation deriving almost entirely from a collective psychosis of terror and intimidation. What is to be observed at this stage, however, is the significant lack of meaning which legal forms and restraints (over which a certain optimism had been raised in the summer of 1934) had undergone. While political and social cohesions were being broken open and prised apart, the Red Army command was presented with the opportunity to cement itself formally into a new hierarchy along more orthodox lines.

In September the Red Army Staff was re-named the General Staff of the Workers-Peasants Red Army.[60] On the same day as that announcement, 22nd, a decree prescribed the introduction of formal distinctions and marks of rank in the Red Army — lieutenant, senior lieutenant, captain, major, colonel, brigade commander (*kombrig*), corps commander (*komkor*), army commander 1st and 2nd grade (*Komandarm* I–II), with Marshal of the Soviet Union becoming the new and most senior rank. The title of 'General' was, as yet, still eschewed by the *Politburo*. Red Army other ranks were to be distinguished by 'Red Army man' (private), section commander, junior platoon commander and senior (sergeant).[61] On 20th November, 1935, a *TsIK* decree conferred upon Budenny, Voroshilov, Yegorov, Blyukher and Tukhachevsky the rank of Marshal of the Soviet Union. The rank of army commander 1st grade was conferred upon the commanders of the Moscow, Leningrad, Belorussian and Ukrainian Military Districts; ten senior commanders and the commanders of five other military districts, the head of the Military Academy (A. I. Kork at this time) and the head of the *VVS* (Alksnis) were given the rank of army commander 2nd grade. Senior ranks for the Political Administration were also introduced, with 15 senior military commissars (the heads of the political departments of military districts) being confirmed in the rank of Army Commissar 2nd grade. Lev Aronstam, head of the political administration of the Far Eastern forces, was similarly included in the appointments to army commissar 2nd grade. Also among the political administration appointments had been three of the naval side — A. S. Grishin, political deputy to the Baltic Fleet commander, G. Gugin of the Black Sea Fleet and G. S. Okunev of the Far Eastern Fleet. Naval command ranks were introduced, with 1st and 2nd grade categories of the senior rank *Flagman* (Flag-officer), 'Admiral' being as yet avoided; Galler (Baltic Fleet commander) and Koshchanov (Black Sea Fleet commander) were appointed Flag-officers 2nd grade, while Kuznetsov, commander of the cruiser *Chervonaya Ukraina*, was promoted to Captain 1st grade. Orlov remained senior naval commander, and Viktorov, Far Eastern Fleet commander, was raised to flag rank. Viktorov represented a somewhat odd case. Until 1921 commander of the Baltic Fleet, in 1924 he had been relieved of all command duties as a consequence of his wife being involved in an espionage case. A submarine specialist, known as a very capable officer, Viktorov had quite restored his fortunes in the Far East.[62]

Not only did the September decree provide for the new table of ranks, but it conferred upon the middle grade and senior command levels a privilege which apparently set the officer corps completely apart from the rest of Soviet society. Immunity from arrest by civil authorities, without the special dispensation of the Defence Commissar himself, was granted to all but the junior officers of the Red Army. Conspicuous attention was paid to improving the material lot of the Red Army commander, including living accommodation, special privileges and financial benefits — changes by no means premature, for the officer corps as a whole had been the loser economically, especially during the 1920's. Prestige and pay were now both falling into the ready grasp of the officer corps, a fillip not only to the presently serving officers, but an inducement to the new officers in the making. The rapid expansion of the armed forces increased the need for officers. As Voroshilov's figures showed, the officer corps prior to the expansion was almost exclusively a veteran body at its higher levels. The last great transfusion of personnel had been during the period of the 'militarising' of the commissars, when political staff had changed over to command duties. And over the ubiquitous commissars, continual troubles were ever in the making. During the early years of the decade, while political subjects had been introduced most extensively into the training courses for commanders, a marked effort had been made to raise the level of the military skill of the commissar, some of whom in 1932 were completely lacking in any formal military education. From March 1932 political workers of this type were obliged to pass the exams of the normal military school. The demands of hard and exacting military training in the new methods and with the new techniques put the political worker in an inferior position to the commander, who was not slow to capitalise in a number of cases on this advantage. By way of asserting themselves, senior commanders began to demand the removal of political deputies who were not to their taste.[63] In a number of cases they were successful. While these social and professional concessions were no doubt made in the interests of increasing the all-round efficiency of the army, and while the command may have been permitted to become more ostentatiously professional, there was no licence for it to become political, in the sense of taking sides. One of the striking features of the period 1930–5 is the absence of any proven organised discontent which strove to become politically effective. Throughout the bitter and terrible years of 1930–3, Stalin had not had to deal with a military opposition, although that is not to suppose that he found the command pliant and in any way submissive. Watched it certainly was, with a degree of interest almost too intense, if the Primakov case is any test. In the face of much-increased military dangers, *raison d'état* prompted effective measures to establish the armed forces on the solid foundations of professionalism and not a collection of political shibboleths. Secret policemen and military commissars alone could not fight the war which appeared to be a danger steadily on the increase. In one sense, the decree of 22nd September had undone ten years of work to keep the officer corps from developing too avid a sense of *esprit de corps*. The process was deliberately reversed, but the gain of military effectiveness had to be set against the possibility of developing over-mighty military subjects. Nothing of this was new to the Soviet regime. For the moment, it appeared that Stalin was prepared to rely upon his command. It was a choice perforce prescribed, for in 1935 there existed no real alternative.

* * * *

Since the end of the Civil War, the Soviet Union had clung, at times almost desperately, to a strategy which augmented her military strength by an attempt at military coalition, or in a cruder form, collusion. The security of the western frontiers had been founded in the division of military labours between Germany and the Soviet Union. Although benevolent feelings toward the German Army had been by no means entirely dissipated among sections of the Soviet military command, and a cleavage of sorts existed as a consequence, making military sense of the *rapprochement* with France was clustered about with difficulty. Stalin had not hidden from Laval, when the latter was in Moscow in May, that a military convention between France and the Soviet Union would be a desirable thing.[64] Laval telegraphed from Moscow that Stalin had agreed with him in looking on the Franco-Soviet pact as a pacific instrument, but in the event of 'peace breaking down', then the arrangement might be analogical to an alliance; the black side must be borne in mind, and it was time to fix certain technical aspects so that they might have full effect. Laval agreed to this suggestion, but only on the condition that a Soviet-Czech agreement was concluded.[65] Reynaud charges Laval with having made of the Pact a dead letter from the very beginning, and thereafter seizing every pretext to complete this nullification. It had been agreed in Moscow that conversations between the French and Soviet Staffs would be opened after a short delay. The delay lengthened. Laval's manœuvres were designed, in neutralising the pact, to prevent placing the issue of peace in Stalin's hands.[66] The agreement was to be understood, not as the Russians appeared to envisage it in terms of automatic commitment and a step to a military convention (operating defensively on the lines of the 1892 convention), but in more formal terms. The condition stipulated by Laval as a necessity to Franco-Soviet military talks — a Soviet-Czech agreement — was speedily forthcoming and with equal speed ratified. Close contact ensued. Although lacking a common Soviet-Czech frontier, the leap which Soviet military forces could make would be with their aviation. In the late summer of 1935 Shaposhnikov travelled to attend the manœuvres of the Czech Army held in Western Slovakia. French, Italian and Czech military observers attended the autumn manœuvres of the Red Army. General Loiseau, who headed the French military mission, was reported in *Krasnaya Zvezda* for 17th September, 1935, as having passed extraordinarily favourable comments on the Soviet tank park, part of which he had seen exercising during the manœuvres of the Kiev Military District, Yakir's command.[67] It appears that the French General was genuinely impressed by what he saw.

To German eyes, Tukhachevsky showed himself to be pronouncedly pro-French. In his first visit to a German house in Moscow since the collaboration had been ended, Tukhachevsky let it be known that General

Köstring, the new German Military Attaché in Moscow (Köstring was merely taking up where he had earlier left off), would be warmly welcomed in Red Army circles. Even at this stage, Tukhachevsky observed, there was great affection for the German Army among Red Army officers — and the German Army was to be complimented on its great progress. Tukhachevsky would not be gainsaid, adding that Germany had everything necessary — a martial spirit, ability, the best technical industry and a capacity to organise. The Red Army could only make slow progress, for *everything* had to be fashioned anew. But if it came to war between Germany and the Soviet Union, Germany would not be meeting the old Russia — the Red Army had learned much and laboured mightily. If only, added Tukhachevsky, both countries enjoyed their friendship and political relations as in the past, they could dictate peace to the world. And yet another but — 'We are Communists and you have need not to forget that we must and will remain Communist.' However, if Germany adopted a different position, nothing need stand in the way of further Soviet-German collaboration. Tukhachevsky described himself as a mere soldier, knowing nothing of politics, but he could not help hoping that Germany and the Soviet Union 'can find themselves again'.[68] From a conversation larded with hints, threats and promises, from a whole collection of 'ifs' and 'ands', this October talk with Tukhachevsky was interpreted in terms of his pro-French orientation. Whatever the personal impression made, there is little doubt that Tukhachevsky was strewing official hints that the Soviet Union would willingly resume relations with Germany, subject to certain conditions. At a November reception in Moscow, German military observers again noted Tukhachevsky's pro-French attitude, but they could not claim that they were ignored.[69]

If Tukhachevsky had veered to a pro-French position, his opposite numbers in France were not noticeably pro-Soviet. Since July 1935 Potemkin, Soviet Ambassador in Paris, had been pressing Fabry for a decision about the military convention. Potemkin brought specific assurances that Moscow was extremely desirous of adhering to and implementing such a convention. Since Laval had slipped out of automatic commitments in the Pact, it was less likely that 'l'automatisme brutal' of a military convention — even expressly defensive — would be acceptable.[70] Observing the trend to procrastination, Potemkin terminated his second talk with Fabry by putting a blunt question — 'Why do you not want a clear military agreement with us?' Fabry countered this and Potemkin's rider that the French had military compacts with other powers (the Rumanians he expressly cited), by insisting that the French government desired peace, while the Soviet government appeared to regard a conflagration in Europe as something, if not desirable, then at least inevitable. Potemkin waved away the fear of war as such, and with a statement compounded of the lugubrious and the prophetic, remarked that the Russia of the Soviets had emerged from the last war — Soviet Europe would emerge from the next.[71] While these conversations bear some witness to the fact that Stalin viewed the potentialities of the Franco-Soviet pact with considerable seriousness, but was willing to take it seriously only if it returned proper dividends, enthusiasm among the French military command was quickly waning. General Maurin, Minister of War, had expressed the opinion that the pact was devoid of military interest, even at the moment of its signing.[72] In Warsaw, the Franco-Soviet Pact had exploded with an impact hardly less ringing than in Berlin itself, but with the signal difference that any serious Franco-Soviet mutual and military assistance (the case, for example, of Russian aid to a France attacked by Germany) would mean inevitably Soviet passage through Poland. There were no Polish illusions on this score; Soviet troops in Poland meant 'passage' turning into permanent occupation.[73]

In the business of setting up a 'tentative encirclement' of Germany, no opportunity had been lost by Stalin in indicating a readiness to resume a friendly relationship with the new regime. Senior Soviet military leaders had talked 'off the cuff' and indeed on the cuff about the spirit of accommodation towards the German Army existing in the Red Army. The latest addition to these remarks had been made by Tukhachevsky, and in no sense could they be regarded as mere impromptu observations. Stalin may well have been under the impression that he had a strong card to play with the German generals, and his own would start the play. The Germans were invited to join the proposed Eastern Pact, while at the same time being pressed by the prospect of the Soviet Union making a real change of sides. If diplomacy and a little journalistic blackmail would not induce a softening of Hitler's hardened anti-Soviet heart, then the game could be intensified through manipulation of the by no means defunct economic ties linking Germany and the Soviet Union. Kandelaki and Friedrichson were handling the economic negotiations (which included proposed Soviet orders for military equipment) in Berlin.[74] For Stalin, the German grant of a 200 million gold mark credit came as proof that big business was indeed the ally of the Soviet Union, and this same ally would restrain Hitler from venturing his hand against the Russians. One of the intelligence reports coming to Artuzov, head of the *NKVD* Foreign Division, did make in the month of August 1935 a comprehensive but pessimistic survey of the question which Krivitsky asserts most troubled Stalin — the source and strength of forces in Germany advocating *rapprochement* with Russia. Artuzov, having presented the report, observed that it made no impact on Stalin's feeling that accord with Germany could be achieved.[75] In the not too distant future Stalin was to employ his official trade negotiator and private agent, David Kandelaki, to put this conviction to the test.

If the contacts with France were a form of re-insurance, there still remained the troubled situation on the Far Eastern frontiers. Tukhachevsky's statement in January 1935 about the separation of the potential fronts, the east from the west, was easier said than done, although double-tracking the Trans-Siberian went on at high speed. Blyukher's forces, assembled in barrack-towns and manning the first-line fixed defences, were growing to some 200,000. 14 rifle divisions, with strong cavalry and expanding mechanised support,* were at his disposal. At the end of 1934, Red Army troops again entered Outer Mongolia, and a force of some 50,000 men, officially the Mongolian People's Republic Army, stiffened up the extreme right flank of the Soviet positions facing the Japanese. A Frontier Defence Force, under control of the *NKVD*, added to the manpower resources, although they were not part of the military command as such. In a number of respects the Far Eastern army was a singular force, drastically but effectively hammered into shape by Blyukher and his staff. Blyukher apparently tolerated little interference by the political staff in what was strictly military business; according to one account, Aronstam, chief of the Political Administration, was not even a member of the Military Soviet of the Far Eastern Army, and a senior commissar who started insisting on his rights was speedily posted away at Blyukher's insistence.[76] Chief of Staff was M. V. Sangurskii (ranked as a corps commander), the 'little Asiatic' who had fought with Blyukher in the days of the South Urals Detachment during the Civil War. Kalmykov, commander of the Special (Kolkhoz) Corps, was evidently another Civil War associate of Blyukher; by all accounts a colourful character, Kalmykov was rivalled in flamboyancy only by another senior corps commander, Pashkovskii. Colourful his commanders may have been (and Blyukher himself was not a little addicted to private panache), but they were nevertheless tough, hard-bitten fighting commanders. The same applied to Lapin, commander of the aviation forces, who had begun his military career in the Civil War in Putna's 27th Division.[77]

Whatever the protests of the military at an act of appeasement, the sale of the Chinese Eastern Railway to the Japanese was finally put in hand and the transaction arranged in March 1935, after twenty-one months of negotiation. But in appraising the effect of the sale of the railway on the prospects for peace in the east, Litvinov turned down a proposal for a 'demilitarisation' which implied withdrawing forces from the frontier.[78] Blyukher's policy had been to man the frontiers and to prevent any dilution of population in the frontier areas, even to the extent of setting up a Jewish

* Estimated at 3 cavalry divisions, up to 950 aircraft and 900 tanks.

state Birobiyan, not far from Khabarovsk. To demilitarise put the Soviet forces at the mercy of the Japanese, who had been expanding the railway net of Manchuria northwards, thereby facilitating rapid concentration against the Soviet frontier. Anchored in their barrack towns, the bulk of the Soviet forces were clustered in three main masses: in the Maritime Provinces (5 rifle divisions, with cavalry),* the Trans-Baikal centred on Chita† (4 rifle divisions with cavalry) and the Amur valley (2 rifle divisions).[79] Mongol troops, stiffened with Red Army detachments, held the right flank. The striking feature of Blyukher's dispositions was that, although designed for defence, they placed him favourably for a concentric offensive driving from the east, north and west in a huge encircling movement. Strong forces would check a Japanese attempt on the Maritime Provinces; the equally powerful formations based about Chita would check an attempt at breaking into the Baikal region. The feverish railway construction on the Soviet side of the border was designed to facilitate rapid movement of troops to threatened sectors, as well as to ease the supply problem. The presence of cavalry, tanks and armoured cars implied that Blyukher would not be out-manœuvred if a mobile war developed on the plains to the west. And to fight in the air, besides the 'aerial artillery' being developed throughout the Red Army, a long-range bomber force could strike out against Japan itself. To the change in the situation the Japanese command did not long remain insensible.‡ By 1934 there were 144,100 men in the Kwantung Army (as compared with 64,900 in 1931); the air squadrons had increased to 15 (making a total of some 150 aircraft). A further 20,000 men and three squadrons joined the Japanese army in Manchuria in 1935.[80] The new plan of offensive operations envisaged the commitment of 24 out of 30 fully equipped divisions against the USSR. The battle in the air would be enormously important during the opening of the operations, which must be moved as rapidly as possible on to Soviet territory. Soviet bomber and submarine bases must be obliterated at the very outset. The main blow would be in an easterly direction, after the success of which a re-deployment would be designed to facilitate a drive on the Lake Baikal area.[81] There were signs in 1935 that the Soviet command was turning its full attention to securing the safety of the Trans-Baikal, at the same time putting on considerable pressure to secure the Soviet hold in Sinkiang,[82] a forward policy

* Reinforced to a total of at least 7 rifle divisions, with 650 tanks.

† At the end of 1935, what had been the original Far Eastern Army's jurisdiction (eastwards from Krasnoyarsk) was split at the Greater Hsingan Mountains, and Trans-Baikal MD (HQ Chita) set up.

‡ *Study of Strategical and Tactical Peculiarities of Far Eastern Russia . . .*, p. 39 also makes it clear that the Japanese General Staff was fully aware of the growing Soviet superiority in potential; in 1934 this was set at 40 divisions (against 31 Japanese), in 1937 at 50 against 22 Japanese.

with military overtones which passed into the active stage at the end of 1933. To set up a separate Trans-Baikal Military District, some of the western garrisons were detached from the Far Eastern Army to provide a nucleus. While that smacked of military logic, nevertheless it had the air of a precaution about it, for it put the 'gate of Siberia' out of the control of the already powerfully concentrated force under Blyukher.[83]

Supplementing the military activities and preparations, the Japanese made widespread use of agents and saboteurs, attempting to weaken and undermine the efficiency of the Soviet forces.[84] Nor were the military idle in probing Soviet defences. In May 1935 a mixed force of Japanese infantry and cavalry clashed with Soviet troops near Grodekovo. On 6th and 12th October there were more attacks.[85] To a Soviet suggestion of a mixed frontier commission to regulate matters, the Japanese made no response. In the middle of December, ten lorry loads of Japanese-Manchurian troops staged a local attack on the Outer Mongolian frontier. While in themselves isolated and on a very small scale, the danger was that a larger calamity might flare up out of such incidents; there was the possibility of blundering into war. The foundation of Soviet policy appears to have been to ensure that the maximum conditions should be established for localising any danger (the sale of the Chinese Eastern Railway was a massive illustration of this technique), while retaining enough military force to meet a full-scale Japanese attack, and under Blyukher so to dispose this force that a strong counter-offensive could be launched, which might mean striking the Japanese on an exposed flank. Viktorov's submarine force, committed to defensive tasks but also a threat to the sea communications of Japan with the mainland of Asia, had grown by the end of 1935 to a minimum of 45 boats, more than doubling the number available to him some two years ago.[86] Finally, the possession of a small but potent strategic bomber force, set apart from the front aviation for use tactically, invested the Soviet command in the Far East with a weapon which inspired a deal of Japanese respect. All the signs indicated the air warfare would play a vitally important role in any large-scale Soviet-Japanese clash.

For both the Russian and Japanese, extensive military operations presented a number of strategic peculiarities. If Blyukher had to maintain a state of immediate readiness on several critical sectors, as well as a constant frontier guard, in anticipation of the several ways in which a small or large scale war might begin, the Japanese could not prevent themselves being beset with the major difficulty of how to bring their operations to a decisive conclusion in view of the immensity of the territory upon which they would be engaged. Both armies had to look to their rear. To man the new industries intended to make Blyukher's forces independent of large-scale supplies from the west, a policy of economic concession had been applied to the Far East, in addition to the forced movement of population to increase the manpower resources.[87] The vital factor was the increase in transportation facilities, indispensable to supplying Blyukher not merely in the material sense but endowing him with increased facilities for putting into practice the surprise and mobility which were cardinal points of his doctrine. While the Japanese paid close attention to measures of 'political sabotage'[88] designed to disrupt Blyukher's rear, the Kwantung Army was obliged to look to the security of its own rear, which involved active consideration of the problem of China. At once withdrawing from Chiang Kai-shek's relentless anti-Communist offensives but advancing towards the rear of the Kwantung Army, Chinese Communist forces had been moving on their 'Long March' in the north-westerly direction, the gigantic strategic retreat which was bringing them into Northern Shensi late in 1935.[89] As Mao Tse-tung's battered and ragged Red troops moved north, the Japanese command intensified their penetration of the vital passage of Inner Mongolia; by the end of the year the Japanese had a tight grip on the provinces of Chahar and Hopei. This further advance was necessitated, from the Japanese point of view, in order to seal off the Chinese Communists moving into the north from the Russians who might move down from the south through Outer Mongolia.[90] The Japanese credited Stalin with a greater revolutionary boldness than appears to have been the case. Soviet strategic calculations for the security of their possessions in the Far East do not appear to have included any tangible connection with the badly-armed and poorly-fed Chinese Red Army men, led by the stubborn and independently minded Mao Tse-tung. Since *raison d'état* now ruled, it was with Nanking rather than northern Shensi that Stalin had entered into formal relations.[91]

At the end of 1935, as the Japanese strengthened their positions on the frontier of Outer Mongolia, military clashes had taken place, with a consequent rise in the temperature of Soviet-Japanese relations. From the Soviet side, the flare-up on the eastern frontier was represented, not so much as a direct threat to the security of the Far East, as a German-Japanese machination aimed at blocking the ratification of the Franco-Soviet Pact by giving substance to certain French misgivings that being embroiled in the Soviet Union's Far Eastern difficulties might be a direct result of the proposed Pact.[92] Gamelin had listened on 21st November to an exposition made by Laval of his policy; Laval had expressed his mistrust of the Pact — and the Russians — adding that he had taken out 'the most dangerous' parts of it.[93] If this was the mine with which Litvinov proposed to neutralise Hitler, then the fuse was being carefully but capably extracted. The military arrangements still lagged far behind even these questionable political cavortings, and without a military convention the Franco-Soviet Pact remained at best merely 'a Platonic gesture'. Faced with the prospect of assault from the west and east, the inescapable answer to the problem which in no way diminished was to maximise the efficiency of the Red Army, to prepare the country to withstand the shocks of war upon its fabric and its resources, to deepen in the west those defences which would absorb the first utterly destructive German echelon depicted with such startling accuracy by Tukhachevsky's article, and to harden in the east the military webs, spun out of railway tracks, which would enmesh the Japanese.

★ ★ ★ ★

Trotsky set the transformation of 1935 in the Red Army at a degree no less than a revolution. Coming from the creator of the Red Army, this was no mere purposeless exaggeration, but it was qualified by the statement that the Red Army had not been wholly immune to the 'process of degeneration' which marked the Soviet regime. These degenerations had found their 'most finished expression' in the armed forces. Certainly in spite of the reforms initiated in 1934, which appeared to give the military chiefs a greater autonomy, at the highest levels bureaucratism appeared to be winning over leadership as such. This situation was in no way different from that prevailing in other Soviet enterprises, but the danger of stultification in the military leadership carried with it enormous consequences. Tukhachevsky, in January 1935, insisted that the key to the problem was to encourage 'nerve', flexibility and daring. On the other hand, the purge of 1933–5 had been designed to bring, not flexibility into society, but a greater degree of conformity to a line dictated from above. Political controls were being tightened over the army, in pursuit of an objective in no particular way connected with improving the efficiency of the army as a combat instrument. But Stalin could no more afford to diminish the effort to bind the army politically into his regime, whatever the loss in military effectiveness, than could Trotsky himself during his rule over the Red Army. The great difference was the operation of this rule at the vitally important top levels; under Trotsky it had been a personal dictatorship of the military, under Stalin so far it had developed only bureaucratically. To step into personal dictatorship over the army, although it might be done with the Party, was set about with special difficulties.

Stalin could not pretend to himself that he was master of the new Marshals and army commanders. Voroshilov and Budenny were undoubtedly his men, almost his own creations, but two men were not the Soviet high command and officer corps. Tukhachevsky, the brain behind the modernisation and a legendary figure in his own right, owed nothing to Stalin. Grouped round Tukhachevsky were men of high talent also, his professional supporters and collaborators, equally far removed from being political creatures. Blyukher, another legend, was of singular independence of mind; he it was who is reported to have demanded of Stalin a slackening of the collectivisation else he refused to take any further responsibility for the defence of the Soviet Far East. Yegorov was a political nonentity, described by Lieutenant-General Sir Giffard Martel as 'a good figurehead';[94] his role appears to have been mainly that of co-ordinator, his admiration for the Germans genuine, and his talents limited rather sharply. In 1935 he was suitably rewarded for having backed Stalin, Voroshilov and Budenny against Tukhachevsky during the furious quarrels of 1920. Further down the scale the mass of commanders were Civil War veterans, their mass being leavened only slightly as yet by the products of the military academies. The massive expansion of the Red Army was to create a new pressure, that of the new cadres upon the old. But in 1935 Stalin had little or no choice of cadres.

The striking feature of the military innovations of 1935 is that they produced the very reverse of what the purges had accomplished during 1933–5 in the state as a whole. This political cautery had been applied to bring the Party into closer alignment with Stalin's rule and leadership. The resistance to the economic programmes initiated under Stalin had been ground down, a whole section of the peasantry politically and economically annihilated, supporters of the former Opposition cowed into acquiescence.[95] The Kirov murder had been used to smash up the Leftists of the Opposition, to bring the leaders to trials momentarily secret. The old intellectuals and administrators were broken up and scattered from influence and position, and in this way the path was opened up to the cadres reared under Stalin. With the settling of rank and privilege on the Red Army, Navy and Air Force command staff, quite the opposite appeared to be happening. There had been little interference with the Party members of the armed forces, not in one but in two purges. The army was set in a world apart, divided by that apparently magic line of immunity from arrest. The senior and middle grades of command were consolidated and hardened with rank, professionalised and conventionalised very markedly.

On the surface, therefore, towards the close of 1935 the relations between Stalin and his military command, between the Army and the Party, seemed to be bereft of major tensions. If Tukhachevsky and his collaborators were becoming increasingly pro-French, such a disposition was not out of place with the current emphasis on collective security and collaboration with the West. There may have been the origins of a deep division between a section of the army command which looked upon alliance with the French as an insurance against German military attack, and Stalin who considered it more a means to coerce Hitler into agreement with him, but there were virtually no signs of this in 1935. Tukhachevsky's talk with his German hosts in 1935 had been curiously ambiguous, and in all a mixture of threat, warning, cajolement and even nostalgia. The most striking feature of the difference of the military approach, if Tukhachevsky's article might be taken as an expression of that, and the political, in which the door to accommodation with Germany was left open, consisted of the realistic appraisal by the military of the threat already in being. In no sense did Tukhachevsky minimise the military danger from Germany; the military core of his argument was sensible and cool, his interpretation of the timing and the present intentions of the German leadership somewhat exaggerated. If Krivitsky is correct in his report on Stalin's reception of the *NKVD* Intelligence on the attitude of Hitler in the summer of 1935, then it is some proof that Stalin failed completely to understand the real significance of the Nazi regime.[96]

In his October conversation Tukhachevsky had not failed to threaten. The threat was not altogether an idle one. A gigantic effort was going into Soviet aviation, the Second Five-Year Plan envisaging the creation of 62 air regiments, and the capacity to put 5,000 machines into front-line service.[97] It was too early to speak of an effective Russian autarky in armaments, but this was the avowed aim.[98] The transportation situation remained, nevertheless, a marked weak spot, accounting for Tukhachevsky's serious reservation about the feasibility of moving large bodies of troops from front to front. Commissar for Communications Lazar Kaganovich had revealed that in 1934 the Soviet railways suffered 62,000 accidents involving damage to 7,000 locomotives. During the first two months of 1935 the accident rate had gone on rising. By the end of the year the *NKVD* had taken over the running of the railway troops and the security supervision of railway operations. The re-disposition of the troops in European Russia was being prepared in order to minimise the effects of deficient rail links and inefficient operation on the operational employment of the Red Army. Some of the fuel supplies for the mechanised units would be moved by road (although that was not a recognition of the superiority of the Russian road, but to relieve congestion). The increase in manpower, the acquisition of more modern weapons, the strengthening of aviation, further progress in heavy industry and the attempt to screw up the efficiency of the transportation system, plus the energetic efforts of the command were making of the Soviet armed forces at the close of 1935 'a dangerous opponent'.[99] It remained to be seen how and at what point Stalin and his *NKVD* officers would construe this as applying to themselves.

CHAPTER THIRTEEN

Plots and Counter-plots

To have maintained the loyalty of the army to the regime during the years of forced collectivisation and increasing political repression was no mean achievement. Much of the credit for such a feat must go to Gamarnik as head of the Political Administration. As for the senior military commanders, whatever the dissatisfactions and anxieties which existed amongst them as a result of Stalin's policies, no degree of dissaffection had developed which rendered the army totally unreliable from Stalin's point of view. Singular precautions had been taken against such an eventuality. The army was wedged in the vice of the Party and the *NKVD*. Stalin had evidently not failed to take his own special measures to supervise the loyalty of the high command. As early as 1932 he introduced one of his own picked agents, Tairov, into Voroshilov's Commissariat with the mission of checking on the reliability of senior officers, Voroshilov included.[1] Strict centralised control and constant attention to inducing political loyalty at all levels appeared to have produced the desired results, to judge by the immunity enjoyed by the armed forces during two successive purges. It seemed as if there were two separate policies applied to military and civilian Communists; the recent concession of immunity from arrest granted to officers widened the divergence of the laws of the Medes and the Persians, which had hitherto been tacit. Conscious of its growing prestige and basking in privileges newly conferred, the command and the army seemed to be girding itself for a war which loomed ahead, indeterminate in time but unavoidable in circumstance. In his report to the Central Executive Committee (of which he had been a member since 1930) Tukhachevsky once again in January, 1936, pointed with the finger of urgency to the rate of German military expansion. The facts and figures which he used to substantiate his argument about the *Drang nach Osten* were ridiculed as 'sheer fantasy' by the German Military Attaché in Moscow.[2] Certainly Tukhachevsky produced figures of a German military effort (in tank production, for example) which invested this potential enemy with formidable and even terrifying strength. This was professional admiration of the *Wehrmacht*, to which substantial sections of the Soviet military command had been addicted and even conditioned, operating in reverse, producing a form of mesmerism which could not be lightly shaken off. Whatever his exaggerations, there seemed to be little doubt that Tukhachevsky was in earnest about his warnings over German military strength.

Proof that the military threat, which the Soviet command supposed to be stemming from Germany, was not taken lightly beyond the public platform lay in the re-disposition of Soviet troops in European Russia. In order to minimise the difficulties which faulty transportation might impose, supply dumps were gradually built up, in a manner not dissimilar to that employed by Blyukher's forces. Stronger forces were moved up to the frontiers, and 90 per cent of the active troops put on a war-footing. Already the Red Army consisted of over 70 per cent cadre as opposed to militia troops. A factor of great importance was effective mobilisation of the reserves; an estimate made by German Intelligence of Soviet improvements in this field pointed to the comparison with the year 1931, when after an eight-week mobilisation period the Red Army Staff could reckon on a coefficient of expansion only in the region of ·6. The Russians aimed at increasing this to 3–4, and had even claimed in 1933 that it had reached the figure 6.[3] In the Leningrad, Belorussian, and Kiev Military Districts (and including the Moscow Military District as reserve), there were not less than 40 rifle divisions and not less than 17 cavalry divisions. The two great concentrations of motor-mechanised forces were located in the Belorussian and Kiev Military Districts. With the Kharkov and North Caucasus Military Districts as a reserve for the potential South-western Front, a further 12 rifle divisions could be added to the regular forces ready for immediate use, favoured also with a greater ease of communications. Such a distribution of Soviet ground forces left no doubt that the West occupied first place as the decisive front, for little more than 10 per cent of the available regular rifle divisions and only a fraction of the motor-mechanised troops were located in the Far East, and for the moment few, if any of the 15–16 new rifle divisions in the process of being raised were destined for Blyukher's command. In addition to the formidable problems of supply which presented themselves, the presence of large forces of tanks and aircraft raised severe problems of technical maintenance. As early as 1933 a Soviet calculation of the man-power requirement to keep one aircraft serviced and fully operational (as well as to provide a replacement) stipulated 125 men, and for one armoured fighting vehicle 70,[4] which was approximately double the Western European equivalents. With a tank force in excess of 4,000 and a front-line air-strength set at a minimum of 5,000 machines, the technical factor and the requirement in technical skills reached major proportions. Just how seriously this could affect the combat performance of the Red Army was to be shown with an unnerving clarity during the autumn manœuvres. Mechanised agriculture, with its tractors and lorries, provided a reserve of tank drivers and mechanics, but this did not remove the necessity for the Red Army turning itself into a technical as well as a tactical training school.[5]

Technical superiority, however, as an end in itself had been specifically rejected along with the idea of an élite army, highly professionalised and separated quite distinctly from the mass of society. The predominant feature of military organisation remained as ever the mass army, into which a growing volume of armament was constantly poured. One of the main characteristics of Tukhachevsky's work was to raise the armament norms to the maximum with respect to aircraft, tanks and artillery. A second was to provide a set of tactical forms which would enable this mass of men and equipment to be used to the greatest effect. In spite of the obvious attempts of the Soviet command to devise something consciously unique as well as effective in military matters, retention of the mass, even with the leavening of the mobile force within it, suggested an adherence to the traditional Russian method of trundling its vast assemblies of men on to the battlefield. The steam-roller was given a more powerful engine and a greater capacity to crush. During this phase of intensive development, what emerged to all effects was not so much a unique army employing the most original of tactics, but a curious blend of the old with the new. In spite of his opinion that trenches were a thing of the past and out of harmony with the doctrinal point that positional warfare was wherever possible to be avoided, fixed fortifications and 'defence belts' formed a part of the defence plan which was evolved under Tukhachevsky. A serious start had been made in 1932–3 with setting up a series of fortified positions in the north, and what was to be labelled 'the Stalin line' was begun not long afterwards, the construction work being directed by Pivovarov.[6] By no means a line, even in the geographic sense, the system incorporated 'deep defensive zones'[7] with forward obstacles and tank-traps, as well as mine-fields and gun-emplacements. Block-houses of varying size and tank-shelters were also set up, the whole providing a defence position in depth — above all, an anti-tank defence based on 'anti-tank zones' (*protivotankovye raiony*). In the Far East Blyukher also waited behind his fixed defences, in places three miles deep and based also on dispersed fortified points,* although these might be classified more as frontier defences in a more limited sense.

* There were also the special 'fortified districts' (*ukreplennye raiony*: abbreviated UR). Para. 258 of *PU-36* defined the function of the URs as (*i*) securing important economic, political and strategic points or districts (*ii*) securing space for deployment and manœuvre (*iii*) covering the flanks of formations operating along the line of the main blow. Each UR was designated with a number. URs were established in the Southern Ussuri at Leninskoe Blagoveshchensk and Borzya-Duariya. The frontier defences were made up of permanent, disappearing and dummy fire-points.

There appeared to be no intention, however, of locking up the Red Army behind fortified walls. The movement of troops towards the frontier districts and the concentration of strong motor-mechanised forces in the three main frontier regions suggested that the Soviet command took the battle for the frontiers, should it develop, very seriously and would be committed from the outset to active offensive operations. While the offensive was to be mounted from depth, the same principle was applied to defence, the depth of which was designed to rob the tank of its full effectiveness, as well as to facilitate the adoption of 'anti-tank zones' and the use of mobile anti-tank reserves. At the heart of everything lay the insistence on fire-power, supplied by an ever-growing strength in artillery, that arm in which the Russians had a tradition of excellence. By a terrible irony, it had been German artillery which had shattered the Russian infantry during the World War, a lesson which the commanders of the Red Army took entirely to heart. Tactical aviation was conceived of primarily as an extension to ground artillery by lifting the gun-platform into the air. Great attention was paid to supplying a force of heavy artillery; by the end of 1933, the Artillery Reserve of the Supreme Command (*ARGK*) was composed of 55·2 per cent heavy artillery. In addition, super heavy artillery (*artilleriya bol'shoi moshchnosti*) — the 152-mm gun and the 203-mm howitzer — made up a further 11 per cent of the total. A similar effort was made to put the heavy guns on wheels (or caterpillar tracks), so that the 'non-stop offensive' might be supported by an artillery which could keep pace with it.

Two forms of supplying the Red Army with its artillery were adopted. The first consisted of the modernisation of older weapons, the second of a planned design and construction policy. Under the modernisation programme, the 76-mm field gun (standard to divisional artillery) was modified from the original Type 1902 to become Type 1902/1930. Sidorenko's innovation consisted largely of increasing the barrel length to 40 calibres and thereby the range from 8,500 metres to 13,290. The 122-mm howitzer (corps artillery) was similarly modernised and designated Type 1910/1930, as was the 107-mm gun. The 152-mm field piece (Artillery Reserve) was a product of modernisation, but the 203-mm howitzer was a Soviet design of 1931 and was later introduced into the Artillery Reserve. The 45-mm anti-tank gun (firing 20 1·43 kilogram armour-piercing rounds per minute) was a product of the early 1930's, as was the 76-mm anti-aircraft gun, together with a fire-control system (PUAZO-1).[8] The summer of 1935 marked an important dividing line in Soviet artillery policy, when in June Stalin, Voroshilov and Ordzhonikidze inspected all-purpose and dual-purpose guns on an artillery training ground near Moscow. Some time after this inspection, a *Politburo* session, with leading designers in attendance, critically appraised present policy. The upshot was the cancellation of orders for the multi-purpose divisional gun, and henceforth an instruction that specific guns for specific tasks — divisional artillery as such, anti-aircraft weapons as such — was to be followed, the new designs to provide for a high rate of fire, manœuvrability, greater ranges and closer grouping of shots.[9]

It was in the *VVS*, however, that progress of a most spectacular order was being made, with re-equipping providing increased potentialities and a higher state of performance. In spite of the specific rejection of Douhet and all that he professed, strategic aviation centred upon the bomber appeared to be enjoying its hey-day within the Soviet command. Khripin had left no room to doubt that long range independent bomber operations would play an important and conspicuous part in the war waged by the *VVS*. The composition of Soviet military aviation underwent a marked and radical change, with the heavy (long-range) bomber and the medium bomber taking greater hold in place of the reconnaissance and light bombing aircraft. While 'front aviation' had its complement of bombers assigned to tactical roles, it was in 1936 that a strategic bomber force, the *TBS*, was organised as such.[10] Khripin emphasised above all that military aviation was an offensive weapon, and could be effectively employed in striking deep into the enemy rear, at his mobilisation, communications and industrial centres. Alksnis and Khripin had ensured that the *VVS* possessed the means to implement this idea. Designer A. N. Tupolev helped materially to provide the long-range machines capable of carrying out these missions. The TB–3 (ANT–6) four-engined heavy bomber, carrying a bomb-load of not less than 2 tons, formed the backbone of the long-range striking force. Tupolev also contributed to the potentialities of front aviation with his SB–2 (ANT–40) all metal light bomber with a speed not exceeding 250 m.p.h. (400 kilometres p.h.) and powered by two M–100 engines. That the bomber was in the ascendant in the *VVS* was to be confirmed by Khripin himself at the end of 1936, when he revealed by that time the figure of 60 per cent for the proportion of bombing aircraft in the total strength of the *VVS*. The four-engined machines of the *TBS* were pointed against Japan and Germany also.

To support this phenomenal activity, the *VVS* could call on four engine and ten aircraft factories in the Soviet Union turning out 4,000 airframes and a reputed 20,000 aero-engines annually.[11] While this represented a large slice of the armaments autarky which was a Soviet aim, quantity was not quite the full story. The Soviet aviation industry remained in a state of considerable dependence on foreign technical sources, principally those of France and the United States of America. Both in matters of design and problems of engines, the gap remained. The I–15 Soviet fighter bore a strong family resemblance to a Breguet design, the I–16 was powered by a Wright Cyclone aero-engine (manufactured under licence). Native Soviet effort had developed the AN–1 engine and perfected it for use in the TB–7 long-range bomber, the engine being a product of the 'Special Experimental Design Bureau' headed by A. D. Charomsky.[12] While Soviet design and aviation pioneering had notable feats to record, constant modernisation and technical innovation were of the uttermost importance, and the need to avail itself so liberally of external assistance represented the Achilles heel of Soviet aviation. In line with the quantity of machines which also dominated the ideas of the *VVS* command — combat aviation was to be employed on a mass scale — a vast campaign to develop 'air-mindedness' in the Soviet Union continued without abatement. *Osoaviakhim*, with its sport (parachute) and flying clubs, carried out important functions in pre-military training. The pilot training programme in 1936 envisaged preparing five pilots for each one specifically required. With the increase in technical resources and trained ground crews, the 'aviation park' had been superseded in favour of the operational deployment of *VVS* units on forward aerodromes, the construction of which was pushed ahead. In the same way that Red Army units had access to supply dumps built up to ensure a minimum period of self-contained supply, so the *VVS* organised its units with a sufficiency of spare-parts, fuel and lubricants with a view to being able to commit its machines to operations with no delay and to maintain operations for a period without additional supply.

While the *VVS* appeared to leap ahead and to be aiming at nothing less than the air hegemony of all Europe, the Soviet naval forces showed no such striking progress. While its technical standard was undoubtedly rising,[13] the accent was on a strictly defensive doctrine among the naval leaders. The *VMF* was very far from being a fully balanced naval force, the emphasis being on coastal defence craft and submarines. By the beginning of 1936 there were not less than 100 and not more than 120 Soviet submarines in existence, some of an older and even obsolete type, but with the noticeable introduction of submarines of heavier displacement.[14] The wind of change, nevertheless, had begun to blow from the direction of the *Politburo*, and it is reported that at the end of 1935 Stalin intervened in naval affairs in a manner not unlike that concerning the Red Army's artillery. From the Pacific Fleet Stalin called together a number of the younger officers to attend a conference in Moscow, where the questions of an ocean-going navy were extensively debated in the presence of Molotov, Voroshilov and Ordzhonikidze.[15] Confirmation that a change of naval policy was pending came from Tukhachevsky in his January report to the *TsIK*, when he mentioned that although in times past the Soviet navy had concentrated mainly upon submarines and smaller surface vessels, greater attention would now be paid to strengthening the surface ships. But more than merely additional ships was at stake, the issue being whether the Soviet navy was to break out of its strategic straitjacket as it had done from the geographic one in its physical expansion in 1933. Orlov, Muklevich and Chief of Staff Ludri had concentrated on raising the technical capacity and efficiency of a defensive force; naval defence was still tied, sensibly enough, to its minefield, coastal battery system and shore-based aircraft. The submarine appeared to be prized for its value as a defensive weapon, although this seemed to apply only with reservations to the Pacific. Nor was there any great amplitude of time in which to pursue the naval debate. If a decisive turn were to be made, and new Soviet battleships, cruisers and destroyers were to make their appearance on the world's oceans, provision for building them would have to be set into the Third Five-Year Plan. Even more immediately, Germany was unshackling herself from naval limitation, and it was no coincidence that at the end of 1935 and the beginning of 1936 the possibility of sending Koshchanov as Naval Attaché to London was being considered.

The real key to success lay with the capabilities and the attainments of the command. Tukhachevsky himself made no secret of this fact, of the importance attaching to the degree to which they could master the intricacies of modern mobile warfare. Higher military education centres had expanded as the Soviet armed forces developed in size and complexity. The Stalin Motorisation and Mechanisation Academy, the Dzerzhinskii Artillery Academy, the Budenny Electro-technical Institute in Leningrad and the Kuibyshev Military Engineering Academy were expansions of the earlier academy frame. In 1936 the General Staff Academy was opened for the express purpose of training very senior commanders. In the Zhukovskii Air Academy, the Command Faculty prepared aviation officers and its technical faculties the large number of specialists required by the expanding *VVS*. The high command itself was not spared its 're-education', although Budenny appears not to have made the new grade.[16] The Civil War veterans had to accustom themselves to a military technique far removed from the infantry-cavalry rushes with which they were familiar. Foreign military literature, both classic and contemporary, had a wide circulation in command circles. Khripin wrote his own introduction to the translation of General Douhet's book on air warfare; in matters of tank warfare, Khalepskii and his collaborators kept well abreast of British experiments[17] and Eimannsberger's pioneer work on tanks and artillery was issued in translation.[18] Side by side with the radical innovations, such as air landing brigades, long-range bombers and the mechanised formations, were traditional conservatism and strategic restrictions. Tukhachevsky's 'nerve' had to be combined with an over-all system which stressed control of the mass by strict centralisation and nothing less than automatism. Having chosen not to exclude the quality troops from the mass, and being as much committed to mass employment of special weapons, the problem remained how to energise the whole. Flexible and capable command at all levels (including a high level of tactical training) was a prime necessity. 'Inter-action' of arms demanded the same. The Soviet offensive appeared to be many-phased and above all sustained, thereby requiring no technical or command breakdowns. In all this uneven patchwork of military designs there were numerous opportunities for acute differences over doctrines and strategy. Some had already been seized upon. Although there is nothing to suggest that at this point military affairs and defence planning were a bone of serious contention between the Red Army high command and Stalin, the latter seemed to have embarked on devious explorations of his own.

* * * *

On 23rd January, Marshal Tukhachevsky was nominated to accompany Litvinov to London in order to attend the funeral of King George V. While Litvinov arrived in London on 26th, Tukhachevsky's journey included an item which gave rise to considerable speculation — a brief halt in Berlin. That break in the journey was used by the Soviet Marshal to seek out his erstwhile companions of the Red Army-*Reichswehr* collaboration, and in particular Blomberg. One year later, in the course of a conversation with Smigly-Rydz in Warsaw, Göring was to bring up the question of Tukhachevsky's 'passing through' Berlin, with a tale which was somewhat embroidered in the telling. Göring informed his Polish host that '. . . not only did he [Hitler] not receive him personally, but he had not allowed anyone from military circles to have any contact with him.'[19] Such retrospective testimony, even with its embellishment, would suggest that Tukhachevsky's descent in Berlin came as no complete surprise. There is at least one significant item which confirms that contact of a tenuous but deliberate nature was sustained between German and Soviet officers. Although the collaboration had lapsed, Seeckt's disciples in the German Army remained interested in possible re-insurance in the east; General Köstring, before taking up his appointment as Military Attaché in Moscow, was instructed by Fritsch and Beck to work — along purely personal lines — for an improvement in relations between the Red and German Armies.[20] That reservoir of good will towards the German generals had certainly not evaporated in the Red Army by the end of 1935. Personal contacts would presumably be subject to personal arrangement. It was enough that Fritsch, Beck and von Stülpnagel should indicate this to Köstring. It was inevitable that none of this should be secret to Stalin.

After his few hours sojourn in Berlin, Tukhachevsky travelled on to London, arriving on 27th January. In London Tukhachevsky made the acquaintance of Gamelin, and also came into contact with Duff Cooper and Lister.[21] After thirteen days, Tukhachevsky left for Paris to take up the invitation extended to him by Gamelin to break his return journey in France. Taking with him Vitovt Putna, Military Attaché in London, Tukhachevsky spent a week as the guest of the French General Staff. His programme was varied and amounted to an inspection of important sectors of French armament, a personal confirmation of what had been reported by the Soviet Military Mission to France in 1935. On that occasion another of Tukhachevsky's intimates, Sedyakin, had played a prominent part. On 11th February, accompanied by Ventsov (Soviet Military Attaché in Paris), the assistant attaché Virilov and Vassilchenko (Soviet Air Attaché), Tukhachevsky inspected aircraft plants; on the following day he inspected the aviation centre at Chartres. Uborevich had by this time joined the Soviet party, and on 14th Uborevich, Tukhachevsky, Putna and Ventsov paid a visit to Havre.[22] Tukhachevsky's presence gave Gamelin the opportunity for closer acquaintance with the commander-designate of the Red Army at war. Gamelin, aware that Tukhachevsky had been a prisoner of war in the company of a number of French officers,* assembled some of them at a small dinner party. In this way Tukhachevsky once again met Fervacque, biographer extraordinary to the Soviet Marshal, and a fellow prisoner. In an atmosphere thus more relaxed, Gamelin and Tukhachevsky approached more serious business. To Gamelin the Soviet commander made no secret of the fact that he would like to see an intensification of the relations between the French and Red Army, nor did he hide the fact that he had, '. . . relations avec des personalités de l'armée allemande'.[23] Such contacts existed, Tukhachevsky pointed out, for no other purpose than to follow the progress being made by the German Army; the Soviet Marshal was of the opinion, Gamelin noted, that the re-occupation of the Rhineland was to be expected as the next item on the German military agenda. Over technical matters, Tukhachevsky showed a keen interest in French tanks and seemed to be impressed by what he saw of French armour, although he counselled Gamelin to get 'many and quickly'. The French general could only reply that he hardly held the purse strings, whereupon Tukhachevsky observed that in this respect the Bolshevik regime conferred a decisive advantage — 'As for me, I get all I ask for'.[24] To Gamelin, Tukhachevsky appeared to be both sure of himself and of his influence.

* Among these officers had been General de Gaulle.

While in France, Tukhachevsky was the object of a speculative interest on the part of the French press, which enlivened its readers with fanciful references to the Soviet Marshal's aristocratic lineage. Nor was Tukhachevsky the soul of that discretion designed to re-assure certain quarters of French opinion. At a celebrated dinner at the Soviet Embassy in Paris, Tukhachevsky came out with nothing less than an attack on the attempts to align the Soviet Union with the mechanism of collective security. To the Rumanian Foreign Minister Titulescu he advised the need to look to Germany for rescue. In a company including Herriot, Paul-Boncour, Politis and Potemkin — and the French journalist Mme Tabouis — Tukhachevsky excelled himself in admiration of German achievements, and in discussing an Air Pact between the powers and Germany repeated to Mme Tabouis, 'Ils sont déjà invincibles!'[25] These words and the whole tone of Tukhachevsky's remarks created no small amount of misgiving. They are all the more incomprehensible in the light of his talk with Gamelin which stressed increasing Franco-Soviet military collaboration. If this was an attempt to rouse influential opinion, it was crude and ill-managed. Nor do the complications of Tukhachevsky's rather sensational foreign tour end here. It has been reported that Admiral Canaris, head of the German *Abwehr*, had proof of even greater indiscretions by Tukhachevsky, namely that he had entered into contact with emissaries of General Miller, the head of the organisation of Tsarist veterans in exile. This Tukhachevsky was supposed to have done while executing his commission abroad at the funeral of King George V.[26] One more mystery surrounds Tukhachevsky's return journey through Berlin. Although it can be established with some certainty that he stopped off for some hours in Berlin on his way to London, his return journey from Paris began on 17th February and his official itinerary gave his date of arrival in Moscow as 19th. The name of Blimiel, German Communist and *NKVD* agent, has been given as the individual who managed to 'slip into' a small and private meeting which Tukhachevsky held in Berlin with Russian emigrés in Germany. The information about Blimiel came from one Ernst Niekisch, himself not unconnected with the *Reichswehr*-Red Army collaboration, one who came into contact with Blimiel when both were in a German prison.[27] Although Blimiel may well have existed, the story of a meeting with Russian emigrés sounds wholly improbable. Out of all the Soviet Marshal's adventures beyond the Soviet frontiers, the one which carries with it most of its own proof is merely the Berlin stop-over in January. If Tukhachevsky had compromised himself so irretrievably (and with such blatant lack of caution), then there would have been no need for a subsequent *NKVD* conspiracy of such complication and ramification that it ranged over all Europe. That Tukhachevsky was shadowed while abroad was as inevitable as the Soviet security system itself and this fact also was not unknown to Tukhachevsky. The tales of illicit contacts rest primarily upon the assumption that Tukhachevsky was desirous at this time of entering into a conspiracy presumed to be anti-Stalinist. No reliable evidence is forthcoming to support this.

The period of Tukhachevsky's journey abroad had been marked also by a fresh outbreak in the Far East at the focal point of Japanese-Soviet struggles — Outer Mongolia. 'The state of virtual war'[28] which existed along the Mongolian-Manchurian border was a consequence of the Japanese attempt to undermine Soviet power in that critical area. Severe crisis had followed upon an incident on 29th January, when Japanese troops had pursued a company of their Manchurian puppet troops, intent upon desertion, on to Soviet territory west of Grodekovo. In the subsequent fighting, Red Army troops suffered casualties including killed. After an extended period of appeasement, however, there were signs that the Soviet attitude was changing. In the Trans-Baikal area, the Soviet command could count upon a considerable strengthening of its position, while the Baikal-Amur railway, rapidly nearing completion, secured for the Far Eastern Army a vital link facilitating easier supply and rapid troop movement. In an interview published on 5th March, 1936, in *Pravda*,[29] Stalin, questioned by Roy Howard, opened with an estimate of the situation in the Far East. Stalin found that, due to the picture being 'insufficiently clear',* he could not pronounce about the possible consequences of the '26th February Incident', a Japanese Army conspiracy aimed at taking over the government. But he passed on a blunt warning that a Japanese attack on Outer Mongolia (the Mongolian People's Republic) would precipitate Soviet 'assistance'. This had already been indicated through diplomatic channels to the Japanese, with a reference to the 'invariably friendly' relations which had existed between the Soviet Union and Outer Mongolia since 1921. 'Positive action' would be the Soviet response to any Japanese attempt to take Ulan Bator by force, a relevant enough warning in view of Japanese troop concentration on the Mongolian border.

Stalin gave pride of place to the 'Japanese zone' as a centre of the war danger, but the second danger spot was in the 'German zone'. 'It is,' Stalin

* By this time the Sorge espionage ring (Sorge, Ozaki, Voukelich, Klausen and Miyagi) was active and operational in the Japanese capital. Sorge aimed to report on Japanese intentions towards the Soviet Union, Japanese military preparations for attack, the role of the Japanese Army in politics, Japanese heavy industry, German-Japanese relations, Japanese policy in Manchuria and China, Japanese policy towards Britain and America, who were thought by the Russians to be a possible support for any Japanese drive into Siberia. There can be no reasonable doubt that a colossal quantity of information found its way to Moscow from Sorge's efforts, based on an infiltration of high-ranking German and Japanese circles. See Hans-Otto Meissner, ***The Man** With Three Faces*, London 1955, which makes use of information from *Intelligence Summary 23* (Washington).

went on, 'difficult to say which is the more threatening'. In contrast with these two major threats, the Italian-Abyssinian war was merely 'an episode'. Although the 'Japanese zone' had been until recently the most active, the emphasis 'may shift to Europe'. As for the German danger, in response to a request to be specific about the position and direction of a possible German attack, Stalin replied that since no direct attack could be launched, a potential aggressor would have to 'borrow' a frontier or frontiers across which to reach out at the Soviet Union.[30] The reference was, without specifying, to Poland, the Baltic states or Finland. The converse was that, in order to be militarily effective in Europe, the Soviet Union had to have rights of passage for troops, and transit routes for aircraft. A week after Stalin's interview was published, the Soviet Union and Outer Mongolia signed at Ulan Bator a pact of mutual assistance. The preamble referred to the 'liberation' of 1921 and confirmed the existence of the 'gentleman's agreement' of 27th November, 1934, which provided for mutual assistance 'in all possible ways'. The pact, signed by Tairov, Amor and Gendun, formally committed the Soviet Union and the Mongolian People's Republic, in the event of an attack upon the territory of either by a third country, to '... adopt all measures that may be necessary' to safeguard their territories — that is, it gave the Red Army a free hand. When published, the agreement called forth both Japanese wrath and Chinese indignation. Even before the diplomatic wrangle began, fighting on some scale had started.

Although at the time of Stalin's interview with Roy Howard incidents had temporarily ceased, at the end of March the Japanese began to make use of their military concentrations on the Mongolian-Manchurian border. On 29th March Japanese and Manchurian puppet troops attacked the frontier position at Adyk-Dolon. Two days later, a strong force of infantry, supported by tanks, artillery, armoured cars and aircraft renewed the assault.* The Japanese force had broken through the resistance offered and turned in the direction of Tamsag-Bulak.[31] Although the Japanese drive was checked, fighting was continuing on Mongolian territory. Neither side, Soviet or Japanese, was under any misapprehension as to the importance of Outer Mongolia. This area underpinned the whole of the Soviet defence system for the western sectors of the Far Eastern frontiers, and Japanese control would have meant speedy access to the Trans-Baikal, thus cutting Blyukher's forces in two and outflanking the fixed defences which hindered the Japanese advance to the east. In addition to the strategic difficulties facing the Soviet command, Barmine records one of a different nature, also born of the fighting on the Mongolian frontier. In expediting a shipment of arms for the Turks, Barmine was anxious to gain advance delivery of tanks. On

* Buir-Nor (Tauran) incident.

applying to Tukhachevsky for these, Barmine was handed a report from Blyukher, indicating that the Red Army had not had favourable experiences with riveted tanks. Vulnerable to anti-tank guns, the riveted tanks had showed up badly under fire and Blyukher recommended a switch to welded tanks.[32] (The T–26S, introduced in 1937, was welded almost throughout).

Stalin's surmise about a shift of emphasis to 'the German zone' proved to be correct. In Paris, Tukhachevsky had spoken to Gamelin about a German move into the demilitarised Rhineland. At dawn on 7th March, German troops began their moves to remilitarise this zone. The challenge was thrown down to France. In the German memorandum of 7th March, the Franco-Soviet Pact was blamed for destroying the basis of Locarno. With this charge Soviet diplomats were to deal in a short while. Even by 9th March, there were sound reasons for a belief in Moscow that no military counter-action would be involved.[33] At the meeting of the Council of the League, on 17th March, Litvinov came out with a comparatively stern speech; he asked whether the League was to condone Germany setting up hegemony over all of Europe.[34] On 19th March, the Soviet Ambassador in London, Maisky, made a speech on the war danger, in which he stressed the Soviet desire to see created — 'in a short space of time' — a peace front capable of talking to an aggressor 'in a language of tanks and machine-guns'.[35] In spite of the misgivings in German quarters about Tukhachevsky's talks with the French Staff and the complaint that these were 'jumping the gun' with respect to the Franco-Soviet Pact, the Red Army was not directly concerned with events on the Franco-German frontier. If Stalin was using the Rhineland as a test of French and British intentions, then the latter scarcely emerged positively from the situation. The greatest anomaly, however, remained Soviet-German relations. The logical outcome of Hitler's denunciation of the Franco-Soviet Pact should have been cutting off any German relations with the Soviet Union. Maisky repeated in his speech of 19th March that the Franco-Soviet Pact was not meant to encircle Germany, that Germany had not taken 'the hand stretched out to her'. No exclusion of Germany was intended. On the same day, Molotov gave an interview to M. Chastenet of *Le Temps*. In the course of this question-and-answer report, Molotov came to the core of the question — Soviet *rapprochement* with Germany. In answer to the question about groups in the German Army desirous of an understanding with the Soviet Union, and the existence of their Soviet counter-parts, Molotov pointed out that some sections of the Soviet *public* were thoroughly roused by Hitler's anti-Soviet remarks, but '. . . *the chief tendency, and the one determining the Soviet Government's policy, thinks an improvement in Soviet-German relations possible*'.[36] This, then, was the real determinant.

If no immediate deterioration had taken place, the Soviet strategic situation had not improved to any degree by the spring of 1936. The German move on the French frontier could produce only two consequences. The first was to block France, even to the extent subsequently of building up a chain of fortifications. The second was to grant Germany liberty of action to operate against Austria, Poland and Czechoslovakia. The prospects for an effective military arrangement to be made out of the Franco-Soviet Pact were considerably dimmed. 'Even Hitler's Germany', to use Molotov's own phrase, must somehow be brought to a direct understanding, to which end Stalin was even now beginning to muster the resources of his secret diplomacy, or, to apply another description, his personal diplomacy. If Tukhachevsky was speaking the language of a *rapprochement* with Germany, when he shocked not a few of the diplomats of Europe at the Embassy dinner in Paris, he was expressing nothing less than the fundamental aim of 'the Soviet Government'. Stalin must have been encouraged by reports of the wish of certain sections of the German military command for an understanding with the Soviet Union, motivated entirely by political reasons but a factor in its own right. There was, therefore, neither blind coincidence nor hapless inconsistency in the fact that the Finnish Ambassador in Moscow, Kivimaki, heard 'that Russia would finish in half an hour the agreement with France if Germany would sign a pact [with Russia].'[37]

* * * *

The Soviet command had to reckon with a decisive change in the balance of power in Europe as a consequence of Hitler's move in the Rhineland. At the same time a vital struggle had been finally and formally joined in north-east Asia. The situation had meanwhile begun to deteriorate on the north-western approaches of the Soviet Union, due to German pressure on Lithuania. The Soviet attempt to gain a joint Soviet-German guarantee of the Baltic states had long ago failed. Subversive Nazi activities in the Baltic states had attracted the investigation of the authorities concerned and the misgivings of the Soviet Union.[38] At all costs the strategic triangle Leningrad-Minsk-Memel had to be held inviolate, else a 'borrowed frontier' could bring about the unmasking of the Soviet defences and expose Soviet air bases to direct threats. Finland's flirtation with Germany posed yet another threat, that of direct pressure on Leningrad and the possibility of attacking the Soviet retirement areas in the rear. The wedge which the Russians could use to keep open the Baltic door was Lithuania, which suddenly ceased to be the object of Hitler's ominous discriminations shortly after the re-occupation of the Rhineland. Although the Baltic states had shown as yet no great fervour in looking to the Soviet Union as their potential guardian, in the spring of 1936 their attitude tilted in a pro-Soviet direction, although there was no lack of Soviet misgiving about the real attitude of these states. Stalin's remarks to Roy Howard about 'borrowed frontiers' had been preceded by hints in the Soviet press about certain Baltic ambiguities. None of this prevented the Chiefs of Staff of Lithuania, Latvia and Estonia from accepting Yegorov's invitation to attend the First of May parade in Moscow, during which time certain talks took place.[39] On 29th April, M. Uritskii, acting head of Military Intelligence, in the course of a conversation with Colonel Maasing (adjutant to the Estonian Chief of Staff), made it plain that Germany intended to incorporate the Baltic states in her eastern drive, and that such a situation would be insupportable for the Soviet Union.[40] Voroshilov made exactly the same points at the reception held on 3rd May, to which remarks General Reek, the Estonian Chief of Staff, replied that Estonia wanted good relations with all, and that an alliance with great powers held the risk for a small country that it would be gobbled up.[41]

Into the possession of German Military Intelligence came a curious and interesting document relating to the possibility of Soviet military assistance to Lithuania and eventual action in the case of a German military intervention. Dated 15th May, 1936, and numbered No. 137/17, the document was a directive to Uborevich, Belorussian Military District commander and was an addition to 'earlier instructions and Mobilisation Plan No. 4'. Fuels and lubricants would be collected from Depot No. 26 in Vitebsk. From Depots Nos. 19–21 a small force of tanks would be readied. Specialists and technicians were to be assembled and instructed by the beginning of July. In the event of any German troops making their appearance in Lithuania, 9 squadrons of aircraft were to be despatched, within six hours of a receipt of the requisite telegram, to Lithuanian aerodromes. Bombing targets for Soviet aircraft had been selected as the railway station and bridges near Tilsit, Insterburg and Eydtkuhnen. Reconnaissance would be carried out to observe if German troops were being transported through the Polish Corridor; constant watch was to be maintained by Marienburg. Photo reconnaissance of Tilsit and Insterburg would be effected without bombing attacks. Other targets would be the harbour and railway installations of Königsberg, and also the rail network of Allenstein. Troops of the Leningrad Military District would make a show of force on the Estonian frontier, while the Baltic Fleet would bar the approach of German ships with mine barriers. During the pre-mobilisation period, all cavalry in Uborevich's command was to be kept in a state of readiness and the motorised and mechanised troops stationed at Polotsk, Minsk, Slutsk and Zhitkovichi — but no unit was to proceed to a point nearer than thirty kilometres to the frontier. Weekly reports on readiness states would be submitted to the Defence

Commissar, to Yegorov, Tukhachevsky and Gamarnik until 15th July.[42]

Rumours of a secret Soviet-Lithuanian agreement were not lacking.[43] But just as Germany might be obliged to borrow frontiers, so the Soviet Union had to borrow space. Any direct transfer of land forces to Lithuania, by means of the shortest route, would have meant a violation of Polish territory. Similarly, the transfer of land forces to the aid of Czechoslovakia implied movement through Poland or Rumania. Soviet air power, however, represented one way of short-circuiting some of the difficulties of awkward neighbours. It was on 25th March, 1936, that the House of Commons heard a statement to the effect that the Czech Government had given assurances that no Soviet-Czech agreement existed for the use of Czech aerodromes by the Soviet Air Force. The summer of 1936 appears to have been the point when Czech-Soviet military collaboration took on a more positive aspect. On 15th July, Alksnis, with a group of senior Soviet aviation officers, arrived in Prague.[44] General Krejčí was to attend the Red Army manœuvres in September (from which he gathered a very favourable impression of the Red Army), while Czechoslovakia became also for the Red Army the source of particular supplies which were not forthcoming from other sources. In the west, therefore, the possession of strong and mobilised aviation and motor-mechanised forces seemed to fit in with what the Soviet command might anticipate by way of their probable employment. With bomber aviation moving to advanced bases, the motorised formations on the Soviet frontier could be used to provide comparatively rapid support, by passage either assured or forcibly taken. Two powerful striking forces could be assembled either from Yakir's group in the south-west or Uborevich's command to the north-west. Thus, accepting the possibility of Soviet activity in Lithuania and the potentiality afforded by Czechoslovakia's well-developed aerodrome system (screened by an efficient army), active offensive operations, directed from East-central Europe, were in theory attractive enough.

The hints about an expansion in Soviet strength in surface ships, while not materialising at once, took the form in the early summer of 1936 of Soviet participation in negotiations with Great Britain over naval armaments. As a lesser naval power, the Soviet Union had not been a party represented at the London Naval Conference of March 1936 on the limitation of naval armaments. With the clash of German and Soviet interests in the Baltic, it was essential to reduce the emergence of a Soviet-German naval race, although there were some who argued that the Anglo-German Naval Agreement of 1935 had given Germany the distinct possibility of naval hegemony in the Baltic. Soviet naval interests were also bound up with Japan, whose withdrawal from the London Conference, on the

COMMAND AND ADMINISTRATION OF THE SOVIET NAVAL FORCES (VMF): 1936

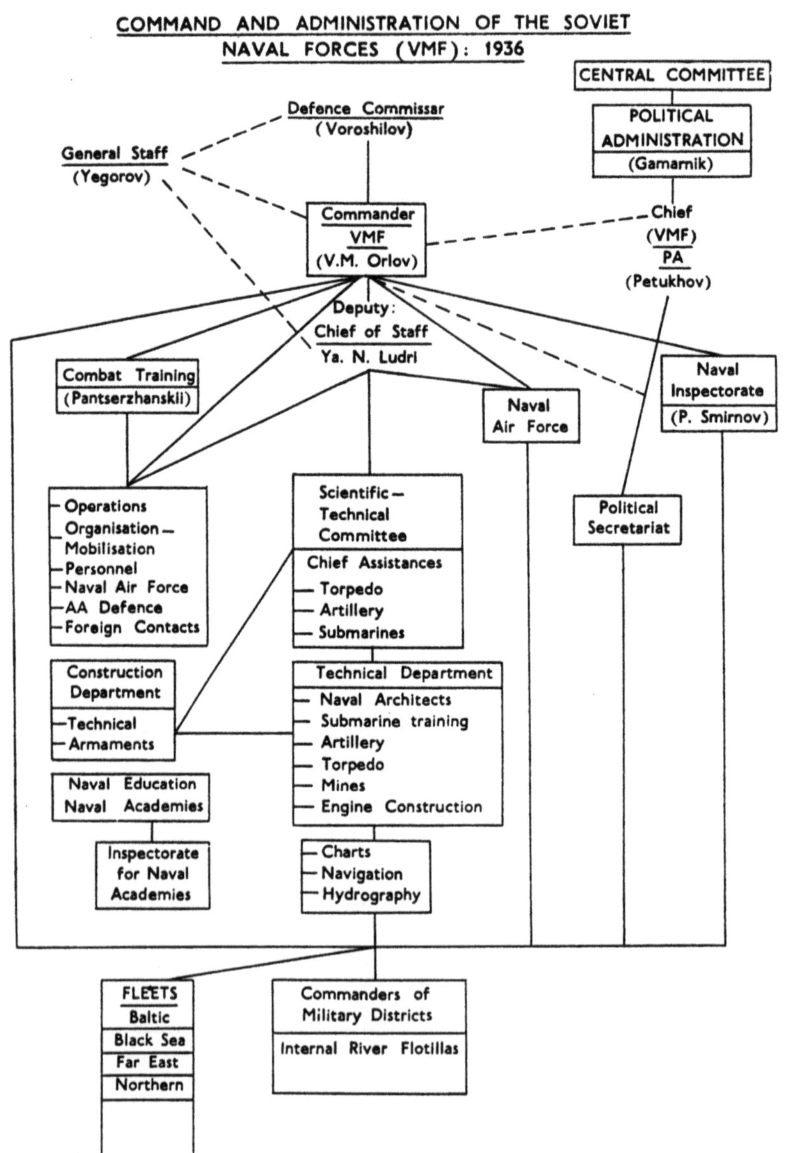

CENTRAL COMMITTEE
POLITICAL ADMINISTRATION
(Gamarnik)
Defence Commissar
(Voroshilov)
General Staff
(Yegorov)
Commander
VMF
(V.M. Orlov)
Chief
(VMF)
PA
(Petukhov)
Deputy:
Chief of Staff
Ya. N. Ludri
Combat Training
(Pantserzhanskii)
Naval
Air Force
Naval
Inspectorate
(P. Smirnov)
Operations
Organisation – Mobilisation
Personnel
Naval Air Force
AA Defence
Foreign Contacts
Scientific – Technical Committee
Chief Assistances
Torpedo
Artillery
Submarines
Political Secretariat
Construction Department
Technical
Armaments
Technical Department
Naval Architects
Submarine training
Artillery
Torpedo
Mines
Engine Construction
Naval Education
Naval Academies
Inspectorate for Naval Academies
Charts
Navigation
Hydrography
FLEETS
Baltic
Black Sea
Far East
Northern
Commanders of Military Districts
Internal River Flotillas

grounds that 'parity' had been refused her, created a serious situation. Germany, on the other hand, refused to commit herself to a qualitative limitation of naval armament until the Soviet Union had likewise committed itself.[45] The Soviet government accepted the British invitation to discuss naval questions, but made from the very beginning two conditions: that any limitation binding on the Soviet Union must also bind Germany,

COMMAND AND STAFF ORGANISATION OF THE BALTIC FLEET: 1936

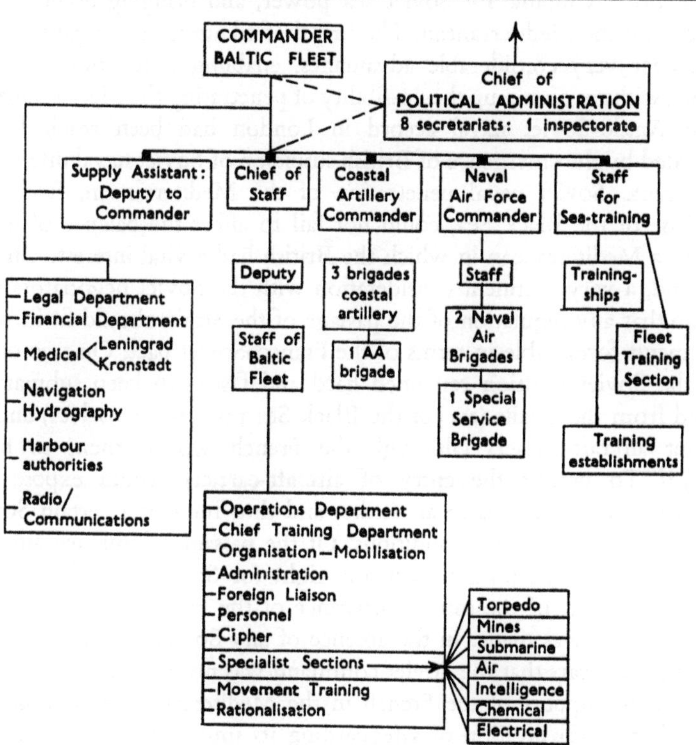

and that if Japan launched upon a naval programme beyond treaty limits the Soviet Union must be free to meet this situation with specific reference to its Far Eastern forces. No objection was raised to these stipulations. Antsipo-Chikunskii, Engineer Flag Officer, was appointed Soviet Naval Attaché to Great Britain. By July an Anglo-Soviet naval agreement was ready and agreement in principle announced. On learning of the terms of the draft treaty, the German government protested, thus making protracted naval negotiations inevitable. While a silent struggle developed over forces in the Baltic, from which point onwards the Soviet Navy pressed the construction of new cruisers, another involved situation concerned the position of Soviet naval power in the Black Sea, coming upon Turkey's request for a revision of the agreement governing the Straits. Under the terms of a close, if somewhat forced Soviet-Turkish friendship, the Soviet Black Sea Fleet could permit the Turks to run that corner of their house, while the prospect of a treaty revision supplied the possibility of events taking a turn favourable for Soviet sea power, and bringing Soviet naval influence into the Mediterranean. The first drafted agreement[46] gave Soviet naval power very considerable advantages, enabling it to command the Black Sea without giving up the possibility of penetrating the Mediterranean.

What Anglo-Soviet naval accord in London had been reached was complicated by the emergence of British suspicion of Soviet naval intentions at Montreux. Soviet naval penetration of the Mediterranean, from the secure base of the Black Sea, could not fail to affect the balance of naval power in a Mediterranean in which the British had a vital interest. On the other hand, a very pertinent consideration with the Soviet negotiators was to ensure that any regulation of the passage of the Straits should fit in with arrangements foreseeable in terms of the Franco-Soviet pact. On two other points the Soviet position remained hard and fast — to keep submarines excluded from the Straits (except the Black Sea powers themselves) and to keep out aircraft-carriers (although the French wished them to have passage).[47] To permit the entry of aircraft-carriers would expose the southern industrial regions to air strikes and thus remove a certain Soviet immunity under prevailing conditions. Of the passage of military aircraft, in spite of French attempts to win the right for Soviet aircraft to travel unrestricted as part of the mutual assistance of the Franco-Soviet Pact, no specific mention was made. In the absence of any Soviet representation on this point, it appears that the Soviet command was not prepared to commit its aviation to support of the French in the Mediterranean and chose the negative but useful position of safeguarding its immunity from air attack in the Black Sea area. Out of the international negotiations, it was apparent that Soviet naval ambitions were growing and every diplomatic lever was pressed to ensure a further escape for Soviet naval units from the geographical trap in which they were fastened. With hints of a more aggressive and dynamic naval policy emerging, and signs that the German challenge in the Baltic was being taken up with all seriousness, the main weight seems to have lain still with ensuring minimum access for Soviet ships as a means of operating under an arrangement consistent with the Franco-Soviet Pact. The Soviet proposals to France on a possible form of mutual military assistance early in 1937 were to prove the priority of this factor.

While these manœuvres, designed to extract the maximum of strategic freedom for the employment of Soviet striking power, were taking place against a wide international background, on the home front the Red Army command was trying to close up its own ranks. This process of consolidation had been given a first and great impetus with the introduction of ranks in the autumn of 1935. The effects upon military morale had been immediate. In April 1936 the wave of concession spread out to include the right to organise Cossack formations within the Red Army, from man-power resources which had formerly been rightly depicted as the scourge of Bolshevism, the feared and hated whip-swinging Cossacks who had been at the centre of one of the fiercest anti-Soviet furnaces of the Civil War.[48] In yet another way the military pressed their soldierly claims — by elbowing aside the political staff. Intensive training in the techniques of mobile war and concentration upon raising technical standards were seized upon (with no small degree of justification) as a pretext for crowding out political indoctrination. The growing tension between the command and political staff did not escape the notice of Gamarnik, who is described as having decided to alleviate the situation by proposing an increase in the authority of the command staff.[49] Under Gamarnik's rule over the Political Administration, the political staff had developed along two lines, divided roughly by the position they occupied in the military-political hierarchy. At the senior levels, Gamarnik's men had become skilled political experts, with the accent on theoretical knowledge and a certain intellectualism. Lower down the scale, the political assistant was trained to do an efficient job but was much more a cog in a huge machine. The Political Administration had been plagued, almost from its inception, by two problem-types, the intellectual and the 'frustrated marshal'. While the latter had been eliminated by the change-over of the mid 1920's, the fractious intellectual had made trouble as late as 1929–30. The bulk of the corps and divisional commanders, veterans of the Civil War and other actions involving the Red Army, who were whipping the complex formations into shape for a war creeping up on them, were not of a calibre or a disposition to suffer gladly either Gamarnik's super-intellectuals or his political cubs. The technical units presented extremely difficult problems; in the *VVS*, a political officer tied to the ground enjoyed little or no prestige, and if in the air (in rare cases), he was perforce first aircrew and secondly a political. If Gamarnik was envisaging a further diminution of the power of the political staff, then he failed to read aright the intentions of Stalin in this matter, although such a scheme did appear to serve best the increase in military efficiency which seemed everywhere to be the order of the day.

In sum, the military effort of 1936 was concentrating upon the maximisation of material and manpower resources, and making a consistent effort to widen the strategic opportunities available to the Soviet command. If necessary, it looked as if the three key points of the whole defensive system — north-west (Lithuania), western (Czechoslovakia) and north-east Asian (Outer Mongolia) — would be defended. The process had already begun in north-east Asia. The most intensive effort was going into Soviet aviation. The way was being prepared for the Soviet navy to take up naval challenges directly and certainly to dispute the Baltic on as well as below the surface. In August, the Red Army was given another transfusion of strength, when the age level for drafting recruits was dropped to nineteen. It was denied that the aim was to increase the Red Army above its present 1,300,000; but, since the new decree provided for the calling up of contingents covering an eighteen-month period for each separate year (thus drafting on 1st September the 1914 class and half of that for 1915), the compound would increase the intake by at least 300,000. For purely practical purposes, the Red Army would number some 1,600,000 men.[50]

Should it come to war, the military command could look upon a situation in which the turbulence associated with collectivisation had begun to settle. While collectivisation had still not been able to yield ample reserves of food-stuffs, the country was no longer throbbing with violence and running with disaffection. The regime, having passed through the crisis of 1930–3, had taken on a more stable aspect, a fact noted with varying degrees of satisfaction or grudging admissions abroad. Transportation was slightly less chaotic, with the emphasis on cutting out as many long hauls as possible. In view of the road-building programme, motorised transport could be considered as a useful adjunct to rail communications, but subject to a greater degree to climatic conditions. Transport of fuel and ammunition, however, by motorised transport (to be employed also in 'cross-country' runs) was a feasible alternative on a limited scale. Supply dumps could tide formations over an initial period; the first phase of operations, therefore, was designed to function from a set supply base.* Extensive pre-military training, besides its value for instructional purposes, also had the virtue of diminishing the shock of transition to purely military conditions. From that point of view, the outstanding feature of the entire Soviet military establishment was its maintenance of a state falling only fractionally short of permanent mobilisation. The real distinction, perhaps, was only between

* In the Soviet Far East, the problem was especially difficult, not to say acute. Grain production did not meet current needs. Petrol had to be brought from the west. No large-scale munitions production had as yet been organised. Bringing in supplies increased the load on the Trans-Siberian. Part of the solution was found in stock-piling, but the Soviet Far Eastern forces remained considerably dependent on European Russia.

those formations on a war-footing and those in conditions of pre-mobilisation. It was not an ideal arrangement. Moreover, while external blockade was not so formidable a problem, the real issue was to develop that superabundance of resources indigenous to the Soviet Union into the autarky which was so essential. Frenzied production, with frequent break-downs and a high wastage rate, might see the Red Army over its short-term problems only. And no article of Soviet military dogma envisaged a short or 'lightning' war.

★ ★ ★ ★

As the military command was going about the business of cementing what to all intents and purposes seemed like a working autonomy in military affairs, the summer of 1936 brought with it a major political upheaval. While in the first part of 1936 the purge, although officially discontinued, had rumbled away with a scrutiny of Party membership, during the same period a Constitution had been pushed increasingly into public prominence, having been mooted in 1935. Into this curious amalgam of re-assurance and terror was thrust, on 29th July, 1936, a top-secret circular letter to all Party committees on '. . . the Terrorist Activity of the Trotskyite, Zinovievite Counter-Revolutionary Bloc'.[51] In the name of 'vigilance', there followed a 'holocaust of denunciations'.[52] On 19th August, 1936, the trial of the 'Trotskyite-Zinovievite Centre' began. Zinoviev, L. B. Kamenev, Mrachkovskii, I. N. Smirnov, Bakayev and Evdokimov were the former Party leaders put on trial; five days later they were sentenced to be shot. Two aspects of this first major show trial of outstanding political figures command attention. The first is that incriminating hints were dropped by the accused, implicating in turn Bukharin, Tomsky, Rykov, Radek and Sokol'nikov, thus virtually announcing a second trial. Buried far from public sight was a second aspect, involving an even deeper conspiracy and touching at the edges of the military command. Mrachkovskii of the accused was a former military man, famed as a partisan commander in the Urals, senior in the Central Asian Military District and the man behind the energetic construction of the *Turksib* railway. The *NKVD* had to take Mrachkovskii in hand, to bend and break him with interrogation until he 'confessed'. Twice Stalin interviewed him in order to ease this 'confession' from him. Obdurate still, Mrachkovskii was an object of special *NKVD* attentions.[53] I. N. Smirnov was brought in to face Mrachkovskii. Smirnov, noted Eastern Front commander in the Civil War, never himself yielded completely. During the trial he tried to disavow his 'confession', but prosecutor Vyshinsky silenced him.

While the *NKVD* prepared Mrachkovskii for a public ordeal, they moved privily against two other men with Red Army connections—Dmitri

Schmidt and Vitovt Putna. Schmidt, son of a poor Jewish shoe-maker and destined to become one of the brilliant if unruly guerrilla commanders in the Civil War, had continued to serve in the Red Army after 1921 as a cavalry commander. A member of the Opposition, in 1927 Schmidt had accosted Stalin in Moscow and 'half-joking, half-serious' subjected the future dictator to an insulting and almost threatening tongue-lashing.[54] Not later than August 1936 the *NKVD* took Schmidt into their special custody.[55] At some later and unknown date, with no unnecessary work on 'confessions', Schmidt was shot. In one sense Schmidt was the first Red Army victim of the *NKVD*, but the case of Putna, intimate of Tukhachevsky and recently Soviet Military Attaché in London, runs a close second. Putna had been implicated by the testimony of the Zinoviev-Kamenev Trial.[56] It is reported that he was already under arrest in August 1936.[57] Mention of so senior a Red Army officer in such a context looked like an unmistakable sign of an intention to act — at a date unspecified — against the military.

Had, then, the gage been finally flung down between the army and the *NKVD*? Matters did not proceed in so direct a manner. The Zinoviev-Kamenev Trial could hardly be reckoned a complete success, from Stalin's point of view. Crude and ill-managed, the technique of the 'show trial' needed obvious improvement. In previous trials the *NKVD* had been marshalling the scape-goats for failure in industry or transport. Now a whole political generation, holding leaders of undeniable stature, had to be obliterated. Resistance to this political massacre appears to have raised itself after this first trial. The 'investigation' of Bukharin and Rykov, incriminated in the August Trial, was publicly called off early in September.[58] According to the evidence supplied by a former Communist Party official of some rank,* the autumn plenum of the Central Committee saw a determined stand by at least three-quarters of the Central Committee members against Stalin and in support of Bukharin. Of the Red Army high command, in addition to Voroshilov and Budenny, Yakir and Gamarnik were Central Committee members; Uborevich, Yegorov, Blyukher Tukhachevsky and Gamarnik's deputy I. A. Bulin were candidate members. With the exception of Budenny and Voroshilov, the Red Army officers voted against Stalin and against Yezhov, who had succeeded Yagoda as head of the *NKVD*.[59] The mention of Yezhov as head of the *NKVD* would place this meeting at some date after September. On 25th September, 1936, Stalin, who was taking a summer vacation with Zhdanov on the Black Sea coast, sent a telegram to Kaganovich, Molotov and other members of the *Politburo*, demanding the appointment of Yezhov as head of the *NKVD* in place of Yagoda, who has '. . . definitely proved himself incapable of

* A. Uralov.

unmasking the Trotskyite-Zinovievite block.' In the same telegram Stalin pointed out that the *NKVD* was four years behind 'in this matter'— indication of a sort that a liquidation timetable existed.[60] Yezhov was appointed on 26th.

Indirect confirmation that something had gone wrong is supplied in a German diplomatic report, dated 28th September, which interpreted the fall of Yagoda as a victory for the army. Tippelskirch wrote that the Zinoviev-Kamenev Trial had been a complete fiasco in foreign eyes and had damaged the Popular Front policy abroad. Yagoda's own hunger for power had not stopped short at the Kremlin and the Red Army; what had been planned to follow the Zinoviev trial was a show trial of the 'Trotskyist commanders' of the Red Army, in which Putna was to play the main role. Tukhachevsky had fallen under a distinct cloud, for he ranked as a 'protector' (*Gönner*) of Putna. During the visit of the British, Czech and French military missions to the Red Army manœuvres, Tukhachevsky had played a rather subordinate role. But now Tukhachevsky was again in full public circulation, and had recovered his old position. Yagoda's fall was followed by the 're-instatement' of Tukhachevsky, and '. . . one hears no more that a trial of the Red commanders shall take place'.[61]

This report bears out the interpretation of Stalin's tactics with regard to the *NKVD*-Red Army question. Armed and ready, the Red Army represented a real check on the power of the *NKVD*, who needed to resist the temptation to become over-mighty subjects. Holding this strange and dangerous balance, Stalin was able to carry through a purge of the *NKVD*, by which Yezhov turned it into the reliable instrument used to carry through the most devastating liquidations. Part of the re-arrangement was loosing the *NKVD* on the army, which may have been planned for 1936 but the scheme fell to pieces through inadequate preparation or bad management. *NKVD* preparations evidently took time and considerable planning and the 'anti-Soviet centres' were thought out in great detail. It remained to fit the chosen victims to the fictitious but politically damaging stories. In this way, the Leningrad *NKVD* informed its selected prisoner that 'you, yourself will not need to invent anything. The *NKVD* will prepare for you a ready outline for every branch of the centre; you will have to study it carefully. . . .'[62] While this might be achieved with certain individuals (and many refused to 'confess' in this style), the problem involved in removing senior army commanders was not quite in the same category. And yet to be dictator absolute, such as he aspired to be, Stalin had to do more than control the armed forces; he had to make them over to himself completely, a point upon which he was to have a strange reminder in the none too distant future. In that sense, the Red Army command — independent of

Stalin, self-created, an equal at least in its own estimation to its political master — was hopelessly and irretrievably guilty of being the ultimate barrier to absolute power. There were indications that upon occasions Stalin had been obliged to accommodate himself to the majority of the high command, and had perhaps even bargained with the man who had blackened his name in connection with the 1920 disaster before Warsaw. If visiting savage and crude vengeance on his former political opponents created adverse opinions abroad (although it inculcated salutary political lessons at home), this could not be compared with striking at the vital interests of the state at the point of its greatest vulnerability, the command of the armed forces. That reported revolt on the Central Committee by the senior officers — which, if it took place, was at best only an empty political demonstration in support of men already doomed — may have finally decided Stalin to proceed with this particular liquidation, to take the step of now applying to the military Communists what had been forced upon the civilians. Putna's contrived incrimination indicated a beginning; either this was merely a first provisional step, or a more ambitious plan to ensnare the military had fallen to pieces.* Whichever was the real clue, there were precautions to be taken and preparations to be made, both of a peculiarly involved nature; in the late autumn of 1936, Yezhov, with his senior assistants Gorb, Pauker, Volovich, Frinovskii and Slutskii, gave such undertakings their greater attention.

★ ★ ★ ★

During the period of the first great trial Stalin also had to decide on the role to be taken by the Soviet Union in yet one more international storm, the civil war in Spain, at once a struggle between the great powers and also 'the laboratory in which modern warfare was first tested out'.[63] During the initial period of the Spanish war, in July and August, 1936, when the worker rising was struggling to deliver a fighting response to the forces rallied by General Franco, any sign of massive intervention on the part of Stalin was lacking.[64] This was, on the surface, all the more strange since he might have moved to the support of the Spanish Communists. Basically Stalin was in a cleft stick; to move in Soviet tanks and guns to support 'the Reds' in Spain would have meant the ultimate isolation of the Soviet Union, with a Communist victory bringing a re-alignment of Germany with Britain, France with Italy, against the Soviet Union.[65] The ideal solution would have been to have France intervene in Spain. In this way, the Popular Front would be strengthened with French Communists taking all the kudos and possibly an even greater share of the divided power; the possibility

* A. Uralov, *The Reign of Stalin*, p. 48, writes that Putna was used by the *NKVD* to obtain a 'statement' that Tukhachevsky was working for British Intelligence.

of a combination of powers against the Soviet Union, virtually uncommitted would be banished. As the Spanish Republicans fought on, and as the French government launched the notion of 'non-intervention', the crisis for Stalin became acute. In one sense, Stalin's policy consisted of a determination to show his availability as an ally. While he had so offered himself to France, this still did not preclude such a policy being applied to Germany also. In spite of the propoganda battle being waged between the Germans and Russians, none of this touched upon the reality of the situation, as viewed from Stalin's eyes. Even now he was making preparations for an overture, furtive in the extreme, to be made to Hitler to open direct Soviet-German negotiations. The first results would soon be showing. It was imperative, therefore, to do nothing to jeopardise an eventual understanding with Hitler, and since Stalin had to demonstrate his worth, to allow the Republicans to perish would ruin his stock, not only with his temporary democratic allies, but with Hitler also. In short, the problem was how to intervene without 'over-intervening'.

It fell upon Krivitsky of Military Intelligence to supply one path out of the trap. On 5th August, *Izvestiya* announced Soviet adherence to the principle of 'non-intervention', and on 23rd communicated news to the French of an arms embargo.[66] At the end of August, Stalin placed before the *Politburo* his plans for the special type of intervention he required.[67] It is significant that Stalin, not Litvinov or even a show of Litvinov, was at work. While officially adopting 'non-intervention', the Soviet Union would render assistance to Spain — under certain conditions. For guns, there must be Spanish gold. Over the Republicans, there must be the tightest hold, amounting to Soviet control of the internal Spanish situation (for the Spanish front was one more extension of the later stages of the struggle between Stalin and Trotsky in exile). As Military Intelligence was mobilised, so was the *NKVD* for operations in Spain. On 14th September Yagoda (still head of the *NKVD*) summoned a special conference to discuss the details.[68] One of these details was an elaborately worked out scheme for the smuggling of arms into Spain. The Red Army was represented at this conference by M. S. Uritskii, acting head of Intelligence; the Red Army would handle the purely military and technical aspect of the Spanish action, to set the types of equipment to be sent and the categories of officers to be despatched — tank, artillery, aviation specialists, and military assistants. In all but military matters, Red Army personnel came under the aegis of the *NKVD*. By way of manpower, Stalin could utilise foreign Communists and have them organised into 'International Brigades'. While this was one substantial and even spectacular form of reinforcement, Red Army assistance was also necessary. Stalin selected Berzin, head of Red Army Military

Intelligence (Uritskii being his replacement due to the new assignment), to direct operations in Spain. As assistant and commissar to Berzin, Stalin attached Stashevskii, a former Red Army officer.[69] Stalin's directive, if so it might be named, took a curious form. *Podal'she ot artillereiskovo ognia!* — 'Keep out of the range of artillery fire!' — was passed on as a warning to exercise the utmost discretion and 'to stay out of the war'.[70]

Berzin, with Stashevskii's assistance, took command of the small and highly specialised Red Army contingent in Spain. Their immediate task was not to try out any other military method but that designed to accomplish the defence of Madrid. Red Army personnel were kept rigidly separate from any Spaniards wherever possible, and, in Krivitsky's description, isolated from any contact with Spanish political groups. *NKVD* surveillance was designed to accomplish that. The main objective was to keep their presence as secret as possible. The International Brigade was used to draw off publicity from Berzin's military staff, and the Brigade commander, under the *nom de guerre* of Kleber, served as a useful deflection by way of creating an artificial mystery. According to Krivitsky, Kleber's real name was Stern, a former prisoner of war lodged in a camp in Siberia. After 1917 Stern joined both the Party and the Red Army, going on to graduate from the Military Academy in 1924. After serving with Red Army Intelligence until 1927, Kleber (or Stern) was assigned to the military section of the *Komintern*, taking a part in the abortive adventures in China.[71] His romantic and fictitious past was concocted and publicly disseminated to conceal his real connection with the Red Army. While Stalin supplied a nucleus of a military command, his hidden arrangements to supply limited and conditional military aid began to show some result. By the end of October the first pieces of Soviet military equipment, transported by a Norwegian ship, had begun to make an appearance in Spain. Aircraft, tanks and artillery, in small quantities but doubly potent in their propaganda value, were employed in the later stages of the battle for Madrid. T–26 tanks appeared; some Soviet artillery was in action.*

* In his recent article, 'Soviet Military Aid to the Spanish Republic in the Civil War 1936–1938' (*The Slavonic and East European Review*, Vol. XXXVIII, No. 91; pp. 536–8 and table), D. C. Watt has presented the information obtained by the German military attaché in Ankara, which presumably came from a German agent with access to Turkish records. The record of shipments of Soviet military aid covers the period September 1936–March 1938. If these details are correct, over 700 tanks were despatched to Spain. Mr Watt observes, however, that the term *Panzerwagen* in the German original can also include armoured cars. The newly published *Ist. Velik. Otechest, Voiny Sov. Soyuza 1941–1945*, Moscow 1960, Vol. 1, p. 113, states that in October 1936, 30 Soviet tankcrew-tank instructors arrived with 50 tanks. The figure supplied in the German table is 58 (under *Panzerwagen*); the figure of 25 (I–15) planes also agrees with the German list. The Soviet volume sets the figure of volunteers at 557 (Soviet personnel); 23 military advisers, 49 instructors, 141 pilots, 107 tank crew, 29 sailors, 106 communications experts, military engineers and doctors, 73 interpreters and other specialists. Neither Zhukov nor Koniev is mentioned as being in Spain, only Malinovskii.

Borkenau saw in the relation between the military and the *NKVD* established by the conference of 14th September a certain independence for the former, in so much as the representatives of the Red Army were in no way 'executive organs' of the *NKVD* in Spain.[72] Yezhov's men acted with odious murderousness, the killings being preceded by a massive penetration into all aspects and levels of the state which Stalin was assisting in so bizarre a fashion. In the International Brigade, the commissars appointed (working as in the Red Army) were 'without exception'[73] agents of the Soviet security service, and the *NKVD* had a tight hold on the commissars nominated by Alvarez del Vayo, the Spanish commander, to purely Spanish units. Stalin had no reason to find fault with the work done by Berzin. Berzin's was the hand that guided both General Miaja and General Kleber in the defence of Madrid. Berzin's military staff, with its Red Army technicians and specialists, never attained any great numerical proportions. Krivitsky's estimate of the maximum is 2,000, with only pilots and tank crews ever committed to action.[74] With the successful defence of Madrid, which brought a momentary flood of prestige to the Communists and the Soviet Union, Stalin could regard one aspect of his policy as definitely accomplished. It was now the turn of the *NKVD* and its commander in Spain, Orlov, to press forward with its policy of killing, kidnapping and outright terrorisation in order to shackle the republic, which Berzin had helped to save.[75] Stalin's second manipulation of the *Komintern* in Spain brought about the same bloodshed and internecine destruction which his first, in China a decade ago, had worked. At a subsequent date, in common with other foreign armies, the Red Army command would have to decide what conclusions should be drawn from the lessons of the fighting in Spain. Towards the end of 1936, however, and as the terror increased at the start of 1937, the military command was occupied with attempts to restrain the *NKVD*. With relations between the Red Army and the *NKVD* already passing into a stage of increasing conflict at home, the Spanish action could only serve to exacerbate this.

In October, M. Coulondre took up his appointment as French Ambassador in the Soviet Union. Before leaving for his post the Ambassador had been given certain instructions and directions, 'précautions oratoires', to use his own phrase;[76] from the mouth of M. Delbos, Foreign Minister, these could be reduced to 'no preventive war', 'no Soviet interference in French internal affairs' and 'possible military aid', should war be inescapable. On the latter point, M. Coulondre could only bear in mind the complete lack of knowledge in French quarters of 'Russian possibilities'. From Admiral Darlan there had been little or no co-operation in the question of an exchange of naval attachés. Once in Moscow, Coulondre had to deal with Litvinov, whom he informed at once that the survival of the Franco-Soviet Pact depended on the Russians refraining from interference in French internal affairs. But the Pact lacked any vitality. Kalinin chided Coulondre over the French failure to co-operate. The Ambassador knew how well founded were the grievances. 'Our technical departments acted . . . with a great deal of irresponsibility.' Having supplied Red Army representatives with lists of war materials available, they had gone back on their word. The French Admiralty revoked its offer of naval guns, the War Ministry supplied merely obsolete artillery. The firm of Creusot had been placed in a totally false situation as a result of these caprices.[77] Not long after Coulondre indulged in a game of hidden purposes with the *NKVD*, in order to convey his views to Stalin, principally on the significance of the *Komintern*, and the transfer of its seat beyond Soviet frontiers. This was rejected as a suggestion on the grounds that the *Komintern* was an instrument of national defence. Affairs in Spain, run to Stalin's special rule, envisaged a particular if dishonourable role for the *Komintern*. The Anti-Comintern Pact of November 1936 signed between Germany, Japan and Italy — and about whose secret protocols Soviet Military Intelligence* kept Stalin remarkably well-informed[78]— made Coulondre's idea even less tenable. Rather Stalin decided, in all secrecy, upon a manœuvre all his own.

For this purpose, which was nothing less than opening direct negotiations with Hitler, Stalin chose the avenue of the Soviet Trade Delegation in Berlin and the person of the Soviet Trade Representative, David Kandelaki. Already the person of Kandelaki, close to Stalin and reputedly a school-fellow of his, had excited some notice in German diplomatic circles. Kandelaki, at a date unspecified in December, approached Schacht at his own request and enquired about the prospects of enlarging Soviet-German trade. Schacht replied that a pre-condition must be an end to Soviet inspired Communist agitation in Germany. After this initial exploration, Kandelaki, with his companion Friedrichson of the *NKVD*, left for Moscow for consultation with Stalin. According to the German documentation, it must have been at the end of December or beginning of January that Kandelaki was given a written draft proposing the opening of Soviet-German negotiations, either through ambassadors or, if the German government so desired, in secret.[79] The paper Kandelaki held in his hand reminded the Germans that this was not the first time an agreement had been suggested from the Soviet side.[80] In some six months, Stalin was to have the high command shot on charges of negotiating with the Germans.

* For Sorge, Hans-Otto Meissner also claims the unlocking of the door to the secrets of the Pact, one of the most effective keys being Sorge's handling of Colonel Ott (German Military Attaché, later Ambassador in Tokyo). It is not at all unlikely that the western and eastern agencies of Soviet Intelligence came upon the details.

There were, however, other straws in the wind, blowing from the direction of Prague. Certain negotiations had also been taking place between Hitler and Beneš. In 1935 Hitler had offered a gaurantee of integrity to Czechoslovakia in return for her neutrality in a Franco-German war. In the conversation recorded by Winston Churchill, Beneš informed him that it was in the 'autumn of 1936' that he was told to be quick in making up his mind as events in Russia were 'pending'. Beneš was in possession of information about a traffic between Berlin, the Soviet Embassy in Prague and Moscow.[81] Via the Soviet Ambassador in Prague, Aleksandrovskii, Beneš passed on to Stalin also news of this illicit traffic. Léon Blum was likewise informed. At the end of 1936 he ceased to press the French military authorities to take steps to fashion a real military solidarity out of the Franco-Soviet Pact, for his son, passing through Prague, had been given a private letter by Beneš for transmission to M. Blum. This letter advised taking up an attitude of extreme caution in dealings with the Soviet General Staff, for Czech Intelligence had stumbled upon the fact that the heads of the Soviet staff were conducting illicit relations with Germany.[82] It was this news, testified Léon Blum, that dealt a mortal blow to his efforts of the past months to give the Franco-Soviet Pact a real meaning. Léon Blum had cause for alarm at the receipt of such news from Beneš, for not only could it not be lightly dismissed coming from this level, but also Czech Intelligence enjoyed a considerable reputation with regard to Soviet affairs.

* * * *

In the event, however, it was to become apparent that Czech Intelligence was not the only foreign intelligence service interested in the Soviet high command. In connection with Putna, the *NKVD* had already shown its hand, but if this presaged an assault on the army, such a proposition seemed to have suffered a check. There entered also, at a date which eludes any precise definition, another intelligence service, the activities of which were to have considerable bearing on the ultimate fate of Tukhachevsky and his fellows. This latter organisation was Reinhard Heydrich's *Sicherheitsdienst* (*SD*), which entered on the scene by virtue of two possible considerations. One valid reason was the enmity existing between the SS leaders in Germany and the high command of the German Army; put more directly, such a condition was narrowed down to Heydrich's own inordinate ambition. In the inclinations of a part of the German military leadership for some sort of understanding with Russia, and the very fact that German senior officers had for not less than twelve years maintained close contact with the Red Army command, Heydrich discerned a means of bringing the army to heel by instituting an enquiry of treason against them.[83] By dragging up 'evidence' derived from the years of Red Army-*Reichswehr* contact, quite a plausible case of conduct prejudicial to the interests of the German state could be presented. Schellenberg, at that time one of Heydrich's lieutenants, has put the origin of Heydrich's intense interest in the Soviet command in a different context. Heydrich had learned from General Skoblin, Russian emigré and deputy to General Miller of the Union of Tsarist Veterans, that Tukhachevsky was engaged upon a conspiracy with the German General Staff with the aim of overthrowing the existing regime in the Soviet Union.[84] Heydrich, aware at once of the possibilities contained within this information, consulted Jahnke, a highly experienced officer who had worked with German Intelligence during the World War and became Hess's expert on intelligence. Jahnke looked somewhat askance at the 'evidence' supplied by Skoblin, warning Heydrich that Skoblin might well be a double agent, working on *NKVD* instructions. Stalin and the *NKVD*, reasoned Jahnke, might well wish to have the incriminating material against the Soviet high command come from an external and non-Soviet source, and also to weaken the German high command by raising suspicions in Heydrich's mind against them.[85] By way of appreciation for an exposition of opinion marked by no small degree of insight, Heydrich at once placed Jahnke under house arrest, suspecting him of too great a sympathy for the German General Staff. Taking this material emanating from Skoblin to Hitler, Heydrich obtained permission to concoct evidence *fully* implicating the German senior officers.[86]

A third version, supplied by an officer of the *Ostabteilung* of the SD,[87] places the origin of the idea of neutralising the Soviet high command and robbing Stalin of any effective political initiative in the mind of Hitler, who was only too willing to fall in with the scheme suggested by Heydrich, once Skoblin's information had worked its influence upon the latter. The actual forgery of the mysterious dossier cannot have been begun before January 1937. Schellenberg's account is noteworthy in as much as it makes reference to documentary material supplied by Skoblin to Heydrich. What is less credible is Schellenberg's account of the burglary organised by Heydrich's squads to break into the offices of the *Abwehr*, the organisation directed by Admiral Canaris, and the archives of the German General Staff.[88] Even less credible is the reported direct approach by Heydrich to Canaris for help in obtaining signatures and materials dating from the period of the Red Army-*Reichswehr* collaboration.[89] What is more likely is that Heydrich, aware of the relative inadequacy of the forgery facilities available in the *Jagowstrasse* head-quarters of the SD *Ostabteilung*, approached Canaris about the assistance which the *Abwehr* could supply over this highly technical matter. It was, however, without the co-operation of Canaris —

who was wary of Heydrich, his men, methods and motives — that Hermann Behrends, another SD officer, was able to obtain the specimen signatures so essential for the operation.* The *Ostabteilung* SD was able to obtain the services of a competent engraver, who could set the signatures of von Seeckt, Hammerstein-Equord, Tukhachevsky and Trotsky on to the incriminating material. All this took time. According to Schellenberg, it was in January 1937 that Heydrich ordered him to prepare a study of the relations between the Red and German armies. While much of the chronology and many of the circumstances remain obscure and a matter of completely contradictory interpretation, over the fact of a German intervention — stage-managed largely by Heydrich — there can be no doubt. Himmler himself gave a curious if lugubrious confirmation of the whole operation at a subsequent date.[90]

Krivitsky supplies one piece of information about the activity of the *NKVD* which ties down part of what was to become a highly-ramified conspiracy against the Soviet military leaders to December 1936, 'the first week of December'. The *NKVD* order, issuing from the head of the Foreign Intelligence Division, directed Krivitsky to assign two of his officers who could 'impersonate German officers', and assign them for *NKVD* duties 'without delay'. In a meeting with the head of the Foreign Division, Krivitsky was given a hint of the course set for opening negotiations with Hitler. The two agents detached from Krivitsky were to be set to work upon an assignment in France.[91] Only later was Krivitsky to see the significance of this demand for his men, and to connect it with the activity of Skoblin; his men were not, however, employed at once. After spending some idle weeks in Paris, they were informed that their mission had been postponed. The fact that Heydrich had received information, or was reported to have received information from a Russian emigré source — and that pin-pointed as Skoblin — raises the question of *NKVD* penetrations of these circles. In times past this had been known to happen, with disastrous consequences. In addition to General Miller's organisation, the Guchkov emigré group was known to harbour sympathies for National Socialism and suspected of contacts with German Intelligence; Krivitsky was to report that the Guchkov group also had been thoroughly penetrated by the *NKVD*.[92] And finally the long fingers of the *NKVD* might well have reached into Czech Intelligence, so that the latter's 'discovery' of suspicious, not to say infamous, conduct on the part of Soviet military leaders could well have been arranged.[93] By the use of such a channel, external and yet within a country known to be friendly to the Soviet Union, any denunciation of the Soviet

* On the question of signatures, *Zweigstelle Dresden* records a loan to the *Wehramt*, Ausl. VI from February–November, 1937, of 11th Infantry Brigade files which contained a specimen of Tukhachevsky's signature as a prisoner-of-war in Germany. See *OKH* Records (Part 1), The National Archives, Washington D.C.

high command would not appear to be the unaided work of the *NKVD*.

It would therefore appear that by the late autumn of 1936, and certainly by December of that year, some machination had been set in motion, the purpose of which was to compromise the Soviet 'military clique' led by Tukhachevsky. It was at the end of 1936 that Léon Blum received alarming news from Beneš.[94] By Christmas Heydrich was either in possession of his information concerning Tukhachevsky, or immersed in planning his moves against the German General Staff, or betwixt both. Krivitsky, according to his own testimony, had received in December an order to place at the disposal of the *NKVD* two officers for an assignment in Paris — although thereafter Krivitsky's story suffers something of a chronological collapse. Berlin, Paris, Prague and Moscow comprised the four points about which some web was being spun, and implicated in the spinning were the *NKVD*, Czech Intelligence, Heydrich's SD and Russian emigré circles in Paris and Berlin. Meanwhile, behind the Soviet frontiers, Yezhov's men loosed one more wave of arrests. By December 1936 preparations must have been far advanced for the trial of Radek, Pyatakov, Muralov, Serebryakov and Sokol'nikov as the main defendants. It fell to Radek, whether as a result of physical or mental intimidation, to name during the January trial not only Putna, but to implicate Tukhachevsky. All this must have been rehearsed towards the very end of 1936. External and internal 'preparation' undertaken by the *NKVD* against the Red Army was about to synchronise.

* * * *

During the autumn of 1936, at a time when his position seemed to be somewhat shaken, Tukhachevsky, together with Voroshilov, Yegorov, Uborevich, Budenny and Khripin, played host to a British military mission which attended the September manœuvres of the Red Army in the Belorussian Military District. A French and Czech mission were also in attendance.[95] Colonel Martel,* present on this occasion, provides a substantial critique of the exercises; it was 'more like a tattoo than manœuvres'.[96] A comparatively small area in relation to the size of forces engaged facilitated the control of troops, ideal for exercising with tanks on a terrain lacking numbers of river obstacles or marshes. What General Blomberg observed in 1928 Colonel Martel noticed in 1936 — that the level of tactical training at the junior officer level left a great deal to be desired. The Soviet ideas on the employment of tanks naturally occupied a place of prime interest, for observers and observed alike. Of the work of Khalepskii, Colonel Martel had only praise. But in the tactical handling of the tanks, as witnessed during these manœuvres-cum-demonstrations, considerable shortcomings

* Lieutenant-General Sir Giffard Martel, K.C.B., K.B.E., D.S.O., M.C.

could be discerned. Radio communication was not generally employed. Poor reconnaissance before tank advances led, even here, to the tank falling too often an easy victim to the anti-tank gun. The infantry-support tanks, large and with some speed but thinly armoured, would have suffered heavy losses if their attacks on defensive positions had been mounted in war. The mechanised formations, engaged in a 'spectacular battle', provided some idea of the use of tanks on a large scale, but 'little skill' was manifested in the way in which these forces were handled, the Red and Blue forces appearing 'just to bump into each other'. Aircraft used in direct support of front operations (although none were employed to bomb objectives in the rear) and parachute descents were other features of the exercises. Summing up, Colonel Martel found the Red Army not dissimilar to its Imperial predecessor in that it combined the old advantage of great physical toughness with the drawback of obvious 'tactical clumsiness'. The Red Army remained a bludgeon, a bludgeon with 'armoured spikes' on its head; the great danger was that a nimble and well-equipped enemy could dodge the blow and make the Russians pay for their clumsiness.[97] Of the Soviet senior officers, Tukhachevsky appeared to be the most able; Yegorov gave the impression of lacking drive, Voroshilov seemed similarly bereft of a strong personality, but Alksnis, Khripin and Khalepskii left a strong impression of knowing their jobs.[98]

In the light of these observations, critical without being exaggerated, the last great service rendered by Tukhachevsky's command group takes on particular meaning. At the close of 1936, the new *Provisional Field Service Regulations* (*PU-36*) were issued under Defence Commissariat Directive No. 245 of 30th December. The initial note announced that *PU-36* would supersede the 1929 regulations — and added a rider that chemical weapons would not be employed unless first directed by an enemy against the Red Army. The 1936 regulations provide a number of insights into the prevailing views of the Soviet command. In the first place, they are of some assistance in showing how far the Red Army command had grasped the essentials of modern war, and secondly in what manner they proposed to conduct their operations. In addition, in the light of what had appeared during the 1936 exercises, they are a commentary on how far the tactical handling of the army lagged behind the tactical possibilities envisaged by the authors of the regulations. In Chapter One (General Principles),* pride of place went at once to the offensive, which alone could produce the 'complete destruction' of the forces and resources of the enemy; the inter-action of all arms, acting along the line of the main blow and in complete depth was a second prerequisite. The employment of each arm must be governed by its particular characteristics and material capacities. Infantry, supported by tanks and

* See Appendix III.

artillery, '. . . by its own decisive actions in the offensive and by maintaining its combat position in defence decides the outcome of the battle.'[99] Artillery supplied the greatest concentration of fire-power, tanks the greatest mobility; in the offensive, tanks and artillery combined smashed open a path for the infantry. Used in conjunction with tanks, it was the task of artillery to destroy the anti-tank capacity of the enemy. In the offensive, *tanks must be employed on a mass scale*. Strategic cavalry would attack enemy flanks and the rear, but such was the capacity of modern fire-power that the cavalry must be prepared to fight dismounted. The mechanised unities

> . . . consisting of tanks, self-propelled artillery and lorry-borne infantry, are able to carry out independent tasks disengaged from other types of troops, or in co-operation with them. Mechanised unities possess great mobility, powerful fire-capacity and great shock power. The basic form of the operation of the mechanised unity in combat consists of the tank attack, which *must be secured by organised artillery fire*. The manœuvre and shock-blow of the mechanised unity must be supported by aviation.[100]

Aviation, in addition to carrying out independent operations, would operate

> . . . in close operational-tactical contact with all types of army formations, carrying out the tasks of striking at the columns and concentrations of enemy troops, striking at his combat resources, different types of transportation (low-flying attack-aircraft and light bombers), bridges (bombers), enemy aviation even on its own aerodromes (fighters, low-flying attack-aircraft and light bombers), and also defend its own troops and their dispositions (fighters). Reconnaissance aviation is one of basic means available to the command for operational and tactical reconnaissance.[101]

Modern technical means of waging war, available to the Red Army, were such as to permit

> . . . the simultaneous destruction of the enemy's combat order throughout the whole depth of his position. The possibilities have grown of rapid change of groupings, of sudden turning movement and investment of the enemy's rear area, cutting off his means of retreat.

In attack the enemy must be surrounded and completely destroyed.[102] Continuous reconnaissance and effective intelligence* were singled out as

* Only one word, *razvedka*, is used to cover both functions. In *The Military Staff* (Military Service Publishing Co., Penn. USA, 1952 Edn.), Colonel Hittle in his discussion of the Soviet staff draws attention (p. 249) to Zenoviev's article on intelligence functions at divisional level. The chief of the divisional intelligence/reconnaissance section was assigned: preparation of the reconnaissance plan, assignment of reconnaissance missions, preparing and forwarding requests for aerial reconnaissance, keeping the enemy situation map, reporting intelligence to the chief of staff and commander, despatching intelligence information to corps, adjacent and lower units. Colonel Hittle points out that the divisional intelligence officer was joined in his work by the political officer, the latter's responsibility falling more into 'what we consider to be counter-intelligence'.

the indispensable condition of success in war, and detailed provisions set out in the chapter dealing with the means of guaranteeing the security of operations, which also included anti-aircraft, anti-chemical and anti-tank defence.[103] The troop commanders were to maintain contact with their reconnaissance units by radio (coded messages), aircraft, armoured cars, light tanks, scout cars, motor-cycles and horses — precisely the 'refinements' which Colonel Martel had observed to be lacking, and from the lack of which he adduced a certain retardation in training and technique.

The principle of 'storm' and 'support' groups was maintained as the basis of the combat order prescribed for operations. Both were echeloned in depth (2–3 echelons). Both the march and combat order would be secured by the prescribed methods of anti-tank, anti-aircraft and anti-chemical defence. In offensive operations, the 'storm group' would be assigned to act in the direction of the main blow. The second storm echelon would support the operations of the first. If success was achieved on one of the offensive sectors, commanders were to direct there all forces and available means, employing the fire of the basic artillery mass and committing parts of the second (and third) echelons and reserves. When the enemy combat order had been shattered by the main blow, the support groups would mount their attacks 'with the main decisive offensive'.[104] The aim was to achieve 'the isolation, complete encirclement and annihilation' of the enemy; tanks, artillery, aviation and mechanised troops (tank-borne infantry — seven men on the top of each tank), used on a large scale, could accomplish simultaneously the turning of one or both enemy flanks, the bursting into the enemy rear with tanks and tank-borne infantry with the aim of cutting off the retreat of the main enemy force; aviation, mechanised and cavalry units would attack columns in retreat. (In the 1936 manœuvres, opportunities had *not* been taken to turn a retirement into a rout by the use of aircraft.) Tank forces were divided, in the divisional tank battalions, into infantry support tanks (TPP) and long-range tanks (TDD), the latter to be used for deep penetrations into enemy positions. Infantry-support tanks in offensive actions operated under the control of the infantry commander. Long-range tanks, according to the tactical situation, operated under the control of the corps or divisional commander. In the same way, the artillery was allotted an infantry (or cavalry) support role (PP/PK) and a long-range (DD) bombardment function, with siege artillery (AR — *Artilleriya razrusheniya*) for the bombardment of heavily fortified positions.

The 1936 regulations contained interesting views on the use of tactical aviation. By definition in Chapter Five, tactical aviation was conceived of as an aerial extension to the means of destruction supplied by infantry and artillery fire — in fact, aerial bombardment, to be applied on *a mass scale* to achieve maximum success. Liaison was to be effected by use of technical means and perfected by 'personal contact between ground force and aviation commanders'.[105] Low-flying ground-attack aviation (*shturmovaya aviatsiya*) was to assault enemy formations entering or leaving the engagement, damage his communications, cover sea-borne landings (or river-crossings), disrupt rear services — railway links, stations, motor-transport — and assist in warding off enemy bomber attacks. Fighter aviation had the basic task of destroying all types of enemy aircraft on the ground and in the air. Light-bomber aviation would operate against enemy troop concentrations, staffs and lines of communication, railways and roads and enemy aviation on its aerodromes. In addition, light-bomber aviation would take part in parachute operations and air-landing work (the SB–2 was used as a troop-carrier at a later date). Aviation was to open an assault on the enemy while on the march, even before he was committed to the meeting engagement; aerial attack on his columns 'will prepare his piece-meal destruction'. Low-flying attack aircraft produced the best results, with machine-gun fire, bombing and the spraying of poison gas; light bombers would augment the bombing and gas attacks. Mechanised unities would also be loosed on these enemy columns. In the meeting engagement aviation would likewise carry out the reconnaissance and spot for the mechanised brigades assigned to effect the destruction of enemy infantry (and cavalry) forces, as well as knock out the artillery.[106]

The emphasis in offensive operations was upon utilising the co-operation of various arms to achieve a simultaneous neutralisation (*podavleniye*) of the entire depth of the enemy defences. Aviation would strike at the enemy rear and his reserves, artillery would disrupt the work and hammer at the whole depth of the tactical disposition of the enemy, long-range tanks would penetrate the depth of the enemy's tactical position, infantry supported by tanks would invade the enemy positions, mechanised and cavalry unities would be hurled deep into the enemy rear, while extensive use of smoke-screens would conceal from the enemy the deployment of the second echelons.[107] A flank attack was designed to open the way to the rear, thus bringing a double pressure to bear upon him. The combat directives would fix the duration of the artillery preparation, the time of the attack to be launched by the long-range tanks and the time of the infantry attack. The time-table must be so devised (and incorporated into the directive) that feasible co-ordination for the given terrain could be implemented between infantry, artillery and tanks. The corps commander would have liaison officers (equipped with radio) with the long-range tank groups and a staff officer in the open to maintain observation of the battle-field and the course of the tank operations. The penetration of the long-range tanks into the depth of the enemy defence positions had 'a decisive significance'; therefore, this must not be frittered away by failure to relate the committing of these tanks to '*the concrete conditions of the tactical situation*'. The strength of enemy anti-tank gunfire, the location of anti-tank obstacles and the nature of the terrain would, to a large degree, determine the choice of the sector to which the long-range tanks would be committed. The DD tank attack would generally be so planned that the infantry and infantry-support tanks could take advantage of the disordering of enemy fire-systems; shortening the gaps between the DD tank echelons and the infantry supported by their tanks 'prevents the enemy establishing a fire-system'. If the main defence line presented terrain difficulties for the tanks, the infantry attack — supported by artillery and tanks — must precede the long-range tank attack; in that contingency, the tanks will exploit the infantry gains. The tank battalion of the DD group would adopt a formation where the tanks were closed up for the assault; the breadth of front, depending on the terrain conditions, artillery disposition and the depth of the tank formation itself, would be 300–1,000 metres (per attacking battalion). The aviation group (AG), during the development of the battle, would be committed to prevent the enemy moving up his reserves and to destroy units attempting to escape encirclement; in order to make full use of the possibilities of aviation, Red Army infantry and tanks in assault should have special agreed and visible recognition marks or signs, which their own aircraft can see.[108] Artillery preparation was aimed at neutralising enemy artillery, destroying or neutralising observation points and strong points (especially concrete fire-points), the neutralisation of machine-gun fire schemes on sectors either not to be assaulted by tanks or inaccessible to their attacks. During the DD tank attack the artillery would provide support designed to paralyse enemy anti-tank guns or to cause substantial reduction in their volume of fire; during the infantry-tank attack, the artillery will support 'with fire and wheel', reducing machine-gun positions and anti-tank guns. Where there were not less than 30–35 guns concentrated per 1 kilometre of front (not including long-range artillery) and up to 2 tank battalions per rifle division, the artillery preparation could be cut to half an hour. With 'an insufficient quantity' of tanks, the artillery preparation would be prolonged to three hours, and even longer if the enemy defence system comprised very strongly fortified positions. In all cases '. . . *the tank attack on the main defence line must be secured by artillery support and cannot proceed without it either in the operations of the main forces or in reconnaissance*'.[109]

Defence ought to be so designed that, as enemy infantry is destroyed before the main defence line, tanks cannot achieve a break-through into the depth of the defensive positions; in the case of a tank break-through, the infantry must be detached and destroyed with rifle and machine-gun fire, the tanks destroyed by artillery fire and tank counter-attacks. Modern defence must be

> . . . above all *anti-tank* [defence], consisting of a fire-system of troop and anti-tank artillery in conjunction with a system of natural and artificially constructed anti-tank obstacles and rapidly placed anti-tank mines and other artificial obstacles. The courage of the defender, the clever utilisation by him of terrain in conjunction with rifle and machine-gun cross-fire, by the disposition of machine-gun units in anti-tank zones, establishes the condition for the desired destruction of the attacking infantry and their being detached from the tanks.[110]

Main defence lines, assault group zones and artillery positions must be selected by virtue of their anti-tank possibilities (lines inaccesible to tanks, flank fire-positions, etc.). The anti-tank zone must be circular to be of any advantage, and the intervening spaces between them ('passages' — *koridory*) must be covered by anti-tank guns firing over open sights. At the main defence line the anti-tank guns would be screened by anti-tank obstacles, in the depth of the position distributed throughout the anti-tank zones. Basic anti-tank zones would be assigned by the divisional commander; supplementary zones may be fixed by the dispositions of the regimental commanders. The infantry must be imbued with the idea that it is not the tank itself, but the infantry following in its wake, which is the greatest threat to them. The battalion area would adopt a circular defensive form. The divisional commander is to direct the divisional artillery barrage on to the main body of the attacking enemy forces, seeking to detach the infantry from the tanks. In the event of a tank break-through into the depth of the defensive positions, the divisional commander would employ his mobile anti-tank reserve against the invading tanks and his own would mount a tank counter-attack. Having thrust the enemy tanks back and having thrown the enemy infantry into confusion, the divisional commander in his turn would counter-attack with his storm-groups and re-establish the position which has been disrupted. All uncommitted forces would be employed in the counter-attack, which would persist until the main line had been re-established. Only the divisional commander, who must report without delay to the corps commander, could order a cessation of the counter-attack.[111]

To disrupt enemy preparations for the offensive, the corps commander may employ 'counter-artillery preparation' (*kontrartilleriiskaya podgotovka*), aimed at infantry being moved up, tanks being moved into position, staff centres and communication networks; 'counter-preparation' ought also to forestall enemy artillery preparation. If reconnaissance indicated disorganisation of the enemy preparations, the divisional commander may mount spoiling attacks with independent detachments, covered by artillery fire, although night attacks offer the greatest security.[112] Defence on a wide front was organised when forces were committed to the defence of a front 'significantly in excess of the normal' (a rifle division defensive front was set at a length of 8–12 kilometres and a depth of 4–6 kilometres, the rifle regiment sector 3–5 kilometres long and 2½–3 kilometres in depth, the battalion area 1½–2½ kilometres long and up to 2 kilometres deep).[113] Wide front defence disposed of a general defensive system, employing instead separate areas set against the probable line of an enemy advance — 'the basis of the defence on a wide front consists of the battalion area' — assigned to throw back the enemy with fire-screens and disrupt the advance of his storm groups. The artillery would be distributed between the regimental sectors and the battalion areas. Mobile defence would be employed when for operational reasons it was possible to relinquish ground in order to gain time and to keep forces intact. It was characterised, not by actions fought 'to the bitter end' (*do kontsa*), but falling back on new defensive lines; the support group in mobile defence would have less than its usual strength, and divisional artillery would be decentralised in its control, guns being distributed to regiments and battalions. Chemical weapons played a notable part, and every opportunity should be taken for delivering 'short blows' at the enemy.[114] In this context, therefore, 'mobile defence' resembled more a delaying action or a series of such actions.

The new regulations embodied a number of specific Soviet features, such as preoccupation with the flank attack and the disruption of the rear, the stress upon the offensive, and a special emphasis upon 'activeness' and 'initiative'. The main contribution of the regulations was the attempt to work out a precise theory for operations — offensive and defensive — conducted in depth. The constant exploitation of the artillery fire-power available was stressed at all times. It was apparent that the tank and the aeroplane had been only imperfectly coupled. With regard to the offensive operations, multi-echeloned and mounted from depth and proceeding into depth, it was apparent that the problem of sustained contact with the enemy was somewhat underestimated; encirclement would facilitate the annihilation of enemy man-power and equipment piece-meal.[115] The difficulties of co-ordination were by no means small, and although the regulations stressed the vital importance of liaison and inter-communication, some of the evidence of the 1936 manœuvres suggests that essential equipment was not abundant and even totally lacking. The use of group-tactics for the infantry made it inevitable that the support groups would be reduced to a certain passivity, both in the offensive and in defence. The infantry tactics were no advance on what they had been seven years ago. The provisions for defence, while taking account of the need for depth also, did not ensure that the small tactical groups — also deficient in the means of inter-communication — could persist in their operations if temporarily cut off by a considerable enemy penetration, since they lacked strength. The tactics of separating the infantry from the tanks in order to deal with each threat separately, while making a neat theory, was to have disastrous consequences when applied.

In spite of the obvious and inevitable imperfections in the new work, the question has to be answered as to what degree of mastery and understanding of the new forms and basic features of contemporary warfare Tukhachevsky and his collaborators had achieved. Increased mobility, while facilitating manœuvre, also accelerated actions at the tactical level, increasing their tempo and curtailing their duration. This was the contribution of motorisation. Mechanisation was employed substantially in the break-through method developed; rapid regrouping and deployment of forces would enable the command to take advantage of any success on the decisive sector. The storm group embodied the greatest concentration of force. Tactical air power was to be utilised to the full to derive from it the benefits of support and protection, extending the notion of depth vertically to cover the enemy's air-space. The 1936 regulations incorporated a doctrine of tank warfare based upon the experiments which had been proceeding for some six years. The tank was utilised both for infantry-support and independent operations, although the latter aspect was more sketchily portrayed in 1936. It was apparent that experimentation was by no means over; what was definitely affirmed was the absolute necessity of artillery support for all forms of tank attack. The long-range tanks, supported by artillery, would be committed with each tank battalion (32 tanks) having a frontage of 300–1,000 metres broad. While emphasising the importance of surprise, speed, mobility and tactical dexterity, the Soviet offensive was not conceived as a 'lightning blow', but as a series of blows, each adding to the power of the offensive, each mounted with careful preparation. Certain features (such as the committing of the DD tanks) called for great tactical skill, a talent not conspicuously displayed in the 1936 manœuvres. Tukhachevsky demanded 'nerve' and initiative. Yet the very operation of the command method seemed to blanket this at subordinate levels. The emphasis lay upon exact implementation of the plan, which had to be almost rigidly specific in order to compensate for the deficiencies in tactical ability and training at the lower levels. The offensive form adopted called for considerable flexibility (especially in the forms of the co-operation of the various arms), and yet the danger was dogmatism and even conservatism. The refinements of equipment which would have facilitated the operational forms envisaged by the

1936 regulations were also lacking, an inhibiting factor which could not be underestimated.

On balance, however, it was a striking piece of work, indicating progress in solving the problems which Tukhachevsky had admitted were besetting the command at the beginning of 1935. But it was the political rather than the military fortunes of Tukhachevsky which were at stake towards the close of 1936.

★ ★ ★ ★

Whatever storm had shaken the military command in the late autumn of 1936 appeared to have settled momentarily by late November, although alarm was stirred up as Yezhov began to slip the purge into high gear and the arrests continued. If there had been an attempt by Party leaders, supported by a section of the military command, to put a brake on the policy of out-and-out terror, then it met with no success. Yet it was not a simple failure, a show of impotence complete. Stalin did not meet the threat or the possibility of resistance to his aim of a grand decimation head-on. Behind the formal and formidable apparatus of the *NKVD* and the police, Stalin had constructed one more secret and utterly reliable purging command of his own,* of which Yezhov was a highly important member. Through these clandestine channels, 'operating behind the back of the normal party organs,'[116] Stalin could strike at will, unencumbered by pleas for moderation. Of equal importance, Yezhov had overhauled the *NKVD*, carrying out a salutary purge of the purgers. The scene was almost set. It is also quite feasible that Tukhachevsky could remain in complete ignorance of the nature of the moves being made against him.

By contrast, in the full glare of publicity, military leaders at the 8th (Extraordinary) Congress of Soviets paraded some of their achievements. Khripin made sensational disclosures about the Soviet Air Force; proclaiming (not without some basis for it) the *VVS* the strongest air force in the world, Khripin announced that the combat strength had quadrupled since 1932, that 60 per cent of the combat machines of the *VVS* were bombers, and that 100,000 pilots would be ready for duty at the end of the year. Orlov announced a sevenfold increase in Soviet submarine strength since 1933, with the trebling of small coastal defence craft.[117] Although statements at the Congress of Soviets concerning the Soviet armed forces tended to be stereotyped, aiming to assure home opinion of the growing military capacity of the Soviet Union and advise would-be aggressors to desist, Khripin's

* A. N. Poskrebyshev headed Stalin's personal secretariat and possibly the Special Department of the Secretariat, and its successor the Secret Department. What relations this had with the *NKVD* remains almost wholly obscure. On Stalin's death, Poskrebyshev vanished.

assertions were little short of sensational. In connection with the new Constitution, which the extraordinary Congress had been summoned to adopt, Tukhachevsky had been named No. 191 of the editing commission. During the 8th Congress, Tukhachevsky played a conspicuous and active role, and on the eve of its opening *Pravda* had published a lengthy article by him on the defence of the Soviet Union.[118]

Official and public favour had certainly not been withdrawn from Tukhachevsky at the close of 1936. But this was no real test. In its own way, the new Constitution provided a clue to the essentials of the situation, for the previous provision forbidding 'non-toilers' to handle arms was now superseded — which is to say that the 'toilers', as a section of society, had undergone considerable transformation. While every effort had been made to increase the worker contingent in the Red Army, it is difficult to say how a mechanic from a collective farm was classed — peasant or worker. The significant point is that collectivisation and mechanisation had blunted the original sharp division between 'worker' and 'peasant'. The very great significance of the 1935 decree on ranks implied that, socially, the Red Army was moving to a form not radically different from that of a 'capitalist' army. Yet, by definition, the Red Army was the armed instrument of the dictatorship of the proletariat. In short, military reorganisation brought with it (as in 1923–4) social problems of some dimension. The issue vitally affected the Soviet officer corps. Trotsky was indubitably correct in seeing 1935 as a revolution in the relation of the army to the state. From this initial consolidation of prestige and privilege, the officer corps was closing itself up, with its special immunities and benefits developing almost into a caste. Nor was the officer corps immune from the wider social effects, deriving basically from the increased technical requirements, in so far that influx to the officer corps was coming from the new intelligentsia. In other spheres of Soviet life Stalin had replaced the older cadres by those reared under his rule. That military cadre, swelling in size with each graduation from the Military Academies, had access only to the lower command posts. Taking Voroshilov's figures of the proportion of Civil War veterans holding senior (divisional and above) command posts in 1933 as one substantially correct, then the 'upper crust' by 1936 — even by conservative estimate — would still be 80 per cent veterans, whose tutoring owed nothing to Stalin. One of the essential preconditions for a successful purge (again as in 1923–4, when the 'Red commanders' played politics for promotion) was a division within the officer corps. If at the end of 1936 there was no actual division, a rift of no small size was in the making.

PART FIVE

THE MILITARY PURGE AND THE RECONSTRUCTION OF THE COMMAND

As for the military men, Trotsky, in speaking of them, mentioned only one name, that of Tukhachevsky, as a man of Bonapartist type, an adventurer, an ambitious man who strove not only for a military but also for a military-political role and who would unquestionably make common cause with us.

> N. N. Krestinsky, at the evening session on 4th March, 1938 during his trial.

And, as you know, we had before the war excellent military cadres which were unquestionably loyal to the Party and the fatherland. . . . There is, however, no doubt that our march . . . towards the preparation of the country's defence would have been much more successful were it not for the tremendous loss in the cadres suffered as a result of the baseless and false mass repressions of 1937–1938.

> N. S. Khrushchev, speech in closed session of the 20th Party Congress, 25th February, 1956.

The victims of the repression were also prominent military leaders, such as Tukhachevsky, Yakir, Uborevich, Kork, Yegorov, Eideman and others. They were the praiseworthy men of our army, especially Tukhachevsky, Yakir and Uborevich . . . I knew comrade Yakir well. I knew Tukhachevsky but not as well as Yakir . . . One must say that Yakir in his time had been regarded by Stalin as of great importance . . . We could also add that at the moment of his being shot Yakir cried out: 'Long live the Party, long live Stalin!' . . . When they told Stalin how Yakir had behaved before his death, Stalin used foul language over Yakir.

> N. S. Khrushchev, closing remarks at 22nd Party Congress, 27th October, 1961.

CHAPTER FOURTEEN

The Killings: 1937

On 23rd January, 1937, the trial opened of the participants in the 'anti-Soviet Trotskyite Centre', in which the principal defendants were Radek, Pyatakov, Muralov, Serebryakov and Sokol'nikov. As in the first great show-trial of 1936, Vyshinsky led for the prosecution. On 24th, in the course of numerous exchanges, Vyshinsky brought Radek to his disclosures about Putna, who had already been implicated by the 1936 trial:

Vyshinsky. Accused Radek, in your testimony you said: 'In 1935 ... in January ... Putna came to me with a request from Tukhachevsky. ...' I want to know in what connection you mention Tukhachevsky's name.

Radek. Tukhachevsky had been commissioned by the government with some task for which he could not find the necessary material. I alone was in possession of this material ... he accordingly sent Putna ... to get this material from me. Of course, Tukhachevsky had no idea either of Putna's role or of my criminal role. ...

...

Vyshinsky. So Putna came to you, having been sent by Tukhachevsky on official business having no bearing whatever on your affairs since he, Tukhachevsky, had no relations with them whatsoever?

Radek. Tukhachevsky never had any relations with them.

...

Vyshinsky. Do I understand you correctly that Putna had dealings with the members of your Trotskyite underground organisation, and that your reference to Tukhachevsky was made in connection with the fact that Putna came on official business on Tukhachevsky's orders?

Radek. I confirm that, and I say that I never had and could not have any dealings with Tukhachevsky connected with counter-revolutionary activities, because I knew Tukhachevsky's attitude to the Party and the government to be that of an absolutely devoted man.[1]

Radek's 'reference'* had meant mentioning Tukhachevsky's name no less

* It has been suggested that Radek bought his own life (he was not sentenced to death) with a bargain stipulating full 'co-operation'. V. and E. Petrov, in their *Empire of Fear*, London 1956, pp. 68–9, state that Radek was killed in 1938 in a prison brawl, when a fellow convict flung him on to the concrete floor. V. Petrov, as an *NKVD* code clerk, received the telegram announcing this.

than ten times in the course of that particular passage. Tukhachevsky's testimonial of loyalty came from a man standing flanked by *NKVD* guards and undergoing trial charged with the gravest crimes against the state. There was clearly some great mischief afoot against the Red Army's commanders, for the only context in which the mention of a name could bring favour was to have that name bracketed on a list of intended 'victims' marked down by these 'terrorists'. It was of no benefit to Tukhachevsky to be absolved politically by Radek.

At the same time a series of re-shuffles in the high command was set in motion. On 27th January the naval command was re-organised, with the Baltic Fleet commander Galler taking over the post of the deputy commander of the Soviet naval forces from Ludri, who was appointed to the head of the Naval Academy. Galler's Chief of Staff in the Baltic Fleet, Zivkov, took over command of the fleet and one of the lecturers at the Naval Academy, I. S. Isakov, took up the post of Chief of Staff to the Baltic Fleet. On 28th January, two new deputies were appointed to Voroshilov, Alksnis and Orlov, appointments which appeared to have no effect on Tukhachevsky's own position, but which had been made almost simultaneously with Radek's bringing Tukhachevsky's name into the trial. Nor were the changes confined to the European commands. In February, Army Commissar 2nd Grade Aronstam was recalled from his post as chief of the Far Eastern political administration and appointed to the position of chief of the Moscow Military District political administration. His successor in the Far East was Corps commander Chachanyan. In the Moscow Military District Aronstam had displaced Army Commissar 2nd Grade Veklichev, who was transferred to head the political administration of the North Caucasus Military District.[2] An important change had already taken place in the senior command of the Leningrad Military District, when at the close of 1936 Corps Commander Primakov, Shaposhnikov's deputy, had been replaced by Germanovich, himself a Corps commander and director at that time of the Stalin Academy of Mechanisation and Motorisation of the Red Army. Like Putna, Primakov's fate remained something of a mystery, for he was not appointed to another command position and presumably was taken into the care of the *NKVD*.[3] Quite the opposite was happening now to what had taken place in the Soviet command some eighteen months ago, when on that occasion the aim had been to consolidate the command and increase its effectiveness. The command was being broken up, dispersed and cross-posted — military and political officers alike. Officers like Aronstam, with five years service in a senior post, were being prised away from their commands and presumably their sources of support. Nor, as the coming weeks would show, was there any conclusive proof that certain of these officers reached their new posts. Primakov is a case in point. Aronstam's eventual successor turned out to be his deputy, Vaineros, while Chachanyan was connected with another duty forming part of the shackling of the command. It was, then, early in 1937 that the key moves in the isolation of the command were being made and soon these would gather momentum.

During the month of February Blyukher's command was also reorganised into the Far Eastern Red Banner Front, which meant in effect separating the Trans-Baikal garrisons from the forces of the Far Eastern army, at least as far as command was concerned. This separation had already been begun in 1935, when the Trans-Baikal Military District was created out of the western garrisons of the Far Eastern Army. The strength of Blyukher's forces had grown to not less than 240,000, made up of 170,000 regular troops, 40,000 *NKVD* (under separate command) and 30,000 of the Kolkhoz Corps and supported by 900 tanks and 400 armoured cars, 1,000 aircraft (80 heavy bombers). In all, Blyukher had 20 rifle divisions and 3 cavalry divisions at his disposal, making up the defence forces of the garrisons of the coastal provinces, the concentration about Blagoveshchensk and the army group to the west. The 40th Rifle Division was in Rasdolnaya, the 26th at Nikolsk-Ussurissk (army corps staff), the 8th Cavalry Division at Grodovka and the 21st Rifle Division at Spassk. The main force of the 2nd Kolkhoz Division was stationed about Smakovka, and the 2nd Rifle Division at Khabarovsk. The 34th Division was settled in the recently-created province of Birobiyan, the 12th Division at Blagovshchensk, the 3rd Kolkhoz Division and the 36th Rifle Division at Chita. Rokossovskii's 15th Cavalry Division was stationed about the Dauriya, and the 57th Rifle Division had its main force at Olovyana and a secondary force at Stretensk.[4] Thus assembled and powerfully armed, Blyukher had a formidable force at his disposal, a deterrent to the Japanese but a force also under a commander of an independent turn of mind. While the re-organisation of early 1937 was some rationalisation of command, there was something of a precaution also about it. Blyukher's wings were being clipped.

The trial of Radek had brought with it the first substantial hint that a move against the military was being contemplated, transferring the hints and rumours set about beyond the Soviet frontiers into a situation developing within these borders. The Radek trial also brought a furious German protest at the way in which Radek had attempted to involve the German Military Attaché. General Köstring at once communicated an official denial of all that had been implied by Radek to the Defence Commissar Voroshilov.[5] While this row blazed up (and in 1939 Stalin was to make a personal apology to General Köstring for so inconveniencing him[6]), the long arm of punishment reached out to Spain, where on 4th February, 1937, General

Kleber was relieved of his command of the International Brigade.[7] He too was assigned to a new command position, this time in Malaga, but was arrested by the *NKVD* and vanished. In Spain the *NKVD* began its relentless extermination of opposition to Stalin, a process resisted with all stubbornness in Catalonia; it was a murderous procedure which called forth the protest of the Red Army representatives Berzin and Stashevskii. In March 1937 Krivitsky reported reading a confidential report from Berzin to Voroshilov on the state of affairs in Spain; Berzin was optimistic about the military situation* and reported favourably on General Miaja, but protested at the behaviour of the *NKVD* which was undermining the basis of Soviet authority in Spain. Berzin demanded the recall of Orlov from Spain.[8] These views, of which Yezhov did not remain in ignorance, were not calculated to smooth the relations between the Red Army and the *NKVD*.

The hints thrown out by the Radek-Pyatakov trial that further liquidations were pending received some confirmation at the February-March plenum of the Central Committee. Stalin made it plain that the purges were to go on, rooting out all subversion, and putting into plain language a reference to the damage which 'spies on the Staff' could do.[9] Krivitsky supplies a description of the scene at this plenary session, at which Bukharin, Rykov and Yagoda were paraded — guarded by *NKVD* troops — before the Central Committee. Demanding more trials, Stalin directed the hysteria against Yagoda, who could only observe mockingly that six months ago he might have arrested them all. Bukharin rose weeping and pleading amidst this turmoil to deny that he had ever participated in a conspiracy against Stalin or the state. Stalin interrupted Bukharin to denounce his behaviour as that unbecoming a revolutionary — that he might prove his innocence in a prison cell. According to this version, Stalin was given an ovation and the prisoners were led back, to the shouts of 'Shoot the traitor!'[10] The military members of the Central Committee would have been present at this appalling scene. There is no indication of how they reacted, either with vote or voice. Voroshilov and Budenny could be expected to support Stalin. If Gamarnik and Yakir, Tukhachevsky and Uborevich tried to check Stalin, their opposition had no effect. If they acquiesced (and Krivitsky's account suggests a mass condemnation) this also did not save them ultimately.[11] It was too late to save Bukharin, however much the military may have desired this. With whatever inaccuracies or distortions Krivitsky has described this session, one point can be agreed on — that the prisoners had seen a show of Stalin's power advancing to the absolute. The time for the army to intervene to check Stalin had been during the first great clash

* In his 'Military Lessons of the Spanish Civil War' (*Foreign Affairs*, October 1937, pp. 34–44) Major-General A. C. Temperley reported that some 200 Soviet tanks were in action.

with the Right in 1929–30, when they might have succeeded in putting Bukharin in power.

Meanwhile Stalin's secret diplomacy was being directed to achieve positive results in Berlin. On 29th January, Kandelaki and Friedrichson once again made their appearance before Dr Schacht, to deliver a verbal undertaking from Stalin and Molotov; the proposal was that the Soviet and German governments should open direct negotiations. Dr Schacht could only ask Kandelaki to pass these 'interesting' comments through the Soviet ambassador to the *Auswärtiges Amt*. Kandelaki, however, pressed Dr Schacht to ascertain whether the Russian proposals might be taken up. Dr Schacht felt that he could only reply to the effect that certain guarantees — such as damping down on *Komintern* agitation — would have to be forthcoming.[12] On 10th February, Neurath saw Hitler about the proposals Kandelaki had made. In a letter of 11th to Dr. Schacht, Neurath began by saying that nothing was known of a Soviet proposal for an agreement with Germany made at the time of the negotiations over the Franco-Soviet Pact. As for seeking a guarantee in the form of having the Russians desist from *Komintern* activities, this seemed to have little practical possibility — indeed, Neurath agreed with Hitler that no practical result could emerge at this juncture by taking up the Russian proposal. However, Neurath continued,

> It would be quite another matter, if things in Russia were to develop further along the lines of an absolute despotism based on the army (*gestüzt auf das Militär*). In that event, we would not, to be sure, let the occasion slip to bring ourselves once more into contact with Russia.[13]

In addition, Neurath passed on the information that the rumours of discord between Stalin and Voroshilov were to be discounted as mere diversionary rumours spread by 'interested circles in Warsaw'. This, then, was the advice passed from one dictator to another — let him be master in his own house, basing his power upon rather than sharing it with the army.

Only a few days after Neurath had written this reply, the Soviet ambassador in Paris, Potemkin, was in the process of conveying to M. Léon Blum the views of the Soviet General Staff — against whom M. Blum had already been warned — on the forms of assistance which might be rendered in the event of a German attack on France or Czechoslovakia. There were two possibilities. If Poland, ally of France, and Rumania, permitted the passage of Soviet troops through their countries, the Soviet Union was ready to act with all arms. If, for 'incomprehensible reasons' Poland and Rumania refused this right, then Soviet assistance would be necessarily curtailed. Troops could be sent by sea to France (a point which Potemkin himself insisted upon) and aviation forces despatched to France and Czechoslovakia.

In both cases, Soviet naval forces would be readied to give assistance. The Soviet Union could also supply France and Czechoslovakia with petrol, food-stuffs, manganese, armaments, engines, tanks and aircraft. The Soviet General Staff, for its part, wished to know what assistance France could render the Soviet Union in the event of its being attacked by Germany, and the scope of this assistance, as well as what military equipment France could supply to the Soviet Union. Potemkin was asked — why is passage through Lithuania not envisaged? The Soviet General Staff replied that passage for Soviet troops had been envisaged through the countries friendly to France, and if other possibilities existed, then it was up to France, acting in concert with the Soviet Union, to prepare them.[14] On 9th April, M. Daladier passed the contents of this exchange to General Gamelin, who made his observations in a note on 10th. As for French aid in the event of a German attack on the Soviet Union, if France herself was not attacked by the bulk of the German forces, this would take the form — subject to particular circumstances, to the provisions of the various mutual assistance pacts and to obligations under the League — of offensive action by all French forces not committed on other fronts or to the defence of overseas possessions. France was unable to supply the Soviet Union with military equipment so far as could be foreseen, since she had need of all of her own production. Concerning the passage of Soviet troops through Poland and Rumania, the French General Staff saw at the moment no solution to this formidable problem and envisaged as the only rapid form of assistance the use of aviation and motorised troops, since both Poland and Rumania would require all their rail transport facilities for their own mobilisation needs.[15] The French were immensely reserved and cautious. General Gamelin and M. Blum had had several talks on the Russian question. Léon Blum testified that the information on the doubtful reliability of the Red Army command coming from Dr Beneš 'paralysed his efforts' to make the Franco-Soviet Pact effective militarily. Already, before the shootings began, the attack on the Red Army leaders had impinged directly on the international scene.

* * * *

Putting the purge into top gear did not, however, meet with a lack of opposition. Ordzhonikidze, whose deputy Pyatakov had recently been tried, evidently tried to intervene in order to put a brake on the *NKVD*, thereby incurring the full displeasure of Beria. Ordzhonikidze had tried to bring Stalin round to his point of view over Beria. This failed manifestly, and Stalin permitted 'the liquidation' of Ordzhonikidze's brother and put no hindrance in the way of Beria bringing Ordzhonikidze 'to such a state' that the latter 'was forced to shoot himself'.[16] One of the consequences of the January trial had also been the temporary disappearance of Tukhachevsky,* but by mid-March he was seen once again and even dined by foreign diplomats.[17] What appears to have finally roused the officers was the extent of *NKVD* interference in the Red Army, and the question of how to curb this. It appeared to outside observers in late March that the Red Army had indeed won this first round, to judge by the re-appearance of Tukhachevsky, and that the strange circumstances of the Yagoda-Tukhachevsky duel of late 1936 had almost repeated themselves. There was indeed a lull in March, although denunciations were on the increase. A likely explanation is that the *NKVD* was undergoing its final overhaul before being sent into action. At a date set by Krivitsky as 18th March — fifteen days after Stalin's speech about the need for further purging and renewed efforts to root out the 'Staff spies' — Yezhov addressed a meeting of senior officers of the *NKVD* 'in the clubroom of the annexe to the Lubyanka building'.[18] Here Yezhov denounced Yagoda, his former chief, as a former Tsarist police spy, as a thief, embezzler and emulator of Fouché. Denunciations of Yagoda's 'spies' in the *NKVD* followed, and Yezhov's demand that no weakness should be shown in the coming intensification of the purge.[19] Krivitsky makes also a second observation on Yezhov, that he was the power behind a formidable security apparatus which was responsible to Stalin alone and which had 'co-existed' for some time with the larger *NKVD* organisations. When Yezhov took full control, he brought with him some 200 men of this personal entourage,[20] the cadre of the force designed to accomplish the complete liquidation of the generation which Stalin had marked down.

Tukhachevsky's position had undoubtedly been shaken. Further protests by the Soviet military command in Spain provided an illustration of how his power had diminished. While Berzin had already made his views known to Voroshilov, in April Stashevskii returned to Moscow to deliver a personal report to Stalin on the situation in Spain. From a military point of view, the position looked relatively favourable; the Italian General Bergonzoli's motorised columns had been pounded to pieces in the famous engagement of Guadalajara which opened on 8th March. On 12th Republican aircraft caught the Italian columns bogged down as a result of heavy rains, and on 13th, using 40 T–26 Soviet tanks, Republican forces had driven the Italians back to their starting line.[21] But Stashevskii had not come to Moscow to discuss military successes, but the methods employed in the rear by the *NKVD*.

* N. Basseches in his *Stalin* (London 1952, p. 302) mentions 'the invention of a strange story' to cover this period. Marshal Tukhachevsky demanded an enquiry into his name being mentioned by Radek. This he obtained, with full Party rehabilitation. The official explanation of Tukhachevsky's final fall linked his extravagant living with the move to the provinces to teach him the simple life. A. Uralov, *The Reign of Stalin*, p. 48, states that Tukhachevsky was re-assured after a talk with Stalin. This seems somewhat improbable.

A 'rock-ribbed Stalinist', Stashevskii sought from Stalin some assurance that this policy might be changed. In a conference with Tukhachevsky, the same point was brought up by Stashevskii, and although the Marshal presumably wished to put a stop to the disastrous policy, he no longer possessed the authority to carry out the necessary disciplining.[22] In Spain, the Red Army had already lost completely to the *NKVD*. To be precise, it was in and over Spain that the Red Army and *NKVD* had locked into combat.

Also at this time, that other hidden element of the situation, the activity of Heydrich's SD, suffered an equal intensification, and the point was about to be reached where the intrigues of a Berlin office would become an inextricable part of the whole circumstance of the case being worked against the Soviet high command. The fact that Heydrich hoped above all to start a treason trial in the *Bendlerstrasse*, to compromise the German military, was given some support by an arrest made by Heydrich on 22nd March, when Ernst Niekisch — confidant of General von Seeckt and friend of Radek — was taken into the custody of the Gestapo.[23] There was also the question of making certain 'improvements' to the documentary material which Heydrich had obtained earlier and which allegedly compromised the Tukhachevsky group of the Red Army high command. Lacking the necessary facilities for skilled forgery, the SD evidently went outside its own immediate circles to obtain the services of a practised engraver. The original material, which had not incriminated any German officers, was given a whole new dimension — a faked correspondence involving the signatures of General von Seeckt, Trotsky, Tukhachevsky, Hammerstein-Equord and Suritz. The margins of the documents were also supplied with appropriate initiallings.[24] Genuine agreements did exist, made at the time of the hey-day of the *Reichswehr*-Red Army collaboration, which would have served admirably as models for any copying and astute alteration. It is by no means clear as to precisely what type of agreement Soviet and German officers had entered into in 1929 and what inducements were offered to hold Germany to the east. An agreement over an exchange of intelligence could be altered into 'espionage'; as the German documents dealing with the collaboration were not infrequently ambiguous and circumlocutory, full of meaning only to the initiated, so retention of a hard core of the genuine would not have been impossible. The finished product was not, as Schellenberg subsequently asserted, 'a remarkably voluminous dossier,'[25] bulk not being one of its features. One of the principal agents behind the compilation was Hermann Behrends of the SD, assisted by another officer attached to that organisation.[26]

The next problem was to get the dossier into Russian hands, in such a manner that the whole affair would retain all its plausibility. The first plan seemingly involved transmission through the Czechs, but this was abandoned as being too risky.[27] In place of this original scheme, the SD turned to exploring the possibilities of effecting delivery through the German Communists and thence to Soviet agents. The idea of any direct trafficking between Heydrich and Yezhov is completely without foundation, but what cannot be dismissed is the circumstantial evidence for a certain collusion between the Gestapo and the *NKVD*. The no-man's-land lay in the strange world of the German Communist underground, over which the Gestapo kept constant surveillance and in which it practised all the arts of penetration. Into this world, patrolled also by the *NKVD*, the SD could introduce its material, advertising a sale of secret papers of interest to the Russians. The SD did indeed fix a price for its goods and enter into a transaction with a German Communist (or Soviet agent), but not after the wildly melodramatic manner depicted by Schellenberg, with his false roubles and aeroplanes. It is also extremely probable that the dossier did travel by way of Prague, but only along the channels of *NKVD* communication.

The SD dossier was ready by April. Although many details concerning its preparation remain obscure, the existence of the forged material cannot be held seriously in doubt. While it would be a fallacy to suppose that Stalin and Yezhov depended on this forgery to accomplish their plans (distinct moves against the military being already apparent before the forgery was complete), the dossier may well have played a very important part in determining the timing of the military purge. This would seem to be the key point about the purge of the high command — not the search for reasons but the explanation of the timing. It is possible that Yagoda had bungled one attempt to bring the military into the *NKVD* net. And it was of the greatest importance that 'evidence' against the proscribed senior officers should come from an external source. The Radek trial had already prepared some of the ground for tales of conspiracy with foreign powers inimical to the Soviet Union. Schellenberg volunteers the information that the dossier reached the Russians in the middle of May 1937.[28] Krivitsky, at a point which may be identified as not later than the beginning of the third week in May, approached Frinovskii for an explanation of the mounting panic in Moscow and arrests in the Soviet officer corps. Frinovskii replied that conspiracy — 'a gigantic conspiracy' — had just been uncovered in the Red Army.[29] Frinovskii might perhaps have added that at last the *NKVD* had within its possession material which could be used against the army, that the poisoned bread cast upon the waters was bringing its final return.

* * * *

Already by April the *NKVD* offensive against the officer corps was beginning to swing into action. Putna and Primakov were by now in detention. Gekker, the corps commander in charge of the foreign liaison department of the Red Army, had inexplicably disappeared in April.[30] Schmidt, who had threatened to 'lop off Stalin's ears', was in an *NKVD* prison and had been for some time.[31] In April, the Red Army newspaper *Krasnaya Zvezda* launched a sharp attack on army commander 2nd grade Kork, head of the Frunze Academy; the head of the Leningrad Military-Political Academy, Ippo, was also singled out for attack.[32] Krivitsky's interpretation that Stalin, confident of an agreement with Germany, could proceed with immunity to decimate the command, and his information that Kandelaki had had an interview with Hitler and bore a draft agreement back to Moscow is not supported by any evidence from German files.[33] The proof to hand would support only the view that the Germans were not encouraging about the prospect for an agreement unless there were 'further developments' in the internal Soviet scene — a hint involving the army. On the other hand, the Kandelaki affair had not petered out in February and contact of some kind was being maintained with Berlin.

On the morning of the May Day parade Tukhachevsky was the first of the military leaders to arrive, walking alone and hands in pockets, at the reviewing stand. A second Marshal, Yegorov, took his place but neither saluted nor glanced at his fellow Marshal. Gamarnik also silently joined the rank. At the conclusion of the parade of the Red Army, Tukhachevsky did not wait for the civilian parade to follow, but hands still in pockets, took advantage of the break to walk away 'out of the Red Square, out of sight'.[34] This public appearance had a parallel in print, when the journal *Bol'shevik* carried Tukhachevsky's commentary on the new *Field Service Regulations* of the Red Army, the *PU–36*, in which Tukhachevsky's ideas had been paramount. The commentary was some indication of how much Tukhachevsky's military ideas had sobered down from the almost fanciful notions with which he had opposed Trotsky during the period of the military debates of 1921–2. Tukhachevsky attacked the idea that a 'special' manœuvrability of the Red Army did in fact exist, and when it was put forward, it was a result of sentimentalising the experiences of the Civil War and ignoring the technique and armaments of potential enemies. The way in which the Red Army had approached the question of its own armaments was a proof that this 'special' manœuvrability had been discounted. Tukhachevsky admitted that the acquisition of quantities of tanks and aircraft had at first given rise to 'a theoretical twist' of the Fuller school. This produced a new manœuvre theory, which argued that the tank, by virtue of its speed, could not be used for co-operation with infantry. It was therefore logical that an attempt should be made to separate the armour into independent tank-formations. This Tukhachevsky criticised for its failure to take into account the power of anti-tank fire, and for the failure to realise that tanks, like infantry, could not operate successfully without massive artillery support. Tukhachevsky singled out Voroshilov for criticism in insisting that the superior morale of the Red Army man would alone bring victory, a 'self-deception' which could bring only unnecessary losses and reverses. Tukhachevsky pointed to the lack of harmony existing in the capitalist countries between the pleading for the small mechanised army and what was actually being done; the French Army — using combinations of tanks, artillery and infantry — was not adopting the ideas of Colonel De Gaulle.* The same thing could be observed with the British Army. While not excluding certain independent operations for tanks, Tukhachevsky defended the idea of the co-operation of all arms as a fundamental of success, insisted upon the need for massive artillery support for tanks and infantry alike, and maintained that the 'harmonic' idea was fully justified in the Red Army and that its tactics ought to be based on this principle.[35]

It was not, however, a military theory which was at stake at this juncture but the very existence of the present command, for the real crisis in the affairs of the Red Army advanced with great rapidity. Even so, it was a blow mounted with no small advertisement of its coming and the gradual build-up of arrests among senior officers hardly conformed to the 'lightning blow', the preventive security strike, in which form the purge is sometimes represented. The critical period can be pinned down to the seven days from 3rd–10th May. Tukhachevsky's appointment to the Soviet delegation attending the coronation ceremonies of King George VI in London was cancelled. Having been so nominated in April, on 3rd May Tukhachevsky's documents had been sent to the British Embassy, but on 4th the British authorities were informed that Tukhachevsky had been taken ill and a visa would no longer be required.[36] Flag Officer 1st grade V. M. Orlov of the Soviet Navy was appointed to fill Tukhachevsky's place in the delegation, which left on 6th. Already on 28th April *Pravda* had published an article on the necessity for the Red Army man to master politics as well as techniques, that the Red Army existed to fight the internal as well as the external enemy. The implications of that article were clearly directed to preparing the way for a drastic political drive in the army, and suggested that Stalin had lost all confidence in the Political Administration. The atmosphere,

* In 'The Armies of Europe' (*Foreign Affairs*, January 1937, p. 246) Captain B. H. Liddell Hart singled out the Red Army for this appraisal: (i) new and old ideas were 'strangely intermingled', with, for example, horsed cavalry racing into tank-infested areas, (ii) many foreign ideas were assimilated without being properly digested, (iii) the actual handling of the tanks by their crews was not equal to the higher tactical handling of armoured forces, (iv) there was an undue disregard for modern fire methods, (v) it would be better to rely on the mechanised forces as such, for there was a risk of communications breaking down in the mass offensive.

thickened with nightmare, denunciation and near panic, was tense in the extreme in early May. The first major blow fell on 10th–11th May, when the threads of the previous months were gathered up into an announcement of the restoration of 'dual command' and of certain changes in the high command. The re-imposition of commissar control was to take the form of setting up of military soviets in Military Districts (with collective command) and the military commissar was to assume his former control functions in military units, training establishments and administrations of the Red Army. The new military appointments came as a greater shock. Marshal Yegorov was relieved of his post as Chief of the General Staff, but appointed First Deputy Commissar of Defence. Army Commander 1st Grade B. M. Shaposhnikov was appointed to the post of Chief of the General Staff (a post in which he had preceded Yegorov in 1931). Army Commander 1st Grade Yakir was transferred from the command of the Kiev Military District to Leningrad. Marshal Tukhachevsky was appointed to the command of the Volga Military District — comprising three territorial divisions and a couple of tank battalions.[37] Tukhachevsky was therefore consigned to the same outpost of disgrace to which Shaposhnikov had been despatched in 1931, when he had momentarily fallen foul of Stalin. Between Shaposhnikov in 1931 and Tukhachevsky in 1937, in connection with the posting to the Volga Military District, lay one vital difference — Shaposhnikov had certainly taken up his menial post. Tukhachevsky had displaced Dybenko as the district commander in Samara (Kuibyshev), yet in the second half of May *Krasnaya Zvezda* was still referring to Dybenko as the area commander.[38] Tukhachevsky, it would seem, never took up his new post. Possibly by 15th and certainly not later than 22nd May, Tukhachevsky was under *NKVD* detention. Frinovskii and his special *NKVD* troops would have been well suited to accomplish this arrest.

Arrests of senior officers proceeded with a momentum of their own. Yakir never reached Leningrad but was also seized by the *NKVD*. Muklevich, who had played such an important part in the technical expansion of the Soviet Navy, was arrested and lodged in the same cell as Bela Kun, the Hungarian revolutionary.[39] Khalepskii had been separated from his tanks and given Yagoda's former assignment in posts and telegraphs. The head of the Volga Military District political administration, corps commander Orlov (who had been recently appointed to this post after many years as deputy head of the Kiev Military District political administration) was relieved of his duties. On 1st June *Krasnaya Zvezda* attacked the Kiev military-political organisation, thus confirming the downfall of Orlov and his former chief in Kiev, Amelin. On 18th May, *Krasnaya Zvezda* reported that Ippo had been transferred to the military soviet of the Central Asian

Military District; on 1st June, he also was denounced for 'political blindness'. Kork of the Frunze Academy was arrested. On 3rd June an article in *Komsomolskaya Pravda* referred to Eideman of *Osoaviakhim* as the former head of that organisation and mentioned Gorshenin as his replacement.[40] Veklichev, who had been transferred from Moscow to the North Caucasus as head of the political administration, was relieved of his duties. On 28th May, *Krasnaya Zvezda* reported the appointment of Army Commissar 2nd grade Mesis (who was formerly head of the Volga District political administration) to the military soviet of the Belorussian Military District, and a certain Pismanik as head of the political administration. Uborevich, Belorussian Military District commander, had vanished, together with Bulin, chief of the political administration and deputy to Gamarnik. Amelin, who had been Yakir's political chief in Kiev, was referred to as the former head of the political administration in *Krasnaya Zvezda* on 2nd June. Shchadenko, formerly of the 1st Cavalry Army and Shaposhnikov's commissar at the Frunze Academy, was appointed to the military soviet of the Kiev Military District.[41]

The axe had fallen on Yan Gamarnik, head of the Red Army Political Administration. His suicide, which was supposed to have taken place on 31st May, was reported on 1st June. Already there had been signs that Stalin had lost complete confidence in the Political Administration as an instrument capable of ensuring support within the armed forces for his policies. The purge, as it gathered momentum in the Red Army, was falling on senior political officers as well as commanders. The decision to re-impose commissar control marked the end of the Tukhachevsky-Gamarnik era, when their policies even before they themselves were swept out of the Red Army. In effect, the Political Administration was treated in a manner no different from the regular military command, and it seems probable that in Stalin's view both had become identified to such a degree that discrimination would have been impossible. Ridding himself of Gamarnik did, nevertheless, pose certain awkward problems for Stalin. There was considerable danger in so mutilating the political apparatus in the armed forces that its comparatively delicate fabric would be shattered. Gamarnik's 'suicide' seems, to say the least, highly questionable. Either he was killed resisting arrest or killed in prison by the *NKVD*.[42] The same technique was used in 1937 as had been employed in 1924 — that previous crisis with many parallels with 1937 — to pull the Political Administration into line; the conference of Party organisations within the armed forces was used to hammer out a new line and to indict the former personnel. On 6th June, *Krasnaya Zvezda* denounced Gamarnik as one of the most dangerous of the 'enemies of the people' and 'a Trotskyist lackey', a counter-revolutionary long engaged in spying and Fascist banditry. Increased revolutionary vigilance was demanded of the commissars, that same vigilance which the former leadership of the Political Administration had failed to show. The very peak of such blindness had been shown by the deputy chief of the North Caucasus Military District political administration, who had discounted the lessons of the trial of the 'Trotskyite Centre' by saying that everything was quite in order in the military-political organisations in his district.

The purge of the political staff was conducted with less secrecy, and indeed was almost a purge within a purge. This had also been a feature of the 1923–4 crisis. The assault on the high command was made with greater secrecy, and the technique had been to break up the cohesion of the higher command levels and to seize individuals at a distance from any support they might have mustered from their troops. Even before this move, a careful thinning out of the staffs of the higher commanders seems to have taken place. Individuals like Muklevich were merely seized and imprisoned. Gekker's fate was similar. In all the welter of cross-postings, only in certain cases was there any proof that the new commander or political officer arrived. The clamour in the press increased. The first stage was almost over.

* * * *

From 1st to 4th June, the Military Soviet attached to the Defence Commissariat held an extraordinary session, at which members of the Soviet government were present. It was here that Yezhov submitted a report on the 'counter-revolutionary and treasonable organisation' which had for a long while conspired within the ranks of the Red Army.[43] The 'case' against the Red Army officers was therefore being presented and put forward as an internal conspiracy, as well as treason. Yezhov was presenting it as work of detection and apprehension, the sudden uncovering of criminal activity. The participation of Voroshilov raises the question of his role in the development of the military purge. At the time, rumour was rife that Voroshilov and Stalin were indulging in a struggle for power, that the position of the Defence Commissar was no more secure than those of his senior officers already under arrest. The rumours lacked any foundation. Stalin was proceeding against a major part of the command but not the whole of it. The adherence of Voroshilov to Stalin's policy was one fact of great importance which made the purge possible. However reluctant the acquiescence, it was nevertheless exactly that. In the equally relevant question of who was *not* purged in the Soviet officer corps, membership of the former 1st Cavalry Army conferred a noticeable immunity, plus Stalin's personal protection of Shaposhnikov.[44] Budenny took over the Moscow Military

District (the former commander Belov being assigned to Uborevich's command). Timoshenko kept the North Caucasus, Shchadenko supervised the Kiev military soviet. Yegorov had been pushed in as Tukhachevsky's replacement. Zhukov was not touched. Apanasenko and Tyulenev survived to be promoted. In June 1937 the 1st Cavalry Army finally and fully revenged itself for the condemnation which Tukhachevsky had heaped upon it after the disastrous outcome of the battle for Warsaw in 1920. Old scores were about to be settled.

On 9th June, Tukhachevsky, Yakir and Uborevich were relieved of their commands. In an official communiqué printed in *Pravda* for 11th June, it was announced that the investigation of the case of Tukhachevsky, Uborevich, Yakir, Eideman, Kork, Primakov and Putna — arrested *at different times* by the *NKVD* — was concluded.[45] The case was to be transferred at once to a special military tribunal of the Supreme Court.* Under the regular president Ulrikh, this special tribunal was reported to consist of Alksnis, Budenny, Blyukher, Shaposhnikov, Belov, Dybenko, Kashirin and Goryachev. Belov had assumed Uborevich's command; Goryachev commanded the special Cossack Corps (soon to be disbanded). Dybenko held the post of Leningrad Military District commander, and had been predecessor to Tukhachevsky on the Volga — he was still reported as that after Tukhachevsky's posting there. Only on 10th June was Yefremov announced as the commander of the Volga district. On 12th June came Voroshilov's order of the day, intimating that the special military tribunal had condemned the arrested officers to death, the sentences being carried out at dawn on 12th. The charges covered treasonable contact with powers unfriendly to the Soviet Union, espionage on behalf of these powers, sabotage of Soviet defence measures and the Red Army, and planning a restoration of capitalism in the Soviet Union. All the accused were found guilty. A second version charged the dead officers with maintaining connections with the Trotskyite-Zinovievite 'terrorists' who had already been tried, with planning the liquidation of Soviet power, with planning the assassination of members of the Party and the government, with the sabotage of Soviet defence measures, with conveying military secrets abroad, and with plotting to cede the Ukraine to a foreign power in return for assistance in the realisation of their plans. All confessed their guilt.[46]

As for the real situation, there is no proof — apart from the official communiqué — that there was any trial of any kind. Krivitsky asserts that, to his certain knowledge, Alksnis was a prisoner of the *NKVD* at a time when

* Besides doubting the whole idea of a trial, A. Barmine dismisses the stories of Tukhachevsky, wounded, being carried to the court-room on a stretcher. He writes (*One Who Survived*, pp. 7–8) that Tukhachevsky's twelve-year old daughter hanged herself and her mother, arrested also, went insane.

he was supposed to be sitting in judgement on his fellow officers.[47] The names of Voroshilov and Yegorov were missing from the court-martial board, a fact which aroused immediate comment. The two announcements bore marked discrepancies. The first was designed for foreign opinion and confined itself to charges of treasonable contact with Germany, sabotage and what amounted to conspiracy. The second, much more melodramatic and diffuse, was aimed to persuade Soviet opinion of the guilt of the executed officers. In both cases, the immense gravity of the charges was designed to consign the accused to the extreme of perdition, to associate their names with the most heinous of crimes against which there could be no recovery of even the faintest reputation.

The question of the guilt of the Red Army officers so charged is not a real one. The whole case rests rather upon the assumption that the elimination of that portion of the command not bound to Stalin would have been necessary at some stage. Not a single item of evidence has emerged to justify the charge of treasonable contact with the Germans.* Even if the accused were desirous of coming to an understanding with Germany, then Kandelaki could bear witness to the fact that this was Stalin's own policy. As for internal conspiracy, even the charges — if such they can be called — were vague in the extreme upon this point. No consistent evidence has been adduced to justify this accusation.[48] An anonymous senior Soviet official has gone on record at this time as saying: 'Obviously, the charges of espionage and treason against the generals should not be taken literally.'[49] If a *coup* had been planned (and the German Army was to show the desperate difficulty of such an undertaking), then it was surprising that Yakir's and Uborevich's motorised troops, Alksnis's aircraft and the Red Army tanks did not succeed. If there had been a military conspiracy on a vast scale, then the government would not have found it so easy to press through the decimation to its dreadful end. If a military strike had been intended, the blow should have fallen with all speed immediately after Radek's trial. Tukhachevsky was an expert on civil war, and lest it be argued he lacked spirit, with the VIIth Red army at Kronstadt in 1921 he had not shown himself averse to blood-letting in a cause. There had been no lack of hints that some action against the army was pending — at the trials, in the press and in the various disappearances of senior officers. In his April talk with Stashevskii, Tukhachevsky could not have failed to discern the crux of the matter. In

* No post-war evidence has come to light to disprove this. F. Thyssen in *I paid Hitler*, London 1941, p. 194, asserts that Werner von Fritsch and Tukhachevsky, both anxious to deal with the dictator in his own country, attempted contact. It is difficult to know where the support for this statement comes from, although there was a contemporary Polish newspaper report that a letter or note from Fritsch had been seized from Tukhachevsky. In Serial 393/212238–241 there is a report dated 23rd July by Joza David on the Red Army, which maintains that Tukhachevsky was in contact with Rosenberg.

short, the essence of the 'Tukhachevsky affair' was the sign of minute care and skilled preparation with which it had been mounted by Stalin and his *NKVD*, rather than the 'lightning blow' against conspiratorial army commanders.

Stalin must, therefore, have had weighty reasons for deciding that the Red Army's best brains and leading personalities were expendable. In liquidating the most independent section of the high command, Stalin rid himself of the last potential source of a leadership which could rival his own, having sent or being in the process of sending his political opponents to the wall. The action was not so much to prevent a conspiracy but to block an eventuality. In addition, the Tukhachevsky-Gamarnik policy was taking such a course — dictated by the interests of military efficiency — that it would have led the army out from under strict political control. With the increasing emphasis on patriotism and nationalism, the army could become identified with the nation and only latterly with the Party.* Stalin's general problem was to manufacture those conditions which would enable a stricter control of the armed forces to be worked without serious detriment to military efficiency. The particular problem was to eliminate a potential source of leadership, to settle with a command which regarded itself as an equal to all comers, which enjoyed not only military but also political position, and which refused to become 'the creature of a political bureaucracy'. On numerous occasions Stalin had been obliged to treat with the command, to concede and retract. The final struggle had been to preserve the Red Army from the attentions of the *NKVD*. Before his own preparations were complete, Stalin appeared to acquiesce even in this; indeed, the support of the Red Army was indispensable to him in curbing the *NKVD* and permitting Yezhov to reform the cadres of repression. But in the final play, the Red Army lost. A crime black enough to cover the Tukhachevsky group with the utmost infamy was needed, together with 'proofs' sufficient to impress external opinion and stifle internal doubts. It is of the greatest significance that a major provision was made to persuade senior Red Army officers of the 'guilt' of the accused. This was the basic precaution. Although the supposed 'trial' may be largely discounted, the same cannot be said for that extraordinary session of the Military Soviet early in June. Here the 'documentary proof', which no doubt included Heydrich's dossier, was presented to Red Army commanders met in special session.[50] This time no antics in the witness box or contradictory

* This has had fairly recent consequences, for the 're-habilitation' of Tukhachevsky was stopped at a time when Zhukov's dismissal was pending. There were evidently two factors at work in blocking a full 're-habilitation' of those killed in 1937–8: (i) the guilt for this was collective, (ii) to complete the re-instatement to their former honour of those like Tukhachevsky may have been an encouragement to serving officers working for greater emancipation from political controls.

stories produced by *NKVD* intimidations, but 'the proof', was produced. This may well have been the master-stroke which did not alienate the army from the regime. If the Tukhachevsky group could not be broken, then it had to be 'framed', to be so completely dishonoured and the conviction of the rightness of this spurious judgement so effectively planted that even in death there could be no rallying to it.*

★ ★ ★ ★

The shootings and arrests, moreover, were not confined to the commands of the Red Army in European Russia. The Radek-Pyatakov Trial of January 1937 had also prepared the ground for punitive actions in the Soviet Far East, since some of the accused had confessed to expediting 'sabotage' on the instructions of the Japanese. These sinister signs began to bear full fruit in May, when drastic action was taken against officials of the railway administration of Eastern Siberia; on 20th, 44 persons were shot for reasons given as Japanese-inspired sabotage, and conveying military secrets to the Japanese.[51] Since the rail communications were of vital importance in imparting real effectiveness to Blyukher's forces, these and subsequent executions could not fail, by virtue of the dislocations so caused, to affect the military performance of Soviet Far Eastern forces, even before the military itself had been touched with its own decimations. And while the executions among the Soviet high command had an undeniable effect in altering unfavourably the estimate in which the Red Army had been held in the west, among potential foe and potential friends alike, the Far East had not been denuded of any of the immediate dangers which faced the Soviet command. To interfere with the military efficiency (or even the impression of that efficiency) of Blyukher's troops was to call in disaster through the Soviet back-door. In no sense could a purge of the Far Eastern military be purely an internal operation devoid of effect on the balance of power.

In China, a new situation was in the making as a result of the events of December 1936, when Chiang Kai-shek had been kidnapped and the infinite intrigue of the 'Sian affair'[52] had led — not to the murder of Chiang Kai-shek by the Chinese Communists — but to the possibility of a limited agreement between the Nationalists and the Communists. Protracted negotiations between these two parties continued throughout the first half of 1937.[53] At the same time, Soviet circles were filled with visible alarm

* There was, nevertheless, a lashing condemnation aimed at Stalin from Raskol'nikov from Bulgaria in an 'open letter', dated 17th August, 1939. The letter accused Stalin of destroying the leaders of the Red Army at the moment of the greatest danger of war, of lying to the nation that the Red Army was becoming stronger, of bringing in dual command and destroying military discipline. For the text, see W. Hermann, 'Die Rehabilitierungen und ihre Grenzen' in *Aus Politik und Zeitgeschichte* (Bonn), for 5th December, 1956.

at the turn which Anglo-Japanese relations were taking; on 10th May, *Pravda* accused London of 'handing over North China to the Japanese', thereby encouraging Japan to direct her energies against the Soviet frontiers in the east.[54] Although there is no evidence whatsoever to support the idea that Moscow had any hand in the Sian *coup*, in April there appeared to be signs that a new Soviet policy towards China was in the making;[55] in Nanking the Soviet ambassador Bogomolov was reported to have made suggestions for a Soviet-Chinese mutual assistance pact.[56] The Chinese Communist Party and the *Kuomintang* were all the while pressing forward their discussions for the organisation of a United Front against the Japanese.

In June, following on the executions among the high command of the Red Army, the purge of commands spread to Blyukher's forces in the Far East. Already by the first half of 1937, the number of arrests in the Soviet Far Eastern and Eastern Siberian areas had been estimated at some 2–300, the full force falling on the railway administration. Now, while Blyukher was still in Moscow and at a time when his name had been associated with the 'trial' and his rank nailed to the condemnation of his fellow-officers, the *NKVD* began its assault on the command and political staff of the Far Eastern Red Banner Front. Vaineros, successor to Aronstam in the Far Eastern Front political administration, was arrested; Sangurskii and Petrushin of the front staff, Valin, chief of intelligence, Sukhomlin, chief of combat training, and staff commissar Rabinovich were seized by the *NKVD*. Mirin, editor of the Far Eastern Military newspaper *Trevoga*, was demoted and sent off to a unit in the Pri-Amur area. Okunev, senior political officer of the Pacific Fleet, was also seized. The purge also extended to the command of the Trans-Baikal Military District.[57] In all, the first phase of the Far Eastern military purge lasted some five weeks, and only lost its initial momentum when Blyukher himself returned to the Far East. The purge of the civil, Party and even security administrations continued, but so compressed was the organisation of the rear of Blyukher's front that civil dislocations were certainly not devoid of military significance.

This first military purge in the Far East did lack, however, the ferocity and intensity exhibited elsewhere in the Red Army. While the fact that Stalin had patently not lost confidence in Blyukher and permitted perhaps only the minimal scope to the *NKVD* may have been of some importance in bringing this about, it is more probable that the situation in the Far East conspired to halt any massacre, for such it was becoming elsewhere. The 'self erasure' by Stalin of the effectiveness of Soviet power must have vastly encouraged the Japanese command. Within that body two main groups had made their appearance — described by Mamoru Shigemitsu as 'the Russia (or Northern) School' and 'the China School'. The preoccupation of the

General Staff, where protagonists of 'the Russia School' predominated, was to bring Japanese equipment up to the standards required in order to engage the Soviet Union. It was therefore inevitable that this group should oppose the idea of any Japanese expansion into the south of China, for it was intended to secure Manchuria primarily and exclude the Russians from North China.[58] Viewed against this background the 'Amur incident'— the 185th of its kind on the Soviet-Manchurian border—assumed a critical importance out of all proportion to the small forces engaged.

On 28th June, Major-General Masaharu Homma, who had attended the coronation celebrations in London and returned to Japan via the Soviet Union, wrote in the paper *Osaka Mainchi* that the recent executions in the Soviet high command had produced a situation in which the Red Army was threatened with disintegration. No longer could it be assumed that the Red Army was in any way a threat to the Japanese. What followed two days after the publication of this view would lend support to the idea that the Japanese command deliberately subjected the Soviet Union to a test of intention, undertaken at a time when Soviet self-inflicted wounds were assuming serious proportions. On 21st June, two small islands in the Amur River had been occupied by Soviet troops (operating some seventy miles below Blagoveshchensk).[59] On 30th June fighting broke out between Soviet and Japanese-Manchurian troops, sundry patrols and gun-boats being involved in the action. While Shigemitsu had already protested to Litvinov over the appearance of Soviet forces on and about 'Manchurian territory', it seemed that a very serious clash had been averted for the moment, and on 2nd July Voroshilov had ordered the withdrawal of Soviet troops and gun-boats. The Japanese also gave an assurance to withdraw. But on 6th July, a company of Japanese troops occupied the Bolshoi Island in the Amur River. In spite of Soviet protest, the Japanese troops stayed and no attempt was made to dislodge them. The Japanese reaction was one of high satisfaction at the outcome of the incident, a proof indeed of the views expressed by Major-General Homma, and a test that the Soviet Union would not commit itself to serious action, at least for the present. The capacity of the Soviet Union to undertake extended military operations in the Far East could be assumed to be 'to no small extent paralysed'.[60]

Following quickly on this episode, on the night of 7th–8th July a company of Japanese infantry, exercising by night some ten miles west of Peking, clashed with troops of the Chinese 29th Army from the small neighbouring town of Wanping. On 8th, the Japanese brought up artillery to shell the town; stubborn Chinese resistance followed a Japanese call for surrender.[61] The 'China Incident', which was to develop into the massive and protracted Sino-Japanese war, had begun. From the outset it was held in Moscow that the 'Incident' could scarcely be localised, and that a major conflagration was looming up. The German view was that a 'military showdown' between China and Japan could only be to the benefit of the Soviet Union, who had a vested interest in having the Japanese engaged elsewhere than upon the eastern frontiers.[62] A Japanese view which reached the Germans pointed out that the 'Soviet Russians were inciting the Chinese', but Japan did not want a clash with Russia 'at this time'. The aim of Japanese action was 'the large-scale and definitive disruption of all lines of communication between Soviet Russia and China'. Should Soviet military intervention occur, the Japanese would strike through Mongolia 'in the direction of Irkutsk'.[63] On 21st August, China concluded — not a mutual assistance pact — but a non-aggression treaty with the Soviet Union, after negotiations which seem to have been lengthy. In Berlin, the Chinese Ambassador gave an assurance that this was not an alliance but merely China securing her rear, and no secret agreement existed. On the other hand, an informal agreement was drawn up whereby the Soviet Union agreed to supply China with a loan of $ (Chinese) 100 million, which would supply 24 Chinese divisions with Soviet equipment.[64]

Stalin, having appreciably disorganised his senior military command, and no doubt prompted by his 1925 maxim that the Soviet Union would be the last to enter any war, returned to a policy of avoiding the provocation of the Japanese. If his policy of providing 'semi-assistance' in Spain was cunning, in China almost the same thing turned out to be merely shabby. By a virtual repetition of the situation of 1924, a Soviet military mission was finally prepared to go to China. This time 'Galin' — Blyukher — remained on Soviet soil,* and his former second-in-command in Canton, A. I. Cherepanov, returned to China as the head of the new Soviet mission. One of the most immediate assistances, however, which the Soviet Union could render was in the way of aircraft; by September, the Chinese were discussing with the Russians the means to prepare ground facilities for Soviet aircraft which would be shipped in via Sinkiang.[65] By the end of 1937 the figure of 200 Soviet aircraft was being mentioned as the first Soviet consignment to China, although as early as November, one report quoted 400 machines (fighters and bombers) and 40 Soviet 'instructors' accompanying them.[66] But by the same date 80 per cent of the volume of war materials reaching China came from German and Italian sources, not the Soviet Union. One contemporary description was that Soviet supplies reached only 'the lowest "decent" limit', and since supplies came in from the north, there was every chance that the Communist 8th Route Army in Shantung might be the

* Generalissimo Chiang Kai-shek in his *Soviet Russia in China* (p. 52) states that he asked Stalin 'several times' after 1932 for Blyukher's services, but this request was denied.

most immediate beneficiary.[67] The niggardliness of Soviet aid and the passivity of the Soviet role raised up pressure for a more direct participation in the war in China.[68] For the moment, faced with a severe crisis in the military command and its resultant effects on the efficiency of the armed forces, Stalin stamped down on such pressures. Later there was to be an apparent change in this limited policy, but once again a ferocious visitation on the Far Eastern forces was to work its crippling influence. The respite, if such it can be called, accorded to Blyukher and his forces was to last but a little while; while the Red Banner Front could not remain immune from the whole effect of the Red Army purge, and had itself suffered losses, the external crisis had acted as some brake.

★ ★ ★ ★

At the centre and in the European commands all the brakes were released in the autumn and winter of 1937. While a crippling blow had been struck at the high command as it had formerly existed, the Soviet officer corps as a whole — 'beginning literally at the company and battalion commander level', to use Khrushchev's own description — was subject to a series of *NKVD* visitations, which resulted in heavy losses. The greatest numerical loss was to be sustained by the command group running through corps and divisional commander down to brigade and regimental level, that is, the group in which Voroshilov had earlier indicated that Civil War veterans predominated. The higher the command level the greater became the proportional loss, although the distinctive feature of this extremely severe purge was that it was extended into a series of eliminations following at intervals; the first great period of elimination lasted from May–June 1937 until the beginning of 1938. The second, which reached its climax in the summer of 1938, was marked by the disappearance of entire staffs and commands of arms and services, hitting the Soviet Navy especially hard. This would tend to support the assumption that the first purge was dominated absolutely and almost wholly motivated by political considerations, and it was in what might be called the second eliminations that conflicts over military and naval doctrine had a very much more obvious role. It is to be noted that the views expressed by Marshal Tukhachevsky in the May 1937 *Bol'shevik* were never officially repudiated; in contrast, Orlov Ludri, Muklevich, Zivkov and Aleksandrov (of the Naval Academy) were denounced for '. . . their twaddle about the possibility or impossibility of supremacy on the seas'.[69] The immediate re-shuffle in May of the high command, when Shaposhnikov and Yegorov were moved into leading positions, merely replaced one set of Civil War (and ex-Imperial) officers by another. Handing over command of the Kremlin guard to an *NKVD* officer was another step taken for reasons of security. The removal of commanders of military districts and the re-imposition of commissar control (the new regulation being formally decreed on 15th August, 1937) were again moves dictated by political considerations; almost half of the military district commanders in these posts on 11th June had been removed by January 1938.[70]

While Stalin evidently issued arrest orders personally in some cases, the *NKVD* thinned the officer corps by the use of denunciations (and not to participate in denunciation was to invite destruction) and the dossiers compiled by the *OO*. Officers disappeared from their positions overnight.[71] Groups of officers in garrisons were rounded up and arrested, being either executed or consigned to prisons and forced labour camps; Khrushchev admitted that in prisons they might be subjected to 'severe tortures', which hazarded their chances of survival.[72] The emptying ranks of the officer corps were filled by means of extremely rapid promotions — one of the reasons why a certain degree of safety existed for Stalin in undertaking the purge. M. Coulondre cited the case of an officer, born in 1905 and called to the colours in 1927, who was cited for decoration and ranked as lieutenant on 22nd October, 1937. Seven days later he was gazetted a squadron commander, commander of one of the three cavalry regiments in the Stalin Division in Moscow.[73] In seven days, this officer (aged twelve at the outbreak of revolution in Russia) attained the rank which required of Zhukov a year of heavy fighting in the Civil War, when he was already a skilled and worthy soldier. There were attempts by senior officers to protect their staffs (Timoshenko appears to have been one); since one way of escape lay in being removed from the centre and attention, officers were posted to distant assignments or put on routine, almost obscure training courses. Despatch to China was one way of being removed from trouble.

There were also certain details concerning the preparation of the 'evidence' against the Tukhachevsky group to be attended to. Soon after the June executions, Heydrich was boasting in German Intelligence circles that the destruction of the Soviet high command was the work of the SD, were the truth but known. There was little danger of the Gestapo-*NKVD* contact being noised abroad, but Krivitsky argues that the great danger of exposure lay with the person possibly in possession of the originals of the material planted by the *NKVD*. He traces a direct connection between this and the disappearance of General Miller in Paris on 22nd September, 1937. Krivitsky also links up the two officers of his who had been detached at the end of 1936 for a special *NKVD* assignment. On the day he vanished General Miller, at the instigation of Skoblin, had gone to keep an appointment with 'two German officers', who also spoke Russian well. General Miller, however, left a note indicating that this might be a trap and conveying a certain suspicion of Skoblin. The General never returned from his luncheon engagement, whereupon his associates came across the note and the reference to Skoblin. The latter managed to break away while he was being questioned by Russian emigrés and made good his escape. He, too, was also never traced, but his wife — arrested as an accessory to General Miller's abduction* — was sentenced to twenty years imprisonment after her investigation and trial in France.[74] It remained only to silence Krivitsky.

Too rational an explanation of the military purge could do little or no justice to the welter of fear and the surge of chaos and confusion which swept upon the Soviet armed forces. Although the evidence would suggest that a form of selectivity was employed, and that the high command was not so much destroyed as neutralised, the very processes of the purge tended to override controls. Frustrated ambitions, old vendettas and long-standing scores, not to mention Stalin's own vast and diseased suspiciousness intensified the irrational element. But already there were hints that some plan of re-organisation lay behind the atomisation of particular command groups. On 30th December, 1937, a separate Naval Commissariat was decreed;[75] Voroshilov was relieved of his powers over the naval establishment. Stalin had grandiose plans for his navy and they were to be realised under a command created by himself. The lack of distinction made between political and command staff, both of which fell victim to the *NKVD*, made it clear that Stalin saw all too clearly that, in an army filled up with a much greater proportion of Party members, the Political Administration was no longer fully effective as a policing instrument. It was necessary to Stalinise it thoroughly. For that assignment Lev Mekhlis, a member of Stalin's personal secretariat and his watch-dog on *Pravda*, was installed at the end of 1937 as chief of the Political Administration. Mekhlis, a military commissar during the Civil War and even then connected with Stalin's entourage, had been sent to boost the flagging operations against Wrangel in the autumn of 1920. Seventeen years later, as the Red Army's chief commissar, he was much experienced in the requirements of Stalinist control.

And, in the very last resort, even while cowing the Red Army and its leaders, Stalin had not forfeited the loyalty of the army. This was the absolute foundation of success and due not merely to chance. While the

* For the letter of General Miller's lawyer to have the ship carrying General Miller stopped in a German port, and the German Consul in Sofia report on a trace of General Miller, see *Politische Bestrebungen der Emigration*, Serial 611/249100 (dated 25th November, 1937) and 249126–7 of 22nd December, 1937, respectively.

first Red Army purge showed signs of being carried out to a pre-determined plan, of equal importance was the indication of astute precaution. There was much less secrecy about the May–June purge than is generally supposed. Opinion both inside and outside the armed forces had been carefully prepared to expect some dire event. To the very maximum Stalin capitalised on the internal differences within the command and the officer corps as a whole. At the extraordinary session of 1st–4th June senior Red Army officers were initiated into the 'justification' for the purge; the assault on the political staff took place at the same time as the All-Army Conference of political organs and personnel. The visible divergence in the announcements of the June executions makes it clear that the persuasion of both external and internal opinion had been taken into consideration.

This was no blind, bloody and aimless killing. On the contrary, it was the most delicate piece of surgery which Stalin carried out on the Soviet body politic. Moreover, as the Soviet armed forces were to discover, the cure was to be not only protracted but almost as arduous as the initial operation.

CHAPTER FIFTEEN

Exeunt Omnes . . .

The elimination of the Tukhachevsky group from the Soviet command had been primarily a political operation. The state, personified by Stalin and his apparatus of repression, had reversed the normal order by itself turning Bonaparte and marching on the soldiers. In destroying a potential opposition and crashing this final barrier to untrammelled power, Stalin had done himself a monumental service.* Breaching the magic circle of the military, he had hurried the fractious, ambitious, independently minded or critical commanders into the oblivion of death or the *NKVD* labour camps. He set out to destroy not only their persons but also their policies and prestige. For that reason, their infamy was concocted and their names daubed with a contrived disgrace. There were, moreover, signs that Stalin had additional purposes to fulfil out of the opportunity which he and his malevolent collaborators had so painstakingly prepared. The attempt to realise these aims was to be a prime illustration of what lay behind these 'crimes against the Fatherland and the Party', of which the erstwhile command stood both accused and condemned. Potent crimes they must have been, for the dead officers apparently went on committing them. The alterations brought about by Stalin were themselves an indication of the enormous pressures of divergence and conflict over strategic doctrine and priorities which had been building up for some time before the onset of the purge. In no case was this more clearly demonstrated than in the circumstances of the re-organisation of the Soviet naval command.

* It was also at this time that Hitler purged the German high command. Blomberg's unsuitable marriage provided a pretext to be rid of him. Himmler produced for Hitler a dossier purporting to prove that Fritsch was guilty of homosexual practices. On 4th February, 1938, the resignations of Blomberg and Fritsch were announced. Hitler himself took over the newly-created *Oberkommando der Wehrmacht*. Sixteen senior generals were retired and forty-four other generals were transferred to new posts. In comparing the German and Russian military purges, there are three points for consideration: (i) both the German and Soviet security services succeeded in compromising the military leadership and beating their rivals down, (ii) both Hitler and Stalin either relied on or worked to secure the junior officers and the rank-and-file, (iii) when faced with a crisis of existence, the German high command failed to take action as much as their Soviet counter-parts failed to do. As the German Army had failed to act in January 1933, so the Red Army had failed in 1929–30. As a comment on the latter, A. Barmine is of the opinion that the Soviet military leaders did not wish to sacrifice national unity by threatening the regime. (On the German Army, see Gordon A. Craig, *The Politics of the Prussian Army 1640–1945*, pp. 481–96).

The Soviet Navy had already lived a hazardous enough life. Its political unreliability had almost occasioned in 1921 its ignominious scuttling. Having tamed the sailors, the next problem was to create an effective fighting force at a time when Soviet technical resources were very limited. German help had been indispensable in giving the Soviet Navy a modern look, and under Orlov and Muklevich, a steady if unspectacular rate of progress had been maintained. The naval command had adhered to a policy of maintaining a relatively small naval force — but with a preponderance of submarines — committed to a defensive role. This represented a realistic view of Soviet technical capacities. It did not, however, correspond to Stalin's grandiose schemes. Technical limitations, advanced as an argument, did not correspond to what Stalin had achieved with his Five-Year Plans; this was dire heresy, contradicting the image of Soviet power which was current. By extension, it was a refutation of Stalin's achievement — 'sabotage', 'a crime against the Party'. Molotov, speaking at the first session of the Supreme Soviet in January 1938 (when the decree on a separate Naval Commissariat was approved), switched the searchlight of publicity on to the new naval policy:

> We take this view: the main thing is that our ship of state should be strong and powerful, and it is — as we know — strong and becoming still stronger. Our Soviet regime is powerful and wishes to be still more powerful, it wishes to be beyond the grasp of enemies. From this we draw the conclusion that we need a powerful Red Army and we need a powerful war-fleet. The powerful Soviet state must have a sea-going and ocean-going fleet, consistent with its interests, worthy of our great task.[1]

To this end the new Naval Commissariat, which had last enjoyed independent existence in 1918, was reformed.

The new Commissar for the Navy was not, however, V. M. Orlov, who had been head of the naval forces in 1937, but P. A. Smirnov, who had been a rather obscure officer of the Naval Inspectorate. The appointment of Smirnov in January 1938 signalled the disgrace of Orlov and his command group. Muklevich had been seized in May 1937 and presumably executed in the summer. Orlov was not shot at once; his biographical entry ends on 28th July, 1938.[2] Orlov's former deputy Ludri (who had been superseded in January 1937), the Baltic Fleet commander Zivkov, Black Sea Fleet commander Koshchanov, Northern Fleet commander Dushkenov, Kadostkii of the Amur Flotilla, Aleksandrov, Stashevich and Petrov of the Naval Academy were liquidated in the course of 1938. Naval officers were seized and removed from ships, naval installations and educational institutions. Only Viktorov survived the purge of fleet commanders. As an 'agent of Fascism', Tukhachevsky's name was finally dragged in to complete the vilification of the Orlov-Muklevich-Ludri group, and Tukhachevsky was to be charged with preventing '. . . the addition to the navy of new surface ships'.[3] This was the extreme of nonsense. In 1936 Tukhachevsky had spoken with approval of the measures taken to increase the strength of Soviet surface forces, to bring the navy on to rather than under the sea.

'The most powerful navy in the world' — that policy was publicly declared and repeated in 1938. The new command was to achieve that goal. Molotov had made it clear that the naval agreements which the Soviet Union had been negotiating in 1936–7 were regarded as unsatisfactory. In 1936 Great Britain and the Soviet Union had arrived at a provisional naval agreement, but German objections delayed the actual signing of an agreement until July 1937. Already the Soviet programme for cruiser building had created a difficulty; the proposed seven 8,000 ton Soviet cruisers were to mount 7·1-inch guns (although the London Treaty stipulated 6·1-inch). The Soviet Union was permitted to proceed with the building (since a calibre alteration would create difficulties in the Soviet armaments industry), and Germany was also able to expand her cruiser programme.[4] In addition, there was provision for the Soviet Union to build or acquire two 16-inch gun battleships.

Smirnov, in spite of a number of speeches in conformity with the requisite Stalin line, seems to have exercised very little power. Real control was vested in the Main Naval Soviet (*Glavnyi Voennyi Soviet Voenno-Morskovo Flota*)[5] which was set up to supervise the work of the Naval Commissariat and at the head of which Stalin set one of his trusted lieutenants, Zhdanov. The Naval Staff was entrusted to Galler, who had formerly commanded the Baltic Fleet and had been promoted to the position of Orlov's deputy in January 1937. There could be no doubt that the new command group, closely supervised by Stalin, had to produce results and with some speed. The idea of the Soviet Union as a great naval power was easier to formulate than to bring about. The notion that the Soviet Navy would definitely limit itself to the task of defending the Soviet shores was abandoned, to be replaced by the idea of taking the war into enemy waters, and this with powerful surface ships. Whatever the imagined achievements of Soviet industry, a capacity to supply this offensive naval facility was demonstrably not one of them. For the Soviet Union to join in the race for naval supremacy had as little point as it had chances of any real success. The former command had certainly not overlooked the possibility of developing a balanced fleet, but this would be one developed in line with the limited tasks assigned to the Soviet naval forces and planned in accordance with existing technical facilities. Quite how this war at sea was now to be carried into enemy waters remained something of a mystery — whether by reliance on the submarine as a commerce-raider or grand forays with powerful surface forces. It seemed to be the possibilities, if not the difficulties of the latter which had caught Stalin's imagination. It was, fundamentally, a move for prestige rather than any precise strategic calculations which inspired the new Soviet *Flottenpolitik*. President Kalinin, in his speech of 2nd July, 1938, in Leningrad, made it clear that the Soviet Union was to enter into naval competition with even the strongest naval powers, not excluding Great Britain — the strongest Socialist country must eclipse the strongest capitalist country — hence the Soviet Navy must overshadow the Royal Navy.[6] Once again the *Komsomol* was mobilised, as it had been in 1925–6, for service with the navy, and the Party composition of the naval forces was stiffened in the style which had been tried and tested some twelve years previously.

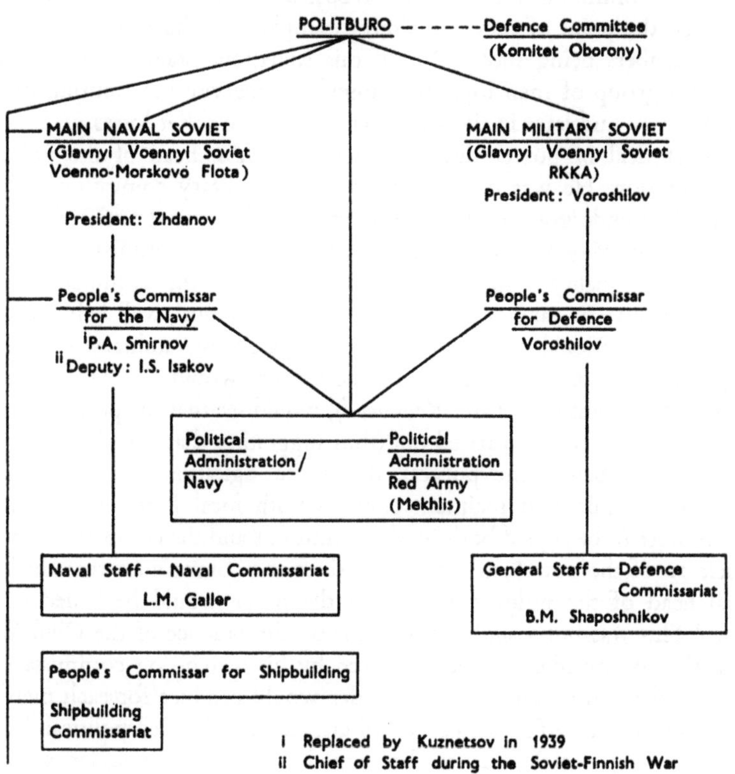

At the same time the command organisation of the Red Army was being overhauled, thus lending some force to the view that the re-organisation which had followed on the June executions was merely provisional. The first step had been to split off the naval command. The second was to modify the organisation of the Defence Commissariat. Much of the independence gained by the 1934 statute was curtailed. A form of dual command, a modified type of collective responsibility, was introduced once again into the Defence Commissariat. On 13th March, the Central Committee adopted a decision to set up a Main Military Soviet (*Glavnyi Voennyi Soviet RKKA*), with a staff of eleven members. Voroshilov was to be chairman of this body, which included Blyukher, Budenny, Mekhlis, Stalin, Shaposhnikov and Shchadenko. The new Soviet's functions were concerned primarily with policy-making in matters concerning the Red Army.[7] The implications of this, however, were rather more sinister. Under the 1934 statute, there had existed the Military Soviet which exercised advisory functions and which had operated under the control of Voroshilov as Defence Commissar. No more was to be heard of this body. It had suffered, or was on the point of suffering almost complete annihilation — 75 out of its 80 members being shot.[8] Out of this ruination, Stalin set up a small command group of men loyal to himself to supervise the running of the Red Army — and later in the year even this was to suffer losses.

A great deal of power devolved upon Mekhlis, head of the Political Administration. He was now the head of the military commissars whose fortunes had undergone a rapid improvement. The 1937 statute, which had been issued in May and confirmed in August, put the commissar back in a position of equality with the commander. With the commander, the commissar was to take responsibility for the political well-being of the unit, for operational and mobilisation preparedness, military discipline, weapon maintenance and supply. The commissar would direct the work of the political organs (Party and *Komsomol*), would see that the programme of political instruction was carried out (thus suggesting that it had been somewhat slighted before the purges), direct the 'agitation and propaganda' work in the unit, and maintain contacts with local Party organisations. Orders were to be signed both by the commissar and the commander under Article 12 of the new Instruction, but since the commander remained the actual head of the military unit, then the order would be issued in his name.[9] This was but a slight refinement on the practice of the Civil War, when the commander had been flanked by his watch-dog commissars. In addition, the commissar and commander would produce for each member of the command staff in the process of attestation a detailed political dossier (*kharakteristika*) which was to be signed by the commander and the commissar alike.* Both would also be responsible for promotions, demotions, awards and distinctions.[10] Above all, the military commissar was entrusted with the task of vigilance — to guard the administration against the incursions of 'enemies of the people, spies, saboteurs and wreckers'. In April 1938 the All-Union Assembly of Political Workers met under the baleful eye of Mekhlis to discuss the priorities of the political programme. Two basic principles were set out; the first demanded an increase and strengthening of the political work in the Red Army, and the second declared unceasing war on the remnants of the 'Bukharinite-Trotskyist rabble', 'spies, saboteurs, assassins and betrayers of the Fatherland.'[11]

The insistence on the need to strengthen political work in the Red Army makes it apparent that this had suffered some eclipse in the later stages of Gamarnik's rule at the Political Administration. The commanders had succeeded in putting the claims of military training first, and relegating the tedious business of political instruction to the background. The new regulations on the role of the commissar tried to draw the commissar into the technical as well as the combat training of the military units. This presupposed a very high level of competence on the part of the commissar, and re-opened all the problems of commander-commissar relationships which seemed to have been settling down into a working arrangement, even if the commissar had had to accept reductions in political work. In spite of the phrase about the equality of the commander and the commissar in the new regulations, in a very real sense the command staff was at the mercy of the commissar, since so much depended on the nature of the political testimonial tacked on to the officer's name. The real function of the commissar had always been surveillance of the command staff of the Red Army (as well as the rank-and-file) and to this he now reverted. Such an arrangement had caused limitless trouble and difficulty in the old Red Army made up of infantry and cavalry; it was to be ultimately disastrous for the efficiency of the Red Army combining highly-complicated and complex modern technical units within its organisation. Tukhachevsky had made it quite plain that the problems of mechanised warfare had imposed a great strain on the command staff of the Red Army. To the intrinsic problems involved, which had only been partially solved, the crude and cumbersome dual command was added, wiping out the gains which the command staff had won in the course of a protracted struggle.

There could be no doubt about the need for such strenuous precaution, since the purge continued without abatement. Although there was a steady momentum of arrests and replacements within the officer corps as a whole, the bulk of which affected officers below the rank of colonel, the elimination

* For an example, see General Appendix on attestation.

within the senior levels of the military command could be divided roughly into two major phases, the second covering the first half of 1938.[12] The military purge kept in step with measures taken against society at large; in line with the purge of the nationalities in the Soviet Union, the national formations which had existed before 1937 were now broken up and their personnel incorporated into the main Red Army. The whole structure of 'extra-territorial' recruitment was at this time swept away. This decision was made formal on 7th March, 1938.[13] A certain relationship between the expansion of the military purge and technical or doctrinal questions can be detected in 1938, but only with difficulty can this be erected into some kind of dividing line. Once again, the question of rational limits to the purge presents insoluble problems. There was, as yet, no stable command group in existence (just as the purge of the Party and administrative machine kept sweeping away old and new incumbents of their positions); it is quite evident that this grim mobility was deliberately sustained, although beyond a certain point the cohesion of the armed forces would be seriously threatened.

In this most bizarre combination of repression and reform, the military districts came in for some considerable attention. In the summer of 1937 collective command had been re-imposed at the military district level with the setting up of military soviets — commander and two commissars. By January 1938 six of the fourteen military district commanders had vanished; as the summer drew to a close, the entire command of military districts (including the Far East) had been changed. Apart from the setting up of the military soviets, which interrupted the previous arrangement under which military district and formation commanders had been directly subordinated to the Defence Commissar, the military district staff remained much what it had been — the district staff itself, a political department, air force commander, commanders of various arms, an officer in charge of supply and the medical and veterinary staff. The change-over to a cadre army on a much expanded scale, however, necessitated changes in the prevailing system of recruitment and mobilisation. Previously, district military commissariats had supervised the operation of corps and divisional mobilisation districts. This had many disadvantages from the point of view of satisfying the increasingly complex needs of the Red Army; it was, above all, a clumsy business. In its place, a new form of organisation set up autonomous military commissariats in the various republics, as well as in regions and towns. The number of district commissariats was gradually increased until it had more than tripled.[14] The extensive purge of the military district commands could therefore be conceivably connected with a wholesale modernisation and overhaul of the military administration at this level.

Upon inspection, the military and naval purge emerges as a number of separate operations, multi-phased and affecting different levels of the command at various times. By March, it appeared that a preliminary stabilisation of the high command had been effected, but while the *Yezhovshchina* raged, there could be safety for no one and immunity for no organisation. At the beginning of March, Bukharin, Rykov, Yagoda, Krestinsky, Rakovsky and Rosengoltz were the principal defendants in what was to be the last of the great trials. It was then that a version of the guilt of the executed senior officers was produced.

* * * *

The trial of the 'Anti-Soviet "Bloc of Rights and Trotskyites" ' opened on 2nd March, with Vyshinsky once more appearing for the prosecution. The trial offered the same spectacle of degradation and humiliation which had been a feature of 1936 and 1937. The charges once more comprised sabotage, terrorism and the attempted overthrow of the Soviet government (Stalin and his colleagues) by force, treasonable contact with Germany and Japan as well as participation in a plot with those powers to dismember the Soviet Union, in return for aid in the internal conspiracy. The indictment, read by the secretary of the court at the morning session on 2nd March, contained under the first count — 'Espionage against the Soviet State and Treason to the Country': Rosengoltz's 'evidence' admitted,

> . . . After I had established contact with TUKHACHEVSKY and RYKOV, I informed the former through KRESTINSKY, and the latter I myself informed, of TROTSKY'S instructions regarding wrecking activities, and both approved of the work I had done.[15]

Events took a dramatic turn during the first examination; while cross-questioning Bessonov, Vyshinsky called on Krestinsky to make the requisite corroboration of Bessonov's evidence of contact with Trotsky. Krestinsky refused and flatly refuted Bessonov. Krestinsky went further:

> . . . The important thing is that I declare that I do not admit myself to be a Trotskyite. I am not a Trotskyite. . . . (after a pause) No, I declare that I am not a Trotskyite.[16]

Krestinsky felt unwell and was allowed to rest. Meanwhile Vyshinsky carried on questioning Bessonov, whose evidence Krestinsky had just challenged. Bessonov claimed that he had talked with Krestinsky in May 1933 when a general outline of a 'Trotskyist' policy was worked out, and that Krestinsky indicated that he — and another person referred to as 'we' — was sounding out contacts with the military circles of the Soviet Union, mentioning the names of Tukhachevsky and Uborevich.[17] The tactics involving agreement with foreign states were developed in the Krestinsky-Trotsky discussions which took place in Meran. Bessonov's evidence, which had drawn in the names of Tukhachevsky and Uborevich, lacked any real consistency; its high-light was the dogmatic assertion of its truth in the face of Krestinsky's sudden and apparently quite spontaneous denial of his original testimony. At the evening session of 2nd March, Vyshinsky opened the examination of Grinko, a former Finance Commissar. The latter, in his description of the type of 'national-fascist' organisation which was created in the Ukraine, brought in the names of Gamarnik and Yakir. Gamarnik was associated with Trotsky's plan to pay out the Ukraine as compensation for 'the military assistance that we were to receive in our fight against Soviet power'. It was 'about the end of 1935' when Grinko made connection with Gamarnik, Pyatakov and Rykov. Once again, Krestinsky flatly denied such 'testimony';

> *Vyshinsky*. How do you explain the fact that Krestinsky is denying everything?
> *Grinko*. I cannot explain it.[18]

So far, the testimony affirmed that the military command had joined the conspiracy in 1933, and the military-political head and a senior officer in the Ukraine were fully implicated towards the end of 1935. Grinko did, however, make qualifications upon his statements which set the date at 'the beginning of 1934', when he formed a comprehensive view of the aims and scope of this 'Right and Trotskyite centre'. The main foundation was 'the military aid of aggressors', and a policy bent on 'undermining the power of defence of the Soviet Union, undermining activities in the army, opening the front in the event of war and provoking this war'.

Grinko's testimony did contain an illuminating passage about the February-March (1937) plenum, which '. . . is connected with the beginning of the crushing of the conspiratorial organisations'. Gamarnik conferred with Bukharin and Rykov after the Radek trial; 'something extraordinary had to be done' to check the *NKVD*; after the plenum 'the question was bluntly raised of removing Yezhov'. Garmanik and Yakir instructed one Ozeryansky to prepare 'a terrorist act' against Yezhov. There is something a little incongruous in the head of the Red Army Political Administration and Army Commander Yakir, one of the most gifted of Soviet military leaders, instructing the Chief of the Department of Savings Banks (for that was Ozeryansky's position) to carry out such a mission.

Rykov, who was called upon to substantiate Grinko's evidence of a 'wrecker's plan' in the Finance Commissariat, supplied a different version of the role of the military. Rykov knew that

> . . . this military group was organised independently of the bloc, independently of shades — Trotskyite or Bukharinite. The military group set itself the object of violently removing the government of the Union and, in particular, it took part in preparations for a Kremlin coup. . . . I learnt of it from Tomsky in 1934.
>
> *Vyshinsky*. In 1934?
>
> *Rykov*. Probably.[19]

Later, at the evening session on 3rd, Rykov produced a much more detailed version of what he called 'the palace *coup*'. During '1933–4', 'individual members' of the Right organisation expressed a preference for a 'palace *coup*' carried out with a specially prepared armed force. Rykov added that even in 1930 'one of the members of the Right organisation' came to him with a fully-worked out plan for such a *coup*. In 1933 'this question' came to the fore. The adherence of Yenukidze and Yagoda to the bloc enabled a start to be made with organising the *coup*:

> . . . I remember that the first piece of information I received was about the group of Kremlin officers and the principal figures here were Yagoda, Peterson, Gorbachov and Yegorov; I have in mind not the Chief of the General Staff — I don't know what he is doing now — but Yegorov the chief of the Kremlin military school. . . . Several times Tomsky informed me about the enlistment through these persons — Yenukidze and Yegorov — of a group of military officials, headed by Tukhachevsky, who also prepared to accept this plan and were working in this direction. He mentioned the names of Uborevich and Kork . . . I cannot speak of the details of this work because it was kept very secret. . . . This group . . . worked independently of the other underground groups and it was the only one.[20]

In corroboration, Bukharin testified that 'the front would be opened to the Germans' in the event of war, adding that Tomsky supplied confirmation of '. . . such an opinion among the military men'. Vyshinsky broke in:

> . . . An opinion or a plan?
>
> *Bukharin*. I would not say a plan. Perhaps it was a plan, but in a very cursory conversation . . . (dots in the text).
>
> *Vyshinsky*. And was Tukhachevsky a member of this group?
>
> *Bukharin*. I have already explained . . . (dots in the text).
>
> *Vyshinsky*. I am asking: Were Tukhachevsky and the military group of conspirators members of your bloc?
>
> *Bukharin*. They were.[21]

Vyshinsky turned finally to Krestinsky, who seemed now ready to play the part assigned to him and to indulge in no more recantation. Krestinsky supplied the proper confirmation of Rykov's testimony on the military group:

> (*Krestinsky*). I know the following about Tukhachevsky's participation. When I met Trotsky in Meran in October 1933, he pointed out to me that . . . we must come to an agreement both with the Rights and with the military group. He paid particular attention to Tukhachevsky, a man with an adventurous bent who lays claim to first place in the army and would probably be ready to take many chances. He asked me to convey this opinion of his to Pyatakov and to talk with Tukhachevsky personally.
>
> *Vyshinsky*. Did you talk to Tukhachevsky?
>
> *Krestinsky*. I had a talk with him in the beginning of 1934, after Pyatakov had spoken to him, and I told him of my talk with Trotsky. Tukhachevsky said that in principle he is favourably disposed not only to the joining of forces but also to the fact that such a task was being posed. But the question, he said, requires deliberation, the possibilities have to be established. . . . I found out from Pyatakov in February 1935 that an agreement had been reached. . . . Subsequently I spoke to Tukhachevsky several times on this subject. This was in the second half of 1935, in 1936 and 1937. . . . During one of the conversations in 1935 he mentioned several people on whose support he relied. He mentioned, among others, Yakir, Uborevich, Kork and Eideman. . . . later on, [during] a very important conversation which took place at the Extraordinary Eighth Congress of Soviets, Tukhachevsky urged the necessity of hastening the *coup*.[22]

Rosengoltz supplied the necessary corroboration.

On the evening of 4th March, Rosengoltz himself was examined and the second examination of Krestinsky concluded. These two testimonies provided more detail of the *coup* and the illicit contacts between the 'conspirators' and foreign powers. Rosengoltz affirmed that 'the chief stake' in 1936 was a military *coup*. But Tukhachevsky showed himself to be a none too competent conspirator: he 'kept on appointing dates for the execution of his criminal plan — an uprising — and postponing them'. Rykov denied that there had been any conversation 'in the lobby of the Council of People's Commissars' about hurrying Tukhachevsky along. Rosengoltz then proceeded to develop his story of the conference with Tukhachevsky 'at the end of March, 1937':

> (*Rosengoltz*). At this conference Tukhachevsky stated that he counted definitely on the possibility of a coup and mentioned the date. He believed that by 15th May, in the first half of May, he would succeed in carrying out this military *coup*.
>
> —Tukhachevsky had a number of variants. One of them, the one on which he counted most, was the possibility for a group of men, his adherents, gathering in his apartment on some pretext or other, making their way into the Kremlin, seizing the Kremlin telephone exchange, and killing the leaders of the Party and the government.[23]

The great difficulty about this argument was that Tukhachevsky was nominated early in April to accompany the Soviet delegation to the coronation ceremonies of King George VI. 'So as not to arouse suspicions', Tukhachevsky was preparing to go to London. But, Krestinsky went on, when he learnt that his appointment had been cancelled, Tukhachevsky 'said that he would start a revolt in the early part of May'. (It was in the early part of May that Tukhachevsky learned of the cancellation of his appointment.) Rosengoltz proceeded to place Gamarnik in the context of this extraordinary, lackadaisical *coup*:

> As regards Gamarnik, the chief point is that Gamarnik told us of his proposal, which apparently had the consent of Tukhachevsky, that it was possible to seize the building of the People's Commissariat of Internal Affairs [*NKVD*] during the military *coup*. Gamarnik assumed that the attack would be carried out by some military unit under his direct command. . . . He calculated that in this affair he would have the support of some of the commanders, especially the dare-devils. I remember that he mentioned the name of Gorbachov.[24]

The testimony supplied by Rosengoltz then proceeded to unfold the story of the secret contacts between the *Reichswehr* and the Red Army. By substituting the word 'espionage' for the genuine collaboration, Rosengoltz could relate what was essentially true and yet have it support the tale which he was required to tell. Rosengoltz, who was in 1924 one of the powers behind Soviet military aviation, admitted to supplying information to General Seeckt about the *VVS*. This was quite true, when Junkers was being pressed to supply aero-engines from its Russian-based factory; what was twisted into a political lie was the connection with Trotsky, who also at that time was not 'spying' but trying to straighten out the complicated situation which had arisen with the Junkers contract. Krestinsky admitted that in 1922 he concluded 'on Trotsky's instructions' an agreement with General Seeckt, 'with the *Reichswehr*, in his person'; Krestinsky enlarged upon his story and produced the evidence about Kopp, making, however, a careful distinction between 'the purely official aspect' and 'the secret Trotskyite aspect, a criminal thing'.[25]

Krestinsky revoked his earlier denials. He confirmed Bessonov's testimony in the required manner, expounding the implications of the Meran meeting with Trotsky. In February 1934 Krestinsky met Tukhachevsky and Rudzutak, obtaining from them 'their acceptance of the line for an understanding with foreign states for their military assistance, for a defeatist policy. . . .' Krestinsky resolved the inconsistency about the hastening of the *coup* by declaring that Trotsky had done this on his own initiative, but had sent instructions 'in a different, roundabout way to Rosengoltz'. There was also the odd point about Tukhachevsky's visit to London and the fixing of the *coup* for early May. In fact, Tukhachevsky had set the *coup* for 'the first half of May'. In this manner, Krestinsky tidied up the loose ends of evidence, so that a certain consistency was attained, but not without making modifications which themselves led to further complications. It remained to be seen what Bukharin would have to say at his examination on 5th.

Bukharin in his testimony went back to the 'Ryutin platform' and the summer of 1932. The 'essential points' of this programme were '. . . a "palace *coup*", terrorism, steering a course for a direct alliance with the Trotskyites'. The idea of an armed blow had occurred to Tomsky and Yenukidze, since the latter had control of the Kremlin guard at this time. The court session was drawing to a close when Bukharin came to speak of the Ryutin programme; he attempted to speak openly of his own ideas and of the implications of his discussions about the Party leadership, but Vyshinsky blocked him at every turn. After a day's recession, the proceedings were resumed on 7th, when Bukharin took up the history of the 'conspiracy'. The Bloc was formed 'at the end of 1932 . . . on the basis of the Ryutin platform'; moreover,

> . . . the formation of the group of conspirators in the Red Army relates to that period. I heard of it from Tomsky, who was directly informed of it by Yenukidze . . . rather I was informed by Tomsky and Yenukidze . . . ; names mentioned to me — I don't vouch that I remember them all exactly — but those I have remembered are Tukhachevsky, Kork, Primakov and Putna.[26]

Bukharin went on so to qualify the idea of action by the military group that it lost almost the whole of its meaning. 'The idea of a *coup d'état*' dates back to 1929–30, as a '*coup d'état* on relatively a very narrow basis'. Bukharin would rather say '. . . that it was an idea of a circumscribed *coup d'état*' — or, '. . . rather of a "palace *coup*".' But it was not 'an armed uprising';

> *Vyshinsky.* Then would it not be better to speak not of a 'palace *coup*' but of an attempt to seize power by means of an armed uprising?
>
> *Bukharin.* No, it is not correct to speak of an armed uprising.
>
> *Vyshinsky.* Why not? You wished to seize power with arms in hand?
>
> *Bukharin.* An armed uprising is a mass affair, while here it was a matter of a narrower . . . (dots in the text).
>
> *Vyshinsky.* What masses? You had no masses with you.
>
> *Bukharin.* Consequently, it is not an uprising.
>
> *Vyshinsky.* An uprising with the aid of a group.
>
> *Bukharin.* If you choose to define an uprising by a group as an uprising, then it is correct.
>
> *Vyshinsky.* In any case, it is more correct than to speak of a 'palace *coup*', which is supposed to take place in some palace.[27]

Bukharin repeatedly affirmed his opposition to the idea of relying on Germany; if Germany did intervene during the war 'to help the counter-revolutionary *coup*', then she would '. . . inevitably put her feet on the table and tear up any preliminary agreement which had been concluded'. Nor could the danger from the military men themselves be ignored, for '. . . a peculiar Bonapartist danger might arise'. And, Bukharin continued,

> . . . Bonapartists — I was thinking particularly of Tukhachevsky — would start out by making short shrift of their allies and so-called inspirers in Napoleon style. In my conversations I always called Tukhachevsky a 'potential little Napoleon' and you know how Napoleon dealt with the so-called ideologists.[28]

To eliminate this danger from the over-mighty soldiers, Bukharin proposed to have them promptly liquidated by bringing charges of defeatism against them.

Yagoda, former chief of the *OGPU*, on the evening of 8th March, produced yet another version of this fantastically complicated plot. Yagoda, having admitted to conversations of a regular nature 'towards the end of 1932' with Yenukidze on the subject of a 'palace *coup*', announced that '. . . the time was of no importance'. Vyshinsky tested Yagoda out on his 'participation':

> *Vyshinsky*. . . . you plead guilty to the fact . . . (that) you pursued the aim of overthrowing the Soviet government and of restoring capitalism. . . .
>
> *Yagoda*. Yes, I do. We set ourselves the task of seizing the Kremlin.
>
> *Vyshinsky*. That for the purpose of overthrowing the government you chose the method of an insurrection timed primarily for the outbreak of war. Is that so?
>
> *Yagoda*. No, it is not so. An armed insurrection — that was nonsense. Only these babblers here could think of that.
>
> *Vyshinsky*. Well, what were you thinking of?
>
> *Yagoda*. Of a 'palace *coup*'. . . . There was one plan, namely, to seize the Kremlin. The time was of no importance.[29]

The burden of Krestinsky's evidence had been to the effect that the time-factor was of critical importance.

The melancholy spectacle was over and Vyshinsky's detestable work done at 4 a.m., on 13th March. Eighteen death sentences, with Bukharin's name heading the list, were passed. Although the names of the commanders who had been publicly condemned (and also despatched in secrecy) were connected with the crimes of the 'Bloc' at appropriate points, the tale of a 'palace *coup*', 'armed uprising', 'circumscribed *coup d'état*' 'armed overthrow of the Soviet government', '*coup d'état* with the help of the armed counter-revolutionary forces' — every variety of description was employed — became increasingly bedraggled. If a conspiracy of such mammoth proportions had existed and had been so well prepared, Stalin's government would either have succumbed or would be fighting desperately for its life. As plotters and organisers of a *coup*, however, Tukhachevsky and his fellows emerged not as monsters but rather incompetent bunglers. The timing of this supposed *coup* — and in any *coup* the timing is vitally important — produced glaring inconsistencies of evidence. The tale became tangled up in obvious improbability when Tukhachevsky was simultaneously to attend a ceremony in London and raise rebellion in Moscow. This presupposed that Tukhachevsky had set the date. But in the light of Krestinsky's evidence, it appeared that even after three years of planning and thinking, Tukhachevsky still could not fix the date. Rykov had the military group working in the deepest secrecy, and the Krestinsky-Rosengoltz account involved the military conspirators in a whole round of meetings and contacts. While Yagoda was storming the Kremlin, presumably at a time chosen quite arbitrarily, and using the one military group involved, Krestinsky, Rosengoltz and Rykov were trying to rush Tukhachevsky into a *coup*, which would take place at a time coincident with a plan previously prepared with the Germans, although Bukharin scoffed at this arrangement and was himself engaged to wipe out the traitors, who were such a Bonapartist danger that they might not let 'ideologists' live. At the same time, the civilian conspirators (and here the omission of the military was marked) were working furiously for foreign intelligence services — German, Japanese, Polish and British. All were the puppets of Trotsky, but it seemed a little unfortunate for the fate of this stupendous plot that vital 'instructions' seemed to go astray.

The whole thing was preposterous, and almost inane. As was intended, the very grotesqueness stripped away any vestige of political reality from men who had once been outstanding political figures. It was the damnation of a generation.

* * * *

The March trial produced no further hints of action against the Red Army command. Yegorov's name had been mentioned, and while that was usually an unfavourable sign, the context was quite neutral this time. Yet while the trial had furnished sensations enough, and added to the misgivings which were being widely felt about the nature of Soviet power and its stability, the European situation deteriorated still further. Hitler annexed Austria. Poland served an ultimatum on Lithuania, which was practically treading on the Soviet doorstep. On 23rd March, Litvinov spoke to the American Ambassador on the implications of the new situation. Litvinov was of the opinion that Germany opposed Poland's attempt to take over

Lithuania, as there were German designs aimed at the Baltic states. Czechoslovakia would 'cause trouble this summer', and there was the danger that Czechoslovakia might 'voluntarily yield to Germany', since she had no confidence in France. There followed an even more ominous statement — 'France has no confidence in the Soviet Union and the Soviet Union has no confidence in France.'[30] Joseph Davies had observed on 17th March that 'this government is going more isolationist than ever before', even though there was proof of the Soviet Union being 'extremely war conscious', and sending out substantial shipments of military supplies and foodstuffs to the Far East.[31]

The Lithuanian situation, in which a vital Soviet interest was involved, did not lead to the war which had been half-expected. While putting pressure on Poland, the Soviet government through Litvinov had advised Lithuania to accede to the Polish demand for a resumption of relations and thus stave off invasion. Meanwhile the Czech-Soviet military conversations, which followed a provisional course at the 1936 manœuvres, were also resumed. The movement of Soviet troops through Poland, although much more acceptable as an alternative to transport through Rumania, was blocked by unyielding Polish hostility. Aviation was the only possible form of immediate assistance which the Soviet Union could render. It appeared that a test of the possibility had already been carried out. Sixty Soviet bombers had landed at the aerodrome of Užhorod in Eastern Slovakia, proving that Soviet machines could use a base in an area least threatened by potential enemy attack. A new air base at Vinnitsa had been developed (bringing Soviet bombers further westward than Kiev). It remained to fit out the Slovak base with fuel dumps and greater technical facilities — a process which had been interrupted by violent denunciation in the German press.[32] M. Coulondre observed in this context that as the Czech crisis became the nodal point of the European situation, so the 'Russian factor' waxed in importance and was reaching its ultimate significance. But 'the Terror remained a horrifying fact'.[33] Above all, the necessary military conventions were lacking. In April, M. Noël travelled to Prague to report at first-hand on the Czech situation of the French government. Beneš reported to M. Noël that no effective military arrangement with the Soviet Union existed; as neither France nor Great Britain had concluded a military convention with the Soviet Union, and since Beneš's policy remained one of 'western orientation', then he too had not pressed for a military understanding.[34] And if the purges as a whole repelled Russia's potential allies, the effect of the decimations in the Red Army and its command had not failed to have an adverse influence on British and French estimates of Soviet military capacity.[35]

Stalin's purge had earlier taken on an isolationist aspect. Foreign consulates in the Soviet Union were being closed down, even the Czech Consulate in Kiev. If there ever had been a genuine 'western element' in the direction of Soviet external policy, it was taking some hard knocks. Litvinov's position was being overshadowed gradually by Stalin's own men; the new Commission for Foreign Affairs, which had been officially set up in January 1938, had Zhdanov at its head, and Mekhlis, Manuilskii, Lozovskii, Khrushchev and Beria among its members. Bogomolov was certainly in prison in February 1938. Yurenev, who had worked very capably on Soviet-Japanese relations, had vanished. There were rumours in the late spring that a special trial of diplomats would be arranged, involving Yurenev (former ambassador in Japan), Antonov-Ovseenko (who had been assigned to Spain) and the former military attachés Colonels Vassiliev, Smirnov and Yakovlev, who had worked in London, Paris and Berlin respectively. No such trial took place; Antonov-Ovseenko was consigned to a prison, Yurenev vanished silently. While the diplomatic apparatus was being re-modelled, the Czech crisis advanced itself to the very centre of European affairs. At once, two Soviet policies seem to have been worked in that tense combination which had marked Soviet foreign policy for some time. *Izvestiya* held out the hope of assistance to the Czechs. Kalinin promised Czech workers that the Soviet government would carry out 'to the last letter' its obligations to Czechoslovakia.[36] While Beneš had admitted that there was no actual military convention under which aid could be rendered, the Czech military attaché in Moscow, Lieutenant-Colonel Dastic, was 'cautious' about the possibilities of Soviet help. The real restraint was the possibility of a war on two fronts. Soviet help could be expected to be set at the absolute minimum, and the absence of a common frontier would provide a convenient excuse.[37] The First of May was a convenient occasion for hurling defiance at enemies to east and west; Naval Commissar Smirnov warned the Japanese against being foolhardy and miscalculating Soviet strength. Defence Commissar Voroshilov spoke of a 'state of mobilisation', of the need for 'further perfecting the fighting capacity of the Red Army as well as raising its political consciousness and technical level'.[38]

In May there had been a further Soviet-Japanese clash on the eastern frontier, but this quietened quickly. Greater quantities of Soviet aid had been going to China and included personnel as well as equipment. Cherepanov's military mission was stepping into the shoes vacated by the German mission to Chiang Kai-shek, Five flights of Soviet aircraft, manned by Soviet pilots, were operating in China.[39] But Dr Tsiang, the Chinese Ambassador in Moscow, had formed a different impression of the basis of Soviet policy in China. In his talk with German diplomats in Hankow at the end of February, when he came to report to Chiang Kai-shek, Dr Tsiang answered the question of why there was not more direct Soviet participation in the Sino-Japanese war, by saying simply: 'Russia cannot.'[40] An extensive tour of the Soviet Union and inspection of Soviet industrial installations had persuaded Dr Tsiang that industry, with the possible exception of armaments, was full of failings. On the very foundations of his policy — agriculture — Stalin had not won, but was compromising and had no other choice. Dr Tsiang saw evidence at first-hand of the frailty of the Soviet transportation system (in April, Lazar Kaganovich again became Commissar for Communications, in addition to his assignment as head of Heavy Industry). It was true that the output of coal, steel, rolled metal and pig-iron was below plan.

The Soviet military mission to China never reached the strength attained in 1925–7. A maximum of 500 is the figure set for the Soviet officers who were attached, not to front-line troops, but to formation headquarters (and in a consultative role only), to tank and artillery schools and to the flying training-centre at Inning. 'Technical consultation', and not the formulation of strategy was the capacity allotted to the Soviet officers by Chiang Kai-shek.[41] Too great a degree of specialisation hampered the wider employment of the Soviet officers, for many were experts on a single Soviet weapon only. In artillery work, the Soviet idea of mass fire-support was out of place in a situation where ammunition was often exceedingly short.[42] China was yet another laboratory into which Soviet personnel were sent to watch the course of the experiments. Soviet aircraft were not transferred outright to the Chinese Air Force. The Soviet air units, reported to be under the command of Asanov,[43] were stationed at points covering the main Chinese bases at Nanking, Hankow, Chungking and in the north-west at Lanchow, the terminal point of a 1,700 mile transport link with the Soviet border.[44] The Japanese, meanwhile, who continued to hold a main force of over twenty divisions ready for possible operations against the Soviet Union, met up with stiff resistance from the Chinese in March–April (in Shantung Province) and for the Suchow operation part of the 'anti-Soviet reserve' was finally committed.[45] The 'China Incident' was settling into protracted war.

And as the European crisis began to march to its zenith, Stalin did not cease to make a complete sacrifice to his attempted political stabilisation through the *Yezhovshchina*. Among the military and civilians alike, the fact of the terror obtruded like a twisted limb. The purge was a weakening factor which neither friend nor foe could overlook. Litvinov's somewhat unusual address to the voters of Leningrad towards the end of June, a speech not given for '. . . any reason or necessity of foreign policy',[46] prepared the way for a complete freedom of choice for Soviet policy. On Czechoslovakia, Litvinov noted,

> . . . we strictly refrain from giving any unsolicited advice to the Czechoslovak Government, for we believe in its peaceful intentions, and . . . that it will itself find reasonable limits for concessions compatible with its prestige . . . that the responsibility for the consequences, in any event, will be borne by the attacking side . . . the Soviet Government, at least, has relieved itself of responsibility for the further development of events . . . the Soviet Union asks nothing for itself, does not wish to impose itself on anybody as partner or ally, but merely agrees to collective co-operation. . . .[47]

While Litvinov was speaking in a language of strange omen, Lev Mekhlis went about another special assignment in the Soviet Far East.

* * * *

At the end of May Mekhlis arrived in Khabarovsk, and a group of military commissars from the Political Administration reserve travelled with him. These were the 'new men', among whom a very junior political assistant had first reached the level of battalion commissar and would soon find himself, at this frenzied rate of promotion, head of one of the departments of the Front political administration.[48] Into Khabarovsk came also one other notable figure, corps commander Frinovskii (holding that rank as head of the Special Sections of the *NKVD* in the Red Army). Like Mekhlis, Frinovskii brought in his baggage train a whole staff of his own, destined to take over the positions of *NKVD* officers whose ranks were also to be torn apart. The arrival of Mekhlis in the Far East was a bad sign, the sinister implication of which was underlined by Frinovskii's presence. The Far Eastern Red Banner Front had already suffered once with the preliminary decimations of the summer of 1937, when sections of the military and political staff had been removed. The purge of the Party and administrative cadres had gone on. The 'Kolkhoz corps' had been disbanded in the winter of 1937–8 and its commanders disposed of. Individual officers were taken off to arrest or execution; Corps Commander Rokossovskii was dragged off, beaten senseless by the *NKVD* and lodged in prison.[49] The 'Mekhlis mission' arrived at a point when arrangements had been made to liquidate the Red Banner Front as such, and to set up in its place three independent Far Eastern armies; two would be based in the Maritime Province and a third in the Pri-Amur. As the military operations of July–August were to show, this fracturing of Blyukher's former Front command had already taken place by that date.[50] In addition, such a move would suggest some kind of collusion between Mekhlis and Voroshilov, designed to bring about the curbing of Blyukher's power.

Blyukher kept Mekhlis at a distance, according him none of the courtesies which had been extended to Gamarnik on his inspection trips. For his part, Mekhlis set up his 'purge GHQ' in the rail coach which had brought him to Khabarovsk. Straightway Mekhlis proceeded to make changes, beginning with the replacement of divisional commissar Kropachev (who was acting head of the Front political administration) by one of the reserve commissars Mekhlis had brought with him. Another 'Mekhlis man' was appointed deputy head, and a third — a singularly truculent fellow — posted as commissar to the staff headquarters in Khabarovsk.[51] Mekhlis got his hands at once on the military newspapers and press by assigning Regimental Commissar Bayev (chief of the press section of the Red Army Political Administration) to the supervision of these activities in the Far East. Frinovskii meanwhile was far from idle, setting about his first task which was the purging of the Far Eastern *NKVD* command. At a trial held at the beginning of June in Khabarovsk, the deputy *NKVD* commander was sentenced to death for 'treason and espionage'.[52] There was nothing very extraordinary in this, since it corresponded to what had been happening in 13 federal and autonomous republics and 26 regions of the Soviet Union, where senior *NKVD* officers were also being liquidated. The turn of the Far East had finally come, in a process which had wiped out 16 of the higher *NKVD* officials who were appointed in November 1935 (shortly after the army's elevations).

In what seems to have been something of a joint operation, Mekhlis and Frinovskii, having put their own houses in order, proceeded to carry out the final full-scale purge of Blyukher's forces. Political and command staff alike were subject to the eliminations. The same pattern showed itself once again — the higher the command level, the greater the proportional loss. Up to regimental level, a reported 40 per cent loss of command and political personnel was incurred. In divisional and corps staffs, the figure rose to 70 per cent, while the Front staff and departments lost over 80 per cent of their officers, and the Far Eastern army was soon to lose a Marshal. *NKVD* lorries or search parties moved about Khabarovsk, while officers' quarters or offices were subject to little short of raids. Arrests, after the time-honoured fashion of the *NKVD*, were usually made at night. Chinese and Korean elements were ruthlessly eliminated. Blyukher's staff, the flower of the Far Eastern army, was scythed down without further ado. Chachanyan, who had been appointed to the Far Eastern military soviet in May 1937 (and a reputable military expert in his own right), was eliminated. Blyukher's official deputy, Divisional Commander Pokus, his supply chief, Gulin, chief of staff Vasentsovich (who had made a rapid ascent of the command ladder as a result of the 1937 purge), Aviation Commander Pumpur (who had served in Spain), the acting political chief, Kropachev, and senior Army Commander Levandovskii (who had formerly commanded the South Caucasus Military District) were all dragged off — either to death or imprisonment — by the *NKVD*.[53] Not all were shot, for Far Eastern officers did make unexpected appearances in command posts during 1941, either on the eve or the immediate morrow of the German attack. But only a minority escaped untouched. New commanders were moved in, among them Corps Commander G. Shtern, who had recently seen service in Spain; Shtern was assigned to the command of what was later designated the 1st Independent Red Banner Far Eastern Army, and was given P. Rychagov as his aviation commander. He was going to need him. Koniev, the former political officer who had transferred to the command staff, and who had completed the command course at the Frunze Academy in 1935, had been in the Far East since 1936. He was one of those who passed through the Stalinist flame unscathed, and took over the Trans-Baikal Military District. For the moment, Blyukher remained untouched. He enjoyed great popularity in the Soviet Union and immense prestige in the Far East. At the end of June, he was standing amidst the shambles of what had been his command. At least he was never accused of 'conspiracy' or 'treason', but he had to reckon with Mekhlis, and in the final clash with that Stalinist agent Blyukher brought about his own destruction.

The first days of July brought about a new complication and one which set the Soviet Union on the path which seemed to lead to war. Not surprisingly, the occasion was provided by a Soviet-Japanese clash over frontiers. The location was a point somewhat to the south of where the borders of Manchuria, the Soviet Maritime Provinces and Korea met (approximately seventy miles to the south-west of Vladivostok). Between Soviet and Korean territory ran the River Tumen-Ula, keeping in a south-easterly direction until it reached the small village of Yangkuanpei, where it swung west and looped for some 5–6,000 metres until it resumed its main course at Podgornaya, another little village. Within this loop, on the eastern bank of the Tumen-Ula, lay high ground, the commanding point of which was the height of Changkufeng (roughly half way between the two villages) reaching 155 metres above sea level. Behind this height lay Lake Khasan, a stretch of water some half mile wide and one mile in length. The fighting which occurred in this area was to determine whether the frontier ran along the ridge of Changkufeng (the Soviet interpretation) or whether, as the Japanese contended, the height lay within Japanese-Manchurian territory. The trouble began on 6th July.

On that day, a reconnaissance party of three Soviet horsemen travelled the area of the height, finding no Japanese troops. Shortly afterwards, a small party of Soviet troops moved on to the height for a brief period, and this was followed after an interval of a few days by Soviet working parties which began to dig in on the western slope. Towards the end of July, a strong force had invested Changkufeng, setting up positions and placing a red flag on the crest. These activities had been closely observed by Japanese patrols to the west, who had seen the increased activity, the barbed-wire obstacles and the flag. The Japanese at first resorted to diplomacy, but on 15th July there was a Soviet rejection of the Japanese demand for the withdrawal of Soviet troops.[54] For the Japanese the position was not without certain complications. In China a major operation was being mounted for the eventual seizure of Wuhan and Hankow. Already the Japanese had drawn on that 'anti-Soviet reserve' which had been created to undertake operations against the Soviet Union at some future date. Japanese forces in Korea hardly matched the standards of the Kwantung Army. Tactically and strategically the Japanese were at a disadvantage. On the other hand, the Russians could not be made a present of the height. On 19th July, after the approval of the Japanese government had been given, Japanese infantry and artillery were moved up to the west bank near the height. On 26th July, after serious deliberation, the Japanese command decided to concentrate its forces on the Tumen opposite the height. The policy was to wait and see.[55]

What the Japanese saw on the morning of 29th July was not re-assuring. On another piece of high ground, named Shachaofeng* and a little more than 1,000 metres due north of Changkufeng, a small party of Soviet troops made their appearance and began to dig in. The commander of the 19th Japanese Infantry Division, General Suetaka, ordered the removal of the intruders. The Soviet version has Lieutenant P. F. Tereshkin and ten frontier guards attacked by 'up to a company' of Japanese troops.[56] Later in the day, Soviet reinforcements moved up from Changkufeng and drove off the Japanese party which had dislodged the Soviet patrol from Shachaofeng. The weather was bad, with fog and rain. During the night, having received permission to engage the Soviet forces, General Suetaka moved a couple of infantry battalions, with artillery and engineers, on to the eastern shore of the river, with the intention of launching a night attack on Changkufeng itself.[57] Both sides built up their forces.

Sharp fighting during the night of 31st July and on 1st August gave the Japanese a tactical victory. The Russians were dislodged from the high ground and the Japanese penetrated four kilometres into Soviet territory.[58] The commander of the 19th Japanese Division asked permission for more

* Shachaofeng is represented as 'Bezymyannaya Heights' and Changkufeng as 'Zaozernaya Heights' on Soviet military maps, an example of which is reproduced here.

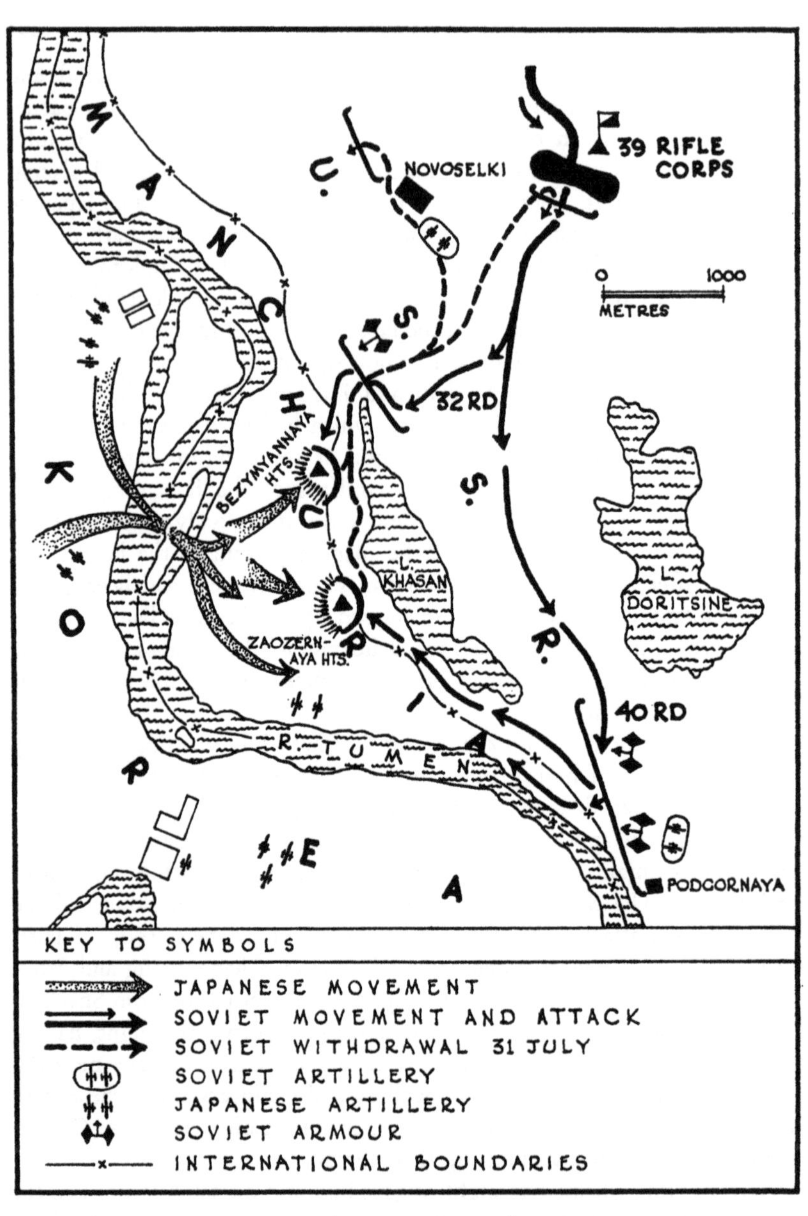

LAKE KHASAN (CHANGKUFENG) OPERATIONS
31 July - 13 August, 1938

troops to be moved over to the heights to repel a possible Soviet counter-attack. Army commander Nakamura refused this request, considering the incident at an end.[59] He was soon to see that this was not the view of the Soviet command, which moved the 40th Rifle Division into the area of operations. Due to bad weather and the haste of the improvised counter-attack, the 40th Division's efforts were unsuccessful. Failure showed that Soviet forces were too weak to carry out the task assigned to them,[60] although the Russians kept up their attacks. On 4th August, in another diplomatic exchange, Litvinov laid down to Shigemitsu the terms on which the fighting might cease — '. . . if the situation existing approximately up to 29 July is restored.'[61]

Throughout the fighting the Soviet press referred to the Far Eastern Red Banner Front, which indicated that Blyukher was in command. But the final stage of the operations was carried out by the 1st Independent Red Banner Far Eastern Army under G. Shtern. Up to 6th August, then, Blyukher was presumably still at his post but was removed either on that date or shortly afterwards.* The fighting on the frontier has been imputed to be the occasion of the final 'show-down' between Mekhlis and Blyukher. Whether Blyukher resisted Mekhlis's interference in the operations, and the latter used this to destroy confidence in Blyukher in Moscow, remains an open question. Alternatively, it is suggested that matters were brought to a head when a Red Army soldier shot down an officer who was behaving 'treasonably'. Mekhlis defended the soldier as an example of 'revolutionary vigilance', while Blyukher had him put under close arrest to await a military tribunal.[62] There is every likelihood that some major clash did occur, or that even the pretext of growing obstinacy on the part of Blyukher was seized upon to 'transfer' him to Moscow. The military action seems to have been initiated by the Russians, and presumably with the approval of Blyukher. That Blyukher was trying to provoke a major conflict with Japan seems to be too sweeping an interpretation.[63] A diversion, aimed at hampering Japanese operations in China, could be a possible explanation. Blyukher took care not to commit himself against the Kwantung Army, but the inferior Army of Korea. On the other hand, there were perfectly valid reasons — on a more local scale — for pursuing a forward military policy. Absolute control of the high ground would deny any effective control of the eastern river bank to the Japanese and make the river the real frontier between Korea and the Maritime Provinces.[64] And there was 'the Amur incident' to be revenged.

Shtern committed the 39th Rifle Corps (40th and 32nd divisions) to the

* The new *Istoriya Velik. Otechestv. Voiny Sov. Soyuza 1941–1945* (Moscow 1960, pp. 232–4, giving an account of the Lake Khasan operations, would confirm this.

rapidly developing operations.* Soviet aircraft carried out front-line sorties, as well as penetrating to targets in the Korean and Manchurian rear — flying some 700 sorties in five days.[65] Japanese air-power was not, however, committed to oppose these Soviet flights. Suetaka, playing with the idea of mounting an offensive into Siberia as the most effective way of employing his increased forces, was ordered not to try this. Precise instructions for careful manœuvring were passed to the Soviet command.[66] Both sides rejected the obvious military solutions in favour of careful arrangements to keep the conflict within bounds. The Soviet counter-attack was planned with artillery, tank and aviation support, and was timed for 6th August; the 32nd division would attack from the north and the 40th from the south. Poor visibility and bad weather on the morning of 6th grounded Soviet aircraft. When it came, the artillery preparation lasted only half an hour (very surprising in view of the detailed artillery arrangements which had been made).[67] The tanks, impeded by marshy ground and checked by Japanese anti-tank guns, were unable to take part in the battle for the heights. The Soviet infantry had to go it alone, straight into the Japanese defences. Not surprisingly the assault failed. Ferocious fighting took place from 7th–9th August. Both sides, in spite of their initial care to limit operations, proceeded to reinforce; Suetaka's division was fully concentrated, and the 104th (Kwantung Army) Division — detailed for service in South China — was ordered to North-east Manchuria.[68] Although on 8th the Japanese intercepted a Soviet signal to headquarters intimating that Russian losses were severe and could be expected to double, Soviet strength was built up to some 27 infantry battalions, several regiments of artillery, plus tanks.[69] The Japanese had now either to reinforce themselves very considerably, or call a halt. They chose the latter course, and a cease-fire was arranged for noon on August 11th.[70]

For an army which had just undergone a drastic purging, the Soviet performance was surprisingly good. Finally abandoning all attempt at finesse, Soviet commanders flung their troops into desperate frontal assaults. To judge by the extremely intensive political preparation of the troops, there were misgivings about morale. On the whole, the process worked. As a test of doctrine, the fighting confirmed the correctness of the basic principles embodied in the 1936 *Field Service Regulations* — it was, therefore, something of a misfortune that most of the authors of the regulations had been shot. Aviation (admittedly without real opposition) had carried out its

* Shtern was appointed commander of the 39th Rifle Corps on 3rd August; the Corps was strengthened to include the 40th RD, 32nd RD, 39th RD and the 2nd Mechanised Brigade (under Colonel A. P. Panfilov). In his report to the front Military Soviet, Shtern reported that not all these formations could concentrate at the same speed, but recommended having all available forces ready for use on 5th August.

predestined mission of attacks 'in the entire depth of the enemy position'. But where the enemy was strongly entrenched and his troops and guns well dug in, aviation alone could not accomplish a real weakening of the defences. It needed massive artillery work to realise the conditions necessary for successful tank and infantry attacks. The plain truth at Lake Khasan was that there were not enough guns. Without proper co-ordination with the artillery, and in the absence of the necessary field engineers, the tanks had been at the mercy of the anti-tank guns. The Soviet tanks had been unable to support the infantry. That 'inter-action', for which Tukhachevsky had constantly pressed, had been lacking during the operations at Lake Khasan. The Soviet infantry paid dearly for this, as well as for the deficiencies in tactical training — especially in the platoons and companies — which had always been a serious drawback in the Red Army.[71] This time the Red Army paid in battle casualties, for the Japanese infantry and gunners were not foreign observers, and Lake Khasan was not manœuvres.

The Japanese were obliged to admit defeat at the hands of the Russians, who had extracted every ounce of advantage from the difficulties facing Japan in China, as well as capitalising on the fact that Germany was deeply involved in the west. But the victors were simultaneously vanquished by the *NKVD*, and Blyukher's command had suffered very severely in this internal and one-sided battle. As for Blyukher himself, there is no way of establishing with any certainty the date on which he was removed from the Far East and despatched to Moscow.* On 9th November, 1938, however, Blyukher was dead.[72] Most probably this proletarian Marshal of the Soviet Union, soldier, diplomat and the lord of Eastern Siberia, was the victim of a persistent and deadly intrigue, from which neither Voroshilov nor Mekhlis emerge with any honour. At the death of Blyukher there were no trumped up charges, no orders of the day, no talk of tribunals — only a complete and utter silence which remained unbroken for some twenty years. It was the epitome of personal vengeance.

★ ★ ★ ★

Secondary, personal intrigues were certainly pursued and played out against the main background of Stalin's policy of bringing the army under tighter control. These personal manœuvres had a counter-part in the struggle taking place in the leadership below the level of the *Politburo*. But the main purpose of clearing out the remnants of the old command and setting up the new men continued throughout the summer of 1938. The crisis in the

* In the entry under A. Y. Golovanov (*Biographic Directory of the USSR*, p. 184) it is stated that Golovanov was commander in 1937 of the special multi-engined aircraft used for bringing arrested persons back to Moscow. This machine was used to bring Blyukher back from the Far East, but no specific date is mentioned.

naval command had not yet been satisfactorily resolved. On 2nd July, in a speech to Leningrad shipyard workers, Kalinin openly proclaimed the priorities of naval policy: 'to outdo England', to build fast, cheaply and well.[73] The rapid construction of sizeable naval vessels was quite obviously beyond the immediate capacities of Soviet yards. Even as it proposed to surpass the Royal Navy, the administration was forced to admit that Soviet shipbuilding facilities lagged appreciably behind those supplying the British fleet. Negotiations were set in motion through a Soviet-American trading agency, run by Molotov's brother-in-law, to have a battleship built in an American yard by an American firm; some $60–100,000,000 in cash would have been involved, with the arrangement providing for American technical aid in building a duplicate battleship in the Soviet Union.[74] The Soviet Union had capable designers of its own, even though several members of the Construction Faculty of the Naval Academy had been ousted; Professor Krylov, an outstanding designer, had not been removed by the purge, but while designers could produce plans, they could not produce shipyards. Naval Commissar Smirnov certainly lacked any kind of independence, and had probably been appointed precisely for his insignificance. Stalin's hand was directly in naval affairs. He wanted quick results, but it is difficult to see what the naval authorities could do but embark on a renovation programme for larger ships. More rapid progress was made with smaller vessels. Smirnov's position was unstable. Misgivings about and even opposition to the naval programme may have prompted more command changes. In the Far East, Kuznetsov took over the fleet command from Viktorov, who finally fell. Kuznetsov's star was rising rapidly, and in the spring of 1939 he finally displaced Smirnov as Naval Commissar and the door was shut tight on twenty years of Soviet naval development.

Soviet military aviation, especially the bomber fleet, still enjoyed a formidable reputation in some quarters in Europe. Very obviously the most immediate aid which the Soviet Union could lend in Europe entailed the use of its strategic aviation, which had been reaching impressive proportions by 1936. In 1938 the situation changed, as a result of the purge and the interpretation of the fighting in Spain. Alksnis and Khripin, under whom the *VVS* had developed its powerful bomber forces and the constant shift in emphasis to the bomber in independent operations, were removed. Khripin vanished. Alksnis, whose name had been associated with the 1937 military tribunal, was displaced from the *VVS* command; he died or was executed in 1940 at the age of forty-three.[75] As with the Navy, the command changes were not unconnected with modifications in the strategic line; the emphasis now shifted to defensive fighter aviation and diminishing the role of the bomber. The designer Tupolev was also in prison, charged with disclosing Soviet aviation secrets abroad; the brain behind the long-range *VVS* bomber designs, with his school, was temporarily eliminated. Not all the commanders sharing Khripin's point of view were eliminated, nor was strategic aviation wholly flung away,[76] although the purge of designers and staffs could only bring deterioration upon the long-range bomber groups. Successor to Alksnis was Corps Commander Loktinov, an officer without apparent distinction, who held his position until September 1939 when he was replaced by Ya. Smushkevich. The latter had made a tremendous reputation as a fighter pilot and commander in the Far East;* of Lithuanian Jewish origin and an infantryman during the Civil War, Smushkevich had been first a commissar in an aviation unit, changing to the command line in 1931. To a man who was essentially nothing more than an aviation brigade commander, although very brave, Stalin assigned control over the Soviet Air Force.

To date the beginning of the decline in the efficiency of Soviet military aviation from the purge may be somewhat misleading. Certainly a very experienced section of the command, which had seen the *VVS* through some of its most difficult days and early technical difficulties, had been deprived of control. Of equal importance with the command problem was the question of how effectively the rate of re-equipping could be maintained. Substantial achievements had been effected by reliance on French and American technical help. The *VVS* depended on constant modernisation. American sources, being increasingly occupied with their own processes of re-armament, began to dry up. In 1938, S. A. Lavochkin began work on his new fighter designs, which were later to achieve great fame. Yet even with the comparative speed with which prototypes were produced, this was still a long way from effective re-equipping. This also was to bring disastrous results in its wake, and was a true commentary on the degree of real autarchy that had been achieved in the armaments and aviation industry. The other complicating factor was the interpretation of the combat lessons of the Spanish Civil War. Soviet bombers — principally Tupolev's SB-2's — had little chance to show their paces, since they operated only on a small scale, without being committed *en masse*. It was a combat test in which the qualifying conditions needed careful and astute evaluation.

The purge of the Far Eastern forces coincided with one more assault on the senior officers. Out of the membership of the military tribunal which was associated with the 'trial' of Tukhachevsky and his companions in June 1937, only two men survived — Budenny and Shaposhnikov. Dybenko, appointed the commander of the Leningrad Military District, was liquidated on 29th July, 1938. Kashirin vanished. Blyukher's fate was being tightly

* Smushkevich has also been identified as the 'General Douglas' of the Spanish Civil War.

sealed. Alksnis had been removed. Goryachev died of natural causes. Yegorov, who had been appointed Voroshilov's deputy, was removed from this position, although he had three more years to live. Yegorov's disappearance brought the tally of purge victims of Marshal's rank to three, three of the five who had held that rank in May 1937. Army Commander 2nd Grade Vatsetis, the first Bolshevik commander-in-chief under Trotsky during the Civil War, was eliminated on 28th July, 1938, the day before Dybenko was shot. The same day Orlov was shot. Berzin and Stashevksii had long been cleaned out of Soviet Military Intelligence. With the purge of the senior officers went a purge of their staffs; in the technical and specialist branches, the eliminations reached right back into the design centres and the training staffs.

The physical annihilation of the Tukhachevsky group in the Red Army command, together with the elimination of officers thoroughly trained in the ideas developed in the years 1933–6, brought inevitable consequence upon the quality of trained military leadership, 'lowering the strategic quality of the Red Army'.[77] With the exception of Shaposhnikov, the new high command was stamped either by mediocrity or lack of experience. Tukhachevsky's theories had been by no means faultless and the training based on them as yet imperfect, but the Marshal's line was undoubtedly correct. At least the problem of mass and mobility was being tackled, and much depended on what line of policy would be adopted towards the Red Army's most distinctive feature, its mechanised forces. The problems of command raised by the greatly increased technical differentiation in the Red Army had not been minimised by Tukhachevsky. At one sweep, however, these were pushed aside by the needs of Stalin's attempted political stabilisation, which presumably counted on the fact that another command could be created to replace the one destroyed. It was a singular calamity that the dominance of mediocrity and inexperience should coincide with a military re-organisation based partly on the incorrect evaluation of the lessons of the fighting in Spain. The idea that independent operations by mechanised forces would play an important part in any future conflict suffered as heavily as that same notion applied to air-power. Drawing incorrect conclusions from the localised actions, or interpreting the mis-application of the weapons as the failure of the weapons themselves was not the monopoly of the Soviet command. French military opinion took a mistaken comfort from the outcome of the battle of Guadalajara. The effect upon the balance of the Red Army which had been contrived previously, however, was to be disastrous. The resultant inferiority could not be ascribed to technical failure; there is no evidence to suggest excessive interference with the corps of tank designers, and the improvements in tank design projected in 1938 were to lead to some excellent machines.[78] Quantity was still at a premium. In the end, however, and in spite of the objections of Shaposhnikov and Zhukov, much of Khalepskii's valuable introductory work was undone.

It was, therefore, with a military command becoming increasingly disordered that the Soviet Union faced the oncoming crisis over Czechoslovakia. In that curious June speech, Litvinov had already washed his hands of any further responsibility, and had performed this action on behalf of Soviet policy. As German pressure increased in the summer of 1938, 'the Russian factors' reached its very maximum importance. But effective Franco-Soviet military conversations had yet to be begun. Poland and Rumania refused transit to Soviet troops, and Litvinov ruled out specifically the idea of the Red Army forcing a passage. The Soviet Union could not appear as an aggressor.[79] This resort to morality began to bear out the German report which suggested that the Soviet Union would find the lack of a common frontier with Czechoslovakia a convenient pretext for limiting its aid. In Moscow, M. Coulondre learned from the Czech Ambassador Fierlinger that 'in the Kremlin' there was no belief that France and Great Britain would be ready to wage war on account of Czechoslovakia, and consequently the Soviet Union should reserve its own attitude.[80] If this was indeed the prevailing view in Soviet ruling circles, then formal promises could be made — as they were made — without the risk of bringing the Soviet Union to the very brink of war, for the machinery of the pacts put the onus on France, which in turn depended on French deference to the British position. On 21st September, in his speech at the League of Nations, Litvinov revealed that two days earlier the Czechs had asked if the Soviet Union would fulfil its obligations under the pact, in the event of France rendering aid. The Soviet Union replied in the affirmative — 'a clear answer in the affirmative'.[81] General Gamelin reported that Voroshilov was informed, through the Soviet Military Attaché in Paris, of the measures being taken by the French; on being asked about a possible Soviet reaction, the Military Attaché replied that there seemed to be every likelihood of Poland committing herself to the side of Germany and closing on Czechoslovakia in order to recover Teschen. In this event, the Soviet Union would have no option but to move rapidly against Poland — a prospect which the Soviet officer visibly relished.[82] On 23rd September, the Soviet Vice-Commissar for Foreign Affairs Potemkin warned that if the Poles proceeded to 'occupy by force part of the territory of the Czechoslovak Republic', then the Soviet Union would denounce its Non-Aggression Pact with Poland.[83] This seemed to be very far from being an idle gesture. If the Poles had actually attacked Czechoslovakia, the Red Army could have moved against Poland with a very fair degree of confidence, since the Soviet view seemed also to be that Germany would not move an inch to pull any Polish chestnuts out of the fire. At one stroke, the Soviet Union could diminish the threat to the Ukraine and probably make some territorial acquisition at the expense of Poland. On 26th September the Soviet Military Attaché in Paris called on General Jeannel, General Gamelin's Chief of Staff (General Gamelin himself being in London), to convey Voroshilov's thanks for the French communication and to report that the Red Army had thirty rifle divisions, a mass of cavalry, numerous tank formations and the bulk of Soviet military aviation ready to intervene in 'the west'.[84] On 28th September, General Gamelin saw the Soviet attaché once again on the eve of his departure for Moscow, and asked him to convey to Marshal Voroshilov the view that it was hoped the Soviet armies would not be launched against Poland without the French being given prior knowledge, as they still hoped to keep Poland 'on our side'.[85] The Soviet armies in the west were deprived of the opportunity of moving on Poland when, on 1st October, Czechoslovakia accepted the terms of the Polish demands. Potemkin was visibly put out at this 'second capitulation'.[86] A Soviet counter-attack on Poland, which would in no way have involved Germany, would have been well within the capacity of the Red Army, weakened as it was by the purge. M. Coulondre had all the while maintained that the Russians did not look upon Poland as 'a front', in the manner in which it was envisaged in the west. It was either a meeting-ground or a battle-ground with Germany. The soundness of that observation was to be proved in the none too distant future. If this was indeed the core of the Soviet military position at the time of the Czechoslovak crisis, then it was a policy as cynical and self-interested as the western powers' was dubious. That there was the highest degree of calculation in Soviet policy had been demonstrated only a few weeks earlier, at Lake Khasan. The inevitable exclusion of the Soviet Union from the Munich settlement completed a self-imposed isolation, and made it imperative for Stalin to proceed with his private policy of negotiating an agreement with Hitler.

* * * *

The *Yezhovshchina*, which had gone careering on to bring about ever greater losses and demoralisations, came quietly to a stop. Already by the beginning of 1938, presumably out of fear that the mass arrests endangered the very survival of the Party as an organised body, there had been an attempt to limit the effects of the terror and institute hearings for those unjustly accused. But 'widespread repression' continued to exist in 1938.[87] The Red Army continued to suffer from that 'repression' along with the rest of society. On Khrushchev's own admission, the military purge was no transitory phenomenon or even a sudden, crippling chastisement to the ambitious or the incompetent, but went on 'during 1937–41'. The question therefore arises at what point the losses to the Red Army officer corps and the high command can be estimated. Seventeen months elapsed between the shooting of the first Soviet Marshal and the last. Both the changes and the actual eliminations in the naval command ran from January 1937 to the summer of 1938, followed by a final re-shuffle. The arrest of senior officers had begun by the late autumn of 1936; the first reinstatements, to judge by Rokossovskii's case, occurred in the late autumn of 1938, although there were Soviet officers lodged in prison right up to the beginning of the Soviet-German War. Any estimate of the military losses made at the time of the contraction of the purge as a whole needs the important qualification that if the tempest was dying down, it was by no means over. Taking the period from the late spring of 1937 to the late autumn of 1938 (and the elimination of Blyukher), the Red Army had lost 3 out of 5 Marshals. All the 11 Deputy Commissars for Defence were eliminated. Of the total membership of the Military Soviet which had been set up in 1934, there were 5 survivors — the other seventy-five perished. By the summer of 1938, all the military district commanders who held that position in June 1937 or who had been appointed to fill places vacated by the first executions had vanished. The head of the Political Administration had been shot. His deputy, Bulin, together with most of the chiefs of political administrations in military districts, vanished.

The former heads of the naval and air forces were removed, the former to be shot in 1938, the latter to die or be liquidated some time later. The naval and air chiefs of staff were eliminated. The purge of naval constructors had a counter-part in the arrest of Tupolev, together with his colleagues and pupils. Of the army commanders holding that rank in May 1937 only two survived — thirteen were shot. Fifty-seven out of 85 corps commanders were shot, as were 110 of the 195 divisional commanders. At brigade commander level, of the original 406 officers in that rank on the eve of the 1937 executions, 220 survived the main blow of the purge. The head of the Frunze Military Academy and the chief of *Osoaviakhim* had been shot. Only one fleet commander survived the naval purge. In the Far Eastern forces, over 80 per cent of the staff were removed, as well as the commander. The higher the command level the greater was the proportional loss. Among the deputy commissars and members of the Military Soviet the loss was 100 per cent and 95 per cent respectively, and climbed to 90 per cent among army commanders. To discover a single connecting characteristic which might account for this decimation of senior officers is apt to be misleading. Among the Marshals, it was not merely a purge of the 'ex-

Imperial officers', for Blyukher was wholly proletarian and an ex-NCO. Ex-officer Shaposhnikov was retained. All were products of the Civil War, but commanders trained in the Civil War — and having little else besides — were retained, and indeed promoted. Distinctions between political and command staff had no effect, since the military-political leadership of the Red Army was affected as drastically as the military command. The only protected group appeared to be former officers of the 1st Cavalry Army, and even that immunity did not stretch to Yegorov. Links with the *Reichswehr* have been construed as the spot which damned, but there were notable exceptions to this, not the least Voroshilov himself. By the end of 1938, only some 39 per cent of the officers at a level running from divisional commander to Marshal of the Soviet Union remained as compared with the position in May 1937.[88]

The greatest numerical loss was borne in the Soviet officer corps from the rank of colonel downwards and extending to company commander level. The extent of the loss is variously estimated. The figure will depend on two things; firstly, the original estimate of the strength of the Soviet officer corps, and secondly the date at which the estimate is to apply (and whether it includes both of the Far Eastern purges). The strength of the Soviet officer corps as a whole could be set reasonably at a maximum of 75–80,000 (which would include naval officers). The highest figure set for the losses reaches 30,000 and the lowest is half of that figure.[89] The discrepancy is considerable, and depends to some degree upon the question of the permanency of the displacement of the officers involved. In the autumn of 1938, rehabilitation commissions were at work setting officers back in the posts from which they had been arbitrarily removed. The bulk of the officers at this level seem to have been imprisoned rather than executed. If the final figure remained 15,000, then that would correspond to the average which occurred in the Party.[90] This figure, however, needs qualification as to the period for the estimate and this is lacking. Allowing for reinstatements but including all the arms and extending the estimate to cover the period from the early summer of 1937 to the late autumn of 1938, then a conservative estimate of 20–25,000 might not be out of place for the real loss incurred. That is to say, between a quarter and a half of the officers of the Soviet armed forces were involved, with varying degrees of misfortune and calamity, in the processes of the military purge. Nevertheless, even if the lowest estimate is accepted, this was by no means a minor operation carried out on the Soviet officer corps, and it was one which left terrible scars.

Numerical calculations, while suggesting the extent of the purge, are not themselves an assessment of the effects, although the physical damage is obvious enough. At the cost of great efforts and many tribulations, the Red

Army had accomplished the education and training of its officer corps. The basic issue of the military re-organisation, both throughout the 1920's and in the first half of the 1930's, had been the problem of command. Soviet officers of all ranks had been sent to school. In February 1937 *Pravda* boasted of Soviet prowess in studies of Clausewitz, Moltke, Schlieffen and Ludendorff, which were taught in military schools.[91] Soviet military literature was rich and suggestive, even if it suffered from an indigestion of too varied a diet of foreign products. Those whose combat experience was drawn from Civil War days were evidently slow to adjust themselves to the new tempo of mechanised warfare, as well as its complexity, but this phenomenon of reluctant adaptation was not unique to the Red Army. If the justification of the purge of the high command was advanced as the elimination of the incompetent, this was patently false. It was precisely the best brains of the Red Army which had been removed from the top. Officers trained in their ideas had also been removed. All this had been effected for the sake of a possibility, that of raising a new senior command, politically reliable and even subservient, and one inclined to adapt itself to Stalin's requirements. The main problem was to create it. From the military academies and even from the *NKVD*, officers were coming forward to make good some of the damage to the officer corps. The commissions of reinstatement were a sign that things had gone too far. Discipline was going to pieces because of the widespread 'denunciations' and the practice of setting one part of the armed forces to spy upon the other. The new officers were taking up their posts under the awkward conditions of dual command, which had never contributed to any sort of military efficiency. Whatever the exact tally of Soviet officers who succumbed in the 1937–8 purge, it had been a loss grievous enough to endanger the entire stability of that body which had already suffered the many disadvantages deriving from a lack of homogeneity and marked differences in professional capability. The way to a homogeneous and Stalinised officer corps might have been wedged open, but this was to take many years to establish. And what the Red Army needed still was not political but tactical training. All the exhortations of the commissars during the fighting at Lake Khasan could not reduce the casualties due to faulty or incomplete training. Soviet soldiers may have died patriotically but they also died unnecessarily. It was to take another military tragedy to drive this lesson in on the army's political masters.

The reconstruction of the officer corps, and the high command especially, depended not only on the degree of destruction which had been brought about but also on the factor of the expansion of the Red Army and Navy. In view of the latter, it was a matter of crucial importance that a sound military policy should be developed and adopted. Some 1,000 officers needed training to take over the senior command and administrative posts which had either fallen vacant or were growing out of the development of the armed forces. The depleted staffs needed reinforcement. The Defence Commissariat was securely in the hands of Stalin's former military comrades and their nominees. Voroshilov was no longer overshadowed by a brilliant deputy, but it remained to be seen whether he did in fact possess the ability to guide the army aright. Ambition he possessed to no small degree, but foreign observers had noted his lack of military knowledge. Great brave phrases came tumbling out of him — as on 7th November, 1938, when he spoke of 'the crushing force of Soviet arms and the heroism of the Red warriors and their commanders' at Lake Khasan — yet sound ideas seemed to elude him. Victory was made to sound easy, 'heroism' fitted into the place of sound training. Reeling off lists of percentage increases in tanks, guns and aircraft did not mean that a system had been devised for their efficient use on the battlefield. Nor did Voroshilov's deputy commissars inspire any great confidence by virtue of their military ability — Budenny, Mekhlis, Shchadenko and the upstart figure of Kulik. Shaposhnikov alone was possessed of a high degree of professional competence, yet his powers were evidently limited even in his position as Chief of the General Staff, when the mechanised formations could be broken up and distributed piece-meal among the rifle divisions against his better judgement. Under Shaposhnikov, however, a new group of talented officers was brought to the fore. Names hitherto either unknown or undistinguished make their appearance at the senior command levels. A. M. Vasilevskii, regimental commander during the Civil War, graduate of the Frunze Academy (at a time when Shaposhnikov was its head), member of the training and inspectorate staff in the Defence Commissariat until 1936 and then a student and graduate of the General Staff Academy, was attached to the General Staff after 1937. I. K. Bagramyan, former cadet of the Imperial Russian Army and Red Army commander in the Civil War, was completing his course at the General Staff Academy. K. A. Meretskov, a volunteer in the Red Army in 1918, and chief of staff in the Belorussian Military District before the purge, took over Shaposhnikov's own command of the Leningrad Military District in 1938. A. A. Grechko, N. F. Vatutin, G. K. Malandin, V. V. Kurasov, A. N. Bogolyubov, I. A. Pliev were undergoing training in the staff academy. I. D. Chernyakovskii, P. P. Poluboyarov, and A. L. Getman underwent advanced training for commands in the tank forces.

Time was running short, but Stalin had schemes of his own to circumvent even this danger. There was, to his mind, one sure way out of the trap of isolation into which the Soviet Union had apparently been forced as a result of the Munich agreement. The Red Army purge, even if it had weakened the armed forces, had extirpated one fundamental danger, which had already in 1927 caused a furious clash as Trotsky criticised Stalin's 'rotten ropes' and asserted the duty of the Opposition to take power to wage a possible war more effectively and efficiently. In the event of the Soviet Union being involved in war and suffering serious initial reverses, the purge ensured that no military command group existed which might be of a mind to seize upon this opportunity to undo Stalin's dictatorship. The sacrifice of a command was worth this security. If it is difficult to discern any particular, dangerous feature common to the purged officers, which might itself afford some explanation for the decimations, in general the previous high command had shown a notable independence of outlook, a singular homogeneity and internal loyalties. The present command exhibited no such characteristics. Since its early days, the Soviet regime had been forced to balance political reliability and military efficiency most precariously. The one inevitably gained, only for the other to suffer. Under Stalin and the particular requirements of his dictatorship, the crisis had become acute and the balance previously achieved was tipped deliberately but disastrously towards political reliability. The interests of the Red Army as a military machine necessitated some restoration, but this was not to come about before the Red Army suffered grim experiences in the fighting it was called upon to do.

CHAPTER SIXTEEN

The Race with Time: 1939–1940

The 17th Party Congress, which met in 1934, had been dignified with the title of 'the Congress of Victors'. Assembling five years later and after the frenzied years of the great purges, the 18th Congress deserves at least the name of the congress of survivors. In this obedient and subservient assembly Stalin could measure much of the extent of his own victory. Yezhov, architect of the *Yezhovshchina*, had been finally displaced and Beria put in command over the *NKVD*. If the name of Yezhov was held in dread in the Red Army, that of Beria would come to have equally infamous connotation and be clustered about with an extreme of hatred among the military. Voroshilov remained the only military member of the *Politburo*, to which Zhdanov and Khrushchev, out of recognition for services rendered, were elected full members. Like the Congress, the *Politburo* was now so constituted as to reflect and represent only the will of Stalin.

The rump of the military command treated the Congress to a formal but not uninformative survey of military policy. Pride of place went to Voroshilov, who produced an impressive tally of percentage increases in the technical equipment available to the Red Army. The fire-power of a Soviet rifle corps could produce by its artillery volley 65 tons of metal per minute; adding the weight of other projectiles (mines, grenades, bullets) this came to the grand total of 78 tons of metal. The cavalry was being strengthened, increasing numerically by over a half since 1934 and with a 43 per cent increase in its artillery power, not to mention special anti-aircraft artillery designed to protect the cavalry against air-attack. Tank regiments attached to the cavalry had been increased by 30 per cent. The tank forces themselves, in addition to being re-equipped, had been completely re-organised. The greatest increase in Soviet artillery had occurred with anti-tank guns, anti-aircraft weapons taking second place. The 'so-called short range artillery' (including mortars) had undergone considerable strengthening. Chemical troops were now double what they were, signal troops had increased and were almost completely mobile. Voroshilov obviously could not pass over dual command in silence. On the contrary, the Defence Commissar launched into a grand eulogy of the commissar, who was '. . . a most responsible figure in the army'. The commissar, Voroshilov went on, had a vital place in the modern army, in which the commander was necessarily preoccupied with combat training and specialist instruction. In battle that 'integral unit' of the commander and the commissar would lead the troops into action; in training, both were responsible for the combat efficiency and material well-being of their units. The commissar had played his vital role in rooting out the traitorous elements in the Soviet armed forces. Political staff had grown with the expanding army; there were now 34,000 political workers compared with 15,000 at the time of the 17th Congress.

In addition to citing Lenin and Stalin as the founts from which correct military-political ideas flowed to ensure victory — as had been proved in the Civil War — Voroshilov dragged in Clausewitz to substantiate this wholly idealised picture of the commander-commissar relationship (which had been exposed by some twenty years' experience). Out of this, out of the fact that commanders and political staff are bound into a 'monolithic collective' with their troops, and since the Red Army is a 'splendidly-trained army', Voroshilov could produce his *quod erat demonstrandum* — 'Comrades, our army is invincible!' The shoddiness of this propaganda and the almost primitive nature of the military notions underlying it were to be shown up drastically in some nine months in Finland.[1]

Shtern and Mekhlis both contributed to the Congress, as did Shaposhnikov and Budenny. Mekhlis, in the course of his political homily, made a number of very interesting points. The military purge was nothing less than the complete 're-Bolshevisation' of the Red Army. The admission of such an aim tends to confirm that the purged commanders had objected to the increased demands of political work in the army, that there had been a real clash between the priorities of military efficiency and political indoctrination. The new commissars — and the implication was to emphasise the contrast with their predecessors — would act with all vigilance as the eyes and ears of the Party, ready to root out any incipient 'treason'. In his treatment of the purge, Mekhlis produced a very illuminating little tale, bearing a moral for his listeners yet indicating the degree to which morale must have suffered at this time. In one Soviet regiment the representative of the Special Section (OO) mentioned to the commissar that he was 'after' a *politruk* by the name of Rybnikov. The commissar explained this in confidence to the Party organisation, who at once expelled Rybnikov since counter-intelligence was on to him. But, explained Mekhlis, the Special Section considered Rybnikov 'a wanted man' only because they were interested in having him work for them; Comrade Rybnikov's 'mental suffering' (which must have been acute) was quite unnecessary, and illustrated how abused the matter of 'vigilance' might be.[2] It would also explain partly why, in action, Soviet officers were numbed into an extreme state of reliance on orders from above, shunning all resource. Shtern, acclaimed as the victor of Lake Khasan, had some additional points to make. The Soviet organisation was strong because it had removed spies and wreckers from its midst; technically, the Red Army was in excellent shape, its training under Voroshilov of the highest standard, its military qualities enhanced by an important political consciousness. The Red Army command had not suffered as a result of the purge of the Tukhachevsky-Gamarnik clique and other 'Trotskyite-Bukharinite' wreckers and spies. On the contrary, these eliminations had actually strengthened the command, which disposed of a high level of military competence at all grades and was both loyal to and the devoted servant of the Soviet state.

Voroshilov and M. M. Kaganovich (Commissar for the Aviation Industry) on the *VVS* produced more percentages and the firm assertion that the threat posed by the bomber did not intimidate the Soviet Union (in which connection there had been more than a doubling of Soviet fighter aircraft forces). Kuznetsov, then Pacific Fleet commander, spoke out for the new naval programme, under which the Soviet Union could and would build '. . . excellent ships of any class and size', some of which had already been built in Soviet yards and were at least equal to, if not in some cases superior to the same types possessed by 'the great naval Powers'. Shipbuilding Commissar Tevosyan produced the story that 'enemies of the people' Tukhachevsky, Orlov and Muklevich had opposed the idea of a powerful Soviet surface fleet and worked to prevent the addition of new surface units to the fleet.[3] Now the position was changed; such dangerous enemies were not in power and the Soviet Navy had embarked upon its ambitious programme. Later in the year, both in speech and writing, Kuznetsov (then Naval Commissar) and Tevosyan were to give the widest publicity to the expanded naval programme, whereby the Soviet fleet would be transformed into 'a most mighty attacking force'.

None of this was especially new. The talk of invincibility and great technical advances sounded well. Shtern delivered a re-assuring address on the results of the fighting at Lake Khasan. The names of the purged officers were dragged in at the appropriate moments to embellish the appropriate arguments. Army-Party relations had not yet settled down properly under the new conditions, although it was clear that the Party could regard itself as the eventual victor; the consolidation of this victory remained the great question under discussion. Difficulties had obviously arisen as a result of the purge going crashing out of control in its later stages. Mekhlis's new commissar staff had to be hurriedly reinforced.[4] As for the remarks about the Red Army's 'invincibility' and the assertions that the command had emerged vigorous and capable after the blood-letting, if the words had any real significance at all, then it was to be that they would have to be eaten ignominiously almost before the year was out.

* * * *

Stalin's report of 10th March to the Congress was, however, quite another matter, containing extremely important views on international affairs. His Marxist analysis led him to conclude that recent events were, in effect, an intensification of the 'imperialist struggle', in which it was now '... a question of the re-division of the world, of spheres of influence and colonies, by military action'.[5] The failure to stand up to the aggressors could not be attributed to weakness vis-à-vis the Fascist states, since the '... non-aggressive, democratic states are unquestionably stronger . . . both economically and militarily'. England and France had rejected collective security, taking up a position of 'non-intervention, a position of neutrality', a dangerous game which in reality boiled down to having 'all the belligerents . . . sink deeply into the mire of war, to encourage them surreptitiously in this . . . to allow them to weaken and exhaust one another . . . egging on the Germans to march farther east, promising them easy pickings and prompting them: "Just start war on the Bolsheviks and everything will be all right".'[6] Over the Carpathian Ukraine there had been 'a suspicious hullabaloo', the object of which seemed to be '. . . to incense the Soviet Union against Germany, to poison the atmosphere and to provoke a conflict with Germany without any visible grounds'. This game of 'non-intervention' was both dangerous and serious. In other words, what Stalin appeared to want was a specific guarantee covering the reliability of the Western powers (he was evidently assured of their economic and military strength); at the same time, a very strong hint had been dropped to Germany that 'no visible grounds' existed to engender conflict between that country and the Soviet Union.[7]

The relevance of Stalin's remarks would be amply demonstrated during the coming six months, and their hidden implications fully unfolded. The crisis came over Poland, which twenty years previously had played so vital a part in bringing capitalist Germany and Communist Russia together. Stalin's March speech had evidently not fallen on deaf ears in Germany.[8] Meanwhile the Soviet government denied that Soviet aid had been promised to Poland and Rumania 'in the event of their becoming victims of aggression', but it was admitted that London had asked Moscow what the Soviet attitude might be if there were an assault on Rumania. This exchange had taken place on 18th March, and the Soviet government had replied with a suggestion for the convening of a conference of the most interested States — Britain, France, Rumania, Poland, Turkey and the Soviet Union. This suggestion, however, the British found 'premature'.[9] The British counter-proposal consisted of a possible formal declaration, to be signed by Great Britain, France, the Soviet Union and Poland, declaring the intention to enter into consultations on steps required to meet a threat to the peace of Europe. Polish objections to this were induced '. . . by a lack of faith that a step of this kind would be adequate'.[10] On 31st March the British Prime Minister delivered on the floor of the House of Commons the declaration, drafted on the afternoon of 30th, that in the event of any action which clearly threatened Polish independence, 'His Majesty's Government would feel themselves bound at once to lend the Polish Government all support in their power.' And a vital part of that support hinged on the Soviet Union.

The British guarantee failed to arouse any immediate Soviet enthusiasm. A mere guarantee was not enough. On 9th April in the French War Ministry a conference, which included M. Daladier, M. Bonnet and Generals Gamelin, Vuillemin, Bührer and Colson, grappled with the question of Polish resistance to the idea of Soviet assistance. M. Bonnet therefore proposed to seek a Soviet declaration on possible aid to Rumania and Poland, and France would transmit these notions to the countries concerned. The French Military Attaché in Moscow was to engage in conversations with Marshal Voroshilov on this matter,[11] while the French Ambassador followed the diplomatic channel. On 14th April, M. Bonnet's plan was submitted in Moscow and the possible text of a joint declaration presented. New British proposals had also been presented to Litvinov in Moscow.[12] The upshot was a set of Soviet counter-proposals which endeavoured 'to combine English and French proposals', submitted on 18th April for the consideration of the British Government. This set of points formed the basis of the Soviet position in the subsequent negotiations with France and Great Britain until the collapse of these talks. The first point covered the possibility of France, Great Britain and the Soviet Union concluding with each other a five- or ten-year agreement, under which they would render forthwith 'all manner of assistance, including that of a military nature' in the event of aggression in Europe against any one of the contracting powers. 'All manner of assistance' was to be undertaken towards Eastern European states between the Baltic and the Black Seas and bordering on the Soviet Union, in the event of aggression against these states. 'Within the shortest period of time' the three major Powers were to settle the 'extent and forms of military assistance' to be applied in these areas. The British Government was 'to explain that assistance recently promised to Poland concerns exclusively aggression on the part of Germany'. In the event of hostilities the three contracting Powers would undertake not to sign a separate peace or enter into any kind of negotiations to this end 'without common consent of the three Powers'. By way of a specially negotiated agreement Turkey should also be included in the scheme of mutual assistance.[13] Upon this, with iron obstinacy, Moscow rested its case. Real flexibility was reserved for Berlin.

Merekalov, the Soviet Ambassador appointed to Berlin in June 1938, made on 17th April his first call on Weizsäcker to discuss 'practical matters'. These touched on deliveries of military items from the Skoda works to the Soviet Union, not in itself a vital question but regarded evidently as a form of test of German willingness to expand economic relations with the east. When Weizsäcker casually mentioned that, even granted good-will, the reports of Anglo-French-Russian negotiations hardly contributed to the establishment of a 'favourable atmosphere' in which to ship war materials to the Soviet Union, Merekalov 'seized on these words to take up political matters'. Weizsäcker was given to understand that 'Russian policy had always moved in a straight line'; that ideological differences had not proved a stumbling block with Soviet-Italian relations, nor need they be with Germany. The Russians had not exploited the present friction between Germany and the Western democracies, 'nor did she desire to do so.'[14] As for Merekalov himself, in the next few days he would be setting off for Moscow.

At this juncture it was becoming more apparent that between the Soviet and the Western democracies' attitudes over the problem of security lay wide gulfs, necessitating either extensive French and British concessions, or a real relaxation of Soviet rigidity. The displacement of Litvinov as Commissar for Foreign Affairs by Molotov on 3rd May made the latter eventuality remote. Stalin's speech in March had indicated a certain weariness with the Western democracies' failure to make firm arrangements to hold the aggressor; Stalin charged them with little short of connivance in some of the aggressors' schemes. If Stalin enunciated any principle of policy at this time, it was that of caution, caution to the point of aggravated mistrust of the intentions of the Western powers, dalliance with whom might leave the Soviet Union poised on the brink of war and militarily and politically uninsured. Two days after Molotov's appointment, Astakhov (Soviet Chargé in Berlin) took the opportunity to point out in Berlin 'the great importance of the personality of Molotov . . . who would have all the greater importance for future Soviet foreign policy'.[15] From Berlin also, M. Coulondre reported that Hitler would try, not a head-on attack, but an outflanking of the Franco-British position, for which purpose he would direct himself to Russia — out of which one might well see the fourth partition of Poland. In addition, Japan's equivocal attitude was a factor in inclining Hitler to play the Russian card.[16]

The British reply to the Soviet counter-proposals of 15th April was delivered to the Soviet government on 9th May.[17] In effect, this reply revived the earlier idea of a Soviet public declaration asserting that Soviet assistance would be forthcoming — if desired — for France and Great Britain if the latter were involved in war as a result of acting under the new obligations towards particular Eastern European states. Molotov gave the Soviet reply six days later. The suggestion was unacceptable, and the reasons given underline the Soviet definition of security which must have been current. The Soviet Union was denied full reciprocity; no obligation was apparent on the part of Great Britain and France to guarantee the Soviet Union should the latter be directly attacked by aggressors, while France, Great Britain and Poland enjoyed this security by virtue of their existing reciprocal arrangements. Estonia, Latvia and Finland were not mentioned, thus exposing the Soviet north-western frontiers to want of any arrangement; the lack of any general guarantee and the absence of this particular security might very well 'provoke aggression' eastwards to the Soviet Union. Molotov repeated the three indispensable conditions for agreement; the conclusion of an effective Franco-Soviet-British pact of mutual assistance, the guarantee to Eastern Europe to extend to Estonia, Latvia and Finland, and a 'concrete agreement' as to the forms and extent of this assistance so guaranteed (that is, a military convention).[18]

Soviet-German contacts were meanwhile proceeding with a show of extreme caution on both sides. On 9th May Astakhov, introducing the new *Tass* representative in Berlin, rather undid his previous statement about the effect of Litvinov's removal and remarked that 'for the time being one could not speak of a reorientation of policy'.[19] Eleven days later the German Ambassador in Moscow was received by Molotov — a friendly Molotov. The conversations turned on the economic negotiations, which had come to a halt; Molotov reminded his visitor that a resumption could take place only if the requisite 'political foundations' had been brought into being. The realisation of these 'better political foundations' was a matter 'that both Governments would have to think about'. Once more in very friendly fashion, but having communicated not a whit more, Molotov took leave of von Schulenburg.[20] The Germans could only 'sit tight'.[21] Molotov had now to consider a new British move on the question of the proposed security pact, which came in the form of a draft treaty jointly presented with the French on 27th May. Reference within this draft to the League of Nations as well as the reservation of the rights of Poland and Rumania evidently once again produced Molotov's most obdurate mood and unyielding negative. No guarantee, Molotov observed, such as the Soviet Union required, was included for Estonia. Nothing of the draft measured up to the Soviet specification for 'concrete' arrangements. The third Soviet stipulation concerning the extent and forms of assistance had received merely scant attention.[22]

Speaking on 31st May in the Supreme Soviet, Molotov publicly waved the carrot and brandished the stick. Soviet tasks in foreign policy he defined as being 'in line with the interests of the non-aggressive countries', but the 'indispensable minimum' of the three Soviet requirements was repeated together with the demand for the principle of reciprocity and 'equality of obligations'. The new Anglo-French proposals were 'a step forward', but so dubious were the reservations that this might be merely 'a fictitious step forward'. Moreover, said Molotov producing his stick, negotiations with the democracies did not preclude 'business dealings' with Germany and Italy.[23] (Already in Berlin the decision 'contrary to the policy previously planned' had been taken to set about 'definite negotiations with the Soviet Union'.[24])

The Far East also fell under the hammer of Molotov's speech, and was the subject of a strong warning to the Japanese and Manchurian authorities that 'in virtue of our treaty with Mongolia, we shall defend its frontiers as energetically as our own . . . patience has its limits'.[25] There was every relevance to these remarks, banal as they might have sounded. More trouble had come to roost on the exposed Soviet frontiers in the east.* A small war had begun to flare ominously on the Mongolian-Manchurian frontier, in the region of the River Khalkhin-Gol (or the frontier area identified as Nomon-Han-Burd-Obo).[26]

Already by January, at a date reported as 14th, Japanese forces had raided the Mongolian frontier near Nomon-Han-Burd-Obo, killing a frontier guard and taking the patrol commander prisoner. In February another Japanese-Manchurian force crossed the frontier (the demarcation of which was in dispute) and penetrated to the eastern bank of the Khalkhin-Gol. At a time when the Soviet government was laying down exact, 'concrete' conditions to the Western democracies about a guarantee of its security and a proper reciprocity, the situation on the eastern frontier had begun to deteriorate rapidly. On 11th May, Soviet-Mongolian frontier troops stationed at Nomon-Han-Burd-Obo — some 8–10 miles to the east of the Khalkhin-Gol — were assaulted by Japanese-Manchurian forces and forced to retire to the river bank. The raiding force of cavalry was some 300 strong and supported by aircraft. Soviet reserves were moved up from Tamsyk-Bulak, 65 miles to the rear in the Mongolian People's Republic. Continued fighting, on a small but intense scale, brought daily clashes from 12th to 22nd May. A frontier clash now developed into a small war as the

* After the Changkufeng/Lake Khasan incident in 1938, Soviet Far Eastern forces were organised into 4 separate commands: 1st Red Banner Army (Ussuri area, HQ at Voroshilov), 2nd Red Banner Army (Amur, HQ Kuibyshevka), Trans-Baikal Military District forces, and 57th Rifle Corps (Outer Mongolia, HQ Ulan-Bator). Japanese Army General Staff estimates of strength: 24 Soviet divisions, 1,900 tanks, 2,000 aircraft.

Japanese towards the end of May brought up stronger forces — elements of 23rd Japanese Infantry Division, a body of Manchurian cavalry under Yamagata (commander of the 64th Regiment/23rd Infantry Division), part of the 64th Regiment itself, a reconnaissance unit, a motorised infantry company, the 8th Cavalry Regiment and detachments of the 1st and 7th Manchurian cavalry.

At dawn on 28th May the Japanese attacked. The Red Army was about to undergo its first extensive international test, challenged by the crack Kwantung Army.

* * * *

The area of these and subsequent operations was bounded on the east by the Mongolian-Manchurian frontier, to the west by the Khalkhin-Gol, with high ground to south and north. Marsh and bog were common, hindering the movement of tanks and armoured cars. Slopes of 15–30° and 45° in some places added to the difficulties of movement. The Khalkhin-Gol, 120–130 metres broad, 2 metres deep and more in places, with a current speed of ·8 metres/per second, flowed north-south, roughly parallel with what was to become the front; bisecting the Khalkhin-Gol almost at the centre of this front was a smaller river, the Khailastyn-Gol, which flowed eastwards towards Nomon-Han-Burd-Obo.

Soviet-Mongolian troops were deployed on the eastern bank of the Khalkhin-Gol and on both sides of the Khailastyn-Gol. On the right bank of the latter were three companies of an infantry battalion and the heavy machine-guns of the 11th Tank Brigade, with the 17th/15th Cavalry Regiments (6th Mongolian Cavalry Division) moved up towards Nomon-Han. On the left bank were two infantry battalions reinforced with heavy machine-guns. These forces held positions stretching for some 10–12 miles. A reserve of one infantry company, a battery of 76-mm guns, an engineer company, and the artillery battalion attached to the 6th Cavalry Division was held on the western bank of the Khalkhin-Gol. In all, Soviet-Mongolian forces consisted of nearly 700 infantry, 260 cavalry, with 58 machine-guns, 14 76-mm guns, 6 anti-tank guns and 39 armoured cars. Japanese infantry and cavalry numbered 2,576, with 75 machine-guns, 8 guns, 10 anti-tank guns, 1 tank and 6–8 armoured cars.[27]

The Japanese attack of 28th was supported by 40 aircraft, which strafed the Soviet-Mongolian positions. The aim of the Japanese operations was to encircle and destroy their opponents on the eastern bank of the Khalkhin-Gol, strengthening their right wing with motorised infantry, which would move down from the north-west and cut off the defending troops from the

Khalkin-Gol. During the fighting on 28th, this drive was checked by the fire of the 76-mm guns, which had been moved over to the eastern bank of the Khalkhin-Gol. At the centre, however, the Japanese succeeded in pushing back the 17th Cavalry Regiment. To counter this thrust, the 149th Soviet regiment, which had been moved up by lorry from Tamsyk-Bulak, was thrown into action towards 7 p.m., but achieved little owing to faulty co-operation with the available artillery support. The battle raged throughout 28th and 29th, with Soviet-Mongolian troops organising a counter-attack, which succeeded in pushing the Japanese back about half a mile in the north-east sector. It was then that the Soviet command blundered. The chief of the operating staff of the 57th Rifle Corps,[28] under whose command the Soviet-Mongolian forces were acting, received information about the movement of Japanese lorries in the direction of the Japanese positions. Assuming this to be a preparation for a new attack, the commander had his troops moved over in retirement to the western bank of the Khalkhin-Gol. Only on 3rd June was this mistake discovered and Soviet-Mongolian units once again moved forward to positions between the Khalkhin-Gol and the frontier line of Nomon-Han-Burd-Obo, from which the Japanese had temporarily retired. Certain units had put up an excellent performance — notably the commander and crews of the 76-mm gun battery, which had been transferred to the eastern bank of the Khalkhin-Gol on the commander's own initiative and used to check the motorised infantry. Otherwise, there had been some serious defects. Intelligence of the enemy's movements had been poor. Stringing out the available forces in a narrow belt over ten miles or so was accompanied by poor co-ordination of units and weak cover for the flanks. The 149th Regiment had been drawn too far back with the result that it was brought into action too late to be really effective. Above all, reinforcements were required. To fill this need the whole of the 11th Tank Brigade, the 7th, 8th and 9th Mechanised Brigades, the 36th Rifle Division* (motorised but minus one of its regiments), a heavy artillery battalion and 100 fighters were transferred to the operational zone. The 8th Mongolian Cavalry Division came in to reinforce the 6th.

Throughout June the Japanese also continued their build-up, although the chief characteristic of operations at this time was both intensification and expansion of air activity. While reliable figures for aircraft committed or lost in these actions are lacking, both sides were certainly using on occasions up to 100 aircraft at a time in their operations. On 27th June, 30 Japanese bombers and 80 fighters attacked targets at some depth in the Soviet rear. Japanese fighter-bombers harried positions nearer the frontier line. Japanese

* Late in 1938 the 36th (Motorised) Rifle Division was transferred from Chita (Trans-Baikal MD) to Ude (Outer Mongolia).

and Soviet reinforcements moved up all the while. The Soviet position was undoubtedly complicated by inferior communications; the nearest rail-head was at Borziya, nearly 400 miles from the operations. Besides having shorter lines of communication, the Japanese had the use of efficient railways and two good earth roads running from Hailar to the Soviet-Mongolian frontier. By the end of the month the Japanese had moved up the whole of the 23rd Infantry Division, the 7th Division, more Manchurian cavalry, 170 guns, 130 tanks and some 250 aircraft. Infantry and cavalry represented some 24,700 men. Soviet-Mongolian forces had grown to 11,100 (infantry and cavalry) with 186 tanks and 266 armoured cars.[29] In the place of the former extended front, the Soviet command decided to hold a powerful bridgehead on the eastern river bank, which would be supported by a strong force in the whole defence zone. For that reason, on 1st–2nd July the 11th Tank Brigade, the 7th Mechanised Brigade and the 24th (Motorised) Rifle Regiment were advanced from their positions at Tamsyk-Bulak. Very heavy fighting, introduced by intensified Japanese air activity, was about to begin, when the Soviet-Mongolian troops would be desperately engaged to maintain their bridgehead on the eastern bank of the river.

The Japanese plan adopted for the operations which began early in July was essentially the same as that used at the end of May. The real threat was to come from the right wing and the intention remained to pin, encircle and annihilate the opposing forces on the eastern bank. To this end, Major-General Kobayashi's force was to drive down from the north-east, crossing the Khalkhin-Gol, seizing the high ground known as Bain-Tsagan on the western bank and switching the direction of the attack southwards — thereby cutting off the retreat of the Soviet-Mongolian forces. A second Japanese force would secure the lateral march of Kobayashi's force and cover the crossing of the latter on the night of 1st-2nd July; on 3rd, the second force would engage the enemy on the eastern bank of the Khalkhin-Gol. On 2nd July, as planned, the attack opened and by the evening up to eighty Japanese tanks were in action, breaking through the positions of the 149th Regiment and the 9th Mechanised Brigade. Japanese tanks came up against the direct fire of Soviet artillery, which halted the attack. But at 2 a.m., on 3rd July, Kobayashi's force began its crossing of the Khalkhin-Gol, which was completed by 8 a.m., at which time the Japanese drove straight for the heights. The Soviet command, not yet having learnt of the Japanese crossing, had meanwhile taken some steps to restore the situation with the 149th Regiment. But in moving to check the second Japanese force, Soviet units clashed headlong with Kobayashi's striking force. The Japanese had seized the Bain-Tsagan high ground, setting up anti-tank guns to beat off Soviet tanks and armoured cars.

An immediate Soviet counter-attack to recapture the high ground was launched. At 11 a.m., the 11th Tank Brigade and the tank battalion attached to the 6th Mongolian Cavalry Division attacked the Japanese off the march. The first battalion of the 11th Brigade struck at the Japanese flank and rear from the north-west, while the other battalions moved in from the west. The swift Japanese investment of the Bain-Tsagan height, however, plus their use of anti-tank guns had given rise to a serious situation. At 7 p.m., on the evening of 3rd Soviet-Mongolian troops, attacking from three sides, made a determined attempt to recover the height. The Japanese beat this off and fighting continued into the night of 3rd–4th July. In the morning strong Japanese air support was used to assist a fresh Japanese attack, which was met by a Soviet counter-attack. By the evening of 4th, Soviet-Mongolian troops were beginning their third attack along the whole length of the front, and still the Japanese had not been dislodged from the height. But finally, towards 3 a.m., on the morning of 5th, the Japanese began to dis-engage and seek once more the eastern bank of the Khalkhin-Gol, making use of the pontoon bridge which had been used in the first crossing. Soviet tanks and armoured cars also making for the eastern bank had to be manhandled through the mud and soft ground of the river banks, while Japanese troops were being engaged in savage hand-to-hand fighting.

The Japanese attempt at a wide turning movement which would have completely outflanked the enemy had failed, but the Soviet forces had only escaped by the skin of their teeth. The Japanese had not succeeded in making effective use of their tanks, while part of the Soviet salvation lay with the success achieved by the tanks of the 11th Brigade, which had encircled the would-be encirclers.[30] Nevertheless, this had been achieved as much by good luck as good management. It was obviously a serious blunder not to have foreseen this possibility, especially in view of the May attack, and to have left Bain-Tsagan wide open and ready for the Japanese. And now the struggle turned on the Soviet bridgehead on the eastern bank, against which the Japanese launched furious attacks as well as harrying units on the western bank. After a brief lull, during which fresh Soviet forces were transferred over the river on to the eastern side, the tempo was again speeded up by a Japanese artillery barrage which began at dawn on 23rd July. Only on 25th did the Japanese attacks finally slacken from their day and night intensity, and a return to the defensive took place. About one mile from the eastern bank the Japanese set about the construction of a fortified line, a necessity before mounting further operations to give them that indispensable absolute control of the eastern side of the river.

Seventy-six days of operations had brought no solution in sight for the Soviet command, except the possibility of a prolonged defensive engagement with inferior forces and the high probability of a Japanese victory. Although the line had been held, there had been signs of a none too competent command and some lack of co-ordination. The only answer seemed to be the release of troops from the interior and a change of command. The answer, it appeared, was G. Zhukov, the corps commander who was assigned to take over the 1st Army Group with the task of defeating the Japanese. Zhukov could have had no illusions about this assignment; failure was out of the question. To win and win decisively, even spectacularly, would alone suffice. With Zhukov came massive reinforcement. Zhukov, with a style for which he was later to become much distinguished, launched his counter-offensive only when he enjoyed a superiority of 1·5 to 1 in infantry, 1·7 to 1 in machine-guns, almost 2 to 1 in artillery and the same in aviation and a fourfold superiority in tanks. Throughout August preparations went ahead with frenzied energy for the counter-stroke against the Japanese, and by 18th Zhukov was almost ready, his operations coinciding with the critical stage to which Soviet negotiations with the Western democracies and the simultaneous sounding out of the Germans had advanced in the summer of 1939.

* * * *

What influence upon the Soviet attitude was worked by the Far Eastern fighting is virtually impossible to discover. Certainly the tension and even armed conflict was no new factor for Soviet calculations. If there were grounds for suspecting the British attitude towards Japan as being one of connivance in Japanese anti-Soviet intentions, there were substantial reasons for fearing the role of Germany also.[31] Two subsequent denials were issued from the Soviet side that difficulties over the Far East were preventing an Anglo-Franco-Soviet agreement; the record of the discussions would bear this out, although the Far Eastern factor did impinge to a more marked degree on German-Soviet talks. Soviet, British and French negotiators were still engaged on the task of battering out, in agonisingly difficult talks, an agreed formula which would satisfy Soviet requirements without sweeping the French and British positions into the nothingness of diplomatic capitulation.[32]

At 5 o'clock on the afternoon of 15th June, the British and French negotiators repaired once again to the Kremlin to face Molotov's barrage of questions on British and French commitments to third states and the attitude of those states. Molotov showed some fear of 'compromising the Soviet position' and entered upon a process of interrogation over the points involved.[33] Molotov made his interpreter Potemkin give the Russian words *naivny* and *duraki* their full and unpleasant meaning — the British and French Governments were treating the Soviet Government as 'simpletons' and 'fools'.[34] Six days later Molotov rejected another set of proposals since they represented 'a repetition of previous proposals made by England and France which . . . have met with serious objections on the part of the Soviet Government'.[35] In the midst of these endlessly involved exchanges, Zhdanov's article of 29th June in *Pravda* struck a strange note; Zhdanov's piece dealt with the delay in the negotiations with France and Great Britain and he admitted into the article an expression of his 'personal opinion in this matter, although my friends do not share it'. The opinion which Zhdanov's friends did not share was that France and Great Britain had no wish for 'a treaty on terms of equality with the USSR, that is, for the only kind of treaty to which a self-respecting State can agree'.[36]

Throughout the first half of July Molotov turned to the question of 'indirect aggression', which produced yet more verbal traps and tangles. It remained, however, 'difficult to get to grips with him [Molotov].'[37] On the strained Western negotiators humiliation had been plentifully heaped, and original positions had to be successively abandoned — 'we have had the feeling that Molotov was convinced from the beginning that we should be forced to abandon it.' Mr Strang recognised clearly that there were two Russian policies, each viable and producing the diplomacy of alternatives; there was the policy of isolation and the policy of accommodation with Germany. The strength of the Russian negotiating position was the realisation that the French and British, pressed by their public opinion, 'shall not dare to face a final breakdown of the negotiations.'[38] On the other hand, it was unlikely that the Russians would have entered on the negotiations at all if they had not seen something to their advantage in a possible Three-Power agreement, although they were moved not by any motive of friendship but sheer necessity. Molotov demanded point-blank an admission of the inseparability of the political and military articles of the proposed pact;[39] on the afternoon of 27th July, Molotov was informed that the British were agreeable to 'immediate initiation' of military talks in Moscow, and the French Ambassador conveyed a similar opinion from the French Government.[40] Molotov wished to see 'how many divisions each party would contribute to the common cause and where they would be located'. Even the dubious gains which had so far been made, however, appeared to be largely dissipated by the awkward incident which was caused by Mr Butler's statement in the House of Commons on 31st July; a Molotov perhaps more intractable than ever chose to regard Mr Butler as having 'represented the Soviet formula as meaning that the Soviet Government wished to infringe the independence of the Baltic states. Soviet Government on the contrary wished to guarantee that independence.'[41] Under this newly gathered cloud the military discussions were finally arranged.

On the night of 9th–10th August, the steamship *City of Exeter* carrying the British and French Military Missions docked in Leningrad. After a brief halt, the party of officers, accompanied by Red Army Major Dragun and Captain Frolov, took the night train to Moscow on 11th, and were greeted on arrival in the Soviet capital by the Deputy Chief of the General Staff Smorodinov, the Deputy Chief of the Naval Staff Alafuzov, the military commandant of Moscow Colonel Suvorov and a diplomatic party. At the Defence Commissariat, the officers of the missions were introduced to Voroshilov and Shaposhnikov and received a friendly enough reception. At the Kremlin, by contrast, where the host was Molotov, the atmosphere was more difficult, although this may well have been only the accident of Molotov's rather curious personality. At an evening reception, the British and French met more Soviet officers — Kuznetsov, Shaposhnikov (whom they had seen earlier), Budenny, Loktinov of the Soviet Air Force, and the commander of the Belorussian Military District, Corps Commander Kovalev. Although language difficulties created an inevitable barrier, the atmosphere here was evidently cordial enough. On the morning of Saturday 12th, the first business meeting of the British, French and Soviet missions was held and work had begun in earnest.[42]

The instructions issued to the British Military Mission gave the officers concerned the status of negotiators only (a point over which Voroshilov was to declare his subsequent disappointment). Political and military agreements were to be confined to Europe only, and although careful note was to be made of any Soviet disclosures of their dispositions or intentions in this area, there was to be no discussion or disclosure of allied intentions in the Far East. The brief, while covering details of the information required of the Russians and providing information on British and French estimates of the possible situations which might develop, also included an estimate of the value of the Russian forces. There was, the brief ran, 'little doubt that the Russian services have suffered as the result of the recent purge . . . discipline, which was formerly good, being now of an indifferent standard . . . it has directly resulted in the disappearance of the few experienced commanders in the U.S.S.R.'. The numerical strength of the Soviet forces was, to some degree, misleading. The Soviet Navy had suffered from the purge — 'young and inexperienced officers have had to assume command of ships and squadrons, their average age being 40 in the case of Flag Officers and 30–35 in the case of commanding officers of ships.' The value of the Red Army for offensive operations had been 'much reduced' by the purge. The value of Soviet military aviation west of Lake Baikal was considered to lie in its producing the possibility of a limited threat from machines based in Poland, Rumania and Turkey, the ability to contain on the western frontier more German air defence units than might otherwise be assigned to this task, and finally the possibility of assisting Polish air defence.[43] On the whole, the view embodied in the brief seemed to envisage only limited possibilities for and from the Soviet forces, the first conditioned by the political strait-jacket into which co-operation was being fastened and the second arising out of the inferior performance level of the various services since the purges, as well as technical and logistical difficulties.[44]

The first few conversations with the Soviet mission produced the impression that '. . . the Soviet military negotiators were really out for business'.[45] The minutes of the first meeting between the Missions on 12th record the Soviet representatives as Marshal Voroshilov, Army Commander 1st Grade Shaposhnikov, Flag Officer 2nd Grade Kuznetsov, Army Commander 2nd Grade Loktinov (Air Force) and Shaposhnikov's deputy Smorodinov. *Général d'Armée* Doumenc led for the French officers and Admiral Drax for the British, with Air Marshal Sir Charles Burnett representing the Royal Air Force and Major-General T. G. Heywood the Army.[46] The British mission lacked written credentials, but Admiral Drax undertook to obtain these forthwith. Meanwhile, in answer to Voroshilov's question about the powers of the 'British Delegation representing the British Armed Forces', the Admiral could only say that he was 'authorised to negotiate a military convention with the French and Soviet Delegations, but not to sign that convention without having obtained the approval of his own Government'. No postponement of the discussions was made because of the British lacking credentials. Rather all plunged into the heart of the matter — definite proposals. Voroshilov, while indicating that the Soviet officers had 'drawn up some plans which they considered went into sufficient detail', wished to learn of the British and French ideas.[47] But, Voroshilov warned, it would not be enough to reach agreement 'merely on principles, i.e. without comparing the plans of the three Delegations'. The British and French must initiate the discussion, after which the Soviet Delegation would produce their plans. This was agreed upon.

Admiral Drax took the chair at the next meeting on 13th, at which General Doumenc was to deliver his exposition of the French plans. Voroshilov at once expressed the hope that the General would deal with the measures proposed by the French to relieve pressure on the Eastern Front (should this prove necessary) as well as arrangements for the Western Front. Shaposhnikov made the observation that all forces — land, sea and air — should be mobilised to combat aggression, and for that reason naval and air plans should be included in the discussion. But it might be as well to begin with the Army, observed Shaposhnikov, 'since the Army aspect of the problem was the one which interested the Soviet Delegation most.' With this agreed, General Doumenc fell to his exposition, dealing with mobilisation, fortification, distribution, material and strategy. Since the figures involved were highly secret, General Doumenc suggested that what was heard might be quite forgotten outside the room. The meeting closed with eight Soviet questions being set down on the analysis given by General Doumenc. At the third meeting (also on 13th) General Doumenc took the chair by the rotation which had been agreed upon; the session was taken up with answering the Soviet questions and with Major-General Heywood giving Voroshilov some precise notion of the pace and purpose of the increase in the strength of the British Army.[48] At the conclusion of the meeting Voroshilov indicated that what he wanted was a daily discussion lasting four hours, whereupon the time of session was fixed at 10 a.m.–2 p.m.

In due turn Marshal Voroshilov presided over the session of 14th. The Soviet Delegation wanted time to study the draft of the principles (submitted by General Doumenc at the last meeting) on which the co-operation of the three Powers might be based. If there were to be a military convention, the principles in this draft would form the basis. In taking up points arising out of the question-and-answer session on the previous day, General Doumenc observed that in the east, the initial front would be 'that of the Polish and Rumanian armies' — there could be an intermediate front, but this was for Voroshilov to decide. Sea communications between the two fronts (Western and Eastern) were important, and so was the matter of joint action of the independent fighter and bomber forces of the three Powers. General Doumenc's explanation failed to satisfy Voroshilov; the part 'it was suggested the Red Army should play' was far from clear. General Doumenc stressed that the enemy must never be allowed to break through the Soviet Western Frontier, and the Red Army would presumably concentrate on that frontier. Roused, Voroshilov retorted that this Front was always manned and furthermore, 'the Fascist Powers would never break through whether the Delegations reached agreement or not.' Voroshilov required to know — what, in the opinion of the British and French Staffs, could the Red Army do in the event of aggression against France or Great Britain, or simultaneously against both? General Doumenc pointed out that Poland was bound to assist France, and that it would be necessary to see how the situation developed; the closest co-operation should be developed between Marshal Voroshilov and General Gamelin to decide when the Red Army should intervene; the Red Army should be ready to intervene 'when it was considered desirable' and also to act against the enemy in the air and against enemy communications with sea and air forces. Voroshilov pointed out that 'though the Red Army is well disposed for the defence of its own frontiers, it is not well disposed for offensive operations'. Let him, in pursuit of this question of how the Red Army might act in case of aggression, put 'precise questions':

> Do the British and French General Staffs think that the Red Army can move across North Poland and in particular the Wilno Salient, and across Galicia in order to make contact with the enemy? Will Soviet troops be allowed to cross Roumanian territory?[49]

With great insistence, Voroshilov made this the 'cardinal point, to which all other points are subordinate'. He was sorry that the Franco-British Delegation had not brought 'an exact answer'. After withdrawing to consider the matter, Major-General Heywood reported on behalf of both Delegations that this was specifically a political question, but on the express wish of Marshal Voroshilov, both Delegations would request their respective governments to address to the Polish and Rumanian Governments questions of the entry of Soviet troops upon their territory, if the Soviet Union became an ally.[50] The Soviet Delegation similarly withdrew, to return with a written statement, signifying a willingness to disclose the Soviet plans for military collaboration. Such disclosures would form the agenda for the next meeting.

Admiral Drax was in the chair on 15th, and the meeting opened with an expression of pleasure that the meetings would continue. Voroshilov took note of the fact that the question of the Red Army's access had been addressed to London and Paris. Shaposhnikov now proceeded to give details of the Soviet plan of deployment for the Western Frontier; in the European part of its territory the Soviet Union will deploy and engage on the Front 120 infantry divisions, 16 cavalry divisions, 5,000 heavy guns and howitzers, 9–10,000 tanks and 5–5,500 fighters and bombers (excluding army co-operation aircraft). These figures were exclusive of air defence troops, garrisons of fortified areas, line of communication, depot and base area troops. An infantry division had a war strength of 19,000 men. The concentration of the Red Army would require 8–10 days, and the improved transportation would permit modification of the concentration along the whole length of the Front. Although nothing 'concrete' had been disclosed about the operational plans of the British and French armies, or the 'United Franco-British Fleet', Shaposhnikov would proceed to give three alternative plans for common action:

First Alternative. If the aggressor bloc attacks England and France

> Here the Soviet Union would engage a force equal to 70 per cent of the armed forces which Britain and France will engage directly against Germany. (If the Franco-British force deployed directly 90 divisions against Germany, the Soviet

Union will then deploy 63 infantry divisions and 6 cavalry divisions). Polish support is considered essential in this case, and permission *must* be obtained by London and Paris for access for Soviet forces.

A Franco-British naval force must close the English Channel and send a 'strong squadron' into the Baltic. England and France *must* obtain from the Baltic states and Finland permission for temporary occupation of naval bases.[51] The action of the Soviet Baltic Fleet would depend on the satisfactory outcome of the naval base question.

Second Alternative. If aggression is directed against Poland and Rumania

Both would employ all their forces to resist attack. Poland must protect Rumania. France and Britain must declare war at once on the aggressor. The Soviet Union can only intervene when permission has been obtained for Soviet forces to operate on and through Polish and Rumanian territory. In this case, the Soviet Union would engage forces equal to 100 per cent of those engaged by France and Britain directly against Germany. Naval plans would be substantially the same, with the Soviet Black Sea Fleet closing the mouth of the Danube and the Bosphorus.

Third Alternative

This covers the eventuality of the principal aggressor using the territory of Finland, Estonia and Latvia to direct attacks on the Soviet Union. In this case, Britain and France *must* declare war at once on the aggressor; Poland, bound by agreement to France and Britain, *must* enter the war against Germany and grant rights of passage to Soviet troops. While the Soviet Union would deploy its total 120 infantry divisions in this case, France and Britain must engage the equivalent of 70 per cent of the forces engaged by the Soviet Union and immediately initiate active operations against the principal aggressor.

If 'Roumania should be dragged in', she must engage all her forces and must be prevailed upon to grant rights of access to Soviet forces.[52]

In this fashion Shaposhnikov drew to the close of his study in the categorical imperative.

London and Paris meanwhile sounded out the Polish and Rumanian Governments on the possibility of granting access to Soviet forces in case of war against Germany.[53] On 18th August the French Military Attaché in Warsaw had seen the Chief of the Polish General Staff and had intimated that 'secret and tacit' agreement would suffice. The Polish General Stachiewicz had 'expressed grave doubts of the *bona fides* of the U.S.S.R.' He 'suspected ulterior motives', he feared that the Soviet intention was merely the occupation of Polish territory, and he doubted the intention to employ Soviet troops in offensive operations.[54] In Moscow the military discussions, drawing themselves painfully through the summer heat, began to strike the rocks of dead-lock on 17th, when Voroshilov suggested that it 'was necessary to adjourn and stop work'; the necessary answers to the Soviet questions on movement through Polish territory were not forthcoming. The Soviet Delegation 'could not recommend to their Government to proceed with the examination of the more concrete details . . .'. Breakdown was nevertheless staved off when the Soviet Delegation did finally agree to a further meeting at 10 a.m., on 21st August.[55] On that day, with Admiral Drax presiding, Voroshilov began by suggesting a break in the talks — 'not for three or four days, but for a longer period'. The reason for this, Voroshilov explained, lay with the autumn manœuvres which were consuming a great deal of the time of the Soviet Delegation, which consisted of 'persons who are at the head of our armed forces'. If affirmative replies were received on the 'cardinal questions' put by the Russians, there could be an earlier meeting; in the case of negative replies, Voroshilov affirmed that, 'I do not see that there will be any chance of meeting again'.[56]

But Marshal Voroshilov and General Doumenc did meet in session once again on 22nd August. By this time, after repeated enquiry of the Poles and insistent representation by the French and British on the question of obtaining 'effective assistance' for Poland, the French felt justified in giving an affirmative answer to Voroshilov's question on his 'cardinal point', since Colonel Beck had admitted that the position would be 'different in time of war'. At 7 p.m., on 22nd General Doumenc saw Voroshilov alone.[57] Voroshilov asked at once to see 'the document' emanating from the French Government and wanted to know if the British Mission had received a reply to the same question. General Doumenc had no document but gave a verbal assurance that his Government had empowered him to 'sign a military convention under which authorisation will be given for the passage of Soviet troops at the points specified . . .'.[58] Voroshilov chose to question this and stated that the position of Poland, Rumania and Great Britain was still unknown — 'Let us', added Voroshilov 'wait until everything has been cleared up'. Because the British and French had allowed the discussions to 'drag on too long', then 'we must not exclude the possibility, during this time, of certain political events. Let us wait'. If the position were cleared up, then a rapid settlement of all problems would be possible, but only on the assumption that 'no political occurrence intervenes'. The reference was plain. That 'political event' to which Voroshilov drew the attention of General Doumenc was nothing less than a Soviet agreement with Germany; the terms of a non-aggression pact were proposed from the Soviet side on 19th August.[59] In a conversation in Berlin on 10th August, Astakhov told Schnurre that the negotiations with England had been begun at a time when 'there had still been no sign of a disposition on the part of Germany to come to an understanding'. Entered into 'without much enthusiasm', these conversations had been considered a form of protection against Germany. Although a positive change in the German attitude had occurred, the negotiations with the Western powers could not be simply broken off when they had been initiated after 'mature consideration'. On 10th Astakhov considered that his government regarded 'the question as completely open'.[60] In the next ten days, as Voroshilov entangled the British and French officers in tortuous negotiation, the question was shut tight.

* * * *

On 21st August, at 5 o'clock in the afternoon, Stalin had Molotov deliver a very conciliatory answer to Hitler's message of 20th, which accepted the Soviet draft of a Non-Aggression Pact but also suggested rapid arrangement for the 'substantial clarification' of relevant questions.[61] To effect this Ribbentrop arrived in Moscow on the afternoon of 23rd. By 8 o'clock the first three-hour conference with Stalin and Molotov had ended; 'the decisive point for the final result' remained the Soviet demand that the ports of Libau and Windau be recognised as within the Soviet sphere of influence. With the greatest despatch Hitler's assent to this was signalled to Moscow.[62] On the night of 23rd–24th August Stalin, Molotov and Ribbentrop, toying with their new Pact, conversed at length, touching towards the close on England and France, as well as the recent military conversations. Both Stalin and Molotov made adverse comments on the British Mission, which had 'never told the Soviet Government what it really wanted'. As for the British themselves, Stalin made eager assent to Ribbentrop's comment that Great Britain was weak and only wished to have others fight for its 'presumptuous world domination'. Stalin observed that the British Army was weak, the Royal Navy no longer deserved its previous reputation and the Royal Air Force was short of pilots. Stalin's recognition of the reputation of the French Army only produced from Ribbentrop a boast of the superior strength of the German Army. To the new Pact (which was dated 23rd) Stalin and Molotov raised numerous glasses in toast. To Ribbentrop Stalin pledged his word of honour that 'the Soviet Union would not betray its partner'.[63] In honouring such a dishonour Stalin ultimately paid in Russian dead.

During the course of the verbal wrestling with Voroshilov and his colleagues, the British Mission had taken note of certain strategic points which would themselves incline the Soviet Union to agreement with Germany, although as late as 16th August the impression remained that the Russians 'wish to come to some agreement with the Allies'. Writing on that day to the Chief of the Air Staff, Air Marshal Sir Charles Burnett suggested Soviet fear of being unable to wait until Germany had overrun Poland and then having to fight Germany on the defensive in their own territory, 'which is not nearly as well protected as they would like us to believe'; this German advance would move up bombers able to strike at Moscow and other cities, the adverse effects of which 'would be immediately translated to those in power'.[64] Even if the air threat was not the one most immediately feared by the Soviet ruling group, it is a reasonable assumption that either they wished to transfer the war away from Soviet territory (by offensive operations) or keep war away altogether. Major-General Heywood in his letter of 17th to the Director of Military Operations and Intelligence (War Office) made this point about offensive operations, from which he deduced that the inviolability of Soviet defences was open to question, that the main intention was to 'keep the battlefield as far away from their own frontier as possible', that a sound military reason prompted the desire to co-operate with a Polish Army not yet defeated, and that 'lack of flexibility due to their weak communications' necessitated a 'definite plan' made up beforehand, so that the requisite force could be concentrated in the area from which it was desired to operate. As for the 'cardinal point' or 'military axiom' about passage through Poland and Rumania, there was no certainty that 'some other cardinal point may not be raised'.[65] A most dubious point was the naval co-operation, and Admiral Drax, while aware of the tangle over Poland, foresaw difficulty in reaching agreement over the Baltic, '. . . for personally I would be willing to send there at the start only a minimum force of destroyers and submarines for the purpose of stiffening and helping the Russian Navy.'[66] Admiral Drax and General Doumenc had a final interview with Voroshilov on 25th August, when the latter confirmed that the changed political situation made further conversations useless. At the farewell Voroshilov burst out with a denunciation of the Poles — 'Were we to have to conquer Poland in order to offer her our help, or were we to go on our knees and offer our help to Poland?'[67] This wrath, simulated or real, hardly explained away the Soviet position. Writing his final report on 28th August, Admiral Drax explained the Soviet dalliance with British and French service chiefs as a move to frighten Germany, and to facilitate through agreement with Germany the acquisition of part of Poland, part of Rumania and certain ports and islands in the Baltic. A second reason advanced was that the Russians hoped that 'we might be persuaded to accept their terms and make a treaty at their dictation'.[68] Major-General Heywood expressed the essence of the Soviet tactic as one lying within a situation where '. . . it seems to have been merely a question of who could make the best offer in the shortest time'.[69]

It was on 17th August that Voroshilov remarked to Admiral Drax and his companions that he 'looked on a European war as a certainty'. Certainly the Soviet aims involved in the intricate double game which was being played had little to do with the preservation of European peace.[70] As early as June Astakhov called on the Bulgarian minister Draganov in Berlin and in an apparently random conversation described the prevailing Soviet attitude as one of hesitation, of vacillation even, with three courses suggesting themselves: the conclusion of a pact with France and Great Britain, dragging out the negotiations, and finally *rapprochement* with Germany, the last being 'closest to the desires of the Soviet Union'.[71] When on 16th August Schulenburg in Moscow conveyed to Molotov Ribbentrop's message about a 'speedy clarification' of German-Soviet relations, the Soviet Commissar for Foreign Affairs was most anxious to learn of three things: the disposition of the German Government to a non-aggression pact with the Soviet Union, the willingness of the German Government 'to influence Japan for the purpose of improvement in Soviet-Japanese relations and settlement of border conflicts', and the possibility of a joint Soviet-German guarantee for the Baltic states. In spite of the speed urged by the Germans, Molotov insisted upon an indispensable 'adequate preparation of the problems mentioned by him'.[72] The bargain, then, was of the utmost calculation. The reference to the Far East suggested that Stalin may have been prompted by the realisation that he might kill his eastern and western birds with one carefully flung stone. Above all, the Nazi-Soviet agreement broke the encirclement which the Soviet Union believed had existed for the better part of the decade. The same agreement further suggested that what the Soviet command most feared was not a war on two fronts but a war on any front. If the August pact did not offer security, at least it supplied the illusion of security. Under such conditions, the military conversations did not collapse over Poland but over the absence from the very beginning of any mutually compatible purposes.[73]

* * * *

In his late night conversation of 23rd–24th August with Ribbentrop, Stalin had mentioned the problem of Japan and the limitations on Soviet patience in the face of 'Japanese provocations'. 'If Japan desired war, she could have it.' German assistance in bringing about an improvement in relations would be 'useful', but Stalin was anxious that it should not appear to be Soviet initiative which prompted this. By this time the counter-offensive on the Khalkhin-Gol had begun and had almost reached the end of its first phase. Early in August very powerful Soviet reinforcements were moved up. The existing formations were incorporated into the 1st Army Group, under its own Military Soviet headed by Corps Commander Zhukov. Army Commander 2nd Grade Shtern commanded a 'front group' based on the Trans-Baikal Military District, designed to co-ordinate Soviet and Mongolian forces. The 82nd* and 57th Rifle Divisions, a regiment of the 152nd Rifle Division, the 6th Tank Brigade, the 85th Anti-aircraft Regiment, 126th Artillery Regiment, the 212th Air-Landing Brigade and several companies of flame-throwing tanks moved up. 720 lorries were used to shuttle some 18,000 men into the operational zone; 2,600 trucks shifted the ammunition and fuel needed for the artillery and tanks. Zhukov set in motion elaborate deception measures to conceal his offensive intent. A hand-book entitled *What the Soviet soldier must know in defence* was liberally handed out. Working parties toiled on defensive positions. Ten days before the attack, lorries stripped of silencers were run along the length of the front to hide the noise of tanks being moved up. Very close ground-air co-operation was developed by pilots studying the terrain with the troops and special reconnaissance groups were formed. Night patrols and air sorties were used to plot enemy positions. Zhukov attached to his own staff twelve liaison officers to supervise operations and maintain contact. As at Lake Khasan, a great effort went into the political preparation of the troops. On the eve of his attack, which he had taken such pains to conceal, Zhukov had 35 Soviet rifle battalions and 20 cavalry squadrons facing 25 Japanese battalions and 17 squadrons; Zhukov disposed of 498 tanks (including some of the new T–34 models[74]), 346 armoured cars and 500 aircraft.

Zhukov's plan called for crushing pressure to be applied on the enemy flanks, with the encirclement and annihilation to be carried out between the eastern bank of the Khalkhin-Gol and the frontier line. For this purpose two assault groups (North and South) were formed, with a third group designed to hold the enemy located in the centre. The Southern Group was composed of the 57th Rifle Division, the 8th Mongolian Cavalry Division, the 8th Mechanised Brigade, the 6th Tank Brigade (minus two battalions), a battalion of the 11th Tank Brigade, with artillery, anti-tank guns and a company of T–130 tanks. The Central Group comprised the 82nd Rifle Division, the 36th (Motorised) Rifle Division and the 5th (mixed) Machine-Gun Brigade. In the Northern Group the strength consisted of the 6th Mongolian Cavalry Division, the 601st Rifle Regiment (detached from the 82nd Rifle Division at the centre), the 7th Mechanised Brigade, two battalions of the 11th Tank Brigade and a battalion of the 6th Brigade, the 82nd Howitzer Regiment and the 87th Anti-Tank Battalion. 1st Army Group reserve was made up of the 212th Air-Landing Brigade, the 9th (Motorised) Rifle Brigade and a battalion of the 6th Tank Brigade. This reserve force was ordered on 20th August to take up positions some 2–3

* 82nd Rifle Division had been moved from the Urals District Army. One other rifle division was also brought from the Urals and despatched to the Trans-Baikal MD.

miles south-west of the Khamar-Daba heights and to be ready to exploit the successes of either assault group. The Southern Group was to mount the main blow, destroying the enemy south of the Khailastyn-Gol, crossing over to the northern bank afterwards to operate in conjunction with the Northern and Central Groups in encircling and annihilating the Japanese forces in the northern sector and cutting off the retreat to the east. The attack would begin with a two and three-quarter hour artillery bombardment, supported by air attack on enemy positions. Extremely detailed artillery arrangements had been worked out for the coming offensive—thereby avoiding the mistake at Lake Khasan.[75] As a result of the small actions fought on 7th–8th August Soviet troops had made some gains on the eastern bank of the Khalkhin-Gol, but not until the night of 18th–19th August were the main forces moved over the river in preparation for 20th. By four days Zhukov beat the Japanese to the offensive. Imperial Edict had assigned to the Japanese 6th Army the task of crushing the Soviet opposition with an offensive timed for 24th, but at 5.45 a.m., on 20th August Zhukov struck first.

At 9 a.m. on 20th the Soviet infantry, supported by tanks and aircraft, went over to the offensive, the front extending for some forty-eight miles. For three days the northern and southern assault groups were engaged in fighting their way to accomplish the initial encirclement of the Japanese, which might have been accomplished earlier but for the strong resistance which the Northern Group, commanded by Colonel Olekseyenko, encountered in the fortified region by the Fui heights. For two days, 21st and 22nd August, fruitless attacks were made on the Japanese positions and only the committing of reserve units (the 9th Mechanised and the 212th Air-Landing Brigade) enabled sufficient force to be brought to bear to accomplish the destruction of the Japanese. And time as well as men had been lost. On 24th the Japanese launched an attack with two infantry regiments supported by aircraft operating from the south-east of Nomon-Han-Burd-Obo, with the object of relieving the pressure on the encircled troops. To meet this threat, the 80th Rifle Regiment (57th Rifle Division), reinforced by the 6th Tank Brigade and a second rifle regiment, was assigned to check the Japanese attack and on 26th directed to launch a flank attack on the intruders. Within the encirclement the Japanese set up strong resistance points, so that Soviet troops had to fight desperately for each trench and gun position.

The fighting on 24th marked the beginning of the second stage of Zhukov's operation, which was concerned with containing the Japanese counter-attacks and battering down resistance in the northern sector. Soviet attacks went forward without regard for casualties; to a divisional commander who reported that his troops were unable to advance further,

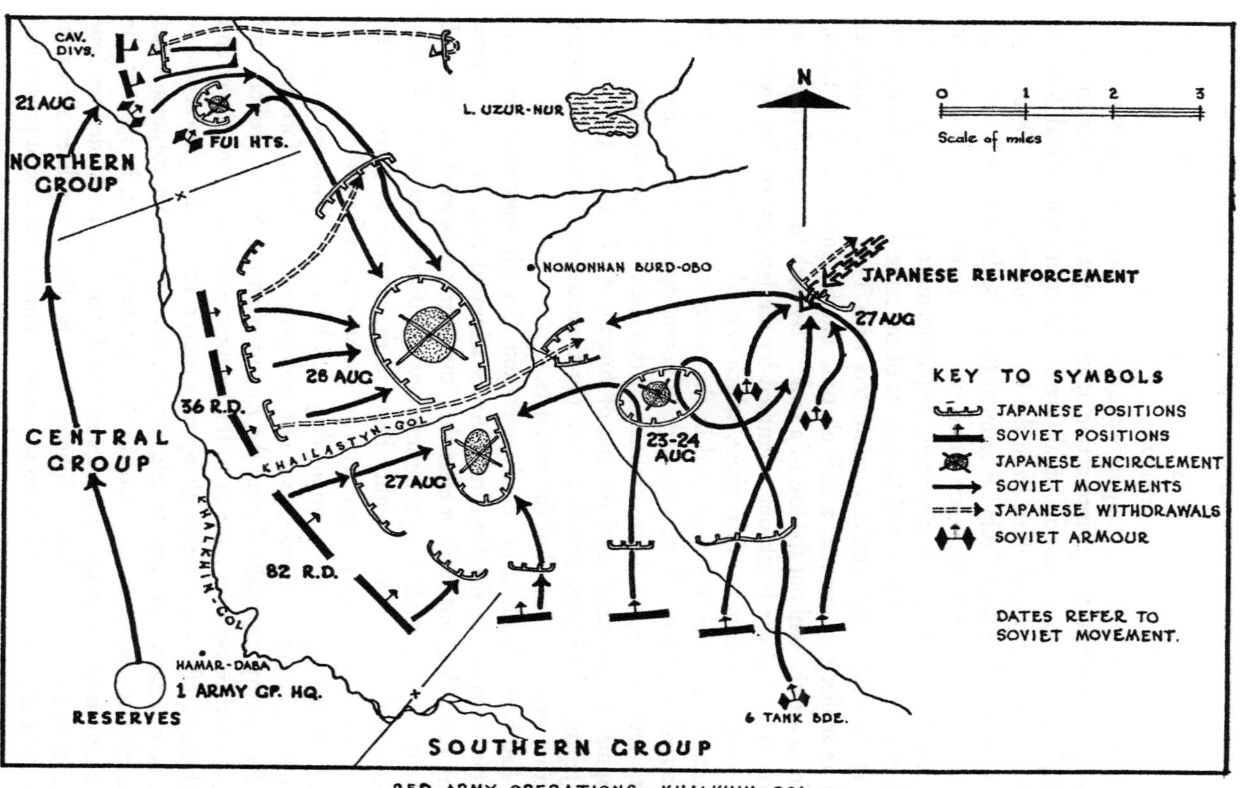

RED ARMY OPERATIONS, KHALKHIN-GOL
20-31 August, 1939

Zhukov gave the order to proceed with his operations or be at once replaced. Zhukov replaced another commander, who was slow in achieving success; in spite of heavy losses, air support was allotted to the second commander, who had to hurl his troops into action again and yet again.[76] Acclaimed a triumph for the co-operation of all arms, the operations called forth a maximum and sustained effort from the Red Army engineers. There were also blunders. The 602nd Rifle Regiment (82nd Rifle Division), operating at the centre on a five-kilometre front, was incorrectly deployed and took five days to sort itself out effectively, requiring more time before it could exploit its successes. The 603rd Regiment of the same division, also operating at the centre and similarly reinforced with T–38 and T–26 tanks as well as artillery, underwent a difficult time but by good use of its tanks, made 14 attacks without the loss of a tank.[77] By 27th the second stage was almost over and the break-out attempted by the Japanese on the night of 27th–28th ushered in the final phase, which was taken up with liquidating resistance about the higher ground in the centre of the front. The 127th and 293rd Regiments of the 57th Rifle Division, operating from the south-west, were assigned to the neutralising of this last and major strong-point; mopping up continued until the end of August. At dawn on 31st August the Japanese had been expelled over the frontier and Soviet-Mongolian territory officially cleared of the intruders.

It had been a brilliant but costly operation. On 5th September the commanding general of the Kwantung Army admitted that the 6th Japanese Army had failed, but made it clear that 'the matter is beyond the limits of a mere frontier conflict', promising new reinforcements to finish this 'mouse-stirring' with one mighty blow in the autumn to come. But the 'mouse-stirring' came to an end with an armistice fixed for 16th September, both sides occupying the positions they held by 1 p.m. (Moscow time) on 15th. The Japanese command was not unimpressed by the performance of the Red Army, especially during the August offensive. Soviet artillery and armour had proved far superior to the Japanese in terms of fire power and mechanised effectives. Although by no means a sustained logistical test, it had been a cause for considerable surprise that the Soviet command had been able to transport and store in the operational zone, in spite of the poor communications and distances involved, the supplies needed for four months of increasingly heavy fighting. Real flexibility had been shown in Soviet tactics. Battle-field innovations and modifications to equipment had been numerous; at first Soviet tanks had been ignited by petrol bottles hurled at them, but subsequently wire nets were put over the tank chassis and the use of the diesel engine cut down the fire risk. Above all, the Red Army had turned out to be tougher than was anticipated.[78] During the first real test of war with tanks, artillery and aircraft used on a large scale, the Soviet command was able to put both theories and equipment to practical tests. One of the crucial points of the earlier experiments had been the difficult business of synchronising the manœuvres of the fast-moving tank forces and the slower infantry. Zhukov's handling of his mechanised forces contributed most substantially to his success. Not lingering to take part in separate battles for isolated strong points and relying on aircraft to inhibit enemy reinforcement of the battle-field, the mechanised forces had made deep penetrations of the enemy defensive positions. In addition to the tanks and artillery which worked together, the third indispensable element was motorised infantry, without which there could be no exploitation of the successes of the mechanised forces operating at a distance from the slower-moving infantry. It was now, however, that the Red Army command was proceeding to disband the seven mechanised corps which had hitherto existed, distributing the tanks in separate battalions to rifle formations as infantry-support tanks. In spite of the reported protests of Shaposhnikov and Zhukov, the idea that the tank could play no independent role on the battle-field triumphed for the moment, when the principal Soviet tank expert Pavlov, who had seen service in Spain, was able to persuade Stalin and Voroshilov of the correctness of this view.[79]

Zhukov had passed the test of Khalkhin-Gol with flying colours. The very creditable performance of the Red Army against the Kwantung Army did, however, attract only a minimum of attention in the west, where the gigantic issues of peace or war overshadowed all else. On the morning of 1st September, German armour and infantry, supported by the *Luftwaffe*, invaded Poland. On the fateful 3rd, Ribbentrop directed an enquiry to Molotov about the movement of Soviet forces 'at the proper time against Polish forces in the Russian sphere of interest. On 5th Molotov promised to give a speedy reply, at the same time confirming that the new Soviet Military Attaché in Berlin, Purkayev, was a 'man of importance', an officer of considerable experience and acquainted with the 'essential features' of the German-Soviet agreements.[80] The question to be arranged was the Red Army's invasion of Poland from the east.

* * * *

On 7th Purkayev was recalled to Moscow for consultations. Two days later the Russians were again approached by their new partners about the date of their military operations against Poland. General Köstring was told in Moscow, according to a message of 9th September, that the Red Army would intervene, and what was equally to the point, there were visible signs that rapid preparations were in hand. The Soviet command had been caught napping by events in Poland, expecting the Poles to put up a prolonged resistance. Molotov had to admit that the Soviet Government was taken 'completely by surprise' by the speed of the German advances; the Red Army had reckoned on having several weeks in which to prepare, and now the Soviet military command found itself 'in a difficult situation' since they required two or three weeks for their own preparations.[81] But with the satisfactory outcome of the Khalkhin-Gol fighting and the elimination of the immediate Japanese threat, on 14th Molotov found it possible to inform the Germans that the Red Army had reached a state of readiness 'sooner than anticipated'. There was every possibility of Soviet military action now occurring earlier than anticipated, although for political reasons there could be no intervention until Warsaw had fallen. By the August Pact, Soviet and German spheres of influence had already been defined; there was a danger that a political vacuum might be created if the Red Army did not act in Eastern Poland. The Soviet decision was welcome to the Germans, since 'it relieves us of the necessity of annihilating the remainder of the Polish Army by pursuing it as far as the Russian boundary'.[82] Molotov confirmed on 16th September that military operations were imminent — 'perhaps even to-morrow or the day after'. Stalin was at that moment conferring with the Red Army command and would in the evening set the day and hour of the advance across the frontier. Such an undertaking had evidently been difficult to arrive at until the Far Eastern front was fully secured; this was very probably a significant part of the 'difficult situation' in which the Soviet military command found itself. It remained only to find a satisfactory pretext, acceptable to the Germans and also making at least a show of plausibility to cover the Red Army invasion.

Front administrations were set up in the Ukrainian and Belorussian commands. Army Commander 2nd Grade M. P. Kovalev took over the Belorussian Front, with the 3rd Army (Corps Commander V. I. Kuznetsov), 11th Army (Divisional Commander N. P. Medvedev), 10th Army (Corps Commander I. G. Zakharin), 4th Army (Divisional Commander V. I. Chuikov), a front command cavalry-mechanised mobile group under Corps Commander I. V. Boldin and the 23rd Independent Rifle Corps. Army Commander 1st Grade Timoshenko took over the Ukrainian Front, with the 5th Army (Divisional Commander I. G. Sovetnikov), 6th Army (Corps Commander F. I. Golikov) and 12th Army (Army Commander 2nd Grade I. V. Tyulenev). Without waiting for the complete concentration of his forces, Kovalev set up three mobile groups: the Polotsk, the Minsk and the Dzerzhinsk. The Ukrainian Front had almost completed its concentration. Timoshenko was ordered to reach the Kovel-Vladimir-Volynsk-Sokal line by 20th September, thereafter pressing on to the River San. To secure a high rate of advance, each army was instructed to form mobile detachments of tanks and cavalry elements. The mobile force of the 6th Army was formed out of the 2nd Cavalry Corps and the 24th Tank Brigade, that of the 5th Army from two tank brigades. Since the 12th Army comprised two (the 4th and 5th) cavalry corps, a tank corps (the 25th) and two independent tank brigades (23rd and 26th), then the whole was operated as a front mobile force. Kovalev's Polotsk group was ordered to drive on Vilna. The Minsk group had Grodno as its final objective. The Dzerzhinsk group was to reach the river Shar by 18th September and then drive on Volkovysk. Speed was essential, in order to catch the Poles in the rear and to push up to the German armies.

At 5.40 a.m., on 17th September, Soviet cavalry and tanks, in the mobile groups, crossed the frontier line and brushed away the resistance of the Polish frontier troops. On the first day of this 'liberation march', for so it was represented during the political lectures which preceded the operations, only small losses were sustained and a distance of some sixty miles covered. Stalin had requested that German aircraft should not fly east of the Bialystok-Brest-Litovsk-Lwow line, to avoid incidents. On the evening of 18th, in conversation with Schulenburg about the despatch of a Soviet mission to Bialystok, Stalin remarked that there were 'certain doubts' as to whether the German High Command would honour the Moscow agreements and respect the demarcation set at the Narew-Vistula-San river lines. Stalin was not calling into question the good faith of the German Government — he referred only to 'the well-known fact that all military men are loath to give up occupied territory'. General Köstring assured Stalin that the German Army would do as the Führer ordered. Soviet troops for their part were given orders to avoid conflict with German troops and to settle incidents without the use of force, but if German troops attempted to check the Red Army, then — 'In the last resort, sweep them away by force'.[83] No major clash did take place, although Soviet and German troops exchanged shots and took casualties in a minor affray. Four days after the armies had met along the dividing line, Stalin asked the German Ambassador in Moscow to call upon him in connection with the final settlement of the Polish question. Nothing of this, affirmed Stalin, must contain within it the seeds of Soviet-German discord. For that reason, he had no wish to see an independent residual Poland. Stalin proposed an exchange. To German acquisitions should be added, from territory lying at present east of the demarcation line, part of the province of Warsaw and that of Lublin. As compensation, the Germans should waive their claims to Lithuania. The whole problem of the Baltic states could be taken up when Ribbentrop visited Moscow to settle the details of the territorial arrangements.[84]

By virtue of the free hand which the treaty with Germany had afforded the Soviet Union, that problem of the Baltic states was already being tackled by Stalin. When proposing his exchange with Germany on 25th September, Stalin had indicated that 'the unstinting support of the German Government' would be required in settling the problem of Estonia, Latvia and Lithuania. Estonia had come first. Foreign Minister Selter, apparently engaged to sign a Soviet-Estonian commercial agreement, faced Molotov who presented him with the draft of a Soviet-Estonian military alliance. Estonia would place naval and air bases at the disposal of the Soviet Union. Selter was not encouraged by Molotov to think that any assistance in resisting Soviet demands would be forthcoming either from Germany or Great Britain. Selter was understandably nervous of Soviet intentions. Colonel Maasing, who evidently attempted to enlist German aid, met with a blank refusal. On 27th the Estonian Chief of Staff indicated that the Russians demanded a naval base at Baltiski and an air base on Estonian islands; Soviet aircraft were much in evidence, but no fire had been opened on them. Selter on the same day wished to inform Ribbentrop that 'under the gravest threat of imminent attack', Estonia was obliged to submit. He would try to make the use of bases applicable only in time of war.[85] In the tense negotiations in Moscow, Selter indicated that it would be out of the question for Estonia to take the side of the Soviet Union in the event of a Soviet-Finnish war. Two hours of fruitless discussion were resolved by Stalin's decision in favour of the Estonian Minister.[86] Latvia and Lithuania fell under the Soviet hammer during the same period. With the Lithuanians, although no specific bases were demanded, an arrangement was arrived at whereby 28,000 Red Army troops would be stationed on Lithuanian soil. While Stalin was willing to adjust the figure of troops (first suggesting 50,000), he was adamant over the principle involved; with the Latvian Foreign Minister Munters he admitted that a division of spheres had already taken place between Germany and the Soviet Union, so that it would be necessary to comply with it. It is reported that Stalin also pointed out that both Germany and Great Britain were ready to attack the Soviet Union, should either win the war now being waged, and there was need to be prepared.[87] On 18th October Soviet forces began to take up their places in the new advanced posts so secured for them.

During the abortive discussion with the British and French missions, Shaposhnikov, in discussing the curious alternative cases envisaged by the Soviet command, specified for naval operations the use of seven ports or bases — Hango (Finland), Ainazi and Libau (Latvia), Habstal, Pärnu, Ösel and Dagö (Estonia). The temporary occupation of the Åland Islands would also be required. With these facilities the Soviet Baltic Fleet could extend its cruiser operations as well as submarine and mine-laying activities along the coast of East Prussia and Pomerania; Soviet submarines would be able to raid the transports carrying raw materials from Sweden to the 'chief aggressor'.[88] While the new pacts with the Baltic states advanced the strategic interests of the Soviet Navy along these lines, the agreement with Germany brought yet another naval question in its train. The German Navy requested the use of repair facilities for German ships and submarines at Murmansk; on 5th October Molotov informed Schulenburg that Murmansk was not 'isolated enough' for these activities, but suggested that Teriberka, east of Murmansk, would meet this requirement. The setting up of equipment and the utilisation of the port could be discussed with Mikoyan (and evidently was on 10th).[89] In this manner a period of renewed collaboration between the German and Soviet navies was ushered in. As before, German plans and designs drew the Russians like a magnet. In December 1939 Admiral Raeder was all in favour of selling the plans and drawings of the *Bismarck* to the Russians.[90]

In the search for bases, however, Stalin sought to distil every drop of advantage from the recent Pact. Inevitably the turn of Finland came, although Soviet policy at first did little more than take up certain loosely hanging threads. In April 1938 the Soviet negotiator Yartsev had demanded for the Soviet Union the right to fortify the Finnish island of Suursaari in return for a guarantee of Finnish territorial integrity, military aid and a commercial agreement. In December Mikoyan offered a commercial agreement on terms intimately connected with 'political rights' and islands in the Gulf of Finland. Litvinov in March 1939 requested the use of four islands (lying between Åland and Leningrad) as observation posts covering the approach to Leningrad; a few days later in Moscow an exchange was proposed, whereby Finland would be ceded 183 square kilometres to the north of Lake Ladoga in return for use of the islands.[91] When the discussions were re-opened in October 1939 matters stood rather differently. At 5 p.m., on 12th October the Finnish representatives Paasikivi, Yrjö-Koskinen, Nykopp and Paasonen met in the Kremlin with Stalin, Molotov, Potemkin and Derevyanskii. The Finns listened to the Soviet requirements; war in Europe demanded that no enemy should have access to the Gulf of Finland. The south of the Gulf was now secured by treaty arranged with Estonia. The north lay open. Finland might well conclude a local treaty of reciprocal aid dealing with the Gulf of Finland. Hango was mentioned as the possible site of a Soviet base on the Finnish coast. There would have to be concessions in Petsamo. To protect Leningrad, the border must be moved to a new line. In the Gulf, Finland must cede islands including Suursaari and Koivisto. Compensation would be forthcoming by turning over parts of Eastern

Karelia to Finland.[92] On 14th a second meeting took place and Stalin made himself plain on the subject of Soviet security. 'We must be able to bar the entrance to the Gulf of Finland' — upon this Stalin developed his argument. Against what enemies? 'England or Germany.' Soviet-German relations were good at the moment, 'but everything in this world may change'. The written proposal asked for a thirty year lease on Hango, which would become a Soviet naval base and be armed with coastal defence guns capable of closing (in conjunction with batteries on the southern shore) the Gulf of Finland. For the protection of the base, the Soviet memorandum suggested the stationing of a force not exceeding 5,000 men — 1 infantry regiment, 2 anti-aircraft batteries, 2 aviation regiments and a tank battalion.[93]

A second conference which opened on 23rd witnessed more of Stalin's explanation. The possibility of military operations on the shores of the Arctic Ocean as well as threats through the Gulf of Finland made rectification at Petsamo of frontier lines in the north equally relevant. Stalin and Molotov mentioned France and Great Britain as possible opponents; Stalin recalled the Civil War period, Yudenich and the operations of British torpedo boats from Koivisto. But, commented one of the Finnish negotiators, '. . . beneath it all . . . one sensed that it was Germany they feared'.[94] At the third conference (the discussion being resumed on 3rd November) the Finnish negotiators rejected the Soviet proposals about Hango and Lappohja Bay. Molotov found the other points unsatisfactory, even though the Finns stressed that their concessions had gone to the farthest limit. At the conclusion of this meeting Molotov let fall ominous words — 'We civilians can see no further in the matter; now it is the turn of the military to have their say.'[95] Negotiations ground to a halt. A bitter anti-Finnish propaganda campaign developed. On 26th November seven artillery rounds were fired by the frontier village of Manaïla — 'the provocatory discharge of artillery . . . directed against Soviet forces,' the Soviet note of protest charged.[96] On 30th November, after a thirty-minute artillery barrage, the Red Army took the offensive against Finland.

* * * *

In his speech to the Supreme Soviet on 31st October, Molotov had publicly proclaimed Soviet proposals to Finland. After this there could be no climbing down. As for war, in spite of Molotov's threatening allusion in November to 'the military', this seemed an unlikely solution although Soviet strength had been built up over some time in the frontier districts. When it did come, the war became the initial responsibility of the Leningrad Military District. This, together with the crude blunder of setting up Kuusinen as head of the 'Democratic Republic of Finland' in the small town of Terijoki, suggested serious Soviet miscalculation about the military and political aspects of their operations in Finland. A quick campaign, which would liberate the Finnish proletariat from the yoke of the Fascist 'military clique', would settle the problem for good. The whole front, running from Leningrad in the south to the Arctic Ocean in the north, stretched some 800 miles and along it were deployed four Soviet armies, a task which must have occupied more than the few days of actual tension preceding the attack. The intentions of the Soviet command were comprehensive enough. The 7th Army under Meretskov, commander of the Leningrad Military District, would strike up the Karelian Isthmus, breach the defences of the 'Mannerheim Line', drive on Viipuri (Vyborg) — and lay open the way to Helsinki. Operating from Petrozavodsk and north of Lake Ladoga, the 8th Army would drive into the flank and rear of the Finnish forces defending the Isthmus and outflank the defensive belt there. Between Kandalaksha in the north and Repola in the south, the 9th Army was ready to begin its drive to the northern edge of the Gulf of Bothnia; the land communications between Finland and Sweden would be severed in this way and Finland would be virtually sliced in two. In the far north the 14th Army would seize the Petsamo district. Enjoying undoubted superiority, applying such a comprehensive plan, choosing a good time for the attack, arguing that the combination of military weakness and internal divisions effectively lowered the capacity to resist — out of this the Soviet idea of a relatively quick decision was not at all fantastic. The Red Army would be liberating rather than fighting.

Blocking the Isthmus stood the 'Mannerheim Line', not at all a line but rather a belt of defences — fire-points, anti-tank traps and barriers, trenches — running from Taipale at the mouth of the River Vuoksi on Lake Ladoga to the Baltic near the fortress of Koivisto. The River Vuoksi formed a third of the belt; land defences were set up linking the river with Lake Ayranaan and Muolaan. Then came the exposed Summa sector, where concrete forts had been constructed. Beyond Summa was one more lake and then Koivisto's guns to cover the flank. The real strong points were the water and marshy ground, about which the defensive positions had been created to utilise the maximum advantages afforded by the terrain. Against these natural and artificial obstacles Meretskov launched the 7th Army. By 6th December the first of his tanks had met up with the Finnish tank-barriers. For the main blow designed to open the way to Viipuri, Meretskov employed two rifle corps (the 19th and 50th) on a seventeen-kilometre front, supported by three tank brigades and a tank battalion, as well as twelve artillery regiments. The 10th Tank Corps was assigned to exploit the break-through when it came. By 15th–16th December this offensive was beginning to gather momentum. Whether from over-confidence or incompetence, Meretskov's offensive was extremely badly prepared. Even a little consultation of Russian history books would have shown the perils of fighting on the Isthmus. In spite of the impressive number of formations (Meretskov had altogether 12 rifle divisions and a tank corps), only 4 of the 9 divisions of the first echelon were properly committed. Tanks and guns were lacking; 19th Corps had 16 guns and 18 tanks to one kilometre of front. The three rifle divisions of 7th Army reserve had not yet finished concentrating. The concentration of forces and support along the line of the main blow was evidently bungled. The troops were by no means trained for the operations they were to conduct. Few gaps were made in the obstacles to assist the tanks. The artillery merely pounded away without any real regard for targets. The co-operation which had been a feature of Khalkhin-Gol was conspicuously lacking. The supply arrangements were far from satisfactory.[97] Mass, frontal attacks were the order of the day. After a thirty-minute barrage, made usually about 3 p.m., Soviet infantry preceded by tanks would assault the Finnish positions. The light and medium tanks fell easy victims to the Finns. A slight modification in the method of attack came with the use of the infantry mass first, the tanks being held as a mobile group ready to irrupt into any gap in the defences prised open by the infantry. These attacks were made more frequently at night, but the Finns switched on searchlights and across the excellent fields of fire formed out of the frozen lakes and rivers poured machine-gun fire into the massed Soviet infantry.[98] On 26–28th December, the Soviet high command called a halt to this slaughter which had yielded next to nothing.

By Petsamo, at the opposite end of the front, a Soviet division had begun to advance down the Arctic Highway on 14th December; having attacked across the strip of territory towards Luostar, on 13th December troops had been landed in Petsamo Sound and the next day began their advance. Finland was sealed off from any relief which might arrive through this port. By January two Soviet divisions were installed, artillery to command the Sound was set up and Soviet mine-layers stood by to close it. North of Nautsi and just ahead of a Finnish defence belt the Russians halted. While the 14th Army enjoyed these limited successes, the 9th met disaster utter and complete. Aiming by its offensive to cut Finland at the 'waist', the 163rd Rifle Division (9th Army) drove for the important road junction of Suomussalmi, advancing along a road built in great secrecy which enabled the Russians to move down from the north. From a southerly direction came elements of the 44th Rifle Division, both divisions effecting a junction at Suomussalmi on 9th December. From the ruined village of Suomussalmi the two Soviet divisions would undertake the second stage of the drive to

Oulu and the Gulf of Bothnia. The Finnish commander Colonel Siilasvuo, disposing of a force markedly inferior in numbers, determined to strike at the junction of the two Soviet divisions. Harrassed by small Finnish battle patrols, the Russians were obliged to quit the ruins of the village. To the east of the village Finnish troops cut the road by which units of the 44th Soviet division had advanced. The 163rd retired its left wing from the village by crossing the ice of Lake Kianta. Siilasvuo, having split his enemy, could now try and stage his own version of Tannenberg. Holding off the 305th Regiment (44th Division) from trying to regain contact with the 163rd Division (this was accomplished by a feint), Siilasvuo turned on the 163rd. As the temperature dropped sharply and grievous cold arrived, fiercer than any known for a quarter of a century, Siilasvuo attacked in flank and rear, striking also at the supply dump in the middle of the frozen lake. Being permitted to withdraw, the 163rd divisional commander carried out an orderly retreat, putting his remaining infantry at the centre of a column protected on either side by a score of tanks. Escaping in this manner, the 163rd was nevertheless finished as an effective force. Siilasvuo turned now to deal with the main body of the 44th Division, advancing to assist the 163rd. Stretched over five miles of road were the divisional artillery, transport and tanks, with the advance force finally in contact with the entrenched 305th Regiment. Blocking the road at the Soviet frontier itself, the Finns worked in four groups, harrying and cutting up the hapless Russians. Cold and hunger added considerably to the casualties inflicted by Finnish machine-gunners and snipers. By 9th January the Finns were mopping up the dreadful battlefield.[99] The 9th Army also suffered a heavy defeat in its attempt to drive on Kemijärvi.

The 8th Army, with six rifle divisions (155th, 139th, 56th, 18th, 168th and the 75th in reserve), operated north of Lake Ladoga. Breaking through on this sector of the front would mean taking Viipuri and 'the Line' in the rear. At the very northern point of the 8th Army front, the 1st Rifle Corps' advance on Ilomantsi was checked. The 18th Rifle Division's drive on Sortavala was checked. The 168th, advancing on the same objective round the shore of Lake Ladoga, was checked. Once again the Finns worked at cutting the supply routes of the Soviet formations. The 18th Division was surrounded. So was the 168th. The 34th Tank Brigade, sent to the relief of the 18th Division, was in its turn sealed off from its supply, surrounded and after fifty-four days of siege the brigade was stormed.[100] The Ladoga front drained Russian men and materials, but it did force the Finns to divert troops from the Isthmus.

By the last week in December the fiasco, redeemed perhaps only by the fatalistic doggedness of the Russian infantry, was plain to see. Out of six

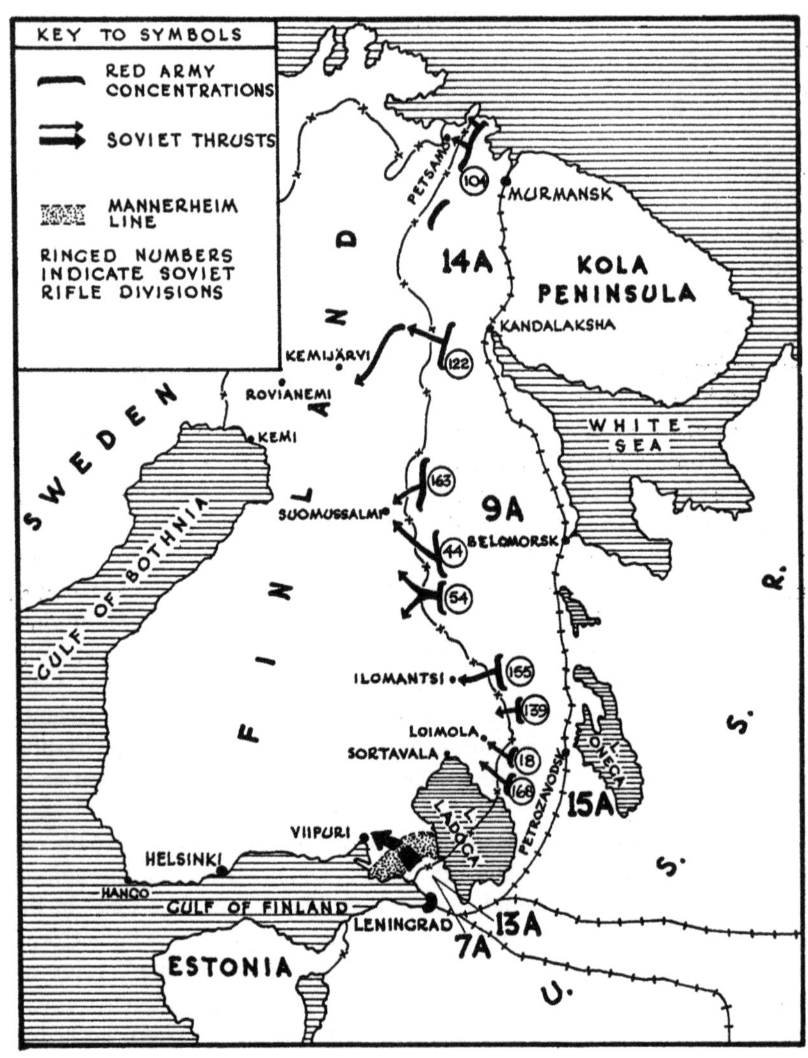
KEY TO SYMBOLS
RED ARMY CONCENTRATIONS
SOVIET THRUSTS
MANNERHEIM LINE
RINGED NUMBERS INDICATE SOVIET RIFLE DIVISIONS
PETSAMO
104
MURMANSK
14A
KOLA PENINSULA
KANDALAKSHA
122
KEMIJÄRVI
ROVIANEMI
KEMI
WHITE SEA
SWEDEN
FINLAND
163
9A
SUOMUSSALMI
44
BELOMORSK
54
GULF OF BOTHNIA
ILOMANTSI
155
139
LOIMOLA
SORTAVALA
18
168
ONEGA
PETROZAVODSK
15A
LADOGA
VIIPURI
HELSINKI
HANGO
GULF OF FINLAND
LENINGRAD
13A
7A
ESTONIA
U. S. S. R.

SOVIET DEPLOYMENT AGAINST FINLAND

offensives attempted, only one far to the north showed any sign of succeeding. After the catastrophe of Suomussalmi, the Red Army's honour had to be retrieved at all costs, although the cost had already been heavy enough. Suomussalmi, although not in itself decisive, revealed the hollowness of Voroshilov's boasts from the rostrum in March. Nor could the war be allowed to drag on indefinitely, for outside intervention could not be entirely discounted. The Soviet Union availed itself both of German neutrality and German help;[101] Admiral Raeder agreed that German steamers proceeding to Northern Sweden could supply Soviet submarines in the Gulf of Bothnia with oil and supplies.[102] Meanwhile the Main Military Soviet had turned its attention to Finland. On 26th December the Soviet armies were re-organised; on the Karelian Isthmus the 13th Army under Corps Commander V. D. Grendal' was added to the 7th. The 8th was re-organised and the 15th Army attached to assist with operations in the region of Loimola. On 28th December a new directive was issued for operations against the Finns. The front commander was required not to rush ahead but to proceed only after adequate preparation had been made. The rear had to be secured against the attacks which had caused such havoc. The directive evidently referred to the campaign conducted by the Russian Army in Finland in 1808–9. Mass attacks were to be discontinued; companies and battalions would be better employed multi-echeloned and using ski-troops for reconnaissance. Artillery fire must be aimed at enemy fire-points. If the pill-boxes of the forward line of the enemy defence were not smashed, then the infantry was not to be committed to an assault. Sending newly arrived divisions or reinforcements straight into action was forbidden. Army staffs would concern themselves with ensuring a satisfactory state in the composition of the troops, their weapons and clothing and acquaintance of the conditions under which they had to fight. Stricter security over orders and greater secrecy of movements and dispositions would now be demanded.[103] As for the command, Voroshilov retained over-all control but Meretskov's former position was much modified by the creation on 7th January, 1940, of the North-Western Front and the nomination of Timoshenko as front commander. A new front, a new command, new methods and new weapons — with these at the beginning of 1940 the Red Army began its second war with Finland.

* * * *

The Soviet Union lost much by failing to win a speedy victory in Finland. Whatever recovery might be effected, it was not possible to obscure the fact that something was amiss with the Red Army; the directive of 28th

December was a catalogue of errors which needed correction. At the end of 1939 the German General Staff rated the Red Army as:

> In quantity a gigantic military instrument. — Commitment of the 'mass'. — Organisation, equipment and means of leadership unsatisfactory. — principles of leadership good. — leadership itself, however, too young and inexperienced. — . . . troops not very uniform. . . . Fighting qualities of the troops in a *heavy* fight, dubious. — The Russian 'mass' is *no* match for an army, with modern equipment and superior leadership.[104]

The Finnish fiasco was squandering some of the gain acquired from the agreement with Germany. Stalin's new strategic frontiers needed fortifying not fighting about. Behind these lines the Red Army could be expanded and modernised, rather than being battered by the Finns. Already the Germans had been staggered by the size of the Soviet military ordering — over a billion *Reichsmark* in value. Stalin early in January made it clear that the Soviet priority was naval artillery,[105] although the discussion covered machines for producing artillery munitions, aircraft (prototypes), as well as periscopes for submarines and related equipment. Of machinery to produce heavy artillery ammunition, Stalin emphasised that the 'Soviet Union was very urgently in need of these machines'.[106] Smashing in the 'Mannerheim Line' during the coming weeks was to be a forthright commentary on that statement.

A turn to complete realism in Soviet policy was implied in the peace feeler of 29th January, which virtually dropped the hopeless political fiction of Kuusinen and his 'democratic republic'. But by early February it was equally plain that the Russians wanted Hango and nothing less than Hango.[107] There were, moreover, other plans relevant to Finland and the Soviet Union afoot. For the British and French two questions — aid to Finland and cutting off German ore supplies in Scandinavia — 'became closely entwined.'[108] General Gamelin on 22nd February submitted, as he had been invited to do, a plan dealing with the possibility of depriving Germany and the Soviet Union of the petrol resources of the Caucasus; this could take the form of attacking German tankers in the Black Sea, striking at the main centres of the industry in the Caucasus and using the Mussulman populations in the area to raise revolts against the Soviet government. This was in addition to an earlier French plan for landing a force at Petsamo.[109] Even while these schemes were receiving their first outlines, Soviet forces facing the 'Mannerheim Line' had been heavily strengthened; ammunition for the artillery, new items of equipment (some of the new KV tanks, armoured sledges, electric digging machines, the Model 1939 improved rifle for the infantry), and excellent divisions such as the 100th and 103rd were moved to the

Isthmus. Although no mean feat of organisation, the Soviet command could proceed without having to reckon on the possibility of large-scale air attack. At 12.45 p.m., on 1st February the Red Army offensive began.

Until 8th Soviet forces more or less carried out probing attacks, maintaining all the while a heavy artillery bombardment and extensive air attacks not only on the Finnish defences but on communications, depots and key towns. The performance of the Soviet air force had been so far disappointing from the point of view of military effectiveness. Now there was evidence of much closer co-ordination with current military operations. The directive of 3rd February laid down the tasks of the North-Western Front. The main effort would be made on the Karelian Isthmus, where the 7th and 13th Red armies were deployed. The 7th Army front ran from the Gulf of Finland to the eastern shore of Lake Muolaanjärvi, a distance of some twenty-three miles. 13th Army operated from that eastern lake shore to Taipale on the western shore of Lake Ladoga, a distance of fifty miles. The Soviet plan envisaged breaking through the main Finnish defence belt on the Isthmus* and reaching a line running from Viipuri through Antrea junction to Keksholm. The main blow was to be in the direction of Viipuri. With its left wing, the 13th Army would mount its main blow in the direction of Antrea junction with a force of not less than five rifle divisions; the right wing would effect a supporting blow with two divisions in the direction of Keksholm. The 7th Army right wing, with a force of not less than nine rifle divisions, would drive on Viipuri, the left wing to the west with not less than two divisions carrying out supporting operations. The line to be attained first ran from the western shore of Lake Ladoga, through Missua, Heinjöki and on to the railway line on the western side of the Isthmus at Kaislakti; 64 per cent of the total forces and artillery were concentrated with the formations aimed at Viipuri. The reserve of each army was set at up to two rifle divisions. Each corps would have two echelons, in the first two divisions, in the second one; divisions would have one or two echelons, rifle regiments one or two, rifle battalions three. Rifle divisions would set up mobile reserves consisting of one ski battalion and one reconnaissance battalion. For the main blow a corps front should be 5–6 kilo-

* Success north of Lake Ladoga would have enabled the Red Army to cut the north-south railway link from Viipuri-Kajaain, outflank the 'Mannerheim Line' and take Viipuri in the rear. The Red Army never accomplished the break-through, but did hold Finnish forces which could have been a vital reinforcement on the Isthmus. These January 1940 offensives north of Ladoga have been described as 'successful feints'. However, their scale and intensity indicate a real intention to attempt this turning of the Finnish defences. In view of failure here, the Soviet high command had no choice but to attempt the head-on attack against the defences of the Isthmus. The apologia for the Red Army and Soviet strategy contained in W. P. and Z. Coates, *The Soviet-Finnish Campaign 1939–1940*, London 1942, is largely undone by recent Soviet 'self-criticism' of what happened in Finland.

metres, a divisional front 2–2½. Artillery preparation would last two or three hours. For destroying pill-boxes special assault groups should be set up and trained; the recommended form of organisation laid down a rifle and machine-gun platoon, a few mortars, two or three snipers, not less than three tanks, one flame-throwing tank, one or two 45-mm guns and a squad of sappers.[110]

Already Soviet artillery had poured a rain of shells, especially in the Summa sector, on the Finnish concrete forts. There was little need to take elaborate measures to screen the guns and Soviet aircraft were able to observe the fire with almost complete freedom. In order to reduce the forts, shells had been put down beside and in front of them, so that some had been literally almost uprooted. On the morning of 11th February the massed Soviet artillery gave the Finnish defences a final battering with pieces ranging from 76-mm to 280-mm. Just before the infantry went in Soviet bombers, working this time according to the rules, showered more high explosive on the Finnish positions. Tanks dragging the armoured sledges brought up infantry to the edge of the Finnish entrenchments, followed by the larger infantry masses. But the interminable bombardments had by no means shattered all the forts, and even when the special assault groups managed to knock them out, the Finns directed artillery and machine-gun fire on the Russians from positions reinforced with timber. In overwhelming these, the Russians faced Finns with bayonets, daggers and grenades. By 13th Soviet troops had prised open a gap in the defences east of Summa;[111] in this fighting the commander of the 123rd Rifle Division (Brigade Commander F. F. Alyabushev) and the commander of the 35th Tank Brigade distinguished themselves. The attacks on the east of the Isthmus met with far less success, although towards the centre Chernyak's 163rd Rifle Division (13th Army) managed to dent the Finnish line. The full fury of the Soviet offensive was accordingly directed to the Summa gap; fresh Soviet units were flung in, the desperate Finnish counter-attacks were ground down with more numbers and more metal. Soviet tanks (of which there were some 980 available) crashed on to and through the Finns who were bereft of any weapons either in working order or sufficient quantity to check them. The 10th Rifle Corps began to push up the western coast, past Summa. On 26th the fortress of Koivisto was encircled, and the whole shattering of the right flank of the Finnish defensive belt was virtually an accomplished fact.

Towards the end of February Timoshenko made his preparations for what was to be the final battle of the war — Viipuri and Viipuri Bay. The 13th Army was to continue smashing through the centre of the defensive belt, while the 7th would drive on Viipuri from the north-east and the south-west. In that latter direction lay a plan of considerable boldness. From 7th

Army reserve the 28th Rifle Corps had been formed and on 3rd March this formation was assigned the task of crossing the ice of the frozen Bay and establishing a bridge-head on the north-western shore and to the west of Viipuri itself. Working round by the eastern shore would be the 10th Corps, aimed at Viipuri as before. By launching mobile columns on hazardous journeys across the ice and striking at the Helsinki side of Viipuri, Timoshenko could hope to achieve a number of telling advantages. The Finnish escape route to the west would be cut. Viipuri would be completely encircled. Most significant of all, in addition to drawing away Finnish troops from the main defensive positions, this approach by the ice turned the Finnish reserve defence line which was designed to compensate for the ruination of the right flank. Also drawing off Finnish strength from the critical sectors were the 8th and 15th Armies operating to the north of Lake Ladoga.

Even so, launching the Soviet columns across the ice was a perilous undertaking. With the few bombers available to them, the Finns blasted Soviet tanks, armoured sledges and infantry columns as they advanced. Blowing up the ice and machine-gunning the Soviet infantry caused heavy casualties, but after three days Soviet troops had a hold on the north-western shore of the Bay and were launching raids on to the islands nearer to Viipuri. From the ice in the Bay Soviet artillery shelled Finnish positions inland. At the same time Finland was facing not only a grave military situation but also the necessity of making an agonising choice between a new Soviet offer to settle the war and the tantalising intimations of forthcoming aid from the Western powers should the Finns request this. France had asked that discussions with the Soviet Union should not be continued. The Soviet Union was well aware of the implications of Western aid and the possibility of being dragged into the wider European war.[112] The situation at the front was all the while deteriorating for the Finns; on 5th March Marshal Mannerheim described the situation on the ice of Viipuri Bay as '. . . impossible, since we are short of men on every hand'.[113] Although Molotov agreed to allow the Finns a little more time in which to decide on the Soviet offer, he intimated that the Red Army demanded to be allowed to advance. A Finnish request for an armistice was turned down flat unless Viipuri and Viipuri Bay were evacuated. To the British and French, the Finnish government directed a plea that the dead-line for requesting their intervention be put off to 12th March. Colonel Paasonen (Finnish Military Attaché in Paris) had meanwhile arrived in Helsinki bringing more news of an Allied expeditionary force and reports of a possible action against Baku, to be set in motion early in April. Secretly a Finnish delegation left for Moscow to talk about possible peace terms; Molotov, Zhdanov and Vasilevskii of the Red Army waited to deliver terms so harsh as to verge on the barbarous.

On the evening of 9th, in Helsinki, the Commander-in-Chief's report was read; it conveyed Lieutenant-General Heinrich's statement on the condition of the Isthmus Army: battalion strengths had fallen below 250 men, severe losses in officers lowered efficiency, machine-guns and anti-tank weapons had been demolished, the Soviet threats off the ice by Viipuri had critically weakened the Finnish defence, and Soviet aircraft made troop movements and maintenance 'decidedly difficult'.[114] Scanty numbers, shortage of ammunition and exhaustion overcame the Finns. The dictated peace was signed on 12th March, the fighting to cease at 11 a.m. on 13th.

★ ★ ★ ★

The Finnish campaign, in which the Soviet Union had skirted the wider war and the Red Army had suffered much from the 'invincibility' which it first showed, precipitated a severe crisis in the highest military circles. The defeats in Finland did at least provide a foundation on which the Red Army recovered some of the ground lost since 1937. The 'lessons' of the war in Finland became the subject of intensive study and considerable controversy. Khalkhin-Gol had not been of the same order. In Finland the Red Army had employed a minimum of 45 rifle divisions (five armies), over 1,500 tanks, 3,000 aircraft and an immense quantity of artillery. The balance sheet was best on its technical side. But leaving aside the political shortsightedness which precipitated the conflict and the initial incompetence of the Voroshilov-Mekhlis clique which literally plunged the Red Army into disaster, there were still serious deficiencies which demanded attention. As ever, there was the question of tactical training. In addition, there had been a colossal failure of Tukhachevsky's 'nerve'. Some of the disasters of the first phase might have been avoided by a show of independence and initiative on the part of the commanders. Since the commander was by no means master in his own house, then this was not surprising. The military purges were not designed to foster independence of spirit. As in the Civil War, dual command could be a very real retarding factor when it came to operations in the field. There was very little evidence of the new ideas which had been developed some time before. Only in the later phase did the *VVS* operations become properly co-ordinated with ground activities. The parachute arm of the Red Army, which had shown its paces earlier, was virtually not used. Only small saboteur groups were dropped. Otherwise mass remained the basic answer to all other situations, and even that had to be set against the artificial condition of complete freedom to run the rear services, since the Finnish Air Force lacked the means to effect real destruction. Not less than 1,200,000 men had been employed by the Red Army in what Zhukov later called the 'acid test', and the drastic modifications in policy might be taken as some indication that the Soviet leadership considered the Red Army had failed to pass it.

At the beginning of May Voroshilov was relieved of his duties as Defence Commissar by a 'promotion' to the post of deputy chairman of the Defence Committee. Voroshilov had been removed to make way for the man of the hour, Timoshenko. The whole question of the Finnish war had been debated by the Main Military Soviet, in sessions which could not have been anything but stormy. The result came ten days after Voroshilov's removal from the Defence Commissariat, when Order No. 120 of 16th May listed the shortcomings which would have to be corrected in the Red Army. Special attention was paid to training troops for operations in difficult conditions, in particular breaking through fortified positions, and offensive operations conducted in winter and wooded areas. At the company/battery and infantry- and artillery-battalion level the lack of proper co-ordination with other arms was especially marked. The officers simply did not know how to use their forces properly nor did they understand the possibilities of other arms. The infantry was not properly trained for close-in fighting, nor could it always take proper advantage of artillery support during the offensive. There was no proper exploitation in the offensive of the heavy machine-gun, mortar, battalion and regimental artillery. The weakest spot in the tank and artillery training was their co-operation with the infantry. As for aviation, there must be an improvement in the poor training for bad-weather flying. The officer corps' training left much to be desired, especially among junior officers. Certain unit and formation staffs had worked badly; in particular, they were criticised for delays in handling information on operations.[115] The more experienced staffs, which had been denuded by the *NKVD* arrests during the purge, might have staved off some of the calamity in Finland.

Pulling the Red Army into shape could not be accomplished without restoring a great deal of the former prestige and freedom of action which had existed before 1937. This was an indispensable condition for which Timoshenko could not forbear to press. But he would have to be careful not to press too far. Although he had been made a Marshal of the Soviet Union on 7th May, 1940, Timoshenko could not fail to realise that another Marshal had lost his head for trying to push military autonomy too far. With Timoshenko, Shaposhnikov and Kulik were also appointed Marshals. Shaposhnikov had supervised the recovery of the former strategic frontiers which Imperial Russia had enjoyed and had evidently advised Stalin very closely on this.[116] Kulik, a Stalinist *arriviste*, had his services in Spain recognised. Stalin brought back the old ranks of General and Admiral, hitherto shunned as too reminiscent of the old regime. In June more than 1,000 officers were promoted to form the new senior command staff of the Red Army, the Navy and Air Force; Zhukov, Meretskov and Tyulenev were appointed full generals. Apanasenko and Gorodovikov became Colonel-Generals (a rank which had not existed in the Imperial Russian Army), Batov, Vatutin, Golikov, Yeremenko, Kirponos, Koniev, Smorodinov, Sokolovskii and Chuikov, with others, were appointed Lieutenant-Generals of the Red Army. No less than 479 senior officers became Major-Generals, including A. I. Antonov, S. S. Biryuzov, A. M. Vasilevskii, D. D. Lelyushenko, K. K. Rokossovskii and F. I. Tolbukhin. Galler, Kuznetsov and Isakov of the naval high command were made Admirals; Tributs (Baltic Fleet) and Yumashev (Pacific Fleet) became Vice-admirals. Officers who had distinguished themselves in Finland were promoted and given responsible assignments — divisional commander Kirponos (whose 70th Rifle Division had done excellent work) became a Colonel-General and later took over the Leningrad Military District, Colonel Khrenov was promoted Lieutenant-General of Red Army Engineers, Colonel Lelyushenko became a Lieutenant-General of the armoured forces, Grendal' rose to Colonel-General of Artillery. The Far Eastern victors were not overlooked. Zhukov became a full general and took over the Kiev Special Military District. G. P. Kravchenko, an aviation major at Khalkhin-Gol, became a Lieutenant-General of Red Army Military Aviation, along with Zhigarev and Zhavoronkov.[117]

Order No. 160 of 16th May also summed up the principles of the new training programme for the Red Army. Combat training was to attain the maximum approximation to combat conditions and requirements. Red Army troops would be trained only in the things necessary for war and only in what they would be required to do on the battle-field. The basic principle must revolve about the absolute necessity to be in a state of 'complete combat readiness' to deal with any enemy. The command staff faced precise tasks; tactical training must be intensified, with special emphasis on 'difficult conditions'. Troops must be exercised by day and night, in all weathers, with hard physical exertion so that sections, units and formations could manœuvre on any terrain. The Red Army would have to learn how to dig in quickly and how to deal with surprise attacks. Timoshenko wanted an army which could fight like the Finns. This strenuous training programme obviously put military matters first. As such, it was a very purposeful attempt to redress the balance in the Red Army which had swung in favour of the Political Administration. The army was commissar-ridden. Voroshilov's picture of the commander and commissar as an 'integral unit' had turned out to be seriously distorted.

Intensive training would be backed up by iron discipline. A new Disciplinary Code was being prepared and was introduced in 1940; in this further round between socialism and militarism, the former now lost a great deal of ground. In 1935 the tendency to transform the officer corps into a caste had been plainly discernible. Although the 1940 Code still shrank from the term 'officer' ('commander' remaining in use), the differentiation of rank and demands for respect for rank were more sharply emphasised. The salute was re-introduced. Courts of Honour for officers (a device of the Imperial Russian Army) came back. Unconditional obedience was stipulated by Article 6; Article 8 required execution of orders 'without reservation, precisely and promptly'.[118] Soviet military discipline was to be 'higher, firmer and marked with severer and harsher requirements than discipline in other armies based upon class subjugation'. 'Fraternisation' between officers and men was over and done with; the 'liberal commander' who courted popularity was a danger to military efficiency, he was 'not a commander but a rag'.[119] The secret of Timoshenko's success in avoiding the all too obvious dangers inherent in any attempt at military reform in the Red Army — a head-on clash with Party and the *NKVD* — seems to have lain not only in the urgency of the situation (the case for reform was plainly undeniable) but also in the method he used. Timoshenko attacked the problem in reverse; although the over-politicalisation of the army was the basic fault, the new Defence Commissar laid down a positive policy of training and discipline. His exchanges with Stalin must have been frank, to say the least. A gale of recrimination had swept the higher levels of the command. The commissars were isolated but not excluded. In the last resort, it could be reduced to the fact that Stalin trusted Timoshenko as he had never trusted Tukhachevsky.

* * * *

With Timoshenko's reforms just beginning, in no sense could the Soviet Union be regarded as ready for war. Three years of degeneration could not be re-couped in a few weeks. For all the talk in Berlin by Astakhov about Soviet policy proceeding in a 'straight line' towards Germany, in the spring of 1939 there seemed to be a real zig-zag. Schulenburg in Moscow recorded the difficulties put in the way of smooth co-operation with Germany; this he put down to Soviet fears that too fervid a show of co-operation might call Soviet 'neutrality' into question. There was a real fear of being forced on some pretext into a large war by the Allies. The sudden termination of the Finnish War fitted into this explanation. Quite suddenly, with the German occupation of Norway, the Soviet attitude changed to one of smiling affability. It could only be assumed that the German invasion had removed the possibility of an Allied occupation, bringing war back into the Baltic. Germany relieved that fear — *Izvestiya*'s article on 11th April sounded like 'one big sigh of relief'.[120]

Shortly afterwards, however, Stalin had to draw in his breath sharply. On the day when the new training plan of the Red Army appeared, German tanks and dive-bombers were unleashing the fury of the *Blitzkrieg* on the Allied armies in France. The unbelievable began to happen. The French Army, in whose reputation Stalin had evidently believed, began to crack. Moscow resisted the unpalatable truth. *Pravda* and *Izvestiya* pinned their faith in an Allied counter-attack, in the military axiom that mechanised divisions did not decide the final result of the operations.[121] Soviet calculations had been based on the premise of a protracted war between Germany and the Allies. The collapse of France and the prospect of the subjugation of Great Britain shattered all this. Complete Allied success would not have served Stalin's interests, but so swift a German domination in the west produced another real fear, that of German attack on the Soviet Union.[122] Real military weakness inhibited Stalin from considering any active part in the war. But German commitments in the west offered a limited opportunity to consolidate still further those strategic frontiers which were being relentlessly sought. On 18th June Molotov offered Schulenburg 'warmest congratulations' on the 'splendid' success of German arms and in the next breath told him of a proposed Soviet action against the Baltic states. Whether the proposed incorporation of these countries in which Red Army garrisons were already stationed was prompted by a desire to forestall Germany or merely an opportunity seized to complete a strategic process begun earlier is difficult to decide.[123] In effect, both were accomplished. Not so long ago, apart from unforeseen difficulties over Finland, time appeared to have been almost entirely in Stalin's favour. If the war were to finish almost at once, then present Soviet opportunities must be exploited to the full. Soviet pressure was directed at once on Rumania and before June was out Red Army troops marched into not only Bessarabia but also Northern Bukovina. The Red Army had reached the Danube and Stalin had, with the incorporation of Northern Bukovina, actually over-stepped the line of partition drawn between Russian and German spheres of interest in August 1939. Russian forces were only a little more than a hundred miles from the Rumanian oil-fields. By sending in a mission to Rumania to assist in the evacuation of *Volksdeutsche* from the annexed provinces, Germany was able nevertheless to begin a process which settled a powerful military influence in Rumania.[124]

In the direction of the Soviet-German frontier strong Russian forces were being massed in the late summer of 1940.* 15 Rifle Divisions were deployed against Finland; there were a further 18–20 in the Baltic states and 22 in Poland. 15 Rifle Divisions, 9 Cavalry Divisions and 10 Mechanised Brigades had been moved into Bessarabia and Northern Bukovina. In the Kiev Special Military District, Zhukov had a force of 20 Rifle Divisions and 5 Cavalry Divisions, while Tyulenev in the Moscow Military District had 10 Rifle Divisions. Out of a total force of 151 Rifle Divisions, 32 Cavalry Divisions and 38 Mechanised Brigades the Japanese in the Far East tied down 34 Rifle and 8 Cavalry Divisions, Turkey required the attention of 6 Rifle Divisions and the Finns 15. The Main Military Soviet could therefore reckon with having at least 90 Rifle and 23 Cavalry Divisions plus 28 Mechanised Brigades for possible operations against Germany. There was, in addition, the threat posed by Soviet aviation.[125] Everything pointed to the existence of a severe tension within the Soviet command during the summer of 1940. By 1st August, in a speech on that date, Molotov summed up the Soviet view of the situation — Germany, in spite of great successes, had not attained her principal objective, 'the termination of the war on terms which she considers desirable.' It was a cool enough statement after the recent Soviet smash-and-grab raids, when tactics appeared to have wobbled into a set of desperate acts.

Although that was by no means an insignificant force assembled to defend the Western frontiers, recent German victories had shown up a method of warfare much in contrast with the present capacities of the Red Army. The new command was already putting the revised military programme into effect, although Shaposhnikov's hand was temporarily taken from the General Staff by a weakening in his health. In August 1940 Meretskov took Shaposhnikov's place for a short time. This change, not without some significance, was eclipsed however by the signal victory which Timoshenko contrived in bringing about the end of dual command. On 12th August unitary command was re-introduced and the Red Army commander became once again 'the sole leader of the fighting forces'. The reform was vital, accompanied as it was a little later by the diminution of the baleful influence of Mekhlis in the Political Administration. At least the influence of the incompetent braggarts had been weakened if not entirely removed.

* In what purports to be the story of a Soviet officer attached to the General Staff, there is an account of Shaposhnikov's attempts to provide a substantial military threat on Germany's eastern frontiers: the *NKVD* supplied Hitler with details of these plans in order to create further confusion in the German command. It remains, at least the part concerning Shaposhnikov, a plausible guess. See Ivan Krylov, *Soviet Staff Officer*, London 1951, pp. 11–23. In Karl Klee, *Dokumente zum Unternehmen 'Seelöwe'*, 'Die geplante deutsche Landung in England 1940', Musterschmidt-Verlag 1959, the only evidence of the Russian factor is taken from Halder. *Besprechung ObdH* (22/7/40), *ibid.*, p. 156, point 7 notes Stalin's 'flirtation' with England, Stalin's game of winning time 'to take what he wants' and his interest in not seeing Germany too strong. Concludes: 'Aber es liegen keine Anzeichen für russische Aktivität uns gegenüber vor.'

Timoshenko displayed his line of argument, and thereby the sort of talk which must have been instrumental in achieving this substantial concession, in mid-October; the training method hitherto adopted, Timoshenko bluntly announced, had been 'altogether wrong'. Nothing could be plainer than that. There was nothing wrong with either the Red Army's loyalty or its technique. But the real fault lay in the failure to master that technique; 'We are against an abstract approach! We are for individual initiative!'[126]

In spite of Timoshenko's disclaimer, there were indeed faults in the technique. After Lake Khasan and Khalkhin-Gol a draft of new *Field Service Regulations* had been made, only to be set aside once the war with Finland showed up the need for even more drastic revision.[127] In August 1940 a special commission took over the task of re-editing, and on 31st October this passed in turn to the Main Commission for Manuals and Regulations. Marshal Budenny was the president of this body, and the Deputy Chief of the General Staff Vatutin, Deputy Chief of the Main Artillery Administration Colonel-General Voronov, Deputy Chief of the Artillery Inspectorate Major-General Govorov, as well as the senior lecturer of the General Staff Academy Lieutenant-General Karbyshev were among its members. Before this new manual was completed, however, the Red Army found itself fighting for its life. Meanwhile the intensive training so recently introduced occupied a great deal of the senior commanders' attention. In all military districts troop exercises and officer training courses went on continuously and did effect some improvement. Timoshenko and his deputies, together with Meretskov and Vatutin, carried out rigorous inspections of the districts and the training methods used. The 70th (Leningrad), the 99th (Kiev), the 137th (Moscow) and the 20th (Trans-Caucasus) rifle divisions were singled out as exemplary formations. Timoshenko evidently found the 99th the best of all and presented its commander Vlasov with an inscribed gold watch.[128] Vlasov was an up and coming man.

While the Red Army attempted to improve its efficiency and decide its tactics, trying also to absorb all the experience purchased so expensively in Finland as well as the lessons demonstrated by the German Army in the west, a parallel effort was made to step up production and mobilise labour. Universal military service came into force in September. In the Aviation Industry Commissariat, where A. I. Shakhurin had taken over when M. M. Kaganovich was sacked earlier in the year, new brooms were hard at work. Both in performance and potentiality, Soviet military aviation had begun to droop. No real success marked Soviet attempts to obtain German prototypes for copying. New Soviet machines did exist, such as the Il–2 armoured ground-attack fighter, the LaGG–3 (of wooden construction), the prototype Yak–1 (I–26) and the MiG–3 — all equipped with the ShVAK

20-mm cannon and the ShKAS machine-gun — but no quantity of these machines had yet been produced. The situation with the new tanks was not dissimilar. Although the KV and T–34 models had appeared, the blight of obsolescence was creeping upon the huge Soviet tank-park. More than that, a frantic effort was being made to re-form the large tank groups, which had been broken down some time ago for distribution among the rifle divisions. German experience in the west showed how mistaken was the view that tanks could not perform independently on the battle-field. Shaposhnikov and Zhukov had been vindicated, although that hardly solved the problem of training and equipping the new formations.

The vital question had become the interpretation of German intentions. As a result of the re-shuffle in the military command, a greater element of realism had been admitted into the conduct of Red Army affairs. This far Stalin was willing to go, and even further to the introduction after September of an anti-German propaganda line in the Soviet forces. This the Germans took to be a recognition of the German intention to attack. Certainly an extremely intensive effort went into re-organising the Red Army, but it was a reform and not a mobilisation. In spite of German troop movements to the east, nothing was to be done until the following spring to erect fortifications in the forward line of the Baltic states. Nothing was done to increase the advanced air-fields upon which a proper deployment of the ground-support aircraft depended. It is doubtful if Red Army formations in the north-west were anywhere near full strength. The measures taken to increase production still fell short of real industrial mobilisation. As much as he sought to defer any decisive conflict, Stalin also fought shy of entry into any coalition. When Molotov visited Berlin in November, Soviet-German relations staggered into ill-concealed difficulties, but in the patched-up arrangement Moscow wriggled out of a suggestion that there should be Soviet adherence to the Axis.[129] Nor was there a neglect of Soviet affirmation of interest in the Balkans, where another barrier against Germany was slowly going up. Yet this game of infinite complication played by Stalin led to a nullification of advantages accruing to him. Although the western frontier was reinforced, the effective deployment of Soviet forces was interfered with to avoid giving 'the slightest provocation' to Hitler. The new equipment which the Red Army desperately needed was not expedited as it might have been. Therein lies the second charge made by the Red Army against Stalin. Working with his accomplices he had killed off many capable commanders who would now have been invaluable to the Red Army. The survivors he actively impeded in their attempts to provide a satisfactory defence for the Soviet frontiers.[130] The chances of an independent military line prevailing were small in the extreme. The purge was still a reality. Seventy senior officers, lodged in prison in Leningrad, were just on the point of being sentenced.[131] Below the *Politburo*, Timoshenko and his fellows might anticipate war, but anticipation fell far short of preparation.

★ ★ ★ ★

On 21st July Hitler, in discussing plans for the invasion of Britain, came to his central point that the latter was confirmed in her resistance by hope of Russia. For his part, Stalin dallied with the English to tie down Germany. Out of the hat of a supposed and strangely convenient Stalinist intrigue with the British, Hitler produced his strategic rabbit — 'tackling the Russian problem'.[132] To tackle meant to destroy, and a preliminary investigation of the possibilities of a campaign in Russia started. Four to six weeks would be required for the German assembly and 80–100 German divisions needed; it was first estimated that the Russians disposed of some 50–75 good divisions. Major-General Marcks, Chief of Staff of the 18th Army, worked out the first plan of campaign.[133] This envisaged the Russians adopting a defensive strategy and joining the blockade; their defence line would be designed to cover the Eastern Ukraine and the interior of European Russia. Forward of the Dnieper, the Red Army would fight only delaying actions. The German objectives would be to cut off the Red Army's retreat into the interior and to push the Russians back beyond the range of mounting air attacks from the east. On 3rd September General Paulus took over the planning from General Marcks and developed the study still further, utilising the results of a war-game in November to frame the very definite proposals for the campaign.

The transfer of German troops to the eastern border had begun in August; 10 infantry and 2 armoured divisions were moved to Poland, 'for the possibility of a necessary rapid action in the interest of a protection of the Rumanian oil fields.'[134] Köstring warned against any under-estimation of the Red Army; in spite of the superficial appearances of the Finnish war, that was not the true measure of Soviet military capacity. Improvements were being made, but Köstring estimated that four years would be needed to bring the Red Army back to its previous level. One salient disadvantage under which the Russians laboured was the difficulty they encountered in moving their motorised formations. On 18th September Halder and Colonel Kinzel (of *Fremde Heere Ost*) noted improvements in the training of lower Russian commands and operational staffs. By the end of November, Halder noted the increase in reports that the Russians were reckoning on war, as well as the fact that troop-training was being intensified. Nor had the Soviet troop concentrations escaped his attention.[135] Lecturing in the presence of Hitler at a *Reichskanzlei* conference on 5th December, Halder observed that to the north of the Pripet marshes a more favourable condition existed for large-scale movements than to the south. For that reason, the main German forces should be put forth north of the Marsh. Directive No. 21 *Operation Barbarossa,* issued from the Führer's Headquarters on 18th December, 1940, ordered the German Armed Forces to be prepared '. . . *to crush Soviet Russia in a quick campaign* (Operation Barbarossa) even before the conclusion of the war against England.' Preparations were to be completed by 15th May, 1941.

The Directive continued:

> I. *General Purpose*
> The mass of the Russian *Army* in Western Russia is to be destroyed in daring operations, by driving forward deep armoured wedges, and the retreat of units capable of combat into the vastness of Russian territory is to be prevented. . . . The ultimate objective of the operation is to establish a defence line against Asiatic Russia from a line running approximately from the Volga River to Archangel . . . the last industrial area left to Russia in the Urals can be eliminated by the Luftwaffe.[136]

Two Army Groups would operate on the northern sector of a zone of operations divided by the Pripet obstacle; '. . . the main effort will be made *north* of this area'. Only after the annihilation of enemy forces fighting in the Baltic and the seizure of Leningrad and Kronstadt, were '. . . the offensive operations aimed at the occupation of . . . Moscow to be pursued'. Army Group South would make its main effort 'in the area from Lublin in the general direction of Kiev'. On the basis of this directive Stalin had precisely 148 days left.

PART SIX

THE BEGINNING OF THE ORDEAL: 1941

The Russians can no longer be taken by surprise.

Graf Alfred von Schlieffen, November 1893.

It is generally known that the development of military art and technique is never so intense as in war. In war, all that is obsolete and ill-adapted to modern warfare is replaced by new and more perfected forms. The moral calibre of the belligerent armies and their adaptability to war conditions is heightened. In order to avoid lagging behind general progress, we need a system of military training which would harden our troops and enhance their combat efficiency. . . .

General of the Red Army G. Zhukov, February 1941.

. . . in the opinion of Soviet circles, rumours of Germany's intention to break the pact and begin an attack on the USSR are devoid of all foundation . . . rumours that the USSR is preparing for war with Germany are lies and provocations. . . .

Izvestiya, 14th June, 1941.

Tactical surprise of the enemy has apparently been achieved along the entire line. . . .

Generaloberst Halder, 22nd June (Sunday), 1941.

CHAPTER SEVENTEEN

'We are being fired on. What shall we do?'

For twenty years the Soviet Union had been preparing for war, ever demanding of its people a state of vigilance and preparedness which might thwart the long-awaited capitalist intervention. In the name of socialism and its suggested grandeurs, giant national sacrifices were demanded for a massive military programme. The influence of the military itself, however, had been sharply curtailed. As a potential rival it had been cut down and kept down. Stalin followed a course which indicated his willingness to accept every single condition which would guarantee the survival of his dictatorship, a rule applied to internal and external policy alike. The pact with Germany had removed one great nightmare, that the Soviet Union might find itself embroiled in war with Hitler's state while the Western maritime powers remained neutral. Great advantages fell to Stalin from an arrangement compounded of mutual perfidies. Party circles watched this apparent triumph as 'pupils proud of the virtuosity of their master'.[1] But now a disturbing paradox impinged itself upon the scene; the farther west that the Soviet frontiers were pushed, the more did that much desired 'security' appear to diminish. Through a combination of miscalculation and incompetence, military as well as political, the Soviet Union had already lumbered into a dangerous situation with Finland. Hitler's insistence that he desired no further war in the Baltic robbed the Russians of the opportunity to put Finland even more at their calculating mercy. Although the frontier had been advanced in the south-west, the German Army was rapidly investing Rumania. After the display of Soviet disquiet and German evasiveness during Molotov's November visit to Berlin, it was no longer possible to pretend that Soviet and German interests were not rampantly divergent in the Balkans. As late as the autumn of 1940 Stalin might have argued that national, military and Party interests coincided generally in his particular arrangements with Germany. The contrived neutralist position meant that the regime would not be subjected to the strain of a general war. The pact had permitted the Soviet Union to recover the old strategic frontiers enjoyed by Imperial Russia, and these victories — with the exception of Finland — could well be counted almost bloodless ones. German assistance was at hand to carry out the complicated tasks involved in building up a powerful navy. The armaments industry benefited from the acquisition of German machinery. But gun-turrets for battleships and shell-producing machinery were no compensation for the passivity which was being forced on Stalin's policy. The Soviet press greeted with official joy the conclusion of a further Soviet-German Trade Agreement, signed on 10th January, 1941, and dealing with reciprocal deliveries. Ten days later Molotov informed Schulenburg that '. . . it would now be in order to turn to purely political issues again'. Turning to the concentration of German troops 'in great numbers' in Rumania, and their readiness to march into Bulgaria, to occupy that country together with Greece and the Straits (a move which the British would try to forestall), Molotov found it necessary to point out that the appearance of any foreign troops in Bulgaria or at the Straits would be 'a violation of the security interests of the USSR'.[2]

The 'purely political issues' which Molotov was anxious to raise concerned the terms of the Soviet-German agreement. The conditions submitted by Moscow for any participation in the Four Power Pact suggested that Stalin would give full freedom to Hitler in the west only if conditions making for a successful prosecution of a war by Germany on the Soviet Union were rubbed out. German troops were to be withdrawn from Finland, Soviet security in the Straits would be guaranteed by a pact with Bulgaria and the grant of bases within range of the Bosphorus and the Dardanelles, the primacy of Soviet interests to the south of Batum and Baku would be clearly recognised, and Japanese claims to coal and oil concessions in Northern Sakhalin were to be waived. If these conditions had been accepted (and the very posing of them was a test of Hitler's intentions), Stalin would have locked up the door to Leningrad, barred the Balkan gate and at the same time have access to the Mediterranean secured. The claim to an exclusive Soviet primacy 'in the general direction of the Persian Gulf' cut the Germans off from control of the oil which they much needed. It was on 17th January that Schulenburg heard the pointed remark of the Soviet Government being 'surprised' at the absence of a reply to these propositions; the Soviet Government 'was counting on an early German reply'.[3] A reply of sorts Hitler had delivered in the course of the Naval Conference of 8th January, when he described Stalin as 'a cold-blooded blackmailer'. If Stalin had deliberately posed these demands as a test of intentions, the subsequent evasive tactics could come only as a confirmation of the worst fears. However fascinated Stalin was by his own cunning, there were other facts which needed serious attention. While German troops were coiling more thickly about the Soviet flanks, in Washington Sumner Welles received from 'sources . . . unquestionably authentic' information that Hitler had decided upon invasion of the Soviet Union in the spring. Soviet Ambassador Umansky was informed of this, and paled visibly at the news.[4] That it was passed to Moscow cannot be doubted, and on 20th March the Soviet Government requested that the information be repeated in a conversation between Sumner Welles and Umansky.[5] To receive warnings, however, was something different from heeding them. In this lies the major Soviet difficulty in explaining that what Hitler sprang upon the Soviet Union had been anticipated yet it was also a catastrophic surprise.[6] The foolish conundrum is used to salvage some reputation from the abysmal result, to retrieve an alibi from a situation in which '. . . Stalin and his commissars showed themselves to be the most completely outwitted bunglers'[7] of the Second World War.

* * * *

Among those commissars were the military and naval chiefs, whose task it was to effect the radical re-organisation of the Red Army and the expansion of the Navy, in order to advance the Soviet forces to a greater combat efficiency. This needed time, but it also required talent. There were, essentially, four major tasks facing Timoshenko and his fellows in dealing with the Red Army: re-organisation, a thorough over-haul of the training programme, the vital question of re-equipping and the equally important question of the re-deployment of Soviet forces in the light of alterations in the frontiers. Soviet military writing affirms the existence of a General Staff plan, but this itself does not mean a co-ordinated military policy. As for 'strategy' and doctrine, Stalin had taken the formulation of these into his own hands. The idea of strategic surprise had been consigned to a kind of Stalinist perdition; war was not considered an immediate possibility.[8] The Red Army had also to recover from that serious blunder, the disbanding of the tank formations. As the rifle division was being streamlined to an establishment in the region of 14,500, hasty assembling of tank and mechanised formations was taking place. Into the five frontier military districts, the new T–34 and KV tanks began their trickle only in April–May, 1941; by June, only 1,475 had arrived (508 KV models, 967 T–34s). 73 per cent of the older machines — BT–5, BT–2, T–28, T–35, T–37, T–38 — were undergoing major or secondary repairs (29 per cent major overhaul).[9] The new formations lacked training as much as tanks; driver-mechanics had had only 1½–2 hours experience of tank-driving, and the command staff lacked, for the most part, any real training in the handling of tank and motorised units. Neither quantity nor quality, therefore, properly distinguished the Soviet tank forces. Even in 1935 theories of *blitzkrieg* warfare had been scorned by Soviet military theorists, but this had not precluded a recognition of the independent role which the tank might play on the battlefield. But 1935 was far away, and the bulk of the armour had been split up among the rifle divisions as infantry support.

In February a change of some significance was effected in the high command. Zhukov, friend and protégé of Timoshenko, displaced Meretskov as

THE RE-ORGANISED RIFLE CORPS AND THE RE-CONSTITUTED MECHANISED CORPS: 1940-1941

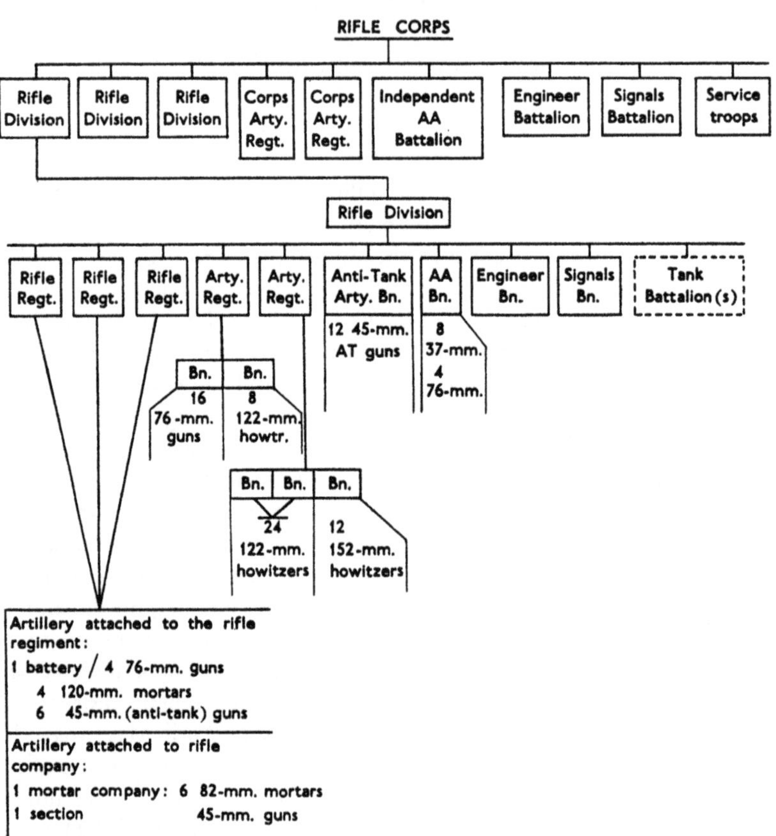

Chief of the General Staff. Kirponos came from Leningrad to take over Zhukov's command in Kiev. Zhukov's appointment coincided with a critical period in the Red Army's affairs. Consequently, some of the blame for the inadequate state of the Soviet defences has been displaced on to his shoulders.[10] It is open to question whether this is just or is merely a political convenience. There were high and forbidding barriers standing in the way of establishing a proper solution to military problems, and how much freedom Zhukov possessed is difficult to assess. What is clear is that the Soviet command had embarked on the re-organisation of the defences of the western frontier, which was now based, from the Barents to the Black Sea, on five military districts — Leningrad, the Baltic Special, the Western Special, the Kiev Special and the Odessa Military Districts. Headquarters of the Special Military Districts were at Riga, Minsk and Kiev. This added one more concentration area — Riga — to the two which Voroshilov had specified to the French and British Missions in 1939. In time of war, three Fronts would be fashioned out of the Special Districts:* the North-Western, the Western and the South-Western. Leningrad would form the Northern and Odessa the Southern Front. The plan of operations, finally drawn up by May, envisaged the five districts taking the brunt of the enemy attack, thus permitting the main body of the Red Army to be mobilised and concentrated. The Soviet General Staff was calculating on the fact that in 'a few days' the frontier districts could be fully manned. In 1939 Shaposhnikov had indicated that full mobilisation and concentration would require 8–20 days. It was therefore to be a battle for the frontiers, in so far that the first stage of a future war was foreseen. Under these circumstances a great deal depended on the proper deployment of the forces in the key western military districts, on an effective mobilisation plan efficiently managed and on the organisation of reserves. In theory at least, and this was to be Stalin's subsequent argument, the Red Army derived a great advantage in taking enemy blows, not on the old line running from Odessa-Kamenev-Podolsk-Minsk-Leningrad, but from Kishinev-Lwow-Brest-Litovsk-Bialystok-Kaunas-Vipurii.[11] How much that advantage was frittered away is disclosed by the state of affairs on this new line.

Before the 1939 pact Soviet frontier forces (which came under *NKVD* control) had been maintained in a state of immediate readiness, with a three-week supply of ammunition, fuel and food.[12] Shaposhnikov informed the British and French officers that fortified areas could be fully manned in 4–6 hours. After the agreement with Germany Stalin apparently lowered his guard. The frontier commands (of which there were eleven, each under the equivalent of a divisional commander) were taken off a state of immediate readiness, having finally only three days' supply allotted to them. As for the preparation of new defence lines, things seem to have gone somewhat awry. In the Baltic states work had begun on frontier fortifications in August 1940, only to be suspended until the spring of 1941 (the harsh winter of 1940–1

* The designation 'Special' was introduced to the west in 1940. Special District and Area Armies appeared to be operational groupings, capable of carrying out operations of limited duration without the mobilisation of extra reserves. A District Army was more of an administrative organisation.

having forced some delay). The new naval bases, which had fallen to the Soviet Navy by the territorial seizures of the summer of 1940, were by no means ready. Having paid such a heavy price for the revised frontiers with Finland, the net result of what had so far been done in the way of fortification and setting up prepared positions remained only 'very weak' defences. The Keksholm and Viipuri fortified districts were not ready — positions were not camouflaged, not properly connected up for signals and not fitted out for the use of field troops. Stalin had made much of the need to close the Gulf of Finland by batteries operating from the northern as well as the southern shore; as yet no proper co-ordination had been established with the coastal batteries on the southern shore.[13]

Serious enough in itself, this failure to capitalise on the advantages of the new line had enormous consequences in the light of the plan for the defence of Leningrad drawn up by the Soviet command. In the event of war in the region of Leningrad, the forces of the Leningrad Military District would form the Northern Front, with the task of holding the most important approaches to Leningrad on the Finnish frontier to the north. A small force made up of a few regiments was to be deployed along the southern shore of the Gulf of Finland to deal with attempted enemy landings. The Baltic Fleet was also committed to denying the Gulf of Riga and the Gulf of Finland to enemy ships and invasion forces. The fixation over attack from Finland left one other possibility — that an enemy force might drive on Leningrad from the south-west — completely out of the calculations.[14] The number of troops available to cover the south-western approaches to Leningrad was therefore dependent on successfully solving the problem of the defence of the Gulf coast-line, which in turn depended on the Special Baltic Military District, and the assumption that the enemy would choose the route apparently covered by the latter in the north-west. The Special Military District contrived out of the Baltic states was responsible for the defence of the southern and south-western shores of the Gulf of Finland, for the bases at Ösel and Dagö, for covering the coast of the Baltic from Riga to Memel and the frontier of Soviet Lithuania with East Prussia; to the north-west of Grodno (at Kopzovo) was the line of demarcation with the Western Military District. As for prepared positions, work had begun on field fortifications running from Kaunas in a north-westerly direction along the River Dubissa and at a second line in the region of Panevezys, presumably designed to cover the junction of Daugavpils (Dvinsk), and provide a position before the River Dvina. The construction of reinforced concrete block-houses had evidently just begun with the spring of 1941.[15]

In March the German command was informed of the noticeable increase in the troop movements in the Western and Baltic Military Districts.[16]

Tanks and infantry were moving into Lithuania, mostly towards Riga. From the Moscow Military District troops were being moved up to Minsk and Smolensk as a reinforcement to the western frontier. In the Western Military District, under the command of General of the Red Army D. G. Pavlov were four Soviet armies apparently deployed to a depth of 250 kilometres. The Western district had a frontage of 450 kilometres, running from north-west of Grodno to Vlodava, where the line of demarcation was set with Kirponos's Kiev District command. While the German eye —

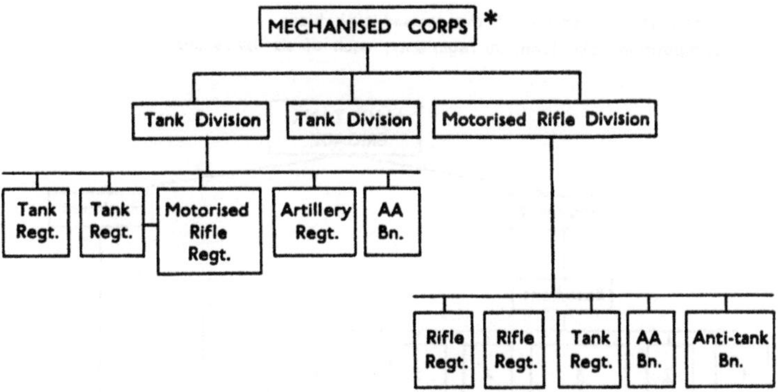

* This type of organisation was adopted during the second stage of the re-organisation of the armoured forces, that is, from March-June, 1941. During this period the few tank corps were retained (15th Tank Corps/ Special Western MD and the 10th Tank Corps/Kiev MD)

a reconnoitring eye kept open by frequent air penetrations — discerned some strengthening of the frontier forces, what was in fact happening on the Soviet side was still far from satisfactory. The rifle divisions which were being moved in were not up to strength (which fell in some cases as low as 6,000) nor were they properly deployed.[17] Pavlov's command, to which was assigned the task of covering the mobilisation, concentration and deployment of the Red Army in Belorussia, was no exception to the prevailing conditions. Pavlov's first echelon consisted of rifle divisions belonging to the covering armies (the 3rd, 10th and 4th, disposed in that order from north to south), with a second echelon built up of mechanised formations. The deployment, such as it was, was designed to cover the approaches to Minsk and Bobruisk, as well as to secure the frontier. Air support would be supplied by the aviation divisions attached to the armies operating in the military district. Right on the frontier were the frontier troops, while the main strength of the first echelon was drawn back as far as forty kilometres, with the second some hundred kilometres still further to the rear. Also at the frontier were engineer troops at work on field fortifications, a labour to which some rifle units of the first echelon were also assigned. Battalion defence positions were being prepared but were not much advanced. At Minsk and Bobruisk were the fortified areas dating back from the period of the old Soviet-Polish frontier. Other urgent matters required attention.

PLANNED ANTI-TANK BRIGADE OF THE ARTILLERY RESERVE OF THE HIGH COMMAND (ARGK)

Function: the repulse of the massed tank blow.
Composition: two identical regiments, each of six battalions.

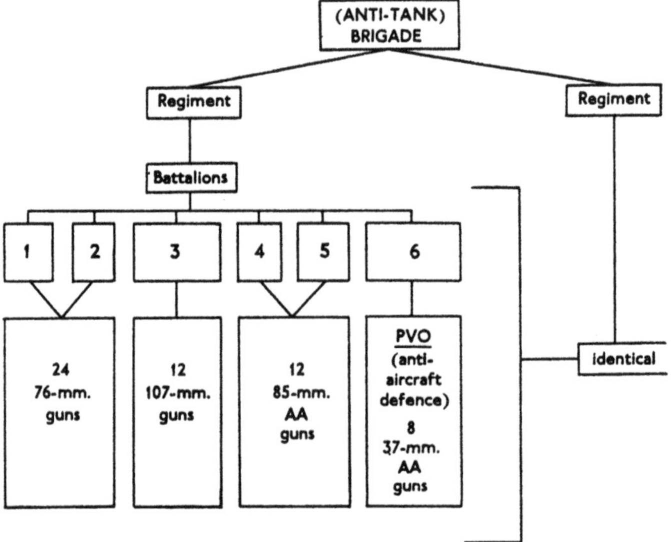

These diagrams are based on the information in *Ist. Velik. Otechest. Voiny Sov. Soyuza 1941-1945*, Vol. 1, Moscow 1960, pp. 456-457

More air-fields were needed. Signal centres had to be set up. Although the broad-gauge railway had been extended since the frontier changes, carrying capacity remained at a low level. The re-equipping of the Red Army inevitably created a certain amount of confusion, even though the quantity of new tanks and aircraft reaching the district was still 'insignificant'.[18]

Nevertheless, from mid-March the Germans were taking account of what appeared to be a preparation for mobilisation on the Baltic coast and a partial mobilisation on the western border.[19] At a time when the situation in the Balkans had deteriorated sharply, some concessions were evidently made to the military point of view. Bulgaria defected from the Slav camp, and German troops entered the country. Timoshenko, who at the end of February spoke of the need for constant readiness to face any surprise attack, was credited with having adopted an aggressive attitude in the face of this further German move.[20] A state of great nervousness came upon Moscow as the crisis in the Balkans advanced. Dissatisfaction over the outcome in Bulgaria was communicated to Sofia, although not directly to Berlin.[21] The German advance into Bulgaria made some kind of Soviet move towards Turkey an immediate necessity; a German-Turkish agreement might well have placed German troops in a very favourable position to mount a blow at the Caucasus. From Molotov the Turkish Minister in Moscow received an assurance of Soviet neutrality in the event of Turkey becoming involved in war with a third power (Germany and her allies). The official communiqué of 25th March which confirmed this relieved the Turks of the fear that Soviet-German complicity might reduce them to the position of the Poles in 1939. But German pressure smashed a possible British-Turkish-Greek united front in the Balkans, a defeat which was of consequence for the Soviet Union also.[22] On the night of 26th–27th March a *coup* in Belgrade threw out the Yugoslav Regency and the Government which had signed its adherence to the Tripartite Pact the previous day. Germany demanded the submission already pledged; the Yugoslav Minister in Moscow Gavrilović (who had in the latter half of 1940 tried to win Soviet support) was informed by Belgrade that a Soviet military convention had been offered.[23] On the evening of 4th April Schulenburg heard from Molotov that the Soviet Union would accept the Yugoslav offer of a non-aggression pact, to be signed almost at once. But on 5th the Yugoslavs learned from Vyshinsky — and it was significant that Molotov did not handle the negotiations — that no military convention had been offered. Only after a desperate fight were the Yugoslavs able to obtain a Russian undertaking that in the event of war not neutrality but 'friendly relations' would prevail. The pact was signed in the early hours of 6th April but dated 5th.[24] To have dated it 6th would have been an open challenge to the Germans, for it was also very early on 6th when the German *blitzkrieg* swept forward into Yugoslavia and Greece.

Farther than a treaty, which accorded some satisfaction to those who demanded an active policy, Stalin would not go. It did not commit him to any breach of his neutralist policy; as in the dead days with Czechoslovakia, the lack of a common frontier provided a useful alibi for inaction. When on 6th Schulenburg gave Molotov official news of the German attack, the Soviet-Yugoslav Pact was simply not mentioned. In spite of indicating its resistance to the encroachments, Moscow had been unable to deflect German advances deep into its declared 'security zone'. War was manifestly not a particle of Stalin's policy, and misadventure in the Balkans failed to shake his intention of neutrality toward Germany.[25] The military, within the limits open to them, took not quite so complacent a view; on 10th April Timoshenko ordered an alert and an increase in the military preparations of units in the west.[26] Although on 11th April *Fremde Heere Ost* signalled the purely defensive aspect of the Russian front,[27] Halder on 7th had been moved to observe that the Russian dispositions 'provoke thought', the rather uncongenial thought that Soviet troops were so disposed as to be able to pass over to the offensive at short notice.[28] On the other hand, they could be taken to mean that the Red Army would make its main defence near the frontier. To consider the possibility of a Soviet offensive was justified if only as a matter of precaution,[29] although any significant signs of this were patently lacking. It was Soviet nervousness rather than aggressiveness which was most marked.

There is no reason to doubt Soviet assertions that the Red Army was in possession of adequate intelligence of German troop movements and concentrations by the border.[30] From the reports of commanders of the military districts facing the frontiers, from the foreign press and 'other sources' it was known that in 'the spring or summer of 1941' Hitler would launch an offensive against the Soviet Union.[31] The April alert in the west might therefore be regarded as a significant measure. 'Other sources' included British as well as American intimations of Hitler's intentions. In London Eden gave Ambassador Maisky* certain warnings, and on 19th April in Moscow Sir Stafford Cripps finally passed on to Vyshinsky the significant details of German troop movements which indicated Hitler's ultimate intentions. On 23rd Vyshinsky informed Cripps that the details supplied by Churchill had been passed to Stalin.[32] (Six months later Stalin was to dismiss this warning with a shrug and the comment that '. . . I did not need any warnings. I knew war would come, but I thought I might gain another six months or so.')[33] The considerable problem remains, therefore, to establish why industry was not placed in a greater state of readiness. A form of industrial mobilisation had already been carried out, and an attempt made to increase productivity, but the new weapons were evidently

* On 13th June, Maisky was informed that in the event of a German attack, Great Britain would be prepared to send a military mission to Moscow and to consider urgent economic needs. The Joint Intelligence Committee produced on 14th June a report dealing with the possible effects of a Russo-German war; Soviet forces were assessed as large, but handicapped by much obsolete equipment, lack of initiative, fear of taking responsibility and bad maintenance. The Chiefs of Staff on 12th June decided to arrange for British heavy and medium bombers to operate against Baku from Mosul. Already at the end of May a possible threat to the Soviet oil-fields in the south had been considered as a means of applying pressure on Russia to refuse concessions to Germany. (See further in J. R. M. Butler, *Grand Strategy*, Vol. II, pp. 542–4.)

not yet reaching the Red Army in any significant quantity. 'The mass output' of military equipment had not as yet been organised, but Voznesenskii speaks of a Soviet precautionary measure 'prior to war' involving a 'mobilisation plan' for ammunition which was scheduled for the second half of 1941 and 1942.[34] The industrial mobilisation plan dealt also with the assignment of special technological missions to plants, and the stockpiling of materials and semi-manufactured items essential for war production in what Voznesenskii calls 'the mobilisation reserves'. The armaments industry was made up of specialised plants, the location of which made it clear that the Red Army was very dependent on factories not as yet strategically dispersed. Infantry weapons came from 30 plants (producing an estimated 50,000 rifles and 6,000 machine-guns per month), the most important being in Tula, Izhevsk, Kovrov, Taganrog, Nizhni Tagil and Zlatoust. Gun-barrels came from Dniepropetrovsk, Mariupol and Kolomna. Infantry ammunition was supplied by 14 plants (estimated monthly production — 60 million rounds of small arms ammunition) and artillery ammunition from 50 factories (17 of which were in Leningrad). Tanks were produced in 42 factories sited in Central Russia, the Urals, Leningrad, Kharkov and Stalingrad. Of the 46 aircraft plants, the three main fuselage building centres were in Moscow; the four principal aero-engine plants were in Moscow, Zaporozhe, Rybinsk and Molotov (in the Urals[35]). Moscow, Leningrad and major industrial centres in the Ukraine were still of paramount importance in the armaments industry.

Khrushchev has himself exposed just how inadequate these precautionary moves were, charging Stalin and his administrators with a failure to carry out a proper and timely mobilisation of industry. Like Voznesenskii, he admits that no mass production of artillery and tanks existed. The mammoth orders for machinery from Germany had already suggested a serious Soviet lack of it. Both old and new machinery was lacking in sufficient quantity. Not enough anti-aircraft guns were being produced; in fact the position was 'especially bad'. Nor was the production of anti-tank ammunition 'organised'.[36] That Soviet industry as a whole was suffering from marked shortcomings could be seen in the attempts of the 18th Party Conference, which met from 15th–20th February, to bring about some improvement. Nevertheless, the precautionary move or the draft mobilisation plan, designed to come into effect as late as 1942, suggests that war was not considered to be an immediate possibility. That such moves were made at all would support the view that war was considered inevitable, with only general notions of what this might imply, although presumably the Soviet Union would have been ready for war by the summer of 1942. The situation, however, was rapidly overtaking what planning there was. The Red Army training programmes for 1941 summer exercises contained evidently no variant that war might occur,[37] although the testimony of Lieutenant-Colonel Tokaev is to the effect that on 16th April General Klokov of the Political Administration made it known to a select group of officers that war was expected 'at any moment' and that the Red Army should not be taken 'unawares'.[38]

The military command, it would appear, had carried out the most rapid re-adjustment to the threats which now lay with much less concealment about the developments of the early spring of 1941. To say that they possessed accurate and valuable intelligence of the German movements would do no damage to truth. But whether they grasped at the import of the German designs or were even uniformly aware of what attack would bring is another matter. Although considerations of strategic defence and withdrawal were 'most weak' in Soviet military doctrine,[39] this had not precluded the working out of a planned defence in depth while Tukhachevsky was in control, evidence of which came from the so-called 'Stalin line'. The problem had been to prevent the development of a threat to the Moscow-Kharkov communications until the mobilisation of the Red Army was complete. In the north, where swamp and forest predominated, the defence problem was easier, but to protect the Ukraine remained a difficult problem. The Dnieper was one barrier in the south, but if that were seized there remained few natural obstacles to impede an advance towards the industrial centres of the Donets basin. Holding the Kiev region would present a threat to an advance on Kharkov; manning the Stalin line west of Kiev with strong forces would mean contributing to both the defence of Moscow and that of the Ukraine. The long line of the western frontier was broken by formidable natural obstacles which favoured the Russian defence, although requiring strong fortification at vital points and the prompt manning of these defences. The Stalin line had been made especially strong in the southern sector and was manned by the pick of the Red Army.[40] Now, in order to invest the new frontier, large forces were being moved forward to the west of the Stalin line, uncovering the main defences in a manner which suggested that an integrated strategic plan simply did not exist. Events would shortly prove that the reaction of the Soviet command to what news it had of German concentrations on the western frontiers had not been to work out any comprehensive scheme of defence. This would suggest an ultimate disbelief in the possibility of a German attack, or the incapacity to prepare such a plan. Soviet opinion presently puts the blame squarely on Stalin. Although Stalin's blunders and abuse of a vast personal power contributed enormously to the fatal outcome, this alibi inflated to gross proportions still does not account for the shortcomings of the military command. It may well be that an ultimate offensive design was being harboured.[41] That, however, could only be carried through at a date yet to be determined and was dependent upon conditions beyond any immediate control. It presupposed a strength and efficiency which the Red Army as yet lacked and was likely to lack for some time, and bore only very indirectly on solving problems connected with immediate dangers.

* * * *

Already Stalin was in receipt of British and American warnings about Hitler's intentions and preparations. What effect these had can only be surmised, but a former Soviet Intelligence officer, Major Ismail Akhmedov, has testified to the fate met by one of Soviet Military Intelligence's own reports. In April a Czech agent by the name of Shkvor reported confirmation of German troop concentrations and the fact that the Skoda works had been ordered by Berlin to halve deliveries of equipment to the Soviet Union. Submitted to the *Politburo*, Stalin wrote in red ink the decision that this was merely 'an English provocation'. The perpetrator of this 'provocation' was to be sought out and punished. Major Akhmedov found himself assigned to this mission and duly travelled to Berlin as 'Georgi Nikolayev'. Arriving at the end of May, the major subsequently took part in the transmission of information on 21st June that war would begin on 22nd. Dekanozov, former *NKVD* chief in Tiflis and now Soviet Ambassador in Berlin, chose not to believe this information and while ordering his intelligence officers to 'forget it', suggested that they join a picnic party next day.[42] It was upon men like Dekanozov that Stalin relied, and indeed why not? He had picked them himself.

Precisely what secret Stalinist game of attempted deception the Beria-Dekanozov element played is quite hidden away. What is abundantly plain is Stalin's attempt to bribe Hitler with exemplary deliveries of food and raw materials from the Soviet Union,[43] which would also help to encourage deliveries of German equipment to assist the armaments programme. This costly scheme was destined to fail, but Stalin had other cards to play. The Yugoslav *débâcle* had precipitated great nervousness both in Moscow and on the western frontiers. At a time when the genuineness of German intentions seems to have been more widely doubted in Soviet circles, Stalin carried through what he must have considered as another of the master-strokes of his diplomacy — the Neutrality Pact with Japan, signed with Matsuoka on 13th April. Stalin seized the occasion of the signing, at a time when rumour of Soviet-German conflict had reached a new peak, to demonstrate his friendly intentions towards Germany. Stalin and Molotov appeared at the railway station from which Matsuoka was taking his departure, to wish the Japanese traveller a pleasant journey. Such considered courtesy included Stalin's request to be presented to Schulenburg and his pointed statement, 'We must remain friends and you must do everything to that end!' To Colonel Krebs, acting Military Attaché, Stalin likewise distributed the favour of his public friendship, having 'first made sure that he was a German', adding, 'We will remain friends with you — in any event.'[44] To the Italian Ambassador, Matsuoka confided that Stalin had assured him of his adherence to the Axis and his opposition to England and America.[45] This was a comforting if misleading statement and well Matsuoka must have known it. Stalin gained the removal of any immediate Japanese threat to the Far Eastern borders, without committing himself — except by a kind of quasi-adherence — to the Axis and without giving Japan an outright guarantee that Soviet support to China would be withdrawn. If Stalin needed Japanese neutrality as the German threat pressed him more closely, so did Japan require Soviet passivity before launching itself against the democratic powers in the Far East. Stalin provided no supplementary agreement. Almost at once the Japanese newspaper *Hochi* attacked the Soviet Government for its refusal to join the Axis and castigated Moscow for gambling on the eventual exhaustion of the partners.[46] Even as the first Japanese disillusionment was setting in, Red Army troops were being transferred from the Far East to European Russia.

The crisis, however, had by no means receded, although with the rapid German military successes in the Balkans, Berlin noticed a 'return of Russia to the previous correct attitude'. Reporting to Hitler in Berlin, Ambassador Schulenburg took great pains to indicate the path of conciliation which the Russians were treading. Schulenburg 'could not believe that Russia would ever attack Germany' and affirmed his conviction that Stalin 'was prepared to make even further concessions to us'.[47] Concentrations of Soviet divisions in the Baltic states could be ascribed to 'the well-known Russian urge for 300 per cent security'. That urge did not extend to exploring alternatives, for the important corollary of confidence in Berlin (albeit of a peculiar nature) remained acute mistrust of London and also Washington; that denied to Soviet policy any possibility of large-scale manœuvre. Until the beginning of May military and diplomatic methods had very generally kept pace with each other, both in tempo being extremely cautious. On 1st May Stalin's and Timoshenko's public statements stressed the maintaining of an aloofness from war with the need to prepare for any eventualities. Stalin took care to maintain Red Army morale, without giving it occasion for extravagant hopes.[48] On 6th May, in a very dramatic move, Stalin himself took over from Molotov the chairmanship of *Sovnarkom*, retaining Molotov as deputy and as Commissar for Foreign Affairs. This singular move was recognised as an attempt to bring Soviet-German relations back on to their regular course. It was an act, reported Schulenburg, of 'extraordinary importance'. Shock at the magnitude of German successes in Yugoslavia and Greece, and divisions of opinion among the military leaders and *Politburo* necessitated Stalin's personal assumption of real and formal control.[49] It signified not the end of concessions but a renewed attempt to placate Germany with even more. At the May Day review the man standing directly next to Stalin was observed to be the Soviet Ambassador in Berlin, Dekanozov, who early in June returned to his post, charged presumably with seeing that Stalin's will was done. The Soviet condemnations refer to the Stalin who held in his hands 'the highest direction of the nation and the Party', so that criticisms of his policy over preparing the Soviet Union for the war which was being planned in Germany may be taken to apply from May onwards. Khrushchev asserts that the leadership was 'conditioned' against information confirming German offensive intentions, and that 'such data was dispatched with fear and assessed with reservation'.[50] On the day on which Stalin took over the direction of the government, 6th May, the Soviet Military Attaché in Berlin Captain Vorontsov reported that Soviet citizen Bozer intimated to the deputy naval attaché that a German attack was scheduled for 14th May, and would take place through Finland and the Baltic states, with heavy paratroop landings in the border areas and raids on Leningrad and Moscow.[51] On 22nd May the deputy military attaché in Berlin, Khlopov, signalled that the German attack was scheduled for 15th June, but 'it is possible that it may begin in the first days of June'.[52]

Stalin's attitude was compounded of complacency, confidence and a form of precautionary nervousness which defeated its own objects. The dismissing of warnings emanating from British and American sources would have its roots in disposing of anything which might impede a further Soviet-German compromise. In explaining Stalin's order that no credence should be given to information about a German attack, Khrushchev asserts that this was done 'in order not to provoke the initiation of military operations'. That would presumably refer to the possibility of an 'accidental war' being triggered off by excessive Soviet zeal in dealing with the tense situation; air activity on both sides had steadily increased during the spring.[53] Troops from the Urals and the Far East were being moved up towards the western frontiers, destined for the Dnieper and Western Dvina,[54] but none of this was being effected with any undue haste. The subdued mobilisation (which could be connected with the summer manœuvres) was itself no unmitigated advantage; the drafts assigned to formations in the frontier areas lacked 'even basic training'[55] in the use of the weapons they would employ. Not one of the basic measures of reform and re-organisation had been completed among the troops stationed in the western frontier districts.[56] According to Khrushchev, some of the fortified districts were actually without any means of defence, since the old weapons were being withdrawn and the new ones had not yet been issued.[57] There could have been no illusions about the fitness of the command staff to wage a modern war on a very extensive scale. The Red Army had not yet recovered from the effects of the purge, which had made such disastrous inroads upon the numbers of trained and experienced officers available. Allied to this debilitation was the weakness imposed by the lack of flexibility in the command, possibly the gravest weakness of all. Reporting from Moscow, Colonel Krebs, German assistant military attaché, found the Soviet higher command decidedly bad, and compared with 1933, the picture was depressing.[58]

What the Military Soviet had achieved, however, was an unmistakable increase in the forces allotted to the western frontier areas, a process which had gone on for an initial period in the spring of 1941 up to the early days in April and then entered a second phase after the middle of May and continued into June. Now armour was being separated from the infantry at long last, although only a handful of tank and mechanised formations had been assembled by May. On 20th May, 1941, the German Army was of the opinion that it was facing in the western frontier areas 121 rifle divisions, 21 cavalry divisions, 5 formations equivalent to armoured divisions and 33 armoured brigades; for further deployment the Red Army also disposed of 11 rifle divisions, 3½ cavalry divisions and 1 armoured brigade.[59] Just as the length of the front caused important modifications in the German plans, so did it appear that the Red Army would avoid frittering away its strength and would concentrate on building up defensive zones. Three main Russian concentrations had already made their appearance; these were in the Baltic states, to the west of Minsk and by Bialystok, and on both sides of the Lwow-Berdichev-Kiev line in the Ukraine. Of these three concentrations, the last two were of major importance and size. Stronger operational reserves were to be observed in the area Shepetovka-Proskurov-Zhitomir, south-west of Minsk and about Pskov. It was impossible for the Red Army to consider adopting the strategy of 1812, being committed to holding the naval and air bases in the Baltic and on the southern flank of the Black Sea and being also dependent on the industries of Leningrad, Moscow and the Ukraine. Soviet strategy could be considered defensive in nature, and although the concentrations on the frontier might be designed merely as deceptions and a means of political pressure, a quick re-deployment appeared to be out of the question in view of the Russian weakness in signals and communications as well as the rigidity of the command. German reconnaissance revealed no evidence of transport preparations for any such re-deployment.

There was also the possibility of a preventive offensive to be considered. This the German Army held to be an unlikely event, since the Soviet high command knew the weaknesses of its own army and since out of political considerations the Russians had not taken advantage of previous German weakness. The course of such an offensive, should it take place, would almost certainly be from the direction of Czernovits-Lwow into Rumania, Hungary and Eastern Galicia, with a supporting operation from Belorussia to Warsaw and East Prussia.[60] What the German Army expected may well have been envisaged in theory by the Soviet command — a strong defence near the frontier, which would involve limited attacks at the beginning of the operations with counter-attacks where the enemy broke through the covering troops. To the rear more powerful and more mobile groups would be utilised to attack the flanks of the German armoured spear-heads; if the Red Army were finally forced back, it would sell its space for time and gather for a final stand on the Dnieper-Dvina line. But this presupposed a definite plan. The Red Army appeared to be caught in a trap of its own making, caught 'between adequate positional and manœuvre strategies.'[61] Soviet accounts make it very clear how undeveloped were the positional fortifications which should have been ready. Also the concentrated deployment near the frontiers could only make manœuvre very difficult. There were very strong forces in the Bialystok-Volkovysk-Brest triangle and nearer Minsk, much stronger than might be suggested by armies *de couverture*. The Soviet command may well have expected the main German drive to develop from the Lublin-Yassy line towards Kiev, in which case they may have anticipated the possibility of striking at the rear of the Lublin forces. On the other hand, the very shape of the new frontiers acquired by the Soviet Union placed an excessive and constricted concentration in some considerable danger in a line from Kobrin to Augustovo. But this is speaking of the concentrations as if they were complete. For whatever purpose they were being assembled, it is clear that they could accomplish nothing, since their assembly was neither organised nor completed. The blame for this is laid upon the requirement of Stalin that no 'provocation' be supplied to the Germans. Divisions had only a few units holding a broad front, or one regiment in position with the main force kept back in barracks or camps some 5–12 miles away. The main forces in the interior of the frontier military districts had, according to one account, been pulled back to distances varying from 150–500 kilometres.[62]

That there was real interference with the business of organising a proper defence of the frontiers Khrushchev purports to show from the case of Kirponos, the able commander of the Kiev Special Military District. At a date specified only as 'shortly before the invasion', Kirponos wrote to

Stalin informing him that the German armies were at the River Bug (where Kirponos had deployed the 5th and 6th Red armies). Kirponos was of the opinion that a German offensive would soon take place and therefore proposed measures for the strengthening of the defences. 300,000 people should be evacuated from the border areas, prepared positions and anti-tank obstacles ought to be set up and made ready. For his pains Kirponos received a reply that this would be a 'provocation', that no preparatory work was to be undertaken at the frontiers and the Germans were to be given no '. . . pretext for the initiation of military action against us.'[63] In Kiev, then, the possibility of a German attack was taken very seriously, and it is some comment on the tightness of the straitjacket into which the Red Army had been thrust that Kirponos should have to consult Stalin over border defences.

Lieutenant-General Vorob'ev adduces the role of 'taking the war into the enemy's territory' as being a powerful inhibition to working out practical defence plans, since offensivism was 'widely diffused'.[64] Nowhere was this better illustrated than over the question of the defence of the Black Sea naval bases. Vorob'ev is of the opinion that Soviet military theory had worked out a doctrine of modern defence which was on the right lines. This applied also to the ideas on the defence of naval bases, which must be defended by the close co-operation of land, sea and air forces. The defence should be deeply echeloned and become progressively stronger with the depth of the defences. Massed artillery and aviation would be employed against strong tank thrusts. The timely preparation of a bridge-head in the region of the base would guarantee the solidity of the defence and the supply of the garrison. Although worked out on paper, these ideas were not realised in practice. In 1941 the Black Sea naval bases, like all the other naval bases, lacked a scheme of land and air defence. Exercises carried out in 1940–1 to test the Black Sea defences, using both land and sea forces, showed that the main base of Sevastopol needed greater security against possible assault by parachute troops and a better system of air-raid warning. Nevertheless the opinion prevailed that the command of the sea exercised by the Black Sea Fleet and the organisation of the coast defence fully secured the bases against attack from the sea. The possibility of an enemy attack on the bases from the land or in the rear was scarcely considered at all.[65] Odessa lacked any defences from the landward approach. Three batteries of coast-defence guns were designed to frustrate enemy landings — a total of 54 guns ranging from 45-mm to 203-mm. The air defence was entrusted to a number of anti-aircraft batteries, one aviation regiment of 20–40 ageing aircraft and 3 flights of Black Sea Fleet naval aviation.[66] The fortification of Odessa began only on 12th July, when the threat from the land had become terribly real.

To attribute to Stalin's final, almost fatal blunders the full responsibility for the weakening at the Soviet frontiers is a distortion deliberate enough to serve present Soviet political purposes and touched with a melodramatic tint to conceal the basic crisis of the system. Basically Stalin's method did not encourage independence of mind in any field. The Red Army and its command was shot through with the failings of the Stalinist system. To assist in preserving that same regime, thousands of officers had been eliminated, and with them had been eliminated their talents and services. It is problematical whether any consistent plan for the defence of the Soviet Union existed even at this late hour. The proposed industrial mobilisation lagged visibly behind the actual requirements of the Red Army. Only 16–17 per cent of the Soviet Air Force had been re-equipped with the new machines.[67] (In February a German estimate set the figures of new machines at 400 out of the total of 3,000 Soviet fighters.)[68] There were certainly schemes for the defence of areas and particular points. Two of them at least, those for Leningrad and the Black Sea bases, excluded all but the most obvious possibilities and the simplest eventualities. There were signs that the issue of quality and quantity was once again troubling the Soviet command; up to 1937 a particular synthesis had been achieved by Tukhachevsky and his officers and there had been signs of an elite army emerging from the mass. Timoshenko now aimed at infusing quality into the Red Army by the introduction of conventional forms of discipline and realistic training. The haste with which tank and mechanised formations were being assembled affirmed that the Red Army command was moving back, admittedly with hesitations and delays, to the criteria which had prevailed before 1937–8. But it was the idea of mass which still predominated, although the requirements were not being fully met, because they were politically inconvenient and economically awkward. The leadership was failing to adhere to 'its own operational requirements'.[69]

* * * *

The thaw came late to Western Russia after the winter. The weather, in combination with the late arrival of the armour which had been employed in the Balkans, caused the initial date set for *Barbarossa* to be set back. The time table for the maximum massing of troops on the Soviet frontiers went into operation on 22nd May.[70] *Aufmarsch Ost* would be represented as a deception exercise connected with the invasion of England. The German Army in the east assembled itself into three large groups: Army Group North (facing the Baltic Military District), Army Group Centre (concentrated against the Western Military District) and Army Group South (running from Vlodava to the mouth of the Danube, and augmented with

Rumanian divisions). On the northern flank of the German armies was the Finnish Army and four German divisions, deployed from the northern shore of the Gulf of Finland to Petsamo. To destroy the Red Army west of the Dnieper, allowing them no escape into the interior, was a condition of both success and safety. The Army High Command considered the northern operational theatre, north of the Pripet Marshes, to be of outstanding importance, for there the German Army might strike ultimately at Moscow. The southern theatre, where the Russians might barricade themselves behind the Dnieper, was less vital. Out of Hitler's choice of primary objectives in Leningrad and the Ukraine, and that of the High Command for Moscow, a compromise plan envisaged seizing the line Leningrad-Orsha-Dnieper, after which the further conduct of operations would be considered.[71] Even upon a first estimate of Russian strength (which was later found to be too small), the German Army knew itself to be outnumbered, not only in men but in machines.*

Covering the frontiers the Red Army had 13 armies from the Barents to the Black Sea. In the Leningrad Military District, running from north of Narva on the Gulf of Finland to Polyarnoe, the 23rd Army held the Vipurii fortified district, the 7th north of Lake Ladoga and the 14th the Murmansk sector. The Leningrad District disposed of some 19 rifle divisions, 3 mechanised brigades, and a mechanised corps in the neighbourhood of Leningrad itself. In the Baltic Special Military District, covered on the frontier by the 8th and 11th armies, were a minimum of 28 divisions and over 1,000 tanks. South of Pskov the second echelon was grouped, with the 27th Army stationed about the Western Dvina. Pavlov's western frontier command disposed of the 3rd, 10th and 4th armies to cover the frontier, with strong forces by Bialystok and Minsk. To each of the covering armies was attached a mechanised corps, but these were not by any means properly concentrated. To cover the frontier of the Kiev Special Military District, Kirponos deployed the 5th, 6th, 26th and 12th armies from Vlodava to Lipkany, with the divisions of the mechanised corps attached to the armies and the 15th Mechanised Corps subordinated to the front command. The two primary Russian concentrations were to be found in the region and to the west of Minsk and in the Ukraine, although the concentration and deployment was not yet completed. By mid-June 10–15 large armoured formations had

* Much is made in Soviet military writing that the Red Army in 1941 was exposed to an enemy enjoying superiority in tanks, in the air and in combat experience. Even now Col. B. S. Telpukhovskii (*op. cit.*, p. 38) gives the combined German and satellite strength as 5 million officers and men, 32,000 guns and mortars, *over 9,000 tanks* and 5,000 aircraft. It can be reckoned, however, that the Red Army enjoyed a superiority of 30 divisions over the Germans and Finns (but excluding the Rumanian armies, Italian corps, etc.). In tanks, taking Stalin's own figure for Soviet sources, the Soviet superiority was at least 7:1. In aircraft, the *Luftwaffe* was outnumbered on the Eastern Front by 4–5: 1.

been assembled and more could be expected within a short space of time.* The mobile operational reserves for the covering armies, which in the western district consisted of a mechanised corps, were very shortly to be exposed as hopelessly inadequate. As for strategic reserves, there is no evidence that any real plan for these as yet existed. The 9th army of the Odessa Military District completed the chain of armies to the south.[72]

As what was so soon to become a gigantic battle-front filled out with forces on both sides, Stalin persisted with his struggle to maintain the peace which slipped swiftly from his grasp. On the day when Hitler assembled his commanders to make his final explanation of the reasons for his Russian venture and to check upon the preparations, *Izvestiya* published what amounted to an invitation to discuss further terms. Stalin was of the opinion that Germany would not attack the Soviet Union in the very near future.[73] The announcement insisted that '. . . according to Soviet data Germany, like the USSR, is also strictly observing the stipulations of the Soviet-German non-aggression pact . . . in the opinion of Soviet circles, rumours of Germany's intention to break the pact and open an attack on the USSR are devoid of all foundation'. 'Lies and provocations' were rumours that the Soviet Union was preparing to attack Germany. 'Clumsy fabrications' were the rumours predicting war between the states. The Soviet Union 'intends to observe the provisions of the Soviet-German non-aggression pact'.[74] This profession of misplaced faith is now universally condemned by Soviet publicists as Stalin's miscalculation. Versions of what actually developed on the frontier itself at this time are most uncommon in Soviet explanations, but one account implicates (not unnaturally) Beria of the *NKVD*, chief of the frontier guards who kept the frontier. Soviet observation posts kept track of German movements; from the Western Bug frontier troops reported on the nightly increases in German artillery. Agents brought

* In addition to the Mechanised Corps and Tank Brigades in the Red Army, since 1940 Tank or Armoured Divisions (2 Tank Regiments, 1 Motorised Rifle Regiment, 1 Artillery Regiment: tank strength, 400) were being introduced. 2 Tank Divisions, 1 Motorised Rifle Division made up a Tank Corps: the Motorised Rifle Division resembled the tank division, but with its ratio of tank and rifle units reversed. Although the figure of 400 tanks is accepted as the maximum for a Soviet tank division, there are references to divisional strength (before action) falling to 280; Soviet sources make this clearly a consequence of the difficulties with re-equipping, so that the complement of BT machines might be met but not that of T-34 and KV machines. Stalin himself recounted that the Soviet tank strength in June 1941 was 24,000 machines organised into 60 tank divisions (or brigades). The Soviet aim was the creation of 20 Tank Corps, but this became an impossible target. Soviet accounts leave no doubt that great confusion attended the organisation and equipping of the armoured forces in the summer of 1941, and there are signal discrepancies in numbers as well as terminology. On 2nd July, 1941, Soviet tank strength was entered in the *Halder Diary* (VI: p. 194) as 15,000 machines in 35 tank divisions, 22 of which had been identified; by the end of 1941 the Germans had identified 65. The divisional organisation was abandoned by the Red Army by October 1941 and replaced by the brigade. See the discussion in Richard M. Ogorkiewicz, *Armour*, 'The development of mechanised forces and their equipment', London 1960, pp. 97–106.

more information. Villagers added to the information so amassed. This was reported without delay to Moscow and personally to Beria, from whom, however, issued only some 'routine order: "Intensify observation".' Soviet frontier troops also intercepted German agents attempting to obtain information about Red Army garrisons, and on 21st June intercepted persons in the neighbourhood of the Brest fortress disguised as Soviet soldiers.[75] Whether that last detail is true remains doubtful, but there can be no doubt that a very considerable body of information had reached Stalin, the Red Army and the *NKVD* about German preparations. Of German intentions, there is no doubt that multiple warnings — from Soviet and non-Soviet sources — were given. On 18th June the Soviet Embassy in London cabled that Sir Stafford Cripps (re-called to London for consultations earlier) was 'deeply convinced' of the inevitability of war, and set the date as 'not later than the middle of June'.[76] Troops still continued with their normal routine. Nothing changed in their political instruction. The frontier troops and the forces of the special military districts received no special orders.

Not until the very final hours of a peace becoming more and more insecure with every minute of its passing did the Red Army command make up its mind that an attack was pending. Reports of this eventuality had been coming in for weeks; from the frontier had come the visual sightings of the *NKVD* frontier guards, from Soviet Military Intelligence more reports, and from non-Soviet sources the warnings about German intentions earlier in the year. In spite of the massacre visited on Soviet Military Intelligence and its agents in 1937–8, the organisation had struggled once more to its feet and was supplying valuable information. In Switzerland, Soviet intelligence had come by the dates involved in the *Operation Barbarossa* timetable.[77] On the night of 21st June, the date on which Soviet Military Intelligence in Berlin had transmitted one more report that the invasion would begin on 22nd, 'a certain German citizen' crossed the border and stated that the German attack was timed for 3 a.m., on 22nd June.[78] (H-hour for *Operation Barbarossa* had in fact been set for 0330 hours on 22nd.) At this final stimulus to belated realisation, Timoshenko and Kuznetsov took steps to alert the Red Army and Navy. At midnight on 21st June, Vice-Admiral F. E. Oktyabrskii and his Chief of Staff Rear-Admiral I. D. Eliseyev received in Sevastopol a signal from the Naval Commissariat ordering a higher state of readiness. The same signal would presumably have gone out to Kronstadt and the northern bases. The Black Sea Fleet had just finished its exercises. Naval aircraft had returned to their aerodromes, ships and submarines to their usual positions in Sevastopol naval base. The practice black-out had been lifted; ships' crews were already ashore. Oktyabrskii ordered at once a 'General Muster', re-imposition of the black-out and the manning of anti-aircraft and coastal defence batteries with readiness to open fire. The Red Army was less fortunate. At about midnight on 21st Timoshenko sent out warning telegrams to the staffs of the military districts, ordering a state of combat readiness for a German offensive expected at dawn on 22nd.[79] The Red Army had therefore some 180 minutes in which to prepare itself to meet the most formidable fighting machine in the world.

Shortly after midnight the Berlin-Moscow international express passed quite normally through Brest-Litovsk. Soon after 2 a.m., General Guderian, who had personally observed on 21st the unoccupied Russian defences on the eastern bank of the River Bug, went to his command post. The German troops awaiting H-hour watched the tail-lights of *Luftwaffe* aircraft vanish as they headed east over the frontier on their way to bomb targets in the Soviet rear. With sky very gradually beginning to lighten after the short summer night, tanks, artillery, infantry and dive-bombers waited away the last few minutes before they fell upon the Red Army.

* * * *

Along almost the entire length of the vast front the German Army achieved tactical surprise. To the south of Brest-Litovsk the bridges over the Bug were intact and undefended. Soviet troops were caught in their camps and barracks. With its aircraft trapped on the ground, the Soviet Air Force suffered grievous initial loss as the *Luftwaffe* worked its destruction. The field fortifications, either incomplete or unmanned, were quickly pierced by German troops. German Army Group Centre intercepted plaintive and desperate Russian wireless signals: 'We are being fired on. What shall we do?', to which their headquarters replied with asperity and reprimand — 'You must be insane. And why is your signal not in code?'[80] German bombers struck at Soviet towns, communication centres, rear installations and naval bases before the Soviet radio made any announcement of war or military operations. At 7.15 a.m., the first order from the Red Army command was sent out dealing with the new situation. It reads very strangely. After reporting air and ground attacks since 4 a.m., the order prescribes:

1. With all their strength and means troops will attack enemy forces and liquidate them in the areas where they have violated the Soviet frontier.
   Unless given special authorisation ground troops will not cross the frontier.
2. Reconnaissance and combat aviation will establish the locations of enemy aviation concentrations and the disposition of his ground forces. With powerful bomber and ground-attack blows [Soviet] aviation will destroy aircraft on enemy aerodromes and bomb the basic groupings of enemy ground forces.

Aviation blows will be mounted to a depth of 100–150 kilometres into German territory.
Königsberg and Memel will be bombed.
There will be no flights over the territory of Finland and Rumania without special instruction.[81]

Strength and Deployment of German Army for 'Barbarossa'

1.	Distribution of forces for 'Barbarossa' on invasion day (less the formations under the command of Military Commander Norway) *N.C.A. (VI): C–39* 80 Infantry Divisions 1 Cavalry Division 17 Armoured Divisions 12 Infantry Divisions (Motorised) 9 Line of Communications Divisions 2 Formations of the 15th Wave 2 Infantry Divisions as Army Reserves. Air Fleets 1, 2, 4.
2.	Deployment *Army Group North* (Field Marshal von Leeb) 18th Army: 16th Army: Fourth Armoured Group (Hoepner) 21 Infantry Divisions, 3 Armoured Divisions, 3 Motorised Divisions. (Finnish Army: 16 Finnish divisions, 4 German divisions) *Army Group Centre* (Field Marshal von Bock) 9th Army: 4th Army: Third Armoured Group (Hoth): Second Armoured Group (Guderian) 30 Infantry Divisions, 9 Armoured Divisions, 7 Motorised Divisions, 1 Cavalry Division. *Army Group South* (Field Marshal von Rundstedt) 6th Army: 17th Army: First Armoured Group (von Kleist). Italian and Hungarian corps, Slovak division, Croat regiment. 25 Infantry Divisions, 5 Armoured Divisions, 3 Motorised Divisions, 4 Mountain Infantry Divisions (11th German-Rumanian Army: 3rd and 4th Rumanian Armies)

A Soviet analysis of the German deployment and military organisation is included in *V.M.V.*, pp. 136–43.
Zhilin, *op. cit.*, p. 25 sets the figure of German tanks at 3,950, more realistic than other Soviet exaggerations.

Organisation of Soviet Frontier Armies: June, 1941

Military District	*Command*	*Frontier Armies*	
LENINGRAD East of Narva Bay, Leningrad, Karelian Isthmus, Soviet-Finnish frontier northwards	Commander: Lt.-Gen. M. M. Popov	14th Army Lt.-Gen. V. A. Frolov	Belomorsk-Murmansk
	Chief of Staff: Maj.-Gen. D. N. Nikishev	7th Army Lt.-Gen. F. D. Gorolenko	N and NE Lake Ladoga
NORTHERN FRONT with hostilities HQ: Leningrad	Commissar: Corps Commissar N. N. Klement'ev/ Political Administration of Military District	23rd Army Lt.-Gen. P. S. Pshennikov	Vipurii-Keksholm. Incl. 10th Mech. Corps on Karelian Isthmus. Note: 10th Mech. Corps (all but 198th Mot. RD) and 70th Rifle Corps transferred to Baltic 27/6/ 1941. Estimated total strength: Up to 19 RDs (not concentrated in 7th Army) 1 Mech. Corps 3 Mech. Brigades.
BALTIC (Special) S and SW shore of Gulf of Finland, defence of Dago, Ösel, Riga Bay to Memel, 300 km. of frontier with E. Prussia	Commander: Col.-Gen. F. I. Kuznetsov	8th Army Maj.-Gen. P. P. Sobennikov	3rd Mech. Corps
	Chief of Staff: Lt.-Gen. P. S. Klenov	11th Army Lt.-Gen. V. I. Morozov	
	Commissar: Corps Commissar P. A. Dibrov	27th Army Maj.-Gen. N. Berzarin	Not a covering army. Under-strength. Advanced to the Dvina.
HQ: Riga NORTH-WESTERN FRONT with hostilities			Second Echelon: Pechory-Pskov-Ostrov. incl. 1st Mech. Corps (1st and 3rd Tank Divs.) 163 Mot. RD, 25th, 30th Cavalry Divs. Estimated total strength: 28 RDs 3 Mech. Corps 4 Cav. Divs. 7 Mech. Brigades 1,000 tanks

[*continued*]

Organisation of Soviet Frontier Armies: June, 1941 (continued)

Military Districts	*Command*	*Frontier Armies*	
WESTERN (Special)	Commander: Army General D. G. Pavlov	3rd Army Lt.-Gen. V. I. Kuznetsov	Grodno
Kopzovo-Vlodava	Chief of Staff: Maj.-Gen. V. E. Klimovskii	10th Army Maj.-Gen. K. D. Golubev	Bialystok
450 km front HQ: Minsk	Commissar: Corps Commissar A. Ya. Fominyi	4th Army Maj.-Gen. A. A. Korobkov	Brest-Litovsk-Pinsk
WESTERN FRONT with hostilities	Deputy Front Commander: Lt.-Gen. V. I. Boldin	Mech. Corps as mobile reserves 11th Mech. Corps/3rd Army Maj.-Gen. A. K. Mostovenko 6th Mech. Corps/10th Army Maj.-Gen. M. G. Khazkelevich (SW of Bialystok) 13th Mech. Corps Maj.-Gen. P. N. Akhlyustin. In region of Bielsk: deficient in tanks. Operated with 10th Army 14th Mech. Corps Maj.-Gen. S. I. Oborin In Pruszany-Kobrin area Note: 6th, 11th Mech. Corps and 6 Cav. Corps (Maj.-Gen. I. S. Nikitin) operated as Mixed Cav.-Mech. Group/3rd and 10th Armies/Sokotki-Lunna area under V. I. Boldin	13th Army: Minsk Lt.-Gen. P. M. Filatov (44th, 2nd Rifle Corps) 7th and 5th Mech. Corps: Bobruisk Interior armies: 13th, 16th, 21st, 22nd Army: Vitebsk, Lt.-Gen. F. A. Yershakov 6 Divs: no tanks or aviation 20th Army Estimated strength for frontier defences: 32 RDs 8 Mech. Corps 2 Cav. Corps (6 Cav. Divs.)
KIEV (Special)	Commander: Col.-Gen. M. P. Kirponos	5th Army Maj.-Gen. of Tank Troops M. I. Potapov	Lutsk
Vlodava-Mogilev-Podolskii	Chief of Staff: Lt.-Gen. M. A. Purkayev	6th Army Lt.-Gen. I. N. Muzychenko	Lwow
HQ: Kiev/Zhitomir	Commissar: Div. Commissar P. E. Rykov	26th Army Lt.-Gen. F. Ya. Kostenko	Borislav

Organisation of Soviet Frontier Armies: June, 1941 (continued)

Military District	*Command*	*Frontier Armies*	
SOUTH-WESTERN FRONT with hostilities		12th Army Maj.-Gen. P. G. Ponedelin	Kamenets-Podolskii/ Czernovits
		Mech. Corps attached to armies: 22 Mech. Corps (5th Army)	Zhitomir Reserve: 19th, 9th Mech. Corps and one rifle corps
		4th Mech Corps (left wing 6th Army)	Proskurov reserve
		15th Mech. Corps (under front command.) 40–120 km. from frontier:	
		Radekhov-Ostrog area	
		8th Mech. Corps (26th Army) 400 km. from frontier	
		Note: 22/6 8th Mech. Corps detached from 26th Army. Ordered to Brody. Used with 15th Mech., 36th and 37th Rifle Corps	
ODESSA Kamenets-Podolskii to Danube mouth. HQ: Odessa-Kishinev SOUTHERN FRONT with hostilities	Commander: Army General I. V. Tyulenev	9th Army (re-grouped after 22nd June) 18th Army	47th Rifle Corps 35th Rifle Corps 2nd Cav. Corps (9th 5th, 72nd Cav. Divs 15th Mot. RD) 2nd, 16th, 18th Mech Corps: Czernovits and Tiraspol Odessa coastal defence forces
Crimea		9th Independent Rifle Corps)	

Soviet statement of strength of first echelon of nine covering armies: 40 Rifle Divisions, 2 Cavalry Divisions.

Average frontage per division: 50 kilometres (on the Prut and in the Carpathians, this became 100–120 kilometres). The regulations laid down a frontage of 8–12 kilometres. Where fortified districts (URs) existed, the frontage was set at 25–30 kilometres, but the URs in the frontier regions were not finished: the field fortifications amounted to only a single line of battalion districts.

Concentration of Soviet Forces along the Line of Advance of German Armoured Groups: Valid to the Morning of 22nd June, 1941

Armoured Groups	*Composition of first echelon*	*Frontage in kilometres*	*Soviet formations on the frontier in the area of Armoured Group offensive*
FOURTH	1st, 6th, 8th *Panzer* Divs. (600 AFVs) 290th, 268th Infantry Divisions	40	125th Rifle Division
THIRD	7th, 12th, 20th *Panzer* Divs. (over 600 AFVs)	50	128th Rifle Division, one regiment of the 188th Rifle Division
SECOND	3rd, 4th, 17th, 18th *Panzer* Divs. (over 800 AFVs)	70	Elements of the 6th, 42nd, 75th Rifle Divisions, 22nd Tank Division (not in state of readiness).
FIRST	299th, 111th, 75th, 57th, 298th, 44th Infantry Divisions*	65	87th, 124th Rifle Divisions

Taken from:

Table, derived from Soviet Defence Ministry archive, *Ist. Velik. Otechest. Voiny Sov. Soyuza 1941–1945*, Moscow 1960, Vol. 1, p. 474. The German strength figures are as presented in this work.

* a footnote to the table, pointing out that in the First Armoured Group the *Panzer* divisions (up to 600 tanks) were distributed directly to the infantry divisions in the first echelon.

Khrushchev again lays the blame on Stalin for thinking that even now Germany intended no war, but that this was merely some insubordination of the German Army. Only at noon was the Soviet Union's entry into war announced over the radio, so that for some six or seven hours a last desperate act of disbelief was performed by Stalin; the strange first order to the Red Army does not mention war, only 'unprecedented aggression'. The point about not crossing the frontier was the final irony in the whole absurdly incorrect estimate of what was happening.

On the Western and North-western Fronts (formed out of the Western and Baltic Special Military Districts) a catastrophic situation developed with terrible rapidity. Having caught Soviet aircraft on their aerodromes,* the *Luftwaffe* flayed the Russian units attempting to assemble for resistance. Since the main strength of many formations in both districts had been held back at some distances, the disorganised forces made nightmare approach marches under this aerial lash. The 3rd Red army under Lieutenant-General V. I. Kuznetsov, holding the right flank of the Western Front, found itself at once in grievous difficulties. Hammered by three divisions of the German VIII Corps, the 56th Rifle Regiment of the 3rd Army fell back to the south-east; the 85th and 27th Rifle Divisions (3rd Army) also fell back, taking up positions on 23rd June to the south and south-west of Grodno. On the left flank of the Western Front, held by the 4th Army, the 49th, 42nd, 6th and 75th Rifle Divisions likewise made to retire. An attempt to assemble the 14th Mechanised Corps (under Major-General S. I. Oborin) in the area of Prushany-Kobrin for a counter-attack failed. The forcing back of 4th Army troops put the 10th Army, holding the centre, in a serious position even on the very first day. The 13th Mechanised Corps under Major-General P. N. Akhlyustin — short of tanks, fuel and ammunition — found itself heavily engaged, and was forced to pull back. The left flank of the 10th Army was heavily pierced; contact was lost with the 4th Army and nothing was known of what was happening in the Brest-Baranovichi direction. Red Army General Pavlov, Front commander, had almost lost control of the situation. On the evening of 22nd, he ordered the 3rd and 10th Army commanders to mount on 23rd a counter-attack with two mechanised and one cavalry corps from south of Grodno, driving north to take the enemy in the flank. The 6th, 11th Mechanised Corps and the 6th Cavalry Corps were accordingly placed under Lieutenant-General I. V. Boldin and formed into a mixed mechanised-cavalry group. But only the 11th Mechanised Corps of Major-General D. K. Mostovenko — attached to 3rd Army — was at the place required. The 6th Mechanised Corps (10th Army) had first to cover some forty-five kilometres, as must the divisions

* By 24th June, Soviet Air Force losses were estimated at 2,000 aircraft.

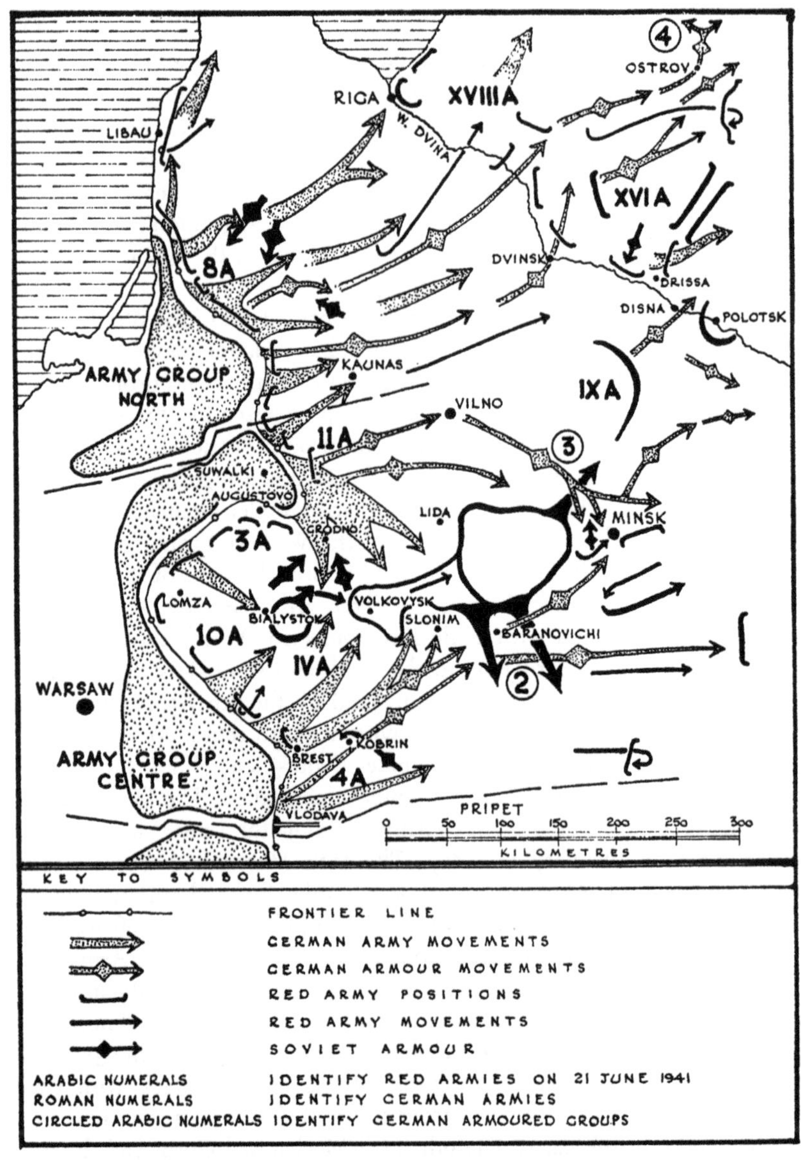

THE BREACHING OF THE WESTERN AND NORTH-WESTERN FRONTIERS

Situation 21 June - 9 July, 1941

of the 6th Cavalry Corps. On the morning of 23rd, only the 11th Mechanised was in position; that morning the *Luftwaffe* caught the 6th Mechanised on the march and the 36th Division of the 6th Cavalry Corps. Both were badly battered. On 24th, the 6th and 11th Mechanised Corps staged their attack, which exhausted itself on 25th, when losses, punishment at the hands of German anti-tank and aviation forces, as well as shortage of fuel and ammunition became too much. General Pavlov's Western Front command began to break into pieces. Contact between the Front staff and the armies fighting at the frontier was frequently lost. No precise information could be obtained about developments on the flanks and in the rear. The signals and supply services rapidly succumbed to disorganisation and chaos; supplies of fuel and ammunition all too often failed. Moreover Pavlov blundered with what arrangements he could make. The Soviet troops to the north-west of Minsk were ordered to move on Lida and were assigned attack missions. This uncovered Minsk to the German forces which had taken Vilna and were driving in the direction of Molodechno-Minsk; meanwhile the 4th Army retired further to the east, having been badly mauled. By Baranovichi the 155th and 121st Rifle Divisions met up with the 143rd, but lacking any unified command, were unable to establish any firm defensive line.

By the evening of 23rd June the Third Armoured Group of Army Group Centre had punched a gap some 130 kilometres wide between the Russian North-western and Western Fronts. At the border on the North-western Front the Fourth Armoured Group had struck at the junction of the 8th and 11th Soviet armies. To restore the situation, the Front command ordered a counter-attack with three tank divisions operating from the south-west of Shauljai and from the east of Rossieni. The attack failed. Soviet troops were forced to retire in a north-easterly direction towards the Western Dvina, uncovering the approach to Dvinsk. The attempt to build up an organised defence from the second echelon of the covering armies on the right bank of the Dvina, between Liwani and Kraslawa, and to use the troops retiring north-eastwards to organise a defence from the mouth of the Dvina to Liwani, met with little success. German troops forced a crossing of the Dvina, and the retirement of the Red Army opened up the Ostrov-Pskov-Luga-Leningrad passages. The right wing of the North-western Front fell back to cover the Riga-Narva-Leningrad line. Almost by the hour the situation deteriorated. Such defence plans as had existed took no account of precisely that threat which was now shaping up with such urgency against Leningrad — a drive from the south-west. On the Northern Front (formed out of the Leningrad Military District), all available forces were concentrated on the Karelian Isthmus and northwards along the Soviet-Finnish frontier. As German pressure continued unabated towards the end of June, with Lithuania and Latvia being wrenched out of the Red Army's grasp, the Northern Front was about to be called upon to fill in the dangerous gap which yawned before Leningrad. Yet lacking any effective reserves, the Northern Front could scarcely meet its existing commitments. The Northern Front was about to be extended to a line from Pskov-Novgorod to meet up with the battered North-western Front.[82] This was merely the introduction to catastrophe.

At the other end of the front, where Field Marshal von Rundstedt's Army Group South, which included General von Kleist's First Armoured Group, had begun operations on 22nd June against the Kiev Special Military District, the Red Army was engaged in agonising battles to check the German thrusts. The weight of the German attack fell upon the left wing, with Kiev as the objective. At once the 5th and 6th Red armies were involved in heavy fighting on what was now Kirponos's South-western Front. Offensives against the 26th and 12th Armies had not yet materialised; in the Odessa Military District, Tyulenev's 9th Army formed itself into the Southern Front. Kirponos quickly took action to organise counter-attacks to check the German advance against his right flank. To the north-east and north-west of Rovno the 19th and 9th Mechanised Corps were moved up from the interior, together with a rifle corps. The 8th Mechanised Corps (detached from the 26th Army), and the 37th Rifle Corps (advanced from the interior) were moved on Brody. For the Rovno area attacks, however, no unified command was established. Already the 22nd Mechanised Corps (5th Army) had suffered heavy losses in counter-attack and fallen back on the River Styr. The 15th Mechanised Corps, attacking from 22nd June in the direction of Radekhov (north-east of Lwow), failed to achieve any substantial success and fell victim to the *Luftwaffe*. Only on 25th did advance units of the 8th Mechanised Corps reach Brody after a 400-kilometre march; on 26th the corps went into action, but lacked contact with other formations and again the *Luftwaffe* tore much of the formation to pieces. Returning to the defensive, the sorely-tried 8th was ordered on 27th to move towards Dubno. The 9th and 19th Mechanised Corps had begun their move towards the front on 22nd–23rd June, getting into action on 25th. The combined forces of the mechanised corps had been intended to strike co-ordinated blows at German spear-heads in the area of Lutsk, Brody, and Dubno, and to restore the situation created by a German irruption at the junction of the 5th and 6th Armies. Halder on 26th June recorded the Russian leadership on this front as 'energetic', mounting flank and frontal attacks, slowing down the German advance and causing heavy losses.[83] On 28th June, Halder recorded the Russian 8th Mechanised Corps as advancing *behind* the German 16th and 11th Divisions.[84] Not only the *Luftwaffe* and von Kleist's tanks did all the damage. Corps Commissar Vashugin, ordered by Kirponos to mount a counter-attack with one and a half tank divisions taken from Vlasov's 4th Corps, took the tanks into a swamp, where they had to be abandoned. Vashugin committed suicide.[85] Fuel, ammunition and spare parts were missing. Above all, it had proved almost impossible to organise an effective command system to co-ordinate the armoured counter-attacks. Even so, Kirponos's armour struck some blows which hurt. The 8th Mechanised Corps, with its wounds bound up, advanced in the rear of the German 11th Armoured Division, created disorder in the German rear between Brody and Dubno. The Russian effort against Army Group South elicited from Halder the remark that Kirponos's command '. . . one must admit, is doing a pretty good job'.[86]

But with German pressure in the direction of Ostrog-Zhitomir increasing, the threat of a deep penetration from the north into the main body of the South-western Front forces could not be ignored. Signs of a Soviet retirement had been observed on 28th–29th June. On 30th, Kirponos was ordered to withdraw his forces to the fortified positions of the 1939 Soviet-Polish frontier. On the evening of 30th Kirponos accordingly gave the order to fall back. His orders were '. . . to organise a stubborn defence with the emphasis on anti-tank artillery weapons'.[87] The junction between the 5th and 6th Armies, which was weakly secured, also had to be reinforced. To accomplish this, rifle units from the Southern Front were brought up to Novograd-Volynsk and Ostrog. On 1st July, however, a Rumanian-German offensive opened against the Southern Front, from which rifle and later mechanised formations were withdrawn to assist the defence of the South-western Front. The right wing of the Southern Front was heavily engaged early in July in the region of Soroki, Orgeyev and Kishinev, with the 2nd Mechanised and 2nd Cavalry Corps attempting to take the attackers in the flank to the north-west of Kishinev. Heavy fighting marked the Soviet withdrawal on the South-western Front during the first week in July. While the First Armoured Group was held for a few days before Novograd-Volynsk, suddenly out of the Pripet Marshes on the northern flank of the German forces a Soviet attack mounted by 2–3 divisions with tanks presented a threat during the first few days of July. After strenuous fighting the threat was eliminated, but not before it had delayed the German advance and was finally held accountable by von Rundstedt for holding him off from an early descent on the Dnieper.[88] Yet for the Red Army the vital problem remained whether or not Kirponos could do as he had been instructed, to organise an effective and timely defence west of Kiev and keep von Rundstedt at bay.

Kirponos, together with his Military Soviet, had been in receipt of his orders from the *Stavka* of the Soviet High Command (*Stavka Glavnovo Komandovaniya Vooruzhennykh Sil SSSR*), the Soviet equivalent of a GHQ which had been set up on 23rd June. By the end of the week the system of government had been delivered of some of the inefficient dualism which marked its operation in time of peace. Stalin had already assumed on 6th May the chairmanship of *Sovnarkom*, thereby compounding Party and governmental functions. On 30th June *Sovnarkom* was swept aside by the creation of the State Defence Committee (*GOKO: Gosudarstvennyi Komitet Oborony*), consisting of Stalin, Molotov, Voroshilov, Malenkov and Beria. The *GOKO* held absolute authority and complete power over governmental, military and administrative organs in the Soviet Union. This was the heart of policy making for the Soviet Union at war, with the *Stavka* acting as a subordinate but complementary body as a kind of 'military Politburo'.[89] The promotions of Malenkov and Beria came at the expense of men who were already members of the *Politburo* — Kaganovich, Mikoyan, Andreyev, Kalinin, Khrushchev and Zhdanov, all of whom were now outranked by Stalin's two new nominees. Of Beria, as always, Stalin had special need, for the *NKVD** had a vital part to play in maintaining internal security and manning the special 'rear security detachments' (*zagraditel'nye otryadi*), the *NKVD* machine-gunners held ready to keep the Red Army from any unauthorised withdrawal. This was a revival of a practice employed during the Civil War and demonstrated also during the bloody operations at Kronstadt in 1921.[90] During the disasters of the autumn of 1941 the Red Army supplied from its own ranks rear security detachments to check panic, but what initial fears there might have been that the troops would not fight were soon dispelled by the stubborn and bitter defence which the Red Army put up against the Germans, fighting as Halder observed 'to the last man', employing 'treacherous methods' in which the Russian did not cease firing until he was dead.

The *Stavka* no doubt owed much in its organisation to Marshal Shaposhnikov. Certainly the form of command followed the lines he had suggested in his earlier study on the 'brain of the army'. The General Staff, which Zhukov headed until October, was subordinate to the *Stavka* and acted as a source of planning and information upon which the *Stavka* could draw at will. Directly subordinated to Stalin and his *GOKO*, the *Stavka* consisted of some dozen or more senior officers, of which the Chief of the General Staff was one and included not only Kuznetsov for naval planning, but also chiefs of services and arms. In August, when Stalin set up the post of Chief of the Rear Services of the Red Army and appointed the Red Army's

* In February 1941 the *NKGB* (People's Commissariat for State Security) was split off from the *NKVD*, but the two were fused again for war-time operation.

Chief of Supply Lieutenant-General A. V. Khrulev to that post, it was in this capacity that General Khrulev sat on the *Stavka*. In the first two or three days of war, High Command intervention had not been much in evidence; lacking strategic reserves on any scale, they had nothing with which to intervene. No plan for a strategic withdrawal was evident. The Red Army had accepted the battles for the frontiers but under the signal disadvantage of the incomplete or awkward deployments existing at the time of the German attack. The possibility of re-deploying to meet the Germans in the direction of their main drives was remote. The first *Stavka* directives demanded a stubborn defence of the main positions, the covering of the important production and population centres and the winning of time. There were signs that the *Stavka* was trying to take under its control the operations at the fronts with a system of command which remained for the moment somewhat decentralised, due most probably to the existing confusion in the command structure as a whole. Even at a very early stage the command of the Red Army had been bludgeoned into little short of chaos, leaving its disastrous mark on operations, signals and supplies.

Although Stalin was by now assured of British and American support and material aid, out of the Far East loomed the threat of possible Japanese intervention at a time when the Soviet western frontiers were beginning to cave in. The Soviet-Japanese Neutrality Pact was merely a scrap of paper and Stalin knew this only too well. The Soviet Far Eastern Front was fully mobilised, and General Apanasenko's twenty-five rifle divisions with armour and aircraft waited to meet the assault on the eastern frontiers which was hourly expected. Japanese reinforcements were moving into Manchuria.[91] Emergency readiness and emergency mobilisation of Kwantung Army aviation units came into effect with the Soviet-German war; the Kwantung Army considerably increased its fighting capacity under the plan devised as the Kwantung Army Special Exercise (*Kan-Toku-En*).[92] Full-scale military and civilian mobilisation in the Far Eastern areas was all that could be done by the Soviet command, with the exception of waiting. Because of the espionage conducted on their behalf in Japan by Sorge, the Soviet government no doubt disposed of accurate information about Japanese intentions. The moment of Sorge's vital importance to Soviet security had not yet come, but come it did as the military situation in the west became critical, and the *Stavka* stood in desperate need of those Red Army troops in the eastern hinterland and on the eastern borders.

At the western borders the *Stavka* was faced with a grave situation, and none more serious than upon the Western Front. To instil a sense of the Draconian upon the Red Army, sentences of death by shooting were passed upon the Western Front commander, General Pavlov, upon his Chief of

Staff, Major-General Klimovskii, and the signals commander, Grigoriev. For 'treasonable activity' Major-General A. A. Korobkov, commander of the 4th Army, was sentenced to death. Rychagov, commander of the aviation on the North-western Front, was also subject to the same sentence, being made to pay for the massive destruction brought about by the *Luftwaffe* on the grounded aircraft. Outclassed and outgunned, the Soviet aircraft were pounced on by the *Luftwaffe* in the air over which it enjoyed complete mastery. For the massacre of Russian bombers, 'floundering . . . in tactically impossible formations,' Kesselring applied the term 'infanticide'.[93] On 23rd June Lieutenant-General Kopets of the *VVS* committed suicide in desperation over a situation where he lost 600 aircraft without having imposed any but a nominal loss on the *Luftwaffe*. 'Ghastly' results came from attempted long-range raids by Soviet bombers following a by now useless operational plan.[94] For the lack of air-cover the Red Army was to pay as heavily as the Allied armies in France. The 'crimes' for which Pavlov, Klimovskii and Korobkov were under sentence of death lay in the 'double battle of Bialystok and Minsk', where three armies and four mechanised corps were trapped in territory some 200 miles long and up to 300 miles deep, bounded in the east by Minsk and to the west by Bialystok, Grodno and Brest-Litovsk. On 25th June the *Stavka* ordered the 3rd and 10th armies, threatened with encirclement, to the Lida-Slonim-Pinsk line. The withdrawal was complicated by the lack of lorries and the shortage of fuel.[95] At Minsk, even now uncovered by Pavlov's attempts to restore the situation further west, P. M. Filatov's 13th Army was assigned to hold the fortified area, already penetrated on 26th by German armour. Halder recorded the taking of Minsk at noon on 28th; the escape route of the 3rd, 10th and elements of the 13th Army to the east was cut. Russian troops trapped in this major encirclement tried furiously to break out, operating with much skill at night and taking advantage of the swamps and wooded country to achieve their purpose. Nevertheless, the Red Army suffered in men and equipment grievous loss,[96] while Guderian hurried for the Beresina and reached for the Dnieper. The *Stavka* decision of 25th June to establish a defence line running from the Western Dvina at Vitebsk, and on the Dnieper to Kremenchug, as well as to place Marshal Budenny in charge of the High Command Reserve Army Group to hold this, signified the realisation that the erstwhile Western Front had been effectively shattered. Further to the east reserve troops were being concentrated to defend the line (behind Smolensk) of Nelidovo-Belyi-the Dnieper-Yelnya and the Desna to Zhukovki. On 2nd July the High Command Reserve was assigned to the forces of the Western Front, where the existing command was relieved of any further direction of military operations. Timoshenko himself took command, with Lieutenant-General G. K. Malandin as his Chief of Staff.

Meanwhile the Soviet troops had been unable to check Guderian's tanks which swept on to the Beresina, securing a bridge-head after heavy fighting on 4th July.

Timoshenko on 6th ordered the 5th and 7th Mechanised Corps to attack the right wing of the Third Armoured Group forces advancing on Vitebsk. Timoshenko's attack was launched from north of Orsha; three days of bitter fighting brought little success. The choice for the direction of the 7th Corps' operations proved unfortunate, necessitating a subsequent switch. Finally the divisions were flung into the attack one by one, taking heavy punishment at the hands of the *Luftwaffe* and suffering again from lack of fuel and ammunition.[97] With General Hoth's tanks pushing by way of Vitebsk and those of Guderian working through Moghilev and Orsha, the 'Stalin line' was already in the process of being breached; on 10th and 11th July Guderian's armour crossed the Dnieper. To the north by Nevel and in the Orsha-Vitebsk area the Germans observed substantial Russian concentrations, with nine divisions in the Gomel area (from which stemmed a road movement almost sixty miles long in the direction of Moghilev).[98] By 11th July, however, a major threat to Smolensk was developing. Stalin demanded of Timoshenko the protracted defence of the city; on 14th, on what appears to have been the direct orders of the *GOKO*, instructions were set out for the defence of the approaches to Smolensk and the operations entrusted to Lieutenant-General M. F. Lukin's 16th Army. Lukin did not succeed with his mission, however, and on 15th German tanks from Guderian's Second Armoured Group were already in the southern outskirts of the city, while Hoth's Third Armoured Group drove down from the north-west. Soviet reinforcements rushed from the Ukraine and the Orel Military District into the vast traffic jam at Smolensk had arrived by 10th July, but had the utmost difficulty in concentrating. They were also fresh troops lacking combat experience. To the north were concentrated some seven divisions in the Velikie-Luki-Nevel area, to the south the nine divisions in the Gomel group; at the centre were the Vitebsk-Orsha-Smolensk forces. In Moghilev, where the Russians held a powerful bridge-head on the Dnieper, Gerasimenko's 13th Army was trapped but continued to fight until 26th July. While the Russians encircled in Orsha and Moghilev attempted a simultaneous break-out to the south and south-east respectively, with the Gomel group Timoshenko launched heavy counter-attacks on the right wing of Guderian's Second Armoured Group. From the *Stavka*, and most likely from Stalin himself, Timoshenko received by telegram the following order: 'Smolensk is not in any event to fall to the enemy.'[99] Such a task was beyond the powers of Timoshenko, whose divisions lacked air cover, sufficient artillery, ammunition and other supplies. But the Russians fought with what Halder called 'savage determination' to check the German advance. Both Russian and German accounts do not fail to underline the crudity of the Red Army's tactics. A captured Soviet order, emanating from the *Stavka*, laid down the need to separate German armour from the infantry by driving attacks between them; from Halder this called forth the comment that such a method required superior equipment and generalship.[100]

On 24th July the *Stavka* split off from the Western Front the 13th and 21st Armies, forming them into a new Central Front under Colonel-General I. F. Kuznetsov; this was aimed at facilitating the operational control of the armies operating in a westerly direction. Already Timoshenko had divided his command into two on the Western Front, setting up new tactical headquarters. Timoshenko operated on the left wing, his Chief of Staff on the right, while Zhukov was charged with the supervision of the High Command reserves being brought up to cover the approaches to Moscow. The situation at Smolensk was critical. Already by 20th July Guderian had reached Yelnya to the south-east of the city, while Hoth curled round past Smolensk to the north-east, reaching Dukhovshchina-Yartsevo. By the end of July the trap was fast closing on Timoshenko's armies. Behind Smolensk small striking forces of 4–5 divisions, drawn from troops holding rear positions, had been assembled and augmented with reserves. Against Hoth's break-through to Dukhovshchina-Yartsevo, Generals Koniev and Rokossovskii used these reserves to halt him at the River Vop and hold one claw from Smolensk. From Belyi a second reserve group attacked in the direction of Dukhovshchina-Smolensk. From the south-west General Kachalov (who was killed in this engagement) attacked in the direction of Roslavl-Pochinek-Smolensk. Army Group Centre did not entirely close the ring round Smolensk, for in addition to desperate Russian resistance, the going was hampered by difficult country. The Smolensk cauldron continued to boil, although by 8th August Guderian had completed the battle for Roslavl and was planning to assault the weak Russian front on either side of the Moscow Highway, rolling it up from Spas Demyansk to Vyazma. At the end of July the Soviet Reserve Front running from Ostashkov to Rzhev and Vyazma had been set up and was being manned with High Command reserves. West of the Desna, Soviet troops continued to fight.

Timoshenko's battle for Smolensk had taken place under the revised command organisation which had been brought into effect on 10th July. The High Command *Stavka*, created on 23rd June, now became the *Stavka* of the Supreme Command (*Stavka Verkhovnovo Glavnokomandovaniya*) with Stalin and Molotov, the Marshals Voroshilov, Timoshenko, Budenny and Shaposhnikov, as well as Chief of the General Staff Zhukov as its members.

Simultaneously this *Stavka* created three major commands, the North-western, the Western and the South-western, confided respectively to Voroshilov, Timoshenko and Budenny. In the north-west (Baltic and Leningrad), Voroshilov's Military Soviet was made up with Zhdanov, in the west Timoshenko's with Bulganin and in the Ukraine Budenny had Khrushchev as the political member of his Military Soviet. The super-commissars were given the military rank of Lieutenant-General. Stalin himself assumed the post of Defence Commissar on 19th July and on 7th August became officially Commander-in-Chief (*Verkhovnyi Glavnokomanduyushchii*). During the same critical period, dual command was re-introduced into the Soviet armed forces on 16th July, a sign as always that the officer corps needed a touch of the Party whip. The new instruction on military commissars re-instated the commissar as 'the representative of the Party and the Government in the Red Army', bearing with the commander 'full responsibility' for the unit's conduct in battle and its 'unflinching readiness to fight to the last drop of blood the enemies of our Native Land (*Rodina*)'. The commissar was to 'warn the Supreme Command and the Government against commanders and political workers [who are] unworthy of the rank of commander and political worker . . . to wage a relentless struggle with cowards, the creators of panic and deserters'.[101] This was the language of the Civil War; the effect could only be to set up between military and political organs that same chronic state of conflict and divided interests which was the natural concomitant of dual command. There were, as yet, no initial mass surrenders by the Red Army;* huge numbers of prisoners were taken by the German Army, certainly, but the monument to the Russian soldiers flung in to die in their masses is the record of their bitter and stubborn resistance to the German advances. Ideologically, the emphasis fell on the 'patriotic war' which the Red Army had been called upon to fight.

The three major commands were meant to correspond to the main German strategic combinations. Timoshenko, the most professional of Stalin's personal soldiers, had already held up the German advance for three weeks. In the north-west and the defence of the approaches to Leningrad, it was up to Voroshilov to show his paces, in a situation which steadily worsened even following upon the disasters of the last five days of June. Already the Northern Front forces were being swung down to defend the south-western approaches to Leningrad. The Chief of Staff of the North-western Front, Lieutenant-General P. S. Klenov, was relieved of his duties

* Voluntary surrenders increased with disorganisation and demoralisation. *Halder Diary* on 28th June (VI: p. 178) reports singularly small number of prisoners but much booty. The unprecedented prisoner-of-war problem is fully examined in G. Fischer, *Soviet Opposition to Stalin*, and L. Schapiro, 'The political background of the Russo-German War' in *The Soviet Army*, pp. 93–100. Both deal with the attitude of the Soviet soldier to the regime.

for incompetence. A new front commander, Major-General P. P. Sobennikov, was appointed (Sobennikov was 8th Army commander) and the Deputy Chief of the General Staff itself, Lieutenant-General N. F. Vatutin, was appointed Chief of Staff to the front. On 9th July Von Leeb's armoured and motorised units reached Ostrov and broke into the Ostrov fortified district (work upon which had been halted in 1940).[102] On 9th Pskov fell, and with it hopes of building up a stable front to check the German advance, moving along the Pskov-Luga road and towards Novgorod. From Shimsk on Lake Ilmen to Narva, along the line of the River Luga, Voroshilov had now to organise a defence against German drives proceeding from along the Baltic Coast and striking up from the south-west. This defence line on the Luga was organised into the Luga Defensive Sector (on Voroshilov's left wing) and the Kingisepp Defensive Sector on his right. Manning the Luga sector were three rifle divisions, a brigade of mountain troops and the cadets from two military schools. On the march from the Northern Front were three divisions of the National Militia (*Divizii Narodnovo Opolcheniya: DNO*), which had been hurriedly recruited by the first week in July.* These scratch but determined units were to be flung in against the superb soldiers of the German Army, battle-wise, confident and under a most able leadership. The Kingisepp sector was held by the 191st Rifle Division and more militia. On 14th July, forward German elements with twenty tanks forced the River Luga near Poreche, meeting no resistance since this part of the line was not yet manned. Exploiting their success, German troops moved forward, meeting up with the 2nd *DNO* on 15th July. On meeting the *Blitzkrieg*, the badly-trained and raw militia men fell back in confusion at the first German blow. Voroshilov, not lacking in personal courage, rallied the defence as best he could in person.[103] On 17th–18th heavy fighting developed on the right wing, where the 191st Division and the militia held the positions. Cadets of the Kirov Infantry School, exhausting their ammunition, perished in hand-to-hand fighting to hold the line. By 21st the Germans were in a position to use their success to threaten the whole Luga defensive line, and to develop a *place d'armes* for an offensive right upon Leningrad.

On the right wing of the North-western Front the 8th Red army, fighting in Estonia, was cut off from the main body of the front. The 8th could still be of service, notwithstanding its worsening plight. Attached now to Northern Front command, these forces were assigned the task of holding

* The *DNO* in Leningrad were originally projected as the *LANO* (Leningrad Militia Army), the Military Soviet of which was formed on 30th June under the direction of Marshal Voroshilov and Lt.-Gen. M. M. Popov. The proposed 15 militia divisions proved impossible without denuding the worker force needed in the factories. At the second session of the *LANO* Military Soviet on 4th July it was resolved to recruit 3 militia divisions by 7th. Each *DNO* was to have 3 regiments, 1 tank battalion and artillery/machine-gun units.

the naval base at Tallinn and exerting pressure on the left wing of the Army Group North. But in a very short time, von Leeb cut the 8th Army into two by striking up to Kunda. From the 23rd Army on the Karelian Isthmus Voroshilov withdrew the 70th Rifle Division and the 10th Mechanised Corps to bolster the Luga defences. Only the 198th Motorised Rifle Division of the 10th Mechanised Corps was left with the 23rd. To bolster morale and stiffen discipline, on 14th Voroshilov and Zhdanov issued an order, full of exhortation and ending with the threat that death by shooting would be meted out for voluntary withdrawals from the line. On 25th July Voroshilov ordered the setting up of commissions for defence construction — on which sat Party officials, the commander of the Leningrad Military District (Lieutenant-General T. I. Shevaldin), scientific experts and the director of the Kirov Factory. The object was to turn Leningrad into a fortress. Tactical and specialist questions concerning the defence lines were to be sorted out by Major-General P. A. Zaitsev, Artillery General V. P. Sviridov and the head of the Northern Front military engineers, Colonel B. V. Vychevskii. By the end of July a million people (more than half youths) were toiling on the defence works.[104] More militia units were drafted. From the worker battalions and sharp-shooter units being formed Voroshilov evidently drew the idea of naming them 'Guards'; the first 'Guards Division' was formed on 20th July. This idea of 'Guards units', which was to have an extremely important influence on the development of the Red Army, was later in the year adopted by Stalin and the *GOKO* for application to cadre units.[105] These first 'Guards', however, lacked much training, had a Red Army cadre of not more than 10 per cent and were used to plug the line.

To build an effective defence out of the Luga positions, the Northern Front commander on 23rd July set out three sectors — the Kingisepp, the Luga and the Eastern Sectors, each directly subordinated to the Front. Major-General V. V. Semashko took over the first (coastal defence guns, 3 rifle divisions and militia), Major-General A. N. Astanin the second (3 rifle divisions and a militia regiment), and Major-General F. I. Starikov the third (a militia division, one mountain brigade and artillery). On 27th July the Luga Operational Groups Staff was disbanded, for by Voroshilov's order the sector troops were incorporated into the 48th Army/North-western Front. The defence could not, owing to the lack of reserves, be organised properly in depth. The Northern Front had used up its reserves when the German offensive opened on 8th August, leaping off from their bridge-heads on the Luga. By 11th a very threatening situation had developed on the Kingisepp sector. The Northern Front command was well-nigh helpless, for on the Karelian Isthmus, to the north of Leningrad, three divisions of 23rd Army were encircled and the left wing of the army endangered. Northern Front commander M. M. Popov had no choice but to send all available forces to help out there, although this weakened the Kingisepp defence. In his report to Marshal Shaposhnikov, the Northern Front Chief of Staff Major-General D. N. Nikishev wrote:

> The difficulty of restoring the situation lies in the fact that neither divisional commanders, army commanders nor front commanders have any reserves at all. Every breach down to the tiniest has to be stopped up with scratch sections or units assembled any old how.[106]

Therein lay the whole desperate situation facing not only the Northern Front command but the entire Red Army and the *Stavka.*

By the middle of August, the defence was being pierced in a number of places. To eliminate these threats reserves were urgently needed, but these had already been expended. The report of the Northern Front Military Soviet of 13th August elaborated on this theme to the Soviet General Staff. The report indicated the main lines of German effort: Narva-Kingisepp-Leningrad, Luga-Leningrad and Keksholm-Leningrad. To suppose that opposition to the German advance could be resisted by militia units just forming up or badly organised, and by units taken from the North-western Front command after they had been pulled out of Lithuania and Latvia 'is completely unjustified'.[107] The *Stavka* responded by rushing to Leningrad three new armies, but as Lieutenant-General A. V. Sukhomlin observed of the raising of the 54th Army, '. . . the army at this time was on wheels' — assembling to the west of Moscow. Also the North-western Front was ordered on 12th August to assault the German forces from Staraya Russa, with the object of bringing pressure on the troops driving on Leningrad. Achieving a limited success, the offensive came to an end on 25th.

With the line all the while contracting about Leningrad, Voroshilov and Zhdanov on 20th August decided to set up the Military Soviet for the Defence of Leningrad. The next day Voroshilov and Zhdanov found themselves called to the telephone linked with the *Stavka.* Stalin was on the line, expressing dissatisfaction that the City Defence Soviet had been set up without his authorisation. He further disliked Voroshilov and Zhdanov joining it once it had been set up. Both explained to Stalin that the new Soviet corresponded to the requirements of the actual situation, that it was a kind of auxiliary organ for implementing defence works. Stalin suggested 'a review of the personnel of the Defence Soviet'. This, needless to say, was done. The new Soviet, which merely complicated the command when there was already the major Military Soviet of the North-western command, lasted exactly nine days, its life from the beginning blighted with Stalinist displeasure.[108] Leningrad faced a very grave situation, menaced by the advance of Army Group North from the west and south-west and the Finnish-German forces operating from the north. The organisation of the defence had shown up critical weaknesses. The Northern Front command had indicated to the *Stavka* that it had now exhausted its game of robbing Peter to pay Paul. The offensive by the 34th and elements of 11th Army from the North-western Front had given only a momentary relief from the heavy pressure. Due to the mistakes of the 34th Army command the success attained at one point could not be exploited.[100] On 23rd August, the *Stavka* split the Northern Front into two, the Karelian under General V. A. Frolov and the Leningrad Front (under M. M. Popov until 5th September, when Voroshilov took over this command). Meanwhile the *Stavka* was rushing two new armies, the 52nd and the 54th, to the eastern bank of the River Volkhov. In fact, what had been the Northern Front had broken to pieces. On 29th August German forces reached Kolpino, and elements broke through to Mga and Schlusselburg. Leningrad was completely sealed off by land.

In the Ukraine, where Kirponos was fighting doggedly to hold Army Group South, Marshal Budenny took up his post as Stalin's military caretaker, retaining Lieutenant-General N. S. Khrushchev as his commissar. On the right wing of the South-western Front the defences had been breached in considerable depth and forward units of the First Armoured Group under von Kleist had reached the Irpen (some 10 miles west of Kiev), which is also to say that the northern wing of Army Group South had smashed into what there was of the 'Stalin line'. The *GOKO* decided on 10th July to unify the South-western and Southern Fronts under the supreme command of Budenny. While pressing upon Kiev, Army Group South decided upon the assault against Berdichev and Belaya Tserkov, to be followed by a southerly and south-easterly movement, which would bring German troops on to the flank and into the rear of the Southern Front. At the same time, the 11th German Army and Rumanian troops would strike on Balta-Pervomaisk and so by-pass Uman. By the middle of July the Soviet line from Fastov-Berdichev-Letichev gave way, and on 18th July the 17th German army and First Armoured Group had attained the line Balaya Tserkov-Kazatin-Vinnitsa-Shmerinka. The loss of Belaya Tserkov put the Southern Front in some jeopardy. To restore the situation in the centre of the South-western Front, the *Stavka* ordered the assembly of fresh forces and immediate attack; the task was assigned to the 26th Army. The German troops were waiting for the 26th Army when it attacked, for on 19th July captured documents indicated that the 26th — with 6 rifle divisions, 2 cavalry divisions operating under 2nd Corps HQ — would be going over to the offensive.[110] This 'irresponsible carelessness' of 26th Army Staff cost the Russians any element of surprise. On 16th July Tyulenev was ordered to abandon Kishinev. Both the right wing of the Southern Front and the left of the South-western were in a serious situation. The latter had lost contact with the staff of the South-western Front and was incorporated into the Southern Front. Tyulenev was ordered to assemble his reserves and to concentrate them in the Uman area. Under the Southern Front command came the defence of Odessa, preparations for which were being made on 12th July. From the 9th Army the 25th and 95th Rifle Divisions were detached under the command of Lieutenant-General N. Y. Chibissov and on 19th July formed, together with calvary units, into the Coastal Army under Lieutenant-General G. P. Safronov.[111] Round Odessa itself work began on a defensive system made up of three lines with a total length of 400 miles, planned to hold 112 battalion defence positions. Meanwhile the 17th German army had cut deeply into the junction of the Southern and South-western Fronts and the advance on Uman continued, with very heavy fighting. The *Stavka* had directed Budenny on 17th–18th July to take up the line Belaya Tserkov-Gaisin-Kamenka to the Dniester, and also to check the First Armoured Group with units of the 5th Army to the north and the 26th to the east. This was intended to hold off the encirclement of the South-western left and the Southern right wing.

Travelling southwards and not being deflected by Red Army attacks launched upon it from Kanev and Cherkassy, the First Armoured Group reached Novo-Ukrainka and the outskirts of Kirovograd at the end of July, by which time the 17th German Army had fought its way to Pervomaisk. The Uman trap had closed on the 6th and 12th Red armies from east and west as the 11th Army of Army Group South fought its way from Balta to Pervomaisk. The withdrawal of Soviet troops from the Uman area towards the River Ingul had been left very late. The Uman débâcle was, however, only an introduction to the catastrophes to come and for which the blame has been laid upon Budenny's ineptness. Certainly in the latter half of July, Budenny and the *Stavka* seemed to be fighting two different battles. On the other hand Halder noted on 26th July that the Russians were still escaping encirclement and showing 'great skill in withdrawing troops from threatened areas', although it was plain that the 26th Army was 'severely compressed'.[112] Not only military dangers faced the Soviet command. Time was desperately needed to cover the evacuation of industrial equipment and personnel to the east, upon which task Khrushchev was engaged in the Ukraine. There was the danger posed by possible political instability, the risk of Ukrainian separatism responding to the opportunity presented by the German invasion. The industrial evacuations and the military operations took place amidst a very considerable disorganisation. If it is difficult to determine Budenny's responsibility for the outcome at Uman, his part in the later and completely disastrous phase of the Ukrainian operations has recently been defended.

While the Smolensk operations were reaching their climax, and as Budenny's armies were cut in two between Uman and Odessa, vital questions concerning the future development of German operations were becoming the subject of dispute between Hitler and his commanders. On 19th July Hitler's *Directive No. 33* envisaged peeling off from Army Group Centre the armoured forces: Hoth's armour would assist von Leeb's Army Group North in its assault on Leningrad by covering its right flank, Guderian's armour and motorised formations would swing south and south-east to co-operate with Army Group South by liquidating the 5th Red army and breaking into the rear of the Soviet South-western Front. This left only infantry to Army Group Centre for its push on Moscow, for which Guderian demanded the highest priority — virtually to rush the disorganised and weakened Russian defences.[113] The upshot of acrid and protracted German high-level discussions was to fritter away valuable time and to win for Hitler acceptance in certain quarters of his plan for the flank operations. It is this which has been described as the real salvation of Moscow. Certainly it sealed Budenny's doom and that of the Ukraine with a spectacular encirclement operation which overwhelmed both.

In view of these German intentions, preparations for which took some time to mature, it was vital for the *Stavka* to prepare the defence of the area to the north-east of Kiev. It is asserted that the *Stavka* had already taken into consideration the possibility of a German advance into the rear of the South-western Front Kiev group through Chernigov, Konotop and Priluki. The proof cited is the formation of the Bryansk Front on 16th August, assigned to Lieutenant-General A. I. Yeremenko and composed of the 50th Army (Major-General M. P. Petrov) and Golubev's 13th Army.[114] The vital task was to prevent the junction of the two German army groups, Centre and South. For this, the *Stavka* devised the plan of moving from the Kiev area elements of the 37th and 26th Armies, as well as the newly-formed 40th Army, up to the River Desna north of Konotop. On 19th the *Stavka*, taking account of the disintegration of the Central Front (which was liquidated on 26th August as Gomel and Starodub fell), assigned to Budenny the task of defending the Dnieper from Loyev to the mouth, defending the Kiev and Dniepopetrovsk fortified districts, and covering by land and air the Donbas and the Northern Caucasus.[115] At this time, with the collapse of the Southern Front, the defence of Odessa — which Halder considered a possible Soviet Tobruk — was a matter of the greatest urgency. The defence of the naval base was to be made into a combined operation; the Naval Commissar Kuznetsov, in receipt of the *Stavka* directive for the last-ditch defence of the base, informed Oktyabrskii that, 'the warships of the base are to support the troops to the last grenade'. The co-operation of the land and naval forces was as yet badly organised, to the degree that Admiral Oktyabrskii was not completely convinced that the Red Army would defend the city and harbour of Odessa.[116]

Subsequent events would tend to support the idea that the Soviet high command had not been able to adjust itself with enough rapidity to the new situation. Both doors which opened on to what was to become the giant encirclement at Kiev had been left ajar. As any attempt to stabilise the Ukrainian front had earlier depended on the effective co-ordination of the Southern and South-western Fronts, so now the staving off of disaster east of the Dnieper depended upon effective domination of the area to the north-east of Kiev and co-operation of the Bryansk and South-western Fronts. Budenny had been given a massive line to defend, but he weakened it by excessive concentration to the south of Kiev. Nevertheless, a considered Soviet military verdict has put the blame for the disaster at Kiev fairly and squarely on Colonel-General I. F. Kuznetsov and Lieutenant-General A. I. Yeremenko of the Central and Bryansk Fronts. The charge against them is failure to take advantage of favourable opportunities to attack the 2nd Army and Second Armoured Group in the flank as they moved south and south-east respectively. Upon the Bryansk Front is heaped special blame for having failed to understand the *Stavka* directives and for having launched badly prepared attacks. As a result, the Kiev concentrations were left unsupported.[117] The blunders, however, were a fatal combination rather than a single incompetence.

The battle for Kiev lasted a month, opening on 25th August when Guderian received his orders to begin striking towards the Ukraine. The 13th Red army had evidently been taken by surprise by Guderian's thrust, for Guderian's 3rd *Panzer* Division succeeded in taking the 750-yard bridge over the Desna to the east of Novgorod-Severskii intact. This was a signal failure on the part of the Bryansk Front. By 9th September Guderian's XXIV *Panzer* Corps had located the Soviet weak spot between Baturin and Konotop. Here the South-western Front 40th Army had blundered. Pushing down to Romny, Guderian's 3rd *Panzer* Division again evidently succeeded in taking the Russians by surprise, to the degree that the latter were unable to take advantage of a strong and well-prepared position.[118] Before Kiev itself, the 6th German Army contained the Soviet troops here, and attacked on the sector south of Loyev. To the south of Kiev, the 38th Red army was holding a 115-mile front on the eastern bank of the Dnieper. On 12th September, von Kleist's First Armoured Group and von Stülpnagel's 17th Army broke out from the Cherkassy-

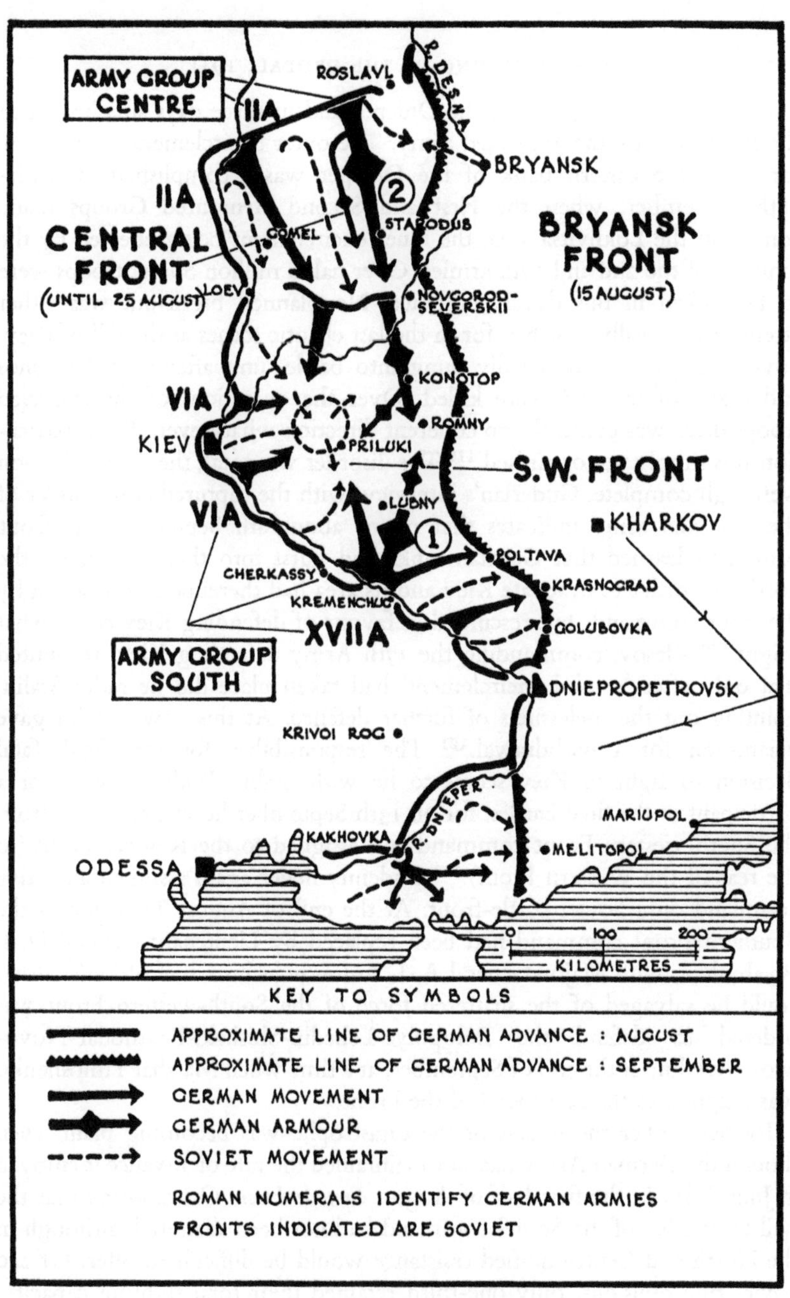
ARMY GROUP CENTRE
ROSLAVL
R. DESNA
IIA
BRYANSK
IIA
2
STARODUB
BRYANSK FRONT
(15 AUGUST)
CENTRAL FRONT
(UNTIL 25 AUGUST)
GOMEL
LOEV
NOVGOROD-SEVERSKII
KONOTOP
VIA
ROMNY
KIEV
PRILUKI
S.W. FRONT
LUBNY
VIA
KHARKOV
1
POLTAVA
CHERKASSY
KRASNOGRAD
KREMENCHUG
GOLUBOVKA
XVIIA
ARMY GROUP SOUTH
DNIEPROPETROVSK
KRIVOI ROG
R. DNIEPER
MARIUPOL
KAKHOVKA
MELITOPOL
ODESSA
0
100
200
KILOMETRES
KEY TO SYMBOLS
APPROXIMATE LINE OF GERMAN ADVANCE : AUGUST
APPROXIMATE LINE OF GERMAN ADVANCE : SEPTEMBER
GERMAN MOVEMENT
GERMAN ARMOUR
SOVIET MOVEMENT
ROMAN NUMERALS IDENTIFY GERMAN ARMIES
FRONTS INDICATED ARE SOVIET

THE KIEV ENCIRCLEMENT
(August-September, 1941)

Kremenchug bridgeheads on the Dnieper and in three days smashed open the front held by the 38th Red army. The outer encirclement of the Kiev forces on the eastern bank of the Dnieper was accomplished on 15th–16th September, when the First and Second Armoured Groups made contact in the Lokhvitsa area, the inner encirclement being effected by the junction of the 2nd and 17th armies. Over half a million Soviet troops were to be locked in this deadly embrace. No planned break-out was either attempted or really possible, for in the last chaotic scenes at the fall of Kiev, Soviet troops were frenziedly flung into battle, unit after unit. Kirponos and many of his staff were killed. Over the operations of the encircled troops there was evidently no coherent direction whatsoever. Their extrication was simply not organised.[119] The disorder was total, the demoralisation well-nigh complete. Guderian's interview with the captured commander of the 5th Red army indicates that on or about 8th September the front command learned that German tanks had burst into their rear from the north. An order to evacuate Kiev and its area had thereupon been given by the front command, but rescinded in favour of defending Kiev come what might.[120] Vlasov, commanding the 37th Army defending Kiev, recounted that only after 'a solid encirclement' had taken place did he radio Stalin, pointing out the uselessness of further defence. At this news, Stalin gave permission for a withdrawal.[121] The responsibility for that final, fatal decision to fight in Kiev seems to lie with Stalin. Budenny was not a participant in the final battles, for on 13th September he was removed from the South-western Front command and assigned to the Reserve Front (to the rear of the Western Front).[122] Budenny never again assumed an active command on a Soviet battle-front. At the end of August Tyulenev of the Southern Front command had been replaced by Lieutenant-General D. I. Ryabyshev, with Major-General A. I. Antonov as his Chief of Staff. What could be salvaged of the shattered force of the South-western Front was ordered to defend the Belopolye-Lebedin-Shishaki-Krasnodar-Novo-Moskovsk line at the end of September, at a time when Marshal Timoshenko was assigned to the command of the Front.

By September the extent of the catastrophe was becoming plain, even though the German Army had not maintained the rate of advance it enjoyed in June–July. In the first half of August *Fremde Heere Ost* reported that the will to combat of the Soviet command had not been shattered, although in the North and Centre unified resistance would be difficult to offer. Of 240 Soviet rifle divisions, only one-third retained their total fighting capacity. For the 40 new divisions in preparation, officers, infantry weapons and artillery were lacking. Of the Soviet armour, most of the 50 armoured divisions which had existed or been assembled were now out of action. The armour had been used 'in bits', without the armoured divisions being grouped and so used in the attack.[123] While the Red Army had launched attack after attack upon the German troops, the *Stavka* could not fail to draw two uncomfortable conclusions from this: that German losses had been grossly over-estimated* and that the Soviet tactics and organisation had been expensively deficient.[124] The Russian attack method involved a three-minute artillery barrage, with the infantry attacking in a mass as much as twelve ranks deep, or else with riflemen on trucks driving abreast with the tanks in a frontal assault on the German firing-line. Securing the rear and flanks received much too little attention. Attacks were launched with inadequate intelligence of enemy dispositions and movements and in spite of what the regulations prescribed, with inadequate preparation, even 'rashness'.[125] Separate and by no means isolated cases of stubborn and tenacious defence could not hide the fact that the Red Army needed drastically new defensive tactics, instead of just stringing out men and guns (in particular the tanks) uniformly along the front. More than that, however, the whole notion of the Red Army as an undifferentiated mass offensive instrument required overhauling. In September the first large-scale moves were made to split up the Red Army into élite and mass formations, to separate the quality out of the quantity. Already in Leningrad with his militia formations Voroshilov had introduced the notion of the 'Guards'. On 18th September, under Defence Commissariat Order No. 308, the 100th, 127th, 153rd and 161st Rifle Divisions became 'Guards Divisions' in the Red Army; by Order No. 318 of 26th September, the 64th, 107th and 120th Rifle Divisions received Guards designation, for proficiency and excellence in combat, organisation, discipline and exemplary order. Guards designation came to be applied also to aviation units, ships and naval units. What is more important perhaps than the designation itself, the Soviet command quickly learned to use these quality troops as such, and to them went the best in available equipment.

At the end of September the *Stavka* ordered a halt to Red Army attacks. At the beginning of September, when Army Group Centre had been stripped of its armour, Timoshenko had taken advantage of this to launch a series of limited attacks on the Western Front by the Yelnaya salient. The Russians claimed that eight German divisions were badly mauled, but this could not affect the situation in the south. The South-western Front on 27th September was instructed to confine itself to defence, and the Southern Front had its proposed attacks cancelled. These were indications that the

* For the first two months of war, the Russians claimed as the German losses: 2 million men (killed and wounded), about 8,000 tanks, over 7,200 aircraft and 10,000 guns. The German Army did not suffer really heavy losses until the end of the year.

Red Army had been badly hurt. Already attempts were being made to re-organise the Red Army, both to adjust it to the situation created by heavy losses in manpower and equipment as well as increasing its tactical efficiency. If the *Stavka* and the *GOKO* labelled this a 're-organisation', in fact they knew it to be a series of desperate and improvised remedies, drastic measures applied to keep the Red Army going until new weapons, new formations and new officers could be gathered to face the German Army with some hope of success. Behind the Soviet statements that commanders failed to understand the 'co-ordination of all arms' lay the unpalatable fact that most commanders could scarcely handle the infantry of the rifle division, not to mention the other arms employed. Where Stalin's earlier purge had cut most deeply, into the corps and divisional commander levels, the command situation was extremely acute. Corps headquarters, of which there were too few, had to operate many divisions. In turn, these depended on a nucleus of skilled officers at army level, who took most of the responsibility. If this top-heavy structure failed to move quickly or collapsed (as it had done with Pavlov in June on the Western Front), then efficiency tumbled into the ruins of disorder and chaos. As divisional commanders lost control, so German Wireless Intercept would pick up the signals of corps and army staffs frantically trying to make radio contact with their divisions. The rifle divisions were perforce cut down in size, due to losses and the need to give a commander a force which he could handle. The mechanised corps were discarded and smaller tactical unities introduced, again because of severe losses in tanks, shortage of new equipment and trained officers. General of Artillery N. N. Voronov was able to persuade Stalin that nothing but the most sweeping change in the artillery organisation could bring any relief to the situation. Like the other arms, the artillery had suffered alarming losses of guns and gun-crews, either killed or taken prisoner. The core of Voronov's programme lay in a vast increase in the production of artillery, but this was a prospect for the future. Voronov proposed for the immediate situation to strip from the rifle divisions one half of their artillery (one regiment) and assemble these guns into a High Command Artillery Reserve, which could be employed as and where required. Because guns and ammunition were short, and since complicated artillery techniques needed time to be mastered, Voronov introduced the principle of putting 'the guns up front where the gunners could see and hit the enemy'.[126] Meanwhile a few mobile rocket-launchers, Kostikov's 'Katyusha', were coming into service. Until the 57-mm anti-tank guns arrived, the 76-mm field gun with the high muzzle velocity could be made to serve the Red Army's needs; and to fill the gaps in the artillery, every effort was put into producing mortars, for which Stalin set up a special Ministry of Mortar Production in November.

The battered Soviet Air Force also needed immediate attention to rescue it from the *Luftwaffe*'s early punishments. By October the Russians had admitted the loss of over 5,000 aircraft. (From the German side, General Bogatsch set Soviet losses on 22nd July at 7,564 machines).[127] The Soviet Air Force had entered the war with outmoded machines and outmoded tactics. For the long-range night raids which the strategic bombers were called upon to perform, the crews lacked the requisite training and the command the necessary skill. Reconnaissance of the target appears to have been lacking. The DB–3 Black Sea Fleet bombers engaged in daylight raids on bases in Rumania lacked a fighter escort and incurred 'unjustified' losses. Bomber squadrons intended for night operations found themselves committed by day and again without fighter escorts. Sustaining enormous losses on the ground, the Soviet I–16 and I–153 machines were shot out of the sky by the *Luftwaffe*'s Me–109's. Once again, but in possibly the most critical form, the problem of quantity and quality faced the Soviet command. It was of little avail to rush quantities of obsolete machines, incapable of carrying out the required tactical functions, to the front. After June–July, the production of the I–16, I–153, SB bomber and the Yak–2 was brought to a halt, and that of the MiG–3, Yak–1 fighters, the Il–2 ground attack aircraft and the Pe–2 light bomber pushed forward. One of the strong men of Soviet military aviation, Novikov, commander of the Leningrad air forces, played a major part in putting the battered squadrons back to fight. The aviation divisions attached to the ground armies were cut down in size, yet another diminution and dilution forced upon the Soviet command by losses and the lack of high-level aviation commanders.

In general, two views prevail to account for the disaster of the first collapse. The first implies that, given the possibility to deploy properly without Stalin's interference before the attack, the Red Army would have been able to withstand the German onslaught with much diminished losses. The second puts the weight of the blame on the failure to mobilise industry in due time. The situation in the early autumn of 1941 was in fact a compound of these two factors.* Certainly the very heavy losses of equipment

* An important study by Col. (now Maj.-Gen.) A. Lagovskii, *Strategiya i Ekonomika* (Moscow 1957, p. 194), argues presently that strategy must fix '. . . the requirement of the armed forces for the waging of the *first year* of military operations' (italics mine). Of 'various methods' used, basic pointers would come from the number of combat days in one year and the number of operations which might be undertaken; statistical data from the last war, adjusted to the present would be of basic importance. Arguing that the 'temporary superiority' obtained by an attacker in the initial phase would not bring victory in a protracted war, Col. V. A. Zakharov writes: 'In the strategic planning of war the correct employment of troops must be estimated not only for the initial period but also for its entire extent. A proper scientific approach to determining the forces of the first and successive strategic echelons, speeds of mobilisation and strategic deployment, the quantity of available forces and reserves, the reinforcement of front-line units and formations with fresh forces for the whole duration of the war is necessary.' (*Marksizm-Leninizm o voine i armii*, Moscow, 1957 and 1958 Edns., p. 262.)

during the summer vastly increased the Red Army's difficulties. The considerable loss of territory involved in the defeats meant a hasty improvisation of the transfer of industries to the east, with industry being faced with the problem of not only supplying but replacing guns, tanks and aircraft.[128] A special Evacuation Soviet, headed by N. M. Shvernik and including A. I. Mikoyan and A. N. Kosygin, was put in charge of moving plants and equipment eastwards; the immediate arrangements were made by the Military Soviets of the fronts and regional administrative bodies. From August to November, either by loss to the enemy or through evacuation, 303 plants turning out ammunition were lost.[129] Production of ammunition fell short of the Red Army's requirements. The concentration upon direct fire guns in re-organising the artillery did also mean that the available ammunition might be more profitably used. As with mortar production, so did the question of tanks fall to a special commissariat, which was first organised in September. The gross underestimation of the needs imposed by war, which was a feature of the national economic mobilisation plan for the third quarter of 1941, came under the corrective of the war economy plan for the fourth quarter of 1941 and for 1942. In organising the mass production of weapons and equipment, it was essential to get the KV, T–34 and T–60 tanks to the front in some quantity. Already the T–34, where it had appeared, had come as an extremely unpleasant shock to the Germans. The Red Army still lacked the new tanks in any effective quantity, but the German Army had seen one of the first ominous signs of possible changes.

To separate the military and industrial aspects of the summer disasters is impossible, for both were part of the general inadequacies displayed by the Stalinist system, recalling all that Trotsky had prophesied in 1927 and summarised as 'rotten ropes'. Only now was the impact of the military purges becoming dreadfully plain, the futile irony of the slaughter standing out garishly as the Red Army reverted increasingly to the ideas which had held sway before the decimations. Orlov and Muklevich had been shot for following a doctrine to which the present naval staff had no option but to revert. Mekhlis, whose own part in inflicting considerable damage on the Red Army was not small, had even in 1939 called attention to the damage which excessive mistrust had done to morale and efficiency. For real discipline there existed now still the product of the terror — the fear of the superior, the obsession with documents, the pervading presence of repression. Troops breaking out of encirclement met not relief in their own lines, but *NKVD* guards and interrogation. To evade capture might mean finally running the risk of being labelled a deserter or a traitor. In rejecting Khrushchev's exaggerated portrait of Stalin at war, the essentials of preoccupation with minutiae and obsessive supervision must be retained. To fight properly, the army would have to be freed of its political baggage train.

* * * *

As the great Kiev encirclement operation was opening into its decisive phase, Hitler issued his *Directive No. 35*, dated 6th September and providing for the rapid strengthening of Army Group Centre, with the aim of destroying Soviet troops east of Smolensk with a pincer movement in the direction of Vyazma. This would be the prelude to the advance on Moscow, Timoshenko's armies having been swept away. While Guderian's back was turned, engaged as he was in the Ukraine, Timoshenko had loosed his blow in the western bend of the Desna. Nor had the Russians neglected to make use of the ten weeks vouchsafed to them by the delay imposed on the German advance in the bitter fighting for Smolensk and the halt called to further offensive operations at the centre by differences in the German command over the further development of operations. Already August and September had slipped away. In the Ukraine the German encirclement operations had been hampered by mud. Autumn had crept upon the battlefield as Army Group Centre resumed its offensive operations. On 2nd October the battle for Moscow had begun in all earnest, by which time Guderian had succeeded in penetrating the Soviet front from the right wing of Army Group Centre.

After Timoshenko's departure for the South-western Front, Colonel-General I. S. Koniev, with General V. D. Sokolovskii as his Chief of Staff, had taken over the Western Front. Part of the Reserve Front force was employed to cover the flanks of the Western and North-western Fronts, although the bulk occupied a defence line in the rear of the Western Front running from Yeltsi-Dorogobuzh; two armies were deployed to cover the Yukhnov approach. Guderian chose as the point of his main effort Glukhov (and thence to Orel), that is, the left flank of the Bryansk Front. The command of the Bryansk Front was in the process of preparing an attack about Glukhov, to improve its tactical position, as Guderian struck.[130] Yeremenko was evidently taken by surprise, but sharp fighting developed at once. On 3rd October Guderian's tanks burst into Orel, with such speed that the trams were still running and the industrial evacuation still incomplete — the streets from the factory to the railway station were filled with dismantled machines and crated tools.[131] Golubev's 13th Army fell back to the north-east. South of Bryansk the way was opening to the encirclement of the Soviet troops holding the first and outermost zone of the defensive belt which the Russians had been trying to consolidate in the past weeks. These were the first locks on the gate to Moscow, now speedily being forced. On the Western Front further breaches were made in the defences, north and south of Vyazma. Throughout this first defensive zone the situation appeared to be developing towards the encirclement of both the left wing of the Western and Reserve Fronts to the west of Vyazma and the left wing of the Bryansk Front to the south of Bryansk itself. On 8th October, in the midst of a crisis beginning to assume very dangerous proportions, Army General G. K. Zhukov took command of the Western Front from Koniev. At the same time the troops of the Reserve Front were incorporated directly into the Western Front. Until now Zhukov had held the post of Chief of the General Staff. Shaposhnikov took over that position, continuing to play his major role in the strategic planning undertaken by the *Stavka*. With Zhukov, one of the ablest heads in the Red Army had taken up the all-important front. That the *Stavka* did consider it all-important may be gauged from the fact that of all Red Army troops engaged from the Baltic to the Black Sea, 40 per cent were concentrated at the western approaches to Moscow.[132]

Near heavily invested Leningrad the situation had lost none of its danger. Blockaded by land, the only access to the city was to be had by air or from Lake Ladoga. Supplies of food, fuel and raw materials held within Leningrad were not extensive; the city was under heavy air attack and artillery bombardment. On 21st June the reserves in Leningrad depots had amounted to 52 days grain-supply, 38 days meat-supply, butter for 47 days and vegetable oil for 29 days. Leningrad could produce weapons — 82-mm and 37-mm mortars, tanks, armoured cars — while there was fuel for the factories, also 50-mm, 76-mm and 85-mm calibre ammunition, naval ammunition and M–13/M–8 rocket projectiles. To increase what was taken in and out by water, the *GOKO* decided on an air-lift, which became the responsibility of the Main Administration of the Civil Air Fleet. Aerial transportation was a vital adjunct to the supply when Lake Ladoga became especially stormy and barges were harried by the *Luftwaffe*. The air-lift was planned to move 100–150 tons every 24 hours, although only 40–45 tons were managed in practice with an air strength of 64 aircraft, of which 20–22 were the average operating strength. In this way guns and artillery ammunition were actually taken out of Leningrad for the use of the troops defending Moscow.[133] At the beginning of October the *GOKO* ordered the evacuation of the technical personnel of the Kirov Factory (a tank-producing works); these men were finally sent to the Chelyabinsk Tractor Works to work on tank production. But the air and water routes were both dangerous and at the mercy of the elements. At the end of September an attempt to break the blockading ring by blows from inside and outside was planned, aimed at destroying the German forces in the Schlusselburg area. From inside the ring, troops of the eastern sector of the Leningrad Front would fight outwards to link up with the 54th Army, subordinated on 26th September to the Leningrad Front command, fighting from outside to reach Mga and Svinyavino. This would have opened up the Leningrad-Vologda railway, which was now severed.

While the Red Army was organising for this offensive timed for 20th October, Army Group North had its own plans and was readying itself

Composition, Strength and Reinforcement of the 54th Army (Leningrad Front): 1st October, 1941

Composition	
Rifle Divisions:	128, 3rd (Guards), 310, 4th (Guards), 294, 286.
Tank Divisions:	21st Tank Division (minus tanks).
Brigades:	16th and 122nd Tank Brigades, 1st Independent Mountain Infantry Brigade.
Artillery:	Two regiments of Corps artillery.

Rifle division strengths	
128th RD:	2,145
3rd Guards:	5,594
310th RD:	3,735
286th RD:	6,016

Weapons		
128th RD:	heavy and light machine-guns	— 12
	82 and 120-mm mortars	— 8
	no guns	
310th RD:	heavy and light machine-guns	— 36
	82 and 120-mm mortars	— 7
	76-mm and other guns	— 27
3rd Guards:	heavy and light machine-guns	— 177
	82 and 120-mm mortars	— 54
	76-mm and other guns	— 32
286th RD:	machine-guns	— 102
	82 and 120-mm mortars	— 5
	76-mm and other guns	— 27

Tank reinforcements: 13th October 16th and 122nd Tank Brigades possessed 52 working tanks, of which 20 were KV and T-34.

No manpower reinforcement in the first half of October.

Average divisional strength: 5,500 men.

for an offensive on Tikhvin, the success of which would cut Leningrad off completely and make a junction with the Finns to the east of Lake Ladoga possible. For the Soviet offensive, eight rifle divisions and not less than 100 KV tanks, plus the mass of the heavy artillery, all the mobile rocket launchers and bomber and fighter aircraft (plus those of the Baltic Fleet) had been earmarked. It was not without something of a struggle that the Baltic Fleet had permitted its guns to fall under the general control of the front command. Now its aircraft were detached for front operations. In fact, although it was intended to gain a local superiority at the points of attack by re-grouping, the Soviet forces were terribly under-manned. The 54th Army holding the Volkhov-Tikhvin area was a case in point, a condition shared by the 4th Army of the *Stavka* reserve, although the strength of the rifle divisions of the 52nd Army (also *Stavka* reserve) averaged 65–70 per cent of their normal combat complement. Of all the forces concentrated to the south of Lake Ladoga, 70 per cent — 6 rifle divisions, 1 tank division (without tanks), 2 tank brigades and 1 mountain infantry brigade — had been concentrated under 54th Army control. On the rest of the 100-mile front were 6 rifle divisions.[134] At dawn on 16th October, the German offensive aimed at Tikhvin opened, striking hard at the defensive position held by the 288th Rifle Division of Klykov's 52nd Army.

On the southern flanks, Army Group South had taken up the offensive, having already delivered its shattering blows in the Ukraine. In breaking through the German encirclement east of the Dnieper, Soviet forces had incurred heavy losses. Odessa had been heavily invested by German-Rumanian troops, but the city had put up a ferocious defence to attempts to seize it. But with the advance of Army Group South to the approaches to the Crimea, Odessa now lay deep in the enemy rear; to save some of the garrison urgently needed elsewhere and to ease the strain on the Black Sea Fleet, at the end of September the *Stavka* ordered the evacuation by stages of the defending forces, to extend over the first sixteen days of October. The Black Sea Fleet naval aviation, which from the first had shown plenty of spirit, had flown 5,328 sorties in connection with the Odessa operations from 15th August until 15th October. The *Stavka* was also faced with the threat which was developing against the Crimea, where work had begun on 3rd July to provide defence positions. On the night of 31st August German troops had forced the Dnieper by Khakovka and continued to advance on Perekop. The force assigned to the defence of the Crimea was F. I. Kuznetsov's 51st Independent Army, but that army had first to be organised and manned. A great deal therefore depended on what strength could be saved from Odessa. To man the defences and fill up the garrisons of the main Crimean bases, the Black Sea Fleet transferred the 8th Naval

Infantry Brigade from Novorossiisk to the peninsula, at the same time organising marine battalions from Black Sea Fleet sailors. That provided 20,000 men with weapons, but apart from this any quantity of weapons and equipment was signally lacking for the defenders of the Crimea. Of the men brought back from Odessa and the Independent Coastal Army, only on 23rd October were they beginning to concentrate by the Ishun positions at the approaches to the Crimea. Army Group South's October offensive caused further destructions on the Southern Front, where, in keeping with the business of sending commander after commander to stem the flood on all fronts, Colonel-General Ya. T. Cherevichenko had taken command on 5th October. Von Kleist's tanks had struck at the right wing of the 12th Army, which gave way. By 7th October the 18th and 9th Red armies were being menaced in the rear — from the east — since stubborn resistance failed to halt von Kleist, who had flung a net of encirclement about these Soviet armies operating by the Sea of Azov. Soviet troops, losing not inconsiderably in the encirclement, fell back on Stalino and Taganrog, the latter falling on 17th October as German troops forced the River Mius. At this stage the *Stavka* had ordered the South-western and Southern Fronts under Timoshenko's over-all command to carry out a withdrawal still further to the east. The object was to rescue available forces, husband reserves and shorten the line.[135] On the South-western Front itself the 6th German Army, hampered now by extensive autumn mud, was fighting its way to Kharkov.

Serious as the situation was on the northern and southern flanks under the two intermediate North-western/Leningrad and South-western commands, a major crisis was developing with great rapidity on the approaches to Moscow, where Zhukov had assumed control. Here, as everywhere else, the shortage of trained men and effective equipment was acute. As in Leningrad the depleted ranks of the Red Army were reinforced with national militia, the Moscow *DNO* formations taking their designation from the district of the city from which they had been raised. Arming these militia-men presented grave difficulties. The military placed at their disposal 5,000 rifles and 210 machine-guns; training weapons from *Osoaviakhim* and even captured weapons from the Civil War days were dragged out to be handed over to these improvised defence forces. One battalion, 675 strong, received 9 heavy machine-guns, 120 (captured) hand grenades, 295 rifles, 145 revolvers and pistols, as well as 2,000 anti-tank 'petrol bottles'.[136] Given some preliminary tactical training, these militia formations were ready for service, but so pressed was the front command that the best militia formations were used to reinforce the first-line troops. After September the militia were drafted as regular divisions into the Red Army; with their training drastically curtailed, these reinforcements were committed knowing little or nothing of organisation or signals.

There is much to suggest that the German offensive begun at the end of September took the Red Army by surprise. This was intimated by prisoners taken during the battles on the Western and Bryansk Fronts. Guderian had certainly surprised the 13th Army. Only 40 per cent of the defence positions were ready; at the best this figure was 80 per cent. With the weather deteriorating, a full-scale drive on Moscow involved very obvious hazards. But at Vyazma and Bryansk the pattern of encirclement which had succeeded by the River Bug succeeded once again. In spite of the continued resistance and local successes which were registered, the Soviet troops were unable to stop the balance tilting disastrously against them. Break-outs from the Vyazma-Bryansk encirclements did succeed, but upon Soviet admission only at the price of heavy losses. Yet if the front commands had been taken somewhat unawares by the German offensive, the *Stavka* seems to have anticipated correctly the threat arising out of the left wing of Army Group Centre. Desperate efforts were made to ready the defence lines by Mozhaisk. Lieutenant-General D. D. Lelyushenko was given command of this force, small in numbers and made up of units from the North- and South-western fronts, as well as reserve units from the Far East. In spite of the escapes and break-outs from encirclement, and considering the losses which had been inflicted on the German Army by four months almost of resistance, Stalin and his *Stavka* had to reckon with the fact that the first-line Red Army of European Russia had been shattered. Losses of equipment had been of staggering proportions. At this late stage, out of what had been an enormous tank-park, the Western Front possessed only 382 tanks,[137] while further losses were incurred in the Vyazma encirclement. If the yard-by-yard resistance of the Red Army had been designed to bleed the German armies white, the attempt at attrition had inflicted grave damage on the Red Army, for so protracted was the resistance that the defenders fell easier victims to the giant encirclements. Chopped up and isolated, the Red Army had been broken to pieces. If the German Army had not succeeded in reaching its strategic objectives within the time originally envisaged, the Red Army had failed to operate a coherent defensive plan which would preserve its armies from destruction in areas known to hold great strategic dangers.

With the defences covering the capital being apparently crushed in towards the middle of October, the prospect of a successful outcome to the battle for Moscow appeared bleak. Between 10th–19th October leadership and populace alike passed through a grave crisis, in which nerves began to give way. Over the *GOKO* and *Politburo* must have spread the shadow of

Brest-Litovsk, the peace which the Bolsheviks had once concluded to save the regime from destruction by German arms. Addressing the Moscow Party *aktiv* with a special report, candidate member of the *Politburo* A. S. Shcherbakov did not conceal the gravity of the situation on this 13th October — 'The battle is drawing near to the limits of our *oblast*. We will not close our eyes: the menace hangs over Moscow.' According to Tokaev, Stalin held his hand over the defence of Moscow until he was assured of the mood of the whole people, an assurance delivered through the countless reports required on this matter from Party officials scattered throughout the Soviet Union. The defence of Moscow to the bitter end had to be balanced against the other claims, those of Leningrad and the south, for which Zhdanov and Beria would plead most earnestly.[138] The rotund and bespectacled Moscow Party secretary Shcherbakov flung himself into organising the last ditch stand in Moscow, raising from Party and non-Party ranks worker battalions to resist the Germans. Although manpower was available, the utilisation of this was limited by the shortage of equipment. It was therefore decided to limit these formations by the supplies which Moscow factories could deliver to them. In some two days, 11,693 recruits had been assembled and the Town Staff of Worker Formations of Moscow organised; at 3 a.m., on 16th a meeting of the commanders in the Moscow Soviet received orders for the dispatch of these units to the front and to defence lines. On 13th the *GOKO* decided upon the construction of a third defence line covering the south-western and western approaches. Almost half a million of the city's inhabitants were to be drafted to digging trenches and setting up obstacles.

The communiqué of 15th October announced that during the night the situation at the front had worsened. At news of the continuation of the German advance, Moscow was thrown into something like a panic. For three days, from 16th–19th, news of the Vyazma defeat caused a mass flight, or attempted flight, when Party officials, bureaucrats and police left their posts and sought the same kind of safety. While the city was stripped of its usual protections, marauders took possession of the streets, looting and plundering. That this ever happened was for long denied by Soviet publicists and hurried out of the histories, but now the admission has been made.[139] On 19th Stalin imposed a state of siege in the city, and order was once again brought back by a show of level-headedness. An organised evacuation was substituted for the impromptu mass exodus which caused such confusion and disarray. While offices were transferred to Kuibyshev, the *GOKO*, the *Stavka* and Stalin remained in Moscow. The military operations, which in Khrushchev's version had suffered disastrously from Stalin's ignorant interference, were put under the direction of Zhukov and Shaposhnikov.

Certainly the wind of change was blowing about the army. Nothing spectacular came of this, only the gradual eroding of the old command which could not escape responsibility for what had happened. The summer and autumn battles had brought on a military purge as opposed to a political purge of the military. There was a growing restlessness with the incompetent and the inept. Voroshilov and Budenny fell back from the leadership of the Red Army. The great and signal strength of the Soviet high command was that it was able to produce that minimum of high calibre commanders capable of steering the Red Army out of total disaster. Voronov's artillery reforms, Novikov's work with the air force were hints of this. Here and there Red Army tactics were touched with a skill which made it apparent, as Guderian put it, that 'they were learning'. Certainly it had been a lesson of terrible proportions.

On the Bryansk Front, where Guderian's armour was moving on from Orel, Colonel Katukov's 4th Tank Brigade went into action south of Mtsensk with a good complement of T–34 tanks. It was here, as his division suffered 'grievous loss', that Guderian saw a convincing demonstration of the superiority of the T–34. Although a small reserve had been employed south-west of Tula, the defence of this town was in the hands of Gorshkov's five worker battalions, stiffened with regular Red Army troops under the military commandant Colonel Melnikov. What was salvaged out of the wreck of the 50th Army on the Bryansk Front came under Major-General Yermakov's command to bolster the Tula defences. To the north-west of Moscow, Kalinin fell on 14th October after a four-day battle. Over what was now designated the Kalinin Front, Koniev took command on 17th, with the assignment of checking the German threat to Moscow from the north. At the Mozhaisk defence line Major-General of Artillery L. A. Govorov took over the 5th Army which had been assembled there. On 20th October, by decision of Stalin and the *GOKO*, all forces operating on the approaches to Moscow were put under Zhukov's control, and the defence of the city itself assigned to the chief of the Moscow garrison, General Artemeyev. This unification of the command over forces which had been severely battered produced, in the Soviet view, 'a positive result' on the right wing and centre of the Western Front. The German attempt to rush Tula failed, and Guderian considered plans to move past the town to the east. Zhukov's line ran by the Volga reservoir, east of Volokolamsk, Naro-Fominsk, the river lines of the Nara and the Oka to Aleksin. Out of early October's disaster to the defences, when Army Group Centre advanced sixty-two miles on a wide front, Zhukov had saved enough of the situation to begin knitting up the broken lines. With rocks of harder resistance standing out of the sea of mud, human and elemental factors contrived to slow the German advance. All Zhukov could do was to fight for time to maintain the margin of a month.

* * * *

For the defence of Moscow, Zhukov disposed of seven armies and finally a cavalry corps. Although apparently a formidable enough tally, what these armies lacked was men, tanks and guns. No more revealing commentary on the impact of the four months of disaster upon the Red Army is supplied than the fact that these desperate battles before Moscow were being fought with worker battalions, the products of a mobilisation from the streets of Moscow itself. In all, some 1,000 aircraft were available (400 of them of the older types). The vicious circle tightened day by day. The gaping cracks in the military power permitted more German advances, which deprived the Soviet command of the factories from which equipment and ammunition might be drawn to keep the Red Army in the field, which in turn would cover the evacuation of plant to the east. In four months the Red Army had suffered hideous loss. In the major encirclement battles before 1st November, 1941, the Germans claimed 2,053,000 prisoners.[140] Of aviation losses, A. S. Shcherbakov admitted in October the destruction of over 5,000 machines. The Red Army's tank forces, which had once been its pride and joy, had been shattered with astronomical loss. Shot up, captured, abandoned and stranded without fuel, the huge Soviet tank-park had been ruinously thinned. The Red Army had lost a large proportion of its guns and its gun-crews. Since huge ammunition dumps had been placed dangerously close to the frontier areas, these had been lost together with many of the means of producing ammunition. Now it is freely admitted by Soviet military commentators that an ammunition shortage prevailed, recalling the fate which befell the Imperial Russian Army and the straits into which it was plunged.

The roots of defeat lay deeper than two weeks of disaster at the frontiers. Present Soviet explanations villify Stalin but absolve the Soviet system. What remains clear is that, for reasons of political convenience and even necessity, the Stalinist *coterie* set aside the total preparedness and 'vigilance' which had appeared as a basic tenet of Bolshevik doctrine. The concentration in Stalin's hands of massive and undisputed power made his personal interpretation of a given situation crucially important. The degeneration which had crept upon the Red Army also owed its origin to previous political necessities. The professional deficiencies of the military, naval and aviation command were revealed in the state of such defence plans as chanced to exist. The post-purge promotions placed men totally unsuited or untrained for high command in key positions. None showed any capacity for large-scale strategic thinking. Even in tactics, the frontier deployments were proof in them of a dull or listless mind. Such was the rigid nature of the Soviet military-political machine that a failure at the top, the absence of planning for a number of possible contingencies, presaged certain dislocation and confusion. Mass, upon which Soviet military confidence rested, became too massive to respond to control and manipulation. As for the separate arguments of military and economic-industrial unpreparedness, they are essentially one; their most 'un-Bolshevik' separation in recent Soviet assessments of 1941 is a means to ward off an otherwise inevitably jolting criticism of the system as a whole.

It was therefore not as strategists or tacticians that the high command made war, but as desperate improvisers. Equally it was not that the Russians had to recover the strategic initiative; rather it was that even now they must learn how to grasp at it at all. Khrushchev charges Stalin with having lost his nerve in the crisis so rapidly precipitated, with having made mischievous and blundering interference with military operations. This would not dispose of the fact that in June and July, the Red Army command lost its head, nor of the repeated shuffles designed to seek out the commanders capable of coping. The July decision to set up three major commands over the North-western, Western and South-western 'directions' (*napravlenie*) failed to produce any of the necessary co-ordination or cohesion. These huge and virtually unmanageable strategic masses succumbed in the space of a few weeks to the smashing blows of the German Army, to their intrinsic unwieldiness and, in the case of Budenny especially, to the ineptness of their commanders. Only Timoshenko, whom the German General Staff had rated in the spring of 1941 as 'outstanding', showed himself capable of adjusting his methods of command to the very exacting situation. But the whole position of the Red Army degenerated at such speed that effective control became impossible. According to a former Soviet Major-General, from the second day of the war the Red Army was 'a hopeless mess'.[141] Stalin held the command to immediate account for this with the shootings of the first Western Front commander, General of the Army Pavlov, his staff and that of the North-western Front. This left other commanders in no doubt of the fate to be meted out to them in the event of failure, even though they were powerless to bring a situation for whose disorders they were not initially responsible under control. General Petrov met congratulation upon his appointment to a front command with the words: 'So now they are going to shoot me *too*.'[142]

Khrushchev charges Stalin with two grievous shortcomings at this time; a loss of nerve in face of the disasters at the front and costly interference with the conduct of operations. Evidence of Stalin's loss of confidence, although not the 'nervousness and hysteria' of which Khrushchev speaks, might be drawn from the astounding if unrealistic remarks addressed by Stalin to Harry L. Hopkins, President Roosevelt's special envoy, on 30th July, to the effect that American troops under American command would be welcome on any part of the Russian front. After the disaster in the Ukraine Stalin, visibly depressed, touched upon the possibility of British troops being sent to the Ukraine. To Sir Stafford Cripps, he admitted the possibility of the German Army taking Moscow, but avowed that it would be defended to the bitter end. The fall of Moscow would not mean the end of Russian resistance but a retirement to the Volga. But the way back would be the agonised labour of many years.[143] Stalin's war leadership at this time seems to have been a curious compound of broad strategic control and minute attention to particular details. In the latter category fell Stalin's admonishment to Voroshilov and Zhdanov for setting up a defence committee in Leningrad without the former's prior agreement. The fact that no proper withdrawal plans existed made movement of troops to even semi-prepared positions a most difficult undertaking; the mounting chaos made any central control rudimentary. It is not that Soviet military doctrine had ignored the need for adaptability when considering the plan of strategic deployment; in 1935 this had been carefully examined in a study of strategic deployment.[144] Under Voroshilov's management, those stipulations had been set aside.

At the same time as he shot the generals held responsible for the collapse at the frontier, Stalin slowly turned to a reconstitution of the Red Army command. The criterion became ability on the battle-field. If it can be dated, the process began about October 1941. Out of the thousand or so higher commanders of the post-1939 period, Stalin began to make his selections. It was to mean that the fate of Moscow was confided to between a dozen and a score of commanders for whom the only thing that mattered was ability to get results. The rest depended on what Hitler and the German General Staff believed to be impossible — the existence and proper use of further Russian reserves. For the Red Army as a whole to recover itself from this morass of defeat, disorganisation, panic and a terrible physical weakening did indeed appear to be an impossibility.

CHAPTER EIGHTEEN

The Battle for Moscow: November–December 1941

With early November came the biting Russian frosts. The chilling hints of the Russian winter at first served to aid the *Wehrmacht*, for the wheels which had been caught in the vast muddy traps of late autumn could now move more easily. The drive on Moscow, which was already in an extremity of danger, could be renewed, although weather conditions were far from favourable and the German casualty lists were carrying the first tallies of severe frost-bite cases. But the German spearheads were once more on the move and the Red Army was committed to a desperate act of defence. The month of November figures in Soviet accounts as the period of greatest danger, both military and economic. Already German troops had penetrated over 500 miles in the north-west, some 600 miles at the centre and 900 miles in a south-easterly direction. Leningrad was tightly invested. As German advances lopped off its coal and electric power resources, Moscow's industrial production suffered an inevitable drop. Occupation of the Donets coal basin robbed the Soviet Union of 57 per cent of its pre-war coal production; 68 per cent of the pig-iron, 58 per cent of the steel, 60 per cent of the aluminium and 38 per cent of the grain production of the Soviet Union had been lost in areas invested by the enemy. Voznesenskii, who was responsible after Stalin and the *GOKO* for war-time economic measures, was of the opinion that November 1941 embodied 'the most critical period' of the whole history of the Soviet war economy. The production of weapons and ammunition had fallen in October and took a disastrous tumble in November. Weapon production was incapable of catching up with the immense losses suffered by the Red Army in the course of the disastrous frontier battles. In November the production of combat aircraft fell to less than a quarter of what it had been in September. Even though the output of artillery ammunition had increased to 2·3 times what it had been in the first half of 1941, the Red Army's ammunition requirement jumped ahead of what could be produced.[1] In November the *GOKO* decided to organise the production in Moscow of the artillery ammunition required by the forces defending the city. This included the manufacture of explosives, which had hitherto not been an item produced in the capital. Although some 200,000 skilled workers were evacuated along with plant from the city, the production of 22-mm, 37-mm, 76-mm (and 76-mm anti-aircraft), 45-mm and 85-mm (anti-aircraft and armour-piercing) shells was intensified. The great limiting factor was the amount of explosive which could be manufactured. In Leningrad intensive reconnaissance and hydrographic research had been designed to explore the usefulness of an 'ice road' across Lake Ladoga. On 20th November, using an M–1 lorry, the Chief of the Rear Services of the Leningrad Front Major-General F. N. Lagunov travelled over the 'road' from Konkorev to Kobona. On 22nd the first convoy of sixty lorries under Major Parchunov travelled the 'road' — a life-line of some fragileness, where the ice thickness was in places only 5½ inches — and opened this crack in the blockade. Horses were used extensively in this work.[2]

Improvisations in this fashion could bring local relief and stave off dire consequence, but they remained local ameliorations. The immense capacity for improvisation remained, nevertheless, a signal advantage for the Russians. Much of the military and economic activity during the initial period of disasters bore that very stamp, including the partisan movement. Stalin, in his 7th July speech, did formally inaugurate this, but the reality fell far behind the speeches. No comprehensive plan for possible guerrilla operations existed prior to the German attack. Groups of Red Army men, cut off by German advances, were bereft of command and control; in fear of possible punishment on return to their own lines and anxious to avoid the rigours of German prison camps, these groups of fighting men degenerated into marauding bands, preying when they could on German supplies. The Communist Party organisation was used to set up small, independent partisan units, but in the absence of adequate supplies of weapons and explosives, as well as wireless sets, this resulted in neither significant result nor co-ordination. A factor of very great importance was the passivity, and in not a few cases the accommodation of the population towards the Germans. In that respect, the blunders of German policy could themselves be held accountable as bringing an extensive pro-Soviet partisan movement into being. Only in December 1941 was a central command of the partisan movement — *GShPD* — set up, although there seems to be considerable evidence of a rudimentary collaboration between guerrilla fighting units and the Red Army at the approaches to Moscow.[3] The partisan movement, upon which the centre was only obtaining the slightest grip, was beset with enormous political problems. Out of the activities of the German *Sicherheitsdienst* and the central Soviet partisan command a new dimension of bestiality and ferocity was to be added to the war on the Eastern Front.

The development of the partisan movement, however, was intimately linked with the aim of the Soviet command in organising a 'national war', which called for a soft-pedalling of the ideological content in the war propaganda.

Stalin was also waging a coalition war, in which his chief tactic even at the outset appeared to be to force from his newly-found allies maximum concessions. To Prime Minister Churchill, Stalin at once directed urgent appeals for munitions and supplies; on 25th July 200 Tomahawk fighters were routed for Russia and the British prepared to meet some of the very considerable Russian demands for rubber. The Moscow Conference, held in September on an Anglo-American-Russian basis, was a strange and difficult affair. On 4th September Stalin wrote to Churchill on the measures needed to bring alleviation to the Soviet Union. At once the 'Second Front' issue raised its head, with Stalin's observation that such a diversion was needed to draw off 30–40 German divisions from the Eastern Front. A second support was needed in the way of supplies; the Soviet Union needed 30,000 tons of aluminium and a monthly minimum of 400 aircraft and 500 tanks (small or medium) as a means of staving off either defeat or such losses as would render Soviet assistance to the 'common cause' a matter for recovery only in the future. Soviet Ambassador Maisky brought the Soviet plea in person to Churchill, but tinged his advocacy with an 'air of menace', so that the British Prime Minister did not forbear to remind Maisky that '. . . you of all people have no right to make reproaches to us'.[4] To secure Iran from Axis penetration, a joint Anglo-Soviet operation in August succeeded in holding that country open as a channel through which supplies were later to be poured into the Soviet Union. With British troops holding west of the Nile and Soviet forces still fighting west of the Don, the Germans were momentarily held off from the oil fields of the Middle East and Southern Russia. Although this was a gain, the measures of military collaboration between Great Britain and the Soviet Union, which Stalin himself proposed, were utterly unrealistic. Upon Churchill Stalin pressed the idea of the despatch of 25–30 British divisions to Arkhangel, or to Southern Russia through Iran. Churchill castigated as absurd and foolish the professional advice which had been tendered to Stalin in support of this scheme. It was obvious that the Russian command was totally ignorant of the problem of transporting large numbers of troops by sea. Even in 1939 their idea of effective coalition warfare (even allowing for certain deliberate political distortions) had been for a definite undertaking to commit a prescribed number of divisions. To this rigidity was once more added that sterile suspiciousness, which introduced into the all-important political factor still further complication. To Churchill's letter of 4th November, suggesting closer contacts in military planning and co-operation, Stalin on 8th returned a 'chilling and evasive' reply.[5] Over the British attitude to declaring war on Finland a crisis loomed and gathered in mid-November. From Stalin's words, there is no doubt about the desperate straits to which he was reduced, the root cause of which, however, lay not in the British having too few ships with which to scatter divisions over many quarters, but in the ruin of his own self-directed strategy from 1939 onwards.

In November Stalin was grievously short of men as well as munitions and weapons. It was at this time that the strength of the Red Army forces on the European fronts fell to 2·3 million, the lowest they ever reached throughout the whole of the Soviet-German war.[6] Trained and fully equipped men were to be found in the Far Eastern garrisons, although the employment of these forces on the European front depended on a careful calculation of the chances of a clash with Japan. To assist with this calculation, Stalin and his command had the invaluable services of Sorge, adviser to the German Ambassador in Tokyo, Ott, and a party to the secrets of such vital importance to the Soviet Union. With Sorge worked Hozumi Ozaki, a member of Prince Konoye's entourage; through the latter Ozaki learned the details of secret Japanese decisions, which were passed in turn to Sorge and thence to Moscow. It is, therefore, safe to assume that Stalin was fully and properly informed of the decisions of the Imperial Conference held on 2nd July, when the Japanese Prime Minister and thirteen military and civilian leaders assembled in the presence of the Emperor. Here the decision to move into Southern French Indo-China, first mooted on 12th June but not finally agreed until 25th, was confirmed. Japan was resuming the advance to the south. Matsuoka had himself described to Shigemitsu the possibility of 'the conflagration' blazing up either in the north or the south. Shigemitsu records Sorge as being 'more accurate',[7] since the Soviet spy indicated that it was to be the south and not the north where the trouble would begin. Japanese action against the Soviet Union would be dependent on the successes achieved by the German Army. Advised in due time of the Japanese intention to move south, Stalin could more easily draw on the Far Eastern manpower which was critically needed on the European front.* The movement of these troops, which had begun before June 1941, speeded up through the late summer and autumn. In this process Panfilov's 316th Rifle Division was assembled and moved out of Central Asia towards the Western Front. From the Far Eastern command altogether 15 rifle divisions, 3 cavalry

* Hans-Otto Meissner in his work on Sorge records that Sorge sent his vital message on 3rd October, giving absolute assurance that the Kwantung Army would not strike north. But the subsequent connection of this information with the employment of Siberian troops does not correspond with the actual course of the Moscow battles, and certainly two million men were not brought from the eastern hinterland.

divisions, 1,700 tanks and 1,500 aircraft were moved westwards — approximately half of the ground strength of the Far Eastern armies. From the Trans-Baikal came 7 rifle, 2 cavalry and 3 air divisions and 2 tank brigades. Outer Mongolia supplied 1 rifle division and 2 tank brigades, the Amur area 2 rifle and 1 air divisions with 1 tank brigade. From the vital Ussuri area 5 rifle and 1 cavalry divisions and 3 tank brigades were pulled out for use in the west. This re-deployment made two measures inevitable and necessary in the Soviet Far East, the re-organisation of the Far Eastern armies and fresh mobilisations to replace the forces now lost to another theatre. Where the First Red Banner Army had hitherto held sway, from Khabarovsk to Vladivostok on the Ussuri front, two new army headquarters were established. On this undulating front the 25th Army (HQ Voroshilov) was assigned to the left flank, the First Red Banner Army held the centre and the 35th Army (HQ Iman) kept the northern sector. The Second Red Banner Army remained in the Kuibyshevka region, while the 15th Army was located in Birobidzan. In the Trans-Baikal, in addition to the area army, there were two important subordinate commands in the 16th Army (Borziya) and the 17th (Ulan-Bator). Total mobilisation in the Soviet Far East brought the Soviet forces up to a strength of 800,000, organised into what the Japanese Army General Staff estimated at 23 rifle divisions, 1,000 tanks and 1,000 aircraft. The numerical aspect was, nevertheless, offset by the fact that the increased Soviet strength represented troops as yet in training.[8]

While the Red Army mobilised those reserves which the German high command thought it could not possibly possess, Stalin entrusted the defence of Moscow to those officers who had shown their abilities in the summer and autumn battles and had managed to survive. The new command group had passed through a short but terrifyingly intense battle-school in the autumn of 1941. The salvation of the Red Army lay perhaps fundamentally in the fact that the Soviet command was able to produce a small but highly talented group of officers capable of adjusting themselves to the demands of the situation. The rise of new officers was itself a hint of the revolt in temper which had taken place against the incompetents who boasted only of their experience in the Civil War. There was nothing spectacular about this transformation of the command. It was, basically, a purge, but one dictated by the requirement of success on the battle-field. The 'linear tactics', by which term the Red Army leadership described the first phase of the Soviet-German war, were themselves described by Stalin at a later date as 'stupid and pernicious'. The art of co-ordination, although repeatedly emphasised since 1933, was only now being properly understood and beginning to be practised. Some of the new men understood what was required; those who did not lay dead after the battles with an experienced enemy in the frontier districts and further in the interior. Dovator had shown his paces in the counter-attacks at Smolensk. Katukov, the victor at Mtsensk, was raised to the rank of general and his tank brigade given the title of 1st Guards Tank Brigade on 11th November, 1941. Rotmistrov, whose few tanks had been smashed to pieces in an unequal combat in the Baltic Military District, had shown energy enough to be entrusted with a new command of armoured units near Moscow. Vlasov, who had fought on in Kiev and then hacked his way through German encirclement, received command of one of the formations covering Moscow. The front command rested with Zhukov, the direction of the *Stavka* with Shaposhnikov and the last vital word with Stalin. Much depended on whether the *Stavka* could dispose of its reserves correctly. In the July battles the Red Army leadership had committed the fatal mistake of advancing to meet the Germans. In this way, front-line forces and reserves had been overwhelmed in fast-moving catastrophes over which the *Stavka* and front command had no control whatsoever, or else the lines with tanks and guns strung out but without strong mobile reserves had been quickly pierced and Red Army troops encircled. Space, although it had itself been one of the weapons with which Stalin and his commanders tried to fight, was running out. With great territorial loss had gone important sections of the Soviet industrial vitals. There could be no more, unless Stalin accepted the prospect of a retirement which would virtually exclude Russia from the war.

* * * *

Although Leningrad had not fallen to the blows of the German Army, the danger of the city being strangled by blockade was inescapably real. One attempt to force open the trap had failed. The threat of a German-Finnish junction on the Svir was also real enough, although decisive success still eluded Army Group North at the end of October. For a fortnight Soviet troops had launched a series of attacks which had not halted the enemy but certainly slowed his progress. With the threat to Tikhvin growing very great at the beginning of November, the 4th Red army commander Yakovlev concentrated his available forces for yet one more counter-attack on the German troops. Yakovlev aimed to mount two co-ordinated attacks, with a force made up of three rifle divisions and one tank division, on the German flanks and rear in the Budogoshch-Gruzino direction. On 1st November the 191st Rifle Division, the 25th Rifle Regiment (44th Rifle Division) and the 4th (Guards) Rifle Division attacked, followed on 4th–6th November by the 92nd Rifle and the 60th Tank Division operating by Sitomlya. Massed artillery fire and tank-supported infantry met the Red Army in a five-day struggle; in this manner the *Wehrmacht* broke the Soviet attack and broke into the junction of the 191st and 4th Rifle Divisions, advancing to overwhelm the Soviet positions on the River Syas. After bitter fighting, Tikhvin fell into German hands on 8th November. The railway link between the Leningrad Front (54th Army) and the interior was now cut. Leningrad's fortunes took a distinct turn for the worse. Yakovlev has come in for criticism for failing to co-ordinate the counter-attack properly and for launching the attack without adequate 'material-technical preparation'. The lack of adequate experience among the rank-and-file and command staff in carrying out offensive operations is also adduced as a cause of failure.[9] Nevertheless, holding the enemy for five days before Sitomlya is counted a definite gain. By 9th, after retiring to the north and north-east of Tikhvin, the 4th Army managed to bring their opponents to a halt, thus holding them off from the River Svir.

Yakovlev was now replaced as commander of the 4th Army by Meretskov, who was moved from the 7th Army on the Karelian Front. On 10th November, the 4th Army was split into four operational groups to simplify the conduct of further operations. Major-General Lyapin took over the Volkhov Operational Group (two regiments of the 292nd Rifle Division, 285, 311th, 310th Rifle Divisions, 6th Naval Infantry Brigade and 16th Tank Brigade), Major-General Pavlovich assumed command of the Northern Operational Group (two rifle regiments, one bridging battalion, the 46th Tank Brigade and the 1067th Rifle Regiment transferred from the 7th Army), Major-General Ivanov took over the Eastern Operational Group (191st Rifle Division, 27th Cavalry Division and the 65th Rifle Division of the *Stavka* reserve, with one tank regiment and one tank battalion), while Yakovlev himself took command of the Southern Operational Group (4th Guards and 92nd Rifle Divisions, one rifle and one tank regiment).[10]

The capture of Tikhvin had been accompanied by the development of a serious threat to Volkhov; by 9th November a gap of nearly forty miles had been opened up between the Tikhvin and Volkhov groups of the 4th Army. The left flank of the Volkhov group (4th Army) lay open, and German penetrations promised to cut off the retreat to the north of the 285th and 311th Rifle Divisions. On 12th November forward German units were only twenty miles from the shore of Lake Ladoga and now the communications of the 54th Red army were in jeopardy. Fedyuninskii, 54th Army commander, received orders on 9th to send a reinforcement to the Volkhov group of the 4th Army, to secure the left flank and rear, as well as to prevent any further German penetration to the north. To accomplish this, Fedyuninskii sent from his right wing on 10th the 16th and 122nd Tank Brigades, the 3rd (Guards) Rifle Division and the 6th Naval Infantry Brigade. That is how Major-General Lyapin's 'Volkhov

Group' took on part of its composition. On 12th November, the position of this 'Volkhov Group' had become precarious; communications between the group and the 4th Army staff (located fifteen miles east of Tikhvin, at Bolshoi Dvor) were severed. The *Stavka* radioed that the 'Volkhov Group' must be severed from the 4th Army and attached to the 54th Army under the control of the Leningrad Front. This was merely a recognition of the actual position. Fedyuninskii was ordered to halt the German attempts to break through to the north and to keep Army Group North from Novaya Ladoga and the shore of the Lake. It was vital to hold the railway station of Voibokalo, against which a special reinforcement of the German left wing had been battering since 9th November. To counter this Fedyuninskii moved up the 122nd Tank Brigade, a battalion of the 1st Mountain Infantry Brigade and elements of the 285th Rifle Division, with which reinforcement he was able to force the Germans on to the defensive.

Although the situation had been scored with severe crisis in the first half of November, Meretskov and Fedyuninskii had succeeded in holding off an enemy break-through into the rear of the Soviet Karelian Front or cutting the 54th Army's communications. The complete investment of Leningrad was so far being held off, and now work was going ahead with the 'ice road' which would afford some relief to the city harrassed by German long-range guns and the *Luftwaffe* and now suffering the first agony of famine. *Stavka* reserves, drawn away from Moscow, played an important part in bringing about the necessary correction to a dangerous situation. The 4th and 52nd Armies had received from the *Stavka* one tank and six rifle divisions. It was obvious from an examination of the strength of these armies before the end of October that they were far from being in a condition to stand up to a determined offensive. By moving four divisions from the Leningrad Front, the Soviet command calculated that it might alter the relationship of forces in the Volkhov-Tikhvin area (taking into consideration the losses suffered by the Germans in the thrusts aimed at Tikhvin and Volkhov). The German troops, moreover, were in a less favourable operational situation, hemmed in on three sides by the Red Army and with their forces dispersed over a wide front, thus limiting their offensive capacities. By mid-November the left flank units of the 54th Army (Leningrad Front) were continuing to hold German attacks on Voibokalo. North and north-east of Tikhvin the 4th Army held its defensive positions while reinforcements came to it, so that offensive operations might be renewed. To the south of 4th Army lay the 52nd Army (288th, 259th, 111th and 267th Rifle Divisions) under Klykov, holding the Malaya Vyshera river line, and south again was the Novgorod Army Group of the North-western Front, with two rifle divisions (305th and 180th) and the 3rd Tank Division — minus tanks. The junction between the 52nd Army and the Novgorod Army Group was held by the 25th Cavalry Division.[11]

Yet the Soviet intention was not confined to the defensive. The *Stavka* reserves were not committed to accomplish a successful defence, but to assist the 4th, 52nd and 54th Armies in going over to the offensive, the operations being designed to liquidate German troops east of the River Volkhov. Three main groups had emerged among the Soviet forces — the 54th at Voibokalo-Volkhov, the 4th at Tikhvin and the 52nd Army at

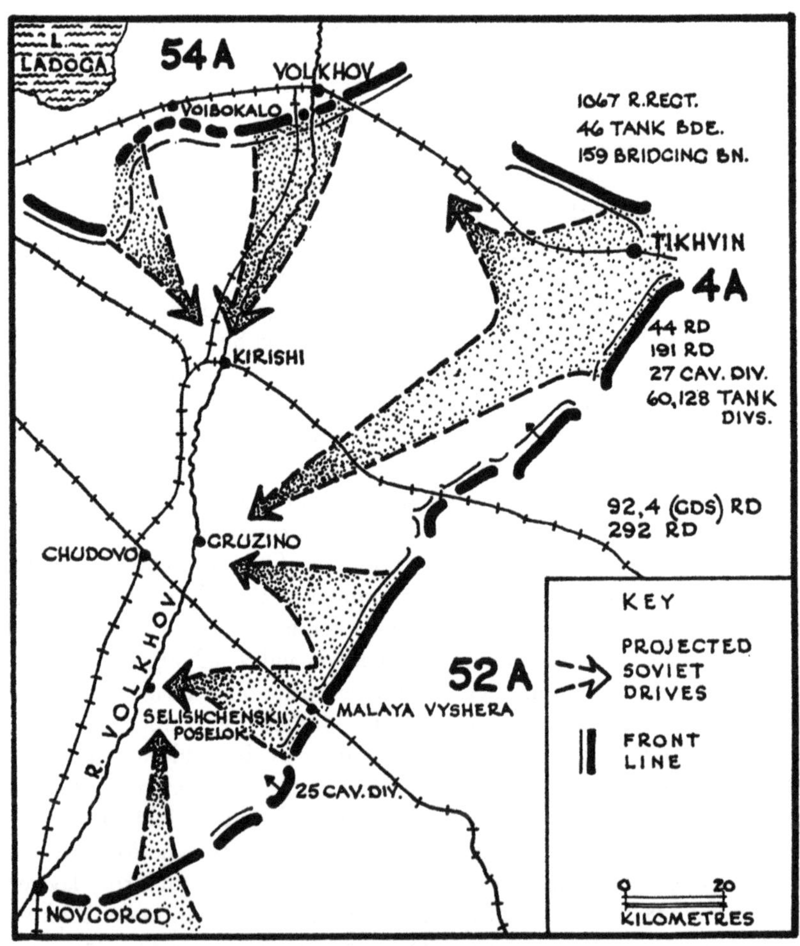

GENERAL SOVIET PLAN FOR TIKHVIN-VOLKHOV OPERATIONS

Malaya Vyshera. The offensive operations were further designed to prevent the transfer of German troops from the north-west to assist the operations against Moscow. The key to the Soviet appreciation of the role of the Volkhov-Tikhvin-Malaya Vyshera operations appears to lie with the actions of the 52nd Army (both the 4th and 52nd Armies were directly subordinated to the *Stavka*). On 12th November, while the 4th Army had only just succeeded in halting the German advance and as the 54th Army was heavily committed south of Voibokalo and Volkhov, Klykov's 52nd Army went over to the offensive. The idea underlying this embodied using forces better prepared for a counter-attack, which by driving on Gruzino and Selishchenskii Poselok could bring Soviet troops into the rear of German forces advancing in the Tikhvin direction. This would facilitate the 4th and 54th Armies' commitment to the offensive operations against Volkhov and Tikhvin, previously ordered by the *Stavka*. Accordingly, at dawn on 12th November, after a two-hour artillery preparation and with air support, 52nd Army rifle units attacked German positions on the Malaya Vyshera. The first day's heavy fighting did not bring the required results. Right flank units of the Novgorod Army Group also failed to win any significant gains. The four days of Soviet attacks, spread over 12th–16th November, were likewise devoid of substantial results. The organisation of the attack evidently left a great deal to be desired. Klykov strung out his four rifle divisions along a thirty-mile front, with only two regiments of the 259th Rifle Division assigned to carrying out the primary task of the whole operation. The artillery support had not been as effective as it might have been. The whole of the 267th Rifle Division had been thrown into action on 12th, with the result that this formation had become split from the outset and existed merely as a collection of units for several days. Frontal attacks on the well-prepared German positions came to nought and ground to a halt. There was nothing for it but to organise another series of attacks, which were prepared in greater secrecy and timed for 18th November.[12]

* * * *

From Tokyo Sorge's remarkable espionage system was furnishing Stalin with invaluable information on the course of German and Japanese policy. In Berlin meanwhile a Soviet intelligence network, manned by Germans and subsequently known as the *Rote Kapelle*, had begun to supply information on German plans and intentions, details obtained from highly-placed sources. Shortly before June, 1941, Harro Schulze-Boysen, an intelligence officer in Göring's Air Ministry and inclined sympathetically towards Soviet Communism, had been selected by Soviet intelligence officers to join Harnack and Kuckhoff in operating a spy-ring in the event of war. Whatever its significance as an anti-Nazi resistance movement, the *Rote Kapelle* carried out an extraordinarily successful and sustained act of espionage on behalf of the Soviet Union. Suffering at first a serious breakdown in radio communication with Moscow (although information on further German movements on the Dnieper was successfully passed on in July), by autumn matters had improved. Utilising their wide and penetrating contacts, the *Rote Kapelle* operators were able to supply the type of information which included such invaluable items as the decision of the German command to postpone its Caucasus offensive until the coming spring, the decision to invest rather than to storm Leningrad, planned German airborne raids (with exact times and places), the planning of an air attack on a convoy from Britain to Russia, disputes within the German high command, as well as data on the strength and location of German forces on the Eastern Front.[13] From Rössler ('Lucy') in Switzerland, the agent who had already supplied an accurate forecast of the date of the German invasion, information of such an accurate and incredibly well-informed nature streamed to Moscow that Soviet suspicions were aroused that this was merely an agent of the *Abwehr* engaged on an elaborate process of 'dis-information' aimed at luring the Soviet command into a giant trap. In what remains an astounding performance, and one finally appreciated by Moscow as genuine, 'Lucy' supplied up-to-date data on the German order of battle, with day-to-day changes, as well as being able to answer Russian enquiries about high-level matters dealing with the German Army. Such was 'Lucy's' role that one former highly valued Soviet agent considered that '. . . in the end Moscow very largely fought the war on Lucy's messages'.[14]

In devising measures to hold the Germans on the flanks, while barring their way to Moscow, Stalin and the *Stavka* were demonstrably not without a considerable quantity of vital information bearing on the state and intentions of the forces opposing them, not to mention the information coming in through the Soviet front commands. Knowledge of German intentions was an indispensable element for success in the revised policy dictated by the *GOKO* in November, when the decision was adopted to transmit available weapons only to those formations operating on the decisive sectors of the front. Since an increasing number of Guards units were committed to these decisive sectors, this amounted to nothing less than supplying tested and élite troops with what weapons were available. At the same time, weapons and ammunition were concentrated in the main directions where the newly-organised strategic reserves were being built up. The number of formations attached to the field armies was slowly growing, although to cut down the time needed to get fresh forces into action, as well as to provide the type of smaller force which the available Soviet commander might best handle, a 'significant number' of independent rifle brigades and independent ski battalions were brought into being.[15] That a change for the better had come over the leadership of the Red Army is confirmed to some degree by the actions being fought out in the Volkhov-Tikhvin area and those contemplated for the south. No longer was the Red Army merely fighting for each piece of ground, but signs of some kind of co-ordination were beginning to make their appearance. It is a Soviet argument that the yard-by-yard resistance of the Soviet troops had made its special contribution to destroying the chances of the German Army to win victory in a lightning campaign. But, by the same admission, it was not enough merely to halt the Germans, although even this possibility hung in the balance in the decisive period of the 1941 campaign, a period set in the last fortnight of November.

Over making a final attempt to reach Moscow at this late date, German opinion had been divided. On the one hand was the argument that Moscow lay almost within reach, on the other the substantial evidence of the weakened condition of the forces destined for the assault. While the German divisions facing Moscow had enjoyed a small respite since the end of October, this same period had been utilised by the *Stavka* to build up the Russian forces defending the city. By mid-November the number of aircraft assigned to the Western Front and to the Moscow anti-aircraft defence force had grown to 1,000. The *Stavka* re-grouped and reinforced the armies about Moscow. By Zagorsk, the 1st Shock Army (*Udarnaya Armiya*) was put under the command of V. I. Kuznetsov, in the Ryazan area the 10th Army was assembled under F. I. Golikov, and at Lobnaya the 20th Army. The Bryansk Front had been liquidated on 10th November, and its available forces distributed between the Western and South-western Fronts. To unify the Western Front command the 30th and 50th Armies (the latter covering Tula) had been incorporated into this front.[16]

On 15th November, the German Army went over to the offensive to make its final bid for the capture of Moscow. The German plan called Guderian's tanks to advance on Tula and then move north-east. Von Kluge's Fourth Army, the bulk of which lay along the Nara, between the Podolsk-Maloyaroslavets and the Moscow-Smolensk roadways, would hold the Russians, while Hoepner's tank and infantry force should advance on the city from the west and north-west. On a line stretching from the north-east of Kalinin to the south of Tula, the German intention was to utilise their favourable positions to crack Soviet resistance by assaulting the flanks. In an effort to impede German preparations, Lieutenant-General I. G. Zakharov's 49th Army had carried out a series of attacks on the right wing of the German Fourth Army in the Serpukhov area, where the German front was thinly held. In spite of creating difficulties for the Germans, the Red Army was unable to ward off the blow which was about to fall upon it. Mud had given way to frost-hardened country as the German offensive gathered momentum, driving on the northern flank in the Klin-Solnechnogorsk direction and to the south on Kashira-Stalinogorsk. On the hundred-mile front to the north-west of Moscow the Red Army was once more engaged in desperate defensive battles. To the north of Volokolamsk, Reinhardt's Third Armoured Group overwhelmed Major-General V. A. Khomenko's 30th Army (Kalinin Front, now incorporated into the Western Front); on 17th November Major-General D. D. Lelyushenko took over command of this army. Rokossovskii's 16th Army, holding the Volokolamsk-Istra sector, was assailed by the Fourth Armoured Group, which at first enjoyed some success. The 30th Army was forced back to the east. On the Volokolamsk highway, at the right wing of the Western Front, the German offensive met up with Panfilov's battle-tested 316th Rifle Division, General Dovator's cavalry and General Katukov's 1st Guards Tank Brigade. Panfilov's men especially distinguished themselves in the fighting for Dubosekovo.* On 18th November the 316th Division was re-designated the 8th Guards Rifle Division; Panfilov himself was killed in action on 19th. To the south, where the Tula defence force was under the command of Major-General A. N. Yermakov, the bitterness of the fighting was no less marked. Guderian's Second Tank Army launched its attack on 18th November, by-passing Tula to the south-east. On the previous day Guderian had learned of the arrival of Siberian troops in the Ryazan-Kolomna area, and the 112th German Infantry Division made contact with them. Fresh Russian troops, Russian tank attacks in the Dedilovo area and a freezing temperature which interfered with the proper working of the German weapons caused a momentary snapping of the German will. On 24th November, having mastered determined Russian resistance and the difficulties created by the rapidly deteriorating weather conditions, Guderian's tanks took Venev. Reinhardt's tanks had meanwhile ground down Lelyushenko's left flank and taken Klin on 23rd November. Splitting the adjacent flanks of the 30th and 16th Armies, German troops forced their way to Dmitrov-Yakhroma-Krasnaya-Polyana-Kryukovo. On 26th–27th November German elements succeeded in crossing to the eastern bank of the Moscow-Volga Canal, thereby presenting a grave threat to Moscow from the north.[17]

The *Stavka* had to take rapid measures to reinforce the right wing of the Western Front. To restore the situation the *Stavka* made use of its reserve in

* This has been the subject of a recent novel in the series *Sovetskii voennyi roman*: A. Bek, *Volokolamskoe shosse* (The Volokolamsk highway), Moscow 1959. This is in the newer critical fashion, and the narrative of the Moscow operations begins with Panfilov listening to a report on the execution of an officer for cowardice.

the shape of Kuznetsov's 1st Shock Army, which was moved up to Dmitrov-Krasnaya Polyana. On 28th, this force put in a counter-attack aimed at throwing the enemy back over the Moscow-Volga Canal. With heavy fighting raging to the north, the *Stavka* had also to counter the German moves aimed at Moscow from the south. From Venev, Guderian could strike at Kashira, and having forced the Oka, drive on Moscow from the south. To block this, the *Stavka* assigned Belov's 2nd Cavalry Corps to the Kashira direction, strengthening his formation with tank and rifle formations. Zhukov and Shaposhnikov committed their reserves with great care but with considerable skill. While in the last week in November, in a temperature which plunged disastrously to bring a ferocious cold,* German forces on the flanks manœuvred as they could in the nightmare conditions to split the Russian defences, and von Kluge was prevailed upon to employ the Fourth Army in an attack towards Moscow along the Nara. On 1st December, north and south of Naro-Fominsk, the Fourth Army attack succeeded in breaking into the flanks of the 33rd Army, and forward German units penetrated some fifteen miles into the Soviet rear. To check this incursion Yefremov's 33rd Army and parts of Golubev's 43rd Army were directed to hold the Germans. As von Kluge launched this final attack, on 30th November General Zhukov, Western Front commander, had submitted to Stalin a report containing an analysis of the situation at the front and a suggested plan for a counter-offensive. This plan, which contained the basic outline of the offensive operations subsequently undertaken by the Red Army, was adopted by Stalin.[18]

* * * *

In the south also Army Group South had renewed its offensive in November. At the end of October, South-western and Southern Front forces had fallen back to a shortened line, with the aim of attacking von Kleist's armoured forces, Timoshenko had begun to build up reserve divisions at Kamensk and to form these into the 37th Army, which was to be assigned as a shock army to the Southern Front command. On 5th November, the German offensive aimed at Shakhty (thereby outflanking the Rostov defences) developed against Major-General F. M. Kharitonov's 9th Army. For a fortnight von Kleist's armour struggled forward against Soviet resistance and mud alternating with ice. By 17th November Kharitonov

* Colonel P. Zhilin, in *Protiv fal'sifikatorov istorii vtoroi mirovoi voiny*, p. 93 produces a record from the Main Administration of the Meteorological Service to the effect that in the Moscow *environs* (Kashira, Dmitrov) the temperatures were: (minimum) October —8·2°, November —17·3°, December —28·8°. This is to disprove the German statements that cold produced 42 degrees of frost, to show that the climate was an obstacle to both sides, and to insist that the Red Army should be given some of the credit for the German check before Moscow.

was holding off von Kleist for the moment, and the preparations to assemble the 37th Army were evidently complete. On 17th, with the German drive now directed at taking Rostov from the north-west, Lieutenant-General A. I. Lopatin put the 37th Army in to counter-attack von Kleist. The German pressure on Rostov increased and on 21st, after heavy fighting, the town was taken. Further north, in the direction of Voroshilovgrad, Major-General K. A. Koroteyev's 12th Army had managed to check the German 17th Army at Golubovka. As on the Leningrad and North-western Fronts the *Stavka*'s idea remained the same, to prevent the withdrawal of German forces from the wings to assist the main drive on Moscow. At the same time, the *Stavka* was transferring forces from Timoshenko's command to replenish the armies defending Moscow. Meanwhile, although the defence of the Crimea had caved in at the end of October as the Ishun positions were breached and the Germans burst into the Peninsula, Sevastopol had been organised for a protracted resistance. The Coastal Army, the strength of which had been depleted by its continuous action, was assigned as part of the Sevastopol defence force; on 9th November the Coastal Army strength was recorded as 8,000.[19] Both the Coastal Army and the 51st Army (the latter moved to cover Kerch) came under the command of Vice-Admiral G. I. Levchenko. The Sevastopol fortified district was divided into four sectors as regards the distribution of the land forces. Colonel Novikov commanded the first (383rd Rifle Regiment, elements of the 2nd Cavalry Division), Colonel Laskin the second (172nd Rifle Division), Major-General Kolomiets the third (15th Rifle Division) and Major-General Vorob'ev the fourth (95th Rifle Division).

It was not Odessa but Sevastopol which became the Soviet Tobruk. The operational plan for the defence of Sevastopol had been worked out before the war, but it had envisaged the main threat coming from sea- or air-borne landings. The emphasis had been laid on powerful coastal gun-batteries, with torpedo-boat, submarine and torpedo-aircraft squadrons organised to ward off enemy blows. The anti-aircraft defence was assigned to the 61st AA Regiment, with a battalion of anti-aircraft machine-guns; on the Crimean aerodromes at Belbek and Eupatoriya were some 200 I–15 and I–16 fighters. On 16th December, 1940, Voroshilov had ordered the preparation of a land-based defence of Sevastopol, but by the summer of 1941 only the site of the defence zone, running up to 5 miles from the naval base, had been selected. In July 1941 a rear defence line against possible German parachute landings had been started, and after noting what had worked at Odessa, the Black Sea Fleet command set to work on creating a deep defensive zone up to ten miles from the harbour, with four strong-points — Shchorgun, Shcherkes-Kermen, Duvankoi and Arantchi. The

Composition of the 9th Soviet Army (Southern Front): For Period 21st October—2nd November, 1941

Southern Front under Colonel-General Ya. T. Cherevichenko, comprising the 12th, 9th, 18th Armies.

9th Army command

Major-General F. M. Kharitonov
Brigade Commissar K. V. Krainyukov
Brigade commander N. P. Ivanov (Chief of Staff)

→ Military Soviet 9th Army

Composition: 21st October	Rifle Divisions	Cavalry Divisions	Corps Artillery
9th Army	30th 150th 339th	35th 56th 66th	648 Regiment

Reinforced by:
136th Rifle Division
2nd, 132nd Tank Brigades

Tank strengths:	38
T–26	11
T–34	20
KV	7

Deployment on (87 km. defensive front) under Directive 30th October 1st and 2nd Echelon, Army reserve

1st Echelon	
30th RD	Major-General M. D. Goncharov
339th RD	Colonel A. M. Pykhtin
66th CD	Colonel V. I. Grigorovich
541st Rifle Retg. (136th RD)	
23rd Rifle Regt. (formerly att. 51st RD)	Major N. V. Merkulov
2nd Echelon	
136th RD	Lieutenant-Colonel E. I. Vasilenko
150th RD	Major-General D. G. Yegorov

(*continued*)

Army Reserve	
Novocherkassk Cavalry School 1 Bn./8th (Guards) Mortar Regt.	Colonel B. A. Boikov

Aviation	
Aviation commander: 20th Mixed Aviation Division 50th Long Range Aviation Division 5th Aviation Reconnaissance Group	Colonel I. T. Batygin subordinated to army command subordinated directly to Front command

Strength: 20th Division (fighters)

11 — I-16
7 — MiG-3
1 — LaGG-3
1 — I-153
50th Division
24 bombers

Strength in machine-guns, artillery, mortars: for 30th October

Light/ heavy MGs	AA MGs	Artillery					Mortars 82- and 120-mm
		37-mm	45-mm	76-mm	122-mm	152-mm	
799	26	5	94	117	55	47	132

Tank forces: to 2nd November
38 tanks, 14 armoured cars increased to 48 tanks (10 transferred from 56th Independent Army/Rostov)
2nd Tank Brigade taken into reserve
132nd Tank Brigade assigned to 136th Rifle Division.

Engineering resources

5 Army pioneer/eng. bns. 5 divisional eng. bns. 13 regimental eng. coys. 3 bridging bns. 1 light ferrying park 3 special assignment coys.	113 tons of explosives 1,700 anti-tank mines 2,300 anti-personnel mines

(*continued*)

Soviet Comparison of Opposing Forces/Donbas-Rostov Operations

German-Italian	*Soviet*
Von Kleist First Armoured Group	*9th Army*
Corps:	3 Rifle Divisions (plus 1 as reinforcement)
14th, 3rd Motorised	3 Cavalry Divisions
49th Mountain Infantry	2 Tank Brigades (as reinforcement)*
Italian Motorised (of *Corpo di Spedizione Italiano*)	(holding left wing, Southern Front. To halt drive on Rostov)
Divisions:	*18th Army*
13th, 14th, 16th *Panzer*	Strength not given
60th Motorised	(holding right wing)
SS *Viking* and *Adolf Hitler*	
198th Infantry	*56th Independent Army*
1st, 4th Mountain Infantry	Being formed in the Rostov area
3 Italian motorised	5 Rifle Divisions
1 Slovak	4 Cavalry Divisions
	1 Tank Brigade
Artillery:	(to cover Rostov from the west and north-west)
60th, 511th Arty. Regts.	
602nd Heavy Arty.	
	37th Army
Average divisional strength:	Being formed in the Kamensk-Krasnodon area
10,000	
(60th Motorised down to 7,000)	6 Rifle Divisions
	2 Tank Brigades
Tank strength: von Kleist in excess of 300 tanks, 100 armoured cars	NOTE: in no case did the strength of a rifle division exceed 7,000.

* On 6th November the 142nd Tank Brigade was assigned from the Front reserve to the 9th Army (together with the 756th Anti-Tank Artillery Regiment and the Armoured Train *Za Rodinu*).

Source: these figures are presented in a recent Soviet military monograph, *Oboronitel'naya operatsiya 9-i Armii (Oktyabr'-Noyabr' 1941 g.)*, (The 9th Army defensive operation October–November, 1941), Moscow 1960. The author, A. K. Oreshkin, is of the opinion that insufficient attention has been paid to the publication of and research into examples where Soviet troops held a wide defensive front with limited man-power and equipment.

construction of a further defence line, twenty miles from Sevastopol, was planned but German troops were hammering at the naval base before this could be prepared.[20] The Coastal Army had gone into action south of the Ishun positions on 24th October, with only half of its complement of men and weapons. On its evacuation from Odessa, this army left behind its horses (there being no room to ship them) and almost all its lorries; the 95th Rifle Division's heavy artillery was dumped into Odessa harbour (there being no cranes to load them), and although 57 Artillery Regiment guns and equipment had reached Sevastopol, these could not be moved from the harbour for lack of horse transport. According to Vorob'ev's own account, Petrov, commander of the Coastal Army, was without instructions about withdrawing, since contact with the front staff had been broken after the German break-through into the Crimea. On 31st October, the military soviet of the Coastal Army was called into session at the village of Ekibash in the 95th Rifle Division's combat zone. All divisional commanders, commissars and chiefs of divisional staffs, brigade staffs, the chief of staff of the army and the chief of the army administration met with Petrov, who decided to withdraw on his own initiative to Sevastopol.[21] The 8,000 men who broke through to Sevastopol were a much needed reinforcement to Vice-Admiral Oktyabrskii, who assumed command of the entire Sevastopol defence. Petrov was subsequently given full command over the land forces which held the naval base after the first German attempt to seize it off the march had failed. The Sevastopol thorn was to dig into the German flesh for 250 days.

While Sevastopol was being sealed off, Stalin was evidently concerned to attempt the destruction of von Kleist's armour and the forces which had seized Rostov, a process which occupied the Soviet command throughout the latter half of November. The *Stavka* plan worked out to meet this requirement envisaged the 37th Army mounting the main blow on a front running from Darevka-Biryukovo, in the direction of Bolshe-Krepinskaya, thus driving into the rear of the German motorised corps operating against Rostov. Left flank divisions of the 18th Army would cover the upper reaches of the River Mius, while the 9th Army would co-ordinate its offensive actions with the 37th in attacking von Kleist. The 12th Army, together with centre and right flank forces of the 18th, was to secure the offensive from the direction of the Donbas. The 56th Independent Army (raised early in November from units of the North-Caucasus Military District and put under the command of Lieutenant-General F. N. Remizov) was to operate in the Rostov-Novocherkassk area, and was divided into western, central and eastern groups to cover its assigned sectors.[22] Although it proved impossible to hold Rostov, on 27th Russian pressure was obliging the German command to relinquish its recent capture. Remizov's troops crossed the Don and began fighting into the southern suburbs of Rostov, while Kharitonov pushed into the north-eastern approaches. The movements of the 37th, 9th and 56th Armies threatened von Kleist with encirclement; the German withdrawal behind the River Mius, while it cost Field-Marshal von Rundstedt his command over Army Group South, was the logical step to take. The recapture of Rostov was the first major success enjoyed by the Red Army since the German invasion. It signalled the first Russian seizure of the initiative and announced the fact that an army, many times beaten on paper, was making a striking recovery.

To the north, where the *Stavka* had already attempted an offensive earlier in November to restore the situation in the Tikhvin-Volkhov area, the 52nd Army renewed its attacks on 18th November to isolate the German garrison at Malaya Vyshera. The frontal attacks having failed, the 52nd Army commander ordered the 259th and 111th Rifle Divisions each to provide a detachment of 500 men ready to operate by night in the German rear. Although the two detachments penetrated to the rear of the German positions, they failed to co-ordinate their actions. On 18th, the 259th and 111th Rifle Divisions made their frontal attack, and for two days fierce battles for houses and strongpoints raged. It was now that the 4th Army launched an attack aimed at Tikhvin, but much depended on the progress which the 52nd Army made with its offensive. The 52nd made slow progress towards the River Bolshaya Vyshera, coming up against the second German defence line. The 52nd's rate of advance did not average, by the end of November, two kilometres per day. Holding the 52nd enabled the German command to move parts of the 61st Infantry Division to meet the threat posed by the 4th Army in the Tikhvin area. The *Stavka* therefore ordered the 52nd to get results and to be quicker about it, so that Russian forces could be advanced to the River Volkhov between Gruzino and Selishchenskii Poselok. Accordingly, the 52nd Army commander issued orders that only light forces were to be utilised in covering the German positions, while the bulk of the rifle divisions were to be employed in gaining the line Gorneshno-Aleksandrovskoe by 7th December. The need to get the 52nd Army to the Volkhov river was dictated by the course of operations nearer to Tikhvin. Taking Gruzino would mean severing the escape route of the German forces engaged at Tikhvin. Only the 267th Rifle Division, however, managed to make any substantial progress, and the *Stavka* was shortly to rain down categorical orders to press on.

The 4th Army had launched its attacks on 19th November, and at first tended to emulate the tactics of the 52nd. The operational plan called for the 4th Army Northern Group to attack from the north and north-west of

Tikhvin and to drive southwards, while the 4th Army Eastern Group would attack from the south-east and move in a north-westerly direction; the junction of these two groups was to effect the encirclement of the enemy's 39th Motorised Corps. Elements of the Eastern Group would also hold German forces to the east of Tikhvin, while the Southern Group's attacks were designed to sever the German escape route to the west and south-west. At first the usual Russian frontal attacks on German fortified positions failed to produce results. Meretskov thereupon made it unmistakably clear to his commanders that he expected them to attempt outflanking manœuvres and an end to the business of tying up most of the Russian troops in front of the German defences.[23] By 23rd November, elements of the Northern and Southern Groups had managed some turning of the German defences, and at this time the German command sent reinforcements to secure their lines of communication. Meretskov now decided to attempt the encirclement of German troops within the Tikhvin area, withdrawing the 60th Tank Division into reserve for possible use against an enemy retirement. From 24th November–3rd December the Tikhvin area was the scene of heavy fighting in difficult conditions of terrain and climate, and only on 3rd December did the 4th Army's Northern Group manage to overcome the resistance of units of the 12th *Panzer* Division, thereby threatening a German retirement in a westerly or north-westerly direction. German counter-attacks pushed the Northern Group back from its gains, checking the threat to German communications north-westwards; the Southern Group, reinforced at the end of November by the 1st Rifle Brigade detached from the 7th Independent Army (Karelian Front), moved slowly on Sitomlya, menacing German communications with Tikhvin from the south-west. The 54th Army, which had been containing German attacks on Volkhov and Voibokalo, made ready at the end of November to go over to the offensive. The main effort of the 54th was to be in the Voibokalo-Kirishi direction, for which purpose the 80th, 311th and 285th Rifle Divisions, the 6th Naval and the 122nd Tank Brigades had been concentrated in the Voibokalo area. This offensive, launched on 3rd December, failed to break the German resistance in the direction chosen; at the end of ten days of fighting, Fedyuninskii decided to use the 115th and 198th Rifle Divisions — transferred from Leningrad — in a flank attack on German troops operating to the south-east of Voibokalo.[24]

A Soviet critique of the first phases of the Tikhvin-Volkhov operations draws attention to the delays imposed upon the Soviet offensive by the faulty instructions issued to the rifle divisions. Frontal attacks on the German strongpoints enabled the German command to move up reserves and shift troops from un-attacked sectors of the front. The small German garrisons were able to hold up comparatively large Soviet forces, whose assault forces were not properly constituted. 4th Army's Eastern Group, the most powerful of the three, possessed only one regiment of the 60th Tank Division, the available tank resources having been equally distributed throughout the army instead of being united into a strong strike and pursuit force. Meretskov had had to attempt this in the middle of the battle. Similarly with the artillery; the 52nd Army command had divided the high command artillery reserve among the rifle divisions at the beginning of the offensive and divisional artillery had been parcelled out to rifle regiments and 'even to battalions'.[25] The lack of reserves available to army and operational group commanders led, in the case of the 4th Army, to the failure to accomplish the encirclement at Tikhvin in the four days from 19th–23rd November. The night operations had been on the whole successful, but the troops were not sufficiently trained in them and operations by night were consequently but little employed.

The Tikhvin-Volkhov operations had still a long way to run before they brought the desired results to the Soviet command. Events near Rostov had taken a more spectacular turn, but both operations at the northern and southern ends of the entire front were aimed at preventing possible German reinforcement of the armies attacking Moscow. Both the northern and southern offensives had been some time under preparation, and might generally be dated in origin to the first half of November. The *Stavka* had assigned a minimum reinforcement to its 4th and 52nd Armies in the north, while Timoshenko, in addition to supplying troops for the defence of Moscow, assembled a shock army from his available forces. But at Moscow the crisis had yet to be resolved.

★ ★ ★ ★

By the beginning of December, the Red Army was fielding some 200 rifle, 35 cavalry and about 40 tank formations against the very formidable Germans. Among the rifle formations were many brigades, and the average strength of a rifle division had fallen much below the war establishment fixed before the outbreak of war. The Soviet tank divisions were approximately the size of a German brigade, and not for some time were corps-type armoured formations re-introduced.* The Soviet plan for a counter-offensive, submitted by Zhukov to Stalin on 30th November, was the product of co-operation between the front commands, the *Stavka* and the

* Although the brigade organisation remained, for reasons of shortage of tanks and the capacities of Soviet commanders, a form from which the Soviet command only slowly departed, by the close of 1942 tank corps were back in the Red Army. Comprising some 300 AFVs, these formations were the Soviet approximation to a western-type armoured division. See Richard M. Ogorkiewicz, *Armour*, p. 101 f., for a discussion on the differentiations in Soviet armoured forces after 1942.

General Staff, and its vital point appears to have rested on an analysis of the strength relationships between the Soviet and German forces. The counter-offensive was to be mounted from three fronts — those of Kalinin, the South-west and the West — the Western Front playing the decisive part. Elements of the right wing of the Western Front were to co-operate with those from the left wing of the Kalinin Front in assaulting the northern wing of Army Group Centre. The Third and Fourth Armoured Groups would therefore be assailed by the 30th, 1st Shock, 20th and 16th Armies, driving on Klin, Solnechnogorsk and Istra. The left wing of the Western Front, in co-operation with the right wing of the South-western Front, was to strike at the southern wing of Army Group Centre, at Guderian's force. The 50th and 10th Armies, as well as the 1st Guards Cavalry Corps, were to drive on Uzlovaya and Bogoroditsk. The central sector of the Western Front (held by the 5th, 33rd and 43rd Armies) was to hold the enemy in the first phase of the offensive near Mozhaisk and Maloyaroslavets, to prevent any attempt to strengthen the wings of the front. In this manner, a wide double encirclement of the German 4th Army as it now stood before Moscow might be accomplished. The military soviet of the Western Front, with Zhukov and Bulganin at its head, had submitted on 30th the basic outlines of this plan envisaging the attacks against the northern and southern wings of Army Group Centre. On 1st December, Shaposhnikov and the *Stavka* issued a directive to Koniev on the Kalinin Front to employ his left wing (29th and 31st Armies) in attacks south-east and south-west of Kalinin to break into the rear of the enemy forces at Klin. For this purpose Koniev, by means of an internal re-organisation, was to organise an assault force consisting of not less than 5–6 rifle divisions. Timoshenko was instructed to do the same with the right-wing forces of his front; the 3rd, 13th and 40th Armies were assigned to the task of destroying enemy forces in the Yelets-Livny area, and by means of an internal re-grouping Timoshenko formed a small number of assault groups to the north and south of Yelets.[26]

In the first few days of December the issue before Moscow hung in a last balance before it tipped decisively. With troops wholly without means of protection against an agonising cold, in conditions where the temperature sealed the moving parts of machine-guns and burst engines, lacking replacements in any strength for the mounting casualties, the German Army made its final lunge at Moscow. Guderian to the south could persist with his attack only so long as the 4th Army at the centre continued its offensive operations. Although a German reconnaissance battalion had penetrated to the south-western fringe of Moscow by 3rd, on 4th von Kluge decided to abandon an attack which had no chance of success. On the night of 5th–6th December Guderian resolved to break off his attack, at a juncture when

Reinhardt's and Hoepner's armoured forces to the north of Moscow were at the end of their resources. By battle, continuous exertion and extreme cold the German drive had been burned out. An official Soviet account sets the moment as that 'most favourable' for the Soviet counter-offensive with the arrival of a German infantry division in Mozhaisk from the rear areas, indicating the exhaustion of the German reserves.[27] On 5th December, as ordered by the *Stavka* at the beginning of the month, Koniev's Kalinin Front went over to the offensive, followed on 6th by Western Front troops and those of the right wing of the South-western Front.

Koniev's left-wing armies (the 31st under Major-General V. A. Yushkevich and the 29th under Lieutenant-General Maslennikov until 11th December, followed by Major-General V. I. Shvetsov) were to avoid a frontal attack on Kalinin itself but to move north-west and south-east to bring them into the left flank of Army Group Centre. The opening move of the Moscow counter-offensive came on 6th December, when right-wing forces of the Western Front struck at Reinhardt's armoured group from the north-west and east of Klin, while the Fourth Armoured Group was assaulted at its junction with the 4th Army. Lelyushenko's 30th Army, V. I. Kuznetsov's 1st Shock Army, Rokossovskii's 16th Army, A. Vlasov's 20th Army and elements of Govorov's 5th Army were engaged in these operations to eliminate the German threat to Moscow from the north and north-west. Abandoning their heavy equipment, impeded in the movement of their tanks and guns by snow, the German armoured groups fell back; on the first day of the offensive Lelyushenko pushed ahead for some eleven miles, bringing his right flank units up to the Leningrad highway and by 9th December having his main force to the north and east of Klin. The 30th and 1st Shock Armies did not, however, manage to complete the encirclement of German forces in this area, although they inflicted considerable losses. On 11th Vlasov's troops fought their way into Solnechnogorsk, while Rokossovskii's 16th Army attacked along the Kryukovo-Dedovsk line, having Istra as its objective. On 8th December, Kryukovo fell to the 8th Guards Panfilov Division and the 1st Guards Tank Brigade; with his weight on the left wing, Rokossovskii drove on to Istra. At the Istra reservoir the retreating Germans opened the sluice gates to impede the Russians. To force the River Istra Rokossovskii formed two assault groups, under the generals Remizov and Katukov, to attack from the north and south of the reservoir. The Germans were finally dislodged from the western bank of the river and the reservoir and fell back westwards. Govorov's 5th Army supported Rokossovskii from the south, while General L. M. Dovator's 2nd Guards Cavalry Corps embarked upon another of its famous deep penetrations, this time breaking through south-west of Zvenigorod with the aim of cutting off the German retreat at Volokolamsk and the River Ruza. It was Zhukov's intention to utilise the 30th and 1st Shock Armies to achieve an encirclement at Klin, while using the remaining forces of his right wing for a pursuit westwards.[28] Once again the Russian frontal attacks on German defensive positions came in for severe criticism and on 13th December Zhukov issued a directive demanding less of the 'vicious tactics' of frontal attacks and more use of outflanking.[29]

On 6th December the left wing of the Western and the right wing of the South-western Front went over to the offensive. It was here that a visibly dangerous situation developed, which threatened the life of the Fourth Army.

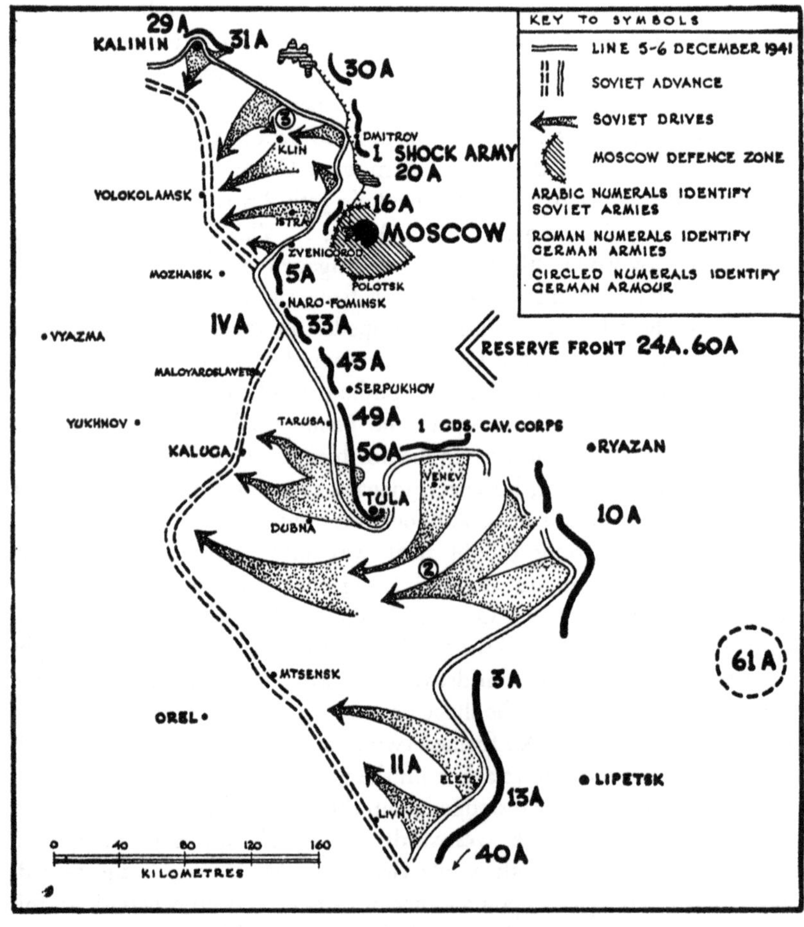

THE MOSCOW COUNTER-OFFENSIVE

Guderian had been aware for some time of the danger to his flank and rear from the Russian reserves concentrated by Ryazan-Kolomna. On 7th December Lieutenant-General F. I. Golikov's 10th Army approached the Kashira-Pavelets railway; these fresh troops of the Western Front moved in the direction of Stalinogorsk, and were aiming a flank attack at Guderian. Simultaneously Major-General P. A. Belov's 1st Guards Cavalry Corps attacked from Mordves to Venev; on 8th Lieutenant-General I. V. Boldin's 50th Army began a powerful drive southwards from the direction of Tula, with the object of severing the German escape route to the west. Boldin was heavily engaged to the south and south-east of Tula, so that by the time his troops began to break through the German defences, the trap had been sprung too late. On the right wing of the South-western Front Major-General A. M. Gorodnyanskii's 13th Army attacked to the north of Yelets, and on the following day Lieutenant-General Ya. F. Kostenko's front group of the 40th Army attacked from Trebuny to the south. Yelets, the important rail junction controlling tracks running in four directions, fell on 9th December, thus eliminating the threats which had developed early in December against the right flank of the 3rd Red army as well as the penetrations between the 3rd and 13th, the 13th and the 40th Red armies. In the course of the heavy fighting which developed on this sector, Soviet troops knocked out the 45th and 95th German infantry divisions of the XXXIV Army Corps, while by a development of the offensive to the north-west the Orel-Tula railway link — Guderian's supply line — was directly menaced.

Between the right flank of the 4th Army and Guderian's Tank Army a gap of some twelve miles had already been opened, with the Russian forces striving to expand it. Lacking reserves with which to attempt a strengthening in the south, and dependent for supplies on the great road running along Yukhnov-Maloyaroslavets-Podolsk, the 4th Army was faced with an extremely serious situation. I. G. Zakharin's 49th Army had been attacking on the Aleksin-Tarusa sector of the river Oka, to the north of Tula; on 14th December these forces took Aleksin and established bridge-heads on the left bank of the Oka at Aleksin and north of Tarusa, the left wing swinging north-west to drive on Maloyaroslavets-Medin. To exploit the possibility of the gap between the two German armies, Zhukov set about forming from Boldin's army a mobile group, command of which was assigned to General V. S. Popov. This group, composed of tanks, infantry and cavalry, was to break into the German rear towards Kaluga, and on 18th December set out through the wooded country along the southern bank of the Oka.[30] With a Soviet force sent out to take one of the main German supply bases, and with Belov's cavalry corps moving in the rear towards that vital supply road, the crisis settling about the 4th Army deepened.

To the north, in the fighting at Kalinin, Koniev's 29th and 31st Armies were moving to encircle five German infantry divisions, while the Western Front 30th Army under Lelyushenko advanced to the Lama and threatened to break into the rear of the German 9th Army. As the German troops pulled back to the south-west the Russians took Kalinin on 16th December, claiming as the cost to the Germans of the Kalinin fighting the destruction of six divisions or half the strength of the 9th Army.[31] The re-capture of Kalinin was an important success, for a direct link was re-opened between the Western and North-western fronts, and the Bologoye-Kalinin-Moscow road and rail links could once more be utilised. With the taking of Kalinin, the *Stavka* decided upon the strengthening of Koniev's left wing, assigning Lelyushenko's 30th Army to this command. Lelyushenko was ordered to employ his left-wing divisions against Staritsa and move with his right against the German lines of communication south-west of Kalinin, but this change came at a time when the 30th was still heavily engaged with Reinhardt's armoured group, so that it proved impossible to switch the 30th at once to break into the rear of the 9th Army.[32] Koniev's left-wing armies, the 29th, 31st, 30th and 39th (assembled about mid-December in the Torzhok area), were subsequently employed in attacking towards Rzhev-Lotoshino.

At the centre of the Western Front, to the south of the Moscow-Smolensk highway, the 33rd and 43rd Armies of the generals Yefremov and Golubev and the 5th under Govorov had been assigned to hold the 4th Army while the assaults on the northern and southern wings took place. Part of Govorov's forces had been used to assist Rokossovskii, and on 13th December Govorov started his advance in the direction of Mozhaisk. The 33rd and 43rd Armies attacked at the centre on 18th December, breaking into the German line, taking Naro-Fominsk, and driving thereafter on Borovsk-Balabanovo-Maloyaroslavets. In threatened Maloyaroslavets, von Kluge and his staff stayed on, planning the withdrawal of elements of the 4th Army from south of the Moscow-Smolensk highway. At this time of growing crisis, von Bock was obliged by illness to relinquish command of Army Group Centre, which passed to von Kluge, but by that turn of events the 4th Army momentarily found itself bereft of a commander. At this time also, as what looked like disaster before Moscow made its impact on the German high command, Hitler himself took over as commander-in-chief from von Brauchitsch.[33]

The Bryansk Front, which had been engulfed in the second German offensive in November, was re-formed on 18th December and put under the command of Colonel-General Ya. V. Cherevichenko. The Front was made up of the 3rd and 13th Armies, detached from the right wing of the South-western Front, and the 61st, transferred from the *Stavka* reserve on

24th December. The Bryansk Front forces were intended to take advantage of the successes of the left wing of the Western Front, opening in the second half of December a drive on Orel. The 13th Army, however, made only slight progress at this time, and the reason adduced for the 'unsatisfactory development of the offensive' is the lack of men and equipment to carry it through. 13th Army is cited as a case in point; by 1st January, 1942, the total strength of this army, which had originally consisted of five rifle divisions, was 11,833 men and 82 guns and mortars of all calibres.[94] The army therefore lacked the complement of one rifle division at normal strength. In action since 6th December in the offensive operations, in twenty-five days the 13th had been very considerably weakened. Although the quality of Soviet rifle divisions varied as much as their strength, it might be assumed that the 13th's five divisions amounted to not less than 30,000 and not more than 45,000 men. Even by the most generous estimate, Soviet losses were still notably high.

In the period from 6th–25th December, Red Army operations against Army Group Centre had liquidated the threat to Moscow. With the danger still far from diminished on its southern flank, the German 4th Army had also been severed by 22nd December from the Third and Fourth Armoured Groups on its northern wing. Hitler's order that the Fourth Army should stand fast seemed to be an invitation for complete disaster to overtake this sorely-tried army.

* * * *

The *Stavka* meanwhile was also directing its attention to the north of the Soviet-German front, where three armies were trying to accomplish the destruction of the German forces in the Tikhvin-Volkhov area. On 17th December the Volkhov Front was formed, with General of the Red Army K. A. Meretskov in command, Brigade Commander G. D. Stel'makh as Chief of Staff and Army Commissar 1st Grade A. I. Zaporozhets as the member of the military soviet. The 4th and 52nd Armies were assigned to the new front. Meretskov's directive for the front operations ordered a development of the offensive along the whole front, the forcing of the River Volkhov, the attainment of the line Lyuban-Cholovo and the establishment of conditions for further offensive operations in a north-westerly direction with the aim of breaking the blockade of Leningrad. The 52nd Army, which had recently come under the lash of the *Stavka's* 'categorical requirements', began to move its 111th Rifle Division northwards on the morning of 18th December and by 21st this force had reached a point not far south of Gruzino. On 23rd, 52nd Army troops reached the Volkhov and for eight days fought for a bridge-head on the left bank, some distance to the north-east of Chudovo. Although the crossing had been managed, the criticism is made that the 52nd Army failed to accomplish one of the most important of its assignments, the timely movement of its troops to Gruzino in order to sever the communications of the German forces at Tikhvin and to prevent their withdrawal to the Volkhov.[35]

The 4th Army recaptured Tikhvin on 9th December. The Northern Group of this army was ordered to pursue the German 12th *Panzer* Division retiring along the Tikhvin-Volkhov road and to co-operate with units of the 54th Army. The Central Group (the Eastern Group having been so designated on 10th) was to move on Budogosh, co-operating with the Southern Group in destroying the XXXIX Motorised Corps. The turning point of the operations in favour of the Soviet troops is set at 15th December, when units of the 4th Guards Rifle Division (Southern Group) took Sitomlya and five days later cut the Luga-Lipovka road.[36] Fedyuninskii at this time had switched the direction of his attack, which at first had been held in check; his assault on the flank of German troops in the Voibokalo area was aimed in the direction of Olomna. After two days of sharp fighting, Fedyuninskii's 115th and 198th Rifle Divisions came upon Olomna by 17th; on 20th this had developed into a serious threat to the left flank of German forces operating to the south of Volkhov, and on that day the 3rd Guards and the 310th Rifle Divisions of Fedyuninskii's left wing at Volkhov attacked. To avoid encirclement to the south-west of Volkhov, German forces retired in that direction to the line of the Kirishi-Mga railway. To increase the possibility of Soviet forces crossing the Volkhov in the direction of Kirishi, the *Stavka* on 22nd despatched the 377th Rifle Division to the 4th Army, simultaneously ordering the 4th Army to act with the 54th in a speedy liquidation of the enemy east of the River Volkhov and south-east of Voibokalo. At the end of December the 54th Army had reached the Mga-Kirishi railway line, fighting for Pogoste and Posadnikov Ostrov. A firm German defence line blocked any further Soviet advance, while difficulties in supply and communications caused the offensive to peter out by Tigoda, Kirishi and Irsa, which were not recaptured.[37]

Only in the Crimea did the German Army find the opportunity to press any offensive action. The object of these operations was the reduction of Sevastopol, to which end almost the entire strength of von Manstein's 11th Army was committed. At 8 a.m. on 17th December German guns opened fire along the length of the Soviet defences. In the ferocious fighting which raged by day and night the Soviet reserves of men and munitions were quickly expended. To restore what was reported as a critical situation, the *Stavka* had ordered the transfer on 20th December of the 79th Independent Rifle Brigade (an officer-training school unit) from Novorossiisk and on 21st that of the 345th Rifle Brigade from Tuapse to Sevastopol. The cruiser *Krasnyi Kavkaz*, the destroyer flotilla leader *Kharkov* with the minelayers *Nezamozhnik* and *Bodryi* were used to transport the troops, while the destroyer *Tashkent* and fast minelayers lifted ammunition from Poti to the besieged naval base. The 79th Brigade went straight into action, winning back the positions which the 388th Rifle Brigade had been forced to relinquish.[38]

To assist the defence of Sevastopol and to establish conditions for an offensive aimed at winning back the Crimea, the *Stavka* in mid-December had ordered the preparation of a sea-borne landing on the Kerch Peninsula. The Trans-Caucasus Front command (Lieutenant-General D. T. Kozlov, Chief of Staff, Major-General F. I. Tolbukhin) were assigned this task, with 21st set as a preliminary date for mounting the invasion. This extremely risky venture, embedded with technical and natural difficulties, was the brain-child of the *Stavka*. However, part of the forces earmarked for the operation had already been sent directly to Sevastopol to relieve the situation brought about by heavy German attacks. The Kerch-Feodosiya operation was nevertheless mounted and carried through from 26th December, 1941, to 2nd January, 1942. The operational plan called for units of the 51st Army and elements of the 44th to be landed on the morning of 26th at the northern and eastern shores of the Kerch Peninsula, with the main strength of the 44th being landed at Feodosiya on 29th. During the period of the operation the Black Sea Fleet and the Azov Flotilla would be subordinated to the command of the Trans-Caucasus Front. From the outset, apart from natural hazards, the operation was beset with difficulties. 51st Army forces were divided up into landing detachments, but not enough ships could be found to transport these men. Vessels had to be commandeered from the local population. In the end, an assortment of 300 barges, fishing-boats, barques and cutters were gathered together, but these were not of a sort which would guarantee a speedy disembarkation of troops under fire from enemy-held beaches. Lack of coal for the ships and a shortage of fuel for the fishing boats meant that only a part of this fleet could actually be used.[39]

On Christmas night the 224th Rifle Division and the 83rd Rifle Brigade (51st Army) were embarked. Ships of the Azov Flotilla began to move to the landing zones. In storms of sleet and snow, with the temperature well below zero, only the 4th Detachment was put ashore, the 1st and 2nd being caught by bad weather and the *Luftwaffe*, the 3rd and 5th failing with the disembarkation. At dawn on 26th, marines from the 4th Detachment got ashore, however, and established a bridge-head by Khrona. On the following day units of the 302nd Rifle Division were landed at Kamysh-Burun. Heavy storms prevented any further landing until 30th, for the attempt to put down units of the 44th Army at Opuk had also failed. Only a few tanks and guns were eventually put ashore, so that instead of the proposed offensive action, the invaders had to fight for their foot-holds. Events took a more favourable turn near Feodosiya, where Black Sea Fleet ships put off the 44th Army; by 31st December, the 157th, 236th Rifle Divisions, 63rd Mountain Troops Division and the 251st Regiment of the 9th Mountain Troops Division had been landed under the fire of German coastal guns. Kerch and Feodosiya were taken, but by 2nd January Soviet troops came up against a firm German defence line and the operation came to a halt. Although the general situation remained unchanged in the Crimea, and in spite of serious mistakes in the ordering of the operation, the Kerch-Feodosiya assault was reckoned to have accomplished its limited aim.[40]

The *Stavka*, however, had envisaged offensive operations of a somewhat greater duration in the Crimea. Together with the recapture of the Crimea, the *Stavka* had also stipulated for the south-western theatre as a whole the recovery of the Donbas.[41] As the leap into the Crimea was caught by the heels in the German defence, the Barvenkovo-Lozovaya operation was in the final stages of its planning and preparation. This was to be mounted by the Southern Front (commanded at this time by Lieutenant-General R. Ya. Malinovskii) and the South-western Front (Lieutenant-General F. Ya. Kostenko). Marshal Timoshenko remained in supreme command of the whole theatre. The basic idea consisted of employing the adjacent wings of the Southern and South-western Fronts to breach the German defences between Balakleya and Artemovsk (north and south of Izyum) and to develop the offensive in the general direction of Zaporozhe. Soviet troops might be brought into the rear of the German Donbas-Taganrog group, whose escape route to the west would be severed. Pushing them on to the Sea of Azov, their elimination would be accomplished in co-operation with the left wing of the Southern Front. Simultaneously units of the South-western Front left wing would strike towards Krasnodar in order to secure the operation from the north and to recapture Kharkov.[42] In what turned out to be an abortive offensive, the plan — ambitious enough — seems not to have been adequately related to the means to hand. Tanks and artillery were in short supply. Cavalry corps, useful in exploiting successes, were evidently extremely deficient in these items. Nor were these formations placed under a unified command, but operated independently and thereby dissipated their power. The supply of fuel, ammunition, and food was not properly planned.[43]

The south-western and north-western operations, as well as the extension of the offensive at the centre, had developed into a general offensive by the Red Army at the end of December. The main effort of the general offensive was located in the centre of the Soviet-German front, and was to be mounted by forces of the Western and Kalinin Fronts operating with the left wing of the North-western Front with the object of destroying Army Group Centre. The general offensive grew out of the Moscow counter-offensive, which itself comprised a complicated series of battles. By 18th December it had been recognised that the German threat to Moscow from the southern flank of Army Group Centre had been eliminated. By 25th the entire threat to Moscow had been dissipated, although not until 22nd January, 1942, was Moscow *oblast* cleared of the enemy. The Russian offensive posed problems of command and leadership which required urgent solution. As in defence Soviet commanders had frequently wasted their strength by faulty disposition, so in attack what power there was again drained away by the failure to concentrate in a manner which provided adequate force in the requisite direction.[44] It was perhaps a final irony that the instructions and directives which Stalin, the *Stavka* and the General Staff prepared for the guidance of the offensive operations should have been based on a very urgent reconsideration of pre-war Soviet military theory. In particular, back came the instruction about the assault or shock group, the use of artillery and tanks *en masse*, and Tukhachevsky's basic theme of the indispensability of the co-operation of all arms and types of troops.[45]

Now also came the time for a modification in the method of supreme command over the operations of the Red Army. At the beginning of the war a form of decentralised high command had existed in the three main theatres set up almost at once and entrusted to Voroshilov, Budenny and Timoshenko. Only Timoshenko survived as a commander of real importance in this arrangement, and the Moscow operations had been directed in what appeared to be the close concert of Stalin, Zhukov, Shaposhnikov and the apparatus of the *Stavka* and the General Staff. The vast and awkward fronts of the summer of 1941 had given way to many more fronts of smaller size. A front operation became part of a strategical operation. The winter of 1941–2 marked an interim stage in the organisation of the higher direction of strategic operations. A part of the original system was still left, while new forms were developing. The *Stavka* operated through the staffs of the various administrations, through the General Staff itself, through the commanders of arms and their staffs, through the central administration of the Defence Commissariat and upon front commanders. In the Tikhvin-Volkhov operations in November–December, 1941, the 4th and 52nd Armies had been in effect a *Stavka* front until the Volkhov Front was set up. In the matter of strategic reserves the *Stavka* was the master, although in the Moscow battle itself Stalin seems to have reserved for himself a final right on this vital question.[46] One indispensable condition of the *Stavka's* completely centralised control and operating technique was that, regardless of its extent, there was only one strategic front.* This facilitated 'concrete direction' by the *Stavka* not only in the preparation but also the conduct of all basic operations.[47] At the time of the Moscow counter-offensive the number of competent higher commanders in the Red Army, at important army or front levels, remained relatively small. Success had turned upon not more than two score of men, while during the summer and autumn the Red Army had run through a veritable roster of senior officers in testing the capacities of commanders in important posts. The first victories helped the Red Army to recover its position vis-à-vis the Party, and the deliberate programme of identifying the army and the nation in a 'patriotic war' also assisted this process. But the Party under Stalin remained the army's master, and control of policy remained with a regime buttressed as ever by the *NKVD* and operated by Stalin's own particularly constricted methods. That frustration, discontent and disgust operated high in the military command levels is shown by Lieutenant-General Vlasov's own career as an organiser of an anti-Stalin liberation movement after his capture by the Germans in 1942. Against the clogging of the command and the manifest mis-use of time in the operation of the political administration, complaint began to be more public at the beginning of 1942. While there was the most obvious need to press forward with tactical training and a much more thorough military preparation of operations, hours and even days were taken up with political lectures. *Politinformatsiya,* talks and lectures combined rudimentary military lessons with instilling the basic line of a 'patriotic war'; 'verbal propaganda' (talks with rank-and-file) and the printed word (army and divisional newspapers, leaflets and posters) covered topics such as 'The sacred Patriotic war of the Soviet people against the Hitlerite bands', 'What Hitler intends for the Slav peoples', 'Fearless destruction of German tanks', 'Vigilant execution of sentry duties', 'Guarding military secrets like the apple of the eye', 'Digging in and camouflaging in order better to strike the enemy' and 'Mutual assistance in combat — the unbreakable tradition of the Red Army fighters'. The Red Army was only at the beginning of its reform through actual war experience and requirements.

* * * *

Not unnaturally, the Soviet record and assessment of the Moscow counter-offensive differ appreciably from the German. There can be little

* For the operations in the Far East in 1945, a second *Glavnoe Komandovanie* (Supreme Command) for Soviet forces/Far East was set up. The commander-in-chief was Marshal A. M. Vasilevskii, Colonel-General I. V. Shikin as member of the Military Soviet, and Colonel-General S. P. Ivanov Chief of Staff.

doubt that the counter-stroke had been under preparation for some time. The main problem was to halt the Germans and gain the strategic initiative, imposing a decisive alteration of the situation in the north-west and before Moscow, as well as the Crimea. Both the north-western and south-western theatres had been strongly activated at the beginning of November in order to prevent the movement of German reserves to the centre. A plan of offensive operations had been worked out for the Tikhvin-Volkhov armies, but the difficulties encountered in holding the German drives imposed upon this original plan a multiplicity of offensive-defensive variations. To accomplish its purposes in the north-west, the *Stavka* despatched a portion of its precious reserves to this theatre, demanding all the while more positive results from the operations being undertaken. Discrepancies in the performance of the forces involved imposed further delays. Not until 7th December was it reckoned that the turning-point had arrived in these more northerly operations. To the south, Timoshenko's recapture of Rostov was the first major Soviet success in counter-attack, the chief effect of which was not so much any radical alteration in the situation as the provocation of a major crisis in the German high command.

When Zhukov and his staff submitted their plan for the Moscow counter-stroke, the German advance on the capital had still not been halted although the going had become agonisingly difficult. With the strength of front-line German units falling, accompanied by losses in equipment and the havoc wrought by the cold, the German and Russian recognition that the taking of Moscow was beyond the capacity of the German Army may have been almost simultaneous. The decisive change at the front, in the reckoning of the Soviet command, came with the movement of the 1st Shock Army, the 20th and 10th Armies as reinforcements to the left and right wings of the Western Front.[48] Since Zhukov's plan called for a series of blows at the northern and southern German 'pockets', the strengthening of the Soviet flanks in order to assault the Third and Fourth *Panzer* Groups as well as Guderian's Tank Army was of prime importance. Inclusive of the formations working on the left wing of the Kalinin Front and the right wing of the South-western Front, the *Stavka* had seventeen armies deployed or in the last stages of concentration for the Moscow counter-offensive. At least one of these armies, the 1st Shock Army, is cited as being under-gunned, possessing a total of 125 pieces, the calibres ranging from 45–76 mm, but none heavier than 76-mm.[49] The size and quality of Soviet rifle divisions varied very considerably; the Moscow armies appear to have enjoyed something like an average of 5 rifle divisions to an army, while the reserve armies were raised on the basis of a rifle corps. As for aviation, it is here that Soviet superiority is recorded as being two-fold — 1,170 Soviet aircraft facing 580 German machines, with the bulk of the Soviet force being composed of I–15, I–16, and I–153 models.[50] The Red Army remained inferior in tank strength (the percentage of inferiority cited suggesting that Zhukov did not dispose of very much more than the 500 machines available to him in mid-November).[51] In the opening phase of the Moscow counter-offensive the Soviet claim is that the Red Army lacked any general superiority in men and equipment, and was actually inferior in tanks* and artillery. The density of guns per kilometre on a rifle division sector designated for a break-through was not more than 15–20 (this figure also includes mortars) and that for tanks, 3–5.[52]

The credit for the main design of the counter-blow must go to General Zhukov and his Chief of Staff, General V. D. Sokolovskii. In attendance on the discussions of the plan, in addition to Lieutenant-General Bulganin as commissar, were Rokossovskii, L. A. Govorov and M. G. Yefremov, with other unspecified commanders. On the planning of the wider aspects of the operation and the co-ordination of the fronts, Marshal Shaposhnikov and the General Staff appear to have worked as the main organising committee. Timoshenko and Koniev had extremely important parts to play in both the forthcoming counter-offensive and the transition to a general offensive. The foundation of success lay, however, in having sufficient strategic reserves available to make the carefully-considered plan work. In this undertaking the Soviet command scored an undoubted success, one which was in marked contrast with the profusion of blunders which had attended the earlier handling of the location and commitment of reserves. In general, these had been either most inadequate or non-existent, or else faulty location had led to their being ground to pieces prematurely. When the German high command believed the Russians to be almost at the end of their resources, fresh forces were in fact being concentrated in great secrecy at the approaches to Moscow. By disregarding all but a dangerously bare minimum of safety regulations, trains succeeded in rushing extra forces from the interior, so that troops mobilised in Siberia and Central Asia could be put into action. Guderian had earlier espied the threat in the making on his learning of the Russian concentration at Ryazan-Kolomna — which was the 10th Army. Stalin's role in the Moscow counter-offensive has been confined by recent reporting to one of mere supervision, to his acceptance and confirmation of the plan submitted by Zhukov. Although Stalin was associated most closely and personally with the battle for Moscow, and while it is inconceivable that the operations could have been launched without his approval, his role was not primarily military but rather formal and even figurative.

* Major-General N. Talenskii, comparing the Moscow and Stalingrad counter-offensives, set Soviet tank strength at Moscow at some 15 brigades, with about 700 machines.

Zhukov, Shaposhnikov and their fellow-planners showed considerable skill in devising the direction of their blows. With the German Army turning to linear defence on a front seriously over-extended, crucified by the cold and lacking any strong operational reserves, the timing of the Soviet counter-stroke was well-chosen, resulting in a formidable assault which the German troops were demonstrably ill-prepared to meet. While one prodigy of spirit was demonstrated by the German troops who stood their ground and faced the Russians, the latter exhibited a remarkable recovery after what had become months of retreat, with disaster piled on disaster. That the Soviet command was concerned for the morale of their men is shown by the great intensification in the work of the Political Administration before the counter-attack. Two themes were hammered into the Soviet troops: that this time the will of the high command must be done, and this time it could be done. As much tactical training as possible appears to have been carried out to increase the co-operation between arms, with the emphasis on tackling German tanks and profitable use of the available artillery.

Above all, the Red Army high command mobilised its talent. The very highest levels of the command contained a small core of extremely capable men, upon whom an increasing responsibility devolved. Zhukov retained the field command on the Western Front during the counter-offensive, and he was supported by a group of army commanders who had learned what art they mastered in a grievously hard school. V. I. Kuznetsov had survived out of the maelstrom of the Western Military District in June 1941 and was now commanding the 1st Shock Army. Rokossovskii's troops had already played a significant part in the operations of the Western Front and especially the later stages of the Battle of Smolensk. Lelyushenko, participant in the Civil War and graduate of the Frunze Academy in the 1920's, had seen considerable service with armoured units in the Far East. Zhukov would therefore know of his capacities. Katukov, who had distinguished himself at Mtsensk, and Remizov from the south were attached to the Western Front command. Dovator, the Jewish cavalry commander who had shown his paces at Smolensk, was assigned another behind-the-lines raiding mission. Vlasov, the stubborn defender of Kiev, was assigned to an important command in the break-through operations. At Tula I. V. Boldin, deputy commander of the Western Military District in June 1941, whose mechanised divisions had been smashed to pieces in the course of his fruitless counter-attacks, took command of the 50th Army. At the centre of the Western Front, L. A. Govorov, Yefremov and Golubev could all muster a record of sustained defensive actions against the German Army. By no reckoning were these men as yet especially skilled commanders, yet they no longer lacked experience nor did they lack ability as a group. As the Soviet offensive broadened in the winter of 1941–2, the silent revolution in the command continued as the purge by battle threw out the incompetents whose claims to authority dated back to the Civil War. There were lessons as grim and relentless to be learned in attack as during the time of the great disasters. The pretence has been swept aside that the first phase of the winter offensive was free from error and miscalculation and an indifferent military performance at times. The Moscow counter-offensive was an act as desperate as any performed at the height of the summer and autumn catastrophes, but with the signal difference that finally the command had hopes of imposing their will upon the situation. Thanks to Zhukov and Shaposhnikov, much assisted by the German command having overreached itself, a coherent and realistic plan was combined with the required minimum of operational skill.

Broader Russian strategy, if this can be said to have existed at this stage of a furious face-to-face struggle with Germany, fell under Stalin's iron hand from the outset. A major effort went into applying pressure upon Great Britain to mount operations in the west designed to draw off the German Army from the east. Although the foundations of economic aid to the Soviet Union had been prepared on a larger scale, in 1941 the problem had been to fix the outlines of political co-operation. Stalin's argument appears to have been constantly quantitive, a crude mathematics of strategy in which the simple sums apparently worked out. By November 1941, as a consequence of one of Stalin's overbearing letters to Prime Minister Churchill, the newly-established co-operation suffered no small crisis. While the Moscow battles raged, Stalin indulged in a most tortuous piece of haggling-cum-intimidation with the Poles, whose military manpower he kept fast in the depths of Russia or held in *NKVD* camps, not to mention the riddle of the Katyn massacres. As the Far Eastern crisis grew to menacing proportions, Stalin also indicated that the Russian intention in this area would be limited to the defensive, as indeed it remained for many long months and through a succession of Allied disasters, until the Yalta bargain was finally struck. Meanwhile the highest priority went to transforming the Soviet-German war into a popular, national war, a process accompanied by a massive and successful drive to enlist abroad an active sympathy which could be employed in the form of useful pressure on Allied governments. Ultimately the scale was tipped for a 'patriotic war' as much by the fundamental miscalculations of the Germans as by the efforts of the Soviet regime to generate a reliable and persistent response. Finally, the gross blunders in the economic preparation, aggravated by the loss through enemy occupation and the movement of plants to the east, had to be made good. Although the production of weapons for 1942 is reported as 25,000 aircraft, 23,500 tanks (of which 13,500 were T–34 machines) and more than 34,000 guns (76-mm, 122-mm and 152-mm),[53] the 1941–2 winter offensive was mounted with demonstrably inadequate supplies of weapons and ammunition. Up to 1945, the Soviet Union had to drag with it the heavy, dead weight of the productive power lost to it by German occupation of major industrial centres in the summer and autumn of 1941. Grave as had been the impact of the German invasion on the military power of the Soviet Union, the deadliest blows had been struck into Russian industrial vitals; in 1945 the Soviet Union was producing 10 per cent less of electric power, 33 per cent less steel, 40 per cent less pig iron, 37·7 per cent less petrol, and 10 per cent less coal than in 1940.[54] Mass without power, and a mass drastically thinned at that, was the inevitable and inescapable form of the first co-ordinated offensive fought by the Red Army in 1941–2.

* * * *

In the end, the Red Army winter offensive achieved only partial success. An uninterrupted offensive had been aimed at denying the German Army the opportunity to establish a firm defensive line, and at accomplishing the destruction of the principal German forces on the main axes; but already by early January one of the ambitious offensive operations, that against the Crimea, had been blunted into the defensive. The major attacks launched by Timoshenko in the south to recover the Donbas and Kharkov failed to develop as they had been envisaged. At the centre, a succession of highly dangerous situations were created which threatened Army Group Centre. In January 1942 the Russians smashed their way into the junction of Army Groups North and Centre; the 27th Army drove on Kholm, while the 3rd and 4th Shock Armies pushed into the gap, swinging south to Velikie Luki. The Soviet intention was to cause the German command to commit its tactical and strategical reserves and thereby cause some inhibition of its future offensive capacity. This enjoyed a degree of success,[55] so that there is some coincidence of Soviet and German military opinion over the fact that the 'indirect result' was greater than the 'direct danger'.[56] The deep Russian flank penetrations were a severe trial of German steadfastness, but in general the Russian tide rolled past rather than into the German defensive positions organised into a series of major and minor 'hedge-hogs'. The capture of Kaluga, taken by the Popov's raiding column at the end of December 1941 after extremely bitter fighting, represented the seizure of a 'hedge-hog' of outstanding importance and has been described as the most notable single success of the Red Army winter offensive.[57] The recapture of Kalinin was a success gained earlier and was a gain which came into the same category as the taking of Kaluga.

The threat to Moscow had been well and truly deflected.* Towards the end of February 1942 the Red Army winter offensive finally began to exhaust itself. In March it came to a halt some forty-five miles east of Smolensk and lay stalled before Orel, Vyazma, Rzhev and Kharkov.

THE PROSPECT

In two major purges, one political and the other military in so far as it was dictated by the terms of the battle-field, the very highest, the senior and the intermediate levels of the command of the Soviet armed forces had been savagely handled. With its talent diminished and its ranks visibly thinned, that command had been launched into a devastating war for which its political masters had made either insufficient or miscalculated preparation. The Red Army was not unique in suffering so disastrously at the hands of the *Wehrmacht*, although the achievement of some 17 *Panzer* divisions of the latter in inflicting the stupendous initial loss on Soviet armour must be accounted one of the most singular military feats ever performed. By the same token, the Red Army counter-stroke before Moscow was an undeniably remarkable undertaking by an army which had been so terribly and continually mauled. Upon Soviet admission, no plan for strategic withdrawal had existed. General Vorob'ev is demonstrably correct in adducing the undue emphasis on the offensive and 'carrying the war into the enemy's territory' as the factor which hampered proper defensive planning. Nor was criticism, however sensible, consistent with retaining grace and favour under Stalin's system. German interrogation of captured Soviet senior officers in 1941 revealed that senior commanders, although convinced of the uselessness or downright stupidity of their operational

* The argument over the Moscow battle centres on whether the German Army fell back or was thrust back. To advance the climate as the chief cause of disaster is a misleading over-simplification. There was no discernible precise 'turning-point', but certainly a critical period, running from mid-November to 5th December, when the German offensive ground to a halt. Of this outcome of the 1941 German campaign in Russia, it might be argued that the initial failure to destroy the Soviet armies west of the Dnieper-Dvina line was itself a factor of outstanding importance. The offensive against Moscow proceeded in rapidly deteriorating weather conditions, with no adequate preparation for meeting the climatic conditions. During August-September, as the German Army diverged from the Moscow direction, the Russians had been able to put the two months to good use. General Blumentritt considered this last 'fatal'. Captain B. H. Liddell Hart stresses that inadequate provision of tracked vehicles reduced mobility, upon which so much depended. Before Moscow itself, the German command seriously under-estimated the Soviet capacity for further resistance. And in the widest context, the political blunders proved to be at least as potent as the military errors, and placed a powerful weapon at the disposal of the Soviet leaders.

orders, had no option but to carry them out to the very letter, and to the end which was bitter beyond their imagining.

In an attempt to cover up what was manifestly the crisis of the entire system, Khrushchev has devised the comprehensive euphemism of Stalin's 'faulty methods of directing the nation and the Party'. Although that was of enormous significance, the crisis over the competing claims of military efficiency and political reliability had been permanent in the Soviet state. Into its preparations for modern war, the Soviet command dragged a bitter legacy of military-political conflict since the Civil War. The inevitable tendency was for the military, at moments of its ascendancy, to seek the efficient non-political army, and to attempt to slip the shackles of political control. At its very best, the Soviet system could manage only the neutralisation of the armed forces in a state subject to an increasing degree of militarisation. At its worst, the politically reliable commissars and the militarily inept but pliant commander combined to render an acceptable but mediocre service to the masters of the regime. The inter-command feuds and the clash of ambitions, features common to *bourgeois* and Communist armed forces alike, made their constant contribution to the internal evolution of the senior command group. Stalin's utilisation of these personal intrigues was one of the guarantees of his success in carrying through the major purge in 1937, and one which he had practised during the major crisis of 1923–5.

After the initial disasters, the Red Army command recovered a little of its nerve and succeeded in gathering its wits, to the degree that it no longer sought merely to defend ground but began to exploit space with planned withdrawals. In November 1942 ill-health caused Shaposhnikov's retirement from the post of Chief of the General Staff, but by that time the organisation and operation of the *Stavka* had become much more stable and the small group of higher commanders invested with exceptional responsibility had acquired further experience. The *Stavka* system worked with an increasing efficiency as the war progressed. To co-ordinate or even execute major operations, *Stavka* 'representatives' went to specified Fronts. Gradually the level of ability among Front commanders increased, to become in many instances most striking; the Front commander enjoyed some latitude in applying the *Stavka*/General Staff plan which had been previously worked out, but the sharp break in freedom of action came at army level, where dilutions of talent made the letter of the law come into rigorous operation. Out of its subordination, the army marched into equality with the Party. For its twenty-three years of existence before the Soviet-German War, the Workers and Peasants Red Army failed to evolve a tradition. For much of that period, its professionalism had been an extraordinary graft of the Prussian by imitation and the Imperial Russian by the force of unexpected circumstance. While 'patriotic war' laid the foundations for a particular tradition, in 1942 the principle of unitary command (*edinonachalie*) was brought back to the Red Army, thereby abolishing the worst inefficiencies of the dual command system. Over its inveterate and real enemy, the *NKVD*, the military command won no comparable victory. Although streamlined in 1943, the organs of surveillance and repression operated according to their original purpose, with only the superficial concession that in war-time these officers wore Red Army uniform.

That excessive and murderous suspiciousness of Stalin, together with the phenomenon of his identifying the safeguarding of his power with the salvation of the Soviet Union — both of which had enormous effects on the military command — may well have been a distortion through an uninhibited personal tyranny of certain features of the Soviet state. Yet before Stalin captured that power, the problem of military organisation had created formidable problems out of the fears of the Party leadership and the dissatisfactions of the soldiers. After Stalin, an outstanding military leader in the person of Zhukov was swept out of his position for infringing the taboos, the formative and testing stages of which have been set out here. In November 1957 the foremost Party journal *Kommunist* delivered its judgement:

> The army of a Socialist country, an army standing guard over the gains of the working masses — all experience teaches us — can only be an army led and educated by the Communist Party.

Zhukov's transgression lay in his taking up 'an incorrect and non-Party position, in his pursuing

> . . . a line of separating our armed forces from the Communist Party, of weakening the Party organisations and essentially of liquidating the political organs in the Soviet Army. His work was quite clearly marked by a tendency to regard the Soviet forces as his own domain. . . .

In this fashion Marshal Zhukov, one-time apprentice to the fur-trade, commander in the 1st Cavalry Army and subsequently the most lauded officer produced by the Red Army, joined company with the early military dissidents of the Civil War, with Svechin in the early 1920's and Frunze beset by doubts on the eve of his untimely death, with Marshal Tukhachevsky and his fellows, with Marshal Timoshenko's cautious representations in 1940, with the anonymous but swelling band of critics during the Soviet-German War.

It was a company which was far from lacking its own distinctions.

* * * *

NOTES

NOTES

Chapter I

1. Cf. Z. A. B. Zeman, *Germany and the Revolution in Russia 1915–1918*, London 1958, *passim*, for documentary evidence from captured German files of the infiltration and attempted disintegration of the Russian war effort.

2. *The Russian Revolution 1917. A personal record by N. N. Sukhanov* (ed. Joel Carmichael), London 1955, p. 113.

3. See Lieutenant-General N. Golovine, *The Russian Army in the World War*, New Haven 1931. Esp. Ch. XI. 'Order No. 1.', p. 250. Also *Velikaya Oktyabr'skaya Revolyutsiya* (The Great October Revolution), Documents and Materials, Moscow 1957, pp. 601–65. Cf. E. I. Martynov, *Tsarskaya Armiya i Fevral'skom perevorote* (The Tsarist Army and the February overthrow of power), Shtab RKKA 1927, pp. 137–8.

4. General A. A. Brusilov, *Moi Vospominaniya* (Recollections), Moscow 1941 (2nd edn.), p. 224.

5. Text of 'Order No. 2.' in *Baltiiskie moryaki v podgotovke i provedenii Velikoi Oktyabr'skoi Sotsialisticheskoi Revolyutsii* (The Baltic sailors in the preparation and the carrying through of the Great October Socialist Revolution), Moscow-Leningrad 1957, Doc. No. 13. pp. 22–3. For the decision to confine it to Petrograd, see *Velik. Oktyabr' Rev., op. cit.*, pp. 223–4. This was signed by Guchkov, War Minister. Cf. L. Trotsky, *The History of the Russian Revolution*, London 1932, Vol. 1. Trotsky connects up three main links in the relations between the soldiers and the Petrograd Soviet through (i) regiments sending their representatives to the Soldiers' Section of the Soviet, (ii) the Executive Committee sending its commissars to the regiments, (iii) each regiment with its elective committee forming a 'sort of lower nucleus of the Soviet'.

6. For accounts by German soldiers, see East German work, A. Nordern, *Zwischen Berlin und Moskau*, Berlin 1954, pp. 53–67. Cf. *Bol'shaya Sov. Entsiklopediya* (The Large Soviet Encyclopedia), 1st Edn., cited as *BSE* (1), Vol. 7, Col. 129 under 'Bratanie' (Fraternisation), contributed by N. Krylenko.

7. See P. Poitevin, *La Mutinerie de La Courtine*, Paris 1938, 199 pp. Also Kh. I. Muratov, *Revolyutsionnoe dvizhenie v russkoi armii v 1917 g*, (Revolutionary movements in the Russian Army in 1917), Moscow 1958, pp. 172–89. For comparison, see study of French Army mutinies, J. C. King, *Generals and Politicians*, California 1951, pp. 172–8.

8. Cf. *Biographic Directory of the USSR*, N.Y. 1958, pp. 374–5 on Malinovskii.

9. See *BSE* (1) Vol. 12, 1928, Cols. 174–6. Gives the date of the creation of the Bolshevik organisation as 23rd March, 1917. The 3 members were Podvoiskii, Sulimov and Bagdat'ev: 48 military units were connected with it initially.

10. For a recent attempt to inflate the role of the Bolsheviks, see S. G. Kapshukov, *Bor'ba Bol'shevistskoi partii za armiyu v period perv. mirov. voiny* (The struggle of the Bolshevik party for the army in the period of the First World War), Moscow 1957, 163 pp.

11. Kh. I. Muratov, *op. cit.*, p. 19.

12. On the Latvian regiments, see F. A. Shurygin, *Rev. dvizhenie soldatskkih mass severnovo fronta v 1917 g* (The revolutionary movement among the troops of the Northern Front 1917), Moscow 1958, pp. 28–30. By far the most valuable study of the Latvian regiments (which is a subject in itself), see a recent Soviet Latvian work by T. Ya. Draudin, *Boevoi Put' Latyshskoi strelkovoi divizii v dni Oktyabrya i v gody Grazh. Voiny (1917-1920)* (The road of combat. The Latvian rifle divisions during the October Days and in the Civil War), Riga 1960, 154 pp. See also *Krasnyi Arkhiv* (The Red Archive), cited as *KA*, for 1927, No. 21, pp. 3–78 for the documents of the command of the Northern Front.

13. See *Baltiiskie moryaki*, *op. cit.*, on the Naval Soviet: Doc. No. 98. p. 87 for N. G. Markin on *Tsentrobalt.*

14. The detailed work on this is S. E. Rabinovich, *Vserossiskaya voennaya konferentsiya Bol'shevikov 1917 g* (The All-Russian Military Conference of the Bolsheviks 1917). Cf. E. Yaroslavskii, *Istoriya VKP(b)*, (History of the All-Russian Communist Party/Bolshevik), Moscow-Leningrad 1930, Vol. 2, p. 131 f. Also A. F. Ilyin Genevsky, *From February to October 1917*, London 1931, pp. 58–9: gives the figure of 160 delegates from about 500 regiments, making 26,000 soldiers 'organised in Communist nuclei'.

15. Cf. L. Schapiro, 'The birth of the Red Army' in *The Soviet Army* (ed. B. H. Liddell Hart), London 1956, p. 25.

16. Golovine, *op. cit.*, p. 105. This was a check on the figures for the Army Supply Department, 20th April, 1917—a one-day census. Men fed: 9,050,924. Of these, 'crowding the rear' (unofficial or legal desertion) amounted on 1st April to 1,844,000. For 1st June, another estimate of these desertions is 3,053,000 (*ibid.*, p. 112).

17. *Ibid.*, p. 274. Telegram of 9th July from the commissars of the XIth Army. Trotsky, *op. cit.*, Vol. 1, pp. 383–99 had some mordant comments on the offensive.

18. Cf. L. Schapiro, *The Origin of the Communist Autocracy*, London 1956, p. 92.

19. Shurygin, *op. cit.*, p. 122. The men were lodged in the Butyrka prison in Moscow. After a hunger-strike, 593 men were sent to hospitals. Some later helped in the Moscow insurrection.

20. Golovine, *op. cit.*, pp. 121–5 has a set of figures for the *recorded* desertions covering 1st March–1st August, 1917: total 365,137. By 1st November 1,500,000 were recorded.

21. Cf. *The History of the Civil War in the USSR* (Collective authorship), N.Y. 1936 (tr. from Russian). See Vol. 1, p. 258. In spite of being a product of the Stalinist period, this work contains useful information. Kornilov's demand for 30,000 stolen revolvers is also recorded here.

22. *Ibid.*, p. 256. Cf. Sukhanov, *op. cit.*, p. 62, for proposals about the militia.

23. Cf. E. Erykalov, *Krasnaya Gvardiya v bor'be za vlast' sovetov* (The Red Guard in the struggle for power to the soviets), Moscow 1957, pp. 8–10. Bubnov, Nevskii, Sverdlov and Dzerzhinskii were active in these early efforts.

24. The numbers quoted vary very widely, with substantial retrospective recruitment in recent Soviet accounts. Cf. *BSE*, 1st Edn., Vol. 34, 1937, Cols. 576–82 with *BSE*, 2nd Edn., Vol. 23, 1953, pp. 232–3. The first *BSE* account is quite useful.

25. Erykalov, *op. cit.*, p. 32, gives the end of August as the date. *History of the Civil War, op. cit.*, p. 263, gives 2nd March as the date for organising militia. Cf. S. Kukushkin, *Moskovskii Sovet v 1917 godu* (The Moscow Soviet in 1917), Moscow 1957, pp. 57–9 gives 27th April as the date for the Red Guard, 15th May for the organisation of regional staffs in the city. Erykalov, p. 33, cites 2nd September as the date for the central staff in Moscow. Detailed study may be found in G. D. Kostomarov and V. Malakhovskii, *Iz istorii Moskovskoi rabochei Krasnoi Gvardii* (From the history of the Moscow Red Guard), Istpart, Moscow, MK. VKP(b) 1930.

26. *Vtoroi vserossiskii S'ezd Sovetov* (The Second All-Russian Congress of Soviets), Moscow 1957 Edn., Questionnaires to the Bolshevik fraction, pp. 229–385.

27. Erykalov, *op. cit.*, p. 39, gives 23,000 Red Guards for Petrograd, listing them by main detachments. Cf. his optimistic remarks on training (p. 41) with a very detailed archival study for the Petrograd Red Guard in *Istoricheskii Arkhiv*, 1957, No. 5, pp. 119–46. This lists units for 22 factories, strengths, arms and training state, and is a great corrective to Erykalov. Cf. I. F. Pobezhimov, *Ustroistvo Sovetskoi Armii* (The building up of the Soviet Army), Moscow 1954, p. 11, citing 10–12,000 for Petrograd and over 3,000 for Moscow. Erykalov has distinguished between armed and unarmed workers, so that would not account for the discrepancy in the figures.

28. Cf. Golovine, *op. cit.*, pp. 238–40. Loss of faith in the Allies 'became apparent by the end of 1915'.

29. George F. Kennan, *Russia Leaves the War*, Vol. 1 of *Soviet-American Relations 1917–1920*, Princeton 1956, pp. 284–5.

30. This brief account is based on W. H. Chamberlin, *The Russian Revolution*, N.Y. 1935, Vol. 1, pp. 306–35.

31. See *Za Vlast' Sovetov* (For power to the Soviets), MK i MGK KPSS, Moscow 1957, p. 152 f.

32. *Ibid.*, p. 166–71.

33. Cf. D. Fedotoff White, *The Growth of the Red Army*, Princeton 1944. This extremely valuable work describes the role of the sailors and mentions, pp. 14–15, the Red Guard as being 'poorly trained and poorly led'.

34. P. E. Dybenko in *BSE* (1), Vol. 23, 1931, Cols. 698–9.

35. *Vtoroi S'ezd, op. cit.*, p. 413.

36. R. Bruce Lockhart, *Memoirs of a British Agent*, London 1950, p. 252.

37. *Vtoroi S'ezd*, Doc. No. 332, p. 415: 'K frontu' (To the front).

38. Muratov, *op. cit.*, p. 321.

39. *Ibid.*, p. 328.

40. *Ibid.*, p. 313, for archives of the Supreme command, Northern Front. The best documentary study is *Razlozhenia armii v 1917 godu* (The dissolution of the Army in 1917), (ed. N. E. Kakurin), Moscow-Leningrad 1925.

41. Muratov, pp. 313–14: Supreme Headquarters Archive. Novitskii later became chief of staff to M. V. Frunze and a trusted 'military specialist' in the Red Army.

42. A. I. Cherepanov, *Pod Pskovom i Narvoi* (By Pskov and the Narva), Moscow 1957, p. 14. Officer cadets were removed from the training schools to reserve battalions.

43. For a Bolshevik view, see A. G. Shlyapnikov, 'Oktyabrskii perevorot i Stavka'

in *KA*, 1925, No. 8, pp. 153–75, contd. in No. 9, pp. 156–70. ('The October revolution and the *Stavka*'.)

44. Reproduced in V. I. Lenin, *Voennaya Perepiska (1917–1920)* (Military Communications 1917–1920), Moscow (1956 Edn.), pp. 11–14.

45. W. H. Chamberlin, *op. cit.*, Vol. 1, p. 346.

46. Version *ibid.*, p. 347.

47. Blyukher appears in Muratov, *op. cit.*, p. 356. Blyukher became the first president of the Chelyabinsk Soviet.

48. See *Dokumenty Vneshnei Politiki SSSR* (Documents on Soviet Foreign Policy), Moscow 1957, Vol. 1, No. 22, pp. 41–2, and No. 25, pp. 45–6.

49. Fedotoff White, *op. cit.*, p. 28, cites his conversation with Behrens (or Berens, Chief of the Naval Staff in 1918), who recalled talks with Lenin, Trotsky and Admiral Altfater on the re-organisation of the armed forces.

50. Cherepanov, *op. cit.*, p. 15. Also W. H. Chamberlin, Vol. 1, p. 489–90 (Appendix). Both decrees are dated 16 (29) December, 1917, and are printed in *Dekrety Sovetskoi vlasti* (Soviet government decrees), Moscow 1957 Edn., Vol. 1, pp. 242–5.

51. See Cherepanov, p. 17, for a lively account of these elections. Cherepanov, an officer of long service with the Red Army, cuts out much of the propaganda in his account and gives a more accurate picture of the confusion and cross-purpose.

52. M. S. Kedrov took charge of the responsible committee at this congress.

53. For a full and excellent analysis of the struggle over Brest-Litovsk, see L. Schapiro, *Communist Autocracy*, *op. cit.*, Ch. VI. See Lenin's questionnaire in his *Sochineniya* (Works), 4th Russian Edn., Vol. 26, pp. 356–7. This is dated 18 (31) December, 1917.

54. This is according to Cherepanov, *op. cit.*, p. 19.

55. The history of this collegiate appears very obscure. The decree announcing its formation appeared on 28th January, 1918, but it had already been working for a month. N. Podvoiskii and K. S. Yeremeyev were among its first members. In late December 1917 a plenary meeting of the Petrograd Soviet had discussed a 'Red Army': see *Istoriya Grazhdanskoi Voiny v SSSR* (The History of the Civil War in the USSR) (Editorial Commission S. F. Naida, G. D. Obichkin, Yu. P. Petrov, A. A. Struchkov, N. I. Shatagin), Vol. 3, Moscow 1957, p. 126. This is the new post-Stalin history designed to 'rectify' the grosser falsifications. Cherepanov, p. 19, refers to a decision of 26th December, 1917, to organise a new army.

56. Cherepanov supplies many versions of the name.

57. Cherepanov, p. 20.

58. *Ibid. Okopnaya Pravda* was a paper published for front-line troops.

59. See V. I. Lenin, *Soch.*, Vol. 26, p. 386.

60. See a more recent history of the Red Army, Col. N. I. Shatagin, *Organizatsiya i stroitel'stvo Sovetskoi Armii v period inostrannoi voennoi interventsii i grazhdanskoi voiny (1918–1920 gg)* (The organisation and formation of the Soviet Army during the period of foreign military intervention and the Civil War 1918–1920), Moscow 1954. This is a misleading and biased book, not yet freed from the Stalinist grip, but marking the return of the historian to the archives. Leaving aside the florid tributes to Stalin, and the foolish nonsense about Trotsky's 'sabotage', the book contains useful informa-

tion on details. See his account of the early January decisions, pp. 27–31, mentioning the meetings of 3rd January (Red Army collegiate) and 8th (Military Organisations). A Technical Staff was formed on 12th January.

61. *Ibid.*, p. 34.

62. These units are cited in M. I. Kapustin, *Soldaty Severnovo fronta v bor'be za vlast' Sovetov* (Soldiers of the Northern front in the struggle for power to the Soviets), Moscow 1957, p. 318.

63. *Dekrety, op. cit.*, Vol. 1, pp. 352–5. Gives the first draft, with its many alterations, followed by the final decree. There are many variations in the printed versions, according to the notes here. Also pp. 357–8 for the *official* announcement of the All-Russian Collegiate for the Formation of the Red Army.

64. Cherepanov, *op. cit.*, o. 25. Adds the rider that no Bolshevik armed force yet existed which could challenge the Germans and the Austrians 'armed to the teeth'.

65. *Ibid.*, pp. 27–8.

66. *Ibid.*, p. 29 f. Cites Order No. 0301 and F. F. Novitskii's action to form Red Army units. There follows a wholesale changing of unit numbers from XIIth Army designations to Red Army regiments and the amalgamation of one unit with another. Based on an archival source.

67. V. I. Lenin, *Soch.*, Vol. 27, p. 36.

68. Ratification of this required a further struggle in the Central Committee. Cf. Doc. 119, p. 119, in Z. A. B. Zeman, *op. cit.*, for 11th March, 1918: '. . . it would perhaps be better not, as yet, to assume that the transition from a war on two fronts to a war on a single front is definitely assured' (Kühlmann).

Chapter II

1. Cf. L. Schapiro, *Communist Autocracy, op. cit.*, Ch. VI, esp. pp. 104–10. Lenin finally composed the internal difficulties, but Bukharin would not be reconciled to the peace which 'threw the Party on to the dung-hill'.

2. Cf. Fedotoff White, *op. cit.*, p. 35.

3. Prisoner-of-war Congresses were held (February, March, April) in Moscow, Siberia, Central Asia. The total number of recruits so gathered is in dispute. See E. Brandstrom, *Among the prisoners of war in Russia and Siberia*, London 1929, pp. 2389–, for the figure of 90,000. A recent detailed Soviet study in *Ist. Arkhiv*, 1957, No. 4, pp. 3–37, on Red Army 'International Groups' lists ex-prisoner organisations for Czech-Slovak, Hungarian, Rumanian and S. Slav Red Army units. In an earlier study, L. Ulyanov in *Proletarskaya Revolyutsiya* (Proletarian Revolution), 1928, pp. 97–102, gives a figure of 50,000, which corresponds roughly to the figure supplied in *Ist. Arkhiv*.

4. N. A. Popov in *Voprosy Istorii* (Problems of History), 1957, No. 10, pp. 102–24: admits (p. 118) to 8–10,000 Chinese men in the Red Army, but not to the 30–40,000 of a Chinese left-wing account. See G. Novogrudskii and A. Dunaevskii, *Tovarishchi Kitaiskie boitsy* (Chinese comrade fighters), Moscow 1959, on Chinese battalions in the Red Army.

5. W. H. Chamberlin, *op. cit.*, Vol. 2, p. 26, for Sytin's report, 8th April, 1918, that Red units in Bryansk would not submit to discipline; telegram, 18th April, that retreating Red forces terrorising railway workers.

6. Shatagin, *op. cit.*, p. 61–2. Moscow set up 'The Extraordinary Staff of the Soviet Army' to plan their units. Baku obviously took the Red Guard as its model. The Red Army Collegiate's *Regulation and Instruction* for new units seems to have been a very ineffective document.

7. *Dekrety Sovetskoi Vlasti* (Decrees of the Soviet government), Vol. 1, Moscow 1957, p. 522–3. Cf. I. F. Pobezhimov, *Ustroistvo Sov. Armii*, *op. cit.*, p. 15, mentions 'The Extraordinary Military Staff' of January 1918 as the precursor to this. See Cherepanov, *op. cit.*, pp. 98–9. See Appendix 1.

8. Instruction in Lenin-Podvoiskii telegram, 1st April, 1918: Lenin, *Voen. Perepis.*, pp. 32–3. See Appendix. Shatagin, p. 62 refers to a special conference group attached to deal with the organisation of the Red Army.

9. Cherepanov, *op. cit.*, p. 96 f. Refers to an extensive memoir of Fishman's on the work of this command group and the contact with Lenin.

10. Shatagin, p. 51 and 52. Adds courses in Oranienbaum, Tver and Kazan, in addition to Moscow and Petrograd.

11. *Dekrety*, Vol. 1, p. 577. See Appendix. This is presumably the body to which Shatagin refers, p. 62. Cf. I. Deutscher, *The Prophet Armed. Trotsky 1879–1921*, London 1954, p. 388: the 'War faction' lacked a real leader to carry out their particular policy, although Radek and Bukharin did anticipate the way in which the Red Army would actually be built — under fire.

12. See *Izvestiya. Nar. Komm. po Voen. Delyam*, 1st Year, 1st May–31st Oct. 1918, Moscow 1918 (Bulletin. People's Commissariat for Military Affairs.)

13. Trotsky had worked as a war correspondent during the Balkan Wars before 1914.

14. I. Deutscher, *The Prophet Armed*, pp. 477–8, note on Trotsky's military writings. Radek's view was that Trotsky had been much impressed by Jean Jaurès work, *L'Armée Nouvelle*.

15. George F. Kennan, *op. cit.*, Vol. 2., 1958, p. 112 f. Also L. Trotsky, *My Life*, London 1930, pp. 306–7, where he writes that General Lavergne's advice was of '... little value'. Other French officers he mentioned were, in his own words, '... more competent in military espionage than military administration.'

16. George F. Kennan, Vol. 2, pp. 136–66, on the history and background of the Legion. See also Lt.-Gen. K. V. Sakharov, *Cheshkie Legiony v' Sibiri* (The Czech Legions in Siberia), Riga 1930. Ann Arbor Microprint.

17. L. D. Trotsky, *Kak voorazhalas' Revolyutsiya* (How the Revolution armed itself), 3 vols. in 5 parts. Moscow 1923–. Quite indispensable. Cited as *KVR*. See speeches, 19th March ('We need an army'), Vol. 1, pp. 25–9; 28th March ('Work discipline and order'), pp. 31–46.

18. Cf. Shatagin, p. 55. See Organisational sketch, Appendix.

19. Trotsky, *KVR*, Vol. 1, pp. 123–5.

20. *Ibid.*, p. 305. Trotsky declared that volunteer recruitment had never been a matter of principle.

21. See mobilisation and recruitment in *Grazhdanskaya Voina 1918–1921* (The Civil War 1918–1920) 3 vols., Moscow 1928– (edited collectively by A. Bubnov, S. S. Kamenev, R. P. Eidemann and M. N. Tukhachevsky). Cited as *GV*. See Vol. 2, N. Movchin on Red Army recruiting, p. 77 and 78.

22. *Ibid.*

23. *Ibid.*, p. 76. This figure is always cited as 'the basic worker force' but it needs extremely careful qualification.

24. Shatagin, p. 63. Yet p. 45 he gives the data supplied by the Red Army Collegiate: 1st April, 153,678 men (*39,000 men at the front*); 20th April, 195,838. Both Movchin and Shatagin adjust their figures, which are not credible in the light of their other incidentally-presented information. It is an attempt to show how massive and spontaneous was the support for the Bolsheviks.

25. Trotsky, *KVR*, Vol. 1. p. 29; speech.

26. Fedotoff White, p. 52, writes that Trotsky '. . . waved a magic wand before their eyes — a marshal's baton'. During the Soviet-German War, 1941–1945 this indeed came to pass on a considerable scale — Marshal Zhukov is perhaps the best example. See *KVR*, Vol. 1, Decree, August 3rd/1918, pp. 174–5 and speech to ex-NCO's, pp. 176–83.

27. Shatagin, p. 51.

28. V. M. Klyatskin, in *Ist. Zapiski* (Historical Papers), Moscow 1956, No. 8, p. 25.

29. *Ibid.*

30. Trotsky, *KVR*, Vol. 1, p. 135. Speech 'O voenspetsakh' (About military specialists) deals with the malicious criticism, as well as the genuine and serious misgivings about the ex-officers.

31. Cf. Deutscher, *The Prophet Armed*, p. 414.

32. See N. Efimov, in *GV*. Vol. 2, p. 93, on Red Army command staff. Klyatskin, p. 16 states that the first NCO mobilisation produced 17,800 men.

33. Efimov, p. 94. Shatagin p. 52 states that 8,000 ex-officers *volunteered* their services in 1918. This figure seems a little excessive.

34. Efimov, p. 95.

35. *Ibid.* Senior Red officers, trained in the shortened War Academy courses, amounted to 638 in 1919 and 1,259 in 1920.

36. *Ibid.*

37. Trotsky, *My Life*, p. 381.

38. See a recent study, I. I. Vlasov, *V. I. Lenin i stroitel'stvo Sov. Armii* (V. I. Lenin and the building up of the Soviet Army), Moscow 1958, pp. 130–44, esp. p. 134 f., for several cases of defection reported in the Red Army archives.

39. See F. Nikonov, in *GV*, Vol. 2, pp. 48–75, on Red Army organisation.

40. *Ibid.* See Organisational table in Appendix.

41. Shatagin, p. 96.

42. *BSE* (1), Vol. 9, 1928, Col. 100.

43. Shatagin, p. 97.

44. Cf. K. G. Fedorov, *VTsIK v pervye gody Sov. Vlasti 1917–1920 gg* (VTsIK in the first years of Soviet power 1917–1920), Moscow 1957, p. 116.

45. Cf. D. Grinishin, *Voennaya Deyatel'nost' V. I. Lenina* (V. I. Lenin's military

activity), Moscow 1957, p. 278 f. This recent work, full of interesting side-lights, nevertheless conforms to the Party line of substituting Lenin for Stalin as the origin of Soviet victory.

46. Trotsky, *KVR*, Vol. 1, p. 414, for Trotsky's formula for stiffening the Red Army.

47. Trotsky, *My Life*, p. 351.

48. *Ibid.*, p. 343. The first to be shot would be the commissar.

49. Cf. S. I. Gusev, *Grazhdanskaya Voina i Krasnaya Armiya* (The Civil War and the Red Army), Moscow-Leningrad 1925, p. 20. This work was re-published in 1958, under the same title, but this was deleted.

50. Deutscher, *The Prophet Armed*, pp. 425–6, for the use made of this by Trotsky's opponents. Smilga and Lashevich brought it to the Central Committee. Trotsky's letter (Dec. 1918) justified the sentence on the executed commissar Panteleyev, and for any other dereliction of duty.

51. Trotsky, *My Life*, p. 373.

52. *Ibid.*, p. 374.

53. Erich Wollenberg, *The Red Army*, London 1938, pp. 157–8.

54. J. Stalin, *Works*, Eng. Edn., Vol. 4, p. 120, uses 'bunglers'. Russian Edn., Vol. 4, p. 118 — '*sapozhniki!*'.

55. Trotsky, *My Life*, p. 378.

56. D. Furmanov, *Chapayev*, London 1935, p. 78. 'That was Chapayev's sore-spot . . . Chapayev could not stomach them.'

57. *BSE* (1), Vol. 12, 1928, Col. 323 f. Refers to the commissar in the French Revolutionary Wars, Decree of the Convention, 15th December, 1792. Also to commissars introduced into the Imperial Russian Army in Manchuria, 14th December, 1900. Commissars played a very important part before November 1917, but there were no commissars in the Red Guard.

58. See N. Sukhanov, *op. cit.*, p. 63; these were 'voluntary and plenipotentiary commissars'.

59. See commissar reports in *Doneseniya komissarov Petrogradskovo VRK* (Reports of the commissars of the Petrograd Military-Revolutionary Committee), Moscow 1957, 333 pp.

60. Shatagin, pp. 148–9.

61. *Ibid.* The course gave instruction in (i) the class struggle (ii) the path to Socialism (iii) the Russian revolution (iv) the idea of Soviet power (v) the Red Army (vi) the technique of agitation.

62. Cf. Fedotoff White, p. 75–6. Also A. Geronimus in *GV*, Vol. 2, pp. 110–29 on political work in the Red Army; a much more analytical account is F. Blumental', *Politicheskaya rabota v voennoe vremya* (Political work in war-time), Moscow-Leningrad 1927, 374 pp. First regulations on the functions of commissars, *KVR*, Vol. 1, pp. 406–7 (for 6th April, 1918). Wollenberg, *op. cit.*, p. 255, Appendix I.

63. K. G. Fedorov, *VTsIK*, *op. cit.*, p. 108.

64. Shatagin, pp. 151–2.

65. See A. Geronimus, *GV*, Vol. 2, p. 110 f.

66. Trotsky, *KVR*, Vol. 1, p. 185, for 11th December, 1918, on the Communist soldiers' responsibility as opposed to privilege.

67. S. I. Gusev to E. D. Stasova, Central Committee secretary, quoted in G. V. Kuzmin, *Grazh. voina i voennaya interventsiya v SSSR* (The Civil War and armed Intervention in the USSR), Moscow 1958, p. 236. No reference given.

68. *Protokoly Petrograd. Konferentsiya Bol'shevikov Krasnoarmeitsev* (Proceedings of the Petrograd Conference of Bolshevik Red Army men), Petrograd 1918, p. 44.

69. E. Putyrskii, in *Ist. Zapiskii*, 1957, No. 61, pp. 294–333, on the Petrograd Military District and Military Commissariat, 1918; Mobilisation figures for men for the Eastern Front, pp. 299–300 and p. 305.

70. Yu. Petrov in *Partiinaya Zhizn'* (Party Life), 1957, No. 10, pp. 35–46; p. 41 states that 'cells' in volunteer units were much stronger. See A. Geronimus, *Partiya i Krasnaya Armiya* (The Party and the Red Army), Moscow 1928. This is a basic work, by a Communist military sociologist. Estimates the 'cells' at 1,400 for the end of 1918. The number of commissars at the fronts in October 1919 amounted to 5,200 (out of a total of 7,700), p. 80. The number of Communists in the army is set at 120,000 (62,000 at the front).

71. Cf. a recent discussion of Soviet writing on political activity in the army. S. F. Naida, *O nekotorykh voprosakh istorii grazh. voiny v SSSR* (On certain questions of the history of the Civil War in the USSR), Moscow 1958, pp. 18–26.

72. L. Schapiro, *Communist Autocracy*, p. 244.

73. J. Stalin, *Works*, Eng. Edn., Vol. 4, 'Report to V. I. Lenin', 19th January, 1919, p. 194.

74. *Ibid.*, Report, pp. 212–3. The 'Personal and Record Card' for recruits, Items 15 and 16 (on class affiliation and training) had been neglected.

75. *Ibid.*, p. 215.

76. *Ibid.*, p. 219.

77. See an important article, B. D. Wolfe, *American Slavic and East European Review*, 1950, Vol. IX, pp. 169–79, on the centralising factor in military affairs and its relation to the national structure of the USSR; pp. 173–4, the clash between the claims of Ukrainian autonomy and Moscow centralism.

78. See V. I. Lenin, *Voen. Perepis*, p. 110, for a draft of a Central Committee project for military unity. See Appendix.

79. S. F. Naida, *op. cit.*, p. 172. Cf. Geronimus, *Partiya i K.A.*, pp. 46–56, on the 8th Congress. Also *Istoriya VKP (b)* (History of the All-Russian Communist Party/ Bolshevik/), Vol. 4, Moscow-Leningrad 1930, p. 414.

80. Naida, p. 173.

81. L. Trotsky, *Stalin* (ed. C. Malamuth), London 1947, p. 302.

82. See Deutscher, *The Prophet Armed*, p. 431.

83. *KPSS v rez* (Party resolutions), 7th Edn., Official Theses, 8th Congress: Point VI, p. 433. (See also *KVR*, Vol. 1, pp. 186–99.)

84. *KPSS v rez*, Point XV, p. 436.

85. *Ibid.*, p. 440.

86. This is the oppositional platform, printed *ibid.*, pp. 440–1.

87. *Vsevobuch*, with Podvoiskii at its head, played a key role in Trotsky's plans (cf.

Theses, 8th Congress). See Berkhin, *Voen. Reforma*, *op. cit.*, p. 83, for early militia plans. February 1919 the 'Regulation on Reserve Troops' was brought out; see Shatagin, pp. 118–20 for details of this and *Vsevobuch* figures. See First *Vsevobuch* Congress report for 1918 (*Otchot o pervom s'ezde po vseobshchemu voennomu obucheniyu: 1918 g*, Moscow 1918, 179 pp.).

88. Published under the aegis of the Military Inspectorate. A hand-book, *Revolyutsionnaya Voina* (Revolutionary War) (ed. K. Podvoiskii and M. Pavlovich), Moscow 1919, 132 pp.

89. Trotsky, *Stalin*, Trotsky to Lenin, 5th (?) October, 1918: p. 288.

90. Marshal Budenny's memoirs: S. M. Budenny, *Proidennyi Put'* (The road we have travelled), Moscow 1958, p. 245.

Chapter III

1. L. Trotsky, *My Life*, pp. 307–8, for tribute to Sklyanskii (drowned near Chicago 1925).

2. Lenin, *Voen. Perepis*, pp. 32–3.

3. W. H. Chamberlin, *op. cit.*, Vol. 2, p. 56, on the rising.

4. *Ibid.*, p. 60. Muraviev sent out telegrams 'declaring war on Germany'.

5. *Ibid.*, for suggestion of Muraviev's suicide. See also Wollenberg, *The Red Army*, p. 68.

6. D. Footman, 'The Red Army on the Eastern Front', St. Antony's Papers on Soviet Affairs (Mimeographed), p. 13. Berzin had warned Vatsetis of the possibility of treachery. Also *Istoricheskii Arkhiv* (Historical Archive), 1958, No. 4, pp. 85–122, on V. V. Kuibyshev at the fronts of the Civil War. Conversation of Podvoiskii and Kuibyshev, 19th June, 1918, on p. 89 f.

7. Trotsky, *My Life*, p. 340, for a very sympathetic portrait of Vatsetis.

8. Trotsky, *Stalin*, p. 310. Here Vatsetis is 'stubborn and cranky'.

9. Trotsky, *My Life*, pp. 338–51, 'The month at Sviyazhsk'.

10. Stalin, *Works*, Eng. Edn., Vol. 4, pp. 123–4.

11. *BSE* (1), Vol. 61, Cols. 843–4.

12. See *GV*, Vol. 1, pp. 136–64. V. Shorin, 'Bor'ba za Ural' (The struggle for the Urals).

13. Cf. Trotsky, *Stalin*, p. 239; Lashevich addicted to the bottle.

14. See P. Fervacque, *Le Chef de l'Armée Rouge — Mikhail Toukatchevski*, Paris 1928. A highly-coloured account of the author's meeting with Tukhachevsky as a prisoner of war, with reference to his ambition, his bizarre Russophilism and his pseudo-philosophy. See also Wollenberg, p. 60.

15. As at the capture of Simbirsk. See *Ist. Arkhiv*, 1958, No. 4, Doc. No. 6, p. 94, Operational Order to Ist Red army, 24th August, 1918, for the offensive on Simbirsk.

16. See Stalin, *Works*, Eng. Edn., Vol. 4, p. 202 f.

17. See M. V. Frunze, *Izbrannye Proizvedeniya* (Selected Works), Moscow 1957 Edn., in two volumes. Here Vol. 1, p. 75–124 for work at the Yaroslavl Commissariat: this gives an excellent picture of the activity and its scope. See Frunze's autobiography,

pp. 69–72. Frunze received consistent honour and was the object of frequent study even during the worst of the Stalinist distortions.

18. Frunze assumed command IVth Army by Order No. 470, 26th December, 1919. His first order to IVth Army, No. 40/9, 31st January, 1919: Frunze, *op. cit.*, Vol. 1, p. 129. Frunze and Novitskii had been warned by Trotsky of the disaffection: see A. M. Spirin, *Razgrom armii Kolchaka* (The destruction of Kolchak's army), Moscow 1957, p. 83.

19. See *Ist. Arkhiv*, 1958, No. 1, pp. 41–76. Covers the period from February–May 1919, with *Glavkom* strategic appreciations and tabular presentations. If these figures are genuine (and there seems little reason to doubt them) they make complete nonsense of the exaggerated claims of other Soviet military-historical accounts of the huge size of the Red Army late in 1918.

20. *Ibid.*, p. 57 and p. 60.

21. *Ibid.*, p. 71. Signed by Sheideman of the Artillery Inspectorate.

22. Trotsky, *Stalin*, p. 310.

23. A. M. Spirin, *op. cit.*, pp. 93–4.

24. *Ibid.*, pp. 127–8.

25. See F. F. Novitskii (Frunze's 'military specialist'), 'Kontranastuplenie Frunze na vostochnom fronte' in *M. V. Frunze. Polkovodcheskaya deyatel'nost'* (M. V. Frunze. Command activity), Moscow 1951. Also M. V. Frunze, *op. cit.*, Vol. 1, pp. 176–7: Report to Commander/Eastern Front No. 01182 for 23rd April, 1919, Operational plan. Cf. *GV*, Vol. 3 (Strategic-operational studies), pp. 176–9. The tendency at present is to raise the stature and role of Frunze as an ideal Communist commander to enormous proportions. Vol. 4 of the new history of the Civil War mentions Frunze (for 1919) 37 times, and Tukhachevsky 5 times; Trotsky is mentioned 9 times.

26. Trotsky, *Stalin*, p. 311, protocol for 18th April. Spirin, p. 133, dates this decision as 29th April (which would fit the circumstances more easily).

27. Trotsky, *Stalin*, p. 312.

28. See M. S. Kedrov (Commissar for the Northern Commune), *Za Sovetskii Sever* (For the Soviet North), Moscow-Leningrad 1927, p. 39, for handsome tribute to A. A. Samoilo. See A. A. Samoilo's autobiography, *Dve Zhizni* (Two lives), Moscow 1958.

29. Kostyayev was then Chief of the Field Staff of the Republic *Revvoensoviet*. 25th May, 1919, protest about Naval Commander, Petrograd; Stalin, *Works*, Vol. 4, p. 269. Trotsky did not oppose the replacement of Kostyayev — only asking a substitute who would not be worse: see *Stalin*, p. 312.

30. See Spirin, *op. cit.*, p. 161–2. Spirin does not flatter Samoilo.

31. See Samoilo, *op. cit.*, p. 250 f., for a very interesting discussion of these struggles; he hated Gusev, and makes him out an intriguer. In 1935 Samoilo tackled Tukhachevsky about the question of the Eastern Front, and — most important — his *kharakteristika* (his vital personal dossier). Samoilo traced his report on the Eastern Front, made on 7th–8th June, 1918, and found it — in 1947 — in the Party archives, not in the Red Army archives, since it had been passed to Lenin. Samoilo wanted the facts straight.

32. See I. S. Kutyakov, *Vasili Ivanovich Chapayev*, Moscow 1958, p. 48. The 25th Chapayev Division (with Kutyakov as a brigade commander) was assigned to take Ufa.

33. Lenin to Gusev, Lashevich, Yurenev, *Voen. Perepis*, pp. 132–3.

34. Spirin, *op. cit.*, p. 182.

35. *Ibid.*, p. 184. Kamenev argues the merits of an Eastern Front plan drawn up on or about 6th. On 12th *Glavkom* again rejected it, ordering a halt on the defensive line.

36. Cf. Deutscher, *The Prophet Armed*, p. 434. See Bertram D. Wolfe, *American Slavic and E. European Review*, Vol. IX, p. 174, for Lenin's signal of 22nd April, 1919, to Vatsetis and to Aralov in Serpukhov. See also the very important V. Antonov-Ovseenko, *Zapiski o Grazhdanskoi Voine* (Notes on the Civil War), 4 vols., Moscow 1933, here Vol. 4, p. 330: Commander-in-Chief's Order, 5th May and order from Moscow.

37. Spirin, p. 184. Cf. D. Grinishin, *Voen. Deyatel'nost V. I. Lenina*, *op. cit.*, p. 322. Trotsky, Stalin, p. 313.

38. Spirin, p. 185.

39. Kashirin: cavalry commander. One of the names cited in connection with the group of officers who are supposed to have passed sentence on Tukhachevsky in 1937.

40. See *GV*, Vol. 1, pp. 190–205, for Eikhe's account of Vth Army operations in Western Siberia. Eikhe later commanded the Vth, but was 26th Divisional commander at this point.

41. See in *Testimony of Kolchak and other Siberian Materials*, *op. cit.*, A. Z. Ovchinnikov, 'Memoirs of the Red partisan movements in the Russian Far East', pp. 265–325.

42. See Ya. Zhigalin, 'Partizanskoe dvizhenie v Zapadnoi Sibirii' (The partisan movement in Western Siberia), *Prol. Rev.*, 1930 No. 11 (106); pp. 98–114.

43. *Ibid.*, p. 113.

44. *Ibid.*, p. 109.

45. Blyukher's official biography: *BSE* (1), Vol. 6, Cols. 537–8. Blyukher disappeared in 1938. The *Malaya Sov. Entsik.* (The Small Soviet Encyclopedia), 1958 Edn., Vol. 1, Col. 1073, gives his date of birth *and* death; 19.11.1889 — 9.11.1938. Blyukher has been most assiduously 're-habilitated'; see *Krasnaya Zvezda* (Red Star), Military Newspaper, 10th August, 1957, for such an eulogy. In detail, *Ist. Arkhiv*, 1958, No. 1, pp. 76–89, on Blyukher's Civil War exploits; on the Composite Detachment, p. 82. This article and documentary collection is continued in *Ist. Arkhiv*, 1958 No. 5, pp. 77–99. This deals largely with the 51st Division in 1920.

46. See Trotsky, *Stalin*, p. 314. See also S. I. Aralov's recent and small booklet, *V. I. Lenin i Krasnaya Armiya* (Lenin and the Red Army), pub. 'Znanie', Moscow 1958, 39 pp. During this re-shuffle, P. P. Lebedev took over the post of Chief of the Field Staff.

47. Trotsky, *Stalin*, pp. 314–5.

48. *Ibid.*, p. 315.

49. This order is quoted in Frunze, Vol. 1, p. 445.

50. Trotsky, *Stalin*, p. 285.

51. I. Deutscher, *The Prophet Armed*, p. 424.

52. Trotsky, *Stalin*, p. 289.

53. See especially N. Markin, 'Stalin and the Red Army' in L. Trotsky, *The Stalin School of Falsification* (Intro. M. Shachtman), N.Y. 1937, pp. 205–14, for the telegrams exchanged about 'the Tsaritsyn opposition'.

54. This is the point of the recent anti-Stalin historiography in the Soviet Union. The 'cult of personality' is further diminished by insisting that the Revolution was saved in the east and not, as Stalinist distortions had pretended, solely in the south — where Stalin was acclaimed the hero. See S. F. Naida, *op. cit.*, pp. 106–12.

55. See Antonov-Ovseenko, *op. cit.*, Vol. 4, *passim.*

56. *Dok. Vneshnei Politiky*, *op. cit.*, Vol. 2, pp. 148–51, for the Soviet note to Rumania, demanding the ceding of Bessarabia.

57. Louis Fischer, *The Soviets in World Affairs*, London 1930, Vol. 1, pp. 194–5. See also Bertram D. Wolfe, *op. cit.*, p. 175.

58. Bertram D. Wolfe, *ibid.*, p. 174.

59. See Antonov-Ovseenko, *op. cit.*, Vol. 4, p. 153 f., for his important memorandum on the peasant question.

60. See I. Deutscher, *The Prophet Armed*, p. 453. Trotsky evidently had Voroshilov in mind for this task, being under the impression — as is here reported from the evidence of the Trotsky Archives — that Voroshilov had been finally won over to his policy.

61. Trotsky, *Stalin*, p. 316.

62. *BSE* (1), Vol. 6, 1927, Cols. 803–4.

63. S. M. Budenny autobiography, *op. cit.*, p. 83. The General's comment: 'Correct. That man knows his drill.'

64. *Ibid.*, p. 105. Trotsky had evidently opposed the formation of cavalry, partly from the view that this might merely be a slavish imitation of Western war technique. By September 1918 he had changed his mind; Deutscher, *The Prophet Armed*, note to p. 483

65. *BSE* (1), Vol. 54, 1946, Col. 259.

66. *BSE, 2nd Edn.*, Vol. 16, pp. 222–3. Dates Zhukov's Red Army service from October 1918.

67. See account in W. H. Chamberlin, *op. cit.*, Vol. 2, pp. 271–2.

68. See Trotsky, *My Life*, Ch. XXXV, on strategic disputes. It is difficult to extricate all the details of this furious controversy. See Lenin, *Voen. Perepis*, pp. 186–7. See D. Grinishin, *op. cit.*, p. 332 f. for discussion of the dates of the decision — with the emphasis on Lenin's influence; what emerges from this account is that Stalin's letter of 15th October, 1919, to Lenin (*Works*, Vol. 4, pp. 285–9) could not have been written at that date, but rather on *15th November*. Grinishin disposes of the myth of 'the Stalin plan' to beat Denikin. See also S. F. Naida, *op. cit.*, pp. 191–214, also disposes of the Stalin myth, placing the authorship of the final plan upon Lenin and the Central Committee. Lenin was obviously greatly concerned over the collapse of the command machinery: see Lenin, *Soch.*, Vol. 35, No. 224 (letter to S. I. Gusev), pp. 356–7. See Appendix. The whole question has received recent attention in *Reshayushchie pobedy Sovetskovo naroda nad interventami i belogvardeitsami v 1919 g.* (Decisive victories of the Soviet people over the Interventionists and White Guardists in 1919), M. 1960: essays edited by S. F. Naida. N. F. Kuz'min contributes the essay on the defeat of Denikin, pp. 121–66. On the strategic disputes (p. 132 f.), the occasion is taken to attack Sklyanskii and to interpret the Lenin letter to Gusev quoted above as an attack on Trotsky. In fact the version retailed corresponds to Trotsky's account,

but it would be impossible to discern Trotsky's real position, since the whole thing is smothered in the phrase 'the directive of the Central Committee' and 'the Soviet government'. Trotsky's criticism of the way in which the reinforcement of the Southern Front had been handled is borne out by the figures of strength published by Kuz'min:

Front	*Infantry and cavalry*	*Machine-guns*	*Artillery*
Eastern	125,000	2,248	445
Western (with XIIth Army)	139,000	2,857	797
Southern	77,000	1,591	433

(*Glavkom* report for 15th June, 1919)

Reinforcement from 15th June–15th July, 1919:
85,000 infantry and cavalry; 1,409 machine-guns; 178 guns.
By 24th July, 1919, 3,282 commanders transferred (1,312 of which were former Imperial NCOs). (Kuz'min, *loc. cit.*, pp. 130–2.)

69. S. M. Budenny, *op. cit.*, p. 321. See also *BSE* (1), Vol. 34, Cols. 9–13, on the Cavalry Army. The latter is in line with the propaganda on Stalin's 'great military perceptiveness', itself debunked in Trotsky, *Stalin*, pp. 274–5.

70. Budenny, p. 180. Budenny was much impressed by the fact that Yegorov led his Red Army troops into action personally. See *BSE* (1), Vol. 24, Cols. 422–3.

71. Trotsky, *Stalin*, pp. 326–7.

72. For the operation as seen by Budenny, pp. 387–407 of his autobiography. Letter to Lenin, *ibid.*, pp. 398–9. See Appendix.

73. S. M. Budenny, *ibid.*, p. 405. Stalin-Ordzhonikidze telephone conversation of 4th is also reproduced.

74. *Ibid.*, pp. 434–6.

75. See Trotsky, *KVR*, Vol. 2, Bk. 1, pp. 115–22, 'Programmy militsii . . .'.

76. Cf. the valuable account in R. Pipes, *The Formation of the Soviet Union*, Cambridge Mass. 1954, p. 181 f. On the campaign against the Basmachis, see 'The Basmachis. The Central Asian Resistance Movement 1918–1924' in *Central Asian Review*, 1959, Vol. III, No. 3, pp. 236–51. For Frunze's activity, see his Vol. 1, *op. cit.*, p. 232 f. Also *Ist. Arkhiv*, 1958, No. 3. pp. 32–41 for 'Iz perepiski M. V. Frunze s V. I. Leninym 1919–1920' (Frunze-Lenin communications of 1919–1920). There is a very informative account of Red Army operations in a recent Soviet memoir: Ya. A. Mel'kumov, *Turkestantsy*, M. 1960 (Series 'Voennye Memuary'). The book begins with a meeting with Frunze and takes the account of military operations in Central Asia to 1930.

77. See Z. Ordzhonikidze, *Put' Bol'shevika* (A Bolshevik's road), Moscow 1956, p. 277.

78. Shatagin, *op. cit.*, p. 144.

79. See I. I. Vakhrameev, *Vo imya Revolyutsii* (In the name of the Revolution), Moscow 1957, pp. 65–8.

80. For the full organisation of this body, see *Dekrety*, *op. cit.*, Vol. 1, p. 573, 'Polozhenie o verkhovno-morskoi sledstvennoi komissii'.

81. V. I. Sapozhnikov, *Podvig Baltiitsev v 1918 godu* (The achievement of the Baltic sailors in 1918), Moscow 1954, p. 30.

82. See J. V. Stalin, *Works*, Vol. 4, p. 271.

83. This date comes from the first recorded formal contact of the *Reichsmarine* with the Soviet naval command, when the latter made a formal request for German naval assistance. This is discussed in greater detail in connection with the German-Soviet military collaboration.

84. Klyatskin, *op. cit.*, p. 32. According to the Red Army archives quoted here, in 1919 one million deserters were recaptured or voluntarily returned to their units.

85. *Ibid.*, p. 36.

86. Shatagin, *op. cit.*, p. 225.

87. See A. Barmine, *One Who Survived*, N.Y. 1945, p. 73, on his posting to the XVIth Red army.

88. Shatagin, p. 222–3.

89. D. Furmanov, *Chapayev*, p. 78.

90. See Fedotoff White, p. 85.

Chapter IV

1. See R. L. Buell, *Poland, Key to Europe*, London 1939, pp. 63–86.

2. See the explanation in W. H. Chamberlin, *op. cit.*, Vol. 2, pp. 259–60.

3. See Soviet documents, presented in *Krasnaya Kniga. Sbornik dokumentov o russko-polskie otnoshenia. 1919–1920* (The Red Book. Diplomatic Documents on Russo-Polish relations 1919–1920), Moscow *GIZ* 1920.

4. Lenin, *Voen. Perepis*, p. 228.

5. On these organisations, see Trotsky, *KVR*, Vol. 2, Bk. 2, pp. 33–91.

6. Lenin, *Voen. Perepis*, pp. 228–9.

7. Marshal J. Piłsudski, *L'Année 1920*, Paris 1929, p. 266. This basic work falls into three parts: (1) Piłsudski's own lively narrative (2) the notes compiled by the Polish General Staff on 1920 and (3) a text of Tukhachevsky's 1923 lecture, to which reference will be made presently. Of the studies of 1920 there are two main comparisons to be made: (i) between Piłsudski and the work of the Soviet military historians Kakurin and Melikov (ii) between Tukhachevsky and Shaposhnikov, presenting front and staff points of view.

8. Cf. *Dok. Vneshnei Politiki SSSR*, Vol. 2, pp. 492–6, 'To all workers, peasants and honest citizens of Russia.'

9. See a recent study by N. F. Kuz'min, *Krushenie poslednovo pokhoda Antanty* (The crushing of the final Entente offensive), Moscow 1958, pp. 133–4. This monograph might be regarded as one of the better recent productions on the history of the Civil War.

10. On Makhno, see W. H. Chamberlin, *op. cit.*, Vol. 2, pp. 232–9. For a sympathetic contemporary account, see P. Arshinov, *Istoriya Makhnovskovo dvizheniya* (A history of the Makhnov movement), Berlin 1923.

11. Cf. Trotsky, *Stalin*, p. 328.

12. N. F. Kuz'min, *op. cit.*, pp. 118–20. Also Piłsudski, *op. cit.*, pp. 23–5, and the note to pp. 266–9 for critical comments.

13. M. N. Tukhachevsky, 'La Marche au délà de la Vistule'. Reproduced as Appendix I in Pitsudski, *ibid.*, p. 209, figures in tabular form. Polish forces are given as 50,700 infantry, 5,800 cavalry.

14. N. F. Kuz'min, *op. cit.*, pp. 123–4.

15. These consisted of: 29th, 6th, 56th Rifle Divisions, 15th Cavalry Division, 18th, 12th, 21st Divisions. Also 22 aviation units.

16. See *Organizacja armji Bolszewickiej* (Organisation of the Bolshevik Army), Warszawa 1920. Stań na d. 1 marca (1920). Naczelne Dowództwo (Szt. Gen): B.W. No. 19785/II, pp. 137–8 for order of battle.

17. Kuz'min, *op. cit.*, p. 127. V. I. Chuikov: Marshal of the Soviet Union.

18. Opinions vary widely on the Soviet May offensive. See a very important study, N. E. Kakurin and V. A. Melikov, *Voina s belopolyakhami* (The War with the White Poles); *Voen.-Ist. Otdel Shtaba RKKA* (Military-Historical Section Red Army Staff), 1925, Ch. 6, with the emphasis upon the failure of the reserves. Piłsudski himself thought it premature, p. 269. This is the point where the Soviet command began to have a higher regard for Polish fighting capacity. Cf. Kuz'min, *op. cit.*, pp. 127–32; uses two studies (i) *Istorichesko-strategicheskii ocherk XVI armii* (Historical-strategic outline of XVIth Army), compiled by XVIth Army Staff, Moghilev 1921, and (ii) E. Shilovskii, *Kontrnastuplenie Krasnoi Armii v Belorussii* (The Red Army counter-offensive in Belorussia), Moscow 1940. Shilovskii, a 'military specialist', is presently an instructor at the Voroshilov Higher War Academy. In spite of Tukhachevsky's disclaimers, the evidence and interpretation would confirm the premature nature of the move. After 14 days of fighting, units of the XVth Army had advanced only 120 kilometres at the most.

19. Lenin, *Voen. Perepis*, p. 240. To Stalin at Kremenchug.

20. *Ibid.*, note to p. 241. Stalin understood that reinforcements were being moved in from Siberia; Blyukher's 51st Division, 3 rifle divisions, 1 cavalry division and more. This did eventually take place.

21. Kuz'min, *op. cit.*,pp. 133–5: Budenny and Voroshilov appealed to Lenin during the 9th Party Congress, (which coincided with the date of Budenny and Voroshilov's summons to Moscow by *Glavkom*) on the question of transfer by rail. Evidently Lenin was prepared to support them against S. S. Kamenev.

22. Cf. General I. V. Tyulenev, *Sovetskaya kavaleriya v boyakh za Rodinu* (Soviet cavalry in the battles for the Fatherland), Moscow 1957, pp. 169–74. Tyulenev was one of Budenny's brigade commanders. Also I. Kutyakov, ' "Kievskie Kanny" 1920 g' ('The Kiev Cannae' in 1920), in *Voina i Revolyutsiya* (War and Revolution), 1932, Vol. 10, p. 42 f. Also I. Kh. Pauka (Commander XIIIth Army), *Razgrom Belopolyakov pod Kievom v 1920 g* (The destruction of the White Poles near Kiev in 1920), Moscow 1938, p. 35, gives South-west Front strength on 26th May (minus 15th Division) 22,400 infantry, 24,000 cavalry, 1,440 machine-guns and 245 guns. Tyulenev gives 25,053 infantry and 18,000 cavalry.

23. Kakurin and Melikov, *op. cit.*, pp. 436–7.

24. Tyulenev, *op. cit.*, pp. 175–6, Order No. 358.

25. Quoted in Kuz'min, p. 147. From the Marx-Lenin Institute Archive. The signal dealt with operations from 30th May until 2nd June.

26. See Deutscher, *The Prophet Armed*, pp. 462–4, for Trotsky's real views as revealed in *The Trotsky Archives*. Trotsky urged a conciliatory attitude to the British. Cf. Stalin, *Works*, Vol. 4, p. 346: Wrangel was not yet ready, so therefore the 'humane' Curzon begged the Bolsheviks to spare him.

27. Kuz'min, *op. cit.*, p. 166; Red Army strength in the Crimea for 1st June amounted to 9,190 riflemen and 3,500 cavalry. See I. S. Korotkov, *Razgrom Vrangelya* (The destruction of Wrangel), 2nd Edn., Moscow 1955, p. 31. On 26th April, Soviet strength was 8,700 infantry, 3,000 cavalry and *about 7,000 operational reserves*. Wrangel: 8,877 infantry, 3,000 cavalry.

28. J. Stalin, *Works*, Vol. 4, p. 346. On 24th June, Stalin denied that Wrangel could smash his way to the rear of the Soviet armies operating against Poland. On 11th July, Stalin had completely changed his tune. With the success of Wrangel, '. . . our successes on the anti-Polish front cannot be lasting.' (*Ibid.*, p. 353.)

29. Cf. W. H. Chamberlin, *op. cit.*, Vol. 2, p. 307.

30. Foreign Office/State Department. German War Documents Project. Film collection *Auswärtiges Amt* (cited as *AA*). See also chapter 'Towards collaboration with the *Reichswehr*', for a further discussion of this problem. See Film Reference Serial K281/K095851–853, Serial 4829/E241391–394, Serial L625/L198972–975. The whole of Serial K281 is invaluable for giving a picture of the 1920 Soviet-German contacts.

31. This has long been a bone of contention. A recent study of Soviet-German relations, G. Freund, *Unholy Alliance*, Russian-German Relations from the Treaty of Brest-Litovsk to the Treaty of Berlin, London 1957, pp. 75–6, disposes quite effectively of this charge of collusion.

32. Memorandum from Seeckt of the *Reichswehr* to the *AA*, dated 26th July, 1920. See L756/L224527–534; also his summary report on the reasons for German neutrality, 21st July, in K196/K037987.

33. See K196/K037988–989, dated 24th July. Major Schubert was also sent as a liaison officer to the Red Army, as it subsequently drew near to the German frontier: see K281/K095894–5. This was fixed by 7th August, the original suggestion having come from Chicherin in a communication to the German Government: see K281/K095996–99, dated for the German file 22nd July.

34. Kakurin and Melikov, *op. cit.*, p. 209. Signal No. 2155.

35. *Ibid.*, p. 210.

36. *Ibid.*, p. 286.

37. *Ibid.*, p. 200.

38. Quoted Piłsudski, p. 263. Documents captured by the Polish Army. Cf. Tukhachevsky (Piłsudski, Appendix I, p. 215); evidently he counted on taking 40,000 deserters from the villages and by forced mobilisations (this had been done on the Eastern Front). This would 'offset . . . the numerical weakness of the units . . . and the desperate state of the central reserves'.

39. There are various estimates of this strength. See Kakurin and Melikov, p. 286, for the figure of nearly 12,000. General Weygand (head of the French Military

Mission to the Polish Army in 1920) in *The Soviet Army*, *op. cit.*, in his account of 1920 gives 'the equivalent of two divisions'. In fact, Soviet divisional strength varied most widely, and the figure given here is the most conservative. The two divisions were the 57th and the 58th.

40. Piłsudski, p. 290.

41. Kuz'min, p. 251, from Red Army Archives. This was a conversation between I. Smilga and S. S. Kamenev.

42. Order No. 4293 to the Western Front, dated 23rd July. Order No. 4344 to the South-western Front, dated 23rd July. See Kakurin and Melikov, *op. cit.*, p. 211.

43. See Piłsudski, *op. cit.*, pp. 298–9. Analysis of Orders No. 4546 and 4554. Also Yegorov to Tukhachevsky, Signal No. 704/4428.

44. *Ibid.*, pp. 137–42 for a fine description of how Piłsudski arrived at this decision—alone — during the night of 5th–6th August. This point needs some clarification of the role of General Weygand and the Polish operations against the Red Army. The legend that General Maxime Weygand, rather than Piłsudski, was the saviour of Poland in 1920 has been fostered by a number of studies both contemporary with the event and of later origin. The Polish National Democrats (opponents of some standing of Piłsudski) and the French Right were the main sources of this myth, both using the name of Weygand for immediate political purposes. Lord D'Abernon, *The Diary of an Ambassador*, Vol. 1, 1929, p. 75 (note), supports the claim to this particular fame for Weygand. The effective demolition of the 'legend of Weygand' has been carried out by Piotr S. Wandycz, 'General Weygand and the Battle of Warsaw of 1920' in *Journal of Central European Affairs*, January 1960, No. 4: pp. 357–66. It appears that General Weygand himself never concealed the fact that 'this is a purely Polish victory' (*ibid.*, p. 363), although relations between Weygand and Piłsudski broke down completely on 18th August.

45. Kakurin and Melikov, *op. cit.*, p. 274. Order No. 4634.

46. There appears to have been a serious dispute between Tukhachevsky and S. S. Kamenev, which lasted from 2nd–10th August. See Piłsudski, *op. cit.*, note 23, p. 305. Kamenev proposed to push forward in the inter-valley of the Bug and the Vistula, where Polish forces were concentrated. Tukhachevsky maintained his idea of the swing to the north.

47. See General Camon, *La manœuvre libératrice du Maréchal Piłsudski contre les Bolchéviks août 1920*, Paris 1920, p. 27.

48. There is some degree of confusion about the date of this directive. See Tukhachevsky (Piłsudski, *op. cit.*, Appendix I, pp. 244–5), for the date given as 8th. In his own text Piłsudski (p. 126) gives the date as 10th, on the basis of other Soviet documents which support this. Kuz'min, *op. cit.*, p. 260 gives it as 10th, quoting Red Army Archives.

49. Kakurin and Melikov, *op. cit.*, pp. 291–2. Order No. 4738, 11th August.

50. Cf. Piłsudski, *op. cit.*, p. 303.

51. Kakurin and Melikov, pp. 295–6.

52. B. Shaposhnikov, *Na Visle. Voenno-istoricheskii ocherk* (On the Vistula. A Military-historical outline), Moscow 1924, p. 97. These orders were: Nos. 4738, 4752, 4766 — in that order of receipt.

53. Kakurin and Melikov, p. 301.

54. *Ibid.* Cf. Tukhachevsky (Piłsudski, Appendix I, pp. 249–50) for the argument that the transfer was quite feasible provided that the Polish Army did not pass over to the offensive.

55. Piłsudski, p. 304.

56. Quoted in S. F. Naida, *op. cit.*, p. 226. From the Central Party Archive, Stalin Collection.

57. Piłsudski, p. 150.

58. See in *GV*, Vol. 2. A. Vol'pe's study, 'Posledovanie v grazhdanskoi voine' (Pursuit during the Civil War), here p. 253.

59. See Major Schubert's report on the military situation in East Prussia — 'the grave of the Russian Army': K195/K037963–73 dated 29th August.

60. See Gai in *GV*, Vol. 1, pp. 295–302 on his 3rd Corps.

61. Trotsky, *Stalin*, p. 329. As Trotsky subsequently observed, before 1930 he was recognised as an opponent of the drive on Warsaw; under the Stalinist falsifications, he became its instigator.

62. Quoted in S. F. Naida, *op. cit.*, p. 228.

63. S. S. Kamenev, in *Voennyi Vestnik* (Military Herald), 1922 No. 12, pp. 7–15.

64. Stalin, *Works*, Vol. 4, p. 352.

65. M. N. Tukhachevsky, *Pokhod za Vislu* (The advance to the Vistula), Moscow 1923. Stenographic record of the lecture. Reproduced in Piłsudski, Appendix I. Piłsudski (pp. 124–5) did not accept Tukhachevsky's own arguments. In essence, Piłsudski argued that Tukhachevsky had been promised command of the southern forces and the western when the line of the River Bug had been crossed. This undertaking was given by *Glavkom*. But *the Bug was not crossed by the southern* forces. To accept Tukhachevsky's argument, said Piłsudski, meant to give Budenny the same right to complain that Tukhachevsky did not aid *him*.

66. *Voina i Revolyutsiya*, 1925 No. 2.: pp. 21–51.

67. A. Yegorov, *L'vov-Varshava 1920 g. Vzaimodeistva frontov* (Lwow-Warsaw 1920. The co-operation of the fronts), Moscow-Leningrad 1929. Cf. General W. Sikorski, *La campagne polono-russe de 1920*, Paris 1928.

68. See *GV*, Vol. 3, pp. 391–470 for critical studies of the 1920 operations. These are unsigned, but bear traces of the work of Tukhachevsky.

69. A. Svechin, *Strategiya* (Strategy), Moscow 1927.

70. These figures are taken from Movchin, *op. cit.*, *GV*, Vol. 2, pp. 88–90.

71. General Tyulenev, *op. cit.*, p. 36 and pp. 210–12. Argues that the real achievement of the 1st Cavalry was in escaping encirclement. General Tyulenev might consult a Polish General Staff study of great value; *Studja taktyczne z historii wojen polskich 1918–1921*, Tom 3, *Działania armji konnej Budiennego 1920* (Polish tactical studies, Vol. 3. The actions of Budenny's cavalry army 1920).

72. Kuz'min, *op. cit.*, p. 281.

73. Cf. W. H. Chamberlin, Vol. 2, p. 324. This was the 'Army of the Regeneration of Russia'.

74. Kuz'min, p. 284.

75. Lenin, *Voen. Perepis*, p. 245.

76. Kuz'min, p. 290.

77. *Ibid.*, p. 291.

78. See Lenin, *Voen. Perepis*, pp. 248 and 249.

79. Kuz'min, p. 293. *RVSR* Orders No. 417, 29th August, and No. 425, 1st September.

80. Cf. Deutscher, *The Prophet Armed*, p. 469.

81. Cf. *Truppenamt* report on the Soviet position for 28th October. Soviet Russia had turned to the defensive. L396/L114391–93. There is also a later report on a conversation with Kopp, who informed the Germans that Soviet Russia was expecting fresh trouble with Poland and was concerned for a repetition of German neutrality. See L665/L209883–4, 24th November.

82. I. S. Korotkov, *op. cit.*, p. 158.

83. Kuz'min, p. 310. Kuz'min states quite positively that Lenin urged Frunze's appointment.

84. *Ibid.*, p. 311. Quotes Sirotinskii's account, a biographical outline of Frunze.

85. Korotkov, p. 175.

86. Kuz'min, p. 315.

87. See Frunze signals to Lenin, No. 472, 14th October, and 17/u D–S of 15th October. Frunze, *op. cit.*, Vol. 1, p. 375. It was to the latter that Lenin replied with his cautionary note: *Voen. Perepis*, p. 255. See also Frunze's conversation with *Glavkom*, 16th October, and his reply to Lenin on 18th October. Vol. 1, pp. 377–8 and p. 380.

88. See Frunze to Lenin, No. 44/s, 29th October. Frunze, Vol. 1, pp. 396–7. Also p. 400 for report 30th October. For Blyukher and the 51st, see the continuation of the first article on Blyukher in the Civil War, in *Ist Arkhiv*, 1958, No. 5, pp. 77–99. The war-diary of the 51st is produced as Doc. No. 3, p. 80 f. Cf. V. Triandafillov in *GV*, Vol. 1, pp. 339–58 on the Perekop operation.

89. Frunze, Vol. 1, p. 427. Order No. 00155/psh, 24th November to the armies of the Southern Front; lists the crimes of Makhno against the Red Army. Orders No. 00181 and 322/sh, 26th and 27th November: general declaration of hostilities against Makhno and dispositions for attack upon him.

90. See *KPSS v rez* (Party resolutions), Vol. 1, p. 586 f., Resolutions on the Military Question. See Trotsky, *KVR*, Vol. 2, Bk. 1, On the militia programme and its academic critics, pp. 115–22; speech on the structure of the Soviet armed forces, 28th November, 1920, *ibid.*, pp. 122–33.

91. See Chapter Six, for detailed discussion of origins of *Reichswehr*-Red Army collaboration.

92. Lenin, *Soch.* (Works), 4th Edn., Vol. 31, p. 445. Speech, 21st December, 1920.

93. Cf. Gordon A. Craig, *The Politics of the Prussian Army*, London 1955, pp. 408–9.

Chapter V

1. Cf. David D. Dallin, *The Rise of Russia in Asia*, London 1950, pp. 168–71. Also L. M. Papin, *Krakh Kolchakovshchiny . . .*, *op. cit.*, p. 142 f.

2. Cf. Vl. D. Vilenskii, Sibiryakov, *Dva goda Krasnoi Akademii Gen. Shtaba 1918–Sentyabr, 1920* (Two years of the Red General Staff Academy), M. 1921, Also N. I. Shatagin, *op. cit.*, p. 225.

3. A. Barmine, *op. cit.*, p. 83, for his recollections as a student in the Academy at that time.

4. *KPSS v rez* (Party resolutions), Vol. 1, 7th Edn., p. 502, Point 13.

5. See I. Deutscher, *The Prophet Armed*, *op. cit.*, on Trotsky's military writings, pp. 478–9.

6. *KVR*, Vol. 2, Bk. 1, p. 115.

7. *Ibid.*, pp. 118–21.

8. See esp. I. Berkhin, *Voennaya Reforma v SSSR (1924–1925)* (Military reform in the USSR 1924–1925), Moscow 1958. This is a very detailed recent study, of great interest but considerable political distortion. Recommended to the staff and students of Soviet military academies. It carries out its 're-habilitation' of military victims of the 1937–8 purges quite successfully. See p. 31, quoting reports of the Field Staff from Red Army archives.

9. *Ibid.*, p. 31.

10. Cf. *ibid.*, pp. 30 and 31. Also L. Schapiro, *Communist Autocracy*, *op. cit.*, pp. 246–7.

11. This description of the phase is in *Dual Command in the Red Army* (ed. I. B. Atkinson), Air University (USA), 1950.

12. These views are embodied in I. Smilga's *Ocherednye voprosy stroitel'stva Krasnoi Armii* (Immediate problems of the building up of the Red Army), Moscow 1921, p. 8 f. Cf. Geronimus, *op. cit.*, p. 123.

13. Berkhin, *op. cit.*, p. 13, quoting the journal *Politrabotnik* (Political Worker), 1921, No. 1, p. 18.

14. See his *Voina Klassov. Stat' 1919–1920 g* (The War of the Classes. Essays 1919–1920), Moscow 1921. See pp. 50–60 for 'Revolution from without'. Also pp. 138–40, Tukhachevsky's letter to Zinoviev of the *Komintern* in 1920. The full text of this original and provocative letter is given as an appendix. See Appendix I.

15. The pamphlet was published abroad as *Die Rote Armee und die Miliz*, Kleine Bibliothek d. Ru. Korrespondenz, No. 51, Leipzig 1921. See Fedotoff White, pp. 196–7, for a full discussion of this. Cf. *Voina Klassov*, pp. 60–78; essay 'The Red Army and the Militia'.

16. The Circular Letter of the Central Committee, 12th January, 1921, announced the liquidation of the fronts and partial demobilisation. A Demobilisation Commission was appointed on 10th November, 1920, reporting on 27th December, 1920, 24th and 28th January, and 4th February and 13th April, 1921.

17. Berkhin, pp. 33–4, quoting *Politrabotnik* 1921, No. 3, p. 8.

18. *KVR*, Vol. 2, Bk. 2, 'On the mobilisation of the industrial proletariat', Central Committee Theses, pp. 43–50.

19. On this dispute, see L. Schapiro, *Communist Autocracy*, pp. 253–8.

20. See Theses in S. I. Gusev, *Grazh. Voin. i K.A*, *op. cit.*, 1925 Edn., pp. 91–6: 1958 Edn., pp. 120–7. Dated January 1921; place given as Kharkov. Gusev wrote the first 15, Frunze the last 6 points. See also Frunze, *op. cit.*, Vol. 2, pp. 3–4.

21. Points 20 and 21 (Frunze).

22. Point 16.

23. See Robert V. Daniels, 'The Kronstadt Revolt of 1921', in *American Slavic and East European Review*, 1951, Vol. 10, No. 4, p. 242. Also L. Schapiro, *Communist Autocracy*, p. 300.

24. L. Schapiro, *ibid.*, p. 299.

25. W. H. Chamberlin, Vol. 2, p. 442.

26. Robert V. Daniels, *loc. cit.*, p. 243.

27. The Kronstadt artillery commander, General Kozlovskii (ex-Imperial officer) did assume command of the defences but played no political role. See Chamberlin, Vol. 2, note to p. 450.

28. A. Barmine, *op. cit.*, p. 95.

29. *Ibid.*, p. 95. Also L. Schapiro, *op. cit.*, note to p. 304 on the executions.

30. Robert V. Daniels, *loc. cit.*, p. 248, mentions that 240 men went over to the rebels on seeing that this was not a 'White Guard plot'.

31. Cf. N. Beglar, 'The Constant Factor in Moscow's Turkish Policy' in *Caucasian Review*, Munich 1955, No. 1, p. 17.

32. See R. Pipes, *Formation of the Soviet Union*, *op. cit.*, pp. 231–2, for an account of the political background and Bolshevik policy. Also S. Bartanyan, *Pobeda Sovetskoi vlasti v Armenii* (The victory of Soviet power in Armenia), Erevan 1959, Ch. VIII and Ch. X for details of the XIth Army.

33. G. Charachidze, 'The Georgian Communist Party and the National Question' in *Caucasian Review*, 1955, No. 1, p. 24.

34. See R. Pipes, *op. cit.*, pp. 234–5; the process precipitated a conflict between Moscow and the men on the spot.

35. Document quoted in G. Charachidze, p. 25.

36. *Ibid.*

37. Charachidze, *loc. cit.*, p. 27. R. Pipes, *op. cit.*, p. 234.

38. Trotsky, *Stalin*, p. 267.

39. *Ibid.*

40. A. Samoilo, *op. cit.*, p. 261. The Georgia operations were also complicated by a rising in Soviet Armenia directed against the Soviet regime.

41. Charachidze, p. 28.

42. *Ibid.*, p. 28.

43. Cf. Geronimus, pp. 130–2.

44. *KPSS v rez* (Party resolutions), Vol. 1, 10th Congress, p. 569; Point 4.

45. *Ibid.*, p. 570. Point 15. In connection with man-power, it was also decided (Point 20 'On the Red Fleet') to bring back those 'sailor-Communists', who had been dispersed in various regions, to naval stations; this reversed Trotsky's previous policy also.

46. Berkhin, p. 84; the existence of a brigade only is more than likely, since no establishment was worked out before 1922. Gives June 1921 as date of setting up brigade.

47. *KPSS v rez*, Vol. 1, p. 571. See also the new regulation on 'cells', in *KPSS o voor. sil.*, *op. cit.*, Central Committee Instruction, 31st October, 1921, pp. 216–27. See esp. Part 8, Points 85–94, for 'cells' in relation to commissar and command staff.

48. The military delegates to the 10th Party Congress voiced their alarm at the dilutions and degeneration in the command staff, but no positive step was taken until the position of commissars was re-defined in 1922.

49. Cf. V. I. Vlasov, *V. I. Lenin i stroitel'stvo Sov. Armii*, *op. cit.*, pp. 164–5.

50. There is an interesting comparison with recent doctrinal discussions in the Soviet armed forces: cf. H. S. Dinerstein, *War and the Soviet Union*, London 1959.

51. Berkhin, *op. cit.*, p. 197.

52. *Ibid.*, p. 158.

53. *Ibid.*, p. 199.

54. *Ibid.*

55. I. Deutscher, *Prophet Armed*, p. 512, cites correspondence of S. S. Kamenev, Shaposhnikov and Smidovich, also Tukhachevsky report of 16 July, 1921. See also P. G. Sofinov, *Ocherki istorii VChK* (Outline of the history of the *Vecheka*), Moscow 1960, pp. 224–7, on the despatch of *Cheka* and *ChON* troops to Tambov, and an account of their role in the military operations.

56. As in Taras-Rodionov, *Proletarskie perspektivy voennovo dela* . . . (Proletarian perspectives of military work . . .), Moscow 1919. Also in *Voenno Delo*.

57. Frunze, *op. cit.*, Vol. 2, pp. 4–22. Originally published in *Armiya i Revolyutsiya*, No. 1, July 1921.

58. *Ibid.*, Vol. 2, p. 19.

59. Cf. N. F. Kuz'min, *Na strazhe mirnovo truda* (*1921–1940 gg.*) (On guard of peaceful work), Moscow 1959, p. 12. This is a recent history of 'the Soviet Army', which, while it cuts every awkward historical corner, incorporates some useful information and details.

60. *Ibid.*, pp. 68–70. Also of importance was the Military-Scientific Society (*VNO*), the first such group being organised by the Party Organisation of the Staff Academy in October 1920. Many other *VNO* were organised in academies and military units.

61. Cf. *KVR*, Vol. 3, Bk. 2, p. 203, for Trotsky on military doctrine, speaking at Academy *VNO*, 1st November, 1921.

62. *Ibid.*, p. 205.

63. *Ibid.*

64. *KVR*, Vol. 3, Bk. 2, pp. 210–40: 'Voennaya doktrina ili mnimo-voennoe doktrinerstvo' (Military doctrine or Pseudo-military doctrinairism).

65. 'Uroki Grazhdanskoi Voiny' (Lessons of the Civil War) in *Grazhdanskaya Voina i Krasnaya Armiya*, 1925 Edn., pp. 51–90. This was dated December, 1921, and written in Kharkov. One difficulty in treating these debates is the extremely vague terminology which is being used (and Trotsky had every justification for attacking this). Gusev here speaks of 'semi-militia' formations — *polumilitsionnyi*, which may mean a half-converted regular division or a half-formed territorial unit, or merely be a derogatory phrase thrown in for effect.

66. See his attack on '. . . unlimited broad plans — very fine, very Communist — but unrealisable'. *Grazh. Voina i K.A.*, 1958 Edn., pp. 128–31. Taken from *Politrabotnik*, 1921, No. 6–7.

67. *Ibid.*, p. 158, from 'Political work in the Red Army', in *Politrabotnik* 1921, No. 15. Cf. also his remarks to the Conference of Chiefs of Political Departments, Military

Districts and Armies, 16th–18th December, 1921. This is a serious criticism of demobilisation policy. Gusev recommends fitting out barracks, improvement in the political schools, improving the Red Army soldier's lot — and strengthening the political apparatus. *Ibid.*, pp. 162–72.

68. See E. H. Carr, *The Bolshevik Revolution 1917–1923*, London 1953, Vol. III, p. 475. Cf. D. Wheatley, *Red Eagle*, London 1938, p. 280. Also *BSE* (1), Vol. 59, 1935, Col. 261 f.

69. Frunze, Vol. 2, pp. 34–61, 'The Military-political education of the Red Army'.

70. *Ibid.*, p. 47. This was an important qualification, a substantial admission and no doubt induced by Trotsky's attack.

71. *Ibid.*, pp. 57–61.

72. *Ibid.*, pp. 61–92.

73. *Ibid.*, p. 81.

74. *KVR*, Vol. 3, Bk. 2, Speech to the military delegates at the 11th Party Congress, pp. 242–71. See pp. 254, 256, 258.

75. *Ibid.*, p. 251.

76. *Ibid.*, p. 248.

77. See *Stenograficheskii otchot vtorovo dnya soveshchania voen. delegat. XI s'ezda RKP(b) 1 Aprelya 1922* (Stenographic report of the second day of the military delegates' meeting, 11th Party Congress . . .), Moscow 1922, p. 88. See also pp. 66–7, 81–2.

78. *KVR*, Vol. 3, Bk. 2, p. 235. See *Protokoly s'ezdov i konferentsii Komm. Partii (b)* (11th Congress), Moscow 1936, pp. 299–311, for a version of Trotsky's speech of 29th March on the Red Army; Frunze and the military delegates will be found, *ibid.*, pp. 522–4.

79. *Stenograf. otchot . . . 1 Aprelya*, p. 66; Tukhachevsky insisted '. . . that means, we taught ourselves out of our own medium'. He was to modify this view subsequently. A useful account of the political implications of the military debate is to be found in L. Trotsky, *The Revolution Betrayed. What is the Soviet Union and where is it going?* (tr. M. Eastman), London 1937, p. 200 f.

80. M. V. Frunze, *op. cit.*, Vol. 2, p. 92, 'Basic military tasks at the present'.

81. *Ibid.*, p. 95.

82. *Ibid.*, p. 96. Frunze stated that the army was still in the hands of the Communists. There was, therefore, no analogy with criticism levelled at *NEP* as an encouragement to a reversion to capitalism. As for Lenin, he had considerable reservations about the 'new' doctrine: cf. Fedotoff White, *op. cit.*, p. 161.

83. Frunze, *ibid.*, Vol. 2, p. 97. Frunze seemed to be disassociating himself from Taras-Rodionov. The idea of a 'complete revolution' was 'merely laughable'.

84. *Ibid.*, p. 105.

85. N. F. Kuz'min, *op. cit.*, p. 14.

86. Berkhin, p. 183, Orders No. 1674/323 and No. 2477/428 respectively. These replaced the original Order No. 220 on organisation and establishments.

87. Berkhin, *ibid.* See also Ya. A. Mel'kumov, *op. cit.*, Part II–III, on the Turkestan formations, which were operational throughout the decade.

88. N. F. Kuz'min, *op. cit.*, pp. 37–8: percentage of artillery strength per 1,000 men rose from 2·4 to 3·2 on the 1921 establishments.

89. Cf. Berkhin, p. 184. These companies were trained in 'group tactics' and were to be equipped with the Fedorov light and the Shosh heavy machine-gun, which, however, were not available in any quantity.

90. Berkhin, *ibid.*, p. 240. It is relevant to notice that the regularisation followed the decision to make a precise financial allocation to the Red Army as well as for aviation and naval forces, which was accepted on 7th August, 1922.

91. From 27, 429 in January, 1922, to 39,599 in October of that same year.

92. Berkhin, pp. 84–5.

93. 'On the Political Apparatus of Territorial Divisions', *PUR* Circular No. 106/31: see Berkhin, p. 88.

94. Berkhin, *ibid.*, p. 86.

95. Not to be connected with S. S. Kamenev of the Red Army command.

96. Cf. I. Deutscher, *The Prophet Unarmed. Trotsky: 1921–1929*, London 1959, p. 98 f.

97. *KPSS v rez.* (Party Resolutions), Vol. 1, p. 725.

98. See Berkhin, p. 55.

99. I. Deutscher, *The Prophet Unarmed*, p. 111.

100. *Ibid.*, p. 241.

101. Cf. Geronimus, *op. cit.*, p. 157.

102. Cf. *KPSS v rez.*, Vol. 1, p. 766.

103. For a recent example of this suppression, relevant to the military collaboration, see *Lokarnskaya Konferentsiya 1925 g* (The 1925 Locarno Conference), Moscow 1959. The German diplomatic items published here and evidently obtained from the Public Records Office in London, have had the passages indicating the existence of a military arrangement cut out, a fact established by comparison with the originals.

Chapter VI

1. Cf. N. Galay, 'The problem of technological progress in totalitarian and free societies', *Bulletin* (Munich), Vol. IV, 1957, No. 11, p. 6.

2. Gordon A. Craig, *op. cit.*, p. 358.

3. *Ibid.*, p. 364.

4. Cf. *Documents on British Foreign Policy*, 1st Series, Vol. III, London, HMSO 1949, 9th October, 1919, interview with von der Goltz, *Die Trommel*, pp. 169–70, also pp. 170–3.

5. E. H. Carr, *The Bolshevik Revolution*, *op. cit.*, Vol. III, p. 310.

6. Cf. *Documents British For. Pol.*, Vol. III, *op. cit.*, Doc. no. 387: General Malcolm to Colonel Twiss, 7th August, 1919.

7. E. H. Carr, *op. cit.*, Vol. III, p. 246.

8. *Documents British For. Pol.*, 1st Series, Vol. II, 1948, pp. 45–6.

9. E. H. Carr, *op. cit.*, pp. 316–7.

10. Cf. L. Kochan, *Russia and the Weimar Republic*, Cambridge 1954, p. 21.

11. See *Auswärtiges Amt* (cited as *AA*): Film Ref. L617/L193234–6. Memo. 10th January, 1920.

12. *AA*. K281/K095851–3. Memo. 16th April, 1920: Kopp-Maltzan conv.

13. *Dok. Vneshnei Politiki SSSR*, *op. cit.*, Vol. 2, Doc. No. 394, pp. 582–3.

14. E. H. Carr, *op. cit.*, p. 327.

15. See *AA*. K281/K096009–10. Memo. Maltzan, 14th July, 1920; Maltzan-Kopp conv. 19th July, K281/K095871–2; also K281/K096012 Chicherin telegram, 23rd July, 1920.

16. Cf. L. Kochan, *op. cit.*, pp. 36–7.

17. *AA*. 2860/D551896.

18. Maltzan-Brockdorff-Rantzau, 6th August, 1920. 9105H/H237050–2. See also letters of 14th and 18th August: 9105H/H236823–4 and H236825–7.

19. J. W. Wheeler-Bennett, *The Nemesis of Power. The German Army in Politics 1918–1945*, London 1953, p. 127. The information comes from Otto Gessler's testimony before the Foreign Affairs Committee of the *Reichstag*, 24th February, 1927.

20. Cf. I. Deutscher, *The Prophet Unarmed*, *op. cit.*, p. 57.

21. Cf. *Reichspräsident*'s protest over the secrecy of the agreement of 6th May, 1921: L617/L193448–9, 53. 8th May, 1920. Further protests: 9th June: L617/L193455.

22. Cf. E. H. Carr, *op. cit.*, pp. 363–4.

23. George W. F. Hallgarten, 'General Hans von Seeckt and Russia, 1920–1922', *Journal of Modern History*, Vol. XXI, 1949, p. 30.

24. See J. Epstein, 'Der Seeckt Plan. Aus unveröffentlichen Dokumenten', *Der Monat*, November 1948, pp. 42–58. Also Arthur L. Smith, 'The German General Staff and Russia, 1919–1926', *Soviet Studies*, 1956, Vol. VIII, No. 2, p. 129. Also Otto Gessler, *Reichswehrpolitik in der Weimarer Zeit*, Stuttgart 1958, p. 199, on Tschunke and *GEFU*.

25. Cf. G. Castellan, 'Reichswehr et Armée Rouge' in *Les Relations Germano-Sovìetiques de 1933 à 1939* (ed. J. Duroselle), Paris 1954, p. 152. Lebedev is printed as 'Lebeden'. The letter of Seeckt to Hasse, noted as 'May', is presumably that of May 1922.

26. See Wiedenfeld telegrams, 14th September, 1921, and 1st October, 1921: K281/K096235, K281/K096288 and K281/K096305.

27. Castellan, *op. cit.*, p. 152.

28. *Ibid.*, p. 158. Also E. H. Carr, *op. cit.*, p. 436, speaks of a tank-factory at Kazan (see also his *German-Soviet relations between the two wars*, Baltimore 1951, p. 61). There is no evidence for this tank-factory. In his third volume of *The Bolshevik Revolution*, p. 368, the same writer denies that the Krupp concession for tractors had any military significance. This would not appear to be borne out by the facts themselves.

29. Hallgarten, *op. cit.*, p. 31, quoting the Hasse diary. G. Freund, *The Unholy Alliance*, London 1957, p. 112, questions the reliability of the Hasse diary. Harold J. Gordon, in a review of G. Freund written for *Journal of Central European Affairs*, 1959, Vol. XIX, No. 1, p. 92, disagrees with this unsupported judgement on Hasse. It would appear that a serious questioning of the validity of this diary would require a substantial proof.

30. Hallgarten, *op. cit.*, p. 31.

31. *Ibid.*, p. 31, argues that the Russians were serious in their intentions, although no real evidence is offered to support this.

32. For a discussion of the Junkers agreement, see Serial 6698H/H105372–4, Simons-Stresemann conversation, 23rd April, 1926. For *Reichswehrministerium* view of the original contract, also Serial 6698H/H105470–2, 473, with Junkers, Generals von Hasse and Wurzbacher. Castellan, *op. cit.*, p. 153 prints the text of the agreement.

33. Cf. L309/L096110 f.: 'Ausführliche Aufzeichnung . . . des deutsch-russischen Vertrages'. This diary, showing evidence of a certain deliberate concoction in parts, is nevertheless a valuable commentary. Begins 11th April, 1922.

34. None of the *AA* files yields up any trace of a military agreement. For Treaty, see 3398/738919–22, for 16th April, 1922. Seeckt, in addition to denying the existence of any military compact in his May (1922) letter to Hasse, provides subsequent indirect evidence that no military agreement was entered into. Cf. E. H. Carr, *German-Soviet relations, op. cit.*, p. 60.

35. Castellan, *op. cit.*, p. 156, quoting *2e Bureau* Report, 'L'infiltration allemande en Russie', (18th November, 1922, 12 pp.). French Intelligence drew not a little of its information from Polish sources, although this particular information may have been independently come by. At a later date, the German files reveal that there was quite a sale of spurious 'information' on Soviet-German arrangements in Helsinki — and thence to the Poles.

36. *Ibid.*

37. Hallgarten, *op. cit.*, p. 32.

38. Berkhin, *Voennaya reforma, op. cit.*, p. 45.

39. See the important study by General H. Speidel (who worked on the staff of *Sondergruppe R.*), 'Reichswehr und Rote Armee', in *Vierteljahrshefte für Zeitgeschichte*, Vol. 1, 1953, pp. 9–45. The aim of this article is to minimise the importance of the contact between the two armies. Several of the dates supplied here are especially vague. It is asserted that the documents dealing with the military collaboration were regularly destroyed. However, the *AA* files contain substantial materials: see in particular 4564H/E162514–164069: *Mil. Angelegenheiten mit Russland*, Büro d. Staatssekretär. Period: 17th March, 1923–18th May, 1930. Here are some fifteen hundred pages of documents, many annotated. See here Speidel, pp. 17–18 and Hallgarten, *op. cit.*, p. 32.

40. Otto-Ernst Schuddekopf, *Heer und Republik*, Quellen zur Politik der Reichswehrführung 1918–1933, Hannover/Frankfurt am Main, 1955, Doc. No. 68, p. 155 f.

41. See *Seeckt. Aus seinem Leben. 1918–1936*, Compiled by General von der Artillerie Dr F. von Rabenau, Leipzig 1941: p. 313. Seeckt wrote: 'Es bestehen, keinerlei politisch-militärisch Abmachungen; aber die Möglichkeit solcher wird geglaubt. . . . Liegt es in unserem Interesse diesen schwachen Nimbus zu zerstören?'

42. For Seeckt paper, see Schuddekopf, *op. cit.*, Doc. No. 69, p. 160 f.

43. See Hans W. Gatzke, 'Russo-German Military Collaboration during the Weimar Republic', *The American Historical Review*, Vol. LXIII, 1958, No. 3, pp. 565–97. This is a very useful and skilful documented study, using Serial 4564H. For the 1923 exchanges, see p. 571.

44. Castellan, *op. cit.*, p. 157.

45. *Ibid.*, p. 158.
46. *Ibid.*
47. Gatzke, *op. cit.*, p. 572.
48. *Ibid.*, p. 574.
49. *Ibid.*, pp. 571–2.
50. Castellan, *op. cit.*, p. 159. Polish and French Intelligence evidently differed in their views about the presence of German officers as instructors in the Red Army at this stage. The conservative French view was evidently more correct. Technicians were different, but identification would have been difficult.
51. Gatzke, p. 576. The Ambassador wanted Major Fischer. Who did actually run *Z. Mo.*, is a point of dispute for this period.
52. See *Militärische Angelegenheiten*, 9542H/671507–8, on the Red Air Force flying-schools.
53. Speidel, *op. cit.*, pp. 22–4, 25, 26, 27.
54. Freund, *op. cit.*, pp. 205–10 has an excellent description of Lipetsk.
55. See *Direktoren 29/a*, 9480H/H276127. Schöndorff is the 'Schandorf' referred to in Castellan, p. 200.
56. Cf. W. Goerlitz, *History of the German General Staff*, N.Y., 1957 Edn., p. 233. Brings no evidence forward to justify this statement, either from the German or Soviet side.
57. See W. v. Blücher, *Deutschlands Weg nach Rapallo*, Wiesbaden 1951, pp. 172–3. Information given to Nansen and passed to the Germans. Blücher states that this agreed with the reductions in Soviet military man-power and asserts that Lebedev, popular in German military circles, was released as Chief of Staff. It is true that at the end of the year Lebedev came under heavy criticism, but seems to have been carrying out the duties of Chief of Staff.
58. See R. Fischer, *Stalin and German Communism*, Harvard 1948, p. 319, 'Blueprint for a German Red Army'.
59. W. G. Krivitsky, *I was Stalin's agent*, London 1940 Edn., p. 56, also p. 58.
60. See *Reichswehr-Russland: AA Geheim-Akten (Handakten)*, 6698H/H111754–763. Conv. Chicherin, Radek, Brockdorff-Rantzau, 13/12/1923.
61. Cf. Gatzke, *op. cit.*, pp. 576–8.
62. The letter is published in Castellan, *op. cit.*, p. 169, as a note, taken from *Vorwärts*, 12 October, 1928.
63. *Mil. Angeleg.* 9542H/671390–2.
64. Printed as Appendix B in Freund, *op. cit.*, pp. 254–8. Dated 9th June, 1924.
65. *Report, Court Proceedings: In the Case of the Anti-Soviet 'Bloc of Rights and Trotskyites'*, Moscow 1938, pp. 268–9, 260, 263, 261 and 259 respectively.

Chapter VII

1. See I. Deutscher, *The Prophet Unarmed*, *op. cit.*, p. 117.
2. *Ibid.*
3. I. B. Berkhin, *Voennaya Reforma*, *op. cit.*, p. 57. Quotes Red Army Central

Archive, Collection No. 32562, Item No. 218, p. 37. Cited as Berkhin in the notes to this chapter.

4. *Ibid.*, p. 58.

5. N. F. Kuz'min, *Na strazhe mirnovo truda (1921–1940)*, *op. cit.*, p. 21. Quotes as source the Central Party Archive, Institute of Marxism-Leninism: Collection No. 17.

6. Cf. Berkhin, *op. cit.*, p. 60. Quotes the same source as Kuz'min, giving the same Central Party Archive reference, but with different section and page numbers.

7. *Ibid.*, p. 386.

8. Cf. *BSE* (1), Vol. 6, 1927, Cols. 763–4.

9. Berkhin, p. 60. Using the Central Party Archive.

10. *Ibid.*, pp. 60–1.

11. *Ibid.*, p. 61. The charge of incompetence against Lebedev was sheer nonsense. He had been negotiating with German senior officers on behalf of the Soviet command. Later he received further responsible posts.

12. *Ibid.*, p. 61.

13. *Ibid.*, p. 62.

14. L. Trotsky, *My Life*, *op. cit.*, p. 436.

15. Berkhin, p. 62.

16. *Ibid.*, p. 63. On the Staff, pp. 63–4.

17. *Ibid.*, p. 64.

18. Cf. Kuz'min, *op. cit.*, p. 26.

19. See *KPSS v rez.* (Party resolutions), Vol. 1, pp. 813–14. According to Berkhin (p. 69), the date of the first decision was 1st April, 1924; evidence quoted from the Central Party Archive.

20. Kuz'min, p. 25, gives date of Sklyanskii's dismissal as 3rd March, 1924. See Berkhin, p. 66. The discrepancy often occurs with reference either to the date of the decision or the date of its official confirmation.

21. Official date quoted in Berkhin, p. 66.

22. *Ibid.*, p. 70. The Military Commission, which had officially terminated its work, seems to have been kept in existence, and used as the basis of other sub-commissions, all operating under the general supervision of S. I. Gusev.

23. For further details of the constitutional arrangement, see Harold J. Berman and Miroslav Kerner, *Soviet Military Law and Administration*, Harvard U.P. 1955, pp. 173–5.

24. Berkhin, pp. 150–1. The Medical and Veterinary administrations were directly subordinated to the *Revvoensoviet* by Order No. 693/128 of 23rd May, 1924.

25. Kuz'min, p. 41.

26. M. V. Frunze, *op. cit.*, Vol. 2, 'Zadachi Akademikov v armii' (The tasks of members of Academies in the army). Here p. 128. Cf. Frunze, *Sochineniya* (Works), Moscow-Leningrad 1926, Vol. 2, p. 32, on the Staff as the 'military brain' (*voennyi mozg*) of the State, as well as the Red Army.

27. *Ibid.*, Vol. 2, 1926 Edn., p. 32.

28. Frunze, Vol. 2, 1957 Edn., p. 150. This is part of a report, delivered to a meeting of political staff, 17th November, 1924, in Moscow; entitled 'The results and perspectives of military organisation. Made in connection with the re-organisation

of 1924'. Later published as 'Na novykh putyakh' (On new paths), Moscow 1925.

29. *Ibid.*, p. 150. By way of comparison, and since this was an example cited by the Soviet command, see a recent interesting study by Capitaine M. Montfort, 'Force et faiblesse des armées de milice'. in *General Military Review*, Nov. 1959: pp. 459–73, discussing the Swiss organisation.

30. Berkhin, p. 154. The reduction amounted to 22·7 per cent. See Appendix.

31. See Frunze, Vol. 2, 1957 Edn., p. 148. Also Berkhin, pp. 166–8.

32. Berkhin, p. 219. Frunze, Vol. 2, p. 329, for an address on the Air Force (5th April, 1925). States that in 1922 90 per cent of the machines were bought abroad, and 50 per cent in 1923. On the diversity of machines, cf. *Militärische Angelegenheiten* (*AA*), 9524H/671507–8, with a list of 20 makes.

33. Berkhin, p. 219.

34. *Ibid.*, p. 224.

35. *Ibid.*, pp. 225–6.

36. I. Deutscher, *The Prophet Unarmed*, pp. 55–6.

37. Berkhin, pp. 233–6 on Navy: figures. Also Fedotoff White, *op. cit.*, pp. 248–9 on Bubnov and the *Komsomol* in the Navy; here makes the point that the usual method of intensive political reconstruction — *spreading* reliable elements — was reversed with the *concentration* of the new politicals. Cf. Berkhin: in the Baltic Fleet, 83 per cent of the petty-officer and artificer group was *Komsomol*. Also Frunze, Vol. 2, 1957 Edn.: *Komsomol* numbered 70,000 (12 per cent Soviet armed forces). See pp. 385, 387.

38. Berkhin, p. 229. 26·28 per cent of the administrative staff were either purged or dismissed.

39. *Ibid.*, p. 233. See Appendix.

40. Cf. Colonel S. Andolenko, 'The Imperial Heritage', in *The Soviet Army*, *op. cit.*, pp. 15–17 and p. 21. Cf. F. D. Khrustov, *Frunze o voinskom vospitanii* (Frunze on Military education), Moscow 1946, 63 pp.

41. Berkhin, p. 153.

42. Cf. *Malaya Sov. Entsik.*, *op. cit.*, 1958 Edn., Vol. 1, p. 799. Baranov's formal appointment to the command of the *VVS* was made some time later.

43. *BSE* (1), Vol. 24, 1932, Cols. 422–3. Berkhin, p. 66.

44. *BSE* (1), Vol. 36, 1938, Col. 133.

45. *BSE* (1), Vol. 6, 1927, Cols. 537–8.

46. *RVSS* Directive No. 989, 30th July, 1924. Title: 'Komandir Raboche-Krest'yanskoi Krasnoi Armii.' Berkhin, p. 263.

47. Frunze made this quite plain. See his Vol. 2, 1957 Edn., p. 145, pp. 220–37, pp. 258–60. For the impossibility of the 1–1½ million army, Vol. 2, p. 378.

48. Berkhin, p. 46.

49. M. V. Frunze, 'Itogi Dekab'rskovo plenuma Revvoensovieta SSSR. Doklad k Voennoi Akademii RKKA' (The results of the December plenum of the Revvoensoviet of the Soviet Union. Report to the Red Army Military Academy. 20th December, 1924), *Voina i Revolyutsiya* (War and Revolution), 1926, No. 10, pp. 88–111.

50. Frunze, Vol. 2, 1957 Edn., p. 371.

51. Berkhin, p. 104.

52. *Ibid.*, p. 102 for procedures in Nizhni Novgorod, Pskov, Yaroslavl, Samara, Saratov.

53. *Ibid.*, p. 102.

54. *Ibid.*, pp. 98–9, and p. 96.

55. *Ibid.*, p. 96.

56. Berkhin, p. 114, cites the figure of 535 roubles as the cost of training one Red Army soldier in a regular unit, compared with 291 roubles for the militia.

57. See Frunze, Vol. 2, 1957 Edn., pp. 365–82 on the cadre army and the militia — a reply to critics. Ironically enough, it uses Trotsky's Theses at the 8th Party Congress as the stages of the defence; on the illiteracy and backwardness, see p. 374 and p. 381.

58. *Ibid.*, Vol. 2, p. 148. Because of the diversity of structure, '. . . we did not have nor can we have either a unified organisation, or a consistent doctrine.'

59. See Berkhin, pp. 188–9. See also Frunze, Vol. 2, p. 148, on 'practical infantry'. While there was an undoubted effort to increase military efficiency, it is most important to bear in mind that even such a matter as the re-shaping of the form of units was wrapped about with inevitable social-political complications, so that it is difficult to speak, even in this apparently technical context, of straightforward reform. The matter is of considerable relevance at present, now that a proposed reform of the Soviet armed forces — a reversion to a territorial system — is being proposed by Khrushchev (first mentioned publicly in January 1960). In his penetrating article, 'Social problems in the Reorganisation of the Soviet Armed Forces', *Bulletin* (Munich), April 1960, pp. 3–16, N. Galay relates this to the period of the Frunze reforms and cites an interesting instruction (reproduced from Colonel N. V. Pyatnitskii, *Krasnaya Armiya SSSR*, Paris 1931) — Instruction No. 107, 10th August, 1925, on the assignment of citizens to branches and units of the armed forces. This showed that a careful study of the social composition of units which had distinguished themselves in the Civil War had been made, relating their combat performance to the strength of the worker contingent within them. Trotsky had made this point early on in the Civil War. The 1925 Instruction fixed, for various arms, the desirable percentage of workers and Party members:

Navy: 50/34 (worker percentage is the first figure), Armoured units: 50/12, Railway troops: 50/12, Air Force: 40/25, Cavalry: 12/10, Artillery: 12/10, Infantry: 8/10.

A Soviet survey, published in 1928, established that elite units in 1920 (8th Cavalry Division, 1st Cavalry Army, 41st, 42nd, 45th and 28th Rifle Divisions) had a worker contingent of 20–26 per cent, while less reliable units had one of under 10 per cent. See N. Galay, p. 9.

60. Cf. League of Nations Armaments Handbook, Vol. 1, p. 774. Also German military reports, *Mil. Angelegenheiten* (*AA*), Serial 9524H/671383 f., on the infantry and artillery re-organisations. The first artillery re-organisation was very quickly modified. See Appendix II.

61. Berkhin, p. 192. These figures do not differ greatly from those supplied in the *League of Nations Armaments Handbook*, except for the fact that there is more detail of the type of division.

62. Cf. *Mil. Angelegenheiten* (*AA*), 9542H/617403–8, 411, 413–14 for Soviet cavalry. See also Berkhin, pp. 201–5. See Appendix.

63. Colonel V. D. Mostovenko, *Tanki* (Tanks), Moscow 1958, p. 73. Kuz'min, *op. cit.*, p. 114, states that in October 1924 an independent tank regiment — consisting of two tank battalions — was created. These were cadre and training units respectively. In 1925 separate light and heavy tank battalions were formed, each with 3 companies comprising 10 tanks. Not until 1928–9 were full experimental units being properly formed — a story connected with the joint Soviet-German tank-school at Kazan.

64. Frunze, Vol. 2, p. 139. The tractor is to play a great part on future battle-fields; the caterpillar tractor can take over gun-towing duties, and be used in many roles — in addition to the well-known 'tanks' — Frunze's inverted commas.

65. *Ibid.*, pp. 154–5. See also p. 154, and p. 270. In 1922 the Red Army was made up of 64 per cent Great Russians, 22 per cent Ukrainians, 4 per cent Belorussians and 10 per cent for all others.

66. See *Central Asian Review*, *op. cit.*, 1959, on *Basmachis*. Enver Pasha, once go-between between the Soviet and German commands, and later leader of the anti-Bolshevik *Basmachis*, was killed on 4th August, 1922. Also the Georgian insurrection of 1924. Frunze, Vol. 2, p. 379 stated that then the Georgian militia units 'behaved beautifully'. On the Georgian Red Army, 1922, see G. K. Ordzhonikidze, *Stat'i i Rechi* (Essays and speeches), Vol. 1, Moscow 1956, pp. 229–40. Ordzhonikidze speaks of 'the Russian Red Army'. Later Soviet commanders were very conscious of the weakening produced in the Austrian army during the World War due to nationality conflicts, and in the Imperial Russian Army during its crisis.

67. See Ordzhonikidze on Georgia. Berkhin, pp. 124–42 for detailed discussion of new plans.

68. Cf. David J. Dallin, *The Rise of Russia in Asia*, London 1950, pp. 191–2. This area was, in effect, the first Soviet satellite.

69. Cf. Berkhin, p. 137. These formations were disbanded during the 1930's, when they rapidly fell out of favour.

70. *Ibid.*, p. 162.

71. Cf. S. I. Gusev, 'Marksizm i voennaya nauka' (Marxism and military science), in *Grazh. Voina i Krasnaya Armiya*, *op. cit.*, 1958 Edn., pp. 184–201. It is anti-Trotsky, and part of a symposium, *Nashi raznoglasiya v voennom dele* (Our differences in the military field), Moscow 1925, published by the press of *Red Star*.

72. See M. V. Frunze, *O kharaktere budushchei voiny* (On the character of a future war) (Introduced by A. Golubev), Moscow 1931 Edn., 126 pp. See also discussion in M. V. Frunze, *Polkovodcheskaya Deyatel'nost'*, *op. cit.*, p. 230 f. This will be discussed also with respect to the formation of a consistent Soviet view of defence requirements.

73. Berkhin, p. 385.

74. *Ibid.*, pp. 388–9.

75. See Frunze, Vol. 2, 1957 Edn., pp. 121–2 on *PUR*, also p. 155 f., pp. 195–220 and in his discussion of unitary command, pp. 289–97. Frunze quite definitely distinguished the 'bourgeois' army, which 'kept out of politics', from the Red Army, which was consciously military-political.

76. Berkhin, p. 406. This conference adopted a special resolution: 'On the urgent

problems of Party structure in the Red Army'. The lowest level of participant was the head of the divisional Political Section and the divisional commissar.

77. *Ibid.*, p. 422. *PUR* Directive No. 256 of 2nd October, 1924, laid out the following curriculum; The Red Army and the Red Army soldier: the triumph of the October Revolution: history of the Civil War and Red Army: Lenin and the Party: general information on the most important capitalist states: worker movements abroad.

78. Cf. I. Deutscher, *The Prophet Unarmed*, p. 162.

79. See *KPSS v rez* (Party Resolutions), Vol. 1, pp. 913–21.

80. I. Deutscher, *The Prophet Unarmed*, p. 241.

81. See *KPSS o voor. sil. Sov. Soyuza, op. cit.*, pp. 268–73. Instruction dated 20th December, 1924.

82. Berkhin, p. 409, also pp. 407–8.

83. Cf. *Ibid.* Frunze, Vol. 2, pp. 220–36 on the militia and work in the village. Much of this was also on the theme of co-ordinating civil and military organs to increase the stability of the militia — especially during its mobilisations.

84. This change had been prepared between March and September. N. F. Kuz'min, *op. cit.*, gives the date of the new Instruction as 8th September, 1925: see p. 60. See later codification in *KPSS v rez* (Party Resolutions), Vol. 2, pp. 134–5 with the status of the political organs in the armed forces in the new *Ustav* (Party Rules), 14th Party Congress (December 1925). See also A. A. Andreyev in stenographic report of the 14th Congress on political work in the armed forces. His basic argument was: those who are responsible for Party work ought to direct it. *XIV s'ezd Vsesoyuz. Komm. Partii. 18–31 dekabr 1925* (14th All-Russian Communist Party Congress), Moscow 1926, Stenographic report, p. 880. Cf. Berman and Kerner, *Soviet Military Law, op. cit.*, p. 182: refers to the change from *PUR* to *PURRKA* (*sic*) as 'between 1924 and 1929'.

85. See *BSE* (1), Vol. 24, 1932, Col. 455. It is to be observed about unitary command that the Chinese People's National-Liberation Army evidently thinks little of this 'achievement'; see N. Galay's excellent study, 'Revisionism, Dogmatism and the Soviet Armed Forces', in *Bulletin* (Munich), Vol. V, 1958, No. 11, pp. 3–13.

86. Berkhin, p. 260.

87. *Ibid.*, p. 315.

88. *Ibid.*

89. *Ibid.*, p. 318. See Appendix.

90. Frunze on the Soviet officer is most revealing. See his Vol. 2, p. 165 — 'The Red Army commander must be not only a technician but a social worker' — and p. 289 f. On attestation, see Berkhin, pp. 321–3.

91. Berkhin, p. 273.

92. *Ibid.*, p. 276.

93. See *BSE* (1), Vol. 12, 1928, Cols. 319–22 on Soviet Military Academies.

94. Berkhin, p. 284.

95. See Frunze, Vol. 2, pp. 172–85 on the question of higher military education. On the re-organisation of the Military Academy faculties, *ibid.*, pp. 180–2.

96. *BSE* (1), Vol. 12, *loc. cit.* See Appendix.

97. Berkhin, p. 285. This was named *Institut Ad'yunktov*.

98. *Ibid.*, p. 291. Berkhin, however, is not strictly accurate nor does he explain whether or not this applies to command staff or administrative centres. There were, in fact, two orders: No. 511 of 15th March, 1923, and No. 820 of 21st April, 1923. Neither was, by any means, the first step. See also note to p. 451 in Raymond L. Garthoff, *How Russia Makes War*, London 1954, *op. cit.*, for writings of 1923 on this theme.

99. Cf. M. V. Frunze, *Polkovod. Deyatel'nost'*, *op. cit.*, pp. 190–242. Frunze, Vol. 2, pp. 289–300. The factors governing the application of the principle are given, p. 295.

100. Berkhin, p. 292. 'O vovlechenii komsostava v politprosvetrabotu.'

101. Quoted in Berkhin, pp. 293–4.

102. *Ibid.*, p. 294.

103. Frunze, Vol. 2, pp. 293–4. Also p. 165: 'The command staff of our army is not homogeneous. Above all it is divided into Party and non-Party.'

104. The regulation of the place of the military commissar meant superseding the *Regulation* of 3rd January, 1922. In its place was erected the *Provisional Regulation* of 1925, relating to commissars; there were several separate steps: *Regulation for Politruks* (*RVS* No. 48, 14th January, 1925), *Regulation for commissars, commanders — in unified command and assistants for political affairs* (*RVS*, 24th November, 1924). The *Provisional Regulation* for commissars was promulgated on 30th July, 1925. What this assigned to the military commissar was not inconsiderable, including the duty of guarding against 'anti-Soviet outbreaks' in the Red Army and Navy.

105. *KPSS o voor. sil. Sov. Soyuza, op. cit.*, pp. 280–1: 'Ob edinonachalii v Krasnoi Armii' (On unitary command in the Red Army). Also Berkhin, pp. 303–4 for No. 234, 'Ob osushchestvlenii edinonachaliya' (On the accomplishment of unitary command).

106. *KPSS o voor. sil.*, p. 281.

107. These are Berkhin's figures, p. 306. They are not lower than usual Soviet figures, but he has set them against the *total* officer-strength, thereby showing the slow rate of application. In view of the restrictions, the role of the attestation boards, the careful regulation of this freedom, and the limited application, it is difficult to see how it can be interpreted as the triumph of the commander over the commissar; cf. Berman and Kerner, *op. cit.*, p. 15, stating that the Frunze-Voroshilov reform '. . . did establish the supremacy of the military commanders over the commissars'. Frunze's reforms scarcely did that, giving the commander only what was due to him, and the Voroshilov 'reforms' were definitely retrogressive. The same study also is in error about the significance of the 'independence' of the *PUR* from the *Revvoensoviet*. The Frunze reform *looks* like the emancipation of the commander, but closer inspection shows it not to be so.

108. L. Trotsky, *Stalin*, p. 418. Cf. B. Bajanov, *Avec Staline dans le Kremlin*, Paris 1930, pp. 108–11, for an account similar to this charge. For what it is worth, see mention of this incident in Maxim Litvinov, *Notes for a Journal* (Ed. E. H. Carr), pp. 19–20. If this was Litvinov, he rejects Trotsky's notion.

109. See Boris Souvarine, *Staline*. Aperçu historique du Bolchévisme, Paris 1937, p. 371. Cites B. Pilniak's play, *Story of an unextinguished moon* — with the sub-title

'The killing of the commander'. Stalin had copies of this seized. Souvarine leaves the Frunze case as undecided.

110. Mentioned by E. Wollenberg, *The Red Army*, *op. cit.*, p. 166.

111. Souvarine, *op. cit.*, p. 371.

112. *BSE* (1), Vol. 23, 1931, Cols. 698–9. Sheideman had kept his artillery post certainly up to 1924, from his first appointment in 1918–19.

113. Berkhin, p. 159.

114. See I. Deutscher, *The Prophet Unarmed*, p. 248.

115. *Ibid.*, p. 257.

116. *KPSS v rez* (Party resolutions), Vol. 2, pp. 160–6. Cf. Souvarine, *op. cit.*, p. 397.

117. *KPSS v rez* (Party Resolutions), Vol. 2, pp. 170–1.

118. Cf. note to I. Deutscher, *The Prophet Unarmed*, p. 264.

119. Berkhin, pp. 162–3.

120. *Ibid.*, pp. 156–8. See Appendix II.

121. *Ibid.*, p. 306.

122. See *Biographical Directory USSR*, *op. cit.*, pp. 291–2.

123. *Ibid.*, p. 312. Printed from a Red Army Central Archive source. It is difficult to disagree with Fedotoff White (p. 240), who interprets this order as a serious reverse for unitary command. On weighing up the various circumscriptions and limitations of this reform, *even* for Party commanders who came off best, it is correct to place the most conservative interpretation upon the progess with command.

124. *BSE* (1), Vol. 12, *loc. cit.* See Appendix.

125. Fedotoff White, *op. cit.*, p. 215.

126. Quoted as footnote in S. I. Gusev, *Grazh. Voina i Krasnaya Armiya*, *op. cit.*, 1958 Edn., p. 199.

127. Berkhin, p. 343, for an account of the meeting of 25th April, 1924.

128. *Vremennyi Polevoi Ustav* (Provisional Field Regulations), 1925. The other regulations involved were: *Boevaya sluzhba pekhoty* (Infantry combat duty), 1924; *Vremennyi boevoi ustav pekhoty. Ch. i* (Provisional Infantry Combat Regulations. Part I); *Vremennyi boevoi ustav konnitsy RKKA. Ch. II* (Provisional Red Army Cavalry Combat Regulations. Part II). A new disciplinary code was also introduced; this replaced that of 1919, which was itself an expurgated edition of the Imperial Russian Army disciplinary manual, St Petersburg 1869, Book XXIII, 4th Edn. This same manual had also been used by the Provisional Government before the Bolsheviks, with the cutting out of phrases such as 'His Imperial Majesty'.

129. Cf. Lt.-Colonel J. D. Hittle, *The Military Staff*, USA, 2nd Edn., 1952, p. 246. Over 100 authors were involved in compiling the new regulations.

130. Frunze, *op. cit.*, Vol. 2, pp. 253–89, 'The Red Army and the defence of the Soviet Union'. Also pp. 340–55, 'Our military structure and the tasks of the Military-Scientific Society (*VNO*)'.

131. J. Stalin, *Works*, English Edn., Vol. 7, pp. 11–14. This speech was printed for the first time twenty-two years after the event, in the 1947 Russian Edition of Stalin's works.

132. *Ibid.*, p. 13.

133. *Ibid.*, p. 14.

134. M. V. Frunze, *op. cit.*, Vol. 2, pp. 343–4.

135. See a recent and important Soviet military-political study, *Vtoraya Mirovaya Voina 1939–1945* (The Second World War 1939–1945) (Under collective authorship), Moscow 1958. This draws attention to the value of the military discussions of the 1920's and singles out Triandafillov for particular comment. See also *Podgotovka Rossii k Imperialisticheskoi Voine* (Russia's preparation for the Imperialist War), Moscow 1926; introductory essay by M. N. Tukhachevsky. Also *BSE* (1), Vol. 12, 1928, Cols. 552–76, Tukhachevsky on 'War as a problem of armed struggle'. Kuz'min, *op. cit.*, quotes on p. 78 from a work *Voprosy sovremennoi strategii* (Problems of contemporary strategy), written by Tukhachevsky and published Moscow, 1926. Tukhachevsky did, however, publish a paper of the same title in a symposium *Voina i Voennoe Iskusstvo v Svete Istoricheskovo Materializma* (War and Military Art in the light of Historical Materialism) (ed. B. Gorev), Moscow 1927. The first publication must have been a separate printing of the essay.

136. A. A. Svechin, *Strategiya* (Strategy), Moscow 1927, *passim*. This is the 2nd Edn.

137. See Film Serial M108/M003868–004047: *Reichswehrministerium-Marineleitung/Russland.* Period 1926–30. This deals with Soviet-German naval collaboration, although there are gaps in the file for 1928 and parts of 1930 and 1931. The original is, in fact, a large ledger, and it might be assumed that the gaps are due to no record having been taken of certain items, but it is more likely that they are recorded elsewhere; this file contains drafts of reports, followed by the typed versions, so that it is more a record book than a file in the proper sense. It does contain, however, unique items. See here frames M003868–9 for *Fragebogen*: 15 items, translated from the Russian.

138. *Ibid.*, frames M003873–7–8. This covers a German naval mission to the Soviet Union, June 1926, and conversations with Zof. These contacts will be further examined in Chapter Nine.

Chapter VIII

1. See 'The Siberian Question', Ch. XV, pp. 340–62 in George F. Kennan, *The Decision to Intervene*, Princeton 1958. Also David J. Dallin, *The rise of Russia in Asia*, *op. cit.*, pp. 156–9.

2. L. M. Papin, *Krakh Kolchakovshchiny . . .*, *op. cit.*, pp. 50–8.

3. *Ibid.*, p. 63. See also David Footman, 'Last days of Kolchak' in *Indiana Slavic Studies*, Vol. II, pp. 1–37.

4. H. K. Norton, *The Far Eastern Republic of Siberia*, London 1923, p. 131.

5. L. M. Papin, *op. cit.*, p. 102.

6. *Ibid.*, pp. 102–8: quotes from a stenographic record of the conversations, published in a journal, *Sibirskie Ogni*, 1927, No. 5.

7. H. K. Norton, *op. cit.*, pp. 134–6. Also L. M. Papin, p. 142.

8. Papin, *op. cit.*, p. 117.

9. H. K. Norton, *op. cit.*, p. 141.

10. L. M. Papin, *op. cit.*, pp. 152–3.

11. *Ibid.*, p. 149.

12. H. K. Norton, *op. cit.*, p. 146.

13. M. I. Gubel'man, *Bor'ba za Sovetskii Dal'nii Vostok 1918–1922* (The struggle for the Soviet Far East 1918–1922), Moscow 1958, p. 200. It has not proved possible to obtain a copy of Gubel'man's life of Lazo published in 1938.

14. *Ibid.*, pp. 202–3. See a recent reprint of Postyshev's memoirs, *Grazhdanskaya Voina na Vostoke Sibiri 1917–1922 gg* (The Civil War in East Siberia 1917–1922), Moscow 1957.

15. M. I. Gubel'man, *op. cit.*, p. 166.

16. *Ibid.*, p. 195. For a wider account of the Japanese punitive expeditions, see H. K. Norton, *op. cit.*, pp. 112–18.

17. Conrad Brandt, *Stalin's Failure in China 1924–1927*, London 1958, pp. 20–1.

18. M. S. Kapitsa, *Sovetsko-Kitaiskie Otnosheniya* (Soviet-Chinese Relations), Moscow 1958, p. 68.

19. For biographical sketches, see 'The Men at the Helm', in H. K. Norton, *op. cit.*, pp. 170–91. On Yurin, pp. 182–3.

20. See text in *Dok. Vneshnei Politiky*, *op. cit.*, Vol. 3, Moscow 1959, No. 110, pp. 213–17.

21. *Ibid.*, p. 324.

22. This version is supplied in M. S. Kapitsa, *op. cit.*, p. 65.

23. *Ibid.* Cf. David J. Dallin, *op. cit.*, p. 190.

24. Dallin, p. 190, puts the membership at not more than 160.

25. M. S. Kapitsa, *op. cit.*, p. 67.

26. G. V. Kuz'min, *Grazh. voina i voennaya interventsiya v SSSR*, *op. cit.*, pp. 338–9. Cf. H. K. Norton, *op. cit.*, pp. 225–6, for further details of the military operations. Norton makes no mention of any revolutionary Mongolian Army, only of Soviet and Republican troops.

27. M. S. Kapitsa, *op. cit.*, p. 67.

28. M. I. Gubel'man, *op. cit.*, pp. 221–2.

29. For the seizure of power, see Norton, pp. 253–4.

30. Letter quoted in M. I. Gubel'man, p. 224.

31. M. I. Gubel'man, *ibid.*, p. 236.

32. David J. Dallin, *op. cit.*, p. 175.

33. Quoted in M. I. Gubel'man, *op. cit.*, pp. 242–3.

34. See the interesting 'Lenin and Asian nationalism: source of an alliance', Ch. 1 in C. Brandt, *op. cit.*, pp. 1–18.

35. *Istoriya sovremennoi Kitaiskoi Revolyutsii* (History of the modern Chinese Revolution) (ed. He Huan-chi, trans. M. F. Yur'ev), Moscow 1959, pp. 77–8. Edgar Snow, *Red Star over China*, London 1946, p. 154.

36. David J. Dallin, *op. cit.*, p. 191.

37. See text in *Sovetsko-Kitaiskie Otnosheniya 1917–1957* (Soviet-Chinese relations 1917–1957), (Documents), Moscow 1959, No. 52, pp. 90–3.

38. C. Brandt, *op. cit.*, p. 33.

39. Text in *Sov.-Kit. Otnosheniya*, (Documents), *op. cit.*, No. 28, pp. 64–5.

40. David J. Dallin, *op. cit.*, p. 212. Also Louis Fischer, *op. cit.*, Vol. 2, p. 633.

41. M. S. Kapitsa, *op. cit.*, p. 105.

42. Also by Borodin, 'towards the end of 1924'. See Louis Fischer, *op. cit.*, Vol. 2, pp. 649–50.

43. F. F. Liu, *A Military History of Modern China 1924–1949*, Princeton 1956, p. 6.

44. *Ibid.*, p. 8.

45. *Ibid.*, p. 9.

46. *Ibid.*, p. 10.

47. M. S. Kapitsa, *op. cit.*, p. 139.

48. F. F. Liu, *op. cit.*, p. 15.

49. *Ibid.*, p. 6.

50. *Ibid.*, p. 16.

51. *Ibid.*, p. 20.

52. Cf. C. Brandt, *op. cit.*, p. 117.

53. David J. Dallin, *op. cit.*, p. 225, for developments in Inner Mongolia.

54. F. F. Liu, *op. cit.*, p. 22.

55. C. Brandt, *op. cit.*, pp. 69–70.

56. Stepanov quoted in Liu, *op. cit.*, pp. 22–3. Louis Fischer, *op. cit.*, Vol. 2, p. 651, states that Chiang Kai-shek's object was to rid Whampoa of Wong Ching-wei, commissar successor to Liao Chung-k'ai, since he favoured the co-operation with the Communists and the Russians.

57. David J. Dallin, *op. cit.*, pp. 225–6.

58. For an account of this, see C. Brandt, *op. cit.*, p. 77.

59. This version is in F. F. Liu, *op. cit.*, p. 37. On Borodin and Blyukher, see Louis Fischer, Vol. 2, pp. 661–2.

60. See R. C. North, *Moscow and the Chinese Communists*, Stanford, California 1953, p. 90.

61. See C. Brandt, *op. cit.*, p. 117 and his note to this.

62. F. F. Liu, *op. cit.*, p. 34.

63. *Ibid.*, p. 38.

64. See *Ist. Arkhiv*, 1959, No. 4, 'Iz istorii Severnovo Pokhoda' (From the history of the Northern Expedition), Blyukher's orders, pp. 101–6.

65. *Ibid.*, p. 126.

66. *Ibid.*, p. 106.

67. See C. Brandt, *op. cit.*, p. 111, and F. F. Liu, *op. cit.*, p. 38.

68. F. F. Liu, *ibid.*, p. 39.

69. C. Brandt, *op. cit.*, p. 113.

70. F. F. Liu, *op. cit.*, p. 41.

71. J. Stalin, *Works*, Eng. Edn., Vol. 9, pp. 259–60. 'Talk with the students of the Sun Yat-sen University, May 13, 1927.'

72. C. Brandt, *op. cit.*, p. 122 — so also did Stalin.

73. Text in David J. Dallin, *op. cit.*, p. 230.

74. M. F. Yur'ev, *Krasnaya Armiya Kitaya* (The Red Army of China), Moscow 1958, p. 13. See C. Brandt, p. 143, for the important qualification that *all* Kuomintang troops revolted, scarcely knowing that they were doing so, merely obeying orders.

75. *Ist. Arkhiv*, *op. cit.*, 1959, No. 4, p. 125.

76. J. Stalin, *Works*, Eng. Edn., Vol. 7, p. 301.

77. David J. Dallin, *op. cit.*, p. 241.

78. Mamoru Shigemitsu, *Japan and her destiny. My struggle for peace* (ed. Major-General F. S. G. Piggott), London 1958, p. 49.

79. David J. Dallin, *op. cit.*, p. 253.

80. See in Dirksen's papers (*AA*) Film Ref. 9481/H276358–9, dated 13th April, 1928, for discussion of Blyukher and his appointment.

81. E. Wollenberg, *The Red Army*, *op. cit.*, p. 192.

82. N. F. Kuz'min, *Na strazhe mirnovo truda 1921–1940*, *op. cit.*, p. 124.

83. Louis Fischer, *op. cit.*, Vol. 2, p. 800.

84. David J. Dallin, *op. cit.*, p. 265. There is in *Notes for a Journal*, *op. cit.*, which purports to be from the pen of Litvinov, an account of the divisions of opinion over action against Chang Hsueh-liang; Litvinov supported Voroshilov's plan to send troops, Molotov and Stalin opposed it. Voroshilov was to go to Chita to decide at what moment action should be taken. Stalin received a Japanese assurance that there would be no interference if Soviet troops did not proceed beyond the meridian 50 kilometres east of Hailar. See *ibid.*, pp. 111–13.

85. Account of the operation in N. F. Kuz'min, *op. cit.*, pp. 126–9.

86. *Ibid.*, p. 130.

87. *Ibid.*, p. 131.

88. *Ibid.*, pp. 130–3.

89. See Saburo Hayashi (in collabn. with Alvin D. Coox), Kōgun *The Japanese Army in the Pacific War*, Marine Corps Assn., USA 1959, p. 3.

90. *International Military Tribunal. Far East*, Judgements, Verdicts. Part A, p. 804.

91. A. Svetlanin (pseud.), *Dal'nevostochnyi zagovor* (The Far Eastern Conspiracy), Possev-Verlag, Frankfurt/Main 1953, p. 101.

Chapter IX

1. See Hans W. Gatzke, 'Russo-German Military Collaboration during the Weimar Republic', *American Historical Review*, *op. cit.*, p. 578. Cf. G. Freund, *Unholy Alliance*, *op. cit.*, pp. 213–15.

2. Hans W. Gatzke, *ibid.*, p. 580.

3. See G. Castellan, in *Les Relations Germano-Soviétiques*, *op. cit.*, p. 194. Also Hans W. Gatzke, p. 580.

4. Relevant passages in *AA* file: Wallroth papers, *Direktoren* files, *Russland Politik* (*Woroschilow*), 5265H/E318692–784. See also military reports, *Militär. Angelegenheiten*, (*Po. 13*), 9524H/E671544 f.

5. See *Russland Politik* (*Woroschilow*), *passim*, Brockdorff-Rantzau protests to Chicherin.

6. See in *Akten betr. Militärische Angelegenheiten mit Russland, Büro von Staatssekretär v. Schubert*, Serial 4564H/E162673–5. Dated 21st January, 1926. Note: in addition to these files dealing with military collaboration, there is also a collection under Dirksen's name. To distinguish them, the relevant name — Schubert or Dirksen — will be

added; where no name is given, the reference covers the *Militär. Angelegenheiten* file of German military reports.

7. See Hans W. Gatzke, *op. cit.*, p. 581.

8. *Militär. Angelegenheiten* (Schubert), 4564H/E162694–9.

9. *Ibid.*

10. See 'Sowjetgranaten' in *Geheim-Akten Russland 1920–1936. (AA). Handakten* 6698H/H106231–398, covering the period December 1926–June 1927. Also C. F. Melville, *The Russian Face of Germany*, An account of the secret military relations between the German and Soviet Russian governments, London 1932, 230 pp. This contains a number of important items about the collaboration, and covers the incident of the grenades; see his appendices.

11. *Manchester Guardian*, 3rd December, 1926. 'Secret plan between Reichswehr officers and Soviet. Startling Disclosures.' I am grateful to the *Manchester Guardian* for assistance in checking a German Intelligence report (6698H/H111749–450) of 14th January, 1927; this suggested that the newspaper revelations were a deliberate Soviet conspiracy (*Machenschaft*), in which a certain Gavrilov, agent of the *Narkomindel* in London, had relayed information on the aircraft, gas and munitions manufacture in Soviet Russia. In Paris, Soviet agents were instructed to pass the same information to 'Comte du Chayllat' and 'Duchesse d'Uzès, rue Murillo 26' and have it passed to General Weygand. There appears to be no foundation for this whatsoever.

12. *Militär. Angelegenheiten* (Schubert), 4564H/E162663–4.

13. *Ibid.*, 'Unternehmungen der Junkerswerke in Russland'. Period: 25th June, 1926–13th August, 1926. Frames 163752–852. See also *Geheim-Akten*, 6698H/H105370–105526.

14. Hans W. Gatzke, *op. cit.*, p. 585.

15. See Film Ref. M108/M003868–004047: *Reichswehrministerium-Marineleitung/Russland*. This is the only file on Soviet-German naval collaboration which has come to light here. It is not, properly speaking, a file, but a ledger containing separate entries, with a gap for 1927–8. See here frame M003901. There are also reports on naval affairs in the Soviet Union, under *Marine-angelegenheiten*, covering German observation of Soviet naval activities; see K299/K105008–58, for the period March 1924–September 1926, including items on the naval installations of Odessa.

16. M108/M003872. *Marineleitung/Russland*.

17. *Ibid.*, M003873 f.

18. *Ibid.*, M003877–9 for Spindler's report (evidently written in Moscow), and M003901–22 for Kinzel.

19. *Ibid.*, M003888–98.

20. *Ibid.*, M003932: *A II. g. Kds. 533/26*. Also M003933–4 for U-boat numbers; one set is illegible.

21. *Ibid.*, M003922–4 and M003899, the latter signed by Spindler.

22. *Ibid.*, M003930–31.

23. A. Barmine, *One who survived*, *op. cit.*, p. 123.

24. M108/M003937–8. *Marineleitung/Russland*.

25. *Ibid.*, M003942.

26. See discussion in Hans W. Gatzke, *op. cit.*, pp. 586–7.

27. Copy in *Militär. Angelegenheiten* (Schubert), 4564H/E163885. *Protokoll*, 26th February, 1927. See also a further collection: *Direktoren 29a/1, Handakten von Herr Min. Dir. von Dirksen. Militär. Angelegenheiten. Russland.* Serial 9481H/276238–508, for period 1926–8. This is continued under Serial 9480H, up to 1931. See here frames 276337–8, /9481H. By using these two collections it is possible in many cases to trace a document with its subsequent annotations and comments; certain of them are duplicated in the *Geheim-Akten*, but these frequently lack notes and comments.

28. Hans W. Gatzke, *op. cit.*, p. 587.

29. *Militär. Angelegenheiten* (Schubert), 4564H/E163867–8, also 163869–70. The point of 'legalisation' was raised by Major Fischer in connection with the disclosures about the gas-experiments in the *Leipziger Volkszeitung;* General Heye was much disturbed about this, and Fischer pointed out that to preserve secrecy '. . . we must think of legalising these connections'. See Major Fischer to Wallroth, 10th January, 1927; in 'Reichswehr und Russland', *Geheim-Akten* 6698H/H111751–3.

30. *Geheim-Akten, ibid.*, H111743–5. Dated 23rd April, 1927.

31. *Militär. Angelegenheiten* (Schubert), 4564H/163880–4. Also *Geheim-Akten*, 6698H/H111738–41.

32. *Geheim-Akten*, 6698H/H111742, 24th May, 1927.

33. *Militär. Angelegenheiten* (Dirksen), 9481H/276437–8, 4th June, 1927.

34. *Ibid.*, 276430–1, Dirksen to Major Behschnitt.

35. *Ibid.*, 276417.

36. Voroshilov's admission to Blomberg; see 9480H/276193.

37. *Militär. Angelegenheiten* (Dirksen), 9481H/276499–500, 3rd June, 1926.

38. *Ibid.*, 276324–5. Table, dated 21st November, 1928.

39. *Ibid.*, 276403–4. Request from Blomberg, dated 14th November, 1927.

40. Colonel-General Heinz Guderian in *The Soviet Army* (ed. B. H. Liddell Hart), *op. cit.*, pp. 128–9. Cf. General Speidel, *op. cit.*, p. 35.

41. *Militär. Angelegenheiten*, 9524H/671612–19.

42. *Ibid.*, 671628–30.

43. For full report on manœuvres, *ibid.*, 671631– 6.

44. Quoted in I. B. Berkhin, *Voennaya Reforma v SSSR 1924–1925*, *op. cit.*, pp. 376–7. Report from Red Army Central Archive.

45. *Militar. Angelegenheiten*, 9524H/671638. German Consulate in Kiev.

46. *Militär. Angelegenheiten* (Dirksen), 9481H/276401–2.

47. *Ibid.*, 276358–9.

48. *Ibid.*, 276341.

49. *Ibid.*, 276271.

50. This flatly contradicts General Speidel, *op. cit.*, p. 36, who complains of a lack of reciprocity in the relationship and the lack of opportunity for German officers to follow the real direction of Soviet military affairs. The *Statistische Abteilung* obviously had a real insight into Soviet military affairs and appraised the Red Army with an insight keener than that of the Soviet command.

51. Mittelberger report, *Militär. Angelegenheiten* (Dirksen), 9481H/276305–9; on Tukhachevsky, 276306 — 'Allgemein wisse man, dass er nur aus Opportunitäts grunden Kommunist sei.' Report dated 10th May, 1928.

52. *Ibid.*, 276307–9.

53. *Militär. Angelegenheiten*, 9524H/671672.

54. *Ibid.*, for full report, 671672–5. Signed by Colonel von Kühlenthal, head of the *Statistische Abteilung*.

55. *Militär. Angelegenheiten* (Dirksen), 9481H/276249.

56. See *Reise des Chefs des Truppenamts nach Russland.* (*August/September 1928*) *Reichswehrministerium Truppenamt*, Nr. 231/28, geh. Kdos. T 3 V. In *Militär. Angelegenheiten* (Dirksen), file for November 1928–1931, Serial 9480H/276183–236. Will be cited as *Blomberg report*, and page numbers quoted. Here pp. 2–3.

57. *Ibid.*, Blomberg report, p. 4.

58. *Ibid.*, pp. 6–7.

59. *Ibid.*, p. 8.

60. *Ibid.*, p. 9.

61. *Ibid.*, pp. 9–11.

62. *Ibid.*, p. 11.

63. *Ibid.*, p. 12.

64. *Ibid.*, p. 13.

65. *Ibid.*, pp. 13–14.

66. *Ibid.*, p. 14.

67. *Ibid.*, p. 18.

68. *Ibid.*, p. 21.

69. *Ibid.*

70. *Ibid.*, pp. 35–8. Opens with an account of the Zhukovskii Military Aviation Academy in Moscow — '. . . ausgezeichnet organisiert'. Reconnaissance and bomber aircraft belong to the 1918 era; Soviet machines have BMW engines in many cases. The Soviet air-force is very conscious of the problem of modernisation; 2 Heinkel single-seat fighters are on order, also 300 BMW 600 H.P. engines and new machine-guns on test. Continues with a description of the Gomel exercises, also use of aircraft in the Kiev exercises (pp. 39–40).

71. *Ibid.*, p. 53.

72. Hans W. Gatzke, *op. cit.*, p. 590.

73. So described in G. Castellan, *Le Réarmement clandestin du Reich 1930–1935*, Paris 1954, p. 197. This contains further valuable information on the Soviet-German collaboration.

74. *Militär. Angelegenheiten* (Dirksen), 9480H/276155–8. See also the pencilled exchanges between Blomberg and Schubert, 22nd February, 1929: *Militär. Angelegenheiten* (Schubert), 4564H/163946.

75. G. Castellan, *Le Réarmement clandestin du Reich*, *op. cit.*, pp. 190–2 on Kazan, using the reports of the French 2e *Bureau*.

76. Cf. *ibid.*, p. 192. On the despatch of tanks, see *Militär. Angelegenheiten* (Schubert), 4564H/163953 — the *Kaufvertrag* whereby the Red Army would be the purchasers of the machines. Also *ibid.*, 163966, Blomberg to Moltke, information that the tanks were shipped at the end of June 1929; six machines were sent in this load.

77. See *BSE* (1), Vol. 53, 1946, Cols. 559–60, on early Soviet tanks and their manufacture. Also V. D. Mostovenko, *Tanki*, *op. cit.*, pp. 80–2.

78. Mostovenko, *ibid.*, p. 83.

79. G. Castellan in *Les Relations Germano-Soviétiques, op. cit.*, p. 195.

80. See *Militär. Angelegenheiten* (Dirksen), 9480H/276155–6 of 18th February, 1929, and 276173–4, 21st January, 1929.

81. *Ibid.*, 276146–7.

82. G. Castellan in *Les relations germano-soviétiques, op. cit.*, p. 195.

83. *Ibid.*, pp. 195–6.

84. *Ibid.*, p. 196. Letter of the French Military Attaché in Berlin, 9th October, 1929.

85. *Militär. Angelegenheiten* (Dirksen), 9480H/276083–8 for Halm's first report on the Red Army, dated 11th July, 1930.

86. Cf. *ibid.*, 276063. Telegram from Colonel Köstring from Moscow; Voroshilov has asked that General Adam of the *Truppenamt* might delay his visit until the Red Army manœuvres. Dated 23rd May, 1931.

87. According to R. Fischer, *Stalin and German Communism, op. cit.*, p. 535.

88. *Militär. Angelegenheiten* (Dirksen), 9481H/276345. Dated 23rd April, 1928.

89. *Militär. Angelegenheiten* (Schubert), 4564H/163984–9.

90. *Ibid.*, 163974–7. See also 163956 f. on Soviet approach to Krupp, 1928.

91. *Ibid.*, 164003–5.

92. *Ibid.*, 164011–13. Dated 7th February, 1930.

93. *Ibid.*, 164023–9.

94. Report rendered by Eltze, *ibid.*, 164053. Dated 12th February, 1930.

95. There are scattered naval items in Serial 9524H and in the continuation of K299 *Marine-Angelegenheiten* in Serial K300/105115 f. Serial M108 does not resume until 1929.

96. See *Militär. Angelegenheiten* (Dirksen), 9480H/276151–2.

97. M108/M003949, *Marineleitung. Russland.*

98. Biography of Vladimir Mitrofanovich Orlov: M108/M003970.

99. M108/M003974–6. See also K300/105107, on visit of Soviet naval mission; Orlov appears as 'Adamhoff', Smirnov as 'Sokolin'. This instruction, dated 15th February, 1930, was circulated to German naval commanders.

100. For report, see M108/M003977–80.

101. This conversation, reproduced here with some slight shortening of the comments but with no alteration of the sense, is reproduced verbatim in M108/M003981–9.

102. *Ibid.*, M004018 f. On officer exchange, Niedermayer sent an item from Moscow to the *Marineleitung* on 14th March, 1930, which answered a query about Soviet officers being sent to Japan for training; 2 officers were detached for 2 years, but Niedermayer communicated the Soviet version that 'no political significance' should be attached to this. See *ibid.*, M003994.

103. *Ibid.*, M004036.

104. G. Castellan in *Les Relations Germano-Soviétiques, op. cit.*, pp. 192–3. Quotes letter of French Military Attaché in Berlin in support of details about Soviet officers.

105. *Ibid.*, French Attaché letters. The *Reichswehr* major is named as Feldgiebel.

106. *Militär. Angelegenheiten* (Dirksen), 9480H/276101.

Chapter X

1. M. V. Frunze, *op. cit.*, Vol. 2, pp. 355–64. Address of 25th May, 1925, on 'War industry — the basis of our defence capability'.

2. J. Stalin, *Works*, Eng. Edn., Vol. 9, p. 328, from *Pravda*, 28th July, 1927. Cf. B. Souvarine's revealing comments in his *Staline*, *op. cit.*, p. 418; '. . . écrit-il [Stalin] sans y croire, car dans les conversations privées, il a le cynisme d'ironiser sur cette fable.'

3. L. Fischer, *The Soviets in World Affairs*, *op. cit.*, Vol. 2, p. 741.

4. D. Fedotoff White, *The Growth of the Red Army*, *op. cit.*, p. 279. This author takes the war-scare more seriously, but is concentrating upon the purely military aspects.

5. See J. Stalin, *Works*, Vol. 10, under 'Joint Plenum of the C.C. and the C.C.C. of the C.P.S.U.(B)', Part IV, p. 44 f. Stalin here disputes the assertion that *he* was a member of the 'Military Opposition'. Trotsky's letter to Ordzhonikidze, pp. 54–5. Stalin completely transforms Trotsky's argument and example into the position that '. . . Trotsky is thinking of starting civil war in the Party at a time when the enemy will be eighty kilometres from the Kremlin' (p. 57).

6. I. Deutscher, *The Prophet Unarmed*, *op. cit.*, p. 350.

7. L. Trotsky, *Stalin*, *op. cit.*, p. 413.

8. See *The Stalin School of Falsification*, *op. cit.*, under 'The War Danger — The Defence Policy and the Opposition', p. 161 f. For the accusation against Voroshilov, *ibid.*, p. 167.

9. *Ibid.*, p. 176, 'Trotsky: The Opposition thinks that the leadership of Stalin makes victory more difficult.'

10. *Ibid.*, in response to Molotov's interjection. Cf. B. Souvarine, *op. cit.*, p. 418.

11. See *KPSS v rez.* (Party resolutions), Vol. 2, pp. 267–74. To p. 270 it is first a history and then a catalogue of the sins of the Opposition.

12. *Ibid.*, pp. 368–70, for the date of the verdict and list of names.

13. B. Souvarine, *op. cit.*, p. 442. In the actual voting strength, I. Deutscher in his *Stalin*, p. 312 adduces a total of four — Stalin, Molotov, and the new men Kuibyshev and Rudzutak.

14. B. Souvarine, *ibid.*, p. 445 and p. 448.

15. Cf. M. Beloff, *The Foreign Policy of Soviet Russia 1929–1941*, London 1947, Vol. 1, Ch. 1, pp. 1–12.

16. Reported in *Russische Geheimdokumente* (*AA*) Serial K284/K098508 under 'Die Aussenpolitik der UdSSR und die Komintern', dated 16th April, 1928. Many of these documents are agents' reports and their reliability is difficult to assess, although this item appears to be a serious attempt to estimate the influence of the *Komintern*.

17. Cf. Lenin, *Soch.* (Works), 4th Edn., Vol. 25, pp. 18–19, speech on the war at the 1st Congress of Soviets, 22nd June, 1917. 'War is nothing but politics, it is a pursuit by these classes of the same ends by different means.' See also R. L. Garthoff's

interesting passage in his *How Russia Makes War*, *op. cit.*, p. 53. For a recent Soviet comment, see an extraordinary and fascinatingly original Soviet study by V. I. Skopin, *Militarizm* (Militarism) (ed. Major-General N. V. Pukhovskii) Moscow 1956, Ch. 20, pp. 325–36.

18. E. Wollenberg, *The Red Army*, *op. cit.*, p. 196. No support is offered for this statement.

19. B. M. Shaposhnikov, *Mozg Armii* (The Brain of the Army). Published in three volumes, Moscow 1927–9. R. L. Garthoff, *op. cit.*, note to bibliography, p. 530, mentions the possibility of a fourth volume which was 'projected and possibly published', but is not available. British holdings appear to contain no trace of a fourth volume.

20. B. M. Shaposhnikov, *op. cit.*, Vol. 1, p. 14.

21. See R. L. Garthoff, *op. cit.*, p. 198, for one of many excellent comments on Shaposhnikov and valuable points on the influence of the Imperial Russian General Staff. Cf. V. I. Skopin, *op. cit.*, pp. 490–2, on the staff and the difference between 'collective' and 'collegiate' military directorates.

22. See discussion in C. Goudima, *L'Armée Rouge dans la Paix et la Guerre*, Paris 1947, pp. 136–7.

23. In *BSE* (1), Vol. 12, 1928, Cols. 576–98. M. N. Tukhachevsky, 'Voina kak problema vooruzhennoi bor'by' ('War as a problem of armed struggle').

24. *Ibid.*, 578.

25. *Ibid.*, 579.

26. *Ibid.*, 597.

27. *Ibid.*, 590.

28. See D. Fedotoff White, 'Soviet Philosophy of War' in *Political Science Quarterly* Vol. 51, 1936, p. 345.

29. *Ibid.*

30. See F. Rotshtein, 'Voina kak sotsialnoe yavlenie' ('War as social phenomenon'), in *BSE* (1), Vol. 12, 1928, Cols. 552–76. An interesting and authoritative recent Soviet study, which invites comparison, is *Marksizm-Leninizm o Voine i Armii* (Marxism-Leninism on War and the Army) (ed. Col. I. N. Levanov), Moscow 1957, 1st Edn., and 1958, 2nd Edn.

31. M. V. Frunze made a close study of the Moroccan operations and military-political relations: see his Vol. 2, *op. cit.*, pp. 392–472. A recent Soviet study, casting this in contemporary terms but also inviting comparison, is V. L. Tyagunenko, *Voiny i kolonii* (Wars and colonies), Moscow 1957.

32. *BSE* (1), Vol. 12, Col. 596.

33. See D. Ryazanov, *Voina i Voennoe Iskusstvo . . .*, *op. cit.*, pp. 20–1.

34. Reported in *Militär. Angelegenheiten* (*AA*), 9524H/E671584.

35. I. Deutscher, *The Prophet Unarmed*, p. 458, for this letter.

36. *Ibid.*, p. 459.

37. *Ibid.*

38. *Ibid.*

39. J. Stalin, *Works*, Vol. 10, p. 310.

40. J. Stalin, Vol. 11, pp. 255–80: 'Industrialisation of the country and the Right

Deviation of the C.P.S.U.(B).' Speech at the Central Committee Plenum, 19th November, 1928. See also *ibid.*, pp. 121–32: reply to Frumkin's letter of 15th June, 1928, attacking Frumkin for singing 'the swan-song' of the Soviet Union and his defeatism over the economic prospects. Stalin wanted greater allocations for industrialisation from the budget.

41. B. Souvarine, *op. cit.*, p. 447.

42. F. Engels, *Anti-Dühring*, Moscow 1954, pp. 230–1.

43. Cf. *KPSS v rez.* (Party resolutions), Vol. 2, p. 277. Plenum of the C.C. and the C.C.C., 21–23/10/1927. Makes this point unmistakably plain in Point 3. Cf. Max Werner, *The Military Strength of the Powers*, London 1939, p. 46, quoting an article by Ventsov on this subject. S. Ventsov was the author of *Narodnoe Khozyaistvo i Oborona SSSR* (The national economy and the defence of the USSR), Moscow 1928.

44. *From the First to the Second Five Year Plan. A Symposium*, Moscow-Leningrad, 1933, p. 351, K. Voroshilov, 'Strengthening the defence of the USSR.'

45. *Ibid.*, pp. 355–6.

46. See *KPSS v rez.* (Party resolutions), Vol. 2, p. 585.

47. Figure quoted in E. Yu. Lokshin, *Ocherk istorii promyshlennosti SSSR* (Outline of the history of Soviet industry), Moscow 1956, p. 276.

48. Figures in *Promyshlennost' SSSR. Statisticheskii Sbornik* (Soviet Industry. Statistical Almanac), Moscow 1957, p. 106. The figures for 1914 were 4,137,000 and 4,466,000 tons of pig-iron and steel respectively.

49. *Ibid.*, p. 42.

50. Quoted in *Soviet Economics* (From the German: *Die Rote Wirtschaft*, ed. Dr G. Dobbert), London 1933, p. 112.

51. *Ibid.*, Dr H. Saller, 'Transportation in the Soviet Union', pp. 197–221. For a more recent and excellent study, see Holland Hunter, *Soviet Transportation Policy*, Harvard U.P. 1957, 'Soviet locational objectives and problems', p. 21 f. and 'Industrialization and Transportation', Ch. 3, pp. 39–72.

52. *Soviet Economics*, p. 207. Cites the average transport distance in the Soviet Union as 585 kilometres (152 for Germany); 1,440 sleepers to the kilometre (1,600 in Germany). Sleepers were not always treated with preservative (7 million untreated laid after 1929–30). Average mileage of a wheel-flange dropped from 35–40,000 kilometres before 1914 to 8–12,000. These figures applied to the First Five-Year Plan period and earlier.

53. *Ibid.*, see Hans Jonas, 'Organisation of Economic Life', pp. 21–51.

54. See Preface to Artur W. Just, *The Red Army*, London 1936.

55. *Ibid.*, p. 19.

56. Figures from *League of Nations Armaments Handbook*, Vol. 5, 1928–9, pp. 829–31.

57. General Blomberg, Report on visit to the Soviet Union (1928), *op. cit.*, pp. 49–51. (Cf. a curious comment on *Osoaviakhim* in Lord Vansittart, *The Mist Procession*, London 1958, p. 286.)

58. This work was V. Melikov, *Marna–1914 — Visla–1920 — Smyrna 1922*, Moscow-Leningrad 1928, 468 pp.

59. In *Zapiski Sektsii po izucheniyu problem voiny pri Komakademii* (Proceedings of

the Section for the study of the problems of war attached to the Communist Academy), Vol. 1, Moscow 1930. See *Prol. Rev.* (Proletarian Revolution), 1930, 10(105), pp. 162–6. See also an interesting series of comments by N. Galay, 'The problem of quantity and quality in the Soviet Armed Forces', *Bulletin*, Munich, October 1956, pp. 3–9; Tukhachevsky was not then Chief of Staff, however, as stated, p. 8.

60. See *KPSS o voor. sil. Sov. Soyuza, op. cit.*, p. 304.

61. *Ibid.*, p. 306.

62. *Ibid.*

63. *Ibid.*, p. 308.

64. *Ibid.*, pp. 309–10.

65. *Ibid.*

66. *Ibid.*, pp. 316–17.

67. *Ibid.*, pp. 314–15.

68. Cf. I. Deutscher, *The Prophet Unarmed*, p. 303.

69. Cf. *BSE* (1), Vol. 14, 1929, Cols. 455–6. Also *MSE*, 4th Edn., Vol. 2, 1958, Cols. 828–9.

70. *KPSS v rez.* (Party resolutions), Vol. 2, pp. 485–94, 16th Party Conference (Moscow), 23rd–29th April, 1929.

71. L. Schapiro, 'The Army and the Party in the Soviet Union', *St Antony's Papers on Soviet Affairs*, (Mimeographed) 1954, p. 10.

72. M. Fainsod, *Smolensk under Soviet Rule*, London 1959, p. 219. Taken from the Captured Smolensk Archive.

73. *Polevoi Ustav 1929* (PU–29), Moscow, Voenizdat 1934. See p. 5, para. 1.

74. *Ibid.*, para. 8.

75. *Ibid.*, para. 63.

76. *Ibid.*, p. 39.

77. See N. F. Kuz'min, *Na strazhe mirnovo truda, op. cit.*, pp. 101–2.

78. Naval regulations: *Boevoi Ustav Voenno-morskikh Sil RKKA*, Moscow 1930. A mine-sweeping manual was ready in 1928.

79. V. Triandafillov, *Kharakter operatsii sovremennykh armii* (The nature of the operations of modern armies), 1st Edn., Moscow 1929; 2nd Edn., 1932, used here and quoted p. 27.

80. On 'the operating art', see *BSE* (1), Vol. 43, 1939, Cols. 179–82. General Svechin supplied this definition of this concept: 'The operating art regulates the achievements of tactics. Battles are not independent phenomena; they are only the essential materials from which operations are made. . . . The operation is a military undertaking of a nature which ceaselessly directs the efforts of the troops in a given region of the battlefield, with the object of achieving the given intermediary aim. . . . The essentials of the operating art are tactics and organisation. . . . Concerning the aim of the operation, the operating art brings out the whole row of tactical tasks and poses a series of problems for the rear administration. . . . the operating art dictates to the tactic the essential line of its work' (*Strategiya*). 'The operating art' grew out of an idea developed in the Imperial Russian Army: see Garthoff, *op. cit.*, note to p. 450.

81. See R. L. Garthoff, *ibid.*, p. 45. Cf. C. Goudima, *op. cit.*, p. 132.

82. *League of Nations Armaments Handbook*, Vol. 5, 1928–9, p. 836.

83. Printed in *KPSS o voor. sil. Sov. Soyuza, op. cit.*, pp. 318–21.

84. *Ibid.*, pp. 320–1.

Chapter XI

1. See *Wreckers on Trial. Trial of the Industrial Party, November–December 1930* London 1931 (also in a German version, *Spione und Saboteure vor dem Volksgericht*... Berlin 1931).

2. Date as entered in his official biography in *BSE* (1).

3. Quoted from Voroshilov's address on the 15th anniversary of the Red Army (February 1933): cited in M. Werner, *The Military Strength of the Powers* (trans. E. Fitzgerald), London 1939, p. 36. A much more restrained and qualified judgement on the years to which Voroshilov was referring will be found in General Yuri Danilov, 'The Red Army', *Foreign Affairs*, October 1928, pp. 96–110.

4. See Appendix on organisation of Soviet armoured forces.

5. Strength quoted in *League of Nations Armaments Handbook*, Vol. 6, p. 851. Also Vol. 14, p. 853.

6. N. F. Kuz'min, *Na strazhe mirnovo truda, op. cit.*, p. 119. Cf. J. M. Mackintosh in *The Soviet Army, op. cit.*, p. 59.

7. *MSE*, Vol. 1 (1958), Col. 283.

8. See analysis in H. J. Berman and M. Kerner, *Soviet Military Law, op. cit.*, p. 176.

9. See discussion in Julian Towster, *Political Power in the U.S.S.R. 1917–1947. The Theory and Structure of Government in the Soviet State*. New York 1948, pp. 162–3.

10. J. Stalin, *Problems of Leninism*, 11th Edn., Moscow 1952, p. 82.

11. *Ibid.*, pp. 89–90.

12. J. Stalin, *Works*, Vol. 11, pp. 24–9. 'Three Distinctive Features of the Red Army' (Speech at the Plenum of the Moscow Soviet, 25th February, 1928).

13. Cf. Richard Wraga, 'Methods and Means of Soviet Foreign Policy' in *Problems of Soviet Foreign Policy*, Munich 1959, pp. 37–8.

14. See L. Kochan, *Russia and the Weimar Republic, op. cit.*, p. 142, quoting *Pravda* for 5th December, 1929.

15. Cf. *Notes for a Journal, op. cit.*, pp. 105–6 for a supposed reaction from Stalin, who believed that the Germans would strike first at the Poles.

16. For text of a joint Soviet-German statement on their relations (13th June, 1930), see *Soviet Documents on Foreign Policy* (ed. Jane Degras), London 1952, Vol. 2, p. 440.

17. Cf. M. Beloff, *op. cit.*, Vol. 1, p. 62.

18. *Ibid.*, p. 63.

19. This version is supplied in *Notes for a Journal*, p. 92. No German documents support this, but it may refer to limited pressure brought by the Soviet command. If there is any foundation to it at all, such an idea makes interesting comparison with the charges levelled against the military in 1937.

20. *IMT* (Nuremberg) Session 31st July, 1946: /SA 236/ examination of Rechberg's

affidavit. (It did not prove possible to find the rejected affidavit itself, only the proceedings.) On A. Rechberg's other plans, see 'A. Rechberg . . . und ähnliche illegale Aktionen zu Herbeiführung einer deustch-französischen Militärallianz, insbes. die Angelegenheit "Klönne".' Serial 2264/124002–146.

21. G. Castellan, *Le Réarmement clandestin*, *op. cit.*, p. 481.

22. *Documents Soviet F.P.*, Vol. 2, pp. 476–7. Cf. M. Beloff, *op. cit.*, p. 20.

23. Cited in L. Kochan, *op. cit.*, pp. 135–6.

24. *Documents Soviet F.P.*, Vol. 2, p. 505.

25. *Ibid.*

26. Cf. M. Beloff, *op. cit.*, p. 21, mentions the draft handed over by M. Patek on 23rd August, but does not state that the draft was rejected.

27. *Documents Soviet F.P.*, Vol. 2, p. 507.

28. L. Kochan, *op. cit.*, p. 153, sees a radical and far-seeing turn in Soviet policy in 1931. Even admitting the sharpness of the turn, not the proposal of an Austro-German Customs Union but the mounting danger in the Far East might be more readily adduced for changes.

29. Cf. *Soviet Documents F.P.*, Vol. 2, pp. 490–2, for credit agreement between Germany and the Soviet Union, 14th April, 1931.

30. G. Castellan, *Le Réarmement clandestin*, *op. cit.*, p. 482. Letter of French Military Attaché in Berlin, 9th April, 1931.

31. *Ibid.*, p. 192. An unconfirmed report mentioned that *Tankabteilungen*, assembled out of Russian equipment but with German military personnel to operate them, were carrying out exercises in the Soviet Union in close contact with similar units in the Red Army. Whether this took place inside or outside the confines of Kazan is not clear, although the implication is that it was in a wider context than Kazan.

32. See Appendix B in M. Beloff, *op. cit.*, on the Soviet Far East, p. 206 f.

33. Cf. R. Storry, *The Double Patriots. A study of Japanese nationalism*, London 1957, pp. 46–53.

34. M. Shigemitsu, *op. cit.*, pp. 70–1.

35. *Ibid.*, pp. 34–5 on Professor Shumei Okawa.

36. See R. Storry, *op. cit.*, p. 71.

37. *IMT/FE* Verdicts and judgements, p. 804.

38. See Kōgun, *op. cit.*, p. 3.

39. Bruce Hopper, 'Soviet Transportation Plans: Winning the East' in *Foreign Affairs*, July 1930: pp. 652–8.

40. Cf. M. Beloff, *op. cit.*, p. 245.

41. Cf. Owen Lattimore, 'The Unknown Frontier of Manchuria' in *Foreign Affairs*, January 1933, pp. 315–33. This very penetrating analysis did locate the place where the large-scale Soviet-Japanese actions of 1939 took place.

42. R. Storry, *op. cit.*, p. 75 f.

43. *Notes for a Journal*, *op. cit.*, pp. 137–8 has a passage in which Stalin disposes of Voroshilov's argument for a preventive movement into Manchuria.

44. M. Gubel'man, *op. cit.*, p. 254.

45. *Documents Soviet F.P.*, Vol. 2, p. 512.

46. *Ibid.*, pp. 514–15.

47. *Ibid.*, pp. 515–17.
48. *Ibid.*, p. 526 f.
49. *Ibid.*, p. 552.
50. M. Shigemitsu, *op. cit.*, pp. 76–7.
51. *IMT/FE op. cit.*, p. 804.
52. Quoted in *Survey of International Affairs* (ed. A. J. Toynbee), London 1932, p. 437. (Cited as *Survey* with relevant year.)
53. For the case of General Su, see *Survey 1932*, pp. 438–9, and *Documents Soviet F.P.*, Vol. 2, pp. 549–50.
54. Cf. Owen Lattimore, *op. cit.*, p. 330.
55. *Documents Soviet F.P.*, Vol. 2, p. 551.
56. M. Beloff, *op. cit.*, p. 87.
57. I. Deutscher, *Stalin*, *op. cit.*, p. 333.
58. *Documents on Soviet F.P.*, Vol. 2, p. 517.
59. J. Stalin, *Works*, Vol. 13, p. 117.
60. *Ibid.*, p. 119.
61. G. Castellan, *Le réarmement clandestin*, *op. cit.*, p. 194.
62. *Official Documents concerning Polish-German and Polish-Soviet Relations 1933–1939. The Polish White Book*, London n.d., p. 171.
63. G. Castellan, *Le réarmement clandestin*, p. 483. Report of the French Military Attaché.
64. *Ibid.*
65. Cf. Raymond L. Garthoff, *How Russia makes war*, *op. cit.*, p. 47.
66. Cf. *Militär. Angelegenheiten* (*AA*), Serial K298/K104940–5000 for January–August 1932.
67. G. Castellan, *Le réarmement clandestin*, p. 484. Quotes the *2e Bureau* survey of the possibilities of this visit. As subsequently emerged, one of the topics of conversation was certainly the future of the station at Lipetsk.
68. Cf. L. Kochan, *op. cit.*, p. 163.
69. Dirksen letter from Moscow: Serial 9352H/E661431.
70. G. Castellan, *Le réarmement clandestin*, p. 485. See also Castellan in *Les Relations Germano-Soviétiques*, *op. cit.*, p. 248.
71. *Relations Germano-Soviétiques*, p. 248.
72. Cf. *Le réarmement clandestin*, p. 486. It is nevertheless significant that the idea of some agreement in 1929 (political if not conspiratorial) is produced by the *2e Bureau*.
73. See Gordon A. Craig, *op. cit.*, p. 453 f.
74. See David J. Dallin, *Russia and Post-war Europe*, New Haven 1945, pp. 61–2.
75. G. Castellan, *Les Relations Germano-Soviétiques*, p. 203, cites the evidence of Köstring that he had been 'put on approval' after Hitler's seizure of power. To judge by his handling of the situation in 1933, Hartmann acquitted himself excellently in the Soviet Union.
76. *Documents on German Foreign Policy 1918–1945*, Series C (1933–1937), Vol. 1, London (HMSO) 1957, p. 22. (Cited as *DGFP*, Series C, vol. number.)
77. *Ibid.*, p. 87.
78. *Ibid.*, p. 259. 'We cannot do without Russia's cover for our rear with respect

to Poland.... It is known that Poland is playing with the idea of a preventive war....' (Minutes of Conference of Ministers, 7th April, 1933.) Cf. Zygmunt J. Gasiorowski, 'The German-Polish Non-Aggression Pact of 1934' in *Journal of Central European Affairs*, April 1955, pp. 10–11.

79. *DGFP*, Series C, Vol. 1, p. 355.

80. *Ibid.*, pp. 467–8.

81. *Ibid.*, pp. 422–3.

82. *Ibid.*, pp. 464–6 for this conversation.

83. *Ibid.*, p. 469.

84. *Ibid.*, p. 467.

85. See *Militärattaché Moskau* (*auch Kowno*) (*AA*) Serial 5892H/E432446–3261, for period January 1933–May 1936. The reports begin only in June 1933; also Vols. 2–3 of the total 1–5 are missing, having been destroyed by fire. Some of the documents in Vol. 5 are also fire-damaged. See here E432509–514, Report No. 154/33.

86. Tukhachevsky-Twardowski conversation, *ibid.*, E432738–740. Report dated 1st November, 1933. The question of the initiative for the break in the collaboration is a matter of some dispute. H. Speidel, *op. cit.*, p. 41, notes that in the summer of 1933 Hitler gave orders to wind up the military activity in the east. Dirksen, and the Hartmann reports, plus the subsequent remarks exchanged between Soviet officers and German diplomats, would support the view that the interruption came first from the Soviet side (in the first week in June) and was followed by a German reprisal, followed by a zig-zag of meetings and exchanges. At no time, however, did the Soviet command shut the door tight on the idea of collaboration (a point which the Germans grasped at once), although quite what was implied in 'co-operation in another form' is difficult to guess.

87. See Enclosure I to Hartmann's Report No. 161/33, 19th September, under 'The situation with regard to German-Russian military policy', *ibid.*, Serial 5892/E432620–30. Hartmann refers to several items received from the *Auswärtiges Amt* and the *Reichswehrministerium*, but it does not appear possible to find these.

88. *Ibid.*, Enclosure I.

89. *Ibid.*, E432646–50 and Enclosure I, E432651–6, dated 26th September, No. 162/33.

90. *Ibid.*, E432740.

91. V. D. Mostovenko, *Tanki*, *op. cit.*, p. 85, offers these figures.

92. See Appendix. See R. M. Ogorkiewicz in *The Soviet Army*, pp. 298–9 on early Soviet tanks.

93. M. Werner, *op. cit.*, p. 88. Werner, while making use of a number of important Soviet military writings (it is G. Isserson here), uses them rather uncritically and cuts out a number of the important qualifications which the Soviet experts themselves placed upon their views.

94. See C. Goudima, *op. cit.*, p. 141.

95. The evidence supplied by Soviet manœuvres must be placed in a special category, as will be seen with respect to 1936. In the first place, the 1933 exercises were on a relatively small scale, and secondly carried out before foreign military observers. Serial 5892H carries a very detailed analysis of the 1933 exercises in the

Orel area, E432665–87, including the time-tables and manœuvre directives. A report on a smaller exercise near Kubinka (July 1933), in E432483–95. The Orel exercises took place from 20th–21st September, 1933. On the whole Hartmann was favourably impressed, but pointed out that the Orel exercises were only on a divisional scale.

96. Cf. M. Werner, *op. cit.*, p. 97, on Soviet views of strategic cavalry; quotes Krivoshein's views on mixed formation of cavalry and mechanised troops, p. 98.

97. Reference to Zhukov's activity at this time in P. Ruslanov, 'Marshal Zhukov' in *The Russian Review*, July 1956, pp. 187–9.

98. Serial 5892/E432459, 4th July, 1933, information on Soviet dispositions.

99. German study, *Betrachtungen über die operativen Verwendung der Baltischen Flotte in Falle eines Krieges mit dem Baltischen Block*, April 1932, 11 pp.

100. Report of Colonel Mendras, quoted in G. Castellan, *Le Réarmement clandestin*, p. 490, Mendras letter No. 44, 1st August, 1933.

101. Captain N. Klado, *The Battle of the Sea of Japan*, London 1906, p. 278.

102. Study *Verwendungsplan der U-boote im Kriege*, 1933 (?).

103. Naval information, *DGFP*, Series C, Vol. 2, pp. 378–9, Hartmann report.

104. W. G. Krivitsky, *op. cit.*, p. 246.

105. E. Wollenberg produced this in his book on the Red Army, but without any particular proof. See I. Deutscher, *Stalin*, *op. cit.*, p. 354.

106. Joseph C. Grew, *Ten Years in Japan*, London 1944, p. 51 (dated 27th September, 1932).

107. *Survey 1933*, p. 520.

108. Information of Soviet dispositions in the Far East, Serial 5892/E432701 and 432703 (information 'gained privately'); also E432890–2 for more detailed information (especially on the forces in Vladivostok). For military aviation, see Report No. 164/33, 17th October, 1933, E432708 f. A comprehensive list of Soviet Aviation Brigades, with their locations, is supplied; an examination of this (assuming it to be correct in its essentials) would confirm that a small striking force of bombers was in the Far East. Not less than 40 bombers conforms to the information on the brigades.

109. *Ibid.*, E432460 f. Information supplied by the German Consul in Vladivostok (Kastner), July 1933. Kastner had made a careful observation of the railway system and the methods for its defence.

110. KŌGUN, *op. cit.*, p. 7.

111. Joseph C. Grew, *op. cit.*, p. 101.

112. *DGFP*, Series C, Vol. 2, p. 183. Hassell to *AA*, 7th December, 1933, reporting on Litvinov's visit to Rome.

113. There is a very useful and well-informed study in 5892/E432938–56 Report No. 1/34, dated 10th January, 1934: 'Kurze militär-politische Beurteilung zur Lage im Fernen Osten.' The Japanese Military Attaché Kawabe made available to his German counter-part some of the information known to the Japanese on the Soviet forces in the Far East, but this item is much more ambitious in its scope than mere retailing of dispositions. Much more difficult is the question of naval forces; see *ibid.*, E432877 (Naval Attaché Baumbach) on submarines in Vladivostok. His information is that the first submarines in Vladivostok were observed in October — 1 medium, 2 small,

but that a total force of 12 submarines was rumoured to be in the Far East. (The Japanese *Nishi-Nishi* on 28th September reported 6 submarines readied, 6 being brought into a state of readiness.) Baumbach submits the following table:

	December, 1933 (Submarines)
Black Sea	8–9
Vladivostok	12
Baltic	16
Under construction	? Leningrad
	? Nikolayevsk

A work of very considerable value dealing with the Soviet military organisation in the Far East is *Study of Strategical and Tactical Peculiarities of Far Eastern Russia and Soviet Far East Forces* (Japanese Special Studies on Manchuria, Vol. XIII). Prepared by Military History Section, HQ. Army Forces Far East. Distributed: Office of the Chief of Military History, Dept. of the Army, Washington (dated January 1955). The various frontier-incidents with Japan are regarded as 'boosters' to the steady development of Soviet strength. The line of argument adopted in this study about the development of Soviet strategy in the Far East does not differ markedly from what is stated subsequently on this theme in the present work, and had been developed without having had the assistance of this invaluable manual.

114. G. Castellan in *Relations Germano-Soviétiques*, p. 204, report of Colonel Mendras.

115. *Ibid.*, p. 205, Colonel Mendras' letter, 25th October, 1933.

116. *DGFP*, Series C, Vol. 2, p. 76.

117. Général Gamelin, *Servir: Le Prologue du Drâme (1930–Août 1939)*, Paris 1946, p. 132. Cf. A. Géraud ('Pertinax'), 'France, Russia and the Pact of Mutual Assistance' in *Foreign Affairs*, January 1935, p. 226 f.

118. Reported in Serial 5892/E432745 f. Report No. 167–33, dated 7th November, 1933, from German Consul in Kiev. Subject: visit of Colonel Mendras, 29th September. Colonel Mendras thought the Red Army 'the aristocracy' of the Soviet Union, and Soviet aviation *very good.* G. Castellan in *Les Relations Germano-Soviétiques*, p. 205, mentions Pierre Cot's visit to Soviet Aviation Factories No. 24 and No. 22 in Moscow and the fact that an effort was made to show the French everything. In his talk with Twardowski, Tukhachevsky admitted this, but added that the French Minister and the French Air Force officers had not seen anything which the Germans had not also been shown down to the last detail.

Chapter XII

1. See Serial 5892H (Military Attaché: Moscow-Kovno) E432503–5, on appointments and changes in the Soviet high command.

2. Cf. I. Deutscher, *Stalin, op. cit.*, p. 364, for the manner of operation of the *Politburo* at this time.

3. See I. F. Pobezhimov, *Ustroistvo Sov. Armii, op. cit.*, p. 98. For the complete

text, see H. J. Berman and M. Kerner, *Documents on Soviet Military Law and Administration*, Cambridge (Mass.) 1955. No. 3. It is important to notice that this statute still forms the basis for the present day definition of functions of the Soviet armed forces and their administration.

4. Berman and Kerner, *op. cit.* (monograph), p. 26.

5. The incident is related in A. Barmine, *op. cit.*, p. 220.

6. *Ibid.*, p. 219.

7. See the budgetary table in *League of Nations Armaments Handbook*, Vol. 14, 1938, p. 848. These figures agree substantially with those presented in other sources.

8. See figures in N. F. Kuz'min, *op. cit.*, p. 185.

9. Presented in composition table, *League of Nations Armaments Handbook*, Vol. 14, 1938, p. 844.

10. K. E. Voroshilov, *Stat'i i rechi* (Writings and speeches), Moscow 1937, p. 576.

11. *Ibid.*, p. 573 and p. 575.

12. See *League of Nations Armaments Handbook*, Vol. 14, p. 845.

13. Cf. L. Schapiro, *op. cit.*, (Mimeograph), pp. 10–11.

14. The instruction is printed in M. Fainsod, *Smolensk under Soviet rule*, *op. cit.*, pp. 329–30.

15. *KPSS v rez.* (Party resolutions), *op. cit.*, Vol. II, p. 785.

16. See Fedotoff White in *Political Science Quarterly*, *op. cit.*, p. 348.

17. See further in M. Fainsod, *How Russia is ruled*, *op. cit.*, p. 365.

18. I. F. Pobezhimov, *op. cit.*, p. 100. The phrases are his.

19. W. G. Krivitsky, *op. cit.*, p. 181. In spite of the sensationalism of Krivitsky's title and the style of presentation as a whole, it is generally agreed that Krivitsky's disclosures are substantially accurate. While many of Krivitsky's points can be checked indirectly or have received subsequent confirmation, the case of Primakov defies both of these verifications. To my knowledge, no similar disclosure has been made in any other source; there would appear to be no valid reason for rejecting Krivitsky's version, but the full circumstances and the timing remain largely obscure.

20. The murder of Kirov has aroused much speculation and its circumstances remain, to say the least, suspicious and smack of peculiar contrivance. See N. S. Khrushchev 'secret speech' (1956), *Manchester Guardian* text: United States Department of State version, p. 12.

21. The phrases and description as in Khrushchev speech, p. 10.

22. *DGFP*, Series C, Vol. 2, p. 319. See pp. 318–32 for the whole: 'Political Report. Subject: The shaping of German-Russian relations.' Secret A90/Moscow, 9th January, 1934.

23. *Ibid.*, p. 352, report dated 13th January, 1934.

24. *Ibid.*, p. 332, report 11th January.

25. *Ibid.*, p. 333. Reference also A90, 9th January. Radek began by saying: 'Do not believe that something has already been decided.'

26. *Ibid.*, p. 334.

27. Cf. *XVII Konf. VKP(b). Stenograf. Otchot.* (17th Congress Russian Communist Party. Stenographic report) Moscow 1934: Voroshilov, pp. 224–36, Blyukher, pp. 629–31, Tukhachevsky, pp. 464–6.

28. W. G. Krivitsky, *op. cit.*, pp. 17–19. While again it is possible to admit Krivitsky's account and his recollection of Berzin, there is no basis for admitting Krivitsky's assumptions or his wider interpretations.

29. See Z. J. Gasiorowski, 'The German-Polish Nonaggression Pact of 1934' in *Journal of Central European Affairs*, April 1955: pp. 26–7.

30. See *The Soviet Union 1935*. Co-operative publishing society of foreign workers in the USSR, Moscow-Leningrad 1935. M. N. Tukhachevsky on national defence: pp. 211–25.

31. *Ibid.*, p. 223.

32. *Ibid.*

33. This was given outside confirmation by a German report: *Die militärpolitische Lage der UdSSR* for 19th November, 1934, and 14th January, 1935.

34. Cf. A. Barmine, *op. cit.*, p. 179.

35. See the important passages in *How Russia Makes War*, *op. cit.*, p. 344. Also *BSE* (1), Vol. 12, 1928, A. Lapchinskii, 'Vozdushnyi boi' (Aerial combat) and 'Vozdushnaya oborona' (Aerial defence), Cols. 455–7 and 436–9. Also A. Shiyukov, *ibid.*, 'Vozdushnyi flot' (The air fleet), Cols. 460–3.

36. See the study in Military Attaché (Moscow-Kovno) Serial 5892H/E432900–2, on Lapchinskii and his work (the 1932 volume rendered into German as *Luftstreitkämpfe im Gefecht und in der Operationen*). Criticises part of Lapchinskii's work for its typical Soviet 'schematising'. It has not proved possible to trace the Soviet original in any accessible collection.

37. *Ibid.*

38. Quoted in M. Werner, *op. cit.*, pp. 86–7.

39. *Soviet Documents on Foreign Policy 1917–1941* (ed. Jane Degras), Vol. 3, pp. 124–6 has a part of the text.

40. A translation into German and full analysis of the Tukhachevsky article, with the German comments, is to be found in Serial 5892H/E433022–32.

41. *Ibid.*, report 12/35, 5th April. For the protest to Litvinov and Gekker, frames E433035 f.

42. See G. Castellan in *Relations Germano-Soviétiques*, *op. cit.*, pp. 254–5.

43. M. Beloff, *op. cit.*, p. 140.

44. For texts see *Documents on International Affairs* (ed. J. W. Wheeler-Bennet), Vol. 1 for 1935 (Pub. R.I.I.A. 1936), p. 253 f.

45. See *Sov. Doc. on For. Pol.*, Vol. 3, pp. 96–7.

46. M. Beloff, *op. cit.*, p. 149.

47. *Sov. Doc. on For. Pol.*, pp. 119–21.

48. *The Polish White Book*, *op. cit.*, p. 26.

49. *Ibid.* Cf. *Les Frontières Européennes de L'U.R.S.S. 1917–1941* (ed. J-B.. Duroselle), Paris 1957; study by B. Goriely, 'L'Union soviétique et la Pologne', pp. 243–5 on Beck's reaction to these overtures.

50. See Military Attaché (Moscow-Kovno) 5892H/E432986–988 on Franco-Soviet military collaboration. Report dated 11th February, 1935.

51. *Sov. Doc. on For. Pol.*, Vol. 3, p. 129. Original from *Pravda*, 29th April, 1935.

52. See M. Beloff, *op. cit.*, pp. 152–4 for a discussion of the implications of the wording of the articles of the Pact.

53. L. Trotsky, *The Revolution Betrayed*, *op. cit.*, p. 205.

54. See analysis in Serial 5892H/E432991–3001, Report 9/35 dated 11th March. The German Military Attaché subjected Gekker to quite a thorough questioning over the significance of these changes. It is by no means an implausible interpretation that a 'pro-French nucleus' was being brought into the foreground.

55. The full text will be found in M. Fainsod, *Smolensk under Soviet Rule*, *op. cit.*, p. 333.

56. *Ibid.*, p. 334.

57. Based on (i) German study, *Potentiel de guerre* (signed by von Stülpnagel) (ii) *League of Nations Armaments Handbook* and (iii) J. M. Mackintosh in *The Soviet Army*, *op. cit.*, p. 61. On Red Army chemical weapons and organisation, see Colonel V. Pozdnyakov, in *The Soviet Army*, pp. 384–5.

58. The first figure is that accepted by German Intelligence. The second was supplied by Guderian in 1935, and repeated in the 2nd (1938) Edn., of his *Die Panzertruppen und ihr Zusammenwirken mit den anderen Waffen*, p. 16.

59. The phrase is M. Fainsod's, in *How Russia is Ruled*, p. 367.

60. Cf. I. F. Pobezhimov, *op. cit.*, p. 98.

61. See *O vvedenii personal'nikh voennikh zvanii nachal'stvuyushchevo sostava RKKA i ob utverzhdenii polozheniya o prokhozhdenii sluzhby komandnym i nachal'stvuyushchevim sostavom RKKA* (On the introduction of personal military ranks of the Red Army command staff and on the confirmation of the position of the length of service of the Red Army command staff), 22nd September, 1935, SNK, TsIK, Moscow (OIZ. NKO), 22 pp.

62. See Serial 5892H/E433107–9, Report 132/35, dated 24th November, 1935. According to this German source, a formal naval command rank system had been secretly in use for some time before its announcement.

63. See L. Schapiro, *op. cit.* (Mimeograph), p. 14.

64. See Paul Reynaud, *Au cœur de la mêlée 1930–1945*, *op. cit.*, p. 78.

65. *Ibid.*

66. *Ibid.*, p. 76.

67. Cf. M. Werner, *op. cit.*, pp. 89–90. Also Paul Reynaud, p. 87: General Loiseau's report was reproduced in *Le Temps*, 20th September, 1935.

68. See Serial 1909H/429959. Dated 26th October.

69. See Serial 5892H/E433081.

70. Cf. Paul Reynaud, *op. cit.*, p. 83, quoting Colonel Fabry.

71. *Ibid.*, p. 83.

72. *Ibid.*, p. 89.

73. Cf. Leon Noël, *L'Agression allemande contre la Pologne*, Paris 1946, pp. 88–9, also p. 119.

74. *DGFP*, Series C, Vol. 3; see Memorandum by official of Department IV, 2nd March, 1935, p. 975.

75. W. G. Krivitsky, *op. cit.*, p. 31.

76. Recounted in A. Svetlanin, *op. cit.*, p. 39.

77. *Ibid.*, p. 93. While this account cannot be relied upon for its political information and interpretation, it has been possible to check the military and biographic details contained in it, and these are substantially correct.

78. *Sov. Doc. on For. Pol.*,Vol. 3, p. 121.

79. Cf. J. M. Mackintosh, 'The Soviet Army in the Far East 1922–1955' in *The Soviet Army, op. cit.*, p. 173.

80. See KŌGUN, *op. cit.*, p. 8 for tables.

81. *Ibid.*

82. See M. Beloff, *op. cit.*, Appendix D, pp. 236–7, on Russia and Sinkiang.

83. A. Svetlanin, *op. cit.*, p. 72.

84. See M. I. Gubel'man, *op. cit.*, p. 250. Cf. Note 23, p. 195, in KŌGUN on Japanese political sabotage and the use of White Russians, Koreans and emigré Polish officers (and later a senior officer of the *NKVD*, Colonel Lyushkov, who deserted to the Japanese).

85. Cf. *Sov. Docs. on For. Pol.*, Vol. 3, p. 147. Also *Documents on International Affairs*, Vol. 1, 1935, pp. 226–7, Molotov's speech of 11th January, 1936, which referred to the incidents in October 1935.

86. See Naval Attaché (Moscow) report 1st December, 1935, in Serial 5892H/E433115.

87. See Appendix B in M. Beloff, *op. cit.* Cf. Walter Pahl, *Wetterzonen der Weltpolitik*, Leipzig 1937, p. 185 f. See p. 195, 'Wachstum der Städte im Osten (1926–1933).'

88. The phrase is from KŌGUN, *loc. cit.*

89. See Edgar Snow, *Red Star Over China*, London 1937, *passim.*

90. Cf. Namoru Shigemitsu, *op. cit.*, p. 94, '. . . it was only a matter of time before it (Soviet Russia) joined forces with Chinese troops to menace Manchukuo.'

91. The view that the Chinese Communist move into Northern China played little or no part in the strategic calculations of the Soviet command is supported in Charles B. McLane, *Soviet Policy and the Chinese Communists 1931–1946*, Columbia 1958, pp. 45–7, on the strategic aspects of the Chinese Communist movement as viewed from the Soviet Union.

92. Cf. M. Beloff, *op. cit.*, p. 176.

93. General Gamelin, *Servir*, *op. cit.*, Vol. 2, p. 180. This private note, recorded at 6 a.m., on 22nd November, 1935, reports Laval as having said of the terms of the Pact, '. . . J'en ai extrait le plus dangereux (?) Mais, tout de même, je méfie d'eux.'

94. Lieutenant-General Sir Giffard Martel, *The Russian Outlook*, London 1947, p. 24. As Colonel Martel, the author met Yegorov in 1936. Cf. German Military Attaché (Serial 5892H/E433081, dated 11th November, 1935) on Yegorov — '. . . in politische Ausserungen immer feige gewesen.'

95. See further in Z. K. Brzezinski, *The Permanent Purge. Politics in Soviet Totalitarianism*, Harvard U.P. 1956, p. 61 f.

96. While Krivitsky's evidence is largely circumstantial and second-hand, there is sufficient material in the captured German documents to qualify the statement in I. Deutscher, *Stalin*, p. 420, that in 1935–7 Stalin 'was genuinely striving for an anti-Hitler coalition'. This point will be more fully examined in the following chapters.

97. L. Trotsky, *The Revolution Betrayed*, *op. cit.*, p. 197.

98. There is an excellent survey of this question in Serial 5892H/E433146 f. under *Die Sowjetrussische Marine an der Jahreswende 1935/36*, compiled by the German Naval Attaché. Much of the report is taken up with an examination of Soviet war potential.

99. The conclusion to *ibid.*

Chapter XIII

1. W. G. Krivitsky, *op. cit.*, p. 142. Tairov was, according to Krivitsky, one of Stalin's adherents during the Tsaritsyn days.

2. See Serial 5892H/E433177, dated 27th January, 1936, on Tukhachevsky's views. For Tukhachevsky's speech, see *The Soviet Union and the Path to Peace 1917–1936*, London 1936, Tukhachevsky to the 2nd Session of the Central Executive Committee of the USSR, 15th January, 1936, pp. 46–56. Apart from its rather wild estimates of German power, the speech is noteworthy for its insistence that the most potent modern weapon has become aviation, and by implication the heavy bomber.

3. See a German study, *Der neue Plan für Krieg, Mobilmachung und Aufmarsch* (*Abwehr/Ost* 684/4.36 *Abw.*), on progress in Soviet mobilisation. While containing some interesting remarks, this and other studies in the same series are markedly inferior to the type of report previously quoted, that compiled by the German Naval Attaché, which is a model of careful compilation and close reasoning.

4. Quoted in M. Werner, *op. cit.*, p. 266, which cites a Soviet estimate in *Voina i Revolyutsiya* (March–April, 1933).

5. Cf. Artur Just, *The Red Army*, *op. cit.*, p. 46, on the deficiencies of the Soviet technical cadres. Werner, p. 270, quotes Soviet sources to show the size of the trained reserves, including 3·3 million men trained as mechanics.

6. Cf. M. Berchin and E. Ben-Horin, *The Red Army*, *op. cit.*, p. 204. (In an interview with a former Red Army officer who worked on these defence constructions in 1935, it became apparent that the term 'line' or 'Stalin line' was something of a misnomer.)

7. See the discussion on positional warfare in R. L. Garthoff, *How Russia Makes War*, p. 92.

8. Cf. I. S. Prochko, *Artilleriya v boyakh za Rodinu*, *op. cit.*, pp. 127–30.

9. N. F. Kuz'min, *op. cit.*, p. 153.

10. *How Russia Makes War*, p. 345.

11. Berchin and Ben-Horin, *op. cit.*, p. 74.

12. See *Biographic Directory of the USSR*, New York, pp. 111–12.

13. See Naval Attaché report, 5892H/E433146 f. In matters of ship and engine construction, there could be no denying Soviet progress. Generally speaking, Soviet naval officers gave the impression of being well-trained and competent.

14. See Appendix III.

15. Reported in *The Soviet Navy* (ed. Commander M. G. Saunders R.N.), *op. cit.*, p. 96. I am grateful to Colonel Kowalewski for giving me the opportunity to discuss with him the political and military ideas of the Soviet command and to take advantage of his first-hand contacts with Soviet military and naval personalities.

16. See under *Budenny*, in *Biographic Directory*.

17. See M. Werner, *op. cit.*, p. 246. Writing in 1935, Khalepskii was citing the British view that tanks could carry out independent operations without infantry support. In 1934 the British were complimented on having 'the most progressive' views on motorisation in '. . . the military literature of any capitalist country'.

18. Translated as *Tankovaya voina* (Tank warfare) (trans. E. Veinraub, intro. K. Stepnii), 10,000 copies. At the same time K. Stepnii edited A. Gromychenko's, *Ocherki taktiki tankovykh chastei* (Outline of tactics of tank units), a Soviet text-book, 20,000 of which were printed.

19. *The Polish White Book*, p. 37.

20. See G. Castellan in *Les Relations Germano-Soviétiques*, pp. 217–18, using evidence from the IMT interrogation of General Köstring.

21. *Ibid.*, p. 224.

22. *Ibid.*

23. General Gamelin, *Servir*, Vol. 2, p. 196.

24. *Ibid.*

25. G. Tabouis, '*Ils m'ont appelée Cassandre*', pp. 248–9.

26. See K. H. Abshagen, *Canaris* (tr. A. H. Brodrick), London 1956, pp. 116–17 (and translator's note). The German edition, Stuttgart 1949, p. 168, has the remark that Canaris knew Tukhachevsky '. . . keineswegs völlig unschuldig erschossen wurde'. This, to say the least, is highly ambiguous.

27. The Blimiel-Niekisch story is related in Ian Colvin, *Chief of Intelligence*, London 1951, pp. 39–40. Niekisch's existence is in no doubt, for Heydrich arrested him in 1937, but the Blimiel story is another matter, and the whole incident without any other circumstantial confirmation whatsoever.

28. See *Survey* (1936), p. 933.

29. Printed in *Sov. Doc. on For. Pol.*, Vol. 3, pp. 164–8.

30. *Ibid.*, p. 165.

31. See *ibid.*, p. 186.

32. A. Barmine, *op. cit.*, p. 226.

33. This view is supported in M. Beloff, *op. cit.*, Vol. 2, p. 50.

34. See *Sov. Doc. on For. Pol.*, Vol. 3, pp. 173–4.

35. *Ibid.*, p. 179.

36. *Ibid.*, p. 184. The italics are mine.

37. See Serial 393/212171–172, Pol. V report, dated 18th May.

38. Account in *The Baltic States. Estonia, Latvia and Lithuania* (Information Dept. R.I.I.A.), O.U.P. 1938, p. 87 f.

39. See *Survey* (1936), p. 536.

40. Reported by Stuart R. Schram in *Les Frontières Européennes . . .*, *op. cit.*, p. 107. The source is the *Stockholms Tidningen*, Estonian edition, 12th December, 1954. Some doubt has been thrown on the reliability of the latter part of this report; there seems to be less reason to call the first part into question.

41. *Ibid.*

42. Von Stülpnagel report (with document). *Generalstab d. Heeres* 918/36 geh. 3 Abt. V, dated 8th August.

43. Cf. R. L. Buell, *Poland. Key to Europe*, *op. cit.*, p. 314.

44. *Survey* (1936), p. 485.

45. *Ibid.*, p. 113.

46. *Ibid.*, p. 617.

47. *Ibid.*, p. 639.

48. See Serial 5892H/E433260, 27th April, Report No. 12/36 on the Cossacks. The 4th, 6th, 10th and 12th Red Army cavalry divisions were to carry the traditional Cossack names. In addition, the 13th Cavalry Division would be raised as the Don Cossack Division.

49. See L. Schapiro, *op. cit.* (Mimeograph), p. 13.

50. See *Survey* (1936), p. 147.

51. M. Fainsod, *Smolensk under Soviet rule*, *op. cit.*, p. 233.

52. *Ibid.*, pp. 233–7, for samples of denunciations.

53. W. G. Krivitsky, *op. cit.*, p. 224, for an account of the interrogation of Mrachkovskii.

54. Recounted in A. Barmine, *op. cit.*, p. 90. The threat was to 'lop off Stalin's ears'.

55. German Military Attaché report, 4th September, 1936. Noted the connection of Putna and Schmidt with Mrachkovskii. Schmidt was a cavalry brigade commander in the Ukraine.

56. See L. Schapiro, *The Communist Party of the Soviet Union*, London 1959, p. 409.

57. 'Balticus', 'The Russian Mystery: Behind the Tukhachevsky Plot' in *Foreign Affairs*, October 1937, note to p. 47.

58. L. Schapiro, *The Communist Party of the Soviet Union*, p. 409.

59. This version is supplied by A. Uralov, *The Reign of Stalin*, London 1953, Ch. IV, pp. 41–7 under 'The Central Committee repudiates Stalin'. The author was a former member of the Communist Party of some considerable standing, but absolute confirmation of this account is lacking.

60. The text is in N. S. Khrushchev, *Secret speech* (text cited), p. 12.

61. See Serial 6487/E486016–120: Report A/2037, 28th September.

62. Details in N. S. Khrushchev, *loc. cit.*, p. 15.

63. F. O. Miksche, *Blitzkrieg*, London, 1941, p. 42.

64. Franz Borkenau, *European Communism*, London 1953, p. 166 f.

65. This is the argument suggested *ibid.* A somewhat different interpretation will be found in I. Deutscher, *Stalin*, p. 424 f. Of the two, the former seems to fit more closely to the instructions which Krivitsky received and the orders he had to carry out.

66. *Sov. Doc. on For. Pol.*, Vol. 3, p. 203.

67. W. G. Krivitsky, *op. cit.*, p. 98. Krivitsky dates this as 28th August. As for the reliability of Krivitsky as a witness here, Franz Borkenau confirms this testimony through the first-hand experience gathered by him in Spain.

68. W. G. Krivitsky, p. 100.

69. *Ibid.*, p. 115.

70. *Ibid.*, pp. 99–100. See note in F. Borkenau, pp. 168–9 on the significance of the phrase.

71. W. G. Krivitsky, p. 116.

72. F. Borkenau, p. 171.

73. *Ibid.*, p. 171.

74. W. G. Krivitsky, p. 114.

75. On the *NKVD* in Spain, see F. Borkenau, p. 174.

76. Robert Coulondre, *De Staline à Hitler Souvenirs de deux Ambassades 1936–1939*, Paris 1950, p. 21.

77. *Ibid.*, p. 35.

78. W. G. Krivitsky, pp. 34–6, on the operation of Soviet Intelligence to obtain information on the Japanese-German negotiations. Litvinov did make reference to the Soviet Union having knowledge of the secret negotiations: *Sov. Doc. on For. Pol.*, Vol. 3, p. 224, speech at the 8th Congress of Soviets, 28th November, 1936.

79. Krivitsky has made reference to the Kandelaki mission (a point which G. Castellan suspected as being without foundation). The details of the Kandelaki mission are to be found in Serial 1907H/429293 f. On 6th February, 1937, Schacht sent to Neurath a deposition about the dealings which he had had with Kandelaki (429298–9), in which it is clear that Kandelaki had begun his work in December 1936.

80. *Ibid.*

81. Winston S. Churchill, *The Second World War*, Vol. 1, 'The Gathering Storm', London 1948, p. 224.

82. See Paul Reynaud, *op. cit.*, p. 97, quoting from Léon Blum's testimony of 18th June, 1947, at the *Commission d'enquête sur les évènements survenus en France 1933–1940*.

83. On Heydrich and the SD, see Gerald Reitlinger, *The SS Alibi of a Nation*, London 1956, pp. 93–5, and sketching some of the background to the SD interest in the *Reichswehr* officers who had worked with the Red Army.

84. Walter Schellenberg, *The Schellenberg Memoirs* (intro. Alan Bullock), London 1956, Chapter Three, 'The Reichswehr and the Red Army'. Not the most reliable of witnesses, there are nevertheless some points of Schellenberg's account which require notice. The first is the mention of Skoblin, and the second the suspicion that Skoblin might be a Soviet agent.

85. *Ibid.*, p. 47. Cf. W. Hagen, *Die Geheime Front*, Nibelungen-Verlag 1950: 'Heydrichs grösster Coup: er liefert Stalin das Material gegen Marschall Tuchatschewski', pp. 54–68. See English version, W. Hoettl (Hagen), *The Secret Front*, London 1953, pp. 79–91. This places Heydrich's contact with Russian emigrés in Paris at 1935 and names Skoblin as a 'double'. Heydrich wished to act against the dangerous tendency of the 'traditional leaning' of the German high command for an alliance with the East; hence he must show that 'military collaboration' was in reality treason. Heydrich's use of the Tukhachevsky affair indicated that he wished to act through Moscow rather than proceed *directly* against a German general.

86. Schellenberg, p. 47. Also Hoettl, p. 82–3.

87. It has proved possible to make certain private enquiries into the German side of the operation, the main object being to ascertain (i) when the intrigue against Tukhachevsky definitely began and (ii) how the material was delivered to the Russians, and at what date. Such an enquiry (much facilitated by a grant from St Antony's College, Oxford, to work in Germany) produced evidence of the SD participation, but failed to have individuals provide accurate information on dates (partly

accounted for by the nature of this operation, where it was difficult to distinguish 'preparation' from 'action').

88. Schellenberg, p. 48.

89. K. H. Abshagen, *op. cit.*, p. 116. Peter Kleist, *Zwischen Hitler und Stalin*, Bonn 1950, p. 213, reports the Canaris-Heydrich contact, but without proof. The story of the actual forging tends to dispose of this also.

90. Himmler, speech at Posen, 4th October, 1943. IMT (Nuremberg), Vol. XXIX, Doc. 1919–PS.

91. W. G. Krivitsky, *op. cit.*, p. 237.

92. *Ibid.*, p. 259. See also G. Castellan, *loc. cit.*, p. 252 on emigré circles.

93. The footnote to Winston S. Churchill, *op. cit.*, Vol. 1, does not dismiss the idea of *NKVD* penetration of Czech Intelligence for its own ulterior purposes.

94. In his memoirs, Beneš has a somewhat different version, suggesting that he heard of the illicit contacts through a slip made by Trautmannsdorff, who was taking part in the negotiations pursued by Berlin with Beneš. See *The Memoirs of Dr Eduard Beneš*, London 1954, note to p. 47. Beneš passed on this information to Aleksandrovskii, Soviet Ambassador in Prague for transmission to Stalin. On Trauttmannsdorff and the Prague negotiations, see Gerhard L. Weinberg, 'Secret Hitler-Beneš negotiations in 1936–1937' in *Journal of Central European Affairs* January 1960, p. 372 esp. Haushofer and Trauttmannsdorff were received by Beneš on 18th December, 1936 and Trauttmannsdorff returned to Prague on 3rd–4th January, 1937. These would appear to be two likely dates, fitting both versions of where Beneš obtained his information.

95. General Schweissguth led the French delegation. Léon Blum had some difficulty in obtaining his report, which tended to refute what General Loiseau had reported in 1935. The French general, even then, reported that he believed the Russian intention to be to deflect a storm directed at the east upon the west; the Soviet aim was to play the role of the United States of America in 1918, the role of arbiter of European destinies: quoted in I. Deutscher, *Stalin*, p. 420 from Georges Bonnet.

96. Lieutenant-General Sir Giffard Martel, *The Russian Outlook*, *op. cit.*, p. 21.

97. *Ibid.*, pp. 23–4.

98. *Ibid.*, pp. 24–6. Voroshilov did not impress by virtue of the knowledge of warfare he had gained in the Civil War.

99. *Vremennyi Polevoi Ustav RKKA 1936* (*PU 36*) (Provisional Field Service Regulations of the Red Army), Para. 7, p. 11. See also Appendix III.

100. *Ibid.*, Para. 7, pp. 13–14. Emphasis as in the original.

101. *Ibid. Shturmovaya aviatsiya* has been translated as 'low-flying ground attack-aviation/aircraft'.

102. *Ibid.*, Para. 9, p. 16.

103. *Ibid.*, Ch. 2, p. 21 f. A certain difficulty is met with the word *Razvedka*, which means both 'reconnaissance' and 'intelligence'. Corps aviation would carry out aerial reconnaissance of the line of the front (at a height of up to 500 metres); one aircraft of corps aviation squadrons should be able to carry out observation of battle-field in an area 10 × 12 kilometres; deep reconnaissance up to 100 kilometres, at a height of not less than 1,500 metres. Mechanised unities would employ recon-

naisance patrols (2–3 machines), up to 2 kilometres in advance of the main force. Directly behind the patrols would be a tank used as a mobile observation post. The brigade would employ a reconnaissance company (special tanks, motorised infantry, observation aircraft), operating 25–35 kilometres in advance of the main body. The nucleus of the company would travel at an average speed of 10–15 kilometres per hour.

104. *Ibid.*, Ch. 5, 'Principles of conducting combat', p. 62.

105. *Ibid.*, p. 66. How this worked in practice was to be seen in the operations in Outer Mongolia in 1939.

106. *Ibid.*, Ch. 6, 'The meeting engagement', p. 85.

107. *Ibid.*, Ch. 7, 'Offensive combat', p. 96.

108. *Ibid.*, pp. 104–7 (Para. 180 f.).

109. *Ibid.*, pp. 111–13.

110. *Ibid.*, Ch. 8, 'Defence', p. 133. See Appendix III.

111. *Ibid.*, Para. 248, p. 149.

112. *Ibid.*, pp. 145–6 on *kontrpodgotovka*. The *kontrpodgotovka* (counter-preparation) is a combination of offensive-defensive blows, designed to upset enemy preparations for an offensive and fully embodying the idea of 'active defence' and ensuring some retention of the initiative. Used on a large scale, the practice of having one formation at battle readiness in defensive positions and a second echeloned formation ready to go over to the immediate attack to disrupt enemy offensive preparations (the attack begun when the *Stavka* supervisor estimated that such an attack was imminent) was developed in 1943 after the Kursk operations.

113. *Ibid.*, pp. 134–5.

114. *Ibid.*, pp. 153–4.

115. R. L. Garthoff, *How Russia Makes War*, p. 107 (and note) has an interesting and important note on the relation of envelopment and encirclement in Soviet offensive manœuvre, making the very significant point that the idea of encirclement was not 'borrowed' by the Russians from the Germans after 1941. Dr Garthoff equates Tukhachevsky's term 'concentric manœuvre' with the notion of double envelopment. This is valuable corrective to many statements seeking an explanation of the forms of Soviet offensive manœuvre merely as a reaction to the success of German methods in 1941. The point is further enlarged in G. Castellan, *Relations Germano-Soviétiques*, p. 213, citing *2e Bureau* studies. It was from that 1934, according to this source, that the 'enveloping manœuvre' had come to occupy a place of primary importance. In March 1935 a *2e Bureau* report was citing the views of Savinov in *Voina i Revolyutsiya* (July 1934) to the effect that the enveloping manœuvre was of outstanding importance, that it lay well within the technical capacity of Soviet arms and that it could be employed in all its amplitude in all theatres. Castellan connects both the Blitzkrieg and Stalingrad (1942) with this idea — the latter correctly, but the former incorrectly. In 1936, Sergeyev and Novoslobodskii both disclaimed undue reliance on surprise and mobility — 'No, suddenness alone will certainly not suffice to determine the result of the preliminary operations' (Sergeyev). '. . . the hopes of those military experts who believe that a future war can be won by a lightning blow . . . are vain' (Novoslobodskii). Cited in M. Werner, *op. cit.*, p. 164.

116. The phrase is L. Schapiro's, *The Communist Party of the Soviet Union, op. cit.*, p. 412. There is certainly a sufficiency of circumstantial evidence to support this view; the military purge is a case in point, and in addition to his secret security apparatus, Stalin also appeared to operate his private diplomatic organisation — seen in action in 1936–7 and again in 1939.

117. See *Survey*, 1936, p. 157.

118. G. Castellan, *loc. cit.*, p. 225.

Chapter XIV

1. See *Report of Court Proceedings in the Case of the Anti-Soviet Trotskyite Centre* (Hearings of 23rd–30th January, 1937), Moscow 1937, p. 146. Z. K. Brzezhinski, *op. cit.*, p. 73, quotes Souvarine's explanation that Radek escaped death by 'convenient disclosures' implicating the Red Army leaders. See Note 23, p. 405, of N. Leites and E. Bernault, *Ritual of Liquidation. The Case of the Moscow Trials*, The Free Press, Ill., 1954, for information indicating that Radek had come round to the idea of full co-operation with the *NKVD* by 5th January, but that his being spared from death was part of a much wider 'agreement', in which Stalin had an eye to the persuasion of European opinion.

2. See Serial 7500H/E540792 f., *Militärangelegenheiten Russland*, dated 7th June, 1937, the file containing only this entry under 'Personalveränderungen in der Leitung der Roten Armee', Tgb. Nr. A/1164. Cf. G. Castellan, *loc. cit.*, p. 225, on the appointments of Alksnis and Orlov.

3. Both Putna and Primakov present very real mysteries. Putna was evidently an exceedingly able officer. The reference to Primakov-Germanovich will be found in Serial 7500H/E540794–795: *Izvestiya* for 5th June reported the expulsion of three 'enemies of the people' including Primakov from the Executive Committee of the Leningrad Soviet. The German report tends to support the opinion that Primakov had been under arrest for some time.

4. See Serial 1702. This information came from the German Ambassador in Afghanistan and was received from the Japanese Military Attaché Major Miyasaki. It is interesting to compare this with information supplied by General Niessel, 'L'U.R.S.S. en Extrême-Orient' in *Revue des Deux Mondes*, Feb. 1937, pp. 567–76. General Niessel gives the figure of 800 tanks and 100 heavy bombers. While giving a somewhat pessimistic estimate of Soviet chances in the Far East, General Niessel was assured that the Japanese would be drawn off from Indo-China.

5. See *Radek Ausweisungen*, Serial 3530H/E021915 f. Radek had mentioned 'a general', and as Köstring was the only foreign general in Moscow, the inference was plain. In addition to Köstring's denials, this serial also has the protest about dragging in Press Attaché Baum.

6. G. Castellan, *loc. cit.*, p. 242, taken from General Köstring's *IMT* evidence.

7. W. G. Krivitsky, *op. cit.*, p. 122.

8. *Ibid.*, p. 124. Orlov was the alias assumed by the *NKVD* chief in Spain.

9. Stalin's March speeches are reproduced in *The Moscow Trial (January 1937) and*

two speeches by Joseph Stalin (compiled by W. P. and Z. K. Coates), Anglo-Russian Parliamentary Committee 1937.

10. W. G. Krivitsky, *op. cit.*, p. 227. Krivitsky has got the date wrong, but it is 1937 and vilifications of Bukharin to which he is undoubtedly referring.

11. Cf. L. Schapiro, *The Communist Party of the Soviet Union, op. cit.*, p. 424. N. S. Khrushchev in his 1956 speech (text cited, p. 13) refers to 'many members' questioning the rightness of the terror, and singles out Postyshev as one who 'most ably' expressed these doubts.

12. Serial 1907H/429299–300.

13. *Ibid.*, 429296–7.

13. *Ibid.*, 429296.

14. Gamelin, *Servir, op. cit.*, Vol. 2, p. 285.

15. *Ibid.*, pp. 286–7.

16. Ordzhonikidze was reported at the time to have been the victim of a heart-attack. See here Khrushchev speech, p. 27.

17. Joseph E. Davies, *Mission to Moscow*, London 1943, pp. 95–6. W. Görlitz, *The German General Staff, op. cit.*, p. 308, mentions that 'in the spring of 1937' Tukhachevsky visited Prague to discuss military co-operation with the Czech government. It is impossible to find any confirmation of this statement, least of all for the next assertion that Tukhachevsky returned via Berlin, having passed on the substance of the conversations to German Intelligence. Beneš was 'profoundly shocked'. This seems an altogether improbable explanation of Tukhachevsky's disappearance from the public scene.

18. W. G. Krivitsky, *op. cit.*, p. 167.

19. *Ibid.*, p. 169.

20. *Ibid.*, p. 166. This would seem to be a very plausible explanation of the *NKVD* re-organisation.

21. See F. O. Miksche, *op. cit.*, p. 36. For this point on mechanised columns in Spain (the evaluation of which was to have a subsequent effect on Red Army organisation), see G. R. Johnston, 'Mechanised columns in Spain', *The Army Quarterly*, Vol. XXXIV, 1937, No. 2, pp. 323–37.

22. W. G. Krivitsky, *op. cit.*, p. 126.

23. Gerald Reitlinger, *op. cit.*, p. 94. Cf. Gordon A. Craig, *op. cit.*, p. 489 f. on the Himmler-Heydrich intrigue against the German Army and its culmination in the Fritsch affair, which misfired.

24. W. Hoettl, *op. cit.*, p. 84.

25. W. Schellenberg, *op. cit.*, p. 48. It certainly took longer than four days to prepare the dossier.

26. W. Hoettl, *op. cit.*, p. 83. It has been possible to confirm this from a private source who was also implicated.

27. *Ibid.*, p. 85. It is here that Schellenberg's version falls apart, and seems to be a mixture of two versions. There appeared to have been no 3 million roubles involved.

28. This piece of Schellenberg information (p. 49) appears to be quite plausible.

29. W. G. Krivitsky, *op. cit.*, p. 253. It is to be noted (i) that Frinovskii volunteered

no information about the source and (ii) Krivitsky never mentions and presumably was ignorant of the SD intervention.

30. Serial 7500H/E540797.

31. *Ibid.*, E540798. This would confirm the earlier German report on the disappearance of this officer.

32. *Ibid.*, E540797.

33. W. G. Krivitsky, *op. cit.*, p. 249. Krivitsky makes a too direct connection between the Kandelaki mission and the military purge, although the two were not unrelated.

34. *Ibid.*, pp. 250–1.

35. See *How Russia Makes War*, *op. cit.*, pp. 84–5 and Berchin and Ben-Horin, *The Red Army*, *op. cit.*, p. 132. The view which Tukhachevsky was putting forward did not at all conflict with his opinions expressed in 1930 during the debate on the Red Army.

36. See Serial 6490H/E486072 in Report No. A/1002, 15th May, 'Veränderungen in der Roten Armee' (German Embassy, Moscow).

37. Cf. G. Castellan, *loc. cit.*, p. 226.

38. Serial 7500H/E540796.

39. W. G. Krivitsky, *op. cit.*, p. 219.

40. Serial 7500H/E540798.

41. *Ibid.*, E540795.

42. The version of Gamarnik's 'suicide' has too many disclaimers for it to be taken seriously. Krivitsky (p. 254) speaks of Stalin's attempts to induce Gamarnik to assist in the destruction of Tukhachevsky, and that these failed. Gamarnik was first denounced, and then most clumsily 'tacked on' to the list of condemned officers. The real effort to obliterate Gamarnik politically came only subsequently, in the Bukharin-Rykov trial of 1938.

43. There is a close examination of the verbal announcements and the reports for June 1937 in G. Castellan, *loc. cit.*, p. 225 f. Castellan cites here an Order of the Day, No. 96 for 12th June, 1937, printed in *Morskoi Sbornik*, No. 7, July, pp. 3–5.

44. Cf. Cyrille Kalinov, *Les Maréchaux soviétiques vous parlent . . .*, Paris 1950, p. 73. While Kalinov is a witness of questionable reliability, his explanation of the origins of undeniable confidence in Shaposhnikov could quite well be true.

45. G. Castellan, *loc. cit.*, p. 227.

46. Both the confession and the question of the guilt of the Soviet officers have produced a wide diversity of views. L. Schapiro, in his valuable chapter on the military purge, in *The Soviet Army*, *op. cit.*, p. 68 f. has an interesting comment taken from a senior Soviet officer who later joined the Vlasov Movement. According to this account, the officer had a conversation with one of the military members of the supposed tribunal, the latter commenting that in effect '. . . the *documentary* evidence produced . . . was overwhelming and convincing'. It is a very likely explanation that this emigré officer heard an account of the 1st–4th June meeting of senior Red Army commanders, where there is much to suggest that this documentary evidence was produced.

47. W. G. Krivitsky, *op. cit.*, p. 255. There are two observations to be made on

this point: (i) an article signed by Alksnis on the *VVS* appeared in *Krasnaya Zvezda* on 14th August, 1937 (which proves nothing) and (ii) Alksnis was listed as a candidate in the elections under the new Constitution, but his name was withdrawn in December 1937. However, neither of these points would invalidate Krivitsky's information.

48. There can be no dispute with L. Schapiro's comment in *The Soviet Army*, *op. cit.*, p. 70 that accounts of a conspiracy are 'scrappy and unconvincing'. They are based largely on the version given in the Bukharin-Rykov trial of 1938. In this connection, it is important to note that the recent 're-habilitation' of Gamarnik completely nullifies the 'evidence' given by Krestinsky in that trial, and which was a version of conspiracy. I. Deutscher, *Stalin*, *op. cit.*, p. 379, states that '. . . all non-Stalinist versions concur in the following: the generals did indeed plan a *coup d'état*'. Joseph E. Davies, *op. cit.*, Despatch No. 457, dated 28th July, 1937, pp. 129–38, argues that the verdict of the 'trial' was justified in the light of the evidence developed at the Bukharin trial (this is done by a subsequent note to the edited despatch); but is an argument of *potential* opposition, not of a *coup*. M. Coulondre, *op. cit.*, pp. 82–3, reports the information of the Lithuanian Minister, who said that Tukhachevsky had put himself at the head of a movement designed to set up a military dictatorship, but one keeping Stalin in power and maintaining the social achievements of the Revolution. This is a very plausible idea, for Tukhachevsky and his fellows were Communists as well as soldiers, but such a plan showed little realisation of the power of the *NKVD* and was scarcely realistic. In addition, M. Coulondre reported his conversation with Potemkin, who said that in February, M. Daladier had taken him aside to mention the information obtained from Beneš; 'in suppressing the traitors, we have shown our fidelity to the Franco-Soviet *entente* . . .' added Potemkin. M. Coulondre arrives at the conclusion that '. . . il paraît donc peu douteux qu'il y ait eu complot militaire'. Nevertheless, the recent 're-habilitations' from the Soviet side tend to diminish this. As the German Army was to show, planning a *coup* is a long, laborious and dangerous business in a state dominated by the security service, and is not to be spoken of lightly.

49. See 'Balticus', *Foreign Affairs*, *loc. cit.* How else can a treason charge be taken but literally? Recent Soviet military literature has certainly made it clear that the slur of 'treason' against Red Army officers is not justified; cf. Marshal Zhukov's speech, 15th July, 1957, at the *Bol'shevik* plant in Leningrad. P. Leverkuehn, *German Military Intelligence*, London 1954, p. 156, disposes of the treason charges against Tukhachevsky. In a close analysis of relevant passages in the Bukharin trial of 1938, G. Castellan, *loc. cit.*, p. 238 f. shows that while the *Reichswehr*-Red Army collaboration was carefully twisted to provide *background* of a kind, and while Voroshilov's June 1937 order had used the term 'spy' or 'espionage' nine times, this description is omitted from the name of Tukhachevsky during the 1938 trial: '. . . juridiquement, l'accusation d'espionage n'est pas formulée contre le maréchal.' A contemporary British publication, *Eight Soviet generals plotted against Peace* ('Friends of the Soviet Union' pubn. 1937, 18 pp.), is one of the best examples of current Communist propaganda on 'the Generals'. F. Thyssen, *I Paid Hitler* (tr. C. Saerchinger), London 1941, p. 194, has a comment on Tukhachevsky and Fritsch attempting to come into contact — 'each desired to overthrow the dictator in his own country' — but this is not supported by any concrete evidence. 'Balticus' in *Foreign Affairs*, *loc. cit.*, is

certainly one of the most useful surveys of contemporary opinion on the 'treason and espionage' question.

50. Cf. Joseph E. Davies, *op. cit.*, p. 136, for adequate confirmation of this meeting.

51. See *Survey* (1937), Vol. 1, pp. 11–22. The name of the Japanese agent was evidently Mr Hiroshima.

52. Edgar Snow, *Red Star over China*, *op. cit.*, p. 415 f.

53. *Ibid.*, p. 432 f.

54. Quoted in M. Beloff, *op. cit.*, Vol. 2, p. 177.

55. Joseph E. Davies, *op. cit.*, pp. 96–7, dated 26th March, 1937; reports that 'a definite understanding' had been arrived at between China and the Soviet Union.

56. See F. F. Liu, *op. cit.*, p. 166. Cf. M. Beloff, *op. cit.*, Vol. 2, note to p. 175, which discusses the implications of Soviet policy in China and confirms Liu's assertion. The underlying Soviet motive was to assist in the unification of China and thereby lessen the chance of war in Asia.

57. Cf. A. Svetlanin, *op. cit.*, pp. 92–3 and J. M. Mackintosh in the *The Soviet Army*, on Soviet forces in the Far East, p. 174.

58. N. Shigemitsu, *op. cit.*, p. 136. Cf. M. Beloff, *op. cit.*, Vol. 2, p. 175, for General Tojo's telegraph message of 9th June, 1937, to the General Staff that it was desirable to eliminate the threat from the 'Nanking regime' first, before attacking the Soviet Union.

59. See *Survey*, 1937, Vol. 1, p. 149 and *Sov. Doc. on For. Pol.*, Vol. 3, pp. 242–3.

60. This is the verdict of the *Survey*, 1937, Vol. 1, p. 150. A note to p. 115 in Joseph E. Davies, *op. cit.*, states that in 1938 he learned from a high Japanese official that these tests of Soviet resistance had been 'deliberately projected'. This is an addition to a despatch on the Amur incident, dated 1st July, 1937.

61. Cf. Richard Storry, *op. cit.*, p. 217 f., on the 'Lukouchiao incident'.

62. *DGFP*, Series D (1937–45), Vol. 1, Ch. IV, No. 463, Berlin, 20th July, 1937, pp. 733–4.

63. *Ibid.*, p. 735, 21st July, 1937, von Hassell conversation in Rome with Japanese Ambassador Sugimura.

64. *Ibid.*, p. 756–7, Gaus memorandum on conversation with Chinese Ambassador, 30th August; it was pointed out to the Ambassador that a non-intervention clause was conspicuous by its absence. Also F. F. Liu, *op. cit.*, p. 167.

65. *DGFP*, Series D, Vol. 1, p. 763.

66. Joseph E. Davies, *op. cit.*, p. 165, for the latter figure.

67. *Survey*, Vol. 1, 1937, p. 231. In fact, it is doubtful if this happened on any appreciable scale.

68. Joseph E. Davies, *op. cit.*, p. 166, reporting information from a Far Eastern 'expert' (in whom Davies obviously placed some confidence) on the arrival of Bogomolov; also second entry on p. 166 on shipments of military supplies. See also in this connection *Red Star Over China*, 'On War with Japan', pp. 98–107, for Edgar Snow's conversation with Mao Tse-tung on 16th July, 1936; the Chinese Communist leader was assured that the Soviet Union '. . . cannot remain passive'. He was to be somewhat undeceived on this score as Soviet policy in Asia unfolded itself. The same

passage is also of interest for Mao Tse-tung's views on the importance of a 'war of manœuvre' and the Chinese Red Army.

69. See David D. Dallin, *The Big Three. The United States, Britain, Russia*, London 1946, p. 74. There is an extremely useful survey to be found here of Soviet naval policy in the section 'The Soviet Navy', pp. 68–78.

70. L. Schapiro, *The Communist Party of the Soviet Union*, *op. cit.*, p. 420.

71. I am grateful to Dr G. Katkov for giving me the opportunity to see certain Soviet emigré accounts, which gave first-hand details of conditions prevailing at this time in the Red Army.

72. N. S. Khrushchev, 1956 speech (text cited, p. 20).

73. See note to R. Coulondre, *op. cit.*, p. 128.

74. See W. G. Krivitsky, *op. cit.*, p. 260. Also G. Castellan, *loc. cit.*, Note 71 to p. 236. See also A. Barmine, *op. cit.*, p. 223, accusing a certain Alexeyeff of being heavily involved in the Tukhachevsky case, and of having published in the emigré journal *Vozrozhdeniye* a statement of Tukhachevsky's treasonable contacts with the German General Staff. Barmine includes the Gestapo story, but reverses its order, by saying that Stalin used the forgeries to convince the Czechoslovak statesmen of the guilt of the Soviet officers.

75. N. F. Kuz'min, *op. cit.*, p. 170. The decree on the new naval organisation was confirmed by the Supreme Soviet, 15th January, 1938: see I. F. Pobezhimov, *op. cit.*, p. 98.

Chapter XV

1. I. F. Pobezhimov, *op. cit.*, pp. 98–9. The speech is also quoted in W. P. and Z. K. Coates, *Why Russia Will Win*. The Soviet Military, Naval and Air Power, London (n.d.), pp. 62–3.

2. See under V. M. Orlov in *MSE*, 3rd Edn., Vol. 6, p. 972.

3. Quoted in David J. Dallin, *The Big Three*, *op. cit.*, p. 74. (See Chapter Thirteen, p. 9, for Tukhachevsky's speech in January 1936 which specifically mentioned the addition of surface units to the Soviet naval forces.)

4. Cf. Joseph E. Davies, *op. cit.*, p. 81, and his conversation with Litvinov on the cruiser programme (Despatch dated 26th March).

5. See N. F. Kuz'min, *op. cit.*, p. 170.

6. David J. Dallin, *op. cit.*, pp. 71–2.

7. N. F. Kuz'min, *op. cit.*, p. 188.

8. This is the figure cited in Raymond L. Garthoff, *How Russia Makes War*, *op. cit.*, p. 220. Dr Garthoff handles his evidence with great care, and there is no reason to doubt this.

9. See Berman and Kerner (monograph), *op. cit.*, p. 15.

10. *Ibid.*, p. 16.

11. I. F. Pobezhimov, *op. cit.*, p. 90. Pobezhimov's book was written before the 'de-Stalinisation' campaign got into its stride (the book was submitted for type-

setting in July 1953), hence his use of a political terminology which has since been much modified and finally abandoned in speaking of the Red Army.

12. Cf. L. Schapiro, *The Communist Party of the Soviet Union*, p. 420. There is much which would substantiate this opinion, although the naval command was under a special duress for a much longer period. In the nightmare conditions of the military purge, it becomes impossible to distinguish a re-shuffle from something much more drastic.

13. See order in *KPSS o voor. sil. SSSR*, *op. cit.*, p. 353. This is the only reference to the period of the purge, the documentation being taken up from 1941. In this way, a great deal of awkward material has been cut out.

14. Cf. N. F. Kuz'min, *op. cit.*, p. 189, on the re-organisation.

15. See *Report of Court Proceedings in the Case of the Anti-Soviet 'Bloc of Rights and Trotskyites' . . . March 2–13, 1938*, Moscow 1938, p. 16. This passage (with capitalisation in the original) comes from the material collected during the preliminary investigations, and is referred to under specific volumes. This statement is from Vol. VI, p. 49.

16. *Ibid.*, pp. 54–5.

17. *Ibid.*, p. 61. Bessonov's testimony is badly confused.

18. *Ibid.*, p. 73.

19. *Ibid.*, p. 84.

20. *Ibid.*, p. 177.

21. *Ibid.*, pp. 188–9.

22. *Ibid.*, p. 197. In connection with this passage, it is useful to compare George Fischer's comment in his *Soviet Opposition to Stalin*. A Case Study in World War II, Cambridge, Mass. 1952, pp. 143–4: '. . . If in some instances organized opposition reached a more advanced stage, these instances must have been tragically few and tragically unsuccessful. Neither the Soviet trial proceedings nor the testimony of Soviet "nonreturners" offers evidence to the contrary.' The conclusion is that an organised opposition did exist (Bukharin's testimony, even though he was frequently silenced by Vyshinsky, would bear this out), but it did not reach 'any significant proportions' before being obliterated by Stalin. Conversations undoubtedly did take place, but as the trial evidence, jaded as it may have been, shows, these were both informal and inconclusive. As for the military side, the opposition movement in the German Army went through agonies of indecision and enormous difficulties of planning and was itself a proof that in a police state, it is not just a question of setting the soldiers to march. The question of where, when and why — and exactly how — are by no means slight or the concern of hotheads.

23. *Ibid.*, p. 253.

24. *Ibid.*, p. 256.

25. *Ibid.*, pp. 268–9. See Chapter Six.

26. *Ibid.*, p. 393.

27. *Ibid.*, p. 395.

28. *Ibid.*, pp. 431–2.

29. *Ibid.*, p. 575.

30. Joseph E. Davies, *op. cit.*, p. 189.

31. *Ibid.*, p. 188. Cf. W. P. and Z. K. Coates, *op. cit.*, pp. 88–9 for information

from Yasuo Mishima on the continuous transport of aircraft parts to the Soviet Far East, and the readying of the 'munitions and electric industries' and food supplies.

32. Reported in R. Coulondre, *op. cit.*, p. 136.

33. Joseph E. Davies, *op. cit.*, p. 197.

34. L. Noël, *op. cit.*, pp. 200–1.

35. Cf. note to p. 127 in M. Beloff, *op. cit.*, Vol. 2.

36. Speech quoted in *Sov. Doc. on For. Pol.*, Vol. 3, p. 279.

37. Schulenburg's report A/796, dated 30th May in *DGFP*, Series D, Vol. 2, pp. 363–4.

38. Quoted in W. P. and Z. K. Coates, *A History of Anglo-Soviet Relations*, London 1943, p. 586.

39. F. F. Liu, *op. cit.*, p. 168.

40. See Serial 3483H/019366–7: Trauttmann report. Dr Tsiang continued 'Russland ist durch und durch verottet'. He would be making the same report to Chiang Kai-shek but in even sharper terms.

41. F. F. Liu, *op. cit.*, p. 170 and attributed to 'a high Chinese source'. There is some direct evidence from the Soviet side in the person of A. Vlasov, who was a member of the Soviet military mission. See George Fischer, *op. cit.*, Appendix I, pp. 170–1, for Vlasov's career in China; Vlasov was Chief of Staff to Cherepanov, and lectured to senior Chinese officers on operational tactics and then took over the position of military adviser to General Yen Hsi-shan. Vlasov carried on as chief military adviser when Cherepanov was recalled and continued in this capacity until Cherepanov's successor arrived.

42. F. F. Liu, *op. cit.*, p. 170.

43. *Ibid.*, p. 168. The name cited may be an incorrect version of Kachanov, who succeeded Cherepanov.

44. *Ibid.*

45. See KŌGUN, *op. cit.*, p. 11.

46. Report in *DGFP*, Series D, Vol. 1, p. 922.

47. *Sov. Doc. on For. Pol.*, Vol. 3, p. 290. See also *DGFP*, *ibid.*, for the German interpretation of this remarkable speech; it was taken as a very 'objective' statement of opinion about German policy and herein lay its chief interest for the German Embassy in Moscow.

48. A. Svetlanin, *op. cit.*, p. 103, claims to have known personally of this case.

49. *Biographical Directory*, *op. cit.*, p. 533, cites the arrest of Rokossovskii for neglecting the material supply of his corps; this was the official excuse. Khrushchev's 1956 speech mentions Rokossovskii as one of the commanders who suffered unjustly, hence the arrest must have been political.

50. Svetlanin, *op. cit.*, p. 105, maintains that the disclosure of the new arrangement was to be at special discretion of the Defence Commissariat, although Far Eastern commanders were acquainted of the proposed decision. This is quite a likely explanation, since the official references to the Far Eastern forces were very guarded.

51. A. Svetlanin, *ibid.*, p. 104. Information from this source is not distinguished by its complete reliability, although it appears to be based on some kind of personal knowledge.

52. See report on the *NKVD* purge in *DGFP*, Series D, Vol. 1, p. 924.

53. These names are supplied by Svetlanin, p. 116. His information on Levandovskii, to the effect that the latter escaped from a Soviet concentration camp and led an anti-Soviet partisan war, is based by admission on a vague rumour and seems to have no real foundation.

54. See *Sov. Doc. on For. Pol.*, Vol. 3, p. 294 for the Soviet-Japanese exchange over map variations.

55. See the most recent study of this action by M. Blumenson, 'The Soviet Power Play at Changkufeng' in *World Politics*, Vol. XII, Jan. 1960, No. 2, pp. 249–64. M. Shigemitsu, *op. cit.*, pp. 158–60 has a very revealing passage on the action. I am much indebted to Dr Alvin D. Coox of Tokyo for his assistance in bringing to my attention evidence, both written and oral, which destroys the usual Soviet case that this was 'Japanese aggression' (so registered in the *IMT/FE*) at Changkufeng, and also for a great deal of information on Khalkhin-Gol (Nomon-Han), the subsequent incident in 1939. It is perhaps more profitable to keep these actions linked.

56. N. F. Kuz'min, *op. cit.*, p. 200 f. has one of the few Soviet accounts of this action. Kuz'min follows the line of 'Japanese aggression' faithfully, on account of which his story has some curious twists. In Soviet accounts, the action is always referred to by the location of Lake Khasan, although 'Changkufeng' has been used here since it is under that name most references will be found. His account of the opening engagement will be found pp. 200–1.

57. M. Blumenson, *loc. cit.*, p. 258. A full study of the Japanese side will be found in Monograph # XI, *Small Wars and Border Problems*, Part 3, Book A: 'Changkufeng Incident' in *Manchurian Research Series*, Japanese Research Division, Office of the Military History Officer, HQ AFFE/8th Army (US).

58. This N. F. Kuz'min's admission, p. 201.

59. M. Blumenson, *loc. cit.*, p. 259.

60. N. F. Kuz'min, *op. cit.*, p. 202. This is where the point about the 'Far Eastern Front' takes on some relevance. Kuz'min refers to the 1st Far Eastern Army. M. I. Gubel'man, *op. cit.*, p. 259, refers to the 1st Pri-Amur Army. The contemporary Soviet press referred to the 'Front', although *Krasnaya Zvezda*, No. 247, for 26th October, 1938, announced the award of the Order of Lenin to G. M. Shtern, corps commander. There was no mention of Blyukher.

61. *Sov. Doc. on For. Pol.*, Vol. 3, p. 297.

62. This version is supplied in A. Svetlanin, *op. cit.*, p. 124 f.

63. This point, supported by evidence from a Soviet deserter (Lyushkov?) is presented in M. Blumenson, pp. 254–5.

64. Remarks about the Japanese desiring a point of control for Possiet Bay (a view advanced by Walter Duranty) are without foundation, and rest on the assumption of complete and utter Japanese aggression. Limited Soviet objectives seem a much more reasonable idea, and one which does not contradict geography.

65. M. Blumenson, *loc. cit.*, p. 260.

66. See N. F. Kuz'min, *op. cit.*, p. 202, on this very important point.

67. *Ibid.*, p. 202. The artillery arrangements are the object of a comment by Clark W. Tinch, 'Quasi-War between Japan and the U.S.S.R., 1937–1939' in *World*

Politics, Volume III, October 1950–July 1951, p. 180, in which he interprets Shtern's comments to mean that there was a shortage of shells. From Kuz'min's comments and criticisms, it would appear that it was *guns*, not shells which were short. This would be borne out by I. S. Prochko, *op. cit.*, p. 141, which speaks of 'great difficulties', of the summer training programme not being completed, and the shortness of the time for the gunners to prepare.

68. M. Blumenson, *loc. cit.*, p. 261.

69. *Ibid.* Up to 100 Soviet tanks must have been committed.

70. See especially M. Shigemitsu, *op. cit.*, pp. 159–60; Shigemitsu carried on the negotiations with Litvinov for a cease-fire, and comments, '. . . I have a shrewd suspicion that Russia knew that their troops had reached the boundary line they claimed. . . .' The Germans, incidentally, vigorously denied that the Japanese had sought their help over the Changkufeng incident (see *DGFP*, Series D, Vol. 1, pp. 896–7).

71. These observations were made by N. F. Kuz'min, p. 209. See M. Blumenson, *loc. cit.*, p. 262, for a note on the casualties: Soviet losses were estimated by the Japanese at 4,500–7,000 and Japanese losses set at 1,500 (but were probably higher). Soviet figures set their own losses at 236 killed and the Japanese 600 killed, 2,500 wounded.

72. *MSE*, 3rd Edn., Vol. 1, 1958, p. 1073. In this connection, see p. 184 of *Biographical Directory*, under A. Y. Golovanov: according to Colonel Tokaev, Golovanov commanded the special multi-engined aircraft used to bring prisoners to Moscow and it was in this fashion that Blyukher was brought from Khabarovsk to Moscow.

73. In this connection, a Shipbuilding Commissariat was set up. The date given for this is frequently 1939, although N. F. Kuz'min, *op. cit.*, p. 170, states that the decision to set up this Commissariat was taken at the same time as that to set up a separate Naval Commissariat (end 1937–beginning 1938), and an expanded building programme was incorporated into the first year (1938) of the Third Five-Year Plan.

74. See discussion with Stalin, Joseph E. Davies, *op. cit.*, pp. 223–4.

75. *MSE*, 3rd Edn., Vol. 1, 1958, p. 283. While by no means conclusive in itself, this edition of the *MSE* has done two things (i) restored the names of military, naval and aviation commanders who had suffered disgrace in the purge (ii) supplied terminal dates to biographical entries. All the officers executed under the June order (1937) have the date 11th June, 1937, entered against their names.

76. See *How Russia Makes War*, *op. cit.*, p. 345, for an important note on the fate of strategic aviation. See also R. Coulondre, *op. cit.*, p. 128.

77. This is the phrase used by M. Werner, *op. cit.*, p. 66. Werner's book has certain uses, but he fails to follow out the logical consequences of this statement and his assessment of the high quality of the Soviet forces is based almost entirely on pre-1937 achievements.

78. Cf. V. D. Mostovenko, *op. cit.*, p. 104 f.

79. R. Coulondre, *op. cit.*, p. 156.

80. *Ibid.*, p. 157.

81. *Sov. Doc. on For. Pol.*, Vol. 3, p. 303.

82. General Gamelin, *op. cit.*, Vol. 2, p. 348.

83. *Sov. Doc. on For. Pol.*, Vol. 3, p. 305.

84. General Gamelin, *op. cit.*, p. 349.

85. *Ibid.*, p. 357.

86. R. Coulondre, *op. cit.*, p. 171.

87. Cf. L. Schapiro, *The Communist Party of the Soviet Union, op. cit.*, p. 431. Khrushchev 1956 speech (text cited), p. 16.

88. The best presentation is to be found in Raymond L. Garthoff, *How Russia Makes War, op. cit.*, pp. 220–1.

89. W. G. Krivitsky, *op. cit.*, p. 255, speaks of the sacrifice of 35,000 officers. Z. K. Brzezinski, *op. cit.*, p. 106, cites a Polish General Staff estimate (without the date) of 15,000. C. Kalinov, *op. cit.*, pp. 20–1 mentions 1,500 senior officers as having been executed, and 4,000 in prison, and speaks of an initial plan to purge 12,000 officers. The reliability of this information is, however, rather questionable. Without giving any figures, Khrushchev reports that '. . . the cadre of leaders who had gained military experience in Spain and in the Far East was almost completely liquidated'.

90. Z. K. Brzezinski, *op. cit.*, p. 106.

91. Quoted in M. Werner, *op. cit.*, p. 262.

Chapter XVI

1. For this speech see *The Land of Socialism Today and Tomorrow*, Moscow 1939, pp. 269–301. Also *18 S'ezd VKP(b) 10–21 Mart, 1939 g. Stenograf. Otchot*, (Stenographic Report, 18th Party Congress) Ogiz 1939, pp. 187–205.

2. See M. Fainsod, *How Russia is Ruled, op. cit.*, p. 414, and the subsequent comment.

3. David J. Dallin, *The Big Three, op. cit.*, p. 74.

4. See *KPSS v rez.* (Party resolutions), Vol. 2, p. 921, for the alterations in the required length of Party service for posts in the political administration.

5. J. Stalin, *Problems of Leninism*, 11th Edn., p. 750.

6. *Ibid.*, pp. 754–5.

7. See the note on Soviet-German contacts in M. Beloff, *op. cit.*, Vol. 2, p. 217. German 'loss of interest in the Ukraine' was one foundation of the subsequent *rapprochement.*

8. *Ibid.*, p. 227. Cf. *Nazi-Soviet Relations 1939–1941* (edited R. J. Sontag and J. S. Stuart), U.S. Dept. of State, 1948, p. 76. (Cited as *N.S.R.*)

9. *Sov. Doc. on For. Pol.*, Vol. 3, p. 324.

10. See *Polish White Book*, p. 71.

11. General Gamelin, *Servir*, Vol. 2, p. 406. The note that this was delayed by the British appears to lack foundation.

12. Lord Strang, *Home and Abroad*, London 1956, p. 163.

13. *Documents on British Foreign Policy 1919–1939*, Third Series, Vol. V, p. 228. (Cited as *DBFP.*)

14. *N.S.R.*, p. 2.

15. *Ibid.*, p. 3.

16. *Le Livre Jaune Français* Documents Diplomatiques 1938–1939, Paris 1939, pp. 153–4.

17. Lord Strang, *op. cit.*, p. 164.

18. *DBFP*, Third Series, Vol. V, p. 639 f. Para. 35 of the memorandum dealing with Anglo-Soviet relations mentions but finds it difficult to assess the chances of a possible Soviet-German agreement.

19. *N.S.R.*, p. 4.

20. *Ibid.*, pp. 5–7.

21. *Ibid.*, p. 7.

22. Lord Strang, *op. cit.*, pp. 168–9.

23. Speech quoted in *Sov. Doc. on For. Pol.*, Vol. 3, p. 337.

24. *N.S.R.*, p. 15.

25. *Sov. Doc. on For. Pol.*, Vol. 3, p. 339.

26. Japanese (and one or two other) accounts use the name Nomon-Han. Soviet accounts stick to Khalkhin-Gol. Colonel S. Shishkin's *Khalkhin-Gol* was the first public treatment of these operations, and may well have been connected with Zhukov's rapid advancement after Stalin's death. It is therefore of some interest to compare that account with N. F. Kuz'min, *op. cit.*, p. 209 f. (published after Zhukov's dismissal). In the latter his name is merely tacked on to the end of the account as a recipient of a decoration. From the Japanese side, Kōgun, *op. cit.*, p. 14, states that a force of 700 Outer Mongolian horsemen crossed the river on 12th May; they were beaten off but attacked again. The definition of 'aggressor' depended, as in 1938, upon the maps being used to set the frontier lines.

27. This information is taken from S. Shishkin, *op. cit.*, on the May operations.

28. The 57th Rifle Corps (HQ: Ulan-Bator) was under *komdiv* N. V. Feklenko, chief of staff *kombrig* A. M. Kushchev; the formation was directly subordinated to Moscow.

29. See Appendix IV.

30. This account is based on both Shishkin and Kuz'min.

31. Although Hans-Otto Meissner states that Sorge failed to give advance warning of Khalkin-Gol (difficult in so much that the incident blew itself up almost locally), he was able to transmit vital information on Japanese policy and decisions. This was obviously a factor in its own right in permitting the Russians to practise 'brinkmanship' with the Japanese and derive full advantage from it.

32. See *DBFP*, Third Series, Vol. VI, pp. 22–3, No. 20 (French draft of a possible three power treaty). Also Annex 2 to No. 35, pp. 39–40. Annex 1 to No. 35 deals in Point 7 with the objections of the three Baltic states to being subject to a guarantee involving the Soviet Union. Events would soon prove how well-founded these fears were.

33. *Ibid.*, No. 103, Moscow, 20th June, 1939, p. 115 f.

34. *Ibid.*, p. 119.

35. *Ibid.*, No. 126, Moscow, 22nd June, p. 143.

36. *Sov. Doc. on For. Pol.*, Vol. 3, p. 352. Sir W. Seeds communication of 24th June (*DBFP* Vol. VI, p. 160 f.) to Viscount Halifax gives a comprehensive analysis of the Soviet attitude.

37. See *DBFP*, Third Series, Vol. VI, p. 422. Letter of Mr Strang to Sir O. Sargent, 20th July, 1939.

38. *Ibid.*

39. *Ibid.*, p. 424. See also p. 331 and pp. 333–6 on the British objections.

40. *Ibid.*, No. 473, pp. 521–5.

41. *Ibid.*, No. 525, pp. 571–2.

42. *DBFP*, Third Series, Vol. VII, p. 35.

43. See Appendix V to Vol. VI, p. 762 f. 'Instructions to the British Military Mission to Moscow August 1939', Annex II, pp. 783–6 includes information on the Soviet Navy and port facilities.

44. *Ibid.*, para. 24, p. 766: the assessment points out that although 'by all the rules of logic' the Soviet transportation system ought to have broken down, it had not done so. Also para. 102, p. 778: the question of Soviet lorries and railway lines crossing the Polish frontier.

45. *DBFP*, Third Series, Vol. VII, p. 558. (This is the summary by M. Roberts on the negotiations, dated 23rd August, 1939, and Item (i) of Appendix II.)

46. *Ibid.*, pp. 561–2. No. 1 of the Minutes of the military discussions, with the composition of the delegations.

47. *Ibid.*, p. 564. There is some discrepancy between the translators' versions of what precisely the Russians wished to know of arrangements with Poland and Turkey.

48. *Ibid.*, p. 567 (Voroshilov's questions) and further for the British replies on the second echelon of the British Field Force.

49. *Ibid.*, p. 573.

50. *Ibid.*, p. 574. General Heywood asked that the answer to the Soviet question be assumed as 'Yes', so that the discussions might continue.

51. *Ibid.*, p. 577. The list of bases corresponded to what the Soviet Union later attempted to take by direct action.

52. *Ibid.*, pp. 576–8. See also No. 34 pp. 32–5, Admiral Drax to Admiral Lord Chatfield on this new 'theory of war . . . the whole idea is, of course, quite childish'

53. See *ibid.*, Nos. 22 and 30.

54. *Ibid.*, p. 61.

55. *Ibid.*, p. 588.

56. *Ibid.*, p. 590.

57. *Ibid.*, p. 609 f.

58. *Ibid.*, p. 609. See in this connection Sir L. B. Namier's *Diplomatic Prelude 1938–1939*, London 1948, pp. 207–10; Paul Reynaud, *op. cit.*, pp. 325–7.

59. *N.S.R.*, p. 66.

60. *Ibid.*, p. 46. Astakhov did nevertheless add that the situation had changed somewhat since the conversations with Germany began.

61. *Ibid.*, p. 66 and p. 68.

62. *Ibid.*, p. 72, done by telephone and telegram.

63. *Ibid.*, p. 76.

64. *DBFP*, Third Series, Vol. VII, p. 599.

65. *Ibid.*, pp. 601–3.

66. *Ibid.*, p. 33. Letter of 16th August.

67. *Ibid.*, pp. 613–14.

68. *Ibid.*, pp. 608–9.

69. *Ibid.*, p. 607. Voroshilov's statement on the military talks professed that the pact with Germany was concluded because the talks broke down. This is quite untrue, as the chronology shows.

70. See M. Beloff, *op. cit.*, Vol. 2, p. 273, on the delay in ratifying the pact with Germany.

71. *N.S.R.*, p. 21.

72. *Ibid.*, pp. 52–3.

73. Cf. Lord Strang, *op. cit.*, pp. 198–9.

74. In addition to the early T–34 models were T–26, BT–7 and BT–7M machines. On relative strengths see Appendix IV. I am grateful to Dr Alvin D. Coox for information on Soviet tanks used in this action.

75. See N. F. Kuz'min, *op. cit.*, p. 215 and 217.

76. Cf. P. Ruslanov, 'Marshal Zhukov' in *The Russian Review*, July 1956, p. 190.

77. See N. F. Kuz'min's examples, *op. cit.*, pp. 222–4.

78. KŌGUN, pp. 15–16.

79. See N. Galai, 'Tank Forces in the Soviet Army', *Bulletin*, Munich October 1954, p. 7 (with reference to Col. Aldan and Col. Antonov in *Prizyv*, Munich 1948, No. 2). See also p. 173 'Vlasov's Biography' in *Soviet Opposition to Stalin*, *op. cit.*, for the responsibility for the disbanding being placed on Kulik. Mis-interpretation of the Spanish lessons is blamed by the authors of *Vtoraya Mirovaya Voina 1939–1945*, *op. cit.*, p. 176 for this serious blunder. However, both A. M. Samsonov in *Velikaya Bitva pod Moskvoi 1941–1942* (The Great Battle by Moscow 1941–1942), Moscow 1958, p. 34 and B. S. Tel'pukhovskii, *Velikaya Otechestvennaya Voina Sov. Soyuza 1941–1945 gg.* (The Great Patriotic War of the Soviet Union 1941–1945), p. 40 date the disbanding of the mechanised corps and the substitution of the tank brigade from 1937.

80. *DGFP*, Series D, Vol. 8, p. 3.

81. *N.S.R.*, p. 91.

82. *DGFP*, Series D, Vol. 8, p. 69.

83. Colonel Antonov in *The Soviet Army*, *op. cit.*, p. 73.

84. *DGFP*, Series D, Vol. 8, p. 130, also pp. 137–9.

85. *Ibid.*, p. 129 and pp. 147–8.

86. Cf. *Les Frontières Européennes de l'U.R.S.S.*, *op. cit.*, p. 156.

87. *Ibid.*, p. 157.

88. Cf. *DBFP*, Third Series, Vol. VII, p. 577. 'Chief aggressor' was later admitted to be Germany.

89. *DGFP*, Series D, Vol. 8, p. 213.

90. *Ibid.*, p. 537. Raeder estimated that it would take the Russians six years to copy them. The plans were not delivered in the end, nor were German cruisers sold.

91. See *Les Frontières Européennes . . . op. cit.*, p. 185. Also Marshal Mannerheim, *Muistelmat* (Memoirs), Helsinki 1952, pp. 137–8, and Väinö Tanner, *The Winter War*, Finland Against Russia 1939–1940, Stanford U.P., 1957, p. 4.

92. V. Tanner, *op. cit.*, p. 25.

93. *Ibid.*, p. 27 and p. 29.

94. *Ibid.*, p. 41.

95. *Ibid.*, pp. 66–7.

96. *Ibid.*, p. 85. It was Zhdanov who was supposed to have engineered the Finnish incident.

97. The criticisms are those of N. F. Kuz'min, *op. cit.*, pp. 237–9.

98. Geoffrey Cox, *The Red Army Moves*, London 1941, pp. 154–6.

99. *Ibid.*, Ch. 18, for a full description. N. F. Kuz'min, *op. cit.*, p. 261, blames defective command for the calamity. Although this action was not in itself decisive, Cox rightly asserts that its real significance was to force the Red Army to recover its prestige. The Leningrad Military District did on 13th January, 1940, take the unusual step of putting out a denial of the large losses and the fate of the 44th Division.

100. G. Cox, *op. cit.*, p. 194. The Soviet troops set themselves up in stockades or 'Mottis'.

101. See Wippert von Blücher in *DGFP*, Series D, Vol. 8, pp. 555–7.

102. *Ibid.*, p. 507 and p. 511.

103. Cited by N. F. Kuz'min, *op. cit.*, p. 239.

104. See *Nazi Conspiracy and Aggression*, Washington 1946, Vol. VI, pp. 981–2, emphasis as in the original.

105. *DGFP*, Series D, Vol. 8, p. 595, under Enclosure 1.

106. *Ibid.*, p. 591.

107. V. Tanner, *op. cit.*, pp. 127–8.

108. J. R. M. Butler, *Grand Strategy*, Vol. II (History of the Second World War) HMSO 1957, p. 106.

109. See Paul Reynaud, *op. cit.*, pp. 368–9. The German White Books Nos. 4 and 6 contained versions of the Allied plans; they will be found as an appendix in F. O. Miksche, *Unconditional Surrender*, The Roots of World War III, London 1952, p. 423 f.

110. N. F. Kuz'min, *op. cit.*, pp. 240–2.

111. G. Cox, *op. cit.*, p. 202, reports that a Finnish reserve battalion gave way and retreated.

112. V. Tanner, *op. cit.*, p. 196. This was Schulenburg's explanation from Moscow: *N.S.R.*, p. 136.

113. V. Tanner, *ibid.*, p. 211.

114. *Ibid.*, p. 227 and p. 231.

115. N. F. Kuz'min, *op. cit.*, pp. 269–70. Although the Red Army was badly reported in the Finnish war, many of the same faults appeared at once in 1941 — especially badly-prepared offensives, bad intelligence and the failure of co-ordination. Soviet criticisms only are presented here.

116. *DGFP*, Series D, Vol. 8, Appendix, p. 942.

117. N. F. Kuz'min, *op. cit.*, pp. 184–5.

118. See Berman and Kerner (monograph), *op. cit.*, p. 52. The Red Army Military Oath had already been changed in January 1939 and saluting on and off duty made compulsory in June.

119. Quoted in David J. Dallin, *Russia and Postwar Europe*, *op. cit.*, p. 30.

120. *N.S.R.*, pp. 138–40.

121. See David J. Dallin, *Soviet Russia's Foreign Policy 1939–1942*, New Haven 1945, p. 251.

122. Cf. *Nazi Conspiracy and Aggression* (cited as *NCA* and volume number), Vol. VI: German Naval High Command File, Hitler 21st July — '. . . Russia views Germany's great successes with tears in her eyes', although there was no Soviet intention to enter the war against Germany (p. 984). Entry 5th June states that Russia fears a German attack after decisive victory; but 'allied victory is *not* desired either'.

123. See David J. Dallin, *Soviet Foreign Policy . . .*, *op. cit.*, p. 241 f. for treatment of the Baltic states.

124. See *NCA* Vol. VI, p. 877.

125. German *Fremde Heere Ost* estimate, for 24th July, 1940.

126. Quoted in David J. Dallin, *Russia and Postwar Europe*, p. 27.

127. A summary of these will be found in N. F. Kuz'min, *op. cit.*, pp. 226–8.

128. 'Vlasov's Biography' *loc. cit.*, p. 173. Kuz'min mentions the 99th Division but naturally not Vlasov.

129. See *N.S.R.*, p. 258 f.

130. See *Vtoraya Mirovaya Voina . . .*, *op. cit.* (cited as *V.M.V.*), pp. 176–8. This is intensely critical of the pre-war state of the Soviet forces, further reference to which will be made later. Charges that a 'significant part' of the skilled cadres were 'annihilated' by the Yezhov-Beria gang 'worming their way into Stalin's confidence'. In this connection German Military Attaché Report (Moscow) 29/10/1940 *Nr. 20 001/40 geh Ausl III b* is relevant; criticised (i) weakness of organisation, (ii) lack of experienced men and training staff, due to the purges: not capable of carrying out large operations in a war of movement: quality of equipment not up to the standards of a western army.

131. See note to p. 228 in K. Z. Brzezinski, *op. cit.*

132. Cf. J. R. M. Butler, *op. cit.*, p. 537. Also *N.S.R.*, pp. 166–8, on the Cripps Mission.

133. See Waldemur Erfurth, *Die Geschichte des Deutschen Generalstabes 1918–1945*, Göttingen 1957, p. 264.

134. *N.C.A.* Vol. VI, p. 987 (German Naval High Command file). On 16th September Ribbentrop instructed Schulenburg to tell Molotov 'casually' about German troop movements into Finland; he was to do this by 21st, if not otherwise ordered.

135. Walter Goerlitz, *op. cit.*, p. 387, argues that Halder, like Hitler, had begun 'to doubt the sincerity of Russian intentions'. On 31st December, 1940, Hitler wrote to Mussolini that he saw no likelihood of Soviet action against Germany while Stalin lived, with the proviso that no major calamity befell Germany.

136. For Halder discussion, *NCA* Vol. IV, pp. 374–5. Halder's notes in *Vortragsnotiz für einen Vortrag des ObdH bei Hitler 5/12/1940* emphasised (i) the mass of the Russian tank force was badly armoured (ii) the Red Army was without effective leadership (iii) in artillery, there were few modern batteries, all else being old material re-conditioned. For Directive 18th December, 1940, see *N.S.R.*, p. 260 f.

Chapter XVII

(Note. In tables and footnotes, reference has been made to *Ist. Velik. Otechest. Voiny Sov. Soyuza 1941–1945*, Moscow 1960, Vol. 1. This is the first volume of a major Soviet history of the 1941–5 Soviet-German War, which is to be completed in six volumes. In full title/volume title, publishers and editorial board, the work is as follows: *Istoriya Velikoi Otechestvennoi Voiny Sovetskovo Soyuza 1941–1945*, Vol. 1: Podgotovka i razvyazyvanie voiny imperialisticheskimi derzhavami. Pub: Institut Marksizma-Leninizma pri Tsk KPSS/ Otdel istorii Velikoi Otechestvennoi Voiny, 1960: Ministerstva Oborony Soyuza SSR, 1960. Editorial commission: P. N. Pospelov (president), V. A. Andreyev, A. I. Antonov, I. Kh. Bagramyan, P. A. Belov, E. A. Boltin (deputy president), M. G. Bragin, F. I. Golikov, A. A. Grechko, I. D. Eliseyev, A. S. Zheltov, P. A. Zhilin, E. M. Zhukov, H. A. Zhuravlev, I. N. Zemskov, L. F. Il'ichev, D. M. Kukin, V. V. Kurasov, A. P. Kuchkin, I. I. Mints, V. P. Moskovskii (deputy president), G. D. Obichkin, Z. S. Osipov, B. N. Polevoi, S. I. Rudenko, A. L. Sidorov, V. D. Sokolovskii, B. S. Tel'pukhovskii, A. A. Timofeevskii, V. M. Khvostov, N. I. Shatagin. In the subsequent notes, this work will be cited in its abbreviated form.)

1. Cf. G. Gafencu, *Préliminaires de la Guerre à l'Est*, De l'Accord de Moscou aux Hostilités en Russie, Paris 1944, p. 185.

2. *N.S.R.*, pp. 270–1.

3. *Ibid.*, p. 270.

4. See Summer Welles, *A Time for Decision*, N.Y., 1944, pp. 168–71: this makes it clear that the American information came from a source which is described as being outside possible Soviet contacts. Cf. David J. Dallin, *Soviet Russia's Foreign Policy 1939–1942*, *op. cit.*, pp. 332–3: describes Umansky as having taken the whole thing 'rather lightly'.

5. See M. Beloff, *op. cit.*, Vol. 2, p. 358.

6. For a discussion of this in connection with 1941, see the valuable Appendix II, 'Trial by Arms: June to December 1941' in *How Russia Makes War*, p. 433 f. The explanation which emerges from *Ist. Velik. Otechest. Voiny Sov. Soyuza 1941–1945*, Moscow 1960, Vol. 1, is that (i) war was certainly not considered an immediate eventuality (ii) the type of deployment plan drawn up by the General Staff envisaged a margin of time of at least 'several days' during which time they could bring their frontier formations up to full strength see: *ibid.*, p. 472, p. 473, p. 476.

7. The phrase is Winston S. Churchill's, *op. cit.*, Vol. III, 'The Grand Alliance', Ch. XX, 'The Soviet Nemesis', p. 316. This is also of the opinion that Stalin threw away the chance of a Soviet-British front in the Balkans after January 1941 and that the Soviet Union under Stalin 'supinely awaited' the German onslaught.

8. See A. M. Samsonov, *Velikaya bitva pod Moskvoi 1941–1942* (The great Moscow battle 1941–1942), Moscow 1956 (Academy of Sciences publn.), p. 36. This is in the line of writings criticising Stalin, but somewhat detached. Based on archives. See also *Ist. Velik. Otechest. Voiny Sov. Soyuza 1941–1945*, Moscow 1960, Vol. 1, 'Soviet military science before the German attack', pp. 436–51. This criticism is made also

with respect to the draft of the *Field Service Regulations* (1939) (see pp. 440–2).

9. *Ist. Velik. Otechest. Voiny, ibid.*, p. 475.

10. See I. M. Shlyapin, M. A. Shvarev, I. Ya. Fomichenko, *Kommunisticheskaya Partiya v period Velikoi Otechestvennoi Voiny* (The Communist Party during the Great Patriotic War), Pub.: Military Publishing House, Ministry of Defence, Moscow 1958, p. 42. This polemical work tries hard to show the Party as the great war-winner. The criticism of Zhukov echoes the great debate carried on 1956 about the responsibility for the catastrophe. Under Stalin, the specious theory of a 'planned retirement' had been carefully cultivated, luring the *Wehrmacht* into the depth of Russia so to destroy it. *Voennyi Vestnik* (Military Herald), 1956, No. 4, pp. 2–9, wrote of the great retreat as unplanned and caused by lack of adequate preparation. Party spokesmen bitterly contested this view, but were unable to gain any retraction of the military point of view. If a realistic view of recent military history was to be taken (and this was vital for the regeneration of Soviet military theory after Stalin's death), it would be useless to perpetuate the purposeless myth propagated under Stalin. It also appears that the Soviet military leadership wished to be absolved of the disgrace which attended the 1941 disasters by pointing out that the military were ham-strung. On 9th May, 1956, *Krasnaya Zvezda* (Red Star) in 'Preparedness and one-man command' attempted to tone down the *Voennyi Vestnik* criticisms, but without substantial success.

11. Cf. Winston S. Churchill, *op. cit.*, Vol. III, p. 342. Stalin produced this argument to justify his pre-1941 policy. Cf. I. F. Pobezhimov, *op. cit.*, p. 86, (writing under the old Stalinist theses) announces that without this advanced frontier, the war would have gone on until 1947 or even later. By what reckoning this is made, Pobezhimov prefers not to say.

12. See Appendix II, *How Russia Makes War*, pp. 434–5.

13. See A. V. Karasev, *Leningradtsy v gody blokady* (Leningraders during the years of blockade), Moscow 1959, p. 26 (Academy of Sciences publn.). This is an extremely useful work, which self-consciously sets out to rectify the inadequate state of histories of the Leningrad siege; an account of the vicissitudes of the writing of these previous accounts (and some that were never finished) will be found, pp. 4–14. This passage illuminates types of records assembled and the inaccuracies of some of their information. The minutes of the Leningrad Military Soviet are lodged in the Defence Ministry archive. Karasev makes extensive use of Collection No. 217, which evidently deals with the military condition and operations of the Baltic and Leningrad MDs.

14. *Ibid.*, p. 27: Defence Ministry Collection No. 217.

15. *Ibid.*, p. 29 quoting a *German* Intelligence report on the state of the Baltic MD defences. *Ist. Velik. Otechest. Voiny Sov. Soyuza 1941–1945*, Moscow 1960, Vol. 1, pp. 477–8, states that a general plan for defence constructions was drawn up in the summer of 1940, but that only by June 1941 had the work been finished in the frontier areas; but that was not to say that the fortifications were manned. According to this statement, by the beginning of June, 1941, only a partial arming of the positions of the first line of defences had occurred in 4 sectors of Vladimir-Volynsk and 5 of the Strumilovsk fortified districts (URs). But since the fire-points were not fully ready, the left-flank sectors of the Vladimir-Volynsk UR were vulnerable. The 1940 plan for overhead signal wires was met by one quarter only, and only 10 per cent of the

underground lines had been put ready. This history also makes the point that the *NKVD* controlled the labour for the construction of aerodromes and forward positions (apart from military personnel); shortage of labour and materials slowed the construction work down.

16. Cf. *Fr. H. Ost (II) Nr. 33/41: Chefsache* 13th March, 1941. Also *Fr. H. Ost* for 20th March, 1941, on troop movements in the Baltic MD.

17. See *V.M.V.*, p. 177. The point of the deployment is discussed in *Ist. Velik. Otechest. Voiny Sov. Soyuza 1941–1945*, Moscow 1960, Vol. 1, p. 474, which admits that the deployment of Soviet troops was not consistent with fending off a sudden surprise attack by German troops: 'Neither an operational nor a tactical grouping of forces was established to repel an enemy blow.'

18. See *Die wichtigsten Operationen des Grossen Vaterländischen Krieges 1941–1945*, (ed. Col. P. A. Zhilin), pub. Verlag des Ministeriums für Nationale Verteidigung (East Germany), 1958, pp. 81–2. This is a translation of *Vazhneishie operatsii Velikoi Otechestvennoi Voiny 1941–1945*, Moscow 1956. Since a copy of the Soviet version was not available to me for extended use, the references are to the East German edition, cited as *Zhilin*.

19. See *N.C.A.*, Vol. VI, p. 955: Russo-German relations/High Command of the German Navy files. Entries for 16th and 17th March.

20. Cf. G. Gafencu, *op. cit.*, p. 171.

21. *N.S.R.*, p. 278.

22. See discussion and footnote in M. Beloff, *op. cit.*, Vol. 2, p. 365.

23. *Ibid.*, p. 366.

24. *Ibid.*, p. 367.

25. *N.C.A.*, Vol. VI, p. 996.

26. *Ibid.*

27. *Fr.*(emde) *H.*(eere) *Ost: Gdso* for 11th April, 1941.

28. *Generaloberst* F. Halder, *Halder Diary* (Printed by AG/Eucom. US Army): Vol. VI (period 21st February–31st July, 1941). Entry 7th April, p. 57.

29. The German concern was for the Rumanian oil-fields. See Keitel's order, *OKW Gdso: Chefsache F.H.Qu.* 26th March, 1941. In ordering increased defence measures, this pointed out: '(1) überraschende feindliche Angriffe sind mit züneh-mender Enttarnung des Aufmarsches Barbarossa *auch schon vor Beginn der Feindselig-keiten möglich.*' Emphasis as in original. Anti-aircraft defences were to be strengthened.

30. Information supplied to Dr Garthoff by a former Soviet staff officer: see *How Russia Makes War*, p. 434. This point is now made by Soviet sources.

31. Cf. *Komm. Part. Velik. Otechest. Voiny, op. cit.*, pp. 40–1.

32. See Winston S. Churchill, 'The Grand Alliance', pp. 319–22, 329. On 3rd April Churchill instructed Cripps to pass information on the movement of German armour to Southern Poland to Stalin.

33. Winston S. Churchill, 'The Hinge of Fate' (Vol. IV of *The Second World War*), p. 443: Stalin to Beaverbrook, October 1941.

34. N. Voznesenskii, *Voennaya ekonomika SSSR v period Otechestvennoi Voiny*, Moscow 1948. See translation *The Economy of the USSR during World War II*, Public Affairs Press USA 1948, p. 42.

35. See *Die Kriegswehrmacht der UdSSR* (German Army study), *AA* collection, Serial 1891H/426090–152, dated 1st January, 1941. A more detailed commentary is to be found in the bulletins *Mitteilungen zur Lage in der Sowjetunion*, originated from *Der Reichsführer SS*, 1939 forwards.

36. N. S. Khrushchev, *Secret speech* (text cited), p. 19. The descriptions are Khrushchev's.

37. See Appendix II, *How Russia Makes War*, p. 435.

38. See note to *ibid.*, p. 504. This also mentions that the Red Army would be the first to attack in August. The explanation for this may well be Stalin's concern for Red Army morale and the need to pacify the soldiers, although the main line of propaganda conducted by the Political Administration was not switched.

39. See *V.M.V.*, 'Soviet military art on the eve of the Great Patriotic War', pp. 165–76.

40. See 'X', 'Policy and Strategy in the War in Russia', *Foreign Affairs*, July 1942, No. 4, pp. 612–13 and p. 619.

41. See *N.C.A.*, Vol. VI, Document C–66, 'Memorandum for Admiral Assmann for his own use, signed "Raeder", 10th January, 1944', pp. 887–91. Raeder here sets out his view of what Stalin's intentions may have been, dismissing the idea that Stalin planned war in the autumn of 1941; Stalin's action depended on the course of the war between Germany and 'the Anglo-Saxon powers'.

42. David J. Dallin, *Soviet Espionage*, New Haven 1955, pp. 132–5. Akhmedov's testimony is from *Hearings before the Internal Security Subcommittee of the Senate Committee on the Judiciary, Interlocking Subversion in Government Departments* (US Senate), p. 1006.

43. Cf. *N.S.R.*, p. 318.

44. *Ibid.*, p. 324.

45. *Ibid.*

46. David J. Dallin, *Soviet Russia's Foreign Policy, op. cit.*, p. 348.

47. *Ibid.*, p. 332.

48. See G. Gafencu, *op. cit.*, p. 234.

49. *N.S.R.*, p. 338.

50. N. S. Khrushchev, *Secret speech* (text cited), p. 18.

51. *Ibid.*, p. 19. The information came from '. . . a certain German officer from Hitler's Headquarters'.

52. *Ibid.*

53. On the air penetrations, see *N.S.R.*, p. 329 and p. 341.

54. A. M. Samsonov, *op. cit.*, p. 35. *Study of strategical and tactical peculiarities . . . Soviet F.E. forces, op. cit.*, Vol. XIII, Japanese Spec. Stud. Manchuria, p. 64, points out that the movement of troops from the Far East had begun in March, 1941. The forces from the Urals were part of a strategic reserve, a third-line force for use either in the east or the west. In the Soviet Far East, all forces east of Lake Baikal were first-line forces for operations against the Japanese, the second-line being the Siberian District Army, west of Lake Baikal. The latter study makes the point that preparations for war in the Soviet Far East 'were more thorough than on the German front'.

55. *V.M.V.*, p. 177.

56. *Ibid.*, p. 176.

57. *Secret speech* (text cited), p. 19.

58. *Halder Diary*, Vol. VI, p. 100.

59. *Fr. H. Ost: Feinbeurteilung* 20th May, 1941.

60. *Ibid.*

61. *How Russia Makes War*, p. 92. This is quite borne out by the discussion of Soviet military science, *Ist. Velik. Otechest. Voiny Sov. Soyuza 1941–1945*, Moscow 1960, Vol. 1, pp. 447–8; this charges that the 'features of manœuvre war' were not fully exploited. Staffs were not trained in the movement of troops, and paid too little attention to securing the army by the use of 'mobile equipment'. Communications were in a serious way. The radio communication units of the high command were considered adequate to maintain communication between the General Staff and the staffs of the fronts; it was assumed that auxiliary lines from the People's Commissariat of Communications would be adequate for the traffic in time of war. The same source makes it very clear how dis-organised were the preparations for positional warfare.

62. *V.M.V.*, p. 179 for these figures.

63. N. S. Khrushchev, *Secret speech* (text cited), p. 19.

64. Lt.-Gen. Vorob'ev, 'The battle for the Black Sea bases 1941–1942' in *Zhilin, op. cit.*, p. 148.

65. *Ibid.*

66. *Ibid.*, p. 150.

67. This figure is supplied in Col. B. S. Tel'pukhovskii, *Velikaya Otechestvennaya Voina Sovetskovo Soyuza 1941–1945 gg.* (The Great Patriotic War of the Soviet Union 1941–1945), Moscow 1959, p. 40.

68. General Konrad of the *Luftwaffe* on the Soviet Air Force: *Halder Diary*, 22nd and 27th February, 1941. This would be 13 per cent, which means a 3–4 per cent increase during the spring, if both the German and Soviet figures are accepted. *Ist. Velik. Otechest. Voiny Sov. Soyuza 1941–1945*, Moscow 1960, Vol. 1, p. 476, adds the training figures for the new machines (which are stated to have formed 22 per cent of the total aviation strength of the frontier districts). For 1st May, 1941, only 72 per cent of the pilots had been trained on the Pe–2, on the LaGG–3 only 32 per cent, and on the MiG–3, about 80 per cent. For the first three months of 1941, pilots in the Baltic MD had an average of 15½ hours flying-time, in the Western MD up to 9, but only 4 hours in the Kiev MD.

69. See Appendix II, *How Russia Makes War*, p. 434.

70. See *N.C.A.*, Vol. VI, 'Time Table Barbarossa', Document C–39, p. 858. Cf. B. H. Liddell Hart, *The Other Side of the Hill*, London 1948, pp. 176–8 on the delays due to the weather and the Balkan operations.

71. The discussion here on the German side is based almost entirely on Vice-Admiral Kurt Assmann, 'The Battle for Moscow, Turning Point of the War' in *Foreign Affairs*, January 1950, No. 2, p. 312.

72. This information is based on *V.M.V.*, and *Zhilin.*

73. Cf. A. M. Samsonov, *op. cit.*, p. 34. This assertion is made generally now in Soviet accounts of the pre-June period, and Stalin is so described in the recent Party history, *Istoriya Komm. Partii Sov. Soyuza, op. cit.*, p. 519.

74. *Sov. Doc. on For. Pol.*, Vol. 3, p. 489.

75. See S. Smirnov, *Brestkaya krepost'* (The Brest fortress), Moscow 1957, p. 22.

76. N. S. Khrushchev, *Secret speech* (text cited), p. 19.

77. For details of the Rado and Rössler intelligence activities, see David. J. Dallin, *Soviet Espionage*, *op. cit.*, p. 195.

78. This version is supplied by N. S. Khrushchev, *loc. cit.*, p. 20.

79. For the naval orders, see N. P. V'yunenko, *Chernomorskii Flot v Velik. Otechest. Voine* (The Black Sea Fleet in the Great Patriotic War), Moscow 1957, p. 27. *V.M.V.*, p. 179 points out that the orders went out to the Red Army 'after it was established' that a German attack was to be expected at dawn. Cf. *Zhilin*, *op. cit.*, p. 49.

80. Signals intercepted by German Army Group Centre: see General Günther Blumentritt's account in Part Two of *The Fatal Decisions*, London 1956.

81. This first operational order is printed in A. V. Karasev, *op. cit.*, pp. 32–3. Khrushchev's account that 'Moscow issued the order that German fire was not to be returned' is very possibly something of a Khrushchev exaggeration.

82. See *V.M.V.*, pp. 183–90 and Zhilin, *op. cit.*, for Col. K. A. Cheremukhin on the Western Front (22nd June–10th July) pp. 78–111 and Col. I. P. Barabashin on the North-western Front, pp. 55–61. A. V. Karasev, *op. cit.*, puts the blame for the Baltic collapse on the shoulders of Lt.-Gen. P. S. Klenov, with his 'weak direction of military operations . . .' (p. 63).

83. *Halder Diary* (VI), p. 173.

84. *Ibid.*, p. 178.

85. See General Vlasov's biography, *loc. cit.* (G. Fischer), p. 173.

86. *Halder Diary* (VI), 27th June, p. 175.

87. *Stavka* directive cited in *V.M.V.*, p. 193.

88. B. H. Liddell Hart, *The Other Side of the Hill*, p. 186.

89. The description is Dr Garthoff's, *How Russia Makes War*, p. 196. On the governmental re-organisation see also L. Schapiro, *The Communist Party of the Soviet Union*, p. 493.

90. See the note on the organisation and strength of these detachments: *How Russia Makes War*, pp. 162–3.

91. The Soviet version of Far Eastern developments and the Japanese mobilisation will be found in D. I. Gol'dberg, *Vneshyaya politika Yaponii* (*Sentyabr' 1939–Dekabr' 1941 g.*) (Japanese Foreign Policy September 1939–December 1941), Moscow 1959, p. 152 f. The bulk of the evidence rests on the Tokyo Trials.

92. Cf. *Air Operations Record Against Soviet Russia* (Japanese Monograph No. 151), Mil. Hist. Secn. HQ Army Forces Far East, Office of the Chief of Military History, Dept. of the Army, Washington, pp. 2–4. Cf. *Study of strategical and tactical peculiarities . . . Soviet F.E. forces*, *op. cit.*, p. 64 f. In *Japanese Intelligence Planning against the USSR* (Japanese Special Studies on Manchuria), Vol. X, Chief. Mil. Hist., Dept. of the Army, Washington, Note 12, p. 108, there is a short discussion of the possibility of Soviet sabotage in Eastern Manchuria, at Tatutzuchuan on 2nd August, when huge stores of fuel and ammunition were blown up. This was interpreted by one Japanese source as a major blow at offensive Japanese plans.

93. The term as used in Kesselring, *The Memoirs of Field-Marshal Kesselring*, London 1953, p. 90.

94. Maj.-Gen. Markoff as quoted in Appendix II, *How Russia Makes War*, p. 430.

95. *V.M.V.*, p. 185.

96. On 8th July the German count was submitted as: 289,874 PWs, 2,585 tanks captured and destroyed, 1,449 guns and 246 aircraft. Army Group Centre estimated that it had crippled 22 rifle, 7 armoured and 6 cavalry divisions, plus 6 mechanised brigades. *Halder Diary* (VI), p. 214.

97. *Zhilin, op. cit.*, p. 92 and pp. 93–5.

98. *Halder Diary* (VI), 12th July, p. 226.

99. *Zhilin, op. cit.*, p. 102. Col. L. L. Dessyatov on the Smolensk defensive battles.

100. *Halder Diary* (VI), 19th July, p. 254.

101. *KPSS o voor. Sil. Sov. Soyuza, op. cit.*, pp. 358–61.

102. A. V. Karasev, *op. cit.*, p. 63.

103. See account in *ibid.*, pp. 64–5.

104. *Ibid.*, pp. 70–1.

105. *Ibid.*, p. 75.

106. *Ibid.*, pp. 98–9.

107. *Ibid.*, p. 101.

108. *Ibid.*, pp. 105–6, quoting from D. V. Pavlov, *Leningrad v blokade*, Moscow 1958.

109. *V.M.V.*, p. 207.

110. *Halder Diary* (VI), 19 July, p. 254, gives the source of this information as a captured document. Cols. L. L. Dessyatov, Zhilin and Solov'ev, discussing the Ukrainian operations in *Zhilin, op. cit.*, p. 117, quote 'documents of the German General Staff' for 18th July as: 'A wireless message of the staff of the 26th Army was intercepted, in which was reported that the attack with four rifle and two cavalry divisions in the region south of Kiev is fixed for to-morrow.'

111. This force consisted of:

95th and 25th RD
1st Cavalry Division
a composite *NKVD* frontier regiment
1st Naval Infantry Regt
54th Infantry Regt/4 artillery battalions
69th Fighter Regiment (*VVS*)
82nd, 70th Independent Naval Aviation Squadrons/Black Sea Fleet.

112. *Halder Diary* (VI), 26 July, p. 270.

113. See discussion in Vice Admiral Kurt Assmann, *loc. cit.*, p. 315. This Admiral Assmann sees as a turning point in the war, a 'Marne miracle' on the Eastern Front, giving the Russians two months grace. On 28th July Halder wrote (*Diary* (VI), p. 278) of the 'absurdity' of the present operations, which will weaken the drive on Moscow.

114. *V.M.V.*, p. 219.

115. *Ibid.*

116. Lt.-Gen. Vorob'ev in *Zhilin, op. cit.*, p. 151.

117. *Ibid.*, p. 130. Colonels Dessyatov, Zhilin and Solov'ev.

118. General H. Guderian's account 'The Battle of Kiev' in his *Panzer Leader*, London 1956 Edn.

119. Stated quite bluntly in *V.M.V.*, p. 220.

120. General Guderian's interrogation of the captured 5th Army commander.

121. General Vlasov's biography, *loc. cit.*, p. 173.

122. Note to *V.M.V.*, p. 227.

123. *Fr. H. Ost: Chefsachen 11th August, 1941*. In the Centre and North it was estimated that the Soviet command could no longer offer a unified resistance. Most of the 50 Russian armoured divisions were assumed destroyed. It was also stated that the Russians suffered from night-blindness due to poor feeding.

124. A comment on this is supplied in Maj.-Gen. Sir John Kennedy, *The Business of War*, London 1957, p. 152, note dictated on 21st July, 1941 — 'The Russians are still extremely optimistic . . . claim to have inflicted a million casualties on the Germans . . . some of German Panzer divisions are reduced to 40 or 50 tanks.'

125. See criticisms in *V.M.V.*, pp. 221–2. It is also to be noted that heavy losses of infantry officers were due to the outmoded combat regulations for infantry which had the officer at the head of his men. These were modified in 1942.

126. See 'Artillery, and Arms of Annihilation' in Col. Louis B. Ely, *The Red Army To-day*, Mil. Service Pub. Co., Harrisburg, Penn. 1953, p. 64.

127. *Halder Diary* (VI), p. 261.

128. This problem, which assumed terrifying proportions for the Soviet command, is the subject of a very serious argument in Col. A. Lagovskii, *Strategiya i Ekonomika* (Strategy and Economics), Moscow 1957, pp. 92–100, on equipment norms needed. Lagovskii uses a statistical analysis based in detail on aircraft sorties and loss.

129. *Komm. Partiya Velik. Otechest. Voiny*, *op. cit.*, p. 52.

130. *V.M.V.*, p. 227.

131. Orel was taken by Guderian's 4th *Panzer* Division.

132. D. Z. Muriev, 'Razgrom Nemetsko-fashistskikh voisk pod Moskvoi v 1941–1942' (Destruction of German-Fascist troops by Moscow in 1941–1942) in *Ist. Zapiski* Vol. 55, 1956, p. 32.

133. A. V. Karasev, *op. cit.*, pp. 132–3. A great deal of information connected with the defence of Leningrad is to be found in S. F. Edlinskii, *Baltiiskii transportnyi flot v Velikoi Otechestvennoi Voine 1941–1945 gg.* (The Baltic transport fleet in the Great Patriotic War 1941–1945), pub. 'Sea Transport', Moscow 1957. See p. 68 f. This work is also valuable for the light it throws on Soviet archives, especially port records.

134. I. P. Barbashin, A. D. Kharitonov, *Boevye deistviya Sovetskoi Armii pod Tikhvin v 1941 godu* (Military operations of the Soviet Army by Tikhvin in 1941), Moscow 1958, p. 19. Single echelon deployment alone was possible owing to the paucity of the forces and the length of the front. Klykov's 52nd Army comprised: 288th RD, 267th RD, 5 artillery regiments, one engineer battalion. Divisional strength was 65–70 per cent of the establishment (14,500). A. V. Karasev, *op. cit.*, pp. 111–12, cites the case of the 55th Army (defending the approaches to Leningrad) and assigned to Maj.-Gen. I. G. Lazarev: this new army had only 10,000 men all told, and an 'insignificant quantity' of guns, mortars and machine-guns.

135. *V.M.V.*, p. 236.

136. A. M. Samsonov, *op. cit.*, pp. 73–4.

137. This figure is supplied, *ibid.*, p. 66.

138. See G. A. Tokaev, *Comrade X*, London 1956, p. 216.

139. As in A. M. Samsonov's study of the defence of Moscow, *op. cit.*, p. 103. In a much more spectacular manner it has been admitted into Soviet novels on the war; in this connection, see a most useful discussion by Reuben Ainsztein, 'The Soviet Russian War Novel since Stalin's Death' in *The Twentieth Century*, April 1960, pp. 328–39.

140. See G. Fischer, *Soviet Opposition to Stalin, op. cit.*, p. 3, quoting a German General Staff report. There is a very full discussion of the question of Soviet prisoners of war and their voluntary surrenders.

141. Maj.-Gen. Markoff quoted in *How Russia Makes War*, p. 252. As Dr Garthoff properly observes, this officer was in a position to know the real situation.

142. *Ibid.*, p. 216. From the diary taken from the body of Security Major Shabalin; communicated to Dr Garthoff by anonymous high-ranking German source.

143. I. Deutscher, *Stalin, op. cit.*, pp. 464–5. It would be difficult to agree with the comments, pp. 494–5, on Stalin as a military leader free from strategic 'bees in his bonnet'. Stalin and Voroshilov had blotted out much of the 'original and experimenting mind' in the Red Army. One of the ironies of the 1937–8 purge of the naval command was that the test of war vindicated the soundness of the purged officers' views and by September 1941 Stalin was turning to the principles firmly developed up to 1937. Stalin's vanity, as much as his excessive suspiciousness, made significant inroads into the development of the Red Army.

144. *How Russia Makes War*, p. 258; from V. Melikov, *Problema Strategicheskovo Razvertyvaniya po Opyta Mirovoi i Grazhdanskoi Voiny* (The problem of strategic deployment in the light of the World War and Civil War), Moscow 1935, Vol. 1, p. 11.

Chapter XVIII

1. See references to Soviet Defence Ministry files, *V.M.V.*, *op. cit.*, pp. 234–5.

2. A. V. Karasev, *op. cit.*, pp. 174–5.

3. See Capt. N. Galay in *The Soviet Army*, *op. cit.*, pp. 162–3.

4. Winston S. Churchill, *op. cit.*, Vol. III, 'The Grand Alliance'. See Ch. XXI *passim* and Ch. XXV, pp. 405–7.

5. *Ibid.*, Ch. XXVIII, p. 469. A Soviet version of the origin of the alliance will be found in a work recently reprinted: V. L. Israelyan, *Diplomaticheskaya Istoriya Velik. Otechest. Voiny* (Diplomatic History of the Great Patriotic War), Moscow 1959, pp. 36–55.

6. Cited by Field-Marshal Erich von Manstein, *The Soviet Army*, p. 141.

7. N. Shigemitsu, *op. cit.*, pp. 244–5.

8. See *Study of Strategical and Tactical Peculiarities of F.E. Russia. . . . op. cit.*, p. 64.

9. Based on I. P. Barbashin and A. D. Kharitonov, *op. cit.*, p. 28.

10. *Ibid.*, pp. 28–9.

11. *Ibid.*, pp. 38–9.
12. *Ibid.*, p. 46 f.
13. The organisation of these Soviet net-works is discussed in detail in David J. Dallin, *Soviet Espionage*, *op. cit.*, p. 246 f.
14. *Ibid.*, p. 196 quoting and discussing A. Foote.
15. *V.M.V.*, *op. cit.*, pp. 245–6.
16. A. M. Samsonov, *op. cit.*, p. 132.
17. *Ibid.*, pp. 136–8.
18. *Ibid.*, p. 170.
19. N. P. V'yunenko, *op. cit.* (Black Sea Fleet), p. 99.
20. *Zhilin*, *op. cit.*, p. 156.
21. *Ibid.*
22. *V.M.V.*, p. 239.
23. I. P. Barbashin and A. D. Kharitonov, *op. cit.*, pp. 61–2.
24. *Ibid.*, p. 68 f.
25. The criticism is to be found *ibid.*, p. 77.
26. *V.M.V.*, pp. 250–1 and A. M. Samsonov, p. 172. It is here that recent Soviet accounts take issue with the idea that the Red Army enjoyed not only a general but a very marked superiority over the German Army. *V.M.V.*, written throughout from Defence Ministry archives, quotes 'archival material' for the following relationship of strengths: on the Kalinin, Western and right wing of the South-western Fronts German superiority in manpower was 1·1, in artillery 1·8 and tanks 1·4. Only in aircraft did the Red Army have any superiority and this was 2:1 in its favour. The point would be much clarified if the Soviet documents so used were printed in full, so that a comparison might be made with German statements.
27. *Zhilin*, *op. cit.*, p. 140. This account records the Soviet estimate that German reserves ready for immediate use had shrunk to 3–4 infantry divisions.
28. *V.M.V.*, p. 253.
29. *Ibid.*, p. 254.
30. A. M. Samsonov, p. 192.
31. *V.M.V.*, p. 255.
32. *Ibid.*, p. 254.
33. See Vice-Admiral Kurt Assmann, *loc. cit.*, p. 323.
34. *V.M.V.*, p. 258.
35. I. P. Barbashin and A. D. Kharitonov, *op. cit.*, p. 60.
36. *Ibid.*, p. 67.
37. *Ibid.*, p. 72. The 55th Army from within the Leningrad perimeter had also been launching a series of attacks designed to improve the situation.
38. N. P. V'yunenko, *op. cit.*, pp. 112–13.
39. See *V M.V.*, p. 263.
40. *Ibid.*, p. 264. The invasion came up against two German infantry divisions, one German and one Rumanian brigade.
41. *Ibid.*, p. 266.
42. *Ibid.*, p. 272.
43. *Ibid.*, p. 275.

44. A. M. Samsonov, p. 204.

45. *V.M.V.*, p. 266.

46. See the statement of Lieutenant-General Bulganin (Zhukov's commissar), in *How Russia Makes War*, p. 167. Bulganin's remarks were inspired by the need to show Stalin as a military leader of genius. In the course of these remarks he observed that Zhukov knew that the *Stavka* had 'large reserves' near Moscow and obviously wanted to use them. Stalin kept them back.

47. See the study in *V.M.V.*, p. 865; see the whole section, analysing the effect of the war on Soviet military art, pp. 851–73.

48. *Ibid.*, p. 278.

49. *Ibid.*

50. *Ibid.*, p. 864.

51. Figure cited in A. Surchenko, *Geroicheskaya oborona Moskvy 1941 g.* (The heroic defence of Moscow 1941), Moscow 1957, p. 61.

52. *V.M.V.*, p. 872. The corresponding figures at the battle of Stalingrad were 40–70 guns and 10–12 tanks. During the 1943–5 offensives, the gun density varied between 120–250 (this figure also included mortars) and infantry-support tanks 15–30.

53. *Ibid.*, p. 847.

54. *Ibid.*, p. 848.

55. An account of the German reserves so committed was printed in *Krasnaya Zvezda*, 8th April, 1942: see the lengthy quotation in Berhcin and Ben-Horin, *The Red Army*, *op. cit.*, pp. 233–5.

56. See General Blumentritt's views in B. H. Liddell Hart, *The Other Side of the Hill*, *op. cit.*, p. 201. *V.M.V.*, p. 281, in summing up the offensive, comes more or less to this conclusion, bringing forward as evidence the fact that the Germans were obliged to commit from December 1941–April 1942 to the Eastern Front 39 divisions and 6 brigades (analysed as follows: 11 Divs/3 Bdes. from Germany, 16 Divs. from France, 4 Divs/2 Bdes. from Rumania, 3 Divs/1 Bde. from Hungary and 2 Divs. from Yugoslavia.)

57. Cf. Major-General J. F. C. Fuller, *The Decisive Battles of the Western World*, London 1956, Vol. III, p. 445.

(NOTE: in *Vtoraya Mirovaya Voina 1939–1945*, cited as *V.M.V.*, the individual Soviet contributors were Col. I. E. Zaitsev (on the planning of Operation *Barbarossa*), Major-General N. A. Fokin (on Soviet military art, organisation and deployment on the eve of the German attack), Col. K. A. Cheremukhin on the course of military operations to 10th September, 1941, Col. A. I. Kuznetsov on the winter offensive 1941–2, and Major-General N. G. Pavlenko on Soviet military art and organisation in the Soviet-German War.)

APPENDIXES

GENERAL APPENDIX

I. Strength and Composition of the Red Army: 1918–1941

1. *Numerical strength*

1918 (May–October)	50–100,000 *trained* effectives (Official figure: 306,000)
1919 (January–February)	343,100 infantry 40,060 cavalry in field armies 137,000 mobilised in military districts (Reports of Vatsetis)
1919 (June)	1,500,000
1920 (1st October)	*5,498,000 mobilised* 2,587,000 in reserve armies 391,000 in Labour Armies 159,000 on all fronts 1,780,000 drawing rations as military Maximum strength for 1920 given as: 5,500,000 of which 800,000 combat effectives (4–500,000 riflemen) (*N. Movchin*)
1921 (1st January) (1st May)	4,110,000 2,614,000
1922 (1st January)	1,590,000
1923 (first half) (1st October)	703,000 dropping to 600,000 566,517
1924 (1st October)	529,865
1925–1934	562,000 (ceiling of cadre force) plus Territorial-militia
1934	940,000
1935–6	1,300,000 (*Note:* 77 per cent regular after 1936)

1. *Numerical strength*—continued

1941 (June)	Total mobilisation estimate: 9,000,000 4,700,000 in European Russia
(November)	Estimated total strength: 6,900,000 2,300,000 on the European fronts

2. *Organisation of the Red Army: estimates of strength*

Note: Varying assessments are presented where necessary. Armed formations of the *OGPU/NKVD* and auxiliary forces (such as railway troops) are also included. The strength of the Special Red Banner Army of the Far East (*OKDVA*) is presented separately for 1933–7 and its strength set off for 1941.

1918–20

Planned: mid-April, 1918	30 Divisions
May, 1918	Revised to 88 Divisions
Directive No. 4 11/9/1918	Planned 47 Rifle Divisions 4 Cavalry Divisions 1 Cavalry Brigade

By 1920

16 Armies: 70 Divisions (widely varying divisional strength): 2 Cavalry Armies

1923–4 ('Mixed military system')

17 Corps: 52 Rifle Divisions: (34 regular 15 territorial 3 national)	10 Cavalry Divisions 8 Independent Cavalry Brigades 1 Detached Territorial Cavalry Brigade

1925–6

19(?) Corps:	77 Rifle Divisions: (31 regular 46 territorial)	11 Cavalry Divisions: (1 territorial) 8 Cavalry Brigades	77 Artillery Regiments 428 Artillery Battalions 1,212 Batteries (3,718 guns)

1928 *Reichswehrministerium/Statistische Abteilung*

Estimate of strength and mobilisation

70 Rifle Divisions: (35 on frontier facing Poland)	3 Cavalry Corps: 6 Cavalry Divisions (frontier defence)	40 Territorial Divisions: (10–12 day mobilisation)	/160 Divisions *Total* after 21 days mobilisation

1929

66 Rifle Divisions:	12 Cavalry Divisions:	66 Artillery Regiments
(29 regular	9 Cavalry Brigades	21 Artillery Battalions
37 territorial)		(Heavy Field Artillery)
	455 cavalry squadrons	
594 infantry battalions	66 detached squadrons	

1930

25 Corps:	70 Rifle Divisions:	13 Cavalry Divisions:	59 Artillery Regiments:
(21 rifle	(29 regular	(10 regular	(31 light
4 cavalry)	41 territorial)	3 territorial)	28 heavy)
		45 Cavalry Brigades:	Plus territorial force
	212 regiments	(36 regular	
	(89 regular	9 territorial)	
	123 territorial)		
	636 battalions		
	9 machine-gun battalions		
	174 artillery batteries		

Engineers

16 battalions (9 bridging)

1933–7

Special Red Banner Army of the Far East

Estimate: 1933–5

11 Rifle Divisions:	3–4 Cavalry Divisions:	Technical: troops	Frontier Defence Force (under *NKVD*) 40–50,000

Military strength: 200,000. Soviet-Mongol forces (extreme right flank) 50–100,000

Estimate (Major Miyasaki): 1937

15 Rifle Divisions:	3 Cavalry Divisions:	Frontier Defence Force: (40,000)	'Kolkhoz Troops' (30,000)

Regular military strength:	240,000
Aircraft:	1,000 (including 80 heavy bombers)
Tanks:	900
Armoured Cars:	400

1935

(i)

27 Corps:	90 Rifle Divisions:	16 Cavalry Divisions:	8 Artillery Brigades
(23 Rifle 4 Cavalry)		6 Independent Cavalry Brigades	(Main reserve)

20–30 Engineer Battalions:
(Main reserve)

Frontier troops: 70,000

Local Defence Militia: 11 regiments, 28 independent battalions, 50 independent companies

Armed Railway Troops: about 80,000

Militarised Factory Protection Units: ?

OGPU/NKVD troops: strength 150,000, organised into rifle and cavalry divisions with tanks and aircraft

Tank park: about 3,000
(German military estimate)

(ii) *1935*

27 Corps:	84 Rifle Divisions:	16 Cavalry Divisions:	125 Artillery Regiments:
(23 Rifle 4 Cavalry)	(26 regular 58 territorial)	6 Independent Cavalry Brigades	25 Heavy Field Artillery

23 Engineer Battalions:	5 Tank Regiments:	10 Railway Regiments:
	12 Independent Tank Battalions	

3 Chemical Warfare Regiments

11 Independent Chemical Warfare Battalions

1936–7

(*Note:* composition 77 per cent regular, 23 per cent territorial.)

34 Corps:	87–90 Rifle Divisions:	32 Cavalry Divisions:	150 Artillery Regiments
(27 rifle 7 cavalry)	261–270 Regiments (Rifle Division war-strength: approx. 14,000)		90 (light 60 heavy)

4(?) Mechanised Corps (for independent operations, as well as assisting break-through)

25 Tank Brigades

1939

108 Rifle Divisions: 30 Cavalry Divisions: approx. 30 Mechanised and Tank Brigades
Forces estimated by British (August 1939) available on western frontier:

	Possible increase
20 Cavalry Divisions	same figure
42 Rifle Divisions	100–110
3 Mechanised Corps	4
17 Mechanised and Tank Brigades	

NOTE. The mechanised corps, of which there were an estimated 7 each with 500 tanks, were being disbanded as a result of incorrect evaluation of the experiences of the Spanish Civil War.
The British military estimate rated a mechanised corps as the equivalent of 'a light armoured division'.

Estimate for the Far East:
32 Rifle Divisions: 5 Cavalry Divisions

1940

20 Armies: 30 Rifle Corps: 9 Cavalry Corps: 30–40 Mechanised Brigades
151 Rifle Divisions 32 Cavalry Divisions

August:

	Rifle Divisions	Cavalry Divisions	Mechanised Brigades
Total	151	32	38
For defence			
Western Frontiers	55	9	10
Soviet Far East	34	8	8
Facing Turkey	6	1	–
Facing Finland	15	–	2

Note: late 1940, the mechanised and tank corps re-introduced.
To each Army Group, 1 Air Fleet attached.

1941

(i) *January*

20 Armies: 150 Rifle Divisions: 9 Cavalry Corps: Minimum of 35–6 Mechanised/ (15 motorised) Tank Brigades
(This estimate proved to be much too low)

(ii) *April*

171 Rifle Divisions: 36 Cavalry Divisions: 3 Armoured Corps: 40 Mechanised/ Tank Brigades

(iii) *June*

Total strength European Russia: 213 divisions. 171–5 Rifle Divisions

(iv) *July* 30–6 Cavalry Divisions

6 Armoured Divisions

180–188 Rifle Divisions: 6 Armoured Divisions: 55–60 Mechanised/Tank Brigades

(v) *1st December, 1941*

12 Army Groups: 45 Armies; 263–5 Rifle Divisions: 40–1 Cavalry Divisions: 50–1 Mechanised/Tank Brigades.
On European Front, facing the German Army:
7 Army Groups: 33 Armies: 200 Rifle Divisions: 35 Cavalry Divisions: 40 Tank Brigades
Soviet Far East: 18 Rifle Divisions: 1 Cavalry Division; 5 Tank Brigades

---

3. *Outline of organisation: Soviet motor-mechanised/mechanised/tank forces.*

1920–2	1 (the 7th) Tank Detachment
1924	1 Independent Tank Regiment
	2 Tank Battalions (1 cadre, 1 training)
1925	Tank Regiment replaced by 1 Independent Heavy and 1 Light Tank Battalion, each with 3 companies of 10 tanks
	Armoured Train Regiment
	3 Armoured Trains and 2 artillery batteries.

1928–9

1 Tank Regiment (MS–1 tanks)
1 Experimental Composite Mechanised Regiment.

1930–2

(*a*) *Independent mechanised and tank unities*

May 1930 1st Mechanised Brigade
2 tank battalions
2 motorised infantry battalions
1 artillery battalion
1 reconnaissance battalion
Re-organised with 3 regiments
1 light (reconnaissance) regiment
1 tank regiment
1 artillery regiment

1932 Mechanised Brigade expanded into a Mechanised Corps:
2 Mechanised Brigades
1 Rifle/machine-gun brigade
1 Independent AA battalion

(*b*) *The Tank Reserve of the Supreme Command* (*TRGK*)

Organised into tank regiments, battalions and companies
(Tank regiment: 2–3 battalions of 2–3 companies)
For break-through and support of main operations

(*c*) *Tank units*

General support roles and co-operation with cavalry.
Independent tank and 'tankette' battalions
'Tankette' and armoured-car companies

Proportion of (*a*), (*b*), (*c*) of Soviet tank and mechanised force:

(*a*) 33·5 per cent
(*b*) 15·5 per cent
(*c*) 51 per cent

(German estimate, on count of machines seen at parades, of tank park, 1933: 2,000)

1935

Estimated: 25 mechanised brigades/or, 15 brigades and 50 regiments
Estimate of Soviet tank park: 10,000 tanks (150,000 military tractors
100,000 military lorries)

NOTE. A 'few' tank and mechanised corps, according to Soviet sources, were created in the 1930's, but 'erroneous interpretation' of the experience of the Spanish Civil War caused them to be disbanded.

1936–7

Mechanised Brigade:

3 Tank battalions (32 tanks in each) Equipped with *BT* tanks
1 Light Tank battalion (reconnaissance)
1 Machine-gun battalion (lorried)

Motor-mechanised Brigade:

2 Tank battalions
1 Light Tank battalion
2 Machine-gun battalions Tank-borne infantry (up to a battalion)
7 men carried on 1 tank

Tank Brigade:

4 Tank battalions (32 tanks in each) Equipped with T–28
distribution in corps and divisions (rifle and cavalry):
Corps: 1 tank regiment
Division: 1 tank battalion, 1 medium tank company, 2 light tank companies.
Also Motor-Mechanised Corps: up to 7, each with 500 tanks (Note: *PU–36* drops the term 'motor-mechanised' for 'mechanised' only.)

1938–9

Disbanding of mechanised corps, distribution of tanks to infantry formations as infantry support tanks. Highest tactical unity: mechanised or tank brigade. Estimated number: 36.

1940–1

Autumn 1940, hasty re-introduction of large armoured formations; planned to have 20 Tank Corps (40–50 tank divisions).

Tank division (1940 establishment): 2 Tank regiments (up to 400 tanks)
1 Motorised infantry regiment
1 Artillery regiment

Tank corps: 2 Tank divisions, 1 motorised rifle division.

Estimated tank park: 20,000 (lowest figure, 15,000: highest 24,000) of which 1,475 KV or T–34 by 15th June, 1941.

Characteristics of principal Soviet tank models

MS–1 (also designated T–18) 1929	5·2 tons, raised to 5·5 later 1 37-mm gun: 1 machine-gun 17 kilometres per hour (increased to 22) Crew: 2 Range: 60–70 miles Air-cooled engine.
T–24 (1930)	18·5 tons 1 45-mm gun: 4 machine-guns Maximum speed: 22 kilometres per hour Crew: 5 M–6 engine, 300 H.P.
Bystrokhodnyi Tank (BT) (Based on American Christie designs) *BT–2* (1931)	 11 tons 1 37-mm gun: 1 DT machine-gun 96 shells and 2,709 MG rounds 13-mm turret armour Crew: 3 Liebert aero-engine: 400 H.P. Range: 100 miles.

Characteristics of principal Soviet tank models—continued

BT–5 (1932)	11·5 tons 1 improved 45-mm gun (optical sight): 1 DT machine-gun Radio 72 rounds (in radio-equipped tank) 115 rounds where no radio M–5 Soviet-produced engine (later BT–5 models equipped with short (16·5 calibres) 76·2-mm gun, 1 DT 7·62-mm machine-gun. So-called 'artillery tanks', for use in second echelon as fire-support for assault tanks. Some BT–5 equipped in 1938 with V–2 Diesel engine.)
BT–7 (1935)	13·8 tons 1 45-mm gun (or short 76·2-mm gun): 1 machine-gun (or anti-aircraft machine-gun) 172–188 rounds (without radio) 132–146 (with radio) Speed (tracked): 53·4 kilometres per hour Range: 150–170 miles. (BT–7M — 1939 series — Diesel-engined, weight 14·65 tons, speed on tracks 62 kilometres p.h.)

(BT–7 models used in Khalkhin-Gol operations, and in Poland, 1939.)

T–26 Influenced by Vickers 6-ton tank T–26A (1931–3 twin-turret model)	8 tons 2 machine-guns (a few with 1 37-mm gun and 1 machine-gun) 90 H.P. engine Speed: 30 kilometres p.h. Range: 60 miles.
T–26B (1933 single-turret)	9·4 tons 1 45-mm gun: 1 machine-gun (some with 1 76·2-mm gun) Radio. 2 searchlights for night operations Serial production provisionally discontinued in mid-1930's, in favour of the T–46.

Characteristics of principal Soviet tank models—continued

T–26S (1937)	Electro-welded in parts 10·3 tons 1 45-mm gun: 1 machine-gun Radio 165 rounds: 3,654 machine-gun rounds Range: 100–130 miles. (T–26 also used as basis for tests with SP guns)
T–28 (Medium tank) (1932)	28 tons Triple-turret: 1 76·2-mm gun, 3–4 machine-guns. In 1938 equipped with L–10 26 calibres long 76·2-mm gun. 70 shells: 7,938 machine-gun rounds Crew: 6 Radio Range: less than 135 miles Speed: 37 kilometres p.h., with M–17L engine of 500 H.P. Modernised after Soviet-Finnish War, weight raised to 31–2 tons, armour thickened.
T–35 (Heavy tank) (1933–1939)	50 tons 1 76·2-mm and 2 45-mm guns: 5 machine-guns 96 76·2-mm shells, 220 45-mm: 10,000 machine-gun rounds Maximum speed: 30 kilometres p.h. Engine: M–17, 500 H.P. Range: nearly 100 miles. (Used early in Soviet-German War)
T–34 (Medium) (1939 — in service 1940)	28 tons 1 76·2-mm gun: 2 machine-guns Water-cooled, 12-cylinder Diesel engine, 500 H.P. (V–2) Crew: 4–5 Speed: 55 kilometres p.h.
KV–1 (Heavy) (Designed earlier than the T–34: introduced 1940.)	43–47 tons 1 76·2-mm gun: 3 machine-guns Water-cooled Diesel engine (V–2), 600 H.P. Crew: 5 Speed: 35 kilometres p.h.
KV–2	As KV-1, with increased weight but with 152-mm howitzer.

II. ATTESTATION: COMMAND AND POLITICAL STAFF, RED ARMY

(A case from captured Soviet military records)

Note: Since much reference has been made to the importance of the political dossier accompanying an officer in his career, and also to the process of attestation, two cases are reproduced here in the form in which they were originally done. Source — captured Soviet military documents, Finland 1939–40. See V. Zenzinov, *Vstrecha s Rossiei* . . . Pis'ma v Krasnuyu Armiyu, N.Y. 1944 Part III.

Name of officer: Senior Lieutenant P. N. Sokol'chuk.

ATTESTATION SHEET

for awarding the next military promotion
Chief of Signals of the 44th Artillery Regiment
Senior Lieutenant SOKOL'CHUK Pavel Nikolayevich

Award next
military rank

....

People's Commissar for
Defence USSR, Marshal of
the Soviet Union

....1939

	ATTESTATION	Decision of senior and middle grade commanders	Decision of District Attestation Commission
Present post: Chief of Signals (Regiment) since 27/3/38 Number of order for appointment: K(iev) M(ilitary) D(istrict) 0237, 1938 Date of birth: 1907 Party status, length of	Personal general educational, political and specialist qualification good. Works hard and successfully to improve himself. Willing and useful commander. Carries out his duties completely satisfactorily. Worthy to be awarded next military rank CAPTAIN		

service: Party member since May, 1932. Party Card No. 0264515 Social origin: Worker Nationality: Ukrainian General Education: lower Military Education: Courses with 6th radio battalion U/MD in 1932 Service with RKKA: from 31/11/1929 Service in the Civil War: None Decorations: Has none. Date, order number for award of previous military rank: NKO SSSR 1938 No. 0143p dated 20/2	Regimental Commander Shamsheyev Acting Military Commissar Politruk Chernov		

Follows attestation for the period 1/1/38 to 28/2/1938, signed by Chief of Staff 44 AR Captain Glagolev (noting conclusion of 1935 attestation)

Decision of senior commanders

Attestation and extract (from 1935 report) agreed
Commander 44 Art. Regt. Major Shamsheyev
Acting Military Commissar Politruk V. Chernov

Decision of Attestation Commission

To draw attention to the personal execution of the instructions of the higher constituted staff

Performs the duties of Chief of Signals Arty. Regt., satisfactorily.

President of the Commission — Major Gurenko
Members: Chief of Political Section, Battalion Commissar Pletsint
Chief of Artillery, Colonel Marushev
Secretary of Party Commission, Politruk Kravets
Plenipotentiary Special Section State Security Administration NKVD (OO UGB NKVD) 44 r. div. Kondratskii
Commander artillery regiment 44 arty. regt., Shamsheyev
Military Commissar 44 arty. regt., Politruk Chernov

31 December 1938

Final decision confirming attestation
dated 8th January, 1939, signed by commander and commissar 44 Rifle Division

Actualisation of the attestation
Enrolment on the list of candidates .... Signatures .... date

Attached: Extract from the 11th session of the Party purge commission in 44 AR, 5–6 November, 1933
Case 4: Sokol'chuk, P.N. . . .
Decision: Sokol'chuk's case — Party membership verified.

Also an *Autobiography*, written by Sokol'chuk, dated 21st February, 1939, and confirmed by chief of staff Captain Glagolev

POLITICAL STAFF
Junior Politruk S. G. Lishchuk

PARTY-CHARACTERISATION
(PART-KHARAKTERISTIKA)

Lishchuk Sidor Grigor'evich, candidate member VKP(b) since 1938, candidate card No. 1144651, born 1911, collective farm worker, Ukrainian, 4th grade education, Red Army since 1933.

During the period of taking part in Party organisational courses for junior Politruks K(iev) S(pecial) M(ilitary) D(istrict) from 15/8/1938 to 15/2/1939 comrade Lishchuk has shown himself to be devoted to the work of the Party and the Soviet government.

Politically steadfast, morally sound, a disciplined candidate to the Party. Political development completely satisfactory. About soc(ial)-economic disciplines he has sound and good valuations.

He has taken part in Party work (carrying out independent assignments), he has worked hard to improve himself. He enjoys authority among the Communists.
Secretary of the praesidium of the Company Party organisation Lavrenov
Members of the praesidium Grigoroshvili
Belousov
Kofman

Confirmed at session of the Party bureau of the Courses /29/1/1939
Secretary Party bureau Kursov
Battalion Commissar Ivchenko

APPENDIX I

(material from the period 1918–20)

On the Supreme Military Soviet

V. I. Lenin to N. I. Podvoiskii. Telegram.

1st April 1918

At the head of the defence affairs of the country will be the Supreme Military Soviet, to which will be entrusted the following tasks:

(*a*) presenting the basic tasks concerning the defence of the country to the military and naval departments;

(*b*) presenting tasks connected with the organisation of the armed forces of the country (army and navy) to the defence departments;

(*c*) unifying the activities of the army and the navy and solving all general questions relating to military and naval departments;

(*d*) the systematic collection of factual information on all military personnel fitted by their professional knowledge and combat experience for appointment to the higher military command.

The staff of the Supreme Military Soviet will be made up of:

1. In the capacity of president — the People's Commissar for Military Affairs;

2. The People's Commissar for Naval Affairs, member of the collegiate of the People's Commissariat for Military Affairs;

3. Two military specialists, possessing a knowledge of military matters and combat experience, and one naval specialist, also possessing a knowledge of military affairs and combat experience.

President of the Soviet of People's Commissars
V. Ul'yanov (Lenin)

V. I. Lenin, *Voen. Perepis*, Moscow 1956, pp. 32–3.

Plan for a military centre to re-organise the army. 9th March, 1919

Decision of the Soviet of People's Commissars. 9th March.

With the undermentioned experienced and skilful military specialists, who have expressed a readiness to work with the Soviet government and under its direction, Yurii Danilov, Vassili Al'tfater and Aleksandr Aledogskii, it is proposed to set up a commission for the presentation if possible not later than 15th March (2nd March) of a plan for the organisation of a military centre for the re-organisation of the army and for the creation of a powerful armed force on the principles of a socialist militia and the universal arming of the workers and the peasants.

President of the Soviet of People's Commissars.
Secretary of the Soviet.

Setting up of the Supreme Military Soviet. Not later than 4th March, 1918

The Supreme Military Soviet consisting of: M. D. Bonch-Bruevich, military director, and two political commissars P. P. Prosh'yan and K. I. Shutko: is entrusted with the direction of all military operations with the unconditional subordination of all military institutions and personnel without exception to the Supreme Military Soviet.

President of the Soviet of People's Commissars
V. UL'YANOV (LENIN)

Dekrety Sov. Vlasti, Vol. 1, 1957, p. 577 and p. 522.

Provisional instruction on the Collegiate of the People's Commissariat for Naval Affairs: 30th April, 1918

(Extract of items No. 4–16 from Nos. 1–23)

4. The Collegiate of the People's Commissariat for Naval Affairs will consist of the People's Commissar for Naval Affairs and four members — two for specialist and two for political matters.
5. The president of the Collegiate of the People's Commissariat for Naval Affairs will be the People's Commissar for Naval Affairs.
6. The People's Commissar for Naval Affairs will be appointed to this post by decree of the Soviet of People's Commissars, with the confirmation of the Central Executive Committee.
7. The People's Commissar for Naval Affairs will be the chief representative of the Government in the Naval Administration.
8. The specialist-members of the Collegiate of the People's Commissariat for Naval Affairs will be chosen by the People's Commissar for Naval Affairs from the command staff of the fleet and appointed by decree of the Soviet of People's Commissars.
9. The specialist-members of the Collegiate of the People's Commissariat for Naval Affairs will be termed the 1st and 2nd naval members.
10. Political affairs-members of the Collegiate of the People's Commissariat for Naval Affairs will be chosen by the People's Commissar for Naval Affairs, appointed by decree of the Soviet of People's Commissars and will be named members of the Collegiate of the People's Commissariat for Naval Affairs.
11. One of the members for political matters in the Collegiate of the People's Commissariat for Naval Affairs, at the selection of the People's Commissar for Naval Affairs, will become Deputy People's Commissar for Naval Affairs and so announced by decree of the Soviet of People's Commissars.
12. The 1st Naval Member of the Collegiate of the People's Commissariat for Naval Affairs will concern himself at the same time with the responsible direction on matters: the functioning of the Naval General Staff, fleet personnel in connection with manning and recruitment, training, service records, naval training-establishments.
13. The 2nd Naval Member of the Collegiate of the People's Commissariat for Naval

Affairs will occupy himself with the responsible direction of technical and supply matters.

14. The Collegiate of the People's Commissariat for Naval Affairs is charged with the responsibility for maintaining the fleets in proper order and in a state of combat readiness.

15. The Collegiate of the People's Commissariat for Naval Affairs will direct the activities of all parts of the administration towards the ends of their establishment.

16. In relation to the fleets in time of peace, and to units, administrations, establishments and institutions of the Naval Administration in general, the Collegiate of the People's Commissariat for Naval Affairs will enjoy the rights of a fleet commander and flag-officer separately of the commander and will moreover have the right: (*a*) to change the existing establishments and instructions, and equally to issue and alter, in case of need, new establishments for units, administrations and institutions, for which the existing establishments make no provision; (*b*) to appoint commanders of squadrons, detachments, brigades, commanding officers for ships in the 1st and 2nd grade and other personnel, enjoying authority with them; in naval administrations, establishments and institutions to name to all appointments not lower than chiefs of sections and units; (*c*) to assign to duty or remove personnel in the latter category, and equally to transfer from one post to another all serving in the fleet and the Naval Administration; (*d*) to dismiss at its discretion all personnel serving in the fleet or the Naval Administration within the Republic or abroad.

Dekrety Sov. Vlasti, Vol. 2, pp. 195–7. For the instruction on the administration of the Baltic Fleet, 29th March ,1918, see *ibid.*, pp. 31–3.

TABLE

Organisation of Military Commissariats at Lower Levels: Okrug (Region), Guberniya (Province), Uyezdnyi (District or County), Volostnyi (Small Rural Township) and Town Commissariats

Region: *OKRUG.*

Department 1. *Commissariat Administration*
Secretariat controlling Guberniya commissariat affairs.

Department 2. *Regional Staff*
Automobile department
Administrative department
Mobilisation
Military Communications
Economic Administration

Department 3. *Political Administration*
Editorial section for orders and announcements
Newspaper section
Educational and agitation section
Personnel
Organisation section

Legal section
Press section
Economic section

Department 4. *Inspectorates*
Infantry
Cavalry
Artillery
Military engineers

Department 5. *Supply and Provisioning Administration*
Veterinary
Food
Technical
Billets and quarters
Artillery
Hygiene and medical

The Standing Council of the Region
Control functions

PROVINCE: *GUBERNIYA*

Headed by a commissar nominated from the centre and 3 section chiefs.
With 10 sections:
Administrative
Agitation-Recruiting
Survey (local resources)
Unit formation and training
Universal military training (*Vsevobuch*)
Supply
Instructor section
Transport
Hygiene and Medical
Veterinary

DISTRICT, COUNTY: *UYEZD*

Headed by a commissar appointed by the Regional Commissariat
Chief of the Political Section is his deputy
Commissariat office
Mobilisation section
Supply
General training
Political

SMALL RURAL TOWNSHIPS: *VOLOSTNYI*

Run by a military commissar
No fixed establishment

Organisation of the Republic Revvoensoviet: by Departments

Department One.	Revvoensoviet Administration.
Sections	(1) military-administrative
	(2) personnel qualifications
	(3) general/routine
	(4) military-economic.
Department Two.	Central Military Supply.
Sections	(1) main administration/provisioning
	(2) artillery administration
	(3) meteorological
	(4) engineering administration
	(5) military-economic administration.
Department Three.	Political (*PUR*)
Department Four.	Military Soviet for Military Regulations/Legal Branch.
Sections	(1) regulations and legal codifications
	(2) budgetary
Department Five.	Financial.
Sections	(1) General financial direction for all departments
	(2) control and supervision
	(3) economic — in co-operation with Department Four
	(4) general/routine
	(5) Press
Department Six.	Field Staff
	(1) Operational Staff
	(2) Command administration: 2 sections
	(i) military-administrative, for lower command staff higher command staff administrative staff
	(ii) general/routine, for general reports (including casualties) accounts information/co-operates with *PUR* archives.
Department Seven.	Military and Naval Inspectorate
Directors	President and Vice-President
Composition	Directorate of Military and Naval Inspection
	Military and naval inspectors to military/naval installations and fronts.
Department Eight.	The All-Russian Supreme Staff
Sections and Administrations	(1) Organisation for army organisation, composition of troops, training, compiling training manuals, regulations and planning
	(2) Mobilisation

for general mobilisation matters, detailed mobilisation measures, strength and manning of fronts, demobilisation

(3) Personnel/Command Staff
lists/numbers of Red Army command staff, other ranks

(4) Military-topographic
mapping corps, 5 units: Northern, Western, South-western, Central Asian, Far Eastern

(5) Main Administration/Universal Military Training (*Vseobuch*)

(6) Main Administration/Military Schools and Education
- (i) personnel
- (ii) financial
- (iii) teaching and organisation: inspectorate for infantry, cavalry, artillery instructional courses

(7) Main Administration/Military stores:
- (i) arms and ammunition stores
- (ii) provision stores
- (iii) control section

Each store with a collection and distribution department.

Department Nine. Military-Revolutionary Tribunal
Introduces regulations for 'comradely courts', pre-front, local and company tribunals.

Department Ten. Military-Hygiene Administration
- (i) administrative
- (ii) medical-sanitation
- (iii) supply
- (iv) evacuation

Organisation People's Commissariat Military Affairs: by Departments

1. Supreme Military Inspectorate
2. Main Administration Military Air Fleet
3. Aviation Council
4. Committee of aerial defence
5. Main Administration Billets and Quarters
6. Main Veterinary Administration
7. Military Repair Administration
8. Supreme Valuation Commission
9. Commission for winding-up military stores
10. Demobilisation Commission
11. Bureau of Military Commissars
12. Central Administration for prisoners and evacuated persons
13. Central Administration of the Proletarian Red Cross
14. Central Collegiate of the Russian Red Cross
15. Armoured forces Administration
16. Military Radio/Telegraphic Administration

Organisation People's Commissariat for Naval Affairs: by Departments

1. Naval General Staff: operational
2. Supreme Naval Staff; naval quartering/personnel department
3. Main Administration Ship Construction
4. Main Administration Naval Economics
5. Main Hydrographic Administration
6. Ship construction section
7. Naval aviation administration
8. Naval schools administration
9. Naval hygiene-sanitation administration
10. Docks/Dry-docks administration

V. I. Lenin to S. I. Gusev. Letter of 16th September, 1919, criticising the Republic *Revvoensoviet* (*RVSR*) for its failure to deal with Denikin and Mamontov.

Comrade Gusev! Having gone deeply into Sklyanskii's letter (on the state of affairs 15/IX) and into the results according to the reports, I am convinced that our RVSR is working badly.

Smoothing things over and smoothing things over — that is bad tactics. The 'game of keeping quiet' is the result.

We have stagnation in our work — it has almost broken down.

You have put some kind of dirty scum in Ol'derog and grandma Pozern on the Siberian Front and 'things are being smoothed over'. Shame on you! And they have started to beat us! We will hold the RVSR responsible for that, if *energetic* measures are not taken! To let victory slip through our fingers — shame.

Stagnation with Mamontov. Apparently delay on delay. You delayed the troops, moving from the north to Voronezh. You delayed with shifting the 21 Division south. You delayed with the automatic machine-guns. You delayed with liaison. Whether *Glavkom* went to Orel on his own or with you — the jobs were not done. You have not established communications with Selivachev, you have not arranged any supervision over him, contrary to the *long-standing* and *direct* requirement of the Central Committee.

As a result there is stagnation both with Mamontov and stagnation around Selivachev (instead of those day-to-day 'victories' promised by the childish little drawings — do you remember those drawings which you showed me? and I said: They have forgotten about the enemy! !).

If Selivachev abandons his post or his divisional commanders change sides, the RVSR will be to blame, for it slept and relaxed, and did not do its job. It is essential to send the best, *most energetic* commissars to the south, but not sleepy-heads.

We are also behindhand with raising troops. We are letting the autumn slip past — while Denikin triples his forces, gets tanks and so on and so on. We can't go on like this. We must transform the *drowsy* tempo into a *brisk* one.

Send me a reply (through L. Al. Fotiev).

Lenin

16.IX.

Apparently our RVSR 'gives out the orders', is not interested or is unable to keep an eye on *putting them into effect*. If that is our general error, then in military affairs that is outright disaster.
(Emphasis as in the original)
V. I. Lenin, *Sochineniya.*, 4th Edn., Vol. 35, 1955, No. 224, pp. 356–7.

S. M. Budenny to V. I. Lenin on the operations of the 1st Cavalry Army. Letter, 1st February, 1920

Bagaevskaya stanitsa on the River Don, 1st February, 1920.

Deeply respected leader, Vladimir Il'ich! Forgive me for addressing myself to you with this letter. I very much wish to see you personally and bow before you as the great leader of all poor peasants and workers. But duty at the front and Denikin's bands prevent me from doing that. I have to inform you, Comrade Lenin, that the Cavalry Army is going through a difficult time. Never yet has anyone beaten my cavalry, like the Whites have beaten it now. And they have beaten it, because the Front Commander has positioned the Cavalry Army in such conditions, that it might perish altogether. It is shameful for me to speak to you about this, but I love the Cavalry Army, yet I love the Revolution still more. And the cavalry is still very necessary to the Revolution. Front Commander Shorin first positioned the cavalry in the Don swamp and obstructed the forcing of the River Don. The enemy profited by this and nearly wiped out all our cavalry. And when the *Revvoensoviet* demanded that the line of advance of the Cavalry Army be changed, Comrade Shorin deprived me of the infantry of the army entrusted to me. He handed two infantry divisions over to the 8th Army, but the Cavalry Army was thrown alone against the enemy and for a second time ended up being severely knocked about. During the whole of my command there were never any tragic events like these. And since only Shorin had the right to decide on the disposition of the army entrusted to me, so calamities poured out. As far back as 26th October, 1919, when I was subordinate to Comrade Shorin, he gave me a task, which damaged our prospects and was beneficial to the enemy. Then I told him about this by telegraph, and he, evidently, he was hurt and remembered it, and now all that is being reflected in our general revolutionary work. To-day I got the assignment of beating the enemy and moving on 60 *versts*, but the neighbouring armies are stationed according to Shorin's directive in the place and in such a way they give the enemy the chance of removing his units from the front and throwing them in against the Cavalry Army. That is a patent crime. I beg you to turn your attention to the Cavalry Army and other armies, else they lay down their lives in vain because of such criminal command.

I give you a firm hand-clasp. Army Commander 1st Cavalry

BUDENNY.

S. M. Budenny, *Proidennyi Put*, pp. 398–9.

M. N. Tukhachevsky's letter to G. Zinoviev, 18th July, 1920

Deeply respected Comrade Zinoviev.

The Second Congress of the Communist International has prompted me to put down in this letter to you a few words on the military question.

The civil war — not a small and not a partisan war — but a large, physically-exhausting civil war, which we have been waging for two and a half years, came as a surprise to us with regard to its extent.

As regards a regular proletarian army the general body of the members of our Party were not prepared.

That lack of preparation of ours for war is making itself felt right up to the present time. The main reason for these blunders lies in the fact that the theoretical form and means of resistance to the bourgeoisie in the period of the socialist revolution have not been investigated. The strategy and tactics of civil wars and imperialist or national wars in one and the same epoch (as regards their form and means) are not the same. Special investigation of the theory of civil war is necessary, in which war the working class, and consequently the Communist Party, as the attacking side, is interested above all else and therefore must be its investigators.

In essence the foundation of a science of civil war consists only of the development of the basic principles of Karl Marx's theory of revolution and from this it is understood what relation the strategy of the civil war has to the programme of our Party. Marx ends up with the dictatorship of the proletariat. The strategy of civil war is a continuation of that theory and examines the military forms and means with which the insurrectionary proletariat protects and expands its dictatorship right up to the withering away of states, classes and armies.

The main principles in the strategy of class, that is, civil war, on which it is fit to base all calculations and which are sharply distinguished from such principles in the strategy of imperialist war, will be as follows:

1. The war can be concluded only with the coming to power of the universal dictatorship of the proletariat, since the world bourgeoisie will not permit the socialist island to live in peace.

2. From the first point it follows that the state, falling under the power of the working class, sets for itself a political aim in war which is not in conformity with its armed forces and military means, but, on the contrary, must create for itself adequate forces for the conquest of the bourgeois states of the whole world.

3. The source of recruitment of the army will consist of the proletariat of the whole world, independent of nationality.

4. The socialist island will never have peaceful frontiers with the bourgeois state. That will always be a front, even though it may be in a latent form.

From these basic principles all the features of the strategy of civil war can be developed.

Taking into account such huge problems, we must more than seriously concern ourselves with the question of war. The *Komintern* must prepare the proletariat with a military point of view for the advent of civil war, for the moment of the world attack with all the armed forces of the proletariat on world armed capital.

Above all we must occupy ourselves with mastering the theory of civil war, especially in the realm of the preparation of a proletarian army and its first operations, we must find a place in the programme of the International for the definition of these military principles. For that it is necessary broadly to familiarise the Communist Parties of Western Europe with the Red Army in the 1918–20 war.

Considering the inevitability of a world civil war in the very near future, we must now set up the General Staff of the *III. Komintern*. The staff's mission — to consider in advance the forces and means of the adversaries in a future civil war in countries even as yet ruled by capitalism.

To avoid those difficulties and crudities, from which we suffered at the creation of our Red Army, it is vital to work out beforehand a plan for the mobilisation of the working class, worker Red officers must be trained in advance, both senior combat chiefs and staff workers must be prepared beforehand.

World civil war need not come as a complete surprise. The working class must be trained for it, so that with the seizing of arms it can be quickly formed into a regular Red Army.

By the way, taking into account the difficulties of training officers from workers in bourgeois countries it is essential for us in Soviet Russia to open a series of military instruction centres and academies of the General Staff to train command staff from workers and Communists of all nationalities in their languages.

It seems to me, that the situation permits of no delay in this undertaking. We are standing on the eve of a civil war, which the *Komintern* will direct on the side of the proletariat. It is no light task to prepare the organs of military control, and for this reason we must undertake their creation on an intensified scale.

With Communist greeting.

Smolensk — M. TUKHACHEVSKY.
18th July, 1920.

M. N. Tukhachevsky, *Voina Klassov*, M. 1921, pp. 138–40.

APPENDIX II

(material from the period 1923–7)

Comparison of the Numerical Composition and Assignment-Groups of the Red Army
1st October, 1923–1st October, 1924

	1st October, 1923		1st October, 1924	
Category	*Numbers. Exclusive of central administration*	%	*Numbers. Inclusive of central administration*	%
Command staff (except Junior)	41,506	8·10	53,754	13·07
Political staff	16,288	3·18	8,003	1·95
Administrative staff	29,550	5·77	23,441	5·69
Medical/Veterinary	11,944	2·33	10,133	2·46
Junior command staff	27,837	5·43	21,273	5·18
Leaders from Red Army ranks	—	—	13,778	3·34
Junior economic/technical staff	—	—	15,617	3·79
Red Army rank-and-file	385,256	75·19	254,646	61·92
Civilians	—	—	10,711	2·60
	512,381		411,356	

Modifications in the Artillery Strength Incorporated in Infantry (Rifle) Divisions

Year	*Divisional Artillery*	*Regimental Artillery*	*Battalion Artillery*	*Divisional guns*				*Mortar 58-mm*
				37-mm Anti-Tank	*76-mm Regiment*	*76-mm Division*	*122-mm Howitzer*	
1923	2 artillery battalions	—	—	—	—	12	12	—
1924	1 light artillery regiment: made up of 1 field and howitzer battalion, plus mountain battery	1 battery regimental artillery	—	—	18	24	12	—
1929	1 artillery regiment: of three artillery battalions	1 artillery battalion: of two batteries	1 section of battalion artillery	9	18	18	18	9

Note. The term *artilleriiskii divizion* has been translated as *artillery battalion.* By directive No. 308 (26th April, 1918) such a battalion had 3 batteries. Directives No. 220 (October, 1918) and No. 487 (March, 1919) also: 3 batteries to a battalion were kept, except for the howitzer battalion, which had only 2 in 1919. After 1923 the artillery battalion was fixed again at 2 batteries, although there were variations on this. In 1927 the artillery regiment did not have a fixed number of artillery battalions within it, and 'artillery groups' — provisional tactical unities — could be set up out of artillery battalions or separate batteries. Further intricacies in the Soviet artillery maze were added by new models and modernisation of old weapons.

PARTY MEMBERSHIP IN THE SOVIET COMMAND STAFF AND UNITARY COMMAND

1. *Percentage of Party membership: 1924–1926*

	1924	1926
Company commanders	41·5	52·0
Regimental commanders	41·0	51·0
Divisional commanders	45·0	54·7
Corps commanders	85·0	85·0

2. *Full unitary command; percentages for Party members of the command staff*

September, 1926

	%
Corps commanders	100
Divisional commanders	54·7
Regimental commanders	36·5
Company commanders	37·7
Heads of Military — Training Institutions	75·5

SOCIAL COMPOSITION OF STUDENTS AT MILITARY ACADEMIES

comparison for the academic years 1924–5 and 1925–6. In percentages

	1924–5			*1925–6*		
	Workers	*Peasants*	*Various*	*Workers*	*Peasants*	*Various*
Military Academy Red Army	20·6	40·0	39·4	38·0	27·0	35·0
Naval Academy	12·9	34·9	52·2	36·0	49·0	15·0
Military Aviation Academy	24·0	38·0	38·0	21·0	45·0	34·0
Military-Political Academy	40·8	14·7	44·5	60·0	18·0	22·0
Military-Technical Artillery	14·2	33·3	52·5	32·0	32·0	36·0
Engineering	32·7	37·2	30·1			

Regular Staff of Higher Military-Educational Institutes, 1925

Social composition

Workers: 8·9% Peasants: 12·6 %Various: 78·5% (including 12·6% ex-nobles)

Party composition

Party members: 11·9% Candidate members: 2% *Komsomol*; 3·8%
Non-Party: 82·3%

Age-groups

Up to 30: 43·4% 30–40: 34·2% 40–50: 17·1% over 50: 5·3%

Educational qualifications

Staff with higher educational qualifications: 23·8%
middle-grade : 41·8%
low-grade : 34·4%

Categorisation of the Red Army Command Staff: 2nd October, 1924

Group	*Category*	*Designation in the Red Army*
Junior	1	Commander of a group
		Commander of a detachment
	2	Assistant to platoon commander
		Warrant-officer/First sergeant of the company
Middle	3	Platoon commander
	4	Assistant to company commander
		Commander of a detached/independent platoon
	5	Company commander
	6	Assistant to battalion commander
		Commander of detached/independent company
Senior	7	Battalion commander
	8	Assistant to regimental commander
		Commander of detached/independent battalion
	9	Regimental commander
Higher-grade	10	Assistant to divisional commander
		Brigade commander
	11	Divisional commander
	12	Corps commander
	13	Assistant to the commander of Military District, Front, Army
		Commander of army (non-detached)
	14	Commander of Military District, Front, Army

STRENGTH AND GENERAL ORGANISATION OF SOVIET CAVALRY: 1ST OCTOBER, 1923

Type of formation	*Over-all number*	*Regi-ments*	*Artillery battalions*	*Detached batteries*	*Detached squadrons Engineers Signals*	*Establish-ment*
Divisions of 4 regiments	4	16	4	—	8	18,940
Divisions of 6 regiments	6	36	6	—	12	23,310
Independent cavalry brigades	8	24	—	8	16*	19,360
Detached Territorial (Militia) brigades	1	3	—	1	2*	2,020
		79	10	9	38	63,630

* Half-squadron strength. Thus, 18 of the 38 detached Engineer/Signals squadrons were of half-squadron strength.

GENERAL COMPOSITION OF ARTILLERY FORCES: 1ST OCTOBER, 1924

Category	*Regiments (artillery)*	*Battalions (artillery)*	*Batteries attached to Battalions*	*Detached batteries*	*Guns*	*Strength (by establish-ment)*
Artillery:						
Attached to infantry divisions	58	116	402	—	2,412	36,106
Attached to cavalry divisions	—	10	30	—	120	4,240
Attached to cavalry brigades	—	—	—	9	54	1,503
Corps artillery	—	20	46	—	276	5,400
Special assignment artillery	1	4	27	5	148	4,695
Training batteries	—	—	—	6	36	1,824
	59	150	505	20	3,046	54,768

NOTE: from the 1st October, 1925, all batteries were converted to an establishment of *six* guns.

GENERAL DISTRIBUTION OF ARTILLERY STRENGTH: 1ST OCTOBER, 1926

Designation	*Artillery regiments*	*Artillery battalions*	*Batteries*	*Detached batteries*	*Guns*
Heavy field artillery: attached to corps or outside corps	7	13	88	—	264
Artillery attached to:					
Infantry divisions	65	378	1,016	—	3,048
Cavalry Corps	—	3	6	—	18
Cavalry Divisions	—	11	44	—	132
Cavalry brigades	—	8	16	—	48
Artillery outside corps and divisions	5	15	42	2	208
	77	428	1,212	2	3,718

NOTE: in 1926 all batteries reverted to an establishment of *three* guns (in order to double the number of batteries).

ORGANISATION OF THE MILITARY ACADEMIES: MILITARY, POLITICAL, AVIATION, NAVAL, TECHNICAL. 1926

1. *Frunze Military Academy of the Red Army*
   Training of higher-grade command staff.
2. *Dzerzhinskii Military-Technical Academy of the Red Army*
   Training of highly-qualified staff in military engineering, specialists in fortification, artillery construction, chemical warfare.
   Faculties: Combat, Mechanical, Chemical, Fortification and Constructional.
3. *Zhukovskii Military Aviation Academy of the Red Army*
   Training of personnel for command and staff duties in military aviation, highly-qualified specialists for engineering and technical duties in aviation.
   Faculties: Engineering, Aviation services (with a naval section).
   Courses for heads of aviation technical units.
4. *Naval Academy*
   Training of highly-qualified personnel in general naval education, hydrography, engine and ship construction, electrotechnical duties, naval armament.
   Faculties: naval (education), armament, hydrography, engine-construction, naval architecture.
   Courses for higher-grade command staff.
5. *Military-Medical Academy*

6. *Military-Political Academy of the Red Army*
   Two faculties: military-political, general education and pedagogic.
   Training of higher-grade political staff, and courses for lecturers giving political instruction in other military-education centres.

GENERAL CURRICULUM

1. Political work in the Red Army
2. Social and economic studies
3. Strategy (instruction on war and the conduct of operations)
4. Tactics (the conduct of operations in combat)
5. Military administration
6. The history of war and of military science
7. Artillery course
8. Military engineering duties
9. Military geography and statistics.

Subjects 1, 3, 4, 5: general to all command courses.
12–15% of the instructional time given to Marxism-Leninism in all faculties.

(See *BSE* (1), Vol. 12, 1928, Cols. 319–322.)

RE-ORGANISATION OF SOVIET INFANTRY: REVVOENSOVIET NO. 1298/203, 7TH OCTOBER, 1924

Composition of the company

3 rifle platoons (32 men in each)
1 machine-gun platoon (2 heavy machine-guns, 14 men)
Administration platoon (7 men)
1 detached heavy machine-gun (5 men)
1 detached light machine-gun (4 men)

Composition of the infantry battalion

3 rifle companies (124 men in each)
1 machine-gun company (54 men)
Battalion artillery platoon (2 guns, 20 men)
Signals (9 men)

Composition of the infantry regiment

Regimental staff (11 men) controlling:

Mounted reconnaissance platoon (21 men)
Signals (32 men)
Musicians (17 men)
Political unit (7 men)
Regimental schools (37 men, regular staff)

Composition

3 infantry battalions
1 regimental artillery battery (6 3-inch guns, 115 men)
Chemical platoon (11 men)
Administrative unit (16 men) with administrative-supply company (99 men)
Veterinary unit (6 men)
Hygiene-medical unit (19 men)

Composition of the infantry division

Divisional staff (34 men)
Detached signals company (125 men)
Political Section/Division (16 men)

Composition

3 infantry regiments (1,781 men in each)
1 artillery regiment (841 men, 4 batteries, 6 guns to a battery)
Independent cavalry squadron (131 men)
Military-administrative/Supply unit (2 men)
Hygiene-medical unit (3 men)

Strength and composition of the artillery corps

Command; 3 men
Corps Staff (30 men)
Independent signals company (232 men)
Corps engineering administration (1 man); with independent sapper battalion (637 men)
Corps artillery administration (2 men); with independent heavy field artillery battalion (2 batteries, 6 guns in each, 342 men)
2 or 3 infantry divisions
Hygiene-medical unit (2 men)
Military-administrative/Supply unit (2 men)

Social Composition and Political Affiliations of Students at the Military Academies: 1927

Academy	*Worker*	*Peasant*	*Various*	*Members and Candidate-Members C.P.*	*Non-Party*
Military	19	49	32	74	26
Technical	17	35	48	58	42
Political	58	23	19	100	—
Aviation	32	38	30	78	22
Naval	22	31	47	69	31

(*BSE* (1), Vol. 12.)

Order No. 390. 12th July, 1926.

Organisation and Definition of the Functions of the Central Military Administration

1. *The Red Army Staff*

To be concerned with all functions relevant to the preparation of the country and the armed forces for war. All organs which hitherto carried out this function in other administrations (Supply, Naval and Air Forces) to be transferred to the Staff. All organs not directly concerned with this, such as Military Topography, to be withdrawn from the Staff.

Organisation of the four Departments of the Red Army Staff

Department 1. Operations.

Strategic planning
Naval defence
Defence construction/engineering
Staff services.

Department 2. Organisation-Mobilisation.

Organisation policy
Organisational deployment in the event of war
Material security of armies
Mobilisation planning.

Department 3. Military communications.

Organisation of means of communication/railways, road transport.

Department 4. Intelligence.

Scientific-Regulations/Manuals Section. Attached to the Staff.
Subordinated to the indirect command of the Chief of Staff, with the assignments of:
research into combat experience
the direction of the composition and publication of combat regulations and manuals.

2. *The Main Directorate of the Red Army*

Invested with the direction of the combat training and Inspectorate apparatus, troop mobilisation, recruiting to the ranks, and routine affairs in the Red Army. Divided into departments, under:

1. Combat training
2. Military Education institutes
3. Military-Topographic
   (with the Red Army Staff retaining the right to assign general tasks)
4. Command
5. Troop mobilisation and recruitment
6. Organisation and military service of troops

7. Re-mount section
8. Inspectorates:
   Artillery
   Cavalry
   Military Communications/Engineers
   Chemical Warfare training.

Attached: a Rifle-Shooting Committee, without regular establishment, operating through Combat Training.

3. *Directorates under the control of the Revvoensoviet SSSR.*

A. *Red Army Supply.*

Concerned with the purchase and procurement of all types of supplies and the actual supply of the Red Army. Divided into departments, under:
Artillery
Military-Technical
Military-Chemical
Military Commissary
Infantry and Rifle Supply
Military-Financial
Attached, an Administrative Section.
Also attached, a Planning Commission, without regular establishment, connected with the Chiefs of Supply, and with the Budgetary Section of the Military-Financial Department.

B. *PU RKKA.* (Political).

NOTE: under the direct supervision of the Central Committee. Technically speaking, it does come under the *RVS SSSR*, but not as a matter of final responsibility.
Departments:
Organisation-distribution
Agitation-propaganda
Information-statistical
Mobilisation
Naval
Press

C. *Naval Forces.*

With the following departments:
Combat training
Technical
Special (Naval) Supply
Hydrographic
Scientific-Technical Committee.

D. *Military Air Force.* (*VVS*)

Departments:
Combat training
Special (Air Force) Supply
Meteorological section
Research Commission into Aeronautics
Inspectorates of the Civil Air Fleet
Scientific-Technical Committee.

E. *Military-Medical.*

G. *Military-Veterinary*

H. Administrations of the People's Commissariat for Military and Naval Affairs and the *Revvoensoviet* USSR itself.

Figures and Percentages of Strength, Party Membership in Red Army Officer-Corps

Strength of command and administrative staff: 1st January, 1923, and 1st October, 1924.

	1923	1924	
Command staff	43,233	40,587	Reduced by 6·1%
Administrative staff	31,677	12,416	Reduced by 61·8%

Composition on the 1st October, 1925

Total officer strength: 76,273. 15% of total Red Army strength.

Percentage by function: Command staff: 58·1%
Political staff: 19·4%
Administrative officers: 18·6%
Medical: 3%
Veterinary: 0·9%

Proletarian affiliation of officer-corps

Percentage among command staff, 1st January, 1923: 13·6%
" " " " , 1st April, 1925 : 20%

Party-membership

1st January, 1923:	22·9% among command staff, 18·8% in administrative staff.
1st April, 1925 :	40·9% (for command and administrative staff combined).

For comparison. Naval staff, 1st October, 1924 and December, 1926.

Year	Workers	Peasants	Various	Members and Candidate-members C.P.	Komsomol	Non-Party
	combined					
1924	45·64		54·36	23·51*	?	over 70%
1926	18·52	47·35	34·13	43·08	1·76	55·16

* NOTE: Proportion of Party members among the *command* staff was 22·5%. Figures represent command-administrative staff as a whole.

(See I. B. Berkhin, *Voennaya Reforma*, pp. 232–3).

N. F. Kuz'min, *Na strazhe mirnovo truda 1921–1940.*

See p. 51. Supplies an alternative set of figures for 1st June, 1924. Command staff only.

Date	Social		Aristocratic affiliations	Various	Political		Non-Party
	Workers	Peasants			C.P. Members	C.P. Candidates	
	combined						
1st June, 1924	46·5		26·2	27·3	20·4	2·5	77·1

Data on the Soviet Officer Corps: 1923–1927

From: Grazhdanskaya voina 1918–1921 (ed. A. S. Bubnov, S. S. Kamenev, R. P. Eideman), Vol. 2, Moscow 1928. See N. Efimov, pp. 91–110, on the command staff of the Red Army.

p. 105.

Social composition: command staff, Red Army

	Workers	*Peasants*	*Various*
1923	13·6	52·7	33·7
1926	16	57·2	26·8

Social composition: by command category

	1924			1926		
	Workers	*Peasants*	*Various*	*Workers*	*Peasants*	*Various*
Higher command staff	6·9	25·3	67·8	7·3	31·2	61·5
Senior command staff	10·1	37·7	52·2	9·3	46	44·7
Middle-grade command staff	17·2	56·1	26·7	18	61·4	20·6

p. 108. *Valid to 15th November, 1927.*

Party composition

	1924	1927
Members VKP(b)	24·4	38·7
Candidate members	6·2	10·9
Komsomol	1·2	5·8
Non-Party	68·2	44·6

Military Experience

	Imperialist War (1914)	*Civil War*	*No combat experience*
1923	14·6	25·8	20·4
1927	3·4	50·8	34·6

Military Education

	Completed military school	*No formal military education*
1923	8·2	13·4
1927	42·1	7·7

APPENDIX III

(materials from the period 1936–7)

Vremennyi Polevoi Ustav RKKA 1936 (PU 36)

NKO SSSR: Moskva 1937.

Provisional Field Service Regulations of the Workers and Peasants Red Army 1936.

People's Commissariat for Defence: Moscow 1937.

(Extracts)

Chapter One: 'General Principles'

Para. 2. The military operations of the Red Army will lead to the annihilation of the enemy. Achieving a decisive victory and the complete shattering of the enemy comprises the basic aim in a war thrust on the Soviet Union.

The sole means of achieving the prescribed aim is battle. Through battle there is accomplished:

(*a*) the destruction of the manpower and the material resources of the enemy,
(*b*) the neutralisation of his spiritual strengths and capacity for resistance.

All battles — offensive and defensive — aim at bringing about the destruction of the enemy. But only *decisive offensive on the main line of advance*, closed with a relentless pursuit, *will lead to the complete annihilation of the manpower and resources of the enemy.*

The constant urge to get to grips with the enemy, with the aim of destroying him, must lie at the basis of the training and activity of every commander and soldier of the Red Army. Without special orders to this effect the enemy must be attacked boldly and with dash wherever he is discovered.

3. *It is nevertheless impossible to be strong everywhere. To guarantee success it is necessary by means of re-grouping men and equipment to obtain decisive superiority over the enemy on the main line of advance*. On secondary sectors only forces to hold the enemy are needed.

4. For the destruction of the enemy, however, it is not enough to have a simple concentration of superior manpower and weapons. It is essential to achieve the *co-operation of all arms, operating on one line of advance, in the entire depth and the co-ordination of the operations of units*, acting in various directions.

5. The methods of conducting the operations will depend on the character of the various periods of the war. The Red Army must be prepared to break stubborn enemy opposition in manœuvre warfare, just as in conditions of its transition to positional defence.

. . .

9. *Modern technical means of warfare permit the achieving of the simultaneous destruction of the enemy combat array in the entire depth of his disposition. The possibilities of rapid changing of grouping, surprise turning movement and the seizure of the enemy rear area with the severing of his retreat are increasing. In attack the enemy must be encircled and completely destroyed.*

10. *Defence must be made insurmountable for the enemy however powerful he might be on a given line of advance.*

Defence must be organised on the basis of a deep disposition of fire-power and units assigned for the counter-blow.

The enemy, weakened in overcoming the depth of the defence, must be destroyed by decisive infantry and tank counter-attack supported by aviation and all the artillery. This itself in defence can bring victory by small forces over an enemy enjoying superiority.

Chapter Five: 'Fundamentals of the Conduct of Operations'

Para. 112. Modern means of neutralisation, primarily tanks, artillery, aviation and tank-borne infantry raids, employed on a large scale, make it possible to organise the simultaneous attack on the enemy throughout the entire depth of his positions, with the aim of isolating, completely encircling and destroying him.

The encirclement of the enemy is brought about:

(*a*) by *outflanking* the enemy on one or both flanks for a decisive attack from the flank or rear of his main forces;
(*b*) by a *break-through* into the enemy rear with tanks and infantry in infantry-carriers, with the task of cutting off the escape route of his main forces;
(*c*) by attack with aircraft, mechanised units and cavalry on enemy columns, attempting to withdraw, with the aim of preventing this retirement.

113. *Divisional tank battalions* comprise *infantry-support tanks* (TPP). Tanks, attached to army formations, depending on their characteristics, are either distributed to the infantry for the reinforcement of TPP groups, or make up groups of *long-range operations tanks* (TDD) for breaking into the depth of the enemy rear.

Infantry-support tanks in offensive combat, as a general rule, by companies and platoons are subordinated to the infantry commanders. In defensive combat the tank battalion is usually subordinated directly to the divisional commander for use in counter-attack and for destroying attacking enemy tanks.

The long-range operations tank group, depending on the tactical situation, is subordinated to the corps or divisional commander.

In the majority of cases the tanks will attack in several echelons.

. . .

116. Aviation is employed for the destruction of those targets which cannot be neutralised by infantry or artillery fire or that of other arms.

To achieve the maximum combat success of the *VVS* it must be used *on a mass scale*, concentrating the forces according to the times and targets which have the greatest tactical importance. As a rule the formation commander assigns to combat aviation missions throughout the whole of the battle with an instruction on the expenditure of resources in sorties.

According to the tactical situation, in the course of the battle, tasks can be fixed for particular sorties.

The success of the co-operation of the *VVS* with the ground forces must be secured by close technical contact and by establishing personal contact between formation and aviation commanders.

The responsibility for locating and equipping landing strips and aerodromes with men and equipment from the ground forces is a daily task of formation commanders of all grades and their staffs.

117. *Ground-attack aviation* carries out the following tasks:

(*a*) prevents the movement to and from the battle-field of enemy troops and destroying them in formation and army rear areas;
(*b*) supplies direct support to its own troops by attacks on the enemy in the various phases of the battle;
(*c*) interrupts communications and enemy conduct of operations by destroying staffs, signal centres and radio stations;
(*d*) enters into battle with airborne or seaborne (riverborne) assaults, destroying them at their place of forming up, during the journey, before their descent and initiation of operations on our territory;
(*e*) interrupts the work of the rear, halting railway traffic, destroying motor-transport communications, destroying dumps, stations, etc.;
(*f*) participates in the warding off of enemy heavy bomber flights.

118. *Fighter aviation* has the basic function of destroying all types of enemy aircraft in the air and on the ground.

Fighter aviation carries out the following tasks:

(*a*) destroys enemy aircraft in the air and on his aerodromes;
(*b*) secures its own troops and fixed objectives from enemy aerial attack;
(*c*) destroys observation and barrage balloons;
(*d*) covers the assembly area of aviation units; escorts the aviation units of the formation on a limited radius of its range and meets these aircraft after the completion of their combat mission;
(*g*) where necessary — protects air-photo reconnaissance and artillery spotting aircraft.

In special circumstances fighter aviation can be used for:

(*a*) attack on ground groups both in position and on the move;
(*b*) reconnaissance missions in the interests of formation as well as aviation commanders.

119. *Light-bomber aviation* is used for operations against the following targets:

(*a*) troop concentrations;
(*b*) organs for the control of troops — staffs and communication nets;
(*c*) supply bases;

(*d*) railway and motor-transportation echelons;
(*e*) enemy aviation on its aerodromes.

In addition, light-bomber aviation may be assigned missions: countering enemy aerial invasion and participating in parachute-landing operations.

120. *Army co-operation aviation* has the basic function of the combat service of the formation, carrying out reconnaissance duties, observation of the battle-field, communications, escorting tanks and spotting artillery fire.

Communications aviation carries out:

(*a*) conveying orders to troops and receiving reports from them;
(*b*) assisting communications between groups of troops;
(*c*) battle-field observation.

(Cf. Dr Raymond L. Garthoff, *How Russia Makes War*, *op. cit.*, p. 325 f. on the statements of the role of Soviet aviation in tactical support of the ground forces in more recent times. It will be seen that the basic ideas were worked out here.)

Chapter Eight: 'Defence'

Para. 224. Defence is employed with the aim:

(*a*) of economy of forces on a wide front for a blow in the decisive line of advance;
(*b*) of winning time for the creation of the necessary grouping of forces for the offensive;
(*c*) of winning time in secondary directions until results on the decisive line of advance;
(*d*) of holding space (regions, borders and roads);
(*e*) of the disordering of the enemy on the offensive for the subsequent transition to the offensive.

The strength of defence consists of the most favourable exploitation of fire-power, terrain, defence works and chemical weapons.

Defence, combined with offensive action or with a subsequent transition to the offensive, especially against the flank of a weakened enemy, can lead to his complete destruction.

(NOTE: the itemised characterisation of defence has received frequent repetition in Soviet military writing since 1936.)

SOVIET SUBMARINE STRENGTH: 1936

(*a*) January, 1936

3 new submarine types:

Large	1,000–1,200 tons	(Type III)	
Medium	840 tons	(Type IX)	
Small	100 tons	(Type VIII)	(6–8 months from keel-laying to completion: Leningrad yards.)

Total submarine strength (December, 1935–January, 1936): 120

Baltic Fleet	50 (a minimum of 40 operational submarines)
Black Sea	20
Far East	45
Northern	5

(*b*) April, 1936 *Black Sea Fleet submarine strength*

L4, L5, L6 (*Dekabrist* class, being completed)
Shch 204
M51, M52, M?, M79, M80, M81 (Molodki Class) (last three undergoing trials)
A2 (old, classified *Holland*)
New submarines: and total strength.

3 large	1,039 tons	(Type I)	
3 large	896 tons	(Type ?)	
3	896 tons	(*Dekabrist* Class)	
3 medium	600 tons	(Type VIII)	
6 small	100 tons	(Type IX)	
4 old	330 tons		22 submarines, although not all operational

Distribution of Soviet submarine force: 1937

Type	*Baltic*	*joint*	*White Sea*	*Far East*	*Black Sea*	*Total*
Pravda		3		—	—	3
Garibaldets	1		—	—	3	4
Yakobinets	—		—	—	3	3
N	5		—	1	—	6
Leninets	3		—	5	3	11
Dekabrist		6	—	—	5	11
Shch 301	4		—	—	—	4
Shch 305	7		—	34	10	51
Shch 312	16		4	—	—	20
Molodki	17		—	29	9	55
Bolshevik (old)	6		—	—	—	6
Holland (old)	—		—	—	4	4

178
without new
construction

APPENDIX IV

(materials from the period 1939–41)

Comparative Soviet-Japanese Strengths: July/August, 1939
Khalkhin-Gol Operations

(i) *11th May, 1939*	*Infantry*	*Cavalry*	*MGs*	*Guns (75-mm and over)*	*Anti-tank guns*	*Tanks*	*Armoured cars*
Soviet-Mongolian	668	260	58	14	6	—	39
Japanese	1,676	900	75	8	10	1	6–8
(ii) *2nd July* Soviet-Mongolian	*c.* 11,000	*c.* 1,000	152	86	23	186	266
Japanese	*c.* 20,000	*c.* 4,700	164	170	98	130	6

(iii) *20th August*	*Infantry and cavalry, machine-guns*		
	Infantry battalions	*Cavalry squadrons*	*Heavy and light machine-guns*
Soviet-Mongolian	35	20	2,255
Japanese	25	17	1,283

	Artillery, mortars, tanks, armoured cars				
	Guns (75-mm and over)	*Anti-tank guns and regimental artillery*	*Mortars*	*Tanks*	*Armoured cars*
Soviet-Mongolian	216 or 266	286	40	496	346
Japanese	135	142	60	120	not known

	Air strengths			
	Fighters	*Light bombers*	*Heavy bombers*	*Total*
Soviet	376 or 311	181	23	581 or 515
Japanese	252	144	54	450 or 303

NOTE. Alternate figures are from N. F. Kuz'min and S. Shishkin. Shiskin's figures appear first.

(iv)	*Soviet distribution of artillery in the Southern, Central and Northern groups: August counter-offensive*					
	Breadth of front (in kilometres)	*Numbers*			*Guns per kilometre of front*	*Guns per kilometre including 45-mm guns*
		76-mm	*122-mm 1910/30*	*122-mm 1909/30*		
Southern	17	20	28	12	3·5	10
Central	30	20	36	—	2 (approx)	9
Northern	15	—	12	12	1·6	8

Soviet Air Force Effectives: 1939 and 1941

(*a*) *French Estimate* 1st January, 1939

Total: 5,200 aircraft

European Russia:	3,750
Central Asia and Siberia:	600
Far East:	850

Naval Aviation: 650 Baltic, 250; Black Sea, 200; Pacific, 200

Quality estimate

Type	Numbers in service	Date and role
R5	1,500	1931 Ground support and reconnaissance
RZ	1,620	1935 As above
SB	500	1935 Light bomber
TsKB	150	1936 Medium bomber
TB3	500	1932 4-engined bomber
TB4		1934
I–15	310	1934 Fighter
I–16	1,085	1935 Fighter

(*b*) *British Military Estimate* 1st August, 1939

(not including Far Eastern forces)

Total: 3,361 machines. 894 long-range bombers, 217 short range
983 fighters, 1,066 reconnaissance and ground support

(*c*) *Statement Army Commander 2nd Grade Loktinov, 17th August, 1939*

Available for operations in the west:

between 5,000 and 5,500 machines, 80% modern

Composition: 55% bombers, 40% fighters and 5% Army co-operation

Production of military aircraft: 900–950 per month (excluding training and civil aircraft)

(See *Les Evènements survenus en France de 1933 à 1935*, Témoignages, Vol. 2, Paris 1947, p. 315.

DBFP, Third Series, Vol. VII, p. 585, and Vol. VI, p. 788)

(*d*) *Luftwaffe estimate*, February 1941.

Fighters and bombers (available in the west): 4–5,000

Ground facilities: 1,100 airfields, 200 serviceable

Parachute troops,

transport aircraft: mostly based on Kiev

Luftwaffe expects to encounter: 1,600 Soviet bombers
4,050 fighters
disposed: north of the Pripet Marshes,
1,530 bomber and reconnaissance aircraft
2,200 fighters
south of the Pripet Marshes
675 bombers and reconnaissance aircraft
1,250 fighters
AA (*PVO*) forces: 300 medium
200 light AA batteries and AA machine-gun batteries.

NOTE. See Raymond L. Garthoff, *How Russia Makes War*. Soviet Military Doctrine Appendix II, p. 429, and Note 20 to this (p. 503). The Soviet press on 5th October, 1941, admitted a *loss* of 5,316 aircraft. Soviet losses up to the end of 1941 were in the region of 8,000. Since an estimated 1,500–2,000 aircraft were still operating, initial Soviet strength must have been in excess of the *Luftwaffe* statement, and 10,000 would therefore be reasonable.

SOURCE MATERIALS AND BIBLIOGRAPHY

THE following is presented only as a compilation of the principal materials employed in the preparation of the present work and is not intended in any way as a complete bibliographical survey of the military or other themes displayed here.

I. SOVIET MATERIALS

NOTE: Soviet monographs based upon or incorporating in any degree archival or other original materials are indicated with an asterisk.

For convenience of reference, the writings of Trotsky relevant to this work are included under the Soviet heading, even though they may have been written in exile.

1. SOVIET MILITARY ORGANISATION

Dekrety Sovetskoi vlasti, Vols. I and II, Moscow 1957–9.

See under headings: Red Army, Fleets, Military Laws and Institutions.

KPSS o vooruzhennykh silakh Sovetskovo Soyuza, Sbornik dokumentov 1917–1958, Moscow 1958.

O vvedenii personal'nikh voennikh zvanii nachal'stvuyushchevo sostava RKKA i ob utverzhdenii polozheniya o prokhozhdenii sluzhby komandnym i nachal'stvuyushchim sostavom RKKA [22nd September, 1935], Moscow, SNK TsIK/OIZ NKO SSSR, 22 pp.

S'ezdy Sovetov Soyuza SSR, soyuznykh i avtonomnykh sovetskikh sotsialisticheskikh respublik Sbornik dokumentov v trekh tomakh 1917–1936 g.g., Vol. I, Moscow 1959.

Voennye voprosy v resheniyakh KPSS 1903–1917 gg. Sbornik dokumentov, Moscow 1960.

VKP(b) a voennoe delo (ed. A. A. Geronimus and V. Orlov), Moscow 1928.

*Berkhin, I. B., *Voennaya reforma v SSSR (1924–1925 gg.)*, Moscow 1958.

Kuz'min, N. F., *Na strazhe mirnovo truda (1921–1940 gg.)*, Moscow 1959.

Nikonov, F., 'Glavneishe momenty organizatsii Krasnoi Armii' in *Grazhdanskaya Voina 1918–1921* (ed. A. S. Bubnov, S. S. Kamenev, R. P. Eideman), Vol. 2, 1928, pp. 48–75.

Morozov, N., *Alfabitnyi ukazatel' sovetskikh uzakonenii i rasporyazhenii po voennomu vedomstvu*, Moscow 1919.

Pobezhimov, I. F., *Ustroistvo Sovetskoi Armii*, Moscow 1954.

Shatagin, N. I., *Organizatsiya i stroitel'stvo Sovetskoi Armii v period inostrannoi interventsii i grazhdanskoi voiny (1918–1920 gg.)*, Moscow 1954.

Trotskii, L., *Kak vooruzhalas' Revolyutsiya*, Vols. I–III, Moscow 1923–5. [This is the basic work for the formative period of the Red Army.]

Vlasov, I. I., *V. I. Lenin i stroitel'stvo Sovetskoi Armii*, Moscow 1958.

See also:

Pyat let voennoi knigi, 1919–24 gg., Moscow 1924.

Zlatomskii, V. A., *Bibliograficheskii ukazatel' po voprosam stroitel'stva vooruzhennikh sil po militsionnoi systeme*, Petrograd 1921.

See also under *Select Articles*.

2. THE POLITICAL ADMINISTRATION: ARMY-PARTY RELATIONS

Blumental', F., *Politicheskaya rabota v voennoe vremya*, Moscow-Leningrad 1927.

—— 'Partiino-politicheskaya rabota v grazhdanskoi voiny 1918–1921' in *Grazhdanskaya Voina 1918–1921*, Vol. 2, pp. 129–41.

Geronimus, A. A., 'Osnovnye momenty razvitya partiino-politicheskovo apparata Krasnoi Armii' in *Grazhdanskaya Voina 1918–1921*, Vol. 2, pp. 110–29.

—— *Partiya a Krasnaya Armiya*, Moscow 1928.

Mishchenko, N., *Partiino-politicheskaya rabota v Krasnoi Armii* Sistematicheskii ukazatel' literatury za 1918–1928, Moscow-Leningrad 1929. [Note: in some collections, this item appears under the name of the editor, F. Blumental'].

Petrov, Yu. P., *Stroitel'stvo partiino-politicheskovo apparata v gody inostrannoi voennoi interventsii i grazhdanskoi voiny*, Moscow 1952.

—— *Voennye komissary v gody grazhdanskoi voiny*, Moscow 1956.

—— *Partiinye mobilizatsii v Krasnuyu Armiyu v 1918–1920 gg.*, Moscow 1956.

Petukhov, I., *Partiinaya organizatsiya i partiinaya rabota v RKKA*, Moscow 1928.

Portyankin, I. A. (Ed.), *Sovetskaya voennaya pechat'* (Istoricheskii ocherk), Moscow 1960.

Suslov, P. V., *Politicheskoe obespechenie sovetsko-pol'skoi kampanii 1920 g.*, Moscow-Leningrad 1930.

See also under *Select Articles*.

3. REGULATIONS, INSTRUCTIONS, MANUALS

Rukovidyashchaya instruktsiya po organizatsii vseobshchevo voennovo obucheniya i formirovaniya reservnikh chastei, Moscow 1918, 35 pp.

Rukovodstvo po bor'be s dezertistvom (*S prilozheniem ankety dezertira*), Moscow 1918, 12 pp.

Polevoi Ustav (Chast' 1: Manevrennaya voina), 1918.

Stroevoi pekhotnyi ustav RKKA (*Stroevoe obuchenie*), 1919.

Ustav vnutrennei sluzhby RKKA, 1918.

Distsiplinarnyi ustav RKKA, January, 1919.

Zapiski po voennoi administratsii dlya sovetskikh kursov po podgotovke komandnovo sostava, 1919.

Sputnik krasnovo komandira, 2nd and enlarged edn., Moscow 1923, 371 pp.

Boevaya sluzhba pekhoty. Rukovodstvo dlya komandnovo sostava RKKA, Moscow 1924.

Vremennyi polevoi ustav RKKA (Chast' 2: Diviziya, korpus), Moscow 1925.

Boevoi ustav pekhoty RKKA (Chast' 2 B.Us.P27), Moscow 1927.

Spravochnik dlya pomoshchnikov komandirov polkov po khozyasitvennoi chasti i zaveduyushchikh khozyaistvom v RKKA po vsem vidam snabzheniya i mirnoe vremiya.

Officially accepted 15th November, 1927. Pub. Moscow-Leningrad 1928.
Podgotovka komsostava RKKA [starshevo i vyshera]: Nauchno-ustavnii otdel Shtaba RKKA, (issued under I. Uborevich's name), Moscow-Leningrad 1928.
Polevoi ustav RKKA (1929), Moscow-Leningrad 1929. (Also 1934 and 1935 Edns.).
Boevoi ustav voenno-vozdushnikh sil RKKA (Kniga 1: Istrebitel'naya aviatsiya), Moscow 1929.
Boevoi ustav voenno-morskikh sil VMF/RKKA, Moscow 1930.
Ustav motomekhanizirovannykh voisk, Moscow VAMM, 1932.
Nastavlenie po samostoyatel'nomu vozhdeniyu krupnykh motomekhanizirovannykh soedinenii, Moscow VAMM, 1932.
Pribory dlya nablyudeniya i dlya upravleniya ognem motomekhanizirovannykh voisk (ed. S. I. Pevnev, B. A. Leninov, I. E. Maron), Moscow VAMM, 1935.
Vremennyi polevoi ustav RKKA 1936 (PU 36), Moscow 1937.
Polevoi ustav Krasnoi Armii/Proekt 1939 g., Moscow 1939.
Vremennoe nastavlenie po vedeniyu morskikh operatsii 1940 g., Moscow 1940.
Polevoi ustav Krasnoi Armii/Proekt 1940 g., Moscow 1940.
Polevoi ustav Krasnoi Armii (proekt 1941 g.), Moscow 1941.

4. Military history and military operations: 1917–1941

(i) *The Revolution and the armed forces*

*Belov, G. A., Struchkov, A. A., Shul'ga, S. I. (ed.), *Doneseniya komissarov Petrogradskovo Voenno-revolyutsionnovo komiteta*, Moscow 1957.
**Bol'shevistskie Voenno-revolyutsionnye komitety*, Moscow 1958.
Erykalov, E., *Krasnaya Gvardiya v bor'be za vlast' Sovetov*, Moscow 1957.
*Kakurin, N. E. (Ed.), *Razlozhenie armii v 1917 godu (sbornik dokumentov)*, Moscow-Leningrad 1925.
*Kapustin, M. I., *Soldaty Severnovo fronta v bor'be za vlast' Sovetov*, Moscow 1957.
Kapshukov, S. G., *Bor'ba Bol'shevistskoi partii za armiyu v period pervoi mirovoi voiny*, Moscow 1957.
Kostomarov, G. D., and Malakhovksii, V., *Iz istorii Moskovskoi rabochei Krasnoi Gvardii*, Moscow, *Istpart* MK VKP(b) 1930.
*Martynov, E. I., *Tsarskaya armiya i fevral'skom perevorote*, Voen.-Ist. Otdel, Shtab RKKA, Moscow 1927.
*Mordvinov, P. N. (ed.), *Baltiiskie moryaki v podgotovke i provedenii Velikoi Oktyabr'skoi sotsialisticheskoi revolyutsii*, Moscow-Leningrad 1957.
*Muratov, Kh. I., *Revolyutsionnoe dvizhenie v russkoi armii v 1917 g.*, Moscow 1958.
*Petrov, N., *Bol'sheviki na Zapadnom fronte v 1917 godu Vospominaniya*, Moscow 1959.
*Rabinovich, S. E., *Vserossiiskaya voennaya konferentsiya Bol'shevikov 1917 g.*, Moscow *Istpart*, 1925.
*Shurygin, F. A., *Revolyutsionnoe dvizhenie soldatskikh mass Severnovo fronta v 1917 godu*, Moscow 1958.
Za vlast' Sovetov, Inst. Ist. Partii MK i MGK KPSS, Moskovskii Rabochii, 1957.

(ii) *The Civil War*

**Grazhdanskaya voina 1918–1921* (ed. A. S. Bubnov, S. S. Kamenev, R. P. Eideman), 3 vols., Moscow 1928–1930:

vol. 1 Boevaya zhizn' Krasnoi Armii
vol. 2 Voennoe iskusstvo Krasnoi Armii
vol. 3 Operativno-strategicheskii ocherk boevykh deistvii Krasnoi Armii.

***History of the Civil War in the USSR:* Vol. 1. *The Prelude of the Great Proletarian Revolution (from the beginning of the War to the beginning of October 1917)* (ed. M. Gorki, V. Molotov, K. Voroshilov, S. Kirov, A. Zhdanov, J. Stalin), (trans.), London 1937.

**Istoriya Grazhdanskoi Voiny v SSSR 1917–1922* (editorial board: S. F. Naida, G. D. Obichkin, Yu. P. Petrov, A. A. Struchkov, N. I. Shatagin), Vol. 3 (November 1917–March 1919), Vol. 4 (March 1919–February 1920), Moscow 1957 and 1959.

Anishev, A., *Ocherki istorii grazhdanskoi voiny 1917–1920 gg.*, Leningrad 1925.

Aralov, S. I., *V. I. Lenin i Krasnaya Armiya*, Moscow 1958.

—— 'Pod rukovodstvom V. I. Lenina' in *Moskvichi na frontakh grazhdanskoi voiny*, Moskovskii Rabochii 1960, pp. 8–31.

Blyukher, V. K., Reminiscence of South Urals Detachment, written originally in 1936 for a history of the 30th Irkutsk Red Banner Rifle Division, now published in *Legendarnyi reid*, Sbornik vospominanii o pokhode yuzhnoural'skikh partizan pod komandovaniem V. K. Blyukhera, Moscow 1959.

**Boevye podvigi chastei Krasnoi Armii (1918–1922 gg.)*, Sbornik dokumentov, Moscow 1957.

Boevoi put' Sovetskikh vooruzhennykh sil, Krasnoznamennaya Ordena Lenina i Ordena Suvorova l-i stepeni Voennaya Akademiya imeni M. V. Frunze, Moscow 1960, Part One, pp. 1–168.

Boltin, E. A., *Kontranastuplenie yuzhnoi gruppy vostochnovo fronta i razgrom Kolchaka (1919 g.)*, Moscow 1949.

Borisenko, I., *Sovetskie respubliki na severnom Kavkaze v 1918 g.*, Vols. I–II, pub., 'Severnyi Kavkaz', Rostov-on-Don 1930.

Cherepanov, A. I., *Pod Pskovoi i Narvoi* Fevral' 1918, Moscow 1957.

Draudin, T. Ya., *Boevoi put' Latyshskoi strelkovoi divizii v dni Oktyabr i v gody Grazhdanskoi Voiny (1917–1920)*, Riga 1960.

Fedorov, A., *Permskaya katastrofa i kontrnastuplenie vostochnovo fronta*, Moscow 1939.

Furmanov, D., *Chapayev*, (Trans.), London 1941.

Grinishin, D., *Voennaya deyatel'nost' V. I. Lenina*, Moscow 1957.

Istorichesko-strategicheskii ocherk XVI armii, Moghilev 1921.

*Korotkov, I. S., *Razgrom Vrangelya*, 2nd Edn., Moscow 1955.

Kuz'min, G. V., *Grazhdanskaya voina i voennaya interventsiya v SSSR*, Moscow 1958.

*Kuz'min, N. F., *Krushenie poslednovo pokhoda Antanty*, Moscow 1958.

Kutyakov, I. S., *Vasilii Ivanovich Chapayev*, Moscow 1958.

Naida, S. F., *O nekotorykh voprosakh istorii grazhdanskoi voiny v SSSR*, Moscow 1958.

*Papin, L. M., *Krakh Kolchakovshchiny i obrazovanie Dal'nevostochnoi Respubliki*, Moscow 1957.

**Reshayushchie pobedy Sovetskovo naroda nad interventami i belogvardeistami v 1919 g.* (Collected essays), Moscow 1960.

Sapozhnikov, V. I., *Podvig Baltiitsev v 1918 godu*, Moscow 1954.

*Shangin, I. S., *Moryaki v boyakh za Sovetskii Sever (1917–1920)*, Moscow 1959.
*Shelestov, D. K., *Bor'ba za vlast' Sovetov na Altae*, Moscow 1959.
Shilovskii, E., *Kontrnastuplenie Krasnoi Armii v Belorussi*, Moscow 1940.
*Spirin, A. M., *Razgrom armii Kolchaka*, Moscow 1957.
*Tarasov, V. V., *Bor'ba s interventami na severe Rossii*, Moscow 1958.
*Tashliev, Sh., *Turkmenistan v period inostrannoi voennoi interventsii i grazhdanskoi voiny (1918–1920 gg.)*, Sbornik dokumentov, Ashkhabad 1957.
*Tsentrarkhiv/*Partizanskoe dvizhenie v Sibirii*, Vol. 1, Moscow-Leningrad 1925.
Tyulenev, I. V., *Sovetskaya kavaleriya v boyakh za Rodinu*, Moscow 1957.
*Vartanyan, S., *Pobeda Sovetskoi vlasti v Armenii*, Erevan 1959.
Vasil'chikov, V. S., *Nachdiv Shchors*, Moscow 1957.
Velikii pokhod armii K. E. Voroshilova ot Luganska k Tsaritsynu, Moscow 1938.
Vetoshkin, M. K., *Stanovlenie vlasti Sovetov na severe RSFSR*, Moscow 1957.
Vilenskii, V. D., *Dva goda Krasnoi Akademii General'novo Shtaba (1918–1920)*, Moscow 1921.
*Yegorov, A. I., *Razgrom Denikina (1919)*, Moscow 1931.
Izvestiya/Narkomvoendel (First Year: 1st May–31st October, 1918), Moscow 1918.
Otchot o pervom s'ezde po vseobshchemu voennomu obucheniyu 1918 g., Moscow 1918, 179 pp. (Report on *Vsevobuch*/Universal Military Training.)

(*iii*) *Soviet-Polish War 1920*

Gai, G. D., *Na Varshavu*, Moscow-Leningrad 1928.
*Kakurin, N. E., and Melikov, V. A., *Voina s Belopolyakami*, Voen.-Ist. Otdel Shtaba RKKA, Moscow 1925.
*Kluyev, L., *Pervaya Konnaya Krasnaya armiya na pol'skom fronte v 1920 godu*, Moscow 1932.
*Kuz'min, N., *Krushenie poslednovo pokhoda Antanty*, Moscow 1958, Ch. IV and V.
Melikov, V., *Marna 1914–Visla 1920–Smirna 1922*, Moscow-Leningrad 1928.
*Pauka, I. Kh., *Razgrom Belopolyakov pod Kievom v 1920 godu*, Moscow 1938.
*Putna, V. K., *K visle i obratno*, Moscow, 1st Edn., 1926, 2nd, 1927.
*Shaposhnikov, B. M., *Na Visle. K istorii kampanii 1920 goda*, Moscow 1924.
*Tukhachevskii, M. N., *Pokhod za Vislu*, Smolensk 1923.
*Yegorov, A. I., *L'vov-Varshava 1920 godu*, Moscow-Leningrad 1929.

(*iv*) *Far East 1921–9*

Gubel'man, M. I., *Bor'ba za Sovetskii Dal'nii Vostok*, Moscow 1958.
Kuz'min, N. F., *Na strazhe mirnovo truda (1921–1940 gg.)*, Ch. V on 1929 operations in Manchuria.

(*v*) *Central Asia 1921–30*

Mel'kumov, Ya. A., *Turkestantsy*, Moscow 1960.

(*vi*) *Far East 1938–9*

Kuz'min, N. F., *Na strazhe mirnovo truda (1921–1940 gg.)*, Ch. VIII on Lake Khasan and Khalkhin-Gol.
*Shishkin, S., *Khalkhin-Gol*, Moscow 1954.
Boevye epizody, Sbornik statei i materialov o sobytyakh u ozera Khasan, Moscow 1939.

(*vii*) *Soviet-Finnish War 1939–40*

Kuz'min, N. F., *Na strazhe mirnovo truda (1921–1940 gg.)*, Ch. IX.

Zinov'ev, I., *Boi v okruzhenii*, Moscow 1941.

Boi v Finlyandii. Vospominaniya uchastnikov, Parts I and II, Moscow 1941.

(*viii*) *Soviet-German War [The Great Patriotic War]: from June 1941 to the Battle of Moscow*

Boevoi put' Sovetskikh vooruzhennykh sil, Moscow 1960, Part Three.

**Istoriya Velikoi Otechestvennoi Voiny Sovetskovo Soyuza 1941–1945*, Vol. 1, 'Podgotovka i razvyazyvanie voiny imperialisticheskimi derzhavami', Moscow 1960. [This is the first of a six-volume Soviet official war history. As an analysis of the course of Soviet pre-war policy, this volume contains considerable material on military operations in the Far East, Poland and Finland. The account of the state of the Red Army and Soviet plans proceeds to the morning of the 22nd June, 1941.]

Ocherki istorii Velikoi Otechestvennoi Voiny 1941–1945 gg., Moscow 1955.

**Vazhneishie operatsii Velikoi Otechestvennoi Voiny 1941–1945 gg.* (ed. Col. P. A. Zhilin), Moscow 1956.

East German edition: *Die wichtigsten operationen des Grossen Vaterländischen Krieges 1941–1945*, Verlag des Ministeriums für Nationale Verteidigung, Berlin 1958.

**Vtoraya Mirovaya Voina 1939–1945*, Voenno-istoricheskii ocherk, Moscow 1958. This work (which has a separate volume of maps) is under the general editorship of Lt.-Gen. S. P. Platonov, Maj.-Gen. N. G. Pavlenko, Col. I. V. Parotkin. See Ch. 3–8.

*Barbashin, I. P. and Kharitonov, A. D., *Boevye deistviya Sovetskoi Armii pod Tikhvinom v 1941 godu*, Moscow 1958.

*Edlinskii, S. F., *Baltiiskii transportnyi flot v Velikoi Otechestvennoi Voine 1941–1945 gg.* (Istoricheskii ocherk), Moscow 1957.

Golikov, S., *Vydayushchiesya pobedy Sovetskoi Armii v Velikoi Otechestvennoi Voine*, 2nd Edn., Moscow 1954.

Isakov, I. S. (Admiral of the Fleet), *The Red Fleet in the Second World War* (Tr. Jack, Hural), London n.d.

*Karasev, A. V., *Leningradtsy v gody blokady, 1941–1943*, Moscow 1959.

Minz, I., *The Army of the Soviet Union*, Moscow FLPH, 1942.

*Oreshkin, A. K., *Oboronitel'naya operatsiya 9-i armii (Oktyabr'–Noyabr' 1941 g.)*, Moscow 1960.

Partizanskie byli (Under the literary editorship of P. P. Petrov and L. M. Subotskii), Moscow 1958.

Strategy and Tactics of the Soviet-German War By Officers of the Red Army and Soviet War Correspondents, Published by authority of 'Soviet War News', London n.d.

*Samsonov, A. M., *Velikaya bitva pod Moskvoi 1941–1942*, Moscow 1958.

Smirnov, S., *Brestkaya krepost'*, Kratkii ocherk geroicheskoi oborony 1941 goda, Moscow 1957.

Surchenko, A., *Geroicheskaya oborona Moskvy 1941 g.*, Moscow 1957.

*Tel'pukhovskii, B. S., *Velikaya Otechestvennaya Voina Sovetskovo Soyuza 1941–1945 gg.*, Moscow 1959.

V'yunenko, N. P., *Chernomorskii flot v Velikoi Otchestvennoi Voine*, Moscow 1957.

V'yunenko, N. P. and Mordvinov, R. N., *Voennye flotilii v Velikoi Otechestvennoi Voine*, Kratkii voenno-istoricheskii ocherk, Moscow 1957.

See also under *Select Articles*.

5. Individual memoirs (also collected speeches, writings)

Antonov-Ovseenko, V., *Zapiski o Grazhdanskoi Voine*, (Vol. 4), Moscow 1933.

—— *V Revolyutsii*, Moscow 1957. [Edited to remove certain 'factual inaccuracies'.]

Bonch-Bruevich, M. V., *Na boevykh postakh fevral'skoi i oktyabr'skoi revolyutsii*, Moscow 1930.

—— *Vsya vlast' Sovetam*, Moscow 1957.

Brusilov, A. A., *Moi vospominaniya*, Moscow, 2nd Edn., 1941. 1st Edn., 1929.

Budennyi, S. M., *Proidennyi put'*, Moscow 1958 (also issued 1959).

Danishevskii K. and Kamenev, S. S., *Vospominaniya o Lenine. Lenin i Grazhdanskaya Voina*, Moscow 1934.

Demidov, M., *Zapiski Krasnoarmeitsa*, Moscow 1958.

Dybenko, P., *Iz nedr Tsarskovo flota k velikomu Oktyab'ru*, Moscow 1928.

—— *Revolyutsionnye Baltiitsy*, Moscow 1959.

Ignat'ev, A. A., *Pyat'desyat let v stroyu*, Vol. 2, Book 5, Moscow 1959 Edn.

Ilyin Genevsky, A. F., *From February to October 1917* (trans.), London 1931.

Kedrov, M. S., *Za Sovetskii Sever*, Moscow-Leningrad 1927.

Ordzhonikidze, G. K., *Stat'i i rechi* Tom 1: 1920–1926, Moscow 1956, pp. 229–240, 'O Krasnoi Armii' (First All-Georgian Congress of Soviets, 3rd March, 1922).

Postyshev, P. P., *Grazhdanskaya voina na vostoke Sibiri (1917–1922 gg.)*, Vospominaniya, Moscow 1957.

Roshal', M. G., *Na putyakh revolyutsii*, Moscow 1957.

Samoilo, A., *Dve zhizni*, Moscow 1958.

Trotsky, L., *My Life. The Rise and Fall of a Dictator*, London 1930. See 'The month at Sviyazhsk', pp. 338–51.

Vakhrameev, I. I., *Vo imya Revolyutsii*, Moscow 1957.

Voroshilov, K. E., *Stat'i i rechi*, Moscow (Partizdat), 1937.

See also *Ot Fevral'ya Oktyabr'yu*, Moscow 1957, for biographic questionnaires completed in 1927 and now published. Section 4 of the questionnaire deals with military activities. See under A. S. Bubnov (pp. 61–7), A. G. Gerasimov (pp. 97–103), P. E. Dybenko (pp. 152–9), M.S. Kedrov (pp. 170–6), N. I. Podvoiskii (p. 148).

See also under *Select Articles*.

6. Military doctrine and military writings (also military-political questions)

A number of periodical references are included here, in order to contain under a particular name the principal sources from which arguments have been taken and used in the text.

Engel's, F., *Izbrannye voennye proizvedeniya*, Moscow, 1957 Edn., in the series *Biblioteka ofitsera*. See introduction, Col., A. Strokov, 'F. Engel's — velikii znatok voennovo dela', pp. v–xxv.

Lagovskii, A., *Strategiya i ekonomika*, Moscow 1957.

Marksizm-Leninizm o voine i armii, Moscow 1957 and 1958: series *Biblioteka ofitsera*. Collective work under the general editorship of Col. I. N. Levanov (chief editor), Col. B. A. Belyi, Col. A. P. Novoselov.

Maryganov, I. V., *Peredovoi kharakter sovetskoi voennoi nauki*, Moscow 1953. [Polish Edn., *O radzieckiej nauce wojennej*, Wyd. Ministerstwa Obrony Narodowej, 1955.]

Rybkin, E. I., *Voina i politika*, Moscow 1959.

*'Sovetskaya voennaya nauka nakanune Otechestvennoi voiny' in *Istoriya Velikoi Otechestvennoi Voiny Sovetskovo Soyuza 1941–1945 gg.*, Moscow 1960, Vol. 1, pp. 436–51.

'Sovetskoe voennoe iskusstvo nakanune Velikoi Otechestvennoi voiny' in *Vtoraya Mirovaya Voina 1939–1945 gg.*, Moscow 1958, pp. 165–76.

Taranchuk, M. V., *O postoyanno deistvuyushchikh faktorakh, reshayushchikh sud'bu voiny*, Moscow 1952.

Alksnis, Ya., 'Podgotovka k voine i voprosy komplektovaniya armii' in *Voina i Revolyutsiya*, 1927 (6), pp. 46–65.

Bubnov, A. S., *Boevaya podgotovka i politicheskaya rabota*, Moscow 1927.

—— *O Krasnoi Armii*, Moscow 1958.

Frunze, M. V., *Sobranie sochinenii*, (Ed. A. S. Bubnov), Vols. I–III, Moscow 1929.

—— *Stat'i i rechi*, Moscow 1936.

—— *Izbrannye proizvedeniya*, Moscow 1940.

—— *Izbrannye proizvedeniya*, Moscow 1951.

—— *Izbrannye proizvedeniya*, (Joint editorship of Col. M. S. Dolgi and Col. N. V. Shiryakin), Vols. I–II, Moscow 1957.

—— *Edinaya voennaya doktrina i Krasnaya Armiya*, Moscow 1921.

—— *Na novykh putyakh*, Moscow 1925.

—— 'Itogi dekabr'skovo plenuma Revvoensoveta SSSR. Doklad k Voennoi Akademii RKKA, 24.12.1924' in *Voina i Revolyutsiya*, 1926 (10), pp. 88–111.

Golubev, A., *M. V. Frunze o kharaktere budushchei voiny*, Moscow 1931.

Gusev, S. I., *Uroki grazhdanskoi voiny*, Moscow 1921. [2nd Edn.]

—— *Grazhdanskaya Voina i Krasnaya Armiya*, Moscow-Leningrad 1925. [Republished in 1958, with certain shortened texts and a preface by N. Kopylov.]

—— 'Marksizm i voennaya nauka (Politika i tekhnika)' in *Nashi raznoglasiya v voennom dele*, Moscow 1925.

Kamenev, S. S., 'O metodakh uchebnoi raboty po taktike v normal'nykh shkolakh i v chastyakh' in *Voina i Revolyutsiya*, 1926 (3), pp. 24–30.

Kapustin, N., *Operativnoe iskusstvo v pozitsionnoi voine*, Moscow-Leningrad 1927.

Lapchinskii, A., *Krasnyi vozdushnyi flot 1918–1928 gg.*, Moscow 1928.

—— 'Vozdushnaya oborona' in *Bol'shaya Sovetskaya Entsiklopediya*, Vol. 12, 1928, Cols. 436–9.

Lebedev, P., *Boevaya podgotovka v territorial'nikh voiskakh*, Moscow 1927.

Lenin, V. I., *Zamechaniya na knigu Klauzevitsa 'O voine i vedenii voiny'*, Moscow 1933.

Podvoiskii, N. I. and Pavlovich, M., (editors), *Revolyutsionnaya voina*, Moscow 1919.

Rotshtein, F., 'Voina kak sotsialnoe yavlenie' in *Bol'shaya Sovetskaya Entsiklopediya*, Vol. 12 (1928), Cols. 552–76.

Shaposhnikov, B. M., *Mozg armii*, Vols. I–III, Moscow 1927–9.
Smilga, I., *Ocherednye voprosy stroitel'stva Krasnoi Armii*, Moscow 1921.
Svechin, A., *Strategiya*, 2nd edn., Moscow 1927.
Triandafillov, V. K., *Kharakter operatsii sovremennykh armii* (ed. N. S. Naumov), 2nd edn., Moscow 1932.
Trotskii, L., *Kak vooruzhalas' Revolyutsiya:*
'Partizanstvo i regulyarniya armiya', Vol. 2, Bk. 1, pp. 59–65.
'Programmy militsii i eë akademicheskii kritik', Vol. 2, Bk. 1, pp. 115–22.
'Stroitel'stvo krasnoi vooruzhennoi sily', Vol. 2, Bk. 1, pp. 122–33.
'Voennaya doktrina ili mnimo-voennoe doktrinerstvo', Vol. 3, Bk. 2, pp. 210–241.
'Voennoe znanie i marksizm' (8th May, 1922), Vol. 3, Bk. 2, pp. 271–93.
—— 'The Red Army and its doctrines' in Ch. VIII, *The Revolution Betrayed. What is the Soviet Union and where is it going?* (trans. M. Eastman), London 1937, pp. 194–205.
Tukhachevskii, M. N., *Voina Klassov. Stat'i 1919–1920 g.*, Otdel Voen. Lit. pri RVSR, Moscow (Gosizdat), 1921.
—— *Die Rote Armee und die Miliz*, Kleine Bibliothek der Russischen Korrespondenzen, No. 51, Leipzig, 1921. [Trans. from *Krasnaya Armiya i militsiya*, Moscow 1921.]
—— *Voprosy vyshevo komandovaniya*, Moscow 1924.
—— Preface to *Novaya organizatsiya mestnovo voennovo upravleniya* (M. Kulchak), Moscow 1926.
—— Introductory essay to *Podgotovka Rossii k imperialisticheskoi voine*, Moscow 1926.
—— *Voprosy sovremennoi strategii*, Moscow 1926.
—— 'Obuchenie vzaimodeistviya (pekhoty i artillerii)', in *Voina i Revolyutsiya*, 1926 (6), pp. 3–8.
—— 'Bor'ba s kontrrevolyutsionnym vosstaniyam', in *Voina i Revolyutsiya*, 1926 (7), pp. 3–17 and (8), pp. 3–15.
—— 'Voina kak problema vooruzhennoi bor'by', in *Bol'shaya Sovetskaya Entsiklopediya*, Vol. 12, 1928, Cols. 576–96.
—— On German war-plans, *Pravda*, 31st March, 1935.
—— Report on National Defence, *The Soviet Union: 1935*, Moscow-Leningrad 1935, pp. 211–25. [English language edn.]
—— Speech to the 2nd Session of the Central Executive Committee of the USSR, in *The Soviet Union and the Path to Peace 1917–1936*, London 1936, pp. 46–56. Speech of 15th January, 1936.
—— *Bol'shevik*, 1937 (9), pp. 46–57, on *PU-36*.
Voina i Voennoe Iskusstvo v Svete Istoricheskovo Materializma (ed. B. Gorev), Moscow 1927.
Zapiski Sektsii po izucheniyu problem voiny pri Komakademii, Vol. 1, Moscow 1930.

Translations of foreign military writings

Dzh. Fuller, *Tanki v Velikoi voine 1941–1918 gg.*, Moscow 1923.
Liddel Gart (Liddell Hart), *Novye puti sovremennykh armii*, Moscow-Leningrad 1930.

Eimansberger, *Tankovaya voina* (trans. E. Veinraub), Moscow 1935.

Due (Douhet), *Gospodstvo v vozdukhe*. Posmertnoe izdanie trudov po voprosam vozdushnoi voiny: I. Gospodstvo v vozdukhe; II. Veroyatnye formy budushchei voiny; III. Podvedenie itogov polemiki po voprosam vozdushnoi voiny; IV. Voina 19...goda (Foreword V. V. Khripin), Moscow 1935.

7. WORKS OF LENIN, TROTSKY AND STALIN

Lenin, V. I., *Sochineniya*, 4th edn.

—— *Voennaya perepiska (1917–1920)*, Moscow 1956.

Leninskii sbornik, Vol. XXXIV.

Trotsky [Trotskii/Trotski], L. D.,

Trotskii, L., *Kak vooruzhalas' Revolutsiya*, Vols. I–III.

Trotsky, L., *History of the Russian Revolution* (trans. M. Eastman), 3 Vols., London 1932–3.

—— *Problems of the Chinese Revolution. With Appendices by Zinoviev, Vuyovich, Nassunov and others*, New York 1932.

—— *The Revolution Betrayed*, London 1937.

—— *The Stalin School of Falsification* (Introduction M. Shachtman), New York 1937. See 'Stalin and the Red Army', pp. 205–31. [*Stalinskaya shkola falsifikatsii i dopolneniya k literature epigonov*, Berlin 1932.]

Trotski, Léon, *La Révolution Trahie. Les Crimes de Staline* (trans. V. Serge), Paris 1937. See 'La décapitation de l'Armée Rouge', pp. 335–53.

Trotski, Leon, *Stalin. An appraisal of the man and his influence* (edited and translated from the Russian by Charles Malamuth), London 1947.

Stalin, I. V., *Sochineniya* [also in English translation as *Works*], Moscow 1947 —. This is a discontinued publication, the last volume being the thirteenth.

Stalin, J. V., *Problems of Leninism*, Moscow FLPH, 1958. From the 11th Russian edition, *Voprosy Leninizma*, Moscow 1952.

Perepiska predsedatelya Soveta ministrov SSSR s prezidentami SShA i prem'er-ministrami Velikobritanii vo vremya Velikoi Otechestvennoi voiny 1941–1945 gg., Vol. 1, Moscow 1957.

On the Great Patriotic War of the Soviet Union (Speeches/Orders), London 1943.

8. COMMUNIST PARTY CONGRESSES, CONFERENCES AND RELATED MATERIALS

VKP(b) v rezolyutsiakh i resheniyakh s'ezdov, konferentsii i plenumov TsK, 1898–1935, 2 vols., 5th Edn., Moscow 1936.

KPSS v rezolyutsiakh i resheniyakh s'ezdov, konferentsii i plenumov TsK, 1898–1953, 2 vols., 7th Edn., Moscow 1953.

KPSS v bor'be za pobedu Velikoi Oktyabr'skoi Revolyutsii, 5 Iyulya–5 Noyabr' 1917 g., Sbornik dokumentov, Moscow 1957.

Vos'moi s'ezd RKP(b). Protokoly, Moscow 1933.

Vos'moi s'ezd RKP(b) 1919 goda. Protokoly, Moscow 1959.

Desyatyi s'ezd RKP(b), Protokoly, Moscow 1921.

Stenograficheskii otchot vtorovo dnya soveshchania voennykh delegatov XI s'ezda RKP(b), 1 Aprelya 1922, Moscow 1922.

XI s'ezda RKP(b), Protokoly, Moscow 1936.
Chetyrnadtsatyi s'ezd VKP(b), Moscow 1926.
Pyatnadtsatyi s'ezd VKP(b), Moscow-Leningrad 1927.
Semnadtsatyi s'ezd VKP(b), Moscow 1934. See pp. 224–36, 464–6, 512–14, 629–31.
O perestroike partiino-politicheskoi raboty. K itogam plenuma TsK VKP(b), 26 Fevral'ya 1937 g., Moscow 1937.
Vosemnadtsatyi s'ezd VKP(b), Moscow 1939. [See also *The Land of Socialism Today and Tommorrow*, Moscow FLPH, 1939.]
The Red Army Today. Speeches delivered at the 18th Congress of the CPSU (B), March 10–21, 1939, Moscow FLPH, 1939.
Popov, N. N., *Outline History of the Communist Party of the Soviet Union*, 2 vols., Moscow FLPH, n.d.
Yaroslavskii, E., *Istoriya VKP(b)*, Vol. 4, Moscow-Leningrad 1930.
Istoriya Kommunisticheskoi Partii Sovetskovo Soyuza (collective authorship under the direction of B. N. Ponomarev), Moscow 1959.

9. TRIAL RECORDS 1936–1938

The Case of the Trotskyite-Zinovievite Centre. Report of Court Proceedings heard before the Military Collegium of the Supreme Court of the USSR, Moscow, August 19–24, 1936. People's Commissariat of Justice of the USSR, Moscow 1936.
The Case of the Anti-Soviet Trotskyite Centre. Report of Court Proceedings heard before the Military Collegium of the Supreme Court of the USSR, Moscow, January 23–30, 1937. People's Commissariat of Justice of the USSR, Moscow 1937.
The Case of the Anti-Soviet 'Bloc of Rights and Trotskyites'. Report of Court Proceedings heard before the Military Collegium of the Supreme Court of the USSR, Moscow, March 2–13, 1938. People's Commissariat of Justice of the USSR, Moscow 1938.

See also N. S. Khrushchev, speech at the 20th Party Congress, 25th February, 1956: *United States Department of State* text. Published as 'The Dethronement of Stalin', *Manchester Guardian*, June 1956, 33 pp.

10. FOREIGN POLICY STATEMENTS AND PRINTED DOCUMENTS

Krasnaya kniga. Sbornik dokumentov o russko-polskie otnoshenia 1918–1920, Moscow 1920. [Also printed in a French version, as *Livre rouge*.]
The Soviet Union and Peace (Introduction H. Barbusse), London 1929.
Litvinov, M. M., *The Foreign Policy of the Soviet Union*, 'Friends of Soviet Russia' publication, 1930.
The Soviet Union and the Path to Peace. Lenin-Stalin-Molotov-Voroshilov-Tukhachevsky. (Speeches and documents 1917–1936), London 1936.
Litvinov, M., *Against Aggression*, London 1939. [Russian edition, *Protiv Agressii*, Moscow 1938.]
Stalin, J., *An interview with the German author Emil Ludwig* (English version), Moscow 1932.

Stalin, Litvinov, Molotov, *Soviet Foreign Policy. Declaration by MM Stalin, Molotov and Litvinov*, Anglo-Russian Parliamentary Committee, 1934. Also *Our Foreign Policy* (English version), Moscow 1934.

Recent documentary publications

Dokumenty vneshnei politiki SSSR, Ministerstvo inostrannykh del SSSR, Vols. I–IV, Moscow 1957 (publication proceeding).

Sovetsko-kitaiskie otnosheniya 1917–1957, Sbornik dokumentov, Moscow 1959.

Lokarnskaya konferentsiya 1925 g., Dokumenty, Ministerstvo inostrannykh del SSSR, Moscow 1959.

Select studies

Gol'dberg, D. I., *Vneshnaya politika Yaponii (Sentyabr' 1939 g.–Dekabr' 1941 g.)*, Moscow 1959.

Israelyan, V. L., *Diplomaticheskaya istoriya Velikoi Otechestvennoi Voiny 1941–1945 gg.* Moscow 1959.

Kapitsa, M. S., *Sovetsko-kitaiskie otnosheniya*, Moscow 1958.

Potemkin, V. P. (ed.), *Istoriya diplomatii*, 3 Vols., Moscow 1941–5. [The first volume of an enlarged, revised edition of *Istoriya diplomatii*, edited by V. A. Zorin, V. S. Semenov, S. D. Skazkin, V. M. Khvostov, appeared in 1959.]

Shtein, B. E., *Burzhuaznye fal'sifikatory istorii (1919–1939)*, Moscow 1951.

NOTE: *Istoriya Velikoi Otechestvennoi Voiny Sovetskovo Soyuza 1941–1945*, Vol. 1, Moscow 1960, Ch. 3, Ch. 4, Ch. 6, Ch. 9(i), contains the current versions of Soviet foreign policy and its relation to the security of the Soviet state.

East German studies

Norden, Albert, *Zwischen Berlin und Moskau. Zur Geschichte der deutsch-sowjetischen Beziehungen*, Dietz Verlag Berlin, 1954.

Rosenfeld, Günter, *Sowjetrussland und Deutschland 1917–1922*, Akademie Verlag, Berlin, 1960.

11. SOVIET INDUSTRY/WAR ECONOMY

Lokshin, E. Yu., *Ocherk istorii promyshlennosti SSSR, (1917–1940)*, Moscow 1956.

Soldatenko, E. I., *Trudovoi podvig Sovetskovo Naroda v Velikoi Otechestvennoi Voine*, Moscow 1954.

Voznesenskii, N., *Voennaya ekonomika SSSR v period Otechestvennoi voiny*, Moscow 1948.

—— *The Economy of the USSR during World War II* (trans.), Public Affairs Press, USA, 1948. Mimeographed.

'Voenno-ekonomicheskie vozmozhnosti SSSR' in *Istoriya Velikoi Otechestvennoi Voiny Sovetskovo Soyuza 1941–1945*, Moscow 1960, Vol. 1, Ch. 9 (2), pp. 405–24.

12. ENCYCLOPEDIA REFERENCE

Bol'shaya Sovetskaya Entsiklopediya, 1st Edn., especially Vol. 12, 1928.

Mal'aya Sovetskaya Entsiklopediya, 4th Edn., for biographical details under individual entry. Publication proceeding.

13. Soviet military law

Chkhikvadze, V. M., *Sovetsko voenno-ugolovnoe pravo*, Ministerstvo Yustitsii SSSR' Moscow 1948. See Ch. III, (i), 'Razvitie sovetskovo voenno-ugolovnovo zakonodatel'stva v period grazhdanskoi i inostrannoi interventsii', pp. 80–92; also Ch. IV, 'Voenno-ugolovnyi zakon', pp. 117–38.

14. Select articles

(*i*) *Documentary materials in periodical publication*

**Krasnyi Arkhiv*

KA 1924 (5), pp. 213–40, 'Verkhovnoe komandovanie v pervye dni revolyutsii'.

KA 1925 (8), pp. 153–75, 1925 (9), pp. 156–70, 'Oktyabr'skii perevorot i Stavka' (A. G. Shlyapnikov).

KA 1926 (17), pp. 36–50, 'Revolyutsionnaya propaganda v armii v 1916–1917 gg.'.

KA 1927 (21), pp. 3–78, 1927 (22), pp. 3–70, 'Fevral'skaya revolyutsiya 1917 g. Dokumenty stavki verkhovnovo komandovaniya i shtaba glavkomandovaniya/ Armiya Severnovo fronta'.

KA 1927 (23), pp. 64–148, 'Moskovskii Voenno-revolyutsionnyi Komitet'.

—— pp. 149–94, 1927 (24), pp. 71–107, 'Oktyabr' na fronte' (Commissar and staff reports).

Also KA 1938 (86), pp. 29–55, Documents on the history of the organisation of the Red Army; 1939 (93), pp. 3–50, M. V. Frunze's defeat of Kolchak (1919); KA 1941 (104), pp. 54–102, Timoshenko's military activities.

**Istoricheskii Arkhiv*

IA 1956 (1), pp. 132–56, 'Otchot Revvoensoveta Respubliki 1917–1919 gg.'.

IA 1957 (1), pp. 129–51, 'Geroizm chastei i soedinnei Krasnoi Armii na vostochnom fronte v 1918–1920 g.'.

IA 1957 (4), pp. 3–37, 'Internatsional'nye gruppy RKP(b) i voinskie formirovaniya v Sovetskoi Rossii (1918–1920)' [Czechoslovak, Hungarian, Chinese international units in the Red Army].

IA 1957 (5), pp. 119–46, 'Iz istorii Krasnoi Gvardii Petrograda'.

IA 1958 (1), pp. 41–76, (2), pp. 36–51, 'Doklady I. I. Vatsetisa V. I. Leninu (Fevral'–Mai 1919 g.).'

IA 1958 (1), pp. 76–89, 'K. V. Blyukher na frontakh grazhdanskoi voiny' [South Urals Composite Detachment].

IA 1958 (3), pp. 32–41, 'Iz perepiski M. V. Frunze s V. I. Leninym (1919–1920 g.)' [Entry into Turkestan].

IA 1958 (4), pp. 85–122, 'V. V. Kuibyshev na vostochnom fronte 1918–1919 g.' [Kuibyshev-Tukhachevskii/1918: Kuibyshev-Novitskii-Frunze/1919].

IA 1958 (5), pp. 77–99, 'K. V. Blyukher na frontakh grazhdanskoi voiny' [1920 operations with 51st Division, including war diary].

IA 1959 (4), pp. 106–36, 'Iz istorii Severnovo pokhoda'. [Reports of Soviet military advisers in China, covering the period 1925–27.]

IA 1960 (3), pp. 61–8, 'Dokument o geroizme voinov Pribaltiki v boyakh za Rodinu (1941 g.)'. [Report of Battalion Commissar Zasepskii to the Political Administration North-west Front on operations in the Baltic area, and dated 28th December, 1941.]

(*ii*) *Select recent periodical items*

NOTE: where *Voprosy Istorii* supplies an English version of the title of an article, it is this which is given here.

Belikov, V. E., 'Partiinaya organizatsiya Petrograda v bor'be protiv Yudenicha letom 1919 g.', *Voprosy Istorii*, 1956, No. 1, pp. 31–45.

Berkhin, I. B., 'The strengthening of part-political organs and the strengthening of political workers in the Red Army, 1924–1925', *Voprosy Istorii*, 1958, No. 2, pp. 23–45.

Boltin, E. A., 'The victory of the Soviet Army before Moscow, 1941', *Voprosy Istorii*, 1957, No. 1, pp. 20–33.

Dykov, I. G., 'The Petrograd Military-Revolutionary Committee — fighting Bolshevik staff of the armed rising in October, 1917', *Voprosy Istorii*, 1957, No. 7, pp. 17–36.

Kirillov, V. S., 'On some aspects of Lenin's military activities in the Civil War', *Voprosy Istorii*, 1957, No. 4, pp. 3–24.

Kuz'min, N. F., Naida, S. F., Petrov, Yu., Shishkin, S., 'O nekotorykh voprosakh istorii grazhdanskoi voiny', *Kommunist*, August 1956, No. 12, pp. 54–72.

Kuz'min, N. F., 'K istorii razgroma belogvardeiskikh voisk Denikina,' *Voprosy Istorii*, 1956, No. 7, pp. 18–33.

Naida, S. F., Petrov, Yu., 'Kommunisticheskaya Partiya — organizator pobedy na vostochnom fronte v 1918 g.', *Vorposy Istorii*, 1956, No. 10, pp. 3–16.

Petrov, Yu., 'Stroitel'stvo partiinykh organizatsii v Krasnoi Armii v period inostrannoi voennoi interventsii i grazhdanskoi voiny (1918–1920 gg.)', *Partiinaya Zhizn'*, May 1957, No. 10, pp. 35–46.

Popov, N. A., 'The role of the Chinese international units in defence of the Soviet Republic in the period of the Civil War (1918–1920)', *Voprosy Istorii*, 1957, No. 10, pp. 109–24.

Spirin, L. M., 'Kommunisticheskaya Partiya — organizator razgroma Kolchaka', *Voprosy Istorii*, 1956, No. 6, pp. 16–32.

II. GERMAN WAR DOCUMENTS PROJECT: FILM COLLECTIONS

Since these sources have been used very selectively, no attempt is made here to follow or reproduce the original German classification. Even in such a collection as the *Geheimakten: Handakten/Russland* (1920–36), the individual files will be cited. Files marked with an asterisk indicate the basic materials employed here, the remainder having been used for reference, background and biographical information. Into the latter category fall the voluminous collections of the *Komintern* files maintained by the *Auswärtiges Amt, Innere Politik* and *Russische Geheimdokumente* collections (grouped chronologically), as well as general files on Soviet-German relations. In addition, German material of a documentary nature has been drawn from *Nazi Conspiracy and Aggression, Documents on German Foreign Policy* (Series C and D), *Trial of the Major*

War Criminals before the International Military Tribunal (Nuremberg), and *Nazi-Soviet Relations 1939–1941* (Department of State).

1. SOVIET-POLISH WAR: EARLY SOVIET-GERMAN CONTACTS

*Serial L679/L213664–4558

*K195–196/K037911–8007 (contains reports of the German military command on the Red Army advance)

Also Serials L617 and K281:

*L617/L193234–8: Hey memorandum on Radek's visit to him (10/1/1920)

*K281/K095851–3: Maltzan memorandum on conversation with Kopp (16/4/1920)

*K281/K096009–10: Maltzan memorandum on conversation with Kopp (14/7/1920)

*K281/K095871–871: ditto (19/7/1920)

*K196/K037987: von Seeckt on basic reasons for German neutrality (21/7/1920)

*L756/L224527–34: von Seeckt on prospect of Russian victory (26/7/1920)

*2860/551567–73: von Seeckt, 'Die militär-politische Lage im Osten'

*K281/K095894–5: Instructions and credentials for Major Schubert to proceed as liaison officer to the Red Army in Poland (7/8/1920)

*K281/K095908–11: Survey of Soviet and German positions, position of Hilger and Kopp (14/8/1920)

*K195/K037963–73: Major Schubert on the military situation in the east. Soviet defeat (29/8/1920)

*L396/L114391–3: *Reichswehrministerium* (T3 Foreign Armies) appraisal of the military-political situation in the east. Soviet Russia on the defensive (29/10/1920)

*L557/L157128–31: von Seeckt-Simons exchange, military position on the eastern frontier (11/12/1920)

*K462/K133327–8: Maltzan-Brodowsky exchange, (*a*) departure of specialists for Russia, (*b*) on raising state of war between Germany and Russia (5/2/1921)

*K304/K105236–9: *Komintern* and Germany, intercepts of telegrams to the Soviet Trade Delegation in Berlin (4/4/1921)

*4829/E241618–25: Soviet-German Agreement (*Abkommen*) (6/5/1921)

*1563/378300–3: *Reichsminister*-Krestinsky, confidential exchange on Soviet-German relations (12/12/1921)

*6698H/H105470–2, 473: *Reichswehrministerium* views on original Junkers contract (original 15/3/1922; this examination dated 23/4/1926)

*3398/738919–22: Treaty of Rapallo/Rathenau-Chicherin (16/4/1922)

*L309/L096163–4: Secret letters to the Treaty/Rathenau-Chicherin (16/4/1922).

2. MILITARY ATTACHE REPORTS ON THE RED ARMY/AIR FORCE/NAVY

*Serial 9524H/671321–704: *Militärangelegenheiten* (Po. 13), Vols. 1, 2, 3, 4, 5, 7 (Vol. 6 missing). Period covered: December 1922–October 1928 and 1932.

*Serial 5892H/E432446–433261: *Militärangelegenheiten* (Kowno-Moskau), Vols. 1, 4, 5 (some of which fire-damaged). Period covered: January 1933–May 1936. Also contain duplicates of Naval Attaché's reports. See Leningrad military exercises (28/6/1933); Death of Lebedev (11/7/1933); Air networks in the USSR (with maps); Visit to camp Kubinka (15/7/1933); Soviet armaments industry (18/7/

1933); High command appointments (autumn 1933); Methods of tactical training of infantry (8/8/1933); Technical tables on Soviet air force machines (8/8/1933); Personalities/High Command (22/8/1933); Report on the closing of the 'installations' (19/9/1933); Farewell dinner for the head of *Z.Mo.* (26/9/1933); Report on Soviet manœuvres (1933); Franco-Soviet military co-operation; Organisation and deployment of Soviet military aviation (listed by air brigades and parks) (17/10/1933); Tukhachevsky-Twardowski on Soviet German military collaboration (7/11/1933); Report on the military situation of the Red Army in the Far East (10/1/1934); French military influence upon and collaboration with the Red Army (11/2/1935); Changes in the high command of the Red Army and their significance (11/3/1935); Promotions to Marshal, Admiral in the Soviet armed forces (24/11/1935).

*Serial 6490H/E486069–74: *Militärangelegenheiten* (Po. 13), dated 15th May, 1937, signed by Ambassador Schulenburg, by title, 'Veränderungen in der Roten Armee'.

*Serial 7500H/E540791–9: further to the above, dated 7th June, 1937, by title, 'Personalveränderungen in der Leitung der Roten Armee'.

*Serial 1891H/426090–152: *Die Kriegswehrmacht der UdSSR (1940)*. Composite report.

3. *Reichswehr*-RED ARMY COLLABORATION

*Serial 4564H/E162514–164069: *Büro des Staatssekretärs;* collection *Militärische Angelegenheiten mit Russland* (17/3/1923–18/5/1930). This is an immensely important collection, which, while duplicating some of the documents in the *Direktoren* collection, contains in many cases the 'action taken or decided' noted on to the document. It is impossible to single out a period for which it is particularly important.

*Serial 9481H/H276239–508, *9480H/H276062–236: *Direktoren* 29a/1 and /3. *Militärische Angelegenheiten* (Dirksen), for the period March 1926–November 1928 and November 1928–32. Blomberg report (*Reise des Chefs des Truppenamts nach Russland.* August/September 1928) in 9480/H276183–236.

*Serial 5265H/E318692–784: *Direktoren 11/4*. Deals with Voroshilov's 'revelations' in the spring of 1926.

* Serial 6698H/H105370–526: Junkers litigation (*Geheimakten/Handakten*).

Serial 6698H/H106231–398: *Sowjetgranaten* (12/1926–6/1927).

Serial 6698H/H111733–763: *Reichswehr und Russland* (12/1923–6/1927).

*Serial K298/K104940–105000: *Militärangelegenheiten* (Po. 13); *Rheinmetall*, for the period January 1932–August 1932. Fire-damaged.

*Serial 8074H/579392–455: *Militärische Kommandierungen und Studienreisen* (4/1928–8/1935). Contains von Bockelberg's report on his visit to the Red Army in 1933 and information on Soviet armaments industry.

4. EARLY REPORTS ON SOVIET NAVAL FORCES AND NAVAL COLLABORATION

*Serial K299/K105008–058, K300: *Russische Marine*, for the period 1924–6, 1928 and items for 1931–2 (on transfer of German submarine experts to the USSR).

*Serial M108: Soviet-German naval contacts.

5. SOVIET FOREIGN POLICY (ALSO SOVIET-GERMAN RELATIONS)

Serial 6698H/H110486–526: *Russland-Japan*, for period 8/1926–9/1928.

Serial 6698H/H116200–117302: *Russland-China* (Part II), for period 7/1929–2/1930. Materials on the Soviet-Chinese dispute.

Serial L267/L199438–613: Soviet-German treaties, for period 6/1926–6/1931.

*Serial 9187H/H249209–607: *Briefwechsel mit dem Herrn Botschafter von Dirksen*, for period March 1931–July 1932.

*Serial 1908H/E429388–761: Soviet-German relations 1932–3; Litvinov conversation with Schleicher and Neurath (27/12/1932); Neurath-Litvinov (1/3/1933); Dirksen-Molotov (4/8/1933).

*Serial 1909H/429825, 429959: Conversations with Tukhachevsky (1933 and 1935).

*Serial 393/212171–2: Kivimaki on Stalin's attitude to the Franco-Soviet Pact (18/5/1936).

Serial 1907H/429294–324: Kandelaki-Schacht-Neurath (December 1936–February 1937). Also item on the Far East.

*Serial 1903H/428428–502, 1822H/416759–885: Soviet-Finnish War (1940).

6. INFORMATION ON THE PURGES

See Serials 6490H and 7500H on the purge in the Red Army, 1937.

*Serial 3540H/E021912–936: *Ausweisungen*/Radek Trial (dealing with allegations against German citizens).

*Serial 3483H/019150–019397: Reports, affidavits and analytical material dealing with the purges, for the period January 1937–March 1938. The affidavits concern the Germans mentioned in the trials.

Serial 600/246921–59: *Strafverfolgungen/Russland.*

Serial 598/246389–803: *Verhaftungslisten* (1936–8). Deals with arrest of Germans in the USSR.

7. THE RUSSIAN EMIGRATION

*Serial 611/248860–249137: *Politische Bestrebungen der Emigration*, for the period May 1936–December 1937. Contains entries on General Miller.

8. MATERIALS ON SOVIET INTERNAL AFFAIRS, *Russische Geheimdokumente* AND ESPIONAGE

Note: Serial 3483H comes under the filing of *Innere Politik.*

*K294/K104220–656: *Innere Politik*, for the period 1926–30.

*K284/K098422–522: *Russische Geheimdokumente*, for the period 1926–8, dealing with internal events through agents' reports.

See also Serial K285, and Serial K283.

See also Serial 5462H for *Geheimberichte*, dealing with Soviet Intelligence, and containing items of an intelligence nature on the USSR (1925–7).

9. THE *Komintern*

Covering the period 1920–34, the *Geheimakten* files on the *Komintern* open with Serial K304/K105223–726 for the period July 1920–June 1924 and run chronologically with each successive serial. A small number of items have been used from the K304 run, dealing with the *Komintern* and the Red Army.

10. MISCELLANEOUS

*Serial 2665H/D527851–988: *Wehramt* studies of the economy of the USSR, figures for the period 1934–9. Maps and tables.

*Serial 1615H/387293–8: *Oberkommando der Wehrmacht* and *Oberkommando der Kriegsmarine* (29/10/1940 and 27/11/1940 respectively) on the Red Army and Soviet-Turkish naval strengths in the Black Sea.

Serial 4506H/124002–146: *A. Rechberg und ähnliche illegale Aktionen zur Herbeiführung einer deutsch-französischen Militarallianz insbes. die Angelegenheit 'Klönne'.*

OTHER GERMAN SOURCES: PRINTED DOCUMENTS AND MEMOIRS/MONOGRAPHS

Documents on German Foreign Policy 1918–1945, London: HMSO, Series D (1937–45), Vol. I, 1949; Vol. VIII, 1954. Series C, Vols. I–III, 1957–9. *Halder Diary* (Printed US Army/Eucom), Vols. VI–VII.

Nazi Conspiracy and Aggression, Office of the U.S. Chief of Counsel for the Prosecution of Axis Criminality, Washington 1946, Vols. V–VI.

Nazi-Soviet Relations 1939–1941, Documents from the Archives of The German Foreign Office (ed. R. J. Sontag and J. S. Beddie), Department of State, 1948.

Trial of the Major War Criminals before the International Military Tribunal, Nuremberg 14th November 1945–1st October 1946, published at Nuremberg, Germany. Reference by volume and document.

White Book (German) No. 6. Also as *Die Geheimakten des Französischen Generalstabes*, Berlin 1940.

Abshagen, K. H., *Canaris*, Stuttgart 1949.

Blücher, W. von, *Deutschlands Weg nach Rapallo*, Wiesbaden 1951.

Blumentritt, Günther, in *The Fatal Decisions*, London 1956.

Dirksen, H. von, *Moskau, Tokyo, London. Erinnerungen und Betrachtungen zu 20 Jahren deutscher Aussenpolitik*, 1919–39, Stuttgart 1949.

Erfurth, W., *Die Geschichte des Deutschen Generalstabes von 1918 bis 1945*, Göttingen 1957.

Gessler, Otto, *Reichswehrpolitik in der Weimarer Zeit*, Stuttgart 1958.

Goerlitz, Walter, *History of the German General Staff 1657–1945* (trans. B. Battershaw), N.Y., 1957.

Guderian, Heinz, *Panzer Leader* (Foreword Captain B. H. Liddell Hart), London 1952.

Hagen, Walter, *Die Geheime Front*, Nibelungen-Verlag, 1950.

Hilger, Gustav (and Meyer, A. C.), *The Incompatible Allies*. A Memoir-History of German-Soviet Relations 1918–1941, N.Y., 1953.

Kleist, Peter, *Zwischen Hitler und Stalin 1939–1945*, Bonn 1950.

Rabenau, F. von, *Seeckt. Aus seinem Leben 1918–1936*, Leipzig 1941.

Schüddekopf, O-E., *Das Heer und Die Republik*, Quellen zur Politik der Reichswehrführung 1918 bis 1945, Hannover und Frankfurt am Main, 1955.

Speidel, Helm, 'Reichswehr und Rote Armee' in *Vierteljahrshefte für Zeitgeschichte*, January 1953, pp. 9–43.

The Memoirs of Field-Marshal Kesselring, London 1953.

The Schellenberg Memoirs (Introduction by Alan Bullock), London 1956.

III. Far East: Japanese Special Studies and Materials on Soviet-Chinese Relations

1. Japanese

Japanese Special Studies on Manchuria

Prepared by Military History Section, Headquarters, Army Forces Far East. Distributed by Office of the Chief of Military History, Department of the Army (US Army), Washington, USA.

—— *Japanese Operational Planning against the USSR* (1955), Vol. I of Special Studies.

—— *Japanese Intelligence Planning against the USSR* (1955), Vol. X.

—— *Study of Strategical and Tactical Peculiarities of Far Eastern Russia and Soviet Far East Forces* (1955), Vol. XIII.

Also:

Hayashi, Saburo (in collaboration with Alvin D. Coox), KŌGUN *The Japanese Army in the Pacific War*, Marine Corps Assn., Quantico, Va., 1959. See 'The Army's Course until World War II'.

Shigemitsu, Mamoru, *Japan and Her Destiny My Struggle for Peace* (ed. Major-General F. S. Piggott and trans. O. White), London 1958.

Togo, Shigenori, *The Cause of Japan* (ed. and trans. Togo Fumihiko and B. B. Blakeney), N.Y. 1956.

See also:

Dallin, David J., *The Rise of Russia in Asia*, London 1950.

Friters, Gerard M., *Outer Mongolia and its International Position*, London 1951.

Jones, F. C., *Japan's New Order in East Asia Its Rise and Fall 1937–45*, London 1954.

Moore, H., *Soviet Far Eastern Policy 1931–1945*, Princeton U.P., 1945.

Norton, H. K., *The Far Eastern Republic of Siberia*, London 1923.

2. The Chinese Revolution, the Soviet Union and China

Documents on Communism, Nationalism and Soviet Advisers in China 1918–1927 (ed. C. Martin Wilbur and Julie Lien-ying How), Columbia U.P., 1956.

Soviet Plot in China (English translations of documents described as having been seized during the raid on the Soviet Embassy in Peking), Peking 1927. [Cf. Mitarevsky, N., *World Wide Soviet Plots*, Tientsin Press Ltd., n.d.]

Chiang Kai-shek, *Soviet Russia in China*, N.Y. 1957.

Brandt, C., *Stalin's Failure in China 1924–1927*, Harvard U.P./O.U.P., 1958.

Liu, F. F., *A Military History of Modern China: 1924–1949*, Princeton 1956.

McLane, Charles B., *Soviet Policy and the Chinese Communists 1931–1946*, Columbia U.P., 1958.

North, R. C., *Moscow and Chinese Communists*, Stanford 1953.

Snow, Edgar, *Red Star over China*, London 1937.
Weigh, Ken Shen, *Russo-Chinese Diplomacy*, Shanghai 1928.

IV. Polish Military Studies of 1920

Organizacja armji bolszewickiej (Stan z r. 1920, według źródel oficjalnych Władz Sowieckich), Warszawa 1920.

Piłsudski, J., *L'Année 1920* (trad. du polonais par le lieut.-col. Ch. Jeze et le commandant J. A. Teslar), Paris 1929. [This includes Tukhachevsky's lecture on the Polish campaign.] An accessible Polish edition is *Rok 1920*, London 1941.

Sikorski, L., *Le Campagne polono-russe de 1920* (trad. par le commandant Larcher. Préface de M. le Maréchal Foch), Paris 1928.

Tactical studies:

Studja taktyczne z historii wojen polskich 1918–1921

—— *Działania armji konnej Budiennego 1920*,

—— *Boj pod Zasławiem. 23 wresnia 1920*. Published by Historical Section/Polish General Staff.

See also

Camon, Gen., *La manœuvre libératrice du Maréchal Pilsudski contre les Bolchéviks, août 1920*, Paris 1929.

V. French Materials

Le Livre Jaune Français Documents Diplomatiques 1938–9, Ministère des Affaires Étrangères, Paris, Imprimerie Nationale, 1939.

Coulondre, Robert (Ambassadeur de France), *De Staline à Hitler Souvenirs de Deux Ambassades 1936–1939*, Paris 1950.

Gamelin, Général, *Servir Le Prologue du Drame (1930–Août 1939)*, Paris 1946.

Reynaud, Paul, *Au cœur de la mêlée 1930–1945* (édition entièrement rénovée de *La France a sauvé l'Europe*), Paris 1951.

Items on Soviet-German military relations incorporating materials from the *Deuxième Bureau:*

Castellan, Georges, 'Reichswehr et Armée Rouge, 1920–1939' in *Les Relation Germano-Soviétiques de 1933 à 1939* (ed. J.-B. Duroselle), Paris 1954, pp. 137–261

—— *Le Réarmement clandestin du Reich 1930–1935*, Vu par le 2ᵉ Bureau de l'État-Major Français, Paris 1954.

VI. British Documents Relating to the Military Conversations in Moscow, 1939

Documents on British Foreign Policy, 1919–1939 (ed. E. L. Woodward and R. Butler), 3rd Series, London, HMSO, Vol. VI (1953) and Vol. VII (1954).

VII. Personal Accounts, Memoirs, Records and Testimonies

(The writings of former Soviet personnel are indicated with an asterisk.)

*Bajanov, B., *Avec Stalin dans le Kremline*, Paris 1930.

*Barmine, Alexander, *One Who Survived* The Life Story of a Russian under the Soviets, N.Y., 1954.

Beneš, Eduard, *Memoirs of Dr Eduard Beneš*, London 1954.

*Bessedovsky, G., *Revelations of a Soviet Diplomat*, London 1931.

Churchill, Winston S., *The Second World War*, London 1948–54. See 'The Gathering Storm', 'The Hinge of Fate' and 'The Grand Alliance'.

Davies, Joseph E., *Mission to Moscow*. A record of confidential dispatches to the State Department . . . , London 1942.

Denikin, General A. I., *The White Army*, London 1930. [Abbreviated English version of his five-volume *Ocherki russkoi smuty*.]

Ironside, Edmund (Field-Marshal Lord Ironside), *Archangel 1918–1919*, London 1953.

Kalinov, Cyrille, *Les Maréchaux soviétiques vous parlent . . .* , Paris 1950. [Of doubtful reliability.]

Kolchak, Admiral, *The Testimony of Kolchak, and other Siberian materials*, Stanford U.P., 1935.

Krivitsky, W. G., *I was Stalin's agent*, London 1940.

Krylov, Ivan, *Soviet staff officer*, London 1951. [Of doubtful reliability.]

**Lenin School for Training of Political Officers of the Soviet Army* (Written by a former instructor), East European Fund, N.Y. 1952.

Lockhart, R. H. Bruce, *Memoirs of a British Agent*, London 1932.

Lyons, Eugene, *Assignment in Utopia*, London 1938.

Mannerheim, Marshal, *Muistelmat*, Helsinki 1952. Also *Mémoires 1882–1946*, Paris 1952.

*Markoff, Alexei (pseud.), former Major-General of Soviet aviation, 'How Russia Almost Lost the War', in *Saturday Evening Post*, Vol. 222, 13th May, 1950.

Martel, Lieutenant-General Sir Giffard, *The Russian Outlook*, London 1947. [First-hand accounts of Soviet manœuvres, 1936.]

Sakharov, K. V. (Lt.-Gen.), *Cheshkie Legiony v Sibiri*, Riga 1930. [Ann Arbor microprint.]

*Svetlanin, A. (pseud.), *Dal'nevostochnyi zagovor*, Possev-Verlag, Frankfurt/Main, 1953.

*Tokaev, G. A., *Comrade X*, London 1956.

*Uralov, A., *The Reign of Stalin*, London 1953.

*Vlasov, General A. A., 'Official Biography', as Appendix I in George Fischer, *Soviet Opposition to Stalin* A case study in World War II, Harvard U.P., 1952.

Weissberg-Cybulski, Alexander, *Hexensabbat* Russland in Schmelztiegel der Säuberungen, Frankfurt am Main 1951. [English title: *Conspiracy of Silence*, American, *The Accused*.]

Zenzinov, V., *Vstrecha s Rossiei. Kak i chem zhivut v Sovetskom Soyuze*, Pisma v Krasnuyu Armiyu 1939–40, N.Y. 1944. [Letters taken from the bodies of Soviet troops killed in Finland, as well as other captured documents on attestation.]

VIII. Select Bibliography

I. THE RED ARMY, THE SOVIET ARMED FORCES AND SOVIET MILITARY ORGANISATION, MILITARY DOCTRINE AND OPERATIONS

Adamheit, T., *Sowjetarmee und Weltrevolution*, Berlin-Leipzig 1942.

Allen, W. E. D., and Muratoff, Paul, *The Russian Campaigns of 1941–43*, (Penguin Books) London 1944.

Atkinson, L. B., *Dual Command in the Red Army 1918–1942*, Air University, Alabama 1950.

Berchin, M., and Ben-Horin, E., *The Red Army*, London 1942.

Berman, Harold J., and Kerner, Miroslav, *Soviet Military Law and Administration*, Harvard U.P., 1955.

—— *Documents on Soviet Military Law and Administration* (companion volume to monograph).

Coates, W. P. and Z., *The Soviet-Finnish Campaign Military and Political 1939–1940*, London 1941.

—— *Why Russia Will Win The Soviet Military, Naval and Air Power*, London n.d.

Cox, Geoffrey, *The Red Army Moves*, London 1941. [Soviet-Finnish War.]

Dallin, David J., *The Big Three The United States, Britain, Russia*, London 1946. See Ch. V on the Soviet Navy.

Dinerstein, H. S., *War and the Soviet Union*, London 1959. See Ch. 2.

Ely, Louis B. (Colonel, U.S. Army), *The Red Army Today*, Military Service Publishing Co., Harrisburg, Pa. 1953.

Footman, David, 'The Red Army on the Eastern Front', *St Antony's Papers on Soviet Affairs*, (Mimeographed) St Antony's College, Oxford n.d.

Garthoff, Raymond L., *How Russia Makes War Soviet Military Doctrine*, London 1954. [A work of fundamental importance.]

Goudima, Constantin, *L'Armée Rouge dans la paix et la guerre*, Paris 1947.

Guillaume, Général A., *La Guerre Germano-Soviétique 1941–1945*, Paris 1949.

Hittle, J. D. (Lt.-Col., US Marine Corps), *The Military Staff Its History and Development*, Military Service Publishing Co., Harrisburg, Pa. 1952. See Ch. 6, 'Generalny Shtab'.

Hooper, Major A. S., *The Soviet-Finnish Campaign*, Private printing, 1940.

Just, Artur W., *The Red Army*, London 1936.

League of Nations: League of Nations Armaments Handbook, 1924–29. See in each annual under Soviet armed forces.

Liddell Hart, B. H. (ed.), *The Soviet Army*, London 1956.

Mitchell, M., *Maritime History of Russia*, London 1949.

Piatnitskii, Col. N. V., *Krasnaya Armiya SSSR*, Paris 1931.

Saunders, Commander M. G., (R.N.) (ed.), *The Soviet Navy*, London 1958.

Schapiro, Leonard, 'The Army and Party in the Soviet Union', *St Antony's Papers on Soviet Affairs*, (Mimeographed) St Antony's College, Oxford, June 1954.

Werner, Max (pseud.), *The Military Strength of the Powers*, London 1939. See under the Red Army and Soviet strategy.

White, D. F., *The Growth of the Red Army*, Princeton 1944. [An indispensable work on the history of the Red Army.]

White, J. B., *Red Russia Arms*, London 1932.

Wollenberg, E., *The Red Army. A Study of the Growth of Soviet Imperialism*, London 1938 (and 1940 edn.).

See also:

La Documentation Française. Notes et Études Documentaires, January 1956; 'La conception soviétique des conflits armés (Documents)', 39 pp.

In connection with the history of the disintegration of the Imperial Russian Army, and the campaigns of the Civil War, see:

Golovine, Lt.-Gen., N. N., *The Russian Army in the World War*, Carnegie Endowment for International Peace, New Haven 1931.

Stewart, George, *The White Armies of Russia. A Chronicle of Counter-Revolution and Allied Intervention*, N.Y. 1933.

2. POLITICAL HISTORY (INCLUDING THE PURGES)

Beck, F., and Godin, W., *Russian purge and the extraction of confession*, N.Y. 1951.

Brzezinski, Z., *The Permanent Purge*, Harvard U.P., 1956.

Carr, E. H., *A History of Soviet Russia*, London 1950 — .
- The Bolshevik Revolution 1917–1923, Vols. I–III
- The Interregnum 1923–24, Vol. IV
- Socialism in One Country 1924–26, Vol. V (in two parts).

Fainsod, Merle, *How Russia is Ruled*, Harvard U.P., 1953.

—— *Smolensk under Soviet Rule*, London 1959. [See on the restrictions of the 1929 purge and the Army-Party relations.]

Leites, Nathan and Bernaut, Elsa, *Ritual of Liquidation. The Case of the Moscow Trials*, Glencoe, Illinois 1954.

Leites, Nathan, *The Operational Code of the Politburo*, N.Y. 1950.

Meissner, Boris, *Sowjetrussland zwischen Revolution und Restauration*, Köln 1956.

Schapiro, L., *The Origin of the Communist Autocracy 1917–1922*, London 1956.

—— *The Communist Party of the Soviet Union*, London 1960.

Scheffer, Paul, *Seven Years in Soviet Russia. With a Retrospect* (trans. from the German), London 1931.

Shachtman, Max, *Behind the Moscow Trials*, N.Y., 1936.

Two semi-documentary works are also of importance for the history of the purges:

The Letter of an Old Bolshevik. A Key to the Moscow Trials (Anonymous, but attributed by some to Rykov), London 1938.

The Case of Leon Trotsky. Report of Hearings on the Charges made against him in the Moscow Trials (J. Dewey as Chairman), London 1937.

3. SOVIET FOREIGN POLICY

NOTE. *Soviet Documents on Foreign Policy 1917–1941* (selected and edited by Jane Degras), Vols. I–III, London 1948–53, is an invaluable aid.

Beloff, M., *The Foreign Policy of Soviet Russia 1929–1941*, Vols. 1–2, London 1947.

Carr, E. H., *German-Soviet Relations between the two World Wars 1919–1939*, Baltimore 1951.

Cattell, David J., *Communism and the Spanish Civil War*, California U.P., 1956.

Coates, W. P., and Zelda, K., *A History of Anglo-Soviet Relations*, London 1943.

Dallin, David J., *Russia and Post-War Europe*, New Haven 1945.

—— *Soviet Russia's Foreign Policy 1939–1942*, New Haven 1942.

—— *Soviet Espionage*, New Haven 1955.

Duroselle, J-B. (ed.), *Les Frontières européennes de l'U.R.S.S., 1917–1941*, Paris 1957.

Fischer, L., *The Soviets in World Affairs. A history of the relations between the Soviet Union and the rest of the world*, 2 vols., London 1930.

Fischer, Ruth, *Stalin and German Communism*, Harvard U.P., 1948.

Freund, Gerald, *Unholy Alliance. Russian-German Relations from the Treaty of Brest-Litovsk to the Treaty of Berlin*, London 1957.

Galay, Nikolai, 'The Influence of Military Factors on Soviet Foreign Policy' in *Problems of Soviet Foreign Policy*, A Symposium for the Institute for the Study of the USSR (11th Institute Conference), Munich 1959.

Kennan, George F., *Soviet-American Relations, 1917–1920*, Vol. II, 'The Decision to Intervene', Princeton 1958.

Kochan, Lionel, *Russia and the Weimer Republic*, Cambridge 1954.

Melville, C. F., *The Russian Face of Germany. An account of the secret military relations between the German and Soviet Russian Governments*, London 1932.

Miliukov, P., *La Politique extérieure des Soviets*, Paris 1936.

Schuman, Frederick L., *Night Over Europe. The Diplomacy of Nemesis 1939–1940*, London 1941. See Ch. VIII.

Taracouzio, I. A., *War and Peace in Soviet Diplomacy*, N.Y. 1940.

Tarulis, A. N., *Soviet Policy and the Baltic States 1918–1940*, University of Notre Dame 1959.

4. BIOGRAPHIES

'Agricola' (A. Baumeister), *Der rote Marschall. Tuchatschewskis Aufstieg und Fall*, Berlin 1939.

Basseches, Nikolaus, *Stalin* (trans. E. W. Dickes), London 1952.

Deutscher, I., *Stalin: A Political Biography*, London 1949.

—— *The Prophet Armed. Trotsky: 1879–1921*, London 1954.

—— *The Prophet Unarmed. Trotsky: 1921–1929*, London 1959.

Ebon, Martin, *Malenkov*, London 1953.

Fervacque, Pierre, *Le Chef de l'Armée Rouge — Mikhail Toukatchevski*, Paris 1928.

Montagu, I., *Soviet Leaders: Voroshilov*, London 1942.

—— *Soviet Leaders: Timoshenko*, London 1942. [British Communist papers.]

Parry, Albert, *Russian Cavalcade. A Military Record*, N.Y. 1944. [Contains biographical sketches of Tukhachevsky, Blyukher, Shaposhnikov, Voroshilov and what was at that time 'The Lesser Galaxy'.]

Pope, A. U., *Maxim Litvinov*, N.Y. 1943.

Souvarine, Boris, *Staline. Aperçu historique du Bolchévisme*, Paris 1935.

Wheatley, Dennis, *Red Eagle. The story of the Russian Revolution and of Klementy*

Efremovitch Voroshilov, London 1938. [Touched with the anti-Trotsky contagion.]

NOTE. Of considerable value for individual biographies is *Biographic Directory of the USSR* (General Editor Wladimir S. Merzalow), compiled by the Institute for the Study of the USSR, Munich, Germany, and published New York 1958.

IX. SELECT ARTICLES

Assmann, Kurt (Vice Admiral), 'The Battle for Moscow. Turning Point of the War', *Foreign Affairs*, January 1950, pp. 309–27.

Baldwin, Hanson W., 'The Soviet Navy', *Foreign Affairs*, July 1955, pp. 587–605.

'Balticus', 'The Russian Mystery: Behind the Tukhachevsky Plot', *Foreign Affairs*, October 1937, pp. 44–64.

Baritz, Joseph J., 'Belorussia and the Kremlin's Strategic Plans', *Belorussian Review*, 1958, No. 6, pp. 82–96.

—— 'The Organisation and Administration of the Soviet Armaments Industry', *Bulletin* (Munich), Vol. IV, November 1957, No. 11, pp. 12–22.

Betts, T. J., 'The Strategy of another Russo-Japanese War', *Foreign Affairs*, July 1934, pp. 592–604.

Daniels, Robert V., 'The Kronstadt Revolt of 1921. A Study in the Dynamics of Revolution', *American Slavic and East European Review*, Vol. X, No. 4, pp. 241–54.

Danilov, Yuri (General), 'The Red Army', *Foreign Affairs*, October 1928, pp. 96–110.

Epstein, Julius, 'Der Seeckt Plan. Aus unveröffentlichen Dokumenten', *Der Monat*, November 1948, pp. 42–58.

Galay (Galai), Nikolai, 'Soviet Naval Forces', *Bulletin* (Munich), Vol. I, August 1954, No. 5, pp. 3–8.

—— 'Tank Forces in the Soviet Army', *Bulletin*, Vol. I, October 1954, No. 7, pp. 3–15.

—— 'Contemporary Soviet Military Literature', *Bulletin*, Vol. II, January 1955, No. 1, pp. 15–23.

—— 'Principles of Command in the Soviet Armed Forces', *Bulletin*, Vol. II, June 1955, No. 6, pp. 11–15.

—— 'New Trends in Soviet Military Doctrine', *Bulletin*, Vol. III, June 1956, No. 6, pp. 3–12.

—— 'The Problem of Quantity and Quality in the Soviet Armed Forces', *Bulletin*, Vol. III, October 1956, No. 10, pp. 3–14.

—— 'The Problem of Technological Progress in Totalitarian and Free Societies', *Bulletin*, Vol. IV, November 1957, No. 11, pp. 3–12.

—— 'Revisionism, Dogmatism and the Soviet Armed Forces', *Bulletin*, Vol. V, November 1958, No. 11, pp. 3–12.

—— 'The Influence of Military Factors on Soviet Foreign Policy', *Bulletin*, Vol. VI, September 1959, No. 9, pp. 3–20.

—— 'Social Problems in the Reorganisation of the Soviet Armed Forces', *Bulletin*, Vol. VII, April 1960, No. 4, pp. 3–15.

Gasiorowski, Zygmunt J., 'The German-Polish Nonaggression Pact of 1934', *Journal of Central European Affairs*, Vol. XV, April 1955, No. 1, pp. 4–29.

Gatzke, Hans W., 'Russo-German Military Collaboration during the Weimar Republic', *The American Historical Review*, 1958, Vol. LXIII, No. 3, pp. 565–97.

Géraud, André, 'France, Russia and the Pact of Mutual Assistance', *Foreign Affairs*, January 1935, pp. 226–36.

Hahlweg, Werner, 'Clausewitz, Lenin and Communist Military Attitudes To-day', *Journal of the Royal United Service Institution*, Vol. CV, May 1960, No. 618, pp. 221–6.

Hallgarten, George W. F., 'General Hans von Seeckt and Russia, 1920–1922', *Journal of Modern History*, Vol. XXI, No. 1, 1949, pp. 28–34.

Hopper, Bruce, 'Soviet Transportation Plans: Winning the East', *Foreign Affairs*, July 1930, pp. 652–8.

—— 'Eastward the Course of the Soviet Empire', *Foreign Affairs*, October 1935, pp. 37–50.

Jacobs, Walter Darnell, 'Limits of Soviet Military Originality', *Revue Militaire Générale/General Military Review/Allgemeine Militärrundschau*, 10, December 1957, pp. 680–90.

Krebs, P., *Chef d'escadrons*, 'Armée et politique', *Revue Militaire Générale*, 10, December 1957, pp. 597–618.

Kreidel, H. *Oberstleutnant*, 'Partisanenkampf im Mittelrussland. Erfahrungen und Erkentnisse', *Revue Militaire Générale*, 7, July 1957, pp. 250–70.

Meister, J., 'Soviet Seapower', *Bulletin*, Vol. VII, January 1960, No. 1, pp. 36–44.

Niessel, *Général*, 'L'U.R.S.S. en Extrême-Orient', *Revue des Deux Mondes*, February 1937, pp. 566–77.

Peltier, *Contre-Amiral*, 'La pensée militaire soviétique', *Revue Militaire Générale*, 10, December 1957, pp. 649–79.

Saint-Chamant, Jean de, 'Après les procès de Moscou — Les contactes Germano-Russes', *Revue des Deux Mondes*, July 1938, pp. 102–17.

Smith, Arthur L., 'The German General Staff and Russia, 1919–1926', *Soviet Studies*, Vol. VIII, October 1956, No. 2, pp. 125–33.

Wandycz, Piotr S., 'General Weygand and the Battle of Warsaw of 1920', *Journal of Central European Affairs*, Vol. XIX, January 1960, No. 4, pp. 357–65.

White, D. Fedotoff, 'Soviet Philosophy of War', *Political Science Quarterly*, Volume Fifty-one, 1936, pp. 321–53.

Wolfe, Bertram D., 'The Influence of Early Military Decisions on the National Structure of the Soviet Union', *American Slavic and East European Review*, Vol. IX, No. 3, pp. 169–79.

'X', 'Russia and Germany. Military and Political Reflections', *Foreign Affairs*, January 1942, pp. 303–24.

BIOGRAPHICAL INDEX TO LEADING MILITARY PERSONALITIES

ALKSNIS, Ya. I.

Born 1897 in Lifland of farm-labourer's family. Party member, 1916. Mobilised, 1917. Active in Western Front Army Committee. In command staff Red Army, spring 1919. Assistant to commander Orlov Military District. Completed Military Academy RKKA, 1924. Completed Military Aviation School, 1926–31. Chief of the Red Air Force (VVS RKKA), 1931–8. Close associate of Tukhachevsky. Arrested 1937. Disappeared. Death given as 1940.

ANTONOV-OVSEENKO, V. A.

Began his revolutionary activity in 1902. Party member, 1902. Finished training as an officer-cadet, St Petersburg, 1904. Revolutionary activity, preparing an armed rising, Russian Poland, 1905. Arrested. After release, worked as president of the Military Organisation of the St Petersburg Party Committee. Participant in the conference of Military Organisations, 1908. Organised a military insurrection in Sevastopol. Arrested, sentenced to twenty years' imprisonment, after his death sentence repealed. Escaped. Worked in Finland. Emigrated to France. Returned to Russia, June 1917. Arrested with Trotsky. One of the prime organisers of the Bolshevik *coup*. The Winter Palace captured by insurgents led by him. Appointed to the Commissariat for Military and Naval Affairs. Directed Soviet operations in the Ukraine. Came into conflict with Trotsky for favouring a decentralised Ukrainian Red Army. Worked in the Ukraine with Bubnov and Podvoiskii. Appointed to the Commissariat for Labour, 1920. Head of the Political Administration, Republic *Revvoensoviet*, 1922–4. Closely associated with Trotsky in his political struggles at the end of 1923. Carried the opposition to the Stalin-Zinoviev-L. Kamenev combination into the garrison 'cells' of Moscow. Possibly directly responsible for Circular No. 200, 1923. Removed from his post in the Political Administration, January 1924. Sent abroad as Soviet diplomatic representative to Czechoslovakia, 1925. Reported shot during the purges of the 1930s. Recently 're-habilitated' after the 20th Party Congress and evidently still living.

ARALOV, S. I.

Born 1880 in Moscow. Party member, 1902. Worked as propagandist. Took part in 1905 revolutionary actions. Worked in the Military Organisation of the Party, 1906. Worked on the organisation of the new Red Army, 1918. A member of the Republic *Revvoensoviet* since its inception. A member of the 'Bureau of Three' — Trotsky, Vatsetis, Aralov — which operated as the nerve centre of the command. Appointed to the *Revvoensoviet* of the South-western Front, also the XIIth and XIVth Red armies. After the war with Poland, assigned to the Commissariat for Foreign Affairs, 1920. Soviet diplomatic representative in Lithuania, Turkey, Latvia. Member of the Collegiate for Foreign Affairs, 1925. Removed from responsible positions under Stalin. Has recently been restored to public notice, contributing several writings on the history of the Civil War.

BARANOV, P. I.

Born 6/9/1892 of St Petersburg worker family. Party member, 1912. Sent to Rumanian Front, 1917. Member Revolutionary Committee VIII Imperial Army. Joined Red Army 1918. Member *Revvoensoviet* of Turkestan and Central Asia. Associated with Frunze. Chief of Red Air Force, 1924–31. Took active part in organising Soviet aviation force and aviation industry. Elected candidate member Central Committee 16th Party Congress. Deputy Commissar for Heavy Industry and Chief of Soviet Aviation Industry, 1931. Killed in accident, when aircraft failed to make landing by instruments, 1933.

BLYUKHER, V. K.

Born 19/11/1889, of poor family. Worked in wagon-factory. Sentenced to 2 years, 8 months, in prison for leading strike, 1910. Mobilised in 1914. Became NCO. Heavily wounded in 1915, released from military service. Party member, 1916. Worked in factory in Kazan. Active in Chelyabinsk Soviet, 1917. Organised Urals armed detachments, 1918. Considerable local military successes. First recipient of 'Order of the Red Banner', September 1918. His troops organised into 51 Division, Eastern Front, employed against Kolchak. In action against Wrangel, storming of Perekop, autumn 1920. Returned to Far East. Commander, Military Minister and President Military Soviet, Far Eastern Republic, 1921–2. Advanced on Vladivostok. Sent as commander and military commissar to Leningrad Military District. Commanded 1st Rifle Corps. Detached for 'special duties', 1924. Head of Soviet military mission to China — *nom de guerre* 'Galin', 1924–7. Not selected as Soviet Military Attaché to Germany, 1928. Possibly implicated in conspiracy; guaranteed by Voroshilov. Commanded operations against Chinese, 1929. Organised Special Far Eastern Army (*ODVA*). Remained in command of Soviet Far East. Raised to rank of Marshal. Candidate member of Central Committee, 1934. Not removed by 1937 purge in Far East, but under restraint. Commanded part of the 1938 operations against the Japanese in the Far East. Disappeared. Date of death or execution given as 9/11/1938.

BUBNOV, A. S.

Born 23/3/1883. Party member, 1903. Member of Ivanovo-Voznesensk Party Committee. Member of Moscow Party Committee, 1907. Arrested, 1908. Released, 1909. Worked on St Petersburg *Pravda*, 1912–13. Member of Petrograd Military-Revolutionary Committee, 1917. Supervised activity for Bolshevik seizure of power. Moved to the Ukraine, fought against Kaledin, end of 1917. Organised partisan units in the Ukraine. Associated with Antonov-Ovseenko and Podvoiskii in Bolshevik work in the Ukraine. Entered the administration of the Ukraine, autumn 1919. Member of the Central Committee of the Communist Party of the Ukraine. President of the Kiev Soviet. Member of the *Revvoensoviet* XIVth Red army, 1919. Took part in the suppression of the Kronstadt rebellion, 1921. Member of the *Revvoensoviet* North Caucasus Military District, also 1st Cavalry Army, 1921–2. Member of the Agitation-Propaganda Section, Central Committee, 1922–3. Member of the Central Committee after the 13th Party Congress. Appointed head of the Political Administration, January 1924. Member of the Soviet Union *Revvoensoviet.* Under the cover-name of 'Kisanka', took part in the Chinese revolution, 1925–6. Replaced by Gamarnik at the head of the Political Administration, 1929. Head of Soviet Education Commissariat, 1929–37. Removed from his posts during the 1937–8 purge. Date of death given as 12/1/1940.

BUDENNY, S. M.

Born 1883, Voronezh province. Moved to the Don. Peasant family. Drafted into the army, 1903. Sent to the cavalry (not the Cossacks). Fought in the Russo-Japanese War. St. Petersburg School of Horsemanship, 1908. Served as sergeant-major of cavalry troop in 1914. Member of the regimental and divisional revolutionary committee, 1917. Organised cavalry detachment to fight for the Reds in the Don, early 1918. Retreated to Tsaritsyn, autumn 1918. Met up with Voroshilov. Party member, 1919. Chief of Staff to new Soviet cavalry division. Took over command of cavalry corps, June 1919. Defeated 2nd Cavalry Corps of Mamontov and Shkuro, 17th November, 1919. Associated with Voroshilov, Stalin, Shchadenko and Yegorov in creating the 1st Cavalry Army, December 1919. Final actions against Denikin, February 1920. Transferred to Polish Front, May 1920. Broke through Polish line, operated in Polish rear, July–August 1920. Failed to co-ordinate action with Tukhachevsky attacking Warsaw. Driven back by the Poles from East Galicia. Employed in operations against Wrangel, autumn 1920. With 1st Cavalry, North Caucasus, May 1921. Appointed assistant on cavalry to Commander-in-Chief, 1922. Appointed Inspector of Red Army cavalry, 1924. Attended Frunze Academy, 1932. Appointed commander of Moscow Military District during the 1937 purge. Deputy Commissar for Defence, 1939. 1st Deputy Commissar for Defence, 1940. Commanded South-western Front against German advance, 1941. Assigned to raising and training troops later in Soviet-German War. Still living. Marshal of the Soviet Union.

DYBENKO, P. E.

Born 16/2/1889, of a poor family in Chernogorsk. Party member, 1912. As sailor in the Baltic Fleet, one of the ring-leaders of mutiny on the battle-ship *Imperator Pavel I*, 1915. President of *Tsentrobalt*, March 1917. Worked against the Provisional Government. Organised naval squads in Helsingfors. Commanded naval squads in action against General Krasnov, November 1917. Commissar for the Navy, November 1917–April 1918. Organised and commanded partisan units in the Ukraine, also the Crimean army, 1918–19. Fought at Tsaritsyn, against Denikin in the Caucasus. Took part in the suppression of the Kronstadt rebellion, 1921. Attended Military Academy, 1922. Commanded the 6th, 5th and 10th Rifle Corps. Chief of the Artillery Administration of the Red Army, 1925. Commander of the Central Asian Military District, 1928: member of the Uzbek, Tadzhik, Central Committees, member of the Central Asian Bureau of the All-Russian Communist Party. Disappeared in the military purge: date of death given as 29/7/1938.

EIDEMAN, R. P.

Born 1895 in Latvia. Attended Forestry Institute in St Petersburg. Called up to Imperial Russian Army, 1916. Joined the Red Army, 1918. Fought against Czechoslovak Legion near Omsk, May 1918. Appointed commander of the Eastern Siberian Flotilla. Named commander of the 16th Rifle Division, beginning of 1919. Commanded the 41st and 46th Divisions against Denikin. Commanded the XIIIth Red army in 1920 in the Perekop operations. Appointed deputy commander of the Ukrainian and Crimean Military Districts, 1921. Commander of the Siberian Military District, 1924. Appointed head of the Frunze Academy, 1925. In close contact with the *Reichswehr*. Succeeded by Shaposhnikov at the Frunze Academy, 1932: appointed head of the Central Soviet of *Osoaviakhim*. Member of the *VTsIK* and *TsIK*. Arrested and shot without trial, May–June 1937.

FRUNZE, M. V.

Born 1885. Father medical assistant, mother peasant-woman. Finished high-school. Entered Polytechnic Institute, St Petersburg. Party member, 1904. Became professional revolutionary. Worked in textile mills, Ivanovo-Voznesensk, May 1905. Took part in December rising in Moscow, 1905. Worked with Gusev. Arrested, imprisoned. Arrested again, July 1915. Fled. Worked in Chita. Escaped arrest. Went to Western Front, agitation among troops. President of Soviet of Peasant Deputies, Minsk, 1917. Member of Front Committee, Western Front. Took part in liquidating Kornilov rising. At head of revolutionary troops, went to assist Bolshevik rising in Moscow, November 1917. Organised Soviet power in Ivanovo-Voznesensk, spring 1918. Worked in Yaroslavl Military Commissariat, organising Red Army units, September 1918. Associated with Novitskii. Sent to Eastern Front, January 1919. Took command of IVth Red army. Operated on southern flank, Eastern Front. Directed army group against Kolchak. Wounded. Sent to Turkestan, 1920. Commanded operations against Wrangel, autumn 1920. Appointed commander Ukrainian troops. Secret military mission to Turkey, December 1921–January 1922. Struggle with Trotsky over doctrines and organisation of the Red Army. Appointed Trotsky's deputy, January 1924. Introduced the 'military reforms' of 1924–5. In effective command of the Red Army. Became Commissar for War, January 1925. Severely ill, late summer 1925. Died 31st October, 1925, possibly a victim of medical murder instigated by Stalin.

GALLER, L. M.

Born 17/11/1883. Naval officer by career. Joined Soviet naval forces, 1918. Commanded a cruiser, mine-laying squadron. Appointed Chief of Staff to Operations Sections, Baltic Fleet. Appointed Deputy Commissar for Defence, 1937. Chief of the Supreme Naval Staff, 1938. Deputy Commissar for the Soviet Naval Forces, 1940.

Commander-in-Chief Soviet Naval Forces for ship construction and naval armament. Head of the Naval Academy for Ship Construction and Armament (the Krylov Academy), 1947. Died 12/7/1950.

GAMARNIK, Ya. B.

Born 1894. Began revolutionary work in 1914, in student organisations. Party member, 1916. Secretary Kiev Party Committee, to November 1917. Organised Odessa, Crimea workers. Military commissar of 58 Division: member *Revvoensoviet*, Southern group, XIIth Red army, 1919. President Odessa and Kiev Party Committee, 1919–23. Sent to Soviet Far East, secretary Far East Party Commission, 1923–8. Candidate member Central Committee, 14th Party Congress. Secretary of the Central Committee, Communist Party of Belorussia: began work in the Red Army, 1928. Member of the Central Committee VKP(b), 1927. Member of Belorussian Military District *Revvoensoviet*, 1st December, 1928. Appointed head of the Political Administration of the Red Army, 1st October, 1929. Member of the *Revvoensoviet* of the Soviet Union, 11th October, 1929. Deputy Commissar for Defence, deputy president of the *Revvoensoviet* USSR, June 1930. Committed suicide, or was killed resisting arrest, 31st May, 1937.

GUSEV, S. I.

Born 1874 in Sapozhok, of a family of petty officials. Moved to Rostov-on-Don as a child. Student in St Petersburg. Returned to Rostov, carrying on revolutionary work. Party work in Odessa, May 1905. Member of Moscow Party Committee, 1906. Secretary of Petrograd Military-Revolutionary Committee, 1917. Appointed to Republic *Revvoensoviet* in July 1919 after service with the Eastern Front *Revvoensoviet* and the Vth and IInd Red armies. Member of the South-eastern and Southern *Revvoensoviet*. Appointed head of the Political Administration, spring 1921. Closely associated with Frunze in plans to reform the Red Army. Opposed to Trotsky's militia plan. Candidate member of the Central Committee, 1921. Worked out schemes for planned political work in the Red Army. Displaced by Antonov-Ovseenko in the Political Administration, 1922. Secretary of the Central Control Commission, 1923. Head of the special commission which undertook a full-scale examination of the Red Army, 1923–4. Appointed head of a special Central Committee commission to enquire into the Red Army, January 1924. Worked on reform plans for the Soviet military establishment, 1924. Transferred to Party Historical Commission, 1926. Press section of the Central Committee, 1928–9. Member of the praesidium of the *Komintern*, 1928–33. Died 10/7/1933.

KONIEV, I. S.

Born 1897, Vologda province. Attended rural elementary school. Took part in underground work, 1914. Party member, 1918. Helped to put down SR rising in Vologda. Attached as military commissar, Armoured Train No. 102: operated against Kolchak. Brigade and divisional commissar, 1920. During military reforms, changed to command staff. Attended Frunze Academy, 1926. Posted as regimental and then divisional commander. Attended training course, Special Faculty, Frunze Academy, 1934–5. Appointed commander in the Special Red Banner Army of the Far East. Post as commander of the Transbaikal Military District, 1938–41. Transferred to the Transcaucasian Military District. Opening of hostilities, Soviet-German War, attached to the Western Special Military District. Took part in the battle for Smolensk. Senior army and front commander during Soviet-German War. Replaced Zhukov as commander-in-chief of the Soviet Ground Forces, 1946. Appointed commander of the Warsaw Pact forces, 1955. Bitterly critical of Zhukov at the time of the latter's dismissal. Enjoys the reputation of being very loyal to the Party. Still living. Marshal of the Soviet Union.

KORK, A. I.

Born 22/7/1887. Officer in the Imperial Russian Army. Completed course at Military Academy, 1914. Lieutenant-Colonel in Imperial Army during the World War. Service with the Red Army officially dated at May 1918. Deputy commander of the VIIth Red army in the defence of Petrograd, 1919. Commanded the XVth Red army, on Tukhachevsky's front, during the war with Poland, 1920. Commanded the VIth Red army against Wrangel, autumn 1920. Head of the Kharkov Military District, May 1921. Deputy to Frunze in the Ukraine and Crimea. In command of the Turkestan Front, 1924. Attached to the army of the Caucasus. Soviet Military Attaché in Berlin, 1928–9. Commander of the Leningrad and Moscow Military Districts, 1930–5. Appointed head of the Frunze Military Academy, 1935. Removed during the 1937 military purge, shot 11/6/1937.

LEBEDEV, P. P.

Born 1872. Completed General Staff Academy course, Imperial Russian Army, 1900. Chief of Staff III Imperial Army during World War. One of first 'military specialists' to volunteer his services to the Red Army. Chief of the Organisation-Mobilisation Section of All-Russian Supreme Staff, 1918. Chief of Staff Eastern Front, April–July 1919. Chief of the Field Staff, Republic *Revvoensoviet*, July 1919–21. Chief of Staff, Red Army, 1921–4. Simultaneously head of the Military Academy, 1922–4. Replaced as Chief of Staff in 1924. Chief of Staff and assistant to the commander of the Ukrainian Military District, 1925. Died 1933.

MEKHLIS, L. Z.

Born on 13/1/1889 in Odessa. Party member, 1918. During the Civil War, military commissar to a brigade and division. One of the senior commissars sent to assist with political agitation in the operations against Wrangel. Attached to the Workers-Peasants Inspectorate (*Rabkrin*), 1921. Worked in the secretariat of the Central Committee. One of Stalin's special personnel entrusted with duties in the political apparatus. Completed the course at the Institute of Red Professors, 1930. Subsequently appointed editor of *Pravda*. Replaced Gamarnik as head of the Red Army Political Administration, 1937. Carried through a drastic purge of the political personnel. Conducted the investigation and purge of the political administration of the Far Eastern Red Banner

Army, 1938. Implicated in the disappearance of Blyukher, 1938. Member of the Central Committee, 1939 (candidate member since 1934). Removed from his post in the Political Administration, September 1940. Attached to the Commission for State Control. Member of the *Orgburo*, 1938–52. Died 13/2/1953.

MUKLEVICH, R. A.

Born 1890. Textile worker. Party member, 1906. Secretary of the Bialystok Party Committee, 1907–9. Called up to the Imperial Navy, 1912. Active in the Bolshevik military organisations, 1917. Military commissar with Red troops fighting the Germans in the north-west, 1918. Secretary of the Vilno Party Committee, 1919. Commissar to the staff of the XVIth Red army, also commissar to the staff of the Western Front, 1920. Deputy Director of the Military Academy, 1921–2. Attached to Military Aviation (*VVS*), 1925–6. Took over effective control of the Soviet navy from Zof, late 1926 or early 1927. Associated with the collaboration with the German *Marineleitung*. Played leading role in the modernisation and reconstruction of Soviet naval forces. Director of Naval Construction. Arrested in the spring of 1937 and shot at some later but unknown date.

NOVIKOV, A. A.

Born 19/11/1900. Took part in the Civil War, Party member, 1920. Remained in Soviet forces, completed the course at the Frunze Academy, 1930. Also attended the Command Faculty of the Zhukovskii Air Academy. Commanded an aviation regiment, division and corps. Chief of Staff of the Leningrad *VVS*, 1938–40. During the Soviet-Finnish War, Chief of Staff *VVS* on the Karelian Front. Commander of the Leningrad *VVS*, 1940–1. Retained command of the Leningrad *VVS* until 1942, when he was appointed head of the Air Force Main Administration. Promoted to Colonel-General. Reported as having played a major part in re-organising Soviet military aviation after the serious set-backs at the hands of the *Luftwaffe*. High command posts throughout the 1941–5 war. Relieved of his command as head of Army Aviation in 1946. Re-appeared in command circles in 1953.

ORDZHONIKIDZE, G. K.

Born 27/10/1886, in Georgia. Joined the Party in 1903. Revolutionary activity in the Caucasus, 1905–7. Arrested 1905, 1912 and 1915. Arrived in Petrograd, 1917. Special Commissar in the Ukraine, 1918. Member of the *Revvoensoviet* of the XIV, XVI Red armies. Worked closely with Stalin in the south, 1920. Member of the Central Committee, 1921. Head of Caucasus Party organisation, 1921–6. Also associated with the Frunze group in the Red Army. President of the Central Control Commission, 1926–30. Member of the *Politburo*, Commissar for Heavy Industry, 1930. As stated by Khrushchev, shot himself because of persecution by Beria. Date of death (officially ascribed to heart-failure) given as 18/2/1937.

ORLOV, V. M.

Born 3/7/1895 in Kherson. Studied in St Petersburg. Joined Imperial Russian Navy as cadet, 1916. Active in the Reval Party organisation, Party member, 1917. Chief of the Political Department of the Baltic Fleet, Deputy Chief of the Political Department of Inland Waterways Administration, Chief of the Political Department of the Volga Waterways, 1918–22. Deputy Head of the Naval Political Administration attached to the *Revvoensoviet*, 1922. Appointed Head of Naval Training/Education. Completed course at the Naval Academy, 1926. Closely connected after 1927 with the collaboration with the *Marineleitung*. Commander of the Black Sea Fleet, 1926–30. Member of the *Revvoensoviet SSSR*, commander of Soviet Naval Forces (*VMF*), 1931–4. Deputy Commissar of Defence, commander of the Soviet naval forces, 1935–7. Disappeared in 1937 in connection with the military purge. Date of death, presumed shot, 28/7/1938.

PRIMAKOV, V. M.

Party member, 1914. Arrested and deported to Siberia 1915. Organiser of the Red Guard, 1917. Cavalry commander, 1918–20. Completed course at the Military Academy, 1922. Assigned to the command of a cavalry corps. Military attaché in Afghanistan, assistant military attaché in Japan. Deputy commander of the North Caucasus Military District to 1935. Deputy commander of the Leningrad Military District, 1935–7. Shot without trial, 11th June 1937.

PUTNA, V. K.

Born 12/3/1893. Joined the Red Army, 1918. Regimental and brigade commander. Commanded the 27th Division during the Soviet-Polish War, 1920. Completed a Higher Command Course, 1923. Head and commissar of the Military Training Administration. Assistant to Red Army Inspectorate. Chief of the Military Educational Institutes Administration. Head of No. 2 Moscow Technical School. Military attaché in Japan, Finland, Germany and Great Britain. Shot without trial, 11th June, 1937.

SHAPOSHNIKOV, B. M.

Born 1882 in Zlatoust. A career-officer in the Imperial Russian Army. Attended the Moscow Military School and the General Staff Academy. Completed his courses before 1914. Assigned during the war to the staff of the Caucasian division, later to the staff of the Caucasian Front. Reached the rank of colonel by 1917. After November 1917 elected to the command of the Caucasian Grenadier Division by the Congress of Military-Revolutionary Committees. Volunteered his services to the Red Army, in which his service is officially dated from May, 1918. Attached to the Operations Section of the Supreme Military Soviet. Carried out staff duties with the Operations Branch of the Field Staff of the Republic *Revvoensoviet*. Took part in planning operations against Denikin: drew up basic plans for the Western Front in February 1920. Subsequently defended the *Glavkom* and his staff and their part in the Warsaw operation. Awarded the Order of the Red Banner, 1921. Assistant to P. P. Lebedev Chief of Staff, 1921–4. Assistant to Frunze, also deputy commander and later commander of the Leningrad Military District, 1925–7. Commander of the Moscow Military District, 1927–8. Chief of Staff, early 1928–June 1931. Advocated the alignment of the Staff with the government in a unified 'war leadership'. His views were developed in a three-volume study, *The Brain of the Army*, 1927–9. Party member, 1930. Temporarily disgraced for praising Trotsky in connection with Soviet military operations. Removed to the Pri-Volga Military District, June 1931. Replaced by Yegorov as Chief of Staff. Appointed head of the Frunze Military Academy, February 1932. His lectures reputedly attended by Stalin and Molotov. Appointed Chief of Staff, 11th May, 1937. Took part in the negotiations with British and French officers in Moscow, early summer 1939. Drew up the plans for the occupation of Eastern Poland, 1939. Assisted in working out a proper plan of campaign for the Finnish operations after the first defeats. Promoted to rank of Marshal of the Soviet Union, 1940. Active in developing the defences of the western border areas, 1940–1. Briefly withdrew from formal occupation of the post of Chief of Staff, August 1940–February 1941. Suffered from severe ill-health. Member of the *Stavka*, as Chief of the General Staff, during the first phase of the Soviet-German War. Retired finally from his post in November, 1942. His retirement dictated by reasons of health. Succeeded by his pupil General Vassilevskii. Chief of the important Historical Administration, a military research and analysis centre of great influence, until his death in 1945. Author of several military works regarded as classics by Soviet authorities. Reputedly Stalin's 'military mentor'. His view of the role and function of the General Staff seems to have generally prevailed. A representative of the severely professional section of the Soviet high command.

TIMOSHENKO, S. K.

Born 1895 in village of Furmanko, Bessarabia. Peasant family. Attended village school. Worked as a barrel-maker. Mobilised 1915. Served as NCO. Took part in revolutionary agitation among the troops. Went to the south at the beginning of 1918. Fought with Red partisans. Turned irregulars into '1st Revolutionary Cavalry-Guards Crimean Regiment'. Entered the Red Army. Fought in Tsaritsyn, autumn 1918. Sent to the staff of 10th Red army under Voroshilov. Commanded 2nd Independent Cavalry Brigade: attached to Budenny's cavalry. Command of the 6th Cavalry Division, 1st November, 1919. Operated in Denikin's rear. Became one of the foremost commanders of the 1st Cavalry Army. Operated at the Zhitomir break-through, Polish Front, June 1920. Fought on the Polish Front. Assumed command of the 4th Cavalry Division, 1st Cavalry Army, August 1920. Took part in operations against Wrangel. Wounded 5 times in the Civil War. Completed a higher command course, Military Academy, 1922. Completed further higher command course for senior officers, 1927. Completed course for commander-commissars, Military-Political Academy, 1930. Deputy commander of troops, Belorussian Military District, 1933. Appointed to Kiev Military District, 1935. Commander of the Northern Caucasus, June 1937. Transferred to the Caucasus, September 1937. Sent to the Kiev

Military District, February 1938. Took part in the Soviet occupation of Poland, 1939. Commanded Karelian troops, Russo-Finnish War, 1939–40. Awarded decoration Hero of the Soviet Union. Promoted to Marshal of the Soviet Union, 7th May, 1940. Took over effective command of the Soviet military establishment from Voroshilov. Put into operation extensive schemes for the modernisation of Red Army training, stricter discipline. Deputy Commissar for Defence, commander of Western Special Military District, July 1941. Organised defence against German advance autumn 1941, in the centre. Commanded first Soviet counter-attacks. Took part in operations of fronts and armies, Soviet-German War. Senior military appointments after 1945. Still living.

TRIANDAFILLOV, V. K.

Born 14/3/1894. Joined the Red Army in 1918. Party member, 1919. Regimental and brigade commander during the Civil War. Completed course at the Military Academy, 1923. Commander of a rifle corps. Deputy Chief of the Red Army Staff, 1925. Chief of the Operations Section, Red Army Staff. Author of a Soviet military classic on the operations of modern armies (1929). Died 12/7/1931.
(NOTE: both Triandafillov and Triandafilov appear to be accepted spellings, but it is the former which appears on this officer's printed works.)

TROTSKY (BRONSHTEIN), L. D. [Military appointments only]

Born 1879 near Elizavetgrad. Agitator, propagandist, revolutionary and journalist. War correspondent in the Balkans, 1913. Returned to Russia, May 1917. Joined Lenin and the Bolsheviks. Took an extremely important part in Bolshevik *coup*. From post of Commissar for Foreign Affairs, made Commissar for War, March 1918. Created the basic outline of the Red Army, its organisation and early command structure. Took part in restoring the situation on the Eastern Front, autumn 1918. Responsible for setting up a centralised military administration, and introducing the 'military specialists'. Came into violent conflict with the Stalin-Voroshilov group at Tsaritsyn. Successfully defended his policy at the 8th Party Congress, 1919. Exponent of the militia system. Conflict with the 'Red commanders' over the militia-regular army issue, also military doctrine. With the end of the Civil War, devoted more energy to reconstruction work. Organised 'Labour armies'. Involved in protracted debate over military organisation and doctrine, 1920–2. Identified with the cause of the 'military specialists'. Violently attacked by Frunze-Gusev group, 1923–4. Ousted from the War Commissariat, first by interference with his staff, subsequently by being replaced by Frunze in 1925. Launched bitter attack on Voroshilov-Stalin handling of defence and military affairs, 1927. Exiled in 1928, banished in 1929. Remained critic of Stalin's defence policies. Assassinated in Mexico, 20th August, 1940. Years of Stalinist propaganda have been unable to dislodge Trotsky's reputation as the creator of the Red Army.

TUKHACHEVSKY, M. N.

Born 1893 of aristocratic but impoverished family. Entered Cadet Corps of the

Imperial Russian Army, 1911. Pupil at the Aleksandrovskii Military Academy. Gazetted as junior lieutenant, 1914. Taken prisoner by the Germans, February 1915. After five unsuccessful attempts at escape, lodged in Ingolstadt. Finally succeeded in reaching Russia, October 1917. Put himself at the disposal of the Bolsheviks, training troops in the Moscow area, spring 1918. Singled out by Trotsky. Party member, April 1918. Given command of the 1st Red army, Eastern Front, facing the Czechs. Took Simbirsk, 12th September, 1918. Commanded the Vth Red army, March 1919. Played outstanding part in the Soviet counter-offensive against Kolchak. Transferred to the Caucasian command, January 1920. First meeting with the 1st Cavalry Army command. Assumed command of the Western Front, April 1920, for operations against the Poles. Commander of the entire Soviet military force operating against Poland, July–August 1920. Carried out his spectacular drive on Warsaw, August 1920. Repulsed, also embroiled in bitter dispute with the 1st Cavalry Army and South-western Front commander. Commanded the VIIth Red army to put down the Kronstadt rebellion, 1921. Commanded the troops putting down the Tambov rising, 1921. Head of the Military Academy, 1922. Opponent of Trotsky's plans for re-organising the Red Army. Supported the idea of a strong regular Red Army. Deputy Chief of the Red Army Staff, 1924. Posted as commander of Belorussian Military District, 1925. Worked on the new *Field Service Regulations*. Urged technical advances. Chief of the Red Army Staff, November, 1926. Replaced in this position by Shaposhnikov, 1928. Commander of the Leningrad Military District. Deputy to Voroshilov, 1931. Chief of Ordnance, responsible for weapon development. Co-operated with General Ludwig on technical questions. Favoured developments in armour, parachute troops, army-aviation co-operation. Worked closely with Alksnis of *VVS*. Visited Germany, attended manœuvres, September 1932. Member of Military Soviet, 1934, a director of this with Gamarnik and Voroshilov. Worked on the new *Field Service Regulations*. A main source of ideas and leadership at this time. Created a Marshal of the Soviet Union, November 1935. Suspected by the Germans of being pro-French. Attended the funeral of King George V, January 1936. Brief visit to Paris. Appointed member of the commission to draw up the Stalin Constitution, December 1936. Mentioned by Radek during his trial, 24th January, 1937. Published his commentary on the new *Regulations*, 1st May, 1937. Demoted to the command of the Pri-Volga Military District, 10th May, 1937. Arrested *en route* by *NKVD*. His execution, without trial, took place on 12th June.

Uborevich, I. P. (Uborevich-Gubarevich, I. P.)

Born 1896 of a peasant family. Mobilised 1915. Completed course at Military Academy, 1916. Party member, 1917. Organised Red Guards on the Rumanian Front, 1917. Led troops against German forces: wounded: escaped from captivity, 1918. Commanded the IXth, XIIIth and XIVth Red armies operating against Denikin and Wrangel, 1919–20. Transferred to the Far East, 1922. One of the supporters of the Frunze reforms. Command of the North Caucasus Military District, 1925. Command of the Moscow Military District, 1928. Sent to Germany for higher command training. Closely connected with German military circles. Deputy president of the

Soviet Union *Revvoensoviet*, 1930. Worked closely with Tukhachevsky in re-organising the Red Army and Soviet defence planning. Commanded the Belorussian Military District. Arrested and shot without trial, June 1937.

VATSETIS, I. I.

Born 11/11/1873 in Courland. Completed course of study at military school, 1907. Course at General Staff Academy, 1909. Served in Imperial Army, 1914–17, reaching the rank of Colonel. Entered the Red Army as a 'military specialist'. Commanded Red troops fighting anti-Bolshevik forces, January 1918. Commanded troops against the Left SR rising, Moscow, 6–7 July, 1918. Nominated commander of the Eastern Front, 10th July, 1918. Worked with Trotsky in organising first Soviet front. Named the first Commander-in-Chief of the new Red Army, September 1918. Dispute with S. S. Kamenev over the course of the offensive against Kolchak, June 1918. Relieved of post as Commander-in-Chief, replaced by S. S. Kamenev, July 1919. Accused of treason and conspiracy, as part of Stalin's intrigue against Trotsky. Appointments in the Republic *Revvoensoviet*, staff and planning, August 1919–21. Critic of Trotsky's militia policy. Appointed lecturer in the Military Academy, 1922. Attached to the Militia Inspectorate of the Red Army. Participant in the dispute over the future organisation of the Red Army, 1928–29. Date of death given as 28/7/1938.

VOROSHILOV, K. E.

Born 1881 in Ukraine. Party member, 1903. Worked in Lugansk German-owned factory. Strike-leader, 1905. Arrested and exiled, 1907. Fled to Baku. Re-arrested 1908. Member of the Petrograd Soviet, March 1917. City Commissar of Petrograd, November 1917. Helped to organise the *Cheka*, end of 1917. Sent to the Ukraine, took command of the Vth Red army. Fought out of encirclement, reaching Tsaritsyn; took over the Xth Red army, July 1918. Organised defence of Tsaritsyn. With Stalin, came into violent conflict with Trotsky. Accused of insubordination. Removed to the Ukraine on Trotsky's orders, end of 1918. Further bitter clashes with Trotsky. Associated with Budenny, Stalin in creation of the 1st Cavalry Army, November 1919. Close association with Stalin. Took part in final actions against Denikin. With the 1st Cavalry Army in war against Poland, 1920. Supported drive in East Galicia, acting against Tukhachevsky's orders. Fought with the 1st Cavalry against Wrangel, autumn 1920. Elected member of the Central Committee, 10th Party Congress. Commander of the North Caucasus Military District, 1921–4. Associated with Frunze in attacks on Trotsky's policy for the Red Army. Commander of the Moscow Military District, 1924. Appointed Commissar for War, November 1925: held this position during the mechanisation of the Red Army. Survived the military purge of 1937–8, giving his support to Stalin. With the re-organisation of the Soviet command in 1934, nominated Commissar for Defence. Virtually relieved of this position in May 1940, when promoted to deputy chairman of the Defence Committee. Timoshenko took over the work of re-organising the Red Army. Commander of the armies of the North-west (Leningrad), July 1941. Assisted by Zhukov in the defence of the city. Removed from operational command posts and transferred to the State Defence Committee (*GOKO*). Head of the Soviet Control Commission in Hungary, 1945–7. After death of Stalin, criticised by Khrushchev at the 20th Party Congress. Given a purely formal position. Still living. Marshal of the Soviet Union. Denounced at 22nd Congress, 1961.

YEGOROV, A. I.

Born 22/10/1883, of peasant family. Did well in examinations in secondary school. Mobilised, 1914. Distinguished for his bravery. Rose to regimental commander, Imperial Russian Army. Joined Left SR's in February, 1917. Arrested for criticism of Kerensky. Attended the 2nd All-Russian Congress of Soviets, November 1917. Worked with Bolshevik military authorities. Sent to the Ukraine to organise Red troops. Arrested, but freed by Bolsheviks. Worked on the setting up of the new Red Army. President of the Higher Attestation Commission, and commissar of the All-Russian Supreme Staff. Joined Communist Party, summer 1918, after abortive Left SR rising. Went to the Southern Front, took over the IXth Red army. Joined Stalin and Voroshilov at Tsaritsyn, late 1918. Heavily wounded in a cavalry attack. Commanded XIVth Red army in Kiev and Bryansk offensive, summer 1919. Commanded Southern Front in offensive against Denikin. Closely associated with the formation of the 1st Cavalry Army. Commanded the South-western Front in Polish war, 1920. In dispute with Tukhachevsky and the Warsaw operation. Remained in the Red Army command staff after the Civil War. Produced his version of the 1920 operations in 1929, defending the 1st Cavalry Army. Chief of Staff of the Red Army, 1931. Associated with the secret military collaboration with Germany. First Deputy Commissar for Defence, 1937. Displaced from the senior command level as a result of the military purge. Date of death given as 10/3/1941.

ZHUKOV, G. K.

Born 1896, Kaluga province. Mobilised 1916. Known as a brave and outstanding NCO. Served with the 10th Novgorod Dragoons Regiment, 10th Cavalry Division. Joined the Red Army, October 1918. Assigned to a Red Army cavalry detachment. Action against the Don Cossacks, near Tsaritsyn, November 1918. Unit included in the 2nd Cavalry Brigade under Timoshenko. Attached to the 1st Cavalry Army. Served with Timoshenko's division throughout the Civil War. Rose to squadron commander. Continued service in 4th Cavalry Division, Timoshenko's 3rd Cavalry Corps, Belorussian Military District. Attended Frunze Academy, 1928–31. Appointed assistant to regimental commander, 6th Cavalry Division, 3rd Cavalry Corps. Commander 4th Cavalry Division, 1934. Began experiments with armoured forces. Commander 3rd Cavalry Corps, 1936. Deputy commander cavalry forces, Belorussian Military District, 1937. Closely associated with Timoshenko. Sent to China with Soviet military mission: observation of Japanese military methods. Took command of Soviet counter-offensive against Kwantung Army, in operations at Khalkhin-Gol, Mongolia, July–August 1939. Defeated Japanese, but at cost of severe Soviet losses. Deputy Commander, Ukrainian Military District. Chief of Staff, Red Army, final stage of Russo-Finnish War, January 1940. Assigned to the command of the Kiev Special Military District. Given the rank of General, May 1940. Took part in the occupation of Bessarabia and the Bukovina. Appointed Chief of Staff, Red Army, January 1941. Sent to assist Voroshilov at defence of Leningrad, October 1941. Took over forces for battle of Moscow. Appointed permanent member, Soviet General Staff, 1942. On the death of Shaposhnikov, appointed 1st Deputy Commander Soviet forces, 1942. Took part in planning front and army actions. Carried out the Berlin operation, 1945. Removed from the lime-light by Stalin to Odessa Military District, later the Urals, 1946–52(?). Brought back secretly to senior command post, 1952(?). Soviet Minister of Defence, 1955. Removed from this post and military duties, after trip to Albania, 27th October, 1957. Accused by the Party of trying to alienate the army from its political leaders. Presumably in retirement. Marshal of the Soviet Union.

ZOF, V. I.

Born December 1889. Party member, 1913. Various command posts during the Civil War. Appointed senior commissar of the Soviet Navy (*VMF*), 1924. Appointed head of the navy and chief commissar, 1925. Conducted many of the negotiations with German naval officers for German technical help, 1926. Member of the Soviet Union *Revvoensoviet*. Assigned to the Collegiate for Communications: president of the Soviet Merchant Marine (*Sovtorgflot*), 1927–9. Deputy Commissar for Communications, 1930. 1st Deputy Commissar for Inland Waterway Transport, 1931. Date of death given as 29/10/1940.

INDEX

Abteilung R. See Sondergruppe R
Abwehr, 413, 434, 638
Adam, General W., 272, 333
AEG, German firm, 147
Aerochemical units and commands, *Osoaviakhim*, 307
Aero-engines, 154, 157, 161, 382; production, 1936, 408; Wright-Cyclone, 409; main producing centres, 1941, 575; *BMW* types ordered, 1928, 712 n. 70; M–6, 270; M–100, 408; AN–1, 409
Afghanistan, 290, 333
Agariev, 222
Aircraft; Soviet strength, 1918, 75; used against Wrangel, 105; arrangements with Junkers, 154, 155; varied stock of, 175; Soviet strength, 1924, 176; production, 304; re-equipment, 382; planned first-line strength, 403; servicing requirement, 1933, 405; strength in Far East, 1939, 517; losses in 1941, 593, 615, 808; fall in production, 1941, 628; Soviet requirement from Britain, 630; Loktinov on monthly production, 1939, 807; British, French estimates of strength, 1939, 807; German estimate of Soviet strength, 1941, 807, 808
Bombers; DB–3 (naval), 615; Pe–2, 615; SB–2 (ANT–40), 408, 440, 501; TB–3 (ANT–6), 408, 807; TB–4, 807; TB–5, 360; TB–7, 409; TsK B, 807
Fighters; I–15, 382, 407, 430, 642, 662, 807; I–16, 382, 408, 615, 642, 662, 807; I–153, 615, 662; LaGG–3, 558; MiG–3, 558, 615; R–5, 807; RZ, 807; Yak–1 (I–26), 558, 615; Yak–2, 615
Ground-attack; Il–2, 558, 615
Airframe manufacture, 408
Air-landing corps, 351, 390, 410. *See also* Parachute troops
Air-lift, Leningrad 1941, organisation and capacity, 618
Air-power, concepts, 382, 383
Aizenberg, G., 221
Akhlyustin, Major-General P. N., 590, 593
Akhmedov, Major I., 577
Alafuzov, Admiral, 524
Albatross Werke, 150
Aledogskii, A., 28, 776
Aleksandrov, Naval Academy instructor, 470, 475
Aleksandrovskii, S. S., 433
Alekseyev, Infantry Inspectorate, 367
Alksnis, Army Commander Ya. I., chief of *VVS*, 327; and *Z. Mo.*, 347; and Soviet bombers, 382; *Komandarm* II, 392, develops *TBS*, 408; in Prague, 419; General Martel on, 437; Deputy Defence Commissar, 450; and 'military tribunal', 1937, 463, 736–7 n. 47; disappearance and death, 500, 502; biography, 835
All-Army Assembly of Cell Secretaries, 1925, 189, 190
All-Army Conference of Political Workers, 1937, 473
All-Russian Assembly of Political Workers
First, 81; Second, 117–18
All-Russian Bureau of Military Commissars, 41, 46, 49
All-Russian Bureau of Military Organisations, 7
All-Russian Collegiate for the Formation of the Red Army, organisation, 18, 674 n. 55; budget, 19; and defence effort, 34; Organisation-Agitation Bureau, 41; issues *Regulation and Instruction*, 676 n. 6
All-Russian Conference of Front and Rear Organisations, *RSDRP(b)*, 43, 672 n. 14
All-Russian Conference of Sailors (Battle-fleets), 76
All-Russian Demobilisation Congress, 17, 18
All-Russian Supreme Staff. *See* Staff
All-Union Assembly of Military Scientific Societies (*VNO*), 1925, 209
All-Union Assembly of Political Workers, 1938, 479
All-Union Conference of Heads of Political Organs, 1924, 188, 189
All-Union Meeting of Red Army Military Instruction Centres, 1925, 194
Allied Supreme Council, 85
Al'tfater, Admiral V., 26, 27, 674 n. 49, 776
Aluminium production, losses in, 1941, 628
Alyabushev, Brigade Commander F. F., 550
Amelin, senior political officer in Kiev, 460
Ammunition-production, 157; location and output of plants, 1941, 575; 303 plants lost, August-November, 1941, 616; in Leningrad, 618
Amor, 415
Amphibious operations, air support stipulated, 317; on Kerch Peninsula, December, 1941, 657–8
Amtschef A (Admiral Brutzer), 274, 275–6, 277
'Amur incident' (1937), 468
Amur Railway, 217

Amur River Flotilla, 241, 361, 475
Anarchists, influence of, 121
Andreyev, A. A., 168, 198, 306, 598, 703 n. 84
Annual mobilisation (*Tersbor*), 180
Anti-aircraft defences, *Luftwaffe* estimate of, 1941, 808
Anti-aircraft guns, production deficiencies in 1941, 575
Anti-Comintern Pact, 432
Anti-tank ammunition, production deficiencies, 1941, 575
Anti-tank brigade, Artillery Reserve High Command, 572
Anti-tank defence, 270, 406, 442
Anti-tank reserves, mobile, 407, 442
Anti-tank zones (*protivtankovye raiony*), 406, 407; in *PU–36*, 442
Antipov-Chikunskii, Engineer Flag Officer, 421
Antonov, Marshal A. I., 554, 612
Antonov-Ovseenko, V. A., 7, 10, 11, 12, 17, 69, 138, 142, 164–5, 168, 171, 186, 490, 835
Apanasenko, General I. R., 183, 463, 554, 599
Apoga, 259
Araki, General, 335
Aralov, S. I., 36, 61, 835–6
'Arcos' raid, 1927, 284
Armament norms, 406
Armenia, 123
Armenian National Army, 123
Armies, formation, units
  Chinese
  Armies: 8th Route (Communist), 469; 29th, 468
  Corps: 1st, 232, 234; 4th, 236; 7th, 235, 236
  Regiments: 1st Training, 230
  German
  Army Groups: North, 583, 588, 605, 609, 620, 633, 635, 665; Centre, 583, 587, 588, 595, 602, 609, 617, 622, 650, 654, 659, 665, 756 n. 96; South, 583, 588, 596, 607, 620, 641, 647
  Armoured Groups: First, 588, 596, 597, 607, 610, 612, 645; Second, 588, 601, 610, 612, 640, 661; Third, 588, 595, 601, 640, 650, 655, 661; Fourth, 588, 595, 640, 650, 655, 661
    Armies: 2nd, 610, 612; 4th, 639, 641, 650, 651, 652, 653, 654, 655; 6th, 610, 621; 9th, 654; 11th, 588, 607, 608; 17th, 607, 608, 610, 612
    Corps: 3rd Motorised, 645; VIII, 593; 14th Motorised, 645; XXIV *Panzer*, 610; XXXIV, 653; 39th Motorised, 648, 656; 49th Mountain Infantry, 645
  Infantry Divisions: 1st Mountain, 645; 4th Mountain, 645; 44th, 592; 45th, 653; 57th, 592; 61st, 647; 75th, 592; 95th, 653; 111th, 592; 112th, 640; 198th, 645; 268th, 592; 290th, 592; 298th, 592; 299th, 592
  Panzer Divisions: 1st, 592; 3rd, 592, 610; 4th, 592; 6th, 592, 596; 7th, 592; 8th, 592; 11th, 596, 597; 12th, 592, 656; 13th, 645; 14th, 645; 16th, 645; 18th, 592; 20th, 592
  SS Divisions: *Viking*, 645; *Adolf Hitler*, 645
  Japanese
  Armies: 6th, 534, 536
  Divisions: 5th, 221; 7th, 520; 19th, 495; 23rd, 518, 520; 104th (Kwantung Army), 498
  Regiments: 1st Manchurian cavalry, 518; 7th Manchurian cavalry, 518; 8th Cavalry, 518; 64th Infantry, 518
  Mongolian (People's Republic: MPR)
  Cavalry Divisions: 6th, 518, 521; 8th, 519, 533
  Regiments: 15th, 518; 17th, 518, 519
  Polish
  Armies: 3rd, 90; 4th, 88; 6th, 94
  Rumanian
  Armies: 3rd, 588; 4th, 588
  Russian
  Imperial Army; Armies: 1st, 20; Vth, 8, 20; XIth, 5; XIIth, 5, 20; Regiments: 436th Novoladozhskii, 5, 19; 479th Khadnikovskii, 19
  Workers-Peasants Red Army (*RKKA*) Civil War designations
    Armies: Ist, 55, 57, 60; IInd, 45, 57, 60, 61, 64; IIIrd, 45, 57, 58, 61, 64, 65, 93, 95, 98, 218; IVth, 57, 59, 60, 61, 93, 98, 100; Vth, 36, 57, 60, 61, 63, 64, 65, 218, 219, 220; VIth, 59, 63, 105, 106; VIIth, 60, 122; VIIIth, 60, 72, 73, 74; IXth, 60, 69, 73, 102, 103, 104, 123; Xth, 60, 67, 68, 73; XIth, 60, 75, 104, 123, 124; XIIth, 60, 89, 90, 93, 94, 95, 96, 97, 101; XIIIth, 72, 91, 102, 105; XIVth, 72, 89, 90, 93, 94, 97; XVth, 87, 88, 89, 93, 98; XVIth, 87, 88, 89, 93, 96, 98; Lettish, 60; Turkestan, 61
    Cavalry Armies: 1st, 67, 71, 72, 73, 74, 85, 89, 90, 93, 94, 95, 97, 98, 99, 102, 105, 106, 126; 2nd, 103, 105, 106, 123
    Cavalry Corps: 1st, 91; 3rd, 93, 98–9, 100
    Cavalry Divisions: 4th, 90; 6th, 71, 90, 97; 8th, 97; 11th, 90; 14th, 90
    Rifle Divisions: 1st Amur, 221; 1st Irkutsk, 219; 15th, 88; 25th, 79; 26th, 65, 218; 30th, 71, 105; 45th, 89; 48th, 94; 51st, 64, 65, 105, 106, 223; 58th, 90
    Cavalry Brigades: Bashkir, 89; Special, 90
    Regiments: 1st, 20; 1st Tallin, 20; 2nd, 20; 4th Lettish, 39; 9th Siberian, 20; 43rd, 88
    Squadrons: No. 4 Armoured Car, 184; 2nd Tank, 184
    Special Far Eastern Red Banner Army (*ODVA/OKDVA*: 1929–37), 65, 240, 241, 242, 244–5, 336, 337, 358, 360, 363
      Rifle Corps: 18th, 241; 19th, 241

Cavalry Divisions: 5th, 360; 8th, 451; 15th, 451
Kolkhoz Divisions: 2nd, 451; 3rd, 451
Rifle Divisions: 1st 'Pacific Ocean', 360; 2nd, 241, 242, 360, 451; 12th, 241, 360, 451; 21st, 241, 242, 243, 360, 451; 34th, 451; 35th, 242, 243, 244, 360; 36th, 242, 243, 360, 451; 40th, 360, 451; 57th, 360, 451
Cavalry Brigades: 5th Detached, 242, 243, 244; 9th, 360
Rifle Regiments: 4th, 242; 5th, 242; 63rd, 243; 106th, 242, 243; 107th, 242, 243; 108th, 242, 243
Red Army Post-1937 designations
Army Groups: 1st, 522, 532–4; Novgorod, 635, 636, 637
Armies: 1st Red Banner, 494, 497, 517; 2nd Red Banner, 517; 3rd, 571, 584, 590, 593, 600, 650, 653, 654; 4th, 538, 571, 584, 590, 593, 595, 600, 620, 633, 634, 635, 636, 637, 647, 648, 649, 655, 656, 659; 5th, 538, 539, 582, 584, 590, 591, 596, 597, 608, 609, 612, 650, 651; 6th, 538, 582, 584, 590, 591, 596, 597; 7th, 543, 544, 547, 549, 550, 584, 589, 634, 648; 8th, 543, 544, 545, 547, 551, 584, 589, 591, 595, 604, 605; 9th, 543, 544–5, 585, 596, 608, 621, 641, 643, 645, 646, 647; 10th, 538, 571, 584, 590, 593, 600, 639, 650, 653, 661, 662; 11th, 538, 584, 589, 595; 12th, 538, 539, 584, 591, 596, 608, 621, 641, 642, 646; 13th, 547, 549, 550, 590, 600, 601, 602, 609, 610, 617, 622, 650, 653, 654, 655; 14th, 544, 584, 589; 15th, 547, 551; 16th, 590, 601, 640, 650, 651; 18th, 591, 621, 643, 645, 646; 20th, 590, 639, 650, 651, 661; 21st, 590, 602; 23rd, 584, 589, 605; 24th, 652; 26th, 584, 590, 591, 596, 607, 698, 609, 756 n. 110; 27th, 584, 589, 665; 29th, 650, 651, 654; 31st, 650, 651, 654; 33rd, 641, 650, 654; 34th, 607; 37th, 609, 612, 641, 642, 645, 646, 647; 38th, 610, 612; 40th, 609, 610, 650, 653; 43rd, 641, 650, 654; 44th, 657, 658; 48th, 605; 49th, 639, 653; 50th, 609, 624, 639, 650, 653, 663; 51st Independent, 620, 642, 657; 52nd, 607, 620, 635, 636, 637, 647, 649, 655, 656, 659, 757 n. 134; 54th, 606, 607, 619, 620, 634, 635, 636, 637, 648, 656; 55th, 737 n. 134; 56th Independent, 644, 645, 646, 647; 60th, 652; 61st, 654; Independent Coastal, 608, 621, 642, 646
Shock Armies: 1st, 639, 641, 650, 651, 652, 661, 663; 3rd, 665; 4th, 665
Cavalry Corps: 1st Guards, 650, 653; 2nd, 539, 591, 597, 641; 2nd Guards, 651; 4th, 539; 5th, 539; 6th, 590, 593, 595
Mechanised Corps: 1st, 589; 2nd, 591, 597; 3rd, 589; 5th, 590, 601; 6th, 590, 593, 594; 7th, 590, 601; 8th, 591, 596, 597; 9th, 591, 596; 10th, 589, 605; 11th, 590, 593, 594; 13th, 590, 593; 14th, 590, 593; 15th, 584, 591, 596; 16th, 591; 18th, 591; 22nd, 591, 596
Rifle Corps: 1st, 545; 2nd, 590; 9th Independent, 591; 19th, 543, 544; 23rd, 538; 28th, 551; 35th, 591; 36th, 591; 37th, 591, 596; 39th, 496, 497, 498; 44th, 590; 47th, 591; 50th, 543; 57th, 517, 519, 745 n. 28; 70th, 589
Tank Corps: 4th, 597; 10th, 543, 571; 15th, 571; 25th, 539
Cavalry Divisions: 1st, 756 n. 111; 2nd, 642; 5th, 591; 9th, 591; 25th, 589, 636; 27th, 634; 30th, 589; 35th, 643; 36th, 595; 56th, 643; 66th, 643; 72nd, 591
Rifle Divisions: 3rd Guards, 619, 634; 4th Guards, 619, 633, 634, 656; 6th, 592, 593; 8th Guards, 631, 640; 9th Mountain, 658; 15th, 591, 642; 18th, 545; 20th, 558; 25th, 608, 756 n. 111; 27th, 593; 30th, 643; 32nd, 497, 498; 36th Motorised, 519; 40th, 497, 498; 42nd, 529, 593; 44th, 545, 633; 49th, 593; 56th, 545; 57th, 533, 534; 63rd Mountain, 658; 64th, 613; 65th, 634; 70th, 558, 605; 80th, 648; 82nd, 533, 536; 85th, 593; 87th, 592; 92nd, 633, 634; 95th, 608, 642, 646, 756 n. 111; 99th, 558; 100th (1st Guards), 548, 613; 103rd, 548; 107th, 613; 111th, 635, 647, 655; 115th, 648, 656; 120th, 613; 121st, 595; 124th, 592; 125th, 592; 127th, 613; 128th, 592, 619; 136th, 643; 137th, 558; 139th, 545; 143rd, 595; 150th, 643; 152nd, 533; 153rd, 613; 155th, 545, 595; 157th, 658; 161st, 613; 163rd, 544–5, 589; 168th, 545; 172nd, 642; 180th, 635; 188th, 592; 191st, 604, 633, 634; 198th, 589, 604, 648, 656; 224th, 657; 236th, 658; 259th, 635, 637, 647; 267th, 635, 637, 647, 757 n. 134; 285th, 634, 638, 648; 286th, 619; 288th, 620, 635, 757 n. 134; 292nd, 634; 294th, 619; 302nd, 657; 305th, 635; 310th, 619, 634, 656; 311th, 634, 648; 316th, 631, 640; 339th, 643; 377th, 656
Tank Divisions: 1st, 589; 3rd, 589; 21st, 619; 22nd, 592; 60th, 633, 648
Air-Landing Brigades: 212th, 533, 534
Mechanised Brigades: 2nd, 498; 7th, 519, 520, 533; 8th, 519, 533; 9th, 519, 520, 534
Naval Infantry Brigades: 6th, 634, 648; 8th, 620–1
Rifle Brigades: 1st, 648; 1st Independent Mountain, 619; 9th Motorised, 533; 79th Independent, 656, 657; 83rd, 657; 345th, 657; 388th, 657
Tank Brigades: 1st Guards, 633, 651; 2nd, 643; 3rd, 635; 4th, 624; 6th, 533, 534;

Armies, formation, units—*contd.*
11th, 518, 519, 520, 521, 533; 16th, 619, 634; 22nd, 619; 23rd Independent, 539; 26th Independent, 539; 34th, 545; 35th, 550; 46th, 634; 122nd, 634, 635, 648; 132nd, 643; 142nd, 645
Rifle Regiments: 24th Motorised, 520; 54th, 756 n. 111; 80th, 534; 127th, 536; 149th, 519, 520; 293rd, 536; 305th, 545; 383rd, 642; 601st, 533; 602nd, 536
Armour, 585, 649
Armoured car battalion, 270
Armoured cars, 136, 137, 270, 518, 520, 522, 533, 644
Armoured fighting vehicles. *See* Tanks
Armoured sledges, 548, 550, 551
Armoured trains, 105, 137; No. 8, 184; *Za Rodinu*, 1941, 645
Army of the Regeneration of Russia, 1920, 689 n. 73
'Army-Party relations', as concept, vii, 301, 368
'Army syndicalism', 44
Aronstam, Army Commissar L., 392, 397, 450, 451, 467
Artemeyev, General, 624
Artillery, 136, 137, 167, 241, 243, 304, 326, 351, 381, 389, 390, 407–8, 430, 438, 510; multi-purpose divisional gun, 408; concentration, in offensive, *PU-36*, 441; *kontrartilleriiskaya podgotovka*, 442; divisional, in mobile defence, 443; *A/DD*, *A/PP/PK*, *AR*, 439; futility of Soviet practice in China, 491; at Lake Khasan, 1938, 498–9; at Khalkhin-Gol, 518, 519, 520, 521, 522, 533, 534, 536, 806; in Finnish War, 544, 549–50, 551; rocket-artillery, 614; Voronov's reorganisation, 614; total strength in 1st Shock Army, 661; density per kilometre on rifle division break-through sector, 662; strength per 1000 men, 695 n. 88; Halder on, 1940, 749 n. 136; comparative density, Moscow & Stalingrad, 760 n. 46; strength in rifle divisions, 1923–9, 787; general composition, 1924, 790; general distribution, 1926, 791
45-mm AT, 407; 57-mm AT, 614; 76-mm AA, 407; 76-mm 1902/30, 361, 407; 122-mm howitzer, 407; 152-mm, 407; 203-mm howitzer, 407
Artillery production, 1942, 665
Artuzov, *NKVD* officer, 380, 396
Asanov, 491. *See also* Kachanov
Assistance in Defence (*OSO*), 307
Astakhov, G., 515, 516, 529, 530, 532, 555
Astanin, Major-General A. N., 605
Attestation, 176, 192, 193, 478–9
Attestation boards, 192, 198
Attestation Commissions, 49
Attestation records, case cited, 773–5
Attrition, as strategic principle, 211, 296, 309
Aurora (cruiser), 11
Aus Politik und Zeitgeschichte, 466
Austria, 417, 488
Auswärtiges Amt, 152, 256, 257, 272, 273, 453
Automobile industry, 303, 356
Aviation: Army co-operation, basic combat functions, *PU-36*, 803; Communications, functions, *PU-36*, 803; Corps, 176; reconnaissance duties, 732 n. 103; Fighter, normal and special tactical functions, 802; Ground-attack, 440; tactical functions, *PU-36*, 802; Light-bomber, tactical functions, 802–3; Naval, 176, 615, 620, 807; 'Strategic' (Army), 176; Strategic, bomber (*TBS*), 408, 500, 501. *See also* Military Air Force (*VVS/RKKA*)
Aviation and Chemical Society (*Aviakhim*), 307
Aviation formations, brigades, regiments/squadrons
Divisions: 20th Mixed, 644; 50th Long Range, 644
Brigades; 18th, 360; 19th, 360
Parks: No. 16, 360; No. 41, 360
Regiments: 69th Fighter, 756 n. 111
Squadrons: 26th Naval, 360; 68th Fighter, 360; 69th Bomber, 360; 70th Naval, 756 n. 111; 82nd Naval, 756 n. 111
Aviation industry, 75, 155, 382; foreign help, 408; modernisation problems, 501; seeks German prototypes, 1940, 548; Shakhurin in command, 558; main plants, 1941, 575; production losses, 1941, 628; output, 1942, 664
Avksent'evskii, Army Commander K. A., 105, 202
Avrov, Petrograd MD commander, 1921, 122
Azov Flotilla, 102; and Kerch landings, 1941, 657

BA–27, armoured car, 270, 350
Bagdat'ev, 671 n. 9
Bagramyan, Marshal I. K., 80, 508
Bakayev, 425
Bakhturov, P. V., 101
Bakinskii, S., 13
Baltic Fleet, 4, 6, 11–12, 33, 46, 76, 77; limited role in Civil War, 78; and Kronstadt rebellion, 121–2; proposed scuttling, 176; Orlov's career in, 275; and defence of Leningrad, 353; strategic tasks, 353–354; Galler as commander, 392; possible combat role, 1936, 418; command and staff organisation, 1936, 421; command re-shuffle, 1937, 450; potential operational role, 1939, 528, 540–1; Tributs assumes command, 554; operational tasks in Baltic defence plan, 570; operational alert, 1941, 586; guns put under Front command, 620

Baltic Fleet Political Directorate (*Pubalt*), 121
Baltiiskii, General A. A., 57, 75
Baluyev, General, 15
Baranov, P. I., chief of *VVS*, 75, 178, 200, 266, 279, 326, 367, 836
Baranov, V. K., 184
Batrak (submarine), 252
Barmine, A., 122, 373, 415, 416, 463, 739 n. 74
Basmachis, 184
Batis, naval commissar, 121
Batov, General, 554
Batygin, Colonel I. I., 644
Bauer, Colonel M., 147, 154, 158, 162
Bayerische Flugzeugwerke, 340
Bayev, Regimental Commissar, 493
Beck, Colonel J., 380, 386, 387, 529
Beck, Colonel-General L., 411, 412
Behrends, H., 435, 436
Behschnitt, Major, 263
Belomorstroi. *See* White Sea Canal
Belov, Major-General P. A., 463, 641, 653
Beneš, Dr E., 433, 436, 454, 490, 732 n. 94, 737 n. 48
Berens (Behrens), Admiral, 255, 674 n. 49
Berg, President Naval Section *VNO*, 275
Beria, L. P., 454, 490, 510, 585, 586, 598, 623
Bernhardi, Lieutenant, 269
Bersol (poison-gas), 157, 162, 250
Berzarin, Major-General N., 589
Berzin, R. I., 90, 98, 256
Berzin, Ya., 256, 357, 380, 429, 430, 431, 452, 455, 502
Bessonov, S. A., 481, 485
Bindseil, Naval Captain, 252
Biographic Directory of the USSR, 499
Biryuzov, Marshal S. S., 554
Bismarck, proposed sale of plans to Russians, 541
Black Sea Fleet, 6, 77, 254, 275; Koshchanov in command, 392; and Turkey, 422; potential operational role, 1939, 528; defence of naval bases, 582; operational alert, 1941, 586–7; and defence of Odessa, 610; naval aviation attacks Rumania, 615; naval aviation and Odessa defence, 620; marine brigades, Crimea, 621; Kerch-Feodosiya operation, 657; submarine strength, 1936–7, 804
Blimiel, 413, 729 n. 27
Blohm und Voss, 150
Blomberg, Field-Marshal W. von, 256, 257, 258, 259, 263–8, 270, 271, 272, 278, 280, 307, 382, 411, 436, 474
Blum, Naval Captain (retired), 253
Blum, L., 433, 436, 453, 454
Blumentritt, General G., 666
Blyukher, Marshal V. K., 15, 64, 682 n. 45; career to 1918, 65; Gurov mentioned as real name, 65; at Perekop, 1920, 106; 'special duties', 1924, 178, 211; replaces Eikhe, 1920, 223; and Dairen Conference, 224; Volochaevka operations, 1922, 224–5; recalled from Far East, 225; as 'Galen', 'Galin' in China, 228; and Whampoa, 229; at Mien-hu, 229–230; opinion of Chiang Kai-shek, 230–231, 232; and Northern Expedition, 234; supports Borodin, 235, 236; role in China, 237; commands *ODVA*, 240–1; Fukdin operation, 1929, 242; remains in Far East, 245; and Voroshilov, 245–6; named for Berlin posting, 261; General Blomberg on, 266; decorated, 335; and Far Eastern crisis, 336, 337; and Stalin, 356; strategic problems, Far East, 361–2; organises staff, 367; at 17th Congress, 379; appointed Marshal, 392; relations with staff, 397; probable operational intentions, 398; strength available, 399; transportation facilities, 400; and Stalin, 402; supply dump system, 405; development of fixed defences, 406; and tanks, 416; strength and deployment, 1937, 451; and 'military tribunal', 1937, 463; Chiang Kai-shek's request for, 469; member Main Military Soviet, 478; and Far Eastern purge, 492–4; possible explanation of disgrace, 497, 743 n. 72; liquidation, November 1938, 499, 501–502, 504, 505, 506; biography, 836
Blyumberg, Zh. K., 57, 61
BMW (*Bayerische Motorenwerke*), 161
Board of Trade, 269
Bock, Field Marshal F. von, 588, 654
Bockelberg, Lieutenant-General A. von, 343, 344, 345–6
Bodryi (minelayer), 657
Bogatsch, *Luftwaffe* General, 615
Bogomolov, D. V., 467, 490
Boikov, Colonel B. A., 644
Boldin, General I. V., 538, 590, 593, 653, 663
Boldyrev, General, 15
Bol'shevik (journal), 458, 470
Bonapartism, 'Bonapartist projects', 138, 189, 298–9, 299–300, 368, 447, 487
Bonch-Bruevich, General M. D., 14, 26, 53, 99, 777
Bonnet, G., 514
Bonin, Naval Captain, 275, 277
Borkenau, F., 431, 730 n. 67
Borodin (artillery expert), 235
Borodin (Gruzenberg), M., 228, 230, 232, 233, 235, 236, 237
Borshchevskii, 122
Bozer, Soviet citizen, 579
Bratman-Brodowski, Soviet plenipotentiary, 261
Braunstein, 41
Brest-Litovsk, Treaty of. *See* Treaties
Bridging battalions, 389

Brockdorff-Rantzau, U. Count von, 150, 156, 157, 158, 161, 162, 247, 248, 249, 250, 251
Brüning, H., 341, 342
Brukhanov, 38
Brusilov, General A. A., 109
Bubnov, A. S., 7, 67, 69, 168, 171, 190, 200, 232, 233, 237, 246, 309, 310, 314
Budenny Electro-Technical Institute, Leningrad, 410
Budenny (Budënnyi), Marshal S. M., 6, 32, 51, 67, 101; military career to 1918, 70; defeats Mamontov, 71–2; and creation of 1st Cavalry Army, 72–3; victory at Rostov-on-Don, 73; letter to Lenin, 1920, 74, 783; with Stalin against Trotsky, 83; transfer to SW Front, 87; protests over cavalry transfer, 89, 686 n. 21; attack on Kiev, 90; and Tukhachevsky, 1920, 97; escapes encirclement, 98; against Wrangel, 106; and disbanding of 1st Cavalry Army, 126; at 11th Congress, 133; on Republic *Revvoensoviet*, 171; on Cavalry Inspectorate, 178; and cavalry organisation, 183; and *RVS*, 1925, 200; preparation of cavalry manual, 207; and Bonapartism, 299; visits French officers, 364; head of Cavalry Inspectorate, 367; appointed Marshal, 392; and Stalin, 401; lacks higher education, 410; and Stalin, 1936, 426; at manoeuvres, 436; at 1937 plenum, 452; to Moscow MD, 462–3; and 'military tribunal', 463, 501; on Main Military Soviet, 478; as Deputy Defence Commissar, 508; at 18th Congress, 511; meets Anglo-French mission, 524; president of Manuals Commission, 558; commands Reserve Army Group, 600; member Supreme Command *Stavka*, 602; takes over SW command, 603, 607; and Uman catastrophe, 608–9; *Stavka* assignment, 609; and Kiev disaster, 612, 626; biography, 837
Bülow, B. W. von, 343
Bukharin, N. I., on 'revolutionary war', 27, 676 n. 13; and Zinoviev, 141; and Stalin, 1925, 201; and Stalin, 1927, 285, 287, 288; on Stalin, 301; and the Right, 315; position after 1936 Trial, 425; 'investigation' of, 426; in 1937, 452; on trial, 1938, 481, 483, 486–7; death-sentence on, 487
Bulganin, Marshal N. A., 73, 603, 650, 662, 760 n. 46
Bulgaria, 566, 573
Bulin, I. A., Deputy Chief of Political Administration, 426, 461, 504
Bulletin (Munich), 132
'Bureau of Three', 36
Bureau of the Revolutionary Committee for the Defence of Petrograd, 26
Burnett, Air Marshal Sir C., 525, 530–1
Buro Tsentralnoi Komendatury (Red Guard), 9
Bussche, Colonel, 263
Butler, R. A., 523

Camouflage, 207
Canaris, Admiral W., 253, 413, 434, 729 n. 26
Capital ships, proposed Soviet purchase of, 500
Categorisation, command, political, administrative staff, 192–3; table of designations, 789
Caucasian Bureau (*Kavburo*), 75, 123
Cavalry, 51, 70–1, 126, 127, 137, 167, 181, 182–3, 206, 326, 337, 350, 360, 389, 405, 438, 439, 510, 518, 520, 521, 683 n. 64, 730 n. 48, 790. *See also* Cossack formations, Strategic Cavalry
Cavalry-mechanised mobile group, 1939, 538
'Cells' (Party collectives), development of, 43–4, 679 n. 70; activities circumscribed, 44–5; and 10th Congress, 126; in territorial-militia scheme, 139; and Circular No. 200, 142; and 1923 crisis, 164–5; ferment in, 166, 168; 'swamping' of, 186, 189; limitations on, 189; enquiry into, 190; of Military Academy, 206; criticism of, 1928, 311–12
Central Army Chemical Polygon (*TsVKhP*), 264
Central Asia, 184, 185, 195, 245
Central Command, Partisan movement (*GShPD*), December, 1941, 629
Central Committee (*TsK*), Russian Communist Party, 36, 45, 47; decision on Urals advance, 64; considers plan against Poland, 87; appoints Stalin to SW Front, 89; on territorial divisions, 139; and Circular No. 200, 142; and Red Army budget, 155; attack on Trotsky, 164; Military Commission of, 166–7; appoints special military commission, 168; hears evidence, 169–70; and changes in military personnel, 171; and Blyukher, 178; fixes military strength, 179; removes Trotsky from *RVS*, 189; and 'cells', 190; direct control over army political apparatus, 190–1; and *PURKKA*, 191; and unitary command, 196; Andreyev's letter on command, 198; appoints Voroshilov and Lashevich, 200; and Leningrad, 201; breaks Zinoviev-Lashevich combination, 201–2; and Military Academy 'cell', 206; expulsion of Trotsky, 286–7, 288; Communist Academy of, 308, 319, 321, 375; and 'cells', 311; issues 'State of Defence', 319; and *VVS*, 375; autumn plenum, 1936, 426, 428; February-

March plenum, 1937, 452; and Main Military Soviet, 478. *See also* Communist Party, Russian; Congresses, Russian Communist Party; Political Administration; *Politburo*
Central Committee of All-Russian Naval Forces (*Tsentroflot*), 76
Central Control Commission (*TsKK*), 141, 164, 190, 202, 286, 287. *See also* Military Commission
Central Powers, The, 20–1, 25
Chachanyan, Corps Commander, 450, 451, 493
Chair of Military Industry, Military Academy, 195
Chang Hsueh-liang, 240, 244
Chang Shi-lin, General, 222
Chang Tso-lin, General, 227, 239, 240
Changchun Conference, 1922, 225
Chapayev, V. I., cavalry commander, 40, 79, 678 n. 56
'Chapayev Division', 89
Charomsky(-ii), A. D., 409
Cheka. *See* Security Organs
Chemical troops, Red Army, 266–7, 279, 389, 510
Chen I, 223
Cheremisov, General, 10, 15
Cherevichenko, Colonel-General Ya. I., 621, 634, 654
Chernov, V., 15
Chernyakovskii, Tank General I. D., 508
Chervonaya Ukraina (cruiser), 392
Chiang Kai-shek, Generalissimo, 178, 227, 228, 229, 230–1, 232–3, 235, 236, 237, 238, 240, 261, 284, 287, 400, 466, 469, 490, 491, 708 n. 56
Chibissov, Lieutenant-General N. Y., 608
Chicherin, G. V., 150, 161, 222, 223, 227, 247, 248, 287, 328, 687 n. 33
Chief of Red Army Supply, 173, 175, 178. *See also* Supply
Chief of Rear Services, Red Army, post created 1941, 598–9
Chief of Naval Forces, *VMF/RKKA*, post created 1924, 176
China, 178, 195, 211, 217, 218, 221–2, 222–3, 226–39 *passim*, 239, 241, 244, 284, 287, 338, 400, 414, 415, 466–7, 468–9, 470, 490–1, 495, 498, 499, 578
Chinese Eastern Railway, 217, 222, 226, 227, 239, 240, 336, 358, 397, 399
Chinese People's National-Liberation Army, 703 n. 85
Chinese Red Army, 237, 738–9 n. 68
Choibalsan, Marshal Kh., 223
Chorkov, head of Zhukovskii Air Academy, 367
Chou En-lai, 229, 234, 237
Christie tank-designs, American, 350
Chu Teh, Marshal, viii, 237
Chubar, V. Ya., 125, 388
Chuikov, Marshal V. I., 88, 538, 554
Churchill, Sir W. S., 433, 574, 630, 664, 752 n. 32
Circular No. 200, 1923, 142, 164, 186
Civil Air Fleet, and Leningrad air-lift 1941, 618
Civil Defence. *See Osoaviakhim*
Civil War, Russian: 1918–22; Tukhachevsky on, 108; 'manoeuvre character' of, 127; Trotsky on lessons of, 128–9; combat experience collated, 128; Gusev on, 129; command staff deficiencies in, 133; 'idealisation of', 134; and Red Army manuals, 207; Blomberg on, 267; as propaganda, 281; Frunze on higher direction of, 283; and 'civil front', 306; Stalin's references to, 1939, 542; recent modifications of Stalinist myths, 674 n. 60, 683 n. 54, 683 n. 68. *See also* Military Operations
Civil War, Spanish, and Soviet Union, 429–31
Clausewitz, Lieutenant-Colonel von, 292, 294, 507, 511
'Clemenceau thesis', propounded by Trotsky, 286
Coal production, 628, 665
Coastal defences, weaknesses in 1941, 570, 582, 583
Cochenhausen, Colonel von, 263
Colonel-General, introduction of rank, 554
Colson, General, 514
Command: elective, 1917, 16; reorganised, 1918, 30; 'dual', 41; Trotsky on, at 8th Congress, 46; problem in navy, 76; collegiate organisation of, 80; and the commissar, 81; attack on 'dual command', 81–2; 'unity of command' (*edinonachalie*), 82; modified 'dual', 117; difficulties in naval forces, 121; debate on, 10th Congress, 126, 693 n. 48; progress in unitary command, 1922–3, 195; forms of unitary, 196; commissars' resistance, 1924, 196–7; and Directive No. 234, 1925, 198; percentage of unitary, 198, 704 n. 107; further progress in unitary form, 204, 788; Voroshilov on, 204–5; unitary in 1928, 309, 311; control and, 313–14; Tukhachevsky on, 381, 411; and *PU-36*, 444; 'dual' restored 1937, 460, 478–9; unitary restored 1940, 557; 'dual' restored July 1941, 603; unitary restored 1942, 668
Command Staff: name 'officer' eschewed, 31; 'military specialists' in, 32; and ex-Imperial NCOs, 32, 677 n. 26 & n. 32; 'Red commanders', 32; training of 'candidate-commanders', 32–3; strength, 1918–20, 33; and Attestation Commissions, 49; on Eastern Front, 57; proletarian cadres for, 79; 'Red command' as political force, 82–3; lack of

Command Staff—*contd.*
homogeneity in, 114; Tukhachevsky on, 134; Radek to Germans on, 153; deficiencies in, 1923, 165; social composition, 166; losses from war and demobilisation, 169; purge of naval, 1924, 176; political, social composition, 1924–6, 797; and title 'Red Army commander', 179; shortages in, 181, 191; and national formations, 184; divergences and divisions in, 191; sub-commission on service in, 192; categorisation of, 192–3; and unitary command, 196; 'Communising' of, 197; and percentage of unitary command, 198, 788; versus the commissar, 204–5, 704 n. 107, 705 n. 123; training in Germany, 258; posting to German units, 265; Blomberg on, 267; political level of, 311; non-Party component, 313; and 1929 purge, 315; and *PU-29*, 316; Party composition of, 319; and *OO*, 368; political composition, 1933, 374, Party membership, 381; reserve officer, 388; formal ranks introduced, 1935, 391–2; material conditions, 392–3; consolidations in, 402; immunity from arrest, 404; education of senior grade, 410; and political staff, 422; need for tactical training, 436; and new military cadres, 446; re-shuffled, 1937, 450–1; beginnings of purge, 460–2; executions in senior level, 463–4; purged in Far East, 1937, 467; losses due to purging, 470–1, 744 n. 89; rapid promotions in, 471; commissar control over, 1938, 478–9; further purging in, 479–80; purge losses in Far East, 493–4; mediocrity in, 502; provisional estimate of total losses in, 505–6; reconstruction of, 507–8; and the commissar, Voroshilov's views, 510–11; training deficiencies in, 533; senior promotions in, 1940, 554; and new disciplinary code, 555; purge continued, 1940, 559; lack of training to handle tank, mobile forces, 567, 754 n. 61; Colonel Krebs on, 1941, 570; death sentences in, 1941, 599–600; shortage of, for corps and divisional staffs, 614; discontents and frustrations within, 660; and new higher command group, 663; purge by battle, 664

Command Staff Administration (Cadres), 341, 388

Commissars (pre-1918), 4; historical precedents, 678 n. 57; reports, October 1917, 10; Bolshevik replacements, 13; after 1917, 41; party affiliations, 42. *See also* Military Commissars; Political Administration

Commission for Foreign Affairs, 490

Committee for Military and Naval Affairs (1917), 12, 17

Communist Academy of Central Committee, Military Section, 308, 319, 321, 375

Communist International. *See Komintern*

Communist League of Youth. *See Komsomol*

Communist Parties, non-Russian; Chinese, 226, 231, 232, 236, 466–7; German, 149, 160, 161, 330, 331, 342; Mongolian, 223

Communist Party, Russian; agitation in Imperial Army, 5–6; and standing army, 6; para-military forces, 1917, 8–9; prepares *coup d'état*, 10–11; and 'revolutionary war', 18; left-wing anti-centralism in, 39; conflicts over military policy, 46–9; Military Opposition, 49–50; early divisions over military policies, 82–3; and militia schemes, 115–16; demands for control over Army political organs, 116, 125; and Kronstadt, 1921, 121–2; and commissars, 125–6; and territorial system, 139; power struggle in and military machine, 140–3, 164–5, 166; membership among naval officers, 1924, 176; Party organisations and militia, 180; rift between civilian and military Party functions, 187; probes Party work in armed forces, 189–91; inner-Party struggle, 1925–6, 201–2; and reduction of Red Army to 'simple militia', 209–10; and Chinese Revolution, 226–8, 231–2, 235–6, 236–7; and war-scare, 1927, 285–6; Stalin-Trotsky struggle, 1927, 286–8, 714 n. 5; Party apparatus and Bonapartism, 299–301; criticism of work, 1928, 311–13; 1929–30 purge in, 314–15; and responsibility for morale, 367; Party penetration and military efficiency, 368–9; strength in Red Army, 1930–4, 373; contrast of military and civilian purging, 1933–4, 374; increases contingents in technical branches of Red Army, 375; problem of control with Communised officer corps, 375–5; and *Osoaviakhim*, 389; effect of purge, 1933–5, 402; and denunciations, 425; and Radek trial, 449–50; conference of Party organs and purge, 1937, 461–2; new political programme in Red Army, 478–9; mass arrests endanger its survival, 504; and defence of Moscow, 1941, 623; and partisan war, 629; attack on Zhukov, 668; and Stalinist distortions of history, 674 n. 55, 683 n. 54 & n. 68; dispute with Army over responsibility for 1941 disasters, 751 n. 10. *See also* Military Commissars; Political Administration; Purges; Trials; Stalin; Trotsky

'Concentric manoeuvre', analogous with double envelopment, 733 n. 115
'Concessions' (1921), military significance of, 151, 152, 153
Congresses, Russian Communist Party; 7th, 27; 8th, 46–9; 9th, 74, 115–16, 132; 10th, 120, 122, 125, 126, 693 n. 48; 11th, 131, 132–3, 133–4; 12th, 140–1; 13th, 187; 14th, 201, 239, 314; 15th, 301, 314; 16th, 304, 314–15, 321, 332, 334; 17th, 375, 379, 510; 18th, 510–11, 512–13; 21st, 447
Congresses of Soviets; 2nd, 11, 12; 3rd, 19; 7th, 74; 3rd (1925), 209; 6th (1931), 332; 7th (1935), 380; 8th Extraordinary (1936), 445
Constitution, 1924, and *RVS SSSR*, 172
'Corngrowers Union', 180
Cossack formations, re-introduced 1936, 422, 423, 730 n. 48
Cot, P., 364, 365
Coulondre, R., 431, 432, 471, 489, 503, 515, 737 n. 48
Courts of Honour, introduced into Red Army, 555
Crato, Major, 259
Cripps, Sir S., 574, 586, 627
Cruiser-building programme, Soviet naval forces, 1937–8, 476
Czechoslovak Legion (1918), 29, 54
Czechoslovakia, 385, 386, 387, 394, 417, 419, 424, 433, 453, 454, 489, 490, 491–2, 503–504

Dairen Conference (1921), 224, 225
Daladier, E., 454, 514, 737 n. 48
Danilov, Yu., 28, 776
Danishevskii, 53
Darlan, Admiral, 431
Dastic, Lieutenant-Colonel, 490
David, J., 464
Davies, J. E., 489
de Gaulle, General C., 412, 459
Defence Committee (*Komitet Oborony*), 477
Dekanozov, V. G., 577, 579
Delbos, Y., 431
Der Kampf der Marine gegen Versailles 1919–1935 (German naval study), 255
Dereluft, mixed Soviet-German air-transportation company, 159
Derevyanskii, 541
Deserters, 78, 93, 139, 685 n. 84
Deutsch, F., 147, 148
Deutschland zwischen Ost und West, 343
Dibrov, Corps Commissar P. A., 589
Die Geschichte des Deutschen Generalstabes 1918–1945, 150
Diplomacy, and war-making, Shaposhnikov on, 294; in relation to war-plan, Tukhachevsky on, 295
Directorate of Political Education (*Glavpolitprosvet*), 125
Dirksen, Dr H. von, 255, 256, 261, 280, 343, 344, 365
Disciplinary codes, 1919, 42; 1940, 555; Soviet replacement of Imperial Russian manual, 705 n. 128
Doihara, Colonel, 336
Dokumente zum Unternehmen 'Seelöwe', 557
Domozhirov, 66
Douhet, General G., 382, 408, 410
'Douhet-ism', 382
Doumenc, General J., 525, 526, 529, 531
Dovator, Major-General L. M., 633, 651, 663
Dovgalevsky(-ii), V. S., 343
Draganov, Bulgarian minister, 532
Dragun, Red Army major, 524
Drax, Admiral Sir R. A. R., 525, 527, 529, 531
Dresden Infantry School, 280, 341
Drunkenness, 311
Dubenskii, deputy head of Zhukovskii Air Academy, 367
Dukhonin, General, 14–15
Dumenko, cavalry commander, 51, 70, 71
Dushkenov, Northern Fleet commander, 475
Dutov, Cossack General, 15, 65
Dve Zhizni, 124
Dybenko, P. E., 12, 76, 77, 122, 200, 460, 463, 501, 502, 837–8
Dzerzhinskii, F. E., 45, 58, 66, 89, 141, 287

East Siberian Soviet Army, 1920, 219
Eden, A. (Earl of Avon), 586, 574
Edgewood Arsenal, 291
Egorov. *See* Yegorov
Eideman, Army Commander R. P., commander XIII Army, 102; in Germany, 259; and *Osoaviakhim*, 307; on Verkhovskii, 309; member of Tukhachevsky command group, 327; command posts, 1932, 340; criticised in 1935, 388; denounced, 461; 'case' and 'trial', 463; mentioned in 1938 Trial, 484; biography, 838
Eikhe, G. K., 61, 73, 220, 223, 682 n. 40
Eimannsberger, General L. von, 410
Electric digging machines, 548
Electric power, production losses in 1941, 665
Eliava, Sh. E., 171
Eliseyev, Rear-Admiral I. D., 586
Eltze, official of *Rheinmetall*, 273, 274
Empire of Fear, 449
Encirclement, tactical methods tested in 1933 manoeuvres, 352
Engels (destroyer), 252
Engels, F., 302, 309
Engineer troops, Red Army, 167, 389
'Enveloping manoeuvre', Savinov on, 1934, 733 n. 115
Enver Pasha, 146–7, 149, 150, 702 n. 66
Estonia, 385, 418, 516, 528, 540

Evacuation Soviet, 1941, 616
Evdokimov, G. E., 141, 425
Extraordinary Commission for Red Army Supply, 38
Extraordinary Military Staff, 1918, 676 n. 7
Extraordinary Plenipotentiary of the Red Army Supply Council, 38
Extraordinary Staff of the Soviet Army, 1918, 676 n. 6
Ezhov. *See* Yezhov

Fabry, J., 395
Factory No. 8 (Soviet-German enterprises), 157; No. 22, 154, 161; No. 24, 154
Faculty of Mechanisation and Motorisation (Leningrad), 333
Faculty of Supply, Military Academy, 195
Falkenhausen, General von, 280
Far Eastern Red Banner Front. *See* Red Banner Front
Far Eastern Regional Party Committee, 221
Far Eastern Republic, 114, 218–19, 220, 221, 222, 223, 224, 225, 226
Far Eastern Republic National Assembly, 224
Far Eastern Soviet of People's Commissars, 218
Fedko, 122
Fedotoff White, D., 17, 113
Fedyuninskii, Major-General I. I., 634, 635, 656
Feklenko, Divisional Commander N. V., 745 n. 28
Feldman, B. M., head of Command Staff Administration, 341, 370, 388
Feng Yu-hsiang, General, 228, 231, 233, 236, 244
Fervacque, P., 412
Field Administration of Aviation Units (*Aviadarm*), 75
Field Staff. *See* Staff
Fierlinger, Z., 503
'Fighting Detachments of the People's Militia' (*BONV*), 9
Filatov, Lieutenant-General P. M., 590, 600
Filipovskii, Infantry Inspectorate, 367
Finland, 290, 385, 415, 417, 516, 528, 540, 541–2, 543–52 *passim*, 631
Fire-control system (*PUAZO–1*), 407
First World War, Soviet study of, 184, 186, 209, 294, 306
Fischer, Colonel, 158, 252, 255, 256, 257, 259, 261, 340, 711 n. 29
Fishman, Ya. M., head of Red Army Chemical Warfare/Chemical Troops, 27, 266, 279, 344, 345, 347, 349
Five-Year Plans
  First, 245, 301, 302, 322; Second, 382, 403; Third, 390, 410
Flegontov, A., 225
Fokker D–XIII aircraft, 159
Fominyi, Corps Commander A. Ya., 590
Foreign Affairs (journal), 452, 459
Foreign Armies (published Moscow, *VNO*, 1926), 248
Fortified districts (*ukreplennyi raion*: *UR*), 167; functions of, 406; manning of, 569; unfinished state of, 1941, 570; of Minsk and Bobruisk, 1941, 572; in relation to divisional frontage, 591; condition of, June 1941, 751–2 n. 15
Forty-Six, The, oppositional group, 142, 164–5
France, 153, 156, 159, 289, 332, 339, 342, 348, 364, 365, 385, 386, 387, 394, 395, 400, 401, 412, 416–17, 428, 429, 432, 433, 453–4, 489, 503–4, 513–14, 515–16, 517, 522–9, 542, 556. *See also* Military Collaboration
Franco, General, 428
Frankel, A., 146
Fremde Heere Ost ('Foreign Armies East': German Military Intelligence on Red Army), 560, 574, 612
Friedrichson, *NKVD* agent, 396, 432, 453
Frinovskii, *NKVD* Corps Commander M., 390, 428, 457, 469, 492, 493
Fritsch, Colonel-General W. von. 411, 412, 464, 474
Frolov, Captain, 524
Frolov, Lieutenant-General V. A., 589, 607
Frontier commands, readiness state lowered 1941, 569
Frontier defences; *tochka* system, Far East, 361; delay with, Baltic Special MD, 1941, 569–70; and field fortifications, Western Special MD, 572; rapidly pierced, 22nd June 1941, 587
Frontier troops (under *NKVD* command), 378, 390, 569, 571, 585, 586
Frunze, M. V., 6, 9, 668; early military experience, 59; assumes command IVth Army, 61, 681 n. 18; role in Eastern Front counter-offensive, 63; praised by Trotsky, 74; as exception among military Communists, 79–80, 681 n. 25; faith in Red Army, 82; command against Wrangel, 1920, 105; asks for 1st Cavalry Army, 106; reform schemes for Red Army, 120; and Central Committee, 125; and disbanding of 1st Cavalry Army, 126; on unified military doctrine, 127; ridiculed by Trotsky, 128; mission to Turkey, 130–1; on military programme, 1922, 131; Theses at 11th Congress, 132, 133, 134–5; for proletarian control of militia, 137; and Military Commission, 166–7; member of special commission, 168; verdict on state of Red Army, 170; successor to Sklyanskii, 171; opportunity as reformer, 172; Chief of Staff, 1924, 173; on importance of the Staff, 173–4; and military administration; 174–5; and *VVS*, *VMF*, 175, 700 n. 32,

and military budget, 177; on command, and the commissar, 177–8; frankness over 'mixed military system', 179; his military-administrative policy, 181; on Soviet infantry, 182, 701 n. 59; and Soviet cavalry, 183, 702 n. 64; on tractors, 184; insists that Red Army not a *Russian* army, 184; views of future war, 186; and Political Administration, 187–8, 702 n. 5; successor to Trotsky as head of Red Army, 189; on Party work and military discipline, 190; and command staff, 192; on the ideal of a Soviet officer, 193, 703 n. 90; temporary head of Military Academy, 194–5; on unitary command, 196; on non-Party officers, 197; issues Directive No. 234, 1925, 198; suspicious circumstances of death, 1925, 199–200; speeds work on manuals, regulations, 207; on Soviet strategy, 208–9; specifies four fundamental characteristics of future war, 210–11; influence of ideas in evolution of Staff, 282; on para-military training, 283; positional warfare, conclusions on shared by Tukhachevsky, 296; inevitable emphasis on man-power, 302; 'Frunze system' modified, 1934, 372; biography, 838
Fuller, Major-General J. F. C., 308, 318, 355, 382
Furmanov, D., military commissar, 40, 79
Fuselage-construction plants, location 1941, 575

Gai, G. D., cavalry commander, 61, 93
'Galen' or 'Galin'. *See* Blyukher
Gallenkamp, Captain, 263
Galler, Admiral L. M., 392, 450, 476, 477, 554, 838–9
Gamarnik, Army Commissar Ya. B., 13, 246, 465, 512; head of Political Administration, 1929, 314; political inclinations, 315; Deputy Defence Commissar, 327; and Far Eastern commissars, 367; position in hierarchy and bureaucracy, 371, 372; and maintenance of Army loyalty, 404; mentioned in possible mobilisation order, 419; influence on development of commissar staff, 423; and Central Committee plenum, 1937, 452; at May Day parade, 1937, 458; 'suicide', and doubtfulness of, 461, 736 n. 42; mentioned at 1938 Trial, 482, 485; 're-habilitation' and vindication of loyalty to state and Party, 737 n. 48; biography, 839
Gamelin, General M. J., 365, 400, 412, 416, 454, 503, 504, 514, 526, 548
Gas-shells and grenades, request for experiments with, 265
Gatovskii, cavalry expert, 114
Gavrilovic, M., 573
Gekker, A. I., head of Red Army Foreign Liaison, 123, 384, 385, 458, 462
Gendun, 415
General Staff of the Red Army. *See* Staff
Georgia, 123–4
Gerasimenko, Lieutenant-General V. F., 601
German Red Army (1923), 160–1
Germanovich, Corps Commander, 450
Germany, 92, 109–10, 144–63 *passim*, 247–82 *passim*, 291, 320, 331, 340, 341, 342, 343, 339–49 *passim*, 363, 365, 378–9, 380, 383–4, 385, 396, 400, 403, 408, 410, 411, 413, 414, 415, 416–17, 419, 421, 428, 432, 433, 453, 454, 464, 469, 476, 488–9, 503, 504, 513, 514, 515, 516–17, 522, 523, 528, 529–30, 530–2, 537–8, 539, 540, 541, 547, 555–6, 557, 559, 560–1, 565–7, 572–3, 577–9, 690 n. 81. *See also* Hitler; Kandelaki; Military Collaboration; Military Operations; *Operation Barbarossa*; Pacts; *Reichswehr*; *Sicherheitsdienst*; Stalin
Geronimus, A. A., 142
Gesellschaft zur Förderung Gewerblicher Unternehmungen (*GEFU*), 151, 158, 212, 250
Gessler, Dr O., 150, 251, 257
Getman, A. L., tank warfare expert, 508
Gittis, V. M., 70, 85, 86, 104
Glavmorput. *See* Northern Sea Route
Göring, H., 386, 411
GOKO. *See* State Defence Committee
Golikov, Marshal F. I., 538, 554, 639, 653
Goloschekin, F. I., 64
Golovanov, Aviation Marshal A., 499, 743 n. 72
Goltz, General R. Count von der, 145
Golubev, Major-General M. D., 643
Gongota Agreement (1920), 220
Gorb, senior *NKVD* officer, 428
Gorbachov, B. S., 843, 845
Gorev, B. I., 308
Gorky(-ii), M., 378
Gorodnyanskii, Major-General A. M., 653
Gorodovikov, Colonel-General O. I., 71, 102, 105, 554
Gorolenko, Lieutenant-General F. D., 589
Gorshenin, reported as head of *Osoaviakhim*, 461
Goryachev, Corps Commander E. I., 463, 502
Govorov, Marshal of Artillery L. A., 558, 624, 651, 654, 662
Grand Strategy (Vol. II), 574
Great Britain, 91, 148, 153, 156, 210, 227, 238, 284, 289, 354, 386, 414, 419, 421, 422, 428, 467, 476, 489, 503, 513–14, 517, 522–9, 540, 542, 556, 560, 573, 574, 578, 630–1, 664
Grechko, Marshal A. A., 508
Greece, 573, 579

Grendal', Colonel-General of Artillery V. D., 547, 554
Grigoriev, Ataman G., 69
Grigoriev, Signals commander Western MD, 1941, 600
Grigorovich, Colonel, V. I., 643
Grinko, G. F., 482
Grishin, A. S., 392
Groener, Lieutenant-General W., 145
'*Grosse Traktoren*'. *See* Tractors
'Group tactics', 136, 206, 695 n. 89. *See also* Rifle troops
Gubel'man, M., 221, 223
Guchkov, A. I., 435
Guderian, Colonel-General H., 347, 390, 587, 600, 601, 602, 609, 610, 612, 617, 622, 624, 639, 640, 653, 662
Gugin, G., senior commissar of Black Sea Fleet, 392
Gulin, Supply chief, Far Eastern forces, 493
Gun-barrels, main production centres for, 1941, 575
Gurov. *See* Blyukher
Gusev, S. I., 43, 57, 61, 63, 66, 104, 105, 120, 125, 129–30, 138, 166, 168, 169, 171, 188, 299, 681 n. 31, 693 n. 65, 693–4 n. 67, 782, 839

Haber, Dr F., 272
Halder, Colonel-General F., 560, 563, 596, 597, 598, 600, 601, 602, 608, 609, 756 n. 113
Halder Diary, 585, 603
Haller, General, 98
Hallmich, Captain, 263
Halm, Major-General, 259, 271, 272
Hammerstein-Equord, Colonel-General K. von, 271, 272, 273–4, 280, 331, 342, 435, 456
Hansard (May 1930), 269
Hartmann, Major O., 263, 343, 344, 345, 346, 347, 348, 364
Hasse, General P. von, 151, 152, 154, 159, 163, 248, 250
Hasse Diary, 153, 696 n. 29
Hata, General S., 335
Hayashi, Colonel S., 337
'Heavy Vehicle Experimental and Test Station', 257
Heeresleitung, 253, 277, 347
Heim Deutscher Angestellter Moskau, 261. *See also Zentrale Moskau*
Heinrich, Lieutenant-General (Finnish Army), 552
Henrys, General P., 91
'Herr Untermann'. *See* Unshlikht
Herriot, E., 343, 365, 413
Hesse, German pilot, 146
Hey, *Auswärtiges Amt* official, 148
Heydrich, R., 433, 434, 435, 456, 457, 471, 731 n. 85
Heye, Colonel-General W., 256, 272, 711 n. 29
Heywood, Major-General T. G., 525, 526, 527 531
Higher Academic Military-Pedagogic Soviet of the Red Army, 128
Higher Attestation Commission, 49, 193, 204
Hilger, G., 92, 148
Himmler, H., 435, 474
Hintze, Admiral, 147, 152, 154
History of the Communist Party of the Soviet Union (Bolsheviks), 122
Hitler, A., 342, 343, 379, 383, 400, 403, 411, 416, 417, 429, 433, 434, 435, 458, 474, 488, 504, 515, 530, 557, 559, 560, 566, 574, 584, 585, 609, 617, 654, 655, 721 n. 86, 749 n. 122 & n. 135
Ho Lun, 237
Hoepner, General, 588, 639, 651
Hoetzendorff, Field Marshal K. von, 293
Homma, Major-General M., 468
Hopkins, Harry L., 627
Hormel, Captain, 275
Hoth, General, 259, 588, 601, 602, 609
Howard, R., 414, 415, 418
Hungary, Soviet Republic of (1919), 64, 69
Hunt Club (Moscow), 114

Ice-breakers (Baltic Fleet), 77
'Ice-road' (Lake Ladoga), 1941, 629
Illiteracy, 182
Imperator Pavel I (battleship), 12
Imperial Austrian Army, 282, 329
Imperial Russian Army; mutiny, 1917, 3; Bolsheviks in, 7; strength, 1917, 9, 672 n. 16; commissars in, 10; General Posokhov on, 13; struggle over *Stavka*, 14–15; demobilisation of, 16; and formation of Red Army, 19; ex-officers and Red Army, 26; characteristics of officer corps, 32; role of ex-NCOs and Red Army, 32; ex-officers and Civil War, 53; Zhukov's service in, 71; similarity of drives on Warsaw, 1830 and 1920, 100; Bagramyan, cadet in, 508; Soviet reference to campaigns of 1808–9, Finnish War, 547; Courts of Honour, introduced into Red Army 1940, 555. *See also* 'Military Specialists'; Shaposhnikov; Tukhachevsky
India, 238
Indriksson, commissar to head of Zhukovskii Air Academy, 367
'Industrial Commission' (German), 146
Industrial evacuation, 1941, 608, 616, 617
Industrial mobilisation, in 1927, 285; partial, spring 1941, 574–5; national economic mobilisation plan, 3rd & 4th quarter 1941, 616
Industrial planning, and the war-plan, Tukhachevsky on, 295
Industrialisation; strategic aspects of, 285, 295; investment and tempo, 301; and defence

requirements, 302, 303; investment in armaments, 1929–41, 304; production costs, 1931, 305; and *STO*, 306; role of the manufacturing licence, 349; and progress in Soviet Far East, 362–3
Infantry forces, Red Army. *See* Rifle troops
Ingenieurskantor voor Scheepsbouw (I.v.S.), 253
Inspector-General of Armaments, 370
Inspectorates: Military-Naval (*Rabkrin*), 141, 164; Cavalry, 178, 367; Militia, 178; Artillery, 367; Infantry, 367; and Red Army Staff, 1934, 370; *VVS*, 388; Naval, 475; Civil Air Fleet, 796
Inspektion der Kraftfahrttruppen, 269
Institute of Junior Scientific Assistants, Military Academy, 195
Instruction on Military Commissars (1922), 195
Instruction on Red Army Military Schools (1925), 194
Intelligence (*razvedka*), functions of divisional intelligence, 438
Intelligence Summary 23(Washington), 414
'International Brigades', formed in Red Army 1918, 675 n. 3 & n. 4; and Spanish Civil War, 429, 430, 431
International Communications Section (*OMS: Komintern*), 160
International Military Tribunal (*IMT*), Nuremberg, 331
Ioffe, A. A., 154, 226, 227, 228
Ippo, head of Leningrad Military-Political Academy, 458, 460–1
Iran, 290, 630
Isakov, Admiral I. S., 450, 477, 554
Istoriya Velikoi Otechestvennoi Voiny Sovetskovo Soyuza 1941–1945 (Vol. 1), 304, 430, 497, 572, 592, 750
Ivanov, Major-General I. I., 634
Ivanov, Captain 1st Class M. V., 77
Ivanov, Brigade Commissar N. P., 643
Ivanov, Colonel-General S. P., 660
Izvestiya (newspaper), 248, 429, 490, 556, 563, 585
Izvolsky(-ii), A., 387

Jahnke, German intelligence expert, 434
Japan, 217, 219, 224, 225, 238, 239, 241, 244, 245, 290, 291, 334, 335, 357–8, 361, 362, 363, 379, 397, 398, 399, 400, 408, 414, 415, 419, 421, 432, 466–7, 468–9, 490, 494–9, 515, 517–18, 518–22, 532, 577–8, 599, 631. *See also* Kwantung Army; Manchuria; Military Operations; Mongolia, Inner and Outer; Pacts; Treaties
Jaurès, J., 676 n. 14
Jeannel, General, 504
Joint Intelligence Committee (British), 574
Junkers, German aircraft firm, 146, 152, 154, 155, 157, 160, 161, 162, 163, 250, 340, 485
Junkers, Professor, 151, 161

Kachalov, General, 602
Kachanov, 741 n. 43
Kadostkii, commander of Amur Flotilla, 475
Kaganovich, L. M., 20, 403, 426, 491, 598
Kaganovich, M. M., 512, 558
Kakurin, N. E., 93, 94, 100
Kaledin, General A. M., 17
Kalinin, M. I., 121, 288, 432, 477, 490, 500, 598
Kalinovskii, K. B., 270
Kalmykov, commander of *Kolkhoz* Corps, 363, 397
Kamenev, L. B., 140, 141, 189, 201, 288, 391, 425
Kamenev, S. S., 57, 61, 80; fortunes as Eastern Front commander, 63; favours advance in the east, 64; becomes Commander-in-Chief, 66; operational plan against Denikin, 69–70; failure, 71; operational plan against Poles, 1920, 86; directive to Yegorov, 89; discussion with Yegorov, 90; optimism over drive on Warsaw, 92; Directive of 23rd July 1920, 93; and Yegorov, Tukhachevsky, 94; difference of opinion with Tukhachevsky, 95, 688 n. 46; orders to Yegorov, 97; explanation of failure in Poland, 99; and member *RVSR*, 171; attached to Inspectorate, 173, 178; member of *RVS SSSR*, 1925, 200; speaks on France, 332
Kandelaki, D., 396, 397, 432, 453, 458, 464, 731 n. 79
Kaplan, Fanya, 54
Kappel, General V. O., 55
Karakhan, L. M., 151, 222, 227, 228, 335
Karbyshev, Lieutenant-General D. M., 61, 558
Kashirin, I. D., cavalry commander, 64, 65, 133, 463, 501, 682 n. 39
Katukov, Colonel-General of Tank Troops M. E., 624, 633, 640, 651, 663
Katyn massacre (Polish prisoners-of-war held in Soviet Union), 1941, 664
'Katyusha', rocket-projectile launcher, 614
Katyushin-Kotov, F. M., 234
Kazan tank-school (Soviet-German), 251, 256, 257, 258, 264, 265, 269, 270, 333, 346, 347
Kazan Veterinary University, 195
Kedrov, M. S., 7, 34, 377
Kemal Ataturk, 130
Kennan, George F., 34
Kerensky(-ii), A. F., 11, 13, 17
Kesselring, Field Marshal, 600
Khalepskii, Army Commander I., head of Red Army armoured forces, 327, 333, 347, 410, 436, 437, 460, 503, 729 n. 17
Khanzhin, General M. V., 61
Kharitonov, Major-General F. M., 641, 643, 647
Kharkov (destroyer flotilla leader), 657

Kharkov Locomotive-Construction Works, 270
Khazkelevich, Major-General M. G., 590
Khinchuk, L., 342, 343
Khlembovskii, General, 8
Khlopov, Soviet Deputy Military Attaché, 579
Khmelev, A., 237
Khmelevskii, Zhukovskii Air Academy command staff, 367
Khomenko, Major-General V. A., 640
Khrenov, Colonel-General of Red Army Engineers A. F., 554
Khripin, V. V., deputy chief of *VVS*, 372, 382, 383, 408, 409, 410, 436, 437, 445, 500, 501
Khrulev, Colonel-General A. V., 599
Khrushchev, N. S., 80, 132, 378, 447, 471, 504, 510, 575, 579, 580, 581, 593, 598, 603, 607, 608, 623, 626, 627, 667, 701 n. 59, 735 n. 11, 744 n. 89, 755 n. 81
Khvesin, T. S., 57, 91
Khvostikov, General, 103
Kikvidze, V. I., cavalry commander, 80
Kinzel, Colonel, 560
Kinzel, Naval Captain, 252, 280
Kirov, S. M., 75, 80, 123, 125, 201, 378, 391
Kirov Infantry School, 604
Kirponos, Colonel-General M. P., 554, 568, 571, 581–2, 584, 590, 596, 597, 607, 612
'Kisanka'. *See* Bubnov
Kivimaki, Finnish Ambassador in Moscow, 417
Klado, Captain, 355
Klausen, M., 414
Kleber, cover-name for Stern, International Brigade commander in Spain, 430, 431, 452
Kleist, Field Marshal von, 588, 607, 621, 641, 642, 646, 647
Klement'ev, Corps Commissar N. N., 589
Klenov, Lieutenant-General P. S., 589, 603–4, 755 n. 82
Klimovskii, Major-General V. E., 590, 600
Klokov, General, 576
Kluge, Field Marshal G. von, 641, 650, 654
Klykov, Lieutenant-General N. K., 620, 635, 637, 757 n. 134
Knox, Major-General Sir A. W. F., 6
Kobayashi, Major-General N., 520
Köpke, G., 256
Köstring, Major-General, 263, 333, 343, 395, 411, 412, 451, 537, 539, 560, 720 n. 5
KŌGUN, 337
Koiso, K., 357
Kolchak, Admiral A. V., 57, 68, 69, 113, 218
Kolomiets, Major-General T. K., 642
Komintern (Communist International), 84; Tukhachevsky's letter on, 1920, 107–8, 118; idea of international general staff rejected, 134; and Ruhr crisis, 1923, 160; German fears of, 161; Zinoviev expelled as president, 202; and Chinese revolution, 221–2, 226; and *Kuomintang*, 227; Blomberg's complaint over, 265; and diplomacy, 290; and Tukhachevsky, 1929, 308; and *KPD*, 330; Kleber's activity in, 430; role in Spain, 431; Coulondre's suggestion on, 432; mentioned in Kandelaki negotiations, 453
Kommunist (Soviet journal), 80, 668
Komsomol, 176, 180, 190, 319, 373, 374, 477, 478, 700 n. 37
Komsomol (Chinese), 232
Komsomolskaya Pravda (newspaper), 461
Koniev, Marshal I. S., 204, 494, 554, 602, 617, 618, 624, 650, 651, 654, 662, 839–40
Konstantinov, Colonel-General M. P., 184
Konstruktionsbüro (Soviet-German), 273, 274
Kopets, Lieutenant-General of Aviation, 600
Kopp, V. E., 92, 147, 148, 149, 150, 151, 163, 239, 247, 485, 690 n. 81
Korea, 217, 336, 495
Kork, Army Commander A. I.; commander XV Army, 1920, 88; commander Western MD, 202; Attaché in Germany, 261; recalled, 1929, 271; and Tukhachevsky group, 327; *Komandarm* II, 392; denounced, 458; arrested, 461; 'case' and 'trial', 463; mentioned in 1938 Trial, 483, 484, 486; biography, 840
Kornilov, General L. G., 8
Korobkov, Major-General A. A., 590, 600
Koroteyev, Major-General K. A., 642
Koshchanov, Black Sea Fleet commander, 392, 410, 475
Koshevnikov, Chief of Command Faculty, Air Academy, 367
Kossior, S. V., 168
Kostenko, Lieutenant-General F. Ya., 590, 653, 658
Kostikov, designer of 'Katyusha', 614
Kostyayev, 63, 681 n. 29
Kosygin, A. N., 616
Kotovskii, G. I., cavalry commander, 80
Kovalev, Army Commander M. P., 524, 538, 539
Koval'skii, V. V., 77
Kovtyukh, E. I., cavalry commander, 80
Kozlov, Lieutenant-General D. T., 657
Kozlovskii, General, 692 n. 27
Krainyukov, Brigade Commissar, K. V., 643
Krasnaya Nov (Soviet journal), 144
Krasnaya Zvezda (Red Army newspaper), 122, 206, 394, 458, 460, 461
Krasnoshchekov (Tobelson), A., 218, 219, 222
Krasnov, General P. N., 12, 67
Krasnyi Kavkaz (cruiser), 657
Krassin, L., 38, 151
Kravchenko, Lieutenant-General of Aviation G. P., 554
Krebs, General, 578, 580

Krejčí, General, 419
Krestinsky(-ii), N. N., 66, 154, 157, 161, 162, 163, 249, 256, 275, 343, 447, 481, 482, 483–4, 485, 486, 487, 488
Krivitsky, W. G., 160, 356, 377, 378, 380, 396, 403, 429, 430, 431, 435, 436, 452, 455, 457, 458, 463, 471, 472, 724 n. 19
Kronstadt rebellion (1921), 120–1, 121–2, 125, 176, 464, 692 n. 30
Kronstadt Soviet Executive Committee, 121
Kropachev, divisional commissar, 493, 494
Krupps, 144, 150, 152, 153, 157, 268, 273
Krylenko, N. V., 5, 7, 12, 14–15, 27
Krylov, professor at Naval Academy, 500
Kühlenthal, Colonel, 271, 272, 281
Kühn, Captain, 269
Kuibyshev, V. V., 15, 61, 75, 80, 125, 141, 378
Kuliev, Ya., divisional commander, 184
Kulik, Marshal G. I., 508, 553
Kulikov, R., 34
Kun, Bela, 105, 460
Kuomintang, 226, 227, 228, 230, 231, 232, 233, 235, 237, 238
Kurasov, V. V., 508
Kurskii, 89
Kutyakov, I. S., cavalry commander, 80, 89
Kushchev, Brigade Commander A. M., 745 n. 28
Kuusinen, O., 542, 548
Kuzmin, commissar, 121
Kuz'min, N. F., 103
Kuznetsov, Colonel-General F. I., 589, 602, 610
Kuznetsov, Admiral N. G., 338; promoted Captain 1st grade, 392; Naval Commissar, 500; on new naval programme, 512; meets Anglo-French military mission, 524, 525; promoted Admiral, 554; alerts naval forces, 22nd June 1941, 586–7; member of *Stavka*, 598; and Odessa defence, 609–10
Kuznetsov, Lieutenant-General V. I., 538, 590, 593, 639, 651, 663
Kwantung Army, 240, 244, 333, 334, 335, 336, 361, 365, 398, 399, 400, 495, 497, 498, 518, 536, 537, 599, 631. *See also* Military Operations
Kwantung Army Special Exercise (*Kan-Toku-En*) 1941, 599

'Labour Armies', 85, 119
Lagovskii, Major-General A., 615, 757 n. 128
Lagunov, Major-General F. N., 629
Lahs, Captain, 253
Lapchinskii, A. N., on tactical aviation, 382–3, 825 n. 36
Lapin, A. I., 241, 397
Larin, Yu., 46, 134
Lashevich, M. M., 10, 27, 46, 57, 63, 141, 170, 200, 201, 202, 203, 678 n. 50
Laskin, Colonel, 642
Latvia, 385, 418, 516, 528, 540
Laval, P., 386, 394, 395, 400
Lavochkin, S. A., 501
Lazarev, Major-General I. G., 757 n. 134
Lazarevich, 154
Lazimir, 68
Lazo, S., 218, 221
Le Temps, 416
League of Nations Armaments Handbook, 389
Lebedev, adjutant to Khalepskii, 333
Lebedev, N. N., 13
Lebedev, General P. P., 36, 56, 80, 89, 149, 152, 153, 159, 169, 177, 178, 279, 367, 698 n. 57, 699 n. 11, 840
Leeb, Field Marshal W. R. von, 588, 604, 609
Legal consultants, 193
Lelyushenko, Colonel-General D. D., 554, 622, 640, 651, 654, 663
Lenin, V. I., 3; and 'sealed train', 5; during 'July days', 5; instruction to Podvoiskii, 11, 776; and Russian armed forces, 17, 674 n. 49; on 'Socialist Army', 18; and 'Left Communists', 27; support over 'military specialists', 34; president of Soviet of Workers and Peasants Defence, 38; Stalin's complaint to, 39; support for Trotsky, 46; wounded, 1918, 55; urges conquest of Urals, 63; requires link with Soviet Hungary, 64; signal from Stalin at Tsaritsyn, 67; concern over N. Caucasus and Don, 68, 69; intervenes in Southern Front dispute, 70, 683 n. 68; Budenny's personal appeal to, 1920, 74, 783; demands blocking of Crimea, 85–6; telegram to Stalin, 1920, 89; comment on 1st Cavalry Army, 99; against continuation of war, 104; and appointment of Frunze, 105; suspects Frunze's optimism, 106; and Frunze-Gusev theses, 1921, 120; instruction on Georgia, 124; caution over 'proletarian military science', 134, 694 n. 82; illness, 139; moves against Stalin, 140; and German connection, 146, 150; attitude over German war industry, 151; persuaded not to have Baltic Fleet scuttled, 176; and Far Eastern Republic, 219, 226; letters to carried by Chiang Kai-shek, 227, 228; interest in and respect for Clausewitz, 292; cited by Voroshilov, 1939, 511
Leningrad; Frunze on threat to, 290; defence plans for, 1932–3, 353; revised defence plan, 1941, 570, 583; Voroshilov and Zhdanov organise defence, July 1941, 605; Stalin and City Defence Soviet, 606; reserve food supplies, 618; air-lift organised, 618; 'ice-road', Lake Ladoga, 629
Leningrad Electrotechnical Institute, 195

Leningrad Militia Army (*LANO*), organised 1941, 604
Leonov, 275
'Letter to Friends' (Trotsky), 1928, 299
Levandovskii, Army Commander M. K., 123, 202, 494, 742 n. 53
Levchenko, Vice-Admiral G. I., 642
Levichev, Soviet Military Attaché, 346, 388
Levin, M., 27
Li Tsung-yen, 236
Liaison, ground-air forces, 440; at Khalkhin-Gol, 533
Liao Chung-k'ai, 229, 230, 231, 708 n. 56
Liddell Hart, Captain B. G., 308, 459, 666
Lipetsk air-base (Soviet-German), 159, 161, 248, 251, 256, 261, 264, 265, 269, 278, 345, 346, 347, 382
'Liquidation-ism', as applied to Political Administration, 187
Lithuania, 290, 333, 385, 417, 418, 424, 454, 488–9, 539, 540
Litvinov, M. M., 239, 256–7, 258, 328, 330, 332, 333, 335, 336, 338, 339, 357, 358, 362, 363, 379, 384, 386, 387, 397, 400, 411, 416, 429, 431, 468, 488, 489, 490, 491–2, 497, 503, 514, 515, 516, 541
Lockhart, Sir R. Bruce, 12
Löwenfeld, Naval Captain, 251
Lohmann, Naval Captain, 251
Loiseau, General, 394, 732 n. 95
Loktinov, Corps Commander, head of *VVS*, 501, 524, 525, 807
Lominadze, B., 237, 338
London Naval Conference (1936), 419
Lopatin, Lieutenant-General A. I., 642
Lozovskii, 490
Luchinskii, General A. A., 184
Ludendorff, General E., 147, 162, 507
Ludri, Ya. N., Chief of Naval Staff, 410, 450, 470, 475
Ludwig ('Herr Ludwig'), General, 272–3, 274, 281, 306, 331, 341
Ludwig, E., 339
Luftwaffe, on the Eastern Front, 584, 587, 593, 594, 596, 600, 601, 615, 618; estimate of Soviet air strength and deployment, 1941, 807–8
Lukin, Lieutenant-General M. F., 601
Luniev, Soviet Military Attaché, 252, 261, 263
Lutskii, A. N., 221
Lutz, Major-General, 269, 347
Lyapin, Major-General, 634
Lyushkov, senior *NKVD* officer, 727 n. 84

Ma, General, 335
Maasing, Colonel, 418, 450
Machine-gun barrels, 273
Machine-guns, monthly production, 1941, 575
Main Administration of the Red Army, 203
Main Administration of the Workers-Peasants Military Air Fleet (1918), 75
Main Commission for Manuals and Regulations, 558
Main Directorate of the General Staff (1918), 34
Main Directorate of Military Education, 33
Main Intelligence Administration of the Red Army (*GRU*). *See* Military Intelligence
Main Military Procuracy (*GVP*), 476
Main Military Soviet (1938), 478, 547, 553, 557
Main Naval Soviet (1938), 476
Main Operating Staff (East Siberian Army), 219
Main Supply Administration (*Glavnachsnab*), 165, 175
Maisky(-ii), I., 416, 574, 630
Makhno, N., 87, 102, 107, 114, 690 n. 89
Maksimovich, 77
Malandin, Colonel-General G. K., 508, 600
Malbrandt, Colonel, 269
Malcolm, General, 146
Malenkov, G. M., 73, 598
Malinovskii, Marshal R. Ya., 4, 132, 430, 658
Maltzan, A. von, 148, 149, 154
Mamontov, E. M., 65
Mamontov, General K. K., 71
Manchester Guardian, 250, 710 n. 11
Manchuria (also 'Manchukuo'), 217, 239, 240, 241, 242–4, 245, 334, 335, 336, 338, 358, 361, 397, 398, 399, 414, 415, 468, 517–18
Mannerheim, Marshal K. G., 551
'Mannerheim line', 543, 548, 549
Manstein, Field Marshal F. E. von, 656
Manuilskii, D. Z., 490
Mao Tse-tung, 400, 738 n. 68
Marat (battleship), 252
Marcks, Major-General, 560
Marineleitung, 213, 251, 252, 254, 255, 274, 275, 277, 280
Maring, *Komintern* agent in China, 226
Marksizm-Leninizm o voine i armii (1957 and 1958 Edn.), 615
Marshal of the Soviet Union, title introduced, 1935, 391
Martel, Lieutenant-General Sir Giffard, 402, 436, 437, 439
Martynov, General, 114
Marxism; and military doctrine, 128–9, 132; assimilation of by command group, 179; and 'military science', 186; Shaposhnikov's use of, 294; and problem of war, 319, 321
Maslennikov, Lieutenant-General I. I., 651
Matsuoka, Y., 577, 578, 631
Maurin, General, 396
Mdivani, B., 123
Mechanics, 406
'Mechanised companies' (1922), 136
Mechanised/motor-mechanised forces, Red Army
  m./m.-m. brigades: composition, 1930, 350; role and composition, 1935, 389–90

m. corps: composition, 1932, 350; disputes over role of, 355–6; disposition of, 353, 405; operational role, *PU–36*, 438; organisation of reconnaissance in, 1936, 732–3 n. 103; disbanding of, 508, 537, 747 n. 79; re-constituted, 1941, 571; as second echelon to frontier armies, 571, 589–91; again disbanded, autumn 1941, 614

m. regiments: organised, 1929, 270. *See also* Tank forces, Red Army; Tanks

Medvedev, N. P., divisional commander, 538

Mein Kampf, 379

Meissner, Hans-Otto, 414, 432, 631

Mekhlis, Army Commissar L. Z., 80, 105, 472, 478–9, 490, 492, 493, 494, 497, 508, 511, 557, 616, 841

Mekhonoshin, K. A., 7, 10, 27, 68

Melikov, V. A., 100, 308

Melnikov, Colonel, 624

Mel'nikov, B., 221, 224

Mendras, Colonel, French Military Attaché in Moscow, 349, 364, 365, 385, 723 n. 118

Men'shov, 61

Menzel, Lieutenant-Colonel, 157

Menzhinskii, V. R., 378

Merekalov, A., 515

Meretskov, Marshal K. A., 543, 544, 547, 554, 557, 558, 568, 634, 635, 649, 655

Merkulov, Major N. V., 643

Merkulov, S., 224

Mesis, Army Commissar 2nd grade, 461

Mezheninov, General S. A., 61, 90, 388

Mezhin, Yu. Yu., 105

Miaja, General, 452

Mikeladze, 51

Mikhailov, V., 61, 308

Mikoyan, A. I., 306, 541, 598, 616

Military Academies; training programme, 1918, 79; re-organisation, 1924–5, 194–5; system re-organised round 6 major centres, 1926, 205; social composition of students, 1924–6, 788; political, social educational composition of teaching staff, 1925, 789; organisation and specialisations, 1926, 791; general curriculum, 792; social composition, political affiliations of students, 1927, 793

Artillery: 79, 194

Dzerzhinskii Military-Technical: 205, 791

Frunze Military: 205, 262, 350, 367, 505, 508, 791

General Staff (1918): 79, 114, 128

General Staff (1936): 410, 508, 558

Military: 194, 195

Military-Administrative: 194

Military-Political: 205, 792

Military Aviation: 194

Military Engineering: 194

Military Medicine: 194

Stalin A. of Mechanisation and Motorisation: 350, 410, 450

Supply: 79

Zhukovskii

Military-Aviation: 205, 367, 410, 712 n. 70, 791. *See also* Chair of Military Industry; Faculty of Supply; Institute of Junior Scientific Assistants; Staff courses; Universities

Military administration: military commissariats, 1918, 20; chaos in, 26; re-organisation of, 30; Commissariat for Military Affairs created, 1918, 34; Military-administrative-supply organisation, Civil War, 35; central military executive formed, 36; supply and mobilisation, 38; centralising policies, 46–7; contradictory elements within, 51–2; investigation into workings of, 1923, 164–5; numerical strength of administrative staff, 1923–4, 167; 'dangerous elements' in, 169; Frunze's criticisms of, 170; new personnel proposed for, 171; preparation of basic reforms in, 1924, 171–2; formal subordination of, 172; and Red Army Administration, 173; position of Red Army Staff, 173–4; 'Communising' of, 174–5; Directive No. 390 (1926) on staff and administration, 203, 794–5; place of Main Military Procuracy, 368; specific functions of Defence Commissariat, 369; operation of administrative system, 369–71; re-organisations, 1938–9, 477–8; creation of autonomous military commissariats, 480. *See also* Military Commissariats; Military Districts; Mobilisation; People's Commissariats; *Revvoensoviet*; Supply

Military Air Force (*VVS/RKKA*); early organisation, Civil War, 75–6; percentage of strength of Red Army, 1922, 137; and opening of Lipetsk air-base, 158–9; 'No. 4 Squadron', of, 159; delivery of aero-engines from Germany, 161; numerical strength, 1923–4, 167; severe criticism of, 1924, 175; re-organisation and differentiation by combat functions, 176; Baranov appointed commander, 178; operational in Manchuria, 1929, 241, 242, 243; combat aircraft production, yearly averages, 1930–7, 304; estimated strength in flights and squadrons, 1930, 326; Alksnis commander of, 327; build-up of strength in Far East, 337; tactical role as 'air artillery', 350–1; deployment in Far East, 360, 722 n. 108; aviation administration and Defence Commissariat, 370; Party mobilisation for flying

Military Air Force (*VVS/RKKA*)—*contd.* and technical schools, 375; re-equipped, 1935, 382; strategic bomber force, 383, German opinion of, 1935, 384; Far Eastern bomber force, 399; plans for expansion, 1935, 403; estimated front-line strength, 1936, 405; Alksnis and Khripin emphasise offensive role, 408; 'aviation park' superseded by operational deployment, 409; possible operational targets, 418; and Czech aerodromes, 419; political staff in, 422; manoeuvres, 1936, 437; tactical role, *PU-36*, 438, 439–40, 801–3; Khripin on percentage of bombers, 445; aviation assistance to China, 469; and possible base in Slovakia, 489; Soviet fighters in China, 490; air cover for Chinese bases, 491; in Lake Khasan fighting, 498–9; Alksnis and Khripin no longer in command, 500; shift to defensive fighter aviation, 500–1, 512; difficulties of re-equipping, 501; Voroshilov, M. M. Kaganovich on, 1939, 512; in fighting at Khalkhin-Gol, 1939, 519, 522, 533, 536–7, 807; British and French estimates of, 1939, 524–5, 807; in Finnish war, 550, 552; need for bad-weather flying training, 1940, 553; slow rate of re-equipping with new fighters, 1941, 583; caught on the ground by the *Luftwaffe*, 22nd June 1941, 587; estimated losses after two days at war, 593; outclassed and outgunned by *Luftwaffe*, 600; losses by October 1941, 615; strength available for Moscow battles, 625, 639; numerical superiority in later Moscow battles, 661–2, 759 n. 26; *Luftwaffe* estimate of strength, 1941, 807; deployment before German attack, 808. *See also* Aero-engines; Aircraft; Alksnis; Aviation; Aviation formations; Aviation industry; Baranov, P. I.; Lavochkin; Lipetsk air-base; Loktinov; Pilots and pilot-training; Smushkevich; Tupolev

Military Collaboration: Soviet Russia/Soviet Union and

China: problem studied by Soviet officers, 1923, 227; military supplies for, 227–8; and Blyukher, Yegorov, 228; work with Whampoa Military Academy, 229; Soviet military mission for, 229–30; and Soviet senior advisers, 230–1; and Canton *coup*, 232; Northern Expedition, 233–4; reports of Soviet officers, 234–5; and Chinese Communists, 235–6; collapse of enterprise, 236–7; and Soviet strategic interests, 237–8; Soviet military aid, 1937, 469; second Soviet military mission, 1937, 469; Soviet aircraft despatched, 490; strength and role of Soviet mission, 491

Czechoslovakia: exchange of officers to manoeuvres, 1936, 419; military conversations resumed, 1938, 489

France: Soviet hints to French visitors, 1933, 364–5; limited officer exchanges, 386; Soviet desire for a military convention, 394; Tukhachevsky-Gamelin talks, 1936, 412; and Rhineland crisis, 416–17; and the Straits, 422; French failure to supply military equipment, 431–2, 433; Potemkin's statement on, 1937, 453; Daladier-Gamelin and, 454; Gamelin-Voroshilov exchanges, 1938, 503–4

Germany: first contacts, 1919, 145–7; Radek's work for, 147–8; and Soviet-Polish war, 148–9; first German missions, 151–2; and 'concessions', 152–3; military arrangements, 153–4; financial aspects of, 154–5; German mission, 1923, 157–8; and aviation, 158–9; and Ruhr crisis, 159–61; difficulties over, 161–2; version of early contacts produced in Trial, 1938, 162–3; new agreements on, 247–50; crisis of 1927, 255–6; German caution, 256–7; Russian reserve, 257–8; officer-exchange, 258; and role of Uborevich, 259; and manoeuvres, 1927, 259–60; Blyukher's possible appointment, 261; German appraisals of Red Army, 261–2; German Intelligence estimates of Soviet capacities and intentions, 262–3; General Blomberg's visit of inspection to 'installations', 263–8; technical help, 268; officer-exchange, 1929, 268–9; development of Kazan tank-school, 269–70; staff collaboration, 271–2; military-industrial aspects, 1929–30, 272–4; phases of collaboration, 277–82; impact of political crisis, 1931–2, 330–3; Colonel Fischer visits Moscow, 339–40; Tukhachevsky travels to Germany, 341–2; onset of Soviet-German crisis, 343–4; General Bockelberg's visit, 344–6; evidence of Soviet obstruction, 346; 'installations' closed, 346–7, 721 n. 86; Smagin-Hartmann talks, 347–8; Tukhachevsky-Twardowski exchanges, 348–9; Yegorov-Twardowski talk, 1934, 378; Voroshilov-Nadolny discussion, 1934, 379; Tukhachevsky's hints on renewal, 1935, 395. *See also* Naval Collaboration

Military commissars (Bolshevik); attached to military commissariats, 30; functions of, 41; origins still subject to debate, 41–2; and Political Administration (*PUR*), 42; status and functions, 42–3; competitions with 'cells', 44; recent Soviet

listing of, 80; in relation to military structure, 82; apparent eclipse of, 117; discussed at 10th Congress, 125–6; personnel reshuffled, 1924, 187; categorisation of, 193; *Instruction* (1922) on, 195; alarm over unitary command, 196; *RVS* on, 197; in relation to commander, 1925, 198–9; transfers to command line, 204; and unitary command, 1925–7, 204–5; opposition by 'Tolmachev group', 315; role specified in *PU–29*, 316–17; senior political staff as Party intellectuals, 375; control functions in communised army, 376; formal ranks introduced, 392; efforts to raise military education of, 393; evolution under Gamarnik, 423; resume former control functions, 1937, 460; new regulations on, 471; further responsibilities of, 1938, 478–9; purged in Far East, 493; Voroshilov's eulogy of, 510–11; wartime regulations on, 1941, 603. *See also* Command; Commissars; Political Administration
Military commissariats, 30, 35, 480, 778–9
Military Commission (Bolshevik), 5
Military Commission (*TsKK*), 141, 164, 165, 166, 169, 171–2, 699 n. 22
Military Districts; preliminary organisation, 1918, 34; investigation into, 164; reforms in, 1924, 174; peasant demonstrations in, 180; administrations of, 185; unitary command in, 195–6; 'repeater command courses' in, 205; military soviets established over, 1937, 460; commanders purged, 1937–8, 480; staff organisation of, 1938, 480; designation 'Special', 569; German movement reported by frontier MDs, 574; lack of specific orders for, June 1941, 586, receive warning telegram, 587; and first Red Army operational order, 22nd June 1941, 587–8
Baltic Special: 569, 570, 583, 593; Belorussian: 341, 350, 353, 367, 390, 392, 405, 419, 436, 461, 508; Central Asian: 185, 202, 245, 460–1; Kharkov: 405; Kiev: 394, 405, 460, 461; Kiev Special: 554, 557, 568, 571, 584, 590–1; Leningrad: 178, 201, 202, 266, 292, 293, 392, 405, 418, 450, 460, 463, 501, 508, 542–3, 569, 570, 584, 589, 605, 748 n. 99; Moscow: 34, 182, 200, 266, 405, 450, 557, 571; North Caucasus: 126, 202, 377, 405, 450, 462, 463; Odessa: 569, 585, 591; Orel: 34, 601; Petrograd: 122; Pri-Volga: 34, 340, 460, 463; Trans-Baikal: 398, 399, 451, 467, 494, 517, 533; Ukraine: 260, 266, 271, 367, 390, 392; Urals: 34; Western: 185, 197–8, 202; Western Siberian/Siberian: 179, 182, 185, 202, 240, 241, 314; Western Special: 569, 570, 571, 583, 584 590, 593, 594–5; Yaroslavl: 34
Military doctrine; early disputes over, 1918, 39; and 'proletarian methods of waging war', 50–1; notions of 'proletarian science of war', 82; and 'science of civil war', 108; Frunze's views on, 1921, 127; Trotsky's counter-arguments, 128–9; Gusev on, 129; Frunze's presentation of, 1922, 131; debated at 11th Congress, 132–4; Tukhachevsky on, 133–4; Frunze's revised views, 135; lack of unified view of, 166; and the tank, 270; coalition warfare, 295; in *PU–29*, 316; offensive and defensive operational methods, 1929, 317; and employment of infantry, 317–18; Triandafillov on, 318; tactical role assigned to tanks, 350–1; operations in depth, 352; disagreements over role of the tank, 355–6; and work of Communist Academy, 375; and tactical aviation, 382–3; assumptions over probable combat forms, 1935, 390; and fixed fortifications, *URs*, 406; General Principles, *PU–36*, 437–8, 800–1; tactical aviation assignments, 438, 439–440, 732 n. 103, 802–3; 'storm' and 'support' infantry groups, 439; co-operation of all arms and neutralisation of defence, 440; defence and defensive systems, 441–2, 443–4, 802, 803; *kontrpodgotovka*, 442–3, 733 n. 112; flaws in infantry tactics, 443–4; utilisation of the tank, 444; Tukhachevsky on tank-operations, 458–9; strategic surprise discounted, 567; 'most weak' in studies of strategic defence, withdrawal, 576; 'offensivism' as inhibition to defence planning, 582; strategic deployment studies ignored, 627; 'linear tactics' as 'stupid and pernicious', 632; Zhukov's demand for less frontal attack, 652; reversion to pre-war ideas, winter 1941, 659; envelopment and encirclement, forms of offensive manoeuvre, 733 n. 115. *See also* Airpower; Aviation; Civil War; Marxism; Military operations; Operating art; Regulations; Reserves; Strategy; War
Military education, 79, 193–5, 205, 259, 410
Military Electro-technical Section (Leningrad Electro-technical Institute), 195
Military ideology, 308
Military Intelligence (*GRU*), 203, 282, 291, 357, 418, 429, 430, 432, 586, 794. *See also* Berzin, Ya.; Krivitsky; *Rote Kapelle*; Sorge; Uritskii
Military intelligentsia, 194, 195, 267

Military literature, non-Soviet, and Red Army, 267, 281, 308, 410, 507
Military Oath (1939), 748 n. 118
Military operations, 1918–41; Civil War: Simbirsk-Kazan, 54–5; Perm catastrophe, 58; Kolchak offensive, 1919, 59–60; Red Army counter-offensive, Eastern Front, 61–3; Urals advance, 64; Soviet operational plans, Ukraine, 66; Denikin offensive, 69, 71; Budenny-Mamontov engagements, 71–2; storming of Bataisk, 73–4; Wrangel's break-out, 102–3; Soviet counter-stroke, 103; reduction of Wrangel, 103–7; Vth Army in Irkutsk, 218; partisans of Trans-Baikal, 221; Ungern Sternberg at Urga, 223; In-Khabarovsk, 1921, 224; Republican Army offensive, 224–5; assault on Spassk, taking of Vladivostok, 225
Soviet-Polish War, 1920: opening phase, 86; first Soviet plan, 86–7; Soviet offensive to Berezina, 88–9; SW Front drive on Kiev, 89–90, 686 n. 22; plan and reinforcement for Warsaw offensive, 90, 92–3; 1st Cavalry Army operations, 93–4, 97; Soviet fronts diverge, 94–5; Polish assembly and counter-blows, 95, 98; Soviet armies defeated, 98–9
Manchuria, 1929: Soviet mobilisations, 240–1; Fukdin-Lakasus, R. Sungari, 241–2; Manchouli-Dalainor, 242–3; Manchouli attack, 243–4; raid on Mishan-Fu, 244
Lake Khasan, 1938: initial incidents, 495–6; Japanese gains, 496–7; Soviet movement, 497; 39th Rifle Corps committed, 497–8; Soviet attacks, 6th August, 498
Khalkhin-Gol, 1939: first incident, 517; opening phase, May, 517–18, 805; Soviet deployment, 518; Japanese attack, May 28th, 518–19; Soviet reinforcement, 519–20, 805–6; Japanese July operation, 520–1; Soviet reinforcement, operational plan, 532–3, 533–4; Soviet August counter-offensive, 534, 536; battle analysis, 536–7
Soviet-Finnish War 1939–40: initial Soviet plan, 543; first offensive fails, 543–4; Suomussalmi, 544–5; Soviet thrusts held, 545; Soviet re-grouping, 547; February (1940) offensive opened, 549; Summa defences breached, 550; Viipuri and Viipuri Bay, 550–1
Soviet-German War 1941–45: Soviet deployment, frontier MDs, 570–1, 581, 584–5, 589–92, 752 n. 17; Soviet alerts, 586–7; first operational order, 587–8; W. Front breached, 593–5; W. and NW Fronts separated, 595; SW Front counter-attacks, 596–7; S. Front, Soroki-Kishinev, 597; 'double battle, Bialystok-Minsk', 600; Smolensk, 600–2; Luga-Kingisepp, 604; 8th Army cut in two, 604–5; German advance on Leningrad, 605–6, 606–7; Ukraine, mid-July, 607; Uman encirclement, 608; Bryansk Front, 609; Kiev encirclement, 610–12, 617; Glukhov-Orel, 617; Leningrad Front, September, 618–19; German offensive, Tikhvin-Volkhov, 620; Odessa evacuation, 620; Crimea-Sea of Azov, 620–1; Vyazma-Bryansk encirclement, 622; Tula-Mozhaisk-Kalinin, 624; Soviet defensive, Tikhvin-Volkhov, 633, 634–7; approaches to Moscow, 17–27th November, 640–1; German drive on Rostov, 641–2; Sevastopol sealed off, 642, 646; Soviet counter-stroke, Rostov, 647; Tikhvin-Volkhov counter-strokes, 647–8, 655–6; final German drive on Moscow, 650–1; Soviet counter-offensive, W. Front, 651–2, 652–3, 654; advance on Mozhaisk, 654; threat to Moscow liquidated, 655; Kerch-Feodosiya landings, 657–8; Barvenkovo-Lozovaya operations, S. Front, 659. *See also Operation Barbarossa*
'Military Opposition', 47, 49, 52, 82
'Military Organisations' (Bolshevik), 5
Military procurators, 193
Military ranks, reintroduced 1935, 391; social significance of, 446
Military Research Commission, 173
Military-Revolutionary Committees (1917), 10–11, 13, 15
Military schools, 193, 194, 373
Military Scientific Society/Societies (*VNO*), 128, 209, 307, 693 n. 60
Military sociology, 308
Military Soviet (Defence Commissariat), 369, 462, 465, 479, 505
Military Soviet (*NRA*), 219–20, 221, 223, 225
'Military specialists' (*Voenspets*), 26, 28, 29, 31–2; Trotsky's arguments for, 33; opposition to, 33; mutiny of, E. Front, 33; mobilisation of, 33–4; disputes over, 39–40; and Bolshevik commissars, 41; Lenin on, 46; struggle over at 8th Congress, 47–8; attacks on by 'Military Opposition', 50; disquiet over militia plans, 109; attack on militia schemes, 115–16; and Staff, 128; attacked by Gusev, 1923, 169; general position, 1924, 179; displacement of, 192; 'monopoly of military knowledge', 206; as military intellectuals, 208; on strategy, 211; and *Reichswehr*, 279; services still necessary, 298; attacked, 1929–30, 308, 309; and 1929 purge, 315; contribution of, 1929, 318
Militia. *See* Workers-Peasants Militia

Militia formations (*DNO*), 1941, 604, 621–2, 623, 624
Miller, General E. K., 413, 434, 435, 471, 472
Minin, S. K., 39, 68, 133
Mirbach, Count W. von, 54
Mirin, editor of *Trevoga*, 467
Mironov, F. K., cavalry commander, 105
Mittelberger, Colonel, 261, 262
'Mixed military system', 132, 179–80, 205, 319, 373
Miyagi, Major, Japanese Military Attaché in Afghanistan, 414
Mobilisation, 31, 33–4, 108, 136–7, 262, 405, 480, 569
'Mobilisation Plan No. 4', 418
Molchanov, General, 224, 225
Molotov, V. M., 125, 288, 306, 332, 343, 350, 386, 409, 416, 417, 426, 453, 475, 476, 515, 516, 517, 522, 523, 530, 532, 537, 538, 540, 541, 542, 551, 556, 557, 559, 565, 566, 573, 577, 598, 602
Moltke, Field Marshal H. Count von, 507
Moltke, H. A. von, 262
Mongolia; Inner, 358, 361; Outer (Mongolian People's Republic: MPR), 185, 217, 222, 223, 226, 227, 231, 238, 241, 245, 335, 338, 358, 397, 400, 414, 415, 424, 517–18, 518–22
Moraht, Dr, 253
Morozov, Lieutenant-General V. I., 589
Mortars, experimental medium, 272; 'so-called short range artillery, 510; production of, 1941, 614, 618
Moscow, German threat to, 1941, 622–3; panic in, 623; air defences strengthened, 639; temperature, winter 1941, 641; plan for Soviet counter-offensive, 649–50; German defeat before, 650–1; clearing of *oblast*, 659
Moscow Conference, Anglo-Soviet, 1941, 630
Moscow garrison, 164, 168, 187
Moscow Institute of Chemical Warfare, 272
Moscow Party Committee, discussion of militia plans, 1921, 119
Mostovenko, Major-General A. K., 590, 593
Movchin, N., 31, 763
Mozg Armii (The Brain of the Army: 3 vols.), 282, 292, 293–5
Mrachkovskii, S. V., 425
Müller, Colonel, 259
Muklevich, R. A., 254, 275, 279, 335, 410, 460, 462, 471, 475, 512, 616, 841
Muralov, N. I., 54, 56, 142, 171, 436, 449
Muraviev, Colonel M. A., 54, 55
Murtazin, M., cavalry commander, 89
Muto, General A., 357
Muzychenko, Lieutenant-General I. N., 590
Myasnikov, A. F., 6, 88, 171

Nadolny, R., 362, 379
Nakamura, Lieutenant-General A., 497
Nakhimson, S. M., 14
Nansen, F., 698 n. 57
Napoleon, 58, 134
'Nation in arms', concept of, 116, 118
National Formations, Red Army, 167, 184–5, 198, 480
National Revolutionary Army (*Kuomintang*), 230, 231, 234, 235
National Revolutionary Army (Mongolian), 223
'National-Socialist Guards' (1918), 19
Nationalism, Great Russian and defensivism, 298
Naval Academy, 194, 275, 450, 470, 475, 500, 791
Naval administration; *Tsentroflot* as initial organ, 76; Commissariat for Naval Affairs (1918), organisation and personnel, 77, 777–8; Party workers for, 169; reforms, 1924, 176; Orlov's career in, 275; and Defence Commissariat, 370; organisation in 1936, 420; separate Naval Commissariat, 1937, 472, 475; Main Naval Soviet created, 1938, 476, 477
Naval Agreements; Anglo-German, 419; Anglo-Soviet, 421, 422, 476
Naval Assistant to Commander-in-Chief, 176
Naval aviation. *See* Aviation
Naval bases, defensive plans for, 1941, 582, 642. *See also* Odessa; Sevastopol
Naval collaboration: Soviet Russia/Union and *Germany*: first contacts, 212, 251–2; German naval mission, 252–3; and German submarine plans, 253; potential assistance in war, 253–4; and Muklevich, 254; German caution in, 255; command contacts, 1929, 274; Soviet naval mission, 275; Orlov-*Amtschef A*, 276; limits of, 277; renewed, 1939, 541; and Finnish War, 547; equipment and machinery, 566. *See also Marineleitung*; Naval equipment; Submarines
Naval commissars, 78, 121
Naval doctrine; interest in strategic, tactical employment of submarines, 212; discussion of, Orlov-*Amtschef A*, 276; combat manual prepared, 318; indecision about sea-power, 354; the submarine and defensivism, 355; debate on ocean-going navy, 409; the strict defensive in doubt, 409–10; desire for ocean-going fleet, 475; change to offensivism, with surface units, 476; and 'a most mighty attacking force', 512
Naval equipment, German and Italian, Soviet interest in, 253, 355, 548
Naval Forces (*VMF/RKKA*); limited role in Civil War, 76–8; social composition of, 120; and Kronstadt rebellion, 1920, 121–2; without combat value, 1923,

Naval Forces (*VMF/RKKA*)—*contd.*
165; stiffened with *Komsomol*, 176, 700 n. 37; excluded from unitary command, 197; contact with *Marineleitung*, 176, 212, 251; and German assistance, 251–5; Orlov's career in, 275; Soviet-German command exchanges, 275–7; Pacific Fleet created, 1933, 338; Northern Fleet created, 353; Baltic Fleet operational assignments, 353–4; and geographic limitations, 354; search for foreign technical help, 354–5; defensive doctrine in, 355; surface ships, submarines, Pacific Fleet, 361, 722–3 n. 113, 804; Far Eastern 'mosquito fleet', 362; Voroshilov suggests French help, 364; hints of policy changes, 409–10; command and administration of, 420; and Naval Agreements, 421, 422, 476; Mediterranean ambitions, 422; Orlov on, 1936, 445; possible motivation for purge in, 470; separated from Red Army, 472; Molotov on, 1938, 475; construction programme, 500; Kuznetsov and Tevosyan on, 1939, 512; British estimate of, 524; projected operations in Shaposhnikov's three 'alternatives', 528, 540–1; new naval bases incomplete, 570; alerted, 21st June 1941, 586–7; and defence of Odessa, Sevastopol, 610, 642, 657; and Kerch-Feodosiya landings, 657–8; submarine strength, 803–4. *See also* Aviation; Baltic Fleet; Black Sea Fleet; *Komsomol*; Naval administration; Naval collaboration; Naval doctrine; Northern Fleet; Pacific Fleet; Submarines
Naval officers, political and social composition, 1924–6, 797
Naval ranks, reintroduced 1935, 392
'Naval specialists' (ex-Imperial officers), 26, 78, 121
Naval Staff, 176, 476, 477
Nazarov, General A. M., 102, 104
NEP. *See* New Economic Policy
'Neumann' (or 'N'). *See* Niedermayer
Neurath, Baron C. von, 453
Nevskii, V. I., 7, 38
New Economic Policy (*NEP*), 125, 299, 694 n. 82
Nezamozhnik (minelayer), 567
Nicolai, Colonel, 110
Niedermayer, Major O., 151, 152, 153, 154, 256, 263, 275, 348, 713 n. 102
Niekisch, E., 413, 456, 729 n. 27
Niessel, General, 65
Nikishev, Major-General D. N., 589, 606
Nikitin (A. N. Chernikov), 234
Nikitin, Major-General I. S., 590
Nikolayev, L., 378
NKGB. *See* Security organs
NKVD. *See* Security organs
Noël, M., 489
Northern Expedition (China), 233, 234, 237, 238
Northern Fleet, organisation and function, 1933, 353; submarine strength, 804
Northern Sea Route (*Glavmorput*), 354
Novikov, Colonel, 642
Novikov, Aviation Marshal A. A., 615, 624, 841
Novitskii, Major-General F. F., 14, 16, 59, 61, 75, 681 n. 18
Novoslobodskii, F., 733 n. 115
Novye puti sovremennykh armii (Soviet translation of Liddell Hart), 308
Nykopp, J., 541

Oboronitel'naya operatsiya 9-i Armii (Soviet monograph), 645
Oborin, Major-General S. I., 590, 593
Odessa, naval base, lack of landward defences, 582; directive for 'last-ditch defence'. 609–10
OGPU. *See* Security organs
Oi, General, 220
Okawa, Japanese official, 334
Okopnaya Pravda (newspaper), 19
Oktyabrskii, Admiral F. E., 586, 610, 646
Okulov, military commissar, 68
Okunev, G. S., senior naval commissar, 392, 467
Oleg (cruiser), 77
Olekseyenko, Colonel, 534
Operating art, 318; Svechin's definition of, 717 n. 80
Operation Barbarossa, initial planning, 560; *Directive No. 21*, 1940, 561; German misgivings over Soviet military posture, 574; German view of Red Army, May 1941, 580; *Aufmarsch Ost*, 583; compromise solution over primary objectives, 584; Soviet Intelligence discovers timetable of, 586; German strength and deployment, 588; *Directive No. 33*, July 1941, 609; Soviet statement of German losses, 613; *Directive No. 35*, September 1941, 617; Soviet intelligence data on, 637–8; German plan for taking Moscow, 639; Rundstedt relieved of command, 657; final drive for Moscow, 650–1; opinion on German defeat before Moscow, 666. *See* Military operations
Oras, 252, 275
Order No. 1, 3
Order No. 2, 4
Ordzhonikidze, G. K., 74, 75, 80, 104, 123, 124, 125, 140, 168, 170, 171, 200, 285, 306, 407, 409, 454, 841
Oreshkin, Colonel A. K., 645
Orlov, corps commander, 460

Orlov, pseudonym of *NKVD* officer, 431, 452
Orlov, Flag Officer V. M., career to 1929, 275; and *Amtschef A*, 275–6, 277, 713 n. 99; and defensive naval doctrine, 355; senior naval commander, 392; and naval defence, 410; on submarines, 445; Deputy Defence Commissar, 450; visits London, 459; strategic views denounced, 470; liquidation, 1938, 475, 502; denounced at 18th Congress, 512; wartime justification of strategic views, 616; biography, 842
Osaka Mainchi (newspaper), 468
Osoaviakhim (Society of Associates for Aviation and Chemical Defence), organisation, membership, 307; and Eidemann, 308, 340; criticism of, 388; reorganised, 389; and 'air-mindedness', 409; Eidemann displaced from, 461; chief shot, 505
Ota, Japanese Ambassador, 358
Ott, General, 432, 631
Ozeryansky(-ii), 482
Ozolin, Ya. I., Amur River Flotilla commander, 241, 242

Paasikivi, J. K., 541
Paasonen, Colonel A., 541, 551
Pacific Fleet, creation of, 1933, 338; submarines in, 355, 410, 804; strength, 1933, 361; 'mosquito fleet', 362; commanders, 392; and Moscow conference, 409; Viktorov replaced, 500; Kuznetsov in command, 512; Yumashev in command, 554
Pacts; Soviet-Polish Non-Aggression, 332–3, 339, 503; Franco-Soviet Non-Aggression, 332, 339, 342; Eastern, 385, 386, 387, 396; Soviet-Czech Mutual Assistance, 387; Franco-Soviet Mutual Assistance, 387, 394–5, 396, 416, 431–2, 433, 453–4; Soviet-Chinese Non-Aggression, 469; Soviet-German Non-Agression, 516, 530, 532, 539, 541, 556, 565, 566, 585; Soviet-Yugoslav, 573; Soviet-Japanese Neutrality, 577–8
Paikes, A. K., 226
Panfilov, Major-General I. V., 631, 640
Panfilov, Colonel A. P., 498
Panteleyev, military commissar, execution of, 678 n. 50
Pantserzhanskii, E. S., senior naval commander, 178, 420
'*Panzerschiff A*' (pocket-battleship), 275
Papen, F. von, 341, 342, 343
Parachute troops, Red Army, 327, 350, 351, 390, 437
Parchunov, Major, 629
Partisan Administration, Far East (1919), 221
Partisans, 64, 65, 87, 129, 218, 221, 225; in 1941, 629
Partizanschina (guerrilla-ism), 38, 44
Partkharakteristika, 'political characterisation' of dossier, 205, 478, 775
Party schools and education in Red Army, standardising of, 1925, 190
Pashkovskii, corps commander, 397
'Passive defence', municipal bodies and, 307
Patek, 333
Pauka, I. Kh., 91
Pauker, senior *NKVD* officer, 428
Paul-Boncour, J., 413
Pavlov, General D. G., 537, 571, 584, 590, 593, 595, 599, 614, 626
Pavlov, P. A., 227
Pavlovich, Major-General A. A., 634
Peace Conference, Paris (1919), 85
'Peasants Red Army of Western Siberia', 65
People's Commissariats; Aviation Industry, 558; Communications, 754 n. 61; Defence, 369, 370, 371, 372, 377, 389, 462, 478; Foreign Affairs, 257; Heavy and Light Industry, 306; Internal Affairs, *NKVD*, *see* Security organs, Military Affairs, 17, 781; Military Education, 34; Military-Naval Affairs (War), 34, 173, 354, 369; Naval (1918), 77, 777–8, 782; Naval (1938), 472, 475, 586; Shipbuilding, 477
People's Revolutionary Army (*NRA*), Far East, 219, 224, 225
Peremytov, Chief of operational staff, S. Front, 1919, 70
Pétain, Marshal H. P., 383
Peterson, Kremlin officer, 483
Petin, General N. N., 90, 173, 178, 202
Petlura, S. V., 69, 86
Petrograd Conference of Soldier-Communists (1918), 43
Petrograd Military Commissariat, 30
Petrograd militia brigade, 138
Petrograd Soviet of Workers and Peasants Deputies (1917), 3, 5, 671 n. 5; discusses a 'Red Army', 674 n. 55
Petrol, shortages in Soviet Far East, 424; production loss, 1941, 665
Petrov, 25
Petrov, Naval Academy staff member, 475
Petrov, Major-General M. P., 609, 626, 646
Petrovskii, G. V., 125
Petrushin, staff officer, Far Eastern Army, 467
Pig-iron production, 1928–30, 304; wartime losses in production, 1941, 628, 665
Pilots and pilot-training, 1936, 409, 445; and new fighters, 1941, 754 n. 68
Piłsudski, Marshal J., 85, 93, 94, 98, 104, 284, 386, 688 n. 44, 689 n. 65
Pirner, Major, 269
Pismanik, reported replacement to Bulin, 1937, 461
Pivovarov, Soviet military engineer, 406
Plan HEI (Japanese), 336

Plan OTSU (Japanese), 336
Planning Commission, attached to *RVS*, 175
Pliev, Colonel-General I. A., 508
Podvoiskii, N. N., 7, 10, 11, 12, 27, 53–4, 69, 671 n. 9, 674 n. 55, 679 n. 87, 776
Poison-gas, 151, 157, 162, 344, 345. *See also* 'Tomka', gas experimental centre
Pokus, divisional commander, 493
Poland, 85, 86–99 *passim*, 104, 148–9, 150, 151, 152, 153, 156, 159, 209, 218, 254, 265, 274, 284, 332, 333, 339, 340, 343, 348, 363, 364, 365, 380, 385, 396, 411, 415, 416, 419, 453, 454, 488, 489, 503–4, 513–14, 515, 516, 527, 528, 529, 531, 537, 538–9, 664, 690 n. 81. *See also* Military operations; Pacts; Treaties
Politburo, and disputes on Eastern Front, 1919, 61; upholds S. S. Kamenev, 70; and Georgia, 1921, 124; and transfer of 1st Cavalry Army, 126; removes Sklyanskii, 170; assault on Zinoviev, Trotsky, 201; criticism of Voroshilov, 286; and reins of policy, 328; and Stalin's 'last word' in, 368; and Political Administration, 370; as 'super-bureaucratisation', 372; considers German events, 1934, 380; concessions to the military, 1935, 391; session on artillery, 407–8; and naval policy, 409; Stalin's telegram demanding appointment of Yezhov, 1936, 426–7; intervention in Spain, 429; leadership struggles in, 499; Voroshilov only military member, 510; Stalin dismisses warning of German attack, 1941, 577; and Stalin's promotions to *GOKO*, 598. *See also* Central Committee, Russian Communist Party; Communist Party, Russian
Politchas ('political hour'), 188
Political Administration (*PUR*, *PURKKA*), viii; *PUR* set up, 1919, 42; struggle with 'cells', 45; and 8th Party Congress, 48; Smilga, head of, and dual command, 81; civilian demands for control of Party work, 109; attack on centralised control of, 116; organisation of, Fronts, Fleets, Armies, 1921, 117; and prelude to Kronstadt rebellion, 121; compromise over at 10th Party Congress, 125; status of *PUR*, 125–6; and 1st Cavalry Army, 126; Gusev's programme, 129–30; Antonov-Ovseenko, head of *PUR*, 138; programme for territorial divisions, 139; Circular No. 200 (1923), 142; crisis in, 1923, 164–5; Bubnov as head of *PUR*, 168; position of, 1924, 172; Order No. 23, 186; re-staffed, 1924, 186–7; new political instruction courses, 188, 703 n. 77; and inner-Party struggle, 188–9; and 'cells', 190; under direct control of Central Committee, 191; as *PURKKA*, 191, 703 n. 84, 795; categorisation of staff, 193; and unitary command, 196; 'Tolmachev group', 197; revised position of, 1926, 203; copied in China, 229; Gamarnik as head, 246; to reduce inefficiency in Red Army, 260; Party-political organisation, 1929, 310; Directive 28015, 1928, 311; internal organisation, 1928, 312; and collectivisation, 313; control function complicated, 314, and Defence Commissariat, 371; nature of control exercised by, 373; and 17th Congress, 375; reduced policing role, 376; ranks introduced into, 392; development of under Gamarnik, 423; senior appointments in, 1937, 450; Stalin's loss of confidence in, 459; purged, 461–2; Mekhlis head of, 472, 478; revised political programme, 1938, 479; Far Eastern staff purged, 1938, 493; purge losses in, 505; numerical strength of political staff, 1939, 511; Klokov on possibility of war, 1941, 576; intensification of work, December 1941, 660, 663. *See also* Antonov-Ovseenko; Bubnov; 'Cells' (Party collectives); Central Committee, Russian Communist Party; Communist Party, Russian; Gamarnik; Gusev; Mekhlis; Military commissars; Political Sections; Smilga
Political Centre (Irkutsk), 218, 219
Political Sections (1918), 42, 77
Politinformatsiya (political lectures) 1941, 660
Politis, 413
Politruks (political assistants), 188, 190, 204, **205**
Polkovnikov, Colonel, 11
Poluboyarov, Colonel-General P. P., 508
Polyakov, tank-regiment commander, 269
Ponedelin, Major-General P. G., 591
Pontoons, pontoon-building, 207
Popov, Lieutenant-General M. M., 589, 604, 606, 607
Popov, General V. S., 653
Popov, N., 221
Popular Front, 428
Poskrebyshev, General A. N., 445
Posokhov, General, 13
Postyshev, P. P., 224
Potapov, Major-General of Tank Troops M. I., 590
Potemkin, V. P., 104, 105, 395, 413, 453, 503, 504, 541, 737 n. 48
'Practical infantry'. *See* Rifle troops
Pravda (newspaper), 5, 140, 199, 285, 383, 387, 414, 446, 459, 463, 467, 472, 507, 523, 556
Pre-mobilisation political indoctrination, militia formations, 180
Presse, *Geheimrat*, 253

Primakov, Corps Commander V. M., 377, 378, 450, 451, 457, 463, 486, 734 n. 3, 842
Prisoner of War Congresses (1918), 25, 675 n. 3
Prisoners-of-war, Russian, as unprecedented problem, 1941, 603; German claims, November, 625; German count, 8th July, 756 n. 96
Procurator of the USSR, 368, 377
Promotion (officers), 193, 205, 471, 554. *See also* Attestation
Prosh'yan, P. P., 26, 777
Protiv fal'sifikatorov istorii Vtoroi Mirovoi Voiny (Soviet essays), 351, 641
Provisional Government (1917), 3, 4, 10
'Provisional Government of the Far Eastern Republic', 219
Provisional Government of the Maritime Provinces, 222
Provisional National-Revolutionary Government of Mongolia, 223
Pshennikov, Lieutenant-General P. S., 589
Pu Yi, 336
Pubalt. See Baltic Fleet Political Directorate
Pumpur, aviation commander, 493
PUR. See Political Administration
Purges; 1923 'military reform' as a purge, 172; of naval officers, 1924, 176; in political apparatus, 1924, 186; in Red Army, 1929, 315, 325; in Red Army, 1933–4, 374; and Kirov killing, 378, 391; in 1936, 425; within *NKVD*, 445; Stalin on, 1937, 452; onset of in Red Army, 1937, 460–2; in railway administration, Siberia, 466; characteristics of military purge, 1937, 472–3, 479–80; naval purge, 1937–8, 475–6; in nationalities, national formations, 480; effect of military purge on non-Soviet opinion, 489, 491; isolationist aspect of, 490; in Far Eastern command, 492–3, 497; effects in aviation command, 500–1; and numerical losses in Red Army, 505–6; military purge as 're-Bolshevisation' of army, 511; military purge remains a reality, 559–60; 'purge by battle', 664. *See also* Security organs; Trials; Yagoda; Yezhov
Purkayev, Colonel-General M. A., 537, 590
PURKKA. See Political Administration
Putna, Army Commander V. K., 200, 261, 271, 275, 286, 333, 397, 412, 426, 427, 428, 433, 436, 449, 450, 457, 463, 486, 842
Pyatakov, G. L., 67, 436, 449, 454, 482
Pykhtin, Colonel A. M., 643

Rabinovich, senior military commissar, Far East, 467
Rada (Ukraine), 20
Radek, K. B., 144, 146, 147, 148, 151, 152, 153, 161, 249, 344, 379, 380, 383, 425, 436, 449, 450, 451, 455, 456, 676 n. 11 & n. 14, 734 n. 1
Radio communication units, High Command, 1941, 754 n. 61
Raeder, Grand Admiral E., 541, 547, 747 n. 90, 753 n. 41
Railway troops, 167, 391, 403
Railways. *See* Transportation
Rakovsky(-ii), Kh. G., 481
Rapallo, Treaty of. *See* Treaties
Raskol'nikov, F. F., 11, 56, 76, 77, 121, 466
Rathenau, W., 146
Razvedka. See Intelligence; Reconnaissance
Rear, organisation of, in rifle formations and units, 1929, 317; Rear Services, Chief of, appointed 1941, 598–9
'Rear security detachments' (*zagraditel'nye otryadi: NKVD* troops), 1941, 598. *See also* Special Assignment Detachments (*ChON*)
Rechberg, A., 331, 718–19 n. 20
Reconnaissance (*razvedka*), Tukhachevsky on, 381; poor quality of, 1936 manoeuvres, 437; stipulations on, *PU–36*, 438–9, 732–3 n. 103; Zhukov's special arrangements for, Khalkhin-Gol, 533; ski-troops for, Finland 1940, 547, 549
Red Air Force. *See* Military Air Force (*VVS/RKKA*)
Red Army. *See* Workers-Peasants Red Army
Red Army Administration, 370, 388
Red Army Staff. *See* Staff
Red Banner Army of the Caucasus (*OKA*), 202
Red Banner Front, Far Eastern forces, as from February 1937; organised, 1937, 451; momentary immunity from purge, 470; purged, 492–4; in action, Lake Khasan, 494–9; four commands of, 517; strength of rifle and cavalry formations, 557; fully mobilised, 1941, 599; formations moved to European Russia, autumn 1941, 631–2; formations moved to west, March 1941, 753 n. 54; estimated strength, 1940, 767. *See also* Blyukher; Military operations, Special Far Eastern Red Banner Army
'Red commander' (*Kraskom*). *See* Command staff
Red Fleet. *See* Naval Forces (*VMF/RKKA*)
Red Guard, 809, 16, 27, 673 n. 25 & n. 27
'Red Revolutionary Army' (1918), 18
Reek, General, 418
'Regulation on Reserve Troops', 1919, 679–80 n. 87
Regulations, combat manuals, military and naval
Vremennyi Polevoi Ustav, 1925, 207
Boevoi Ustav, to be published, 1924, 207; list, 705 n. 128

Regulations, combat manuals, military and naval—*contd.*
PU–29, 208, 316–18
Boevoi Ustav Voenno-morskikh sil RKKA, 1930, 319, 717 n. 78
Ustav motomekhanizirovannykh voisk, Nastavlenie po samostayetl'nomu vozhdeniyu krupnykh motomekhanizirovannykh soedinenni, 1932, 351
Vremennyi Polevoi Ustav (*PU–36*), 443–4, 458–9, 498; general principles, 437–8; aviation, 438; reconnaissance, 438–9; combat order, 439; aviation combat roles, 439–40; tank echelons, 440–1, artillery, 441; defence, 441–3; 'General Principles', 800–1; 'Fundamentals of the Conduct of Operations', 801–2; 'Defence', 803
PU: projected but unfinished, 1939–40, 558
Reibnitz, General, 147
Reichswehr, ix, 92, 110, 143, 145, 151, 152, 153, 155, 156, 157, 158, 159, 160, 161, 163, 246, 247, 248, 249, 250, 252, 256, 257, 258, 259, 262, 263, 265, 267, 268, 270, 271, 273, 281, 291, 331, 333, 340, 341, 342, 343–9, 364, 365, 367, 378, 380, 411, 413, 434, 457, 485, 506. *See also* Military collaboration; Seeckt; *Sondergruppe R*
Reichswehrministerium, 110, 151, 152, 157, 161, 249, 250, 258, 262, 346
Reimer, Naval Captain, 252
Reinhardt, Colonel-General, 640, 651, 654
Reinstatement or 're-habilitation' commissions, 1938, 506, 507
Remizov, Lieutenant-General F. N., 646, 647, 651, 663
Reserves (manpower), pre-military training for, 30; and recruiting districts, 49; in Polish campaign, 1920, 89, 98; strength, reserve armies, 101; and operations against Wrangel, 107; reserve group, strength of in infantry attacks, *PU–29*, 318; in Far East, 363; reserve officers, training of, 388; tank-drivers and mechanics, 406, 728 n. 5; strategic, lack of, 1941, 599; of High Command, and Zhukov, Smolensk, 602; total absence of, Northern Front, 606; Colonel Zakharov on, 615; problematical existence of, 1941, 627; formed into 37th Army by Timoshenko, 641; expended in Crimea, 656; and Stalin's control, battle for Moscow, 659, 760 n. 46; moved by *Stavka* to Tikhvin-Volkhov operations, 661
Revolutionary Committees (*Revkom*), 38; in Georgia, 124
Revolutionary military officer cadres, internationalised, Tukhachevsky on, 108
Revolutionary Military Soviet (*RVS*). *See Revvoensoviet*
Revolutionary Tribunals, punitive organs, 38, 39
Revvoensoviet (*RVS*)
RVS/Armies: organisation of, 38; of 1st Cavalry Army, 72
RVS/Fronts: organisation of, 38; of Southern Front, Gusev on, 43; of Eastern Front, disputes in, 61–3, 64
RVS/Military Districts, 185
Revvoensoviet Respubliki (*RVSR*); organisation of, 34, 780–1; controls Red Army security organs, 45; attacked by Stalin-Dzerzhinskii, 45–6; criticised at 8th Party Congress, 48; personnel, 56; personnel re-shuffled, 66; orders over 'Curzon line' being crossed, 92–3; and disbanding of 1st Cavalry Army, 126; in Zinoviev's plans, 141; criticism of, 1923, 169; attacked by Uborevich, 169–70; new appointments to, 1923, 171; on unitary command, 195–6; Lenin's critical letter on, 1919, 782–3
Revvoensoviet/USSR (*RVS SSSR*); formal position of, 1924, 172; Planning Commission, 175; as new command group, 178; and 'Red Army commander', 179; and Military Districts, 185; removal of Trotsky from, 189; and *PURKKA*, 191; on officer service, 192; and command assignments, 193; on military education, 194; Directives on commander, 196; plenum on commissars, 197; new command group in, 1925, 200; competence of, 203; organisational form copied in China, 230; and *ODVA*, 240; and *Reichswehr*, 258; Gamarnik appointed to, 314, 327; Alksnis appointed to, 327; powers of, 328; in 1933, 366; dissolved, 1934, 368
Reynaud, P., 394
Rheinmetall, German firm, 273, 274, 282, 373
Ribbentrop, J. von, 530, 532, 537, 539
Rifle troops, Red Army; strength, 1919, 59; divisional establishment, 1921, 136; percentage of Red Army, 1922, 137; numerical strength, 1923–4, 167; first- and second-line divisional strengths, 181; composition and re-organisation, 182, 792–3; combat manual for, 207; in Manchuria, 1929, 242–3; and defence, Tukhachevsky on, 296; and *PU–29*, 317; combat employment of, 317–18; strength, 1930, 326; in Far East, 336, 360; air support for, 382–3; strength, 1935, 389; deployment in European Russia, 1936, 405; tank-borne, 439; and *PU–36*, 443–4; tactics and combat performance, Lake Khasan, 1938, 498–9; Voroshilov on, 1939, 510;

at Khalkhin-Gol, 1939, 518, 519, 520, 521, 533, 534, 537, 805–6; potential strength to be deployed, Shaposhnikov on, 527; deployment and combat performance in Finland, 543, 544, 545, 546, 547, 549, 550, 551; training deficiencies, 1940, 553; realistic training programme needed, 554; new divisional establishment, 567; rifle corps, organisation, 568; under-manned formations, 1941, 571; inefficient tactics, 1941, 613
Rifles, production, 1930–37, annual averages, 304; Model 1939 introduced, 548; monthly production, 1941, 575
Robinson, Colonel R., 146
Rocket-projectile launcher. *See* 'Katyusha'
Rocket-projectiles, M–13/M–8, production of, Leningrad, 618
Rockinson, reported as Chief of Staff, Red Army Chemical Troops, 345
Rössler, R. ('Lucy'), Soviet Intelligence operator, 638
Rogachev, V., 228, 230, 232
Rogovskii, head of Artillery Inspectorate, 367
Rokossovskii, Marshal K. K., 71, 360, 451, 492, 505, 554, 602, 640, 651, 654, 662, 663, 741 n. 49
Rosenberg, A., 344, 348, 379, 464
Rosenblatt, Soviet negotiator, 155
Rosengoltz, A. P., 56, 157, 160, 163, 248, 481, 484–5, 488
Rote Kapelle, 637, 638
Rotmistrov, Marshal of Tank Troops P. A., 633
Roy, N. N., 236
Royal Air Force, Stalin on, 530
Royal Navy, 77, 477, 500; Stalin on, 530
Rozwadowski, General, 91, 95
RSDRP(b). *See* Communist Party, Russian
Rubtsov, B., 225
Rudnev, N. A., 13
Rudzutak, Ya. E., 485
Rumania, 64, 69, 84, 92, 93, 290, 419, 453, 454, 503, 513, 516, 527, 528, 529, 531, 556, 566
Rundstedt, Field Marshal K. G. von, 588, 597, 647
Russo-Japanese War (1905), 217, 334
Ryabyshev, Lieutenant-General D. I., 612
Ryazanov, D. B., 297–8
Rybnikov, *politruk* cited by Mekhlis, 511
Rychagov, P., aviation commander, 494, 600
Rykov, A. I., 38, 66, 247, 285, 315, 425, 426, 452, 481, 482, 483, 488
Rykov, Divisional Commissar P. E., 590
'Ryutin platform', 338, 486

Sachsenberg, 152
Safronov, Lieutenant-General G. P., 608
Saluting, reintroduced, 1940, 555
Samoilo, General A. A., 34, 63, 80, 124, 681 n. 31
San Fu-yan, 25
Sangurskii, Corps Commander V. M., 397, 467
Sapronov, T. V., 168
Savinkov, B. V., 54
Sazonov, S., 387
Schacht, Dr H., 432, 453
Scheidemann, 250
Schellenberg, W., 434, 435, 456, 457
Schleicher, General K. von, 151, 331, 341, 342
Schlieffen, Count A. von, 507, 563
Schmidt, Brigade Commander D., 426, 458, 730 n. 55
Schmitz, Professor, 272, 273
Schmolcke, Lieutenant-Colonel, 259
Schnurre, Dr K., 529
Schöndorff, Captain, 159
Schubert, Major, 150, 152, 158, 249, 255, 256, 687 n. 33
Schüssler, Naval Captain, 255
Schulenburg, Count W. von, 516, 532, 539, 541, 555, 556, 573, 578, 579
Schulze-Boysen, H., 637
Schweissguth, General, 732 n. 95
'Screens' (*zavesy*), 1918, 26, 27, 34
Second International, 116, 118
Secret Department (Secretariat), 445
Security organs
Cheka: 45, 110, 122
OGPU: 199, 203; rivalry with armed forces, 204; as repressive agent, 300, 314; militarised formations of, 357; internal espionage, 367–8; becomes *NKVD*, 368, 376
NKVD: and command organs, 376–7; and 'Primakov case', 377–8; Kirov murder, 378; Foreign Intelligence Division and Germany, 380; and *Osoaviakhim*, 389; Frinovskii and militarised formations, 390–1; intelligence on Germany, 396; commands frontier force, Far East, 397; control over railways, 403; in relation to army, 404; Blimiel and, 413; pressure on Mrachkovskii, 425; and 'show trial', 426; Yezhov head of, 426–7; checked by army, 427; and Putna, 428; in Spain, 429, 430, 431, 452, 456; Skoblin case, 434, 435; increased arrests, December 1936, 436; Yezhov and 'purging command', 445, 455; and Primakov, 1937, 450; circumstances of *SD* dossier, 455, 456–7; arrest of Yakir, Tukhachevsky, 460; arrests in Red Army command, 463; first Far Eastern purge, 1937, 466, 467; purges Far East *NKVD*, 492, 493; purges Blyukher's command, 493–4; officers drafted into Red Army, 507; Beria replaces Yezhov, 510; orders to frontier troops, 1941, 585–6; *NKGB* and *NKVD* fused, 1941, 598; interrogation of escaping

Security organs: *NKVD—contd.*
Red Army troops, 616; wartime rivalry with Red Army, 668; control of labour for defence construction, 1941, 751–2 n. 15. *See also* Beria; Purges; Special Sections; Trials; Yagoda; Yezhov
Sedyakin, Corps Commander A., 327, 341, 385, 412
Seeckt, Colonel-General H. von, 92, 110, 145, 146, 147, 149, 150, 151, 152, 153, 156, 160, 161, 162, 163, 249, 256, 318, 344, 411, 435, 456, 485, 697 n. 41
Selivachev, V. I., 70, 782
Selter, K., 540
Semashko, Major-General V. V., 605
Semenov, General G. M., 219, 220, 221, 222
Serebryakov, L. P., 436, 449
Sergeyev, E. N., 88
Seryshev, S. M., 221, 224
Sevastopol, naval base, test of defences, 1940–1, 582; work on landward defences, 642; defensive forces and sectors, 642; Oktyabrskii in command, 646; *Stavka* reinforcements to, 656 ·
Shakhurin, A. I., 558
Shaposhnikov, Marshal B. M., fortunes in 1917, 17; early service with Field Staff, 36, 56; important contributions to Red Army of, 80; operational plan against the Poles, 1920, 86; on Tukhachevsky's first offensive, 1920, 89; and Budenny-Voroshilov, 89; on Lwow operation, 94; on August Directives, 97, 688 n. 52; assessment of Polish campaign, 100, 109; assistant to Chief of Staff, 173; and new command group, 179; commander Leningrad MD, 202; Blomberg on, 266; *Mozg Armii*, 282, 292, 293–5; on state machine, 296; and morale, 306; at 16th Party Congress, 321; Party member, 325–6; demoted 1931, 340–1; head of Frunze Academy, 350, 367; professionalism of, 371; at Czech manoeuvres, 394; Chief of General Staff 1937, 460, 470, 508; protection of, 462, 736 n. 44; and 'military tribunal', 463, 501; member of Main Military Soviet, 478; relation to new command, 502; and tank forces, 503, 508, 537, 559; immunity in purge, 506; at 18th Congress, 511; and Anglo-French Military Mission, 1939, 524, 525, 526, 527; expounds three strategic alternatives, 527–8, 540–1; appointed Marshal, 1940, 553; temporary retirement, 557; on mobilisation of Red Army, 569; and *Stavka*, 1941, 598, 602; General Nikishev's report to, 606; and General Staff, 618; defence of Moscow, 623, 633, 641, 659; directive to Koniev, 650; co-ordination of fronts, 662; choice of main blows, 663; retires as Chief of General Staff, 667; biography, 842–3
Shatagin, N. I., 31
Shchadenko, E. A., 68, 72, 74, 105, 183, 461, 479, 508
Shchastnyi, Admiral, 77
Shcherbakov, A. S., 623, 625
Sherstobitov, 77
Shevaldin, Lieutenant-General T. I., 605
Shidehara, K., 239, 334, 335
Shigemitsu, M., 467, 468, 497, 631, 743 n. 70
Shikin, Colonel-General I. V., 660
Shilov, D. S., 221
Shilovskii, General E., 384, 686 n. 18
Shimada, 224
ShKAS machine-gun, aircraft armament, 559
Shkvor, Czech agent of Soviet Intelligence, 1941, 577
Shlyapnikov, A. I., 68
Shorin, V. I., 57, 61, 70, 71, 73, 74, 80, 783
Shtern, Army Commander G. M., 494, 497, 498, 511, 512, 532–3, 742 n. 60, 742–3 n. 67
Shutko, K. I., 26, 777
ShVAK 20-mm cannon, aircraft armament, 559
Shvernik, N. M., 80, 141, 168, 616
Shvetsov, Major-General V. I., 651
Siberian Revolutionary Committee (*Sibrevkom*), 219
Sibirtsev, V. M., 221
Sicherheitsdienst (*SD: Ostabteilung*), and preparation of dossier on Red Army 'treason', 433, 434, 435, 436, 456, 457, 471; *SD* in Russia, 1941, 629
Sidorenko, artillery designer, 407
Sieburg, Naval Captain, 277
Signal lines, overhead and underground, 1940 plan for, 751–2 n. 15; proposed use of auxiliary lines, 1941, 754 n. 61
Siilasvuo, Colonel, 545
Sikorski, General W., 98, 101
Simon, Sir, J., 383
Sinkiang, 335, 398–9, 469
Sirotinskii, S. A., adjutant to Frunze, 105
Sklyanskii, E., deputy to Trotsky, 14, 53–4, 66, 86, 124, 149, 170, 171, 177, 228, 278, 699 n. 20, 782
Skoblin, General, 434, 435, 471, 472, 731 n. 84
Slavonic and East European Review (London), 430
Slutskii, senior *NKVD* officer, 426
Smagin, 346, 347, 348
Smigly-Rydz, Marshal E., 411
Smilga, I., 63, 66, 81–2, 99, 118, 678 n. 50
Smirnov, I. N., 56, 65, 73, 93, 425
Smirnov, P. A., head of *VMF*, 475, 476, 477, 490, 500
Smirnov, V. M., 27, 47
Smoke-screens, tactical use of, 1936, 440

Smorodinov, Lieutenant-General, 524, 525, 554
Smushkevich, Lieutenant-General of Red Army Aviation Ya. I., 501
Snesarev, General, 70
Sobennikov, Major-General P. P., 589, 604
Society of Associates for Aviation and Chemical Defence. *See Osoaviakhim*
Society of Friends of the Air Force (*ODVF*), 307
Society of Sun Yat-sen, 232
Sokol'nikov, G. Ya., 47, 70, 74, 425, 436, 449
Sokolov, N. D., 3
Sokolovskii, Marshal V. D., 554, 617, 662
Sollogub, N. V., 88
Sondergruppe R, 110, 150, 154, 161
Sorge, R., 414, 432, 599, 631, 637, 745 n. 31
South Manchuria Railway East Asia Research Institute, 334
Sovetnikov, General I. G., 538
Sovetsko-kitaiskaya druzhba (Soviet journal), 227
Soviet Air Force. *See* Military Air Force (*VVS/RKKA*)
Soviet Cadet Corps, suggested but rejected, 205
Soviet Navy. *See* Naval Forces (*VMF/RKKA*)
Soviet Opposition to Stalin (monograph), 603
Soviet Red Cross, 307
Soviet Russia in China (Chiang Kai-shek), 469
Soviet Staff Officer (emigré account), 557
Soviet of Baltic Fleet Commissars, 77
Soviet of Labour and Defence (*STO*), 285, 305–6
Soviet of People's Commissars (*Sovnarkom*), 12, 27, 31, 36, 157, 369, 579, 598
Soviet of Red Army Training and Preparation, 182
Soviet of Workers and Peasants Defence, 38
Sovnarkom. See Soviet of People's Commissars
Sovremennaya imperialisticheskaya voennaya ideologiya (Soviet symposium), 308
Sowjetrussland und Deutschland 1917–1922 (East German publication), 145, 159
Spain, 428, 429, 430, 431, 451, 452, 455, 456
Spalock, 152
Special Assignment Detachments (*ChON*), 167
Special Department of the Secretariat, 445
Special Experimental Design Bureau, 409
Special Far Eastern Air Fleet, 337, 360, 382, 399
Special Far Eastern Red Banner Army (*ODVA: OKDVA*), 65, 240, 241, 242, 244–5, 336, 337, 358, 360, 363. *See also* Red Banner Front
Special Kolkhoz Corps, *ODVA/OKDVA* reserve formations, 363, 397, 451, 492
Special Sections (*Osobyi Otdel: OO*), counter-intelligence organs, 45, 203, 314, 368, 376, 471, 492, 511
Speidel, General H., 159, 280
Spindler, Admiral, 212, 252, 253
Spiridonova, M. A., 27
Stachiewicz, General, 528
Staff (1918–41)
  All-Russian Supreme Staff (*Vserosglavshtab*): 33, 34, 37, 38, 46, 54, 78, 114–15, 116, 128, 780
  Field Staff (*Polevoi Shtab*): 36, 48, 86, 103, 116, 124, 128, 780
    of Red Army (*Shtab RKKA*): vii, 128, 165, 169, 170, 173, 182, 200, 203, 211, 213, 241, 260, 271, 282, 283, 291, 292, 319, 340, 341, 370, 371, 391, 405, 794. *See also* Military Intelligence (*GRU*)
  General Staff (*Generalnyi Shtab RKKA*): vii, 372, 388, 391, 433, 454, 557, 568, 569, 598, 618, 650, 659, 662, 667. *See also* State Defence Committee; *Stavka*/High Command and Supreme Command
Staff courses, in 1919, 79; Senior and 'repeater' courses, 1925–6, 205
Staff functions, defined 1924, 173; Frunze on, 174; re-defined 1926, 203, 794; as 'military brain', 282; Shaposhnikov's *Mozg Armii*, 292, 293–5
Stalin (Djugashvili) Marshal I. V., ix–x; member of Soviet of Workers and Peasants Defence, 38; on ex-officers, 39; reports on Perm catastrophe, 45–6, 58; at 8th Party Congress, 47; protests to Lenin over Trotsky, 55–6; protests over Kostyayev, 63; presses for dismissal of Vatsetis, 66–7; recalled by Trotsky, 68; meets Budenny, 70; and 1st Cavalry Army, 72; blamed by Trotsky for Tukhachevsky's unemployment, 73; support for Budenny over dispute in Bataisk fighting, 74; as 'super-commissar', 80; directs discord against Trotsky, 83; on Wrangel, 86, 687 n. 28; and planning against Poles, 87; telegram from Lenin, 89, 686 n. 20; analyses 1st Cavalry Army failure, 90; opposes subordination to Tukhachevsky, 98; attacks Smilga and is attacked by Trotsky, 10th Party Congress, 99; tactical moves against Trotsky, 119; triumvirate formed, 140; survives crisis of career, 140–1; on Red Army, 1923, 170; and 1924 Constitution, 172; in relation to new command group, 178, 179; control of Party machine, 187; proposed as War Commissar, 189; implicated in Frunze's death, 199, 704–705 n. 109; preference over new War Commissar, 200; finds new political allies, 201; assault on opposition, 1926, 202; secret speech, 1925, 209–10; and Chiang Kai-shek, 228; relations with *Kuomintang*, 231; and Bubnov's mission to China, 232–3; keeps Borodin in Wuhan, 235; on Shanghai, Wuhan, 236;

Stalin—*contd.*
sends Lominadze to China, 237; 'Asiatic view' of, 238; on Japan, 239; and Blyukher, 240; 1925 speech and military policies, 247; Shaposhnikov's views and, 282; intensifies 'war scare', 1927, 284, 714 n. 2; struggle with opposition, 284–5; attacked by Trotsky, 286–7; Bukharin on, 288; Trotsky on, 1928, 300; industrialisation question, 301, 715–16 n. 40; activates *STO*, 306; command group, 321; and centralisation, 327; on strategy, tactics, 329; Rechberg on, 331; on France, 332; and Rapallo, 333; on Soviet Far East, 334; attitude over Far Eastern crisis, 336; 'plot' against, 338–9; interview with E. Ludwig, 339; reported attendance at Shaposhnikov's lectures, 350; and mechanisation, 356; plays off army and secret police, 357; on defence, 1934, 358; significance of 'last word' in *Politburo*, 368; grip on the military, 371; control exercised by, 372; disposes of armed force outside the military, 377, 391; decree to *NKVD* after Kirov killing, 378; Radek on, 1934, 379; attitude to Germany, 379–80, 383; receives Simon-Eden, 386; on *Osoaviakhim*, 388; enforced reliance on existing military command, 393; view of Franco-Soviet Pact, 394; feeling for accord with Germany, 396; no overt support for Chinese Communists, 400; little choice of cadres, 1935, 402; Krivitsky's views on, 403; supervises loyalty of high command, 404; inspects artillery, 407; intervenes in naval affairs, 409; intelligence of Tukhachevsky, 412; on international situation, 1936, 414–15; possible attitude over Rhineland crisis and Germany, 416, 417; attitude over commissars, 423; Schmidt's 'threats' to, and their consequence, 426; demands appointment of Yezhov, 426–7; tactics in *NKVD*-Red Army issue, 427; possible decision to liquidate high command, 428; and Spanish Civil War, 428–31; despatches Kandelaki mission, 432; reported to have received information from Beneš, 433; formation of special 'purging command', 445; independence of military command from, 446; 'inconveniences' Köstring, 451; states that purges must go on, 1937, 452; course of Kandelaki mission, 453; Ordzhonikidze's pleas to, 454; Stashevskii's request to, 456; evident loss of confidence in Political Administration, 461; support of Voroshilov for, 1937, 462; and military purge, 464, 465, 471, 474; Raskol'nikov's denunciation of, 466; momentary restraint over Far Eastern purge, 467; denies Chiang Kai-shek's requests for Blyukher, 469; personal issue of arrest orders, 471; suspiciousness intensifies irrationality of purge, 472; grandiose schemes for navy, 474, 475; and Main Naval Soviet, 476; member of Main Military Soviet, 478; Dr Tsiang's opinion on, 491; influence on naval policy, 500; and Munich crisis, 504, 508; reliance on new command, 509; supporters in *Politburo*, 510; cited by Voroshilov, 511; on world situation, March 1939, 513, 515; and Nazi-Soviet Pact, 530, 532; on 'Japanese provocations', 532; and tanks, 537; orders invasion of Poland, 538; doubts over German intentions, 539; and Baltic States, 540; negotiates with Finns, 1939, 541–2; on military-industrial orders placed in Germany, 548; and Timoshenko, 555; reaction to German victories, 1940, 556; Halder on, 557; and defence preparations, 559; Hitler on, 560, 566; and German policy, 565–6; warned of German attack, 566–7; subsequent arguments over value of new frontier line, 569; and frittering away of advantages, 570; attitude over Yugoslavia, 1941, 573–4; warned of German attack by Prime Minister Churchill, 574, 752 n. 32; Khrushchev's criticisms of, 575, 579, 581, 593, 623, 626, 627, 667; blamed for inadequate planning in 1941, 576, 579, 583, 585, 625, 751 n. 10; dismisses attack warnings as 'provocation', 577, 753 n. 41; demonstration over Matsuoka, 577–8; chairman of *Sovnarkom*, 578–9; blamed for incomplete military concentration, 581; Kirponos to, 581–2; on Soviet tank-strength, 584, 585; opinion on possibility of German attack, June 1941, 585; receives multiple warnings of attack, 586; forms *GOKO*, 598; and defence of Smolensk, 601; becomes Defence Commissar and C-in-C, 603; displeasure over Leningrad Defence Soviet, 606, 627; Vlasov's radio signal to, 612; and artillery reorganisation, 614; Tokaev on, 623; remains in Moscow, 623; assigns Moscow command to Zhukov, 624; apparent loss of confidence, 626–7; inaugurates partisan movement, 629; letter to Prime Minister Churchill, 630–1; and evaluation of Japanese threat, 631, 637; on 'linear tactics', 632; intelligence available on German moves and intentions,

638; adopts Zhukov's plans for Moscow counter-stroke, 641, 649; and Rostov counter-stroke, 646; directives for offensive operations, 659; role in Moscow defence, 662, 760 n. 46; and military-political strategy, 664; purge technique, 667; identifies own power with salvation of USSR, 668; question of 'strategic bees in bonnet', 758 n. 143
'Stalin line', system of defence works, 406, 576, 607, 728 n. 6
Stalingrad Tractor Works, 305
'Stalinist military science', 129
Starikov, Major-General F. I., 605
Stashevich, member of Naval Academy, 475
Stashevskii, 430, 452, 455, 456, 464, 502
State Defence Committee (*GOKO*), formation and powers of, 1941, 598; and defence of Smolensk, 601; and 'Guards' units, 604; unifies South and South-western Fronts, 607; and reorganisation of Red Army, 614; problem of Leningrad air-lift, 618; authorises third Moscow defence line, 623; assigns Moscow command to Zhukov, 624; organises artillery production in Moscow, 628; assigns equipment to vital sectors only, 638
Statistische Abteilung, disguised intelligence organ of *Reichswehr*, 262, 271, 280, 711 n. 50
Stavka (1918), 18
Stavka (1941)
  of High Command (23rd June 1941): membership and functions, 598–9; and Western Front, 25th June, 600; and Smolensk defensive operation, 601; forms Central Front, 602
  of Supreme Command (July 1941): organised, 602; sets up three major commands, 603; and Leningrad defence, August, 606; splits Northern Front, 607; and South-western Front, July, 607; and Uman catastrophe, 608; assignment to Budenny, 609; lesson of faulty tactical methods, 613; re-organisation of Red Army, 614; and Leningrad defence, 618; orders evacuation of Odessa, 620; authorises with-drawal behind Mius, 621; anticipation of threat from Army Group Centre, 622; and 'Volkhov Group', 635; regroups armies by Moscow, 639; and German drive on Moscow from south, 641; transfers forces from Timoshenko, 642; plan for destruction of First Armoured Group, 646; categorical orders to 52nd Army, 647, 655; directive to Koniev, 650, 651; strength-ens Koniev's left wing, 654; and Tikhvin-Volkhov operations, 655–6; transfers troops to Sevastopol, 656: orders Kerch amphibious operation, 657; method of operating, 659–60; total deployment for Moscow opera-tions, 661; further wartime evolution, 667–8
Steel-production, 1928–30, 304; losses in, 1941, 628, 665
Stel'makh, Brigade Commander G. D., 655
Stepanov, 232
Stern. *See* Kleber
Stock-piling, raw materials and semi-manu-factured items, 1941, 575
Stopani, 123
Strang, W. (Lord Strang), 523
Strategic cavalry, 183, 206, 352, 438
Strategiya i Ekonomika (Soviet monograph), 615
Strategy; of civil war, 108; offensive-defensive, debated, 132–4; limitations on Soviet choice of, 208–9; attritional, Svechin on, 211; in China, 233, 238; possible Soviet-German naval, 1926, 254; and military-political relationships, 282; and the technical factor, 284; 'military assumptions' and, 289; to prevent anti-Soviet coalitions, 209; war and political objectives, 294–5; strategic objectives and diplomacy, 295; social and economic foundations of, 296; defen-sive, Ryazanov on, 1927, 297–8; Stalin on, 329; Stalinist, interpretations of, 330, 334; naval, 1933, 353; Japanese, in potential war against USSR, 361, 363; peculiarities of, in Far East, 399–400; naval, and emergence of new views, 1937–8, 475–7; first phase of Soviet, Finnish war, 543–4; apologia for failure of, Finnish war, 549; German views on probable Soviet strategic intentions, 1940, 1941, 560, 580; positional and manoeuvre, Red Army caught between, 581; German in Russia, compromise over primary objectives, 584; and Moscow offensive, 1941, 609; Lagovskii on, 615; Stalin's control of, 1941, 664. *See also* Marxism; Military doctrine; Military operations; War
Stresemann, G., 249, 256, 257
Stülpnagel, General J. von, 151, 348, 412, 610
Su Ping-wen, General, 337
Submarines, Soviet interest in, ix, 212; Soviet-German exchanges over, 252; receipt of German designs, 253; in Pacific, 1933, 338, 722–3 n. 113; possible tactical assignments, 355; strength in Pacific, 399; Soviet strength, 1936–7, 409, 803–4; as a defensive weapon, 410; Orlov on, 445; to be supplied by German ships, Finnish war, 547; Soviet submarine types, 803, 804

Suetaka, General, 495, 498
Sukhe-Bator, 223
Sukhomlin, chief of combat training, Far Eastern forces, 467
Sukhomlin, Lieutenant-General A. V., 606
Sukhorukov, V. T., 345
Sulimov, 671 n. 9
Sun Chuan-fang, 235
Sun Yat-sen, 226, 227, 228, 229
Supply, 165, 171, 173, 175, 317, 318, 405; norms and procedures, 175; dumps, 405, 409, 424; Administration (1926), functions and departments, 794; Special Air Force, 794
Supreme Court, Military Collegium, 368, 376, 377
Supreme Military Soviet (1918), 26, 34, 36, 53; Lenin's instruction on, 776; personnel and functions, 777
Supreme Naval Committee of Enquiry, 77
Supreme Soviet, 132, 475, 517
Supreme Soviet for National Defence, 26
'Supreme Staff of the Partisans of the Red Army' (1919), 64
Suritz, Soviet Ambassador in Germany, 456
Suvorov, Colonel, 524
Suvorov, Field Marshal, Prince A., 177
Suzuki, Colonel, 336
Svechin, Major-General A. A., 36, 101, 114, 116, 129, 211, 293, 308, 309
Sverdlov, Ya. M., 26, 27, 79
Sviridov, General of Artillery V. P., 605
Syrtsov, S. I., 338
Sytin, General, 68

Taalat Pasha, 146
Tabouis, Mme G., 413
Tachanka, peasant cart with machine-gun, 50
Tairov, 404, 415
Talenskii, Major-General N. A., 662
Tambov peasant insurrection (1920–21), 114, 120, 125, 127
Tanaka, General G., 239, 240
Tankabteilungen (Soviet-German), 719 n. 31
Tank design, 184, 270, 503
Tank-drivers, 406; lack of experience, 1941, 567
Tank forces, Red Army; Soviet interest in the tank, 270; tactical assignments, *PU–29*, 317; long-range tank groups (*TDD*), 317, 351, 439, 801; infantry-support (*TPP*), 317, 350, 439, 801; grouped into three types, 350, 769; and the *bystrokhodnyi tank* (*BT*), 350, 351, 355, 390; disputes over, 355–6; and the shock army, 365; tank brigades, composition, 1935, 390; servicing requirement, 1933, 405; machines employed in Spain, 430, 452, 455; in 1936 manoeuvres, 437; tactical assignments, *PU–36*, 439, 440–1, 801; independent operations, Tukhachevsky on, 458–9; in Lake Khasan fighting, 498, 499; estimated strength in Far East, 1939, 517; in action at Khalkhin-Gol, 518, 519, 520, 521, 522, 533, 534, 536–7; and mobile groups for invasion of Poland, 538, 539; operations against the Finns, 544, 545, 550, 551, 552; tank formations re-assembled, 559, 567; Tank Divisions and Corps, organisation and strength, 585; losses in armoured divisions, German estimate, August 1941, 613; requirements from Britain, 1941, 630; brigade organisation introduced, 1941, 649; brigade strengths, Moscow 1941, 662; comparative strengths, Moscow-Stalingrad, 760 n. 52; outline of organisation, 768–70. *See also* Mechanised/motor-mechanised forces, Red Army; Tanks
Tank-park, in 1933, 365, 769; in 1935, 389, 394, 769; in 1936, 405; obsolescence in, 559; Western Front, autumn 1941, 622; estimated, 15th June 1941, 770
Tank-production, 153, 270, 303, 304; 42 factories for, 1941, 575; special commissariat for, 1941, 616; in 1942, 664–5
Tank Reserve of Supreme Command (*TRGK*), 350, 769
Tanks, characteristics of Soviet models, 1929–1940, 770–2; BT–2, 567, 771; BT–5, 567, 771; BT–7, 771; KV–1, 548, 559, 567, 616, 619, 620, 643, 665, 771; KV–2, 772; MS–1 (T–18), 184, 241, 242, 270, 350, 770; T–19 (tankette), 270; T–20 (tankette), 270; T–24, 270, 770; T–26, 350, 430, 455, 771; T–26A, 350; T–26B, 771; T–26S, 772; T–28, 390, 567, 772; T–34, 533, 559, 567, 616, 619, 624, 643, 665, 772; T–35, 567, 772; T–37, 567; T–38, 536, 567; T–60, 616; T–130, 533
Tashkent (destroyer), 355, 657
TBS, heavy bomber force of *VVS*, 408
Techel, Dr, 253
Technical Bureau (for tank-study), 184
Technical Staff, for proposed Red Army, 1918, 674–5 n. 60
Telpukhovskii, Colonel B. S., 584
Temperley, Major-General A. C., 452
'Temporary Revolutionary Committee', Kronstadt 1921, 121
Teng Yen-ta, 234, 235
Tereshkin, Lieutenant P. F., 495
'Territorial military units'. *See* Workers-Peasants Militia
'Teuchmann'. *See* Schubert
Tevosyan, Shipbuilding Commissar, 512
The Decision to Intervene (Vol. II of *American-Soviet Relations, 1917–20*), 34
The Man with Three Faces, 414
The Military Staff (2nd Edn.), 438

The Prophet Unarmed, Trotsky 1921–29, 231
'The Regular Army and Militia', Frunze's paper, 1922, 131
The Reign of Stalin, 428, 455
The Soviet-Finnish Campaign 1939–1940, 549
Thomas, Colonel, 345
Thomsen, Colonel, 150, 151, 254, 257
Thyssen, F., 464
Timoshenko, Marshal S. K., career to 1918, 71; and 6th Cavalry Division, 1920, 97; deputy to Uborevich, 350; association with Zhukov, 353; to N. Caucasus MD, 1937, 463; protects staff, 471; Ukrainian Front commander, invasion of Poland, 1939, 538; North-western Front commander, Finnish operations, 547; Viipuri Bay operations, 1940, 550–1; appointed Marshal, 553; new training programmes, 554–5, 558, 583; possible anticipation of war, 560; main tasks in military re-organisation, 567; orders alert in west, spring 1941, 574; public statement on readiness, 578; alerts Red Army too late, 586; warning telegrams to MDs, 587; first operational order, 587–8; takes over from Pavlov, 600; defence of Smolensk, 601–2; takes over Western theatre, 603; commands South-western Front, 612; limited attacks on Western Front, 613, 617; withdrawal authorised, 621; earlier German opinion of, 626; builds up 37th Army, 641; ordered to form assault force, 650; commands south-western counter-blows, 658; survives as authoritative commander, 659; biography, 843–4
Tippelskirch, W. von, 427
Titulescu, N., 413
Tochka defensive system, 361
Todorskii, Lieutenant-General A. I., 227
Tokaev, G., 576, 623
Tokuma Kikan, Special Service Organ, Kwantung Army, 335
Tolbukhin, Marshal F. I., 554, 657
'Tolmachev group', dissident military commissars, 197
Tolmachev Military-Political Institute, 194
'Tomka' (Volsk) gas-warfare centre (Soviet-German), 264, 344, 345
Tomsky(-ii), M. P., 201, 285, 315, 425, 483, 486
Town Staff of Worker Formations, Moscow 1941, 623
Tracer-bullets, 272
Tractor industry, 303, 305
Tractors, 152, 153, 161, 184, 273, 304, 390, 696 n. 28, 702, n. 64
Transportation; *Inland Waterways*: limitations, 305; *Belomorstroi*, 353, 354; *Railways*: and Warsaw offensive, 1920, 98; and militia system, 132; capacity in western frontier areas, 1928, 262; long-distance traffic, 305, 424, 716 n. 52; in Soviet Far East, 334, 337, 360, 361, 397, 398, 400, 401; internal movement of forces, 381–2; *NKVD* supervision of, 403; faultiness of, 405; dislocations due to purging administration, 466; Dr Tsiang on, 491; and Red Army concentration, 527; broad-gauge extension, Belorussia, 572; British view of, 1939, 746 n. 44; Baikal-Amur (BAM), 414; Trans-Siberian, 334, 360, 397, 424; Turksib, 335, 425; *Road*: 1% properly surfaced, 305; proposed movement of fuel, 403, 424; motorised transport, 424; transport lorries and Khalkhin-Gol, 533
Trautmann, 272
Treaties; Brest-Litovsk, 16, 20–1, 144, 675 n. 68; Rapallo, 153, 154, 156, 330, 332, 333, 347; Soviet-Japanese (1925), 239
Trevoga (Far Eastern military newspaper), 467
Trials; 'Industrial Party', 1930, 325, 332; Zinoviev-Kamenev, 1935, 391; 'Trotskyite-Zinovievite Centre', 1936, 425, 426, 427; 'Anti-Soviet Trotskyite Centre' 1937, 449–50, 451, 462, 466; Khabarovsk, June 1938, 493; 'Anti-Soviet "Bloc of Rights and Trotskyites" ', 162–3, 481–8, 740 n. 22
Triandafillov, V. K., on Polish campaign, 1920, 100; on modern operations, 318; recent Soviet attention to, 706 n. 135; biography, 844
Tributs, Admiral V. F., 554
Trotsky(-ii: Bronshtein), L. D., role in Bolshevik *coup*, 10–11; early re-organisation of armed forces, 17, 674 n. 49; Commissar for War, 21; and Supreme Military Soviet, 26; qualifications as War Commissar, 28, 676 n. 13; possible use of Allied help, 29, 676 n. 15; handling of Czechoslovak Legion, 29; military reforms, 30; on 'military specialists', 31–2; use of ex-NCOs, 32; reprisals against ex-officers, 33; head of *RVSR*, 36; member of Soviet of Workers-Peasants Defence, 38; imposition of death-penalty, 39, 678 n. 50; on military theories, 39; clash with Stalin, 1918, 40; on Red Army and the Imperial Army, 40–1; centralisation of political organs, 42; criticised by Gusev, 43; attacked over Perm catastrophe, 45–6, 58; Lenin's support for, 46; programme at 8th Party Congress, 47–8; militia programme at 9th Party Congress, 49–50; attack on Voroshilov, 51; at Sviyazhsk, 55; selects Tukhachevsky, 57; involved in

Trotsky—*contd.*
Eastern Front disputes, 61; fears over Urals advance, 64; offers resignation, 66; on Voroshilov, 68, 683 n. 60; strategy for Ukraine, 69, 683 n. 68; and cavalry, 70, 683 n. 64; protests over Ukrainian operations, 71; Tukhachevsky's complaint to, 73; on transition to militia, 74; on military commissars, 81; opposed by 'Red command', 82; as organiser of Red Army, 83; militarisation of labour, 85; opposes optimism over Polish campaign, 87; and reinforcements for Stalin, 1920, 89; warns against Warsaw drive, 97, 687 n. 26, 689 n. 61; attacks Stalin, 98; on militia, 109; opposes export of revolution, 113; on militia, 9th Party Congress programme, 115–16; opposed by Tukhachevsky, 118–19; attacked by Stalin-Zinoviev, 119; and Frunze-Gusev reforms, 120; explanation of Kronstadt, 120; misrepresented by Zinoviev, 121; and Georgia, 124; criticised, 126, 127; on military doctrine, 128–9; clashes with Frunze, Gusev, 130; answered by Frunze, 131; at 11th Party Congress, 132–4; and 'Red command', 135–6; success for territorial formation, 139; attack by triumvirate, 140–1, 142; and Kopp, 147, 148; supposed signal to Kopp, 1920, 149; and German military assistance, 150; on possible German-Polish conflict, 1923, 160; talk with Brockdorff-Rantzau, 161–2, 247; Vyshinsky on, 163; attacked, 1923, 164; indicted by Military Commission, 166; leaves Moscow, 163; attacked by Voroshilov, 170; ousted from Red Army leadership, 171; misrepresented, 172; and Baltic Fleet, 176; compared with Frunze, 177; military opponents, 179; on peasants, 180; and inner-Party struggle, 188–9; removed from *RVS*, 189; attitude over military commissars, 198; opinion of Frunze's death, 199; at 14th Party Congress, 201; and 'new Opposition', 201–2; expelled from *Politburo*, 202; validity of arguments, 208; 'permanent revolution', exponent, 210; approval over Far Eastern negotiations, 219; contacted by Chiang Kai-shek, 227, 228; policy for China, 231, 233; on Blyukher, 237; criticism of defence policies, 1927, 285–6, 616; 'Clemenceau thesis', 286, 509; on implications of 'defence of Soviet Union', 286–7; expelled from Party, 287–8; deportation, 288; and coalition warfare, 295; on Soviet Bonapartism, 298–9, 300–1; on Red Army, 1935, 387, 401; struggle with Stalin, extended into Spanish Civil War, 429; 'signature' on SD dossier, 435, 456; mentioned in 1938 Trial, 481, 484, 485; biography, military appointments, 844

Troyanovsky(-ii), A., 357, 362

Truppenamt, 52, 151, 152, 156, 263

Tschunke, Major F., 150, 151, 157

Tsiang, Dr, 490, 491

Tukhachevsky(-ii), Marshal M. N., at Simbirsk, 1918, 55; 1st Army commander, 57; career up to 1918, 57–8; personality, 58, 680 n. 14; commands Vth Army, 61; and Samoilo, 63; successful advance in the east, 64; transferred to Southern Front, 73; meets Budenny and Voroshilov, 74; commander of N. Caucasus, 75; deleted from recent list of Soviet commanders, 80; strength on Western Front, 1920, 87; modifies operational plan, 88; justification of initial offensive, 89, 686 n. 18; regroups forces, 91; total force available, Polish operations, 93, 687 n. 38; refuses troops to Yegorov, 94; moves 'secret army', 94–5; dispute with S. S. Kamenev, 95, 688 n. 46; directive for Warsaw battle, 96, 688 n. 48; defeated before Warsaw, 98; and Stalin's charge, 99; lecture on Polish war (1923), 99–100, 689 n. 54 & n. 65; for a renewal of war, 1920, 104; proposals to *Komintern*, letter to Zinoviev, 107–8, 784; command at Kronstadt, 110; director of Staff Academy, 114; opposes militia scheme, 119–20; crushes Kronstadt rebellion, 122; and *Kavburo*, 123; command during Tambov risings, 127; offensivism criticised, 128; views on 11th Party Congress, 133–4, 694 n. 79; critised by Frunze, 135; on Red Army, 1923, 170; assistant to Chief of Staff, 173; and Red Army manuals, 178; position within command group, 179; head of Red Army Staff, 200; implied criticism of Voroshilov, 207; and Eikhe, 1920, 220; possibly returned to Staff, 1929, 241; Muklevich's service under, 254; Mittelberger on, 262, 711 n. 51; Blomberg's talk with, 266; and *Reichswehr* collaboration, 279; not a signatory to protest over Voroshilov, 286; position vis-à-vis Shaposhnikov, 292, 293; on modern war, 295–6; on political interference with the military, 296–7; stress on internationalism, 297–8; on location of war-industry, 303; and morale, 306; exponent of the mass army, 308; attacks Svechin, 308–9; must equate mass and mobility, 321; influence, 327; visit to Germany, 1932,

341–2; meets von Bockelberg, 343–4; on 'installations', 344–5; talk with Twardowski, 346–7; absent from *Z.Mo.* dinner, 347; denies 'leak' over collaboration, 348, 723 n. 118; and the new Red Army, 349–50; as centre of 'command group', 350; on manoeuvre and mobility, 351; involved in disputes over the tank, 355–6; supposed bargain with Stalin over mechanisation, 356; meets Colonel Mendras, 364; as compared with Yegorov, 371; as mere 'functionary', 372; on Red Army, 1935, 381–2; on German military threat, 383–4; Gekker on, 385; and Sedyakin, 388; appointed Marshal, 392; considered pro-French by Germans, 394; call on Germans in Moscow, 395; position in 1935, 401; ambiguity of views and opinions, 1935, 402–3; and planning of 'defence belts', 406; on naval forces, 1936, 409–10; stress on command capability, 410; visits London, 1936, 411; in France, 412–13; supposed conspiratorial contacts, 413–414; and welded tanks, 415–16; and Central Committee, 1936, 426; 're-instated' in 1936 but pressure on Putna, 427, 428; 'signature' for SD dossier, 435, 456; machination to compromise the Marshal and his 'clique', 436; Colonel Martel's opinion of, 437; demand for 'nerve' vitiated by command method, 444; political fortunes at stake, 445; at 8th Congress of Soviets, 1936, 446; Krestinsky's 'testimony' on, 447; implicated in 1937 Trial by Radek, 449–50; and 1937 Central Committee plenum, 1937, 452; re-appearance in March, 1937, 455, 735 n. 17; conference with Stashevskii, 456; commentary on *PU–36*, 458–9, 470; London journey cancelled, 459; arrested, 460; 'case' and 'trial', 463, 464, 737 n. 48 & n. 49, 739 n. 74; difficulties of 're-habilitation', 465; as 'agent of Fascism', 475–6; mentioned in 1938 Trial, 481, 482, 483, 484, 486; and supposed *coup*, 1938 Trial versions, 488; inherent soundness of military ideas, 502; denounced at 18th Party Congress, 512; previous plans for defence in depth and 1941 situation, 576; ideas partially re-adopted, 583; military ideas revived in 1941, 659; biography, 844–5

Tupolev, A. N., 382, 408, 500–1, 505

Turkey, 75, 123–4, 130–1, 146–7, 290, 291, 333, 354, 422, 513, 573

Tsentrobalt, 6, 77

Twardowski, F. von, 346, 348, 364, 378

Twiss, Colonel, 146

Tyagunov, head of Faculty of Motorisation and Mechanisation (Leningrad), 333

Tyulenev, General I. V., 102, 367, 463, 538, 554, 557, 591, 607, 608, 612, 689 n. 71

U–boat plans, delivered to Russians, 253

Uborevich, Army Commander I. P., commander of XIVth Army, 1920, 90; commander of XIIIth Army, 103; criticises military administration, 1923, 169–70; commander of N. Caucasus MD, 202; commander in Far East, 1922, 225; attached to *Reichswehr*, 258–9; seconded to German staff, 1929, 271; part in military-industrial collaboration, 272, 273; on war of revenge, 274; in Dresden, 280; contact with Hammerstein-Equord, 280; and Tukhachevsky group, 327; commands Belorussian MD, 341, 367; in France, 412; mentioned in possible mobilisation order, 418; commands north-western striking force, 419; and Central Committee plenum, 1936, 426; at 1936 manoeuvres, 436; and Central Committee plenum, 1937, 452; vanishes, 1937, 461; 'case' and 'trial', 463; mentioned, 1938 Trial, 482, 484; biography, 845–6

Ufimskaya avantyura Kolchaka Mart–Aprel' 1919 (Soviet monograph), 61

Uglanov, N. A., 201

Ulagai, General, 103, 104

Ulrikh, V. V., President of Military Collegium, Supreme Court, 463

Umansky(-ii), S., 566–7, 750 n. 4

Ungern Sternberg, R. F., 222, 223

Union of Tsarist Veterans, 434

Unit administration, 175, 260

United States of America, 218, 219, 223, 225, 239, 241, 362, 414, 500, 566–7

Universal Military Training. *See Vsevobuch*

Universities, military faculties and sections, 195

Unshlikht, I. S., 85, 168, 170, 171, 173, 178, 200, 248, 249, 252, 253, 256, 257, 292, 315

'Untermann' ('Herr U'). *See* Unshlikht

Uralov, A., 426, 428, 455

Urals-Siberian Bureau, 64

Uritskii, M. S., 27, 122, 418, 429

Ustinov, 157

Vaineros, senior military commissar, 451, 467

Vakhrameev, I. I., 77

Valin, chief of intelligence, Red Banner Front, 467

Vasentsovich, 493

Vashugin, Corps Commissar, 597

Vasilenko, Lieutenant-Colonel E. I., 643

Vasil'ev, 61

Vasilevskii, Marshal A. M., 508, 551, 554, 660

Vasiliev, 121

Vassilchenko, Soviet Air Attaché, 412
Vassilenko, head of Infantry Inspectorate, 367
Vassiliev, 490
Vatsetis, Army Commander I. I., 36, 46, 54, 55, 59, 61, 63, 64, 66, 67, 115, 178, 211, 298, 502, 846
Vatutin, General N. F., 508, 558, 604
Vayo, Alvarez del, 431
Vedenichev, Lieutenant-General of Tank Troops N., 351
Veklichev, Army Commissar, 450, 461
Velichko, General, 114
Ventsov, S. S., Soviet Military Attaché, 385, 412
Verkhovskii, General A. I., 9, 114, 211, 308, 309, 318
Vikorist, Rear-Admiral Ya. E., 34
Viktorov, Flag-Officer, commander of Pacific Fleet, 361, 392, 399, 475, 500
Vinogradov, Soviet Attaché, 342
Virilov, 412
Vlasov, Lieutenant-General A. A., 558, 597, 612, 633, 651, 660, 663, 741 n. 41
Voenki, small armed Bolshevik bands, 1917, 8
Voennaya nauka i revolyutsiya (Soviet military journal), 128
Voennyi Vestnik (Soviet military journal), 128
Voikov, assassination of, 284
Voina i politika (Soviet monograph), 294
Voitinsky(-ii), G., 221
Volovich, senior *NKVD* officer, 428
Volunteer Army, 15, 102
Vorob'ev, Lieutenant-General V., 582, 642, 646, 666
Voronov, Colonel-General N. N., 558, 614, 624
Vorontsov, Captain, Soviet Military Attaché, 579
Voroshilov, Marshal K. E., on Lugansk town defence committee, 1917, 9; commands Vth Ukrainian Army, 21; obstructionist attitude at Tsaritsyn, 39, 40; Stalin's indirect support for, 47; Trotsky's disparagement of, 51; associated with Stalin, Budenny, 67; clashes with Trotsky, 68; meeting with Budenny, 70; member of *RVS*, 1st Cavalry Army, 72; meets Tukhachevsky, 74; aids Stalin against Trotsky, 83; protests over cavalry move, 89, 686 n. 21; cavalry offensive, 1920, 90, 91; association with 1st Cavalry command, 101; at and on Kronstadt, 122; and Central Committee, 125; protests over disbanding of 1st Cavalry Army, 126; at 11th Party Congress, 132, 133; contact with Zinoviev, 141; attack on Trotsky, 168, 170; commander of Moscow MD, 171, 178; member *RVS*, 171; and cavalry organisation, 183; commission on political work, 187; successor to Frunze, 200; fitness for new post, 200–1; position in 1926, 202; centralisation scheme, 203; on unitary command, 204–5; criticised by Tukhachevsky, 207; and Manchuria crisis, 241; relations with Blyukher, 245–6; implicated in 'revelations', 1926, 248; loses control of collaboration matters, 257; drives through agreement on 'installations', 258; on demand for German manuals, 259; inspection report on Ukrainian MD, 260; Blomberg on, 264–5; asks about German intentions, 265, 277–8; desire for armaments base, 268; contact with senior German officers, 271, 272, 713 n. 86; deals with General Ludwig, 273; despatches naval mission to Germany, 275; relation with Halm, 280; reliance on human element, 284; criticised as incompetent, 286; attacked by Trotsky, 286–7; supports Stalin, 288; address to *Komintern* agents, 290; contrives removal of Tukhachevsky, 293; and Bonapartism, 299; on military equipment, 302–3; member *STO*, 306; on Right Opposition, 315; and *PU–29*, 316; on the military commissar, 316–17; association with Uborevich, 326; place in Stalin's command, 327; request to Köstring, 333; in Soviet Far East, 335; talk with Dirksen, 33; and closing of 'installations', 347, 348; on new weapons, 351; hints on foreign technical help for *VMF*, 354–5; on the tank, 1933, 356; and French help, 364; receives German condolences on death of Lebedev, 367; Defence Commissar, 369; increased powers, 371; exercises strict control, 372; on command staff, 374; obtains release of Primakov, 377; reported 'liberal' tendency, 378; talk with Nadolny, 379; favours pro-German orientation, 385; controls *VVS* Inspectorate, 388; appointed Marshal, 392; implications of statistics on command staff, 393; a Stalin man, 401; kept under surveillance, 404; and artillery policy, 407; present at debate on naval policy, 409; on Baltic states, 418; and supposed mobilisation order, 418–19; supports Stalin, 1936, 426; host to British military mission, 1936, 436; Colonel Martel's opinion of, 437; receives protest on 1937 Trial from Köstring, 451; Berzin's confidential report to, 1937, 452, 455; and Central Committee plenum, 452; criticised by Tukhachevsky, 459; and Red Army purge, 462, 464, 737 n. 49; orders over 'Amur incident', 468; president of Main Military Soviet, 478;

speech, May Day, 1938, 490; implicated in Blyukher affair, 492, 499; exchanges with General Gamelin, 503, 504; as exception, other officers having been purged, 506; ability for high command, 508; only military member of *Politburo*, 510; on dual command, 510–11; on *VVS*, 512; to be approached by French Military Attaché, 514; negotiations with Anglo-French military mission, 524, 525, 526, 527, 528–9; sees General Doumenc alone, 529; final interview with French and British senior officers, 531; and disbanding of mechanised formations, 537; over-all command, Finnish operations, 547; becomes Deputy Chairman, Defence Committee, 553; member of *GOKO*, 1941, 598; member of Supreme Command *Stavka*, 602; takes over North-western command, 603; rallies defence, Luga sector, 604; sets up 'Guards' units, 605; criticised by Stalin over Leningrad Defence Soviet, 627; initial orders over Sevastopol defences, 642; biography, 846–7

Voskanov, G. K., 90, 97

Vostretsov, S. S., 242

Voukelich, 414

Voznesenskii, N. A., 575, 628

Vsevobuch (Universal Military Training), 38, 49, 115, 306, 679–80 n. 87

Vsevolodov, N. D., 69

Vuillemin, General, 514

Vychevskii, Colonel B. V., 605

Vyshinsky(-ii), A. A., 163, 425, 449, 481, 482, 483, 484, 486, 487, 573, 574

Wallroth, 250

War, between bourgeois state and socialist island, Tukhachevsky on, 108; in 'small' (partisan) form, 127, 361; problems of 'revolutionary' form, 128, 133, 210; 'Communist doctrine' of, 129; offensive aim in, 1922, 133; and technical factor, 207, 210; in the future, Frunze's views, 210–11; and Japanese planning against the USSR, 254; against Poland, contingency of, 262–3, 265; and 'total leadership', 282; war-scarce, 1927, 284–6; not in itself an object of Soviet policy, 289; higher direction and planning of, 291; General Staff as directorate of, 293; Shaposhnikov on, 293–5; and diplomacy, 294; coalition warfare, 295; Tukhachevsky's view of higher direction of, 295; and defensive techniques, 296; future form of, argued 1928, 296–7, 327; as social (class) phenomenon, 297; and the 'civil front', 306; and *PU–29*, 316; future form, speculation over 1933, 352; and the 'battle for the frontiers', Soviet views, 352, 384, 407, 569; without declaration, Shilovskii's views, 384; assumptions over possible combat forms, 1935, 390; and Soviet operational plan, 1941, 569; *Blitzkrieg* theories discounted by Soviet writers, 733 n. 115

Civil war: 'science of', Tukhachevsky on, 108; in the capitalist rear, 297

'Imperialist war': as opposed to class or civil war, 108; 'positional' character of, 127; persistent propaganda against, 291; and colonialism, 297

'Patriotic war' (also synonym for Soviet-German War): ideological emphasis on, 1941, 603; German miscalculation as stimulus to, 664, 666

War games, 207

War Industry Main Directorate (*GUVP*), 184, 292

War Ministry, operated by Bolsheviks, 1917, 17

War-plan, Voroshilov on, ix, 288; Tukhachevsky on, 295; railways in, 305

Washington Conference, 224, 225

Weapon-production, 304, 575

Wehrkreis No. II, 280

Weimar Republic, 160, 330

Weizsäcker, E., 515

Welles, Sumner, 566–7

Werth, Naval Captain, 253

Wetzell, General, 249, 255, 256

Weygand, General M., 91, 95, 385, 688 n. 44

Whampoa Military Academy, 229, 230, 232, 708 n. 56

White Sea Canal (*Belomorstroi*), 353

Wireless equipment, 272

Wirth, Chancellor, 156

Wirtschaftskontor (*WIKO*), 251

With the Russian Army, 1914–1917 (Vol. II), 6

Witzell, Naval Captain, 277

Wong Ching-wei, 708 n. 56

Workers-Peasants Inspectorate (*Rabkrin*), 140, 141, 306

Workers-Peasants Militia, suggested at 8th Party Congress, 48; formulated, 9th Party Congress, 49–50; Trotsky on, 1919, 74; clashes over, 83; increasing differences over, 109; transition to, discussed at 9th Party Congress, 115; criticised, 118; accepted as experiment, 119; first militia brigade, 125; Gusev on, 129; Frunze on, 131–2; territorial system, 138; political work in, 139; persistent misgivings over, 180; in relation to *Osoaviakhim*, 388; and cadre forces, 405

Workers-Peasants Red Army (*RKKA*), vii, viii, ix; wide variety of names for, 1918, 18–19; decree on *RKKA*, 19; decentralisation in, 19–20; organisation of first

Workers-Peasants Red Army (*RKKA*)—*contd.* units, 20, 675 n. 66; 'International battalions', 25, 675 n. 3; Chinese units in, 25, 675 n. 4; transition from volunteerism, 30–1; organised mobilisations for, 31; strength, 1918, 31, 677 n. 23 & 24; problem of officering, 31–2; planned strength, 1918, 33; and 'military specialists', 33–4; military districts organised, 34; *RVSR*, 36; early characteristics of, 40; and Political Administration, 42; 'cells' in, 44–5; centralised control, 46–7; combat strength, Eastern Front, 1919, 59; total combat strength, table, 1919, 60; strength of worker element, 78; and struggle over 'dual command', 81–3; strength deployed against Poles, 87, 88, 93; divisional strengths, Polish campaign, 100, 687 n. 39; total strength, 1920, 101; strength deployed against Wrangel, 105, 106, 687 n. 27; peasant-worker tie endangered, 109; disputes over organisation of, 115; arguments for a regular army, 118; and experimental militia units, 119; Frunze; Gusev programme for, 120, 691 n. 20, and decisions of 10th Party Congress. 125; Frunze on, 127; Red Army Staff created, 128; political work in, 129–30; 'mixed military establishment', 132; effects of demobilisation on, 136, 693–4 n. 67; composition, 1922, 136–7; and territorial system, 139; political issues in, 1923, 142; and agreement with *Reichswehr*, 155; investigation into, 1923, 164–5; 'instability' in, 165; composition, 1923–4, 167, 786; further enquiry into, 1923, 168; 'unfit for combat', 169; Frunze's criticisms of, 170; new command appointments in, 171; Order No. 446/96 on reform, 173; and Staff, 173–4; aviation units, 175, 176; and operation of 'mixed military system', 179–80; territorial training, 180–1; strength, 181; infantry re-organisation, 182–3, 792–3; cavalry re-organisation, 183–4, 788; tanks and armoured-car forces, 184; National Formations, 184–185; and Military Districts, 185; and Political Administration, 186–7; involved in inner-Party struggle, 188–9; 'cells' in, 1924–5, 189–90; and *PURKKA*, 191; command staff, 191–2, 788, 796–9; categorisation of command staff, 192–3, 789; Military Academies of, 194, 788, 791–3; unitary command in, 1925–7, 196–9, 788; administrative re-organisation, 1926, 203–4, 794–6; commander fails to triumph in unitary command, 204–5; manuals, regulations, 207; general position of, 1923–5, 212–13; creation of *ODVA*, 240; Manchurian operations, 1929, 241–4; Red Army officers in Germany, 258–9; German opinion of, 260; Voroshilov's criticisms, 260; Mittelberger report on, 261–2; German estimate of combat strength, 1928, 262; and possible Soviet operational intentions, 262–3; General Blomberg's report on visit to, 263–8; German officers with, 1929, 269; British tanks ordered for, 269–70; 'mechanised unities' in, 1929, 270; value of *Reichswehr* assistance to, 281; and war-scare, 1927, 285; weapon production for, annual averages 1930–1937, 304; para-military training and, 307–8; and heresy of small élite armies, 308–9; political indoctrination in, 311–12; purge in, 1929, 315; and *PU–29*, 316–18; contribution of ex-Imperial officers, 318; military intelligentsia and, 318–19; impact of technical changes, 319; field strength, 1930, 326; Stalin on, 329; in Far East, 336, 337; and *Reichswehr*, 1933, 343–9; mention of Japanese officers seconded to, 348; German assistance, 349–50; mechanised and tank forces, 1933, 350–3, 355–6; deployment in Far East, 360; reserves in Far East, special arrangements for, 363; senior command group, 1933, 366–7; and Defence Commissariat, 369–70; impact of military reforms, 1934, 370–2; bureaucratism in, 372; budget, 1934, 372; social and political composition, 1930–4, 373–4; purge in, 374; Tukhachevsky on, 380–2; ground-support tactical aviation, 382–3; French officers to, 386; Trotsky on, 1935, 387, 401; field strength, 1935, 389; development of tank, mechanised, motor-mechanised forces, 389–90; motorisation in, 390; military ranks introduced, 1935, 391; expansion in Far East, 397–8, 734 n. 4; re-deployed, 1936, 405; technical requirements, 405–6; new artillery specifications, 407–8; and higher military education, 410; possible mobilisation order for, 1936, 418; Cossack formations re-introduced, 422, 730 n. 48; man-power, 1936, 424; contingent in Spain, 430–1; manoeuvres, 1936, 436–7; and *PU–36*, 437–45, 800–3; social revolution embodied in, 446; strength in Far East, 1937, 451; Tukhachevsky on internal differences of opinion over doctrine, 458–9; onset of military purge, 1937, 459–60; arrests of senior officers and commissars, 460–2; and 'trial' of high command, 463–6;

preliminary purge in Far East forces, 1937, 467–8; and 'Amur incident', 468; further eliminations in Red Army, 470–2; Stalin still retains loyalty of, 472–3; and Main Military Soviet, 1938, 478; 'vigilance' is entrusted to military commissar, 478–9; administrative reforms, 480; purge of Far Eastern forces, 1938, 492–4; and Lake Khasan fighting, 1938, 497–9; forces available 'in the west', Munich crisis, 504; losses in commanders due to purge, 505–6, 744 n. 89; statements on at 18th Party Congress, 1939, 510–11, 512–13; strength in Far East, Japanese estimate, 1939, 517; in Khalkhin-Gol operations, 1939, 517–18, 518–22, 532–7, 805–6; British estimate of, 524; deployment and concentration, Shaposhnikov's disclosures, 527; mobilisation for Polish invasion, 538–9; combat methods, operations and shortcomings, Finland 1939–40, 543, 544, 545, 547, 548–52, 748 n. 115; German assessment of, 548, 749 n. 130; Order No. 120 on shortcomings in Finnish operations, 553; senior command promotions, 1940, 553–4; new disciplinary code, 555; occupies Bessarabia, N. Bukovina, 556; strength and deployment, 1940, 557; more realistic training for, 558; and charges of incompetence against Stalin, 559; infantry and armoured formations re-organised, 1941, 567–8; operational plan for, 569, 750 n. 6; and defence plan for Baltic states, 570; frontier deployment, spring 1941, 571–2; British assessment of, 1941, 574; slow delivery of new weapons to, 574–5; training programmes do not include variant of possible war, 576–7; no consideration of strategic defence and withdrawal for, 576; maintenance of morale, 578; troops moved from Far East to European Russia, 579, 753 n. 54; German view of strength and possible operational employment, 580–1; affected by too uncritical an offensivism, 582; covering armies, frontier districts, 1941, 584–5; strength and organisation of armoured forces, 585; alerted, midnight 21st June 1941, 586–7; first operational order to, 587–8; Order of Battle, frontier armies, 589–92; and frontier MDs smashed, 593–7; *NKVD* machine-gunners hold from unauthorised withdrawal, 598; Chief of Rear Services for, 598–9; fully mobilised, Far East, 599; death-sentences in, 599–600; encircled, Bialystok-Minsk, 600; at Smolensk, 601–2; no initial mass surrenders in, 603; and idea of 'Guards' units, 605; smashed in Ukraine, 607–12; German estimate of losses, view of defective tactics, 612–13; creation of 'Guards Divisions', 613; offensive attacks halted, 613–14; artillery re-organisation, 614; short of tanks, ammunition, essential equipment, 616; real impact of purge is becoming plain, 617; organises for October offensive, Leningrad Front, 619; reinforced with *DNO*, 621; taken by surprise by German September offensive, 622; 'they are learning', 624; losses, men and equipment, by autumn 1941, 625; rapidity of degeneration of its position, 626; reconstitution of command, 627; and co-operation with partisans, 629; lowest strength ever in Soviet-German War, 631; strength, Far East, 632; slight improvement in leadership of, 632–3; Tikhvin-Volkhov fighting, defensive phase, 633–7; weapons, men for decisive sectors only, 638; independent rifle brigades formed, 639; desperate fighting, approaches to Moscow, 640–1; comparison, Soviet and German-Italian forces, Donbas/Rostov operations, 645; strength fielded, December 1941, 649; takes offensive before Moscow, 651–5; attacks, Tikhvin-Volkhov, 655–6; Kerkch-Feodosiya landings, 657–8; general offensive, December, 1941–January, 1942, 658–9; political instruction in, 660; high command mobilises its talent, 663; winter offensive achieves only partial success, 665–6; command begins to recover nerve, 667; unitary command brought back, 668; strength and composition table, 1918–41, 763–8; organisation of Red Army motor-mechanised, mechanised, tank forces, 768–70; tank models in, 770–2; attestation procedure for, 773–5. *See also* Armies, formations, units; Artillery; Aviation; Budenny; Cavalry; Command; Command staff; Commissars; Communist Party, Russian; Frunze; Lenin, Mechanised/motor-mechanised forces; Military Academies; Military administration; Military collaboration; Military commissars; Military doctrine; Military operations; 'Military specialists'; Political Administration; Purges; Regulations, combat manuals; Rifle troops; Shaposhnikov; Special Sections (*OO*); Stalin; Tank forces; Tanks; Trotsky; Tukhachevsky; Voroshilov; Workers-Peasants Militia

Wrangel, General P. N., 73, 86, 91, 92, 94, 97, 99, 101, 102, 103, 104, 105, 106, 113, 223

Wu Pei-fu, Marshal, 233, 234
Wurzbacher, General, 105

Yagoda, G. G., head of *NKVD*, 378, 426, 427, 429, 452, 455, 457, 481, 483, 487, 488
Yakir, Army Commander I. E., career to 1918, 80; commands 'Fastov army group', 1920, 89; work in Military Education Administration, 178; and new command group, 179; commands Ukrainian, Pri-Volga MD, 202; signs criticism of Voroshilov, 286; member of Tukhachevsky 'group', 327; commands Ukrainian MD, 367; commands Kiev MD, 394; commands south-western striking force, 419; and Central Committee plenum, 1936, 426; and plenum, 1937, 452; 'posted' to Leningrad MD, 1937, 460; 'case' and 'trial', 463; mentioned, 1938 Trial, 482, 484
Yakovenko, Soviet Military Attaché, 333, 340, 341, 346
Yakovlev, Lieutenant-General V. F., 633, 634
Yamagata, Japanese cavalry commander, 518
Yartsev, B., 541
Yefremov, General M. G., 463, 641, 654, 662, 663
Yegor'ev, V. N., 70
Yegorov, chief of Kremlin military school, 483
Yegorov, Marshal A. I., 70, 71, 109; military career to 1918, 72–3; commander South-western Front, 89; to take precautionary measures against Rumania, 92; forces available, 93; ambiguous strategic assignment, 94; account of Polish campaign (1929), 100–1; associated with special military commission, 168; on need for reform, 170; command posts, 1924, 178; in Peking, 228; Chief of Staff, 340; invited to Germany, 341; to be visited by General Lutz, 347; and *Reichswehr* collaboration, 364; remains Chief of Staff, 370; limited talents of, 371; talk with Twardowski, 378; counted pro-German, 385; and Sedyakin, 388; appointed Marshal, 392; 'a good figurehead', 402; invitation to Baltic states senior officers, 418; and possible mobilisation order, 419; as candidate member of Central Committee, 1936, 426; host to British military mission, 1936, 436; appears to lack drive, 437; at May Day parade, 1937, 458; relieved of post, 460; replaces Tukhachevsky, 463, 470; not on 'court-martial' board, 464; mentioned, 1938 Trial, 483, 488; disappearance, 502, 506; biography, 847
Yegorov, Major-General D. G., 643
Yenukidze, A. S., 483, 486, 487
Yeremenko, Marshal A. I., 554, 609, 610, 617
Yeremeyev, K. E., 27
Yermakov, Major-General A. N., 624, 640
Yeroshchenko, Soviet tank-regiment commander, 269
Yershakov, Lieutenant-General F. A., 590
Yezhov, N. I., head of *NKVD*, 426, 427, 431, 445, 452, 455, 457, 462, 465, 482, 510
Yoshizawa, 336
Young Plan, 330
Yrjö-Koskinen, A. S., 541
Yudenich, General N. N., 66, 71
Yugoslavia, 573, 577, 579
Yumashev, Admiral I. S., Pacific Fleet commander, 554
Yurenev, K., 56, 362, 490
Yurin, 222
Yushkevich, Major-General V. A., 651

Z. Mo. See Zentrale Moskau
Zaitsev, Major-General, P. A., 605
Zakharin, Lieutenant-General I. G., 538, 639, 653
Zakharov, Colonel V. A., 615
Zaporozhets, Army Commissar A. I., 655
Zedin, K. Ya., 77
Zenoviev, on intelligence functions at divisional level, 438
Zentrale Moskau (*Z.Mo.*), 158, 251, 261, 263, 347
Zhavoronkov, Lieutenant-General of Red Army Aviation S. F., 554
Zhdanov, A. A., 426, 476, 477, 490, 510, 523, 551, 598, 603, 605, 606, 623, 627, 748 n. 96
Zheleznyakov, A. G., 77
Zhigarev, Marshal of Aviation P. F., 554
Zhloba, D. P., cavalry commander, 91
Zhukov, Marshal G. K., viii, 4, 245, 471, 503; enters Red Army, 1918, 71, 683 n. 66; as with Trotsky, Tukhachevsky, charged with 'de-politicalising' army, 170; outstanding service in Belorussia; MD, 352–3; escapes purge, 1937, 463; and 'rehabilitation' of Tukhachevsky, 465; command at Khalkhin-Gol, 1939, 522, 532, 533, 534, 536, 537; on Finland as 'the acid test', 552–3; promoted full General, 554; view over tanks vindicated, 559; on training, 563; Chief of General Staff, 1941, 568; now blamed for 1941 disasters, 568–9; and General Staff-*Stavka* relation, 598; commands High Command reserves, 601; member of Supreme Command *Stavka*, 602; commands Western Front, 618, 621, 623, 624, 633; forces available to, 625; and plan for Moscow counter-offensive, 641, 649; detailed plan for Moscow operations, 650, 661; criticises 'vicious tactics', 652; forms mobile group from 50th Army, 653; and direction of

Moscow operations, 659; strength of tank force, 662; and choice of main blows, 663; dismissal, 1957, 668; biography, 847–8
Zhuravlev, P. N., 221
Zinoviev, G. E., 'warns' Trotsky, 47; letter from Tukhachevsky, 107, 784–5; attacks Trotsky, 119; and Kronstadt, 1921, 121; member of triumvirate, 140, 189; moves against Stalin, 141; Frunze's supposed support for, 199; favours Lashevich for War Commissar, 200; at 14th Party Congress, 201; expelled from *Politburo*, 202; defeated by Stalin, 285, 287; tried, 1935, 391; shot, 1936, 425
Zinoviev, G. V., 61
Zivkov, Chief of Staff, Baltic Fleet, 450, 470, 475
Zof, V. I., head of *VMF*, 178, 212, 252, 254, 848
Zoldan, 382
Zotov, S. A., cavalry commander, 101
Zweigstelle Dresden (*OKH* Records), 435

Lightning Source UK Ltd.
Milton Keynes UK
UKHW02f2214210918
329338UK00005B/57/P

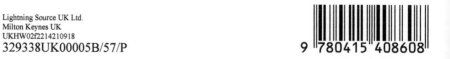